HANDBOOK OF ENVIRONMENTAL PSYCHOLOGY

Volume Two

HANDBOOK OF ENVIRONMENTAL PSYCHOLOGY

Edited by

DANIEL STOKOLS
University of California, Irvine

IRWIN ALTMAN
University of Utah

A Wiley-Interscience Publication

JOHN WILEY & SONS

New York / Chichester / Brisbane / Toronto / Singapore

Library of Congress Cataloging in Publication Data:

Handbook of environmental psychology.

    "A Wiley-Interscience publication."
    Includes bibliographies and indexes.
    1. Environmental psychology.   I. Stokols, Daniel.
II. Altman, Irwin. [DNLM: 1. Behavior. 2. Environment.
3. Psychology. BF 353 H236]

BF353.H26 1987   155.9   86–19081
ISBN 0-471-63017-9 (v. II)
ISBN 0-471-86631-8 (Two-volume set)

Printed in the United States of America

10 9 8 7 6 5 4 3 2 1

CONTRIBUTORS

JOHN AIELLO
Department of Psychology
Douglass College
New Brunswick, New Jersey

IRWIN ALTMAN
Department of Psychology
University of Utah
Salt Lake City, Utah

ROGER G. BARKER
Department of Psychology
University of Kansas
Oskaloosa, Kansas

ANDREW BAUM
Department of Medical Psychology
Uniformed Services University of the
    Health Sciences
Bethesda, Maryland

BARBARA B. BROWN
Department of Family and Consumer Studies
University of Utah
Salt Lake City, Utah

DAVID CANTER
Department of Psychology
University of Surrey
Guildford, Surrey
United Kingdom

FRANCES CARP
Wright Institute
Berkeley, California

JANET REIZENSTEIN CARPMAN
Carpman Grant Associates
Ann Arbor, Michigan

SHELDON COHEN
Department of Psychology
Carnegie-Mellon University
Pittsburgh, Pennsylvania

KENNETH CRAIK
Institute of Personality Assessment and Research
University of California
Berkeley, California

KAREN CRONICK
Instituto de Psicologia
Universidad Central de Venezuela
Caracas, Venezuela

IAN DONALD
Department of Psychology
University of Surrey
Guildford, Surrey
United Kingdom

GARY W. EVANS
Program in Social Ecology
University of California
Irvine, California

PETER B. EVERETT
College of Human Development
Pennsylvania State University
University Park, Pennsylvania

NICKOLAUS FEIMER
The Quaker Oats Company
Chicago, Illinois

BARUCH FISCHHOFF
Decision Research
Eugene, Oregon

E. SCOTT GELLER
Department of Psychology
Virginia Tech
Blacksburg, Virginia

REGINALD G. GOLLEDGE
Department of Geography
University of California
Santa Barbara, California

CARL F. GRAUMANN
Psychologisches Institut
Universitat Heidelberg
Heidelberg, Federal Republic of Germany

PAUL V. GUMP
Department of Psychology
University of Kansas
Lawrence, Kansas

avi CONTRIBUTORS

GENICHI HAGINO
Department of Psychology
Komazawa University
Tokyo, Japan

ROB HALL
School of Behavioral Sciences
Macquarie University
North Ryde, New South Wales, Australia

HARRY HEFT
Department of Psychology
Denison University
Granville, Ohio

MATI HEIDMETS
Department of Psychology
Tallinn Pedagogic Institute
Tallinn, Estonian S.S.R., U.S.S.R.

CHARLES J. HOLAHAN
Department of Psychology
University of Texas
Austin, Texas

DENISE JODELET
Laboratoire de Psychologie Sociale
Ecole des Hautes Etudes en Sciences Sociale
Paris, France

RICHARD KNOPF
Arizona State University
Phoenix, Arizona

ANDRÉ KREMER
Psychologish Laboratorium
Katholieke Universiteit
Nijmegen, The Netherlands

LENELIS KRUSE
Schwerpunkt Okologische Psychologie
Fern Universitat
Hagen, Federal Republic of Germany

JURI KRUUSVALL
Environmental Psychology Research Unit
Tallinn Pedagogic Institute
Tallinn, Estonian S.S.R., U.S.S.R.

RIKARD KÜLLER
Lund Institute of Technology
School of Architecture
Lund, Sweden

BRIAN R. LITTLE
Department of Psychology
Carleton University
Ottawa, Ontario, Canada

WILLIAM MICHELSON
Department of Sociology
University of Toronto
Toronto, Ontario, Canada

MAMORU MOCHIZUKI
School of Liberal Arts
International College of Commerce and Economics
Saitama, Japan

GARY T. MOORE
School of Architecture and Urban Planning
University of Wisconsin
Milwaukee, Wisconsin

TOOMAS NIIT
Department of Sociology
Institute of History
Tallinn, Estonian S.S.R., U.S.S.R.

STUART OSKAMP
Department of Psychology
Claremont Graduate School
Claremont, California

PAUL PAULUS
Department of Psychology
University of Texas
Arlington, Texas

DAVID PITT
Department of Horticulture
University of Maryland
College Park, Maryland

HAROLD M. PROSHANSKY
Graduate School and University Center
City University of New York
New York, New York

BARBARA ROGOFF
Department of Psychology
University of Utah
Salt Lake City, Utah

JAMES A. RUSSELL
Department of Psychology
University of British Columbia
Vancouver, British Columbia, Canada

SUSAN SAEGERT
Environmental Psychology Program
Graduate School and University Center
City University of New York
New York, New York

EUCLIDES SÁNCHEZ
Instituto de Psicologia
Universidad Central de Venezuela
Caracas, Venezuela

PAUL SLOVIC
Decision Research
Eugene, Oregon

JACALYN SNODGRASS
Department of Psychology
University of British Columbia
Vancouver, British Columbia, Canada

ROBERT SOMMER
Department of Psychology
University of California
Davis, California

PAUL C. STERN
National Academy of Sciences
Washington, D.C.

DANIEL STOKOLS
Program in Social Ecology
University of California
Irvine, California

PETER STRINGER
The Queen's University of Belfast
Belfast, Northern Ireland

PETER SUEDFELD
Psychology Department
University of British Columbia
Vancouver, British Columbia, Canada

ERIC SUNDSTROM
Department of Psychology
University of Tennessee
Knoxville, Tennessee

OLA SVENSON
Department of Psychology
University of Stockholm
Stockholm, Sweden

RALPH B. TAYLOR
Criminal Justice Department
Temple University
Philadelphia, Pennsylvania

ROSS THORNE
School of Architecture
The University of Sydney
Sydney, New South Wales, Australia

JEROME TOGNOLI
C.W. Post Center
Long Island University
Brooklyn, New York

ABRAHAM WANDERSMAN
Department of Psychology
University of South Carolina
Columbia, South Carolina

SEYMOUR WAPNER
Department of Psychology
Clark University
Worcester, Massachusetts

BARRY G. WATSON
Toronto Transit Commission
Toronto, Ontario, Canada

ESTHER WIESENFELD
Instituto de Psicologia
Universidad Central de Venezuela
Caracas, Venezuela

ALLAN W. WICKER
Department of Psychology
Claremont Graduate School
Claremont, California

GARY H. WINKEL
Environmental Psychology Program
Graduate School and University Center
City University of New York
New York, New York

JOACHIM F. WOHLWILL
Department of Individual and Family Studies
College of Human Development
Pennsylvania State University
University Park, Pennsylvania

TAKIJI YAMAMOTO
Hiroshima University
Hiroshima, Japan

CRAIG ZIMRING
College of Architecture
Georgia Institute of Technology
Atlanta, Georgia

ERVIN ZUBE
School for Renewable Natural Resources
University of Arizona
Tucson, Arizona

CONTENTS OF VOLUME TWO

CONTENTS OF VOLUME ONE

PART 4

APPLICATIONS OF ENVIRONMENTAL PSYCHOLOGY TO COMMUNITY PROBLEMS

Chapter 23

ENVIRONMENTAL ASSESSMENT

Kenneth H. Craik, *Institute of Personality Assessment and Research, University of California, Berkeley, California*

Nickolaus R. Feimer, *Marketing Information Department, The Quaker Oats Company, Chicago, Illinois*

23.1. THE DEVELOPMENT AND EVOLUTION OF ENVIRONMENTAL ASSESSMENT

Environmental assessment is a general conceptual and methodological framework for describing and predicting how attributes of places relate to a wide range of cognitive, affective, and behavioral responses. The approach recognizes that the manner in which places are used and evaluated represents important scientific questions and societal concerns that require systematic and objective appraisal. Additionally, the approach assumes that establishing dependable predictive relations between descriptive attributes of places and how they are evaluated and used provides the grounds for advancing our under-

standing of environment–behavior transactions and affords the basis for improving the planning, design, and management of our environment.

The questions addressed by environmental assessment are straightforward and compelling. Which descriptive attributes of campgrounds predict how frequently they are used? Which descriptive attributes of school buildings predict how often they are vandalized? Which descriptive attributes of river valley settings predict how they are evaluated on scenic quality? Which descriptive attributes of housing units for the elderly predict how satisfactory they are judged by the residents?

The scientific-intellectual structure within which these questions are considered and addressed requires a detailed exposition and generates a wide-ranging research agenda (Craik, 1977). However, its concepts, issues, options, and applications derive from a basically pragmatic point of view.

23.1.1. Environmental Assessment in Environmental Psychology

Studies within the environmental assessment framework can be readily traced back through the 1960s and made an important contribution to the body of research findings that led to the emergence of environmental psychology as a distinct field of inquiry in 1970 (Craik, 1970; Proshansky, Ittelson, & Rivlin, 1970; Wohlwill, 1970). Among these early classics in environmental assessment can be included the research on adjustment to flood hazards (Burton & Kates, 1964; Kates, 1963); why buildings are differentially known in Ciudad Guayana (Appleyard, 1969); Adirondack campground use (Shafer & Thompson, 1968); neighborhood preferences (Peterson, 1967); and landscape assessment (Fines, 1969; Kiemstedt, 1968; Linton, 1968; Litton & Twiss, 1967; Shafer, Hamilton, Schmidt, 1969). During that period, the development of descriptive and evaluative assessment techniques had also begun (Craik, 1968; Kasmar, 1970; Lowenthal, 1972; Moos, 1975; Stern, 1970).

The Psychological Assessment Paradigm

As this research area developed within environmental psychology, its bearing on general issues in psychological assessment has become more evident (Craik, 1971, 1981b; Daniel, 1976; Daniel & Vining, 1983). Indeed, environmental assessment can be usefully treated as a new extension of psychological assessment, a research paradigm with over four decades of refinement and hard-earned conceptual and methodological guidelines and insights.

The general assessment paradigm consists of three components: (1) a multidimensional taxonomic model providing descriptive and predictive variables, (2) a set of criterion or outcome variables, and (3) a repertory of self-critical concepts and multivariate statistical techniques for gauging the validity and utility of predictions. Although its most familiar applications are in personnel selection, educational measurement, psychodiagnosis, and personality assessment (Anastasi, 1982; Cronbach, 1984; Dunnette, 1966; Meehl, 1973; Megargee, 1966), it constitutes a general framework with wider relevance (Butcher & Spielberger, 1983, 1984; Jackson & Messick, 1967; McReynolds, 1968, 1971, 1975; 1978, 1981; Spielberger & Butcher, 1982, 1983).

Theory and Assessment

Advances in environmental assessment have yielded techniques for assessing environments along a wide array of descriptive and predictive variables. Many of these assessment variables derive from theoretical sources and assumptions. One conceptual and methodological orientation holds that distinctions among environments that have become encoded within the natural language provide an important guide for environmental assessment. Thus, instruments such as the Environmental Descriptor Scales and the Landscape Adjective Check List draw on terms and constructs from everyday language (see Table 23.1). Personality theory has been a second important source of environmental assessment variables (Walsh, 1973). Thus, Murray's (1938) classification of human needs has inspired the College Characteristics Index and the Social Climate Scales, whereas Holland's (1966) theory of vocational preference types has generated the Environmental Assessment Technique (see Table 23.1). A third example is the behavior setting survey—a method of environmental assessment that is integrally situated within the broader framework of ecological psychology (Barker, 1968).

Other sources for environmental assessment variables include the general aim of comprehensive descriptive coverage, as in the case of the Regional Q-sort Deck and the Technical Neighborhood Assessment Indices, and the measurement systems of relevant disciplines, as in the case of geomorphological dimensions of floodplains (see Table 23.1). Regardless of its source, however, every assessment variable represents a construct and calls for ongoing conceptual analysis and elaboration. Indeed, this theoretically oriented process is a central component of the general psychological assessment paradigm (see the section on construct validity).

23.1.2. Environmental Assessment in Environmental Planning, Design, and Management

Contemporary environments are not static. Perhaps no part of the earth is immune from the continuing process of human-influenced environmental change. In modern industrial societies, this process is institutionalized in the form of regulations, legislation, agencies, professions, and decision-making procedures. The process of environmental planning, design, and management can be viewed within Campbell's (1965) formulation of sociocultural evolution. The multitude of specific plans, designs, and management practices generated by society can be

Table 23.1. Environmental Assessment Instruments

Observer-Based Environmental Assessment Instruments

College Characteristics Index (Stern, 1963, 1970)
Environmental Descriptor Scales (Kasmar, 1970)
Environmental Q Set (Block, 1971)
Group Dimensions Description Questionnaire (Hemphill, 1956; Pheysey & Payne, 1970)
Landscape Adjective Check List (Craik, 1971)
Organizational Climate Description Scales (George & Bishop, 1971; Halpin & Crofts, 1963)
Regional Q-sort Deck (Craik, 1983)
Social Climate Scales (Moos, 1974, 1975)
University Residence Environment Scale (Gerst & Moos, 1972)
Perceived Neighborhood Quality Scales (Carp & Carp, 1982b)

Technical Environmental Assessment Instruments

Water Quality Index (Coughlin, 1976)
Environmental Noise Measures (U.S. Environmental Protection Agency, 1974)
MITRE Air Quality Index (MAQI) (Thomas, 1972)
Air Quality: Aerosol Light Scattering (Stewart, Middleton, & Ely, 1983)
Indoor Air Monitoring Program (Wallace et al., 1984)
Geomorphological Dimensions of Floodplains (Burton, 1962)
Technical Neighborhood Assessment Indices (Carp & Carp, 1982a)
Behavior Setting Survey (Barker, 1968)
Structural Indices for Work Organizations (Pugh, Hickson, & Hinings, 1969)
Environmental Assessment Technique (Astin & Holland, 1961)

considered as efforts to achieve a fitting environmental adaptation (Craik, 1983). The process of sociocultural evolution provides consistent selection criteria to identify, among these new forms, the alternatives that meet the criteria of functional adaptation. Societal mechanisms such as legitimacy, imitation, and diffusion come into play to retain the selected variants and eliminate others. Additional mechanisms such as sanctions, policies, legislation, codes, and guidelines promote the preservation and duplication of the selected variants.

Environmental assessment provides a systematic means of facilitating sociocultural evolution. Evaluative assessments of places appraise the extent to which they meet explicitly measured standards of performance and effectiveness. Descriptive and predictive assessments identify specific attributes of the plans, designs, and management of places that relate to variation in criterion measures.

Thus five steps can be identified in an environmental assessment program. First, a sample of places from a given category or domain of places is drawn. Second, a criterion assessment of the sample of places is conducted. The expectation is that the places will display significant variation in the criterion index. Third, a descriptive assessment of the same sample of places is conducted, entailing an array of attributes. Fourth, the descriptive attributes are related to the criteria. These relationships provide a

preliminary indication regarding potential predictors of the criterion measures. Fifth, cross-validation of the predictive relations on a new sample of places is required to establish the generality of the findings. In many instances, new plans, designs, and management practices for places can be presented in preconstruction simulation, permitting descriptive, evaluative, or both forms of assessment at that point in the development process. In these cases, follow-up cross-validation of findings under postconstruction conditions offers an important check on the predictive validity of findings.

23.1.3. Environmental Units and Environmental Quality

The assessment model entails a population of environmental entities that can be reliably and meaningfully appraised on evaluative criteria. Once they are specified, the approach seeks to assess descriptive attributes of the entities that possess dependable and generalizable validity in predicting the evaluative criteria.

The issue of environmental taxonomy remains unsettled. A wealth of potential units of analysis is at hand, drawn from ordinary language terms (e.g., office, park, alley), broader taxonomic categories (e.g., residential, institutional, urban), and conceptual systems (e.g., behavior settings). Scientific discussion points to a need for conceptual clarification (e.g., Moos, 1973; Pervin, 1978), whereas scientific analysis of the perceptual/cognitive categories of laypersons remains largely unexplored (e.g., Craik, 1981a; Tversky & Hemenway, 1983; Ward & Russell, 1981).

Although an integrative taxonomic framework is a worthy goal, the current varied and flexible ad hoc usages do not stand in the way of applications of the assessment model. The only requirement is the selection and consistent use of a given unit of analysis that designates a population or class of environmental entities for assessment. For ease of exposition, the term *place* will be employed as a general designation for the environmental unit (Craik, 1971).

Within the assessment model, the criteria are typically evaluative, indexing some facet of environmental quality. However, nonevaluative criterion measures are accommodated equally well by the psychological assessment paradigm. Thus, for example, in Appleyard's (1969) study of why buildings are differentially known to the population of Ciudad Guayana, the criterion measure of each building's frequency of appearance on map sketches of the city is relatively neutral from an evaluative standpoint. The variable serves primarily as a cognitive, rather than evaluative, criterion within this application of the assessment model. Furthermore, certain variables such as the Russell-Pratt dimensions of pleasantness and arousing quality (Russell & Pratt, 1980) might function as criterion variables in one application and as descriptive or predictor variables in another application, depending on the scientific aims of the study. Thus both evaluative and nonevaluative criteria have a place within the environmental assessment paradigm.

The identification of criterion variables, however, usually implicates values and valuation, which can be encompassed by the general construct of *environmental quality*. The process requires a conceptual analysis of the construct of environmental quality, as it applies to the class of units under analysis. For most classes of environmental entities, the construct of environmental quality is itself multidimensional and complex. In the case of residential quality, for example, research has shown that the unit varies among persons but usually includes some part of the neighborhood as well as the residential structure (Marans, 1976). A wide range of components are subsumed under the construct of *residential quality*. For example, based on interviews regarding this construct and a review of prior research, Carp and Carp (1982b) employed an array of 147 attributes, yielding 15 factor dimensions.

The main point is that the clarification of the meaning of environmental quality is typically a fundamental and preliminary step in the application of the assessment model (Craik & Zube, 1976). In many domains of environmental assessment research, this basic form of analysis has not received sufficient attention. Systematic analysis is warranted, focusing on individuals' notions of environmental quality drawn from personal experience. For each class of environmental entities, surveys of representative samples of laypersons and experts can assist in clarifying the salient constituent elements of the construct—environmental quality for that domain.

The conceptual analysis of environmental quality provides a basis for illustrating the establishment of comprehensive, standard sets of indicators for appraising specific places. Environmental quality indices (EQIs) can be founded on public health and economic considerations such as air quality and water quality indices or derived from observer-based evaluations of the everyday physical environment in the form of perceived environmental quality indices (PEQIs) (Craik & Zube, 1976).

In addition to providing a source of criterion variables within the application of the environmental assessment model, EQIs serve important policy and monitoring functions. Following on the U.S. National Environmental Policy Act of 1969 (NEPA), EQIs have been generated to monitor the effectiveness of environmental protection programs, to gauge the environmental impacts of proposed public and private projects, and to communicate trends in environmental quality to public officials and citizens. The process of conceptual analysis entailed in the development of adequate EQIs can also serve to clarify the goals of environmental policy.

23.2. EVALUATIVE, DESCRIPTIVE, AND PREDICTIVE ENVIRONMENTAL ASSESSMENTS

The methodological issues raised by evaluative assessments, descriptive assessments, and predictive assessments will be reviewed in that order. A number of specific technical issues are shared by the three forms of assessments, especially by evaluative and descriptive assessments. These topics will be examined in a later section.

23.2.1. Evaluative Environmental Assessments

Two traditions have enriched our understanding of evaluative environmental assessments. Within the fields of environmental planning, design, and management, postconstruction evaluations of the places yielded by specific projects have become a valued activity (Conyne & Clack, 1981; Friedmann, Zimring, & Zube, 1978; Zeisel, 1981; Zimring & Reizenstein, 1980). They highlighted the complexity of establishing appropriate and comprehensive criterion variables.

At one level, the intentions of the initiators and designers of a project can be determined and the extent of their realization gauged in the evaluative assessment. But in addition, each project has a community of users, managers, and other affected individuals who can also serve as a source for the derivation and appraisal of relevant criterion variables (Cooper, 1972, 1975; Friedmann et al., 1978; Zeisel & Griffin, 1975). Evaluative environmental assessments of the postconstruction kind represent a special form of evaluation research (Campbell, 1975; Cook & Reichardt, 1979), and both researchers and users must be alert to the administrative pressures and potential biases inherent in them (Campbell, 1969, 1975). A sensible framework for conducting these case studies in evaluative assessment has emerged (Friedmann et al., 1978), with analysis of cumulative findings from postconstruction case studies providing a basis for some generalizations (Cooper, 1972, 1975).

The second tradition in evaluative environmental assessment has sought to identify comprehensive and standard sets of criteria for appraising specific classes of environmental entities or places. This approach has grown out of the more direct extension of the psychological assessment paradigm to environmental psychology (Craik, 1971, 1981b; Moos, 1973, 1975). It has also been influenced by the search for techniques for systematic monitoring of levels of environmental quality on a broader scale than individual planning and design projects (Craik & Zube, 1976). The use of large samples of assessed places permits the application of multivariate statistical analyses and more readily interpreted claims to generality. Examples of this approach can be found in research on scenic (Daniel & Vining, 1983; Feimer, 1983; Zube, Sell, & Taylor, 1982) and residential quality (Canter, Sanchez-Robles, & Watts, 1974; Carp & Carp, 1982a, 1982b). Yet as the postconstruction case study tradition has demonstrated, every place has its own distinctive set of appropriate evaluative criteria, and some of this individuality of place may be lost in the use of standard EQIs. Both traditions have important contributions to offer, and each has important implications that must be recognized.

Evaluative environmental assessment also entails a general set of procedural issues. First, when a sample of places is evaluatively assessed, the possibility of supplementing the appraisals of on-site observers with those of touring panels is raised. Second, the role of simulated presentations takes on more pragmatic importance when a sample of places is assessed than when a case study evaluation is undertaken. Third, under some circumstances, the instructional set provided to those persons contributing evaluative assessments may be important. For example, they may be asked to provide preferential judgments that record their personal likes and dislikes concerning the places being assessed, or they may be asked to record comparative appraisals, that is, evaluations made with regard to some implicit or explicit standard of comparison (Craik & McKechnie, 1974). Although this distinction is conceptually clear, empirical tests of it within landscape assessment research have not clearly documented its significance (Daniel & Vining, 1983). However, the distinction may warrant attention in contexts that lack the unusually high consensus found in scenic quality judgments, for example, in assessments of residential quality (Craik & McKechnie, 1974; Craik & Zube, 1976).

23.2.2. Descriptive Environmental Assessments

A spirit of taxonomic venturesomeness is appropriate to the field of environmental assessment. Places are complex and multidimensional entities. The fund of available attributes and measures for describing places is large and heterogeneous; many potentially useful descriptive characteristics have not been fully explored. Without doubt, comprehensive descriptive assessments of places is an open-ended, multivariate endeavor.

The field of environmental assessment should take on the mission of scientific caretaker for the abiding question of how best to describe places. The task is not simply to settle on a specific set of standard procedures and techniques. The question itself will be undergoing continuing refinement and reformulation as environmental psychology advances and develops. The future vitality of environmental assessment depends not only on a devotion to its scientific aims but on drawing upon a larger appreciation of places and a fascination with the subtle variations among them.

Buckminster Fuller was well known for his probing of architectural students about seemingly irrelevant descriptive properties of their designs, for example, how much a particular building would weigh if it were constructed. Craik (1972) has urged the adoption of ceremonial recognitions of the character of places. For example, he proposes that public eulogies be commissioned for places that will be destroyed by new construction, as a prerequisite for building permits. Indeed the literature on the appreciation of places has grown substantially in recent years (Lowenthal & Bowden, 1976; Lynch, 1972; Relph, 1976; Tuan, 1977). Continuing progress and innovation in the systematic, standardized descriptive assessment of places must depend in part on the intrinsic motivation provided by the connoisseur's delight in the character and diversity of places.

Technical and Observational Environmental Assessments

Within the context of systematic approaches to descriptive environmental assessment, a major procedural distinction can be drawn between technical assessments and observational assessments (Craik, 1981b) (Table 23.1). Technical assessments are based on an explicit technical system of measurement. These technical systems of measurement can range from standard metrics of weights and measures to those of geomorphology and those of organizational science. Observational assessments are based on consensual impressions in an ordinary language framework made by panels of observers of the places being assessed. Technical assessments are sometimes termed *objective* and observational assessments termed *subjective*. However, this distinction is not useful. Observational as well as technical environmental assessments aspire to the objectivity gained by reproducible measures that meet the goals of adequate reliability, sensitivity, validity, and utility (Craik & Feimer, 1979; Daniel, 1976).

Technical assessments draw on measurement systems from other fields and do not require individual exposition. However, the breadth of relevant technical systems is noteworthy (Canter & Stringer, 1975; Craik, 1971, 1981; Holahan, 1982). For example, some investigators have employed indexes of organizational structure (Astin & Holland, 1961; Jones & James, 1979; Pugh et al., 1969), density (Loo, 1978), and community characteristics (Barker & Schoggen, 1973). Geomorphological dimensions (Burton, Kates, & White, 1978) and land use taxonomies (Zube, Pitt, & Anderson, 1975) have also been found to be appropriate as well as indexes of air and water quality and noise (Barker, 1976; Coughlin, 1976; Stewart et al., 1983; Weinstein, 1976a). Within interior settings, furniture arrangement (Laumann & House, 1970; Mahrabian & Diamond, 1971), lighting (Hendrick, Martyniuk, Spencer, & Flynn, 1977), floor level (Fanning, 1967), ambient temperature

(Berglund, 1977), color (Sivik, 1974), and standard metrics for length and volume have served in descriptive environmental assessments.

A special marginal case in the distinction between technical and observational assessment arises when observers are asked to estimate technical indices. This exercise has been used to illustrate the shared properties of reliability and sensitivity of measurement that can be demonstrated for observational as well as technical indices (Dawes, 1977). Within the environmental realm, research has attempted to gauge how well observers can estimate physically based air quality (Barker, 1976) and water quality (Coughlin, 1976) indices. Because these latter indices measure the presence–absence of culturally identified pollutants, Craik and Zube (1976) have suggested the term *observer-based pollution indices* (OBPIs). They are to be distinguished from *perceived environmental quality indices* (PEQIs), which relate direct experience of places to constructs of environmental quality.

A more central concern of observational environmental assessment is the use of panels of human judges to measure descriptive attributes of places along dimensions drawn from ordinary language. These descriptive assessments have generated several standard techniques (Table 23.1) and raise a number of issues regarding their meanings and proper measurement procedures. However, if adequate reliability, sensitivity, validity, and utility can be demonstrated, observational assessment offers a measurement system independent of and complementary to other technical environmental assessment systems.

Issues in Observational Environmental Assessment

This approach to assessment makes use of the ability of human observers to differentiate among places consensually, along a wide variety of descriptive dimensions that embody meaning within a sociocultural framework. A full understanding of the scope, nature, and potential of this capacity is itself a major item on the research agenda for environmental cognition and perception (Leff, 1978; Ward & Russell, 1981)

In the meantime, standard procedures have been devised to facilitate the observational assessment of places. In Table 23.1, an array of these techniques is listed to illustrate the wide range of intended uses and applications. Other procedures can be considered quasi-standard, in that the item content of adjective check lists, rating scales, and Q-sort decks vary, depending on researchers' specific aims. The various applications of the semantic differential technique exemplify this practice (Bechtel, 1975; Hershberger, 1972).

Nevertheless, a common set of conceptual, methodological, and interpretational issues bear on any observational environmental assessment. To review and discuss these issues, we will take a hypothetical assessment of 40 places by a panel of observers on the descriptive dimensions of active, beautiful, craggy, light, and spacious.

The analysis of the description of places as "active," "beautiful," "craggy," "light," and "spacious" can be focused in two ways. The statements can be treated as assertions of individual observers, or *trait attributions*, and studied within the context of environmental perception. However, if consensus among observers prevails, then the statements can also be treated as *trait designations*, or potentially useful characterizations of the places described (Craik, 1971, 1981b).

MEANINGS OF ENVIRONMENTAL TRAIT DESIGNATIONS

As trait designations, observer-based descriptions of places constitute an important component of environmental assessment. The interpretation of their meanings and the methodological issues they present are similar to those that have been more thoroughly examined in the case of observational trait descriptions within personality assessment. A formulation of these meanings presented by Wiggins (1973) suggests a framework for considering observational descriptive assessments of places.

LEXICAL MEANING.   One source of meaning for descriptive environmental terms is *lexical meaning*, or the set of synonyms for a given term found in a standard dictionary. Lexical meaning can play a procedural role in environmental assessment. For example, in establishing a descriptive checklist for a domain of places, the potential adjectives number in the thousands. A criterion of minimal synonymic overlap and lexical redundancy can be employed as one selection rule.

AFFECTIVE AND PERCEPTUAL/COGNITIVE MEANING.   Most descriptive terms in ordinary language possess affective or emotional overtones. Ward and Russell (1981) have distinguished between *affective meaning* and *perceptual/cognitive meaning*. The affective meaning of environments has been conceptualized as a two-dimensional bipolar space defined by eight affective variables falling in the following circular order: pleasant, exciting, arousing, distressing, unpleasant, gloomy, sleepy, and relaxing (Russell & Pratt, 1980). Alternatively, the same space can be defined by two orthogonal bipolar dimensions: pleasant–unpleasant and arousing–sleepy (Russell, Ward, & Pratt, 1981).

The perceptual/cognitive aspects of environmental meaning (e.g., scale, man-made versus natural, vertical versus horizontal) offer a more complex and less well-understood structure (Ward & Russell, 1981). Furthermore, interpretation of the structure of perceptual/cognitive descriptions of places requires attention to whether the observed correlations among descriptors represent empirical associations, cause and effect connections, or conceptual-definitional relations (Craik, 1981; Daniel & Ittelson, 1981; Russell & Ward, 1981).

IMPLICATIVE MEANING.   *Implicative meaning* refers to the cognitive relations that are found among descriptors that are not lexically synonymous. That is, it addresses the question of expected covariations across places in general. Conditional probability judgments provide one approach to exploring implicative meaning (Wiggins, 1973). An example of the format within the environmental context would be:

Given that a place is *spacious*, how likely is it that the place will also be *light*?

Respondents are asked to record their judgments on rating scales with categories corresponding to probability of occurrence. Note that this method of probing implicative meaning does not entail the presentation of any specific places or sample of places to the panels of judges. The focus is on general expectations conveyed by the descriptive terms and their relationships.

Surprisingly little attention has been granted to the exploration of implicative environmental meaning, although conceptual frameworks are available to guide the study of environmental inference (Craik, 1981). For example, Brunswik's (1956) lens model and conceptual orientation of probabilistic functionalism offer a means of exploring cue–cue inferences (e.g., Craik & Appleyard, 1980). In their exploration of basic object categories, Rosch and her associates (Rosch & Mervis, 1975; Rosch, Mervis, Gray, Johnson, & Boyes-Braem, 1976) provide an approach to the analysis of cue-category linkages in cognitive representations of the environment (e.g., Tversky & Hemenway, 1983).

SEMANTIC MEANING.   *Semantic meaning* refers to the relations between terms and the places to which they refer. The demonstration of adequate consensual and differentiating assignment of descriptive terms to places establishes the semantic meaning of the descriptors. That is, semantic meaning derives from how the descriptive terms are used in their applications to the assessment of specific places and from the evidence marshaled that observer assessments reflect characteristics of places. Several empirical forms of documentation of semantic meaning are available: observer reliability, sensitivity of measurement, and the structural features among assessed environmental dimensions.

SENSITIVITY AND GENERALIZABILITY OF OBSERVATIONAL ENVIRONMENTAL ASSESSMENTS

Suppose a sample of 40 rural settings is descriptively assessed on the dimensions of active, beautiful, craggy, light, and spacious, based on on-site ratings by a touring panel of 20 observers. The first question to consider is the extent to which the composite ratings of each dimension display sensitivity of measurement, that is, differentiation among the places assessed. A descriptive environmental construct that yields the same index for all places possesses little value for characterizing them. Within the context of analysis of variance, a main effect for place or setting is a desirable measurement feature. Ample evidence exists to demonstrate the general capacity of observational environmental assessments to achieve sensitivity in measurement (Kasmar, 1970; Oostendorp & Berlyne, 1978a, 1978b; Seaton & Collins, 1972; Ward & Russell, 1981).

The second question is whether the assessment of the sample of places is dependable. That is, to what extent can we count on the observed ratings to generalize across observers, rating formats, and occasions. Relative independence of observational environmental assessments from the nature of the specific observers making the descriptions, the specific rating formats used (e.g., 5-point versus 7-point scales), the way in which the place is presented to the observers (e.g., on-site versus simulated presentations), and the specific time at which the ratings are recorded is also a desirable measurement property. All of these facets of observational assessment can affect the impressions observers form of places. Indeed, research on environmental perception is dedicated to advancing our detailed knowledge of these effects and processes (Craik, 1970, 1977; Ittelson, 1973). The primary consideration in observational environmental assessment is that the proportion of variance accounted for by these facets is not excessively large in relation to the main effects for places. Ap-

propriate research designs and coefficients of generalizability are available to gauge the sensitivity and reliability of measurement (Cronbach, Rajaratnam, & Gleser, 1963; Cronbach, Gleser, Nanda, & Rajaratnam, 1972; Guilford, 1954; Wiggins, 1973).

As in the case of observational assessment of persons (Block, 1961; Horowitz, Inouye, & Siegelman, 1979), adequately dependable observational assessments of places typically require the pooling or averaging of judgments made independently by several observers (Daniel & Vining, 1983; Feimer, Smardon, & Craik, 1981; Smardon, Feimer, Craik, & Sheppard, 1983). These composite reliabilities for panels of observers can be estimated with regard to the relative standing of places on descriptive dimensions (e.g., whether observers agree in the rank ordering of places on the attribute) or in terms of absolute agreement among observers (e.g., whether they agree on the assignment of specific rating values to places) (Tinsley & Weiss, 1975).

Observational assessments of places can meet rigorous standards of sensitivity and reliability of measurement. Evidence is available to support this assertion, but further testing of it is appropriate as the technical standards of environmental assessment mature (Craik & Feimer, 1979).

STRUCTURAL FEATURES AMONG ASSESSED ENVIRONMENTAL DIMENSIONS

In our hypothetical assessment of 40 rural places on the dimensions of active, beautiful, craggy, light, and spacious, the sensitivity and dependability of each environmental dimension would warrant examination. A next step might be to consider the intercorrelations among the composite ratings of the 40 rural places for the five dimensions. A correlation matrix of this kind raises two interpretational issues. One bears on the *convergent and discriminant validity* of the five constructs; the other concerns what has been termed the *systematic distortion hypothesis*.

CONVERGENT AND DISCRIMINANT VALIDITY.   In their formulation of convergent and discriminant validity, Campbell and Fiske (1959) argue that the conceptual formulation of a descriptive attribute usually includes the implicit or explicit proposition that the attribute can be observed under more than one measurement condition and that it can be meaningfully differentiated from other attributes. The first property—convergent validity—refers to the dependable and generalizable assessment of the attribute across conditions of observers, instruments, media of presentation, and occasions. The second property—discriminant validity—refers to the extent to which each attribute provides nonredundant information about the entities being assessed.

To gauge convergent and discriminant validity of attributes, or descriptive constructs, a heteroattribute, heteromethod correlational matrix must be generated. The research design requires (1) a set of attributes, (2) a set of measurement conditions, and (3) a sample of assessed entities. Let us assume that our sample of 40 rural places was assessed on the attributes of active, beautiful, craggy, light, and spacious, under the following conditions of measurement: (1) a touring panel visited each place for 1 day and assessed it using a 9-point rating scale, (2) another touring panel visited each place for 1 day and assessed it using a paired comparison method, and (3) local residents of each place assessed it using a 9-point scale. Alternatively, one panel might have viewed a color film tour of each place and assessed it on a 9-point scale. The heteroattribute, heteromethod matrix presented in Table 23.2 could be generated from the assessment data.

Several features of Table 23.2 are noteworthy. The subset of correlations gauging convergent validity are identified as the off-main diagonals within the matrix (cv). These coefficients represent the pairwise cross-method correlations for each individual variable. These correlations should be high and significantly different from zero, demonstrating that the relative ordering of the 40 rural places on the descriptive attributes is generalizable across methods of assessment. The main diagonal consists of the reliabilities of the measures for each method (rr) (these are in parentheses in Table 23.2). Because the magnitude of a validity coefficient is bounded by the reliabilities of the measures on which it is based (Guilford, 1954; Nunnally, 1978), the entries of the main diagonal provide an index of the attainable magnitudes for the coefficients gauging convergent validity. Thus for any set of measures to attain appreciable levels of convergent validity, reliabilities must be high. Minimally, reliabilities should be greater than +.75 and preferably greater than +.90.

The remaining off-diagonal entries in the convergent-discriminant validity matrix provide the basis for an appraisal of discriminant validity. To demonstrate discriminant validity, the convergent validity correlations must be greater than the other off-diagonal correlations in the matrix (wm, cm), which represent correlations among various other attributes and methods. Discriminant validity concerns the differentiation among measured constructs and requires evidence of nonredundancy in the descriptive information they provide about assessed places. The specific magnitude and pattern of covariation expected among descriptive attributes depends, in part, on the conceptual formulation of the constructs involved. Thus, for example, moderate correlations between light and spacious might be anticipated across many assessed places, but consistent correlations in the +.90 to +.95 range might raise a question about the conceptual distinctiveness and independent assessment value of the two constructs.

A final feature of the convergent-discriminant validity matrix that merits brief mention is the appraisal of method variance. The correlations between distinct constructs measured by the same method (wm) (the areas of Table 23.2 that are bounded by triangles) provide evidence of the degree to which measurement is a function of the measurement technique itself, rather than the meaningful representation of some underlying attribute of the environment. In any case, where the attribute-within method coefficients approach or are larger in magnitude than the convergent validity coefficients, much of the variability is characterized by variance associated with the measurement system in general, rather than by differentiable constructs.

SYSTEMATIC DISTORTION HYPOTHESIS. We have discussed two kinds of correlation matrices for our five descriptive attributes: active, beautiful, craggy, light, and spacious. The first matrix would be generated to reflect the implicative meaning of the descriptive constructs. In this case, conditional probability judgments would be gathered from panels, without any presentation of specific places. The second matrix would be the obtained intercorrelations of the five descriptive attributes, across the sample of 40 rural places, based upon the results from, say, the local residents.

Within the field of observational assessment of persons, the relation between these two kinds of correlation matrices has itself given rise to controversial issues. These issues are treated under various terms referring to some aspect of the findings at issue or processes presumably accounting for them, including the *halo effect* (Cooper, 1981), *illusory correlations* (Chapman, 1967), *conceptual similarity* (Mulaik, 1964), and the *systematic distortion hypothesis* (Shweder & D'Andrade, 1980). To a lesser degree, this same issue of the relationship between the implicative meaning of descriptive constructs and their observed empirical interrelationships has been the subject of concern and debate in the environment–behavior literature as well (see Craik, 1981a; Danford

Table 23.2 Hetero-attribute, Hetero-method Matrix [a]

Method	Attribute	Touring Panel Paired Comparisons					Touring Panel Rating Scale					Local Residents Rating Scale				
		Active	Beautiful	Craggy	Light	Spacious	Active	Beautiful	Craggy	Light	Spacious	Active	Beautiful	Craggy	Light	Spacious
Touring Panel Paired Comparisons	Active	(.rr)														
	Beautiful	.wm	(.rr)													
	Craggy	.wm	.wm	(.rr)												
	Light	.wm	.wm	.wm	(.rr)											
	Spacious	.wm	.wm	.wm	.wm	(.rr)										
Touring Panel Rating Scale	Active	.cv	.cm	.cm	.cm	.cm	(.rr)									
	Beautiful	.cm	.cv	.cm	.cm	.cm	.wm	(.rr)								
	Craggy	.cm	.cm	.cv	.cm	.cm	.wm	.wm	(.rr)							
	Light	.cm	.cm	.cm	.cv	.cm	.wm	.wm	.wm	(.rr)						
	Spacious	.cm	.cm	.cm	.cm	.cv	.wm	.wm	.wm	.wm	(.rr)					
Local Residents Rating Scale	Active	.cv	.cm	.cm	.cm	.cm	.cv	.cm	.cm	.cm	.cm	(.rr)				
	Beautiful	.cm	.cv	.cm	.cm	.cm	.cm	.cv	.cm	.cm	.cm	.wm	(.rr)			
	Craggy	.cm	.cm	.cv	.cm	.cm	.cm	.cm	.cv	.cm	.cm	.wm	.wm	(.rr)		
	Light	.cm	.cm	.cm	.cv	.cm	.cm	.cm	.cm	.cv	.cm	.wm	.wm	.wm	(.rr)	
	Spacious	.cm	.cm	.cm	.cm	.cv	.cm	.cm	.cm	.cm	.cv	.wm	.wm	.wm	.wm	(.rr)

[a] cm = cross-method; cv = convergent validity; rr = reliability; wm = within method.

900

& Willems, 1975; Daniel & Ittelson, 1981; Russell & Ward, 1981; Ward & Russell, 1981).

On the one hand, some degree of match between the two sets of matrices is a necessary, but not sufficient, condition, if the terms are to describe relations among attributes of places (Wiggins, 1973). A language system having evolutionary adaptive value would be expected to generate implicative meanings that match "real-world" relations (Block, Weiss, & Thorne, 1979). On the other hand, any given set of empirical, obtained relations among attributes across a sample of specific persons or places may be systematically biased toward implicative meaning. Thus if observers on a touring panel are not presented with adequate information about how active the places are or fail to attend to these features, they may, through recourse to implicative meanings, infer from their judgment on other attributes what the standing of places on the attribute of *active* is likely to be. Or, more generally, their memory for features relevant to each and all of the five attributes may shift away from what was or could have been observed and toward what the implicative meaning of the descriptive constructs would suggest about their relations.

The systematic distortion hypothesis is plausible. Indeed, most formulations of perception as an active cognition-saturated process (e.g., Ittelson, 1973; Leff, 1978) suggest that within everyday life, "on site" so to speak, we are constantly making inferences about broader attributes of places from narrower cues and that the research agenda for environmental perception and cognition calls for detailed examination of these processes (Craik, 1981; Craik & Appleyard, 1980; Groat, 1982; Krampen, 1979; Leff & Gordon, 1980; Leff, Gordon, & Ferguson, 1974). However, the assumption and demonstration that perception is inference laden in itself does not support the systematic distortion hypothesis. It is equally plausible that countervailing inference processes neutralize any tendency toward *systematic* distortion in the direction of implicative meaning (Cooper, 1981).

Little research has been directed to this issue within environmental perception. Two conclusions seem warranted from the considerable attention paid to the systematic distortion hypothesis within personality assessment. First, because both positions expect a match between the correlational matrices among attributes generated from implicative meanings and from observational assessments of samples of specific entities, no amount of replications of this similarity will settle or clarify the issue. Second, within observational personality assessment, con-

vincing evidence demonstrating the phenomenon of systematic distortion toward implicative meaning has been difficult to generate, and the few relevant data sets have been open to counterarguments (e.g., Block et al., 1979; Shweder & D'Andrade, 1979).

Controversy regarding the status and interpretation of the match between implicative and assessed correlation matrices among constructs has been viewed as a paradigm clash (Ward & Russell, 1981). From one perspective, the match simply suggests that the implicative structure represents a valid cognitive generalization regarding "real-world" relations. From another standpoint, the match indicates an artifactual component to the observer-based assessed structure. This disagreement will be difficult to resolve if it springs from incommensurate paradigms (Kuhn, 1962) entailing differing basic assumptions, valued methods, and research agendas. However, the debate over the match between implicative and assessed structures can only be examined fully within a wider framework that acknowledges the role of semantic meaning, sensitivity and generalizability of measurement, and construct validity. Perhaps when these issues are clearly delineated within the context of psychological assessment, the appearance of a paradigm clash may be found to be illusory.

CONSTRUCT VALIDITY

Environmental assessment cannot progress if researchers eschew theoretical formulations and conceptual analysis. Observational and technical assessments of places entail *constructs* about the nature of environments. Even the appraisal of adequacy of measurement in the assessment of places inescapably requires attention to the analysis of constructs and the interrelations among constructs.

Figure 23.1 presents the construct point of view in psychological assessment (Cronbach & Meehl, 1955; Torgerson, 1958; Wiggins, 1973). The lines represent operational definitions of indicants of constructs, whereas the double lines connect indicants to constructs. Thus the results of our touring panel's assessment of 40 rural places provide indicants (C'_{1-5}) of constructs of active (C_1), beautiful (C_2), craggy (C_3), light (C_4) and spacious (C_5). To appraise the adequacy of the generalizability of the measures across occasions, for example, we must articulate the degree of stability entailed by the constructs of active or of light.

The single solid lines connecting the constructs represent selected definitional or theoretical relations among constructs. To gauge the adequacy of the discriminant validity of our indicants of these five con-

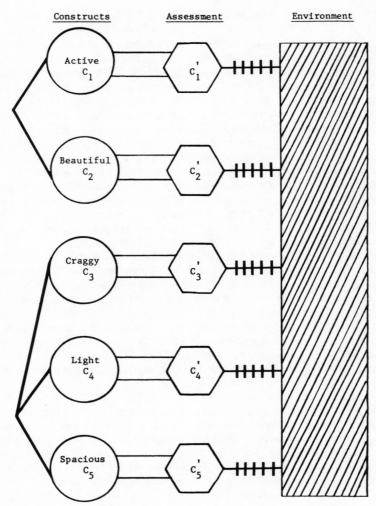

Figure 23.1. Construct point of view in environmental assessment.

structs, we must posit the conceptual relations *among* the constructs. For example, do the constructs of light and spacious lead us to anticipate that their real-world covariation is moderately high, slight, or entirely independent?

These illustrations draw on our example of observational assessment, which employs panels of observers applying ordinary language terms to samples of places. But what about the relation of this form of environmental assessment to other technical assessment systems such as those drawn from the metrics of weights and measures, geomorphology, organizational behavior, or ecological psychology? This question remains the most controversial and least resolved issue in environmental assessment.

A construct might be measured by two or more indicant systems. Thus Dawes (1977) demonstrates that panels of observers and the metrics of length provide close to completely convergent assessments for the heights of a sample of psychology faculty members. Zube and colleagues (1975) have shown that a set of geomorphological and land use indices converges, to a lesser extent, with assessments of scenic quality of a sample of New England settings made by a panel of observers. But because convergence across measurement systems is typically far from complete, conceptual issues cannot be avoided. For example, should the indicants drawn from one measurement system have conceptual priority? That is, the physical measure may take precedence in assessing height, whereas the observer assessment is considered an estimate. The panel judgments of scenic quality may constitute the criterion, whereas geomorphological and land use indices offer potentially useful predictors. But what about constructs such as *spacious* or *active*? It is clear that some cases require individual analyses and formulations of the specific constructs involved, with neither one taking precedence over the other unless dictated by empirical or logistical constraints.

A broader position asserts that other technical systems of assessment always hold priority over observer-based assessments. This stance implies that even constructs that can be measured with consensus and sensitivity by observational assessment have standing only when technical indicants are readily available or conceptually feasible to check on or "validate" them. This issue bears on a considerable number of constructs potentially relevant to environmental description. For example, although some scientists hold out the ultimate feasibility of physical/mathematical indicants for constructs such as *craggy*, the present state of ecological optics and physics does not afford such transformations (Gibson, 1959, 1966). Explorations of the metrics of form (Michels & Zusne, 1965) and the "new psychophysics" of other descriptive constructs (Attneave, 1962; Hochberg & McAlister, 1958) have found that physical indicants are far from simple and require complex, nonlinear combinations of simply measurable physical variables. These indicants must then be thoroughly cross-validated and conceptualized (Weinstein, 1976b).

One orientation to this issue is that the interpretational problems presented by the various levels of meanings in observational assessments suggest that such assessments have "nothing (or virtually nothing) to do with the environment" (Daniel & Ittelson, 1981-) and that their validity must be called into question (Danford & Willems, 1975). Based on this position, their use is a source of futility in environmental psychology and a basis for a crisis in the field.

An alternative orientation (Craik, 1981; Ward & Russell, 1981) sees observer-based indicants of environmental constructs as basic data of environmental psychology. This orientation views observational assessments as sharing issues of measurement common to other technical systems (Craik & Feimer, 1979) and refers to a hard-earned array of sophisticated concepts and methods for interpreting the findings they generate (Craik, 1971, 1981; Wiggins, 1973).

In summary, construct validity raises the question of whether the indicant system measures what it purports to measure. To address it, we must give more conceptual attention to descriptive and evaluative constructs in environmental assessment. Promising developments can be found (Carp & Carp, 1982b; Daniel & Vining, 1983; Wohlwill, 1983).

23.2.3. Predictive Environmental Assessments and Utility in Applied Contexts

Two principal kinds of prediction are supported by environmental assessment: predictions based on empirical generalizations and simulation-based predictions.

Predictions Based on Empirical Generalizations

When descriptive and evaluative environmental assessments are available on a sample of places, the basis is established for seeking empirical generalizations. Thus the question can be addressed: What descriptive attributes of places tend to covary with evaluative appraisal of them?

These potential predictors of evaluative assessments of places can be derived from either technical or observational descriptive assessments. Thus Zube and colleagues (1975) identified correlates of the criterion *scenic quality*, based on technical assessments of landform and land use (e.g., relative evaluation), and Appleyard (1969) established correlates of a criterion measure for buildings in Ciudad Guayana (how well known they were), based on observational assessments (e.g., form qualities).

The development of predictive knowledge based on empirical generalizations does not require the use of simulation techniques. Shafer and Thompson (1968) identified potential predictors of the frequency of use of campsites within the Adirondack State Park in New York State based on on-site technical assessments (e.g., distance to the edge of the nearest lake). However, Shafer and associates (Shafer, 1969; Shafer et al., 1969; Shafer & Tooby, 1973) have also identified potential predictors of landscape preferences based on technical assessments (e.g., perimeter of immediate vegetation) that did use simulated (photographic) presentations of the scenes. The recourse of simulation techniques is logistical (e.g., convenience, cost) rather than necessary in this research approach. That is, presumably their descriptive content measures refer to attributes of the on-site vistas and could be assessed on-site.

Claims for empirical generalizations require the

confirmation of extended replications. Multivariate statistical analyses especially raise the possibility of capitalizing on chance relations within complex data sets and thus call for cross-validational analyses (Weinstein, 1976b). Furthermore, empirical generalizations developed through the use of simulation techniques depend on specific tests of their relevance to on-site relationships or on general evidence of the psychological effectiveness of the simulations used.

The search for empirical generalizations, their exploration, and their function as a probe to theoretical formulation constitute basic processes in scientific research. Gauging the practical utility of empirical generalizations derived from environmental assessments evokes additional issues related to the specific contexts of their application.

It is instructive to consider the comparison between the decision contexts of personnel selection and environmental selection. In personnel selection, a large number of persons are typically assessed, and a smaller number are selected for positions whose predicted criterion placement is above a specified cutting score. The gathering of descriptive assessments is more readily accomplished (e.g., a few hours of testing and information recording), whereas evaluative assessments are more difficult (e.g., several months of trial performance of all candidates in the position at issue). Finally, the descriptive attributes of the persons (e.g., intelligence, manual dexterity, interpersonal effectiveness) are not readily manipulated and are seen as only somewhat professionally manipulable (e.g., training programs).

In contrast, the applied contexts of environmental assessment typically entail a smaller sample of places (or alternative forms, designs, or plans for proposed places) and often only one final candidate or option is sought in the selection process. Typically, the gathering of evaluative assessments is readily achieved, whereas descriptive environmental assessment is more time-consuming and demanding. Finally, the descriptive attributes of places (e.g., wall color, amount of vegetation cover) are at least somewhat manipulable and, indeed, are seen as professionally manipulable.

In personnel selection, the application of assessment results has generated a number of decision tools such as selection ratios, optimal cutting scores on the predicted criterion measures, base rates, and sequential classification strategies (Cronbach & Gleser, 1965; Wiggins, 1973). In environmental decision contexts, these aids to decision making can be employed when large numbers of varied places are being considered for selection or other attention (e.g., preservation, rehabilitation). These environ-

mental decision contexts might include the management of large tracts of land (such as those under the jurisdiction of the U.S. Forest Service and U.S. Bureau of Land Management), urban preservation and rehabilitation programs, and the planning and design of residential units.

In other cases, the utility of empirical generalizations linking descriptive attributes to evaluative criteria can be found in their function as a source for general standards and guidelines. These generalizations can be derived directly from large-scale analyses (e.g., Carp & Carp, 1982b) or from inductive analyses of large numbers of case studies (e.g., Cooper, 1972). The rationale for these undertakings is that although evaluative assessments are often more readily gathered than descriptive assessments, it is those aspects of places referred to by descriptive predictors that are considered or manipulated in the planning, design, and management of places.

Within this perspective, three final points about the use of empirical generalizations in environmental decision making warrant notice. First, guidelines and standards based on technical predictors of environmental criteria may be seen as, or become, constraints on the originality of planners and designers. Thus provision for an open system of potential predictors is important, provided that the new descriptive attributes to be considered are shown to display criterion relevance. Second, the utility of observer-based descriptive attributes and predictors has been challenged. It is held that environmental constructs that have observer-based measures but no completely convergent technical measures fail to provide guidance for environmental planning, design, and management. However, suppose, for example, that *cozy* is found to be a predictor of a criterion in an assessment of restaurants and *cohesive* is found to be a criterion predictor in an assessment of psychiatric wards. Although direct alternative technical measures of these observer-based descriptive attributes may not be available, the craft wisdom of interior design and of ward management may provide a number of strategies and different avenues to the generation of these qualities in places. Thus the descriptive correlates would provide useful information for decision making. Finally, in the case of both technical and observational predictors of criterion measures, the magnitude of predictive validity is likely to remain modest. That is, some aspects of environmental quality will not be captured by the predictors available. Therefore, too tightly circumscribed standards and selection guidelines, over a long term, pose a danger of eliminating important elements of environmental quality.

Simulation-Based Prediction

The environmental planning, design, and management professions deal with the manipulation of the environment and the creation of new and novel places. Predictions based on empirical generalizations gained in scientific research can guide the formulation of specific environmental transformations. However, these predictive assertions hold over the general trend and not necessarily for the particular case, especially for a place embodying a complex configuration of multiple descriptive attributes. Yet assessing the potential impacts of specific new places is an important phase of environmental decision making in everyday professional contexts. Postoccupancy evaluative assessments can be conducted to appraise specific projects. However, at that point the commitment of resources has already been made, although some mitigation of negative impacts and fine tuning are often still feasible.

Simulation-based predictions make forecasts of a potential place's attributes and impacts possible at the prechange (e.g., preconstruction, premanagement) stage of the decision-making process (Appleyard & Craik, 1978; McKechnie, 1977; Sheppard, 1982a, 1982b; Zube, 1980). Some form of project simulation (e.g., sketches) has traditionally been part of the planning and design process (Appleyard, 1977; Cuff, 1982). More recent technical advances in environmental simulation, including modelscope and videotape techniques and computer graphics, hold the promise of improvements within the planning and design stage.

The combination of environmental assessment and environmental simulation also offers a means of increasing public participation in the decision-making process (Appleyard & Craik, 1974; Bosselmann & Craik, in press). An illustration of these procedures is a visual impact assessment of alternate designs and alignments for a bridge that will carry an interstate highway (I-220) over Cross Lake, in the vicinity of Shreveport, Louisiana, in the southeastern United States. Based on a visual resource inventory of the area, three-dimensional scale models of the bridge alternatives were constructed, and a representative sample of viewing points from around the lakeside was selected for visual simulation. Use of the modelscope apparatus permitted 16-mm motion picture filming of eye-level views of the "before" and "after" scenes for the alternatives. Eight samples of residents located at different vantage points around the lakeshore plus samples of recreational users of the lake and potential commuters on the highway were recruited through survey sampling procedures to participate in special environmental assessment sessions in Shreveport. These observational assessments entailed judgments of the natural beauty of the scenes, degree of visual intrusion of the bridge, and personal preferences for the options and related dimensions (Atkins & Blair, 1983). The aim of a visual assessment of this kind is not to select an alternative but to provide a forecast of viewer response at the prechange stage and an accounting of public preferences, as a means of informing the decision-making process.

The use of structured assessment sessions and recruited samples seeks to maximize the representativeness of visual impact assessment findings. Simulated previews of proposed projects can be disseminated in less structured contexts as well, such as at public hearings and on television. Environmental simulation techniques can also be used to (1) illustrate basic planning issues such as zoning ordinances (Bosselmann & Gerdes, 1980), (2) facilitate public participation in the early planning and design process that generates alternatives (Appleyard, Bosselmann, Klock, & Schmidt, 1979), (3) communicate to the public new, untried possibilities such as the use of diverters and controllers in managing traffic in residential neighborhoods (Appleyard, 1981; Bosselmann & O'Hare, 1983), and (4) examine land use compatibility judgments for projects systematically varied in descriptive attributes such as color, size, and texture (Wohlwill, 1978).

APPRAISING THE EFFECTIVENESS OF ENVIRONMENTAL SIMULATION

Environmental simulation provides a means of conveying complex, large-scale environments to individuals without the necessity of direct, in situ presentation. The chief advantages of simulation over direct presentation of environmental settings are threefold: (1) convenient presentation of a complex environment without the need of transporting observers to the setting, (2) the capability of gauging responses to environments that do not yet exist, and (3) the opportunity for systematic experimental manipulation of the environment (Appleyard, 1977; Craik, 1983; Feimer, 1984; McKechnie, 1977).

The importance of these factors lies largely in their potential for achieving economic efficiency in environmental design and for providing a better understanding of the nature of human–environment interaction. First, as distance between one location and the setting of interest becomes greater, the time and expense of transporting observers to the setting, for either research or applied purposes, increases substantially. In many cases, some form of simulation may achieve significant savings. Second, the possibility of accurately forecasting human responses to the large-scale environment through simulation has important economic, social, and psychological implications, by facilitating public review and participation and by anticipating negative public reactions to projects. Finally, the opportunity for experimental manipulation of environmental settings provides an unparalleled opportunity for advances in our understanding of the relationship between physical features of the large-scale environment and their psychological impact.

The use of simulation-based predictions in the environmental decision-making process requires the assumption that responses to the simulated places are comparable to and forecast responses to real or "actual" places with sufficient accuracy. The question "How good is the simulation?" is central to the use of simulation-based predictions and is no less important when simulation is used for logistical reasons in efforts to establish empirical generalizations.

Some progress has been made in analyzing the nature of the question posed by the appraisal of environmental simulation effectiveness (Bosselmann & Craik, in press, McKechnie, 1977; Sheppard, 1982a, 1982b). Before turning to empirical findings on simulation appraisal, consideration of the structure and boundaries of the problem is warranted.

The question "How good is environmental simulation?" generates a formidable research agenda. The complexity of what this research does address must be appreciated, and the issues that it does not address must be recognized (Bosselmann & Craik, in press).

Typical applications of environmental simulation include (1) the presentation of a proposed place to the general public at an environmental hearing and (2) the presentation of systematically selected places to participants in an environmental psychological research project. Almost always in the first case, and often in the second, the places are new to the observers. Thus the research question can be rephrased as "How well do responses to the simulation predict first impressions of real-world places?" The predictive value of first-time impressions, whether based on direct or simulated presentations, in forecasting later adaptations, accommodations, and use–activity patterns regarding places is an important scientific topic but is not a directly related issue of simulation appraisal.

Even this limited reformulation of the research question has many facets and, as a central topic in the study of environmental perception, must be placed within that framework. Any specific appraisal of environmental simulation raises the issue of the generalizability of findings across (1) types of simulation, (2) conditions of encounter with places, (3) categories of places, (4) populations of observers, and (5) modes of response. Finally, the data analytic strategies available in this kind of research offer different ways of gauging the effectiveness of simulation (Bosselmann & Craik, in press; Craik, 1983). For example, the overall congruence of the descriptive and evaluative responses to a place yielded by direct and simulated presentations can be estimated. Or any significant contrasts between direct and simulated conditions in the mean levels of specific descriptive and evaluative responses can be delineated. Or the simulation effects, if any, can be placed in a comparative context, gauging their relative magnitude against those effects due to characteristics of the observers, prior familiarity with the places, and so forth.

In applications within environmental planning and design, an additional procedural option arises in the appraisal of simulation effectiveness. In that context, a proposed place can be selected, a simulation of it developed, impressions of the place based on the simulation gathered, and later, when the project has been implemented, on-site impressions of the place can also be gathered. The problem posed by this research design is that the planning and design process is incremental and subject to ever-changing financial and institutional modifications. What is depicted in simulation at Time 1 may not be what is eventually implemented at Time 2. Thus the psychological effectiveness of simulation and the accuracy and completeness of information for generating simulations of the proposed place can be confounded. The concurrent comparison of simulated and on-site responses to available places forms a clearer basis for gauging the psychological effectiveness of environmental simulation. However, the issue of accuracy of information for developing simulations in the planning and design context does potentially limit the utility of environmental simulation in the decision-making process and warrants further study (Sheppard, 1982a, 1982b).

Note must also be taken of what the question "How good is environmental simulation?" is not about. Simulation appraisal studies are not aimed at resolving issues regarding the nature of the processes involved in environmental perception and cognition. Danford and associates (Danford & Willems, 1975; Danford, Starr, & Willems, 1979; Starr & Danford, 1978) report highly similar descriptions of a law school building when based on some form of presentation and on information about the function and location of a building (e.g., law school, student club). In addition, no differentiation in descriptions was found when three kinds of information were presented regarding the function of the building (i.e., law school, community mental health center, general architectural setting). Daniel and Ittelson (1981) and Lowenthal and Riel (1972) have reported similar relationships among descriptive variables when based on on-site or simulated presentations. These studies address important questions concerning observational assessment discussed earlier in this chapter but not questions specific to simulation appraisal. The issues include the veridicality of implicative meaning, the degree of stereotypic accuracy of cognitive categories related to the environment, and the extent of differentiation prevailing among environmental cognitive categories. All of these processes presumably bear on the perception and cognition of places when directly presented via on-site visits as well as when presented via simulation. Inferential processes are at work in forming on-site impressions of places as well as in forming impressions based on simulations. These issues are not distinctively related to environmental simulation or its appraisal.

Nevertheless, Danford and Willems (1975) hold that the similarity of descriptions of the law school building across the conditions of (1) verbal label only, (2) on-site tour, and (3) photo-slide tour points to a lack of discriminant validity of observational assessments and undermines any appraisal of simulation based on the similarity of results for the on-site tour and photo-slide tour. However, the analysis of convergent and discriminant validity (Campbell & Fiske, 1959) deals with constructs and their measurement and not with simulation appraisal. That is, across different measurement methods for *a sample* of entities, the set of measures of the same construct should intercorrelate highly, whereas the conceptually anticipated pattern of differentiations *among constructs* should be found across the set of measurement methods. Simulation techniques can constitute a source of variability of methods in the analysis of convergent and discriminant validity, but the constructs are at issue, not the simulation techniques. Having studied only one place, Danford and associates could not conduct convergent and discriminant analyses.

In the appraisal of environmental simulation, the degree of comparability of responses to on-site and simulated presentations of places is at issue. When comparable findings are obtained, they do warrant critical scrutiny. One possible source of artifactual comparability is lack of sensitivity of measurement. That is, if the measures display no variability across a sample of places, all assessed on-site, for example,

then lack of variability between on-site and simulated places is probably not informative. Sensitivity of measurement is gauged through adequate differential assessments for a sample of places encountered via a given medium of presentation. Requiring differences across media of presentation as evidence of measurement adequacy, as Danford and Willems (1975) seem to call for, clearly begs the very question of simulation appraisal. Because the Danford and Willems (1975) data set is based on a single place, it would also not permit estimation of sensitivity. Ward and Russell (1981), for example, report evidence of sensitivity of measurement for the data set used in the Daniel and Ittelson (1981) analysis of conceptual similarity.

EMPIRICAL STUDIES OF SIMULATION EFFECTIVENESS

The range of environmental simulation media available for both applied and research purposes is broad and includes such media as artists' or architects' drawings or schematics, scale models, photographs or photo slides, computer-constructed images (displayed as sketches and in video or photo presentation), and techniques combining some of these methods such as photo rendition and model scopes (Appleyard, 1977; Appleyard & Craik, 1978; Bosselmann & Craik, in press; Craik, 1968, 1971; McKechnie, 1977; Sheppard, 1982b; U.S. Department of Interior, Bureau of Land Management, 1980) (Table 23.3). The latter two techniques, combining aspects of other simulation methods, are particularly promising because of their capability of vividly representing environments that either no longer exist due to modification or are planned but do not yet exist. Photo rendition consists of the superimposition or removal of built or natural features of the environment through the application of dyes, paints, and multiple exposure photography. Model scopes consist of either single perspective, multiple perspective, or motion picture photography of scale models. Other methods that allow pre- and postconstruction comparisons are presently less capable of providing perceptually realistic representations, often providing a "cartoonish" or "artistic" appearance (e.g., computer-constructed images, artist and architects' sketches and drawings).

McKechnie has presented a scheme for characterizing the various forms of environmental simulation along two dimensions: (1) conceptual-perceptual and (2) static-dynamic. The conceptual-perceptual dimension refers to the degree to which the simulation provides the same sensory stimulation that would be experienced in the actual environment from a given

Table 23.3. Varieties of Environmental Simulation

Maps
Floor plans
Sketches, renderings, perspective drawings
Photographs (prints, photo slides; black-white, color; single, multiple sequence)
Photo renderings, photo montages
Film (black-white, color)
Videotape (black-white, color)
Models (miniaturized, full-scale)
Modelscope images (photographs, photo slides, films, videotapes)
Computer graphics (images displayed as sketches, videotapes)

position or perspective. At the perceptual pole of this continuum, simulation media attempt to "reproduce" iconic representation, although often perceptual simulation focuses on only one modality—typically vision. Examples of simulations falling on the perceptual end of the continuum include two-dimensional sketches by artists, architects, and computers, photographs or films, and scale models. The conceptual pole of the conceptual-perceptual continuum represents a relatively high level of abstraction in the representation of the environment, normally consisting of highly stylized and abstract qualities. Maps, floor plans, and verbal descriptions are examples of conceptual simulations.

The static-dynamic dimension of McKechnie's model represents the degree to which simulation offers single, unitary perspectives of the environment, or changing multiple-perspective views. At the extreme of the static pole of the continuum, the environment would be represented by a single perspective such as a single sketch, computer simulation, or photograph. As one moves toward the dynamic pole, the number and frequency of perspectives increase, until at the extreme, apparent motion may be provided, as through films or videos of movement through the actual environments or scale models.

A third dimension—scale—might usefully extend McKechnie's taxonomy for environmental simulations. Particularly in the case of physical models, scale represents an important dimension of variation among simulations. A physical model can range from very small scale (e.g., thumb-sized buildings) to full scale mock-up versions of proposed or experimental environments. Another example is the case of photographic simulations, which can be presented in the form of small prints or full-wall slide projections.

In terms of McKechnie's (1977) taxonomy, the literature in environmental psychology has focused primarily on perceptual (iconic) representations, and although appraisals of both static and dynamic media have been conducted, the greater emphasis has been on static modes of simulation. This literature is reviewed briefly next with successive consideration of static and dynamic simulation techniques.

STATIC SIMULATIONS

PHOTOGRAPHIC REPRESENTATIONS. Research concerning the effectiveness of static modes of simulation has focused primarily on an appraisal of the congruence in descriptive and evaluative responses between direct, on-site presentations, and presentations of photographs or photo slides, models, and sketches. Within this class of media, the greatest emphasis has been given to an appraisal of the effectiveness of color photographs and photo slides. Most studies to date (e.g., Brush, 1979; Daniel & Boster, 1976; Garling, 1970; Hershberger & Cass, 1974; Shafer & Richards, 1974; Zube et al., 1975) indicate relatively high levels of correspondence in responses to color photographs or photo slides and on-site presentations, both for natural settings and those with evidence of human influences (ranging from vegetation manipulation to buildings and other human artifacts). Studies comparing on-site responses to single or multiple color photographs or photo slides of the same sites have reported product-moment and rank-order correlation coefficients ranging from +.67 to +.98 (Brush, 1979; Daniel & Boster, 1976; Hershberger & Cass, 1974; Shafer & Richards, 1974; Zube et al., 1975), indicating an appreciable degree of simulation effectiveness for the response domains examined.

Although both single and multiple photographs and photo slides appear to be effective in simulating environmental settings, it is reasonable to expect differences between single and multiple photographic representations and between photo slides and prints. Differences between single and multiple photographic representations might be expected on two accounts. First, single photos are limited in terms of field of view and perspective. Individuals observing a place on-site are almost always free to look and move about somewhat, giving them a variety of views and perspectives, even of a relatively small focal point. Multiple photos, presumably, would be better able to represent these differential views and perspectives. In addition, the increase in reliability resulting from the composite indices constructed for multiple photo comparisons is likely to yield higher congruence coefficients.

Differences between photo slides and prints would be expected largely because of the difference in visual angle and resolution. Photoprints are typically presented on a small surface size, usually no larger than 8" × 10" (.56 sq ft), whereas photo slides are often projected on a much larger surface of several square feet (e.g., a relatively small projection area of 2' × 2' 11.5" for a 35-mm photo slide yields 6 sq ft). Thus the larger surface area of projected transparencies is much closer to actual scale than that of most photographic prints, and consequently, higher congruence might be expected between on-site responses and those to projected transparencies than between on-site responses and photographic prints.

Research findings concerning both of these issues are somewhat ambiguous at present. There are few studies that have reported on these issues, and widely divergent measures, analyses, and samples of settings make comparisons across studies tenuous. Where multiple versus single photographic representations are concerned, the range of variation in coefficients of congruence is similar for both forms of simulation. Congruence estimates for single photographic representations range from +.67 to +.97 (Brush, 1979; Hershberger & Cass, 1974; Shafer & Richards, 1974; Zube et al., 1975) and those for multiple representations from +.79 to +.98 (Daniel & Boster, 1976; Hershberger & Cass, 1974). Hershberger and Cass (1974), providing comparisons for a range of media, including single and multiple photographic representations of eight housing developments, report average congruence coefficients between on-site and simulation ratings ranging from +.72 to +.79. However, specific comparisons between single and multiple representations were not reported. On the whole, the findings from this collection of studies suggest that both single and multiple photographic representations of sites provide adequate simulation effectiveness in terms of the congruence for these descriptive and evaluative responses.

Evidence concerning differences between photographs and photo slides is no more informative. Direct comparisons are typically not afforded because only one mode of photographic representation is used in a given study. Across studies, the range of coefficients reported for photographs (Shafer & Richards, 1974; Zube et al., 1975) and projected photo slides (Brush, 1979; Hershberger & Cass, 1974; Shafer & Richards, 1974) approximates the same narrow band reported for comparisons of single and multiple photographic representations. However, there is one study that does permit a direct comparison of color photographs and projected photo slides. Shafer and Richards (1974) compared responses to semantic differential ratings of eight sites by independent groups of photography students assigned to one of three presentation conditions: (1) on-site, (2) photograph, and (3) projected transparency. After factor analyzing the semantic differential scales of the on-site appraisals for each site, they compared the two simulation media by examining the overlap in their distributions with those of on-site appraisals, using the scales representing the factors of each site. The proportion of agreement between the on-site and two simulation conditions range from 16 to 100% for the photographic transparency condition and from 11 to 100% for the photograph condition. The average proportion of agreement between the on-site and the simulation conditions was 50% and 38% for the photographic transparencies and photographs, respectively, suggesting that generally, projected photo slides provide somewhat better simulations than do photographs.

A final issue concerns the use of color versus black-white photographic representations. Color is obviously an important environmental feature that can usually be adequately represented in color photographs and photo slides. The evidence concerning this issue is scant.

Seaton and Collins (1972) gauged the effects of presentation media on semantic differential responses to four buildings on the University of British Columbia campus. The media used were (1) on-site, (2) color photographs, (3) black-white photographs, and (4) scale models. Analysis of variance reveals a main effect for a building, indicating differential effects for variation in settings and, thus, sensitivity of measurement. A building by medium interaction is also significant. In comparing the pattern of means across buildings and media, Seaton and Collins infer that color photographs are more realistic than either black-white photographs or scale models and that both of the latter media tend to blur differences among buildings. Howard, Mylarski, and Sauer (1972), on the other hand, report a comparison of on-site semantic differential ratings for six building interior spaces with both color and black-white photo slides. One-way analysis of variance for simulation modes reveals few significant differences (17.9%). Howard and associates attribute most of those effects to differences between the on-site and the two simulation conditions, concluding that although meaningful differences among media exist, there is little difference between color and black-white photo slides. The question of how great the differences between color and black-white photographic representations are remains very much at issue.

SKETCHES AND SCALE MODELS. Despite the pervasive use of sketches and scale models in architecture and environmental design, little emphasis has been given to an exploration of the efficacy of these simulation media. An exception is the use of models in mixed mode simulations such as model scopes which will be discussed subsequently in the section on dynamic simulation. Evidence concerning the effectiveness of scale models standing on their own comes from studies by Seaton and Collins (1972) and Lau (1970). The Seaton and Collins (1972) study, discussed previously, suggests that models and black-white photographs appear to provide less discrimination among buildings than do color photographs and on-site presentations, although the degree of these differences is not ascertained. Lau (1970), in a study of the effects of indoor illumination under conditions of direct presentation and a one-sixth scale model, found that ratings of pleasantness and gloom are highly congruent under both conditions (reported r's = +.90 and +.96, respectively). It appears that scale models may be effective simulations, but their range and degree of efficacy are clearly at issue.

Research concerning the effectiveness of sketches, or renderings, of environmental settings must also be inferred from the findings of a limited number of studies. One of these (Garling, 1970) consists of a comparison of judged size and depth under four viewing conditions: (1) on-site, (2) color photograph, (3) detailed perspective drawing, and (4) nondetailed perspective drawing. The obtained relationship of judged size and depth to actual measures of those dimensions is virtually the same under different simulation conditions, namely a negatively accelerating power function. However, a metric directly comparing the congruence of responses in the various conditions was not presented but rather was inferred from the similarity of the obtained power functions.

Another pair of studies provides a comparison of sketches with other simulation media but does not offer a comparison with on-site experience. Schomaker (1978) compared scenic beauty ratings of 48 color photo slides to black-white, hand-drawn sketches made from the slides. He found that although ratings tended to be lower for the sketches, the two sets of ratings were highly correlated (r = +.78). Killeen and Buhyoff (1983) report a comparison of preference judgments for three landscape scenes presented in one of three modes: (1) color photo slide, (2) artist black-white sketch of topographic features, and (3) computer-generated black-white graphic sketches of topographic features. Preferences for sketches and photo slides are significantly correlated (r = +.71) as are preferences for the artist's sketches and the computer-generated sketches (r = +.85). However, preferences for the photo slides and the computer-generated sketches are not significantly correlated. Given that only topographic features were represented by simulations in the Killeen and Buhyoff study (i.e., color and vegetative form were missing), it is not surprising that the two sketch conditions are more highly correlated than the sketch–photograph comparisons.

Whether or not congruence of responses would be as high for sketches and on-site evaluations as it is for hand-drawn sketches and photo slides remains an open question. Because photo slides and sketches are more similar to one another than they are to real settings in at least two respects, namely scale and surface dimensionality (i.e., photo slides and sketches are two-dimensional surfaces, whereas real settings are three-dimensional), it is reasonable to expect less congruence between sketches and on-site evaluations than between sketches and photo slides.

DYNAMIC SIMULATION

Research concerning dynamic modes of simulation has focused largely on the effectiveness of motion picture film or videotape displays of actual environments or scale models. Although few studies including a systematic appraisal of these media have emerged, the small number available suggest that both films and videotape displays result in descriptive and evaluative responses that are comparable to those obtained for direct, on-site presentations (Craik, 1983; Feimer, 1984; Hershberger & Cass, 1974). However, evidence concerning the comparability of cognitive and behavioral responses under these simulation media is less clear, as is their general comparative effectiveness with other simulation media.

Among the first published studies appraising motion picture films and video displays as simulation media is an analysis by Hershberger and Cass (1974). They compared a variety of media, including color slides, color and black-white Super 8 film, and black-white videotape. They found that all media were comparable to on-site evaluations, with average correlations of semantic differential responses to eight housing developments ranging from +.72 to +.79. Although films and video presentations may provide fuller and more complex information, findings on the appraisal of their effectiveness fall within a range similar to that found for static modes of simulation.

A comprehensive evaluation of the effects of dynamic simulation media on descriptive and evaluative responses comes from the Berkeley Environmental Simulation Laboratory (Appleyard & Craik, 1978; Bryant, 1984; Bosselmann & Craik, in press; Craik, 1983; Feimer, 1984). This facility consists of a periscope-type lens probe that can be guided through a scale model to simulate movement through the environment using computer-controlled stop-frame cinematography (for more complete descriptions, see Appleyard & Craik, 1978; Bosselmann & Craik, in press; McKechnie, 1977). The initial appraisal of this model-scope technique consisted of a comparison of observer responses to a geographical locale in northern California for four media of presentation: (1) direct on-site automobile tour, (2) film of automobile tour, (3) film of simulated automobile tour through scale model, and (4) black-white video of simulated automobile tour through scale model. In a comparison of descriptive and evaluative responses using a wide variety of posttour measures, Craik (1983) reports a high degree of congruence among media. For example, cross-media correlations of mean placement for 67 items of the Regional Q-Sort Deck, a technique assessing descriptive responses to an environmental context (e.g., has spectacular views, has residences well separated from one another, is a dangerous place for children) ranged from +.93 to +.98. Similarly, cross-media correlations of mean ratings for 28 items assessing satisfaction with residential attributes of the tour area were also high, ranging from +.89 to +.96. Finally, Feimer (1984), in a comparison of factors affecting perceptions of the tour area, found that media alone never accounted for more than 3% of the variance in any of three factorially derived cross-procedure variables (general evaluation, attractiveness, activity level).

Despite the high communality in responses across media reported by Craik (1983) and Feimer (1984), some differences did emerge. Craik reports an array of specific differences between the direct, on-site automobile tour and the other media. In general, the pattern of differences observed suggests that, in contrast to the on-site automobile tour: (1) the simulation media create somewhat less pleasant and alert mood states, (2) the scale-model tour conditions result in somewhat less satisfactory appraisal of factors relating to maintenance, attractiveness, and environmental quality than the on-site tour, and (3) the black-white model video results in somewhat less accurate comprehension of content and detail concerning physical attributes and spatial characteristics.

These findings are consistent with those of Feimer (1984) concerning the set of cross-procedural variables. In reference to media effects alone, Feimer found that (1) the direct, on-site automobile tour resulted in a more favorable evaluation of the site than did the model film and the model video, (2) the film of the automobile tour resulted in a more favorable evaluation of the site than did the model video, and (3) the model video condition resulted in a lower perceived activity level than did the other media conditions, which did not differ significantly from one another. The pattern of findings reported in these two studies suggests that, on the whole, as the medium of presentation becomes more impoverished, individuals may respond somewhat less favorably to the display and begin to miss some detailed aspects of the environment being represented.

The research on dynamic simulation media described to this point has focused largely on descriptive and evaluative responses, with little emphasis on cognitive and behavioral responses. Few studies have used cognitive and behavioral measures. However, for measures of performance on spatial orientation tasks (i.e., recognition, map placement, number of points in map sketches), Bryant (1984) found significant decreases for simulation (model film, model video) compared to direct auto tour presentations.

In a similar study, Baggen and Feimer (1984) compared scaled interpoint distance estimates and route configuration responses under conditions of (1) an automobile tour of an area, (2) a film of an automobile tour (i.e., simulation with apparent motion), and (3) sequential multiple photo slide presentations simulating a tour (i.e., simulation without apparent motion). They found that the automobile tour and film resulted in greater response accuracy than did the slide presentations, but there were no differences between the auto tour and the film of the auto tour.

In both of these studies, the tour area was presented only once to the research participants (Craik, 1983). Perhaps repeated presentations of the tour would attenuate these differences in spatial cognition (Kozlowski & Bryant, 1977), but this possibility remains to be tested.

A study of driver simulation by Edwards, Hahn, and Fleishman (1977) compared the performance of taxi drivers in real-world driving experience with their performance in two driving simulators representing similar driving conditions. One simulator consisted of the presentation of a silent film while the subject was seated in a mock-up cab and the other of a sound film in a mock-up cab that included coordinated motion. They found that simulator driving "errors" in such factors as speed, steering, signaling, and braking were uncorrelated with actual street performance. Although conclusions concerning the effectiveness of dynamic simulations for cognitive and behavioral criteria based on these studies are clearly premature, it does appear that environmental simulation may not provide as high a level of comparability for those types of measures as it does for descriptive and evaluative responses.

Finally, note can be taken of the borderline case of the use of full-scale mock-up versions of proposed environments in preconstruction evaluation (King, Marans, & Solomon, 1982) and in user participation in the planning and design process (Lawrence, 1982). These settings fall between the categories of actual environments and simulations. However, because they occur in laboratory or temporary contexts and may not be fully detailed in their materials, their use raises the same issues of descriptive, evaluative, and behavioral comparability as those generated by application of the perceptual forms of environmental simulations reviewed in this section. Furthermore, their full-scale, three-dimensional character opens up interesting possibilities for extending the study of behavioral equivalence between simulated and ordinary-use environments.

23.3. ENVIRONMENTAL ASSESSMENT AS SCIENCE AND PRACTICE

Within environmental psychology, the task of environmental assessment is often encountered while en route to some other destination. Any research study that manipulates, contrasts, or specifies environmental characteristics entails the informal or formal use of environmental assessment. Many applied contexts for environmental psychology such as visual impact assessments and postoccupancy evaluations also require implicit or explicit uses of environmental assessment.

Informed application of environmental assessment as a technique presupposes a grasp of its logical and strategic foundations. This brief review of the structure of concepts, methods, and issues reveals environmental assessment to be an important substantive area of scientific research within environmental psychology.

Constructs and their measurement are closely in-

terlinked in any environmental assessment. Yet attention to the conceptual analysis of descriptive and evaluative constructs has been inadequate, especially with regard to those constructs drawn from ordinary language.

Close conceptual analyses must be joined to empirical research that is more programmatic in design and cumulative in outcome. Much more must be learned about the extent to which assessments of places generalize across contexts, occasions, methods, and, if appropriate, observers. The move toward standard methods of assessment warrants encouragement. However, lack of consensus or simply the variety of relevant environmental units of analysis may continue to fragment research in this area into subfields dealing with, for example, landscape assessment, residential assessment, organizational assessment, and so forth. In any event, the agenda of needed empirical research remains formidable. The paucity of scientific findings on the psychological effectiveness and functioning of simulation techniques amply illustrates this point.

The role that environmental assessment plays in practical decision making is a function of changing societal forces. In the United States, the legislative and administrative mandates flowing from the National Environmental Policy Act (NEPA) and its offshoots created a function for environmental assessment in monitoring environmental quality, evaluating projects and programs, and providing feedback to officials and the public. Subsequent trends in society may expand, diminish, or change these opportunities for application.

Nevertheless, environmental assessment offers potential usefulness at stages throughout the planning and design process. Environmental assessments based on preconstruction simulations can provide guidance in the selection of plans and designs. Postoccupancy environmental assessments can contribute to empirical generalizations that also offer selection guidelines for subsequent decision contexts. Greater attention to sensitivity of measurement, generalizability, and validity will advance the level of technical standards in applied environmental assessment and its utility. Because applied environmental assessment can itself be viewed as a sociocultural innovation, the utility and pragmatic value of its use in the environmental decision-making processes of society must be adequately established and documented.

REFERENCES

Anastasi, A. (1982). *Psychological testing* (5the ed.). New York: Macmillan.

Appleyard, D. (1969). Why buildings are known: A predictive tool for architects and planners. *Environment and Behavior, 1,* 131–156.

Appleyard, D. (1977). Understanding professional media: Issues, theory and a research agenda. In I. Altman & J.F. Wohlwill (Eds.), *Human behavior and environment* (Vol. 2). New York: Plenum.

Appleyard, D. (1981). *Livable streets.* Berkeley, CA: University of California Press.

Appleyard, D., Bosselmann, P., Klock, R., & Schmidt, A. (1979). Periscoping future scenes: How to use an environmental simulation lab. *Landscape Architecture, 69,* 487–488, 508–510.

Appleyard, D., & Craik, K.H. (1974). The Berkeley Environmental Simulation Project: Its use in environmental impact assessment. In T.G. Dickert & K.R. Domeny (Eds.), *Environmental impact assessment: Guidelines and commentary* (pp. 121–126). Berkeley, CA: University of California, University Extension.

Appleyard, D., & Craik, K.H. (1978). The Berkeley Environmental Simulation Laboratory and its research programme. *International Review of Applied Psychology, 27,* 53–55.

Astin, A.W., & Holland, J.L. (1961). The environmental assessment technique: A way to measure college environments. *Journal of Educational Psychology, 52,* 308–316.

Atkins, J.T., & Blair, W.G.E. (1983). Visual impacts of highway alternatives. *Garten & Landschaft, 8,* 632–635.

Attneave, F. (1962). Perception and related areas. In S. Koch (Ed.), *Psychology: A study of a science. Vol. 4* (pp. 619–659). New York: McGraw-Hill.

Baggen, E.A., & Feimer, N.R. (1984). *The effects of environmental simulation of the development of cognitive representations.* Paper presented at the 92nd annual convention of the American Psychological Association, Toronto, Canada.

Barker, M.L. (1976). Planning for environmental indices: Observer appraisals of air quality. In K.H. Craik & E.H. Zube (Eds.), *Perceiving environmental quality: Research and applications* (pp. 175–204). New York: Plenum.

Barker, R.G. (1968). *Ecological psychology.* Stanford, CA: Stanford University Press.

Barker, R.G., & Schoggen, P. (1973). *Qualities of community life.* San Francisco: Jossey-Bass.

Bechtel, R.B. (1975). The semantic differential and other paper and pencil tests: A caution against yielding too early to temptation. In W. Michelson (Eds.), *Behavioral research methods in environmental design.* Stroudsburg, PA: Dowden, Hutchinson, & Ross.

Berglund, B. (1977). Quantitative approaches in environmental studies. *International Journal of Psychology, 12,* 111–123.

Block, J. (1961). *The Q-sort method in personality assessment and psychiatric research.* Palo Alto, CA: Consulting Psychologists Press.

Block, J. (1971). *Lives through time.* Berkeley, CA: Bancroft.

Block, J., Weiss, D.S., & Thorne, A. How relevant is a semantic similarity interpretation of personality ratings? *Journal of Personality and Social Psychology, 37,* 1055–1074.

Bosselmann, P., & Craik, K.H. (in press). Perceptual simulations of environments. In R.B. Bechtel, R.W. Marans, & W. Michelson (Eds.), *Behavioral research methods in environmental design.* New York: Van Nostrand.

Bosselmann, P., & Gerdes, H. (1980). Film and video in the planning process. *American Planning Journal, 46,* 12–14.

Bosselmann, P., & O'Hare, T. (1983). Traffic in urban American neighbourhoods: The influence of Buchanan. *Built Environment, 9,* 127–139.

Brunswik, E. (1956). *Perception and the representative design of psychological experiments* (2nd ed.). Berkeley, CA: University of California Press.

Brush, R.O. (1979). The attractiveness of woodlands: Perceptions of forest landowners in Massachusetts. *Forest Science, 25,* 495–506.

Bryant, K.J. (1984). *Geographical spatial orientation ability and the representation of real-world and simulated environments.* Unpublished doctoral dissertation, University of California, Berkeley.

Burton, I. (1962). *Types of agricultural occupance of flood plains in the United States* (Research Paper No. 75). Chicago: University of Chicago, Department of Geography.

Burton, I., & Kates, R.W. (1964). The perception of natural hazards in resource management. *Natural Resources Journal, 3,* 412–441.

Burton, I., Kates, R.W., & White, G.F. (1978). *The environment as hazard.* New York: Oxford University Press.

Butcher, J.N., & Spielberger, C.D. (Eds.). (1983, 1984). *Advances in personality assessment* (Vols. 2 & 4). Hillsdale, NJ: Erlbaum.

Campbell, D.T. (1965). Variation and selective retention in socio-cultural evolution. In H.R. Barringer, G.I. Blanksten, & R.W. Mack (Eds.), *Social change in developing areas.* Cambridge, England: Schenkman.

Campbell, D.T. (1969). Reforms as experiments. *American Psychologist, 24,* 409–429.

Campbell, D.T. (1975). Assessing the impact of planned social change. In G.M. Lyons (Ed.), *Social research and public policy.* Hanover, NH: Dartmouth College, Public Affairs Center.

Campbell, D.T., & Fiske, D.W. (1959). Convergent and discriminant validation by the multitrait-multimethod matrix. *Psychological Bulletin, 56,* 81–105.

Canter, D., Sanchez-Robles, J.C., & Watts, N. (1974). A scale for the cross-cultural evaluation of houses. In D. Canter & T. Lee (Eds.), *Psychology and the built environment.* New York: Wiley.

Canter, D., & Stringer, P. (1975). *Environmental interaction*. New York: International Universities Press.

Carp, F.M., & Carp, A. (1982a). A role for technical environmental assessment in perceptions of environmental quality and well-being. *Journal of Environmental Psychology, 2*, 171–192.

Carp, F.M., & Carp, A. (1982b). Perceived environmental quality of neighborhoods: Development of assessment scales and their relation to age and gender. *Journal of Environmental Psychology, 2*, 295–312.

Chapman, L.J. (1967). Illusory correlations in observational report. *Journal of Verbal Learning and Verbal Behavior, 6*, 151–155.

Conyne, R.K., & Clack, R.J. (1981). *Environmental assessment and design: A new tool for the applied behavioral scientist*. New York: Praeger.

Cook, T.D., & Reichardt, C.S. (1979). *Qualitative and quantitative methods in evaluation research*. Beverly Hills, CA: Sage.

Cooper, C. (1972). Residential dissatisfaction in multi-family housing. In W.M. Smith (Ed.), *Behavior, design and policy: Aspects of human habitats* (pp. 119–146). Green Bay: University of Wisconsin.

Cooper, C. (1975). *Easter Hill Village: Some social implications of design*. New York: Free Press.

Cooper, W.H. (1981). Ubiquitous halo. *Psychological Bulletin, 90*, 218–244.

Coughlin, R.E. (1976). The perception and valuation of water quality: A review of research method and findings. In K.H. Craik & E.H. Zube (Eds.), *Perceiving environmental quality: Research and applications* (pp. 205–228). New York: Plenum.

Craik, K.H. (1968). The comprehension of the everyday physical environment. *Journal of the American Institute of Planners, 34*, 29–37.

Craik, K.H. (1970). Environmental psychology. In K.H. Craik, B. Kleinmuntz, R.L. Rosnow, R. Rosenthal, J.A. Cheyne, & R.H. Walters (Eds.), *New directions in psychology, 4* (pp. 1–122). New York: Holt, Rinehart, & Winston.

Craik, K.H. (1971). The assessment of places. In P. McReynolds (Ed.), *Advances in psychological assessment* (Vol. 2, pp. 40–62). Palo Alto, CA: Science and Behavior Books.

Craik, K.H. (1972). The individual and the physical environment: Assessment strategies in environmental psychology. In W.M. Smith (Ed.), *Behavior, design, and policy: Aspects of human habitats* (pp. 95–118). Green Bay: University of Wisconsin.

Craik, K.H. (1977). Multiple scientific paradigms in environmental psychology. *International Journal of Psychology, 12*, 147–157.

Craik, K.H. (1981a). Comments on "The psychological representation of molar physical environments," by Ward & Russell. *Journal of Experimental Psychology: General, 110*, 158–162.

Craik, K.H. (1981b). Environmental assessment and situational analysis. In D. Magnusson (Ed.), *Toward a psychology of situations* (pp. 37–48). Hillsdale, NJ: Erlbaum.

Craik, K.H. (1983). The psychology of the large-scale environment. In N.R. Feimer & E.S. Geller (Eds.), *Environmental psychology: Directions and perspectives* (pp. 67–105). New York: Praeger.

Craik, K.H., & Appleyard, D. (1980). Streets of San Francisco: Brunswik's lens model applied to urban inference and assessment. *Journal of Social Issues, 36*, 72–85.

Craik, K.H., & Feimer, N.R. (1979). Setting technical standards for visual assessment procedures. In G. Elsner & R.C. Smardon (Eds.), *Our national landscape* (pp. 286–295). Berkeley, CA: U.S. Forest Service.

Craik, K.H., & McKechnie, G.H. (1974). *Perception of environmental quality: Preferential judgments versus comparative appraisals*. Berkeley, CA: Institute of Personality Assessment and Research.

Craik, K.H., & Zube, E.H. (Eds.). (1976). *Perceiving environmental quality: Research and applications*. New York: Plenum.

Cronbach, L.J. (1984). *Essentials of psychological testing* (4th ed.). New York: Harper & Row.

Cronbach, L.J., & Gleser, G.C. (1965). *Psychological tests and personnel decisions* (2nd ed.). Urbana: University of Illinois Press.

Cronbach, L.J., Gleser, G.C., Nanda, H., & Rajaratnam, N. (1972). *The dependability of behavioral measurements*. New York: Wiley.

Cronbach, L.J., & Meehl, P.E. (1955). Construct validity in psychological tests. *Psychological Bulletin, 52*, 281–302.

Cronbach, L.J., Rajaratnam, N., & Gleser, G.C. (1963). Theory of generalizability: A liberalization of reliability theory. *British Journal of Statistical Psychology, 16*, 137–163.

Cuff, D.C. (1982). *Negotiating architecture: A study of architects and clients in design practice*. Unpublished doctoral dissertation, University of California, Berkeley.

Danford, S., Starr, N., & Willems, E.P. (1979). The case against subjective, cognitive report in environmental design research: A critical test: In A.D. Seidel & S. Danford (Eds.), *Environmental design: Research, theory and application* (pp. 181–189). Washington, DC: Environmental Design Research Association.

Danford, S., & Willems, E.P. (1975). Subjective responses to architectural displays: A question of validity. *Environment and Behavior, 7*, 486–516.

Daniel, T.C. (1976). Criteria for development and application of perceived environmental quality indices. In K.H. Craik & E.H. Zube (Eds.), *Perceiving environmental quality: Research and applications* (pp. 27–46). New York: Plenum.

Daniel, T.C., & Boster, R.S. (1976). *Measuring landscape esthetics: The scenic beauty estimation method* (Research Paper RM-167). Ft. Collins, CO: U.S. Forest Service, Rocky Mountain Forest and Range Experiment Station.

Daniel, T.C., & Ittelson, W.H. (1981). Conditions for environmental perception research: Reactions to Ward and Russell. *Journal of Experimental Psychology: General, 110,* 153–157.

Daniel, T.C., & Vining, J. (1983). Methodological issues in the assessment of landscape quality. In I. Altman & J.F. Wohlwill (Eds.), *Behavior and the natural environment* (pp. 39–84). New York: Plenum.

Dawes, R.M. (1977). Suppose we measured height with rating scales instead of rulers. *Applied Psychological Measurement, 1,* 267–274.

Dunnette, M.D. (1966). *Personnel selection and placement.* Belmont, CA: Wadsworth.

Edwards, D.S., Hahn, C.P., & Fleishman, E.A., (1977). Evaluation of laboratory methods for the study of driver behavior: Relationship between simulator and street performance. *Journal of Applied Psychology, 62,* 559–566.

Fanning, D.M. (1967). Families in flats. *British Medical Journal, 4,* 382–386.

Feimer, N.R. (1983). Environmental perception and cognition in rural contexts. In A.W. Childs & G.B. Melton (Eds.), *Rural psychology* (pp. 113–150). New York: Plenum.

Feimer, N.R. (1984). Environmental perception: The effects of media, evaluative context and observer sample. *Journal of Environmental Psychology, 4,* 61–80.

Feimer, N.R., Smardon, R.C., & Craik, K.H. (1981). Evaluating the effectiveness of observer-based visual resource and impact assessment methods. *Landscape Research, 6,* 12–16.

Fines, K.D. (1969). Landscape evaluations—A research project in East Sussex. *Regional Studies, 2,* 41–55.

Friedman, A., Zimring, C., & Zube, E.H. (1978). *Environmental design evaluation.* New York: Plenum.

Garling, T. (1970). Studies in visual perception of architectural spaces and rooms IV. The relation of judged depth to judged size of space under different viewing conditions. *Journal of Scandinavian Psychology, 11,* 133–145.

George, J.R., & Bishop, L.K. (1971). Relationship of organizational structure and teacher personality characteristics to organizational climate. *Administrative Science Quarterly, 16,* 467–475.

Gerst, M., & Moos, R.H. (1972). The social ecology of university student residences. *Journal of Educational Psychology, 63,* 513–535.

Gibson, J.J. (1959). Perception as a function of stimulation. In S. Koch (Ed.), *Psychology: A study of a science* (Vol. 1). New York: McGraw-Hill.

Gibson, J.J. (1966). *The senses considered as perceptual systems.* Boston, MA: Houghton Mifflin.

Groat, L. (1982). Meaning in post-modern architecture: An examination using the multiple sorting task. *Journal of Environmental Psychology, 2,* 3–22.

Guilford, J.P. (1954). *Psychometric methods.* New York: McGraw-Hill.

Halpin, A.W.,& Crofts, D.B. (1963). The organizational climate of schools. *Administrators Notebook, 11,* 1–4.

Hemphill, K.K. (1956). *Group dimensions: A manual for their measurement.* Columbus: Ohio State University.

Hendrick, C., Martyniuk, O., Spencer, T.J., & Flynn, J.E. (1977). Procedures for investigating the effect of light on impression: Simulation of a real space by slides. *Environment and Behavior, 9,* 491–510.

Hershberger, R.G. (1972). Toward a set of semantic scales to measure the meaning of architectural environments. In W.J. Mitchell (Ed.), *Environmental design: Research and practice* (pp. 6-4-1–6-4-10). Los Angeles: University of California Press.

Hershberger, R.G., & Cass, R.C. (1974). Predicting user response to buildings. In D.H. Carson (Ed.), *Man-environment interactions: Evaluations and applications* (Pt. 2). Stroudsburg, PA: Dowden, Hutchinson, & Ross.

Hochberg, J., & McAlister, E. (1958). A quantitative approach to "figural goodness." In D.C. Beardlee & M. Wertheimer (Eds.), *Readings in perception* (pp. 188–193). New York: Van Nostrand.

Holahan, C.J. (1982). *Environmental psychology.* New York: Random House.

Holland, J.L. (1966). *The psychology of vocational choice.* Waltham, MA: Blaisdell.

Horowitz, L., Inouye, D., & Siegelman, E.Y. (1979). On averaging judges' ratings to increase their correlation with an external criterion. *Journal on Consulting and Clinical Psychology, 47,* 453–458.

Howard, R.B., Mylnarski, F.G., & Sauer, G.C., Jr. (1972). A comparative analysis of affective responses to real and represented environments. In W.J. Mitchell (Ed.), *Environmental design: Research and practice* (pp. 6-6-1–6-6-8). Los Angeles: University of California Press.

Ittelson, W.H. (1973). Environment perception and contemporary perceptual theory. In W.H. Ittelson (Ed.), *Environment and cognition.* New York: Seminar Press.

Jackson, D.N., & Messick, S. (Eds.). (1967). *Problems in human assessment.* New York: McGraw-Hill.

Jones, A.P., & James, L.R. (1979). Psychological climate: Dimensions and relationships of individual and aggregated work environment perceptions. *Organizational Behavior and Human Performance, 23,* 201-250.

Kasmar, J.V. (1970). The development of a usable lexicon of environmental descriptors. *Environment and Behavior, 2,* 153–169.

Kates, R.W. (1963). Perceptual regions and regional perception in flood plain management. *Papers and Proceedings of the Regional Science Association, 11*, 217–228.

Kiemstedt, H. (1968). *The evaluation of the natural components of the landscape for leisure*. Paper presented at the Congress of the International Federation of Landscape Architects.

Killeen, K., & Buhyoff, G. (1983). The relation of landscape preference to abstract topography. *Journal of Environmental Management, 17*, 381–392.

King, J., Marans, R.W., & Solomon, L.A. (1982). *Pre-construction evaluation: A report on the full scale mock-up and evaluation of hospital rooms*. Ann Arbor: University of Michigan, Architectural Research Laboratory.

Kozlowski, L.T., & Bryant, K.J. (1977). Sense of direction, spatial orientation and cognitive maps. *Journal of Experimental Psychology: Human Perception and Performance, 3*, 590–598.

Krampen, M. (1979). *Meaning in the urban environment*. London: Pion.

Kuhn, T.S. (1962). *The structure of scientific revolutions*. Chicago, IL: University of Chicago Press.

Lau, J. J-R. (1970). Differences between full-size and scale model rooms in the assessment of lighting quality. In D.V. Canter (Ed.), *Architectural psychology* (pp. 43–48). London: Royal Institute of British Architects Publications.

Laumann, E.O., & House, J.S. (1970). Living room styles and social attributes: The patterning of material artifacts in a modern urban community. *Sociology and Social Research, 54*, 321–342.

Lawrence, R.J. (1982). A psychological-spatial approach for architectural design and research. *Journal of Environmental Design, 2*, 37–52.

Leff, H.L. (1978). *Experience, environment and human potentials*. New York: Oxford University Press.

Leff, H.L., & Gordon, L.R. (1980). Environmental cognitive sets: Longitudinal study. *Environment and Behavior, 12*, 291–328.

Leff, H.L., Gordon, L.R., & Ferguson, J.G. (1974). Cognitive set and environmental awareness. *Environment and Behavior, 6*, 395–447.

Linton, D.L. (1968). The assessment of scenery as a natural resource. *Scottish Geographical Magazine, 84*, 219–238.

Litton, R.B., Jr., & Twiss, R.H. (1967). The forest landscape: Some elements of visual analysis. In *Proceedings of the Society of American Foresters: 1966* (pp. 212–214). Washington, DC: Society of American Foresters.

Loo, C.M. (1978). Behavior problem indices: The differential effects of spatial density on low and high scores. *Environment and Behavior, 10*, 489–510.

Lowenthal, D. (1972). Research in environmental perception and behavior: Perspectives on current problems. *Environment and Behavior, 4*, 333–342.

Lowenthal, D., & Bowden, M.J. (Eds.). (1976). *Geog-*

raphies of the mind. New York: Oxford University Press.

Lowenthal, D., & Riel, M. (1972). The nature of perceived and imagined environments. *Environment and Behavior, 4*, 189–202.

Lynch, K. (1972). *What time is this place?* Cambridge, MA: MIT Press.

McKechnie, G.E. (1977). Simulation techniques in environmental psychology. In D. Stokols (Ed.), *Perspectives on environment and behavior: Theory, research and applications* (pp. 169–190). New York: Plenum.

McReynolds, P. (Ed.). (1968, 1971, 1975). *Advances in psychological assessment* (Vols. 1–3). Palo Alto, CA: Science and Behavior Books.

McReynolds, P. (Ed.). (1978, 1981). *Advances in psychological assessment* (Vols. 4–5). San Francisco, CA: Jossey-Bass.

Marans, R.W. (1976). Perceived quality of residential environments: Some methodological issues. In K.H. Craik & E.H. Zube (Eds.), *Perceiving environmental quality: Research and applications* (pp. 123–148). New York: Plenum.

Meehl, P.E. (1973). *Psychodiagnosis: Selected papers*. Minneapolis: University of Minnesota Press.

Megargee, E.I. (Ed.). (1966). *Research in clinical assessment*. New York: Harper & Row.

Mehrabian, A., & Diamond, S.G. (1971). Effects of furniture arrangement, props and personality on social interaction. *Journal of Personality and Social Psychology, 20*, 18–30.

Michels, K.M., & Zusne, L. (1965). Metrics of visual form. *Psychological Bulletin, 63*, 74–86.

Moos, R.H. (1973). Conceptualizations of human environments. *American Psychologist, 28*, 652–665.

Moos, R.H. (1974). *The Social Climate Scales: An overview*. Palo Alto, CA: Consulting Psychologists Press.

Moos, R.H. (1975). Assessment and impact of social climates. In P. McReynolds (Ed.), *Advances in psychological assessment* (Vol. 3). San Francisco, CA: Jossey-Bass.

Mulaik, S.A. (1964) Are personality factors raters' conceptual factors? *Journal of Consulting Psychology, 28*, 506–511.

Murray, H.A. (1938). *Explorations in personality*. New York: Oxford University Press.

Nunnally, J. (1978). *Psychometric theory*. New York: McGraw-Hill.

Oostendorp, A., & Berlyne, D.E. (1978a). Dimensions in the perception of architecture: I. Identification and interpretation of dimensions of similarity. *Scandinavian Journal of Psychology, 12*, 73–82.

Oostendorp, A., & Berlyne, D.E. (1978b). Dimensions in the perception of architecture: III. Multidimensional preference scaling. *Scandinavian Journal of Psychology, 19*, 145–150.

Pervin, L.A. (1978). Definitions, measurements, and classifications of stimuli, situations, and environments. *Human Ecology, 6*, 71–105.

Peterson, G.L. (1967). A model for preference: quantitative analysis of the perception of the visual appearance of neighborhoods. *Journal of Regional Science, 7*, 19–31.

Pheysey, D.C., & Payne, R.L. (1970). The Hemphill group dimensions description questionnaire: A British industrial application. *Human Relations, 23*,, 473–497.

Proshansky, H.M., Ittelson, W.H., & Rivlin, L.G. (Eds.). (1970). *Environmental psychology: People and their physical settings*. New York: Holt, Rinehart & Winston.

Pugh, D.S., Hickson, D.J., & Hinings, C.R. (1969). An empirical taxonomy of work organization structures. *Administrative Science Quarterly, 14*, 115–126.

Relph, E.C. (1976). *Place and placelessness*. London: Pion.

Rosch, E., Mervis, C.B.(1975). Family resenblances: Studies in the internal structure of categories. *Cognitive Psychology, 7*, 573–605.

Rosch, E., Mervis, C.B., Gray, W.D., Johnson, D.M., & Boyes-Braem, P. (1976). Basic objects in natural categories. *Cognitive Psychology, 8*, 382–439.

Russell, J.A., & Pratt, G. (1980). A description of the affective quality attributed to environments. *Journal of Personality and Social Relations, 38*, 311–322.

Russell, J.A., & Ward, L.M. (1981). On the psychological reality of environmental meaning: Reply to Daniel and Ittelson. *Journal of Experimental Psychology: General, 110*, 163–168.

Russell, J.A., Ward, L.M., & Pratt, G. (1981). The affective quality attributed to environments. *Environment and Behavior, 13*, 259–288.

Seaton, R.W., & Collins, J.B. (1972). Validity and reliability of ratings of simulated buildings. In W.S. Mitchell (Ed.), *Environmental design: Research and practice*. Los Angeles: University of California Press.

Schomaker, J.H. (1978). Measurement of preferences for proposed landscape modifications. *Landscape Research, 3*, 5–8.

Shafer, E.L., Jr. (1969). Natural landscape preferences: A predictive model. A reply. *Journal of Leisure Research, 1*, 197–198.

Shafer, E.L., Jr., Hamilton, J.F., Jr., & Schmidt, E.A. (1969). Natural landscape preference: A predictive model. *Journal of Leisure Research, 1*, 1–19.

Shafer, E.L., Jr., & Richards, T.A. (1974). *A comparison of viewer reactions to outdoor scenes and photographs of those scenes* (Research Paper NE-302). Upper Darby, PA: U.S. Forest Service, Northeast Range and Experiment Station.

Shafer, E.L., Jr., & Thompson, R.C. (1968). Models that describe use of Adirondack campgrounds. *Forest Science, 14*, 383–391.

Shafer, E.L., Jr., & Tooby, M. (1973). Landscape preference: An international replication. *Journal of Leisure Research, 5*, 60–65.

Sheppard, S.R.J. (1982a). *Landscape portrayals: Their use, accuracy and validity in simulating proposed landscape changes*. Unpublished doctoral dissertation, University of California, Berkeley.

Sheppard, S.R.J. (1982b). Predictive landscape portrayals: A selective research review. *Landscape Journal, 1*, 9–14.

Shweder, R.A., & D'Andrade, R.G. (1979). Accurate reflection or systematic distortion? A reply to Block, Weiss, and Thorne. *Journal of Personality and Social Psychology, 37*, 1075–1084.

Shweder, R.A., & D'Andrade, R.G. (1980). The systematic distortion hypothesis. In R.A. Shweder & D.W. Fiske (Eds.), *New directions for methodology of behavioral science: Fallible judgment in behavioral research*. San Francisco, CA: Jossey-Bass.

Sivik, L. (1974). Colour meaning and perceptual colour dimensions: A study of exterior colours. *Goteborg Psychological Reports, 4*(11).

Smardon, R.C., Feimer, N.R., Craik, K.H., & Sheppard, S.R.J. (1983). Assessing the reliability, validity and generalizability of observer-based visual impact assessment methods for the western United States. In R.D. Rowe & L.G. Chestnut (Eds.), *Managing air quality and scenic quality at national parks and wilderness areas* (pp. 84–102). Boulder, CO: Westwood.

Spielberger, C.D., & Butcher, J.N. (Eds.). (1982, 1983). *Advances in personality assessment* (Vols. 1 & 3). Hillsdale, NJ: Erlbaum.

Starr, N., & Danford, S. (1978). The invalidity of subjective ratings of the physical environment. In W.E. Rogers & W.H. Ittelson (Eds.), *New directions in environmental design research* (pp. 428–443). Washington, DC: Environmental Design Research Association.

Stern, G.G. (1963). *Scoring instructions and college norms: Activities Index and College Characteristics Index*. Syracuse, NY: Syracuse University, Psychological Research Center.

Stern, G.G. (1970). *People in context: The measurement of environmental interaction in school and society*. New York: Wiley.

Stewart, T.R., Middleton, P., & Ely, D. (1983). Urban air quality judgments: Reliability and validity. *Journal of Environmental Psychology, 3*, 129–146.

Thomas, W.A. (Ed.). (1972). *Indicators of environmental quality*. New York: Plenum.

Tinsley, H.E.A., & Weiss, D.J. (1975). Interrater reliability and agreement of subjective judgments. *Journal of Consulting Psychology, 22*, 358–376.

Torgerson, W.S. (1958). *Theory and methods of scaling*. New York: Wiley.

Tuan, Y. (1977). *Space and place: The perspective of experience*. Minneapolis: University of Minnesota.

Tversky, B., & Hemenway, K. (1983). Categories of environmental scenes. *Cognitive Psychology, 15*, 121–149.

U.S. Department of Interior, Bureau of Land Management.

(1980). *Visual simulation techniques* (Stock No. 024-011-0016-6). Washington, DC: U.S. Government Printing Office.

U.S. Environmental Protection Agency (1974). *Information on levels of environmental noise requisite to protect public health and welfare with an adequate margin for safety* (EPA Rep. 550/9-74-004). Washington, DC: U.S. Government Printing Office.

Wallace, L., Bromberg, S., Pellizzari, E., Hartwell, T., Zelon, H., & Sheldon, L. (1984). Plan and preliminary results of U.S. EPA's Indoor Air Monitoring Program. In B. Berglund, T. Lindvall, & J. Sundell (Eds.), *Indoor air: Vol. 1. Recent advances in the health sciences and technology*. Stockholm: Swedish Council for Building Research.

Walsh, W.B. (1973). *Theories of person-environment interaction: Implications for the college student*. Iowa City, IA: American College Testing (ACT) Publications.

Ward, L.M., & Russell, J.A. (1981). The psychological representation of molar physical environments. *Journal of Experimental Psychology: General, 110*, 121–152.

Weinstein, N.D. (1976a). Human evaluations of environmental noise. In K.H. Craik & E.H. Zube (Eds.), *Perceiving environmental quality: Research and applications* (pp. 229–252). New York: Plenum.

Weinstein, N.D. (1976b). The statistical prediction of environmental preferences: Problems of validity and application. *Environment and Behavior, 8*, 611–626.

Wiggins, J.S. (1973). *Personality and prediction: Principles of personality assessment*. Reading, MA: Addison-Wesley.

Wohlwill, J.F. (1970). The emerging discipline of environmental psychology. *American Psychologist, 25*, 303–312.

Wohlwill, J.F. (1978). What belongs where: Research on fittingness of man-made structures in natural settings: *Landscape Research, 3*, 3–5.

Wohlwill, J.F. (1983). The concept of nature: A psychologist's view. In I. Altman & J.F. Wohlwill (Eds.). *Behavior and the natural environment* (pp. 5–38). New York: Plenum.

Zeisel, J. (1981). *Inquiry by design: Tools for environment-behavior research*. Monterey, CA: Brooks/Cole.

Zeisel, J., & Griffen, M. (1975). *Charlesview Housing: A diagnostic evaluation*. Cambridge, MA: Harvard University, Graduate School of Design.

Zimring, C.M., & Reizenstein, J.E. (1980). Post-occupancy evaluation: An overview. *Environment and Behavior, 12*, 429–450.

Zube, E.H. (1980). *Environmental evaluation: Perception and public policy*. New York: Cambridge University Press.

Zube, E.H., Pitts, D.G., & Anderson, T.W. (1975). Perception and prediction of scenic resource values in the north-east. In E.H. Zube, R.O. Brush, & J. Fabos (Eds.), *Landscape assessment: Values, perceptions and resources* (pp. 151–167). Stroudsburg, PA: Dowden, Hutchinson, & Ross.

Zube, E.H., Sell, J.L., & Taylor, J.G. (1982). Landscape perception: Research, application and theory. *Landscape Planning, 9*, 1–33.

Chapter 24

DESIGN FOR SPECIAL POPULATIONS: MENTALLY RETARDED PERSONS, CHILDREN, HOSPITAL VISITORS

Craig Zimring, *College of Architecture, Georgia Institute of Technology, Atlanta, Georgia*

Janet Reizenstein Carpman, *Carpman Grant Associates, Ann Arbor, Michigan*

William Michelson, *Department of Sociology, University of Toronto, Toronto, Canada*

24.1. INTRODUCTION

All people are touched by the policies and practices of environmental design, obviously some in more complex and profound ways than others. Similarly, in a given situation, all of us consider ourselves special; in any particular person–environment transaction, it is the actor involved who feels profoundly affected. Yet when it comes to the interaction of design and human populations, some populations have characteristics that add an extra dimension to design considerations. Design may have to be oriented to a special population's unique needs. Or a special population may have unique outcomes to even sensitive design.

Special is a relatively neutral term, not necessarily reflecting only or any one of several dimensions, including minority status, handicap, poverty, or other potentially contributing characteristics. Populations may be special on many different grounds. Similarly,

design occurs at many levels and in numerous substantive applications. Hence the interplay involved in
design for specific populations occurs within the specific situations of a huge array of intersecting population subgroups and settings.

To attempt encyclopedic coverage of all aspects of
design for special populations within the bounds of
this chapter would be self-defeating, not only in
terms of available space but due to the uneven state
of knowledge across so many concerns and situations. Our approach to design for special populations
is more conceptual.

We shall start by exploring the nature of special
populations—and how they relate to conventional
paradigms in environmental psychology. We shall then
illustrate person–environment considerations regarding three extremely different special populations that
represent three different categories of relationship to
design (and with which the authors are personally
familiar through their work). Finally, we shall note
some common methodological issues facing researchers directing their attention to these and potentially
many more such applications.

24.2. DESIGN RESEARCH PARADIGMS AND SPECIAL POPULATIONS: A MODEL FOR APPROACHING PERSON–ENVIRONMENT RELATIONS

Central to this chapter is the concept of *person–
environment fit* (see French, Rodgers, & Cobb,
1974). Every person has a range of needs at any
given minute such as psychological needs for social
interaction or solitude, stimulation or relaxation,
safety or challenge, and physiological needs for food,
water, and physical comfort. All of these must be
satisfied within a permissive physical setting, although the setting does not determine most activities. But viewed from the perspective of an individual wishing to fulfill a need, not every environment provides an adequate fit, and greater or lesser
amounts of behavior are spent seeking a fit between
a form of needed expression and an appropriate setting for it. This fit may be achieved by modifications
to both needs and to environments (see Baum,
Singer, & Baum, 1982).

If one takes fit from the point of view of the environmental designer, he or she intends a particular
design product (whether a plan or a building) to accommodate a certain range of intended behaviors, although not excluding others that may not be primary
but that are still necessary. For example, a new office

design should facilitate white-collar work but not
exclude the possibility of conviviality, eating lunch, or
easy maintenance. Another way of thinking about
person–environment fit from this point of view is
with respect to the concept of congruence (Michelson, 1970). One asks, in terms of possibility, what
behaviors are congruent with a physical design or
plan. The designer's intent is to provide products that
are congruent in all conceivable ways with what relevant user groups are expected to be doing. Looking
at the larger set of factors that bridges environment
and behavior (which would have to include many of
the other topics in this handbook such as perception,
cognition, behavior setting characteristics, and culture), it is evident that creating an environment that
is congruent for a given set of activities is a necessary but not sufficient cause for the appearance of expected behavior.

The experience of fit for the individual is not
necessarily the same as that of congruence in the design of environment. An environment that proves
congruent in terms of the intended behaviors of a
targeted population may not fit a person who was not
targeted but is there anyway, or an unanticipated personal need of a targeted person.

Both fit and congruence have their opposite
states: misfit and incongruence. A large body of research suggests that when these occur, psychological
and physiological stress may also occur (Baum,
Singer, & Baum, 1982). For example, unwanted social interaction caused by long-term crowding may
lead to greater aggressiveness (Baum & Vallins,
1977) and lowered grades in college students (Karlin,
McFarland, Aiello, & Epstein, 1976). Getting lost
may lead to psychological discomfort and heightened
heart rate and other indicators of physiological arousal (Zimring, 1981). A particular misfit may be substantially unrelated to planning considerations, but it
can nonetheless undermine the success of an environment by creating human distress among participants within it.

It is possible for instances of person–environment
misfit to produce direct, serious physical consequences. For example, lengthy exposure to extreme
heat or cold can cause physiological damage. However, in most cases the implications of misfit are
mediated by a range of situational and psychological
factors such as personality, past experience, and
available coping strategies. Lazarus (1966) and
others (see Baum, Singer, & Baum, 1982; Evans,
Chapter 15, this volume, for reviews) have suggested
that the consequences of threatened misfit are related to the appraisals the individual makes about the

seriousness of the threat and of the advisability of alternative coping strategies. Although the research results are somewhat equivocal, some studies have found that simply providing the perception of control over a stressor reduces its negative impacts (see, e.g., Glass & Singer, 1972). Other studies have found that the amount and quality of information about the misfit affects its interpretation and the choice of coping strategies (Baum, Singer, & Baum, 1982). Nonetheless, designs that require considerable human adaptation for the accomplishment of congruence and the avoidance of misfit (and especially when adaptation becomes expensive or of limited utility) involve greater personal and collective costs than those designs that readily accommodate what is deemed to be necessary and desirable by a given set of occupants or users.

In our view, there are three important and largely independent dimensions underlying an environment's congruence and a person's fit: *user abilities and needs* (personal and/or group-related), *design characteristics of the physical environment,* and *organizational and management considerations* that bridge the two.

User abilities and needs, has a direct bearing on our consideration of special populations. Different segments of the population vary enormously in terms of the behavioral demands they place on environments, including and beyond those that represent the primary function of such environments. In addition, an environment that proves congruent for some segments of the population may prove incongruent for others because of one or more basic subgroup differences not pertinent to the targeted activity per se.

Even without taking into consideration the enormous variability of segments of the population and their needs, the latter two dimensions present a tremendous variety of considerations. *Design characteristics of the physical environment,* for example, include several levels of scale. At a low level, the near (or ergonomic) environment, well-designed controls may allow an appliance to be used easily, whereas hard-to-manipulate or confusing controls may make the appliance difficult or impossible to use. At the scale of a room, for example, a kitchen can be helpful or frustrating, depending on the match of its design with the needs of a particular user. At the building scale, a complex layout may cause people to get lost, whereas a simple plan may increase competence; an institutional-appearing building may foster different attitudes than a more homelike one. In the block or neighborhood, the degree that spaces are allocated for outdoor activities such as play and gardening will have a major bearing on their performance. At the urban scale, land use patterns, viewed in terms of how clustered or dispersed particular land uses are with respect to others and to the homes of those who use them, together with the forms and paths of transportation, can limit or enhance what can be done within a day or lesser time period of availability (Hägerstrand, 1970; Mårtensson, 1979). Other macrofeatures such as residential segregation or integration, the presence of landmarks, and the presence or absence of clearly delineated subsegments of the city may all affect the image and use of it.

Organizational and management considerations present immediate conditions under which behavior is to take place within an environment. These include objectives and roles, task definitions and approved procedures, timetables, fares and other forms of monetary costs to users, signage, and, most generally, cultural prescriptions or proscriptions. For example, the Renaissance Center in Detroit is in many respects a highly complex structure that occasional users like tourists have found disorienting; new owners have made a system of signage their key to the elimination of incongruence. Second, as Chapter 26 in this volume indicates, fare and associated incentive structures are considered key intervening mechanisms between the existence of public transit and its use. Finally, the ability to pursue desired recreational or commercial activities on a given day may reflect the interaction of the opening and closing hours with respect to hours of employment, regardless of a rational urban design (cf. Lenntorp, 1976).

An example may clarify the approach. Many cities are concerned with making their subway systems usable by disabled people and are facing a particular problem: How may visually impaired people purchase tickets at ticket machines? In this case, person–environment fit occurs when the need of the person to purchase an appropriate ticket is satisfied, and solutions have been proposed that involve all three of the previously mentioned dimensions. Some cities alter the *physical environment* by providing cane-detectable paths to ticket machines and by installing talking machines. Other cities alter *individual abilities* either by training visually impaired travelers about station layout or by providing them tactile maps or electronic travel aids. Some cities produce person–environment fit through in *organizational change:* They send visually impaired people monthly passes to the subway. Person–environment fit may be achieved by considering any, or all, of the three dimensions.

To this point, however, we have not gone into detail about characteristic subdivisions within the population nor about their interface with design practices. This is now necessary in order to understand design for special populations.

24.2.1. Special Populations

Although the previous discussion is necessary to our analyses of design for special populations, it is not sufficient for our understanding of what is special. This has to be understood as a function of two variables in design: the extent that a population group is formally *targeted* as potentially using an environment and the extent that it meets *customary assumptions about environmental capability.*

Targeting

Targeting is the extent to which persons that use or want to use an environment had their behavioral needs explicitly considered in the design and management of this environment. This view assumes the division of labor noted nearly a century ago by urban sociologists as accompanying modern, urbanized societies (cf. Fischer, 1976). For example, until the nineteenth century, almost all homes were built by the prospective occupants or were crafted for them (Fitch, 1973). Lack of fit would reflect poverty or powerlessness but not a remoteness from the design scene. In the years since, however, financial concentration and technological advances have increased the scale of design projects and separated designer and user by a welter of bureaucracies (Zeisel, 1975). Housing is now only rarely custom-designed by an architect for an individual user. Most housing is now built speculatively with support from financial institutions (with their own conservative design prerequisites for loans) and targeted for users who will only appear after construction, seldom having any contact with the designers. Public buildings are negotiated by offices of public works, as surrogates for employees and public users. City plans are more likely to be considered as subject to public (i.e., user) opinion and influence, but it is difficult to argue that the public input has much precedent as a potent influence in comparison to professional, political, and economic interests (see, for example, Meyerson & Banfield, 1955; Michelson, 1976).

Targeting a user group varies in the amount of guesswork involved. In some forms of housing, an understanding of the market and the need to follow strict financial eligibility criteria make possible a relatively reliable prediction of subsequent users; knowledge or research about them helps to create a con-

gruent design. In other situations, conditions may be more volatile, leading to inexact predictions or to heterogeneous user groups. In some institutional settings and in large public environments, there will be multiple user groups, including socially diverse subcultures, employees and customers, and different degrees of use (e.g., primary vs. secondary users, frequent vs. occasional users, year-round vs. seasonal users, etc.). Public transit systems customarily plan for enhanced use by the type of person who is found to use them rather than for other segments of the population contributing disproportionately low use (Michelson, 1983).

Substituting in certain respects for one-to-one contact between designer and user has been the development of both formal and informal sets of standards regarding various levels of the environment, from plumbing and wiring to dwelling size and configuration, to residential density on a site to land use mixtures, to park and recreation access, and so forth. These standards are intended to ensure no less than the minimum acceptable situations for what professionals and public officials view as the average citizen. The effects of some standards (such as FHA in the United States and NHA in Canada) have been pervasive. Those accompanying government housing loans after World War II, for example, had far-reaching effects on the extent and relatively uniform design of suburban single-family housing, built to the virtual exclusion of alternatives for about 20 years.

Designers are not necessarily callous, but their structural removal from their ultimate clients and the need to target the latter in the process of design ends up in a situation where some users or potential users have simply not been considered very explicitly. And although congruence in design is, in any case, not determinative regarding behavior, it is less likely that a person or group whose behaviors were not considered fully in the design process will find a person–environment fit in the particular environment. To take an example we shall pursue subsequently, hospital patients and employees are more likely to have their design needs considered in contemporary design than are visitors to a hospital. But, however remote the latter might be from the main workings of a hospital, the degree of congruence the design of a hospital makes available for visitors' activities and sensibilities is highly salient to such persons, who are undergoing temporary mental and emotional stress that may be transmitted in kind back to patients—the primary users.

Customary Assumptions

Nonetheless, all targeted persons will not react to or treat a given environment the same. Customary assumptions are made about users of a designed place or aspect of city infrastructure in regard to the strength, sensory capabilities, means of access, time commitment, literacy, language capability, financial resources, and more. Certain minimum levels of environmental competence are assumed. Communities, for example, which place primary emphasis on travel in the private automobile (and which therefore stress rational networks of roads and parking facilities) make the customary assumption that everyone has the economic and physical capacity to drive, or knows someone who can take him or her or can afford taxis. Populations, however, are sufficiently diverse that there are always segments of the population who do not meet customary assumptions. In this example, elderly and very poor residents are highly deprived as a result of not meeting customary assumptions, and lack of targeting means women and children are often frustrated.

How a group that differs from the modal person or group in a setting is treated depends partly on the philosophy behind design or planning. In some municipalities, states, and nations, design and planning are oriented to make possible participation by the greatest part of the population; the customary assumptions are consciously (usually by law) widened to include the handicapped, the illiterate, and the poor. Wheelchair accessibility, for example, has become standard design procedure in certain jurisdictions, and even as far back as the building of the New York subway, color codes were adopted to enable use by those unable to read. Airports and highways are increasingly fitted with picture signs giving universal information without the need to know the local language. In other jurisdictions, however, customary assumptions are more restrictive. If those not meeting them are considered worthy and in need of services that customary assumptions do not permit, separate programs are created, usually on a restricted scale reflecting the degree of perceived size and influence of the targeted group. Institutions for those unable to meet the customary assumptions of the "normal" world have been an outgrowth for those with physical, sensory, or mental handicaps. Many American public transit systems are said to represent a stopgap means of travel for the poor and otherwise choiceless, with less efficiency and flexibility than is enjoyed by those able to drive. The tension between relatively universalistic and restrictive philosophies about customary assumptions may be seen in current debates about deinstitutionalization.

Targeting, Customary Assumptions, and the Identification of Special Populations

Figure 24.1 indicates a simple fourfold classification, according to whether a type of person or group is targeted in the design process or not and whether this person or group meets customary assumptions about the various forms of competence.

Box 1 is the conventional, "normal" design situation, in which relevant populations are typically targeted and where no special considerations about environmental competence appear necessary. Current standards appear to be appropriate criteria for many design decisions in this case. Nonetheless, one must constantly question whether this situation is ever found in its pure form. Is an environment ever utilized only by those with mainstream competencies in all aspects of their physical and social conditions? Or do environments become restricted to such users as a result of their design and/or organization? Such a category may have historical precedents in practice and in theoretical research, but a theme of this chapter is to make clear the number and types of subgroups that need to be integrated into such considerations rather than omitted from thought.

Categories of persons failing to meet customary assumptions are nonetheless explicitly targeted in the creation of various forms of institutions, at the least. These include the sick, the extremely handicapped, the aged, and the retarded. Lawbreakers are provided with jails. Young people are provided with day-care centers and schools. Poor families are provided with public housing (usually no resemblance to what is built for those fulfilling customary assumptions about amount and source of income).

We consider these populations and others as well that would fit into Box 2 in Figure 24.1 to be *special populations* because special care must be taken with respect to their nonmodal characteristics, to ensure that the designs that target them fully and accurately recognize the ways in which they diverge from customary assumptions gained from more modal groups.

Children, for example, need bathrooms near the base of high-rise apartments because they often cannot "wait" for the duration of elevator rides to their own apartments. This is a design consideration not generally needed or recognized by the adult population.

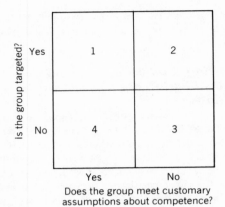

Figure 24.1. Targeting and customary assumptions about populations.

Pioneering research by Gans (1962) and Fried (1963) established that working-class Italian-Americans in the West End of Boston, for whom urban renewal was formally expected to facilitate better housing, had a long-term attachment to their neighborhood. This was what made their betterment process psychosomatically destructive—a clear misfit unlike the better known pattern of the more common middle-class organization man (Whyte, 1956).

It is necessary to ensure that adequate recognition be taken of ways in which customary assumptions do apply and should be incorporated, so that desirable degrees of "normalization" will not be compromised. Prisons, for example, which concentrate exclusively on control and punishment, without considering the development of means of legitimate livelihood or the maintenance of ties to loved ones among prisoners, promote additional rehabilitative problems relating to the special characteristics of inmates, rather than facilitating the gradual assumption by prisoners of more accepted characteristics.

Persons who do not fit the existing customary assumptions underlying design or who have characteristics requiring special attention are often called "vulnerable," in addition to "special." As we have indicated by example, vulnerability may come from a variety of sources. These include physical and organic causes such as illness, accident, retardation, handicap, and sensory deficits such as blindness or deafness. These also include life-cycle causes associated with size, strength, and agility—affecting the very young and the very old most directly—and gender. These include structural sources such as poverty and penology, and cultural sources such as nonmodal values and associated behavioral needs, literacy, and language. Indeed, how customary assumptions are made by groups in power about racial or ethnic minorities (or even de facto majorities) is important to the use of environments by the latter.

Vulnerability is sometimes permanent but often temporary. Everybody is vulnerable at one or more times in his or her life, and some people find themselves vulnerable at one time from more than one source. For this reason, it is essential that designers seek to incorporate the fullest and most accurate understandings of the various forms of vulnerabilities into their plans and designs, whether inclusive or exclusive, and that design researchers assess both the unique and the shared characteristics of the kinds of special populations. Vulnerability is integral, not exogenous to every normal society and to all of us.

Many environmental researchers have responded and are devoting their energies to the needs of vulnerable groups who have been targeted. At the time of this writing, for example, a national news service has picked up the invention by Preiser and his colleagues of an unobtrusive electronic track to assist blind persons to find their way through large public buildings. This invention came at the request of the director of a newly remodeled student union, who wanted to consider needs of blind students for orientation (Krasnow, 1984).

We will discuss the situation of mentally retarded persons to illustrate this general category later in the chapter. Special populations, including the vulnerable, extend beyond targeted populations not meeting customary assumptions. Some vulnerable populations are not fully recognized to the extent that they are such and hence are not sufficiently taken as a target in design. Box 3 in Figure 24.1 represents this category. Because certain parts of the population do not have differences associated with stigma and/or the consideration of institutionalization, the uniqueness of their characteristics is less obvious or overt and therefore not targeted. For example, left-handed people have faced difficulties for years at the ergonomic level, and very tall people are seldom recognized by institutional furniture. Very short people lack sufficient visibility in certain automobile designs.

People do not have to be a minority to be forgotten in design. Numerous writers have pointed out how women, a majority, have not been targeted in certain major aspects of urban design (see Saegert, Chapter 4, this volume). The great trend toward suburbanization was nominally in the interests of "familism" (Bell, 1968). The common postwar building pattern and the means of transportation attached to it led to men being able to commute efficiently by car between an office or factory at the heart of activity to a new home offering peace and quiet in the evenings. Younger children were offered room to play relatively safely out-of-doors. Women, however, were left isolated from virtually all forms of activities but housekeeping and child care. Neighboring became an adaptation but not a direct substitution for a wide range of incongruent activities nor a stimulus to feelings of control. (See, e.g., Fava, 1980; Michelson, 1970; Wekerle, 1979; Whyte, 1956.)

Even with huge increases in maternal employment and single parenthood, to the extent that only about 30% of American families are estimated to fit the traditional structure of husband, nonemployed wife, and minor children (Hayghe, 1982), there has been a lag in explicit recognition of how women differ from men as a basis for planning the urban context. Although women, for example, do cut down on their devotion of time to housework and child care when employed, they nonetheless remain primarily responsible for most such tasks. Employed women are not only faced with the commitment of time to jobs and associated travel, they are often hampered by unequal distribution of family transportation resources. The net result of this is that they often have a more time-consuming load of responsibilities than do men, especially when children are young. Of particular salience in the urban context to women in this situation are the (now inappropriate) locations and restrictive hours of day-care centers, the proximity clustering, and hours of commercial and institutional services, and the organization of transportation. This last is a source of considerable misfit for women in view of their pressing schedules and considerations of personal safety; yet it reflects diminished choice (Michelson, 1985). Despite their numerical size, women as a group are considered vulnerable because the total load of daily responsibilities that so many carry, together with the relatively low economic resources they often bring to bear as individuals, bring about more difficult outcomes, including daily stress and marital disharmony (Michelson, 1985). Kamerman underscores the situation of women in this category in the title of a book, *Parenting in an Unresponsive Society* (1980).

When examining the accumulation of spaces, ways to get about between them, and the rules and timetables associated with their use, it is hardly an exaggeration to observe that the customary assumptions behind design reflect the situation primarily of mature, white, economically able, healthy males with wives at home to dedicate themselves to family health and welfare during standard business hours.

This, indeed, leaves many subsegments of the population who do not meet such customary assumptions and who are not explicitly targeted and, thus are, in our view, special populations in terms of design considerations. This divergence from customary expectations was illustrated by a popular cartoon serial in which a lady blackmailer was caught because she stopped on an urban street at night to make a telephone call; the police stopped to investigate because they did not think a woman would do that unless there were a problem!

The place of children in urban design also illustrates this category well, insofar as schools and other child-care and educational institutions represent only the least part of children's environments. The need to incorporate into design the many other environments and related considerations relevant to children is largely latent. We shall expand on this as a major illustration later in the chapter.

The fourth and final box in Figure 24.1, which we view as urging attention to special populations, is Box 4. Here the population groups involved do not diverge significantly from customary assumptions along the various dimensions of necessary potency, but yet these groups are not targeted regarding certain environmental uses. During the late 1960s, protests on many university campuses often included the feeling that students were not at the center of consideration in campus planning. Even though university students are not particularly vulnerable in most typical respects, a lack of fit regarding their needs as students was said to produce considerable alienation. Sommer (1974), for example, describes a modern, new university campus with clean, handsome buildings, situated in a lush parklike atmosphere, where positive feelings about the educational experience disappear the second one enters the classrooms inside, which are bleak, artificially lit, colorless, uncomfortable, and without apparent aesthetic or accoustical design. It may be unusual for the primary users to be negligibly targeted, but in the context of design practices, this would make students worthy of special attention. This would make them a special population, even if not vulnerable on the basis of their personal attributes.

What is more customary is the situation of a group that may not be at the heart of the primary activity of an enterprise or institution but that is nonetheless an integral part of it. More peripheral functions or lower status may result in a neglect of adequate targeting of the needs of such a group. In universities and many other growing professional and technological work settings, the commonly recognized output reflects the efforts of various categories of professionals and managers: scientists, technicians, executives, and other specialists. Clerical workers, whose contribution may be a step or two away from the cutting edge of the operation, are nonetheless essential to its functioning. Yet their work environments typically take third place to that of their co-workers and indeed to the machinery that they themselves operate. Nevertheless, everyone else's productivity is in certain ways affected by the misfits clerical workers encounter. (The example we mentioned about design for hospital visitors fits this category and will be developed in depth as an illustration.)

In sum, although all vulnerable populations are special in some ways, requiring special consideration even in properly targeted design, the concept of special populations in design is broader. It refers to those that at any time need extra attention either because they are not typically and explicitly viewed in terms of the necessary behaviors to be included and/or because they have characteristics (grounded in many possible physical, mental, and social differences from customary assumptions about competence for environmental behavior) that put special requirements on the design of environments or that result in unique outcomes from these environments.

It can be lucidly argued that the thrust of this chapter is no different from environmental psychology as a whole. Is not the field addressed to creating knowledge for sensitive design in all circumstances? Yes and no. It is our argument that designers and psychologists alike should be continuously aware of the range of population groups and their needs in design. And no one would publicly deny this. Yet, this field, like so many others, addresses itself to certain processual and substantive pursuits that do not concentrate on the disaggregation of populations. Work, for example, on processes like perception, cognition, and development does not generally take the analysis of subgroup differences to their logical extreme, in theory or practice. The same can be said for research on particular users of institutions like schools and transportation, for integrative paradigms like ecological psychology, and for favorite outcomes like stress.

Although we thus do not identify any single phenomenon to be designated as special nor maintain watertight boundaries between our fourfold cross-classification categories in Figure 24.1, our intent is to make explicit the variety of populations that at present ought to be considered special regarding design, within a framework that facilitates an understanding of why special populations should be of par-

ticular concern to designers and researchers. The next section involves an in-depth look at the kinds of considerations that are involved in three different special groups, to serve as examples of the relevance and representative content of such a focus.

In the following pages we examine three special populations in some depth: mentally retarded persons, children, and hospital visitors. These groups have different relationships between targeting, customary assumptions, congruence, and fit. Although mentally retarded persons by definition are limited in their cognitive and life skills, they are often victims of misconceptions about their inabilities to behave normally and to develop. As a result, even when designs such as large institutions are presumably targeted for them, misfit may occur. And much recent research has been devoted to exploring the relationship between abilities and necessary targeting. Children, though a well-liked group, are targeted in only a small range of environments such as schools and playgrounds. Many other settings such as the home or public streets fit their needs poorly. In addition, many of the customary assumptions that are embedded in most environmental designs such as that users will be strong, tall, literate, and affluent do not apply to children. Hospital visitors—a "temporary" special population—have not commonly been targeted because little is known about their requirements and because their needs may conflict with groups who are targeted such as physicians.

24.3. MENTALLY RETARDED PERSONS

Mentally retarded persons are a special population distinguished by their vulnerability: As individuals and as a group they often lack the training, ability, or power to determine their own fate. They can be described by Box 2 in Figure 24.1: They are sometimes targeted in design but do not meet customary assumptions of environmental competence. As a result, mentally retarded persons are often provided with environments incongruent with their needs for development. Although environments for mentally retarded people have seldom been discussed explicitly in environmental psychological terms, the debate among policymakers, designers, and others about appropriate models of care has often revolved around such issues. For example, questions have been asked such as how viable are large institutions for housing mentally retarded persons? What are the critical dimensions of living environments for such individuals?

Within the past century and a half public attitudes

toward mentally retarded people have undergone several significant shifts. Mentally retarded people have been seen as objects of dread, reverence, menace, charity, obligation, and love, and these attitudes have been reflected in the environments provided mentally retarded people and in the level and orientation of their care (Heal, Seligman, & Switzky, 1978; Wolfensberger, 1972). Previously cared for at home or crowded into poorhouses or lunatic asylums, in the 1840s and 1850s mentally retarded people began to be "targeted" by being housed in separate institutions in Europe and the United States. Facilities in Europe were dominated by the antiurban neoromantic thinkers of the day. In an effort at rehabilitation, mentally retarded residents were given a short-term regimen of simple diet, clean air, and exercise (Heal et al., 1978). In the United States, Samuel Gridley Howe adapted the European model to American needs and produced a boarding school where students spent their school-age years, returning home during vacations and after their studies were completed (Heal et al., 1978).

These early goals of preparing mentally retarded people for reentry into society were quickly subverted: Parental and social pressures caused institutions to grow and become custodial (Wolfensberger, 1972). By 1900 there were 25 state institutions housing over 15,000 residents in plantationlike settings complete with active farms, dairies, and "villages" of dormitories. Residents were classified according to age, sex, and mental abilities. By 1925 there were 50,000 mentally retarded people institutionalized in state facilities, and this reached a peak of over 200,000 in 1967 with over 135 facilities, which had a median capacity of over 1000 residents (Scheerenberger, 1978). Since 1967, this has decreased to 150,000 or less, with the reduction mostly due to discharge of higher functioning residents (Scheerenberger, 1978; Willer, Scheerenberger, & Intaglia, 1980).

This deinstitutionalization reflects the impact of several trends. First, over the past decades the definition of "mental retardation" has become more precise. Although still a somewhat crude classification, it has evolved from a vague notion of subnormal functioning, which might in fact have represented lack of education, senility, or dyslexia, to a definition where the person must be both very low in intelligence as measured by a standard intelligence test *and* have very poor everyday adaptive functioning (Grossman, 1977). A considerable proportion of the people institutionalized in the 1960s and before are now not considered mentally retarded.

In addition, the concept of *normalization* has had considerable influence on the deinstitutionalization of mentally retarded people. Normalization is defined in current accreditation standards as "the use of méans that are as culturally normative as possible to elicit and maintain behavior that is as culturally normative as possible, taking into account local and subcultural differences" (Joint Commission on Accreditation of Hospitals, 1971, p. 1). Developed in Scandinavia (see, e.g., Bednar, 1977; Nirje, 1969), this concept has recently been wholeheartedly adopted in the United States. (Even in 1983, some 10 years after its broad U.S. acceptance, it is difficult to find a single issue of a professional journal in mental retardation without normalization being discussed.) Normalization has motivated the recent creation of a large number of group homes, foster homes, and other "community settings," with a recent survey finding over 6000 group homes in the United States alone (Janicki, Mayada, & Epple, 1983). The normalization principle has at its core an analysis of the causes of social stigmatization: a theory about why some groups such as mentally retarded people are labeled *different, strange, subnormal,* or *intimidating.* Advocates of this position argue that, rather than flowing from some immutable physical characteristic, these labels come from the physical isolation of some groups and their relegation to abnormal and inferior standards of treatment (Wolfensberger, 1972). Particular attention has been focused on the destructive impacts of large custodial institutions, where residents lack the freedoms enjoyed by most people in everyday society: Residents wake up at a common hour, independent of their individual needs or schedule, go to sleep at the same time, eat the same food at a prearranged hour, wear assigned (and often castoff) clothing, live and work in the same building (see, e.g., Gunzberg, 1973). It is argued that this routine is dulling and limits development and may in fact cause many of the bizarre behaviors normally associated with mental retardation.

It is also argued that the physical isolation of mentally retarded people deprives others of the opportunity for everyday contact with them and makes it difficult for mentally retarded people to be viewed by society as individuals who are diverse and nonthreatening. As it has been adopted in the United States, normalization has several underlying axioms and assumptions (Butler & Bjaanes, 1978):

1. It is the right of everyone to have patterns of everyday life that are as similar to the mainstream as possible, such as having a sexual and romantic life, a physical separation be-

tween work and living, a homelike living environment, and so on.

2. Institutions are inherently incapable of supporting growth and development and as a result should be used only for people requiring medical support.

3. Smaller, more homelike community facilities are inherently more supportive of development by residents.

These statements have interesting environmental psychological implications. The first is an ethical position that is independent of any real-world implications—normalization should be accomplished because it is "right," regardless of an impact on residents or society (Knight, Zimring, & Kent, 1977). However, the last two are environmental psychological hypotheses: Institutions have negative impacts on residents' behavior and well-being, and community facilities have salutary ones.

Based on these principles and because they can be less expensive to run than large institutions, small group homes and other community-oriented living facilities have burgeoned, but the empirical evidence supporting them is limited and provides a mixed picture (Landesman-Dwyer, 1984). In the next several sections, we will consider this evidence and some necessary further research.

24.3.1. Research on Environments for Mentally Retarded People

In this review we will consider research of primary interest to environmental psychologists, research linking the behavior of mentally retarded people to their physical setting. However, as the model described previously would suggest, it is impossible to ignore the third dimension affecting environmental competence—social and organizational dimensions. Especially for mentally retarded people, who tend to be dependent on care providers, the style and orientation of treatment are critically important. However, because of the scope of this chapter, we will only consider research that links treatment to environment and resident behavior. Also, because of the scope of this chapter we will not cover the impact of physical disability in depth.

Ergonomic Studies

Early theoretical discussions of normalization stressed the importance of the near environment, of normal door handles, and bed design and furnishings to therapeutic progress by mentally retarded people (see, e.g., Dybwad, 1970; A. Gunzberg, 1968; Norris, 1969). H. Gunzberg (1973), although emphasizing the importance of training practices, also stressed the importance of hot and cold taps for hot water, hooks for hanging clothes, and domestic-type furniture. Gunzberg and others see at least two kinds of advantages as resulting from designs like those found in everyday settings: development of the individual because he or she is dealing with a more stimulating and variegated environment and an alteration of attitudes by staff and community because symbols of inferiority and stigmatization are eliminated.

The rapid proliferation of group homes with normal furnishings is testimony to the persuasiveness of such arguments. However, there have been relatively few empirical studies considering the impacts of normalized settings and even fewer specifically focusing on ergonomic elements. In one exception, Reizenstein and McBride (1977) evaluated a small village for mentally retarded people that housed residents in two small houses and had a sheltered workshop and meetinghouse on the campus. Although Reizenstein and McBride performed no numerical analysis, their interviews suggested that the generally positive attitude of staff was due at least in part to the homelike furnishings. Similarly, in a larger study, Bakos and colleagues (1979) studied group homes for psychiatric patients and for mentally retarded people and found that small-scale ergonomic issues such as provision of adequate storage were very important in predicting resident satisfaction.

In a similar study, Wineman and Zimring (1986) evaluated 16 group homes for adult mentally retarded people by observing and interviewing residents and staff. Their results suggest that the fit between the physical design of the home and the specific treatment objectives of the house managers is an important variable in predicting the effectiveness of treatment. For example, several homes have active training programs in cooking, yet have small one-or-two-person kitchens that make training very difficult. When asked about the important features of the house, overall normality was seldom mentioned; rather, the staff focused on issues such as the logical and simple design of cooking controls and the durability of flooring materials.

In sum, the results of the handful of available ergonomic studies are suggestive but hardly definitive. Also, these studies lack an empirical analysis of the physical, ergonomic environment—it is unclear which of the precise dimensions of the environment are the most important. However, there is a recurring theme: Ergonomic designs that are simple, durable, and well-designed can increase the competence of mentally retarded people. (This conclusion is even more significant for multiply-handicapped mentally retarded people, who may have mobility, vision, hearing or coordination problems.)

Research on the Nature of Living Environments

In comparison to the relatively small amount of research considering ergonomic qualities of settings, there is a relatively large literature examining the nature and impact of environments more generally.

As we have suggested, the assumption that the sum total of the experience of living in a large institution is harmful has been a major influence in deinstitutionalization. Typically, a resident of such a facility may sleep on a ward with from 4 to 25 other residents, and the entire facility may house 1000 residents or more. All residents generally wake up, eat, and sleep at the same time; training opportunities are limited, and staff themselves may be poorly trained and unmotivated. However, the consensus about the destructiveness of institutions is often based on ideology rather than data, and it is unclear which of many factors—size of ward or institution, rigidity of routine, and so forth—affect residents and in what ways. As a result, several studies have focused on institutional change, where traditional institutions were altered to provide smaller wards or more control over individual space.

In addition, the rapid growth of community living facilities has generated a number of studies looking at the impacts of moves to community settings or comparing the impacts of different sizes and types of facilities. Although the results of these studies are complex, they seem to indicate that common intuitive descriptors of environments such as "institution" or "community alternative" are not well-defined and are not good predictors of the well-being of mentally retarded people or of the quality of care they receive (Landesman-Dwyer, 1981).

RESEARCH ON INSTITUTIONAL CHANGE
Several researchers have studied the impact on residents and staff of the alteration of large institutions. These studies have been motivated both by an interest in identifying key elements of institutional environments and by an interest in demonstrating to decision makers that institutional reform has practical impacts on residents and staff.

Three past large, longitudinal, observational studies suggest that the transition to smaller, more easily controllable institutional settings may have positive impacts on residents. Zimring, Weitzer, and Knight (1982) studied design changes at a large state institution. Because of a court mandate, the facility was gradually renovating 40-year-old "cottages" that each housed 55 residents into somewhat more homelike facilities. The staggered renovation schedule allowed for a multiple baseline research design, with some groups in unrenovated buildings serving as natural controls for those in renovated ones. Whereas there was not random assignment of residents to buildings, groups were matched on key demographic variables such as IQ and length of institutionalization, and the 2½-year data collection period allowed multiple measures to be recorded on most of the mentally retarded residents, with within-subject comparisons.

Ninety-two randomly selected residents and 33 staff were observed using structured behavior mapping techniques. In addition, several other measures were used such as analysis of resident records, interviews, participant observation, analysis of critical incidents, experimental simulation of the acoustic environment, and measurement of light, heat, and noise (see Knight, Weitzer, & Zimring, 1978; Zimring, Weitzer, & Knight, 1982, for more detail).

The renovation schedule allowed the comparison between the traditional institution—which had undifferentiated sleeping wards for 25 residents and hard, unadorned dayhalls—with three renovated schemes: *modular units*, where hospital doors on their sides were used as 4½-ft-high partitions to create semiprivate spaces in the existing dayhalls and dorms; a *suite-type arrangement*, where 3 three-to-four-person bedrooms were clustered around a small lounge; and a *college-dorm*-type renovation of a 1968 building that provided two wings of single and double bedrooms flanking a central bathroom-and-lounge core.

Although the architects and administrators felt that the suite arrangement would be best because of its grouping of residents into small clusters and its more homelike appearance, the college-dorm arrangement was most positive by far. In that design, even very low-functioning nonverbal residents were more alert and less withdrawn. Higher functioning residents were more verbal and less aggressive and were more positive in their verbalizations. Results of the interviews, participant observation, and other methods suggested these impacts were not apparently due to the "normalization" of the setting, at least as interpreted by the architects and administration. Rather the changes could be explained, at least in part, by the increase in *opportunity for control* of social interaction provided by physical characteristics such as the dorm's single and double bedrooms, its corridors that provided semiprivate areas under the control of a small group, and other clear territorial markers such as fire doors that separated the hallways and indicated they "belonged" to residents on the given hallway.

In a similar study, MacEachron (1983) studied 289 mentally retarded people in a large state facility. Residents were assigned to 15 homogeneous sampling groups. From within each group, residents were randomly assigned to one of two settings: 15 new cottages on the grounds or the existing traditional wards. Residents were evaluated after 1 year using the Adaptive Behavior Scale (ABS), a diagnostic test administered by building staff or supervisors (Nihira, Foster, Shellhaas, & Leland, 1974). In addition, MacEachron recorded much information about each setting (size, staff–client ratio, etc.) and administered standard instruments to assess treatment orientation and "normality" of setting. Her results were complex. She found that whereas only 7 of the 15 experimental groups in the cottages had statistically higher means than their controls on adaptive behavior, the overall pattern of means revealed a positive change from institution to cottages. When she disaggregated her data, she found three measures to be the best environmental predictors of positive differences in adaptive behavior: greater ability for the physical environment to be used by people at their own discretion (a dimension similar to the "opportunity for control" found to be important in the Zimring, Weitzer, & Knight, 1982, study); management practices that were more resident-oriented as opposed to being institution-oriented; and participation in programs. The strongest predictor overall of adaptive behavior was IQ.

In a third study, Landesman-Dwyer (1984, 1985) compared the adaptive behaviors of mentally retarded residents who moved into new duplexes on the grounds of a large institution to others who remained in the traditional institution. Because of the policies of the facility, some residents were randomly assigned to settings, whereas others were assigned to the new settings for clinical reasons. Landesman-Dwyer and her research group used a 69-category code to observe 160 residents for a 2-year period— from 1 year prior to the move to 1 year after. Her findings were somewhat equivocal, with only limited behavioral changes occurring after the move to the duplexes. The largest change was a significant increase in TV watching. She did find that residents with different initial behavioral patterns reacted differently to the move. For example, the group who were most social at the outset were originally paid most attention by staff, but they lost this distinction by the end of the observation.

In a similar study, Hemming, Lavender, and Pill (1981) arrived at somewhat different results. They compared 50 mentally retarded people who stayed in a large facility to a matched sample who moved to small bungalows on the hospital grounds. All residents were assessed periodically for 3 years using the ABS, and the treatment orientation was assessed using the Child Management Scale developed by King, Raynes, and Tizard (1971). They found treatment in the bungalows to be more resident-oriented than that in the traditional dorms. Residents in the bungalows significantly increased their levels of positive adaptive behaviors.

Taken together, these studies of institutional change suggest that a general improvement in the living environment, including providing smaller groups of residents and new surroundings, generally seems to aid adaptive behavior in residents. Although it is hard to separate specific elements, several of the studies suggest that an increase in the opportunity for personal control by residents may be a contributor to improvement in adaptive behavior.

COMPARISONS BETWEEN "COMMUNITY ALTERNATIVES" AND "INSTITUTIONS"

Although the superiority of "community" facilities over large institutions is well-accepted on moral grounds, until recently little data have been available to judge this supposition. However, several studies suggest that greater growth in adaptive skills does occur in community settings but that it is unclear what the relevant dimensions of "community" and "institution" are.

For example, two studies compared matched samples of people living in community settings to those living in institutions and found differences favoring community living. Schroeder and Henes (1978) tested the adaptive functioning of 19 mentally retarded people in four group homes and of a matched sample in an institution, and retested this group 1 year later. They found that the community group had progressed significantly further, with most of the difference due to improvements in communications skills. Similarly, Conroy, Efthimiou, and Lemanowicz (1982) compared 70 people who moved to community settings to a matched sample who remained in the institution. The movers improved their adaptive behavior as measured by the ABS, whereas the people who remained in institutions did not. (Given the potential inferential problems that may occur with quasi-experiments, including situations where matching may have unanticipated consequences, these studies need to be approached somewhat cautiously.)

Whereas the preceding studies discovered fairly general progress, Kleinberg and Galligan (1983) found patterns of improvements in adaptive behaviors after 20 mentally retarded adults moved to community residences: Significant improvement in adaptive behaviors occurred only among behaviors already in the residents' repertoires such as socializing and not in others that they did not currently employ such as self-direction. This is similar to findings of other researchers such as Aanes and Moen (1976) and Fiorelli and Thurman (1979). Kleinberg and Galligan (1983) concluded that this pattern of improvement was due to the everyday life patterns of the residences that required a large amount of domestic activities and hence these behaviors were in the repertoires of many residents. However, activity and social interaction improvement in realms such as vocational skills are not likely to occur without conscious training because they were not normally present in the homes. Kleinberg and Galligan (1983) suggest that the quality and orientation of training may be more important than whether a facility is located in the community or in an institution.

A possible contaminating factor in research focusing on the impacts of moves from institutions to the community is the impact of the move itself. Several earlier studies of institutionalized elderly people being involuntarily relocated have suggested that such a move may be extremely stressful and may in fact result in a higher death rate (see, e.g., Aldrich & Mendkoff, 1963; Bourestom & Tars, 1974; Jasnau, 1967; Heller, 1982, provides a careful review). Such dramatic effects in geriatric populations raise questions about the impacts of moving on younger mentally retarded people. The literature does not provide evidence of increased mortality, but several studies show some negative impacts on adaptive functioning. Cohen, Conroy, Fraser, Snelbecker, and Spreat (1977) administered the ABS to 92 severely and profoundly retarded people who moved from a large (1100-resident) state facility to a somewhat smaller (150-resident) one. They found that higher functioning residents became more withdrawn after the move and decreased their language functioning, whereas lower functioning residents actually improved in domestic activity, self-direction, and responsibility; however, they also increased maladaptive behaviors. In contrast, Carsrud, Carsrud, Henderson, Alisch, and Fowler (1979) found that profoundly retarded residents decreased their adaptive behavior after relocation. Preparation may at least partially ameliorate these effects. Weinstock, Wulkan, Colon, Coleman, and Goncalves (1979) found that when residents were provided a tour and extensive explanation of the new facility prior to the move they showed no difference in adaptive behavior from a matched sample remaining in the institution.

Population, environmental, and treatment differences may account for the effects found in these sev-

eral studies. A number of studies have found differential reactivity to environments for people with varying intellectual and functional abilities (see, e.g., Hull & Thompson, 1980; Landesman-Dwyer, Stein, & Sackett, 1978; MacEachron, 1983; Zimring, Weitzer, & Knight, 1982), and the relocation studies have examined individuals with somewhat different abilities. The Weinstock and colleagues (1979) research, particularly, involved capable residents, and such a preparation procedure may be less effective for lower functioning individuals. Evidence from other, nonretarded populations suggests that people predisposed to depression or neurosis have more severe reactions to relocation (Heller, 1982). We are unaware of studies of relocation of mentally retarded people that have examined these variables. Also, Heller (1982) suggests that for nonretarded people the impact of moving may be mediated by the perception of the relative quality of the new and old settings. Whereas the Weinstock and colleagues (1979) research suggests that this mediator may affect at least some mentally retarded people, its generality has yet to be determined.

To summarize the research on comparisons between community alternatives and institutions, it appears that community alternatives often foster greater improvements in adaptive behavior, and particularly in self-help, socialization, and communication. However, it remains unclear which of the many differences between those setting types are most important, although several studies suggest that the everyday domestic patterns required in these facilities may account for many of the differences. Interpretation of this research is complicated by the disruptive impacts of the relocation itself.

STUDIES OF COMMUNITY RESIDENCES

Several studies have examined differences between community facilities and have found that environmental differences affect behavior. For example, in a large study of 245 mentally retarded residents of 87 family-care homes, Eyman, Demaine, and Lei (1979) examined the relationship of PASS 3 ratings of the normalization of the residence to three consecutive annual ABS ratings of the residents. Using path analysis, they found that high PASS 3 facility scores on location of services, comfort, and appearance seemed to predict significant positive changes in personal self-sufficiency by residents. In an observational study of 406 residents and staff living in 20 group homes in the state of Washington, Landesman-Dwyer, Stein, and Sackett (1978) found that residents in older buildings left the residence more often than did residents of buildings built specially as group homes. Also, group homes that were owned as part of a chain had more inactivity by residents than did homes under single ownership.

In a study that included both group homes for psychiatric patients and group homes for mentally retarded people, Bakos and his colleagues (Bakos et al., 1979) studied 15 residences using observation, questionnaires, interviews, and other methods. They found that a more resident-oriented treatment arrangement predicted several positive differences in resident behaviors, including more cooperation and more talking with others. One longitudinal study has found, however, that the positive results indicated by Landesman-Dwyer and her colleagues and by Bakos and his colleagues may not persist. Birenbaum (1980) observed that as residents lived in the community for several years they made progressively fewer visits outside the home and had a more constrained range of activities.

In addition, several research efforts have examined differences between group homes and family-care homes with mixed results. Baker, Seltzer, and Seltzer (1974) studied a range of living alternatives and found that residents in group homes were given more in-home responsibility and were more likely to have contact with the community than were family-care residents. Schreerenberger and Felsenthal (1977) found that family-care homes tend to have a structured schedule. Willer and Intaglia (1982) noted that family-care residents displayed fewer behavioral problems than did group home residents but were also more passive and less assertive. (It would seem plausible that this finding might result from a lower amount of activity in family-care homes.)

In sum, there seems to be evidence for the differential impact on residents of different community-living alternatives. Good comfort and appearance seem to be related to improved self-sufficiency by residents. Difference in treatment such as orientation of care also seems to affect resident behavior. However, the research literature does not yet allow a critical question to be answered: What environmental and treatment qualities allow the salutory effects of a group residence to *persist?*

SIZE
Size, defined as overall capacity or the size of the living unit, enters into most discussions of environments for retarded people, with the most general conclusion being that settings that are larger are dehumanizing and impersonal and have a negative impact on residents. (Without acknowledging the link, many discussions of size of living environments for

mentally retarded people describe large settings in terms similar to those that ecological psychologists use in describing "overmanned" settings: The individual's contribution is devalued; each person performs fewer activities, and so on.) However, the research on overall capacity of the facility has not borne this out (see Balla, 1976; Baroff, 1980; Landesman-Dwyer, 1981, for reviews). Most studies considering size have found that whereas there were differences between general types of facilities—such as group homes versus large public institutions—there were no consistent relationships between size and quality of care or resident behavior within type.

For example, King and colleagues (1971) developed a Child Management Scale to assess the treatment orientation of a setting (resident-oriented vs. institution-oriented). In a field study of 10 institutions including a large array of facility types (children's homes, hospitals, hostels, etc.), they found great differences between types—hostels were much more resident-oriented than hospitals—but that the differences within type were apparently unrelated to overall capacity. In any case, there is no necessity to infer that size is related to the relationship between number of persons and number of valued roles to be fulfilled in an institution, even though this ratio was found to vary by size in studies of overmanning in schools (Barker & Gump, 1964).

McCormick, Balla, and Ziegler (1975) used the Child Management Scale to compare four size classes of facilities: large central institutions (with a population of over 1000 residents); medium-sized regional centers (150 to 300 residents); small regional centers (10 to 116 residents); and, group homes (7 to 57 residents). As in the King et al. (1971) study, they found dramatic differences between facility types, yet few differences attributable to size within type. However, they did find that the *size of the living unit* (defined as number of residents) predicted orientation of care, with smaller units being more resident-oriented. This finding is corroborated by Witt (1981), who found that the social maturity of a group of 95 mentally retarded residents increased when ward populations were decreased from 30 to 14.

An interesting question about research considering the impact on resident progress of environmental qualities such as size is what baseline growth to expect. Balla, Butterfield, and Ziegler (1974) studied 103 mentally retarded children in four institutions ranging in size from 2012 residents to 383 residents. They found overall improvements in mental age in all settings over time but no relationship to the size of the facility.

An overall conclusion of research focusing on size is that within a facility type, overall size is not a reliable predictor of treatment orientation or quality of care. In fact, in an observational study of 20 group homes in the State of Washington, Landesman-Dwyer, Sackett & Kleinman (1980) found that residents in larger group homes were actually more social than those in smaller settings. Bjaanes and Butler (1974) obtained similar results when they compared the behavior of 10 individuals in two group homes. And in a study of 160 facilities in southern California ranging in size from 1 to 95 residents, Butler and Bjaanes (1978) noted that smaller facilities were often actually less therapeutic than larger ones because they tended to take less advantage of outside resources. Size of the individual living unit does seem to be important, with smaller units generally contributing to increases in adaptive behavior by residents and treatment practices that are more resident-oriented by staff.

Summary and Conclusions: Research on Environments for Mentally Retarded Persons

This research can be viewed from the perspective of the three-dimensional model we have described previously, where the impact of the environment on behavior can be defined in terms of individual needs and abilities, design of the physical environment, and social and temporal organizational factors. For mentally retarded people, individual needs and abilities have been demonstrated to affect environment–behavior interaction in a variety of complex ways. In terms of predictor variables, many studies have found that IQ is a significant predictor of the effects of normalization of living facilities on residents. As for outcome variables, several research efforts have shown that living in smaller, more homelike, community facilities can have positive impacts on adaptive behaviors and primarily on communication and socialization. One training program that improved residents' skill prior to relocation found that the training ameliorated the negative impacts of the move (Weinstock et al., 1979).

This research has also focused on the design of the physical environment. Whereas several authors have attempted to catalog the physical qualities of normality or institutionalization (see, e.g., Gunzberg, 1968; Pederson, 1970; Rivlin, 1978; Rivlin, Bogert, & Cirillo, 1981), empirical research has only recently begun to untangle the critical issues. As we have discussed before, studies comparing significantly different building types such as large institutions with small group homes have emerged with reasonably consistent findings: Community living enhances growth in adaptive behavior. However, it is difficult to separate the effects of physical environmental differences from those caused by varying approaches to training. Several studies have suggested that the overall size of a facility may be less important than the size of a living unit. Several works have also suggested that ergonomic qualities of environments may be important: the simplicity of controls, availability of props, and so on. In addition, several research efforts have found that a critical aspect of environments for mentally retarded people is the extent to which they support the control of social interaction by residents. Even for people labeled *severely* or *profoundly retarded,* it is important to provide private rooms and well-marked, controllable semiprivate spaces.

A number of social and organizational factors have emerged as well, and in fact, some researchers have proposed that treatment orientation by staff may be more important than physical symbols of normalization. However, the relationship between physical environment and treatment is not always what had been expected: Larger community facilities may have more community contact than do smaller ones. Also, there is, apparently at least in some residences, a decrease in community contact over time.

Research on environments for mentally retarded people is marred by serious methodological and inferential problems. Because of ethical and therapeutic concerns, few studies have employed random assignment, sample sizes tend to be small, and causal inferences are difficult to make (see Cook & Campbell, 1979). A larger number of studies has used matching, but matching may have serious unpredictable systematic effects on the results, depending on the relationship of the matching variables to the predictor and outcome variables. More attention needs to be given to these inferential problems, and wherever possible experimental or even quasi-experimental design should be employed (Cook & Campbell, 1979).

There are several significant points of interaction between the three dimensions. The design of the physical environment provides or eliminates training opportunities; it allows mentally retarded people to operate independently or only with help; and it establishes mentally retarded people as equals or as inferiors. What remains is to better understand the relationship between specific needs and abilities, specific physical settings, and specific social and temporal factors. Studies such as those by Zimring, Weitzer, and Knight (1982) suggest that whereas nonretarded people may thrive in suite-type settings, mentally retarded people, who may be less socially skilled, may require more concrete ways to control social interaction: private rooms, closable doors defining semiprivate space, and so on. In other words, to actually understand person–environment fit, we need to develop a taxonomy of person, situation, and environment. The old labels of *institution* or *community* are not of much value in targeting environments for this special population, and neither are the customary assumptions that accompany the labels *retarded* or *normal*. Some progress has been made in considering behavioral profiles or in environmental checklists, but we need to know more.

24.4. CHILDREN

Children receive no end of attention, at home, in municipal budgets, and in this handbook. Chapter 6 by Wohlwill and Heft provides valuable detail on linkages between various levels of the environment and aspects of children's development. Children do not represent a special population far from the public eye, and there is no need in this chapter to contribute at any length to the identification of children for emergent studies.

It is for this precise reason, however, that some discussion of children is necessary in this context. They have been targeted (indeed, spotlighted) with respect to schools and, to a less thorough extent, playgrounds. This is not in itself unfair. School-age children spend a major part of the typical weekday in such institutional environments, and when school time is considered in conjunction with the time needed for normal self-maintenance activities (e.g., eating, sleeping), the typical schooldays of young people have relatively few degrees of freedom (Michelson, 1984). Similarly, it has been said that children's work is play; schools aside, the adult emphasis on playgrounds is not misplaced—as far as such a focus has gone. But for all their influence, schools represent only a fraction of the environments to which children are exposed. Medrich and colleagues (1982), for example, provide valuable detail on the salience and varieties of nonschool environments in which children spend weekday time, not to speak of periods like weekends and vacations that almost totally omit the school environment. Insofar as typical designs do not cover a spectrum of stages in children's development and hence are used selectively by age, children can and do exercise the freedom to bypass playgrounds for other places to play

(Gump, 1975; Pollowy, 1977). Once beyond schools and playgrounds, children, no matter how revered and numerous, are surprisingly untargeted in design, and most customary assumptions about design do not reflect their special characteristics. Many aspects of the environments to which children are exposed reflect a need to view them as the kind of special population that fits Box 3 in Figure 24.1.

Therefore, this section of the chapter will focus on children in the restricted but important perspective of the kinds of representative misfits that appear in the person–environment relationships of a group that is so large and nominally prominent.

24.4.1. Targeting Children

Some of the explanation behind the situations in which children are not targeted undoubtedly lies in a now-obsolete assumption—that beyond the degree that they are covered by municipal obligations concerning public education and park design, children are fully and adequately cared for within nuclear families. Presumably, this includes congruent environments as well.

This assumption is incomplete in a number of ways. First, the individual family is not in a position to order or control most aspects of the urban environment outside the four walls of its dwelling unit (or, under favorable circumstances, the boundaries of its garden). As children grow, increasing time is spent, unless this is impossible, in neighborhood and (during progressive teenage years) wider urban and metropolitan settings. Even at home, though, there are characteristic sources of misfit. Children have a much greater susceptibility to accidents involving common aspects of home environment and products (paint chips, stairways, stoves, poisons, etc.) than do adults, who are often oblivious of the range of child-specific hazards. Research has shown as well that children typically get allocated space at home on a residual basis—after parents have staked out prime space for their own activities. This includes the smallest, often shared bedrooms, and places to study or play like kitchens that no one else has preempted (and less likely shielded in terms of sight or sound from others) (Keller, 1977; Socialdepartmentet, 1975).

But even if one could assume ideal environments for children within the home, the recent trends toward widespread maternal employment mean changes in where children spend their time. Recent work on the use of time and space by children of women who vary in degree of employment shows that the greatest differences in the nature and locus of daily life according to their mother's employment status occur in the youngest children (Michelson, 1985). When the mother has a full-time job, a young child is, not surprisingly, much more likely to spend a significant part of the day away from home, including periods of travel that reflect the centralization of the child-care setting utilized. Ironically, little public attention has been devoted to design and services for this age group in North America. It is the presence of educational institutions, among other factors, that helps to minimize differences by maternal employment as children grow older. Nonetheless, when older children have mothers working full-time, they are, in the absence of lunchtime and/or afterschool services, more likely to return to an empty house, in which girls usually remain alone and from which boys more likely go outside or to friends' homes—both beyond parental supervision and control (Michelson, 1985).

24.4.2. Customary Assumptions and Children

Some of the major defining characteristics of children mean not only that they fail to meet customary assumptions about the minimum competence needed to deal with many aspects of the contemporary environment but that they are vulnerable in that process.

1. Children start out small and weak. This makes it hard to open doors, climb onto buses, reach elevator buttons, and indeed as much as see adequately where they are going.
2. They have no prior experience in coping with their surroundings. Even if they were strong enough to manipulate their environments, they have to comprehend where to go, how to act under particular circumstances, and how to deal with other people.
3. They seldom have much money. Hence they lack the independent capability to participate in either market or nonprofit activities requiring payment, nor can they purchase ways of adapting to environments other than through older persons.
4. Certain capabilities to deal with environments are withheld on an age-graded basis. Driving a car, for example, is seldom sanctioned before the age of 16, often later. Voting for municipal and other officials and property ownership (requiring the ability to enter into a legal contract) are generally reserved for the age of 18 or later.
5. Hence children are typically unable to influence urban decision making and management except

through the initiatives of others (most likely their parents). By themselves, they lack power and control over most environmental situations.

Such a situation with respect to the environment is, unfortunately, not unique to children. Other special groups like the elderly, the handicapped, and various other "minority" groups share one or more of these deviations from customary assumptions about environmental competence. Children, nonetheless, take on an added dimension of salience in this regard because the environment with which they so relate served as the setting for their formative years. When, for example, one learns early that most aspects of the environment are not controllable, to what extent can a conversion of view occur when more control becomes legally and socially possible with age? Parental example becomes a major force in the absence of personal experience for good and ill.

Although the relative lack of targeting for children and the meeting of customary assumptions by children can be understood on their own in a relatively straightforward manner, it is in combination that the nature and variety of person–environment misfits involving children can be most clearly viewed.

24.4.3. Children as an Untargeted, Noncustomary Special Population

Several examples are offered here to give some idea of the flavor and variety of effects on children who often represent a special population that is not sufficiently targeted nor meeting customary assumptions.

Automobile Accidents

Children's relationship to automobile accidents is a case in point. An accident is a clear-cut, severe outcome of a person–environment misfit. The auto-related environment obviously is not appropriate for children's existence or activities when an accident occurs. Not least is this the case because accidents are randomly distributed in neither time nor space (Bunge et al., 1975; National Academy of Sciences, 1976). There are predictable locations where accidents occur most frequently, reflecting where the paths of children and vehicles literally overlap by intent (e.g., pickup points for school buses and car pools) and where children meet fast or heavy traffic by surprise (e.g., from behind tall bushes and fences or by engagement in an activity that makes unexpected incursions into traffic lanes such as cycling or ballplaying). Sandels (1974) concluded from her research that children lack the developmental skills up to about the age of 12 to react as rationally to oncoming cars as do adults. Therefore adult schemes that emphasize the education of children regarding traffic safety miss both a dimension of vulnerability among children and the need of physical barriers to regulate the separation of children and cars where they expect to meet and the need to remove barriers to vision where these jeopardize life and limb.

Statistics, moreover, indicate that, beyond the number and the degree of predictability of such pedestrian accidents encountered by children, they suffer even more accidents and deaths as passengers (Michelson & Roberts, 1979). Automobile design, for example, which has focused on restraining devices for adults is a prime example of nontargeting for children.[1] Recent manufacturing of kiddie seats and the impetus for their use come from different sources than auto design more generally.

Pollution Standards

Although on the surface quite different, pollution standards represent another potentially life-threatening situation where children are not sufficiently targeted and do not meet customary assumptions. Pollution standards, although welcome, typically fail to be calibrated to the characteristics of children exposed to polluted air and soil, nor to the circumstances under which they come in contact with the pollutants. Los Angeles, for example, does set a lower threshold to warn so-called sensitive people about air that might be found unhealthful before other segments of the population might be affected. Yet children, who are generally more sensitive because they are smaller, tend to inhale more pollution because their routines involve active movement in outside play. They tend to come into contact more with heavier pollutants such as lead from the automobile exhaust because they are shorter. And they come into contact with pollutants in the soil because they are more likely to play in and around dirt (Kane, 1976). To be more effective, environmental pollution regulators would have to target children more explicitly, taking into consideration the systematic ways by which children violate customary assumptions about the degree and means of exposure as well as degrees of organic vulnerability.

Institutional Scale

Economists, stressing savings that can be realized through larger scales of enterprises and greater centralization, have fostered political initiatives for building large, comprehensive facilities and institutions, while closing existing settings that are small or de-

clining in user populations. Consolidated schools and relatively large, distant day-care centers are examples of this trend that are pertinent to children.

These economists and politicians have adult taxpayers as their targets, when thinking about this form of environmental intervention. Ecological psychologists indicate that it is unlikely that these economists had children as their targets because the interests of children appear better served by smaller institutions. Barker and Gump (1964) found that children are more engaged in small schools because standard institutional patterns of activity are more likely to require the participation of individuals, whose talents are expanded and rewarded in the process. In the big school, alienation is more likely insofar as students (like citizens in an increasingly large-scale world) must compete with others for the privilege of playing a needed or wanted role. Many more children are likely to feel on the outside under such conditions, which saps their involvement in the core of what they have to do (see Wicker, Chapter 16, this volume).

Small institutions are also of relevance to children with respect specifically to children's environmental competence. It is geographically more feasible to have small institutions more decentralized in space— hence closer to children's homes. Given the limited control children have in the sphere of travel, proximate facilities fit children's capabilities better. Long commutes such as accompany major consolidated schools in rural areas or legislated busing in some large metropolitan areas are physically and mentally debilitating, and they necessarily take time from other activities.

Daycare Location

Work in Toronto on the child-care settings of employed mothers produced a not very surprising finding that day-care centers, the most centralized alternative, are typically located significantly farther from home than home daycare and care from grandparents. The direction of travel is typically something of a diversion from the route from home to work, though not a dramatic detour. Nonetheless, mothers' tension in their daily travel was found mildly though significantly related to how much extra distance the child-care dropoff added to the daily commute, not the total length of travel from home to work or distance from home to place of child care (Michelson, 1984).

Play Areas

Finally, one can turn to the realm of play to observe how even as a target with respect to conventional playground planning, children escape from the view of designers in ways that reflect children's failure to meet customary assumptions. Throughout the sensitive research on people's orientations to the physical environment that made up so much of his life's work, Lynch made penetrating observations on children's de facto use of space, together with some understandings of accompanying rationales. He noted that children frequently utilize what he called *hidden environments* (1977)—places like back alleys and vacant lots left in a vacuum by adults. Unable to exercise control or enjoy relative privacy in formally appropriate land uses by virtue of being children, they turn to making places that are out of mind and somewhat out of sight into their own turf, without the need to hassle with anyone about the programming of activities on such sites. Younger children do not necessarily turn in that direction, because their stage of development usually falls within the parameters of supervised play. But as schoolchildren go beyond the immediate environment of parents and siblings, their play needs keep pace with the spatial and social expansions of their lives.

Adventure playgrounds, for example, are advocated to reflect the need of older children to program their play environments with personal initiatives and continuity. In the typical adventure playground, the young person utilizes building supplies and tools, made available in lieu of the fixed play equipment. He or she works on long-term projects that can be individual but are more likely to be done in conjunction with friends on the site. Small structures and play equipment are most frequently built. An adult supervisor is considered necessary given the nature of the resources, but this person usually keeps in the background. It is ironic but perhaps not surprising that as the recommended functional equivalent of the hidden environment, the adventure playground is heartily disliked by adult neighbors and (in consequence) by political leaders due to its disorderly appearance, even though it has been found to reflect preteenage children's normally nontargeted and special needs (Cooper, 1970; Spivack, 1969).

Thus children may be well recognized and liked as a group, but they nonetheless require considerable attention in many diverse respects in response to the lack of adequate recognition of ways in which they diverge from customary assumptions, when indeed targeting goes beyond a few, selected contexts.

24.5. HOSPITAL VISITORS

Consistent with the definition provided earlier in this chapter, hospital visitors can be considered a special population. Their needs have typically not been considered in hospital design or management—they have not been targeted—and the environment, as it has been designed for other hospital users, is not necessarily congruent with their needs: It does not meet customary assumptions.

24.5.1. Targeting

There are at least three reasons why hospital visitors have not been targeted. Although large in absolute numbers, individuals are hospital visitors, in most cases, for limited periods of time. Thus visitors, as a group, are typically not organized in any formal way. Neither are they usually represented in the hospital organization, probably because they are not seen as having political or economic power. Thus in the case of a design project, hospital client representatives typically focus on staff and patients and consider visitors in a somewhat token way, if at all (such as providing waiting areas).

A second reason why visitors have not been targeted may be that their needs conflict with needs of other, more powerful user groups. For example, during the course of design of a new intensive care unit, physicians argued that a visitor waiting area should be eliminated and the space used instead for clinical purposes (Carpman & Grant, 1984a).

Even if a hospital would like to target its visitor population as design users, it is limited by the state of the art. There is only a very small amount of information about the design needs and preferences of hospital visitors, and the majority of this work has focused on one large, midwestern, teaching hospital (Reizenstein, Grant, & Vaitkus, 1981).

24.5.2. Importance

Despite the fact that hospital visitors have not had their behavioral needs explicitly considered in the design and management of the environment in the past, it is important that these be considered in future work. Visitors play valuable roles in the hospital setting—roles that it is in the interest of hospitals to recognize and promote.

What is most important is that visitors attend to the psychosocial needs of patients, needs that are often not attended to by staff as they care for the patient's physiological requirements. Visitors also implicitly remind patients of their status as human beings, as contrasted with medical personnel who may, although unwittingly, focus only on a leg or a heart or an infection. Visitors can actually save time for the nursing staff by performing various care tasks for the patient. Even small requests like filling a water pitcher or adjusting a pillow may save a staff member a trip to the patient's room.

Furthermore, hospitals are becoming increasingly conscious of competing for patient dollars and of the necessity to market their services (Carpman, Grant, & Simmons, 1986). Hospital visitors are natural targets for hospitals' marketing interests because they themselves are potential patients and because their hospital experience may influence friends' or family's choice of health-care facilities. Thus it is in the hospital's direct economic interest to foster good public relations with their visitors.

24.5.3. Special Circumstances

Hospitals are often designed to accommodate their most frequent users: medical staff. However, visitors' environmental needs are not necessarily congruent with an environment designed to meet staff requirements. Although individual characteristics and circumstances may vary, some commonalities frequently include:

1. Hospital visitors are often in an environment unfamiliar to them.
2. Many visitors are worried about the friend or relative who is sick.
3. Visitors may be away from home and experiencing disruption of their normal daily routine.
4. Many visitors find hospitals to be frightening places (Carpman, Grant, & Simmons, 1984a).

These circumstances may work together to render the individual less able to cope than normal. For example, finding one's way and making sense of unfamiliar terminology that might be challenging or enjoyable in another setting (such as a trip to the zoo) may be disturbing and stressful here (Carpman, Grant, & Simmons, 1984b).

24.5.4. Temporary Vulnerability

Hospital visitors are a particularly interesting special population to examine for several reasons. One is that their vulnerability, although very intense, is temporary. Becoming a visitor is a role one takes on with the hospitalization of a friend or relative. It is usually not considered as one's primary distinguishing characteristic, as is often the case with other special populations such as blind, elderly, or developmentally disabled people.

Of course, there are a number of groups whose environmental vulnerability is temporary. Some of these groups are vulnerable by virtue of a physiological condition such as hospital inpatients, pregnant women, or people using crutches. Other potentially and temporarily environmentally vulnerable people are those who, for various reasons, take on a stressful role such as hospital visitors. In fact, one might speculate that large numbers of people are temporarily environmentally vulnerable. Although difficult to measure precisely, it is possible that there may be extremely large numbers of people suffering from temporary physical disabilities or emotional stress at any given time. People with bad backs that impair walking, those with head colds that diminish hearing, those having experienced a recent business setback or a divorce, would all be included in this classification. Temporary environmental vulnerability is not only a new way of looking at special populations; it may involve far more people than had been previously thought.

24.5.5. Why Focus on Hospital Visitors?

We concentrate here on hospital visitors for several reasons. Because it is a role that takes place in one type of setting, relationships between visitors' behaviors and attitudes and the physical environment are circumscribed to a degree that makes limited description possible. By comparison, discussing the environmental interactions of a newly divorced person would be far more involved, covering many different settings and situations. Second, it is a role that many people have experienced—some multiple times. Thus focusing on hospital visitors as special populations in relation to the physical environment may enable the reader to see a familiar situation in a new way. Third, hospital visitors are a temporary special population that has begun to be studied by environmental psychologists and whose environmental relationships have not been widely reported elsewhere. This small body of information, some of which is data-based and some informed speculation, can serve as a sample approach to understanding the environmental issues surrounding one type of special population.

24.5.6. Experiences Common to Hospital Visitors

Hospital visitors are obviously not a homogeneous group, as most special populations are not. Because virtually anyone can take on this role, visitors vary according to demographic measures such as age, sex, education, and the like. They also vary with regard to the particular patient situation they confront. The patient may or may not be a close relative or friend and may or may not be seriously ill. Obviously, those visiting a close relative who is severely ill are likely to experience the hospital differently than will those visiting a professional colleague hospitalized for minor surgery.

Given these differences and the fact that environmental conditions vary widely among hospitals, there are some experiences that can probably be thought of as common to many hospital visitors. One study at the University of Michigan Hospital asked visitors if various aspects of their experience caused them stress as they defined the term (Reizenstein et al., 1981). Various aspects of the experience itself and of the related physical environments were said by respondents to cause them "a lot of stress," "some stress," or "no stress." This study of 106 randomly sampled hospital visitors found that many activities, from disrupting the typical home or work routine, to finding a place to park, worrying about the patient, to finding a comfortable place to wait, were all considered stressful to varying degrees. A particular source of stress was finding the way through the unfamiliar and often confusing physical environment (Carpman & Vaitkus, in preparation; Hill, 1958; Zimring, 1981).

The Michigan study of visitor activity patterns found that these visitors spent time throughout the hospital: in waiting areas, corridors, and in public spaces such as the lobby, cafeteria, or gift shop, in addition to spending time in the patient room. However, unlike the inpatient—whose spatial base in the hospital is the patient room and who is seen as a legitimate user of other examination, treatment, and public spaces in the hospital—visitors often feel that they do not belong in any part of the hospital, unless their patient is in a private room (Reizenstein et al., 1981).

Reizenstein and colleagues (1981) described a pattern of how close relatives or friends of severely ill patients often see their role. Although they are extremely concerned about the patient's well-being and would like to be able to assist in some way, typically hospital routine does not allow for this. Although it has been speculated that the presence of caring visitors is therapeutic for most patients, often hospital staff, in an effort to get their own jobs done efficiently, think of visitors as extraneous—people who mean well but who get in the way. This attitude as well as nonverbal environmental "messages" that may be interpreted by visitors as having symbolic meaning convey the idea that visitors do not belong in the hospital. (Small, smoky waiting areas or un-

comfortable chairs by the patient's bedside are examples of environmental attributes that can be interpreted in symbolic as well as in literal ways.)

Reizenstein and colleagues (1981) also found that the visitors they studied seemed to internalize this view and tried not to call attention to themselves or to their own needs while in the hospital. They dubbed this the *invisible visitor syndrome.* Interviewers found that many visitors not only go along with the conception of themselves as invisible, but they seem to encourage it:

> I would say that they are forgotten and they feel forgotten. But they think that's the way it should be. They say, "But the hospital is not here for visitors, it's here for patients," as if it had to be either or.
>
> "If I'm good, if I'm quiet, if I don't ask for anything for myself, the patient will get better." That's all they want—for the patient to get better and get out of the hospital. And they feel that anything they do to draw attention to themselves will detract from that. (p. 1)

The same researchers report that many visitors experience a sort of nameless anger at their situation, yet have no target for their anger. What many visitors do not appear to understand is that in order to continue to offer support to the patient, they themselves need good care during the stressful hospitalization period.

Often compounding the feeling of helplessness that goes along with not being able to make the patient well, for the Michigan visitors, is a feeling of ignorance about how to find various services within the hospital and within the surrounding community. These visitors often craved information about hospital policies and amenities, as well as information about eating places, drugstores, and inexpensive places to stay overnight (Reizenstein et al., 1981).

These same researchers report that shared hardships often lead to shared understanding. The occurrence of small communities of visitors was one of the more positive findings about the visitor situation. Sharing small waiting spaces and common stressful situations, often over long periods of time, seemed to lead visitors on some units to regularly talk with one another (Reizenstein et al., 1981).

Hospital visitors are often ignored by larger organizations than the hospitals themselves. For example, in contrast to the carefully kept statistics on hospital patients, little or no local, regional, or national statistical information exists about hospital visitors (Reizenstein et al., 1981). Although visitors spend large numbers of hours in the hospital and perform valuable functions, including lending physical and emotional support for the patient, they have also been virtually ignored in the literature. A few articles focus on visitors' needs (Idea forum, 1981; Hoover, 1979; Traylor, 1979; Van Dyke, 1980; Welsh, 1982), and only a very few empirical studies of visitors have been undertaken (Bernstein, Manchester, & Weaver, 1980; Nicklin, 1979; Molter, 1979; Reizenstein et al., 1981).

24.5.7. Design Research on Hospital Visitors

Two applied hospital environmental design research programs in American hospitals have focused on visitors, at least in part. Bellevue Hospital Center, in New York City, uses environmental design research in its renovation projects, and the University of Michigan Hospital, in Ann Arbor, Michigan, used environmental design research as direct input to its $285-million Replacement Hospital Program.

The Bellevue program focuses on identifying users' needs (patients, visitors, and staff) relevant to renovation of various hospital departments. This information is conveyed to the project's designers, and a small staff steering committee comprised of representatives from each relevant service works with the designers. After the project is completed and about 6 months after occupants have settled in, the researchers evaluate the new design, using criteria based on the problems and goals originally agreed on. Users are also asked their personal opinions about the design and its effect on their productivity (for staff) or emotional state (patients or visitors). Minor changes are made in the design, if evaluation findings uncover any important and correctable problems (Olsen, 1982).

At the University of Michigan, the Patient and Visitor Participation (PVP) Project combined empirical research and advocacy in order to influence the design process for the Replacement Hospital Program in such a way that the resulting design and related policies accommodate the needs of patients and visitors. The key conceptual idea underlying the PVP Project is that hospital patients' and visitors' design needs grow out of a desire to reduce the stress inherent in the hospital environment. The Project gathered data from over 3200 patients and visitors and over 1200 staff in 33 different studies, resulting in reports, literature reviews, design guidelines, and a full-length book. The PVP Project has offered hospital designers and administrators both a process for involving hospital consumers in design and a body of knowledge about their needs. The majority of design-related recommendations growing out of this project had direct

impact on the design of a new adult general hospital and an outpatient services facility (Carpman, 1983; Reizenstein & Grant, 1982a).

24.5.8. Environmental Design Issues Relevant to Hospital Visitors

The Michigan PVP Project has proposed that four environmental design issues are most relevant to hospital visitors: wayfinding, physical comfort, privacy and personal territory, and symbolic meaning (Steele, 1973). These constructs have also been used to examine the relationships of acute-care inpatients to the physical environment (Shumaker & Reizenstein, 1982).

Wayfinding

Wayfinding, the "actual behavior people employ in finding important locations in the environment" (Zimring, 1981), is likely to be a particularly significant environmentally related issue to hospital visitors.[2] Characteristics of the visit, the setting, and management policies often combine to make wayfinding unusually stressful. Most visitors tend to be unfamiliar with the detailed layout of the hospital. Visitors often spend most of their time in one small part of the hospital, usually the patient room and closest waiting area. As a result, they tend not to experience enough of the environment to be able to develop a coherent cognitive map.

Hospital buildings often add to wayfinding difficulties because many are large and complex and have experienced incremental growth over the years. The resulting layout is often a patchwork design that is difficult to negotiate, even for staff. The stress resulting from hospitalization of a loved one, as reported by the Michigan visitors, compounded by the change in normal work routine and family responsibilities, appears to leave visitors without many of their normal coping mechanisms. To expend precious energy on finding their way within the hospital was seen by many of these visitors as an unnecessary insult (Reizenstein et al., 1981; Reizenstein & Grant, 1982b). The problem is exacerbated by the fact that many hospitals do not have a comprehensive and understandable way-finding system (Carpman, Grant, & Simmons, 1984b; Weisman, 1982). Such a system would include clear and well-placed signs, portable directions in the form of clear maps, directories and "You-Are-Here" maps posted at key decision points, as well as staff trained to give clear, consistent directions.

Although wayfinding has been hypothesized as a significant cause of environmentally induced stress, there are few empirical studies that examine way-finding behavior and attitudes in detail. (One exception is Weisman, 1981.) In the Michigan visitor study, wayfinding accounted for a large portion of visitors' "total measured stress" (Carpman & Vaitkus, in preparation).[3]

It is clear that systematic research on the wayfinding patterns and needs of hospital visitors is at an early stage of development. As with the other design and behavior issues described here, wayfinding is a topic of interest to both basic and applied researchers. Wayfinding by first-time or unfamiliar users under stress in a large, complex building is a potential opportunity for researchers to learn more about environmental cognition: how people process enough information to enable them to reach a particular destination and what accounts for differences in how information is processed (Downs, 1979).

For those interested in application of the admittedly limited state of the art to present design problems, specific suggestions for increasing the ease of wayfinding for hospital visitors include (1) design hospital buildings in ways so that they are able to be understood by first-time users (Weisman, 1982), (2) enable people to familiarize themselves with the hospital layout before they arrive by sending maps and photographs as part of an introductory package, (3) design and maintain a good signage system, using terms understood by laypersons (e.g., "Ear, Nose and Throat," instead of otorhinolaryngology), mount signs where people can see them, use letter sizes large enough to read at a distance, place signs frequently enough so that people will be reassured that they are going the right way, (4) use other means for directing people, including directories, "You-Are-Here" maps (Levine, 1982), and verbal directions given by staff who have been briefed about the importance of visitor wayfinding (Olsen, Winkel, & Pershing, 1982), and (5) consider operating a visitor information center where directions, policies, and other information of interest to visitors is available and specially directed at their needs (Carpman et al., 1984b).

Physical Comfort

Although physical comfort is something many visitors are likely to be willing to forgo, a comfortably designed environment may at least partially mitigate the stress of the hospital visit. Here we broadly interpret the construct of physical comfort to include such things as noise, lighting, body positioning, odors, food, and sleep that can be directly affected by the physical environment, alone or in combination with operating policies.

Noise is one aspect of the hospital setting that can be problematic for hospital visitors. Of those visiting patients in semiprivate or multiple bed rooms, slightly over half the visitors sampled in the PVP Project visitor study reported that they would like to have more acoustical privacy when visiting the patient. Nearly 70% of visitors who came alone felt this way, compared with 49% of visitors who came in a group. Approximately the same number reported being disturbed by noise emanating from the room or from the hallway "frequently" or "sometimes" (Reizenstein et al., 1981). Interviewers working on this study reported that to some visitors, noise, such as staff laughter, may be perceived as an additional reminder of their own emotionally stressful situation. Furthermore, noise from staff conversations, from other patients, or from unfamiliar machinery may be interpreted as fearful by some visitors.

Further basic research is needed on noise in hospitals. Questions that need to be addressed include: What impacts do various types and volumes of sound have on hospital visitors? What individual, social, and environmental factors account for interpretations of various sounds as disturbing?

Design approaches to noise reduction include using sound-attenuating surfaces such as carpeting, ceiling materials, wall materials, and furnishings (Simmons et al., 1982). "White noise" machines that produce sounds resembling wind, surf, or rain have been used in some hospitals to screen out extraneous noise (White noise machines, 1982). Operational policies about the volume and location of conversations between staff members can also reduce the noise problem.

Lighting is another environmental design feature that can lead to visitors' discomfort. Lighting intensity, distribution, and glare can be problematic in the hospital setting. For example, in a visitors' waiting area, lighting might be so bright that people complain of headaches after sitting there for more than a few minutes, or it might be so dim that visitors are unable to read. Lighting might be distributed badly — bright enough for reading by the receptionist's desk but too dim elsewhere in the room. Finally, lighting works in conjunction with other environmental design features, including floor materials and window treatments. Glare can be a particular problem when lighting is reflected by a shiny floor or when it shines through a window and cannot be controlled by shades or curtains (Flynn & Segil, 1970; Hayward & Birenbaum, 1980; Lam, 1977).

Hospital lighting is another topic needing research attention. How are different combinations of technical factors (including color, intensity, and distribution) interpreted by hospital visitors? Which ones are seen as stimulating, restful, comforting, or disturbing? How are these effects influenced by other environmental variables such as room size and color?

Lighting issues also need special attention by lighting designers or by those with expertise in how lighting affects behavior. Hospitals may be able to reduce the intensity of lighting in public areas and thus create a warmer, less institutional ambience. They can also try using indirect rather than direct lighting, task rather than ambient lighting, and warm-toned fluorescents rather than cool-toned fluorescents (Carpman & Grant, 1984a).

Body positioning can be an additional source of physical discomfort for hospital visitors. Visitors spend much of their time sitting while in the hospital. Thus the design of seating can greatly add to visitors' comfort (Carpman & Grant, 1984b). Another environmental design feature related to body positioning is the location of television sets in patient rooms. Wall-hung TVs may enable visitors to comfortably watch TV with the patients, whereas small TVs on extending arms may cause visitors to have to twist or lean uncomfortably (Carpman & Grant, 1984c).

Research on types of body positioning and their relation to environmental design is likely to continue to come from the specialty of ergonomics. Because much about human physiological requirements is already known, a potential avenue for research is on the decision-making processes of furniture and equipment manufacturers. One interesting question to explore concerns the role that scientific findings play in influencing these decisions (Carpman, 1983).

The need for uncomfortable body positioning can be reduced by the selection of seating specially designed for human comfort. A good way to be reasonably confident that manufacturers' claims are valid is to actually test a number of sample seats by having real or surrogate visitors sit on them for long periods of time and record their reactions (Carpman & Grant, 1984b; Reizenstein & Grant, 1983).

Odors are another environmentally related feature that can lead to discomfort on the part of visitors. A number of different hospital smells were mentioned by Michigan visitors as disturbing; however, cigarette smoke was the single most disturbing smell reported (Reizenstein & Grant, 1982b). Many hospital visitors in this study requested separation of smokers and nonsmokers and complained vociferously about having to share the same spaces (Carpman & Grant, 1984a).

Odor is usually a subtle aspect of the physical environment, yet one typically negatively associated with hospitals. Researchers might investigate differ-

ent types of hospital odors, the intensities necessary for recognition, the range of visitors' responses to these, and associations of present smells with past experiences.

Odors in the hospital environment can be made less noticeable by choosing materials that do not retain odors, by frequent housekeeping, and by good ventilation. The problem of smoker/nonsmoker compatibility can be approached through design (provide separate waiting areas for each), through policy (designate certain areas for smokers and others for nonsmokers), or through mechanical devices such as special ventilators (Reizenstein & Grant, 1981b).

Food is an obvious, although often forgotten, source of solace for hospital visitors, and having their access to food impeded in some way can be a considerable source of frustration and annoyance (Reizenstein & Grant, 1982b). Many food-related issues are operational ones, yet there are many design issues related to food, including types of food services available and their respective sizes, locations, and layouts.

Design can influence visitors' comfort in eating: where the food services are located, how the first-time user can negotiate these spaces and mechanisms in order to eat in the patient's room. Hospital policies regarding when and where visitors are able to eat also play an important role in their food-related comfort (Reizenstein & Grant, 1981b).

A place to sleep is another aspect of physical comfort needed by those visitors who come from a long distance or who want to keep constant watch over the patient. Although many visitors seem endlessly adaptable in their abilities to sleep sitting up or on the floor in waiting rooms, these adverse conditions are likely to add to their overall self-reported stress (Reizenstein & Grant, 1982b; Simmons, Reizenstein, & Grant, 1982).

Overnight accommodations can be provided through special design features such as Murphy beds (that fold out from the wall), cots in the patient room, and couches or bench seating in waiting areas. Provision of inexpensive accommodations near the hospital are another alternative (Carpman, Grant & Simmons, 1984a; Reizenstein & Grant, 1981b).

Privacy and Personal Territory

Visitors surveyed in the PVP Project studies (Reizenstein et al., 1981; Reizenstein & Grant, 1982b) and those observed in a number of other hospitals (Carpman & Grant, 1984a) request a degree of choice and control over social contact, particularly with regard to visual and acoustical privacy for conversations (Altman, 1975). Many of these same visitors also requested some space in the hospital that they might, at least temporarily, consider their own.

In the Michigan study, although visitors of patients in private rooms did not mention visual or acoustical privacy as a problem, about half the visitors of patients in semiprivate or multiple bed rooms would have liked more acoustical privacy. They were concerned, not only about not having others overhear their conversations, but also they were sometimes unwitting listeners to various medical or personal conversations. These visitors' desires for conversational privacy also extend to the telephone. Whether they use the phone in the patient's room or a public telephone elsewhere in the hospital, acoustical privacy is important to them (Reizenstein et al., 1981).

Researchers at the University of Michigan also found that in hospital waiting areas, visitors often wished to discuss personal matters with other friends or family (Reizenstein & Grant, 1982b). Seating type and arrangement as well as the presence of screening devices and sound-absorbing materials are likely to influence how private visitors feel in this setting. Visitors also often reported a desire to talk privately with the patient's physician. Environmental design can affect this type of conversational privacy in terms of the types of conference spaces provided (such as hallways, open waiting areas, screened waiting areas, conference rooms) and the amount of actual and perceived visual and acoustical separation in each. The Michigan research also showed a desire on the part of some visitors to have some area where they could store belongings such as winter coats, hats, and boots (Reizenstein et al., 1981).

It is clear that existing findings about hospital visitors' concepts of privacy and personal territory are rudimentary at best. However, these concepts and settings can serve as an impetus for future research. Basic researchers may be interested in how different types of visitors define and regulate visual and acoustical privacy. Do they put up with what are for them uncomfortable situations, as the "invisible visitor" syndrome would suggest? How do individual, social, and environmental factors affect these attitudes and behaviors? Similarly, what areas in the hospital do visitors see as their territories? How do they mark or defend these? What factors account for differences in these behaviors?

Applied researchers may wish to implement and test various hypothesized approaches to design and management directed at providing hospital visitors with optimal levels of privacy and personal territory. For example, it has been suggested that visitor waiting areas need to be large enough so that several small groups can be seated together, somewhat separated from other groups; that sound-absorbing materials be used in these spaces; and that operational policies and housekeeping practice should recognize the function of these small groupings and leave them in place, rather than returning all seats to some fixed location (Carpman & Grant, 1984a).

Presently untested but potentially useful approaches to providing a sense of territory for hospital visitors include providing coat storage in patient rooms and waiting areas; providing basic amenities such as drinking fountains, bathrooms, and public telephones near where visitors wait; and making available to visitors a place to change clothes, put on makeup, or even take a shower (Reizenstein & Grant, 1981b).

Symbolic Meaning

One of the currently unmeasured, yet potentially powerful effects of the physical environment on the behavior and attitudes of hospital visitors is its symbolic meaning. Although the various interpretations that visitors might make presently fall more into the realm of informed speculation than quantitative data-based findings, it is an issue worthy of attention by both researchers and designers.

Shumaker and Reizenstein (1982) speculated about the symbolic meaning of hospital design for inpatients. These authors hypothesized that for patients, the image of the hospital's physical environment was one contributing factor to an overall impression of the hospital. They argue that this image also plays a part in influencing how patients see themselves: "Design can reflect the idea that a patient's needs are natural, anticipated and important, or that these needs are deviant and unimportant" (p. 212). They also suggest that symbolic meaning can be grossly classified according to positive and negative messages.

One can extrapolate from their ideas to focus on the symbolic meaning of the hospital's physical environment for visitors. A positive symbolic message associated with a special visitor center might be: "We have thought about and planned for your needs." A negative symbolic message associated with a tiny, out-of-the-way waiting area might be: "We acknowledge your presence, but your needs are simply not one of our high priorities."

In addition to the types of messages communicated by the physical environment, Shumaker and Reizenstein (1982) describe the phenomenon of "unfulfilled environmental expectations," based on an assumption that aesthetics and function work in tandem—that a visually attractive setting will also function well for its users. "Unfulfilled" environmental expectations are involved where an environment is aesthetically pleasing but functions poorly. A beautiful hospital lobby with sparse, uncomfortable seating is one example of this phenomenon.

Applying these ideas to hospital visitors, it is possible to speculate on the symbolic meaning that the hospital environment may have at different levels of scale. The location of the hospital (type of neighborhood, ease of access); ease and proximity of parking; and the size, massing, and exterior design of the hospital buildings may all communicate powerful messages to visitors even before they reach the front door. Visitors may pick up on cues that "tell" them about the hospital's connection to the community; how concerned it is about the public's needs (such as parking); and about its humaneness and competence as an institution.

Once inside the front door, the proximity of a monitored information desk and the tone, clarity, and frequency of signs may serve as a second set of symbolic messages as visitors make their way to the patient's room. Symbolic messages may communicate to visitors about the importance of their needs for information and about their status as hospital users. Once on the patient floor, the visitor is likely to spend time both in the patient's room and in public areas such as waiting rooms, cafeterias, or gift shops. In these spaces, a third set of symbolic meanings may be imparted to the visitor. Provisions for the visitor in the patient room (such as coat storage and comfortable seating) may communicate about how the hospital regards the importance of the visitor's role in the patient's recovery. The decor and furnishings in hospital waiting areas may also "speak" to visitors about the value the hospital places on their comfort. The location, size, and way-finding aids that point out other public areas like a coffee shop or gift shop communicate to visitors when they are welcome, whether their needs have been anticipated, and whether they are considered part of the hospital community.

Symbolic meaning, like other constructs relating to the effects of the hospital environment on visitors, has not yet been clarified by a body of systematic research. However, this is another potentially interesting and important issue at which future research can be targeted. What is the nature of the different messages communicated to visitors by the hospital environment (including the lobby, waiting areas, corridors, patient room, and other spaces)? What individual or situational factors account for different interpretations of the same design? What de-

sign features might account for different messages being communicated (e.g., does the presence of carpeting significantly change the image of a visitor waiting area?).

24.6. SUMMARY

In this chapter we have presented a framework for approaching design for special populations defined in terms of person–environment fit. At all scales of design, from product design to regional planning, designers attempt to provide environments that are congruent with the needs and activities of users. Congruence is achieved by considering and manipulating three important and largely independent dimensions: personal and group-related user abilities and needs, design characteristics of the physical environment at a range of spatial scales, and organizational and management considerations. The degree to which fit has been achieved for special populations is at least partially a function of the degree to which a group has been targeted in design by having its needs explicitly considered and the degree to which the group meets customary assumptions about environmental capability.

In this chapter, we have considered three special populations who represent different types of person–environment fit, who have been targeted in different ways, and who represent a wide range of customary assumptions—mentally retarded persons, children, and hospital visitors.

Although special institutions have been built for mentally retarded people since the 1840s, recent research suggests that customary assumptions that mentally retarded people are unable to develop normally and do not require or desire life patterns of everyday society are incorrect. However, assumptions that settings will have salutary effects on residents simply because they are smaller, community-based, and more homelike in appearance are oversimplified. The research in the area is beset by methodological and inferential problems: Random assignment is seldom used, and sample sizes are often small. Nonetheless, several studies suggest some characteristics of settings that may aid residents and staff in achieving person–environment fit—designs of the near environment like those found in everyday society, smaller living units (the research about overall facility size is equivocal), and units that provide hierarchies of space and straightforward ways for socially inadept residents to control social contact. As with the elderly, mentally retarded people seem to be adversely affected by involuntary relocation from their residence. Further research is needed to specify the relevant abilities and needs of this special population, the key aspects of the physical setting (rather than imprecise descriptors such as "institutional"), and the most important management and organizational issues bridging the first two issues.

Children have been targeted with respect to schools and, to a less thorough extent, playgrounds. However, because children do not meet customary standards of environmental competence—they are small and weak, inexperienced, lack money, lack certain abilities such as driving skill and voting rights and hence lack direct influence on decision making—they are subject to many situations where they face serious misfit—for example, traffic-filled streets where children play, air pollution where children suffer more than adults, child-care settings that are poorly located for working mothers, and adventure playgrounds that are rejected by the community. A further understanding of the three dimensions just described as well as the larger social and political context that has created these misfits is necessary before a resolution is possible.

Hospital visitors, though a large group, have not been targeted in hospital design, and the degree to which they meet customary assumptions about environmental competence has not been well researched. Several studies suggest several environmental design issues relevant to hospital visitors: wayfinding, physical comfort, privacy and personal territory, and symbolic meaning. Although most information on these topics comes from a single large research program, several preliminary strategies can be proposed for resolving misfits such as providing comprehensible building layouts, clear jargon-free signs and a clear introduction to the hospital, providing glare-free lighting, comfortable seating, food, and places to sleep and for private conversations, and generally providing symbols in the hospital's design that suggest the visitor is important.

NOTES

1. When Michelson bought a Big 3 car 6 years ago, no one in his dealership had even seen or sold a kiddie seat in their showroom. The national office finally clarified that the ones this company made, or at least nominally distributed, did not meet Canadian government standards. So they sold nothing at all.

2. Wayfinding includes that trip to the hospital, the trip from the parking area or bus stop to the entry, trips to vari-

ous destinations within the hospital, the return trip to the parking area or bus stop, and the trip home (Carpman et al., 1986).

3. Total measured stress included parking wayfinding, being away from household responsibilities, being away from work, worrying about the patient, worrying about hospital costs, being around sick people, not being able to have questions answered, finding a comfortable place to wait, lack of privacy in the patient's room, and worrying about arrangements for the future.

REFERENCES

Aanes, D., & Moen, M. (1976). Adaptive behavior changes of group home residents. *Mental Retardation, 14,* (4), 36–40.

Aldrich, C.I., & Mendkoff, E. (1963). Relocation of the aged and disabled: A mortality study. *Journal of the American Geriatrics Society, 11,* 185–194.

Altman, I. (1975). *The environment and social behavior.* Monterey, CA: Brooks/Cole.

Baker, B.L., Seltzer, G.B., & Seltzer, M.M. (1974). *As close as possible: Community residences for retarded adults.* Boston: Little, Brown.

Bakos, M., Bozic, R., Chapin, D., Gandrus, J., Kahn, S., Mateer, W., & Newman, S. (1979). *Group homes: A study of community residential environments.* Cleveland, OH: ARC.

Balla, D.A. (1976). Relationship of institution size to quality of core: A review of the literature. *American Journal of Mental Deficiency, 81,* 117–124.

Balla, D.A., Butterfield, E.C., & Ziegler, E. (1974). Effects of institutionalization on retarded children: A longitudinal cross-institutional investigation. *American Journal of Mental Deficiency, 78,* 530–579.

Barker, R., & Gump, P. (1964). *Big school, small school,* Stanford, CA: Stanford University Press.

Baroff, G.S. (1980). On "size" and the quality of residential care: A second look. *Mental Retardation, 18,* 113–117.

Baum, A., Singer, J.E., & Baum, C.S. (1982). Stress and the environment. In G. Evans (Ed.), *Environmental stress.* NY: Cambridge University Press.

Baum, A., & Valins, S. (1977). *Architecture and social behavior: Psychological studies in social density.* Hillsdale, NJ: Erlbaum.

Bednar, M.J. (Ed.). (1977). *Barrier-free environments.* Stroudsburg, PA: Dowden, Hutchinson, & Ross.

Bell, W. (1968). The city, the suburb, and a theory of social choice. In S. Greer et al (Eds.), *The New Urbanization.* New York: St. Martin's.

Bernstein, R.A., Manchester, R.A., & Weaver, L.A. (1980). The effect of visiting on psychiatric patients in a general hospital. *Community Mental Health Journal,* 6, 235–240.

Birenbaum, A. (1980). Social adaptation of the developmentally disabled adult in the community. In H.J. Cohen, D. Klingler, & J.A. Eisler (Eds.), *Urban community care for the developmentally disabled.* Springfield, IL: Thomas.

Bjaanes, A.T., & Butler, E.W. Environmental variation in community care facilities for mentally retarded persons. *American Journal of Mental Deficiency,* 78, 429–439.

Bourestom, N.C., & Tars, S. (1974). Alterations in life patterns following nursing home relocation. *Gerontologist,* 14, 506–510.

Bunge, W.W. et al. (1975). *The Canadian alternative: Survival expeditions and urban change* (Geographical Monograph no. 2). Toronto, Canada: York University.

Butler, E.W., & Bjaanes, A.T. (1978). Activities and use of time by retarded persons in community care facilities. In G.P. Sackett (Ed.), *Observing behavior: Vol. 1. Theory and applications in mental retardation.* Baltimore, MD: University Park Press.

Carpman, J.R. (1983). *Influencing design decisions: An analysis of the impact of the Patient and Visitor Participation Project on the University of Michigan Replacement Hospital Program.* (University Microfilms, Number 84-02, 256.)

Carpman, J.R., & Grant, M.A. (1984a). *Patient and Visitor Participation Project.* Unpublished Working Notes (1980–1984), Ann Arbor, MI: Office of the Replacement Hospital Program.

Carpman, J.R., & Grant, M.A. (1984b). *Executive summary, Report #27: Waiting area seating study* (Unpub. Rep.) Ann Arbor, MI: Office of the Replacement Hospital Program.

Carpman, J.R., & Grant, M.A. (1984c). *Executive Summary, Report #11: TV's in hospitals: Behavior and preferences* (Unpub. Rep.) Ann Arbor, MI: Office of the Replacement Hospital Program.

Carpman, J.R., Grant, M.A., & Simmons, D.A. (1983–84). Wayfinding in the hospital environment: The impact of various floor numbering alternatives. *Journal of Environmental Systems,* 13(4), 353–364.

Carpman, J.R., Grant, M.A., & Simmons, D.A. (1984a). Overnight accommodations for visitors and outpatients: A nationwide study. *Health Care Strategic Management,* 2(6), 9–14.

Carpman, J.R., Grant, M.A., & Simmons, D.A. (1984b). *No more mazes: Research about design for wayfinding in hospitals.* Ann Arbor, MI: Office of the Replacement Hospital Program.

Carpman, J.R., Grant, M.A., & Simmons, D.A. (1986). Design that cares: Planning health facilities for patients and visitors. Chicago: American Hospital Publishing, Inc.

Carpman, J.R., & Vaitkus, M.A. [Hospital visitors and environmental stress]. Paper in progress.

Carsrud, A.L., Carsrud, K.B., Henderson, C.J., Alisch, C.J., & Fowler, A.U. (1979). Effects of social and environmental change on institutionalized mentally retarded persons: The relocation syndrome reconsidered. *American Journal of Mental Deficiency,* 84, 266–272.

Cohen, H., Conroy, J.Q., Fraser, D.W., Snelbecker, G.E., & Spreat, S. (1977). Behavioral effects of inter-institutional relocation of mentally retarded residents. *American Journal of Mental Deficiency,* 82, 12–18.

Conroy, J., Efthimiou, J., & Lemanowicz, J. (1982). A matched comparison of the developmental growth of institutionalized and deinstitutionalized mentally retarded clients. *American Journal of Mental Deficiency,* 86, 581–587.

Cook, T., & Campbell, D. (1979). *Quasi-experimentation design and analysis for field settings.* Skokie, IL: Rand McNally.

Cooper, C. (1970). Adventure playgrounds. *Landscape Architecture,* 61, 18–29, 88–91.

Downs, R. (1979). Mazes, minds and maps. In D. Pollet & P. Haskell (Eds.), *Sign Systems for Libraries.* New York: Bowker.

Dybwad, G. (1970). Architecture's role in revitalizing the field of mental retardation. *Journal of Mental Subnormality,* 16, 45–48.

Eyman, R.K., Demaine, G.C., & Lei, T. (1979). Relationship between community environments and resident changes in adaptive behavior: A path model. *American Journal of Mental Deficiency,* 83, 330–338.

Fava, S.F. (1980). Women's place in the new Suburbia. In G.R. Wekerle et al. (Eds.), *New Space for Women.* Boulder, CO: Westview.

Fiorelli, J., & Thurman, K. (1979). Client behavior in more and less normalized residential settings. *Education and Training in the Mentally Retarded,* 14, 85–94.

Fischer, C. (1976). *The urban experience.* New York: Harcourt Brace Jovanovich.

Fitch, J.M. (1973). *American building I: The historical forces that shaped it.* New York: Schoken.

Flynn, J.E., & Segil, A.W. (1970). *Architectural interior systems: lighting, air conditioning, acoustics.* New York: Van Nostrand Reinhold.

French, J.P., Rodgers, W., & Cobb, S. (1974). Adjustment as person-environment fit. In G.V. Coelho, D.A. Hamburg, & J.E. Adams (Eds.), *Coping and adaptation.* New York: Basic Books.

Fried, M. (1963). Grieving for a lost home. In L.J. Duhl (Ed.), *The urban condition.* New York: Basic Books.

Gans, H.J. (1962). *The urban villagers.* New York: Free Press.

Glass, D.C., & Singer, J.E. (1972). *Urban stress.* New York: Academic.

Grossman, H.J. (Ed.). (1977). *Manual on terminology and classification in mental retardation* (rev. ed.). Washington, DC: American Association on Mental Deficiency.

Gump, P. (1975). *Ecological psychology and children.* Chicago: University of Chicago Press.

Gunzberg, A.L. (1968). Architecture and mental subnormality: II. Sensory experiences in architecture for the mentally subnormal child. *Journal of Mental Subnormality, 14,* 57–58.

Gunzburg, H.C. (1973). The physical environment of the mentally handicapped VIII: 39 steps leading towards normalized living practices for the mentally handicapped. *British Journal of Mental Subnormality, 19,* 91–99.

Hägerstrand, T. (1970). What about people in regional science? *Papers of the Regional Science Association, 24,* 7–21.

Hayghe, H. (1982). Dual earner families: Their economics and demographic characteristics. In J. Aldous (Ed.), *Two paychecks: Life in dual earner families.* Beverly Hills, CA: Sage.

Hayward, D.G., & Birenbaum, L. (1980). Lighting and human behavior. *Proceedings of 19th C.I.E. Congress* (pp. 283–286). Paris: Commission Internationale de l'Eclairage.

Heal, L.W., Seligman, C.K., Switzky, H.N. (1978). Research on community residential alternatives for the mentally retarded. In N.R. Ellis (Ed.), *International review of research in mental retardation (vol. 9).* New York: Academic.

Heller, T. (1982). The effects of involuntary residential relocation: A review. *American Journal of Community Psychology, 10,* 471–492.

Hemming, H., Lavender, T., & Pill, R. (1981). Quality of life of mentally retarded adults transferred from large institutions to new small units. *American Journal of Mental Deficiency, 86,* 157–169.

Hill, R. (1958). Generic features of families under stress. *Social Casework, 39,* 2–3.

Hoover, M.J. (1979, July 16). Intensive care for relatives. *Hospitals,* p. 219.

Hull, J.T., & Thompson, J.C. (1980). Predicting adaptive functioning of mentally retarded persons in community settings. *American Journal of Mental Deficiency, 85,* 253–261.

Idea forum: Sharing meals. (1981, July). *Hospitals,* 36.

Janicki, M.P., Mayada, T., & Epple, W.A. (1983). Availability of group homes for persons with mental retardation in the United States. *Mental Retardation, 21,* 45–51.

Jasnau, K.F. (1967). Individualized vs. mass transfer of nonpsychotic geriatric patients from mental hospitals to nursing homes with special reference to the death rate. *Journal of the American Geriatrics Society, 15,* 280–284.

Joint Commission on Accreditation of Hospitals. (1971). *Standards for residential facilities for the mentally retarded.* Chicago: Joint Commission on Accreditation of Hospitals.

Kamerman, S.B. (1980). *Parenting in an unresponsive society.* New York: Free Press.

Kane, D.N. (1976). Bad air for children. *Environment, 18,* 26–34.

Karlin, R.A., McFarland, D., Aiello, J.R., & Epstein, Y.M. (1976). Normative mediation of reactions to crowding. *Environmental Psychology and Non-Verbal Behavior, 1,* 30–40.

Keller, S. (1977, September). [Panel discussion]. Annual meeting of the American Sociological Association, Chicago.

King, R.D., Raynes, N.V., & Tizard, J. (1971). *Patterns of residential care: Sociological studies in institutions for handicapped children.* London: Routledge & Kegan Paul.

Kleinberg, J., & Galligan, B. (1983). Effects of deinstitutionalization on adaptive behavior of mentally retarded adults. *American Journal of Mental Deficiency, 88,* 21–27.

Knight, R.C., Weitzer, W., & Zimring, C. (1978). *Opportunity for control and the built environment: The E.L.E.M.R. Project.* Amherst, MA: University of Massachusetts, Environmental Institute.

Knight, R.C., Zimring, C.M., & Kent, M. (1977). Normalization as a social-physical system. In M.J. Bednar (Ed.), *Barrier-free environments.* Stroudsburg, PA: Dowden, Hutchinson, & Ross.

Krasnow, I. (1984, May 19). Electronic tracks provide 'road map' for sightless. *Los Angeles Times,* Pt. 1-A, p. 8.

Lam, W.M.C. (1977). *Perception and lighting as formgivers for architecture.* New York: McGraw-Hill.

Landesman-Dwyer, S. (1981). Living in the community. *American Journal of Mental Deficiency, 86,* 223–234.

Landesman-Dwyer, S. (1984). Residential environments and the social behavior of handicapped individuals. In M. Lewis (Ed.), *Beyond the dyad.* New York: Plenum.

Landesman-Dwyer, S. (1985). The changing structure and function of institutions: A search for optimal group care environments. In S. Landesman-Dwyer & P. Vietze (Eds.), *The Social ecology of residential environments: Person x setting transactions in mental retardation.* Baltimore, MD: University Park Press.

Landesman-Dwyer, S., Sackett, G.P., & Kleinman, J.S. (1980). Relationship of size to resident and staff behavior in small community residences. *American Journal of Mental Deficiency, 85,* 6–17.

Landesman-Dwyer, S., Stein, J.G., & Sackett, G.P. (1978). A behavioral and ecological study of group homes. In G.P. Sackett (Ed.), *Observing behavior: Vol. 1. Theory and applications in mental retardation.* Baltimore, MD: University Park Press.

Lazarus, R.S. (1966). *Psychological stress and the coping process.* New York: McGraw-Hill.

Lenntorp, B. (1976). *Paths in space-time environments: A time-geographic study of movement possibilities of individuals* (Lund Series in Geography, No. 44). Lund, Sweden: Gleerup.

Levine, M. (1982). You-are-here maps: Psychological considerations. *Environment and Behavior, 14,* 221–237.

Lynch, K. (1977). *Growing up in cities.* Cambridge, MA & Paris: MIT Press, UNESCO.

MacEachron, A.E. (1983). Institutional reform and adaptive functioning of mentally retarded persons: A field experiment. *American Journal of Mental Deficiency, 88,* 2–12.

Märtensson, S. (1979). *On the formation of biographies* (Lund Studies in Geography, No. 47). Lund, Sweden: Gleerup.

McCormick, M., Balla, D., & Ziegler, E. (1975). Resident-care practices in institutions for retarded persons: A cross-institutional, cross-cultural study. *American Journal of Mental Deficiency, 80,* 1–17.

Medrich, E., Roizen, J., Rubin, V., & Buckley, S. (1982). *The serious business of growing up.* Berkeley: University of California Press.

Meyerson, M., & Banfield, E. (1975). *Politics, planning, and the public interest.* New York: Free Press.

Michelson, W. (1970). *Man and his urban environment: A sociological approach.* Reading, MA: Addison-Wesley.

Michelson, W. (1976). Planning and the amelioration of urban areas. In K.P. Schwirian et al., *Contemporary topics in urban sociology* (pp. 562–633). Morristown, NJ: General Learning Press.

Michelson, W. (1983). *The impact of changing women's roles on transportation needs and usage* (Rep. No. CA-11-0024-1). Springfield, VA: National Technical Information Service.

Michelson, W. (1985). *From sun to sun: Daily obligations and community structure in the lives of employed women and their families.* Totowa, NJ: Rowman & Allenheld.

Michelson, W., & Roberts, E. (1979). Children and the urban physical environment. In W. Michelson, S.V. Levine, & A.R. Spina, *The child in the city: changes and challenges.* Toronto, Canada: University of Toronto Press.

Molter, N.C. (1979). Needs of relatives of critically ill patients: A descriptive study. *Heart and Lung, 8,* 332–339.

National Academy of Sciences. (1976). *Toward a national policy for children and families.* Washington, DC: Author.

Nicklin, W.M. (1979, April). The role of the family in the emergency department. *Canadian Nurse,* pp. 41–43.

Nihira, K., Foster, R., Shellhaas, M., & Leland, H. (1974). *AAMD Adaptive Behavior Scales* (rev. ed.). Washington, DC: American Association on Mental Deficiency.

Nirje, B. (1969). The normalization principle and its human management implications. In R. Kugel & W. Wolfensberger (eds.) *Changing patterns of residential services for the mentally retarded.* Washington, DC: President's Committee on Mental Retardation.

Norris, D. (1969). Architecture and mental subnormality: V. The environmental needs of the severely retarded. *Journal of Mental Subnormality, 15,* 45–50.

Olsen, R.V. (1982, November 16). Hospital bases new designs on documented functional needs of its patients, staff. *Hospitals,* pp. 33–34.

Olsen, R.V., Winkel, G., & Pershing, A. (1982, November). Lighting system greets and guides visitors. *Hospitals,* 56–57.

Pederson, J. (1970). The physical environment of the mentally handicapped. I. Progress in building for the mentally handicapped. *Journal of Mental Subnormality, 16,* 121–125.

Pollowy, A. (1977). *The urban nest.* Stroudsburg, PA: Dowden, Hutchinson, & Ross.

Reizenstein, J.E., & Grant, M.A. (1981a). *Report #1: Schematic design of the inpatient room* (Unpub. Rep.). Ann Arbor: University of Michigan, Office of Hospital Planning, Research and Development.

Reizenstein, J.E., & Grant, M.A. (1981b). *Report #4a: Hospital patient and visitor issues: currently unmet needs and suggested solutions* (Unpub. Rep.). Ann Arbor: University of Michigan, Office of Hospital Planning, Research and Development.

Reizenstein, J.E., & Grant, M.A. (1982a). *From hospital research to hospital design: The Patient and Visitor Participation Project.* Ann Arbor: University of Michigan, Office of Hospital Planning, Research and Development.

Reizenstein, J.E., & Grant, M.A. (1982b). *Report #6: Spontaneous design suggestions by patients and visitors* (Unpub. Rep.). Ann Arbor: University of Michigan, Office of Hospital Planning, Research and Development.

Reizenstein, J.E., & Grant, M.A. (1983). *Report #22: Executive Summary: Outdoor seating evaluation* (Unpub. Rep.). Ann Arbor: University of Michigan, Office of Hospital Planning, Research and Development.

Reizenstein, J.E., Grant, M.A., & Vaitkus, M.A. (1981). *Report #4: Visitor activities and schematic design preferences* (Unpub. Rep.). Ann Arbor: University of Michigan, Office of Hospital Planning, Research and Development.

Reizenstein, J.E., & McBride, W.A. (1977). *Designing for mentally retarded people* (PB291-895/AS). Springfield, VA: National Technical Information Service.

Rivlin, L. (1978, Winter). Institutionalization reconsidered. *Centerpoint.*

Rivlin, L.G., Bogert, V., & Cirillo, R. (1981, April). *Uncoupling institutional indicators.* Paper presented at the 12th annual conference of the Environmental Design Research Association, Ames, IA.

Sandels, S. (1974). *The Skandia report II: Why are children injured in traffic? Can we prevent child accidents in traffic?* Stockholm, Sweden: Skandia Insurance Co.

Schreerenberger, R.C. (1978). Public residential services for the mentally retarded. In N.R. Ellis (Ed.), *International review of research in mental retardation* (vol. 9). New York: Academic.

Schreerenberger, R.C., & Felsenthal, D. (1977). Community settings for mentally retarded persons: Satisfaction and activities. *Mental Retardation, 15,* 3–7.

Schroeder, S.R., & Henes, C. (1978). Assessment of progress of institutionalized and deinstitutionalized retarded adults: A watched-control comparison. *Mental Retardation, 16,* 147–148.

Shumaker, S.A., & Reizenstein, J.E. (1982). Environmental factors affecting inpatient stress in acute care hospitals. In G.W. Evans (Ed.), *Environmental stress.* New York: Cambridge University Press.

Simmons, D., Reizenstein, J.E., & Grant, M.A. (1982). Carpeting in hospitals: A review of the literature. *Dimensions in Health Services, 59,* 18–21.

Socialdepartmentet (Sweden). (1975). *Barnens Livsmiljo [Children's Living Space].* Stockholm, Sweden: Statens Offentliga Utredninga.

Sommer, R. (1974). *Tight Spaces.* Englewood Cliffs, NJ: Prentice-Hall.

Spivack, M. (1969). The political collapse of a playground. *Landscape Architecture, 59,* 288–291.

Steele, F.I. (1973). *Physical settings and organization development.* Reading, MA: Rand McNally.

Steinfeld, E. (1979). *Access to the built environment: A review of the literature.* Washington, DC: U.S. Department of Housing and Urban Development, Office of Policy Development and Research.

Traylor, B. (1979, May). St. Thomas Hospital operates lodge for patients' families. *Hospital Progress,* p. 24.

Van Dyke, C., Sr. (1980, August). Family-centered health care recognizes needs of patients, families, employees. *Hospital Progress,* pp. 54–68.

Weinstock, A., Wulkan, P., Colon, C.J., Coleman, J., & Goncalves, S. (1979). Stress inoculation and interinstitutional transfer of mentally retarded individuals. *American Journal of Mental Deficiency, 83,* 385–390.

Weisman, G.D. (1981). Evaluating architectural legibility: Wayfinding in the built environment. *Environment and Behavior, 13,* 189–204.

Weisman, G.D. (1982). Evaluating architectural legibility: Design considerations in housing environments for the elderly. In V. Regnier & J. Pynoos (Eds.), *Housing for the elderly: Satisfaction and preferences.* New York: Garland.

Wekerle, G. (1979). *A woman's place is in the city* (No. 102). Cambridge, MA: Lincoln Institute of Land Policy, Land Policy Round Table Basic Concept Series.

Wekerle, G., Peterson, R., & Morley, D. (Eds.). (1980). *New space for women.* Boulder, CO: Westview.

Welsh, J. (1982, March–April). Family lodging. *Group Practice Journal,* pp. 28–32.

White noise machines helping users get to sleep. (1982, February 14). *Ann Arbor News.*

Whyte, W.H., Jr. (1956). *The organization man.* Garden City, NY: Doubleday, Anchor Books.

Willer, B., & Intaglia, J. (1982). Comparison of family-care and group homes as alternatives to institutions. *American Journal of Mental Deficiency, 86,* 588–595.

Willer, B., Schreerenberger, R.C., & Intaglia, J. (1980). Deinstitutionalization and mentally retarded persons. In A.R. Novak & L. Heal (Eds.), *Integration of developmentally disabled individuals into the community.* Baltimore, MD: Brookes.

Wineman, J.D., & Zimring, C.M. (1986). *Group homes for the mentally retarded* (Final Rep.). Washington, DC: National Endowment for the Arts.

Witt, S.J. (1981). Increase in adaptive behavior level after residence in an intermediate care facility for mentally retarded persons. *Mental Retardation, 19,* 75–79.

Wolfensberger, W. (1972). *The principle of normalization in human services.* Toronto, Canada: National Institute on Mental Retardation.

Zeisel, J. (1975). *Sociology and architectural design. Social Science Frontiers, Vol. 6.* New York: Russell Sage Foundation.

Zeisel, J. (1981). *Inquiry by design.* Monterey, CA: Brooks/Cole.

Zimring, C.M. (1981). Stress and the designed environment. *Journal of Social Issues, 37,* 145–171.

Zimring, C.M., Weitzer, W., & Knight, R.C. (1982). Opportunity for control and the designed environment: The case of an institution for the developmentally disabled. In A. Baum & J. Singer (Eds.), *Advances in environmental psychology: Vol. 4. Environment and health.* Hillsdale, NJ: Erlbaum.

Chapter 25

TOWARD AN ENVIRONMENTAL PSYCHOLOGY OF DISORDER: DELINQUENCY, CRIME, AND FEAR OF CRIME

Ralph B. Taylor, *Department of Criminal Justice, Temple University, Philadelphia, PA*

Sociology...has recognized that there are neighborhoods in cities which many people know to be dangerous; these are the functional equivalent of the unexplored areas covered by the olden-days cartographers' rubric: Here be Dragons.
DAMER, 1974

When you live on a dead end street, you gotta be tough and strong.
COLWELL-WINFIELD BLUES BAND

25.1. INTRODUCTION

Crime, delinquency, and fear are unevenly distributed in space. Evidence regarding this nonuniform arrangement has been accumulating since the first half of the nineteenth century when European cartographers such as Guerry, labeled by Morris (1957) as the first social ecologist, collected data linking crime to environmental characteristics. And with the advent of surveys on crime-related issues in the last 20 years, we have found that fear of crime is higher in some places than in others (e.g., cities vs. rural areas). The well-established nature of this patterning has drawn the interest of social scientists from a range of fields. Consequently the spatial structuring of crime, delinquency, and fear of crime has been of interest to criminologists, sociologists, geographers, and economists. Consequently one might well wonder: What could environmental psychologists possibly contribute to this already investigator-crowded area of inquiry?

And, indeed, that central query is one with which I intend to grapple in this chapter. What I see as perhaps the key issue in this area of inquiry is: What does an environmental psychological perspective bring to the study of delinquency, crime, and fear of crime that has been lacking in other theoretical perspectives? Obviously the inclusion of this chapter in this volume suggests that environmental psychology does have a contribution to make and that that contribution is multifaceted. More specifically, the nature of this contribution is as follows:

Two well-developed theoretical perspectives in environmental psychology—human territoriality and behavior-setting theory—can provide excellent answers regarding why there is more crime, delinquency, and fear of crime in some places than in others.

Environmental psychology contributes a distinct unit of analysis or level of focus on these issues; it considers small groups and individuals (Stokols, 1977) in, and as part and parcel of, their larger social and physical contexts (Stokols, 1983). This center of attention is unique to environmental psychology.

Environmental psychology is committed to understanding the role of the physical environment, as both a factor contributing to delinquency, crime, and fear of crime, and as a feature influenced by these matters.

Thus in contrast to economists, criminologists, and

geographers who are often concerned with larger scale, areal-level dynamics, environmental psychologists have a more fine-grained concern with individuals and small groups. In contrast to sociologists who have treated the physical environment only as a clue to social facts (Dunlap & Catton, 1983), environmental psychologists are wedded to understanding all the roles that the physical environment may play in any given set of causal processes. In short, there is a place, or, to state it even more strongly, an urgent need for an environmental psychological perspective on these matters. There are significant theoretical and empirical gaps in the work on crime, delinquency, and fear of crime that environmental psychologists can help close.

Consequently the first part of this chapter develops an environmental psychological perspective on issues of delinquency, crime, and fear of crime. I admit at the outset that other, equally tenable environmental psychological perspectives on these issues could, and probably should, be developed. The framework proposed here by no means exhausts the ways that environmental psychologists can construe these issues. But at least it gives us a starting point.

Once we have such a perspective in hand, we can use it as a lens to examine work already completed in this area. Accordingly the next section reviews theories and related findings in the areas of crime, delinquency, and fear of crime, which touch on, or have implications for, the role of the physical environment. My theoretical and empirical review is not exhaustive but rather seeks to provide a familiarizing outline. Where appropriate, theoretical deficits are illuminated. And once the theory and research in an area has been considered, each theory will be examined from the previously described environmental psychological perspective to see how the theory might be altered and developed to incorporate the insights of the latter. Although perhaps too visionary, these suggestions are nonetheless of considerable importance; they indicate the lines along which more powerful, truly multidisciplinary perspectives on these social problems might be developed.

Following the review and reconsideration of work in these areas, I attend to more recent studies that have, either implicitly or avowedly, been more environmental psychological in nature due to their more careful consideration of person–place bonds: the attitudes, sentiments, expectations, and involvements linking a person or group to his, her, or their place of residence. Despite some false starts in this vein, we have considerable theoretical refinement and empirical support that have emerged in just the last 8 to 10 years.

The two final sections contain a caution and an exhortation. The caution is a partial list of the theoretical difficulties and methodological limits that beset research in this area. The enumeration is not meant to dissuade people from this area of inquiry but rather to help them develop more informed lines of attack. The exhortation discusses some research futures. What kinds of issues have yet to be considered, and what are the possibilities of developing appropriate models for such inquiries? The possibilities of, and mandate for, action research are considered.

25.2. TOWARD AN ENVIRONMENTAL PSYCHOLOGY OF DISORDER

In this section, I weave together several theoretical strands to develop an environmental psychological perspective on disorder. The disorder continuum is introduced and explained. The main indexes of disorder that are the focus of this chapter— crime, delinquency, and fear of crime—are related to that larger continuum. The nature of disorder suggests that theory on human territoriality can be fruitfully applied, and I outline the theory of human territoriality. The territorial perspective forces an explicitly spatial concern, the implications of which are explored, as well as a focus on the possible roles of the physical environment, which are discussed. By linking the territorial perspective with behavior-setting theory (Wicker, 1979, Chapter 16, this volume), the temporal and spatial distribution of disorder can be more clearly understood. Finally the environmental psychological perspective is confronted with some sociological (or perhaps philosophical) questions, in order to ascertain the limitations of the perspective.

25.2.1. Disorder Continuum

Crime and delinquency are not isolated issues divorced from other problems and concerns with which individuals and communities must deal. Rather crime and delinquency are perceived and experienced as part of a large web of social problems (Podolefsky, 1983; Podolefsky & DuBow, 1981). Crime and delinquency in middle- and upper-class areas are viewed as stemming from, and contributing to, the larger breakdown in society of the moral order, whereas in lower income areas they are viewed (partially) as responses to the inequitable treatment and blocked opportunities experienced by such groupings (e.g., lack of employment opportunities or recreational facilities). Crime and delinquency are phenomenologically linked to larger difficulties and problems. The latter

link is particularly apparent in the case of collective or political disorders such as riots and terrorist attacks but is also made in the case of isolated incidents (e.g., vandalism; Fisher & Baron, 1982) that are perpetrated by and experienced by individuals or small groups.

Also reflecting these same social problems are less serious events and conditions that, although less serious than crimes per se, nonetheless point to the same societal processes in the eyes of the residents. These less serious matters include "street hassles" such as insulting remarks or threats from deranged individuals, chronic social situations such as wayward kids or teens, winos, street bums, and panhandlers hanging out, and instances of physical deterioration or lack of upkeep such as vacant houses and lots, littered yards or playgrounds, accumulations of trash and garbage, and graffiti. These social and physical conditions suggest that one is surrounded by moral outcasts (Rainwater, 1966), individuals who neither respect nor can be coerced by formal agents to respect the public order.

Consequently, in urban and suburban areas, people can be confronted with a range of disorders, varying from violent robbery or murder or assault to vandals smashing car windows, to requests for money from winos, to kids jumping the back fence to retrieve an errant ball. This continuum is suggested in Figure 25-1. Most serious are actual crimes, particularly those involving person-to-person violence. Less serious are property crimes and FBI Part II, nonserious crimes. Crimes have been rated on seriousness (cf. Gottfredson, Young, & Laufer, 1980), and people in the main can agree on which crimes are more or less serious.

At the midrange on the disorder scale are incidents that have the potential for interpersonal vio-

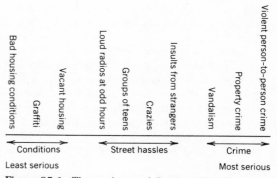

Figure 25.1. The continuum of disorder. *Note:* The appropriate scale for this continuum is not clear. It may well be a logarithmic one.

lence, altercation, or simple disagreement. These incidents are threatening due to their unpredictability. When one encounters some wayward teens or unstable people, it is always difficult to predict how the interaction will go. This is because one is uncertain whether or not these others will follow accepted (in the eyes of ego) norms of public behavior (Wilson, 1975). The incidents themselves suggest the norms will probably not be observed. Such incidents are of a moderately serious nature. Delinquent acts could come under this category. Finally least serious are chronic social and physical conditions indicative of the unraveling of society: people hanging out who should not be and signals of physical deterioration. These are of an even less serious nature than day-to-day stressors such as street hassles because the direct immediate threat to the ego is minimal. However, the conditions may have significant implications for the long-term stability and viability of the neighborhood.

The reasons, to recap, for treating these matters as tied together on a continuum, are several. First, in the eyes of residents, these may often be interpreted as indicative of the same underlying processes: the progressive breakdown of the moral order and the inability of officials to stem this deterioration. Second, these events vary in perceived seriousness, ranging from very serious to only minimally serious. Third, all of these events are capable of inspiring fear in the perceiver. We will turn to the links between the events and fear momentarily. And finally all of the events and conditions represented on the disorder continuum are potentially relevant to territorial control. Thus although the continuum is somewhat speculative, several sound reasons for its proposal can be offered.

Crime and other events and conditions on the disorder continuum are capable of inspiring fear. The amount of fear generated, however, depends on several factors. These parameters will be illuminated more fully when we discuss theory and research on fear of crime; therefore they are only touched on briefly here.

Events or conditions indicative of disorder are more fear-inspiring the more serious they are. Perhaps even more importantly, where the incident takes place, or where the condition occurs, is also of considerable import. Why this is so has to do with the nature of territorial functioning. Also important is the extent to which they recur regularly in the same place or type of place. Predictability diminishes the threatening impact.

As mentioned before, incidents and conditions reflective of disorder are potentially amenable to prevention or reduction by means of resident territorial control. The nature of human territorial functioning must now be described.

25.2.2. Human Territorial Functioning

Human territorial functioning[1] refers to an interlocked system of attitudes, sentiments and behaviors, regarding small-scale or delimited spaces of the environment, concerned with who has access to the spaces in question and what activities go on there, and with the expression of the occupants' linkage to the space. Human territorial functioning is in some respects analogous to, but most definitely not homologous with, territorial functioning in primates or other animals (Suttles, 1972). It is not an instinct ("closed" or "open") but is a set of goal-directed attitudes and behaviors. It is an open system of responding to and at the same time shaping and expressing the social, physical, and cultural context. Although traditionally linked with aggression and dominance, territorial functioning can also serve to smooth relations within and between groups. Territorial functioning is also place-specific. Territorial behaviors demonstrated in a particular location are crucially dependent on the actual physical characteristics of the location and the perceived characteristics or "meaning" of the site. Consequently territorial functioning cannot be investigated without specific reference to particular locations.

The functions of territoriality naturally suggest it as one informal means by which social control is exercised. Social control is a venerable item in the sociological lexicon that has been variously used and is thus to some extent problematic (Meier, 1982). Our use of the term here centers around informal social control "as a mechanism to ensure compliance with norms" (Meier, 1982, p. 35). Although territoriality has other functions as well, this aspect of the system is the one that is of central interest here.

The emergence of norms is part and parcel of the standing pattern of behavior, or program, on a particular street block.[2] The street block, in other words, functions as a behavior setting. But before clarifying that point, it is necessary to examine more closely the spatial distribution of territorial functioning.

From the perspective of each individual household, a gradient of territorial functioning can be observed. Such functioning is stronger in spaces that are more proximal to the home. Stronger functioning suggests that: the individual feels more responsible for things that happen there, can more easily determine who does and who does not belong there or who will be encountered there, and is less tolerant of problems or annoyances or stressors. Territorial functioning is stronger in these more proximal spaces because these locations are more central to the daily life of the individual and household. Stated differently: In terms of general well-being and mental health impacts on the individual and household, events occurring in the front or backyard are more important than events occurring on the sidewalk in front of the house or the alley behind the house, which are more important than events happening on the street block, which in turn are more important than events happening elsewhere in the neighborhood, and which are more important than events happening outside the neighborhood. Moving away from the most central of all places—the home (Rainwater, 1966)—one crosses a series of mental boundaries or psychological cliffs, passing into locations where particular events, *et ceteris paribus,* are of decreasing importance for the safety, security, and well-being of the individual and his or her household. Rowdy young men standing drinking beer are much less of a threat if they are three blocks away rather than on your corner. The closer they are the more they must be encountered, or at least seen, in the daily round. Consequently if we could construct an individuocentric, psychographic map representing the strength of territorial cognitions of individual households on a block, we would have, on either side of the street, a row of "mounds," the peak of each centering on each particular household, and sloping downhill to the yard, sidewalk, streets, and alleys. The cognitions weaken the further from home the space in question.

And, as importantly, the cognitions are weaker with respect to locations that are heavily used, more public thoroughfares. Thus territorial control is weakest surrounding locations such as playgrounds, alleys (Brower, 1980), small corner shops, commercial strips or nodes (McPherson, Silloway & Frey, 1983), institutional land use (Suttles, 1968), or even heavily trafficked streets (Appleyard, 1981). Control is weaker not only because such locations lack natural guardians (Cohen & Felson, 1979) or are less surveillable but also because such locations are more decidedly public and open to all, more heavily used by a wider variety of people coming from a greater distance; thus they are anonymous. These "valleys" in the topography of territorial control, as viewed from the resident point of view, represent interstitial spaces that should perhaps be avoided at particular times. Of course, and as shall be explored further

later, what may be a dangerous area for residents may represent opportunity to delinquents, potential offenders, or marginal members of the local society.

To clarify a previously mentioned point about territorial functioning: It is an open system. Consequently, as the social climate on a block varies (from fractious to harmonious), strength, scope, and configuration of territorial functioning vary also. As social climate becomes colder and/or stability in the larger neighborhood decreases, territorial control is further restricted, and residents are less able to influence events outside the home (Taylor, Gottfredson, & Brower, 1981).

The focus on territorial functioning as a system regulating interactions between residents (insiders) and strangers or miscreants (outsiders) should not obscure the role of the system in influencing resident-to-resident attitudes and interactions. Territorial markers and behaviors play an important role in this respect. Daily or routine maintenance, upkeep, and beautification activities such as washing steps, sweeping sidewalks, trimming lawns and bushes, painting, and planting flowers all send a "nonverbal" message (Rapoport, 1982) to other residents. The message is that "I'm invested in where I live, I care, I'm a good neighbor, and I can be counted on to assist in meeting local needs or emergencies that may arise." Such messages are decoded by others as indexes of reassurance. In cases where such signs are lacking, residents may mistrust or at least be wary and unsure of other residents. To the extent that these territorial behaviors are widely shared on a block, they approach the status of a norm, such that failure to adhere to the norm may result in directives from others, or possibly even censure (Gans, 1967). As in the classic deviance experiment by Schachter (1951), others may try to convince the errant individual to go along with the group, and, should that fail, ultimately give up on the person. To the extent that the appropriate territorial behaviors are widely disregarded, fear instead of trust may ensue. This is a topic that has been explored by several fear of crime models and will be discussed later. Widespread disrepair, lack of upkeep or maintenance, improper garbage disposal, and so on may lead one to conclude that one is living among moral outcasts and that therefore one is potentially in danger. Nearest neighbors may even be the most threatening because they know the most about one: times of coming and going, recent major purchases, and so on.

Thus territorial functioning is relevant not only to serious incidents on the disorder continuum where there is the possibility of interpersonal confrontation but is also relevant to physical conditions on the less serious end of the disorder continuum.

25.2.3. Street Blocks as Behavior Settings

This section outlines reasons why it is justified and fruitful to think of street blocks as behavior settings (Barker, 1968; Wicker, 1979). This treatment of behavior settings agrees, in several respects, with Wicker's treatment (Chapter 16, this volume) of behavior settings as dynamic, fluctuating, open systems, which emerge from and help structure local social life.

There are several reasons for suggesting that the street block is a behavior setting, including a standing pattern of behavior, or program, and a circumjacent physical milieu. First, the street block is physically bounded. At the ends it is traversed by two cross streets, marking its boundaries. The sides are bounded by the housefronts, or, to extend it somewhat more, the backs of backyards, or alleys. The physical environment thus surrounds and encloses the setting. The boundaries are, of course, not completely impermeable. Nonetheless, for residents, generally speaking, events occurring within the setting are of more importance to them than events occurring outside of the setting—all else being equal. The physical surround acts as a loose boundary, defining the arena of resident-to-resident interaction.

Nested within the setting are smaller scale synomorphs, which are also to some extent physically delineated. These include individual front and backyards and driveways. Less delineated but equally important as synomorphs are stretches of sidewalk or alley in front or behind particular dwelling units or single commercial establishments. Multiple commercial establishments or public amenities such as parks or playgrounds may be interspersed between residential behavior settings.

A standing pattern of behavior or program exists in that particular activities recur on a routine basis— daily (e.g., walking the dog), weekly (e.g., mowing the lawn), monthly (e.g., waiting for welfare or unemployment checks and going to the local store to cash them), or yearly (e.g., outdoor Christmas decorations), or on an occurrence basis (e.g., shoveling walk after a snow). These activities are not advertised, like basketball games, in local newspapers but they are predictable and routinized, and residents can inform one about these regularities. The regularities are also supported by the physical environment, as when groups of men sitting out in lower income

neighborhoods switch sides of the street to stay in the shade during summer.

The linkage between physical setting and setting program is also apparent when we consider teen or young adult segments of the setting population or groups that may be viewed as marginal by the residents. The interstices in the larger fabric of territorial control become points of convergence for small groups or gangs. In the interstices, where control is weak and surveillance is minimal, such groups are less likely to be bothered by regular residents and less likely to be perceived as bothersome. They shoot crap in the alley, drink or smoke on the playground, and hang out in front of the corner store. The (as perceived by resident) marginal activities are taking place in the peripheral areas of the setting or in the ambiguous areas between settings.

Physical environment and program are also linked in that territorial markers and cues serve as nonverbal messages (Rapoport, 1982), suggesting to people what kinds of behaviors are expected in particular locations. A block with well-kept-up houses, trimmed lawns, and immaculate flower beds indicates that residents care and that outsiders or passersby should likewise respect the locale. They should behave in an appropriate "guestlike" role.

Further, levels of participation in the program can be distinguished, as in traditional ecological psychology. On a block, some people may be heavily involved in various activities such as organizing meetings or cleanup campaigns or just spreading rumors, whereas others may be peripherally involved. In the case of stable corner groups, some individuals may hang out regularly with the group or club, whereas others are involved only on an intermittent basis.

The notion of a program implies agreement on what behaviors are acceptable and when and where they are acceptable; it implies setting- or synomorph-specific norms. Working on cars may be acceptable in the alley, but not out front, for example. A "bum" sitting on the curb may not be acceptable at any time. The clarity of these norms varies, depending on the nature and homogeneity of the block population and the stability of the surrounding neighborhood context. Norms will be less clear and/or less widely shared in heterogeneous blocks or in changing neighborhoods or in neighborhoods with high turnover rates. But although the clarity and latitude of the norms may vary, they still do operate from block to block, and reflect the underlying programs.

Finally, street blocks have deviation-countering and vetoing mechanisms. These mechanisms are part and parcel of territorial control such as instances where people are told to leave or get out or to be less noisy. Individuals or groups are told that they are not conforming to what is expected.

For all of these preceding reasons—circumjacent physical milieu, standing pattern of behavior or program, links between physical environment and program, levels of participation, and deviation-countering and vetoing mechanisms—residential street blocks qualify as bona fide behavior settings. The territorial system reinforces and clarifies the setting program. Territorial reactions to behaviors outside of the program function as deviation-countering or vetoing mechanisms. Territorial markers and cues further increase the legibility and coherence of the setting by promoting trust and cohesiveness among residents and communicating clear expectations to outsiders.

To return then to our disorder continuum, events and conditions that range from moderately serious to less serious are responded to as threats to the block behavior setting, and these responses are part and parcel of the territorial system. Moderately serious crimes (e.g., assault, burglary), but probably not very serious crimes, can be deterred by this territorial system.

25.3. TOWARD A PLURALISTIC PERSPECTIVE: DISORDER AND TERRITORIALITY FROM THE VIEW OF THE DISORDERLY

Now comes a difficult task. So far I have suggested that the nature of territorial functioning and its spatial distribution, particularly when street blocks are treated as behavior settings, provide powerful tools for understanding why events and conditions along the disorder continuum are more prevalent in some locations than others. All of this territorial synthesis, however, has been from the resident point of view. How are these dynamics to be understood from the perspective of those who are viewed by the residents as disorderly? How do we make sense of this from the view of corner gangs, loiterers, and delinquent youth? Based on extensive theorizing and empirical work with delinquents or gangs (Cloward, 1959; Ley & Cybriwsky, 1974; Miller, 1958; Suttles, 1968; Whyte, 1943), the following suggestions can be made.

First, the routine conduct of the disorderly or delinquent is not viewed by they themselves, as disorderly. Regularly occurring behaviors such as purse snatches, breaking into cars, or "getting high" may be viewed as legitimate ways to get "thrills" (Miller,

1958).[3] "Hanging" or "hanging out," which involves talking with peers, swapping stories of exploits, and matches of verbal wits, is regarded as routine and acceptable.

Perhaps what is more important is that where these activities occur is a reflection of the overarching texture of territorial control. It makes sense for such groups to hang out and carry out their activities in locations and at times where and when resident control and surveillance is minimal; in short, to gather and carry on in the territorial interstices. There are several factors that make such locations desirable activity nodes for the individuals and groups involved. First, in such locations the likelihood of their being confronted or "hassled" by residents is minimal. There is less threat of being forced to move elsewhere because residents have less concern for such locations. Consequently in these interstitial areas a larger number of persons can gather, and they can be noisier or more exuberant than they could be elsewhere. These interstitial areas include places such as corners, alleys, playgrounds, and around stores, bars, or institutional land uses. In such locations, the individuals or groups have greater behavioral freedom. Third, many of these locations ensure significant opportunities for interaction or "thrills." In the case of a corner store, for example, during operating hours there are always people coming and going. Thus one has a good chance of greeting, and perhaps chatting with, a large number of local acquaintances. There is lots of "action." Persons met can be badgered into buying something at the store or sharing what has been bought. There are also significant criminal opportunities. Such locations may draw older women or older men, who can afterward be followed and purses snatched or robbed on the street. Areas around commercial establishments are often not supervised by proprietors during hours of operation and in many instances lack natural guardians when the store is closed. Finally these individuals and groups may feel that their "hanging" contributes to the stability of the locale in that they can keep an eye on who is coming and going and be sure that other groups that "don't belong" are not allowed, or, if allowed, that they are closely watched. These "corner" groups have their own "system" of territorial control.

Related to this control are territorial markers. What may be graffiti from the view of residents are signs of gang control and possession, in the eyes of the markers (Ley & Cybriwsky, 1974). This is more true in cities such as Philadelphia, New York, and Newark where groups are stronger. But vandalizing buildings and property can, in nonterritorial gang instances, be included under the category of activities that provide a "thrill" (Greenberger & Allen, 1980).

By adopting the perspective of the disorderly we can see that on or around a particular street block there is a contrast between what is defined by stable, committed residents as outside the purview of the standing pattern of behavior, and what is viewed by teens or delinquents or marginal members of the group as part of their standing pattern of behavior. What is viewed as troublesome by the first is viewed as acceptable and indeed legitimate (as long as one avoids getting into serious trouble) by the second group.

What are the implications then of these two competing orders? The first implication is that conflict, which may be more or less frequent or more or less serious, is inevitable. There is a continual give-and-take between the residents and those whom they view as troublesome. This conflict is more intense in areas where the resident population is more sociodemographically heterogeneous. In such locales, the residents' setting program is more diffuse and more open to challenge; territorial control is weaker or more spotty (spatially). Nonetheless in many locations an equilibrium can be achieved between these two orders. This equilibrium is achieved by a spatial and temporal sorting process. The residents accept that at certain times of day, and in certain places, certain marginal groups can be found. After dark, one group may gather at the corner store and sit on the mailbox. On weekend evenings when the weather is warm enough, another group may gather on the playground to "get high," knowing that as long as they do not make noise they will not be hassled. Another group may gather on an intermittent basis for a crap game at the end of the alley, obscured from view by large garages between the alley and the backs of the houses. This temporal and spatial sorting is in response to the topography of territorial control. In short, there is a loose kind of mutual accommodation that goes on between the two orders, resulting in an imprecise equilibrium.

25.3.1. Change, Disequilibrium, and Fear of Crime

The equilibrium can be disturbed in two ways. First, residents may wish to expand their domain of territorial control, feeling they have a right to do away with annoyances. In such actions, there is the possibility that residents may seek to exercise too much territorial control. They may seek to exclude those who are merely different or nonconforming, as opposed to those who are genuinely troublesome. In fact, this was one of the problems in the first half of this century with neighborhood covenants, which often sought to exclude blacks or Jews from buying into a neighborhood (Isaacs, 1948). Such attempts to expand the zone of adherence to the block-setting program require considerable effort because collective action is required. Such a move has limited chances of success. And negative side effects can ensue when the targets of the controllers decide to retaliate. In other words, it is difficult to conceive of how the map of territorial control can be successfully applied to the interstitial areas between blocks and between neighborhoods. Opportunity areas of disorder and delinquency, then, are probably not erasable.[4]

A second way the loose equilibrium between order and disorder can be disrupted is when an area experiences a change in the composition of its population, as in the case of gentrification or racial succession, or when an area experiences significant physical or other land use changes such as the building of a shopping mall or highway, demolition or construction of other buildings, or increased vacant units.

Consider for example the sequence of events depicted in Figure 25.2. An interstitial area, along a major artery that is also a neighborhood boundary, is depicted. The location, type of land use, and traffic pattern make this an opportunity area for disorder. At Time 1, a corner store is vacant. People may hang out there and perhaps bother or even attack passersby. Proprietors and residents may not "hassle" those who hang out there unless the group becomes too troublesome. Because the stores close early and residents avoid the area after dark, the group is tolerated and has free reign after that time.

But imagine that the situation changes somewhat, as is shown in the diagram at Time 2. Due to economic recession and changing neighborhood composition, the small commercial area is less viable, and one or two more stores are forced to close their doors. It could also be the case that in the row of houses behind the store vacancies increase somewhat, as one or two slumlords decide that their properties are unsalable and that "fixup" would be too costly. So they abandon the units. Remaining tenants are evicted, and the units are boarded up. Some individuals may get a crowbar though and pry some of these boards off, so the vacant units may be used as shelter by a couple of homeless men and as a rendezvous for some drug pushers.

What these ecological changes bring about is an expansion in the number and size of the opportunity-for-disorder areas. Along the main artery, individuals

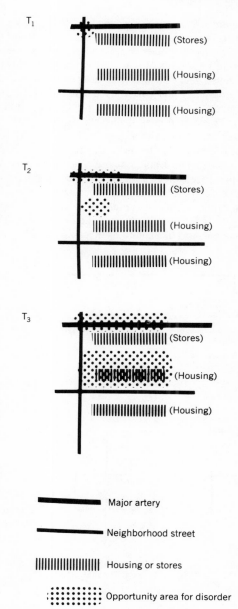

Figure 25.2. Growth of opportunity for disorder areas. *Note:* Top row of housing is comprised of stores. Middle row of houses are partially abandoned at T_1 and become progressively abandoned. Bottom row of houses are residential units, occupied at all three points in time.

feel free to hang out in a larger area because there are fewer proprietors. Part of the alley between the closed stores and the vacant housing units now becomes a good place to hang out also because that area is not under surveillance; it has no natural guardians anymore.

At Time 3, a few months later, the situation has deteriorated even further. Almost all the commercial stores on the strip are now closed, having been burned out by an arsonist. More slumlords have abandoned properties in the row of houses behind the stores, such that almost all the properties are vacant. Consequently the opportunity areas for disorder have spread even further. The entire block in front of the stores has been "taken over" by a local group, and they range freely up and down. Similarly in the alley behind they can meet, have parties or fights, or just "do nothing" because there are no natural guardians on either side. Bums may take to sitting on the steps on the front of the vacant houses during the day. What the residents in the stable group of residential units opposite have experienced is the ecological erosion of their behavior setting and the standing pattern of behavior. The interstices or "gaps" between viable behavior settings have expanded.[5] The order on their own block, to which they have been accustomed, has faded within only a few months time. The equilibrium between order and resident-perceived disorder has given away to the expansion of disorder.

And it is exactly this process of disequilibration that explains fear of crime. When residents in a particular locale perceive a shrinking of territorial control and an expansion of the interstitial opportunity areas for disorder, there is an increase in their community concern and apprehension about their own safety. The spatial extent of actual territorial control has shrunk to less than the expected extent, based on past experience. It is this discrepancy, and expanding of disorder beyond the interstices where its presence was accepted, that is stress-producing and induces concern. To put it more bluntly: It is not only what events and conditions occur that reflect disorder that is important—more crucial is where these instances are observed, how close it is to home, and how the locus has changed.

25.3.2. Implications Regarding Physical Environment

In the weaving of the preceding territorial behavior setting perspective on disorder, allusions to the pertinent roles of the physical environment have surfaced several times. In this subsection, I integrate and summarize these roles.

First, following Rapoport's (1982) suggestion that the physical environment carries nonverbal messages, elements in the physical environment such as territorial markers or traces from territorial behaviors can communicate information to insiders and outsiders (Altman & Chemers, 1978). To insiders, messages of investment are sent to indicate that one is a good neighbor (Mann, 1954), that one is trustworthy and committed to the area. Other residents not only decode such messages but reciprocate as well. Messages of defense are also sent to outsiders or potential miscreants suggesting what kinds of behaviors will and will not be tolerated. If outsiders respect these signs or infringe on them only to find them backed up by the natural guardians (e.g., someone coming out the door as soon as a fence is jumped over), then the territorial control will persist. There will be no weakening of the behavior setting program. If, however, signs are intruded on and found not backed up, then territorial control will wane, and the behavior setting program may unravel somewhat. How these two processes, one involving

insiders and one involving outsiders, might work over time is depicted in Figure 25.3.

The third way the physical environment is relevant to disorder occurs at a more macrolevel of analysis: Land use defines which areas are private or semiprivate property and which are public or open to the community (stores, churches, playgrounds, and so on). These land uses define where the "gaps" between the behavior settings will occur and thus where opportunity areas for disorderly conduct can be established. This is so for several reasons: (1) public spaces are less central to residents and thus of less concern; (2) public spaces by definition draw outsiders and strangers, thereby producing a confusing mix of users; this high quotient of strangers may make one less inclined to exercise territorial control

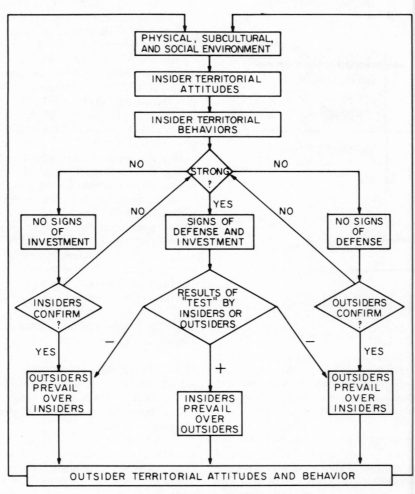

Figure 25.3. Territorial signs and communication.

and/or make the exercise of such less effective; and (3) these public spaces lack natural guardians.

From the perspective of the potential miscreants, physical environment is relevant in two ways. First, locations around public amenities draw foot traffic ("action") and potential targets of crime. The locations represent opportunities for entertainment and for gain. Second, because the spaces are interstitial, activities there are likely not to be surveilled because residents are too distant or their visual access is blocked. Or if these marginal individuals are surveilled, they are less likely to be bothered by leaders or participants in the local setting program because of their location in a nonproximal, noncentral space.

25.3.3. Summary

To summarize the environmental psychological approach to disorder, I have presented the following points. Street blocks are behavior settings. Territorial functioning is one means by which the setting program is communicated and enforced. In spaces less central to a household or outside of the behavior setting, residents will be more tolerant of what they perceive as disorderly conduct. From the viewpoint of those labeled as *miscreants* by residents, these interstitial and peripheral locations provide opportunities for peer contact and "thrills." When this spatially sorted equilibrium between residents and those they view as troublesome is upset by larger social or ecological transitions or by local land use changes, the block setting program can be threatened and fear can develop.

25.4. PAST THEORY AND RESEARCH REVIEWED AND RECONSIDERED FROM AN ENVIRONMENTAL PSYCHOLOGY PERSPECTIVE

In the following sections, theory and research relevant to crime, delinquency, and fear of crime are reviewed, along with selected results from each. Work on where offenders and delinquents live is reviewed first, followed by work on where crime is committed and work on fear. No claim is made regarding exhaustive treatment. Each theory is presented, criticized when the flaws are relevant to the main thrust of the chapter, and empirically supported. Then I attempt to view each theory from the environmental psychological perspective that has already been developed. The purpose of this reexamination is not to

see if these theories come up short but, rather, to see what the possibilities are for building even stronger theories that integrate and utilize an environmental psychological perspective. Some may label such an endeavor as gross miscegenation. I would prefer to view it as an attempt to forge more powerful, truly multidisciplinary models.

25.4.1. Offender and Delinquent Locations

Several sociological theories have centered around issues of offender and delinquent locations, or areas. The focus here has been on mapping, describing and explaining why some sections of urban areas "produce" a greater percentage of the offender or delinquent population.

Human Ecology

Human ecology is an attempt to understand urban life by applying the concepts of plant and animal biology (Park, 1915, p. 936; see also Michelson, 1970, Chapter 1). Humans are viewed as subgroups residing within ecological niches or communities that are "territorially organized" (Park, 1936, p. 4). The subgroup is tied to the area ("more or less completely rooted to the soil it occupies") with the individuals therein living in relationships of "mutual interdependence." There is constant competition between communities, resulting in a (rough) dominance ordering across areas, with dominance being indexed by land values (Park, 1936, p. 8).

> The principle of dominance, operating within the limits posed by the terrain and other natural features of the locations, tends to determine the general ecological pattern of the city and the functional relation of each of the different areas of the city to all others.

Communities, or natural areas, however, go through change. These series of changes, set in motion by larger scale forces such as city growth or decay or population changes, mean that a particular area will experience a series of changes or developments labeled *succession*. Prior to each change, each natural area achieves a homeostasis that is then eroded and ultimately replaced by a new stage or order. Thus an area will experience different waves of immigrants, or ethnic neighborhoods will be cleared or abandoned and devolve into a transition zone area (Preston, 1966), ultimately to be engulfed by an expanding central business district.

Human ecology was the mainspring of the Chicago school of sociology and has proven one of the most fruitful perspectives in that discipline (Hawley, 1981). At the same time, the perspective has been cogently criticized. Probably the most incisive critique has been offered by Alihan (1938). Among her criticisms are the following.

1. Human ecologists expand the concept of environment so dramatically that the boundary between organism and environment is hopelessly blurred. Environment includes physical, cultural, social, and institutional matters.

2. If environment includes social and technological aspects, as the human ecologists admit, the processes of competition must lose their ecological significance, and therefore the monistic emphasis on competition is not justified. The nature of human competition is radically different from competition in animal and plant communities.

3. Their use of terms such as *dominance* and *succession* is a distortion of the original ecological meanings.

4. There is a lack of regard for volitional factors. People are not so rooted that they cannot freely move into or out of areas.

5. There are discrepancies or gaps between the descriptive and the interpretive phases of the human ecologists' work; the data do not support the theory.

Much delinquency research has been ecological in nature, although only a portion of the ecological delinquency research has been theoretically tied to the human ecological school. The main contributions of this school are (1) that crime and delinquency persist at high levels in some areas of the city, (2) these consistently high levels persist in the same locations due to large-scale community-level forces and transactions, and (3) aberrant ecological change and increasing delinquency are linked. On this first point it has been established for some time that criminals and delinquents are concentrated more in some locations of the city than in others and that those areas where they reside are physically "poorer" than the conditions elsewhere in the city. Mayhew observed this in the mid-nineteenth century, Burt (1925) reaffirmed it in the early part of this century, and the evidence has mounted since.

Shaw (1929; Shaw & McKay, 1942/1969) observed it in Chicago for both delinquents and adult offenders. More than any other delinquency researcher, he has attempted to interpret his findings in the theoretical framework of human ecology. Shaw remarked (1929, pp. 119, 203) that the spatial distributions of delinquents and adult offenders were similar. Physically deteriorated places of juvenile residence

were concentrated in the transition zone adjacent to the central business district and near industrial areas. In interpreting these results (pp. 204–205), he felt that physical deterioration was probably best interpreted as a symptom of an area undergoing transition, due to patterns of city growth, from residential to commercial or industrial land use.

These "natural" transition processes translate to actual people acting in the following manner. City growth often results in the expansion of the central business district (CBD) as increasing services and jobs accompany population growth. In residential areas proximate to the CBD, investors expect that the CBD expansion can be translated into profitable real estate transactions. Consequently speculators move into an area and do much buying and selling of real estate. Because properties are only held for a short period of time, they are not improved or even kept up. The housing deteriorates, and properties are subdivided into low-rent apartments and rooming houses. The areas, until transformed into commercial zones, house low-income and transient populations. These "disintegrative forces" undermine traditional norms and processes of social control, making delinquency more likely.

> It has been quite common in discussions of delinquency to attribute causal significance to such conditions as poor housing, overcrowding, low living standards, low educational standards and so on. But these conditions themselves probably reflect a type of community life. By treating them one treats only symptoms of more basic processes. (Shaw, 1929, p. 205) (See also Lind, 1930).

This last point is particularly important. Physical environment is interpreted as an index of a larger social fact— social disorganization. This leap from the physical to the social is fully in keeping with a very strong sociological tradition (Dunlap & Catton, 1983). But it may be erroneous. When I review this theory from an environmental psychological perspective, I will give more attention to possible roles of the physical environment.

Shaw (e.g., 1929, p. 210) also observed that the same areas—in this case square mile areas—were likely to maintain a high rate of delinquency over an extended period of time (30 years). This stability of high delinquency areas has also been observed in other cities. Murray (1982), for example, found that the areas in Baltimore pinpointed by Lander (1954) as "producing" high rates of delinquents continued to do so in 1980.[6]

The covariates of high delinquency-producing

areas are difficult to interpret theoretically. Take the case of substandard housing, for example, Leaving aside how it may be important in its own right as a factor contributing to delinquency, the condition could be interpreted as reflecting relative socioeconomic deprivation or as reflecting the social disorganization resulting from succession and ecological instability, as suggested by the human ecological school. Before discussing the ecological work that attempts to decide between these two explanations, sociogenic theories of delinquency need to be described.

Sociological, or Sociogenic, Theories

Sociological, or as Gibbons (1976) calls them, sociogenic, theories of crime and delinquency causation look to forces, opportunities, and facts outside of the person, and in his or her immediate social or cultural environment, in order to explain why delinquency and crime occur. Although most of the theories have been couched in terms of individual-level processes, some have also been used to explain why certain areas become or remain criminal or delinquent locations.[7] (This is in contrast to the geographic and economic perspectives that focus on where delinquent or criminal acts have occurred as opposed to where delinquents or criminals live. Most accept that offender and offense locations can be different because potential offenders will be drawn to targets of opportunity, and these targets are not necessarily close to where they live (Baldwin & Bottoms, 1976). There are those (e.g., Turner, 1969), however, who argue that they may be similar.) The theories are as follows.

Anomie theory, deriving from the works of Durkheim (1951) and Merton (1957), states that social structure closes off access (means) to accepted societal goals for certain social groups or classes. This results in a disjunction between societally accepted means (go to school, study hard, get a job, work hard) to achieving these ends (be successful, move up, get rich) and the socially structured or defined means accessible to particular social groups. Society tells people what to be but blocks access to the appropriate means. Consequently recognizing this,[8] members of those groups experience anomie (literally normlessness) and turn to other means to achieve these goals. Crime and delinquency, for example, may bring material rewards (Black, 1970) or social status (Miller, 1958).

Differential association theory (Sutherland & Cressey, 1974) and *cultural transmission theory* (Shaw & McKay, 1942) both seek to explain the persistence of

certain locales as delinquency and crime-breeding areas. Differential association theory says that in certain parts of the city a subculture of deviance has evolved and that persons residing in those areas have a much lower probability of coming into contact with law-abiding acts and attitudes. The deviant subcultural transmission approach suggests that unconventional acts and norms become accepted as the dominant norms by persons living in those areas and are transmitted from one generation to the next. Or in the words of Henry Mayhew (1862; cited in Morris, 1957, p. 61): "Thousands of our felons are trained from their infancy in the bosom of crime; a large proportion of them are born in the homes of habitual thieves and other persons of bad character, and are familiarized with vice from their earliest years." These theories, however, do not seek to explain how or why these delinquency or criminality areas become established in the first place.

These two theoretical perspectives are integrated in Cloward and Ohlin's (1960) opportunity theory. They emphasize that persons in delinquent or criminal areas experience differential access to legitimate and illegitimate means of attaining societally accepted goals (e.g., money), with illegitimate means predominating. Or, to focus only on illegitimate modes of access, these means may be much more widely available in some areas, thus fostering the chances of delinquent and criminal behavior being successful (Cloward, 1959). Therefore, given blocked access to legal or conventional means of status attainment and the relative predominance of persons pursuing unconventional or delinquent means, criminals and delinquents result.

Early Ecological Delinquency Area Research and Problems of Interpretation

With these various theoretical perspectives in mind, we can now turn to the early ecological empirical work on delinquency areas, subsequent to Shaw and McKay's own work, and consider how these findings might fit a social disorganization, anomie, or relative socioeconomic deprivation type of model. [Although the previously described theories indicate that anomie is more likely to result from relative deprivation than social disorganization, a Durkheimian case can also be made that disorganization and the disruption of any remaining mechanical solidarity bonds (i.e., clan or family-based) would also lead to anomie if not replaced with adequate bonds of organic solidarity.] We will see that ecological factors are very difficult to interpret theoretically in an unambiguous way. And there are other problems with the ecological research as well. In light of these questions, the utility of this research may be minimal.

Lander (1954) correlated census tract variables with delinquency rates based on court cases. Zero-order correlations between these rates and physical variables such as overcrowding and substandard housing were very high, around .7. But at the same time the rates correlated well, around .7 again, with sociodemographics such as percentage nonwhite population and percentage of rental occupancy. Lander interpreted these latter sociodemographics as indicative of social instability. The pattern of higher order partials and factor analyses led him to conclude that anomie, social instability, and lack of social control, rather than low SES and relative deprivation, were the "cause" of delinquency.

Bordua (1958–1959) in Detroit subsequently attempted and reported achieving replication of Lander's results. Again although the zero-order correlations between delinquency rates and a host of census tract variables (percentage owner-occupied, overcrowded households, substandard housing, percentage nonwhite) were very strong (.5–.6), the pattern of higher order partials led him to conclude that anomie, and to some extent overcrowding, were the responsible causal factors. In Indianapolis, Chilton (1964) failed to find that delinquency was more closely tied to anomie than to SES factors. He concluded, again based on higher order partials because many of the zero-order correlations were strong, that substandard housing, rental (i.e., transient) households, and to some extent low SES were the responsible causal agents.

Chilton also reanalyzed the Lander and Bordua data subjecting it to different analyses. This reexamination called into question the anomie construct and clearly pointed to a higher order (i.e., net of other variables) association between overcrowded housing units and delinquency.

These early studies later came in for heavy criticism. Rosen and Turner (1967) critiqued them on the grounds that multiple regression was inappropriate for the analysis of ecological data because nonadditivity (interaction effects) probably existed in the data. They suggested that predictive attributes analysis, which seeks such conditional effects, was more appropriate. Their analysis of Philadelphia ecological data supported their assertion.

Perhaps more widely known are Gordon's (1967) criticisms of these works. He criticized higher order partialling carried out when there is no theoretical context to specify relevant control variables. Such procedures commit what he called the *partialling fallacy*. He also argued that such a procedure made no sense when "valid covariation" was partialled out. He questioned the construct validity of variables reflective of anomie. He concluded that SES was the major covariate of delinquency.

Taking into account these criticisms, Chilton and Dussich (1974) reanalyzed their original Indianapolis data. They did new factor analyses and carried out predictive attributes analysis, a social area analysis (cf. Shevky & Bell, 1955), and analysis of covariance. They concluded that low SES and delinquency were linked. Perhaps more importantly (p. 81), they said that "delinquency referrals are related to the racial composition and living arrangements of these areas, but that the importance of these factors is not independent of the economic situation." In other words, substandard or overcrowded housing is more of a potential causative factor for those segments of the population that are already at risk due to other factors, for example, being nonwhite, than it is for other segments. Environmental insults may therefore be more deleterious for some groups than for others.

Morris (1957) analyzed delinquency areas in Croydon and also found very strong ties between poor housing (i.e., overcrowding) and delinquency rates. Much more valuable though was his suggestion regarding the processes underlying this descriptive relationship.

> The efficiency of the family as an effective agency of social control must inevitably be impaired when relationships within it are subjected to stress. These factors may arise from…factors which are predominantly economic. Undoubtedly among the most important of these is housing. (p. 168).

Thus:

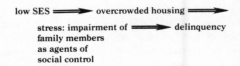

Although Morris' data provide only hints that the preceding sequence may be operating, supporting evidence is available from other studies. Loring (1956) found that controlling for social class, households were more likely to be referred to public agencies (courts, welfare agencies, and so on), if role density within the household was higher. (Role density means an increasingly diverse array of kin or relatives.) And Mitchell (1971) discovered in his Hong

Kong study that as apartment density increased, parents sent their children out of the apartment more frequently and were less likely to know the outside location of the children. Thus the process proposed by Morris to explain the crowded/substandard housing-delinquency link appears worthwhile. Perhaps its most useful feature is that it admits that sociological facts in part determine physical conditions but then goes on to emphasize that the physical conditions have their own consequences.

Subsequent Ecological Work

Studies subsequent to the aforementioned, although more careful in their treatment of aggregate data, or melding aggregate data with case study information, continue to find links between areas that produce high rates of delinquencies or offenders and substandard housing. Herbert (1977b) discovered this for delinquents in Cardiff, Cartwright and Howard (1966) with gang delinquents in Chicago, and Baldwin and Bottoms (1976) found this for adult offenders in Sheffield. Because a poor social as well as physical environment continues to characterize these areas, the question still remains as to which is relatively more important. (For a discussion of other problems with work in this area see Baldwin (1975, 1979).)

As Thrasher (1927) found years ago, delinquent locations are "bad" areas of town, which are interstitial in character—that is, they have a mixed ambience, being neither residential nor industrial, and often lie "between" the boundaries of more stable communities. Shannon (1982), in his analysis of several cohorts of delinquents in Racine (Wisconsin), has noted that this continues to be the case. He also discovered some slight evidence that changes in areas (e.g., increasing mixed land use) was later followed by increasing delinquency. [Kobrin & Schuerman (1982) in Los Angeles found that land use changes also eventuated in more juvenile offenses.] One reason for the delinquency-producing qualities of these mixed areas is the number of potential targets they contain and lack of guardians.

Conclusions: Problems and Possibilities in Delinquency and Crime Location Theory and Research

Given the foregoing, what can we conclude? First, it is abundantly clear that there are serious conceptual and methodological problems with ecological delinquency research. This research tells us nothing about individual-level relationships unless we want to commit the ecological fallacy (Robinson, 1950;

Thorndike, 1939) and impute areal-level relations to individuals.[9] Because various aspects of the environment intercorrelate more strongly at higher levels of analysis, it is exceedingly difficult to untangle this covariation and isolate particular variables as uniquely linked to delinquency or offender rates. Constructing links between areal physical and sociodemographic parameters (e.g., percentage substandard housing, percentage rental population) and social facts such as anomie or social disorganization is a tenuous artistic enterprise at best, and misleading at worst. It may well be impossible to adequately operationalize these social facts that are produced by larger scale metropolitan and intercommunity dynamics by relying solely on ecological data.

But second, despite these limits, problems, and vagaries, two general points are clear from the research. A delinquency or offender area, once established, appears to have considerable "staying power," retaining those qualities over a span of time from one to four decades. Numerous reasons have been proposed to explain such persistence. These explanations have variously focused on internal dynamics (proximity to opportunities, interstitial or transition zone qualities, physical isolation), external social forces (such as labeling by other residents or housing officials), or external pressures due to growth. With regard to the labeling hypothesis, Savelsberg (1982) has reviewed several studies and has suggested that spatially identifiable groups through labeling and discriminatory practices become "objectively disadvantaged" in terms of access to employment, education, and services, thereby setting the conditions for crime and delinquency. Damer (1974) has also used a labeling perspective to explain how areas get and maintain a "bad" reputation. We therefore have indications how such an area forms in the first place and why it persists. Herbert (1977a; see also 1980) has also proposed a "cycle of disadvantage" model that explains delinquency area persistence through several aspects of disadvantage, all of which work together and reinforce one another in several ways.

Areas that produce higher rates of delinquency or offenders also contain a greater prevalence of substandard or dilapidated housing. And this link may be stronger for some groups than for others. As Morris has suggested (1957), and much research has indicated (Baum & Paulus, Chapter 14, this volume), overcrowded conditions may cause stress and interfere with effective interpersonal functioning, dampening the efficiency of parents or other adults as agents of social control. Or it may drive children out of and away from the home in attempts to gain privacy or at least distance from other family members. As we will clarify later, there are several possible ways an environmental psychological perspective could be used to clarify these links.

Returning, then, to the environmental psychological perspective mapped out earlier, how might this be integrated with the extant theory and research on delinquent and offender location?

We can start our theoretical integration with the general recognition that changes happening in a neighborhood or a community, perhaps as the result of larger scale urban processes (growth, succession, decline, and so on), will "filter down" to impact territorial dynamics at the block level. These impacts may be several. First, if the area is in the process of change, or even if it is a socially unstable area with a high rate of turnover, this factor impedes effective territorial functioning in outdoor spaces in several ways.

1. Given a high rate of turnover, it is very difficult for any one particular stable resident to keep track of who belongs or who does not belong in an area. Basic distinctions between "insiders" and "outsiders" become blurred. Territorial access control hinges on the ability to make exactly these kinds of discriminations. Imagine two residents who may be sitting out on their front steps. Two doors down three older men may also be sitting but are loud and carrying on. The first resident suggests they go over and tell the rowdies to move on, but the second resident says she thinks two of the three are new renters who have recently moved in. Given that a typical street block (at least in Baltimore) may contain 30 to 60 addresses and that each address in a rental area may include two to six households, even if we only assume an average household size of four, this is 240 to 1440 people of which one must keep track. And if a large portion of the population is constantly moving in and moving out, the exercise of territorial control will be crippled, due to the difficulties in achieving a rudimentary categorization of other people as either belonging or not belonging in the setting. Support for this proposal has been gained from an investigation of the links between neighborhood context and territorial functioning (Taylor et al., 1981).

2. In light of this instability and illegibility of the social context, residents may restrict their domain of territorial concern. Instead of worrying about what is happening on the entire block, they may restrict their attention and vigilance to a smaller area and perhaps worry only about events up to a couple of doors away. This results then, at the block level, in an overall weakening of the texture of territorial control. For any particular patch of outdoor space there are fewer available "eyes" (Jacobs, 1961). Taylor et al. (1981) also provided supportive evidence for this suggestion. In increasingly unstable neighborhoods, attitudes of territorial responsibility extended a shorter distance from the home.

3. Increasing instability means that it will be more difficult for a clearly defined, widely adhered-to standing pattern of behavior to become established. With people constantly coming and going, the program itself is strained, and people become less familiar with it. Thus there may be less respect for what is agreed on as appropriate behavior, and those actual agreements may devolve over time. The process is analogous to successively putting complete new crews on a ship, but never giving them enough time to learn in detail about the ship's operation; their only teachers are the crew that preceded them. Eventually, after a few turnovers, the ship would not be running too well; a similar situation might obtain for the setting program on blocks in unstable areas.

Or to state the point differently, there will be increasing divergence from the original setting program. Because deviation-countering and vetoing mechanisms are crippled due to social overload, illegibility of social context, and the constriction of territorial functioning, the divergence is not redressed. Consequently the norms progressively degrade or become more diffuse. If we assume that residents recognize these developments, it is easy also to understand how fear of crime develops.

The same processes may also deleteriously influence the development of stable corner gangs. With constant turnover, the group structure (cf. Whyte, 1943) may be less well defined, resulting in a diminution of peer pressure and leadership authority. Whether this then results in more or less delinquent acts is difficult to say, but it undoubtedly provides a less meaningful gang context.

4. Instability means that it is more difficult to establish local social ties. Deutschberger (1946) found that in changing as compared to stable areas, local social networks shrank because losses from the network were not replaced. And these local ties are an important supporter of territorial functioning (Newman & Franck, 1982; Taylor et al., 1981). The lack of social supports further detracts from the possibilities of effective territorial functioning.

The preceding points illustrate how social instability may cripple territorial functioning and the setting program. To tie these processes in to the "production" of delinquents (and later criminals), we need only invoke learning processes. In these more unstable areas, residents will be less likely to intervene if they witness a delinquent act (Hackler, Ho, & Urquhart-Ross, 1974; Maccoby, Johnson, & Church, 1958). The youth learns that he can get away with it. In Miller's (1958) language, he can get his "thrills" and not get in "trouble." Given reinforcement and no punishment, the behaviors are repeated.

Second, in addition to social instability, the ecological delinquency research has clearly indicated deteriorated or substandard housing as a covariate of delinquency-producing areas. It is worthwhile to consider how these also might influence territorial functioning at the block level.

1. Lower quality housing is likely to be rental housing, and the lower quality it is the more likely it is to be subdivided into progressively smaller and increasingly inadequate units. Given such a housing condition, residents are not likely to engage in significant territorial marking. They do not identify with nor do they want others to identify them with such conditions. Consequently, at the block level, there is a paucity of upkeep, beautification, embellishments, and territorial markers. The signs that can carry potential messages from the insiders to the outsiders—that say "we care about where we live and you had better behave"—are missing. The physical cues to the setting program (cf. Wicker, 1979, Chapter 4) are missing, resulting in even less adherence to the standing pattern of behavior.

2. When people see the low housing quality that others are living in and the environmental problems that accompany dilapidated housing, they may be likely to conclude that they are living in the midst of moral outcasts (Rainwater, 1966). This attribution will further deepen co-resident distrust and suspicion. (This theme is explained more fully in the section on fear.) Co-resident ties, which can support individual territorial functioning and underpin effective collective territorial action, become even more difficult to establish. So again, territorial functioning is crippled. People are not visibly invested in their environment (and they would probably add, rightly so), and they perceive that their fellow residents are not either. Given such lack of commitment, and potential threat from others, it is not surprising that the local program devolves. Getting involved in local events raises the possibility of retaliation from unpredictable others and cooperating with "unknowns." (The latter may also have negative consequences.)

In sum, an environmental psychological perspective, grounded in territorial and behavior-setting theories, could be very well integrated with insights from research on delinquent and offender areas. Such integration provides a description of multilevel processes, linking areal dynamics with events at the small-group and individual level. Such integration may therefore provide a much more powerful analysis of the where and why of delinquency and offender areas.

25.4.2. Understanding Where Crimes Occur

Once a delinquent or offender has been "raised," he or she must go somewhere to commit a crime. An important question is where these criminal or delinquent acts occur. Theory and research in this area, to which economists and geographers as well as sociologists have contributed, is substantial, and three levels of inquiry, of increasing sophistication, can be discerned. At the simplest level, the question is: Where do crimes occur? In what kinds of areas, or what kinds of specific locations? At a somewhat more complex level the question is: If going to commit a crime is like going to work, what does the journey to crime look like? How far do people go? Do they go farther depending on the type of crime they want to commit? And last, the most complex level of inquiry is concerned with the relationship between offender locations and offense locations. How is where the offender lives different from where he or she goes to commit a crime? This last level of inquiry represents the most wholistic approach to the question of crime location.

Opportunity and Cost Approaches
Crime needs a target. In the case of property offenses—residential and commercial burglary, larceny—the location of the targets is fixed geographically by land use. Thus the expectation has been, and data have supported the commonsensical notion, that certain types of crimes happen where there are more opportunities or targets for those types of activities. White (1932), who examined both offender and offense areas, found that high offense areas had much of their land devoted to business use. "The point to be made, in view of these facts, is that crime is associated with business and is found in the center of cities because that is where the greatest concentration of business is found" (p. 502). Percentage of business land use explained 31% of the variation in felonies.

Schmid (1960a, 1960b), in an exhaustive Seattle study noted links between robbery and presence of commercial and business establishments.

O'Donnell and Lydgate (1980) carried out a census of all types of land uses in Honolulu and correlated land uses with crime. Resource factors such as retailing, restaurants, and entertainment were associated with robbery and larceny. Fraud was associated with tourist business. Perhaps what is more interesting and less expected was the association of physical resources with potentially violent person-to-person crimes such as robbery, assault, and disorderly conduct.

The role of opportunities in relation to crime has led some to suggest that opportunities rather than population factors should be used as the denominator for developing crime rates. Boggs (1965) examined 12 crimes in St. Louis and proposed an opportunity denominator for each (e.g., square footage of land in streets for street robbery, pairs of persons for homicide and assault, the business-residential land use ratio for business robbery, commercial burglary, and grand larceny). These crime-specific occurrence rates were distributed very differently over the city than standard crime rates and for several rates showed low or modestly negative associations with standard crime rates at the census tract level. Using physical opportunities therefore provides a very different spatial "portrait" of crime.

Subsequent studies reviewed by Harries (1981) have also used opportunity denominators, revealing different spatial distributions of crimes. Two problems noted by Harries (1981) with opportunity rates are (1) the difficulty and/or cost of obtaining valid geographic data for very small areas (e.g., police reporting areas) and (2) if opportunities are used as the denominator for a crime rate, it is not clear how one can control for population characteristics in developing these rates.

Harries (1978, 1981) explored the advantages gained by using alternative denominators in Oklahoma City and Tulsa. Opportunity-based rates showed a much more dispersed crime pattern than did standard crime rates. Harries also determined that opportunity denominators were capturing new information not contained in standard population denominators. He suggested, however, that opportunity-based denominators should only be used for specific subclasses of offenses (e.g., commercial burglary), not broad crime categories.

The link between crime and opportunities is solid (e.g., Dunn, 1980, p. 12) but not perfect. This has led to the consideration of factors (i.e., costs) that would make available opportunities less attractive. One such potential cost is the possibility of police action. Rengert (1980) tested a model that incorporated opportunities and potential costs. Areas with a higher potential cost to the offender were those where police had a higher clearance rate. The percentage of cleared cases was used as the measure of police efficiency. Using abandoned homes (opportunities) and police efficiency (costs), Rengert was able to predict 58% of the variation in crimes of arson and vandalism in 22 Philadelphia police districts.

Costs as well as opportunity factors were considered by Fabrikant (1979) in his analysis of Los Angeles data. Using data from juvenile cases, he found that comparative police efficiency (relative clearance rates) influenced crimes, but the strength of the deterrent impact varied across crimes, being stronger for "outside" crimes such as robbery, which is street-oriented. The implication, then, is that changes in relative efficiency across police areas will result in a change in the distribution of robberies. Robbers will redistribute themselves to avoid areas of high police surveillance or high police efficiency. Such redistribution, however, may not occur as much as Fabrikant suggests. The time involved in travel to and from a crime is also a cost and something offenders seek to minimize.

A markedly different approach to opportunities has been taken by Carter and Hill (1978, 1979). They have argued that if differences in opportunities exist, criminals are "aware" of this and build up images of these areas based on these differences. Thus images should covary with crime. Graphically one may illustrate this as follows:

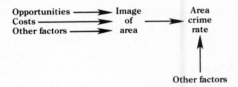

Carter and Hill used a modified semantic differential technique with convicted property offenders ($n = 83$) and a noncriminal sample. Three perceptual dimensions emerged (high status, hard vs. easy mark, and familiarity). Criminals' images based on these three factors explained over 70% of the variation in crime rates. An important next step in this research would be the linking of image with actual physical and social characteristics.

Focusing on behavioral instead of physical factors, Cohen and Felson (1979) have suggested that the opportunity/cost ratio for crime may be higher in areas that lack natural guardians, for example, a neighborhood of young professionals where in most households husband and wife both work and thus are both away from the house during the day. Such areas lack natural guardians—people who would see and perhaps even report suspicious activity—thereby making property crimes such as burglary more likely in an area.

Thus predominance of offenses in a locale reflects opportunities and costs. The former depends on the types of land use and users in an area; the latter refers to formal (i.e., police-based) as well as informal (i.e., resident-based) responses. These informal responses are influenced by a host of factors such as occupational patterns. Although offenders appear to be aware of opportunity and cost factors in subareas, it is hard to know, given the "friction" of distance and varying motivations depending on type of crime, the extent to which they actually maximize the opportunity/cost ratio.

Areal Patterns of Offense–Offender Links

Felons live some place and commit crimes elsewhere. This simple fact has led to interest in the "trip to crime," or the spatial dynamics of offender travel behavior.

DISTANCE

Early work in this area was concerned with the distance between offender residence and offense site. Since White's (1932) early work, it has been confirmed that felons do not travel that far—anywhere from less than half a mile to a mile and a half or two miles depending on the type of offense and the age of the offender. Violent, as compared to property, offenses are more likely to occur closer to home (McIver, 1981; Rhodes & Conly, 1981), and juveniles travel less far than older offenders (Turner, 1969; Baldwin & Bottoms, 1976). Crimes that require less readily available targets (e.g., armed robberies require a store) are associated with longer trip distances (Capone & Nichols, 1976).

RELATIVIZED OPPORTUNITY

Concern about the relations between offender residences and offense sites has given rise to the concept of relativized opportunities structures. That is, in relative terms, how much more attractive or available are opportunities at the crime site as compared to where the offender lives. Rengert (1981), however, criticizes the opportunities model because it does not consider "opportunities for whom." For an opportunity to count, there must be felons nearby whose working radius the crime site is within, and they

must, through their daily activity patterns and so on, become aware of this. Thus Rengert suggested actual or effective [to use Gans', (1968) distinction between potential and effective environment] opportunities were a function of the existence of nearby felons, ease of access, and existence of targets. Using well-known regional science "density potential" models, he tested his thesis on burglaries in different areas of Philadelphia.[10] Areas attracted more burglars if they had more residential units and had higher housing values. Outlying areas of the city were particularly attractive to burglars—due in part to wealthier homes. Katzman (1981), also using a density potential model in Dallas, found that higher neighborhood housing values attracted more property crime. The presence of adjacent poorer populations also contributed to an area's crime rate. Thus this approach confirms the utility of examining opportunities in relation to the distribution of offenders. A crime opportunity is meaningless unless there are nearby offenders to take advantage of it.

Perhaps more interesting has been the question of whether where offenders live is different in terms of areal characteristics, from where they commit their crimes. Rhodes and Conly (1981) addressed this question in a Washington, DC, study that innovatively merged lot-level, physical, land use information available citywide with offender files. They found that offense areas were more transitional, and heavily used for business purposes, as compared to DC land use in general, and as compared to areas where the offenders lived.[11] Thus offenders were moving out of their immediate environment to take advantage of nearby crime sites that were more attractive due to their land use pattern and (presumably) accompanying street activity pattern. This agrees with Suttles' (1968) description of dangerous no-man's-lands in Chicago such as around construction sites or large institutions or factories. Offenders appeared to avoid heavily residential areas fitting Greenberg, Rohe, and Williams' (1982) findings. There was also less movement into small business areas, supporting Jacob's (1961) suggestions about the positive values of such areas.

In sum, then, offenders seek out areas with which they are somewhat familiar in terms of the local ecology, which afford opportunities, and which due to land use and accompanying anonymity and activity patterns lack local or "built-in" guardians.

Specific Locational Factors

Complementing the work on areal factors associated with crime opportunities has been a smaller body of work concerned with specific features associated with crime incidence. There is a host of soft, rather impressionistic evidence that crimes are more likely to happen on streets with certain types of characteristics. For example, Morris (1957, p. 124) reported in his analysis of Croydon data that the streets "which were poorly lit, shaded by trees or with few passers-by . . . were commonly the scene of indecent exposures and assaults." Harder evidence is also available. Bevis and Nutter (1977), for example, observed that type of street layout (closed vs. through) was associated with burglary rates. Thus some types of streets tend to be more crime-prone than others.

With regard to commercial establishments, McPherson and Silloway (1980) found that bars and adult entertainment establishments "generated" nearby street crime but only for certain types of bars and certain types of entertainment establishments. And when they examined crime in small commercial centers, they found that the types of businesses present had a strong impact on the crime rate (McPherson, Silloway, & Frey, 1983).

Physical environment features associated with armed robbery of convenience stores were examined by Duffala (1976), using data from Tallahassee. He assumed that armed robbers would be fairly rational in their casing of targets because they do travel farther than unarmed robbers to do a job and thus would be more responsive to various environmental features. He found that the more frequently, as compared to less frequently, robbed stores were located on lightly traveled streets, with fewer surrounding commercial activities, and thus by implication, fewer surrounding eyes on the street. Although businesses represent opportunities, how many of these opportunities actually become crime targets depends on the type of business, type of clientele, and surrounding activity patterns.

These studies confirm that commercial areas afford viable crime opportunities and shed new light on how these opportunities may work. The commercial area's vulnerability is determined in part by surrounding land use and traffic patterns and its own orderly or disorderly appearance as well as by the nature of the surrounding population. Further, these areas "generate" street crime. In the case of bars, the problem may be between customers. In the case of other establishments, the area may serve as a "lair" due to its anonymity and/or lack of caring by tenants or nearby residents, where unwitting passersthrough can be accosted. Links between commercial areas, processes of neighborhood stability and change, and attitudes of proprietors and customers toward the areas need to be examined. Some possible links along these lines will be discussed later.

Conclusions, Problems, and Possibilities

The work in this area has suggested several points regarding the geography of crime. Offenders are drawn to opportunities as crime loci, but opportunities must be proximate to a large population of potential offenders who can take "advantage" of the opportunities because, on average, offenders do not travel far. The environmental "image" offenders have of an area is associated with the extent to which the area is victimized. Further, crime or offense areas appear to be different from areas where offenders live. Moving to a more specific level of analysis (Brantingham, Dyreson, & Brantingham, 1976), specific types of nonresidential land uses appear to "generate" crime, as a function of the kind of clientele they attract, who can subsequently play the role of either potential offender or potential victim. Thus at a subareal as well as the areal level we can also speak of areas of relative opportunity.

Although these general relationships are promising, several significant gaps in this literature remain. Generally speaking, the process by which offenders get "linked up" to particular opportunities or opportunity areas is yet unclarified. Carter and Hill's (1978, 1979) notion of an area developing an "image" is particularly interesting in this regard. How does this image develop? Is it the case that offenders initially "case" an area, using a set of cues, and then try out their luck, and, if successful, pass the word on to fellow offenders? In interviews with actual offenders (Bennett & Wright, 1984; David, 1974; Letkemann, 1973; Reppetto, 1974), it is suggested that offenders do make such assessments of areas and particular sites and that there is communication between felons involved in similar endeavors. If this is the case, it would be invaluable to know more about the cues offenders use when assessing an area. Two sets of factors may be relevant: features pertinent to the potential opportunity (amount of benefits possible) and features pertinent to potential costs such as surveillability of location, police coverage, presence of safety devices, and perhaps territorial cues indicating investment or vigilance on the part of residents. Offenders may be alert to "clues" in these two areas. The Rhodes and Conly (1981) study particularly underscores this latter point—that offenders committing street assault move into areas where ongoing construction and large-scale nonresidential land uses decrease the likelihood that other passersby, who could act as witnesses or interveners, would be around. Finally the question also arises regarding the actual route taken between origin (offense residence) and destination (crime location). Will the offender seek to route himself or herself along major, heavily trafficked thoroughfares where he or she is likely to be anonymous? This is another aspect of the entire process that needs to be examined thoroughly.

Given the preceding sequence, we can turn to our central inquiry and ask how might this process be folded into and illuminated by an environmental psychological perspective such as the territorial one we have described.

Basically our environmental psychological perspective serves to clarify the types of physical elements in the environment, in addition to location and types of opportunities, to which the potential offender might be attuned. These physical elements would be the signs of upkeep, beautification, and maintenance that reflect strong territorial functioning and high levels of attachment to place (Shumaker & Taylor, 1983). From these the potential offender would infer populations who are vigilant, care about their locale, and are ready and able to confront or do something about intruders or suspicious persons. To the extent that the potential offender infers strong territorial functioning, or high levels of attachment, he or she may anticipate a greater possibility of being detected or apprehended should he or she decide to attempt an offense. Thus the physical observables reflecting territorial functioning or attachment would reduce the anticipated benefit–cost ratio and thereby make the area a less attractive locale to operate in.

Other relevant physical factors may include features such as lighting and volume of traffic on the street, which would lower the salience of the potential offender, and ease of access to a main road for speedy egress. Some of these may also influence resident territorial functioning. With regard to street traffic, Appleyard (1981) indicated that its volume may reduce the time residents spend out front, or the extent to which they are involved with events on the front. With regard to pedestrian traffic, Baum, Davis, and Aiello (1978) found that high levels of foot traffic were associated with residents using their front yards less and less informal chatting between neighbors out front. By implication, then, the pedestrian traffic would also dampen territorial functioning. Thus other factors, above and beyond the resident-generated physical territorial elements, some of which may impact territorial functioning, will shift

anticipated benefit–cost ratios. In other words, in addition to physical factors, the computation of the anticipated benefit–cost ratio is probably also influenced by behavioral factors.

More specifically, I would suggest that the potential offender is somewhat attuned to the scope and coherence of block behavior settings in a neighborhood. He or she is aware, albeit perhaps in a somewhat fuzzy fashion, of the bounds of accepted behavior in various locales and has an idea of what will be "noticed" by residents as opposed to what will not stick out. He or she can gauge the extent to which clear, mutually agreed-on demarcations between insiders and outsiders are made by residents, based on the mix of people he or she observes and the observed responses of residents themselves.

In short, potential offenders may be aware of and sensitive to the extent to which residents in a neighborhood or on a block function as natural guardians. The social and physical evidence he or she uses to make this determination are the reflections of residents' territorial functioning. This input influences the anticipated benefit–cost ratios of committing an offense such as aggravated assault or burglary, by leading the potential offender to estimate that it is more or less likely that he or she will be detected, pursued, or apprehended. Consequently this information influences the images that are formed of particular areas and the desirability of various alternative sites (particular blocks, particular households) within an area. In short, the territorial behavior setting focus allows us to pinpoint specific possible factors that link an offender to a particular target area.

Another way the territorial perspective is helpful is in clarifying why crime target areas may be especially vulnerable. If we focus simply on street crime such as assaults or purse snatching, we know some of the reasons why they happen around nonresidential or commercial land uses. People are attracted to these locations; they go there to shop or drink or be entertained or eat. Consequently these commercial areas act as nodes, drawing pedestrian traffic, resulting in a higher rate of potential targets per time unit. But in addition to the target rate, other factors may be relevant as well. Because small commercial areas are by definition open to the public, no group of "insiders" can establish behavior-setting programs of acceptable behavior. There are some legal remedies that can be invoked such as no loitering within 50 ft of a building, but these are by and large of minimal help. In short, it is difficult if not impossible to establish a delineated setting program when there is a large fraction of commercial land use. Or to state the point differently, commercial areas are not within the territorial purview of a particular group. Residents abutting small commercial areas recognize this (McPherson et al., 1983) and have minimal expectations of control or jurisdiction over such locations. The predominantly commercial areas are by definition interstitial in a territorial sense, falling between zones of resident-based territorial functioning. This point is not only pertinent for understanding street crime around commercial areas, but it also helps us understand why street crimes occur in no-man's-land, the "transitional areas" described by Rhodes and Conly (1981) where, due to type of land use (institutional, temporary housing) or changes in land use (construction or demolition areas), the natural guardians are lacking, and we have "holes" in the fabric of territorial functioning.

The territorial-behavior setting perspective clarifies linkages between offenders and offense areas, delineating a specific set of cues and processes shaping these linkages.

25.4.3. Crime as an Influence on the Physical Environment

Once an offender or delinquent has been "produced" by an area and once that delinquent or offender has chosen and traveled to a particular locale to commit an offense, several consequences ensue. One that will be taken up in the following section is elevated fear of crime, or perceived risk on the part of residents, or heightened levels of behavioral protection. In this section, however, we focus on how the environment itself may be a "victim" of crime. The environment may be a victim of crime in the following way. Crime may be thought of as one element that, along with many others, may "add up" to result in some overall particular quality of life. Crime counts as a negative factor, or disamenity. Or alternatively, we can think of public safety as an amenity or public good, which crime reduces in size. Other amenities include good versus bad schools, large, adequate housing versus smaller or substandard housing, adequate versus inadequate public services such as refuse collection, and so on. All else being equal, a neighborhood with more crime is a less desirable place to live, and a neighborhood with less crime (more safety) is a more desirable place to live. Thus we might expect that as crime goes up in an area, fewer people want to live there. In economic terms, this is a "softening" of the market as the supply–demand ratio increases. Consequently we would expect house prices to fall. And indeed, several studies indicate that crime does serve to depress house values.

Dubin and Goodman (1982; see also Goodman, in press) examined house sales price for 1765 house sales in Baltimore City and Baltimore County. Controlling for characteristics of the house sold and for racial composition, crime had a significant dampening impact on house prices. In the city sample, three independent crime dimensions (nonviolent crime to property, violent crime, and "shopping center" crime) all had substantial and significant impacts. A one (standard) unit change on all three of the crime dimensions implied a house value loss of over $7000. In the county sample, crime impacts were less sizable but still significant for one dimension (violent crime).

Gray and Joelson (1979) examined links between crime and house values and rents in Minneapolis, at the census tract level. Controlling for other neighborhood characteristics, they found that burglary and vandalism depressed house prices. Dollar costs (lost house values) of burglary varied from an average of $336 to $3000 across the various tracts. Vandalism costs varied from an average of $117 to $2100. Crime also depressed mean rents. Hellman and Haroff (1979), in a census tract analysis in Boston, also found a price-depressing effect for crime. These studies move us closer to understanding the role of crime in neighborhood deterioration. They suggest that safety (a relatively crime-free environment) is part of assessed (Miller, 1981) and actual value.

This relationship suggests several short-term and long-term consequences. In the short term, by detracting from the economic viability and desirability of an area, higher crime may "push" people out. People may reconsider buying into a higher crime area or may be more desirous of leaving such an area. Unfortunately the "push" hypothesis has not borne up. Rather than being "pushed" out of high crime areas, it appears that people are "pulled" or drawn toward relatively safe environments. Katzman (1980), for example, found that low as compared to high property crime neighborhoods in Dallas were more attractive to mobile families, particularly if those families had children or were from a higher income bracket. "Crime appears as less important an influence on the likelihood of out-movement than on the likelihood of in-movement" (p. 288). Other studies with individuals (Skogan & Maxfield, 1981, Chapter 4), areas (Guterbock, 1976), and Standard Metropolitan Statistical Areas (SMSAs) (Frey, 1979) have come to the same conclusion. Thus it is not the case that increasing crime drives people out of an area but rather that increasing crime rates reduce the relative attractiveness of a location, thereby increasing the relative attractiveness of safer areas, making the latter more desirable as destination points.

A long-term consequence of crime as a disamenity might be that crime, by "softening" the housing market in an area, makes the housing in that area "filter down" faster, that is, makes it likely that current owners will be replaced more quickly by lower income groups. Results from longitudinal assessments, however, have suggested that the causal process is somewhat different than this. Kobrin and Schuerman (1982), in a longitudinal study of areas in Los Angeles using census data from several decades, found that changes in land use later led to changes in areas' populations, and this in turn was followed by an increase in crime. In other words, after land use and population changes occurred, then crime increased.

Thus even though crime is clearly a disamenity, resulting in decreased house prices, what one might expect to be the short-and long-term consequences of this victimization of environment are not supported by research. Crime does not appear to be something that residents flee from, nor does it, by itself, in the long run, appear to speed up processes of neighborhood dissolution. It is clear, then, that more attention is needed to sort out what these consequences are.

How might this research be integrated into the environmental psychological perspective proposed? Crime may be a disamenity in the following fashion. As crime increases in an area, the system of territorial markers and behaviors is bound to disintegrate (cf. Jacobs, 1961). People will be out less, watching out less, and, if their markers are increasingly disrespected as crime increases in the area, the markers (flowers, decorations, etc.) will no longer be put out. The territorial system will be ignored and overridden and subsequently, unless residents mount a concerted collective effort, will progressively be withdrawn. So it may not be the case, dependent on the realistic alternatives that people have available to them, that crime makes people more desirable of leaving, but it may be the case that crime leads to further physical deterioration and increased fear, and progressively less clear block setting programs, as the resident-generated territorial system weakens.

25.4.4. Fear of Crime and the Physical Environment

Theory

Fear of crime has been discussed for some time as part of a reaction or response to crime (DuBow, McCabe, & Kaplan, 1979). Other reactions to crime include behavioral restriction and community crime prevention. Explicit in this terminology is the assumption that crime brings about these fear reactions; crime is the stimulus, fear the response.

Unfortunately, this logic has foundered on the fact that fear of crime is much more widespread than crime itself, which, fortunately, is still a relatively rare event. Consequently researchers have sought other factors that could diminish this slippage. This has basically given rise to a search for a crime "multiplier." Two theories have taken this approach. [For a comparison of various theories, see Taylor and Hale (in press).]

The indirect victimization theory suggests that local interpersonal channels of communication create "indirect" victims of crime. A person is victimized, others hear about it, and they are indirectly victimized because the information increases their fear, anxiety, and concern levels. This theory has received some empirical support (Skogan & Maxfield, 1981; Tyler, 1980), suggesting that local channels of communication do serve to spread bad news. The results of these investigations, although they bring crime and fear levels into a greater degree of correspondence, do not completely eliminate the slippage.

Another theory that attempts to bring these matters into line focuses on the local physical as well as social environment. Drawing on a symbolic interactionist perspective, Hunter (1978) argues that residents desire to observe others producing behavior in public places that is supportive of the public norms. These norms may vary from area to area, but each community has its own set of shared subcultural norms (Fischer, 1975). Further, Hunter suggests that these norms are not totally subject to local whim or preference but rather are circumscribed by concepts of "citizenship," which link residents to each other and to the state. These citizen–state obligations and the power of the state to define rights and duties circumscribe the range of acceptable norms. Thus people expect public order from each other, and this is related to and embedded within the individual–state connections of citizenship. (The similarities between this line of reasoning and Wilson's, 1975, are several. He suggested that what bothered people most about crime was the implication that people could no longer be counted on to observe accepted norms of behavior in public spaces.)

Social signs of civility include matters such as people not being noisy, politeness in public space encounters, and assistance in times of need. Social signs of incivility include individuals or groups drinking or getting drunk or dealing drugs in public places, "street" or "hey, honey" hassles, rowdy children out of their parents' control, and arguments or disputes between neighbors. Physical signs of civility include well-trimmed lawns and bushes and yards, clean steps and sidewalks and alleys, well-painted houses, clean windows, and unlittered, maintained public facilities or playgrounds. Physical signs of incivility include vacant or abandoned houses, poorly maintained housing, vacant lots that are overgrown or littered with trash and junk, autos in disrepair, littered alleys, scattered bulk trash such as refrigerators or stoves, and so on.

Physical and social signs of incivility are expected at the territorial boundaries between different segments of the social order (Suttles, 1968), that is, between different racial or ethnic or class-based territorial groupings. But when communities experience decline or drastic change (succession in Park's terminology), the physical and social incivilities will become more prevalent, spreading beyond the boundaries. And it is this awareness of social and physical incivilities, decoded as clues to holes or gaps in the social order, that inspires fear. Graphically Hunter (1978) portrays his model as follows (double arrows indicate dominant causal pathways):

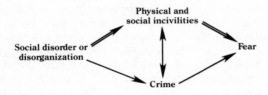

Because physical and social incivilities are more ubiquitous and more frequently experienced than crime, this explains why fear levels are higher than crime rates warrant and why across areas and persons fear and crime are only modestly associated. Further, Hunter suggests that the continued existence and spread of social and physical incivilities serves to further undermine residents' belief in the legitimacy or potency of the state. These signs are "living testimony" to the inadequacy of policing, housing enforcement, sanitation crews, and so on. Perhaps what is more important is a significant assumption in Hunter's incivilities thesis. For fear to be aroused, residents must make an inference from the general to the particular. They must deduce that because the area as a whole is becoming progressively disorderly, they themselves are personally at risk; that some harm could come to them. Finally the major "driver" in Hunter's thesis is social disorganization, as brought about by human ecological processes. By invoking this large-scale concept, Hunter

harks back to the much earlier work of Shaw and McKay. And an important question is whether or not these processes can be adequately measured.[12]

Wilson and Kelling (1982) have used a related line of reasoning to argue strongly that police should be more involved in maintaining the public order that is desired by community residents. They suggest that foot patrols can and do do this effectively in many instances. An experiment in Newark suggested that foot patrols reduce fear levels and result in more effective police–citizen interactions because officers are more familiar with the locale and with whom they are dealing. [For a more thorough discussion of the relevant theoretical and empirical work, see Greene and Taylor (1986).]

Wilson and Kelling's (1982, p. 32) causal reasoning about the links between physical and social incivilities and crime is slightly different from the logic proposed by Hunter. These authors suggest that the growing incivilities lead to behavioral restriction and withdrawal on the part of residents and a reluctance to "get involved" or to attempt to regulate others' behaviors. At that point "such an area is vulnerable to criminal invasion." To depict it graphically:

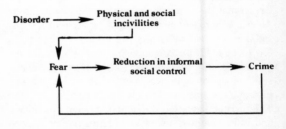

This model is different from Hunter's thesis in that fear, by reducing informal social control, leads to increased crime. Thus (1) crime and incivilities are indirectly instead of directly linked, and (2) fear may cause more crime as well as things working the other way around.

The incivilities hypothesis, in either guise, is appealing. It focuses on contextual characteristics that, potentially, provide very powerful explanations of the fear–crime link. And in contrast to earlier models, it expands still further the scope of potential causal factors.

Research

Empirical work to date has purportedly supported the incivilities thesis. Lewis and Maxfield (1980), in a study of 12 neighborhoods, found that high fear levels were most prominent in areas with high crime levels and high levels of perceived social and physical incivilities. Skogan and Maxfield (1981), using data from the same study, reported a strong positive neighborhood-level correlation between perceived social and physical incivilities and fear levels. These data are limited, however, in that perceived as opposed to objectively assessed incivilities were measured.

When objective measures are used, the results are much less supportive of the thesis. In a secondary analysis of the Greenberg, Rohe, and Williams (1982) Atlanta data set, Taylor and Hale (in press) used measures of on-block physical incivilities, such as vacant houses, to predict individual fear levels. The physical features had few significant impacts. In a Baltimore study of 66 neighborhoods (Taylor, Gottfredson, & Shumaker, 1984; Taylor, Shumaker & Gottfredson, 1985), residents in each locale were interviewed, and 20% of all street blocks were reliably coded by teams of raters. Although the assessments provided a very clear-cut social and physical incivility factor, this feature, after controlling for socioeconomic characteristics, had minimal impact on fear. The authors, however, hypothesized and found that incivilities did have an impact on fear in moderate income neighborhoods. So although linked to perceived social and physical problems, fear of crime is not linked to objective characteristics across the board, although it may be linked in some kinds of neighborhoods.

The implications of this are several. First, the link of fear with perceived social and physical problems supports Garofalo and Laub's (1978) suggestion that "fear of crime" is more than "fear" of "crime." It suggests that community concern, an awareness of community deterioration, is bound up in this affect as well. Second, and perhaps what is more important for an environmental psychologist, it appears that the link between perceived and actual incivilities is by no means straightforward. Rather it appears to be a complex and perhaps Brunswikian probabilistic relationship (cf. Craik & Appleyard, 1980). Some people may be more sensitive to the implications of a deteriorating environment (e.g., those in moderate income neighborhoods that have uncertain futures) than others. In short, the implications of the deterioration of the physical environment for fear levels are not yet clear.

Possibilities

If we turn to the proposed environmental psychological perspective, I would suggest that there are several ways it can help us clarify links between physical environment and fear. First, fear of crime is a reflection of the loss of territorial control, of the breakdown of an orderly setting program. In fact, at the block level, fear of crime and territorial cognitions reflecting a lack of territorial control correlate better than .7 (Taylor et al., 1984).

Second, the impact of physical incivilities depends on how perceivers explain their causes. In the case of vacant houses or lots or units that are not kept up, residents may infer that either local residents are the cause or that forces external to local groupings such as the city bureaucracy or slumlords are to blame. If the latter attribution is made, it may have a negative impact on self-perceptions, as Rainwater (1966) has suggested, or it may not. People may feel that they are being discriminated against, rather than deciding that they are moral outcasts. So if an attribution to extraneighborhood factors is made, the physical deterioration may not be fear-inspiring. I would suspect that this kind of attribution would be made in lower income, predominantly rental areas, where vacancies and dilapidation may be the most widespread.

If, on the other hand, residents attribute an internal cause (within-neighborhood cause) to the physical deterioration, then this is a different matter altogether. If they decide that physical deterioration is coming about because people care less about where they live and the area is going downhill, this would be fear-inspiring. It would indicate that territorial functioning, and concomitantly the setting program, are disintegrating. As territorial markers reassuring residents of each other's mutual trustworthiness are replaced by signs of decay, mistrust will increase. Internal attributions such as these are most likely to be made in neighborhoods that have at least a modicum of homeownership (e.g., at least 30 to 40% owner-occupied housing units). In such areas, physical incivilities are likely to be less prevalent than in the lowest income areas but are likely to have more of an impact. What this adds up to then is a nonlinear relationship between physical incivilities and fear; the impact of the physical degeneration depends on how it is interpreted. If viewed as a breakdown in resident-generated territorial control, it will cause concern. This conditional relationship has been empirically supported (see Taylor, Shumaker, & Gottfredson, 1985).

A third point from a territorial perspective concerns the spatial relationship between the physical incivilities and the person whose fear may be increased. Focusing for the moment on one respondent, whether or not physical deterioration such as a vacant boarded-up house increases his or her fear levels depends upon how close that house is. If it is next door, the person may be extremely concerned due to the possibility of rats attracted by the garbage thrown in or the possibility of a fire being set. The proximity translates into a direct threat to the perceiver's own household and well-being. If the vacant house is located further away but still on the same street block, it is less of a cause for worry, but it is still troublesome. The perceiver must pass by it in his or her daily rounds, and it constitutes an eyesore and a reminder of the lack of viability of the respondent's own neighborhood. If the vacant house is still further away, it may be only of minimal concern. If it is far enough away so that it can be avoided in the daily round of activities, the perceiver can convince himself or herself that what goes on "over there" cannot happen on his or her block. The spatial dynamics, therefore, may also influence impacts on fear.

These considerations all add up to a highly conditional relationship between physical decline and fear of crime. The decline must be interpreted as a reflection of decreased concern, investment, or commitment on the part of residents themselves, and it must be proximate, in order to result in a sense of decreased territorial control, which is reflected in more fear. Thus the environmental psychological perspective we have developed allows the specification of how and when this physical environment–fear linkage may hold.

25.4.5. Summary

In the foregoing sections we have examined theory and research pertinent to several aspects of disorder. We have considered where offenders and delinquents are likely to reside, what kind of target areas they pick and why, and what the impacts of crimes actually committed are. In each area, we have suggested that extant theories can be considerably enhanced by an integration with an environmental psychological perspective. The integration results in a clearer statement of the micro-level causal processes suggested by these theories. The integration also, in some cases, results in an expansion to multilevel models. Consequently the question of whether or not environmental psychology has anything unique to contribute to these areas of inquiry can, on the basis of these considerations, be answered resoundingly in the affirmative. The following section drives this point home more strongly by considering work al-

ready done that has used an environmental psychological approach.

25.5. WORK REFLECTING THE BEGINNING OF AN ENVIRONMENTAL PSYCHOLOGY OF DISORDER

In this section, theoretical and empirical work that explicitly draws on concepts from environmental psychology to determine where crime occurs and where fear or problem levels are lower is considered. The most recent work receives the most attention. Work is reviewed according to the level of analysis, moving from the site level to work at the street-block level, and subsequently to the neighborhood level.

In a theoretical sense, much of this latter work stands in the shadow of (and some might say, on the shoulders of) Newman's (1972) work on defensible space. Although there are several excellent reviews of theory and research in the area (Mayhew, 1979; Merry 1981a, 1981b; Taylor, Gottfredson, & Brower, 1980) some prefatory remarks regarding the theory and research are warranted.

The theory as originally formulated was a strong reaction against the design and planning practices of public housing projects in the 1950s and 1960s. High-rise buildings with hundreds of units were situated in "superblocks," surrounded by undifferentiated landscaping, and far from public streets. Newman (1972) suggested that these very design practices that were praised by architects contributed to crime levels. The large number of people in a building, the large, undifferentiated outdoor areas, and the lack of surveillance, for example, made it difficult for people to exercise their "natural policing function." Newman felt that if exterior spaces could be segmented and redesigned in such a way as to unlease natural territorial instincts, then residents themselves would begin to take care of things more, and crime would decrease. Graphically his original theory was:

$$\text{Design} \rightarrow \begin{array}{c}\text{Stronger} \\ \text{territorial} \\ \text{functioning}\end{array} \rightarrow \text{Less crime}$$

He maintained that his research in New York City housing projects linking certain design features with lower crime rates supported his notion. It is worthwhile to consider just a couple of limits of this early theory and research. (For more, see Taylor, Gottfredson, & Brower, 1980, or the other reviews.) First, Newman's view of human territorial functioning is very global, nonplace specific, and oversimplified. Second, his early research failed to measure the crucial hypothesized mediating variable—territorial functioning. Both of these limitations were addressed in subsequent work. These flaws notwithstanding, the pioneering nature of this early work cannot be dismissed.

25.5.1. Site Level

At the level of the individual site or household, it appears that offenders and residents alike may perceive and be responsive to territorial markers and behavioral traces. Brown (Brown & Altman, 1983) compared burglarized and nonburglarized households in suburban settings and observed that nonvictimized sites displayed more territorial markers and signs of activities. She has suggested, based in part on this evidence, that as the burglar approaches a particular household he or she must penetrate through a series of increasingly "strong" territories, and whether or not he or she chooses to do that depends on the observable territorial cues (Brown & Altman, 1978, 1981). Although actual burglar perceptions have not yet been measured, it makes sense to suggest that burglars would take physical features into account.

What is more clearly established is that residents are aware of and "decode" territorial cues as influencing potential intruders and shaping resident responses to incursions. A study using abstract pictures found that fences, and to a lesser extent flowers, would deter intrusions (Brower, Dockett, & Taylor, 1983). Also flowers were an indication of a safer, better quality block. Respondents felt that if a fence was present, a resident would respond more vigorously to an intruder because an incursion would be harder to justify. Comparing residents in low versus high problem areas, in the latter case redundant territorial cues were viewed as necessary to deter invasions (confirming Brower, 1980). Thus residents and perhaps burglars understand the role of on-site territorial markers. More work needs to be done with offenders to clarify the exact cues that are relevant, and how they are weighed in the decision-making process.

25.5.2. Street-Block Level

At the street-block or group level, territorial functioning can have a deterrent impact on crime and fear. Such functioning can be supported by local social climate and by physical factors. A study of 63 street blocks in Baltimore found that blocks with more extensive real and symbolic barriers and where residents knew one another better and where residents felt more responsible for what happened on the sidewalk and in the alley had less street crime and less fear (Taylor, Gottfredson, & Brower, 1984). Further it appeared that social ties undergirded territorial functioning. A similar result was obtained in a study of 60 + public housing sites across the country. Newman and Franck (1980, 1982) found that design features such as fewer households per doorway encouraged informal outdoor socializing and control over adjoining outdoor spaces, which in turn was associated with less crime and fear. Therefore, at the block or project level, in a broad range of residential environments, territorial functioning, supported by physical factors and group dynamics, serves to dampen incidents of and negative reactions to disorder.

25.5.3. Neighborhood Level

At the neighborhood level, several studies suggest that links between design and disorder are indirect and are dependent on other contextual factors. Merry (1981a, 1981b) has highlighted the role of cultural factors. In her study of a multiethnic public housing area, she found that many potentially defensible areas were left undefended because Chinese members of the community perceived that they were dominated or outnumbered by members of other ethnic groups, even though they were not. In a demonstration project in Hartford (Fowler & Mangione, 1979), entrances to and traffic through a neighborhood were altered so as to make the streets less anonymous and "turn them back" to the residents themselves. When coupled with a local organizing initiative, these steps appeared effective in reducing crime and fear. When local organizing efforts faded, crime appeared to creep back up (Fowler & Mangione, 1981). So again, as at the block level, physical factors alone are not sufficient to guarantee order; but if coupled with other social or cultural dynamics, they can be effective.

Potentially relevant also to the maintenance of neighborhood order is attachment to place (Shumaker & Taylor, 1983). In a study of 66 Baltimore neighborhoods Taylor et al. (1984) found that fear was lower in neighborhoods where attachment to locale was stronger. Person–place bonds, net of actual crime or physical deterioration levels, influenced perceptions of disorder. The more general implication of this linkage is that impacts of events indicative of disorder are conditioned by overall sentiments regarding locale.

25.5.4. Summary

This recent work indicates that concepts of human territoriality and related processes such as attachment to place are helpful in understanding links between physical environment, social environment, crime, and fear. In just a short period of time, relatively sophisticated and powerful models have been developed. These models have been applied to issues of disorder at the site, block, and neighborhood levels and should continue to be useful. The utility of these models confirms that environmental psychological models have a significant place to occupy in the armanentarium of conceptual tools applied to problems of disorder.

25.6. A CAUTIONARY NOTE

The tone throughout has been largely exhortatory and upbeat, suggesting in several ways how a particular environmental psychological perspective could be conjoined with other theoretical areas to provide more powerful, truly multidisciplinary perspectives on various issues of disorder. It is necessary, so that we will not be accused of a Panglossian stance, to trundle out some of the particular difficulties that confront researchers in this area. These problems are already familiar to criminal justice and criminology researchers.

First of all, there is a dearth of large-scale, easily available data bases with which to work. For crime, there are the *Uniform Crime Reports,* issued yearly, but these only report results at the city level. This means that to obtain specific, localized crime data, one must develop a good working relationship with the local police department. Crime data themselves, however, are in many ways problematic (Skogan, 1981, but cf. Hindelang, 1974). Reported crime, for example, is less than true crime. Incidences of true crime may be better approximated using victimization survey data such as is contained in the National Crime Survey (NCS). But in the NCS, no specific geographic codes are available. Thus one cannot transfer NCS victimization reports, for example, onto a census of a city. One might decide to go out and do one's own victimization survey. Several problems crop up here, however, due to the rarity of crime. Many people must be surveyed in order to develop a stable victimization rate (Skogan, 1981). Depending on the

type of crime of interest, anywhere from several hundred to several thousand persons must be interviewed before it will be possible to have a good estimate of the rate. Further because rates are low and thus unstable, they have large standard errors. Consequently it may be difficult to ascertain whether or not two areas have significantly different victimization rates. The smaller the areas compared (e.g., blocks vs. neighborhoods), the more difficult it is to make these discriminations. These difficulties do not surround fear data because everyone has some fear level. Thus there are real problems in developing good crime or victimization measures and relating them to specific environmental factors.

Another problem with crime statistics, and with official delinquency statistics, is that they may be biased, reporting a greater proportion of the incidence of each in the lower social classes. Although in the area of crime several studies have supported their nonbiased nature (e.g., Black, 1970; Hindelang, 1978), the question is by no means settled.

In the area of delinquency reporting, research results suggest that for some purposes, official delinquency data may not be biased (Hindelang et al., 1981, p. 207).

Over the last decade the delinquency research community has been increasingly polarized between those who felt official data were adequate and self-report inadequate and those who felt the reverse. This split was deepened, in part, by the fact that the two different groups kept finding different "predictors" of delinquency. For example, the "official" group claimed that the links between low social class and high delinquency rates were strong, whereas self-report studies failed to find this. (It turned out as discussed earlier that part of this problem was the ecological approach of the former and the individual-level approach of the latter.) Hindelang et al. (1981) found, in a large-scale study, that the self-report method was by and large valid. People were likely to report crimes known to officials, as well as those not known. The validity of the measure, however, was differential across subgroups of the population and was lowest for black males—the group with the highest official delinquency rate. But self-report data from black males, although invalid for some purposes (e.g., black–white comparisons), may be valid for other purposes (e.g., understanding the etiology of delinquency in black males (Hindelang et al., 1981, pp. 213–214). The validity of the data, either based on official statistics or self-report, depends on the uses to which it is put.

A conceptual and statistical problem in this area that requires very careful attention is the aggregation problem (Cronbach, 1976; Hannan, 1971; Taylor, 1982, pp. 307–310). Residents living on the same block may be more like one another, in their attitudes toward the immediate environment, than people living on different blocks. Residents living in one neighborhood may be more like one another than residents living in different neighborhoods. Consequently these similarities must be taken into account by decomposing the data (centering by appropriate means). Otherwise, misleading correlations may result.

A couple of final theoretical issues deserve to be highlighted. First, crime and delinquency are both labels applied to an extraordinary range of behaviors. In the case of delinquency, for example, Gibbons (1976, pp. 97–98) has remarked that "there must be something radically different about gang delinquents, sex offenders, petty 'hidden' offenders, juvenile arsonists, hyper-aggressive delinquents, and other lawbreakers who are lumped together under the term 'delinquent.'" It is not surprising therefore that numerous attempts have been made to develop typologies of delinquents and delinquent behavior. (For a discussion of these approaches, and their pros and cons, see Gibbons, 1976, pp. 99–100, especially Footnote 72.)

In crime, the problem is somewhat simpler because the range of behaviors is more restricted. The FBI has definitions for eight "serious" or Part I offenses. Typically, an ecological researcher will focus on one of these or add them all up to make a "crime" scale or divide them into "property crimes" and "personal crimes." The main point for the theoretician and the researcher is to carefully state, in conceptual terms, why predictors will be linked to particular types of crimes, or particular types of delinquencies.

Second, researchers cannot be sociologically naive regarding the causes and consequences of disorder. What I mean by this is that the existing social order may "cause" disorder and at the same time have a "need" for disorder to exist. There are many possible interpretations of the causes of disorder. It can be interpreted in the Marxist context of conflict, class struggle, and resistance to domination (Sumner, 1977; Taylor, Walton, & Young, 1973). Or it could be viewed as a commitment to an autonomous set of values (Miller, 1958), or a subdominant value orientation (Kluckholn & Strodtbeck, 1961), or as a result of commitment to dominant societal goals but with access only to illegitimate means (Cloward, 1959).

Other interpretations are possible as well. The main point of these different views, whether we subscribe to a Marxist perspective or some other orientation, is that it is possible that the very structure of society and its inequities somehow cause disorder.

At the same time, society may have a need to observe disorder. Durkheim (1960) has suggested that by defining certain people as delinquent or criminal, society is indicating what the norms of acceptable behavior are. People who pass those bounds deserve to be rejected because they are deviant (statistically speaking), and this rejection clearly keeps a reminder of what is and what is not tolerated before society. The situation only becomes problematic when those who are rejected constitute too large a portion of the society. If such a situation developed, Durkheim suggested, society will redefine the boundary between acceptable and unacceptable behaviors, in favor of increased leniency. Society needs to label some people and behaviors as disorderly, so that its own order is clarified by juxtaposition.

Translating these considerations into spatial terms suggests several interesting thoughts. If society is causing and/or needs to define certain segments of the population as deviant, delinquent, or criminal, these individuals are going to be connected to particular locations. At the neighborhood level, this means that individuals from outside of a particular area, including those connected with public service such as housing officials or police will be labeling locations within an area as crime- or delinquent-infested (Damer, 1974). These sociotypes (Triandis, 1977) justify reduced levels of service delivery to these areas. The concentration as opposed to dispersement of such labeled individuals and areas "serves" the public at large because (1) they can avoid such locations, and (2) such locations enhance, by comparison, the quality of upper scale areas.

At a more microscale level, this line of reasoning suggests that if certain people are to be labeled as delinquent or otherwise marginal members of society, they will need, claim, and be granted locations where they can carry on. In other words, suppose society is, in effect, allocating interstitial areas to those groups and individuals whose behavior has been defined as out of bounds. This process of societal allocation and individual or group claiming could be reciprocal, complementary, and systemlike. The out-group is relegated to interstitial areas where, to some extent they are out of sight, and where they are less likely to disturb the most central, close-to-home spaces in the residential environment. And at the same time, these groups claim these spaces with graffiti, litter, and broken bottles, indicating that they have been there and could well return, thereby discouraging others belonging to main-line society from mingling. The fear of dangerous places then serves to maintain a separation between members of society and those who are defined as beyond the bounds. This concentration of outsiders in interstitial areas better serves the local society than deconcentration of outsiders could. In the former case the security of close-to-home territories can be more easily maintained. The gathering of outsiders in interstitial areas only becomes problematic when these spaces are very close to central territories.

The implications of this line of reasoning for issues of territorial control are several. First, it suggests that the interstitial areas are functional. Lapses in territorial control such as occur between block behavior settings help to more clearly define those settings and to protect them from potential deviant pressures. If loud radios and drinking are going on in the park, they will be less likely to happen in front of one's door. Second, attempts to close gaps in territorial functioning, to fill in the interstices, may be bound to fail. The outsiders may simply gather somewhere else—a place where control is minimal—and go through the process of claiming that. In short, attempts to expand the block behavior setting may result only in displacement. (Although this would be a gain for the persons living close to the first location, it is neither a gain or a loss from the perspective of the larger area.)

These comments should not be interpreted as either a defense of current levels of disorder extant in residential neighborhoods, nor should they be viewed as disparagement of attempts to reduce levels of disorder. The main point being made is that, sociologically, the topography of territorial control cuts more than one way and that the perspective of the orderly should not automatically take precedent over potential perspectives from the viewpoint of the disorderly, or over the perspective of the society as a whole. Future theoretical refinements should not lose sight of a pluralistic approach. Although this commitment may make conceptual clarification more cumbersome, it may result, ultimately, in theory that has more external validity.

25.7. RESEARCH FUTURES

Where will the environmental psychology of disorder lead? What theoretical avenues will be pursued?

Throughout we have described various possible theoretical integrations that can be achieved, working with the theories of human territoriality and behavior settings. In this section, we will indicate some further clarifications that are needed regarding territorial functioning in block settings and then move on to consider some more abstract issues deserving of attention.

An important issue will be to develop more complete descriptions of how territorial functioning operates in block settings. These processes are potentially rich in texture. If observations are carried out in systematically related locations, for example, in urban versus suburban areas, in stable versus changing neighborhoods, the links between extrasetting context and setting functioning can be more carefully delineated. These observations will also be useful in more closely delineating where territorial processes leave off and where other processes such as attachment or stress responses come into play. There is a very real danger of expanding the concept of territorial functioning so much that it becomes useless. This danger can and should be avoided by bounding, or indicating the limits, of these processes.

Such in-depth descriptive work can be more useful if it is longitudinal. An investigation over time (e.g., Bechtel, 1977) would help to delineate more carefully how particular individuals play various roles in the block program and perhaps even give clues to the various motivations underlying participation (or penetration) in the setting at a particular locale. Once this background leads to particular hypotheses about individuals in settings, then they could possibly be tested using cross-sectional study designs. Examinations over time may also provide clues about untangling the causal chain involving fear, informal control, and crime, and determining how they feed into one another. Thus descriptive work, over time in a range of settings, may be most useful in further fleshing out the environmental psychological perspective proposed in this chapter.

There may also be a place for experimentation. In fact, field experiments may be the most straightforward way of further elucidating the spatial distribution of territorial behaviors. For example, certain contaminants can be placed at various points in or adjoining a setting, and residents' responses observed. Worchel and Lollis's (1982) technique of depositing small bags of litter may be one useful approach, although others certainly should be tried. It is important to know the topography across synomorphs inside the behavior setting, and outside the behavior setting, of territorial behaviors.

A pressing question deserving attention is the perspective of the delinquent or the potential offender. Carter and Hill's (1979) work in this regard is a very promising start, and consideration of criminals' image of an area needs to be explored at the finer levels of block and site. Many of the methods of environmental cognition could be applied to such an inquiry. Further light must be shed on these processes if we are to understand the etiology of disorder.

Although the preceding points are by no means an exhaustive listing of the needed amplifications for a more complete theory of territorial block settings and disorder, they at least indicate some of the more important loose ends of the theoretical perspective that need to be resolved.

Turning to more abstract matters, there are several aspects of the issue of disorder that deserve pursuing. The discussion in this chapter has turned on fear of crime, delinquency, and crime as indexes of disorder. This is a very limited set of indexes, to be sure. These indexes could be expanded in several dimensions. For example, how are collective disorders such as looting, burning, and so on ecologically patterned? Are the patternings similar to crime? Georges' (1975) finding that buildings burnt in Newark during collective disorders tended to be along main thoroughfares and Crenson's (1983) suggestion that looting targets during the 1979 Baltimore snowstorm tended to be on neighborhood boundaries would suggest there may be similarities between collective disorders and incidents perpetrated by individuals. The same kinds of locations may be susceptible to both types of violence. As yet there has been minimal attention paid to possible links between the geography of collective disorders and the geography of crime. If the disorder continuum is to gain validity, a broader set of indexes will be needed, and for these different indexes researchers will have to demonstrate similar types of causes.

A second issue deserving attention is multilevel processes. How are neighborhood dynamics linked to block dynamics, and how are block dynamics in turn linked to individual or household processes? Research to date has tended to stay focused at one particular level. But in actuality, larger scale processes influence lower scale processes and vice versa.

A sketchy example may clarify these connections. Consider an inner city neighborhood, which was once stable lower middle-class ethnic, which has recently changed to being racially mixed. With increasing demand for affordable starter houses and only more expensive housing elsewhere, the neighborhood may suddenly experience an influx of gentrifying "Yuppies" (young urban professionals). This may make the area a more desirable target for offenders because there is more to steal. Thus the neighborhood may experience an increase in property crime.

At the block level these market processes, in one case, may have resulted in a more heterogeneous population, with resentment between longer term, blue-collar Catholic residents, lower middle-class blacks, and gentrifiers. Some new gentrifiers, more used to advocating for themselves and expecting a higher quality environment given their background, may try to mobilize people around a community crime prevention effort. But due to diversity, the effort may fail. The recently increased diversity may also increase co-resident distrust, further dampening territorial functioning. Individual perceptions of, and responses to, these dynamics may depend upon one's confidence in the neighborhood and particular group membership.

The example begins to convey the kind of complex but significant causal connections that can occur across levels. These links need to be drawn into a more wholistic picture of disorder.

Acknowledgments

The author is indebted to Irv Altman, Joachim Savelsberg, and two anonymous reviewers for many helpful comments on an earlier draft. Discussions with Sidney Brower, Steve Gottfredson, and Sally Shumaker have provided or facilitated the evolution of many ideas contained herein. Suzanne McKibbin heroically handled the typing.

NOTES

1. For more details on the theory of territorial functioning see Altman (1975), Edney (1974, 1976a, 1976b), Sundstrom (1977), Taylor (1978), Taylor & Brower (1985).

2. A street block refers to the spaces encompassed by the houses on two sides of a street, bounded at the ends by two cross streets.

3. Several years ago some student fieldworkers involved in a research project were working in a low-income neighborhood. At a stoplight, local youths were trying to gain entrance to stopped trucks, via rear doors. The assessors informed one driver who pursued the youths. Later the youths came back and asked the students: "What right do you have messing with our fun? We do this every day."

4. One might argue that places providing opportunity for disorder can be eliminated by policies such as age-segre-

gated housing policies. Newman (1979) has proposed an idea somewhat along these lines. The problem remains, however, that even if miscreant individuals or youth were "zoned" out of an area, they would still be likely to migrate to another area in search of purse-snatch or robbery targets.

5. The expansion of the opportunity areas for disorders assumes that there is an available and waiting "supply" of disorderly youth who will move in and make use of the space, for which there is a "demand." The correctness of this assumption varies from neighborhood to neighborhood but may be more correct in neighborhoods that have, or are surrounded by, more sizable youth or lower income populations.

6. Murray (1982) also found some "new" delinquency areas that had not shown up in 1940; these were in the northwest section of the city where, from 1960 to 1970 black populations had largely replaced the prior Jewish population.

7. For the labels applied to some of the theories here, I follow Schmid (1960b).

8. As one person described by Liebow (1967) in his study of inner-city black men said, "A hard working dishwasher just becomes a hard working dishwasher."

9. The problem of changing relations at varying levels of analysis is illustrated in the debate on the low SES–delinquency debate. Gordon has concluded that "the association between delinquency and socioeconomic status is quite unambiguously very strong" (Gordon, 1967, p. 927; see also Gordon, 1976). But as Hindelang, Hirschi, and Weis (1981, p. 184) point out, almost all of the research that has found the SES-delinquency link has been ecological, and "the consistency and strength of the ecological SES–official delinquency relationships are beyond dispute." But the error has creeped in in that "the dominance of ecological research on the SES–official delinquency relation has resulted in the findings of this research being relied upon as evidence about the individual-level relationship, despite its obvious tangential relevance to this question." Reexamination at the individual level of both official delinquency and self-report delinquency studies reveals that studies that use either or both measures show a very weak to nonexistent link between SES and delinquency (Hindelang et al., 1981, pp. 186–197).

10. Density potential models ask, for each of a range of points in a geographic space, what is the potential of that point given surrounding conditions. Contributions from other points to a point's potential are weighted by proximity. Thus one might ask for various potential commercial sites for an expensive store in the city, what is the potential market, as defined by households in adjacent areas with incomes of over $30,000. Or, in our case, for the subpopulations of small stores ("stop and rob") in various locales, what is each locale's potential "market" of offenders living nearby?

11. Transitional areas had temporary lodgings or construction or demolition.

12. The incivilities thesis, although little about it has been published, has been extraordinarily influential in research and policymaker circles in the area of criminal justice and crime prevention.

REFERENCES

Alihan, M.A. (1938). *Social ecology: A critical analysis.* New York: Columbia University Press.

Altman, I. (1975). *The environment and social behavior.* Monterey, CA: Brooks/Cole.

Altman, I., & Chemers, M.M. (1980). *Culture and environment.* Monterey, CA: Brooks/Cole.

Appleyard, D. (1981). *Livable streets.* Berkeley, CA: University of California Press.

Baldwin, J. (1975). British areal studies of crime: An assessment. *British Journal of Criminology, 15,* 211–227.

Baldwin, J. (1979). Ecological and areal studies in Great Britain and the United States. In N. Morris & M. Tonry (Eds.), *Crime and justice: An annual review of research* (Vol. 1). Chicago: University of Chicago Press.

Baldwin, J., & Bottoms, A.E. (1976). *The urban criminal.* London: Tavistock.

Barker, R.G. (1968). *Ecological psychology.* Stanford, CA: Stanford University Press.

Baum, A., Davis, A.G., & Aiello, J.R. (1978). Crowding and neighborhood mediation of urban density. *Journal of Population, 1,* 266–279.

Bechtel, R.B. (1977). *Enclosing behavior.* Stroudsburg, PA: Dowden, Hutchinson, & Ross.

Bennett, T., & Wright, J. (1984). *Burglars on burglary.* London: Gower.

Bevis, C., & Nutter, J.B. (1977). *Changing street layouts to reduce residential burglary (Crime Prevention Through Environmental Design Panel).* Paper presented at the meeting of the American Society of Criminology, Atlanta, GA.

Black, D.J. (1970). Productions of crime rates. *American Sociological Review, 35,* 899–908.

Boggs, S. (1965). Urban crime patterns. *American Sociological Review, 30,* 899–908.

Bordua, D.J. (1958). Juvenile delinquency and 'anomie': An attempt at replication. *Social Problems, 6,* 230–238.

Brower, S. (1980). Territory in urban settings. In I. Altman, A. Rapoport, & J.F. Wohlwill (Eds.), *Human behavior and environment: Advances in theory and research: Vol. 4. Environment and culture.* New York: Plenum.

Brower, S., Dockett, K., & Taylor, R.B. (1983). Residents' perceptions of site-level features. *Environment and Behavior, 15,* 419–437.

Brown, B.B., & Altman, I. (1978). Territoriality and residential burglary: A conceptual framework. In *Crime*

Prevention Through Environmental Design Theory Compendium. Arlington, VA: Westinghouse.

Brown, B.B., & Altman, I. (1981). Territoriality and residential crime: A conceptual framework. In P.J. Brantingham & P.L. Brantingham (Eds.), *Environmental criminology.* Beverly Hills, CA: Sage.

Brown, B.B., & Altman, I. (1983). Territoriality, defensible space, and residential burglary: An environmental analysis. *Journal of Environmental Psychology, 3,* 203–220.

Burt, C. (1925). *The young delinquent.* London: University of London Press.

Capone, D.L., & Nichols, W.W., Jr. (1976). Urban structure and criminal mobility. *American Behavioral Scientist, 20*(2), 199–213.

Carter, R.L., & Hill, K.Q. (1978). Criminals' and noncriminals' perceptions of urban crime. *Criminology, 16,* 353–371.

Carter, R.L., & Hill, K.Q. (1979). *The criminal's image of the city.* New York: Pergamon.

Cartwright, D.S., & Howard, K.I. (1966). Multivariate analysis of gang delinquency: I. Ecologic influences. *Multivariate Behavioral Research, 1,* 321–371.

Chilton, R.J. (1964). Continuity in delinquency area research: A comparison of studies for Baltimore, Detroit, and Indianapolis. *American Sociological Review, 29,* 71–83.

Chilton, R.J., & Dussich, J. (1974). Methodological issues in delinquency research: Some alternative analysis of geographically distributed data. *Social Forces, 53,* 73–82.

Cloward, R.A. (1959). Illegitimate means, anomie, and deviant behavior. *American Sociological Review, 24,* 164–176.

Cloward, R.A., & Ohlin, L.E. (1960). *Delinquency and opportunity.* New York: Free Press.

Cohen, L.E., & Felson, M. (1979). Social change and crime rate trends. *American Sociological Review, 44,* 588–608.

Craik, K.H., & Appleyard, D. (1980). Streets of San Francisco: Brunswik's lens model applied to urban inference and assessment. *Journal of Social Issues, 36,* 72–85.

Crenson, M. (1983). *Neighborhood politics.* Cambridge, MA: Harvard University Press.

Cronbach, L. (1976). Research on classrooms and schools: Formulation of questions, design, and analysis (Occasional Paper). Stanford, CA: Stanford University, Stanford Evaluation Consortium.

Damer, S. (1974). Wine alley: The sociology of a dreadful enclosure. *Sociological Review, 22,* 221–248.

David, P.R. (1974). *The world of the burglar.* Albuquerque: University of New Mexico Press.

Deutschberger, P. (1946). Interaction patterns in changing neighborhoods. *Sociometry, 9,* 303–315.

Dubin, R.A., & Goodman, A.C. (1982). Valuation of education and crime neighborhood characteristics through hedonic housing prices. *Population and Environment, 5,* 166–181.

Dubow, F.L., McCabe, F., & Kaplan, G. (1979). *Reactions to crime: A critical review of the literature.* Washington, DC: U.S. Government Printing Office.

Duffala, D.C. (1976). Convenience stores, armed robbery and physical environment features. *American Behavioral Scientist, 20*(2), 227–245.

Dunlap, R.E., & Catton, W.R., Jr. (1983). What environmental sociologists have in common. (Whether concerned with "built" or "natural" environments.) *Sociological Inquiry, 53,* 113–135.

Dunn, C.J. (1980). The social area structure of suburban crime. In D.E. Georges-Abeyie & K.D. Harries (Eds.), *Crime: A Spatial perspective.* New York: Columbia University Press.

Durkheim, E. (1951). *Suicide.* New York: Free Press.

Durkheim, E. (1960). *On the division of labor in society.* New York: Macmillan. (Original work published 1893)

Edney, J.J. (1974). Human territoriality. *Psychological Bulletin, 81,* 959–975.

Edney, J.J. (1976a). Human territoriality: Comment on functional properties. *Environment and Behavior, 8,* 31–47.

Edney, J.J. (1976b). The psychological role of property rights in human behavior. *Environment and Planning A, 8,* 811–822.

Fabrikant, R. (1979). The distribution of criminal offenses in an urban environment: A spatial analysis of crime spillovers and of juvenile offenders. *American Journal of Economics and Sociology, 38,* 31–47.

Fischer, C.S. (1975). Toward a subcultural theory of urbanism. *American Journal of Sociology, 80,* 1319–1341.

Fisher, J.D., & Baron, R.M. (1982). An equity-based model of vandalism. *Population and Environment, 5,* 182–200.

Fowler, F.J., & Mangione, T. (1979). *Reducing residential crime and fear.* Washington, DC: National Institute of Justice.

Fowler, F.J., & Mangione, T.W. (1981). *An experimental effort to reduce crime and fear of crime in an urban residential neighborhood: Re-evaluation of the Hartford neighborhood crime prevention program* (Draft Executive Summary). Boston, MA: Harvard University/Massachusetts Institute of Technology, Center for Survey Research.

Frey, W.H. (1979). Central city white flight: Racial and nonracial causes. *American Sociological Review, 44,* 425–448.

Gans, H. (1967). *The Levittowners.* New York: Pantheon.

Gans, H. (1968). *People and plans.* New York: Basic Books.

Garofalo, J., & Laub, J. (1978). The fear of crime: Broadening our perspective. *Victimology, 3,* 242–253.

Georges, D.E. (1975). The ecology of urban unrest in the city of Newark, New Jersey during the 1907 riots. *Journal of Environmental Systems, 5,* 203–228.

Gibbons, D.C. (1976). *Delinquent behavior* (2nd ed.). Englewood Cliffs, NJ: Prentice-Hall.

Goodman, A.C. (in press). Neighborhood characteristics and house prices. In R.B. Taylor (Ed.), *Urban neighborhoods.* New York: Praeger.

Gordon, R.A. (1967). Issues in the ecological study of delinquency. *American Sociological Review, 32,* 927–944.

Gordon, R.A. (1976). Prevalence: The race datum in delinquency measurement and its implications for the theory of delinquency. In M.W. Klein (Ed.), *The juvenile justice system* (pp. 201–284). Beverly Hills, CA: Sage.

Gottfredson, S.D., Young, K.L., & Laufer, W.S. (1980). Additivity and interactions in offense seriousness scales. *Journal of Research in Crime and Delinquency, 17,* 26–41.

Gray, C.M., & Joelson, M.R. (1979). Neighborhood crime and the demand for central city housing. In C.M. Gray (Ed.), *The costs of crime* (pp. 47–60). Beverly Hills, CA: Sage.

Greenberger, D.B., & Allen, V.C. (1980). Destruction and complexity: An application of aesthetic theory. *Personality and Social Psychology Bulletin, 6,* 479–483.

Greene, J.R., & Taylor, R.B. (1986). A closer look at community policing. Paper presented at the annual meetings of the Academy of Criminal Justice Sciences, Orlando, FL.

Guterbock, T.M. (1976). The push hypothesis: Minority presence, crime, and urban deconcentration. In B. Schwartz (Ed.), *The changing face of the suburbs* (pp. 137–161). Chicago: University of Chicago Press.

Hackler, J.C., Ho, K., & Urquhart-Ross, C. (1974). The willingness to intervene: Differing community characteristics. *Social Problems, 21,* 328–344.

Hannan, M.T. (1971). *Aggregation and disaggregation in sociology.* Lexington, MA: Lexington Books.

Harries, K.D. (1978, December). *Local crime rates* (Unpub. Final Rep.). Stillwater: Oklahoma State University, Department of Geography.

Harries, K.D. (1980). *Crime and environment.* Springfield, IL: Thomas.

Harries, K.D. (1981). Alternative denominators in conventional crime rates. In P.J. Brantingham & P.L. Brantingham (Eds.), *Environmental criminology* (pp. 147–166). Beverly Hills, CA: Sage.

Hawley, A.H. (1981). Human ecology. *American Behavioral Scientist, 24,* 423–444.

Hellman, D.A., Haroff, J.L. (1979). The impact of crime on urban residential property values. *Urban Studies, 16,* 105–112.

Herbert, D.E. (1977a). Crime delinquency, and the urban environment. *Progress in Human Geography, 1,* 208–239.

Herbert, D.E. (1977b). An areal and ecological analysis of delinquency research: Cardiff, 1966 and 1971. *Tijdschrift voor Economische and Sociale Geographie, 68,* 83–99.

Herbert, D.E. (1980). Urban crime and spatial perspectives. The British experience. In D.E. Georges-Abeyie & K.D. Harries (Eds.), *Crime: A spatial perspective* (pp. 26–46). New York: Columbia University Press.

Hindelang, M.J. (1974). The uniform crime reports revisited. *Journal of Criminal Justice, 2,* 1–18.

Hindelang, M.J. (1978). Race and involvement in common law personal crimes. *American Sociological Review, 43,* 93–109.

Hindelang, M.J., Hirschi, T., & Weis, J.G. (1981). *Measuring delinquency.* Beverly Hills, CA: Sage.

Hunter, A. (1978). *Symbols of incivility.* Paper presented at the meeting of the American Society of Criminology, Dallas, TX.

Isaacs, R.R. (1948). The neighborhood theory: An analysis of its adequacy. *Journal of the American Institute of Planners, 14,* 15–23.

Jacobs, J. (1961). *The death and life of great American cities.* New York: Vintage.

Katzman, M.T. (1980). The contribution of crime to urban decline. *Urban Studies, 17,* 277–286.

Katzman, M.T. (1981). The supply of criminals: A geo-economic examination. In S. Hakim & G.F. Rengert (Eds.), *Crime spillover* (pp. 119–134). Beverly Hills, CA: Sage.

Kluckholn, F.R., & Strodtbeck, J. (1961). Variation in value orientations. Evanston, IL: Row, Peterson.

Kobrin, J., & Schuerman, L.A. (1982). *Interaction between neighborhood change and criminal activity.* Los Angeles: University of Southern California, Social Science Research Institute.

Lander, B. (1954). *Towards an understanding of juvenile delinquency.* New York: Columbia University Press.

Letkemann, P. (1973). *Crime as work.* Englewood, NJ: Prentice-Hall.

Lewis, D.A., & Maxfield, M.G. (1980). Fear in the neighborhoods: An investigation of the impact of crime. *Journal of Research in Crime and Delinquency, 17,* 160–189.

Ley, D., & Cybriwsky, R. (1974). The spatial ecology of stripped cars. *Environment and Behavior, 6,* 653–668.

Liebow, E. (1967). *Tally's corner.* Boston, MA: Little, Brown.

Lind, A.W. (1930). Some ecological patterns of community disorganization in Honolulu. *American Journal of Sociology, 36,* 206–220.

Loring, W.C. (1956). Housing characteristics and social disorganization. *Social Problems, 3,* 160–173.

Maccoby, E.E., Johnson, J.P., & Church, R.M. (1958). Community integration and the social control of juvenile delinquency. *Journal of Social Issues, 14,* 38–51.

Mann, P.H. (1954). The concept of neighborliness. *American Journal of Sociology, 60,* 163–168.

Mayhew, P. (1979). Defensible space: The current status of a crime prevention theory. *Howard Journal of Penology and Crime Prevention, 18,* 150–159.

McIver, J.P. (1981). Criminal mobility: A review of empirical studies. In S. Hakim & G.F. Rengert (Eds.), *Crime spillover* (pp. 20–47). Beverly Hills, CA: Sage.

McPherson, M., & Silloway, G. (1980, October). *Analysis of the relationship between adult entertainment establishments, crime, and housing values.* Minneapolis: Minnesota Crime Prevention Center.

McPherson, M., Silloway, G., & Frey, D.L. (1983). *Crime, fear, and control in neighborhood commercial centers* (Grant No. 80-IJ-CX-0073). Minneapolis: Minnesota Crime Prevention Center.

Meier, R.F. (1982). Perspectives on the concept of social control. *Annual Review of Sociology, 8,* 35–55.

Merry, S.E. (1981a). Defensible space undefended: Social factors in crime control through environmental design. *Urban Affairs Quarterly, 16,* 397–422.

Merry, S.E. (1981b). *Urban danger: Life in a neighborhood of strangers.* Philadelphia: Temple University Press.

Merton, R.K. (1957). *Social theory and social structure.* Glencoe, IL: Free Press.

Michelson, W. (1970). *Man and his urban environment.* Reading, MA: Addison-Wesley.

Miller, E.S. (1981). Crimes's threat to land value and neighborhood vitality. In P.J. Brantingham & P.L. Brantingham (Eds.), *Environmental criminology* (pp. 111–118). Beverly Hills, CA: Sage.

Miller, W.B. (1958). Lower class culture as a generating milieu of gang delinquency. *Journal of Social Issues, 14,* 5–19.

Mitchell, R.W. (1971). Some social implications of high density housing. *American Sociological Review, 36,* 18–29.

Morris, T. (1957). *The criminal area: A study in social ecology.* London: Routledge & Kegan Paul.

Murray, M.A. (1982). *An urban area analysis of delinquency.* Unpublished master's thesis, Johns Hopkins University, Baltimore, MD.

Newman, O. (1972). *Defensible space.* New York: Macmillan.

Newman, O. (1979). *Community of interest.* New York: Doubleday.

Newman, O., & Franck, K. (1980). *Factors influencing crime and instability in urban housing developments.* Washington, DC: U.S. Government Printing Office.

Newman, O., & Franck, K. (1982). The effects of building size on personal crime and fear of crime. *Population and Environment, 5,* 203–220.

O'Donnell, C.R., & Lydgate, T. (1980). The relationship of crimes to physical resources. *Environment and Behavior, 12,* 207–230.

Park, R.E. (1915). The city: Suggestions for the investigation of human behavior in the urban environment. *American Journal of Sociology, 20,* 577–612.

Park, R.E. (1936). Human ecology. *American Journal of Sociology, 42,* 1–15.

Podolefsky, A. (1983). *Case studies in community crime prevention.* Springfield, IL: Thomas.

Podolefsky, A., & DuBow, F. (1981). Strategies for community crime prevention. Springfield, IL: Thomas.

Preston, R.E. (1966). The zone in transition: A study of urban land use patterns. *Economic Geography, 42,* 236–260.

Rainwater, L. (1966). Fear and house-as-haven in the lower class. *Journal of the American Institute of Planners, 32,* 23–31.

Rapoport, A. (1982). *The meaning of the built environment.* Beverly Hills, CA: Sage.

Rengert, G.F. (1980). Spatial aspects of criminal behavior. In D.E. Georges-Abeyie & K.D. Harries (Eds.), *Crime: A spatial perspective* (pp. 47–57). New York: Columbia University Press.

Reppetto, T.A. (1974). *Residential crime.* Cambridge, MA: Ballinger.

Rhodes, W.M., & Conly, C. (1981). Crime and mobility: An empirical study. In P.J. Brantingham & P.L. Brantingham (Eds.), *Environmental criminology* (pp. 167–188). Beverly Hills, CA: Sage.

Robinson, W.S. (1950). Ecological correlations and the behavior of individuals. *American Sociological Review, 15,* 351–357.

Rosen, L.H., & Turner, S.H. (1967). An evaluation of the Lander approach to ecology of delinquency. *Social Problems, 15,* 189–200.

Savelsberg, J. (1984). Socio-spatial attributes of social problems: The case of deviance and crime. *Population Environment, 7,* 163–181.

Schachter, S. (1951). Deviation, rejection and communication. *Journal of Abnormal and Social Psychology, 46,* 190–207.

Schmid, C.F. (1960a). Urban crime areas: Part I. *American Sociological Review, 25,* 527–542.

Schmid, C.F. (1960b). Urban crime areas: Part II. *American Sociological Review, 25,* 655–678.

Shannon, L.W. (1982). The relationship of juvenile delinquency and adult crime to the changing ecological structure of the city (Preliminary Exec. Rep.). Iowa City: Iowa Urban Community Research Center.

Shaw, C.R. (1929). *Delinquency areas: A study of the geographic distribution of school truants, juvenile delinquents, and adult offenders in Chicago.* Chicago: University of Chicago Press.

Shaw, C.R., & McKay, H.D. (1942). *Juvenile delinquency*

and urban areas. Chicago: University of Chicago Press.

Shevky, E., & Bell, W. (1955). *Social area analysis.* Stanford, CA: Stanford University Press.

Shumaker, S.A., & Taylor, R.B. (1983). Toward a clarification of people-place relationships: A model of attachment to place. In N. Feimer & E.S. Geller (Eds.), *Environmental psychology: Directions and perspectives* (pp. 219–251). New York: Praeger.

Skogan, W.G. (1976). Crime and crime rates. In W. Skogan (Ed.), *Sample surveys of the victims of crime* (pp. 105–120). Cambridge, MA: Ballinger.

Skogan, W.G. (1981). *Issues in the measurement of victimization.* Washington, DC: U.S. Government Printing Office.

Skogan, W.G., & Maxfield, M.G. (1981). *Coping with crime.* Beverly Hills, CA: Sage.

Stokols, D. (1977). Origins and direction of environment-behavior research. In D. Stokols (Ed.), *Perspectives on environment and behavior* (pp. 5–36). New York: Plenum.

Stokols, D. (1983). *Scientific and policy challenges of a contextually oriented psychology.* Presidential address presented at the meeting of Division 34, American Psychological Association, Anaheim, CA.

Sumner, C. (1977). Marxism and deviancy theory. In P. Wiles (Ed.), *The sociology of crime and delinquency* (pp. 159–174). New York: Harper & Row.

Sundstrom, E. (1977). Interpersonal behavior and the physical environment. In L. Wrightsman (Ed.), *Social psychology* (pp. 510–549). Monterey, CA: Brooks/Coke.

Sutherland, E.H., & Cressey, D.R. (1955). *Principles of criminology.* Philadelphia: Lippincott.

Suttles, G.D. (1968). *The social order of the slum.* Chicago: University of Chicago Press.

Suttles, G.D. (1972). *The social construction of communities.* Chicago: University of Chicago Press.

Taylor, R.B. (1978). Human territoriality: A review and a model for future research. *Cornell Journal of Social Relations, 13,* 125–151.

Taylor, R.B. (1982). The neighborhood physical environment and stress. In G.W. Evans (Ed.), *Environmental stress* (pp. 286–324). New York: Cambridge University Press.

Taylor, R.B., & Brower, S. (1985). Home and near-home territories. In I. Altman & C. Werner (Eds.), *Human behavior and environment: Current theory and research: Vol. 8. Home environments.* New York: Plenum.

Taylor, R.B., Gottfredson, S., & Brower, S. (1980). The defensibility of defensible space. In T. Hirschi & M. Gottfredson (Eds.), *Understanding crime.* Beverly Hills: Sage.

Taylor, R.B., Gottfredson, S.D., & Brower, S. (1981). Territorial cognitions and social climate in urban neighborhoods. *Basic and Applied Social Psychology, 2,* 289–303.

Taylor, R.B., Gottfredson, S., & Brower, S. (1984). Understanding block crime and fear. *Journal of Research in Crime and Delinquency, 21,* 303–331.

Taylor, R.B., Gottfredson, S.D., & Shumaker, S.A. (1984). *Neighborhood responses to disorder* (Unpub. Final Rep.). Baltimore, MD: Johns Hopkins University, Center for Metropolitan Planning and Research.

Taylor, R.B., & Hale, M.M. (in press). Testing alternative models of fear of crime. *Journal of Criminal Law & Criminology.*

Taylor, R.B., Shumaker, S.A., & Gottfredson, S.D. (1985). Neighborhood-level links between physical features and local sentiments: Deterioration, fear of crime and confidence. *Journal of Architectural Planning and Research, 2,* 261–275.

Taylor, I., Walton, P., & Young, J. (1973). *The new criminology.* London: Routledge & Kegan Paul.

Thorndike, G.L. (1939). On the fallacy of imputing the correlations found for groups to the individuals in smaller groups composing them. *American Journal of Psychology, 52,* 122–124.

Thrasher, F.M. (1927). *The gang: A study of 1,313 gangs in Chicago.* Chicago: University of Chicago Press.

Triandis, H.C. (1977). *Interpersonal behavior.* Monterey, CA: Brooks/Cole.

Turner, S. (1969). The ecology of delinquency. In T. Sellin & M.E. Wolfgang (Eds.), *Delinquency: Selected studies.* New York: Wolfgang.

Tyler, T.R. (1980). Impact of directly and indirectly experienced events: The origin of crime-related judgments and behaviors. *Journal of Personality and Social Psychology, 39,* 13–28.

White, R.C. (1932). The relation of felonies to environmental factors in Indianapolis. *Social Forces, 46,* 525–541.

Whyte, W.F. (1943). *Street corner society.* Chicago: University of Chicago Press.

Wicker, A.W. (1979). *Introduction to ecological psychology.* Monterey, CA: Brooks/Cole.

Wicker, A.W. (1987). Behavior settings reconsidered: Temporal stages, resources, internal dynamics, context. In D. Stokols & I. Altman (Eds.), *Handbook of environmental psychology.* New York: Wiley.

Wilson, J.Q. (1975). *Thinking about crime.* New York: Basic Books.

Wilson, J.Q., & Kelling, G.L. (1982). Broken windows: The police and neighborhood safety. *The Atlantic, 249*(3), 29–38.

Worchel, S., & Lollis, M. (1982). Reactions to territorial contamination as a function of culture. *Personality and Social Psychology Bulletin, 8,* 370–375.

Chapter 26

PSYCHOLOGICAL CONTRIBUTIONS TO TRANSPORTATION

Peter B. Everett, *Division of Man-Environment Relations, Pennsylvania State University, University Park, Pennsylvania*

Barry G. Watson, *Toronto Transit Commission, Toronto, Ontario, Canada*

26.1. INTRODUCTION

26.1.1. Chapter Purpose

Many concerns within the field of transportation require attention from the behavioral sciences. Methods for encouraging the use of mass transit, reducing labor-management conflicts, improving travel safety, and the development of strategies for involving citizens in transportation planning are but a few examples. The discipline of psychology has contributed much to transportation, yet many untapped areas of opportunity remain. It is the purpose of this chapter to present a selected overview of the types of contributions psychology has made and is making to transportation and then to suggest areas for future opportunity. Before embarking on this task, it is first

appropriate to present a very brief history of transportation. This historical backdrop will help illustrate why transportation and psychology have a developing and promising relationship that has been and should be mutually beneficial.

26.1.2. History of Transportation

The transportation services that first played an important role were guided by the straightforward forces of technology and business. Those who were involved in the day-to-day and long-range decisions of transportation firms and organizations had little reason to be concerned about how they might best serve the needs of the people because they operated at a point where demand far exceeded supply and at a time when there were few alternatives, if any, to the services they offered. Roadway systems, for example, either evolved or were built on the basis of decisions by a small number of influential individuals.

Over time economic, regulatory, and social forces changed this situation to the extent that understanding people's attitudes, needs, and behaviors was critical to the successful operation of a modern transportation system.

The environmental movement was a dominant force with regard to the inclusion of social and behavioral factors in transportation construction. The passing of the National Environmental Protection Act in 1971 and its requirement for social impact assessment fostered an increasing number of transportation activities for psychologists, sociologists, and economists.

The automobile manufacturing industry itself saw a similar increase in the breadth of influencing issues as the public showed a greater concern for safety. This resulted in a broader based approach that included, for example, information on the behavioral issues in seat belt usage.

All modes of public transportation including air, rail, and bus experienced a similar broadening of perspectives. Consider three influences in the urban transportation arena. As ownership of private automobiles increased, urban mass transportation systems were no longer in a position where they could be guaranteed a captive market (Smerk, 1974). Some private transit operators found relief by turning to the practice of marketing that showed the advantage of first determining what the customer finds attractive, and then, within the limitations of the organization, concentrating production on that service. Extensive survey research has been, and continues to be, carried out to determine travel patterns of various populations, representative demographics, and the variables that influence the decision to travel at all as well as the mode chosen.

In many situations, the financial plight in which private urban bus firms found themselves was so dire that government intervention was inevitable. The economic assistance and protected monopolies they received were accompanied by regulatory obligations that required that these organizations take care to provide services to the population in an equitable manner as well as attending to the special needs of politically and socially identified groups. This balancing of the previous technological emphasis has created substantial demand for additional information from social and behavioral scientists.

Various formulas and measurement strategies were developed to determine how tax dollars should be distributed and how service should be allocated across political jurisdictions. Massive amounts of money have been provided to study the special needs of the elderly and handicapped and to determine how their needs can best be met.

Another force that encouraged the application of social science to transportation was the general disillusionment of society with the ineffectiveness of exclusively technological solutions to social problems. Increasing concern about the environment and the future quality of urban life forced political decision makers to develop new programs to support behavioral solutions to problems where the "technological fix" had failed. The "conservation" (a behavioral solution) theme for the resolution of the energy problems of the 1970s is a good example.

26.1.3. An Opportunity for Psychology

The evolution of an eclectic approach to transportation has yielded a prime opportunity for psychological contribution. Many transportation professionals clearly perceive a need for a broader based approach, and the desire for behavioral expertise is strongly expressed (Hartgen, 1981).

It is reasonable to understand the need for psychological input to transportation endeavors. Transportation is indeed a most pervasive behavior. Everyone participates in it in one way or another. Further, the aggregate phenomenon of transportation could be viewed as the summing of the transportation behaviors of individuals. Psychological theory and methods are, therefore, appropriate to transportation applications. This has been recognized by a number of psychologists, sociologists, and human factors experts who have argued that transportation systems need to be considered from a human perspective rather than from an exclusively technological view (Appleyard, 1979; Chermajeff, 1968; Craik, 1969; Galer, 1979; Gutman, 1968; Hartgen, 1978; Kogi, 1979; Kreindler, 1979).

Beyond noting that transportation is a phenomenon that can be addressed by psychology and that it is a pervasive behavior, it must be stressed that it is not a trivial behavior nor does the transportation system have a trivial impact on behavior! Many hours of the week are spent by a majority of the world's population in transportation activities. One-sixth of the U.S. and Canadian populations is directly employed in the production and maintenance of transportation systems. Severe social and behavioral problems often emerge as a result of poor access to needed transportation and/or forced relocation (Fried, 1963) as a result of the construction of a new highway or airport. A significant proportion of our national budget is spent on transportation. The ability to maintain employment and friendship patterns is heavily reliant on transportation access. Our quality of life, ranging from residential selection, environmental pollution, resource depletion, to environmental stress, is significantly impacted by transportation. The list is large. Transportation is a field rich with opportunities, challenge, and significance for the field of psychology.

26.1.4. Chapter Organization

The chapter will proceed in the following manner. First, a sampling of the many applications psychology has made to transportation will be discussed. It is not the intent of this overview section to review exhaustively the many studies that have been carried out. Instead, the chapter will attempt to present a sampling of the many diverse applications of psychology to transportation. Following the general overview, a more detailed case study analysis will be presented that will outline how a particular psychological approach (learning theory) has been applied to a particular transportation problem (increasing the use of mass transit).

After the review of psychological contributions to transportation, the chapter will then focus on a qualitative assessment of the current levels of psychological contributions to transportation issues. These comments will be followed by suggestions as to the most appropriate futures for psychological input.

Then the chapter will point out some institutional barriers, cautions, and advice that must be attended to in order to promote the psychological orientation to the field of transportation.

26.2. CURRENT CONTRIBUTIONS OF PSYCHOLOGY TO TRANSPORTATION

26.2.1. A Framework for Analysis

There are so many issues and divisions within the field of transportation and different psychological theories and approaches that it is difficult to decide how to categorize psychology and transportation so that some semblance of a systematic analysis of their joining can be carried out. However, some categorization of transportation issues and psychological approaches must be chosen. What follows is a categorization that provides a framework from which an analysis may proceed. Others (e.g., Hartgen, 1981; Michaels, 1980) have categorized the interactions between transportation and the behavioral sciences in different formats.

Transportation Issues

For the analysis presented in this chapter, the field of transportation has been divided into three functional areas: policy and planning, vehicle and facility design, and management.

The first area—*transportation policy and planning*— includes the broad, long-range decisions that influence all aspects of the design, implementation, and operation of a transportation system. Transportation policy is exemplified by the decision in 1978 to deregulate the airlines in the United States. Planning involves the development of a strategy for the allocation of resources so that a certain goal (often generated by policy) may be obtained.

The second area—*transportation vehicle and facility design*—is a function that usually takes place after policy decisions have been made and the planning function completed. Facility and vehicle design endeavors specify in detail the physical parameters of a transportation construction undertaking. Transportation vehicles include airplanes, cars, escalators, trains, bicycles, boats, and so forth. Facility design includes facilities (other than the vehicles themselves) that are constructed to provide service to transportation vehicles and customers and/or employees. These facilities include airline terminals, bus stations, bus stops, subway terminals, park and ride lots, ticket counters, maintenance buildings, bridges, tunnels, employee lounges, waiting rooms, parking garages, service stations, highway rest areas, and so forth.

The third area—*transportation management*—is distinct from policy and planning. Management is a function that occurs on a day-to-day basis once a policy decision has been made, a plan developed, and the transportation system implemented and operating. Management includes attention to issues such as accounting, finance, labor, operations, short-term planning decisions that affect the ongoing operation of an implemented transportation system, and marketing.

Psychological Approaches

The field of psychology has been subdivided into four divisions for the analysis to be presented in this chapter. As was the case for the transportation field, the divisions presented are arbitrary, yet they yield a framework that provides a heuristic for the analyses presented here. The psychological divisions include physiological and perceptual psychology, personality and social psychology, learning theory and behavior change methodology, and developmental psychology. It should be noted that the physiological and perceptual area also includes work in human factors, ergonomics, and industrial engineering. The developmental division represents more than a focus on a particular age or developmental stage but includes a broad life span perspective. The authors have chosen not to include a particular psychological category for environmental psychology. This is the case because all of the individual areas mentioned (e.g., physiological, perceptual, social, personality, learning theory, and developmental) constitute environmental psychology when they are applied to the real world physical phenomenon of transportation.

It is now the task of this chapter to present an overview by means of examples of how the different psychological perspectives have been applied to the three areas of transportation.

26.2.2 The General Analysis

Table 26.1 is a matrix that illustrates the type of work (as depicted in the cells of the table) that has been initiated by the different psychological approaches to various transportation issues. The table is not exhaustive and is presented primarily to illustrate the range of applications. These examples will be discussed in more detail next.

Psychological Contributions to Transportation Policy and Planning

The active area of psychological contribution to transportation policy and planning has evolved primarily from the physiological and perceptual and the personality and social areas as opposed to those evolving from learning theory and developmental psychology. The physiological and perceptual areas have contributed significantly through the work in human factors engineering. Whether or not the research was specifically carried out because of a policy or planning issue or whether the research was first carried out and then the findings migrated into policy and planning decisions is an issue that is difficult to assess. Whatever the case, there is much physiological and perceptual research that has found its way into policy and planning issues. For example, research by authors such as Leibowitz and Owens (1977), Mourant and Rockwell (1970), and Shinar, McDowell, and Rockwell (1977) have delineated the relationship of visual functioning and car driving. For example, Liebowitz and Owens documented that focal, high-resolution vision cannot operate well at night and that drivers obtain their main visual input from ambient or peripheral vision when it is dark. The peripheral vision detects location, motion, and locomotion, but hazard detection is lost due to the decrement in focal

vision. This leads to a situation where drivers exceed a safe speed. The output of these studies and others like them has helped form transportation policy in regard to standards for day and night highway signage and has provided input into the planning function by allowing professionals to understand safety requirements for highway curve alignments.

Other researchers in the human factors area have focused on an understanding of driver fatigue. Before 1957, there was little work in this regard. Dureman and Boden (1972) determined that heart rate tends to decrease with driving time. This normalization of heart rate leads to a decrease in driving skills. Others such as Mackie and Miller (1978) and Harris and Mackie (1972) have conducted studies that relate bus and truck driver safety behaviors to variables such as the regularity of schedules and the hours of service. Mackie and Miller found that 20% of a sample of long-distance truck drivers' logs showed at least one driving day of over 15 hours out of the previous 6 days. The implications of this finding on fatigue are obvious. A review by McDonald (1984) relates truck driver fatigue to many variables, including hours and schedules of work, noise, vibration, temperature and ventilation, exposure to carbon monoxide, drivers' assessment of their occupational conditions, and various aspects of their career such as type of truck driving (e.g., long-distance versus local), prestige, and proportion of swing shift work relative to regular hours. Works such as these have helped to form policy in regard to standards and laws that specify the length of driver shifts for long-distance highway travel. Olsen (1981) has reviewed many physiological and perceptual studies that have contributed to highway safety policy and planning issues.

Social psychological approaches to transportation policy and planning are illustrated by two categories of research. First, we have the many and varied studies that have attempted to assess the social impact of a planned or implemented transportation system on citizens. In a classic study, the impact of forced relocation because of highway construction in Boston was graphically illustrated (Fried, 1963). Large proportions of both men and women were depressed several years after the forced relocation. The stronger the affiliation with the original neighborhood, the greater the relocation grief. Llewellyn (1981) has reviewed many of the social impacts/costs of urban transportation innovations. Two of the major impacts are the relocation that Fried researched and the impact of transportation noise. Crook and Langdon (1974) found that aircraft noise created

Table 26.1. A Matrix Illustrating the Type of Work Carried Out by the Joining of Psychological Approaches to Transportation Issues.

Transportation Issues

	Policy and Planning	Vehicle and Facility Design	Management
Physiological and Perceptual	Vision and driving skills Driver fatigue and safety standards Information signage	Comfort Vehicle crowding Vision and driving skills Information signage	Advertising evaluation Stress management Public information
Personality and Social	Social impact assessment Transportation and stress Demand modeling	Vehicle crowding Security on transit	Market segmentation Stress management Employee selection Public information
Learning Theory and Behavior Change	Highway enforcement strategies Mode change incentives	Security on transit	Safe driving incentives Mode change incentives Productivity incentives
Developmental	Security on transit Market segmentation	Security on transit Vehicle design for special populations	Special services for elderly Security on transit

Psychological Approaches

speech interference, although not impacting teaching techniques in a school near London airport. In a well-controlled study of third and fourth graders in the Los Angeles International Airport air corridor, Cohen, Evans, Krantz, and Stokols (1980) found that noisy environments elevated children's blood pressure, reduced their puzzle-solving abilities, and decreased their ability to cope with distractions. Yet the aircraft noise did not affect their reading or math skills.

Because of active construction in urban transportation systems, several psychologists are now involved in the social impact assessment of these endeavors. This is exemplified by the work of Baldassare (1981) that reviews the social impact of the Bay Area Rapid Transit System (BART) on nearby residents. In general, residents responded with a neutral or favorable rating of BART. Particular problems were noted in regard to noise, shadows, vibrations, traffic, and parking. Respondents rated these problems differently, depending on many personal variables such as their proximity to BART, their use of it, and whether they had just moved close to it. Although there seems to be much individual work evolving in the social impact assessment area, Llewellyn, Bunten, Goodman, Hare, Mach, and Swisher

noted in 1975 that the guidelines for this work are "hopelessly muddled." Twelve years later, this situation has not significantly improved.

An area of research carried out by Stokols and Novaco (1981) falls somewhere between the physiological and perceptual area and the social psychological area. In this research, the authors found that subjects' psychological and physiological well-being was somewhat dependent on commuting distances and time (*impedance* in the authors' terminology). Greater impedance led to elevated blood pressures. An interesting finding was that Type A personalities (people that are more time-dependent, want to control their environment) were less bothered by high impedance commutes than Type B personalities. Stokols and Novaco note that this may be a function of the person's (and his or her personality type) "fit" with a given environment. An intense, long commute may "fit" Type A and be totally out of context for the more "laid back" Type B. Among the authors' many findings, they conclude that not only does personality modify reactions to impedance, but person–environment fit (e.g., satisfaction with residential location) plays an important role.

The second and major application of sociopsychological approaches to transportation evolves from the large area of research that has been carried out in an attempt to predict travel demand. Travel demand prediction is a function normally carried out in transportation planning. Demand modeling has moved from what has been termed *aggregate demand modeling* to *disaggregate demand modeling*. Disaggregate demand modeling involves the development of a predictive model of travel behavior based on the behavior of individuals, whereas aggregate demand modeling uses predictors such as general demographic, economic, and life-style indicators. The work of the following authors is representative. Dobson, Golob, and Gustafson (1974) have used multidimensional scaling approaches of consumer preferences to predict usage of public transportation. The model yielded data that showed certain population segments would respond to different public transit attributes. To some, it was cost savings, whereas others were less concerned with cost but more interested in energy conservation. Golob, Horowitz, and Wachs (1979) researched the relationship between attitudes and behavior in regard to predicting travel demand. In this work, attitudes are viewed as the "mediators" of behavior that predisposes one to an actual travel decision. Golob and colleagues used a cognitive dissonance perspective to determine what attributes of auto and transit were most salient to auto versus transit users. Auto users and transit users rated various attributes of their own travel mode and the mode they did not use. The greater the difference in ratings, the greater the dissonance and supposedly the importance of the variable. The highly dissonant variables would be appropriate ones to focus on in a transit marketing campaign.

Levin (1979) has developed another attitudinal modeling approach for use in transportation research and predicting travel demand. Rather than have individuals respond to single transportation attributes, Levin had them rate a set of attributes in a context (e.g., an express bus, at a $6 fare, with reserved seats, leaving downtown every half hour). This technique is viewed as an improvement because it measures objective system attributes (i.e., what the bus is really like) as opposed to single attributes. A review by Levin and Louviere (1981) illustrates the many and varied approaches to predicting travel demand that evolve from attitudinal and preference research. This strong base from attitudinal theory is the reason for categorizing this area of transportation application under the social psychological category.

Learning theory approaches to transportation policy and planning issues are exemplified by two areas of application. First, there is the research that attempts to relate different highway traffic enforcement strategies to driving behavior. Second, there are the studies designed to change travel behaviors by reinforcement strategies. Although the research on enforcement did not really evolve from learning theory, the types of variables manipulated are clearly those suggested by learning theorists. For example, Hauer and Cooper (1977) documented the effectiveness of increased enforcement in reducing accidents in Toronto, Canada. Although difficult to track because of many changing variables (e.g., weather, time of year, amount of traffic, enforcement behaviors of different police officers), Hauer and Cooper (1977) credited a 3% reduction in accidents to increased enforcement of traffic rules. It is, however, surprising how little is known in regard to the relationship between traffic laws, enforcement, and their impact on highway speed and accidents. As Dart (1977) has noted, much more research is needed. One would hope that there would be a significant increase in research on enforcement and behavior because of the heightened interest in developing policy to deal with drinking and driving.

The use of reinforcers to change travel behavior is evident both in the transportation policy and planning areas and the management section discussed later. In the management area, reinforcers are typically used to increase the usage of an existing transportation system. There are, however, examples of applying learning theory to the transportation planning function. This work is exemplified by a situation where an environment is designed from the very initial planning phases so that it will reinforce a certain travel behavior. The design of a highway system that has specific lanes set aside for car pools is a good case in point. It is the intent of such car pool lanes, from the very initial planning stages, to allow the car poolers to travel in a much less congested lane, and thus, at an increased speed. The plan was to "reinforce behavior" by increased travel speeds inherent in the highway design for car poolers. A documentation of the results of such planned incentive programs is discussed by Rose and Hinds (1976). These authors cite data from a high occupancy vehicle (HOV) lane opened in Dade County, Florida. Although the results are somewhat contaminated by the simultaneous addition of increased bus service, the impact was still significant. Passengers per vehicle (for all lanes of the highway) rose from an average of 1.30 to 1.45 persons. Forty-seven percent of the bus riders in the HOV lane noted that they rode the bus because of reduced travel time. However, others have noted other reinforcement contingencies operating in HOV lanes. Cars with drivers only often stop at bus stops to pick up riders and thus qualify for a HOV. This decreases bus ridership and thus the overall energy impact of a HOV lane. Another incentive for rider sharing that is often considered in the initial planning stages of transportation facilities is illustrated by those plans that set aside preferred parking facilities for car poolers. Such programs carried out by Hallmark Cards and the McDonnell-Douglas Corporation have contributed to a 50% increase in car pooling (Pratsch, 1975).

Developmental approaches have been recently applied to transportation policy and planning issues because of the need to attend to the transportation needs of all of our population segments. For example, there has been much research, from all areas of social science, that attempts to develop policy and planning guidelines for the handicapped. In a study by Pagano, McKnight, and Dichter-Figurea (1983), it was found that the elderly and handicapped perceived more "transportation quality" from larger, private sector providers rather than small, public sector ones. One would expect that with increased governmental concern for policy in regard to the elderly that we would see more psychological research with respect to policy and planning guidelines for developing transportation environments for this segment of our population. One past study (Patterson & Ralston, 1983) determined that the elderly's fear of crime does indeed deter them from using public transit. The study suggests policy decisions that could potentially reduce this fear. Increased visibility of police protection was one suggestion. Additionally, one would hope that we would be able to develop more specific policy and planning guidelines, based on good empirical research, for the design and management of transportation environments for children. For example, in a Norwegian study, Houg (1982) documented the travel needs of children, their fears and insecurities in regard to travel, and then suggested transportation policies appropriate for children. Another document that discusses children and transportation is a special issue of the *Childhood City Newsletter* that was published in 1981.

Two studies have focused on the travel needs of women and the resulting policy and planning implications. As a result of the rapid increase in female participation in the work force and of the growing number of households headed by women, Michelson (1983) documented the travel needs and usage of this population segment. The study found that not only were transportation issues of concern, but changes were required in hours of operation of service facilities such as banks, provision of more child-care facilities was needed, and an increase in flexible work

hours would ease the difficulty of women scheduling their daily activities. In a study focused on the public transit needs of women, Moore (1982) discovered that large transit and planning agencies in five major U.S. cities had very little data on this subject. In order to develop transportation policy, carry out the planning process, and then develop alternatives, the travel needs of women deserve considerably more attention.

To summarize, physiological and perceptual approaches to transportation policy and planning issues are fairly common as evidenced by the examples given. The major contribution to policy and planning has, however, come from personality and social approaches because of their natural relationship to this transportation area. That is to say, these psychological perspectives have clearly identifiable links to transportation policy (e.g., the work on transportation and stress) and transportation planning (e.g., the work in social impact assessment and demand modeling). Learning theory and developmental approaches have been applied to issues of transportation policy and planning much less. This is the case for learning theory because it is a comparatively new approach to applied areas and also because it lends itself better to the more dynamic "on line" issues (e.g., management) as opposed to planning and policy development. Developmental approaches have received little attention to date primarily because of a lack of concern for different age groups. However, now with heightened concern for groups of all kinds (male/female, young/old, black/white, etc.), developmental approaches should certainly receive more attention in regard to transportation policy and planning.

Psychological Contributions to Transportation Vehicle and Facility Design

Psychology has made a wide range of contributions to vehicle and facility design for all modes of transportation. In the area of urban transportation, the provision of an acceptable environment for passengers is an important concern when designing vehicles. Perceptions of passenger comfort have been shown to have a significant impact on modal choice (Golob, Canty, & Gustafson, 1972; Nicolaidis, 1975; Osborne, 1978). In order to make a transportation mode feasible, one must understand how to design the system to be attractive to potential users.

Generally, passenger comfort has fallen within the problem domain of the human factors expert. The classic ergonomic question of attempting to fit the transportation environment to the passenger has traditionally included such issues as humidity, ventilation, illumination, noise, vibration, acceleration, and seat characteristics (McCormick, 1976), although some consideration has been given to the sociological aspects of comfort (Davis & Levine, 1967). These authors conclude that public transit, in particular, is a uniquely nonsocial environment where one's main purpose is to leave. In contrast to other means of transport such as ocean liners and to a somewhat lesser extent, aircraft and private automobiles, public transportation only subjects one to a series of uncomfortable waits and a paucity of things to do.

Much of the work that has led to the determination of which factors in the public transportation environment contribute to discomfort has come from studies of the passenger perception of ride quality (Golob et al., 1972; Nicolaidis, 1975). Such investigations are psychologically based and involve uni- or multidimensional scaling techniques or some form of factor analysis to determine the most salient perceptions of the public transportation experience.

Similar studies on perception of passenger comfort have been carried out in virtually all travel modes, including automobiles, private and commercial aircraft (Richards & Jacobson, 1975, 1977), and intercity trains (Wichansky, 1979). Wichansky points out that comfort can be viewed as the overall reaction to all aspects of the ride in a vehicle and not just to components such as motion, seating, and lighting.

One element that has emerged from the comfort studies is crowding. Original work that attempted to incorporate this factor into facility or vehicle design generally did not go beyond a measure of density in which some calculated body ellipse is taken as a standard of comfort.

Beyond the focused ergonomic studies, psychologists have looked at the broader psychological factors effecting urban travel by examining the response to crowding in transit vehicles (Yancey, 1972). By showing subjects photographs of bus interiors with differing numbers of people, significant differences in ratings on stress-related scales and measures of hostility were found. There was no evidence to suggest that people adapt to these conditions or that their perceptions were influenced by how much exposure they may previously have had with similar conditions.

Research on the multitude of factors that influence one's perception of crowding clearly establishes that crowding is not solely determined by spatial density and may vary independently of the number of persons per area (Stokols, 1972, 1976). The same number of people in the same area may or may not feel crowded, depending on what the participants had intended to do and on the meaning of that space for the individuals occupying it.

Based on the work of Milgram (1970) that describes the psychological and sociological experiences of living in cities, some have suggested that an important dimension of the crowding experience is the aversive nature of overstimulation (Milgram, 1970). In the transit setting, a wide variety of stimuli emanate from other passengers. Added to the already noisy environment, this overload may be too much for the passenger to bear. Milgram has suggested a range of behavioral strategies that people develop in order to limit the amount of information, and some researchers have explored the behaviors that transit patrons in particular use to deal with crowded situations. McCauley, Coleman, and DeFusco, (1977) looked at the willingness of commuters to make eye contact with strangers and found that a person was much less inclined to meet the eye of another in a crowded city transit station than in a less crowded suburban terminal. These behaviors were seen by the experimenters as being indicative of an attempt at short-term adaptation to interpersonal overload.

Considerations of this type have been applied by designers in mock-up situations in order to determine the seat configurations for transit vehicles. One proposal was to shift the axis of the seat to the longitudinal axis of the vehicle (Lepper & Moorhead, 1970). Although such applications of the theoretical perspective of information and visual contact are appealing, there remains to be conducted any evaluation of seating orientation to demonstrate that this variable is sufficient to have any significant impact on either modal choice or overall passenger comfort.

Some research has shown that the freedom of choice and opportunity to exercise control over one's environment may be crucial elements in the negative consequences of crowding (Glass & Singer, 1972). A study conducted on Swedish commuter trains demonstrated the importance of control over seat choice (Singer, Lundberg, & Frankenhaeuser, 1978). Subjects who boarded trains at various points on the line into the city were asked to rate their annoyance with conditions of crowding. Although the train became more crowded as the trip continued, those who were on for a shorter period indicated more negative reactions and stress as measured by a urine analysis than those who were on the train from the beginning. Apparently, the time of exposure to the stress of traveling is not as important as the context or conditions under which the trip occurred. It is reasonable to assume that because the train was generally more crowded during the second half of the trip, greater opportunity for seat selection, the ability to arrange coats and parcels, and the freedom to choose with whom to sit were potent factors in reducing the stress of the trip. So crucial was such control that it outweighed trip length by a factor of 2 when overall aversiveness of the trip was measured. Similar results were found by Lundberg (1976). Indications of stress were found to be more related to the environment within the train than to the amount of time spent on the train. Control over the situation on the train was implicated as the major determinant of stressfulness. It was assumed that control and density were highly related in that an increase in the number of people in each car corresponded to a decrease in the availability of seats, a reduction in the freedom of choice as to whom a passenger would sit with, and other issues of control. The investigation indicated that even small changes in crowdedness are associated with physiological arousal.

Research has also been carried out on the passenger concerns of transit stations but to a considerably lesser extent. For the most part, attention to the passenger has been through a mathematical modeling approach where traffic flow has been studied. Human factors research strategies have contributed to the understanding of cuing in train stations (Stilitz, 1969). Groups of people lining up to buy tickets in the London underground were observed within a range of station layouts. This was used to recommend specific changes to smooth passenger flow with favorable implications for user satisfaction and understanding of a complex environment.

Studies on passenger processing have sometimes focused on some specific elements of a transportation station. Fulton and Stroud (1981) examined passenger response to turnstiles in order to identify points of hesitation in their use.

Security issues have recently been of great concern within the urban environment with a concentration, to some extent, in public transportation systems, whether urban or intercity. This was particularly highlighted with regard to specific demographic segments including women (Office of Civil Rights, USDOT, 1982) and the elderly (Patterson & Ralston, 1983). Although some research (Pearce, 1980) has shown that at least nonemergency assistance can be expected in these situations, others have suggested guidelines to improve the real and perceived security of these environments (Feldman & Vellenga, 1977). Feldman and Vellenga suggest that the perceived security problem can be addressed in ways other than conventional policy methods. Alter-

natives provided include communications and education programs to increase awareness of sources of aid as well as to promote solidarity among passengers who might be inclined to stand idly by when others are in need of assistance.

The study of signage has been a highly significant area in highway engineering. Human factors and perceptual psychologists have developed reliable methodologies for determining the effectiveness of various presentations of different messages for drivers as well as symbolic signage for all sorts of travelers (Collins, 1982, Mackett-Stout, & Dewar, 1981). In an application of these approaches Dewar, Ells, and Cooper (1977) studied the signs leading to major points within the Toronto International Airport. The researchers used opinion surveys and field observation to evaluate the existing signage before using reaction time and glance legibility within a laboratory to evaluate potential improvements. The improvements were implemented and evaluated by field observation and opinion surveys. This demonstrated both the validity of the laboratory methods and the success of the research approach to solving a navigation problem. Application of these methodologies and principles has not been as extensive in public transportation facilities. Most work within these facilities is carried out by architects and graphic designers, although psychologists are beginning to focus on this area. Beck (1984) considered the wayfinding problems of riders in several large U.S. subway systems. By analyzing the errors riders made in selecting train platforms, Beck developed several design recommendations that emphasize an architectural differentiation of areas of the station that serve different destinations and that maintain sightlines between critical external landmarks and choice points within the station.

Human factors specialists, applying principles from perceptual and physiological psychology, have dealt with the driver–vehicle interface in vehicle and highway system design. Olsen (1981) reviewed many important contributions in this area, including the relationship between the visual environment and highway safety. He concluded that although much had been learned, there was need for more realistic approaches and solutions for the more pressing problems in this complex area. As he pointed out, "Advances in measurements of component and operator reliability have made space flight possible, but drivers still go through red lights and auto brakes still fail without warning the ordinary driver" (p. 160).

Thus to summarize, psychological input to vehicle and facility design has been significant. Most of this work has evolved out of the human factors work that has studied the interface between man and machine. There are large literatures discussing human factors and automobile design and safety, jet cockpit layout and reaction time, train operator seat design and fatigue, and so forth.

It has been the intent of this section to highlight some of the newer areas of psychological contribution to vehicle and facility design. Paramount among these is the research focusing on ride quality and comfort with a subset focusing on the public transportation environment. An emerging literature is focusing in particular on the design of transit vehicle interiors and stress induced by passenger density and control of one's environment in the transit vehicle. Other research has begun to pinpoint the design variables that help reduce the perception of crime in transit vehicles and stations, whereas a final area discussed noted the emerging studies that relate customers' navigational abilities in major transit stations to architectural parameters.

Psychological Contributions to Transportation Management

Managers of transportation systems are continuously confronted with problems involving human behavior, whether it is the behavior of customers or of employees. Not surprisingly, research from various areas of psychology has been brought to bear on management problems.

In the ideal case, management issues involving consumer behavior are formalized as the marketing function within an organization. This function is specifically charged with ensuring an understanding of the needs, attitudes, and behaviors of the consumer so that the firm is in the best position to provide its service or product.

Because marketing focuses on the behavior of the consumer, there tends to be great overlap with many of the other functional areas within the transportation area. For example, an active area within urban transportation has been the development of various trip-generation and modal assignment models to forecast the route a traveler will take and the extent to which individuals will use public transportation or the private automobile (see the discussion on demand modeling). These tend to be multivariate models that take into account a wide range of social and demographic variables as well as characteristics of the particular transportation service being offered. Previously, the bulk of this work was done by engineers, and the responsibility for application of the models frequently resides within the planning area. Increasingly, however, psychologists such as Levin and Louviere (1981) have been predicting travel behavior

based on behavioral demand models. As discussed previously their work (and that of others) uses sophisticated attitudinal scaling techniques to determine what are salient variables to the transportation consumer. These data are then often used to develop marketing programs.

Market segmentation evolves from work such as that of Levin and Louviere. This involves application of multivariate techniques to discriminate groups of individuals along dimensions that personality and social psychology have suggested as important in the perception of transportation systems. The development of these behavioral science principles by marketers has helped transportation providers (commercial carriers and equipment manufacturers alike) develop highly specific services and products that firms can then deliver in a cost-effective manner (Kotler, 1976).

Marketers of transportation products and services have benefited from the application of life span concepts of developmental psychology. These concepts have helped define market segments based on age. Marketers are recognizing that a consumer's need for transportation changes dramatically as the individual ages. Building on these principles, firms and organizations are not only able to operate more efficiently but are able to improve the extent to which they meet the needs of the individual.

Physiological psychologists have also had some impact on one aspect of marketing management—the evaluation of advertising programs. Although not applied broadly, advances are being made in the development of physiological measures of arousal and attention that are likely, in the near future, to provide improved measures of advertising effectiveness (Olson & Ray, 1983).

One specific area of public transit marketing where psychological research has played an active role is the development of public information. The design and distribution of public information has been a problem of continuing frustration for the transit industry. How does the provision of schedule and routing information relate to the individual's choice of public transportation over the private auto? If the availability of information is important in this decision, what is the most effective way of presenting the information? One study (Hall, 1983) showed that mistakes in reading maps resulted in lost travel time or walking effort with significant implications for choice of one mode over another.

General studies on modal choice have demonstrated that the more frequently a bus operates on a particular route, the more likely an individual is to ride it. Obviously, having to wait for a bus deters use. It follows that the more information one has about vehicle schedules, the more likely he or she would use it. Although several studies have provided support for this, it has been difficult to demonstrate that the effect was not due to other causes. In the case of large quasi-experimental situations, external factors such as regional growth may have caused the ridership increase. In other situations, the ridership change may have simply been due to the promotional effect of the manipulation. That is, by disseminating schedule information, people may simply use transit more often simply because they became aware of transit rather than a better schedule promoting ridership.

So remains a task to quantify the conditions under which increased information changes travel decisions. For example, is the importance of information different for discretionary trips than for trips that must be made? Is it different in poor weather versus good weather? Does it depend on how frequently travel services are offered?

The other side of the public information question focuses on how best to provide the information. Although issues of cost enter at this point, the psychologist focuses his or her concern on how effectively an individual uses information to navigate through a transit environment. For example, Geehan and Deslauriers (1978) approached the problem by asking respondents to take imaginary trips using the information aids of five medium-sized Ontario cities. On the average, only 51% of those tested accurately planned a transit trip.

Concern over the difficulty of traveling in New York prompted an evaluative study where university students new to the city rode the subway to predetermined destinations with only the subway map to guide them (Bronzaft, Dobrow, & O'Hanlon, 1976). The students were instructed not to ask for help and to keep a "travel log" of the decisions they made, problems encountered, effective responses, and amount of time the trip took. All students eventually completed the task, but none of them did so in the most efficient manner. They often waited for trains that did not run on that day or did not stop at that station. Though this study does demonstrate the difficulty of navigating in subway systems, the results have limited external validity due to the unique nature of the New York subway system and the limited number of subjects (eight) who participated.

One of the first studies using a systematic approach to determine which information aids and which of their attributes actually increase the accuracy of transit trip planning was conducted using actual route pamphlets from 19 transit authorities in the United States (Everett, Anderson, & Makranczy,

1977). Under laboratory conditions, university students were asked to make three separate transit trips utilizing a different pamphlet each time. Overall, only 41% of the participants successfully completed the transit trips. Results indicated that the greatest accuracy was obtained with two-color single route pamphlets that included features such as bus stop designations.

Following this line of reasoning, Garland, Haynes, and Grubb (1979) published research evaluating the system map component of information aids. Specifically, they examined the effect of color coding and street detail on making an imaginary transit trip. College students received a detailed city street map and one of four different transit system maps—a black-and-white, highly detailed map containing most of the city streets; this same map with color-coded bus routes; a black-and-white system map including only those streets along which a route operated; and finally, a black-and-white map depicting major city streets and bus routes. In this last condition, the names of minor streets were excluded, even if the street was along the bus route. These four maps formed two categories for comparison; the first two addressed the effect of color coding combined with a high level of detail, and the second two examined a moderate level of detail when major city streets are included. It was found that the color-coded, highly detailed map yielded the most accuracy and that students felt less frustrated with the task and were more confident than with the black-and-white detailed map.

Several extensive studies have been conducted on the critical elements of timetables by Bartram (1980) and Sprent, Bartram, and Crawshaw (1982). Subjects were given trip planning tasks and timed to completion. It was found that fewer errors were made using horizontal formats (where the bus stops are listed horizontally on the time table page) than vertical formats. The superiority of this format was explained as being more compatible because it followed "well-established population stereotypes."

These psychological studies assessing the function of public transit timetables evolve from many psychological theories and approaches. Theories and findings of perceptual psychology help determine the physical design parameters (e.g., print size) and user comprehension. Personality, social and developmental theories, and research could help assess which market segments (individuals) would be influenced by different information systems. Learning theory lends knowledge to how people understand a user information system and how this understanding can be enhanced (modified). Other literature such as the research on cognitive mapping of urban configurations (see Lynch, 1960, and Golledge, Chapter 5, this volume) should in the future add appropriate theoretical perspectives to the transit information problems.

As noted earlier, the management of employee behavior is also an important area in transportation management. Behavioral science contributions have been evident in strategies for employee selection (Baehr, Penny, & Fromel, 1980) and labor negotiations (Landy & Trumbo, 1980). Physiological and social perspectives were recently integrated in a review of the role of stress in determining the satisfaction transportation workers experience in their jobs (Spicher, 1982). This synthesis points to the multidimensional nature of the stress response as well as the need to strike a balance between selecting employees who can deal with stress on the one hand and modifying the environment on the other. Past work by Jacobs, Shapiro, and Ray (1983) suggests that variables such as changes in the size of an organizational unit will have a significant impact on the reduction of bus driver absenteeism. Large organizations tended to have much higher rates of absenteeism than small ones because, according to the authors, they lacked accountability and deindividualized the work place.

Learning theory and behavior change strategies have been broadly applied in a number of problem areas involving employees. An intercity bus carrier used reinforcement schedules to increase productivity among maintenance workers, and incentive programs have been used extensively among managers of large fleets to encourage safe driving. Feeney (1973) showed that incentives and feedback have significant impacts on the productivity of workers in the packaging department of Emery Air Freight. In work by Geller (1982), incentives were used to "manage" the seat belt usage of employees of a munitions plant. Incentives (an opportunity to win a lottery prize) increased seat belt usage 38% above baseline conditions, whereas general information and program awareness only yielded an 11% increase. Examples of learning theory applied to changing travel behavior are discussed later in Section 26.1.3, A Detailed Case Study.

There seems to be a fairly uniform, yet moderate, utilization of all psychological approaches to transportation management issues. This is probably the case because management is indeed an area that explicitly deals with behavior. A significant area of management—marketing—is even more directly linked to psychology, as the stated goal of marketing is to change behavior. Personality, social, and developmental approaches have been used to determine market segments and to develop marketing campaigns for these groups. An emerging area involves the use of physiological psychology to assess the impacts of advertising campaigns designed to market a transportation product or service. Consumer information, an important component of a public transportation marketing campaign, has begun to see contributions from all areas of psychology, yet for only the last 5 to 6 years. Issues of employee hiring and relations have received contributions from many areas of psychology (mainly personality and learning theory), and finally, learning theory has been applied to the task of changing consumer travel behaviors.

Although these psychological contributions to management are across the board and credible, many of the examples cited are new and need further attention (e.g., employee selection and satisfaction and travel behavior change strategies). The merging of psychology and transportation management will increase significantly as management requires more rigorous methods (evolving from behavior science theory and research) for dealing with management issues in an increasingly complex environment.

26.2.3. A Detailed Case Study—A Learning Theory Approach to Encourage Transit Patronage

The preceding section outlined, in brief form, the many and varied different types of psychological perspectives that have been applied to a variety of transportation issues. In this section of the chapter, a more detailed analysis of one psychological approach to a particular transportation issue will be addressed. Specifically, a review of how learning theory (reinforcement theory in particular) has been applied to the task of increasing the patronage of public transportation will be presented. This case study represents an application of learning theory to the transportation management section described previously.

Before reviewing the studies that specifically attempted to encourage the use of public transportation, it is appropriate to analyze from a reinforcement theory perspective why certain urban travel behaviors exist. Table 26.2 presents an overview of the analysis. The left-hand margin of the table is labeled *Behavior (Responses)*, and it has been divided into two subcategories. The first is "car driving" and the second is "using transit." The top margin of the table is labeled *Consequences Contingent on Behavior*, and it has also been divided into two categories. The first is "reinforcing" consequences, and the second is "punishing" consequences. In the cells of the table, numbered from 1 to 4, several consequences of a

Table 26.2. A Reinforcement Theory Model of Transit Ridership

Consequences Contingent on Behavior

	Reinforcing	Punishing
Car Driving	1. Short travel time Prestige Arrival/departure flexibility Exhilaration Privacy Route selection Cargo capacity Predictability Delayed costs	2. Congestion Gas and maintenance costs
Using Transit	3. Making friends Reading time	4. Exposure to weather Discomfort Noise Dirt Surly personnel Long walk to stops Danger (crime) Immediate costs Unpredictability Min. cargo capacity Min. route selection Crowded Min. arrival/departure flexibility Low prestige Long travel time

Behavior (Responses)

given behavior (car driving or using transit) have been listed. Although at this time these consequences have not been systematically documented and are simply placed here for the purpose of illustration, it is reasonably safe to assume that reality is fairly accurately portrayed.

As Table 26.2 illustrates, there are many reinforcing events contingent on car driving and few contingent on using public transportation. Conversely, few punishing consequences follow car driving, whereas the use of public transportation results in many. This table presents a psychological environment of reinforcers and punishers that most likely have a strong influence on car driving and the use of transit. It is interesting to note that this environment was probably not designed by psychologists but rather by engineers, politicians, and planners. But it is very much a psychological environment, and if it is desirable to reduce car driving and increase the use of transit, then this environment must be altered according to the principles of reinforcement theory.

A strategy for reducing the amount of car driving would be to decrease the number of reinforcing events contingent on car driving (Cell 1 consequences in Table 26.2) and to increase the punishing consequences (Cell 2). Similarly, the use of public transportation could be encouraged by increasing the number of reinforcing consequences (Cell 3) and by decreasing the punishing consequences (Cell 4) for using transit. If the situation allowed it and an individual and/or agency had the ability to manipulate the consequences in all the cells of Table 26.2, it would be advisable to favor certain types of strategies. It is the position taken in this chapter that the reduction of reinforcing consequences for car driving is not politically acceptable. Withdrawing reinforcing events constitutes a reduction in quality of life. Additionally, this strategy is a rather open-ended one, as there is no specificity as to what behavior might occur.

The allocation of more punishing events contingent on car driving is also not a favored manipulation. These Cell 2 manipulations have two problems. First, the design of a more punishing environment has both ethical and political problems. Second, punishment procedures specify which behavior should not occur, but there is no assurance of what behavior will occur as a result of implementing such a procedure. For example, a highway speed control program that utilizes increased ticketing of speeders promotes legal driving in the presence of police cars or radar traps. However, unspecified and indeed undesirable behaviors may be generated by a punishment procedure. Individuals may simply shift their travel from the interstate highways to the back roads where the likelihood of a ticket is much reduced. Similarly, other individuals may purchase a CB radio. Thus by their ability to pinpoint the location of the police, they can actually increase their highway speed when they are in another location. According to reinforcement theory, and indeed in reality, the establishment of a punishment procedure automatically sets up a negative reinforcement procedure—yet for behaviors that are unspecified. In other words, any behavior that avoids the punishing event (a speeding ticket), whether it is the purchase of a CB radio or driving on a backcountry road, is negatively reinforced.

The most favored manipulations for encouraging the use of public transportation and to discourage the use of private cars reside in Cells 3 and 4 of Table 26.2. The reduction in punishing consequences for public transit use is certainly a worthy strategy as it should be politically well received and indeed encourage appropriate behavior. It does, however, have a problem in that it does not specify exactly what behavior should occur. Cell 3 manipulations are the most preferred. The use of reinforcement is politically acceptable, as in reality it enhances the quality of life by making a more reinforcing environment. It is also theoretically the most appropriate because the reinforcing consequences can be made contingent on particular behaviors, thus assuring which behaviors would be increased.

An example of a study designed to increase the patronage of public transportation by reinforcing transit usage (Cell 3 manipulations) was carried out by Deslauriers and Everett in 1977. The target behavior of interest was patronage of a university campus bus system. Patrons were reinforced with a token on two different schedules of reinforcement (reinforcement for every rider or reinforcement on a random basis for an average of every third rider). These tokens could be exchanged (in various quantities) for discounts on a variety of merchandise in many of the local town's stores.

Figure 26.1 illustrates the results of this experiment. It was carried out using two types of controls

(control buses that were not treated during the experimental days and the ridership on the experimental buses during baseline conditions). During conditions of no token reinforcement, ridership stayed at control levels. However, during conditions of continuous reinforcement, a 27% ridership increase was realized, and when one out of every third rider (on a random basis) was reinforced, a 30% increase in ridership was obtained. The variable reinforcement schedule proved to be economically realistic. The ridership and fare box revenue gains in addition to the merchant contributions to the token exchange almost offset the management costs of running such a procedure.

Applications of the Deslauriers and Everett (1977) campus bus study have been extended to major urban areas. In the city of Spokane, Washington, patrons on the entire 100-bus system receive tokens that are redeemable for goods and services at over 200 business establishments in the Spokane regional area. The participating merchants bear the full cost of the token exchange in order to gain the marketing benefits of being involved in the program and as a mechanism to entice customers into their stores. Although ridership gains in the Spokane project have been minimal, the program has been called a success because of the tremendous involvement of the pri-

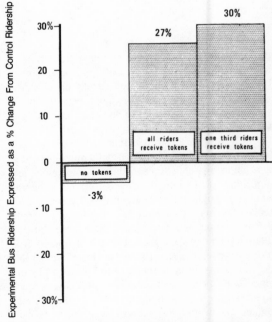

Figure 26.1. Changes in bus ridership under conditions of continuous reinforcement and variable reinforcement.

vate sector in providing public transportation marketing. It is estimated that the Spokane merchants are annually passing on to the patrons of the bus system over $200,000 of economic value in token exchange. This procedure may indeed have obviated a ridership decline in Spokane, one that many transit systems experienced in the early 1980s because of the decreasing price of gasoline for private cars.

The token reinforcement principle has also been implemented in Bridgeport, Connecticut, Seattle, Washington, and Portland, Oregon. These three cities operate a program that is somewhat different than that in Spokane. In Spokane, the reinforcement (the token) is contingent on boarding a bus and purchasing a single bus ride. In Seattle, Bridgeport, and Portland, the receipt of a token is contingent on purchasing a transit pass. In Bridgeport, a booklet of tokens (coupons) is included with the purchase of a monthly transit pass. In Seattle and Portland, the concept has been taken a bit further. The monthly transit pass also serves as the token, and it may be shown at a variety of business establishments in exchange for discounts. In other words, the monthly "flash pass" not only permits one to ride the bus in Seattle and Portland but also allows discounts on meals at a variety of restaurants, reduced fares at several movies, bargain rates at health spas, reduced ticket prices for the performing arts, and discounts at several retail establishments. As of 1985, the Seattle program has led to a 37% increase in pass sales. The Seattle and Portland experiences are unique in that they have attempted to make the program very much "upscale." A very overt attempt was made to have the "backup" reinforcers be clearly of high quality and prestigious. The restaurants involved are some of the cities' best, and the addition of the performing arts option was a very overt strategy. It is envisioned that more programs such as those in Spokane, Bridgeport, Portland, and Seattle will evolve as public and private agencies cooperate in an effort to solve urban problems. Indeed, just recently the State of New Jersey announced a merchant reimbursement to transit pass holders in the entire state and involving over 1800 retail establishments.

It is of paramount importance that these programs (such as in Spokane, Portland, and Seattle) be structured so that they foster "reciprocal reinforcement." In such an arrangement, all parties that are involved in a reinforcement program must receive benefits in relationship to their costs if one expects them to participate over the long run. In the example of these cities, each transit patron benefits by gaining upward to $100 per month of economic value at the establishments of the participating merchants. The transit system benefits by realizing increased ridership and, in turn, fare box revenues. And finally, the private sector benefits by the very tangible results of increased patronage and sales. Additionally, the private sector receives the less tangible results of a more vital urban area because of increased transit usage that promotes the reduction of air pollution, energy consumption, and congestion.

Examples of the effects of punishment removal on public transportation patronage are many. The most typical example involves the elimination of a transit fare. The booklet titled *Low Fare, Free Fare Transit* by Goodman and Green (1977) summarizes much of this work. Transit systems have typically offered free transit on all vehicles within a prescribed area of the city (commonly the central business district) for any time of the day or have offered free transit in the entire city during the less popular off-peak hours of the day. Ridership increases in these programs have been significant.

In a closely monitored experiment, Everett, Gurtler, and Hildebrand (1978) were able to increase ridership to 50% above baseline conditions by offering free transit. In another experiment, Everett, Deslauriers, Newsom, and Anderson (1978) found that the contingency between the receipt of free transit and the behavior of using transit was an important relationship. A control group was given 12 tickets for free bus rides. Two weeks later they were given 12 more tickets for free bus rides regardless of how many of the first tickets were used. However, for the treatment group, a second batch of 12 tickets was dependent on the rate of use of the first 12 tickets. For each ticket that the treatment group used of the original 12, they received an additional ticket within 2 weeks' time. The contingent "free transit" condition increased ridership to a level of 178% more than the noncontingent "free transit" control group.

The reinforcement theory approach to the task of increasing public transportation patronage is a relatively recent endeavor, and many additional avenues of exploration could prove profitable. It would be important to further examine the effects of various different parameters of reinforcement schedules. Additionally, very little research has been pursued as to the nature of reinforcement. Most of the studies cited here and those carried out in practice have manipulated only monetary reinforcers. It would be appropriate to pursue research that delineated the effects of other tangible reinforcers and intangible reinforcers such as "prestige" for using public transportation.

Another viable avenue of research involves determining the effects of modeling on public transportation ridership. It has been shown (Geller, Winett, & Everett, 1982) that modeling has had good successes in changing energy consumptive behaviors in the private home.

This section has been an attempt to outline in somewhat more detail how a particular area of psychology, reinforcement theory, has been applied to a particular transportation concern—that of increasing the patronage of public transportation. It is evident that there is a close relationship between this area of psychology and the needs of the transportation industry. As discussed before, many more applications of reinforcement theory to the task of increasing public transportation patronage could and should be explored. Additionally, there are many other areas of transportation that the principles of reinforcement theory could be applied to. For example, Geller (1982) has been investigating the effects of reinforcement principles on the use of seat belts. Some have suggested that reinforcement theory principles could be used for the control of traffic speeds. Still others have talked about the use of reinforcement principles for decreasing the consumption of gasoline by private automobiles during an energy shortage (see Foxx & Hake, 1977; Geller et al., 1982, for details). The opportunities are many, and they only need to be taken.

26.3. ASSESSMENT OF CURRENT AND POTENTIAL CONTRIBUTIONS OF PSYCHOLOGY TO TRANSPORTATION

Many different examples of the various types of psychological approaches to different transportation issues have been discussed. It is the purpose of this section of the chapter to give the reader an assessment of how well psychology is doing in its applications to transportation problems. This can best be carried out by first presenting Table 26.3. As in Table 26.1, the left-hand margin lists the various psychological approaches that were discussed in this chapter. The top margin lists the various, different transportation issues. In each of the cells, a sign has been placed that symbolizes the level of utilization, to date, of the various different psychological approaches. A *0* signifies that a given psychological approach was little used, *1* signifies moderate utilization, and *2* symbolizes much utilization.

As of this writing, the numbers that have been placed in the cells have not been empirically deter-

mined. They are merely an estimate of the authors' perceptions of the level of utilization of the various psychological approaches. Additionally, one could certainly debate whether or not the categories of transportation issues and/or psychological approaches are appropriate, complete, and/or redundant. It is admitted that further work is needed in order to develop a more valid table (26.3). Whatever the case, it stands as a valuable and instructive heuristic for understanding the current status of the utilization of psychology for dealing with transportation issues.

Physiological and perceptual psychologies have been used somewhat in transportation policy and planning but most used in vehicle and facility design. This high level of utilization for vehicle and facility design is primarily a result of the work carried out on human factors and vehicle design. Some applications of physiological and perceptual approaches have been made to management. Examples include applications to problems of worker stress and physiological approaches applied to the task of assessing the impact of a transportation marketing strategy.

Personality and social psychological approaches have been used most commonly in transportation policy and planning and management. The use of these approaches for policy and planning is typified by the survey research that is used for social impact assessment and demand modeling. This area of psychology has been routinely applied in the management area. Personality assessment is a very common way of judging employee "fit" for a certain type of transportation job. Fairly sophisticated testing batteries have been developed to assess whether an individual would make a good bus driver, airline pilot, and so forth. Personality and social psychologies have been used very little for facility and vehicle design.

Transportation marketing, a subarea of management, is the only area that has received a moderate amount of contributions from learning theory and behavior change strategies. The use of reinforcement theory strategies to change travel behaviors (outlined previously in this chapter) is a good example of how this psychological approach has been used. There is, however, a growing literature that illustrates how behavior change strategies have been used in other management areas. For example, Emery Air Freight (Feeney, 1973) developed a reinforcement procedure to increase worker productivity in the packaging section of their business, and United Airlines ("Productivity Gains," 1978) has used reinforcement procedures to increase airline ticket sales by their telephone agents.

Developmental approaches have been used pretty

Table 26.3. Matrix Illustrating the Utilization of Psychological Approaches to Transportation Issues.[a]

Transportation Issues

Psychological Approaches	Policy and Planning	Vehicle and Facility Design	Management
Physiological and Perceptual	1	2	1
Personality and Social	2	0	1
Learning Theory and Behavior Change	0	0	1
Developmental	1	1	1

[a]Numbers in the cells refer to the level of utilization to date: 0 = little utilization; 1 = moderate utilization; and 2 = much utilization.

much across the board for all transportation issues. This is the case because there is always the need to attend to different age groups regardless of the issue: policy and planning, vehicle and facility design, or management.

The question of whether the scores in each of the individual cells should be increased or decreased is an important one that deserves much thought and additional experience. However, at this point in time, the position is taken that the utilization for the entire table is somewhat low. Although Table 26.3 illustrates that psychology is moderately utilized, one must realize that this score is a result of reviewing primarily the transportation literature. If one were to review the "psychological abstracts" in order to determine the number of psychological studies that have focused on transportation behaviors versus other behaviors a totally different overview would result. In fact, without even embarking on this task, it would be a reasonable guess that there is proportionately little evidence of psychological contribution to transportation issues. It is indeed odd that the majority of psychologists have focused on minority behaviors (e.g., deviant behaviors) while avoiding such a common, everyday phenomenon as transportation behavior.

The field of transportation has also been slow in incorporating psychology. The reasons for this are threefold. First, the field of transportation was traditionally the purview of engineers (see section 26.1.2 on the history of transportation). The incorporation of psychological perspectives and the realized need for this orientation has been a recent phenomenon. Second, on the realization that transportation could benefit from a social science perspective, the transportation professionals first turned to the fields of economics and sociology. Transportation was viewed as a social behavior occurring in the aggregate, and accordingly aggregate theories of behavior were applied. Only recently have practitioners in the field realized that it might also be appropriate to gain an understanding of society's travel behaviors by analyzing the travel behaviors of individuals. This shift from an aggregate perspective to an individual perspective is evident by the change from aggregate demand modeling to the current interest in what is termed *disaggregate demand modeling* (see previous section on demand modeling). Finally, professionals in the field of transportation viewed behavior from a rather simplistic "mechanistic" model. Because of this orientation, they are often befuddled by the ambiguities and inability of psychology to accurately predict a behavior. This mechanistic perspective on human behavior is probably a result of the majority of professionals in transportation having an engineering background. This training is highly quantitative and yields an expectation of precision. This leads to a level of frustration when dealing with a field of study (psychology) that is less precise and indeed may never be as precise as engineering because of the difficulty of measuring such a complex phenomenon as human behavior.

In sum, the studies cited in this chapter show that there have been many psychological contributions to transportation issues over the past 15 to 20 years. Yet in the context of what psychology could contribute to areas such as social impact assessment, demand modeling, travel behavior change strategies, the transportation needs of different age groups, and so forth, the contributions are to date only a beginning. This slow start is in part due to psychology's focusing on more traditional areas of endeavor and the history and tradition of the transportation field that promoted a focus on the engineering and business aspects of a transportation undertaking. Now, however, as transportation issues have become much more complex, the perceived and real needs for multidisciplinary inputs are apparent. And psychology can make a significant input—especially in many areas that have not received much concentration. According to the perspectives presented in Table 26.3, transportation management issues could use additional input from psychology as well as attention from learning theory to policy and planning issues. A developmental perspective could be applied across many areas of transportation endeavors. For example, with the increase of working mothers, their transportation concerns are significant (Michelson, 1983).

26.4. INSTITUTIONAL BARRIERS, CAUTIONS, AND ADVICE

In order to facilitate the contributions of psychological theory and methods to transportation issues, a number of points are identified here that are intended to serve as cautions and advice to those embarking on such an endeavor.

26.4.1. Sensitivity to Transportation Priorities

Psychologists should be careful to maintain a particular sensitivity to the transportation field when determining application priorities. What may appear to be a particularly elegant application or an area ripe for theoretical development may not be an important area to the transportation manager. Because meaningful applications can only be achieved with the cooperation of practitioners, their priorities must be kept foremost in mind. If we are to achieve meaningful applications of behavioral science to transportation problems, it is encumbent on the participants to close this "applicability gap." Although this is a long-standing problem for behavioral scientists working in applied areas, researchers should recognize that public sector or corporate management is generally more constrained in the type of projects they can support. Their budget justifications need to be specific in regard to the benefits to be derived. Academics, on the other hand, may have more flexibility in choosing the transportation problems they address.

With the appropriate understanding of one another, the transportation practitioner and the behavioral science researcher can indeed join in an effort that deals with a significant social and environmental concern while simultaneously advancing behavioral science research methods, findings, and theory.

In assessing those areas that may be of high priority, one must understanding what benefits will accrue to the manager or political decision maker as well as to the transportation operation. Benefits should be considered for both the short term and long term. Applications with distant, intangible benefits are much less likely to be appreciated than those that address an immediate problem. Researchers should not be hesitant to participate in objective cost–benefit analyses in order to determine the worth of a project, nor should they feel that such an exercise is beyond their sense of academic purity. It is important, however, for psychologists to "stretch" the transportation practitioners' perspective a bit at times and demonstrate that an issue not previously perceived by them may indeed be an important area of concern. The work of Stokols and his colleagues (e.g., Stokols & Novaco, 1981) that documents the level of stress associated with commuting patterns is a good example. Previous to this work, little attention from the transportation field was given to this very important area.

At times, academic psychologists may have to accept the notion that many valuable applications may contribute only indirectly to the further understanding of environment–behavior phenomena. Those who see theory building as a main prerequisite for participation in real-world issues may find themselves limited at times to inconsequential problems.

Researchers should be prepared to see the academic benefits as field validation in a broad sense and not necessarily a large-scale, rigorous psychological experiment. Although the latter can often be achieved, it should be seen as a dispensable objective when the added burden imposed by the experiment risks the loss of management cooperation or increases the costs and effort to a level that does not justify the benefits. On the other hand, implementation of psychological strategies in a real-world, open-ended setting often leads to the most severe test of basic theory. This test, because of its severity, strengthens an understanding of theory and psychological phenomena.

Indeed, often a real-world application expands one's understanding of basic theory in a manner not possible in laboratory situations. New theoretical insights and perspectives are often gained. For example, in the reinforcement-based studies on bus ridership, it was observed that one of the most basic and broadly used incentive procedures for changing behavior involved the distribution of coupons to potential buyers. These coupons allowed a discount on a certain item, but reinforcement theory had no terminology for this procedure. It could be categorized as a "response cost reduction" procedure. A rather awkward name for such a common real-world implementation. Some work is needed to match reinforcement theory with reality. Coupon procedures are very widely used in retailing as an incentive. Yet reinforcement theory has no good term for it, nor has it reached its parameters.

The balance shows, at least to us, that applied research certainly has its costs in time, frustration, and so forth. But these are clearly minor, relative to the potential societal payoffs and possible improvements to basic behavioral science theory that results from good applied research.

26.4.2. Sensitivity to the Interdisciplinary Nature of the Field

It is advisable that psychologists also be sensitive to the fact that the transportation field is inherently interdisciplinary. Engineers, planners, economists, and business or public administrators typically hold well-established positions within the organizations in this field. What the behavioral scientist has come to see as his or her primary territory—human behavior—is generally seen by the other players as traditionally falling within their jurisdiction. For example, civil engineers have developed sophisticated mathematical models of behavior that attempt to predict whether an individual will choose to make a trip by transit or private auto based on social and demographic variables. Yet, for example, some psychologists provide a corresponding analysis that predicts the choice based on the relative magnitude of the reinforcers available. It is hoped that the most effective model will be an integration of the two perspectives.

Psychologists wishing to work in transportation must acknowledge the contributions of other professionals while educating them as to the potential of their own perspective in order to gain the trust necessary to work together harmoniously and productively. Indeed, psychologists have had a good history of interdisciplinary endeavors in dealing with applied problems. This orientation will certainly help them with a field as multifaceted as transportation.

Psychologists may play a wide range of roles within the transportation field. On the most overt end of the continuum, psychologists may act as consultants to management. In this role, they must appreciate that those with whom they will be dealing are likely to be engineers or business administrators who may not fully understand the perspective of the behavioral scientist. In this respect, a certain amount of self-marketing or selling is in order.

On the other end of the continuum, psychologists can participate through outside groups who promote the cause of the user through political channels. In this way, the astute psychologist can help the group propose workable, effective ways of achieving their goals through behaviorally oriented solutions to problems that transportation management also want solved. From this vantage point, the psychologist can be effective in advocating socially desirable behavior and in promoting behavioral solutions to environment problems.

26.5. POSTSCRIPT

Many areas of application for psychology to transportation have not been discussed at all in this chapter (e.g., space travel), whereas other areas have received only brief mention (e.g., social impact assessment). Transportation is a tremendously broad field, so the intent of this chapter has been to highlight some of the areas of application. The picture is certainly broader than what was presented here. It is hoped, as a result of this brief review, that the reader has a feel for the full range of possible nodes at which psychology and transportation may join.

The sum total of the psychological contributions to transportation constitute an environmental psychological approach. Environmental psychology is not a particular theory or set of theories but many perspectives of psychology applied to "real-world physical environmental" problems. Transportation is a real-world physical environmental phenomenon that provides an excellent context for environmental psychology. Indeed, starting with much of the human factors work and transportation safety, psychology has been contributing to transportation long before the term *environmental psychology* was coined. But as psychology has broadened, a multiperspective, multitheory area such as environmental psychology has evolved over the past 15 to 20 years and as transportation issues and concerns are clearly perceived as complex and needing inputs beyond the physical, the technical, and the managerial, the joining of psychology and transportation provides many opportunities for future research and application. Although many areas of transportation have received significant contributions from psychology (e.g., human factors of vehicle design), some have hardly been addressed at all (e.g., learning theory contributions to policy and planning, personality and social contributions to vehicle and facility design, and a developmental perspective to all areas of transportation). The opportunities are apparent, and it is our perspective that the transportation field welcomes the contribution.

Psychology is certainly a broad field, ranging from studies of brain chemistry to the assessment of worker performance. Yet transportation is a broader field, ranging from highway construction to space flight financing. Thus the task of relating the two in a comprehensive manner has endless boundaries and perhaps was an overly ambitious task for this chapter. It was decided at the outset, however, to discuss some examples of psychological contributions to transportation rather than exhaustive or even uniformly representative ones. In many cases, our bias toward urban public transportation was evident. Whatever the case, a "snapshot" has been presented. This view was taken from the framework presented in Table 26.1 that lists four psychological approaches to three transportation issue areas. As is the case for the examples we have given, one may take issue with this framework. But it is nevertheless one that provides a useful heuristic for organizing the joining of these two fields. It also may provide, at a future date, the basis for developing a conceptual framework for relating behavior to transportation. At this time, no comprehensive framework exists, only the many separate psychological perspectives applied to particular transportation problems. Indeed, it is time to gain a broader understanding of the past and potential merging of these fields. It is hoped that this attempt will facilitate such an effort.

REFERENCES

Appleyard, D. (1979). Transportation as a social environment. In P. Stringer & H. Wenzel (Eds.), *Transportation planning for a better environment*. New York: Plenum.

Baehr, M.E., Penny, R.E., & Fromel, E.C. (1980). *Validation and analysis of selection procedures for male and female bus operators* (UMTA-MA-06—0011-77-1). Washington, DC: Urban Mass Transportation Administration.

Baldassare, M. (1981). The effects of a modern rapid-transit system on nearby residents: A case study of BART in the San Francisco Area. In I. Altman, J.F. Wohlwill, & P.B. Everett (Eds.), *Transportation and behavior* (pp. 203–238). New York: Plenum.

Bartram, D.J. (1980). Comprehending spatial information: The relative efficiency of different methods of presenting information about bus routes. *Journal of Applied Psychology, 65*(1), 103–110.

Beck, R. (1984). *Designing for passenger information needs*. Paper presented at the annual meeting of the Transportation Research Board, Washington, DC.

Bronzaft, A.L., Dobrow, S.B., & O'Hanlon, T.J. (1976). Spatial orientation in a subway system. *Environment and Behavior, 8*(4), 575–594.

Chermajeff, P. (1968). Orientation in the transit environment. *Journal of the Franklin Institute, 286*(5), 477–490.

Childhood City Newsletter. (1981, August). No. 2.

Cohen, S., Evans, G.W., Krantz, D.S., & Stokols, D. (1980). Physiological, motivational and cognitive effects of aircraft noise on children. *American Psychologist, 35*, 231–243.

Collins, B.L. (1982). *The development and evaluation of effective symbol signs* (NBS Building Science Series 141). Washington, DC: National Bureau of Standards.

Craik, K.H. (1969). Transportation and the person. *High Speed Ground Transportation Journal, 3*(1), 86–91.

Crook, M.A., & Langdon, F.J. (1974). The effect of aircraft noise on schools in the vicinity of London Airport. *Journal of Sound and Vibration, 34*, 241–248.

Dart, O.K. (1977). Effects of the 88.5 km/h (55 mph) speed limit and its enforcement on traffic speeds and accidents. *Transportation Research Record, 643*, 23–32.

Davis, M., & Levine, S. (1967). Toward a sociology of public transit. *Social Problems, 15*(1), 84–91.

Deslauriers, B.C., & Everett, P.B. (1977). Effects of intermittent and continuous token reinforcement on bus ridership. *Journal of Applied Psychology, 62*, 369–375.

Dewar, R.E., Ells, J.G., & Cooper, P.J. (1977, June). Evaluation of roadway guide signs at a large airport. *Transport Engineering*, pp. 19–23.

Dobson, R., Golob, T.F., & Gustafson, R.L. (1974). Multidimensional scaling of consumer preferences for a public transportation system: An application of two approaches. *Socio-Economic Planning Sciences, 8*, 23–26.

Dureman, E.I., & Boden, C. (1972). Fatigue in simulated car driving. *Ergonomics, 15*, 299–308.

Everett, P.B., Anderson, V.B., & Makranczy, U. (1977). Transit route pamphlets: Do they work? *Transit Journal, 3*, 59–79.

Everett, P.B., Deslauriers, B.C., Newsom, T., & Anderson, V.B. (1978). The differential effect of two free ride dissemination procedures on bus ridership. *Transportation Research, 12*, 1–7.

Everett, P.B., Gurtler, M.D., & Hildebrand, M.G. (1978). *Free transit: How much—How long?* Unpublished manuscript, Pennsylvania State University, University Park.

Feeney, R. (1973, Winter). At Emery Air Freight: Positive reinforcement boosts performance. *Organizational Dynamics*, pp. 41–50.

Feldman, L.P., & Vellenga, D.B. (1977). The role of security in marketing urban mass transportation. *High Speed Ground Transportation Journal, 11*(2), 157–172.

Foxx, R.M., & Hake, D.F. (1977). Gasoline conservation: A procedure for measuring and reducing the driving of college students. *Journal of Applied Behavior Analysis, 10*, 61–74.

Fried, M. (1963). Grieving for a lost home. In L.J. Duhl (Ed.), *The urban condition.* New York: Basic Books.

Fulton, E.J., & Stroud, P.G. (1981). Ergonomic design of ticket barriers for use by the travelling public. *Applied Ergonomics, 12*(4), 203–207.

Galer, I.A.R. (1979). The role of psychology in the design and evaluation of transport systems. *Ergonomics, 22*(2), 129–133.

Garland, H.C. Haynes, J.J., & Grubb, G.C. (1979). Transit map color coding and street detail: Effects on trip planning performance. *Environment and Behavior, 11,* 162–184.

Geehan, T.E., & Deslauriers, B.C. (1978). Transit route guides—An investigation and analysis. *Bus Ride, 14,* 56–58.

Geller, E.S. (1982). Rewarding safety belt usage at an industrial setting; Tests of treatment generality and response maintenance. *Journal of Applied Behavior Analysis, 15*(2), 375–406.

Geller, E.S., Winett, R.A., & Everett, P.B. (1982). *Preserving the environment: New strategies for behavior change.* New York: Pergamon.

Glass, D.C., & Singer, J.E. (1972). *Urban stress.* New York: Academic.

Golob, T.F., Canty, E.T., & Gustafson, R.L. (1972). An analysis of consumer preferences for a public transportation system. *Transportation Research, 6,* 81–102.

Golob, T.F., Horowitz, A.D., & Wachs, M. (1979). Attitude-behavior relationships in travel demand modeling. In D.A. Hensher & P.R. Stopher (Eds.), *Behavioural travel modeling.* London: Croom Helm.

Goodman, K.M., & Green, M.A. (1977). *Low fare, free fare transit* (NTIS 52-0002-77-1). Washington, DC: Urban Mass Transportation Administration.

Gutman, R. (1968). Urban transporters as human environments. *Journal of the Franklin Institute, 286*(5), 533–541.

Hall, R.W. (1983). Traveler route choice: Travel time implications of improved information and adaptive decisions. *Transportation Research, 17a*(3), 201–214.

Harris, W., & Mackie, R.R. (1972, March). *A study of the relationships among fatigue, hours of service, and safety of operations of truck and bus drivers* (Rep. No. BMCS-RD-71-2). Goleta, CA: Human Factors Research.

Hartgen, D.T. (1978). *Applications of behavioral sciences to issues in transportation planning.* Albany: New York State Department of Transportation, Planning and Research Unit.

Hartgen, D.T. (1981). Transportation and the behavioral sciences. In I. Altman, J.F. Wohlwill, & P.B. Everett (Eds.), *Transportation and behavior.* New York: Plenum.

Hauer, E., & Cooper, P.J. (1977). Effectiveness of selective enforcement in reducing accidents in metropolitan Toronto. *Transportation Research Record, 643,* 18–22.

Houg, T.G. (1982). Children in traffic. *H Transport og Velferd, 10,* 1–14.

Jacobs, R.R., Shapiro, K.L., & Ray, W.J. (1983). *Operator absence in the transit industry* (UMTA-Pa-11-0028-83-1). Washington, DC: Urban Mass Transportation Administration.

Kogi, K. (1979) Passenger requirements and ergonomics in public transit. *Ergonomics, 22*(6), 631–639.

Kotler, P. (1976). *Marketing management: Analysis, planning and control.* Englewood Cliffs, NJ: Prentice-Hall.

Kreindler, M.L. (1979). *The applicability of behavior theory to transportation.* Paper presented at the annual meetings of the Transportation Research Board, Washington, DC.

Landy, F.J., & Trumbo, D.A. (1980). *Psychology of work behavior.* Homewood, IL: Dorsey.

Leibowitz, H.W., & Owens, D.A. (1977). Nighttime driving accidents and selective visual degradation. *Science, 197,* 422–423.

Lepper, R., & Moorhead, R. (1970). Urban transit vehicle design ride satisfaction. In J. Archea and C. Eastman (Eds.). *EDRA Two, Proceedings of the Second Annual Environmental Design Research Association Conference* (pp. 182–191). Stroudsburg, PA: Dowden, Hutchinson, & Ross.

Levin, I.P. (1979). The development of attitudinal modeling approaches in transportation research. In D.A. Hensher & P.R. Stopher (Eds.), *Behavioural travel modeling.* London: Croom Helm.

Levin, I.P., & Louviere, J.J. (1981). Psychology and travel demand modeling. In I. Altman, J.F. Wohlwill, & P.B. Everett (Eds.), *Transportation and behavior.* New York: Plenum.

Llewellyn, L.G. (1981). Social cost of urban transportation. In I. Altman, J.F. Wohlwill, & P.B. Everett (Eds.), *Transportation and behavior.* New York: Plenum.

Llewellyn, L.G., Bunten, E., Goodman, C., Hare, R., Mach, R., & Swisher, R. (1975). The role of social impact assessment in highway planning. *Environment and Behavior, 7,* 285–306.

Lundberg, U. (1976). Urban commuting: Crowdedness and catecholamine excretion. *Journal of Human Stress, 2,* 26–32.

Lynch, K. (1960). *The image of the city.* Cambridge, MA: MIT Press.

Mackett-Stout, J., & Dewar, R. (1981). Evaluation of symbolic information signs. *Human Factors, 23*(2), 139–151.

Mackie, R.R., & Miller, J.C. (1978). *Effects of hours of service, regularity of schedules, and cargo loading on truck and bus driver fatigue* (DOT-HS-5-01142 and NTIS PB 78-290957). Goleta, CA: Human Factors Research.

McCauley, C., Coleman, G., & DeFusco, P. (1977). Commuters' eye contact with strangers in city and suburban train stations: Evidence of short-term adaption to interpersonal overload in the city. *Environmental Psychology and Non-Verbal Communications, 2,* 215–225.

McCormick, E.J. (1976). *Human factors in engineering and design.* New York: McGraw-Hill.

McDonald, N. (1984). *Fatigue, safety and the truck driver.* London, New York: Taylor and Francis.

Michaels, R.M. (1980). Applications of behavioral science to transportation. In R.M. Michaels (Ed.), *Transportation planning and policy making: Behavioral science contributions.* New York: Praeger.

Michelson, W. (1983). *The impact of changing women's roles on transportation needs and usage* (UMTA-CA-11-0024-84-1 and NTIS PB 84-182591). Washington, DC: Urban Mass Transportation Administration.

Milgram, S. (1970). The experience of living in cities. *Science, 167,* 1461–1468.

Moore, C.B. (1982). *Travel patterns and transit needs of women* (Vol. 1, UMTA-DC-06-0282-83-1 and NTIS PB 84-139716). Washington, DC: Urban Mass Transportation Administration.

Mourant, R.R., & Rockwell, T.H. (1970). Mapping eye-movement patterns to the visual scene in driving: An exploratory study. *Human Factors, 12,* 81–88.

Nicolaidis, G.C. (1975). Quantification of the comfort variable. *Transportation Research, 9,* 55–66.

Office of Civil Rights. (1982). *Travel patterns and transit needs of women.* Washington, DC: Urban Mass Transportation Administration.

Olsen, R.A. (1981). Human factors engineering and highway safety. In I. Altman, J.F. Wohlwill, & P.B. Everett (Eds.), *Transportation and Behavior* (pp. 131–167). New York: Plenum.

Olson, J.C., & Ray, W.J. (1983). *Using brainwave measures to assess advertising effectiveness* (Working Paper 83-108). Boston: Marketing Science Institute.

Osborne, D.J. (1978). Techniques available for the assessment of passenger comfort. *Applied Ergonomics, 9*(1), 45–49.

Pagano, A.M., McKnight, C., & Dichter-Figurea, M. (1983, May). *Quality of service in special transportation for the elderly and handicapped* (UMTA-IL-11-0028-83-2 and NTIS PB83-255604). Chicago: University of Illinois, Urban Transportation Center.

Patterson, A.H., & Ralston, P.A. (1983). *Fear of crime and fear of public transportation among the elderly* (UMTA-PA-11-0026-84-1 and NTIS PB84-145739). Washington, DC: Urban Mass Transportation Administration.

Pearce, P.L. (1980). Strangers, travelers and Greyhound terminals: A study of small-scale helping behaviors. *Journal of Personality and Social Psychology, 38*(6), 935–940.

Pratsch, L. (1975, January). *Carpool and buspool matching guide* (4th ed.). Washington, DC: Federal Highway Administration.

Productivity gains from a pat on the back. (1978, January 23). *BusinessWeek,* 56–57.

Richards, L.G., & Jacobson, I.D. (1975). Ride quality evaluation I: Questionnaire studies of airline passenger comfort. *Ergonomics, 18,* 129–150.

Richards, L.G., & Jacobson, I.D. (1977). Ride quality assessment I: Questionnaire results of a second flight programme. *Ergonomics, 20,* 499–519.

Rose, H.S., & Hinds, D.H. (1976). South Dixie Highway contraflow bus and car-pool lane demonstration project. *Transportation Research Record, 606,* 18–22.

Shinar, D., McDowell, E.D., & Rockwell, T.H. (1977). Eye-movements in curve negotiations. *Human Factors, 19,* 63–71.

Singer, J.E., Lundberg, U., & Frankenhauser, M. (1978). Stress on the train: A study of urban commuting. In A. Baum, J. Singer, & S. Valins (Eds.), *Advances in environmental psychology* (Vol. 1). Hillsdale, NJ: Erlbaum.

Smerk, G. (1974). *Urban mass transportation: A dozen years of federal policy.* Bloomington: Indiana University Press.

Spicher, R.E. (1982). *Review of literature related to bus operator stress* (NCTRP Rep. 33-1). Washington, DC: Transportation Research Board.

Sprent, N., Bartram, D., & Crawshaw, C.M. (1982). Intelligibility of bus timetables. In D.J. Osborne & J.A. Levis (Eds.), *Human factors in transport research.* London: Academic.

Stilitz, I.B. (1969). The role of static pedestrian groups in crowded spaces. *Ergonomics, 12*(6), 821–839.

Stokols, D. (1972). On the distinction between density and crowding: Some implications for future research. *Psychological Review, 79,* 275–278.

Stokols, D. (1976). The experience of crowding in primary and secondary environments. *Environment and Behavior, 8,* 49–86.

Stokols, D., & Novaco, R.W. (1981). Transportation and well-being. In I. Altman, J.F. Wohlwill, & P.B. Everett (Eds.), *Transportation and behavior.* New York: Plenum.

Wichansky, A.M. (1979). *The effects of the ride environment on intercity train passenger activities.* Paper presented at the annual meetings of the Transportation Research Board, Washington, D.C

Yancey, L.L. (1972). *Psychological factors affecting urban travel: Responses to crowding in transit vehicles* (PB-215-625). Tallahassee, FL: Florida State University, Transportation Centre.

Chapter 27

MANAGEMENT OF NATURAL ENVIRONMENTS

David G. Pitt, *Department of Horticulture, University of Maryland, College Park, Maryland*

Ervin H. Zube, *School of Renewable Natural Resources, University of Arizona, Tucson, Arizona*

27.1. DEFINITIONS AND DIRECTIONS

Throughout much of American history the concept of natural environment has been synonymous with wilderness. Wilderness was the medium from which an economic livelihood was wrested; it was a frontier to be conquered, and at times, it was a source of aesthetic and spiritual inspiration. In both a historical and contemporary perspective, the wilderness connotation of natural environment has been defined largely by exclusion to include "the vast domain of organic and inorganic matter that is not a product of human activity or intervention" (Wohlwill, 1983, p. 7).

As environmental settings for human behavior or as objects of attraction to an individual, the connotation of natural environments as large areas that are unadorned with intruding human artifacts can be distinguished from human-made environments into which nature or natural elements have been introduced. In large part, the distinction rests with the perceptions, intentions, and expectations of individuals as they engage in activities in the two types of settings (Wohlwill, 1983). For example, as much as in any other city in the United States, Washington, DC, is a city of trees and natural elements. Yet few Washingtonians would equate their perceptions of the behavioral settings found in the District of Columbia with their perceptions of settings found in state and national park and forest systems in the adjacent states of Maryland and Virginia.

The discussion of environmental management presented in this chapter focuses on the social and behavioral issues inherent in the management of those natural environments in which humans are more of a visitor than an ever-present force (including but not limited to officially designated wilderness areas). Other chapters in this volume (e.g., Slovic, Fischhoff, Svenson, & Slovic, Chapter 29; Little, Chapter 7; Craik & Feimer, Chapter 23) address various aspects of the social and behavioral implications of nature in the built environment. And the role of nature in the urban context has been reviewed elsewhere (R. Kaplan, 1983).

Emphasis is also placed in this chapter on those social and behavioral issues that have evolved out of management of natural environments contained within the federal estate in the United States. This emphasis reflects the fact that policies adopted for the management of natural environments within the federal domain have often set the stage for the subsequent adoption of management policies on other public lands and occasionally on private land. For example, state activity in the preservation of large natural areas as state parks did not emerge until after federal policies toward national parks had evolved. The development of state agencies to manage state-owned land did not occur until after the Forest Service had emerged within the U.S. Department of Agriculture as the lead agency responsible for managing the resources within what is now the National Forest System.

Much of this chapter focuses on an examination of the social and behavioral causes and implications of public policy for the management of natural environments. Policy is "a purposive course of action followed by an actor or set of actors in dealing with a problem or matter of concern" (Anderson, 1979, p. 3). It involves a pattern of behavior over time. The pattern of behaviors inherent in any public policy both affect and are affected by elements in the sociopolitical environment within which the policy is cast. Policies that manipulate natural environments for various purposes express normative values of concerned and involved actors with respect to objects and systems in the natural environment.

In addition to being a manifestation of publicly held values and perceptions toward the natural environment, public policy also serves as an administrative framework that guides the implementation of on-the-ground management practices. For example, a decision to alter the density and diversity of vegetative species within a specific environment, such that the growth and development of commercially valuable trees are favored, reflects a particular balance of values and perceptions. Among the different types of values that might have flowed from alternative uses of this specific environment, a balance has been struck that favors economic use of the vegetation to provide wood and fiber products. This balance reflects physical properties of the environment, the social context within which these physical properties exist, various perceptions of the socioeconomic values these properties possess, and the ability of various political interest groups to manipulate the value-balancing process in their favor. Once the balance is struck, it sets the stage for implementation of management practices (e.g., clear cutting or thinning the stand). The implementation of such management practices may substantially alter the structure and function of the natural environment either as a setting for human behavior or as an object of attraction to the individual. Thus a central theme throughout this chapter involves an examination of the interaction between the values and behaviors implied by public policy for the management of natural environments and the values and behaviors that are perceived or that actually occur in natural environments.

Changes in policy reflect changes in the perception and imagery used to describe natural environments. A late nineteenth-, early twentieth-century feud between Gifford Pinchot and John Muir focused on differing perceptions of natural environment and set the stage for much of the conservation-versus-preservation policy conflicts that have characterized management of natural environments in the United States during the twentieth century. Muir's transcendentalist perspective assigned to natural environments certain religious and aesthetic qualities that produced beneficial effects on those who allow the power of nature to overshadow themselves (Petulla, 1977, p. 232). Pinchot's utilitarian perspective viewed the natural environment as the bestower of natural resources that are to be used to accomplish the inherently contradictory goal of providing "the greatest good for the greatest number for the longest time" (Dana & Fairfax, 1980, p. 1).

Running parallel to the evolution of environmental imagery during the last three centuries, dramatic increases in world population and per-capita resource consumption in the developed nations have also profoundly influenced the development of public policy for the management of natural environments. Although natural environments contain components that are renewable flow resources (e.g., vegetation, water), the environment, itself, as a setting for human behavior or as an object of attraction to the individual is generally conceptualized as a stock resource whose supply is finite and whose rate of replacement is beyond the control of humans. The psychological aspects of scarcity and the management of scarce environmental resources in a scenario of rising demands for a finite supply of resources are discussed elsewhere in this volume (see Oskamp & Stern, Chapter 28).

The combined effects of an expanded and more diverse imagery associated with natural environments, an increasing population growth rate, and an increasing rate of per-capita consumption have resulted in a larger group of more diverse individuals demanding an increasingly more complex array of final goods and services from the natural environment. Individuals using natural environments are no longer from a single or small number of demographic or socioeconomic sectors of society. Similarly, the intentions and expectations of users with respect to natural environments now range from the harvesting or extraction of renewable and nonrenewable resources for economic gain to passive enjoyment of aesthetic values in natural environments.

The exploration of the environmental management implications of this increasing growth and diversification of uses and groups of users serves as an organizational theme for the remaining portions of this chapter. The growth and diversification of uses and user groups have produced a range of environmental management policy eras in the United States that varies from an initial stage of land disposal and environmental exploitation through landscape preservation, conservation, multiple use and reclamation of abused environments to a broadly based concept of environmental planning and management.

The first part of this chapter examines each policy era in more detail; it explores the prevailing environmental perceptions that helped shape policy, examines the range of uses and user groups whose values were reflected in a public policy during each era, and evaluates the impact of each era's policies on natural environments as settings for human behavior or objects of attractions. Subsequently, the conflicting environmental values and aspirations that are brought to the management arena are examined. Conflict is examined first as it exists among different types of groups and individuals who use natural environments and second as it exists between the values and perceptions of users and those professionals responsible for managing natural environments. Partly as a by-product of managers' inability to accommodate the range of environmental perceptions held by diverse groups of users, a concomitant increased demand for involvement of concerned publics in management decision making has drastically altered the way managers go about their jobs of managing natural environments. The emergence and growth of public involvement in the management of natural environments is examined as a technique for broadening the range of values considered in management decision making and assisting managers as they attempt to balance the conflicting and often incompatible demands being placed on natural environments.

Management of natural environments in the twentieth century has been most profoundly marked by the desire, and later the necessity, to consider environmental values that are not directly associated with the consumption of a specific commodity. This noncommodity orientation includes recreational use value, aesthetic value, and wildlife values not directly associated with hunting and fishing. Aspects of the nonconsumptive orientation toward use and management of natural environments explored in the final sections of this chapter include the identification of aesthetic values, management of recreational behavior within constraints imposed by the environment's carrying capacity, and management of deviant and depreciative behaviors in natural environments.

27.2. ERAS OF ENVIRONMENTAL MANAGEMENT: PUBLIC POLICY REFLECTIONS OF CHANGING ENVIRONMENTAL VALUES AND PERCEPTIONS

27.2.1. Disposal

For nearly the first 100 years of the country's existence, the primary land management objective was disposal of public lands. The new nation was land-rich and money-poor. It had incurred a substantial debt in financing the Revolutionary War. Land sales provided a feasible means of raising money to pay off this debt. Land grants were made to the states and railroads and for canal projects to stimulate development of large sparsely or uninhabited sections of the country. The Homestead and cognate acts, starting in 1862, stimulated settlement and promoted an agrarian economy (Coggins & Wilkinson, 1981). The pervasive policy of land disposal provided unlimited opportunities for exploitation of other land-based resources. Attitudes of "consume the resource" and "move on to conquer new lands" prevailed. From the earliest years of the nation, the availability of plentiful and cheap land provided no incentive for conservation-oriented behavior in agricultural practices. Agricultural and grazing practices that ignored soil conservation measures prevailed throughout the period of the Homestead Acts leading to degradation and destruction of tens of thousands of acres (Petulla, 1977, p. 284).

A prime example of such land abuse is the "tragedy of the commons" (Hardin, 1968) on grazing lands in the West. Without public land management policies, it was in each rancher's interest to graze as many cattle as possible leading to overstocking, widespread degradation of plant cover and soils, and intensified violence among competitors for the same grazing lands. It was not until the enactment of the Taylor Grazing Act of 1934 that control was exercised on the prevailing abusive uses of unreserved and unappropriated federal lands.

27.2.2. Preservation

Several important events took place in the decade following the Civil War that signaled changing attitudes toward management of natural environments and in particular to the depreciative behaviors associated with the era of resource exploitation. George Perkins Marsh, in his seminal work *Man and Nature*, published in 1864, cautioned that "man

has too long forgotten that the earth was given to him for usufruct alone, not for consumption, still less for profligate waste" (1864, p. 36). Marsh, a widely traveled New Englander, had observed the effects of humans' long-term habitation and abuse of the Mediterranean landscape. He called for scientific management of forests that protected natural processes and that recognized natural environments as integrated systems. In the second edition, published in 1874, Marsh suggested designating large tracts of land to be preserved as public parks. His book was widely read in the United States and Europe and contributed to the cause of scientific forest management in America during the 1870s and 1880s.

Coincidental with the publication of *Man and Nature* in 1864, Congress ceded Yosemite Valley to the State of California to be preserved for public use and enjoyment. This action was followed in 1872 by the establishment of Yellowstone National Park, the first national park in America and the world. Preservation of these unique landscapes indicated a growing awareness among a small group of influential individuals of the need to address a broader array of resource values than had been the practice in the past. These landscapes also served as symbols of national pride. America lacked the cultural achievements of Europe, symbolized by its monuments and buildings, and found in Yellowstone and subsequent parks such as Sequoia, Mount Rainier, and General Grant symbols of greatness that, when compared with counterpart landscapes in Europe, could be described as bigger, better, and more majestic. Nevertheless, economic values could not be ignored in seeking authorization for national parks. It was necessary to convince Congress that these landscapes were not only outstandingly beautiful and unique within the world but also essentially worthless for realizing economic gain (Runte, 1979, pp. 48–51). The value conflicts between commodity and noncommodity interests that prevail today have a long history.

The National Park Service was created in 1916 to manage a growing number of parks and monuments and was charged with responsibility "to conserve the scenery and the natural and historic objects and wildlife therein and to provide for the enjoyment of the same in such a manner and by such a means as will leave them unimpaired for the enjoyment of future generations" (Dana & Fairfax, 1980, p. 109). This action set forth a continuing and inherently conflicting management dilemma of preserving resources while providing for user enjoyment.

In less than a century, the perceptions of wildlife as an economic resource to provide food for the table shifted and encompassed aesthetic, existence, recreational, and scientific values. A national Wildlife Refuge System was established in 1966. The Endangered Species Act of 1973 provided a powerful tool for the preservation of all wildlife, plants, and animals and dramatized an impressive shift in public perceptions of wildlife.

The Wilderness Act of 1964 was promoted by preservationists and recreationists who became distrustful of professional managers' and agencies' management practices on designated wilderness areas and their failure to subject management decisions to public review. Opponents of the wilderness block tended to represent local or western grazing, lumber, power, mining, and irrigation interests and viewed the act as "locking up" valuable resources. Proponents tended to represent national interests with a strong urban, eastern orientation. The final bill represented a compromise between preservation and economic development interests. The debate over wilderness designation has continued, however, throughout the several inventory and review processes of these roadless areas on public lands.

27.2.3. Conservation

Marsh's concern for proper forest management began to be recognized in the United States by the end of the nineteenth century. Pinchot, who became chief of the Division of Forestry in 1898, embarked on an aggressive program of conservation aimed at timber production and watershed management. The conservation movement, with which Pinchot was strongly associated, was promoted by leaders in science and related professions and drew on European concepts of scientific forest management. Wise use and scientific management were the mottoes. Pinchot also introduced the concept of multiple use, trying to accommodate grazing interests along with timber production and watershed protection.

The conservation movement was a reaction to the abusive behavior toward the natural environment of the preceding century. It marked a major shift in public policy away from land disposal to an emphasis on the establishment of reservations with the initiation of a cadre of professional managers and the beginnings of scientific management of natural environments. The policy of reservation was not without debate. Strong opposition was voiced by western states with interests in timber, grazing, minerals, and water during Theodore Roosevelt's term as president. Professional management was frequently viewed as an infringement on users' rights and as an attempt to

lock up the resources. Debate has continued, off and on over the years, with the most recent going under the rubric of the "Sagebrush Rebellion." Among the supporters of the rebellion were the same interests that voiced opposition during Roosevelt's time.

27.2.4. Multiple Use

Increased mobility of the American public in post-World War II years brought about increased demands for outdoor recreation in national and state parks and forests. The task of "conserving the scenery" in national parks was made more difficult as more and more persons used lands that were not managed for such intensive recreational uses and thus contributed to their degradation. The multiple-use management concept of Pinchot that addressed commodity values of timber, grazing, and water in the national forests and that was predominately under the purview of professionals was expanded by public demand to include noncommodity values including recreation, scenery, wilderness, and wildlife. Enactment of the Multiple Use and Sustained Yield Act of 1960 provided the Forest Service with statutory authority to manage forestlands for this broadened array of resource values. However, the managers had little training or experience in managing these new resource values.

Controversies between national forest managers and local populations during the 1960s and 1970s about clear-cutting of timber, notably on the Bitterroot National Forest in Montana and the Monogahela National Forest in West Virginia led to the enactment of the National Forest Management Act of 1976 (NFMA). Local concerns about damage to fishing streams, impaired scenic vistas, harm to wildlife, and soil erosion prompted citizens groups to call for investigations of forest management practices (Robinson, 1975). Investigations of the allegations concluded there had been inadequate multiple-use planning, inattention to road construction, landscape design, and wildlife needs, and lack of attention to public needs and discussions of those needs. The NFMA now mandates land-use planning and public involvement in developing plans.

27.2.5. Recreation

The Outdoor Recreation Resources Review Commission (1962) was established by Congress in 1958 in response to a growing urban population's demands for greater access to and use of natural environments. The commission studied the outdoor recreation wants and needs of the American people, determined the availability of resources to satisfy those needs, and recommended policies and programs. Of particular significance here are the recommendations that led in 1968 to the enactment of the Recreation and Scenic Trails System and the Wild and Scenic Rivers Systems Acts. Managers of these resources were not only confronted with the use–preservation dilemma but also with mixed ownership problems, including providing access through private lands to public areas.

27.2.6. Natural Beauty

Another significant shift in policy was signaled in President Johnson's message to Congress of February 8, 1965. Johnson called for a conservation movement that went beyond the classical concepts of protection and development and included "a creative conservation of restoration and innovation." He called for a conservation that was not concerned with nature alone "but with the total relationship between man and the world around him." This address marked the beginning of the Johnson Administration's natural beauty program, a program that went well beyond efforts to protect areas of natural beauty and addressed landscape reclamation programs, highway design, billboard and automobile junkyard control, parks and open space, and other aspects of both environmental design and visual blight in America. Some of the components of this natural beauty program grew out of the Outdoor Recreation Resources Review Commission report, whereas others heralded the ensuing environmental movement.

27.2.7. Reclamation

Reclamation of environments was a primary target of the environmental movement including water and air quality. Water and air quality were not only problems of urban and industrial areas but also of remote natural environments. In the Clean Air Act Amendments of 1977, Congress stated one of the purposes of the prevention of significant deterioration of air quality was "to preserve, protect, and enhance the air quality in national parks, national wilderness areas, national monuments, national seashores, and other areas of special national or regional natural, recreational, scenic or historic value."

27.2.8. Environmental Era

The National Environmental Policy Act of 1969 (NEPA) was signed into law by President Nixon on January 1, 1970. There were a number of provisions in the act that precipitated major changes in natural environmental management practices and procedures, including the broadening of disciplinary participation in project analyses, the inclusion of systematic approaches to inventory and evaluation of amenity resources such as scenery and recreation, and the broadening of public participation. The framework was set by NEPA for a more open and interdisciplinary approach to environmental planning and decision making. Perhaps the most important consequence of NEPA was the change in the way in which many institutions, both private and public, approached the tasks of planning and managing natural environments. Requirements for environmental impact assessments suggested comprehensive rather than limited perspective approaches and provided for public access to information and the planning and decision-making process.

27.3. MANAGEMENT IN AN ERA OF CONFLICTING ENVIRONMENTAL VALUES

The changing pattern of environmental management policy over the last two centuries, and specifically since the 1940s, has presented managers—those having responsibility for the care, control, and manipulation of natural environments—with new problems in addition to redefinition of long-standing responsibilities. The interest here is in those new problems and redefined responsibilities that have significant social and behavioral implications.

An overriding change that has occurred is the enormously expanded role that natural environments play in providing noncommodity benefits and services for an essentially urban and suburban population—a change that has taken place in most developed countries. Managers can no longer operate within a user network made up of foresters, ranchers, hydrologists, and others interested in the commodity benefits to be obtained from natural environments. Users now include hikers, campers, picnickers, bird watchers, sport hunters and fishermen, archaeologists, ecologists, skiers, snowmobilers, off-road vehicle drivers, pleasure drivers, and wildlife biologists. They include persons of all ages with varying levels of mobility capabilities, many of whom participate in formal organizations that exist to advance their particular and special interests. Competition for the use of resources among these sometimes disparate groups espousing widely divergent values and advocating uses that can be incompatible or environmentally destructive is keen and difficult to resolve.

Resolution of competition and conflict among uses and users has been a management problem at least since Pinchot implemented the multiple-use concept and tried to resolve the sometimes competing interests of ranchers, foresters, and hydrologists. Two factors make the contemporary resolution of environmental value conflicts more difficult than in Pinchot's era: (1) the array of values that must be considered has grown significantly in the twentieth century; and (2) the personal and even the professional value orientations of environmental managers are now more likely to conflict with the value orientations of those individuals and groups using the environment. The social and behavioral dimensions of each of these two sources of conflict, along with their respective implications for environmental management, are examined separately.

27.3.1. Conflict among Uses and User Groups

Competitive relationships and conflict among uses, users, and managers of natural environments have been a fact of life for a long time. The lore of the West is laced with stories of conflicts for land between cattlemen and sheepmen, ranchers and farmers, and over water rights among ranchers, farmers, and miners. The more publicized conflicts of recent years have been between and among commodity interests, noncommodity interests, and professional managers.

Each decade since the 1920s has seen an increase in the number and size of conservation and environmental interest groups and the development of more politically active coalitions among groups. Multiple-use management policy mandates have added support to their causes, particularly in addressing noncommodity uses and values. In a very general sense, there have emerged three major interest groups: commodity, noncommodity, and professional. A study by Culhane (1981) focused on attitudinal differences among the interest groups on three major conflict issues: timber management/clear-cutting, range management, and wilderness. Using a multidimensional scale, Culhane identified three discrete groupings on an Environmental-Utilitarian scale. He defined individuals with scores at the low end of the scale as utilitarians, those in the middle range as progressive conservationists, and those at the upper end as environmentalists or preservationists. Mean group values for the major commodity interests—timber, livestock, and minerals—ranged from -.59 to -.76. Environmental groups' values, including the Sierra Club and wilderness

organizations, ranged from +1.2 to +1.6, whereas mean values for Forest Service and Bureau of Land Management professionals were +.51. Culhane concluded that environmentalists see agencies capitulating to commodity interests, and commodity interests see agencies capitulating to environmentalists.

Motorized and nonmotorized approaches to recreation represent another much discussed conflict situation. Both Presidents Nixon and Carter issued Executive Orders (11644 and 11989, respectively) directing federal agencies to manage the distribution and use of off-road vehicles (ORVs) with an emphasis on resource protection. Motorized approaches to recreation involve a higher per-capita commitment of resources (e.g., energy) and also increase the potential per-capita impact on environmental degradation than do nonmotorized approaches (Catton, 1983). Although there has been a significant amount of research done on the impact of ORVs on some ecosystems, notably coastal dunes, there has been little done on user conflicts (Kemsley, 1980). Survey research undertaken for the Bureau of Land Management for the California Desert Master Plan suggests that there is a general anti-ORV public attitude (Field Research Corporation, 1977). Although a significant minority of visitors (25 to 30%) reported participation in motorcycle riding, dune buggying, and four-wheel driving, these are activities that the greatest numbers of visitors to the desert (40%) found most objectionable. Culhane (1981) also found that ORV recreationists have few friends among other specific interest groups: Timber interests fear ORV drivers will become involved in accidents on logging roads; stockmen believe ORVs scare cattle; and backcountry hikers view ORVs as offensive to their recreational experiences.

Differences between motorized and nonmotorized recreationists involve more than competition for recreational space, however, and include motivations for participating in selected activities. Jackson and Wong (1982) note that cross-country skiers desire solitude, tranquility, and an undisturbed natural environment, whereas snowmobilers seek adventure and sociability. Furthermore, the nature of the competition between motorized and nonmotorized recreationists is often asymmetrical. The disturbance to the nonmotorized recreationist's experience by the presence of a motorized recreationist is far greater than the impact of a nonmotorized individual on a motorized recreationist (Catton, 1983; Heberlein, 1977). As discussed subsequently in this chapter, preventing the potential displacement of nonmotorized recreation from certain natural environments as a result of contact with motorized recreationists has been a major theme of outdoor recreation resource management.

Ernetaz (1980) suggests that managers are likely to side with the anti-ORV interest groups and see nonmotorized dispersed recreation as acceptable because the activity would be less destructive of the environment. He attributes this dominant management perspective to the fact that most managers have biological sciences backgrounds and hence emphasize protection of the resource over social and psychological benefits accruing from recreational activities.

27.3.2. Conflict between Managers and Users

Environmental managers are usually educated and trained in one of several professions, including forestry, wildlife and fisheries biology, range management, watershed management, and natural resources conservation. The pursuit of a body of professional knowledge that purports to be able to solve resource management problems provides a perspective of professional elitism in which managers view themselves as uniquely qualified to resolve problems relating to the management of natural environments (Bolle, 1971; Twight & Catton, 1975).

A manager's professional training equips him or her with yet another perspective. If trained as a forester, many managers tend to look at a natural environment in terms of the board feet of lumber it will produce or with an abiding concern for the silvicultural health of the plant community. As a wildlife biologist, a manager's perspective may be biased by basic concerns for animal habitat. Watershed hydrologists may view the same environment from the perspective of cubic feet of surface water yields. These professional biases frequently collide with one another when management prescriptions are prepared for a given environment.

A final perspective-establishing consequence of a manager's professional training is the commodity orientation (e.g., board feet of lumber) of the education that often ignores defining a natural environment as a setting for human behavior or as an object of attraction to an individual. Even when curricula include courses in environmental psychology, environmental sociology, resource economics, outdoor recreation, or landscape architecture, professions that are most likely to consider the behavioral consequences of environmental management, pursuit of such information is often viewed as secondary in importance to primary concerns for sustained yields of timber, huntable game, and so forth (Twight & Catton, 1975). This commodity bias is often a source of conflict. For example, U.S. Forest Service employees viewed timber harvesting as a more legitimate use of the forest than recreation, and they see recreation as posing unnecessary constraints on harvest practices (Bultena & Hendee, 1972).

Historically, managers' training served them well in their professional endeavors. Demands for use of natural environments focused principally on commodity-based issues. The small amount of noncommodity use that occurred involved individuals who respected and often shared the manager's perspectives (Burch, 1976). However, the growth of noncommodity use of natural environments has forced the manager into a sometimes confrontational engagement with users seeking aesthetic, recreational, and other noncommodity values in the environment.

The 1960s, 1970s and early 1980s have witnessed several research efforts aimed toward identifying the nature and source of the differences between users and managers. Differences have been observed between users' and managers' perceptions of recreational environments. For example, two distinct groups of wilderness users in Minnesota's Boundary Waters Canoe Area (BWCA) held distinctly different perceptions of the areal dimensions of the Boundary Waters wilderness area, and both sets of perceptions were considerably different from the area's actual dimensions (one being larger and the other smaller) (Lucas, 1966). Positive user and negative manager dispositions toward convenience facilities were also observed among canoeists and managers in the BWCA (Peterson, 1974). Managers were also favorable in their attitudes toward hunting, beaver trapping, and the use of motors, whereas canoeists objected to all three (Peterson, 1974). In the Pacific Northwest, campers and campground managers agreed on a common set of goals for the camping experience, but they disagreed on the appropriateness of various activities as means for achieving these goals. Reflecting a stronger tendency toward social interaction and a set of behavioral norms formed in an urban environment, campers were easily able to meet their desires for isolation and contact with the natural environment in a highly developed campground. For the manager, such experiences were viewed as inconsistent with privacy and environmental interaction goals (Clark, Hendee, & Campbell, 1971). Neither campers in highly developed campgrounds nor those in dispersed road campsites shared the manager's concern for noise, litter, actions of other recreationists and forest users, vandalism, and theft (Clark et al., 1971; Downing & Clark, 1979).

In North Carolina's Shenandoah National Park, managers were able to accurately predict user motivations for park visitation. At the Cape Hatteras National Seashore, however, manager's predictions of user motivations were frequently in error for both pedestrian and off-road vehicle (ORV) users. Managers consistently underestimated the importance to both pedestrians and ORV users of scenery, in-group contact, and escaping personal or social pressure. And they consistently overestimated the importance of meeting new people and getting physical exercise (Wellman, Dawson, & Roggenback, 1982). A possible explanation for the dichotomous success of managers in predicting user motivations focuses on the extent to which an environment is reflective of the contemplative ideal of outdoor recreation as originally set forth in the writings of Frederick Law Olmsted. Wellman and colleagues (1982) suggest that managers of environments similar in character to Yosemite and Yellowstone national parks, where the contemplative ideal of natural scenery was first developed and nurtured, will be more in tune with user motivations than will managers of less traditional wilderness and recreation areas. Other explanations of recreation area managers' inability to predict user motivation revolve around differences in the rural demographic orientation of managers versus the users' urban orientation (Clark, et al., 1971) and the tendency of managers to pay closest heed to vocal conservationist groups having purist environmental philosophies (Hendee & Harris, 1970).

27.3.3. Uses, Users, and Managers

Competitive and conflicting relationships within and among user groups and managers represent, in large part, conflicts among environmental value orientations. The enormous growth in demand for noncommodity uses has made the manager's task far more complex than simply managing biological and physical resources — an orientation that professional training in environmental management tends to retain. In recent decades, however, environmental management has become people management as well as resource management. Many managers consequently find themselves in the middle of competing and conflicting interests that they are mandated by policy to consider but are ill-equipped by training to resolve.

Competition and conflict among users also stems from beliefs about appropriate uses of natural environments and, in the case of public lands, about the public's rights of access to those lands. Conflict arises over competition for use of the same resource by different interests, especially when at least one of the interests proposes a consumptive use of the resource. Conflict also emerges among nonconsumptive uses when the conduct of one activity significantly diminishes the quality of the experience involved in other activities. Greater understanding of the diversity and intensity of value orientations among users, more effective techniques for users to participate in the management decision-making process, and the development and use of behaviorally relevant resource management strategies can all help the manager in resolving or accommodating competitive and conflicting demands.

27.4. BROADENING THE SET OF VALUES CONSIDERED IN ENVIRONMENTAL MANAGEMENT DECISION MAKING THROUGH PUBLIC INVOLVEMENT

The emergence of noncommodity uses for natural environments has increased competition and conflict among alternative user groups as well as conflict between users and managers. The struggle between and among users and managers has produced an expanded role for interested publics or interest groups to play in environmental planning and management decision making. Although it would be naive to assume that users had no role in influencing management decisions in the past, that role was almost always unofficial, occasionally surreptitious and involved only those with specific commodity interests such as grazing, timber harvest, water management, and mining. In many instances, management must now not only accommodate but also identify and seek participation of all interested and affected groups. In the absence of policy directions for weighing the various and competing uses, which is frequently the case, managers are confronted with both the tasks of determining appropriate modes of participation and resolving the strongly stated values of special interest groups.

Prior to the Federal Administrative Procedures Act of 1946 (FAPA), participation of the public in federal environmental decision making was conducted largely on an ad-hoc basis or through the use of advisory boards, committees, or organizations. For example, 1939 amendments to the Taylor Grazing

Act of 1934 established advisory boards in each of the Grazing Service's (now known as the Bureau of Land Management, or BLM) range districts (Laitala, 1975). Such boards were initially dominated by livestock interests, and until the 1960s they maintained veto power over the allocation of livestock grazing leases. Prior to 1950, when grazing permittees on lands in the National Forest System were allowed to petition for the establishment of local advisory boards, the U.S. Forest Service (USFS) relied heavily for public input on local grazing associations that were formed either voluntarily or at the instigation of the USFS (Culhane, 1981).

The FAPA established a federal norm for public participation that affected environmental management well into the 1970s. Participation specifications under this act include requirements that federal agencies post public notice of an intention to establish or change rules or regulations and offer opportunity for public comment either in written or verbal form through adjudicatory and public hearings. Although the 1968 Freedom of Information Act and 1977 "government sunshine act" have improved public access to government documents and procedures, the policy established by the FAPA placed the burden of participation squarely on the public. Public involvement in rule making was

> Confined to specified form at limited points in administrative proceedings (usually late in policy development); and the public was left to its own resources in attempting to apprehend the substance and procedure attending important decisions. (Rosenbaum, 1978, p. 82)

The operating procedures specified by the FAPA served as the public participation model for both the 1964 Wilderness Act and the NEPA of 1969 (Garcia, 1980).

The decade of the 1960s witnessed a broadening of federal agency participation mandates from simply allowing the public to be involved in public policy considerations to requiring that agencies actively recruit participants as well as encourage and facilitate participation (Rosenbaum, 1978). The environmental movement was considerably slower in attaining national policy issue status, however, than was true for the social movements surrounding poverty, housing, and transportation. Consequently, it was not until passage of the Federal Water Pollution Control Act Amendments of 1972 (FWPCA) that the mandate for aggressive and "public friendly" participation reached the environmental management arena. Under this law, public participation must be "provided for, encouraged and assisted" in water quality planning and policy and rule making. The phrase *provided for, encouraged and assisted* was interpreted by the Environmental Protection Agency to mean pursuing and instructing the public about citizen participation, water pollution, and what remedies exist (Garcia, 1980). This form of participation was extended to Bureau of Land Management (BLM) activities by the 1976 Federal Land Policy and Management Act (FLPMA) and to the USFS by 11 specific references to public involvement in the NFMA. The USFS also initiated in the early 1970s a broadly based participatory strategy in the conduct of its Roadless Area Review and Evaluation (RARE) of land units for possible expansion of the National Wilderness Preservation System (Culhane, 1981; Hendee, 1977).

As more and more people have placed increasingly more complex and often contradictory demands on the finite supply of resources contained in natural environments, public involvement has become an integral component of environmental management decision making. It provides managers with a forum wherein the range of environmental values affecting a particular decision may be identified and debated.

Just as the range of values impinging on management decisions has broadened in the twentieth century to encompass noncommodity as well as an expanded set of commodity values, so there also has been a broadening of the techniques managers use for considering environmental values. The pre-1950 grazing district advisory boards wielded considerable power in their partnership relationship (Arnstein, 1969) with the fledgling and undermanned BLM (and its predecessor, the Grazing Service). Yet the value system reflected in the decisions of these boards narrowly represented the interests of only stockmen. Through the creation of grazing associations, the USFS was able to deal with groups of permittees rather than individual permittees. And the grazing associations facilitated the diffusion of USFS norms and management policies as well as the adoption of intensive range management practices and improvements. In short, the grazing associations' existence was as important to the USFS as a means of educating and altering rancher attitudes, implementing agency policy, and co-opting antagonistic perspectives (Burke, 1968) as it was to the USFS permittees as a means of expressing their views to management.

Although the public becomes involved in environmental management decision making under the FAPA only if it sincerely desires to do so, the participation model emanating from the act enables consideration of a much broader set of perspectives than that possible in the advisory committee model. This broadening of the participatory basis for public involvement paralleled the diversification of the environmental user's characteristics and desires during the 1950s, 1960s, and 1970s. The effect of this broadened base of value representation on the formulation and especially the implementation of public policy for managing natural environments is manifest in the myriad of litigation emanating from NEPA, a law that used the FAPA participation model (Anderson, 1973; Wenner, 1982). Indeed, in the early 1970s, the field operations of the USFS southern region came to an abrupt halt in the aftermath of litigation resulting from the Monogahela controversy (Dana & Fairfax, 1980).

The desire to avoid the financial and administrative costs of litigation has prompted many environmental management agencies to seek a broader base of support for their decisions. This generally translates into strategies for identifying parties likely to be impacted by a decision and seeking the representation of affected parties' values in the decision-making process, and it is reflected in the public involvement mandates of the FLPMA and the NFMA. Because environmental managers are often legally accountable for the quality of the environments they manage, it is improbable that the public would ever attain Arnstein's (1969) "citizen control" or Burke's (1969) "community power" level of participation in management decision making. On face value, current public participation mandates as developed in the FWPCA and the NFMA can be viewed as specifications for a form of partnership in which the public assists the agency in developing and evaluating policies and rules and regulations. Although environmental management agencies cannot and will not conduct plebiscites on controversial issues,˙ they can obtain, through various participatory mechanisms, special information concerning public preferences and priorities in land management. The fine tuning of management programs with public preferences will decrease the gulf of perspectives presently existing between managers and the public and help build a legitimate base of political support for agency programs (Fairfax, 1975). The success of management agencies in identifying and balancing pertinent value orientations is reflected in Culhane's (1981) survey findings that environmentalists believe both the USFS and the BLM to be pawns of the commodity oriented interest groups, whereas forest, mining, and cattle industry groups see the two agencies as siding with environmentalists.

27.5. IDENTIFICATION OF AESTHETIC VALUES

The expansion of recreational and other noncommodity uses of natural environments and the NEPA requirements that "presently unquantified environmental amenities and values...be given appropriate consideration in decision making" has stimulated a considerable body of research in the identification of aesthetic and other amenity values that are derived from natural environments. This broad field of research in environmental perception and cognition has had two major objectives: (1) development of a theory of landscape perception to better explain the meaning of human–environment interactions; and (2) development of pragmatic models of the perception process that will enable environmental managers to consider human perceptions of landscape in the environmental plans they formulate and human response to the management practices they prescribe and implement (Sell, Taylor, & Zube, 1984). This is an issue that has received international attention with the greatest emphasis, however, in the United States and the United Kingdom. Past comprehensive reviews of this research as conducted by geographers, foresters, and environmental designers as well as psychologists can be found in Daniel and Vining (1983), Penning-Rowsell (1981), Porteous (1982), and Zube and colleagues (1982), the last of which documents the exponential growth of landscape perception research in the mid to late 1970s.

27.5.1. Approaches to the Study of Aesthetic Values

The assessment of aesthetic values in the natural environment involves a transaction between an observer who is experiencing the environment and the environment that is being experienced. Inherently, the assessment of aesthetic values insists on a perceptual experience. Aesthetic values are neither a direct function of the environmental characteristics being perceived, nor are they a product of the individual involved in the perceptual experience. Rather, human experience, knowledge, expectation, and sociocultural context interact with environmental elements and environments as entities to produce an outcome that affects both the human and the environment (Zube, Sell, & Taylor, 1982). Furthermore, the physical context in which the environment is perceived (e.g., from above versus below, at different speeds of travel) can alter the nature of the perceptual experience (Litton, Tetlow, Sorensen, & Beatty, 1974).

Numerous approaches have been devised to study the nature of environmental perception and to incorporate the aesthetic values that result from the perceptual process into natural resources management strategies. Zube and colleagues (1982) and Daniel and Vining (1983) have classified these perceptually based methods into four and five paradigms, respectively.

In Zube's *expert* paradigm (which Daniel and Vining divide into *ecological* and *formal aesthetic* components), highly trained experts employ principles of ecology, design, and natural resources management to the description, evaluation, and often the management of aesthetic resources. The expert paradigm assumes that the perceptions of professionals are valid surrogates for the perceptions of the publics they serve and that people's environmental perceptions can be validly interpreted through the systematic formulation of conceptual relationships (which may or may not have been empirically tested) between characteristics of the environment and characteristics of the individual (Laurie, 1975; Litton, 1968, 1972). This paradigm was dominant in the earliest efforts to develop inventory and evaluation techniques for including aesthetic values in management decision making in environments ranging in scale from several states (e.g., Zube, 1973) to several acres of a national forest (e.g., Litton, 1968).

The *psychophysical* paradigm (the term is used equivalently by Zube and colleagues and Daniel & Vining) developed shortly after the expert paradigm and continues to occupy a significant position in the research literature. This work stems primarily from the stimulus–response tradition of classical psychophysics. Psychophysical models of perception attempt "to determine mathematical relationships between physical characteristics of landscape and perceptual judgments of human observers" (Daniel & Vining, 1983, p. 56) and are exemplified by studies that obtain comparative observer landscape ratings and associate these with specific quantified physical attributes of the environment (Daniel & Boster, 1976; Heberlein & Dunwiddie, 1979). The attributes such as kind and size of vegetative cover, amount of surface water, and size and complexity of landforms and cultural artifacts are frequently identified by the researcher in collaboration with the manager, and

they represent those attributes that can be manipulated in the management process. Perceptual judgment ratings are regressed on physical environmental attributes with the objective of producing predictive models of aesthetic judgment. The models yield numerical data with specified confidence levels— numbers that can be used by managers in making management decisions. Psychophysical models developed to date fall into two broad classes: those predicting perceptual response to sweeping vistas of the environment (Buhyoff, Wellman, & Daniel, 1982; Brush & Shafer, 1975; Shafer, Hamilton, & Schmidt, 1969; Zube, Pitt, & Anderson, 1974) and those predicting perceptual response to more discrete scenes encountered within the environment (Arthur, 1977; Brush, 1979; Daniel & Schroeder, 1979; Echelberger, 1979; Patey & Evans, 1979).

Zube's *cognitive* paradigm (called *psychological* by Daniel and Vining) attempts to explore and interpret the meaning of the environment in the perceptually based aesthetic experience. Cognitive models are similar to psychophysical models in that the former are based on judgments of individuals within an environmental context. They vary from psychophysical models in that cognitive models attempt to relate human judgment to psychological dimensions manifest in or attached to the landscape rather than physical characteristics of the landscape. Although psychophysical models might relate human judgments of environmental aesthetics to such physical factors as presence and extent of water and/or tree cover, cognitive models attempt to establish relationships between aesthetic judgment and such psychological concepts as perceived complexity (S. Kaplan, 1975, 1979; S. Kaplan, R. Kaplan, & Wendt, 1972; Wohlwill, 1968), fittingness and compatability of adjacent land uses (Hendrix & Fabos, 1975; Wohlwill, 1979; Wohlwill & Harris, 1980), perceived naturalness (R. Kaplan, 1978; S. Kaplan et al., 1972; Zube, Pitt, & Anderson, 1975; Ulrich, 1979, 1981), and mystery, legibility, and coherence (S. Kaplan, 1975, 1979). Researchers in the cognitive paradigm have measured autonomic response to the environment (Gratzer & McDowell, 1971; Ulrich, 1979, 1981) as well as the more traditional paper-and-pencil or verbal response.

The *experiential* paradigm (called *phenomenological* by Daniel and Vining) strives to understand human–environment interactions and draws in part on historical and cultural geography and literary traditions and on unstructured phenomenological exploration (Lowenthal, 1978; Seamon, 1979; Tuan, 1977). Research provides detailed pictures of everday behaviors in holistic environments, and it is from the researcher's interpretation of habitual behavior patterns of individuals in the environment that aesthetic values are inferred. Depth of understanding of the behaviors of a limited number of persons is gained, but external validity and generalizability are lost. Methodologically, the experiential paradigm is distinguished from either the cognitive or the psychophysical approaches by the absence of experimental or quasi-experimental designs and the reliance on historical interpretation, case studies, and anecdotal accounts of behavior.

To a large extent, the expert and psychophysical paradigms have focused on the development of perception models that can be applied directly to environmental management, whereas the cognitive and experiential paradigms have been more concerned with developing a theoretical understanding of the meanings of landscapes to humans. For example, both the USFS and the BLM have developed expert paradigm models to inventory and evaluate the aesthetic values of the natural environments they manage. In addition to this model development activity, both the USFS and the BLM have funded research programs designed to develop psychophysical models of aesthetic judgment in natural environments. As management agencies, the USFS and the BLM are interested in relating perceived aesthetic values to physical parameters over which they have managerial authority. To date, there has been little interaction among the four paradigms, and neither management agency has been able to relate its managerial authority to such psychological properties as mystery or fittingness. However, as reports continue to appear that challenge the current assumptions of the expert paradigm as a model for managing the interaction of people with the environments (Feimer, Craik, Smardon, & Sheppard, 1979; Feimer, Smardon, & Craik, 1981), and as the physical dimensions of relevant psychological variables in this transaction are uncovered (Ulrich, 1983; Wohlwill, 1976), the linkages between and among the paradigms will become more apparent. Management models will be revised and based on explicit investigations of human–environment interactions.

27.5.2. Psychological Correlates of Aesthetic Value in Natural Environments

The principal focus of much of the research on aesthetic values, especially within the cognitive paradigm, has been the identification and interpretation of those features, characteristics, and qualities of the environment that are related to perceived aesthetic value. Findings of this research as well as patterns among the findings have been comprehensively reviewed by Wohlwill (1976) and more recently by Ulrich (1983).

An early theme investigated in the aesthetic value research emerged out of the writings of Berlyne (1960, 1971) and Vitz (1966) on the arousal and exploratory behavior that results from the presentation of stimuli containing various amounts of complexity and the relationships of this behavior to aesthetic preferences. Of specific interest has been Berlyne's hypothesis and findings (with subjects viewing random line patterns) of an inverted U-shaped relationship between the stimulus complexity and aesthetic preferences for the stimulus. However, as Wohlwill (1976) notes, Berlyne's concept of stimulus complexity deals almost entirely with complexity in a structural sense, using abstract line stimuli—not from the perspective of stimulus content. Given that environments are rich in meaning and the conveyance of this meaning is an integral component of the perceptual experience (Ittelson, 1973), it is not surprising that adaptations of Berlyne's stimulus complexity hypothesis to the environment have failed to support the specified inverted U-shaped relationship. S. Kaplan and colleagues (1972) were unable to produce the hypothetical inverted U-shaped relationship between preference and complexity for either urbanized or natural scenes; rather they found a linear and positive relationship between complexity and aesthetic preference in both content domains. Others have found significant relationships between scenic value and several measures of landform diversity but not between scenic value and land cover and vegetative diversity (Anderson, Zube, & MacConnell, 1976; Zube, Pitt, & Anderson, 1974). The scenic value judgments of USFS landscape architects were unrelated to their judgments of complexity (Feimer et al., 1981). Enough additional studies have produced either a linear relationship or no relationship between complexity and scenic value to lead Wohlwill to conclude (1976, p. 50) "that complexity...plays an uncertain role at best." Wohlwill suggests that preference for complexity is likely to be a product of experience, to fluctuate across a diurnal cycle, and be multidimensional in nature.

The importance of stimulus content to the perception of environmental aesthetics is exemplified by the findings of Wohlwill (1976), Hendrix and Fabos (1975), and Zube and colleagues (1975) that the scenic value of landscape is inversely related to the extent of perceived incompatibility among land uses in a scene. Similarly, context and the extent to which an element is congruent with its context in terms of contrasting visual qualities (e.g., color, texture, size, or shape) or contrasting design styles have been empirically linked to scenic value (Wohlwill, 1979; Wohlwill & Harris, 1980; Zube et al., 1975). Content is also implicated as an important determinant of aesthetic value by the repeated finding of a preference for natural versus human-made landscapes (Coughlin & Goldstein, 1970; R. Kaplan, 1978; S. Kaplan et al., 1972) and a preference within human-made settings for the presence of natural elements (Brush & Palmer, 1979; Thayer & Atwood, 1978). Correlations between semantic scale description of landscape on either a high/low scenic value scale or a beautiful–ugly scale and a natural/human-made scale range between .50 and .60, and rank–order correlations of .61 and .74 are reported between rankings of landscapes based on naturalism and rankings based on scenic value (Anderson et al., 1976; Zube et al., 1975). Furthermore, the changing of labels that describe landscape from a naturalistic tone (e.g., forest or lake) to a human-made tone (e.g., plantation or reservoir) significantly lowered scenic value assessments even though the label was the only variable changed in the presentation (Anderson, 1981; Hodgson & Thayer, 1980). Finally, Ulrich (1979) reports findings of anxiety and sadness when subjects are presented with urban scenes and a decreasing level of anxiety and increasing level of positive affective response when natural scenes are presented. He notes (1981) low galvanic skin response and high alpha brain waves related to the viewing of natural scenes and the opposite physiological responses for urban scenes. These studies of compatibility, congruity, and naturalism underline the importance of environmental content to the perception of aesthetic value.

At least two theoretical approaches to environmental aesthetics directly implicate the spatial patterning of open fields and forests as determinants of aesthetic value. S. Kaplan (1975, 1979) suggests that environmental perception involves the processing of visual field information presented in both a two-dimensional pictorial context as well as the three-dimensional spatial context that is so well developed among primates. In both contexts, humans have a desire to "make sense" or recognize the environment and become involved with it in an attempt to be able to better predict future happenings.

In a two-dimensional context, making sense is manifest in the organization of elements that lend a sense of coherence to readily identifiable components of the picture plane. Involvement, in the two-dimensional context, relates to the complexity, diversity, or richness of the elements that make up the visual array. In the three-dimensional spatial realm, involvement relates to mystery—the concept of being able and feeling compelled to enter the scene to gain further information. Environments high in mystery provide the promise or lure of additional information, as when a river rounds a bend, and they contain continuity to facilitate gathering additional information. Making sense of the spatial complex of the environment, or what S. Kaplan refers to as *legibility*, involves orientation and wayfinding. Legible landscapes are readable; they contain well-developed spaces wherein organization is enhanced through the use of depth, "focality," or directed attention (Ulrich, 1983), smooth ground plane textures, and landmarks.

The patterning of spatial qualities, which in S. Kaplan's (1975, 1979) framework provides the cognitive properties of legibility and mystery in the landscape, is in Appleton's theoretical approach (1975a) a manifestation of three types of symbolism, including hazards, prospects, and refuges. Hazards are symbolized as animate or inanimate threats occasioned by some external incident; natural and artificial impediments (e.g., expansive water bodies or walls) that do not, of themselves, initiate an immediate threat; and chronic deficiencies that threaten the satisfaction of a creature's biological needs. Prospects are symbolized by conditions that afford opportunities to view the landscape and the hazards it beholds. Refuges provide opportunities wherein a creature may escape the impending peril that accompanies any of the hazards and remove itself from the view of animate objects likely to generate a potential hazard. Prospect and hazard arouse attention and tension in the perception of landscape, and refuge provides opportunities to resolve the conflicts and anxieties that are aroused by the prospect and the hazard. Landscapes, in which hazards dominate the scene, will produce considerably different aesthetic experience than those characterized as prospect- or refuge-dominant.

Prospects manifest themselves in the form of scenes wherein the viewer's vantage point is elevated in relation to the surrounding landscape and wherein broad panoramas, directed vistas and deflected vistas of adjacent areas are evident. The prospect provides the opportunity to see or survey the surrounding countryside. Hazards are manifest in such landscape elements as broad expanses of water or walls that may impede locomotion, vertical drops that threaten a catastrophic fall, or meteorological phenomenon.

Refuges facilitate escape from hazard or the prospect of being seen and the impending hazard this might evoke. As such, accessibility is important to the successful employment of a refuge. Refuges are manifest in the undulation of forest and field edges, the presence of a visual foil that penetrates an open area (as in an island or finger of vegetation that exists within an open field), and the penetration of a solid barrier by several openings. The juxtaposition of a prospect and refuge facilitates what for Appleton (1975a) is a major objective of human survival—to see without being seen.

Both Appleton (1975a) and S. Kaplan (1975, 1979) assign crucial aesthetic importance to the interplay of mass and space in the landscape. It is from the modulation of mass and space that the existence and prospect of information crucial to survival (i.e., the presence of hazards) is gleaned. To be legible, the organization of mass and space must be orderly such that the presence and location of refuges are discernible. Several empirical studies support the theoretical importance of mass and space relationships. Pupillary eye movement studies of natural environments have found a tendency for fixations to focus on the forest–field interface (Gratzer & McDowell, 1971). Vegetative perimeters are reported as major contributors to the prediction of landscape scenic value (Shafer, et al., 1969). In a study employing photomontage techniques in which the relationship of mass to space was systematically varied, scenic preferences were highest for landscapes possessing between 35 and 65% open areas (Burns & Rundell, 1969). Kaplan's dimensions of coherence, complexity, and mystery have been shown to be orthogonal dimensions of aesthetic value in the landscape (R. Kaplan, 1973), and when entered as predictors of aesthetic value they have produced a coefficient of determination of .64 (R. Kaplan, 1975). Preferences for parklike landscapes consisting of large expanses of mowed grass and groves of trees and shrubs are evident (R. Kaplan, 1977; Rabinowitz & Coughlin, 1970), and other authors (Brush, 1979; Daniel & Boster, 1976) find a preference for the thinned, visually penetrable grove with canopied spaces over a fully stocked stand in which visual penetration and spatial development are limited.

Considerable interest has recently focused on the issue of familiarity or habituation and its role in aesthetic value determination. Repeated exposure to the same environment may lead to either the development of a symbolic association with the setting, or it may lead to a diminishing of the intensity and quality of aesthetic response (Ulrich, 1983). Dubos (1968, p.

200) suggests, for example, that "for animals as well as for man, the kind of environment which is most satisfactory is one that they have shaped to fit their needs." Habituation to the familiar may take the form of physiological adaptation [e.g., the short-legged, long-trunked, barrel-chested, and broad-handed adaptations of perennially forest-dwelling people to their specific habitat (Dubos, 1968)]; cultural adaptation as in the development of rich vocabularies relating to specific peculiarities of a given habitat (e.g., the rich snow vocabulary of Eskimos) (Dansereau, 1975); or the development of deep-seated environmental preferences as evidenced by Turnbull's (1962) studies of Central African pygmies and the extreme anxiety and disorientation they experience when removed from their forested habitat.

Empirical investigations of the effect of familiarity on the perception of aesthetic value in natural environments have produced mixed results. Sonnenfeld (1967) reports differences in the landscape preferences of Alaskan Eskimos, non-Eskimo residents of Alaska, and residents of Delaware. He found subjects' preferences strongest for landscapes most similar to their home-type environment. The familiarity issue that Sonnenfeld's (1967) findings pose has received considerable attention by researchers. Numerous experimental psychologists (Kunst-Wilson & Zajonc, 1980; Moreland & Zajonc, 1977; Wilson, 1979) working with human perception of abstract visual and auditory patterns report the existence of an exposure effect— that is, even when stimuli are presented so quickly as to be unrecognizable, subjects, in subsequent evaluations of preference, will consistently rate those stimuli to which they have been exposed as being better liked than those to which they have not been exposed. Nieman (1980) finds this preference for the familiar also to explain variability in the visual quality perceptions of residents of New York State's coastal zone. Similarly, Hammitt (1981) reports an increase in subjects' visual quality perception of a bog environment as a result of direct exposure to the environment and finds the postexposure visual quality perceptions of repeat visitors to be higher than those of the first-time visitor.

In contrast to these findings of a landscape familiarity affect in aesthetic preferences, Wellman and Buhyoff (1980) and Pitt, Zube, and Palmer (1980) report contradictory evidence. Wellman and Buhyoff showed slides of mountainous regions from the Rocky Mountain and the Appalachian regions to subjects residing in Virginia and Utah. They found no systematic preference for the physiographic region in which subjects resided. In comparing the perceptions of lifelong residents of Wichita, Kansas, to photographs of rural New England, Pitt and colleagues (1980) found strong correlations ($r > .80$) between the Kansans' perceptions and those of subjects from New England, including individuals whose towns and immediately surrounding environments had been depicted in the photographs.

The distinction between Hammitt's (1981) support for familiarity and Wellman and Buhyoff's (1980) and Pitt and colleagues' (1980) refutation of familiarity suggest a need for further investigation of landscape presentation media (Craik, 1968). Hammitt's studies involved in-situ studies, and he notes that the familiarity effect was not induced when the study was conducted via black-and-white photographic media. Wellman and Buhyoff used color slides and Pitt and colleagues employed color photographs. Although the reliability and validity of photographic techniques (both slides and photos) as landscape simulation devices is well documented (Daniel & Boster, 1976; Pitt & Zube, 1979; Shafer & Richards, 1974; Zube et al., 1975), it may be that in these studies of familiarity effects, photo simulation has not captured the ambience of the on-site visit.

An issue related to familiarity is the perceptual set that is evoked by information contained in the stimulus presentation format. Empirically, at least two authors have been able to manipulate the perception of aesthetic value by changing the title of a stimulus from one conveying a naturalistic tone to one conveying a stronger cultural influence in the landscape. Hodgson and Thayer (1980) were able to significantly alter the Wilcoxon Rank Sum of 4 photographs embedded within a set of 15 photographs by changing their labels from *lake*, *pond*, *stream bank*, and *forest growth* to *reservoir, irrigation, road cut,* and *tree farm*, respectively. In a related study, Anderson (1981) reports that the application of labels to photographs consistently altered their perceived scenic value and that labels such as *national park* or *wilderness area* consistently increased the perceived value, whereas consistent value reductions were the consequence of the application of lables such as *commercial timber stand* and *leased grazing area*. In both studies, the application of labels implying a stronger human influence consistently (with the exception of Anderson's ambiguous *recreation area* term) lowered perceived value. This finding is consistent with a pronaturalism bias reported in the perception literature by several authors (Carls, 1974; Kaplan et al., 1972; Zube et al., 1974; Zube & Pitt, 1981). Buhyoff and Leuschner (1978) report that they were able to significantly alter subjects' scenic value perceptions simply by informing subjects that the interesting orangish pattern present in a scene was produced by a beetle infestation.

From 1965 to 1970, an international study was undertaken to investigate alternative measures to enhance the scenic beauty and aspects of public safety at the American side of Niagara Falls (Zube, 1980). The alternatives considered for aesthetic enhancement included removal of fallen rock at the base of the falls, raising the water level of the pool at the base to cover some of the rock, and increasing the flow of water over the falls. An operating scale model of the falls had been constructed, allowing each alternative to be simulated and photographed. Several public hearings were held, and a 12-page brochure was published to illustrate the alternatives and the estimated costs for implementing each. However, the brochure did not describe the natural history of the falls or the erosion process exemplified by the falls that is responsible for the rocks at the base. On September 9, 1973, *The New York Times* carried a 9-page feature article on the study emphasizing the erosion process and reproduced the questionnaire. Over 75,000 responses were received. Responses to the brochure were strongly supportive of some form of alteration to enhance scenic quality, whereas responses to *The New York Times* article were overwhelmingly against any change. In the presence of these conflicting responses resulting from different information sets, the American Falls International Board decided to accept the process of change as a natural feature of the falls.

The studies of the role information plays in establishing a perceptual set further implicate the central role of environmental content to determining aesthetic value. They further suggest the shortcomings inherent in those expert paradigm models of aesthetic value that attempt to conceptualize aesthetics on the basis of ecological or design principles to the exclusion of environmental content. Because the information provided about an environment can alter perception of aesthetic value in that environment and because people with varying levels of familiarity or experience with a given environment bring different sets of information to the perceptual experience, some knowledge of an individual's environmental experiences is crucial to a full explanation of his or her perception of aesthetic value. The importance of an individual's experiences with landscape are directly implicated by reports of systematic variation in perceived aesthetic value of landscape as a function of socioeconomic status, ethnicity (Zube & Pitt, 1981), and age (Zube, Pitt, & Evans, 1983).

Finally, a nearly universal finding has been the positive effect of the presence of water on the aesthetic value of natural environments (Shafer et al., 1969; Ulrich, 1983; Zube et al., 1975). Several authors attribute the aesthetic significance of water to its central biological role in life (Appleton, 1975a; Dubos, 1980; Ulrich, 1983). Such significance is associated with what Appleton calls the *habitat theory* of landscape aesthetics. Habitat theory ascribes aesthetic significance to those landscapes and those elements within the environment that afford the opportunity for achieving basic biological needs. The central role of water in meeting basic biological needs is reflected, then, in people's universal appreciation of its presence in the landscape.

27.5.3. Looking to the Future

Aesthetic values are an issue in most management problems that have accompanied the expansion of noncommunity uses of natural environments. A substantial volume of research has been conducted in response to this situation. Nevertheless, there are a number of questions, theoretical and applied, that remain unanswered or, at best, inadequately addressed.

In a past review, Daniel and Vining (1983) evaluated several approaches to assessment of aesthetic values in terms of validity, reliability, sensitivity, and utility. Following their evaluation, the psychophysical and cognitive approaches were found to provide valid and reliable data. The experiential is most sensitive to variations in person and landscapes but lacks in reliability, and the expert approach has been the most useful in applications. However, the reliability and validity of the expert approach has been questioned in several studies (Feimer et al., 1979, 1981). This evaluation suggests that none of the approaches, as currently employed, are entirely adequate for providing aesthetic values information for managers. Furthermore, in the absence of a general overarching theory of environmental aesthetics (Appleton, 1975b; Porteous, 1982; Wohlwill, 1976), it is not possible to make comparisons across studies and approaches and to aggregate findings to enhance their utility. It is exactly this type of cross-paradigm integration that is needed if the research is to have utility to environmental managers and planners (Porteous, 1982).

The greater utilization of the expert approach can be attributed to a number of factors, including the relative ease of using the talents of in-house staff, managers' confidence in professional judgments, the utiliza-

tion of multiprofessional planning teams that reinforce the role of the professional, and the relatively higher cost of conducting landscape assessment studies utilizing representative samples of interested publics or the public at large.

Use of the expert paradigm tends to produce nominal or ordinal data. Current practices in large-scale planning and management studies, however, are becoming highly quantitative, employing linear programming and similar modes of analysis that require interval or ratio scales of measurement. Therefore, commensurability of data becomes a serious constraint on the effective inclusion of aesthetic values in environmental management decision making when the values emanate strictly from an expert paradigm model. Assuming for the moment that the issue of reliability can be resolved, the expert approach as practiced in the past can continue to have utility for smaller scale local management decisions involving assessments of amenity values at an individual site or among several sites. At the larger scale, however, ratio and interval scale data will be required if aesthetic values are to be considered as integral components in the decision-making process rather than as constraints on decisions that primarily relate to commodity values.

Craik and Zube (1976) have suggested the concept of Perceived Environmental Quality Indices (PEQI) as a way of achieving standard, reliable measures of the quality of the experienced environment. Among the identified potential uses and contributions of PEQIs are (1) for assessing "aspects of environmental quality that intrinsically involve the interplay between the human observer and the environment (e.g., scenic quality)"; and (2) gauging "the extent of congruence between perceptions of environmental quality and physical PEQIs" (pp. 5–6). The development of PEQIs would discriminate between comparative appraisals that involve the use, implicit or explicit, of standards of comparison and preferential judgments that express personal, subjective responses to specific environments. Within such a system, it would be possible to systematically assess the convergence of lay and expert perceptions as well as their convergence with PEQI that are traditionally used by experts.

With notable exceptions (Zube & Pitt, 1981; Zube et al., 1983), much of the environmental aesthetics research to date is characterized by high levels of agreement among participants about the most beautiful or satisfying landscapes. If these findings prevail over broader cross-sections of the public, particularly in terms of comparative appraisals, the PEQI concept could make a valuable contribution to decisionmakers' information needs, particularly if it entailed a more quantitative approach. Small groups of experts and/or lay persons serving as touring panels could provide valid and reliable values information and serve as a potential avenue for public participation in environmental management decision making. Such procedures would both broaden the base of interest group involvement in decision making and guarantee the use of aesthetic values as they emanate from the process of actually experiencing the environment.

27.6. CARRYING CAPACITY AS AN APPROACH TO MANAGING RECREATIONAL BEHAVIOR IN NATURAL ENVIRONMENTS

One of the implications of an expanded noncommodity orientation to the use of natural environments, particularly since World War II, has been a surge in the use of natural environments as settings for various forms of recreational behaviors. For the National Park Service, expansion of the recreational use of natural environments became a public policy objective to help the service develop a political constituency that would support its existence and operations (Dana & Fairfax, 1980). Managers in more traditionally commodity-oriented agencies such as the USFS have been less zealous in their acceptance of the recreational use mandate initially thrust on them by the Multiple Use and Sustained Yield Act and subsequently reaffirmed by the National Forest Management Act (Bultena & Hendee, 1972).

The present public policy posture with respect to recreational use of natural environments was initially spelled out in a section of the National Parks Act of 1916 originally written by the landscape architect Frederick Law Olmsted, Jr.:

> To conserve the scenery and the natural and historic objects and the wildlife therein and to provide for the enjoyment of same in such manner and by such means as will leave them unimpaired for the enjoyment of the future generations (Dana & Fairfax, 1980, p. 109).

Thus recreational uses were to be promoted to encourage present enjoyment of the natural environment but not beyond the extent to which the environment would be unable to provide for the enjoyment of future generations. Herein lies an explicit concern for intergenerational equity in the allocation of natural environments and uses of the environment such that the future stream of benefits flowing from these uses will not be diminished by present use.

The past two decades in environmental management have witnessed a voluminous outpouring of literature that has attempted to define and operationalize various adaptations of a management strategy known as *carrying capacity* as a mechanism to balance present and future levels of recreational use of natural environments. Original conceptualizations of carrying capacity in range and wildlife management were founded on the premise that a given natural environment will be able to sustain a population of animals that is relatively constant and identifiable before adverse impacts will be manifest on either the environment or present or future animal populations (Catton, 1983). Adaptations of carrying capacity to managing the interaction of humans and natural environments similarly assume the existence of a relationship between the physical and biotic characteristics of any given natural environment and that environment's capacity to support human use over time. Just as excesses of animals on rangeland can lead to environmental deterioration and/or adverse population dynamics, so also can excesses of humans result in the degradation of environmental resource values, lowering of the quality of the human–environment interaction or fostering of competition and conflicts over the use of particular resources or places.

As originally developed, the concept of carrying capacity is based on management objectives concerning the types of animals to be managed and desirable population levels to be maintained. The capability of the habitat to sustain desired population levels and the effects of management actions can then be evaluated based on environmental characteristics and known patterns of species behavior. The definition of recreational carrying capacity, however, is complicated considerably by the necessity to consider not only management objectives and the effects of use on environmental quality but also the effects of use on user desires and expectations (Lime & Stankey, 1971; Lime, 1979). In this context of management objectives, *recreational carrying capacity* has variously been defined as the level of use at which the quality of the use experience and the environment remain constant (Wagar, 1964); " the character of use that can be supported over a specific time by an area developed at a certain level without causing excessive damage to either the physical environment or the experience for the visitor" (Lime & Stankey, 1971, p. 175); and the level of use at which unacceptable changes occur in the ecological and social qualities of a recreational opportunity (Frissel & Stankey, 1972). The exact meanings of "quality of use experience and the environment," "excessive damage to either the physical environment or the experience for the visitor," or "unacceptable changes in the ecological and social qualities of a recreational opportunity" must be interpreted in terms of established management objectives for the environment.

27.6.1. Dimensions of Recreational Carrying Capacity

A natural environment's recreational carrying capacity can be defined from four perspectives: physical, ecological, facilities, and social (Heberlein, 1977). For example, in determining the appropriate level of camping in a forest, the physical carrying capacity is a function of the total hectares in the forest divided by a hectare per party campsite requirement. This function represents a theoretical maximum that is seldom given serious consideration in resource management because its achievement is constrained by definitions of ecological, facilities, or social carrying capacity as well as management objectives. Ecologically, *carrying capacity* might be defined as that level of camping at which a specified level of soil compaction or erosion occurs, and it will be profoundly affected by the manner in which the camping activity is conducted (e.g., car camping versus backpacking) (Catton, 1983). The facility carrying capacity of the forest is realized when all of the facilities provided for the campers (e.g., parking lots, campsites, etc.) are in use. Finally, the social capacity of the forest for camping occurs at that level or character of use as it exists when the quality of the camping experience begins to deteriorate.

The perspective a manager assumes in defining carrying capacity as well as the recreational use a manager considers will alter the definition he or she develops for a given natural environment. Different perspectives and different uses or mixes of uses will produce different definitions of carrying capacity. The existence of four different carrying capacity concepts poses a potential dilemma for the manager who must ultimately decide which concept or combination of concepts to employ in allocating use. Furthermore, the availability of operating resources often impacts the level of use that can be sustained by an environment over time (Driver & Brown, 1983).

This dilemma is further complicated by the fact that users often are not aware of the interrelationships among different concepts of carrying capacity and that these interrelationships are part of the bases on which management decisions are made. In the Selway-Bitterroot Wilderness in Idaho and Montana,

a sizable majority of hikers reportedly were well satisfied with trail conditions in spite of the fact that some of the trails were severely eroded (Lucas, 1979). Similarly, correlations between campers' perceptions of campsite physical conditions and actual measurements of physical deterioration were reportedly weak (Knudson & Curry, 1981; Merriam & Smith, 1974); and Boundary Waters Canoe Area visitor satisfaction was only minimally affected by campsite conditions in which 85% of the ground cover vegetation had been destroyed by human use (Frissel & Duncan, 1965). Although there is some evidence supporting the notion that longtime users of an environment are more aware of environmental deterioration (Vaske, Donnelly, & Heberlein, 1980), the apparent obliviousness of most users to environmental change suggests that they may not readily perceive and/or understand the rationale for management decisions based solely on ecological carrying capacity considerations. Thus once managers have completed the task of developing composite use determinations that recognize the ecological, facilities, and social dimensions of the human–environment interaction, they must be prepared to explain their rationale to the public.

Social carrying capacity implies the existence of relationships between the quality and the character of the human–environment interaction. Defining the behavioral quality of this interaction is a multidimensional problem that involves consideration of, among other factors, the level of use, the type of use, and the spatial-temporal patterns of use (Stankey, 1973). Initial attempts to define the quality of the interactional experience (Cicchetti & Smith, 1973; Fisher & Krutilla, 1972) borrowed rather directly from the range management concept of carrying capacity. Essentially, these studies posited an inverse relationship between the quality of a recreational experience and the density of recreationists in the environment. Subsequent field tests of the hypothesis have found density of recreationists encountered to be related to campsite preferences of Illinois campers (Carls, 1974) but poor predictors of satisfaction among river recreationists in the Grand Canyon (Shelby & Nielsen, 1976b), Wisconsin (Heberlein & Vaske, 1977), Vermont (Manning & Ciali, 1980), and Maryland (Pitt, Chaney, & Colton, 1981). Empirical investigations of the relationship between perceived crowding and user satisfaction have found mixed results. Eighty-six percent of the variance in the attractiveness estimates of Vermont ski resorts was explained by perceived length of slopes and perceived level of crowding (Ewing & Kulka, 1979), and a willingness to trade additional visits for less crowding was found among British recreationists (Price, 1979). However, among river recreationists in the Grand Canyon (Shelby & Nielsen, 1976a), Wisconsin (Heberlein & Vaske, 1977), and Maryland (Colton, Pitt, Morgan, III, & Chaney, 1979), relationships between perceived crowding and satisfaction were not significant.

A number of reasons for the poor predictive strength of the density and crowding satisfaction models have been offered. Heberlein and Shelby (1977) explain the poor fit in terms of cognitive dissonance, displacement, product shift, and the multidimensionality of satisfaction. Recreational behaviors are essentially voluntary and self-selected. People chose activities that are in accordance with normative beliefs about "having a good time." Thus recreationists will rationalize the existence of a good time regardless of the conditions encountered, especially if having a good time involves a sizable investment of time or money. Under their displacement explanation, Heberlein and Shelby suggest that individuals who are truly sensitive to high-density relationships may have already moved out of the environment being studied to a less intensively used area—a phenomenon observed among recreationists on the Lower St. Croix and Upper Mississippi rivers in Wisconsin (Becker, Niemann, & Gates, 1981). As densities increase, Heberlein and Shelby suggest that changes occur in recreationists' normative beliefs of what constitutes an appropriate level of contact. This results in a product shift toward and acceptance of the higher density conditions. Finally, Heberlein and Shelby note that the overall enjoyment derived from a recreational experience is multidimensional and may involve consideration of an individual's expectations for the experience, benefits gained from the experience, as well as the social interaction that occurred during the experience.

The theoretical differentiation of crowding from density (Altman, 1975; Rapoport, 1975; Stokols, 1972) has led several authors (Heberlein, 1977; Shreyer & Roggenbuck, 1978; Wagar, 1964) to hypothesize that the relationship between density and enjoyment is moderated by the types of use(s) involved. The importance of type of use is manifest in a relationship of asymmetrical antipathy (Heberlein, 1977) among recreationists. In general, given an identical number of interpersonal or interparty contacts, recreationists employing higher levels of technology in their activities (motorboats as opposed to canoes, horseback as opposed to hiking, motorized river rafts as opposed to paddle rafts) tend to disrupt the experiences of their lower technology counterparts

more than the low-technology recreationists disrupt high-technology recreationists (Lucas, 1964; Shelby & Nielsen, 1976b; Stankey, 1973). A displacement of the low-technology recreationist (whose environmental impact is least) often occurs (Catton, 1983). Furthermore, the work of Cohen, Sladen, & Bennett (1975), Desor (1972), and Lee (1975), wherein the nature of the activity and the affiliation of people involved in the activity moderated the relationship between density and crowding, corroborate Wagar's (1964) supposition that outdoor activities will vary in their sensitivity to densities. The role of expected psychological outcomes in moderating the density–satisfaction relationship is evidenced by the differential crowding sensitivities of white water rafters with varying experience expectations (Shreyer & Roggenbuck, 1978). Sources of variation in the development of an individual's expectations with respect to density and psychological outcomes are variously ascribed to initial experiences with an activity (Nielsen, Shelby, & Hass, 1977), length of involvement in the activity (Foster & Jackson, 1979; Heberlein & Dunwiddie, 1979; Vaske, et al., 1980), and personality traits (Driver & Knopf, 1977).

Other factors have also been found to moderate the density–satisfaction relationship in recreational experiences. Epstein and Karlin's findings (1975) that persons in the center of a group are more likely to feel crowded than those at the group's periphery have been replicated among campers at the Katwai National Monument in Alaska (Womble & Studebaker, 1981). Although measures of actual vegetative screening were unrelated to perceptions of campground crowding, the perceived existence of campsite separation by campsite occupants moderated occupants' perceptions of crowding (Foster & Jackson, 1979). The proximity of Chesapeake Bay boaters to various levels of density moderated their perception of satisfaction, and increasing the numbers of boats in the distance was positively related to satisfaction, whereas increasing the numbers of boats within 300 ft. of an observation boat was inversely related to satisfaction (Pitt et al., 1981). Landscape scenic value has been found to be an important determinant of satisfaction among river floaters in Texas (Ditton, Graefe, & Fedler, 1981) and hikers in wilderness areas in the northeastern United States (Shafer & Mietz, 1969). A number of studies have reported that recreationists were more disturbed by the litter they encountered in natural environments than by the number of people they encountered (Lee, 1975; Stankey, 1973). Finally, noise (Womble & Studebaker, 1981) and the size of the parties involved in an encounter affected wilderness users' perceptions of the encounter (Stankey, 1973). Preferences were consistently expressed for several small-group encounters over one large-group encounter.

Time is a critical dimension in any definition of recreational carrying capacity. Inherently, managers of natural environments must consider issues of intergenerational equity in determining appropriate levels and mixes of recreational uses. These equity issues relate to an environment's resiliency, its ability to assimilate the abusive impacts of use, and its regenerative capacities once abusive impacts have occurred (Wager, 1964). The cumulative effects of these environmental properties impact an environment's ability to sustain continued use over time and retain its ability to satisfy the needs of future generations. They are properties that are often neglected in much of the current recreational carrying capacity literature (Catton, 1983).

Various authors have also described the changing concepts of recreational use of natural environments that have occurred over time (Clark, Hendee, & Campbell, 1971; Lucas, 1967; Nash, 1977). These changes are, in part, reflected in the shifts in resource management policy described earlier in this chapter. Definitions of social carrying capacity must be kept flexible enough to allow recalibration as changes occur in the values, preferences, and expectations on which they are based. Otherwise, managers will find themselves managing for a set of conditions that are no longer socially desirable.

Time also brings about changes in technology. Nash's (1977) chronicle of river running through the Grand Canyon illustrates that technological innovation (e.g., the development of inflatable rubber rafts) can open untapped markets for recreation demand. In addition, the snowmobile/cross-country skiing conflict (West, 1980) illustrates how technological innovations (in the form of snowmobile development) can create new sources of user conflict that ultimately affect the definition of social carrying capacity.

Although there are a myriad of factors that go into making a carrying capacity decision, the implementation of most of these decisions ultimately implies that somebody's personal liberty to use a natural environment is going to be restricted for the betterment of society. This is a concept that is often difficult to grasp in the context of managing for public goals. A tendency often exists to want to allow everyone to use everything. Such policies run counter to maintenance of the long-run quality of the environment and the human–environment experience. Several authors (Brown et al., 1978; Clark & Stankey, 1979; Driver & Brown, 1978; Palmer, 1979) have proposed that environmental characteristics be evaluated in terms of their ability to provide desired psychological outcomes of recreational experiences and that specific environments be managed in a coordinated regional perspective to facilitate the attainment of specific outcomes. This targeting of psychological outcomes to environmental characteristics is the underlying rationale of the Recreational Opportunity Spectrum (Brown, Driver & McConnel, 1978; Clark & Stankey, 1979; Driver & Brown, 1978), an environmental planning and management system currently being adapted to much of the public domain in the United States.

In summary, *carrying capacity* can be defined as a means to an end—the long-term maintenance of quality natural environments and human–environment experiences. It is multidimensional in nature, depending on a number of factors, including the capabilities of natural systems, the availability of user facilities, the types and levels of uses involved, the qualitative and quantitative character of user interactions, externalities associated with uses, expected outcomes or benefits to be derived by the users, user expectations with respect to events occurring during the experience, and operational definitions of acceptable impacts and changes in both environmental quality and user experiences. No single definition of carrying capacity exists for any given environment. Rather, carrying capacity must be viewed as a set of limitations on individual freedoms that may change over time.

27.6.2. Management Approaches to Carrying Capacity

Once an environmental manager has determined that the institution of some form of recreational use limitation is necessary, he or she can achieve this objective by any of three overlapping courses of action: (1) more intensive management of the site where the use is to occur, (2) direct regulation of visitor behavior, and (3) modification of user behavior by means of information management and user involvement (Lime & Stankey, 1971).

Site management techniques focus on improving the environment's ecological capacity to accommodate use. Such techniques may involve various surface treatments and vegetative and soil management approaches designed to "harden" the site where use occurs, design approaches that channel circulation and use into more resilient or hardened parts of the environment, and capital improvements approaches wherein new facilities are developed in underutilized portions of the environment to draw people out of the overused areas (Lime, 1979).

Overt management approaches to the direct regulation of user behavior may take any of several forms, including spatial and/or temporal zoning of use, restrictions of use intensity, restrictions on certain activities, and increased enforcement of user regulations (Lime, 1979). Use zoning is designed to reduce the problems associated with the negative externalities of adjacent incompatible uses such as cross-country skiing and snowmobiling. Use intensity restrictions are designed to decrease the number of users in an environment and may take the form of rotating use among parts of the environment (e.g., periodic closing of trails, roads, campgrounds, etc.) to permit natural systems to rejuvenate themselves, restricting physical access into the environment, rationing the use of the environment among potential users, limiting party size, fixing user itineraries, and requiring demonstration of environmental skills and knowledge (Lime, 1979; Stankey, 1973; Stankey & Baden, 1977).

Information and education programs have been used as alternatives to overt approaches to managing the carrying capacity of recreational areas. In many instances, the more subtle techniques of education and dissemination of information are more appropriate than the heavy-handedness of direct regulation in preventing environmental and/or user experience deterioration (Lime & Stankey, 1971). These approaches generally have three objectives: (1) informing users about the recreational resource, current levels of use, and opportunities for experiencing different psychological outcomes as aids in user decision making, (2) making the users more sensitive to the potential impacts their behaviors might have on natural systems, and (3) giving the manager and the user an opportunity to exchange information concerning user needs and management activities.

Information programs have been demonstrated to be effective modifiers of recreational use of natural environments (Brown & Hunt, 1969). Significant relationships have been reported between wilderness users' understanding of the environmental implications of their behaviors and their self-reported propensity to perform environmentally depreciative behaviors (Robertson, 1981). These findings suggest that information and education programs are likely to moderate the rate of abusive behavior. Brochures describing entry points, time of visit, or usual intensity

of use of different trails have been used in a number of wilderness areas in an attempt to distribute users and reduce crowding. User studies in Yellowstone National Park (Krumpe, 1979) and the Boundary Waters Canoe Area (Lime & Lucas, 1977) indicate that this kind of information is employed by a significant number of users. However, Canon, Adler, and Leonard (1979) report that campers who received a brochure explaining the rationale for backcountry regulations tended to camp at a greater distance from the trails, but contrary to regulations, continued to select only previously used sites. Roggenbuck and Berrier (1982) suggest that backcountry information is most effective (1) with users who have little experience in the area, (2) when it contains more than just use levels, and (3) when it is delivered to the user as soon as possible. Work with wilderness campers suggests, however, that not all recreationists will favorably receive such efforts as increased signing or distribution of information pamphlets. Some recreationists, in fact, may view the effects of these programs as creating rather than resolving problems of overuse and user conflict.

Other forms of behavioral modification have focused on user involvement in resource management and increasing information flow among user groups. The involvement of suspected snowmobiling vandals in a surveillance program reduced abuse of a series of vandalized country homes. The involvement of organized user groups (e.g., snowmobile associations, etc.) in resource management has been found to promote self-regulation of problematic behavior, can be used to instill greater sensitivity to the environmental consequences of behavior, and often provides volunteer assistance in environmental rehabilitation (Sanderson, 1980).

The Green Mountain Club caretaker program provided managers with accurate visitor use records on Vermont's Long Trail in addition to informing hikers of trail conditions and opportunities and providing education about the ecological fragility of the trail (Plumley, Peet, & Leonard, 1978). In the Pacific Northwest, exchange of perspectives and ideas among snowmobilers and cross-country skiers has lead to the sharing of expertise among these two normally conflicting interest groups. Snowmobilers now groom ski trails and race courses and assist in search and rescue efforts. Skiers provide avalanche awareness and winter survival skills talks for snowmobilers (Ernetaz, 1980).

The techniques for managing recreational behavior in natural environments vary in terms of how their costs and benefits are distributed throughout society and in terms of their acceptance by the publics who recreate in natural environments. Yet they all have the common goals of facilitating the achievement of those psychological expectations and outcomes associated with the recreational experience and sustaining the quality of the environmental setting in which the recreational behaviors occur.

27.7. MANAGING DEPRECIATIVE AND DEVIANT BEHAVIOR IN NATURAL ENVIRONMENTS

Public policies such as the National Parks Act or the Multiple Use and Sustained Yield Act, that foster human use and enjoyment of natural environments for noncommodity values inherently force the natural resource manager to eventually reckon with the fact that some uses of natural environments will involve behavior that is normally considered unacceptable by societal norms. Deviant and depreciative behaviors in natural environments, like those in any environment, involve actions committed against people (assault, murder, rape, etc.) and those directed toward property (theft, vandalism, etc.). Because many resource managers have found themselves deeply involved in investigations of rape, suicide, murder, and grand theft (Hoots, 1976), some agencies now routinely send their resource managers to law enforcement academies (Morrison, 1976). But felonious criminal behavior in natural environments is more typically investigated and resolved through traditional law enforcement mechanisms. However, because misdemeanors, especially those committed against property, often involve destruction of the natural environments that managers are responsible for maintaining, a substantial amount of environmental management activity has recently been devoted to preventing misdemeanors, principally the prevention and control of littering and vandalism. In addition to eliminating the destructive environmental consequences of littering and vandalism (Hinds, 1976), managers also hope to diminish the fiscal impact of litter pickup and vandalism replacement programs.

27.7.1. Vandalism: Otherwise Acceptable Behavior in an Inappropriate Context

Numerous authors have examined the types and causes of vandalism (Christensen & Clark, 1978; Cohen, 1973; Samp, 1976; Sokol, 1976; Wells, 1971; Williams, 1976). A common thread within this literature is the contention that acts of vandalism do not differ qualitatively from other, acceptable types of behaviors. Williams (1976) notes that at the same time that society carefully preserves the cliff inscriptions of American Indians, publicly supports the reshaping and preservation of Mount Rushmore's cliffs, marvels at the human-made tunnel cut through a giant sequoia tree, it also becomes outraged when rock outcrops are defaced by a spray paint artist or trees are initialed by knife-wielding whittlers. Indeed, the Boston Tea Party, a vandalistic foray aboard British merchant ships, is celebrated as a harbinger of the American Revolution (Wells, 1971). The felling of a tree for winter firewood in an established fuelwood cut area involves the same set of overt behaviors as does the felling of the same tree species in a park. In one context, the behavior is permitted and even encouraged, whereas in another context, the behavior may result in incarceration. Thus in the right context, what might otherwise be considered appropriate behavior becomes an act of vandalism.

Frequently the change in context that identifies an acceptable behavior as an act of vandalism involves the enactment of a law or regulation. It may involve only a change in perspective from that of the general public to that of the resource manager. Given the well-documented and previously noted discrepancies between the perspectives of managers and users on resource management issues (see e.g., Clark et al., 1971; Twight & Catton, 1975) and the difficulty of informing resource users of regulation changes (Fazio & Gilbert, 1974; Ross & Moeller, 1974), Williams (1976) suggests that some vandalism is inevitable.

However, even when the behavioral norms are clearly understood by both the environmental manager and the user of natural environments, vandalism will still occur. Christensen and Clark (1978) note that vandalistic behavior often has little to do with the social, physical or management context in which it occurs; it is more dependent on the psychological makeup of the individuals involved and the sociological context in which they exist. Vandalism may be a product of financial need, an expression of social protest, revenge, hatred, or self-actualization, or a manifestation of territorial behavior (as when an individual or group paints or otherwise marks its turf) (Cohen, 1973; Miller, 1976; Sokol, 1976). Vandalism is often associated with and can even be an integral part of spontaneous play between people of all ages. The group interaction and competition inherent in many forms of play lead to various types of actions that are not necessarily perceived as vandalistic by the play participants (Williams, 1976). Vandalism with play may be associated with (1) an object that simply wears out gradually over time and its final and ultimate demise is considered an act of vandalism, (2) conflict vandalism in which the vandalized object "got in the way" of some form of play behavior and was removed to facilitate a desired behavior, (3) leverage vandalism in which long leverlike objects are used to pry open or pry loose other objects simply to discover how well the lever works, (4) curiosity vandalism in which a window on a building is smashed to see what is inside, (5) irresistible temptation vandalism wherein a birch tree is broken in the process of discovering how far it will bend, or bottles are thrown off cliffs to watch them smash on the rocks below, and (6) no-other-way-to-do-it vandalism in which the individual urinates next to a comfort station because the door of the building is locked (Samp, 1976).

27.7.2. Management Approaches to Vandalism and Littering

In the past 20 years, a number of management strategies have been advanced for preventing and controlling the problems associated with vandalism and littering, including (1) improved design and maintenance of the physical environment, (2) improved and expanded information and education programs, (3) controlled access into natural environments, (4) removal of highly vandalized objects, (5) improved detection of vandalism and littering and enforcement of vandalism and littering regulations, and (6) stronger involvement of the public in prevention of vandalism and littering.

Design solutions focused initially on the creation of "vandal-proof" facilities. Product literature is replete with vandal-proof claims. Numerous articles report on modifications that have improved the structural strength of facilities and reduced the impetus for vandalism (see e.g., Cook, 1976; Danielian, 1976). However, the vandal's technology seems always to outpace the designer's ingenuity, resulting in facility obsolescence even before completion of construction (Clark, 1976).

Newman's (1972) notions on defensible space and Sommer's (1972) concepts on design responsiveness to user needs have captivated the attention of authors on facility design. Reports of a 22% reduction in vandalism in Washington, DC, due to the installation of sodium vapor outdoor lights, have resulted in calls for increased night lighting of heavily used environments (Einolander, 1976). Magill (1976) suggests

that vandalism can be reduced with park designs that facilitate rather than restrict or frustrate normal patterns of user behavior, improve visibility, foster community surveillance by users, and encourage user interaction at a coherent scale. Hoots (1976) notes that the predominance of nuclear-family-oriented campsite designs in a national forest that is frequented by Mexican-American extended families has been the source of many user-manager conflicts and the suspected cause of subsequently occurring vandalism.

Several authors suggest a link between maintenance and vandalism (Kenline, 1976; Magill, 1976; Sutton, 1976; Ward, 1973) or littering (Finnie, 1973; Iso-Ahola & Niblock, 1981; Reiter & Samuel, 1980). Highly vandalized facilities are reported as being derelict, incomplete, or badly kept, exuding a sentiment that nobody really cares what happens (Kenline, 1976). Further, it is hypothesized that if maintenance programs and budgets can stay abreast of the incidence of vandalism, the physical incentive for vandalism (i.e., already broken-down facilities) will be removed resulting in an overall reduction in vandalistic behavior (Magill, 1976; Sutton, 1976; Ward, 1973).

The management approach of information and education maintains that vandalism and littering occur because environmental users are misinformed about behavioral norms in a given setting. Heightened levels of information and educational messages will thereby indirectly result in a decrease in vandalism. Williams (1976) notes that in situations where users are unfamiliar with management regulations and when these regulations prohibit behavior that might otherwise be acceptable, information programs are especially important. Suggestions for conveying this information include strong use of graphics and the avoidance of intimidating language (Reynolds, 1976), although the differences in litter reduction resulting from use of punishment-oriented, freedom-threatening messages and language emphasizing cooperation have not proven significant (Reich & Robertson, 1979; Reiter & Samuel, 1980). In an island setting, vandalism was significantly reduced as a result of an intensive but subtle information campaign that explained not only what was expected of the user but why such expectations had been established (in terms of environmental protection). After initiation of the program, the only reported acts of vandalism were committed by users who had not been exposed to the program (Sutton, 1976). On the other hand, only moderate amounts of litter reduction were observed as a result of antilitter programs in a theater and campground setting (Clark, Hendee, &

Burgess, 1972), and mixed results in litter reduction were obtained from having campers sign an antilittering petition (Iso-Ahola & Niblock, 1981).

To the extent that vandalism is a product of uninformed users who are not normally predisposed toward vandalistic behavior, information and education programs are likely to be successful in reducing vandalism. The programs help establish a social and informational context within which the consequences of behavior can be evaluated, and they help reinforce an existing set of attitudes leading to higher consistency between attitude and behavior. However, protest vandalism, retaliatory vandalism, and hatred/aggression vandalism occur independent of the users' knowledge of rules and regulations. In the case of retaliatory vandalism, it may very well occur as a result of knowing and understanding a regulation. Given that protest, retaliatory, and aggressive vandalism all involve transference of behavior from one object (e.g., a regulation-enforcing ranger) to another (a picnic table), it is likely that the salient set of attitudes linking affect to overt behavior are not at all being explored or influenced by the information and education program. In fact, the culprit's attitude toward the object from which the behavior has been transferred may conflict with the attitude being developed in the information and education program and block the link between the vandalism attitude and the vandalism behavior. Thus as suggested by Clark (1976), it is unlikely that programs designed to heighten information levels or reinforce attitudes toward vandalism per se will be successful in preventing protest, retaliatory, and aggressive forms of vandalism.

Litter accumulation was significantly reduced in campsites used by recreationists who signed a petition supporting a statement that every effort should be made to keep the state park and recreation areas clean and free of litter. The reduction in total litter was evident, however, only in campgrounds that were relatively clean when the campers arrived. No significant reductions in litter accumulation were evident in heavily littered campgrounds assigned to recreationists who had signed the petition, supporting the notion that cleanliness breeds cleanliness (Iso-Ahola & Niblock, 1981). These findings replicate in a natural environment results obtained from littering research in more urbanized contexts (Finnie, 1973). Cone and Hayes (1980) provide a substantial review of the research on the litter problem with a primary emphasis on the built and urban environment.

The regulation of human access into natural environments has been hypothesized and implemented as a mechanism for controlling vandalism and littering. By requiring campers to register immediately on entering a campground, Hoots (1976) suggests that a psychological benefit accrues to the manager. The user's identity has been established and he or she could be subsequently held accountable for any acts of vandalism committed in the campground he or she has been "permitted" to use. In addition, the granting of a permit allows managers to allocate use within the environment and gives them the opportunity to explain behavioral norms in the setting and make explicit any permit conditions that would otherwise have to remain implicit. Entrance fee structures have also been advanced as a means of controlling vandalism on the grounds that requiring a monetary outlay for use of an environment increases the user's commitment to properly maintaining the environment. Skills testing (e.g., requiring a hunter safety course completion as a condition to hunting license issuance) is perceived as a means of limiting use to the serious recreationist who is assumed to have a strong commitment toward environmental conservation.

Virtually none of these environmental access regulations has ever been tested for its effectiveness in preventing vandalism or littering. In fact, although several factors mitigate against direct interpretation of the findings, some evidence exists to suggest that vandalism is higher in fee-requiring areas than in non-fee areas. Clark (1976) suggests that requiring a fee may establish a mind set of "well, I've paid for it, now I'm going to use it." Because many forms of vandalism have causes that are entirely external to the experiencing of an activity or set of activities in a given natural environment, it is unlikely that limiting access to any particular type of user will affect the incidence of vandalism.

Occasionally, vandalism becomes so frequent and its impact so severe that heavily vandalized objects are physically removed or sealed off from public contact and entrance into heavily vandalized environments is prohibited. Although such actions may be necessary to protect valuable natural or cultural objects, it is unlikely that they will reduce the rate of vandalism. Whyte (1980) has found the erection of protective fencing to prohibit physical access to public fountains does not eliminate physical use of the fountains (wading, swimming, etc.). Similarly, attempts to use popular trails and campgrounds continue long after such facilities are closed (whether for vandalism-related causes or as means to protect the environment from overuse). Such closures may result in increased vandalism as users retaliate against managers who have denied or attempted to deny their access to established territories.

Improved detection of vandalistic behavior and enforcement of environmental regulations have been postulated as deterrents to vandalism (Clark, 1976; Einolander, 1976). To be successful, vandalism detection and enforcement programs must make the potential vandal realize that he or she will be seen, caught, and punished. For example, the imposition of $500 fines and 30-day jail sentences for hunting rule violations soon brought an end to a deer- and elk-poaching problem (Drynan, 1977). All three components (i.e., detection, apprehension, and conviction) are equally important. Many existing programs lack one or more of these elements and consequently are ineffective (Jeffrey, 1971). Detection and enforcement programs need not rely entirely on traditional law enforcement mechanisms. The USFS, for example, has instituted a program in which volunteer senior citizens serve as campground hosts. Part of their job involves campground surveillance as a means of deterring vandalistic behavior and detecting it as soon as it occurs (Hoots, 1976). These campground host programs have been successful in reducing vandalism as well as increasing voluntary compliance with other campground regulations (Clark, 1976). As noted earlier, design solutions that embody Newman's (1972) concepts of defensible space will also help in the detection and deterrence of vandalism (Magill, 1976).

A number of authors (Clark, 1976; Clark et al., 1972; Hampton, 1976; Hoots, 1976) have suggested that the involvement of the public (both those engaging in vandalism and those affected by it) can be a successful approach to controlling vandalism and littering. In California, a cooperative program between the USFS and the U.S. Magistrate's Office allows first-time vandalism offenders involving misdemeanor crimes committed in national forests to perform restitution for their crimes in the forest. Such restitution often involves repair of damage done by vandals. Although the program has not reduced the incidence of vandalism in the forests (McEwen, 1976), the number of program enrollees committing second offenses is less than 10% (Hampton, 1976). The involvement of snowmobilers suspected of vandalizing recreation cabins in a cabin surveillance program eliminated the vandalism; and after several youths suspected of destroying bird cages of endangered species in a Spanish forest were involved in constructing new cages, destruction ceased (Clark, 1976). The provision of incentives (e.g., money, con-

servation patches to children) to the public for engaging in antilittering behavior has been an effective mechanism for not only encouraging proper litter disposal but also in reducing litter counts on the ground (Clark et al., 1972).

27.8. SUMMARY AND CONCLUSIONS

The focus of this chapter has been on social and behavioral issues inherent in the management of natural environments. Natural environments were defined as those in which humans are visitors rather than having a permanent presence and as places that exhibit little evidence "of human activity or intervention." Emphasis was placed on public policy as an indicator of changing social values with respect to natural environments and on changing social and behavioral issues encountered by managers as a function of changing policy. Policy was discussed over a number of eras, from those focusing on resource disposal through preservation, conservation, multiple use, recreation, natural beauty, and reclamation, to the environmental era of the 1960s and 1970s. A dominant theme throughout this evolution of policy has been the continuing growth of noncommodity values and uses of natural environments.

Noncommodity values and uses presented commodity-oriented managers with a new set of management issues, including resolving conflicts between and among users and managers, developing techniques for assessing noncommodity values, providing for greater public participation in planning and management decision making, and confronting the challenge of managing people and behavior (both desirable and undesirable) as well as resources. For most of these issues, managers have been poorly prepared by their professional training and initial experience.

Research has made notable contributions to the resolution of a number of these issues. There have been productive working relationships among managers and researchers in some areas such as in trying to resolve carrying capacity and deviant behavior problems. In other areas, however, it is less clear as to whether research findings have found their way into management practices and prescriptions. And these are also areas that have not been addressed by researchers involved in the study of human–natural environment interactions.

An emerging area of public concern is the conversion of natural environments to urban and suburban environments. It is estimated that nearly 3 million acres of rural land per year are converted to urban and other uses (Fletcher & Little, 1982). The noncommodity values of these lands are rarely considered in arriving at decisions about which lands should be converted and to what uses. The absence of valid and reliable data in a form compatible for decision making will seriously hinder the effectiveness of citizen interest groups.

The age and ethnic structure of the U.S. population is shifting. Significant increases in the older cohort and in the Hispanic population are predicted over the next three-plus decades. It seems likely that this shift will again place a different, or at least modified, set of demands on noncommodity uses of natural areas. In spite of the previously discussed body of research on aesthetic values, the elderly and minorities are conspicuously absent from the populations that have been studied. A past study found the elderly to have different landscape preferences from young and middle-aged adults (Zube et al., 1983). A fairly consistent finding in aesthetic values research has been a marked preference for natural landscapes over those showing signs of human intervention. The elderly adults' scenic quality assessments, however, were not significantly affected by the degree of naturalism in scenes being evaluated. If the aesthetic values of the elderly, Hispanics, and other minorities are also to be considered in management, additional study is warranted.

Noncommodity values have received a considerable amount of research attention but merit much more in the future. As the enthusiasm of the environmental era of the 1960s and 1970s is tempered throughout the world by the economic concerns of the 1980s, it appears evident that even more convincing arguments will be required to maintain aesthetic concerns as one of the priority considerations in management decisions. There are increasing demands for natural areas to be managed for commodity products and values. The commodity–noncommodity value arguments that surfaced with proposals for the first national parks have persisted over time. Greater understanding and documentation of the noncommodity psychological and experiential benefits provided by natural areas are required for balance in the commodity–noncommodity arena of competition. Much attention has been directed, for example, to identifying the most scenic or most preferred environments, but little has been directed to why they are important. What has been accepted as a statement of faith will likely not be adequate in the future.

In summary, a number of priorities exist for future research. They represent both a continuation of present directions and the pursuit of new directions. Among the present directions discussed in this chapter, research in the areas of carrying capacity assessment, perceived aesthetic values, and depreciative and deviant behavior will undoubtedly be of continuing importance to managers of natural environments. Rapid population growth in many of the western states with large areas of natural landscapes and a growing vacation and tourism industry increases demands for the nonconsumptive use of natural environments. Among those users are likely to be an increasing number of individuals who have had little, if any, prior experience in natural environments and hence no idea of expected behavioral norms. Because many of the nonconsumptive values of natural environments are inextricably linked to user expectation and experience level, development of behaviorally based models of resource management will continue to be of primary importance. Furthermore, the increasing demands for noncommodity uses at a time when society is demanding greater productivity of commodity outputs will sustain the need for research in the area of conflict management among competing users and managers.

New directions for research include a more comprehensive assessment of the relative importance of noncommodity values among the broad array of all natural environment values. Many management models continue to treat commodity and noncommodity values separately. Yet the Bitterroot and Monogahela decisions of the 1960s and 1970s illustrate that managers must integrate commodity and noncommodity orientations if an optimal and comprehensive balance of environmental values is to be achieved. Of additional importance is the variability of ranking of perceived values among different sectors of the population and in different regions and places within those regions. Included in this issue is the identification of noncommodity values in transitional landscapes, those areas of the natural environment that are being converted to urban and suburban environments. Research concerned with carrying capacity assessment, deviant behavior, and perceived aesthetic value must also be concerned with the expansion of its study population base to include, in the study of noncommodity values, the perceptions of the elderly, Hispanics, and other minorities. These are sectors of the population that have only rarely been included in research to date. Nevertheless, as the age and ethnic structure shifts to include ever-increasing numbers of elderly, Hispanics, and other minorities, demands on natural environments may change and particularly in natural environments proximate to urban areas.

REFERENCES

Altman, I. (1975). *The environment and social behavior.* Monterey, CA: Brooks/Cole.

Anderson, F.R. (1973). *NEPA in the courts.* Baltimore, MD: Johns Hopkins University Press.

Anderson, J.E. (1979). *Public policy making.* New York: Holt, Rinehart and Winston.

Anderson, L.M. (1981). Land use designations affect perceptions of scenic beauty in forest landscapes. *Forest Science, 27*(2), 392–400.

Anderson, T.W., Zube, E.H., & MacConnell, W.P. (1976). Predicting scenic values. In E.H. Zube (Ed.), *Studies in landscape perception* (pp. 6–69). Amherst, MA: University of Massachusetts, Institute for Man and Environment.

Appleton, J. (1975a). *The experience of landscape.* New York: Wiley.

Appleton, J. (1975b). Landscape evaluation: The theoretical vacuum. *Transactions of the Institute of British Geographers, 66*, 120–123.

Arnstein, S.R. (1969). A ladder of citizen participation. *Journal of the American Institute of Planners, 35*(4), 216–224.

Arthur, L.M. (1977). Predicting scenic beauty of forest environments: Some empirical tests. *Forest Science, 23*, 151–159.

Becker, R.H., Niemann, B.J., & Gates, W.A. (1981). Displacement of users within a river system: Social and environmental trade-offs. In D.W. Lime & D.R. Field (Tech. Coords.), *Some recent products of river recreation research* (General Tech. Rep. No. NC-63, pp. 33–39). St. Paul, MN: U.S. Department of Agriculture, North Central Forest Experiment Station.

Berlyne, D.E. (1960). *Conflict, arousal and curiosity.* New York: McGraw-Hill.

Berlyne, D.E. (1971). *Aesthetics and psychobiology.* New York: Appleton-Century-Crofts.

Bolle, A.W. (1971). Public participation and environmental quality. *Natural Resources Journal, 11*(3), 497–505.

Brown, P.J., Driver, B.L., & McConnel, C. (1978). The opportunity spectrum concept and behavioral information in outdoor recreation resource supply inventories: Background and applications. In H.G. Lund, V.J. LaBan, P.F. Ffolliott, & D.W. Robinson (Eds.), *Integrated inventories of renewable natural resources: Proceedings of the workshop* (General Tech. Rep. No. RM-55, pp. 73–84). Fort Collins, CO: U.S. Department of Agriculture, Rocky Mountain Forest and Range Experiment Station.

Brown, P.J., & Hunt, J.D. (1969). The influence of information signs on visitor distribution and use. *Journal of Leisure Research, 1*, 79–83.

Brush, R.O. (1979). The attractiveness of woodlands: Perceptions of forest landowners in Massachusetts. *Forest Science, 25*, 495–506.

Brush, R.O., & Palmer, J.F. (1979). Measuring the impact of urbanization on scenic quality: Land use change in the northeast. In G. Elsner & R.S. Smardon (Tech. Coords.), *Our national landscape* (General Tech. Rep. No. PSW-35, pp. 358–364). Berkeley, CA: U.S. Department of Agriculture, Pacific Southwest Forest and Range Experiment Station.

Brush, R.O., & Shafer, E.L. (1975). Application of a landscape preference model to land management. In E.H. Zube, R.O. Brush, & J.G. Fabos (Eds.), *Landscape assessment: Values, perceptions and resources*, (pp. 168–182). Stroudsburg, PA: Dowden, Hutchinson, & Ross.

Buhyoff, G.J., & Leuschner, W.A. (1978). Estimating psychological disutility from damaged forest stands. *Forest Science, 26*, 227–230.

Buhyoff, G.J., Wellman, J.D., & Daniel, T.C. (1982). Predicting scenic quality for mountain pine beetle and western spruce bud worm damaged forest vistas. *Forest Science, 28*, 827–838.

Bultena, G.C., & Hendee, J.C. (1972). Foresters' views of interest group positions on forest policy. *Journal of Forestry, 70*, 337–342.

Burch, W.R. (1976). Who participates—A sociological interpretation of natural resource decisions. *Natural Resources Journal, 16*, 41–54.

Burke, E.M. (1968). Citizen participation strategies. *Journal of the American Institute of Planners, 34*, 287–294.

Burns, W.T., & Rundell, D.D. (1969). *A test of visual preferences in a rural New England landscape.* Unpublished master's thesis, University of Massachusetts, Amherst.

Canon, L.K., Adler, S., & Leonard, R.E. (1979). Factors affecting dispersion of backcountry campsites. (Note No. NE-276, p. 6). Broomall, PA: U.S. Department of Agriculture, Northeastern Forest Experiment Station.

Carls, E.G. (1974). The effects of people and man-induced conditions on preferences for outdoor recreation. *Journal of Leisure Research, 6*, 113–124.

Catton, W.R., Jr. (1983). Social and behavioral aspects of carrying capacity in natural environments. In I. Altman & J.F. Wohlwill (Eds.), *Human behavior and environment: Vol. 6. Behavior and the natural environment*, (pp. 269–306). New York: Plenum.

Christensen, H.H., & Clark, R.N. (1978). Understanding and controlling vandalism and other rule violations in urban recreation areas. In *Proceedings of the National Urban Forestry Conference*. Washington, DC: U.S. Department of Agriculture, Forest Service.

Cicchetti, C.J., & Smith, K.V. (1973). Congestion, quality deterioration, and optional use: Wilderness recreation in the Spanish Peaks Primitive Area. *Social Science Research, 2*, 15–30.

Clark, R.N. (1976). Control of vandalism in recreation areas—Fact, fiction or folklore? In *Vandalism and outdoor recreation* (General Tech. Rep. No. PSW-17, pp. 62–72). Berkeley, CA: U.S. Department of Agriculture, Pacific Southwest Forest and Range Experiment Station.

Clark, R.N., Hendee, J.C., & Burgess, R.L. (1972). The experimental control of littering. *Journal of Environmental Education, 4*, 2.

Clark, R.N., Hendee, J.C., & Campbell, F.L. (1971). Values, beliefs and conflicts in modern camping culture. *Journal of Leisure Research, 3*, 143–159.

Clark, R.N., & Stankey, G.H. (1979). The recreational opportunity spectrum: A framework for planning, management and research (General Tech. Rep. No. PNW-98, ,p. 32). Portland, OR: U.S. Department of Agriculture, Pacific Northwest Forest and Range Experiment Station.

Coggins, G.C., & Wilkinson, C.F. (1981). *Federal public land and resources law*. Mineola, NY: Foundation Press.

Cohen, J.L., Sladen, B., & Bennett, B. (1975). The effects of situational variables on judgments of crowding. *Sociometry, 38*, 278–281.

Cohen, S. (1973). Property destruction: Motives and meanings. In C. Ward (Ed.), *Vandalism* (pp. 23–53). New York: Van Nostrand Rheinhold.

Colton, C.W., Pitt, D.G., Morgan, J.M., III, & Chaney, T.H. (1979). Behaviors and perceptions of recreational boaters. In *Proceedings of the First Annual Conference on Recreation Planning and Development* (pp. 171–182). New York: American Society of Civil Engineers.

Cone, J.D., & Hayes, S.C. (1980). *Environmental Problems: Behavioral solutions*. Monterey, CA: Brooks/Cole.

Cook, B. (1976). Design of campground facilities. In *Vandalism and outdoor recreation* (General Tech. Rep. No. PSW-17, pp. 37–39). Berkeley, CA: U.S. Department of Agriculture, Pacific Southwest Forest and Range Experiment Station.

Coughlin, R.E., & Goldstein, K.A. (1970). *The extent of agreement among observers on environmental attractiveness* (Discussion Series No. 37). Philadelphia, PA: Regional Science Research Institute.

Craik, K.H. (1968). The comprehension of the everyday physical environment. *Journal of the American Institute of Planners, 32*(1), 29–37.

Craik, K.H., & Zube, E.H. (Eds.). (1976). *Perceiving environmental quality*. New York: Plenum.

Culhane, P.J. (1981). *Public lands politics*. Baltimore, MD: John Hopkins University Press.

Dana, S.T., & Fairfax, S.K. (1980). *Forest and range policy*. New York: McGraw-Hill.

Daniel, T.C., & Boster, R.S. (1976). Measuring landscape aesthetics: The Scenic Beauty Estimation Method (Research Paper No. RM-167, p. 66). Fort Collins, CO: U.S. Department of Agriculture, Rocky Mountain Forest and Range Experiment Station.

Daniel, T.C., & Schroeder, H. (1979). Scenic beauty estimation model: Predicting perceived beauty of forest landscapes. In G.H. Elsner & R.C. Smardon (Tech. Coords.), *Our national landscape*. (General Tech. Rep. PSW-35, pp. 514–523). Berkeley, CA: U.S. Department of Agriculture, Pacific Southwest Forest and Range Experiment Station.

Daniel, T.C., & Vining, J. (1983). Methodological issues in the assessment of visual landscape quality. In I. Altman & J. Wohlwill (Eds.), *Human behavior and the environment: Vol. 6. Behavior and the natural environment* (pp. 38–84). New York: Plenum.

Danielian, A.C. (1976). Design vs. vandalism. In *Vandalism and outdoor recreation* (General Tech. Rep. No. PSW-17, pp. 39–42). Berkeley, CA: U.S. Department of Agriculture, Pacific Southwest Forest and Range Experiment Station.

Dansereau, P. (1975). *Inscape and landscape*. New York: Columbia University Press.

Desor, J.A. (1972). Toward a psychological theory of crowding. *Journal of Personality and Social Psychology, 21*, 79–83.

Ditton, R.B., Graefe, A.R., & Fedler, A.J. (1981). Recreational satisfaction at Buffalo National River: Some measurement concerns. In D.W. Lime & D.R. Field (Tech. Coords.), *Some Recent Products of River Recreation Research* (General Tech. Rep. No. NC-63, pp. 9–18). St. Paul, MN: U.S. Department of Agriculture, North Central Forest Experiment Station.

Downing, K., & Clark, R.N. (1979). Users' and managers' perceptions of dispersed recreation impacts: A focus on roaded forest lands. In R. Ittner, D.R. Potter, J.K. Agee & L. Anschell (Eds.), *Recreational impacts on wildlands* (R-6-001-1979, pp. 18–23). Seattle, WA: U.S. Department of Agriculture, Forest Service.

Driver, B.L., & Brown, P.J. (1978). The opportunity spectrum concept and behavioral information in outdoor recreation resource supply inventories: A rationale. In H.G. Lund, V.J. LaBan, P.F. Ffolliott, & D.W. Robinson (Eds.), *Integrated inventories of renewable natural resources* (General Tech. Rep. No. RM-55, pp. 24–32). Fort Collins, CO: U.S. Department of Agriculture, Rocky Mountain Forest and Range Experiment Station.

Driver, B.L., & Brown, P.J. (1983). Contributions of behavioral scientists to recreation resource management. In I. Altman & J.F. Wohlwill (Eds.), *Human behavior and environment: Vol. 6. Behavior and the natural environment* (pp. 307–339). New York: Plenum.

Driver, B.L., & Knopf, R.C. (1977). Personality, outdoor recreation and expected consequences. *Environment and Behavior, 9*, 169–195.

Drynan, T. (1977). Perspective of the problem by the state police. In *Proceedings: Theft and vandalism in the woods*. Portland, OR: Oregon Forest Protection Association.

Dubos, R. (1968). *So Human an Animal*. New York: Scribners.

Dubos, R. (1980). *The Wooing of Earth*. New York: Scribners.

Echelberger, H.E. (1979). The semantic differential in landscape research. In G.H. Elsner & R.C. Smardon (Tech. Coords.). *Our National Landscape* (General Tech. Rep. No. PSW-35, pp. 524–531). Berkeley, CA: U.S. Department of Agriculture, Pacific Southwest Forest and Range Experiment Station.

Einolander, J.C. (1976). Vandalism at "Red Rock." In *Vandalism and Outdoor Recreation* (General Tech. Rep. No. PSW-17, pp. 25–27). Berkeley, CA: U.S. Department of Agriculture, Pacific Southwest Forest and Range Experiment Station.

Epstein, Y.M., & Karlin, R.A. (1975). Effects of acute experimental crowding. *Journal of Applied Social Psychology*, 5, 34–43.

Ernetaz, R.V. (1980). Management—The solution to the problem. In R.N.L. Andrews & P.F. Nowak (Eds.), *Off-road vehicles: A management challenge* (pp. 211–219). Ann Arbor: University of Michigan.

Ewing, G.O., & Kulka, T. (1979). Revealed and stated preference analysis of ski resort attractiveness. *Leisure Sciences*, 2, 249–275.

Fairfax, S.K. (1975). Public involvement and the Forest Service. *Journal of Forestry*, 73, 657–659.

Fazio, J.R., & Gilbert, D.L. (1974). Mandatory wilderness permits: Some indicators of success. *Journal of Forestry*, 72, 753–756.

Feimer, N.R., Craik, K.H., Smardon, R.C., & Sheppard, S.R.J. (1979). Appraising the reliability of visual impact assessment methods. In G.H. Elsner & R.C. Smardon (Tech. Coords.), *Our National Landscape* (General Tech. Rep. No. PSW-35, pp. 288–295). Berkeley, CA: U.S. Department of Agriculture, Pacific Southwest Forest and Range Experiment Station.

Feimer, N.R., Smardon, R.C., & Craik, K.H. (1981). Evaluating the effectiveness of observer based visual resource and impact assessment methods. *Landscape Research*, 6(1), 12–16.

Field Research Corporation. (1977). *California public opinion and behavior regarding the California desert*. San Francisco, CA: Author.

Finnie, W.C. (1973). Field experiments in litter control. *Environment and Behavior*, 5, 123–143.

Fisher, A.C., & Krutilla, J.V. (1972). Determination of optimal capacity of resource-based recreation facilities. *Natural Resources Journal*, 12, 417–444.

Fletcher, W.W., & Little, E.E. (1982). *The American cropland crisis*. Bethesda, MD: American Land Forum.

Foster, R.J., & Jackson, E.L. (1979). Factors associated with camping satisfaction in Alberta provincial park campgrounds. *Journal of Leisure Research*, 11, 292–306.

Frissell, S.S., & Duncan, D.P. (1965). Campsite preference and deterioration in the Quetico-Superior canoe country. *Journal of Forestry*, 63, 256–260.

Frissell, S.S., & Stankey, G.H. (1972). Wilderness environmental quality: Search for social and ecological harmony. In *Proceedings, Society of American Foresters Annual Meeting* (pp. 170–183). Washington, DC: Society of American Foresters.

Garcia, M.Y.W. (1980). *Citizen participation in Forest Service planning in Arizona*. Unpublished doctoral dissertation, Tucson: University of Arizona.

Gratzer, M.A., & McDowell, R.D. (1971). *Adaptation of an eye movement recorder to aesthetic environmental mensuration* (Research Rep. No. 36). Storrs, CT: University of Connecticut, Agricultural Experiment Station.

Hammit, W.E. (1981). The familiarity-preference component of on-site recreational experiences. *Leisure Sciences*, 4, 177–193.

Hampton, G. (1976). Creative justice. In *Vandalism and outdoor recreation* (General Tech. Rep. No. PSW-17, pp. 30–32). Berkeley, CA: U.S. Department of Agriculture, Pacific Southwest Forest and Range Experiment Station.

Hardin, G. (1968). The tragedy of the commons. *Science*, 162, 1243–1248.

Heberlein, T.A. (1977). Density, crowding, and satisfaction: Sociological studies for determining carrying capacities. In *River recreation management and research* (General Tech. Rep. NC-28, pp. 67–76). St. Paul, MN: U.S. Department of Agriculture, North Central Forest Experiment Station.

Heberlein, T.A., & Dunwiddie, P. (1979). Systematic observation of use levels, campsite selection and visitor characteristics at a high mountain lake. *Journal of Leisure Research*, 11, 306–316.

Heberlein, T.A., & Shelby, B. (1977). Camping capacity, values and the satisfaction model: A reply to Greist. *Journal of Leisure Research*, 9, 142–148.

Heberlein, T.A., & Vaske, J.J. (1977). *Crowding and visitor conflict on the Bois Brule River* (Tech. Rep. No. WIS-WRC-77-04). Madison: University of Wisconsin.

Hendee, J.C. (1977). Public involvement in the U.S. Forest Service Roadless-area Review: Lessons from a case study. In D.W. Sewell & T. Coppock (Eds.), *Public participation in planning* (pp. 89–103). New York: Wiley.

Hendee, J.C., & Harris, R.W. (1970). Foresters' perceptions of the wilderness-user attitudes and preferences. *Journal of Forestry*, 68, 759–762.

Hendrix, W.G., & Fabos, J.G. (1975). Visual land use compatability as a significant contributor to visual resource quality. *International Journal of Environmental Studies*, 8, 21–28.

Hinds, T.E. (1976). *Aspen mortality in Rocky Mountain campgrounds* (Research Paper No. RM-164, p. 20). Ft. Collins, CO: U.S. Department of Agriculture, Rocky Mountain Forest and Range Experiment Station.

Hodgson, R.W., & Thayer, R.L. (1980). Implied human influence reduces landscape beauty. *Landscape Planning*, 7, 171–179.

Hoots, T.A. (1976). Vandalism and law enforcement on National Forest lands. In *Vandalism and outdoor recreation*. (General Tech. Rep. No. PSW-17, pp. 20–23). Berkeley, CA: U.S. Department of Agriculture, Pacific Southwest Forest and Range Experiment Station.

Iso-Ahola, S.E., & Niblock, L.A. (1981). Reducing litter through the signed petition: A field experiment in the campground. [Abstract]. In *Abstracts from the 1981 Sym-*

posium on Leisure Research (p. 77). Washington, DC: National Recreation and Parks Association.

Ittelson, W.H. (1973). *Environment and cognition.* New York: Seminar Press.

Jackson, E.L., & Wong, R.A.G. (1982). Perceived conflict between urban cross-country skiers and snowmobilers in Alberta. *Journal of Leisure Research, 14,* 47–62.

Jeffrey, C.R. (1971). *Crime prevention through environmental design.* Beverly Hills, CA: Sage.

Kaplan, R. (1973). Predictors of environmental preference: Designers and "clients." In W.F.E. Preiser (Ed.), *EDRA 4: Environmental design research* (pp. 265–274). Stroudsburg, PA: Dowden, Hutchinson, & Ross.

Kaplan, R. (1975). Some methods and strategies in the prediction of preference. In E.H. Zube, R.O. Brush, & J.C. Fabos (Eds.), *Landscape assessment: Values, perceptions and resources* (pp. 118–129). Stroudsburg, PA: Dowden, Hutchinson, & Ross.

Kaplan, R. (1977). Preference and everyday nature: Method and application. In D. Stokols (Ed.), *Perspectives on environment and behavior: Theory, research and application.* New York: Plenum.

Kaplan, R. (1978). The green experience. In S. Kaplan & R. Kaplan (Eds.), *Humanscape* (pp. 186–193). North Scituate, MA: Duxbury.

Kaplan, R. (1983). The role of nature in the urban context. In I. Altman & J.F. Wohlwill (Eds.), *Human behavior and environment. Vol. 6. Behavior and the natural environment* (pp. 127–161). New York: Plenum.

Kaplan, S. (1975). An informal model for the prediction of preference. In E.H. Zube, R.O. Brush, & J.G. Fabos (Eds.), *Landscape assessment: Values, perception and resources* (pp. 92–101). Stroudsburg, PA: Dowden, Hutchinson, & Ross.

Kaplan, S. (1979). Perception and landscape: Conceptions and misconceptions. In G.H. Elsner & R.C. Smardon (Tech. Coords.), *Our national landscape* (General Tech. Rep. No. PSW-35, pp. 241–248). Berkeley, CA: U.S. Department of Agriculture, Pacific Southwest Forest and Range Experiment Station.

Kaplan, S., Kaplan, R., & Wendt, J.S. (1972). Rated preference and complexity for natural and urban visual material. *Perception and Psychophysics, 12,* 354–356.

Kemsley, W. (1980). ORV user conflicts. In R.N.L. Andrews & P.F. Nowak (Eds.), *Off-road vehicles: A management challenge,* (pp. 234–238). Ann Arbor: University of Michigan.

Kenline, G.A. (1976). Vandalism—An overview. In *Vandalism and outdoor recreation* (General Tech. Rep. No. PSW-17, pp. 6–9). Berkeley, CA: U.S. Department of Agriculture, Pacific Southwest Forest and Range Experiment Station.

Knudson, D.M., & Curry, E.B. (1981). Campers' perceptions of site deterioration and crowding. *Journal of Forestry, 79,* 92–94.

Krumpe, E.E. (1979). *Redistributing backcountry use by a behaviorally based communications device.* Unpublished doctoral dissertation, Ft. Collins: Colorado State University.

Kunst-Wilson, W.R., & Zajonc, R.B. (1980). Affective discrimination of stimuli that cannot be recognized. *Science, 207,* 557–558.

Laitala, L.M. (1975). Are advisory boards really necessary? *Our Public Land, 25*(3), 17–22.

Laurie, I.C. (1975). Aesthetic factors in visual evaluation. In E.H. Zube, R.O. Brush, & J.G. Fabos (Eds.), *Landscape assessment: Values, perception and resources* (pp. 102–117). Stroudsburg, PA: Dowden, Hutchinson, & Ross.

Lee, R.G. (1975). *The management of human components in the Yosemite National Park ecosystem.* Yosemite, CA: Yosemite Institute.

Lime, D.W. (1979). Carrying capacity. *Trends in Rivers and Trails, 16*(2), 37–40.

Lime, D.W., & Lucas, R.C. (1977). Good information improves the wilderness experience. *Naturalist, 28*(4), 18–21.

Lime, D.W., & Stankey, G.H. (1971). Carrying capacity: Maintaining outdoor recreation quality. In *Forest Recreation Symposium Proceedings* (pp. 174–184). Upper Darby, PA: U.S. Department of Agriculture, Forest Service, Northeast Forest Experiment Station.

Linton, D. (1968). The assessment of scenery as a natural resource. *Scottish Geographical Magazine, 84,* 219–293.

Litton, R.B. (1968). *Forest landscape description and inventories—a basis for land planning and design.* (Research paper No. PSW-49). Berkeley, CA: U.S. Department of Agriculture, Pacific Southwest Forest and Range Experiment Station.

Litton, R.B. (1972). Aesthetic dimensions of the landscape. In J.V. Krutilla (Ed.), *Natural environments: Studies in theoretical and applied analysis* (pp. 262–291). Baltimore, MD: Johns Hopkins University Press.

Litton, R.B., Jr., Tetlow, R.J., Sorensen, J., & Beatty, R.A. (1974). *Water and landscape: An aesthetic overview of the role of water in the landscape.* Port Washington, NY: Port Washington Press.

Lowenthal, D. (1978). Finding valued landscapes. *Progress in Human Geography, 2,* 373–418.

Lucas, R.C. (1964). *The recreational capacity of the Quetico-Superior area* (Research Paper No. LS-15, p. 34). St. Paul, MN: U.S. Department of Agriculture, Lake States Forest Experiment Station.

Lucas, R.C. (1966). The contribution of environmental research to wilderness policy decisions. *Journal of Social Issues, 22*(4), 116–126.

Lucas, R.C. (1967). *The changing recreational use of the Boundary Waters Canoe Area* (Research Note No. NC-42, p. 4). St. Paul, MN: U.S. Department of Agriculture, North Central Forest Experiment Station.

Lucas, R.C. (1979). Perceptions of non-motorized recreational impacts: A review of research findings. In R. Ittner, D.R. Potter, J.K. Agee, & L. Anschell (Eds.), *Recreational impacts on wildlands* (R-6-001-1979, pp. 24–31). Portland, OR: U.S. Department of Agriculture, Forest Service.

Magill, A.W. (1976). The message of vandalism. In *Vandalism and outdoor recreation* (General Tech. Rep. No. PSW-17, pp. 50–54). Berkeley, CA: U.S. Department of Agriculture, Pacific Southwest Forest and Range Experiment Station.

Manning, R.E., & Ciali, C.P. (1980). Recreation density and user satisfaction: A further exploration of the satisfaction model. *Journal of Leisure Research, 12,* 329–343.

Marsh, G.P. (1864). *Man and nature.* New York: Scribner's.

McEwen, W.W. (1976). A magistrate's view of vandalism. In *Vandalism and outdoor recreation* (General Tech. Rep. No. PSW-17, pp. 29–30). Berkeley, CA: U.S. Department of Agriculture, Pacific Southwest Forest and Range Experiment Station.

Merriam, L.C., Jr., & Smith, C.K. (1974). Visitor impact on newly developed campsites in the Boundary Waters Canoe Area. *Journal of Forestry, 72,* 627–630.

Miller, T. (1976). Vandalism in California state parks. In *Vandalism and outdoor recreation* (General Tech. Rep. No. PSW-17, pp. 14–15). Berkeley, CA: U.S. Department of Agriculture, Pacific Southwest Forest and Range Experiment Station.

Moreland, R.L., & Zajonc, R.B. (1977). Is stimulus recognition a necessary condition for the occurrence of exposure effects? *Journal of Personality and Social Psychology, 35,* 191–199.

Morrison, J. (1976). Vandalism: The California state park approach. In *Vandalism and outdoor recreation* (General Tech. Rep. No. PSW-17, pp. 23–25). Berkeley, CA: U.S. Department of Agriculture, Pacific Southwest Forest and Range Experiment Station.

Nash, R. (1977). River recreation: History and future. In *River Recreation Management and Research Symposium Proceedings* (General Tech. Rep. No. NC-28, pp. 2–7). St. Paul, MN: U.S. Department of Agriculture, North Central Forest Experiment Station.

Newman, O. (1972). *Defensible space: Crime prevention through urban design.* New York: Mcmillan.

Nielsen, J.M., Shelby, B., & Hass, J.E. (1977). Sociological carrying capacity and the last settler syndrome. *Pacific Sociological Review, 20,* 568–581.

Nieman, T.J. (1980). The visual environment of the New York coastal zone: User preferences and perceptions. *Coastal Zone Management Journal, 8,* 45–62.

Outdoor Recreation Resources Review Commission. (1962). *Outdoor recreation for America.* Washington, DC: U.S. Government Printing Office.

Palmer, J.F (1979). The conceptual typing of trail environments: A tool for recreation research and management. In T.C. Daniel, E.H. Zube, & B.L. Driver (Tech. Coords.). *Assessing amenity resource values* (General Tech. Rep. No. RM-68, pp. 14–21). Fort Collins, CO: U.S. Department of Agriculture, Rocky Mountain Forest and Range Experiment Station.

Patey, R.C., & Evans, R.M. (1979). Identification of scenically preferred forest landscapes. In G.H. Elsner & R.C. Smardon (Tech. Coords.), *Our national landscape* (General Tech. Rep. No. PSW-35, pp. 532–538). Berkeley, CA: U.S. Department of Agriculture, Pacific Southwest Forest and Range Experiment Station.

Penning-Rowsell, E.C. (1981). Fluctuating fortunes in gauging landscape value. *Progress in Human Geography, 5,* 25–41.

Peterson, G.L. (1974). A comparison of the sentiments and perceptions of wilderness managers and canoeists in the Boundary Waters Canoe Area. *Journal of Leisure Research, 6,* 194–206.

Petulla, J.M. (1977). *American environmental history.* San Francisco: Boyd and Fraser.

Pitt, D.G., Chaney, T.H., & Colton, C.W. (1981). A perceptually based definition of valued boating environments on the tributaries of the Chesapeake Bay. *Landscape Research, 5*(3), 19–21.

Pitt, D.G., & Zube, E.H. (1979). The Q-Sort method: Use in landscape assessment research and landscape planning. In G.H. Elsner & R.C. Smardon (Tech. Coords.), *Our national landscape* (General Tech. Rep. No. PSW-35, pp. 227–234). Berkeley, CA: U.S. Department of Agriculture, Pacific Southwest Forest and Range Experiment Station.

Pitt, D.G., Zube, E.H., & Palmer, J.F. (1980, August). *Regional and demographic perspectives on landscape perception.* Paper presented at the annual meeting of the Council of Educators on Landscape Architecture, Madison, WI.

Plumley, H.J., Peet, H.T., & Leonard, R.E. (1978). *Records of backcountry use can assist trail managers* (Research Paper No. NE-414, p. 19). Broomal, PA: U.S. Department of Agriculture, Northeastern Forest Experiment Station.

Porteous, D. (1982). Approaches to environmental aesthetics. *Environmental Psychology, 2,* 53–66.

Price, C. (1979). Public preference and the management of recreational congestion. *Regional Studies, 13,* 125–139.

Rabinowitz, C.B., & Coughlin, R.E. (1970). *Analysis of landscape character relevant to preference,* (Discussion Series No. 30). Philadelphia: Regional Sciences Research Institute.

Rapoport, A. (1975). Toward a redefinition of density. *Environment and Behavior, 7,* 133–157.

Reich, J.W., & Robertson, J.C. (1979). Reactance and normal appeal in anti-littering messages. *Journal of Applied Social Psychology, 9,* 91–101.

Reiter, S.N., & Samuel, W. (1980). Littering as a function of prior litter and the presence or absence of prohibitive signs. *Journal of Applied Social Psychology, 10,* 45–55.

Reynolds, H.E. (1976). Preventive planning to reduce vandalism. In *Vandalism and Outdoor Recreation* (General Tech. Rep. No. PSW-17, pp. 42–46). Berkeley, CA: U.S. Department of Agriculture, Southwest Forest and Range Experiment Station.

Robertson, R.D. (1981). *An investigation of visitor behavior in wilderness areas.* Unpublished doctoral dissertation, Iowa City: University of Iowa.

Robinson, G.O. (1975). *The Forest Service.* Baltimore, MD: Johns Hopkins University Press.

Roggenbuck, J.W., & Berrier, D.L. (1982). A comparison of the effectiveness of two communication strategies in dispersing wilderness campers. *Journal of Leisure Research, 14,* 77–89.

Rosenbaum, W.A. (1978). Public involvement as reform and ritual: The development of federal participation programs. In S. Langton (Ed.), *Citizen participation in America* (pp. 81–96). Lexington, MA: Lexington Books.

Ross, T.L., & Moeller, G.H. (1974). Communicating roles in recreation areas. (Research Paper No. NE-297). Upper Darby, PA: U.S. Department of Agriculture, Northeastern Forest Experiment Station.

Runte, A. (1979). *National parks: The American experience.* Lincoln, NB: University of Nebraska Press.

Samp, R. (1976). Vandalism in a city park. In *Vandalism and outdoor recreation* (General Tech. Rep. No. PSW-17, pp. 15–17). Berkeley, CA: U.S. Department of Agriculture, Pacific Southwest Forest and Range Experiment Station.

Sanderson, D.W. (1980). Improving the management of two-wheeled vehicles: Education. In R.N.L. Andrews & P.F. Nowak (Eds.), *Off-road vehicles: A management challenge* (pp. 270–273). Ann Arbor, MI: University of Michigan.

Seamon, D. (1979). *A geography of the life world.* New York: St. Martin's.

Sell, J.L., Taylor, J.G., & Zube, E.H. (1984). Toward a theoretical framework for landscape perception. In T. Saarinin, D. Searnon, & J. Sell (Eds.), *Environmental perception and behavior: Inventory and prospect.* Chicago: University of Chicago, Department of Geography.

Shafer, E.L., Jr., Hamilton, J.F., Jr., & Schmidt, E.A. (1969). Natural landscape preferences: A predictive model. *Journal of Leisure Research, 1,* 1–19.

Shafer, E.L., Jr., & Mietz, J. (1969). Aesthetic and emotional experiences rate high with northeast wilderness hikers. *Environment and Behavior, 1,* 187–198.

Shafer, E.L., Jr., & Richards, T.A. (1974). *A comparison of viewer reactions to outdoor scenes and photographs of those scenes* (Research Paper No. NE-302, p. 26). Upper Darby, PA: U.S. Department of Agriculture, Northeastern Forest Experiment Station.

Shelby, B., & Nielsen, J.M. (1976a). *Motors and oars in the Grand Canyon* (River Contract Study Final Rep., Part 2).

Boulder, CO: Human Ecological Research Service.

Shelby, B., & Nielsen, J.M. (1976b). *Use levels and crowding in the Grand Canyon* (River Contract Study Final Rep., Part 3). Boulder, CO: Human Ecological Research Service.

Shreyer, R., & Roggenbuck, J.W. (1978). The influence of experience expectations on crowding perceptions and social-psychological carrying capacities. *Leisure Sciences, 1,* 373–394.

Sokol, R.J. (1976). A psychoanalytic view of vandalism. In *Vandalism and Outdoor Recreation* (General Tech. Rep. No. PSW-17, pp. 54–58). Berkeley, CA: U.S. Department of Agriculture, Southwest Forest and Range Experiment Station.

Sommer, R. (1972). *Design awareness.* Corte Madera, CA: Rinehart.

Sonnenfeld, J. (1967). Environmental perception and adaptation level in the Arctic. In D. Lowenthal (Ed.), *Environmental perception and behavior* (Research Paper No. 109, pp. 42–59). Chicago: University of Chicago, Department of Geography.

Stankey, G.H. (1973). *Visitor perception of wilderness recreation carrying capacity* (Research Paper No. INT-142, p. 62). Ogden, UT: U.S. Department of Agriculture, Intermountain Forest and Range Experiment Station.

Stankey, G.H., & Baden, J. (1977). *Rationing wilderness use: Methods, problems and guidelines* (Research Paper No. INT-192, p. 20). Ogden, UT: U.S. Department of Agriculture, Intermountain Forest and Range Experiment Station.

Stokols, D. (1972). On the distinction between density and crowding: Some implications for future research. *Psychological Review, 79,* 275–277.

Sutton, R.W. (1976). Vandalism in the Channel Islands National Monument. In *Vandalism and outdoor recreation* (General Tech. Rep. No. PSW-17, pp. 12–14). Berkeley, CA: U.S. Department of Agriculture, Pacific Southwest Forest and Range Experiment Station.

Thayer, R.L., Jr., & Atwood, B.G. (1978). Plants, complexity and pleasure in urban and suburban environments. *Environmental Psychology and Nonverbal Behavior, 3,* 67–76.

Tuan, Y.F. (1977). *Space and place: The perspective of experience.* Minneapolis: University of Minnesota Press.

Turnbull, C.M. (1962). *The Forest People.* New York: Anchor.

Twight, B.W., & Catton, W.R., Jr. (1975). The politics of images: Forest managers vs. recreation publics. *Natural Resources Journal, 15,* 297–306.

Ulrich, R.S. (1979). Visual landscapes and psychological well-being. *Landscape Research, 4,* 17–23.

Ulrich, R.S. (1981). Natural versus urban scenes: Some psychological effects. *Environment and Behavior, 13,* 523–556.

Ulrich, R.S. (1983). Aesthetics and affective response to natural environment. In I. Altman & J.F. Wohlwill (Eds.),

Human behavior and environment: Vol. 6. Behavior and the natural environment (pp. 85–125). New York: Plenum.

Vaske, J.J., Donnelly, M.P., & Heberlein, T.A. (1980). Perceptions of crowding and resource quality by early and more recent visitors. *Leisure Sciences, 3*, 367–381.

Vitz, P.C. (1966). Preference for different amounts of stimulus complexity. *Behavioral Science, 11*, 105–114.

Wagar, A. (1964). *The carrying capacity of wildlands for recreation* (Forest Science Monograph 7-1964). Washington, DC: Society of American Foresters.

Ward, C. (Ed.). (1973). *Vandalism.* New York: Van Nostrand Rheinhold.

Wellman, J.D., & Buhyoff, G.J. (1980). Effects of regional familiarity on landscape preferences. *Journal of Environmental Management, 11*, 105–110.

Wellman, J.D., Dawson, M.S., & Roggenback, J.W. (1982). Park managers' predictions of the motivations of visitors to two National Park Service areas. *Journal of Leisure Research, 14*, 1–15.

Wells, E. (1971). *Vandalism and violence: Innovative strategies reduce costs to schools.* Washington, DC: National Schoo Public Relations Association.

Wenner, L.M. (1982). *The environmental decade in the courts.* Bloomington: University of Indiana Press.

West, P.C. (1980). *Summary and conclusion: Snowmobiles.* In R.N.L. Andrews & P.F. Nowak (Eds.), *Off-road vehicles: A management challenge* (pp. 282–285). Ann Arbor: University of Michigan.

Whyte, W.H. (1980). *The social life of small urban spaces.* Washington, DC: Conservation Foundation.

Williams, M.L. (1976). Vandals aren't all bad. In *Vandalism and outdoor recreation* (General Tech. Rep. No. PSW-17, pp. 46–50). Berkeley, CA: U.S. Department of Agriculture, Pacific Southwest Forest and Range Experiment Station.

Wilson, W.R. (1979). Feeling more than we can know: Exposure effects without learning. *Journal of Personality and Social Psychology, 37*, 811–821.

Wohlwill, J.F. (1968). Amount of stimulus exploration and preference as differential functions of stimulus complexity. *Perception and Psychophysics, 4*, 307–312.

Wohlwill, J.F. (1976). Environmental aesthetics: The environment as source of affect. In I. Altman & J.F. Wohlwill

(Eds.), *Human behavior and environment* (Vol. 1, pp. 37–86). New York: Plenum.

Wohlwill, J.F. (1979). What belongs where: Research on fittingness of man-made structures in natural settings. In T.C. Daniel, E. H. Zube, & B.L. Driver (Tech. Coords.), *Assessing amenity values* (General Tech. Rep. No. RM-68, pp. 48–57). Fort Collins, CO: U.S. Department of Agriculture, Rocky Mountain Forest and Range Experiment Station.

Wohlwill, J.F. (1983). The concept of nature. In I. Altman & J.F. Wohlwill (Eds.), *Human behavior and environment: Vol. 6. Behavior and the natural environment* (pp. 5–37). New York: Plenum.

Wohlwill, J.F., & Harris, G. (1980). Response to congruity or contrast for man-made features in natural recreation settings. *Leisure Sciences, 3*, 349–365.

Womble, P. & Studebaker, S. (1981). Crowding in a national park campground. Katwai National Monument in Alaska. *Environment and Behavior, 13*, 557–573.

Zube, E.H. (1973). Rating every day rural landscapes of the Northeastern U.S. *Landscape Architecture, 63*, 92–97.

Zube, E.H. (1980). *Environmental evaluation: Perception and public policy.* Monterey, CA: Brooks/Cole.

Zube, E.H., & Pitt, D.G. (1981). Cross-cultural perceptions of scenic and heritage landscapes. *Landscape Planning, 8*, 69–87.

Zube, E.H., Pitt, D.G., & Anderson, T.W. (1974). *Perception and measurement of scenic resources in the southern Connecticut River Valley* (Publication No. R-74-1). Amherst, MA: University of Massachusetts, Institute for Man and Environment.

Zube, E.H., Pitt, D.G., & Anderson, T.W. (1975). Perception and prediction of scenic resource values of the northeast. In E.H. Zube, R.O. Brush, & J.G. Fabos (Eds.), *Landscape assessment: Values, perceptions and resources* (pp. 151–167). Stroudsberg, PA: Dowden, Hutchinson, & Ross.

Zube, E.H., Pitt, D.G., & Evans, G.W. (1983). A lifespan developmental study of landscape assessment. *Journal of Environmental Psychology, 3*, 115–128.

Zube, E.H., Sell, J.L., & Taylor, J.G. (1982). Landscape perception: Research application and theory. *Landscape Planning, 9*, 1–33.

Chapter 28

MANAGING SCARCE ENVIRONMENTAL RESOURCES

Paul C. Stern, *Commission on Behavioral and Social Sciences and Education, National Research Council, Washington, DC*

Stuart Oskamp, *Department of Psychology, Claremont Graduate School, Claremont, California*

Note. Our contributions to this chapter have been essentially equal, and the order of authorship was decided by a coin toss.

Environmental resources problems that are currently threatening our world include runaway population growth, land erosion, declining food harvests, exhaustion of mineral deposits, shrinking petroleum reserves, air pollution, failing water supplies, dangerous water quality, acid rain, solid waste disposal, litter control, toxic wastes, and nuclear wastes. This chapter first briefly reviews the threats to earth's environmental resources, then selectively summarizes psychological research findings in seven resource problem areas, and finally discusses in detail the prospects for psychologically oriented research to help reduce these environmental problems.

28.1. BACKGROUND

28.1.1. The Status of Environmental Resources

Useful volumes that stress society's environmental impacts and resource problems include Davis (1979), Ehrlich, Ehrlich, and Holdren (1977), Humphrey and Buttel (1982), Watt (1982), and Welch and Miewald (1982). Perhaps the most compelling warning about the ecological limits on many sorts of human activities came in the *Global 2000 Report to the President* (U.S. Council on Environmental Quality [USCEQ],1980). This monumental compilation of data and projections concerning world conditions through the end of this century stated very gloomy conclusions:

> If present trends continue, the world in 2000 will be more crowded, more polluted, less stable ecologically, and more vulnerable to disruption than the world we live in now. Serious stresses involving population, resources, and environment are clearly visible ahead. Despite greater material output, the world's people will be poorer in many ways than they are today. (USCEQ, 1980, p. 1)

Some researchers have questioned this conclusion about 2000, a few have even argued that a future of world prosperity is likely with unchecked population growth (Simon & Kahn, 1984), but most observers reject such extreme positions (Brown, 1985). For example, a recent National Research Council report (1986), which concludes that population growth does not necessarily have a negative effect on economic growth, also acknowledges that population growth will exacerbate problems in sustaining renewable resources, improving education, controlling pollution, and reducing income inequality. Even if improved technology and economic adjustments forestall some of the consequences predicted in *Global 2000* for fairly long periods, environmental resource problems will continue to be with us. As some become less serious, others will become worse. And because of the interrelations of environmental problems, discussed in the following sections, we judge that as a class, resource problems will continue to increase in seriousness.

Population

Global 2000 projected more than a 50% increase in the world's population, from 4 billion in 1975 to 6^1/$_3$ billion in 2000, with 90% of this growth occurring in the poorest countries. Population levels predicted for 2030 approach the estimated maximum carrying ca-

pacity of our planet, and the carrying capacity of some local areas such as sub-Saharan Africa has already been exceeded. Already in the early 1970s, when food supplies were relatively abundant, about half a billion people in the poorer nations of the Third World were estimated to be below the United Nations standard of minimum adequate food intake, and this figure could rise to 1.3 billion by the year 2000 (USCEQ, 1980, p. 17). The population explosion is an important contributing factor in every one of the world's environmental resource problems.

Land

When land is overused or improperly used, it erodes rapidly and loses much of its life support capacity—a process that precipitated the collapse of the Mayan civilization in Central American about A.D. 900 (Deevy et al., 1979). Overuse of the land often begins with deforestation, when trees are cut down for building materials or firewood, or to provide cropland. Since 1900, worldwide deforestation has been drastic, particularly in the half of the earth's forests that are located in the poorer nations of the tropic and subtropic regions. About 2% of Asia's tropical forests are being leveled each year, and "by 2020, virtually all of the physically accessible forest in the LDCs is expected to have been cut" (USCEQ, 1980, p. 26).

Following deforestation, many other harmful changes occur. Rain falling on cut-over land runs off rapidly, causing periodic floods such as the devastating ones that killed over 300,000 people in India, Pakistan, and Bangladesh in the 1970s (Brown, 1981). The rapid runoff fails to recharge underground aquifers, increases soil erosion, carries topsoil into the rivers, and leaves destructive silt deposts in lakes, harbors, and reservoirs, drastically reducing their useful life.

In the tropical moist forests, the soils are relatively thin and not well suited for growing crops, and clearing these areas can quickly transform them into deserts. Each year throughout the world, an area the size of Maine is changing from useful land into desert. The tropical rain forests are the world's most complex ecosystems, and another drastic effect of their destruction is extinction of the great majority of the biological species that they contain (USCEQ, 1980).

Even on excellent land, intensive farming often leads to severe loss of topsoil. For instance, in the United States, topsoil is being lost twice as fast as it can be replaced by nature. In addition, spreading urban and suburban populations with their homes, highways, and factories take over some of the best farmland each year—a million acres a year in the United States alone (Brown, 1981; USCEQ, 1980).

Food

As the earth's human population spurted in the 1970s, the productive capacity of many of the earth's biological systems began to fall behind population growth. As a result, on a per-capita basis, the worldwide catch of ocean fish and the total production of mutton, beef, forest products, and grains all peaked in the 1970s, and all of these except grains declined nearly 10% by about 1980. Projecting these trends ahead in time, it is predicted that the world's per-capita catch of fish will decrease at least 30% from A.D. 1970 to 2000 (Brown, 1981, 1983; USCEQ, 1980).

Since the 1930s, the world has become highly dependent on grain exports from the United States and Canada, which are now essential to about 100 Third World countries. World food reserves, stated in terms of days of world consumption, decreased from over 100 days in 1960 to only 40 days in 1980 (Brown, 1981). A single bad harvest season for the United States and Canada would have disastrous consequences, converting chronic malnutrition into full-fledged famine in many countries.

Minerals

An often overlooked fact is that all of earth's physical resources are ultimately finite in amount, and recoverable world supplies of some natural resources such as tungsten are nearing exhaustion (Davis, 1979; Ehrlich et al., 1977). Yet in the United States, we wastefully discard about 70% of all metals after their initial use, rather than recycling them for further use. Recycling can save not only the minerals themselves and the costs of purchasing and importing them, but also vast amounts of energy. for instance, processing recycled aluminum requires only 4% of the energy used in smelting the virgin ore; and for copper, the figure is only about 10% (Hayes, 1978).

As convenient, high-grade mineral deposits are used up, production from lower grade sources yields sharply diminishing amounts of additional output, requires greatly increasing amounts of energy, and creates much more extensive environmental degradation, with accompanying serious impacts on human life. Substitution of more abundant materials for scarce ones such as plastics for metals also has limits. Some materials such as structural steel and chromium, an ingredient in steel, have no adequate substitutes at present. Most substitutes are not as satisfactory in all respects as the original material, and their cost is often higher. Recycling could help to minimize these problems, but our society has many business and governmental practices that impose strong institutional barriers to recycling (Davis, 1979; Ehrlich et al., 1977; Welch & Miewald, 1983).

Energy

The dependence of the whole world, both industrialized nations and Third World countries, on supplies of oil and gas was dramatically demonstrated by the disruptions following the Arab oil embargo in 1973-1974 and the Iranian Revolution in 1979. Oil price increases were a major factor in the worldwide inflation of the 1970s and early 1980s, and oil imports for some nations such as Brazil and India cost more than 50% of their export income by 1982 ("The Arms Race," 1982). As illustrated by the petroleum price gyrations of 1984–1986, projections of future petroleum supply and demand are perilous because the entire international energy situation is unstable and likely to change unexpectedly in coming years (Gibbons & Chandler, 1981; Landsberg, 1982; Nye, 1981; Wildavsky & Tenenbaum, 1981). It is clear, however, that a long-term decline in petroleum supply has begun and will become more serious in the decades ahead ("An Atlas," 1981; Flavin, 1984; Gever, Kaufmann, Skole, & Vorosmarty, 1984; Kash & Rycroft, 1984).

Energy problems are closely linked to many other crucial aspects of the world system (Yergin & Hillenbrand, 1982). Escalating fuel costs have threatened to bankrupt poorer nations, and the resulting national defaults on loans could cause the international financial system to collapse. Threats to petroleum supplies could easily lead to worldwide warfare, carrying the risks of nuclear escalation and even destruction of all human civilization (Deese & Nye, 1981). Power plants and electricity distribution grids are vulnerable to accidental disruption or terrorist attacks (Alexander & Ebinger, 1982; Basdekas, 1982; Cottrell, 1981; Harding, 1983; Lovins & Lovins, 1982). Nuclear power carries the dangers of proliferating nuclear weapons and potential nuclear terrorism (U.S. General Accounting Office, 1982), as well as the major unsolved problems of nuclear waste disposal and decommissioning of nuclear power plants after their 30- to 50-year useful lifetime (Hindman, 1984; La Porte, 1981, U.S. General Accounting Office, 1977).

The Atmosphere

Probably the most catastrophic potential problem affecting the atmosphere is the "greenhouse effect." It results from heavy use of fossil fuels, which is gradually increasing the amount of carbon dioxide in the atmosphere and thereby warming the earth (Bernard,

1981; USCEQ, 1980). Even a slight warming of a few degrees Fahrenheit could markedly change the earth's climatic zones for a period of many centuries, creating deserts in current farmlands, melting the polar icecaps, and inundating the coastal areas of the world (Ehrlich et al., 1977; Hoffman & Barth, 1983; Lovins, Lovins, Krause, & Bach, 1981; Weaver, 1981). There is some disturbing evidence that the polar icecap is already melting at greatly increased rates (Brownstein & Easton, 1982).

There are several other serious dangers to the atmosphere. Jet planes and spray cans both threaten to diminish the stratospheric ozone layer, which absorbs ultraviolet radiation and thus protects humans from skin cancer and many plants and animals from serious injury (National Research Council, 1975; USCEQ, 1980). Acid rain has recently changed the balance of thousands of lakes in the United States, Canada, Scandinavia, and other nations so much that all fish life in them has died, and crop and forest growth has also been stunted. The acids come from oxides of sulfur and nitrogen in the air, another result of burning fossil fuels, particularly coal (Boyle & Boyle, 1983; Marshall, 1982; National Research Council, 1981, 1983; USCEQ, 1980).

Other air pollutants, including fine particles of solid matter, ozone, carbon monoxide, and gaseous hydrocarbons, contribute to respiratory ailments and under some circumstances can even cause death, as in episodes of "killer smog" in Pennsylvania and in London, England, around 1950. Recent reviews have summarized the effects of air pollution on human health (Lave & Seskin, 1977) and on behavior (Evans & Jacobs, 1981). Over half the U.S. population is exposed to unhealthy air quality (USCEQ, 1978). However, the federal Clean Air Act Amendments, passed in 1970, have been successful in decreasing air pollution. Noxious discharges from stationary sources such as factories have been markedly reduced, and progressive improvements in automobile engines have cut emission many-fold while at the same time dramatically increasing fuel efficiency ("Environmental Regulations," 1982).

Water

The two major problems concerning water resources are the supply of water and its quality. Historically, water has been cheap and plentiful in most areas of the United States, but with mass urbanization and widespread adoption of irrigated agriculture, that situation has begun to change. Both California and New Jersey have suffered major recent droughts (Jubak, 1982). Many areas of the United States such as California's San Joaquin Valley and the Great Plains' Ogallala Aquifer region have been withdrawing more water from underground souces thab is available to recharge them; the consequences include a falling water table, failing wells, and subsiding land (Brown, 1981; "Ebbing of the Ogallala," 1982).

One result of the heavy use of water for irrigation is buildup of salts in the soil, making it progressively less productive. Agricultural practices often produce water pollution from nitrogen and phosphorus fertilizers, causing eutrophication of lakes, massive growth of algae, and die-off of fish species. Another problem is contamination by pesticides like DDT, some of which accumulate as they are passed through the food chain and can have a variety of serious long-term physiological effects (Ehrlich et al., 1977; USCEQ, 1980).

The many sources of water pollution have been summarized by Hayes (1979). Water-borne bacteria can cause cholera, typhoid, and dysentery epidemics, and insufficient treatment of sewage in many U.S. communities is responsible for spreading diseases such as hepatitis. Over 20 million Americans work with highly toxic chemicals on their jobs (Anderson, 1982). Industrial waste products and surface runoff of rainfall into storm sewers are major sources of toxic chemicals and poisonous heavy metals in rivers and lakes, and consequently in drinking water. Across the United States from Long Island to the San Joaquin Valley, the Environmental Protection Agency has found about 20% of public drinking water supplies contaminated by industrial chemicals (Marinelli, 1983). Thermal discharges (temperature increases), oil spills in harbors and oceans, and radioactive elements in water are other forms of pollution that are very little controlled (Ehrlich et al., 1977; USCEQ, 1980).

In 1972, Congress passed a Clean Water Act and in 1974 a Safe Drinking Water Act, aimed at reducing the many water-borne health hazards. Despite the resulting progress in cleaning up both drinking water and water recreation sites, the major sources of water pollution in the United States are still far from being adequately controlled (Ehrlich et al., 1977; "Environmental Regulations," 1982; USCEQ, 1975).

Solid Wastes

An average U.S. citizen produces about three-quarters of a ton of solid waste each year, and the total cost to the nation for disposing of all these wastes is over $4 billion per year (Purcell, 1981). Almost all solid wastes are disposed of in landfills, but in most urban areas available landfill sites are nearing exhaustion, and costs of waste management are second only to education expenditures in many city budgets. Thus, many schemes for recycling or use of trash are becoming ever more attractive (Hayes, 1978).

Toxic wastes, like the 20,000 tons of chemicals dumped in the Love Canal disposal site in Niagara Falls, can have serious health effects but have typically been handled very carelessly (Epstein, Brown, & Pope, 1982; Levine, 1982). Despite passage of the 1980 "superfund" law to clean up the worst toxic dumps, the Environmental Protection Agency delayed in setting up standards and procedures, and much illegal midnight roadside dumping is still continuing. It will be a gigantic task to clean up contaminated dumps, rivers, and harbors such as the 40-mile stretch of the Hudson River impregnated with poisonous PCBs, the dioxin contamination in the community of Times Beach, Missouri, and the highly toxic insecticide Kepone dumped in Virginia's James River estuary (Davis & Lester, 1984; "Environmental Regulations," 1982; USCEQ, 1980).

Connections among Resource Problems

In any given area of the world, the plants, animals, and nonliving environment make up an *ecosystem* that is intricately interdependent—the fate of any given species can affect or be affected by the welfare of other species. The principle of ecological interdependence has been increasingly recognized in recent years by scientists and authors from many different backgrounds. Among the first to proclaim approaching "limits to growth" were Meadows, Meadows, Randers, and Behrens (1972), who warned that efforts to solve any single environmental problem in isolation would collide with other ecological limits. Though the adequacy of their models and predictions was strongly criticized (Cole, Freeman, Jahoda, & Parritt, 1973), many other authors have issued similar warnings since then (Catto, 1980; Miles, 1974; Ophuls, 1977; Schnalberg, 1980). Some environmental optimists remain on the other side (Kahn, 1979; Simon, 1981; Simon & Kahn, 1984), but most authorities have begun seeking guidelines for developing a "sustainable society" in which human population and human degradation of the environment will stabilize or fall to a sustainable level rather than continuing to climb (Brown, 1981, 1984; Goldsmith, 1978; Pirages, 1977; Renshaw, 1974; Valaskakis, Sindell, Smith, & Fitzpatrick-Martin, 1979).

The Need for Ecological Responsibility

A sustainable society will require ecologically responsible patterns of human behavior (Lipsey, 1977b)—

ones in which the emphasis is on conserving natural resources and preventing degradation of the environment. There are many examples of such approaches, both familiar and novel: water conservation, recycling of minerals and paper, frugal life-styles, careful disposal or destruction of toxic wastes, organic agriculture, and advanced technological means of reducing air and water pollution. Though such approaches are available and in scattered use, their future widespread adoption faces great uncertainties.

Energy conservation is particularly important because levels of energy use are closely tied to other resource problems. Technological schemes for energy *production,* like synfuel development or nuclear plant construction, are extremely slow, expensive, and environmentally harmful (Komanoff & Van Loon, 1982; Lash & King, 1983; Olsen, 1982; "Setback for Synfuel," 1982). By contrast, conservation can reduce energy use relatively quickly, easily, cheaply, and without the need for new technology (Gibbons & chandler, 1981). These advantages of conservation are admitted even by production-oriented industry sources (e.g., National Petroleum Council, 1974). Conservation can be considered as a *source of energy,* just like oil, coal, or nuclear fuels—one that has been largely untapped but thar, in the United States, is potentially large enough to more than replace all oil imports (Stobaugh & Yergin, 1979). Japan provides an outstanding example of an effective national energy conservation program, having reduced per-capital oil consumption 20% in 10 years ("At the End," 1983).

The *soft energy path* (Lovins, 1977) is an example of an energy strategy designed to conserve natural resources and minimize harmful environmental impacts. It emphasizes renewable energy sources such as sun, wind, and biomass in a diverse mix of decentralized, small-scale facilities, which are easy to use, efficient in energy use, and which match the type of energy used (e.g., heat, fluids, electricity) to the end-use needs (i.e., the tasks to be done). This approach conserves fossil fuels for uses for which substitutes are not available (transportation and chemical raw materials) and limits the use of electricity, one of the most expensive forms of energy, to the functions where it is necessary such as lighting and electric motors.

Recent research findings indicate that the amount of energy needed to run expanding national economies under a soft-path strategy would be substantially below the quantities that have been consumed recently in the industrialized nations (Johansson, Steen, Bogren, & Fredriksson, 1983; Lovins et al., 1981; Office of Technology Assessment, 1982; USCEQ, 1979). This conclusion contradicts the formerly held view that GNP and the total expenditure of energy were closely linked (Morrison & Lodwick, 1981). Partly as a result of conservation measures, total U.S. energy use peaked in 1979, reversing a long-term uptrend, and dropped by more than 12% in the next 3 years (Hershey, 1981; Landsberg, 1982; U.S. Department of Energy, 1983). Similarly, U.S. electricity consumption fell 2% in 1982, the first decrease since World War II. Nevertheless, oil imports in 1983 were still over one-third of U.S. oil consumption, leaving the nation, like most other industrialized countries, dangerously vulnerable to oil supply disruptions (Kash & Rycroft, 1984; "Over a Barrel," 1983).

28.1.2. The Role of Psychological Approaches

The environmental resource problems mentioned in the preceding section are often thought of as solely technical and engineering challenges, dependent for their solution on the expertise of physicists, engineers, and other "hard" scientists. Although the scientific and technical challenges are significant, every one of the previously mentioned problems also involves human behavior in a central and important way. Some environmental problems could be ameliorated by changing the behavior of a few key decision makers (e.g., corporation presidents or legislators). For others, it is necessary to change the behavior of millions of individuals. Even where there are clear technological solutions to environmental problems, social and psychological factors are still ivolved: In some instances, people must be willing to provide political support; in others, they must have the motivation and knowledge necessary to adopt new technologies. Thus psychologists and other social scientists have important roles to play in helping to manage our environmental resources.

The public information campaign culminating in Earth Day in 1970 was a watershed event that sensitized many social scientists as well as common citizens to the importance of environmental problems. Some applied psychologists began to conduct research on those problems (Burgess, Clark, & Hendee, 1971; Geller, Wylie, & Farris, 1971), and Maloney and Ward (1973) declared that the environmental crisis was a "crisis of maladaptive behavior." Since then, environmental sociology has developed as a problem-oriented subdiscipline (e.g., Dunlap & Catton, 1979; Humphrey & Buttel, 1982; Schnaiberg, 1980). Similarly, political scientists (e.g.,

Heilbroner, 1974; Ophuls, 1977), economists (e.g., Daly, 1977; Dorfman & Dorfman, 1977; Olson & Landsberg, 1973), and other social scientists have directed considerable attention to environmental problems.

We believe that these perspectives all have contributions to make to managing environmental problems and that their contributions are interrelated. We will not attempt to discuss all the research and theory in the social and behavioral sciences that bears on environmental problems, but to focus narrowly on research termed *environmental psychology* would be too restrictive. We have chosen instead to define our domain loosely as the contributions of psychologically oriented or psychologically informed research to managing environmental problems. Thus we include research done by people who consider themselves psychologists (environmental or otherwise) as well as other research that draws on psychological concepts or methods. We have chosen not to review psychologically oriented research on population issues even though child bearing and migration have clear implications for environmental resources and are obviously behavioral. Our choice of scope, then, is somewhat arbitrary. But we believe our choice suits the problem area, and problem-centered enterprises cannot often be defined by disciplinary or theoretical categories.

Most of the early and enthusiastic research efforts by psychologists were derived from psychological concepts in relative isolation from the practical issues of policymaking. The focus of these studies seems to have been determined by the need to study something easy to measure or by intuitive judgments about which environmental problems were urgent, rather than by systematic analysis of particular environmental problems. As a result, much of the research had limited applicability. It demonstrated the relevance of psychological constructs to environmental problems, but it did so in ways that often had little practical potential for alleviating major resource problems. Behaviors with much greater potential were ignored (Stern & Gardner, 1981b, 1981c).

Many of the early studies were also impractical as guides to policy. For example, some researchers offered cash rebates for energy conservation that were worth more than the energy saved. Others tested the effectiveness of antilittering messages by printing them on handbills and counting which ones were littered most often. Although such studies can provide convincing demonstrations of reinforcement principles (e.g., Hayes & Cone, 1977) or reactance theory (e.g., Reich & Robertson, 1979), they are not very helpful as empirical bases for policy. Furthermore, some policymakers see such studies as proof of the irrelevance of psychological research.

With experience, researchers can avoid such naive approaches and make practical contributions to environmental policy; they are beginning to do so. (Getting these contributions used in policymaking is a separate problem, which is discussed in a later section.) In our view, the best way to proceed is to study carefully the particular environmental problem of concern before trying to apply psychological theories. For a psychologist, the key questions about an environmental problem are the following: (1) which actors can make an important difference by ameliorating, exacerbating, or preventing the problem? and (2) for each type of actor, which actions have a large impact on the problem? Asking these questions requires a researcher to examine the environmental problem before applying theory but to do so in a way that makes psychological theory relevant.

The major types of actors include consumers of goods and services with environmental implications, producers of those goods and services, intermediaries such as bankers and engineers, whose decisions constrain what will be produced and consumed, and policymakers. Each of these influences the others, but sometimes more can be accomplished by influencing one type of actor than another. More was accomplished, for example, by forcing automobile manufacturers to adhere to average fuel economy standards than could have been done by any conceivable effort to directly change the behavior of automobile purchasers.

Actions also fall into generic categories. Some affect resources directly: driving a car, throwing out trash, turning on a light, and so forth. Other actions affect resources indirectly by creating or selecting the buildings and equipment that, subject to other behavior, use resources and create pollution. The choice of a residence determines a household's heating and cooling requirements and the amount of traveling household members must do. The purchase of an electric arc furnace affects how much energy and raw materials it will take to make steel. And choices about buildings and equipment are made not only by those who purchase them but by the manufacturers as well. If there are no energy-efficient refrigerators or returnable containers on the market, people can neither buy nor use them. (For a report on available energy-efficient appliances, see American Council for an Energy Efficient Economy, 1984.)

In terms of resource use, initial choices about buildings and equipment usually make more differ-ence than everyday practices affecting their use. This is the case for household energy consumption (Stern & Gardner, 1981a, 1981c) and appears to be a more general principle. Stern and Gardner (1981b) concluded that actions that "prevent" environmental problems usually have a greater potential effect than actions that "cure" them. For example, air pollution and energy consumption can generally be decreased more effectively by purchasing a fuel-efficient vehicle than by carefully operating and maintaining an inefficient one,[1] and solid waste is likely to be reduced more by minimizing the use of paper packaging than by reclaiming and reprocessing used paper. This "prevention" principle underlines the importance for resource management of major consumer purchases, a class of behavior that has been given relatively little attention by psychologists.

The principle of prevention also underlines the importance of a third class of actions: ones that set the context for choices about the construction and manufacture of buildings and equipment and about their use. These include public policies that reward or require more (or less) resource-efficient manufacturing practices; land use policies that encourage or discourage development along mass transit corridors; the setting of standard practices in engineering, architecture, banking, and other professions in ways that influence the resource efficiency of buildings and equipment; educational strategies designed to raise the level of environmental knowledge and awareness in the next generation; public pressure to influence policies in these and related areas; and so forth. Such context-setting activities can sometimes have a greater long-term effect on resource use than any other type of behavior.

To find the most effective ways to solve environmental problems, it is necessary to survey the range of actors and actions to see where the greatest potential for change lies. Psychologically oriented researchers should choose their activities after a combined assessment of what they have to offer and where change would be most helpful. This sort of problem-centered approach has been developed in recent years by psychologists working on environmental problems in a policy context and has been advocated and described before (Geller, Winett, & Everett, 1982; Stern & Gardner, 1981b, 1981c; Winett & Neale, 1979).

There are three major differences between a problem-centered approach and one that is more deductive in origin. First, a primary focus on the problem directs psychologists' attention to issues that policy officials view as important, and thus increases the likelihood that reasearch outcomes will be recognized as relevant. Second, a problem-centered approach is inevitably interdisciplinary—it stimulates researchers to draw on theories and variables from various subdisciplines of psychology and even from other disciplines. Third, and most important for the content of research, a problem-centered approach redirects attention toward actors and actions that psychologists have largely overlooked.

For example, psychologists have been more likely to study the behavior of individuals than the behavior of corporations. But individuals and households account for only about one-third of U.S. energy consumption (Stern & Gardner, 1981c), and for most types of solid waste and air pollutants, their contribution is of similar or smaller magnitude (Stern & Gardner, 1981b). Thus corporations make a greater direct contribution to environmental problems than individuals, and it is worth examining whether more can be done to alleviate these problems by modifying corporate rather than individual behavior. When indirect resource use and context-setting are considered, the role of individuals is even smaller. Many other actors have important effects on environmental problems by context-setting and indirect resource use: politicians, technological researchers and designers, manufacturers and builders, lenders of capital, environmental organizations, and organizations that standardize, advertise, and market products whose use affects the environment. People may be able to stop pollution, as the ad says, but they cannot stop much of it without changing its institutional context. Recognition of this fact suggests that political and organizational psychologists, who have not yet addressed environmental problems, might have an important contribution to make by studying resource use by business, industry, and government and by examining the forces that set the context for resource use. Interdisciplinary research on the role of attitudes and values in social and political change also emerges as important, as part of the study of context-setting.

A problem-oriented approach would also shift psychologists' research focus from the common, frequently repeated actions they have usually studied to less frequent but more important behaviors. As we have noted, the actions that make the most difference are usually the infrequent ones that "prevent" resource use such as the adoption of major policies, the construction of buildings and equipment, and the purchase of automobiles, homes, and major appliances. Studies by consumer psychologists of indirect

resource use (i.e., individual and organizational purchases) are relevant to understanding and changing these actions.

28.2. CURRENT RESEARCH

This major section follows a problem-centered organization scheme, summarizing research findings related to seven areas of environmental problems: environmental attitudes, litter control, recycling and solid wastes, conservation of land and biological resources, water conservation, environmental pollution, and energy conservation. However, we first briefly describe six research approaches that partially crosscut the substantive problem areas and that can be used to study various kinds of research questions about environmental resource problems.

28.2.1. Major Research Traditions

The first of these approaches is the social psychological study of attitudes. This approach is used in public opinion surveys (Farhar, Unseld, Vories, & Crews, 1980; Lowe, Pinhey, & Grimes, 1980), in measurement studies that develop scales of environmental attitudes and behavior (Heberlein, 1981; Maloney & Ward, 1973; Van Liere & Dunlap, 1981), in research on the causes and correlates of "pro-ecology" behavior (Lipsey, 1977a; Van Liere & Dunlap, 1980; Weigel, 1977), and in a host of studies on the correspondence between environmental attitudes and behaviors (e.g., Becker, Seligman, Fazio, & Darley, 1981; Weigel & Newman, 1976).

The second research tradition is the social psychological study of attitude change. Unlike the first approach, this research is primarily experimental, emphasizing independent variables such as social influence and public commitment (cf. Cook & Berrenberg, 1981; McClelland & Canter, 1981). Much of this research has been done in laboratory settings and has focused on beliefs, attitudes, or intentions as the dependent variables, but an increasing number of studies are being conducted in field settings, often measuring behavior change or other objective outcomes.

The third research tradition, also an experimental one, is applied behavior analysis (see Russell and Snodgrass, Chapter 8, this volume), whose adherents have conducted many experimental studies, in several of the environmental problem areas, on methods of modifying environmentally destructive behavior and promoting more constructive habits (cf. Cone & Hayes, 1980; Geller et al., 1982).

Another approach, one having roots in many disciplines, focuses on the commons dilemma and related situations, in which a public resource is overused and depleted by individuals who are each motivated to maximize their own outcomes (Edney, 1980; Edney & Harper, 1978; Hardin & Baden, 1977; Stroebe & Frey, 1982). Economists and political scientists have worked both conceptually and experimentally on "collective action" or the "free-rider problem" (Bohm, 1972; Olson, 1965; Sweeney, 1973). A biologist popularized the *tragedy of the commons* metaphor (Hardin, 1968), whereas psychologists commonly use the term *social traps* (Brechner & Linder, 1981; Platt, 1973). Within psychology, the typical research method in this area has been laboratory simulations using game-theory concepts (e.g., Dawes, 1980; Linder, 1982).

Another research tradition, stemming mainly from sociology and communication research, studies factors affecting the diffusion of innovations or ideas as they are gradually adopted by more and more members of a population. A review of this approach in the area of energy conservation is provided by Darley and Beniger (1981).

A final approach is the relatively new field of evaluation research, applying systematic observation and measurement to describe the success of government and organizational programs (Rossi, Freeman, & Wright, 1979). One of its typical features is the use of benefit–cost analysis, which is particularly crucial for programs affecting large-scale environmental issues (Fischhoff, 1977; Thompson, 1980). When important decisions to exploit an irreplaceable resource are made under typical real-world conditions of uncertainty about the result, the decision process ought to be conservative and the required benefit–cost ratio should be set well above 1.0 (Miller, 1981–1982). Yet when decision-makers approach ecological problems that have unknown limits (e.g., toxic waste disposal or destruction of natural ecological communities), they typically do so in overly simplistic ways, failing to consider many of the interacting factors (Edmunds, 1980). Benefit–cost analyses have much more typically been applied to resource-conserving policies than to resource-consuming innovations.

Though social science research on environmental resource issues began only around 1970, several summaries and reviews are available on various aspects of the subject (Cone & Hayes, 1980; Geller et al., 1982; Lipsey, 1977a; Zube, 1980). In particular, the crucial problems of energy use have motivated much research and a number of useful summaries (Baum & Singer, 1981; "Consumer Behavior," 1981; "Consumer Behaviour," 1983; McDougall, Claxton, Ritchie, & Anderson, 1981; Oskamp, 1983; Seligman & Becker, 1981; Shippee, 1980; Stern & Gardner, 1981b, 1981c).

28.2.2. Environmental Attitudes

Environmental attitudes, though not a resource problem in themselves, merit scientific study for several reasons. First, it is useful to know whether there are broad, general orientations that link together attitudes on various environmental resource problems. Second, attitudes may be related to people's environmentally relevant actions. Third, regardless of their relation to behavior, people's attitudes about specific environmental issues are of interest in their own right and are often cited in public-policy debates.

Assessment of Attitudes

Inspired by the "environmental movement" of the 1960s and 1970s, several social scientists have constructed scales for measuring environmental knowledge, attitudes, and/or actions (Antil & Bennett, 1979; Dunlap & Van Liere, 1978a, 1978b; Lipsey, 1980; Lounsbury & Tornatzky, 1977; Maloney, Ward, & Braucht, 1975; Weigel & Weigel, 1978). These scales were often validated by showing that they differentiated members of environmental organizations from the general public. More recently, critical analyses of some of these scales have appeared (Heberlein, 1981; Van Liere & Dunlap, 1981), showing that the various diverse measures are not equivalent and occasionally are barely even correlated. However, data from a statewide representative sample showed correlations above +.5 among attitudes toward pollution, resource use, and environmental regulations, but lower correlations with scales of population concerns and self-reported environmental behavior (Van Liere & Dunlap, 1981). Thus there is some evidence for a construct of general environmental attitudes.

Some researchers have investigated the personality and demographic characteristics associated with environmental concern (Arbuthnot, 1977; Borden & Francis, 1978; Trigg, Perlman, Perry, & Janisse, 1976; Weigel, 1977) or with more specific aspects of environmental issues such as nuclear or solar power

(Dunlap & Olsen, 1984; Webber, 1982). In general, people who are concerned about environmental quality are likely to be somewhat younger, better educated, and more liberal politically than individuals who are less concerned (Van Liere & Dunlap, 1980). However, there is an exception to this pattern in urban areas like Chicago, where the highest levels of concern about pollution are apt to be found among residents of poor, nonwhite, high-density neighborhoods that have lots of solid waste and poor garbage disposal service (Cutter, 1981). Women are apt to report more concern about pollution and the need for environmental regulations than men do (Cornwell, 1982; Van Liere & Dunlap, 1980), and they are more distrustful of nuclear energy in particular (Farhar et al., 1980; Nelkin, 1981).

A growing number of studies have focused on people's judgments of the risks involved in various technologies (Fischhoff, Lichtenstein, Slovic, Derby, & Keeney, 1981; also see Pitt and Zube, Chapter 27, this volume). For instance, Slovic, Fischhoff, and Lichtenstein (1981) pointed out the special perceptual characteristics of nuclear hazards and the long path that dangerous technologies must travel before they gain public acceptance. People who are relatively accepting of societal risks from new technologies tend to be more politically conservative, pro-business, and accepting of risk in their individual activities than those who oppose such societal risks (Craik, Dake, & Buss, 1982). In general, the American public has become steadily more negative to nuclear energy since about 1973 ("Opinion Roundup," 1983; Rothman & Lichter, 1983), whereas it still maintains a highly positive attitude toward solar power (Farhar-Pilgrim & Unseld, 1982).

Public Opinion

The average American's score on measures of environmental concern increased rapidly during the growth of the environmental movement in the late 1960s. Downs's (1972) theory of an "issue-attention cycle" would predict a subsequent fall-off of public interest in the environment. A few studies have reported that environmental concern peaked in 1970 and declined thereafter, but most surveys have found it remaining at a continuing high level among the U.S. populace (Dunlap, 1985; Harris, 1982; Heberlein, 1981; Ladd, 1982; Lowe et al., 1980; Mitchell, 1979; President's Council on Environmental Quality, 1980). For example, national samples polled annually by the National Opinion Research Center (1978) between 1973 and 1978 consistently showed majorities who believed the United States was spending too little on "improving and protecting the environment."

Though surveys in several European countries found most people to be unaware of the causes and consequences of environmental pollution (Kromm, Probald, & Wall, 1973), in the 1980s, concern for environmental degradation has become a prominent electoral issue in several European countries as well as in the United States.

Looking more specifically at energy issues, there has also been dispute over how concerned Americans are about them. In the late 1970s, some authors emphasized that many Americans still doubted that there was an energy crisis (e.g., Richman, 1979). However, the people who held that viewpoint were a distinct minority. Consistently, in polls taken since the Arab oil embargo of 1973–1974 through the period of the Iranian Revolution in 1979 and the Iran-Iraq War in the early 1980s, about half of U.S. citizens said they believed the energy crisis was real and serious, and another quarter accepted that idea with some doubts or reservations, leaving only about one-quarter of the population who were still completely unconvinced of the problem (de Boer, 1977; Farhar, Weis, Unseld, & Burns, 1979; Fusso, 1978; "Public Changing Views," 1979; Olsen, 1981). The "oil glut" of the mid-1980s temporarily relieved many people's anxieties, with the result that for awhile little public opinion research was done on the topic, but it did not change the long-range resource picture.

In the early 1980s, the people who believed in the seriousness of the energy crisis were apt to be relatively young and above average in education, income, and occupational status—approximately the same groups that were high in general environmental concern (Durand, Klemmack, & Roff, 1980; Farhar et al., 1980; Strand, 1981). There is still much public ignorance of steps that are effective in conserving energy (Kempton, Harris, Keith, & Weihl, 1985). and rather widespread public attitudes of cynicism, materialism, and faith in technology may diminish concern for energy conservation (Milstein, 1979).

Attitudes and Behavior

Space does not allow a full treatment of this topic here. The evidence from many types of research indicates that attitudes and behavior can each influence the other and that other variables often mediate the relationship (Kelman, 1980). (This reciprocal, bidirectional form of causal relationship is incorporated in Table 28.1, and it is also touched on in Russell and Snodgrass, Chapter 8, in this volume.) In this area, there is much need for more longitudinal research, which would more fully clarify the causal patterns. For managing environmental resource problems, the crucial questions are: Do environmental attitudes predict related behavior? Can such attitudes be changed in ways that will affect related behavior? If so, how?

In general, there is evidence of positive relationships between ecological attitudes and environmentally protective actions (e.g., Bruvold, 1972; Heberlein & Black, 1981; Humphrey, Bord, Hammond, & Mann, 1977; McGuinness, Jones, & Cole, 1977; Weigel, Vernon, & Tognacci, 1974). However, such findings do not establish the existence of a causal relationship, and some researchers, particularly applied behavior analysts, have argued that environmental concern does not even predict behavior that should be related to it (e.g., Geller et al., 1982). They particularly emphasize the failure of many experimental interventions using verbal communication to change environmentally relevant behavior. However, these failures seem largely due to four factors: (1) the ineffectiveness of the communication techniques that are typically employed (Ester & Winett, 1982), (2) the fact that attitudes and beliefs are embedded in personal values and social contexts that are hard to change (e.g., Heberlein, 1981), (3) the fact that attitudes formed through direct personal experience with the attitude object are likely to be relatively clear and confidently held and therefore hard to change (Fazio & Zanna, 1978), and (4) the frequent mismatch in specificity between attitude measures, which are usually general, and behavioral indexes, which are usually specific. Several studies have shown that neither general environmental concern nor belief in the seriousness of the energy crisis is sufficient to ensure that people will take specific personal actions to conserve energy (Farhar et al., 1979; Heslop, Moran, & Cousineau, 1981; Sears, Tyler, Citrin, & Kinder, 1978), but many other studies show that under certain circumstances there are positive relationships between energy beliefs and actions (e.g., Jensen & Schroeder, 1983; Leonard-Barton, 1981; Murphy, Laczniak, & Robinson, 1979).

When attitudes and behaviors are measured at the same level of specificity or generality, much greater correspondence has been found (Ajzen & Fishbein, 1977; Fishbein & Ajzen, 1975; Schuman & Johnson, 1976), and this general principle has been confirmed in several studies of environmental issues (Heberlein & Black, 1976; Weigel & Newman, 1976; Weigel et al., 1974). For example, high levels of energy use for household heating and cooling have been found to be predicted by beliefs that home temperature is important for personal health and comfort, but not by levels of belief in the urgency of the "energy crisis" (Becker et al., 1981; Seligman, Kriss, Darley, Fazio, Becker, & Pryor, 1979). Similarly, individuals' re-

ported votes on a nuclear power initiative in Oregon were correlated more highly with their specific attitude toward the initiative than with their attitude toward nuclear power in general (Bowman & Fishbein, 1978). (The issue of the amount of correspondence between attitudes and behavior is developed further in the subsequent section on energy conservation and is represented schematically in Table 28.1.)

A related point, which is important to understanding of the environmental attitude–behavior relationship issue, is that the many types of proenvironmental *behavior* are not highly correlated among themselves. In a factor analysis of many self-reported "ecologically responsible" actions, Lipsey (1980) found many weak factors composed of rather heterogeneous behaviors, instead of a single general factor or a few major group factors. Similarly, Leonard-Barton (1981) found six factors in her short scale of "voluntary simplicity" actions. In a study of suburban residents, several of the reported energy-saving home-maintenance actions were found not to be closely interrelated, and the same was true for energy-saving transportation behaviors, though there was a greater degree of consistency among several recycling actions and among several environmentally protective consumer-buying behaviors (Tracy & Oskamp, 1983–1984). Even within a single environmental arena, such as residential energy conservation, particular attitudes and beliefs are more closely related to some behaviors than to others. For example, people who feel a sense of moral obligation to improve home energy efficiency have been found to be more likely to make low-cost energy improvements in their homes but not to make more expensive investments (Black, Stern, & Elworth, 1985; Stern, Black, & Elworth, 1982, 1983). The differences among various resource-using behaviors have not only theoretical interest but also important policy implications for mounting governmental or commercial campaigns for resource conservation.

Measurement Issues

A limitation of most attitude–behavior studies is that they accept the respondents' self-reports about environmentally relevant actions at face value. Though self-reports are sometimes quite valid (Beck, Doctors, & Hammond, 1980; Warriner, McDougall, & Claxton, 1984), this procedure can lead to two potential difficulties. First, good intentions may not be carried into action, or self-reports may be exaggerated. For example, a follow-up study of an energy informational workshop showed that the subsequent energy-conservation actions of people who had voluntarily attended the workshop were almost negligible in spite of their enthusiastic postworkshop attitudes and intentions to conserve (Geller, 1981). A second problem is that proenvironmental actions may not have appreciable effects. Though energy-conserving actions often do reduce actual energy use, as would be expected (Verhallen & van Raaij, 1981), in other cases actions taken to promote conservation may be mistaken or ineffective. Some studies have measured actual household energy savings and found them to be much less than would be expected from technical calculations based on participants' reports of energy-conserving actions (Hirst, Hu, Taylor, Thayer, & Groeneman, 1983; Olsen & Cluett, 1979). Some of the reasons for this are technical: Energy use data are sometimes unreliable, and technical calculations make the unrealistic assumption that home insulation and other improvements are always installed properly and used effectively (Hirst et al., 1983). These examples illustrate a point made at greater length in the later section on energy conservation research: There are many links, and loose connections between links, in the causal chain leading from background factors through attitudes, knowledge, and intentions to environmentally protective actions and outcomes (see Table 28.1). Thus self-reports of conservation intentions and actions should be considered with cautious skepticism rather than being automatically accepted as valid indicators of behavior, much less of conservation outcomes. It follows that more studies should use objective measures of environment-related behaviors and outcomes (e.g., actual thermostat settings, or energy meter readings).

Converting Attitudes to Actions

The foregoing material on attitude–behavior relationships demonstrates that the appropriate question about environmental attitudes and behavior is: Which attitudes affect which behaviors, and under what conditions? A review by Olsen (1981) has concluded that two of the strongest factors stimulating energy-conservation actions are (1) awareness of personal consequences of the energy crisis (e.g., belief that home insulation will cut one's own heating bills, or being inconvenienced by having waited in long gas lines), and (2) awareness of a social norm for conservation, particularly if it is internalized as a personal norm (e.g., feeling personally responsible for helping to solve the energy crisis). The latter point suggests that a person's basic values should be important influences on environmentally protective behaviors, and this hypothesis has been supported in several studies of values using measurement techniques such as Rokeach's (1967) Value Survey (Dunlap, Grieneeks, & Rokeach, 1983; Leonard-Barton, 1981; Leonard-

Barton & Rogers, 1979; Neuman, 1982). Dunlap and colleagues (1983) found that recyclers espoused more of Maslow's (1970) "higher order" or self-actualization values such as a world of beauty, inner harmony, and an exciting life, whereas demographically similar members of the general public were more likely to hold safety and security values such as salvation, national security, and world peace. These findings of significant relationships between basic values and specific environmentally relevant behavior seem particularly striking in view of the point made in the preceding paragraph about the generally loose linkages in the causal chain between attitudes and specific actions. It seems likely that attitudes which are closely related to a person's basic values will be the ones most apt to be carried into behavior.

Another implication of the important role of social norms in environmentally relevant behavior is that people's identification with larger social groups should be influential in promoting ecological responsibility. This view is typical of the analyses of such resource problems as the "tragedy of the commons" or "social traps" (Hardin, 1968; Platt, 1973), which stress that environmental crises result from individuals acting in their own narrowly defined self-interest, but that they can be avoided by getting people to act in the collective interest. One way to do this is to offer incentives to individuals for prosocial behavior (Olson, 1965). But concern for the common welfare can be internalized and prosocial behavior induced by events that make social interdependence impossible to ignore. This was demonstrated experimentally in the boys' camp studies by Sherif, Harvey, White, Hood, and Sherif (1961), and it is seen in reactions to local emergency or disaster situations such as the Santa Barbara Channel oil discharge (Molotch, 1971). It has been proposed that this principle could be usefully implemented by increasing local control of resources on which communities depend for satisfaction of essential needs (e.g., increasing community influence on a local factory that is a large employer but also a major air or water polluter) (Stern, 1978, Stern & Kirkpatrick, 1977). There are numerous instances where large groups of individuals limited their consumption for the collective good when local resource crises occurred (e.g., Acton & Mowill, 1975; Agras, Jacob, & Lebedeck, 1980; Berk, Cooley, LaCivita, Parker, Sredl, & Brewer, 1980; Stobaugh & Yergin, 1979, pp. 144–146).

An Environmentally Relevant Theory of Behavior

A theoretical formulation that links concern for the welfare of others to environmentally relevant action is

Schwartz's (1970, 1977) theory of the activation of personal moral norms. It posits that a moral norm is activated in an individual when he or she becomes aware of adverse consequences (AC) to others from some action or event and ascribes responsibility (AR) for averting those consequences to himself or herself. The resulting norm is experienced as a sense of moral obligation to act in ways that will help to prevent or repair the harm to others. Several correlational or path-analytic studies have provided evidence that this norm-activation process can influence environmentally relevant behaviors (Black, 1978; Black & Heberlein, 1977; Black et al., 1985; Stern et al., 1982; Van Liere & Dunlap, 1978). Experimental studies to test the theory have not been conducted in the environmental area, except for one with negative results (Heberlein, 1975), but a number have supported its applicability to a range of other behaviors (Schwartz, 1977). One experimental study of energy beliefs and intentions has supported Schwartz's defensive denial hypothesis that prosocial norms will *not* be activated in situations where the personal costs are perceived as too high (Tyler, Orwin, & Schurer, 1982).

The norm-activation theory has important practical implications for understanding how environmentally relevant behavior comes about and how it can lead to political action. For example, it suggests that dissemination of scientific evidence that environmental pollutants harm human health, combined with information linking certain cases of cancer to the past activities of particular corporations or government agencies, should lead to the activation of moral norms in large segments of the public. This in turn might lead to political or community action. Recent public and legislative reaction after the disasters at Love Canal, Three Mile Island, Times Beach, and similar pollution sites appears to display these theoretically specified processes of moral norm arousal and morally instigated action (Levine, 1982; Molotch, 1971; Walsh, 1981), and a preliminary test of the hypothesis supports a relationship between the AC and AR variables and judgments about the moral obligations of government and industry with respect to hazardous chemicals (Stern, Dietz, & Black, 1986).

The other side of the coin is that information which minimizes adverse consequences and denies or diffuses responsibility will tend to prevent activation of moral norms. Many industrial corporations seem to be acting in accord with this principle when, in public statements and advertising campaigns, they attempt to convince the public that nothing in life is risk-free, that chemicals make life better, that pesticide use is necessary to save crops, or that ties between particular pollutants and cancer are unproven. Claims of this type downplay the adverse social consequences (AC) of chemical manufacture, pesticide use, electricity generation, and the like. Some other familiar claims pertain to the AR side of the theory. For instance, statements that levels of toxic substances are within allowable limits ascribe responsibility for any outcomes to regulatory agencies, and claims that cancer is due to life-style factors ascribe responsibility for adverse outcomes to the sick people themselves. Setting aside the merits of the arguments for and against such claims, it is possible to examine public pronouncements about pollution and toxic wastes as a struggle over the moral norms of the citizenry. At stake are corporate profits, political power, environmental quality, and public health.

We turn now from research on attitudes to consider findings in specific areas of environmental impacts and resource problems, beginning with the area of litter control.

28.2.3. Litter Control

Litter reduction was the first aspect of environmental resources to be studied experimentally. Beginning about 1970, a steady stream of studies has appeared, mostly carried out by applied behavior analysts, and several thorough reviews of this literature are available (Cone & Hayes, 1980; Geller, 1980; Geller et al., 1982). The settings for this kind of research have ranged from movie theaters, football stadiums, parks, and outdoor recreation areas, to streets and highways and areas around and inside buildings. The methods of measuring the litter present have been highly variable, including counts of specified types and sizes of items, total weight or volume measures of collected trash, photographic records of litter in standard size areas, "planting" marked pieces of certain types of trash, and observing and counting people's actual littering actions.

Behavior analysts distinguish between *antecedent strategies*—stimulus events occurring before the target behavior and designed to change its probability—and *consequence strategies*—pleasant or unpleasant events occurring after and contingent on the target behavior (see Russell and Snodgrass, Chapter 8, this volume, for a fuller discussion). In terms of public-policy impact, the most important target behavior would probably be to influence manufacturers of consumer goods to use packaging materials that minimize littering and/or are biodegradable—an example of the "prevention rather than cure" principle discussed earlier. However, the antilittering campaigns described in the psychological literature have been aimed at influencing individual consumers' behavior.

A majority of the experimental studies have used antecedent strategies to try to decrease littering or encourage cleaning-up behavior. The most common technique of this type is a "prompt" on a sign or handbill (or in media publicity) requesting a particular nonlittering or pickup behavior. Such studies have shown variable results ranging from good success to actual increases in littering (apparently due to psychological reactance [Brehm, 1966; Reich & Robertson, 1979]). Requests are more effective when they are polite and when they state a specific desired action rather than a general admonition such as "please dispose of properly" (Geller, Witmer, & Orebaugh, 1976). Other antecedent variables include the number and placement of trash receptacles, attractive design of trash receptacles, offering litter bags to people in the setting, and presence of a human "model" who displays the desired behavior. Studies varying the amount of litter already in an area show that "litter begets litter" (though exceptions have been found in scenic forest areas [Crump, Nunes, & Crossman, 1977]). This typical finding indicates that modeling of undesirable behavior or disinhibition of normal social restraints can increase littering behavior.

Studies using antecedent strategies without any reinforcing consequences have frequently succeeded in decreasing littering but not in increasing litter pickup (Geller et al., 1982). However, reviewers have stressed the poor design of intervention strategies and weak independent variables used in many of these studies (e.g., one-shot interventions; only written messages [Ester & Winett, 1982; Geller, 1980]). These authors have suggested several ways to make interventions more effective (e.g., attention to the specificity, proximity, and convenience of the requested behavior and the salience, intrusiveness, and repetition of the message). What is particularly needed is more use of modeling as an intervention and more effective and repeated use of mass media communication strategies. Well-designed antecedent strategies are usually cheaper to implement than consequence strategies and are highly appropriate for use in large-scale government or commercial programs. In one particularly influential antecedent study using modeling, giving Chicago dog owners a "pooper scooper" for picking up their pets' feces and demonstrating its use led not only to a reduction in dog feces in the area but also to police adoption of the system, large-scale media publicity, and eventual support for a city ordinance requiring owners to carry

a "pooper scooper" when walking their dogs (Jason, Zolik, & Matese, 1979).

Another group of litter-control studies have manipulated the consequences of littering or litter pickup actions (frequently a more powerful intervention than an antecedent strategy), usually in combination with at least an antecedent announcement of the litter-control program. Consequence strategies in this area rely mainly on reinforcement, including attention and social approval as well as money, toys, food coupons, or chances in a drawing or lottery. In various settings, such interventions have produced from 32 to 95% reduction in litter (Geller et al., 1982). One interesting approach is a "talking trash can" containing a tape-recorded message that says "thank you" whenever the lid is pushed open (Silver, 1974), but this technique has not been systematically evaluated.

Some antecedent and most consequence procedures are costly, time-consuming, or laborious to administer, and as a result most of the research has been limited to short-term experimental demonstrations lasting a few months at most. Experimental studies using cash payments or other tangible rewards have frequently had costs greater than their maximum possible savings, and they also raise doubts about whether any savings achieved will continue after the rewards are terminated. In addition, they are most effective with small children, raising the question of exploitation. And rewards have sometimes produced undesired side effects such as importation of refuse in order to win prizes based on the weight or volume of trash collected, or the dumping of trash from one yard to another when rewards were contingent on cleanup of one particular area. Thus most research using tangible rewards does not offer a firm basis for public policy. However, a few studies have developed simple and convenient item-marking techniques and have been notably cost-effective in showing the possibility of substantially reducing paid trash-collection crews (e.g., Bacon-Prue, Blount, Pickering, & Drabman, 1980).

An important need in litter-control research is for more long-term studies and studies of communitywide programs, investigating their continuing impact and breadth of effectiveness. Studies using attractively decorated trash cans and lasting for several months have shown moderate reductions in the amount of nearby litter (Finnie, 1973; O'Neill, Blanck, & Joyner, 1980). However, a similar 10-month study in a shopping mall found increased deposits of trash in the attractive cans but no reduction in total mall littering (Geller, Brasted, & Mann, 1980). Convenient combinations of ashtrays and trash cans did, however, markedly increase the amount and appropriateness of the items deposited. Two communitywide campaigns studied in Murfreesboro, Tennessee, showed a 32% reduction in city litter resulting from a commercially sponsored children's "litter hunt" and a similar decrease following a coordinated publicity program in the city paper (McNees, Schnelle, Gendrich, Thomas, & Beagle, 1979; Schnelle, McNees, Thomas, Gendrich, & Beagle, 1980). However, the former study did not have a postcampaign follow-up, and the latter study showed a return to baseline levels of litter a month after the newspaper publicity ended.

The only widespread, continuing litter-control program that has been described in the psychological literature is the nationwide, highly structured Clean Community System (CCS) model promoted by the organization called Keep America Beautiful, Inc. (Geller et al., 1982). It has been adopted by over 200 U.S. cities and has spread to parts of six other countries. The model has many specified stages and an elaborate organizational framework of committees and teams all designed to promote cooperation between local government, business, and civic groups in carrying out community action to solve waste-management problems, including litter. One side effect of this heavy community emphasis is to deemphasize prevention programs aimed at manufacturers of consumer products such as mandatory regulations regarding packaging. Though the CCS scheme uses many principles of applied behavior analysis, it also includes attitude surveys and stresses goals of attitude change at least as much as behavior change. The CCS model has been adapted for use in energy conservation campaigns, and its procedural strengths and weaknesses have been analyzed in detail by Geller and colleagues (1982), but apparently it has not yet been evaluated by careful empirical research.

28.2.4. Recycling and Solid Wastes

From a behavioral perspective, there are several solid-waste problems because different types of solid waste are generated by different actors in different ways and because once they are generated, different behaviors are appropriate for cleaning up the wastes. Each of several, very different classes of solid waste is important. Mining, extracting, and agriculture account for 92% of all U.S. solid waste (Committee on Environmental Improvement, 1978), but the other 8% present very significant problems as well. The 3% of wastes from industrial sources include radioactive substances and toxic chemicals that have stimulated acute public concern because of the threats they pose to water supplies and public health. The

5% of waste from municipal sources represent serious logistical and political problems and one of the largest budget items for many municipalities. A finer grained analysis shows that within each major class of solid waste, there are subclasses that vary substantially in the ways they are produced, the ways they can be reduced or disposed of, and the problems they cause for segments of society. Such analyses have been done—at least for municipal wastes (Geller et al., 1982; Stern & Gardner, 1981b).

Solid-waste problems can be handled by simple disposal, by resource recovery, or by waste reduction at the source; different behaviors are involved in each. *Disposal* is the familiar method for handling municipal solid waste, and the familiar behaviors are those of filling and moving trash cans and filling, driving, and emptying garbage trucks. *Resource recovery* involves reprocessing discarded goods to capture the material or energy they contain (e.g., burning trash to generate electricity or reprocessing bottles to make new glass). *Recycling* is a form of resource recovery in which waste is used to make new material of the same kind (e.g., aluminum cans). Resource recovery requires separating reusable waste from other waste, and this can be accomplished either by sophisticated electro-mechanical separation technology or by hand sorting at or near the source of the waste. Geller and colleagues (1982) discuss these methods as "high technology" versus "low technology," respectively, noting the important role for psychological research in the low-technology approach. Whereas high-technology methods (for instance, recovery of methane gas from decomposing garbage, or separation and burning of trash to generate electricity) are extremely expensive to install and operate (LaBreque, 1977), low-technology approaches are relatively cheap and efficient and often increase local employment.

Waste reduction means decreasing the total amount of disposed material. It can be accomplished (1) by individuals, through reusing products (e.g., buying refillable rather than throwaway containers), repairing rather than replacing belongings, choosing longer lasting new products, or buying used equipment such as reconditioned auto parts; and (2) by organizations, through designing products for a longer useful life, decreasing the use of packaging materials, or making manufacturing processes less energy- and materials-intensive. These widely varying approaches to waste reduction obviously require different behaviors from different actors.

From the viewpoint of environmental quality and resource conservation, waste reduction is generally preferable to resource recovery, which in turn is generally preferable to simple disposal (Wahl & Allison, 1975; U.S. Environmental Protection Agency, 1977). This is an instance of the more general prevention-versus-cure principle already mentioned. Because prevention is not always practicable, however, an optimal waste management program must involve both waste reduction and resource recovery (Geller et al., 1982; Wahl & Allison, 1975). Stern and Gardner (1981b) discuss the appropriateness of these strategies for the various types of municipal waste, and Davis and Lester (1985) describe hazardous-waste policy issues that are prominent at the local, state, national, or international levels.

Research on recycling behavior began in the early 1970s and has been less common than litter-control studies; a review by Geller and colleagues (1982) found only 14 studies through 1979. Most of the social research on recycling, as on litter control, has featured a behavior analysis perspective, partly because there are clear-cut and objective criterion measures of recycling that are convenient for behavioral study. Almost all the studies have been done in residential, school, or office settings. A large majority have focused on recycling paper, mostly newspaper, because of its ready salability. It is surprising that only a handful have involved bottles or cans. Recently, however, they seem to be getting more attention (e.g., Luyben & Cummings, 1981–1982; McCaul & Kopp, 1982).

Among the antecedent strategies used in recycling studies have been flyers and signs, added collection boxes, and verbal appeals. In various studies, these have produced anywhere from slight to 100% or greater increases in the target behaviors; however, a common finding is that no more than 10 to 15% of the eligible individuals participate, even in successful recycling programs. Many studies have combined antecedent strategies with consequences such as toys, payments, raffle coupons, contests, public feedback, or other rewards. In general, these combinations have produced much greater amounts of recycled material, sometimes more than ten times as much. However, they have usually found the same low levels of individual participation, except for two studies that developed 30 and 50% participation, possibly due to the combination of a predisposed group, multiple interventions, and a desirable incentive (Hamad, Bettinger, Cooper, & Semb, 1979; Jacobs & Bailey, 1979).

There are two major problems in applying the findings of these recycling studies. First, most of them have been short-term experimental demonstrations ranging from a few weeks to 8 months in length; therefore more long-term studies of ongoing community recycling programs are badly needed. Second, most research has not considered the cost-effectiveness issue, and in some studies that have done so, the costs of the experimental intervention exceeded its benefits (one welcome exception was Hamad et al., 1979). Hence more attention is needed to intervention techniques that will pay their own way. Of the few studies done in conjunction with community recycling programs, one that used a combination of personal appeals, written requests, and provision of recycling bags obtained a self-reported participation rate of nearly 90% (Arbuthnot, Tedeschi, Wayner, Turner, Kressel, & Rush, 1977). However, even studies that have shown substantial objectively measured increases in participation in community recycling programs (e.g., Jacobs & Bailey, 1979, 1982–1983) have generally reported unfavorable balances in their cost–benefit analyses. An encouraging exception was an office program for saving high-grade wastepaper at the Environmental Protection Agency's Washington, DC headquarters. In the first year, it earned $11,000 with only minor expenses (Environmental Action Foundation, 1977). A similar program in a university office setting was also promising, though not fully evaluated (Humphrey et al., 1977).

It is unfortunate that very few low-technology community recycling programs have been designed with input from experimental research findings or psychological consultants. In general, there seems to be little appreciation of the crucial role of social and behavioral variables in creating or reducing problems of waste management (Geller et al., 1982). Based on the available research findings, steps in planning an effective waste-reduction program should include assessing what materials are most important to save, designing a convenient area or container for them, establishing waste-reduction goals, developing written and visual appeals for attitude and behavior change, and utilizing commitment, models, incentives, and public and individual feedback to promote sustained conservation efforts (Cook & Berrenberg, 1981; Winett & Geller, 1982).

Another area of research that needs much more emphasis is description and evaluation of large-scale resource recovery programs in settings such as industry or waste-disposal agencies (Winett & Geller, 1982). Among the few reports on such programs that have appeared in the psychological literature are papers describing the recycling or waste-reduction programs of certain large industrial corporations (Eldridge, LeMasters, & Szypot, 1978; Peterson, 1975;

Reynolds, 1979; Schwegler, 1979; Shirley, 1979; Stoerzinger, Johnston, Pisor, & Craig, 1978). There are many reasons that such programs have been relatively slow to develop; laws, government regulations, and local ordinances, as well as union pressures and routine corporation practices, have all erected many barriers to greater reuse of waste materials in our society (Bentsen, 1979; Walter, 1979). Organized attempts to change such laws, regulations, and practices might be some of the most effective steps possible toward creating a conserving society.

Even better for the environment than recycling waste materials is reducing the production of waste at its source. As one simple example, in England most shoppers use durable cloth or mesh shopping bags, and in some areas of the United States refunds for reusing paper shopping bags have been successfully offered (e.g., Greene, 1975). The largest-scale waste avoidance measures in effect in this country are the "bottle bills," requiring reusable soft drink and beer bottles and mandatory bottle deposits—laws which are in effect in at least nine states. Despite beverage industry protests concerning the costs and inconvenience of recycling, there is strong evidence that these bills have been environmentally and economically beneficial. For instance, they have reduced beverage-container litter by about 65%, decreased bottlers' purchases of containers about 80%, and increased local employment (Knapp, 1982; Levitt & Leventhal, 1984; Rose, 1982–1983; Savage & Richmond, 1974; Skinner, 1975; Waggoner, 1976).

28.2.5. Conservation of Land and Biological Resources

This traditional aspect of conservationism includes programs to prevent soil erosion, overgrazing, overcutting of forests, depletion of fisheries and game supplies, extinction of species, and so on. Other than the archival data on these resource problems summarized at the beginning of this chapter, there appears to be almost no psychological literature on them. However, rural sociologists have studied the diffusion of soil conservation techniques; biologists have investigated the results of forestry and game management practices; and the commons dilemma has been used as a model for understanding depletion of fisheries (Wilson, 1977). Yard cuttings and food waste comprise more than one-third of municipal waste (Wahl & Allison, 1975), and these products can be kept out of landfills and employed usefully to enrich garden soil by processing them in backyard compost piles. Geller has demonstrated the feasibil-

ity for suburban dwellers of a related technique—vermicomposting—using a small kitchen worm-bin that can cleanly and conveniently handle all of a normal family's food wastes (Geller et al., 1982). It is clear that psychological analysis and research could be usefully applied to many of these conservation problems and techniques.

28.2.6. Water Conservation

About 85% of the water consumed in the United States goes to agriculture, often at heavily subsidized low prices (Murray & Reeves, 1977). Agricultural water demand could be tremendously reduced by raising water prices to a break-even level and encouraging farmers to grow less thirsty crops and/or adopt drip irrigation techniques (Ehrlich et al., 1977). Water use by industry could also be markedly decreased by recirculation methods. Residential water use represents less than 5% of total U.S. consumption, but it, too, offers major opportunities for conservation (Milne, 1976). Household water heating alone takes one-sixth of residential energy consumption and accounts for 4% of national energy use, showing the close linkages between energy and other resource use. Toilets account for nearly half of indoor residential water consumption, and baths and showers take another 30%, but there are cheap and practical water-saving devices for toilets, and flow restrictors for shower heads can reduce their water consumption by one-half or more. In total, over one-third of household indoor water use could be easily and cheaply saved by installation of a few simple devices. With greater expenditures and the reuse of gray water (waste water from washing and baths), it is possible to reduce household water consumption nearly to zero (Milne, 1976).

There are a number of interlocking institutional and cultural circumstances that combine to deter individuals and organizations from adopting water-saving practices (Cone & Hayes, 1980). Among them are billing systems of municipal water districts (usually declining block rates, which encourage heavy use), local building and plumbing codes and state water laws and regulations, traditional manufacturing and sales procedures, and traditional building–trades union practices (both of which discourage new products or conservation techniques), consumers' lack of knowledge of the actual costs of water use, and lack of knowledge of new conservation devices and practices. In this situation, further education and feedback about water consumption can be useful to consumers, but efforts to alter institutional factors such as water rate structures, legislative and regulatory codes, and manufacturing and distribution practices are at least as important in promoting water conservation effectively.

As yet, water conservation has received very little attention from psychological researchers, as is demonstrated by two review chapters (Cone & Hayes, 1980; Winkler, 1982). An Australian study using Fishbein and Ajzen's (1975) model showed that social norms and age, as well as conservation attitudes, were important factors in accounting for intentions to conserve water (Kantola, Syme, & Campbell, 1982). Studies of actual water consumption during the 1976–1978 California drought showed that communities were able to reduce water use about 30% from previous levels (Agras et al., 1980). Both price increases and educational and regulatory measures were found to decrease residential water use, and their effects on agricultural users were substantially greater than on domestic users, yielding as much as a 60% drop in consumption (Berk et al., 1980). McGarry (1978) reported that in Washington, DC, the introduction of an *increasing* block rate for water reduced residential consumption about 13%. A study in Perth, Australia, found six self-report factors that combined to predict over 90% of the variance in household water consumption. However, neither weekly feedback nor an economically realistic experimental rebate of $1.00 a week per kiloliter of reduction in water use was effective in decreasing water consumption below that of a control group (Syme, Kantola, Reed, & Winkler, 1979; Winkler, Syme, & Thomas, 1979). Similar nonsignificant conservation effects were found in a U.S. study that used a behavioral approach featuring daily feedback as well as an educational-informational approach (Geller, Erickson, & Buttram, 1983). In the same study, an "engineering approach" consisting of the installation of four low-cost water conservation devices in participants' homes did produce a significant drop in water use. However, the saving was much smaller than expected from manufacturers' literature and laboratory tests, suggesting that people may have "compensated" for the expected water conservation by increased consumption (e.g., by taking longer showers). A later phase of the study found that giving householders the same devices together with installation instructions resulted in only a 30% to 40% rate of installation and therefore far less potential for water conservation.

In studying and attempting to influence the demand for water, a novel approach termed *behavioral economics* has combined psychological principles and experimental interventions with an analytical framework and variables familiar to economists (Winkler & Winett, 1982). For instance, direct individual measurement of household water consumption has been used to correct previous econometric estimates of the price elasticity of demand for water (Winkler et al., 1979). This interdisciplinary approach is an excellent demonstration that each field can contribute methods and variables that will broaden understanding of the issue and increase the validity of findings and interpretations.

Even more than in the litter-control and waste-reduction areas, the limited research on water conservation has almost all been done with residential users, and investigation of industrial, commercial, and agricultural settings is badly needed. One experimental research paradigm that is applicable is the "social trap" or commons dilemma, and Berk and colleagues' (1980) findings indicate that the dilemma of the commons can be partially overridden by information and moral appeals.

28.2.7. Environmental Pollution

Past reviews have summarized the effects of air pollution on human health (Lave & Seskin, 1977) and on behavior (Evans & Jacobs, 1981). Despite the importance of air pollution as an environmental stressor, its effects have been studied very little by psychologists, and efforts to control air quality have received even less research attention. Some attitude surveys about air pollution have found that people with higher levels of concern are more likely to advocate government controls on pollution (Medalia, 1964). Evans and Jacobs suggest that people's responses to air pollution, including attempts to control it, can be understood in terms of the psychological constructs of *perceived control* and *adaptation*. Adaptation levels appear to be involved because people who migrated from clear air to smoggy locations have been found to be more worried about the smog than those who came from other polluted areas (Evans, Jacobs, & Frager, 1979; Wohlwill, 1974).

Economists have recommended attacking pollution by means of taxes, price incentives, and effluent charges (e.g., Kneese & Schultze, 1975; Marcus, Sommers, & Morris, 1982). A few studies have begun to evaluate the implementation processes and objective impacts of air quality control programs—for example, Knoepfel and Weidner's (1982) multination European study. However, we have not found any psychological research aimed at controlling water pollution or toxic wastes. Of course, the general research on environmental attitudes and environmentally responsible behavior is tangentially relevant (e.g., Lipsey, 1977b), as is research on the demographic correlates of the relevant attitudes (Hamilton, 1985a, 1985b) and on the structure of those attitudes (Stern et al., 1986). Recently, some psychologists have begun to study toxic waste problems in terms of people's risk perception and acceptance of risks, and also in terms of their behavior and reactions following emergencies such as the nuclear accident at Three Mile Island (e.g., Fischhoff et al., 1981; Sills, Wolf, & Shelanski, 1981; Slovic et al., 1981; Sundstrom, Lounsbury, DeVault, & Peele, 1981; Walsh, 1981). (See Pitt and Zube, Chapter 27 this volume for a fuller treatment of this approach.)

28.2.8. Energy Conservation

When the ecological implications of energy use are considered, energy forms are not all alike. As an environmental policy goal, "energy conservation" refers not merely to using less, but especially to less use of depletable energy resources and of technologies having major negative consequences for the environment (Stern & Aronson, 1984, chapter 2). That implies reductions in the use of fossil fuels and uranium and in processes involving mineral extraction, combustion, or the creation of radioactive or toxic by-products. But because the vast majority of energy use in the United States involves just such sources and technologies, it is a fairly accurate simplification to consider all present reductions in energy use as roughly equivalent in their environmental implications. Granted this simplification, energy use is more easily reducible to a common metric than solid-waste problems are. Thus it makes sense to examine energy use as a single phenomenon and to ask which actors and which behaviors are most responsible for it and which can best reduce it.

Stern and Gardner (1981c) have presented such an analysis for energy use in the United States. Roughly one-third of energy use is attributable to direct consumption by households; the industrial and commercial sectors of the economy account for the rest. Although the importance of household behavior is increased by its indirect effect on commercial and industrial energy use, the power of households to affect national energy use indirectly is limited by manufacturers' decisions about which products to market and by the investments of intermediaries—such as builders, developers, and building owners—in appliances, furnaces, and building "shells." Because intermediaries usually do not pay for the energy used

in the equipment and buildings they buy, they have less interest in energy efficiency than the users of the buildings or equipment. The first systematic attempt to identify behavioral factors in organizations' and intermediaries' influence on energy use was completed by a committee of the National Academy of Sciences (Stern & Aronson, 1984, chapter 5).

In short, households are not the predominant energy users in the United States, and they should not be expected to be the predominant energy savers. More energy savings can often be achieved by business and industry or by changing public policy than by changing individual behavior directly. The best examples of the latter point are the federal regulations governing automobile fuel economy and exhaust emissions.

As discussed earlier in this chapter, "prevention" is usually a more effective approach to energy conservation than "cure." One implication for households is that purchase of energy-using or energy-saving technology is an especially important class of behavior. This is particularly true because investments in prevention—that is, in energy-efficient technology—are likely to be perceived as improvements in "quality of life," whereas many versions of cure, which involve behavioral changes, are frequently perceived as sacrifices.

Research on psychological factors in energy conservation has been reviewed by several writers (e.g., Baum & Singer, 1981; Geller et al., 1982; McDougall et al., 1981; Oskamp, 1983; Seligman & Becker, 1981; Shippee, 1980; Stern & Gardner, 1980). This work has derived largely from the paradigms of applied behavior analysis and experimental social psychology (Stern & Gardner, 1981c), though there has also been a history of survey research (Farhar et al., 1979; Olsen, 1981). Like the solid-waste research, behavioral energy studies have focused almost exclusively on the behavior of individuals and households and on only a limited range of behaviors.

Energy-Using Behavior in the Home

ANALYTICAL STUDIES
The first attempts to understand the psychological dimensions of energy-saving action in the home consisted of surveys, analyzed correlationally. These generally related self-reported energy-saving actions to other variables, most of which were nonpsychological: household income, family size, educational level, appliance ownership, the age and size of dwelling unit, and so forth. Early surveys often included attitudinal measures as well, most often "belief in the

energy crisis." Correlations between these attitudes or other variables and energy-related action were often weak, unreliable, or even nonexistent (Farhar et al., 1979; Olsen, 1981). Recently, however, more sophisticated research designs have been developing knowledge by departing in several ways from the simple correlational approach, as discussed previously in the section on environmental attitudes.

First, researchers have utilized relevant theories more extensively. Understanding of general attitude theory (e.g., Schuman & Johnson, 1976) has led more researchers to measure attitudes at levels of specificity appropriate to the energy-saving actions they are believed to affect. Some researchers have drawn on theory about the diffusion of innovations (Rogers with Shoemaker, 1971) and found that communication about energy with neighbors and associates influences adoption of energy-efficient technologies in the home (Darley, 1978; Leonard-Barton, 1980). Others, following Schwartz's norm-activation model (1970, 1977), found that specific energy-related beliefs influence personal norms about energy and that these in turn influence behavior, sometimes powerfully (Black, 1978; Black et al., 1985; Stern, Black, & Elworth, 1982, 1983). The Fishbein attitude model (Fishbein & Ajzen, 1975) has also been used to demonstrate the role of behavioral intention and related variables in energy-saving action (Macey & Brown, 1983) and the effect of attitudes about solar energy on intentions to adopt residential solar energy systems (Keating & Rosa, 1982).

Second, researchers have used multivariate analytic techniques to assess the interactions of social and psychological influences with physical, demographic, and economic constraints. For example, it has been found that personal norms have more effect on energy-saving activities when the activities are relatively inexpensive, practicable for the particular household, and easy to perform (Black et al., 1985; Stern et al., 1983). Such findings, though not surprising in retrospect, begin to specify the relationships among psychological, structural, and economic influences on conservation; this work provides a basis for interdisciplinary research.

Third, researchers have begun to develop and test theoretical models to differentiate the effects of variables operating at different points in presumed causal chains (e.g., Black et al., 1985; Heberlein & Warriner, 1983; Leonard-Barton & Rogers, 1979; Macey & Brown, 1983; Verhallen & van Raaij, 1981). This work generally supports a multistage causal model such as illustrated in Table 28.1. In such a model, causality moves from top to bottom, with each variable acting as a possible influence—direct or indirect—on those at levels below. Some feedback loops operate in the reverse direction. One of these is learning: Observable effects of action on such outcomes as energy bills and comfort can affect specific attitudes and beliefs about energy saving and, through that, can change subsequent behavior. In another kind of feedback, energy-saving behavior directly affects general attitudes and beliefs through processes such as self-justification or dissonance reduction. For policy purposes, it is important to note that people justify their behavior as a function of the amount of their personal effort, regardless of whether energy savings result. In fact, effortful action that produces little effect is likely to have the strongest positive effect on attitudes. Thus behavior can influence attitudes independently of its effect on resource use.

The model in Table 28.1 has heuristic value. It can clarify the relationships among the various measures often used in energy studies. It emphasizes, for example, that energy use is not behavior but rather an *outcome of behavior*—a point sometimes overlooked (covered at greater length in Russell and Snodgrass, Chapter 8, this volume). It also helps one understand the typical failure to find correlations between income and energy-conserving action or between general attitudes and energy use. Many variables intervene, and in many studies these are left unmeasured.

The model also has implications for policy analysis. It suggests, for example, that the effect of motivational policies such as price increases and tax credits will be mediated by the intervening variables of consumer attitudes and knowledge—and if knowledge is insufficient or attitudes inappropriate, such policies may be ineffective. There is, in fact, evidence that many people are stubbornly misinformed about which actions save them energy in their homes (Kempton et al., 1985) and that partly for this reason, price signals are not optimally effective by themselves (Stern & Aronson, 1984). The model also suggests that policies that shorten a causal chain can be effective. For example, giving feedback about energy use ties behavior more closely to an observable effect and thus facilitates learning.

EXPERIMENTAL STUDIES
Dozens of experimental studies have used communications of various kinds to influence energy-saving behavior directly—to encourage people to turn off lights, take shorter showers, and so on. The results

Table 28.1. An Approximate Causal Model of Resource Use with Examples from Residential Energy Consumption

Level of Causality	Type of Variable	Examples
8	Background factors	Income, education, number of household members, local temperature conditions
7	Structural factors Institutional factors	Size of dwelling unit, appliance ownership Owner/renter status, direct or indirect payment for energy
6	Recent events	Difficulty paying energy bills, experience with shortages, fuel price increases
5	General attitudes General beliefs	Concern about national energy situation Belief households can help with national energy problem
4	Specific attitudes	Sense of personal obligation to use energy efficiently
	Specific beliefs	Belief that using less heat threatens family health
	Specific knowledge	Knowledge that water heater is a major energy user
3	Behavioral commitment	Commitment to cut household energy use 15%
	Behavioral intention	Intention to install a solar heating system
2	Resource-using behavior Resource-saving behavior	Length of time air conditioner is kept on Insulating attic, lowering winter thermostat setting
1	Resource use	Kilowatt-hours per month
0	Observable effects	Lower energy costs, elimination of drafts, family quarrels over thermostat

(Diagram at left: "Self-Justification" brackets levels 5, 4, and 2; "Learning" brackets levels 4, 3, 2, and 0.)

have been similar to those found when similar messages have been directed at solving litter problems. Such *exhortations* or *prompts* have limited effect, but tend to be better accepted when specific, salient, and proximate to the target behavior (Ester & Winett, 1982; Geller et al., 1982). *Modeling* techniques have been used occasionally in experiments and show promise for shaping some specific behaviors (Aronson & O'Leary, 1983) and as part of more comprehensive influence programs (Winett, Hatcher, Fort, Leckliter, Love, Riley, & Fishback, 1982).

There have also been efforts to influence action indirectly with communications that impart *knowledge of how to save* energy. But offering such information has often proved ineffective (for an exception, see Craig & McCann, 1978). This is probably due in part to poor design of the communication programs (Ester & Winett, 1982; Stern & Aronson, 1984).

Like prompts, information can be made more effective if it is specific, relevant, and so forth, but energy information is unlike prompts in that credibility is a major problem (e.g., Craig & McCann, 1978; Stern & Aronson, 1984; Wildavsky & Tenenbaum, 1981). The failure of most energy information programs may also be a function of the fact that they rarely attempt to get a behavioral commitment (Table 28.1 shows a theoretical connection among knowledge, commitment, and action). Analyses of some existing energy information programs, particularly those involving home energy audits, suggest that those that involve energy users actively in the process are more likely to influence action (see Stern & Aronson, 1984).

No single factor accounts for most of the difference between failure and success in energy conservation programs based on communication. Successful programs seem to rely on a *combination of ingredients*. One highly successful experimental program is illustrative. Winett and his colleagues (1982) used a combination of videotaped modeling, instruction about the insulating value of clothing, behavioral adaptation techniques for adjusting ambient temperature, a carefully constructed script that defined energy savings in terms of efficiency rather than "conservation," and, in some experimental conditions, feedback of energy consumption. The study achieved the greatest energy savings yet reported from purely behavioral changes—over 25% in some experimental treatments—under both winter and summer conditions. The program's great success was no doubt attributable to the way it combined several methods of influence and attended to a variety of issues at once: the symbolic meaning of energy, the physiological need for adaptation to changed environments, the need for specific rather than general instructions, and so forth. The existence of economic motives to conserve was probably also necessary for success, for a similar intervention for water conservation failed in a context of low-cost water (Geller et al., 1983). Another experiment which produced short-term energy savings combined the motivational effects of cognitive dissonance with information on how to reduce electricity use (Kantola, Syme, & Campbell, 1984). By contrast to these systematic approaches, most experimental research and public action involving communications for energy conservation has been very narrow in conception.

A few experiments have been conducted to change behavior by securing *behavioral commitment.* Pallak and his colleagues (1980) demonstrated that long-lasting energy savings could be achieved merely by securing from householders a public commitment to save energy, and a program that involved people by having them "self-monitor" and record their energy use on a regular basis produced a smaller but equally long-lasting effect. Becker (1978) showed that energy-use feedback was more effective when combined with a commitment to make a substantial energy saving, and Katzev and Johnson (1983, 1984) reported evidence that a standard foot-in-the-door manipulation could also produce energy savings.

Researchers have experimented with offering *tangible rewards* for energy conservation. As in the solid-waste and litter-control literatures, the rewards have taken the form of money, prizes, and lottery tickets, and they have been given to both individuals and groups. A number of reward systems have been demonstrated to produce statistically significant reductions in energy use, but the costs of the experimental programs have often exceeded the value of the resources saved, and the effects have been short-lived

(see Geller et al., 1982). For policy purposes, it is important to recognize the economic equivalence of a reward and a change in energy price. Experimental rewards and price changes seem to produce effects of similar magnitude when their effects are measured under similar conditions (Winkler & Winett, 1982).

A uniquely psychological contribution to energy conservation policy, stemming from principles of learning theory, is the research on energy use *feedback.* Learning depends on knowledge of results, but unlike other types of learning, knowledge of results about one's energy use is not readily forthcoming in the real world. Most householders learn how much energy they have used only after a long delay—when they receive the monthly or bimonthly utility bill. Also, the information in the bill is very hard to interpret, because energy bills measure not only behavior change but weather, length of day, and various other factors. In the context of Table 28.1, the links from behavior to this information (which is a type of observable effect) and back to energy use are weak. Furthermore, most householders do not even look at the energy use information on the bill; what is most salient to them is dollar cost (Kempton & Montgomery, 1982). Thus special efforts to provide frequent and specific feedback about energy use should help people learn to conserve energy by shortening the causal path from behavior through its effects and back to beliefs about the effects of behavior.

Reviews of the many experimental studies of residential energy use feedback (Ellis & Gaskell, 1978; Seligman, Becker, & Darley, 1981; Shippee, 1980; Winett & Neale, 1979; Winkler & Winett, 1982) find that this procedure can produce savings of up to 20% of household energy use through changes in the ways residents use already existing equipment in the home. The effectiveness of feedback depends on at least four conditions: (1) that the feedback is believable, that is, roughly related to behavior, (2) that the feedback is frequent enough to give people knowledge of the effects of behaviors undertaken to save energy (daily feedback is usually effective, but even monthly feedback has sometimes proven effective [Hayes & Cone, 1981; Russo, 1977]), (3) that the household has made a commitment to saving energy or has set an ambitious and explicit conservation goal, and (4) that energy costs are a reasonably high proportion of the household budget. The first two conditions suggest that the effectiveness of feedback depends on its value as a form of information. Related to this idea are the arguments that feedback works because it makes energy more "visible" to users and because it can provide more credible information than one might get from a utility or a government agency (Stern & Aronson, 1984). Some studies have experimented with feedback devices and displays to make the information more available and interpretable (e.g., Becker & Seligman, 1978). The importance of commitment and cost suggests that the success of feedback also depends on the presence of motivating factors at other levels of the causal model in Table 28.1: behavioral commitment and recent or background events. Discussions of the informational and motivational properties of feedback can be found in the literature (Ellis & Gaskell, 1978; Seligman et al., 1981).

Other Energy Conservation Research

The bulk of psychological research on energy conservation has dealt with residential energy use and the habits of individuals. Yet the great bulk of the potential for energy savings in the United States lies elsewhere—in household purchase decisions, in the actions of intermediaries whose decisions affect the ways others use energy, in the behavior of corporate energy users, and in public policy choices. Psychologically informed research has recently begun to explore this territory, and this work displays some new and promising trends.

HOUSEHOLD INVESTMENTS IN ENERGY-EFFICIENT TECHNOLOGY

Much energy can be saved by investments in home insulation, major furnace improvements, solar water heaters, passive solar heating, fuel-efficient automobiles, and other technologies. Some studies have used the multivariate analytic methods already mentioned to identify psychological and social influences on energy-efficient investments. The variables affecting household investments appear to be different from those that influence changes of habits (Black et al., 1985; Stern et al., 1983). In particular, expensive and effortful activities, which include the major investments such as insulation, are influenced by background factors such as home ownership more than by attitudes, norms, or energy costs. Less constrained behaviors, which include minor investments as well as many behavioral adjustments, are influenced more strongly by personal norms about energy use. Several variables have been found to influence household investments, including communication with neighbors and associates (Darley, 1978; Leonard-Barton, 1980); beliefs, attitudes, and norms regarding energy efficiency (Black et al., 1985); and the mechanical ability of household members (Leonard-Barton, 1979). In addition, attitudes about

solar energy as well as beliefs about its costs and benefits influence intentions to install residential solar energy systems (Keating & Rosa, 1982).

Theories about the diffusion of innovation seem particularly useful for understanding household purchases of energy-saving equipment (e.g., Darley, 1978; Darley & Beniger, 1981; Leonard-Barton, 1980; Savinar, 1981; Sawyer, 1982). For example, people who have installed active solar energy systems in their homes fit the typical profile of early adopters (Sawyer, 1982); this suggests a potential for much wider acceptance of these technologies. Diffusion theory has also been used to suggest policies to accelerate adoption of energy-saving equipment (Darley & Beniger, 1981; Stern & Aronson, 1984).

So far, there has been little experimental work to test the effectiveness of particular psychological variables as influences on household energy investments. One example is the work of Yates (1982), who has applied prospect theory, a recent development in cognitive psychology (Kahneman & Tversky, 1979), to the design of persuasive communications about solar water heaters and insulating jackets for water heaters. Another is the work of Miller and Ford (1985), who found that varying the source of a direct-mail appeal for participants in a major weatherization program changed the rate of participation by about a factor of three. Further experimental work on household investments holds great potential because of the magnitude of energy savings possible. One area where psychological expertise may be especially useful is in the design and implementation of energy-efficiency rating and labeling systems for appliances and buildings (see, e.g., Seligman & Hutton, 1981). Here the type of rating (pass-fail certification versus various numerical ratings) and the format of labels are likely to make much difference in the extent to which people use the information conveyed by a rating or a label. Both existing theory and field experimentation techniques could help create effective labels and ratings.

INTERMEDIARIES

Although energy use is affected in important ways by many intermediaries (Stern & Aronson, 1984), the psychologically informed research in this area has been limited to work on energy conservation in multifamily buildings, where developers' and owners' decisions affect energy use by building occupants. This situation creates special barriers to energy conservation. When energy is billed to the occupants, owners lack the incentive to save and may not invest in insulation and more efficient appliances. Occupants have an incentive to save but are unlikely to invest because they would be improving someone else's property. When energy costs are included in rent (when the building is "master-metered"), building owners have an incentive to improve energy efficiency but may not do so because occupants lack incentives to behave in energy-saving ways. Part of the problem is that of "collective action": Each occupant stands to gain only a small portion of the value of the energy he or she may save because, even if the savings are eventually reflected in lower rents, the savings achieved are divided many ways.

A number of studies have attacked the collective action problem in master-metered buildings by structuring incentives for individuals. Methods have included individual metering (McClelland, 1980; Nelson, 1981), cash rewards (e.g., Walker, 1979), and mathematical systems to divide the energy costs so that they appear on the rent bill (McClelland, 1980). Other researchers have guaranteed incentives to groups such as by offering a prize to all occupants if some energy-saving target is reached (e.g., McClelland & Belsten, 1980; McClelland & Cook, 1980; Newsom & Makranczy, 1978; Slavin, Wodarski, & Blackburn, 1981). These studies show that incentive systems are effective with some uses of energy, producing savings of up to 25% and more when individual metering is applied only to appliances and lights (McClelland, 1980). These effects are produced by changes in the occupants' behavior, however, rather than by improvements in the efficiency of equipment. Thus the energy savings may involve personal sacrifice. Furthermore, individual metering requires costly equipment and might even be a net energy waster because it removes the owner's incentive to make the building more energy-efficient; this possibility has not yet received much attention.

CONSERVATION IN THE INDUSTRIAL AND COMMERCIAL SECTORS

Energy savings amounting to 40% or more have been reported by individual companies within most of the major energy-using industries and in nearly every part of the commercial/service sector of the economy (Oskamp, 1981). However, the average saving achieved has been much lower. Because the economics of energy efficiency is more or less constant within each industry, the variation between similar firms is probably due largely to behavioral or organizational factors. Only a few studies exist, however, of the behavioral dimension of energy use and conservation in the industrial and commercial sectors of the economy. In one survey, Oskamp (1981) found that

energy conservation efforts began earlier and were more extensive and successful in larger chemical firms than in smaller ones. Successful programs were also associated with support from top management, use of energy accounting systems, existence of an energy manager with authority, and encouragement of employee involvement. In a study of the retail industry, Mills (1981) found that more energy management steps were taken by larger firms and by firms in which top managers believed that an energy crisis existed, that there was significant potential for their firms to save energy, that the energy future was uncertain, and that government programs would not be helpful. These findings, of course, are only suggestive. Additional research and policy suggestions have been developed on the basis of a review of literature on organizational behavior (Stern & Aronson, 1984, Chapter 5; Winett & Geller, 1982). (The topic of *conservation in the transportation sector* is discussed in detail in Pitt and Zube, Chapter 27, this volume, so is not included here.)

PUBLIC POLICY CHOICES

It is clear that energy conservation is greatly affected by policy decisions that set the context for energy use. Policies change energy prices, regulate production processes or building practices, alter incentives for investment, affect the disposable income of individuals and organizations, provide information, support energy research and development, and so forth. This is an area where psychologically oriented researchers have done relatively little work. Research on rebates for conservation has clear implications for pricing and tax policies. In addition, some researchers have offered specific suggestions for policies and programs that might encourage energy conservation. For example, Geller and his colleagues (1982) have devised and tried out a community-based energy conservation program derived from behavior analytic principles. Stern, Black, and Elworth (1981) have reviewed residential energy conservation programs and offered a series of policy recommendations. A multinational study of consumer energy policies has been undertaken by an international group of social and behavioral scientists (Joerges, 1981), and two National Academy of Sciences reports (Stern & Aronson, 1984; Stern, 1985) have offered a number of suggestions derived from psychological research for the design and implementation of information-based and incentive-based conservation programs. The National Academy group, for example, recommended policies to put information into a form easily assimilated into energy users' cognitive frameworks and their ordinary decision processes. One recommendation was for the development of "simple, understandable indices of energy efficiency, comparable to miles-per-gallon, for appliances, furnaces, and building shells." A related recommendation concerned improving utility billing practices to make bills more effective as feedback. In addition, policy recommendations were offered for making energy audits more effective as communications, for institutional changes to increase the credibility of conservation programs, for simplifying the administration of incentive programs to make them more attractive, and for diffusing energy-saving practices among energy users. Although these suggestions address policy and program design issues from a psychological viewpoint, they have not yet been tested systematically under field conditions.

Evaluation of Energy Conservation Programs

Some of the most important direct contributions made by psychologically oriented research to energy conservation policy have come from evaluation research, and this contribution has been increasing in recent years as some electric and gas utility companies have expanded their conservation programs. These organizations have the resources and often the interest to evaluate their programs rather thoroughly. However, a meta-evaluation of much of their typical research demonstrated that they rarely used adequate evaluation research designs (White et al., 1984). Furthermore, only a small proportion of the organized energy conservation efforts that have been mounted by governments, utilities, and community groups have been formally evaluated.

The usual purpose of evaluations has been to demonstrate the effectiveness of programs, and in many cases insufficient resources have been provided to employ evaluation research professionals or their best techniques. Much of the early research was of poor technical quality, observing neither behavior nor energy use directly. Even among studies that collected reliable data on energy use, most failed to ask questions that would help explain a program's success or failure. Generalizations can be made, however, from the better quality research.

Purely informational programs have been rather ineffective in promoting energy savings. These programs have usually operated from the implicit (and incorrect) assumption that if people are simply presented with better information about what actions will benefit them by saving energy and money, they will act accordingly. The programs have offered much information but have generally done little to make

their messages attractive, clear, simple, relevant, and/or credible (Ester & Winett, 1982; Geller et al., 1982; Stern & Aronson, 1984). They also typically rely on influencing people through a single exposure to the program. As a result of these deficiencies, informational programs have not been notably successful in influencing the behavior even of those who are exposed to the information offered (e.g., Hirst, Berry, & Soderstrom, 1981; Hutton, 1982; McDougall, Claxton, & Ritchie, 1983). They fare especially poorly in reaching and influencing low-income, elderly, or non-English-speaking potential clients (Hirst et al., 1981; Stern et al., 1981).

Studies indicate that several behavioral and social variables mediate the effectiveness of these programs. These variables include the quality of communication between programs and clients, the use of multiple contacts with clients, the credibility of sponsoring organizations, consumer protection guarantees, and convenience for clients (U.S. General Accounting Office, 1981; Hirst et al., 1981; Stern & Aronson, 1984; Stern et al., 1981). Attention to such variables in addition to the technical and economic factors usually emphasized in program planning would help considerably in making the programs more effective.

The stronger conservation programs rely on more than information. For example, programs designed within provisions of the Residential Conservation Service, which operated under the National Energy Conservation Policy Act of 1978 between that date and 1985, have offered householders a package of services including a detailed, in-person home energy audit, assistance with financing of recommended energy-saving measures, assistance with finding competent contractors, and inspection of contractors' work. Careful studies have demonstrated that at least some of these package programs effectively save energy for participants (Hirst et al., 1983; Hirst, 1984; Stern et al., 1981). A study of one of the programs (Stern et al., 1981) identified noneconomic features that were central to its effectiveness. The most important of these were the program's consumer protection guarantees and its convenience; financial advantages were much less important to program participants. Because of the importance of noneconomic variables to the success of conservation programs, psychologically informed researchers can make an important contribution through well-conceived evaluation research.

Conservation programs that rely on financial incentives have recently been the subject of evaluation studies (Hirst, 1984; Stern et al., 1986). Although these evaluations put most of their methodological emphasis on measuring outcomes (participation rates and measures of energy savings), examination of the process variables shows that nonfinancial aspects of the programs can make more difference to the outcome than the size of the incentive offered. Participation rates typically vary by a factor of 10 when several different utility companies offer the same incentive to households in the same climatic zone (Stern et al., 1986). The reasons for the widespread variation seem to lie in differences in marketing and implementation strategies—the same kinds of variables that influence the effectiveness of informational programs.

It is worth reemphasizing that evaluation research is rarely funded for making its most useful contribution—gaining knowledge for designing or improving programs. Usually its purpose is to provide a summative judgment of the success or cost-effectiveness of a program rather than for "formative" evaluation. To learn from an energy program's experience, it is necessary to do more than quantify the energy savings attributable to it. One must also understand the factors in the program and its environment responsible for its overall performance. Thus evaluation studies should examine a range of psychological, social, and organizational variables in the program's design and implementation, in addition to energy variables. Recently, a few such "progress evaluations" of energy conservation programs have appeared (Lerman & Bronfman, 1984; Lerman, Bronfman, & Tonn, 1983). More extensive work of this type would be valuable. But the sparse funding of evaluation research may not allow for the necessary expansion of the research goals. Psychologically oriented researchers have had only limited success, at least in the United States, in convincing policymakers or program managers on this point.

28.3. PROSPECTS FOR PSYCHOLOGICAL CONTRIBUTIONS

28.3.1. The Bias toward Technology and "Hard" Science

In contrast to technological "solutions," psychological approaches to solving resource problems face a variety of serious external obstacles. Because environmental resource problems are direct outcomes of the use of science and technology, most people expect improvements in the problems also to come from those spheres—few initially think social or behavioral

scientists possess relevant expertise. The alternative perspective, that sees scientific and technological development as social choice, that looks to social science for enlightenment and social institutions for solutions, is much less influential (for discussions of this view, see Schnaiberg, 1980; Stretton, 1976).

The technological view of environmental problems is reinforced by our cadre of environmental experts. These people, usually physical and biological scientists or engineers, make up the scientific staffs of companies and agencies that make decisions about resource management. By training, environmental experts think in terms of physical and biological transformations and their technological applications—they see technologies as more controllable than people, and they direct policy toward technological innovations and technological solutions. Thus they are as a rule more oriented toward industrial production than toward understanding the environmental effects of this production, and more inclined to solve energy problems through production than conservation (Morell, 1981; Schnaiberg, 1980). Through their influence and that of the companies that profit from technological development, policy tends to ignore the human implications of technology. Further, policymakers are left without the expertise to cope with human problems when they arise (cf. Nader & Milleron, 1979; Schnaiberg, 1980, chapter 6). Although some environmental experts have learned from experience that people are more than an obstacle to technological progress, these remain a minority (Dietz, Stern, & Rycroft, 1984).

The U.S. Department of Energy exemplifies the situation. A survey in March 1981 found that only 85 of the department's staff of 19,972 claimed any social science background or reported that they were working on social-science-related issues. These included only 1 claiming an academic background in psychology, 6 with backgrounds in sociology, and none with a background in anthropology (Office of Program Coordination, 1981). The department's conservation efforts have been mainly technological, consisting of research and development on electric cars, cogeneration systems, energy-efficient light bulbs, and so forth. The social dimension of conservation policy has been neglected even where it is most obvious—in policies to influence the separate decisions of millions of energy users. Despite criticism of this approach (U.S. General Accounting Office, 1981), the department has done very little to develop social science expertise.[2]

One effect of the technological view is a failure to understand the importance of evaluation research methodology. People with technical backgrounds often think of resource conservation as a set of engineering problems and of consumers' motives as primarily financial. There is little appreciation of the various behavioral, social, and institutional factors on which programs and policies depend for their success. As a result, policymakers learn less from evaluation research than they might and miss opportunities to improve their programs or policies.

In the technological culture of energy and environmental management, social science is further hampered by the perception that it is "soft." (For an illuminating discussion of the way the social perception and status of "hard" science and social science are influenced by the role of science and technology in corporate production, see Schnaiberg, 1980, chapter 6.) The scientists and engineers who dominate the environmental field value hardheadedness, hard science, hardware, and hard energy technology. It has been suggested that the sexual symbolism of hard and soft in the male-dominated environmental policy culture probably compounds the problem—especially in energy policy, where the hard-versus-soft distinction has polarized debate (Kempton & Downey, 1982).

In addition, psychologically based policies are commonly seen as "behavior modification" and thus inappropriate for government. This perception seems paradoxical to a psychologist: Persuasion attempts are considered to be behavior modification, whereas tax credits and price increases—prototypical Skinnerian consequence procedures—are considered ideal policy instruments and not behavior modification. Thus in 1978, the U.S. Congress approved conservation tax credits that would cost billions of dollars in lost tax receipts, but in 1979, it denied a request from the Department of Energy for $50 million for paid advertising for energy conservation. (Paid government advertising was only considered appropriate for military recruitment.) The common Washington, DC, image of social science as behavior modification must be changed if social science—even applied to purposes other than persuasion—is to become acceptable in policy circles.

A psychological perspective is also opposed because some of the environmental management strategies it suggests threaten the professional and budgetary interests of hard scientists and technologists working in the field or those of corporations in the resource management business. For example, Geller and his colleagues (1982, chapter 4) argue persuasively for a low-technology approach to resource recovery—one that relies on consumers to sort trash and garbage for separate disposal. If such an approach can be made effective, it would obviate the need to develop technologies that separate or process mixed trash, and it would erode the market for complex resource recovery facilities. In this context, it is worth noting that separation of residential solid waste was routine in Los Angeles until the 1960s and is currently practiced in other U.S. cities.

Ignoring behavioral and social issues in environmental policy has costs. When these issues are important, policies err and decision makers are surprised. When policymakers are confronted with an "impossible" nuclear reactor accident, or the nonresponse of energy users to free expert advice on how to save energy in the home, or unruly behavior in gasoline lines, or public demonstrations of outrage over the siting of toxic waste dumps, they sometimes call behavioral scientists— belatedly—to explain the unexpected behavior or to propose solutions to the problems. But because social research on environmental problems has not been given much time or support, behavioral scientists are not always ready to give useful advice. Moreover, the best use of social and behavioral science may be for designing policy to prevent social problems rather than for curing them, but this use of social science is especially uncommon.

28.3.2. Psychology's Disciplinary Blinders

The barriers to a psychological contribution to environmental policy are not all erected from one side. The training and culture of psychology militates against psychologists examining environmental problems in terms relevant to environmental policy. Psychologists get greater professional rewards from "pure" research than "applied" research, and when they do applied work, most of the rewards come from the development, extension, and testing of psychological theory rather than from problem-centered or interdisciplinary efforts. Thus when psychologists are concerned with environmental problems, they often try to combine personal and professional interests by using environmental problems as vehicles for research on some issue in psychological theory. The professional imperative that dictates this approach accounts for many of the gaps and limitations of the existing literature. Psychologists have authored excellent field demonstrations of behavioral principles, the Fishbein attitude model, dissonance theory, and other psychological paradigms—using environmental issues for content. But this approach short-circuits analysis of the environmental problems. As a result, researchers often overstate the importance of their work for solving major world problems. A successful demonstration of a theoretically relevant intervention is not nearly enough to assure a policy success.

The theory-based strategy also leads psychologists to overlook promising lines of research. Infrequent events are rarely studied because both theory and measurement techniques are weak, and political and organizational behaviors are rarely studied because theory is lacking in the subdisciplines of most psychologists who have studied environmental problems. As a result, insufficient research has been done on the environmental effects of people's major life choices, their collective and political actions, and the behavior of corporations, governments, and other major social institutions. Critical environmental problems such as soil erosion, water pollution, and the management of hazardous chemicals have been almost completely neglected by psychologists as a result. Similarly, in the study of energy conservation and solid-waste management in households, research has emphasized habitual behaviors—those for which changes are most easy to quantify—and neglected infrequent behaviors that are often more important from the standpoint of the environmental problem (Stern & Gardner, 1981b, 1981c).

We do not mean to denigrate the importance of applied research that is tied closely to theory. It is essential for theory building, and it can have practical value, especially where successful field demonstrations can be quickly replicated (for examples in environmental policy, see Geller et al., 1982; Heberlein & Baumgartner, 1985; McClelland & Belsten, 1980; good examples from outside the environmental policy area are presented by Varela, 1971). However, because most psychologists have chosen behaviors to study on grounds of theoretical relevance or methodological convenience rather than practical importance, much of their work is of marginal or no relevance to environmental policy, and it is seen as such by the policy community. In the next section, we discuss what might be done to change this situation.

28.3.3. An Integrated Approach to the Human Side of Environmental Problems

Environmental problems are interdisciplinary in nature. This is why government agencies, environmental management firms, and academic environmental policy programs employ physicists, biologists, engineers, economists, and various other specialists. Most of these organizations, however, have not been interdisciplinary enough: They have usually failed to include behavioral and social scientists. Psychologists, for their part, must also become more interdisciplinary to be of use in solving resource management problems. They need to collaborate not only with natural scientists and technologists but also with other social and behavioral scientists. The social and behavioral science disciplines share a similar general perspective that can illuminate many environmental policy issues. This contribution can be expressed more forcefully after collaboration, and psychology stands to learn from the process.

Improving Policy Analysis

With the exception of much of economics, the behavioral and social sciences share a general perspective that emphasizes what a National Research Council study has called "the human dimension...the rich mixture of cultural practices, social interactions, and human feelings that influence the behavior of individuals, social groups, and institutions" (Stern & Aronson, 1984, p. 2). This view contrasts with the usual emphasis of environmental policy analysts on scientific and technological processes and on the actions of the market and the national government. For example, in contrast to the view that people invest in energy efficiency because the technologies exist and save energy and money, behavioral scientists hypothesize that people invest because they have heard from people they trust that the investment will pay or because their friends have already made investments and are satisfied with the results (Stern & Aronson, 1984). Such social processes tend to be overlooked in environmental policy analysis. Interdisciplinary research showing how processes like these play essential roles in solving environmental problems may bring policymakers to take notice of an important but neglected set of issues.

The National Research Council report on *Energy Use: The Human Dimension* (Stern & Aronson, 1984) illustrates what a general behavioral and social science perspective can contribute. That report identified important neglected issues affecting energy policy: energy users' understandable skepticism about information, people's responses to losing part of their control over their own lives, the difficulty of perceiving price "signals" amid the noise, and a variety of reasons that government-produced information does not get used. Suggestions were offered for improving policies and programs by taking these and other behavioral and social factors more fully into account. The suggestions drew on knowledge in several subdisciplines of psychology and the social sciences:

learning, social influence, decision making, organizational behavior and administration, diffusion of innovation within social networks, and so forth. The combination of several approaches produced a more comprehensive set of suggestions than psychology alone would have been able to generate.

This sort of interdisciplinary collaboration may generate clear and compelling problem formulations that would command the attention of policymakers in a receptive political climate. But no single discipline is likely to address the many human aspects of most environmental policy problems. A few examples illustrate this point.

1. Policies to encourage residential energy conservation obviously depend on understanding of household energy use. Behavioral science is relevant because insulation, indoor and outdoor temperatures, installed appliances, house size and configuration, and other structural factors typically account for less than half the variance in energy use among homes (e.g., Vine et al., 1982). Recently, researchers from various disciplines have been pooling their knowledge and improving understanding of the multiple determinants of energy-related behavior. The new models allow for interactions among variables of interest to different disciplines (e.g., Black et al., 1985; Heberlein & Warriner, 1983; Leonard-Barton, 1979; Verhallen & van Raaij, 1981). A generic model, of which most of these are variants, is presented in Table 28.1.

2. Environmental regulation is a social process as well as a technical one. Regulation cannot be instituted or maintained without continued public support and acceptance, a perception of fairness, and the successful resolution of conflicts of political, economic, and regional interests. Psychologists know about some of these processes: attitude formation, for example, and attribution of responsibility (e.g., for damage to public health). They can study the way public attitudes are influenced by changing events and technologies. But if psychologists attempted to suggest policies based on such knowledge, they would be neglecting other important issues. Public opposition to policies is not only the sum of attitudes but is organized in social movements and political interest groups. Also attitudes are translated into social action only through a political process that generates policy and an implementation process that determines whether policy will have its desired effects. The best knowledge of these processes comes from outside psychology. To make useful policy suggestions, then, psychologists must combine their insights with those of social scientists who understand collective and institutional processes better.

3. Resource problems pose some major societal choices. Lovins (1977) describes one as the choice between "hard" (centralized and hardware-intensive) versus "soft" (dispersed, small-scale) energy systems. Lovins and others argue that this technological choice will be critical for the economy, for the nature of the political system, and for the range of people's future individual choices. The argument demands attention from social and behavioral science, but psychological knowledge can probably play only a small part. Analogous social questions can be asked about policy choices regarding waste disposal, food production, and the development of land for urban or industrial purposes; in all of these, there are key psychological aspects.

4. Many communities have addressed their resource problems through local action. Because these efforts depend in part on individual decisions, group cohesiveness, and cooperation, psychological expertise is relevant. But communities are more than small groups: Class and ethnic conflict, local politics and economics, and outside economic and political influences all greatly influence their every activity. The questions are much more than psychological.

Improving Theory and Methods

The social sciences also have much to teach each other in the realm of theory and methodology. One example is the parallel literatures existing in different disciplines on the commons dilemma, the n-person prisoners' dilemma, and social traps. As mentioned earlier, the first work in those areas was done not by psychologists but by economists and political scientists, who refer to the topic as "collective action" or the "free-rider problem" (Olson, 1965) and who have generated a body of empirical literature (e.g., Bohm, 1972; Sweeney, 1973). Research in several social science disciplines has followed from the metaphor of the commons, originally popularized by a biologist (Hardin, 1968; Hardin & Baden, 1977). As researchers learn each other's terminologies and read each other's works, more progress and less duplication of research and theory might occur.

A similar situation exists with the study of what economists for decades have called incentives and disincentives. For just as long, psychologists have investigated the same phenomena with a more elaborated language and theory of reinforcement and punishment (see Russell and Snodgrass, Chapter 8, this volume, for a full discussion), but until recently the two groups had not read each other's works. Now it appears that the experimental methods of psychology and the multivariate analytic methods of economics are complementary. Used in conjunction, they may estimate the behavioral response to changing prices or other incentive systems more accurately than either method alone (Battalio, Kagel, Winkler, & Winett, 1979; Rachlin, Kagel, & Battalio, 1980; Winkler & Winett, 1982).

The possibilities for mutual learning between psychology and economics go beyond the issue of tangible incentives. One strength of a psychological approach to resource problems is that it emphasizes that resource use depends on more than tangible incentives, and that even the effects of tangible incentives are mediated by psychological and social processes. This view is implicit in Table 28.1, and its implications in relation to economic analyses have been elaborated elsewhere (Stern, 1986). Psychological approaches can offer insight into the processes that underlie economic parameters such as elasticity and discount rate, and thus increase economists' understanding of responses to prices and incentives. In return, economics challenges psychology to tighten its own conceptualizations. For example, a number of psychological variables such as knowledge about resources, beliefs in the efficacy of particular conservation actions, comprehension of available information, and trust in information sources can all be put under a single rubric of "information" and treated as an economic activity that has costs. Economists have begun, without much benefit of psychological theory, to build models of consumer choice based on this simplifying assumption (Hirshleifer & Riley, 1979; Wilde, 1980). Although a psychologist may find such models naive, psychological analysis may be advanced by examining them—or modifying or reconstructing them—to build more useful formalizations of psychological concepts.

The process of communication, on which many environmental policies and programs rely, has also been studied from several disciplinary perspectives. In psychology, relevant constructs include persuasion, credibility, expertise, information processing, cognitive heuristics, and the framing of alternatives. Sociologists more often think in terms of diffusion of innovation or the position of people in social networks and the larger social structure. Marketers draw on both these disciplines but add expertise in the use of media and an understanding of the differences between the commercial marketing of products and the "social marketing" (Bloom & Novelli, 1981) of ideas intended for the public good. It is clear that the disciplines can learn from each other—and policy can benefit from the collaboration.

28.3.4. Research Needs

Because scientists are notoriously independent of mind, it would be futile for us to map a grand plan for social and behavioral research on environmental problems. Instead, we highlight some potential research activities that we believe score well on at least one of the following three criteria: They build on extensive research, including experimental studies and field demonstrations; they might substantially mitigate an environmental problem if successful; or they contribute to theory or method by testing or elaborating them in a new way, widening their applicability, or synthesizing concepts across disciplines.

Cumulative Research

Psychologically oriented researchers have the most solid empirical ground to stand on when they focus on residential energy conservation or on litter control or recycling at the individual level—but there is need for additional analytic research. More work on energy use is needed because energy efficiency is being promoted as an alternative to building electric generating plants. Planners need to forecast the effects of energy conservation a decade ahead because they need that much time to get a new power plant operating. To forecast demand, they need to understand the intervening behavior. There is, for example, a likelihood that people who invest in improved energy efficiency will take some of their savings in the form of increased comfort, thus decreasing energy savings (Hirst et al., 1983). This is one reason engineering data are insufficient for predicting energy savings from known improvements in equipment. (For a discussion of the behavioral issues see Stern [1985].)

Psychological research can also aid energy demand forecasting in other ways. Long-range energy demand modeling has not been a notable success (e.g., Koreisha & Stobaugh, 1979). One likely reason is that energy use conditions are changing rapidly; therefore past relationships no longer hold. Where simple economic assumptions have not performed well in predicting behavioral responses to changing prices and government policies, psychological assumptions might do better. A psychological approach might frame the question in terms of attention: What gets energy users to notice a change in price or the availability of a government program? It would also raise questions about attitudes and values: In what ways is energy use tied to individual self-esteem? Are values of "voluntary simplicity" (Elgin, 1981; Leonard-Barton, 1981) gaining ground, and if they are, under what conditions are they likely to be expressed as changes in energy demand? Some of these issues are influenced by demographic factors such as position in the family life cycle (Zimmerman, 1980), which should be included in demand forecasting. (For a discussion of psychological issues in formal energy demand analysis see Stern [1984].)

Another important area for analytical work concerns people's understanding of their own resource use. For example, people systematically misjudge the amount of energy used in various home activities, and these errors are resistant to ordinary information campaigns (Becker, Seligman, & Darley, 1979; Kempton et al., 1985; Mettler-Meibom & Wichmann, 1982). People overestimate energy use for lights and appliances that are visible and that must be actuated for each use. They underestimate it for water heaters and other uses that occur invisibly and without throwing a switch. Because of these biases, people often use ineffective means to save energy and may give up their efforts when these actions have no effect. Furthermore, people tend to think of their energy use in dollars per month rather than in units more relevant for energy conservation such as therms per degree-day (Kempton & Montgomery, 1982). However, when rising prices motivate people to save energy, they also keep home energy bills from falling—and people perceive their conservation efforts as ineffective. Such analyses have policy implications. Programs might be designed to make energy more "visible" to energy users (Stern & Aronson, 1984). Feedback is an example of this approach, as would be more informative utility billing systems and energy meters or signaling devices located in people's living spaces instead of their basements.

Existing programs of experimental research on resource problems should be extended further. Where techniques for energy conservation or waste management and prevention have proved successful in small pilot demonstrations, they should be tested in longitudinal research on real programs run by governments, utilities, or community groups. Where analytic research or program evaluations produce new hypotheses about what might work, these should be tested in small field experiments. Not all possible experiments, of course, are equally worthwhile. The applied research goal is to influence significant target behaviors and actual policy settings. There is no need for more studies comparing the effects of different messages on turning off classroom lights. If communications are to be tested, they should be aimed at influencing environmentally significant behaviors.

Program and Policy Evaluation

Through formative and summative evaluation research, psychologically oriented researchers can play an important role in designing and implementing environmental policy. They can provide convincing quantitative evidence of the effects of policies and programs, identify social and behavioral factors responsible for those effects, and design procedures for revising and improving policy actions.

Psychologically oriented researchers have already become involved in summative evaluation of energy conservation programs, and they could similarly evaluate the effects of "bottle bills," energy tax credits, pollution fee schemes, and various other policy experiments. For optimal effect, methodologists should be involved from the design stages of a program or policy to ensure that data will be available to permit conclusive evaluation. The Wisconsin time-of-use electricity pricing experiment is a good example of such research. The social psychologists involved in this project were instrumental in convincing state and utility officials to accept a true experimental design, even though random assignment of households to electricity rates was potentially controversial. To assure fairness as well as rigor in the experimental method, juries of potential participants were empaneled to pass on the fairness of the experimental conditions before anyone was exposed to them (Black, 1979). The resulting design proved acceptable, and the results were methodologically solid. Furthermore, interdisciplinary collaboration produced a data set that has been useful for assessing the relative roles of economic, psychological, and other factors in influencing energy users' responses to the experiment (Black, 1978; Heberlein & Warriner, 1983).

Psychological researchers can contribute to summative evaluation even if not involved in the research design. A psychological perspective can help make sense of program failures or inconsistent performance in the same program when implemented by different organizations. For an example from residential energy conservation, see Stern and colleagues (1986).

Formative evaluation research is an important area for contribution because knowledge of how a program's effects were produced provides a basis for changing the program or designing a more effective new one. The challenge is to measure the variables that will turn out to be important. Some general knowledge exists. Whenever a policy attempts to influence the decisions of many dispersed actors, persuasion and communication are important factors. And when a policy depends on the use of information, credibility, attention, motivation, and information processing are also critical.

But there is also great variability. For example, the success of a community recycling or energy program may depend critically on financial resources, communication techniques, management skills, political support, the availability of skilled volunteers, or the cooperation of well-respected local organizations or individuals. Different variables will be crucial in different communities. In a given instance, behavioral and social scientists can anticipate some important factors, but other issues are more likely to be anticipated by the people or organizations the policy or program will affect. This suggests that formative evaluation studies should be designed collaboratively by social scientists, program managers and users, and other groups and institutions the program may affect.

Advice to psychologically oriented researchers about program and policy evaluation assumes that serious evaluation efforts will take place. This assumption is questionable because, as we noted, decisions to evaluate and to allocate sufficient resources to evaluation are political decisions. Government "social programs" have been routinely subjected to evaluation, but environmental policies and programs have not. Some exceptions have been returnable bottle legislation (see Geller et al., 1982, for a brief review) and residential energy conservation programs (e.g., Hirst, 1984; Hirst, Berry, & Soderstrom, 1981; McDougall et al., 1983; Seligman & Hutton, 1981; Stern et al., 1986). The public needs to be convinced that serious formative evaluation of environmental policies is in the interest of all affected citizens.

Interventions for Maximum Effect

Psychological research has often neglected areas where the greatest potential lies for ameliorating environmental problems: industrial pollution and energy use, government policy, and so forth. Such inattention is appropriate if there is little that psychological concepts can offer. It is often argued, for example, that businesses act on the basis of economic self-interest and are not subject to psychological influences. However, business decisions are affected by organizational aspirations, rules and routines, management

structure, social influence among firms, leaders' personalities and attitudes, and other noneconomic factors (e.g., March, 1982; Simon, 1979). Such factors may affect organizational use of energy (Stern & Aronson, 1984, chapter 5), but little is known about how much difference they make or about the potential of particular organizational interventions to affect resource use. Because of the large magnitude of resources at stake, further behavioral research on resource use by industrial organizations is needed.

We suggest three other areas where psychologically based research is promising because of the magnitude of the potential effect. Energy use in multioccupant buildings poses one of the most difficult practical problems in energy conservation because of the unusual structure of incentives in this sector. The problem's social implications may be even more serious than its environmental effects because rental housing occupants are disproportionately poor. Already, the poorest households are paying 30% of their income for residential energy, and the percentage rises when energy prices increase (Energy Information Administration, 1982).

Behavioral research may also have a large impact in fine-tuning important institutional innovations. A good example is the recent attempt to develop rating systems for the energy efficiency of homes and mobile homes, similar to those used now for automobiles. A successful rating system could alter the whole residential real estate industry. It could cause builders and architects to compete for high ratings, as automobile manufacturers have done. It could lead mortgage lenders to lend more money for energy-efficient homes on the grounds that owners would have more money available for mortgage payments. This would make efficient homes more salable and give sellers a strong incentive to make the homes more energy-efficient before selling. But this would come about only if the rating system were reliable, credible, and understandable to users. A little help from psychologists with the last two points could make a tremendous difference—and the problems are not trivial. No index of the energy efficiency of a home is as easy to understand as the miles-per-gallon index for automobiles. Estimates of annual energy costs would be understandable, but they are unreliable because they depend too much on behavior: An estimate could easily be 50% off in either direction (Sonderegger, 1978; Vine et al., 1982). Alternatives such as simple certification or a 10-point rating scale may be understandable but could be misleading. It is not obvious which system is best. Careful empirical research is required, and psychologists who know something about how people use information should be an important part of the research effort. The relevant behavioral questions are discussed at greater length in Stern (1985, chapter 5).

Another innovation in which seemingly small adjustments might have a large effect is in utility billing practices. Utilities have detailed information about energy consumption that they could easily simplify and transmit to their customers on a regular basis. With careful research to develop an effective delivery format, this information might be very useful to energy users in their conservation efforts. Of course, there are problems—some utilities will not want to promote decreased sales, and some energy users will not trust the utilities' motives—but the potential is great enough to justify a research effort.

Frontiers of Research

Several areas of environmental policy research are worthy of exploration for their scientific or theoretical importance to psychology, even though their potential to solve environmental problems remains uncertain. One such area is the study of public support of and pressure for environmental regulation. Cognitive psychologists in this field have already contributed, both to policy analysis and to psychology (e.g., Slovic, Fischhoff, & Lichtenstein, 1982). We have also noted that Schwartz's (1970, 1977) model of the activation of moral norms can be extended from individual altruistic acts to the study of public pressure for environmental protection laws (Stern, Dietz, & Black, 1986). Such an extension would begin to draw connections between social psychological literatures on altruism and attitude–behavior relationships and the sociological literatures on social change and collective behavior (e.g., Smelser, 1962; Turner & Killian, 1972).

A second frontier area is the study of community-based efforts at environmental management. Despite thousands of such efforts over the past decade in energy management alone (Center for Renewable Resources, 1980), there are virtually no studies of the social and political conditions that influence their outcomes (Stern & Aronson, 1984). This area is theoretically important because local efforts to manage scarce resources more effectively are, in effect, field experiments on solving the commons dilemma. In particular, they are attempts to develop collective solutions to the dilemma, an approach that attacks the root of the tragedy in individual rationality (Stern, 1978). The commons dilemma further touches on several important issues that cut across social scientific disciplines, including the tension between scar-

city and ideals of equality (Edney, 1981), the roles of individual and social forces in social control, and the distinction between public and private spheres of action.

A third frontier is the study of economic behavior. Resource use is partly economic behavior, but the economic assumptions about behavior that dominate analysis of energy and environmental issues are often incomplete or misleading (e.g., Freedman, Rothenberg, & Sutch, 1983; Stern & Aronson, 1984; Stern, 1986; Zerega, 1981). For a more general criticism, see, for example, Scitovsky (1976), Simon (1979), and Titmuss (1971). Some economists recognize this and add detail to their models, occasionally applying psychological insights to questions of economic action. Others use methods from experimental psychology (e.g., Battalio et al., 1979; Winkler & Winett, 1982). This cross-fertilization stands to bring "mundane realism" (Aronson & Carlsmith, 1968) into an economics dominated by a generally sterile body of mathematical models (Leontief, 1982). Psychology also stands to gain by coming to grips with economic constructs and employing, modifying, or challenging them. Behavior analysts have begun to integrate economic concepts into their analyses (e.g., Rachlin et al., 1980), but other psychologists are slower to recognize that important behaviors are not merely the result of free choice and the interpersonal influences of small groups—they are constrained by factors of cost and scarcity in the economist's sense. For example, economic constructs are relevant in the debate over the place of "external" variables in attitude-behavior theory (Fishbein, 1980; Triandis, 1980). Further analysis of the interactive effects of psychological and economic variables on resource use is likely both to advance behavioral science and to improve environmental policy.

A fourth frontier area is the study of the development and change of values and "life-styles." It has been frequently asserted that ecological resource scarcity threatens central value bases of growth-oriented capitalist society, particularly the values placed on consumption as an end in itself and on the domination of humanity over nature (e.g., Odum, 1974; Ophuls, 1977). In this view, major value changes must occur if the civilization is to adapt and survive. Some have argued that such value changes have already begun (e.g., Elgin, 1981; Yankelovich, 1982), whereas others have declared that the required changes need not be so far-reaching (e.g., Olsen, 1981). This question points to a need for ways of assessing and predicting value change. It also underlines some central but neglected issues in social psychology such as the interrelationship between individual values and attitudes and socially shared values, the process of change in social norms, and the processes by which individuals' whole attitude structures change (e.g., sudden conversion versus more gradual change; the effect of behavior on attitudes; change in individual attitudes versus underlying values). Although there is debate over the causal efficacy of value change for solving resource problems (see Russell and Snodgrass, Chapter 8, this volume; Humphrey & Buttel, 1982), the "environmental crisis" creates important opportunities for extending theoretical social psychology.

28.4. CONCLUSION

Although environmental problems are the direct result of physical, biological, and ecological processes, it is people and their social institutions that ultimately set these processes in motion. It is only by changing social behavior that imminent threats to humanity and its environment can be controlled. Thus psychology and the other social and behavioral sciences can help solve the world's pressing ecological resource problems. But they have difficulties in conducting the needed research and even greater difficulties in influencing policy. Research is difficult because psychologists must first learn something about physical and biological processes. Influence is hard to attain because technical and economic perspectives dominate in environmental policy analysis and because psychology is seen as irrelevant or even politically undesirable. To conclude the chapter, we argue that the opportunities involved in psychological research on environmental problems are sufficient to justify some extraordinary efforts.

There is much left to do. A relatively small number of researchers have made notable progress in understanding some environmentally relevant behaviors of individuals, in developing strategies to change those behaviors, and in evaluating some environmental policies and programs. However, several areas of human action with major environmental implications have received far too little attention—particularly individual investment in resource-conserving capital equipment, corporate behavior, and collective action in communities and political systems.

Psychology as a discipline and psychologists as individuals can be enriched by interdisciplinary work on environmental problems. This can compensate for the professional risk psychologists take by becoming interdisciplinary and "applied." We have shown how work on environmental problems can make important contributions to the psychology of attitudes and values, the theory of psychological conflicts such as "social traps," the study of social movements and group processes at the community level, and the understanding of behaviors with an economic component. In some of these areas, significant contributions to psychology have already been made. In addition, contact with the perspectives and concepts of other social science disciplines can yield fresh insights on psychological constructs and on the discipline itself.

The society needs to incorporate the perspectives of psychology and related disciplines in environmental policymaking. Although physical and biological scientists are indispensable for setting policy goals, they lack the conceptual tools of behavioral and social science for analyzing how social systems can be changed to achieve those goals. In our view, environmental policies dominated by the technological and economic perspectives are often doomed to founder on problems of implementation. For instance, carefully designed technologies will sometimes provoke widespread public opposition; incentives designed to motivate economically rational decision makers will often be ineffective on real people; and many people will ignore even the best technical information. Society cannot afford to keep adopting policies that are technically elegant and economically rational but psychologically naive or politically unrealistic. In the environmental sphere, such policies allow ecological degradation to continue apace. Policymakers need to become more sensitive to psychological and social processes, and social scientists need to take more initiative in trying to make policymakers listen.

Speedy and persistent action on environmental resource problems is urgently needed. This realization has influenced some psychologists to apply their training to environmental problems, and their experience has shown that psychological research can make a contribution. We urge more psychologists to join the research effort for the rewards it can bring to them as scientists, to the discipline, and to the society. We also urge psychologists to use their trained sensibilities about individual and social behavior in their role as citizens. Environmental policies and programs are often proposed without consideration of their human implications, and even nonexperts who have a sense of social process can make valuable contributions by questioning policies when they seem to be based on unrealistic assumptions about the way people will respond.

NOTES

1. An exception to this general rule may occur when energy-inefficient or polluting equipment is replaced before the end of its useful life (Winett & Geller, 1981). Scrapping old equipment creates solid waste and is a failure to get full use of the energy "embodied" in the discarded equipment.

2. On two occasions, in 1981 and 1984, funds for behavioral and social research were included in the Department of Energy's budget. A $1 million item was voted by Congress in the 1981 budget but eliminated by rescission before being spent; a $400,000 item for behavioral research on conservation in buildings was proposed by the Reagan Administration in 1984 but not accepted by Congress. Despite setbacks, interest remains within some Department of Energy offices.

REFERENCES

Acton, J.P., & Mowill, R.S. (1975). *Conserving electricity by ordinance: A statistical analysis.* Santa Monica, CA: Rand Corporation.

Agras, W.S., Jacob, R.G., & Lebedeck, M. (1980). The California drought: A quasi-experimental analysis of social policy. *Journal of Applied Behavior Analysis, 13,* 561–570.

Ajzen, I., & Fishbein, M. (1977). Attitude-behavior relations: A theoretical evaluation and review of empirical research. *Psychological Bulletin, 84,* 888–918.

Alexander, Y., & Ebinger, C.K. (Eds.). (1982). *Political terrorism and energy: The threat and response.* New York: Praeger.

American Council for an Energy Efficient Economy. (1984). *The most energy efficient appliances.* Washington, DC: Author.

Anderson, A. (1982, July). Neurotoxic follies. *Psychology Today,* pp. 30–42.

Antil, J.H., & Bennett, P.D. (1979). Construction and validation of a scale to measure socially responsible consumption behavior. In K.E. Henion & T.C. Kinnear (Eds.), *The conserver society.* Chicago: American Marketing Association.

Arbuthnot, J. (1977). The roles of attitudinal and personality variables in the prediction of environmental behavior and knowledge. *Environment and Behavior, 9,* 217–232.

Arbuthnot, J., Tedeschi, R., Wayner, M., Turner, J., Kressel, S., & Rush, R. (1977). The induction of sustained recycling behavior through the foot-in-the-door technique. *Journal of Environmental Systems, 6,* 353–366.

The arms race, energy, and development: The issues merge. (1982, December). *F.A.S. Public Interest Report,* pp. 1–2.

Aronson, E., & Carlsmith, J.M. (1968). Experimentation in social psychology. In G. Lindzey & E. Aronson (Eds.), *The handbook of social psychology* (2nd ed.). Reading, MA: Addison-Wesley.

Aronson, E., & O'Leary, M. (1983). The relative effectiveness of models and prompts on energy conservation: A field experiment in a shower room. *Journal of Environmental Systems, 12,* 219–224.

An atlas of America's energy resources. (1981, February). *National Geographic,* pp. 58–69.

Bacon-Prue, A., Blount, R., Pickering, D., & Drabman, R. (1980). An evaluation of three litter control procedures—Trash receptacles, paid workers, and the marked item technique. *Journal of Applied Behavior Analysis, 13,* 165–170.

Basdekas, D.L. (1982, April 5). Inside NRC. *New York Times.*

Battalio, R.C., Kagel, J.H., Winkler, R.C., & Winett, R.A. (1979). Residential electricity demand: An experimental study. *Review of Economics and Statistics, 61,* 180–189.

Baum, A., & Singer, J.E. (Eds.). (1981). *Advances in environmental psychology: Vol. 3. Energy: Psychological perspectives.* Hillsdale, NJ: Erlbaum.

Beck, P., Doctors, S.I., & Hammond, P.Y. (1980). *Individual energy conservation behaviors.* Cambridge, MA: Oelgeschlager, Gunn & Hain.

Becker, L.J. (1978). The joint effect of feedback and goal setting on performance: A field study of residential energy conservation. *Journal of Applied Psychology, 63,* 428–433.

Becker, L.J., & Seligman, C. (1978). Reducing air conditioning waste by signalling it is cool outside. *Personality and Social Psychology Bulletin, 4,* 412–415.

Becker, L.J., Seligman, C., & Darley, J.M. (1979). *Psychological strategies to reduce energy consumption* (Project Summary Report prepared for the U.S. Department of Energy). Princeton, NJ: Princeton University, Center for Energy and Environmental Studies.

Becker, L.J., Seligman, C., Fazio, R.H., & Darley, J.M. (1981). Relating attitudes to residential energy use. *Environment and Behavior, 13,* 590–609.

Bentsen, L. (1979). A sensible approach to resource conservation. In K.E. Henion & T.C. Kinnear (Eds.), *The conserver society.* Chicago: American Marketing Association.

Berk, R.A., Cooley, T.F., LaCivita, C.J., Parker, S., Sredl, K., & Brewer, M. (1980). Reducing consumption in periods of acute scarcity: The case of water. *Social Science Research, 9,* 99–120.

Bernard, H.W., Jr. (1981). *The greenhouse effect.* New York: Harper & Row.

Black, J.S. (1978). *Attitudinal, normative, and economic fac-*

tors in early response to an energy-use field experiment. Unpublished doctoral dissertation, University of Wisconsin, Department of Sociology, Madison.

Black, J.S. (1979, September). *The role of social scientists in field experiments on energy.* Paper presented at the meeting of the American Psychological Association, New York.

Black, J.S., & Heberlein, T.A. (1977). *Emergent norms and environmental action: Reciprocal causation of personal and perceived social norms in the purchase of lead-free gasoline.* Unpublished manuscript, University of Wisconsin, College of Agricultural and Life Sciences, Madison.

Black, J.S., Stern, P.C., & Elworth, J.T. (1985). Personal and contextual influences on household energy adaptations. *Journal of Applied Psychology, 70,* 3–21.

Bloom, P.N., & Novelli, W.D. (1981). *Problems and challenges in social marketing.* Unpublished manuscript, Marketing Science Institute, Cambridge, MA.

Bohm, P. (1972). Estimating demand for public goods: An experiment. *European Economic Review, 3,* 111–130.

Borden, R.J., & Francis, J.L. (1978). Who cares about ecology? Personality and sex differences in environmental concern. *Journal of Personality, 46,* 190–203.

Bowman, C.H., & Fishbein, M. (1978). Understanding public reaction to energy proposals: An application of the Fishbein model. *Journal of Applied Social Psychology, 8,* 319–340.

Boyle, R.H., & Boyle, R.A. (1983). Acid rain. *Amicus Journal, 4*(3), 22–37.

Brechner, K.C., & Linder, D.E. (1981). A social trap analysis of energy distribution systems. In A. Baum & J.E. Singer (Eds.), *Advances in environmental psychology: Vol. 3. Energy: Psychological perspectives.* Hillsdale, NJ: Erlbaum.

Brehm, J.W. (1966). *A theory of psychological reactance.* New York: Academic.

Brehm, S., & Brehm, J.W. (1981). *Psychological reactance: A theory of freedom and control* (2nd ed.). New York: Academic.

Brown, L.R. (1981). *Building a sustainable society.* New York: Norton.

Brown, L.R. (1983). *Population policies for a new economic era* (Worldwatch Paper No. 53). Washington, DC: Worldwatch Institute.

Brown, L.R. (1985). *State of the world 1985.* New York: Norton.

Brownstein, R., & Easton, N. (1982). The greenhouse effect: A doomsday scenario? *Amicus Journal, 3*(3), 10–11.

Bruvold, W.H. (1972). Consistency among attitudes, beliefs and behavior. *Journal of Social Psychology, 86,* 127–134.

Burgess, R.L., Clark, R.N., & Hendee, J.C. (1971). An ex-perimental analysis of anti-littering procedures. *Journal of Applied Behavior Analysis, 4,* 71–75.

Catton, W.R., Jr. (1980). *Overshoot: The ecological basis of revolutionary change.* Urbana: University of Illinois Press.

Center for Renewable Resources. (1980). *Renewable resources: A national catalog of model projects* (4 Vols.). Washington, DC: U.S. Department of Energy.

Cole, H.S.D., Freeman, C., Jahoda, M., & Parritt, K.L.R. (1973). *Models of doom: A critique of The Limits to Growth.* New York: Universe.

Committee on Environmental Improvement. (1978). *Cleaning our environment: A chemical perspective* (2nd ed.). Washington, DC: American Chemical Society.

Cone, J.D., & Hayes, S.C. (1980). *Environmental problems/Behavioral solutions.* Monterey, CA: Brooks/Cole.

Consumer behaviour and energy policy. (1983). [Special issues]. *Journal of Economic Psychology, 3*(3,4), 4(1,2).

Consumer behavior and energy use. (1981) [Special issue]. *Journal of Consumer Research, 8,* 233–354.

Cook, S.W., & Berrenberg, J.L. (1981). Approaches to encouraging conservation behavior: A review and conceptual framework. *Journal of Social Issues, 37*(2), 73–107.

Cornwell, M.L. (1982, Fall). Sex differences in environmental concern. *Environmental Sociology,* No. 31, pp. 9–11.

Cottrell, A. (1981). *How safe is nuclear energy?* London: Heinemann Educational Books.

Craig, C.S., & McCann, J.M. (1978). Assessing communication effects on energy conservation. *Journal of Consumer Research, 5,* 82–88.

Craik, K.H., Dake, K.M., & Buss, D.M. (1982, August). *Individual differences in the perception of technological hazard.* Paper presented at the meeting of the American Psychological Association, Washington, DC.

Crump, S.L., Nunes, D.L., & Crossman, E.K. (1977). The effects of litter on littering behavior in a forest environment. *Environment and Behavior, 9,* 137–146.

Cutter, S.C. (1981). Community concern for pollution: Social and environmental influences. *Environment and Behavior, 13,* 105–124.

Daly, H.E. (1977). *Steady-state economics.* San Francisco: Freeman.

Darley, J.M. (1978). Energy conservation techniques as innovations and their diffusion. *Energy and Buildings, 1,* 339–343.

Darley, J.M., & Beniger, J.R. (1981). Diffusion of energy-conserving innovations. *Journal of Social Issues, 37*(2), 150–171.

Davis, C.E., & Lester, J.P. (1985). Hazardous waste politics and policy: A symposium. *Policy Studies Journal, 14,* 47–168.

Davis, W.J. (1979). *The seventh year: Industrial civilization in transition.* New York: Norton.

Dawes, R.M. (1980). Social dilemmas. *Annual Review of Psychology, 31,* 169–193.

de Boer, C. (1977). The polls: Nuclear energy. *Public Opinion Quarterly, 41,* 402–411.

Deese, D.A., & Nye, J.S. (Eds.). (1981). *Energy and security.* Cambridge, MA: Ballinger.

Deevey, E.S., Rice, D.S., Rice, P.M., Vaughan, H.H., Brenner, M., & Flannery, M.S. (1979). Mayan urbanism: Impact on a tropical karst environment. *Science, 206,* 298–306.

Dietz, T., Stern, P.C., & Rycroft, R.W. (1984, August). *Why is everybody so excited? The origins of environmental conflict as viewed by a national elite.* Paper presented at the meeting of the American Sociological Association, San Antonio.

Dorfman, R., & Dorfman, N.S. (1977). *Economics of the environment: Selected readings* (2nd ed.). New York: Norton.

Downs, A. (1972, Summer). Up and down with ecology: The issue-attention cycle. *Public Interest, 28,* 38–50.

Dunlap, R.E. (1985, July/August). Public opinion: Behind the transformation. *EPA Journal,* pp. 15–17.

Dunlap, R.E., & Catton, W.R., Jr. (1979). Environmental sociology. *Annual Review of Sociology, 5,* 243–273.

Dunlap, R.E., Grieneeks, J.K., & Rokeach, M. (1983). Human values and pro-environmental behavior. In W.D. Conn (Ed.), *Energy and material resources: Attitudes, values, and public policy. AAAS Selected Symposium 75.* Boulder, CO: Westview.

Dunlap, R.E., & Olsen, M.E. (1984). Hard-path versus soft-path advocates: A study of energy activists. *Policy Studies Journal, 13,* 413–428.

Dunlap, R.E., & Van Liere, K.D. (1978a). *Environmental concern: A bibliography of empirical studies and brief appraisal of the literature* (Public Administration Series Bibliography P-44). Monticello, IL: Vance Bibliographies.

Dunlap, R.E., & Van Liere, K.D. (1978b). The "new environmental paradigm": A proposed measuring instrument and preliminary results. *Journal of Environmental Education, 9,* 10–19.

Durand, R.M., Klemmack, D.L., & Roff, L.L. (1980). An examination of cohort differences in perceptions of the energy crisis. *Journal of Psychology, 106,* 3–12.

Ebbing of the Ogallala: The great watering hole beneath the Great Plains is going dry. (1982, May 10). *Time,* pp. 98–99.

Edmunds, S.W. (1980). Environmental policy: Bounded rationality applied to unbounded ecological problems. *Policy Studies Journal, 9,* 359–369.

Edney, J.J. (1980). The commons problem: Alternative perspectives. *American Psychologist, 35,* 131–150.

Edney, J.J. (1981). Paradoxes on the commons: Scarcity and the problem of equality. *Journal of Community Psychology, 9,* 3–34.

Edney, J.J., & Harper, C.S. (1978). The commons dilemma: A review of contributions from psychology. *Environmental Management, 2,* 491–507.

Egan, J.R. (1982, February/March). To err is human factors. *Technology Review,* pp. 23–39.

Ehrlich, P.R., Ehrlich, A.H., & Holdren, J.P. (1977). *Ecoscience: Population, resources, environment.* San Francisco: Freeman.

Eldridge, L., LeMasters, S., & Szypot, B. (1978). A performance feedback intervention to reduce waste: Performance data and participant responses. *Journal of Organizational Behavior Management, 1,* 258–267.

Elgin, D. (1981). *Voluntary simplicity.* New York: Morrow.

Ellis, P., & Gaskell, G. (1978). *A review of social research on the individual energy consumer.* Unpublished manuscript, London School of Economics and Political Science, Department of Social Psychology, London.

At the end of a floating pipeline. (1983, August 1). *Time,* p. 43.

Energy Information Administration. (1982). *Residential energy consumption survey: Consumption and expenditures April 1980 through March 1981. Part I: National Data* (DOE/EIA-0321/1). Washington, DC: U.S. Department of Energy.

Environmental Action Foundation. (1977). Paper profits. *Garbage guide* (No. 9). Washington, DC: Author.

Environmental regulations. (1982, March). *F.A.S. Public Interest Report,* pp. 1–16.

Epstein, S.S., Brown, L.O., & Pope, C. (1982). *Hazardous waste in America.* San Francisco: Sierra Club Books.

Ester, P.A., & Winett, R.A. (1982). Toward more effective antecedent strategies for environmental programs. *Journal of Environmental Systems, 11,* 201–221.

Evans, G.W., & Jacobs, S.V. (1981). Air pollution and human behavior. *Journal of Social Issues, 37*(1), 95–125.

Evans, G.W., Jacobs, S.V., & Frager, N. (1979, September). *Human adaptation to photochemical smog.* Paper presented at the meeting of the American Psychological Association, New York.

Farhar, B.C., Unseld, C.T., Vories, R., & Crews, R. (1980). Public opinion about energy. *Annual Review of Energy, 5,* 141–172.

Farhar, B.C., Weis, P., Unseld, C.T., & Burns, B.A. (1979). *Public opinion about energy: A literature review.* Golden, CO: Solar Energy Research Institute.

Farhar-Pilgrim, B., & Unseld, C.T. (1982). *America's solar potential: A national consumer study.* New York: Praeger.

Fazio, R.H., & Zanna, M.P. (1978). Attitudinal qualities relating to the strength of the attitude-behavior relationship. *Journal of Experimental Social Psychology, 14,* 398–408.

Finnie, W.C. (1973). Field experiments in litter control. *Environment and Behavior, 5,* 123–144.

Fischhoff, B. (1977). Cost benefit analysis and the art of motorcycle maintenance. *Policy Sciences, 8,* 177–202.

Fischhoff, B., Lichtenstein, S., Slovic, P., Derby, S.L., & Keeney, R.L. (1981). *Acceptable risk.* Cambridge, England: Cambridge University Press.

Fishbein, M. (1980). A theory of reasoned action: Some applications and implications. In M.M. Page (Ed.), *1979 Nebraska Symposium on Motivation.* Lincoln: University of Nebraska Press.

Fishbein, M., & Ajzen, I. (1975). *Belief, attitude, intention, and behavior: An introduction to theory and research.* Reading, MA: Addison-Wesley.

Flavin, C. (1985). *World oil: Coping with the dangers of success* (Worldwatch Paper No. 66). Washington, DC: Worldwatch Institute.

Freedman, D., Rothenberg, T., & Sutch, R. (1983). On energy policy models. *Journal of Business and Economic Statistics, 1,* 24–32.

Fusso, T.E. (1978). The polls: The energy crisis in perspective. *Public Opinion Quarterly, 42,* 127–136.

Geller, E.S. (1980). Applications of behavioral analysis for litter control. In D. Glenwick & L. Jason (Eds.), *Behavioral community psychology: Progress and prospects.* New York: Praeger.

Geller, E.S. (1981). Evaluating energy conservation programs: Is verbal report enough? *Journal of Consumer Research, 8,* 331–335.

Geller, E.S., Brasted, W., & Mann, M. (1980). Waste receptable designs as interventions for litter control. *Journal of Environmental Systems, 9,* 145–160.

Geller, E.S., Erickson, J.B., & Buttram, B.A. (1983). Attempts to promote residential water conservation with educational, behavioral and engineering strategies. *Population and Environment: Behavior and Social Issues, 6,* 96–112.

Geller, E.S., Winett, R.A., & Everett, P.B. (1982). *Preserving the environment: Strategies for behavior change.* New York: Pergamon.

Geller, E.S., Witmer, J.F., & Orebaugh, A.L. (1976). Instructions as a determinant of paper-disposal behaviors. *Environment and Behavior, 8,* 417–438.

Geller, E.S., Wylie, R.C., & Farris, J.C. (1971). An attempt at applying prompting and reinforcement toward pollution control. *Proceedings of the 79th Annual Convention of the American Psychological Association, 6,* 701–702.

Gever, J., Kaufmann, R., Skole, D., & Vorosmarty, C. (1985). *Beyond oil: The threat to food and fuel in the coming decades.* Cambridge, MA: Ballinger.

Gibbons, J.H., & Chandler, W.U. (1981). *Energy: The conservation revolution.* New York: Plenum.

Goldsmith, E. (1978). *The stable society.* Wadebridge, Cornwall, England: Wadebridge Press.

Greene, A.K. (1975). Bring 'em back, repack and save. In *Proceedings, 1975 conference on waste reduction.* Washington, DC: U.S. Environmental Protection Agency.

Hamad, C.D., Bettinger, R., Cooper, D., & Semb, G. (1979). *Using behavioral procedures to establish an elementary school paper recycling program.* Unpublished manuscript, University of Kansas, Department of Psychology, Lawrence.

Hamilton, L.C. (1985a). Concern about toxic wastes: Three demographic predictors. *Sociological Perspectives, 28,* 463–486.

Hamilton, L.C. (1985b). Who cares about water pollution? Opinions in a small-town crisis. *Sociological Inquiry, 55,* 170–181.

Hardin, G. (1968). The tragedy of the commons. *Science, 162,* 1243–1248.

Hardin, G., & Baden, J. (1977). *Managing the commons.* San Francisco: Freeman.

Harding, J. (1983, February/March). Bombs rock Koeberg nuclear station. *Not Man Apart, 13*(2), 16.

Harris, L. (1982, Winter). Hands off the Clean Air Act: A message to Washington. *Amicus Journal, 3*(3), 27–30.

Hayes, D. (1978). *Repairs, reuse, recycling— First steps toward a sustainable society* (Worldwatch Paper No. 23). Washington, DC: Worldwatch Institute.

Hayes, D. (1979). *Pollution: The neglected dimensions* (Worldwatch Paper No. 27). Washington, DC: Worldwatch Institute.

Hayes, S.C., & Cone, J.D. (1977). Reducing residential electrical use: Payments, information, and feedback. *Journal of Applied Behavior Analysis, 10,* 425–435.

Hayes, S.C., & Cone, J.D. (1981). Reduction of residential consumption of electricity through simple monthly feedback. *Journal of Applied Behavior Analysis, 14,* 81–88.

Heberlein, T.A. (1975). Conservation information: The energy crisis and electricity consumption in an apartment complex. *Energy Systems and Policy, 1,* 105–117.

Heberlein, T.A. (1981). Environmental attitudes. *Zeitschrift für Umweltpolitik, 2,* 241–270.

Heberlein, T.A., & Baumgartner, R.M. (1985, April). *Changing attitudes and electricity consumption in a time-of-use experiment.* Paper presented at the International Conference on Consumer Behaviour and Energy Policy, Versailles, France.

Heberlein, T.A., & Black, J.S. (1976). Attitudinal specificity and the prediction of behavior in a field setting. *Journal of Personality and Social Psychology, 33,* 474–479.

Heberlein, T.A., & Black, J.S. (1981). Cognitive consistency and environmental action. *Environment and Behavior, 13,* 717–734.

Heberlein, T.A., & Warriner, G.K. (1983). The influence of price and attitude on shifting residential electricity consumption from on to off-peak periods. *Journal of Economic Psychology, 4,* 107–130.

Heilbroner, R.L. (1974). *An inquiry into the human prospect.* New York: Norton.

Hershey, R.D., Jr. (1981, October 11). Winning the war on energy. *New York Times,* Section 3, pp. 1, 17.

Heslop, L.A., Moran, L., & Cousineau, A. (1981). "Consciousness" in energy conservation behavior: An exploratory study. *Journal of Consumer Research, 8,* 299–305.

Hindman, S. (1984, March). Do nukes go to heaven? *Environmental Action,* pp. 18–22.

Hirshleifer, J., & Riley, J. (1979). The analytics of uncertainty and information—An expository survey. *Journal of Economic Literature, 17,* 1375–1421.

Hirst, E. (1984). Household energy conservation: A review of the federal Residential Conservation Service. *Public Administration Review, 44,* 421–430.

Hirst, E., Berry, L., & Soderstrom, J. (1981). Review of utility home energy audit programs. *Energy, 6,* 621–630.

Hirst, E., Hu, P.S., Taylor, E.F., Jr., Thayer, K.M., & Groeneman, S. (1983, September). *The residential conservation service in Connecticut: Evaluation of the CONN SAVE Program.* Oak Ridge, TN: Oak Ridge National Laboratory.

Hoffman, J.S., & Barth, M.C. (1983). Carbon dioxide: Are we ignoring a vital environmental issue? *Amicus Journal, 5*(1), 24–28.

Humphrey, C.R., Bord, R.J., Hammond, M.M., & Mann, S.H. (1977). Attitudes and conditions for cooperation in a paper recycling program. *Environment and Behavior, 9,* 107–124.

Humphrey, C.R., & Buttel, F.R. (1982). *Environment, energy, and society.* Belmont, CA: Wadsworth.

Hutton, R.B. (1982). Advertising and the Department of Energy's campaign for energy conservation. *Journal of Advertising, 11*(2), 27–39.

Jacobs, H.E., & Bailey, J.S. (1979). *The Leon County recycling program: The development of an empirically derived communitywide resource recovery program.* Paper presented at the meeting of the Association for Behavior Analysis, Dearborn, MI.

Jacobs, H.E., & Bailey, J.S. (1982–1983). Evaluating participation in a residential recycling program. *Journal of Environmental Systems, 12,* 141–152.

Jason, L.A., Zolik, E.S., & Matese, F. (1979). Prompting dog owners to pick up dog droppings. *American Journal of Community Psychology, 7,* 339–351.

Jensen, T.D., & Schroeder, D.A. (1983, August). *Predicting winter thermostat settings from residents' attitudes and behavioral intentions.* Paper presented at the meeting

of the American Psychological Association, Anaheim, CA.

Joerges, B. (1981, November). *Consumer Energy Conservation Policies. A Multi-National Study. Second Interim Report.* Berlin: International Institute for Environment and Society, Science Center.

Johansson, T.B., Steen, P., Bogren, E., & Fredricksson, R. (1983). Sweden beyond oil: The efficient use of energy. *Science, 219,* 355–361.

Jubak, J. (1982, June). The drying of America. *Environmental Action, 14*(1), 20–23.

Kahn, H. (1979). *World economic development.* New York: Morrow.

Kahneman, D., & Tversky, A. (1979). Prospect theory: An analysis of decisions under risk. *Econometrica, 47,* 263–291.

Kameron, J. (1979). Changing attitudes as a strategy for energy conservation: Lessons from the environmental movement. *Ramapo Papers, 2*(3), 36–62.

Kantola, S.J., Syme, G.J., & Campbell, N.A. (1982). The role of individual differences and external variables in a test of the sufficiency of Fishbein's model to explain behavioral intentions to conserve water. *Journal of Applied Social Psychology, 12,* 70–83.

Kantola, S.J., Syme, G.J., & Campbell, N.A. (1984). Cognitive dissonance and energy conservation. *Journal of Applied Psychology, 69,* 416–421.

Kash, D.E., & Rycroft, R.W. (1984). *U.S. energy policy: Crisis and complacency.* Norman: University of Oklahoma Press.

Katzev, R.D., & Johnson, T.R. (1983). A social psychological analysis of residential electricity consumption: The impact of minimal justification techniques. *Journal of Economic Psychology, 3,* 267–284.

Katzev, R.D., & Johnson, T.R. (1984). Comparing the effects of monetary incentives and foot-in-the-door strategies in promoting residential energy conservation. *Journal of Applied Social Psychology, 14,* 12–27.

Keating, K.M., & Rosa, E. (1982, August). *Policy-relevant variables in homeowners' decisions to adopt solar energy systems.* Paper presented at the Summer Study of the American Council for an Energy-Efficient Society, Santa Cruz, CA.

Kelman, H.C. (1980). The role of action in attitude change. In M.M. Page (Ed.), *Nebraska symposium on motivation* (Vol. 27). Lincoln: University of Nebraska Press.

Kempton, W., & Downey, G. (Co-chairs). (1982, December). *Energy policy.* Symposium at the annual meeting of the American Anthropological Association, Washington, DC.

Kempton, W., Harris, C.K., Keith, J.G., & Weihl, J.S. (1985). Do consumers know "what works" in energy conservation? *Marriage and Family Review, 9,* 115–133.

Kempton, W., & Montgomery, L. (1982). Folk quantification of energy. *Energy, 7,* 817–827.

Knapp, D. (1982). *Resource recovery: What recycling can do.* Berkeley, CA: Materials World Publishing.

Kneese, A.V., & Schultze, C.L. (1975). *Pollution, prices, and public policy.* Washington, DC: Brookings Institution.

Knoepfel, P., & Weidner, H. (1982). Implementing air quality control programs in Europe: Some results of a comparative study. *Policy Studies Journal, 11,* 103–115.

Komanoff, C., & Van Loon, E.E. (1982, Spring). "Too cheap to meter" or "too costly to build"? (How nuclear power has priced itself out of the market). *Nucleus, 4*(1), 3–7.

Koreisha, S., & Stobaugh, R. (1979). Limits to models. In R. Stobaugh & D. Yergin (Eds.). *Energy future.* New York: Random House.

Kromm, D.E., Probald, F., & Wall, G. (1973). An international comparison of response to air pollution. *Journal of Environmental Management, 1,* 363–375.

LaBreque, M. (1977, June). Garbage—Refuse or resource? *Popular Science,* pp. 95–98, 166.

Ladd, E.C. (1982, February/March). Clearing the air: Public opinion and public policy on the environment. *Public Opinion, 5*(1), 16–20.

Landsberg, H.H. (1982). Relaxed energy outlook masks continuing uncertainties. *Science, 218,* 973–974.

La Porte, T.R. (1981). Managing nuclear waste. *Society, 18*(5), 57–65.

Lash, J., & King, L. (Eds.). (1983). *The synfuels manual.* New York: National Resources Defense Council.

Lave, L.B., & Seskin, E.P. (1977). *Air pollution and human health.* Baltimore, MD: Johns Hopkins University Press.

Leonard-Barton, D. (1979, October). *Public acceptance of energy use management.* Paper presented at the International Conference on Energy Use Management, Los Angeles, CA.

Leonard-Barton, D. (1980, September). *The role of interpersonal communication networks in the diffusion of energy conserving practices and technologies.* Paper presented at the International Conference of Consumer Behavior and Energy Policy, Banff, Alberta, Canada.

Leonard-Barton, D. (1981). Voluntary simplicity lifestyles and energy conservation. *Journal of Consumer Research, 8,* 243–252.

Leonard-Barton, D., & Rogers, E.M. (1979). *Adoption of energy conservation among California homeowners.* Paper presented at the meeting of the International Communication Association, Philadelphia, PA.

Leontief, W. (1982). Academic economics. *Science, 217,* 104–107.

Lerman, D.I, Bronfman, B.H., & Tonn, B. (1983). *Process evaluation of the Bonneville Power Administration Resi-*

dential Weatherization Pilot Program (ORNL/CON-138). Oak Ridge, TN: Oak Ridge National Laboratory.

Lerman, D.I., & Bronfman, B.H. (1984). *Process evaluation of the Bonneville Power Administration Interim Residential Weatherization Program* (ORNL/CON-158). Oak Ridge, TN: Oak Ridge National Laboratory.

Levine, A.G. (1982). *Love Canal: Science, politics, and people.* Lexington, MA: Lexington Books.

Levitt, L., & Leventhal, G. (1984, August). *Litter reduction: How effective is the New York State bottle bill?* Paper presented at the meeting of the American Psychological Association, Toronto, Canada.

Linder, D. (1982). Social trap analogs: The tragedy of the commons in the laboratory. In V.J. Derlega & J. Grzelak (Eds.), *Cooperation and helping behavior.* New York: Academic.

Lipsey, M.W. (1977a). Attitudes toward the environment and pollution. In S. Oskamp, *Attitudes and opinions.* Englewood Cliffs, NJ: Prentice-Hall.

Lipsey, M.W. (1977b). Personal antecedents and consequences of ecologically responsible behavior. *JSAS Catalog of Selected Documents in Psychology, 7,* (Ms. No. 1521).

Lipsey, M.W. (1980, May). *The structure of ecologically responsible behavior.* Paper presented at the meeting of the Western Psychological Association, Honolulu, HI.

Lounsbury, J., & Tornatzky, L.G. (1977). A scale for assessing attitudes toward environmental quality. *Journal of Social Psychology, 101,* 299–305.

Lovins, A.B. (1977). *Soft energy paths: Toward a durable peace.* Cambridge, MA: Ballinger.

Lovins, A.B., & Lovins, L.H. (1982). *Brittle power: Energy strategy for national security.* Andover, MA: Brick House.

Lovins, A.B., Lovins, L.H., Krause, F., & Bach, W. (1981). *Least-cost energy: Solving the CO_2 problem.* Andover, MA: Brick House.

Lowe, G.D., Pinhey, T.K., & Grimes, M.D. (1980). Public support for environmental protection: New evidence from national surveys. *Pacific Sociological Review, 23,* 423–445.

Luyben, P.D., & Cummings, S. (1981–1982). Motivating beverage container recycling on a college campus. *Journal of Environmental Systems, 11,* 235–245.

Macey, S.M., & Brown, M.A. (1983). Residential energy conservation: The role of past experience in repetitive household behavior. *Environment and Behavior, 15,* 123–141.

Maloney, M.P., & Ward, M.P. (1973). Ecology: Let's hear from the people. *American Psychologist, 28,* 583–586.

Maloney, M.P., Ward, M.P., & Braucht, G.N. (1975). A revised scale for the measurement of ecological attitudes and knowledge. *American Psychologist, 30,* 787–790.

March, J.G. (1982, January). *Theories of choice and the making of decisions.* Lecture delivered at the annual meeting of the American Association for the Advancement of Science, Washington, DC.

Marcus, A.A., Sommers, P., & Morris, F.A. (1982). Alternative arrangements for cost effective pollution abatement: The need for implementation analysis. *Policy Studies Review, 1,* 477–483.

Marinelli, J. (1983). It came from beneath Long Island. *Environmental Action, 14*(9), 8–12.

Marshall, E. (1982). Air pollution clouds U.S.–Canadian relations. *Science, 217,* 1118–1119.

Maslow, A.H. (1970). *Motivation and Personality* (2nd ed.). New York: Harper & Row.

McCaul, K.D., & Kopp, J.T. (1982). Effects of goal setting and commitment on increasing metal recycling. *Journal of Applied Psychology, 67,* 377–379.

McClelland, L. (1980). *Encouraging energy conservation in multifamily housing: RUBS and other methods of allocating energy costs to residents. Executive summary and list of contents.* Boulder, CO: University of Colorado, Institute of Behavioral Science.

McClelland, L., & Belsten, L. (1980). Promoting energy conservation in university dormitories by physical, policy, and resident behavior changes. *Journal of Environmental Systems, 9,* 29–38.

McClelland, L., & Canter, R.J. (1981). Psychological research on energy consumption: Contexts, approaches, methods. In A. Baum & J.E. Singer (Eds.), *Advances in environmental psychology: Vol. 3. Energy: Psychological perspectives.* Hillsdale, NJ: Erlbaum.

McClelland, L., & Cook, S.W. (1980). Promoting energy conservation in master-metered apartments through financial incentives. *Journal of Applied Social Psychology, 10,* 19–31.

McDougall, G.H.G., Claxton, J.D., & Ritchie, J.R.B. (1983). Residential home audits: An empirical analysis of the ENER$AVE program. *Journal of Environmental Systems, 12,* 265–278.

McDougall, G.H.G., Claxton, J.D., Ritchie, J.R.B., & Anderson, C.D. (1981). Consumer energy research: A review. *Journal of Consumer Research, 8,* 343–354.

McGarry, R.S. (1978). *Water and sewer conservation oriented rate structure.* Paper presented at the National Conference on Water Conservation and Municipal Wastewater Flow Reduction, Chicago.

McGuinness, J., Jones, A.P., & Cole, S.G. (1977). Attitudinal correlates of recycling behavior. *Journal of Applied Psychology, 62,* 376–384.

McNees, M.P., Schnelle, J.F., Gendrich, J., Thomas, M.M., & Beagle, G. (1979). McDonald's litter hunt: A community litter control system for youth. *Environment and Behavior, 11,* 131–138.

Meadows, D.H., Meadows, D.L., Randers, J., & Behrens, W.W., III. (1972). *The limits to growth.* New York: Universe.

Medalia, N.Z. (1964). Air pollution as a socio-environmental health problem: A survey report. *Journal of Health and Human Behavior, 5,* 154–165.

Mettler-Meibom, B., & Wichmann, B. (1982). The influence of information and attitudes toward energy conservation on behavior. In H. Schaefer (Ed.), *Einfluss des Verbraucherverhaltens auf den Energiebedarf Privater Haushalte.* Berlin: Springer-Verlag. (M. Stommel, Trans.).

Miles, R.E., Jr. (1976). *Awakening from the American dream: The social and political limits to growth.* New York: Universe.

Miller, E.M. (1981–1982). The decision to exploit an irreplaceable resource in an uncertain world. *Journal of Environmental Systems, 11,* 125–130.

Miller, R.D., & Ford, J.M. (1985). *Shared savings in the residential market: A public/private partnership for energy conservation.* Baltimore, MD: Energy Task Force, Urban Consortium for Technology Initiatives.

Mills, M.K. (1981, September). *Energy conservation and the retail industry: Public policy implications.* Unpublished manuscript, University of Southern California, Department of Marketing, Los Angeles.

Milne, M. (1976). *Residential water conservation* (Report No. 35). Davis: California Water Resources Center.

Milstein, J.S. (1979). The conserver society? Consumers' attitudes and behaviors regarding energy conservation. In K.E. Henion & T.C. Kinnear (Eds.), *The conserver society.* Chicago: American Marketing Assocation.

Mitchell, R.C. (1979, August/September). Silent spring/solid majorities. *Public Opinion, 2*(4), 16–20, 55.

Molotch, H. (1971). The radicalization of everyone? In P. Orleans & W.R. Ellis, Jr. (Eds.), *Race, change, and urban society.* Beverly Hills, CA: Sage.

Morell, D. (1981). Energy conservation and public policy: If it's such a good idea, why don't we do more of it? *Journal of Social Issues, 37*(4), 8–30.

Morrison, D., & Lodwick, D. (1981). The social impacts of soft and hard energy systems: The Lovins' claims as a social science challenge. *Annual Review of Energy, 6,* 357–378.

Murphy, P.E., Laczniak, G.R., & Robinson, R.K. (1979). An attitudinal and a behavioral index of energy conservation. In K.E. Henion & T.C. Kinnear (Eds.), *The conserver society.* Chicago: American Marketing Association.

Murray, C.R., & Reeves, E.B. (1977). *Estimated use of water in the United States in 1975* (Circular No. 765). Arlington, VA: U.S. Geological Survey.

Nader, L., & Milleron, N. (1979). Dimension of the "people problem" in energy research and "the" factual basis of dispersed energy futures. *Energy, 4,* 953–967.

National Opinion Research Center. (1978). *General social surveys, 1972–1978: Cumulative codebook.* Chicago: Author.

National Petroleum Council, Committee on Energy Conservation. (1975). *Potential for energy conservation in the United States: 1979–1985.* Washington, DC: Author.

National Research Council. (1975). *Environmental impact of stratospheric flight: Biological and climatic effects of aircraft emissions in the stratosphere.* Washington, DC: Author.

National Research Council. (1986). *Population growth and economic development: Policy questions.* Washington, DC: National Academy Press.

National Research Council, Committee on the Atmosphere and the Biosphere. (1981). *Atmosphere-biosphere interactions: Toward a better understanding of the ecological consequences of fossil fuel combustion.* Washington, DC: National Academy Press.

National Research Council, Committee on Atmospheric Transport and Chemical Transformation in Acid Precipitation. (1983). *Acid deposition: Atmospheric processes in eastern North America.* Washington, DC: Author.

Nelkin, D. Nuclear power as a feminist issue. (1981). *Environment, 23*(1), 14–20, 38–39.

Nelson, S.H. (1981, January). *Energy savings attributable to switching from master metering to individual metering of electricity.* (ANL/EES-TM-124). Argonne, IL: Argonne National Laboratory.

Neuman, K.A. (1982, September). *Human values: Do they make a difference in individuals' commitment to energy conservation?* Paper presented at the 2nd International Conference on Consumer Behavior and Energy Policy, Noordwijkerhout, Netherlands.

Newsom, T.J., & Makranczy, U.J. (1978). Reducing electricity consumption of residents living in mass-metered dormitory complexes. *Journal of Environmental Systems, 7,* 215–235.

Nye, J.S. (1981). Energy and security. In D.A. Deese & J.S. Nye (Eds.), *Energy and security.* Cambridge, MA: Ballinger.

Odum, H.T. (1973). Energy, ecology, and economics. *Ambio, 2,* 220–227.

Office of Program Coordination. (1981). *Directory of social science expertise in the Department of Energy: A guide to agency staff trained or working in the social sciences.* Washington: U.S. Department of Energy, Office of Environment.

Office of Technology Assessment. (1982). *Energy efficiency of buildings in cities.* Washington, DC: U.S. Government Printing Office.

Olsen, D. (1982, June 10). The Washington Public Power Supply System: The story so far. *Public Utilities Fortnightly, 109*(12), 15–26.

Olsen, M.E. (1981). Consumers' attitudes toward energy conservation. *Journal of Social Issues, 37*(2), 108–131.

Olsen, M.E., & Cluett, C. (1979). *Evaluation of the Seattle City Light neighborhood energy conservation program.* Seattle, WA: Battelle Human Affairs Research Centers.

Olson, M. (1965). *The logic of collective action.* Cambridge, MA: Harvard University Press.

Olson, M., & Landsberg, H. (Eds.). (1973). *The no-growth society.* New York: Norton.

O'Neill, G.W., Blanck, L.S., & Joyner, M.A. (1980). The use of stimulus control over littering in a natural setting. *Journal of Applied Behavior Analysis, 13,* 379–381.

Ophuls, W. (1977). *Ecology and the politics of scarcity: Prologue to a political theory of the steady state.* San Francisco: Freeman.

Opinion roundup. (1983, June/July). *Public Opinion, 6*(3), 27–37.

Oskamp, S. (1981). Energy conservation by industrial and commercial users: Two surveys. *Journal of Environmental Systems, 10,* 201–213.

Oskamp, S. (1983). Psychology's role in the conserving society. *Population and Environment, 6,* 255–293.

Over a barrel: Ready for oil shock? (1983, October 3). *Time,* p. 16.

Pallak, M.S., Cook, D.A., & Sullivan, J.J. (1980). Commitment and energy conservation. In L. Bickman (Ed.), *Applied Social Psychology Annual* (Vol. 1). Beverly Hills, CA: Sage.

Peterson, J.R. (1975). Environmental protection and productivity. *Proceedings, 1975 conference on waste reduction.* Washington, DC: U.S. Environmental Protection Agency.

Pirages, D.C. (Ed.). (1977). *The sustainable society.* New York: Praeger.

Platt, J. (1973). Social traps. *American Psychologist, 28,* 641–651.

President's Council on Environmental Quality. (1980). *Public opinion on environmental issues: Results of a national public opinion survey.* Washington, DC: U.S. Government Printing Office.

Public changing views on seriousness of energy situation. (1979, September). *Gallup Opinion Index* (Report No. 170, pp. 15–26).

Purcell, A.H. (1981, February). The world's trashiest people: Will they clean up their act or throw away their future? *Futurist,* pp. 51–59.

Rachlin, H., Kagel, J.H., & Battalio, R.C. (1980). Substitutability in time allocation. *Psychological Review, 87,* 355–374.

Reich, J., & Robertson, J.L. (1979). Reactance and norm appeal in anti-littering messages. *Journal of Applied Social Psychology, 9,* 91–101.

Renshaw, E.F. (1976). *The end of progress: Adjusting to a no-growth economy.* North Scituate, MA: Duxbury.

Reynolds, D.P. (1979). Recycling at Reynolds Metals. In K.E. Henion & T.C. Kinnear (Eds.), *The conserver society.* Chicago: American Marketing Association.

Richman, A. (1979). The polls: Public attitudes toward the energy crisis. *Public Opinion Quarterly, 43,* 576–585.

Rogers, E.M., with Shoemaker, F. (1971). *The communication of innovations*. New York: Free Press.

Rokeach, M. (1967). *Value survey*. Sunnyvale, CA: Halgren Tests.

Rose, D. (1982–1983). National beverage container deposit legislation: A cost-benefit analysis. *Journal of Environmental Systems, 12*, 71–84.

Rossi, P.H., Freeman, H.E., & Wright, S.R. (1979). *Evaluation: A systematic approach*. Beverly Hills, CA: Sage.

Rothman, S., & Lichter, S.R. (1983, August/September). The nuclear energy debate: Scientists, the media and the public. *Public Opinion, 5*(4), 47–52.

Russo, J.E. (1977). A proposal to increase energy conservation through provision of consumption and cost information to consumers. In B.A. Greenberg & D.N. Bellenger (Eds.). *Contemporary marketing thought: 1977 educators' proceedings*. Chicago: American Marketers Association.

Savage, J.F., & Richmond, H.R., III. (1974). Oregon's bottle bill: A riproaring success. *OSPIRG Reports*. Portland: Oregon Student Public Interest Research Group.

Savinar, J. (1981). *Social psychological factors in the decision to adopt residential solar technology*. Unpublished doctoral dissertation, Claremont Graduate School, Claremont, CA.

Sawyer, S. (1982). Leaders in change: Solar energy owners and the implications for future adoption rates. *Technological Forecasting and Social Change, 21*, 201–211.

Schnaiberg, A. (1980). *The environment: From surplus to scarcity*. New York: Oxford.

Schnelle, J.F., McNees, M.P., Thomas, M.M., Gendrich, J.G., & Beagle, G.P. (1980). Prompting behavior change in the community: Use of mass media techniques. *Environment and Behavior, 12*, 157–166.

Schuman, H., & Johnson, M.D. (1976). Attitudes and behavior. *Annual Review of Sociology, 2*, 161–207.

Schwartz, S.H. (1970). Moral decision making and behavior. In J. Macauley & L. Berkowitz (Eds.), *Altruism and helping behavior*. New York: Academic.

Schwartz, S.H. (1977). Normative influences on altruism. In L. Berkowitz (Ed.), *Advances in experimental social psychology* (Vol. 10). New York: Academic.

Schwegler, R.E. (1979). Historical sketch of resource recovery and status of energy retrieval from waste. In K.E. Henion & T.C. Kinnear (Eds.), *The conserver society*. Chicago: American Marketing Association.

Scitovsky, T. (1976). *The joyless economy*. New York: Oxford.

Sears, D.O., Tyler, T.R., Citrin, J., & Kinder, D.R. (1978). Political system support and public response to the energy crisis. *American Journal of Political Science, 22*, 56–82.

Seligman, C., & Becker, L.J. (Eds.). (1981). Energy conservation. *Journal of Social Issues, 37*(2), 1–171.

Seligman, C., Becker, L.J., & Darley, J.M. (1981). Encouraging residential energy conservation through feedback. In A. Baum & J.E. Singer (Eds.), *Advances in environmental psychology: Vol. 3. Energy: Psychological perspectives*. Hillsdale, NJ: Erlbaum.

Seligman, C., & Hutton, R.B. (1981). Evaluating energy conservation programs. *Journal of Social Issues, 37*(2), 51–72.

Seligman, C., Kriss, M., Darley, J.M., Fazio, R.H., Becker, L.J., & Pryor, J.B. (1979). Predicting summer energy consumption from homeowners' attitudes. *Journal of Applied Social Psychology, 9*, 70–90.

Setback for synfuel: Exxon shuts down its shale project. (1982, May 17). *Time*, pp. 58–59.

Sherif, M., Harvey, O.J., White, B.J., Hood, W.E., & Sherif, C.W. (1961). *Intergroup conflict and cooperation: The Robber's Cave experiment*. Norman: University of Oklahoma Book Exchange.

Shippee, G.E. (1980). Energy consumption and conservation psychology: A review and conceptual analysis. *Environmental Management, 4*, 297–314.

Shirley, F.L. (1979). Recycling: Yesterday's image builder is today's insurance policy. In K.E. Henion & T.C. Kinnear (Eds.), *The conserver society*. Chicago: American Marketing Association.

Sills, D.L., Wolf, C.P., & Shelanski, V.B. (Eds.). (1981). *The accident at Three Mile Island: The human dimensions*. Boulder, CO: Westview.

Silver, R.R. (1974, March 17). Arthur, talking ashcan, "eats" C.W. Post trash. *New York Times*.

Simon, H.A. (1979). Rational decision making in business organizations. *American Economic Review, 69*, 493–513.

Simon, J.L. (1981). *The ultimate resource*. Princeton, NJ: Princeton University Press.

Simon, J.L., & Kahn, H. (Eds.). (1984). *The resourceful earth: A response to Global 2000*. Oxford, England: Blackwell.

Skinner, J.H. (1975). Effects of reuse and recycling of beverage containers. *Proceedings, 1975 conference on waste reduction*. Washington, DC: U.S. Environmental Protection Agency,.

Slavin, R.E., Wodarski, J.S., & Blackburn, B.L. (1981). A group contingency for electricity conservation in master-metered apartments. *Journal of Applied Behavior Analysis, 14*, 357–363.

Slovic, P., Fischhoff, B., & Lichtenstein, S. (1981). Perception and acceptability of risk from energy systems. In A. Baum & J.E. Singer (Eds.), *Advances in environmental psychology: Vol. 3. Energy: Psychological perspectives*. Hillsdale, NJ: Erlbaum.

Slovic, P., Fischhoff, B., & Lichtenstein, S. (1982). Facts versus fears: Understanding perceived risk. In D. Kahneman, P. Slovic, & A. Tversky (Eds.), *Judgment under uncertainty: Heuristics and biases*. Cambridge, England: Cambridge University Press.

Smelser, N. (1962). *Theory of collective behavior.* New York: Free Press.

Sonderegger, R.C. (1978). Movers and stayers: The resident's contribution to variation across houses in energy consumption for space heating. In R.H. Socolow (Ed.), *Saving energy in the home: Princeton's experiments at Twin Rivers.* Cambridge, MA: Ballinger.

Stern, P.C. (1978). When do people act to maintain common resources? A reformulated psychological question for our times. *International Journal of Psychology, 13,* 149–158.

Stern, P.C. (Ed.). (1984). *Improving energy demand analysis.* Washington, DC: National Academy Press.

Stern, P.C. (Ed.). (1985). *Energy efficiency in buildings: Behavioral issues.* Washington, DC: National Academy Press.

Stern, P.C. (1986). Blind spots in policy analysis: What economics doesn't say about energy use. *Journal of Policy Analysis and Management, 5*(2), 200–227.

Stern, P.C., & Aronson, E. (Eds.). (1984). *Energy use: The human dimension.* San Francisco: Freeman.

Stern, P.C., Aronson, E., Darley, J.M., Hill, D.H., Hirst, E., Kempton, W., & Wilbanks, T.J. (1986). The effectiveness of incentives for residential energy conservation. *Evaluation Review 10*(2), 147–176.

Stern, P.C., Black, J.S., & Elworth, J.T. (1981). *Home energy conservation: Issues and programs for the 1980s.* Mount Vernon, NY: Consumers Union Foundation.

Stern, P.C., Black, J.S., & Elworth, J.T. (1982). *Influences on household energy adaptations.* Paper presented at the meeting of the American Association for the Advancement of Science, Washington, DC.

Stern, P.C., Black, J.S., & Elworth, J.T. (1983). Adaptations to changing energy conditions among Massachusetts households. *Energy, 8,* 515–523.

Stern, P.C., Dietz, T., & Black, J.S. (1986). Support for environmental protection: The role of moral norms. *Population and Environment 8*(1).

Stern, P.C., & Gardner, G.T. (1980). Energy research in psychology: A review and critique. *Social Science Energy Review, 3*(1), 1–71.

Stern, P.C., & Gardner, G.T. (1981a). Habits, hardware, and energy conservation. *American Psychologist, 36,* 426–428.

Stern, P.C., & Gardner, G.T. (1981b). The place of behavior change in the management of environmental problems. *Zeitschrift für Umweltpolitik, 2,* 213–239.

Stern, P.C., & Gardner, G.T. (1981c). Psychological research and energy policy. *American Psychologist, 36,* 329–342.

Stern, P.C., & Kirkpatrick, E.M. (1977). Energy behavior. *Environment, 19*(9), 10–15.

Stobaugh, R., & Yergin, D. (Eds.). (1979). *Energy future: Report of the energy project at the Harvard Business School.* New York: Random House.

Stoerzinger, A., Johnston, J.M., Pisor, K., & Craig, M.

(1978). Implementation and evaluation of a feedback system for employees in a salvage operation. *Journal of Organizational Behavior Management, 1,* 268–281.

Strand, P.J. (1981). The energy issue: Partisan characteristics. *Environment and Behavior, 13,* 509–519.

Stretton, H. (1976). *Capitalism, socialism, and the environment.* Cambridge, England: Cambridge University Press.

Stroebe, W., & Frey, B.S. (1982). Self-interest and collective action: The economics and psychology of public goods. *British Journal of Social Psychology, 21,* 121–137.

Sundstrom, E., Lounsbury, J.W., DeVault, R.C., & Peele, E. (1981). Acceptance of a nuclear power plant: Applications of the expectancy-value model. In A. Baum & J.E. Singer (Eds.), *Advances in environmental psychology: Vol. 3. Energy: Psychological perspectives.* Hillsdale, NJ: Erlbaum.

Sweeney, J.W., Jr. (1973). An experimental investigation of the free-rider problem. *Social Science Research, 2,* 277–292.

Syme, G.J., Kantola, S.J., Reed, T.R., & Winkler, R.C. (1979). Psychological studies of water consumption. In *Hydrology and water resources symposium.* Perth, Australia: Institute of Engineers.

Thompson, M. (1980). *Benefit-cost analysis for program evaluation.* Beverly Hills, CA: Sage.

Titmuss, R.M. (1971). *The gift relationship: From human blood to social policy.* New York: Vintage.

Tracy, A.P., & Oskamp, S. (1983–1984). Relationships among ecologically responsible behaviors. *Journal of Environmental Systems, 13,* 115–126.

Triandis, H.C. (1980). Values, attitudes, and interpersonal behavior. In M.M. Page (Ed.). *1979 Nebraska Symposium on Motivation.* Lincoln: University of Nebraska Press.

Trigg, L.J., Perlman, D., Perry, R.P., & Janisse, M.P. (1976). Anti-pollution behavior as a function of perceived outcome and internal-external locus of control. *Environment and Behavior, 8,* 307–313.

Turner, R., & Killian, L. (1972). *Collective behavior* (2nd ed.). Englewood Cliffs, NJ: Prentice-Hall.

Tyler, T.R., Orwin, R., & Schurer, L. (1982). Defensive denial and high cost prosocial behavior. *Basic and Applied Social Psychology, 3,* 267–281.

U.S. Council on Environmental Quality. (1975). *Environmental quality, 1975.* Washington, DC: U.S. Government Printing Office.

U.S. Council on Environmental Quality. (1978, December). *Environmental quality: The ninth annual report of the Council on Environmental Quality.* Washington, DC: U.S. Government Printing Office.

U.S. Council on Environmental Quality. (1979). *The good news about energy.* Washington, DC: U.S. Government Printing Office.

U.S. Council on Environmental Quality & U.S. Department of State. (1980). *The global 2000 report to the President: Entering the twenty-first century.* Washington, DC: U.S. Government Printing Office.

U.S. Department of Energy. (1983, February). *Monthly Energy Review.*

U.S. Environmental Protection Agency. (1977). *Fourth report to Congress: Resource recovery and waste reduction* (Report No. SW-600). Washington, DC: Author.

U.S. General Accounting Office. (1977, June 16). *Cleaning up the remains of nuclear facilities—A multibillion dollar problem.* Washington, DC: Author.

U.S. General Accounting Office (1981, February 11). *Residential energy conservation outreach activities—A new federal approach needed.* Washington, DC: Author.

U.S. General Accounting Office. (1982, August 2). *Obstacles to U.S. ability to control and track weapons-grade uranium supplied abroad.* Washington, DC: Author.

Valaskakis, K., Sindell, P.S., Smith, J.G., & Fitzpatrick-Martin, I. (1979). *The conserver society.* New York: Harper & Row.

Van Liere, K.D., & Dunlap, R.E. (1978). Moral norms and environmental behavior: An application of Schwartz's norm-activation model to yard burning. *Journal of Applied Social Psychology, 8,* 174–188.

Van Liere, K.D., & Dunlap, R.E. (1980). The social bases of environmental concern: A review of hypotheses, explanations, and empirical evidence. *Public Opinion Quarterly, 44,* 43–59.

Van Liere, K.D., & Dunlap, R.E. (1981). Environmental concern: Does it make a difference how it's measured? *Environment and Behavior, 13,* 651–676.

Varela, J.A. (1971). *Psychological solutions to social problems: An introduction to social technology.* New York: Academic.

Verhallen, T.M.M., & van Raaij, W.F. (1981). Household behavior and the use of natural gas for home heating. *Journal of Consumer Research, 8,* 253–257.

Vine, E.L., Craig, P.P., Cramer, J.C., Dietz, T.M., Hackett, B.M., Kowalczyk, D.J., & Levine, M.D. (1982). The applicability of energy models to occupied houses: Summer electric use in Davis. *Energy, 7,* 909–925.

Waggoner, D. (1976, September). The Oregon bottle bill—Facts and fantasies. *Environment Action Bulletin,* pp. 2–3.

Wahl, D., & Allison, G. (1975). *Reduce? Targets, means and impacts of source reduction.* Washington, DC: League of Women Voters, Education Fund.

Walker, J.M. (1979). Energy demand behavior in a master-metered apartment complex: An experimental analysis. *Journal of Applied Psychology, 64,* 190–196.

Walsh, E.J. (1981). Resource mobilization and citizen protest in communities around Three Mile Island. *Social Problems, 29,* 1–21.

Walter, D.K. (1979). The Department of Energy program

for the recovery of energy and materials from urban waste. In K.E. Henion & T.C. Kinnear (Eds.), *The conserver society.* Chicago: American Marketing Association.

Warriner, G.K., McDougall, G.H.G., & Claxton, J.D. (1984). Any data or none at all? Living with inaccuracies in self-reports of residential energy consumption. *Environment and Behavior, 16,* 503–526.

Watt, K. (1982). *Understanding the environment.* Newton, MA: Allyn & Bacon.

Weaver, K.F. (1981, February). America's thirst for imported oil: Our energy predicament. *National Geographic,* pp. 2–23.

Webber, D.J. (1982). Is nuclear power just another environmental issue? An analysis of California voters. *Environment and Behavior, 14,* 72–83.

Weigel, R.H. (1977). Ideological and demographic correlates of proecology behavior. *Journal of Social Psychology, 103,* 39–47.

Weigel, R.H., & Newman, L.S. (1976). Increasing attitude-behavior correspondence by broadening the scope of the behavioral measure. *Journal of Personality and Social Psychology, 33,* 793–802.

Weigel, R.H., Vernon, D.T.A., & Tognacci, L.N. (1974). Specificity of the attitude as a determinant of attitude-behavior congruence. *Journal of Personality and Social Psychology, 30,* 724–728.

Weigel, R.H., & Weigel, J. (1978). Environmental concern: The development of a measure. *Environment and Behavior, 10,* 3–15.

Welch, S., & Miewald, R. (Eds.). (1983). *Scarce natural resources: The challenge to public policymaking.* Beverly Hills, CA: Sage.

White, L.T., Archer, D., Aronson, E., Condelli, L., Curbow, B., McLeod, B., Pettigrew, T.F., & Yates, S. (1984). Energy conservation research of California's utilities: A meta-evaluation. *Evaluation Review, 8,* 167–186.

Wildavsky, A., & Tenenbaum, E. (1981). *The politics of mistrust: Estimating American oil and gas resources.* Beverly Hills, CA: Sage.

Wilde, L.L. (1980). The economics of consumer information acquisition. *Journal of Business, 53*(3), pt. 2, S143–S157.

Wilson, J.A. (1977). A test of the tragedy of the commons. In G. Hardin & J. Baden (Eds.), *Managing the commons.* San Francisco: Freeman.

Winett, R.A., & Geller, E.S. (1981). Comment on "Psychological research and energy policy." *American Psychologist, 36,* 425–426.

Winett, R.A., & Geller, E.S. (1982). Resource management in organizational settings. In L.W. Frederiksen (Ed.), *Handbook of organizational behavior management.* New York: Wiley.

Winett, R.A., Hatcher, J.W., Fort, T.R., Leckliter, E.N., Love, S.Q., Riley, A.W., & Fishback, J.F. (1982). The effects of videotape modeling and daily feedback on residential electricity conservation, home temperature and humidity, perceived comfort, and clothing worn: Winter and summer. *Journal of Applied Behavior Analysis, 15,* 381–402.

Winett, R.A., & Neale, M.S. (1979). Psychological framework for energy conservation in buildings: Strategies, outcomes, directions. *Energy and Buildings, 2,* 101–116.

Winkler, R.C. (1982). Water conservation. In E.S. Geller, R.A. Winett, & P.B. Everett. *Preserving the environment: New strategies for behavior change.* New York: Pergamon.

Winkler, R.C., Syme, G.J., & Thomas, J.F. (1979). Social factors and water consumption. In *Hydrology and water resources symposium.* Perth, Australia: Institute of Engineers.

Winkler, R.C., & Winett, R.A. (1982). Behavioral interventions in resource conservation: A systems approach based on behavioral economics. *American Psychologist, 37,* 421–435.

Wohlwill, J.F. (1974). Human response to levels of environmental stimulation. *Human Ecology, 2,* 127–147.

Yankelovich, D. (1982). *New rules.* New York: Bantam.

Yates, S. (1982). *Using prospect theory to create persuasive communications about solar water heaters and insulation.* Unpublished doctoral dissertation, University of California, Santa Cruz, CA.

Yergin, D., & Hillenbrand, M. (Eds.). (1982). *Global insecurity.* Boston: Houghton Mifflin.

Zerega, A.M. (1981). Transportation energy conservation policy: Implications for social science research. *Journal of Social Issues, 37*(2), 31–50.

Zimmerman, C.A. (1980, September). *Energy for travel: Household travel patterns by life cycle stage.* Paper presented at the International Conference on Consumer Behavior and Energy Policy, Banff, Alberta, Canada.

Zube, E.H. (1980). *Environmental evaluation: Perception and public policy.* Monterey, CA: Brooks/Cole.

Chapter 29

ACTIVE RESPONSES TO ENVIRONMENTAL HAZARDS: PERCEPTIONS AND DECISION MAKING

Baruch Fischhoff, *Decision Research, Eugene, Oregon*

Ola Svenson, *Department of Psychology, University of Stockholm, Stockholm, Sweden*

Paul Slovic, *Decision Research, Eugene, Oregon*

29.1. INTRODUCTION

Environmental psychology can seem like the study of how people are pummeled by the events of everyday life. Investigators have shown how noise interferes with the ability to learn, how work place pressures diminish the quality of nonworking life, and how crowding strains the fabric of interpersonal relations. On a superficial level, such studies may be accused of contributing to the malaise of modern life, showing problems but not solutions. In principle, one can respond to that charge by arguing that the studies merely reveal problems that already exist. In prac-

tice, one can point to the attention environmental psychologists have given to solutions that individuals may attempt to implement (e.g., ear protectors, job enhancement). Moreover, the existence of the studies in itself facilitates action, by clarifying the relative importance of different problems and by enabling people to demonstrate the environmental burden that they bear.

This chapter moves to center stage the question of active responses to environmental hazards. It asks how people assess the risks posed (and the benefits offered) by hazardous activities and technologies as well as how they decide what to do about them. At one level, the goal of this research is purely descriptive, characterizing an important class of person–environment interactions. Underlying much of the research discussed here and the framework used to present it, however, is a second goal: facilitating people's responses to environmental hazards. The research aims to help people decide when and how to act. It also hopes to make environmental psychology more useful, by clarifying what new information people need in order to take effective action and determining how existing knowledge can be made most useful for them.

29.1.1. Framework

The perspective adopted here examines how an individual decides what, if anything, should be done about an environmental hazard. That decision could concern a personal action (e.g., whether to wear a seat belt), a collective action (e.g., how a country should respond to pollutants coming from a neighbor), or the link between personal and collective action (e.g., whether to sign a petition regarding an environmental issue). Whatever the topic, decision making should, according to almost all theories of deliberative decision making, involve the following steps:

1. Identify all possible courses of action (including, perhaps, inaction)
2. Evaluate the attractiveness or aversiveness of the consequences that may arise if each course of action is adopted
3. Assess the likelihood of each consequence actually being realized (should each possible course of action be adopted)
4. Integrate these evaluations and assessments in order to select the best course of action

Used descriptively, this framework asks how people approach each of these steps: What action options do they consider, what consequences are important to them, and so on. In this regard, the great attraction of the decision-making perspective is the enormous flexibility of the language it provides. Few choices of action or theories of deliberative action cannot be cast in these terms. The framework is, moreover, theoretically neutral. It makes no predictions about how people implement the framework, beyond ascribing a central role to deliberative thought in the choice of action. The flexibility is exploited by many specific theories of decision making with

explicit predictions about how people implement the framework (Feather, 1982).

Used prescriptively, the framework aims to help people make better decisions. In order to do so, it focuses attention on aspects of decision making in which people experience difficulty (and, hence, could use help). This applied interest often leads to a particular kind of description, in which behavior is characterized as deviations from optimal decision making. There may or may not be an attempt to account for those deviations in terms of a descriptive theory of decision making. In either case, deviations are sought because they show opportunities for investigators to help the deviants (e.g., by improving the display of risk information). Thus usefulness is an added constraint on the kinds of accounts that are sought.

The following sections consider the research tools available for examining how people address each component of the decision-making model, along with representative results that each has produced. In doing so, our primary loyalty will be to the problem of responding to environmental hazards, rather than to the literature, describing existing studies of these responses. That will prompt consideration of some attractive tools that have never been applied to environmental problems. As a result, possible studies will at times have equal status alongside ones that have already been conducted.

29.1.2. Background

A brief history of the area might help set the context regarding who the currently active parties are and why they have chosen particular research strategies. Psychologists' interest in how people respond to environmental hazards has paralleled the public's own growing interest in those hazards. In part, psychologists have responded to events themselves, in order to satisfy their own curiosity or to help the public respond more effectively. In part, psychologists have responded to requests for advice from hazard managers, putting their expertise at the service of individuals whose job it is to cope with the public's concerns (e.g., regulators, politicians, technology developers). As will be argued later, research has often been shaped strongly by what these clients believed the problem to be and what they wanted to know about it. The hidden story of much research has been the gradual discovery that the presenting symptoms of an environmental problem, as described by these clients, have often disguised a rather different "deep structure" in the public's responses to it.

With the rise of the environmental movement, hazard managers have increasingly had to contend with lay intervenors having strong opinions about how technologies should be managed. In some cases, the public's opinions have been viewed as legitimate concerns to be incorporated in social policy. In other cases, though, they have been viewed as obstacles to overcome, in order to let the hazard managers proceed with their plans. Whatever its motivation, the desire to know what the public wants has stimulated demand for the services of attitude researchers, who are able to draw on the methodological resources of survey research (e.g., Eiser & van der Pligt, 1979; Harris, 1980; Otway & Fishbein, 1976; Pokorny, 1982; Prescott-Clarke, 1982; Thomas & Baillie, 1982). When lay and expert perceptions of the environment diverge, what the experts frequently really want to know is: "Why is the public so crazy?" This perspective led managers to behavioral decision theorists, whose studies of how people interpret and respond to uncertain events often contrast observed behavior with some notion of "rational" decision making (e.g., John, von Winterfeldt, & Edwards, 1983; Slovic, Fischhoff, & Lichtenstein, 1979; Vlek & Stallen, 1980). In turning to environmental issues, these investigators have exploited the intellectual capital created by psychological theories that treat risk as a general phenomenon, which is encountered in situations as diverse as gambling, medicine, investment, and motor performance (e.g., Coombs & Avrunin, 1977; Pitz & Sachs, 1984; Pollatsek & Tversky, 1970; Slovic, Fischhoff, & Lichtenstein, 1977). The recent interest in hazards of human origin was preceded by interest in people's responses to natural hazards, undertaken by economists, sociologists, anthropologists, and geographers (e.g, Bowonder, 1980; Burton, Kates, & White, 1978; Kunreuther, Ginsberg, Miller, Sagi, Slovic, Borkin, & Katz, 1978; Mileti, 1980; Whyte, 1977; Wolfenstein, 1957). Although these researchers were concerned primarily with the impact of hazards on larger social units, they often found it useful (even essential) to establish how individuals in those communities perceive and prepare for hazards. For example, geographers have studied how farmers perceive the periodicity of droughts (Kates, 1978); economists have looked at home owner's predictions of flood damage in order to explain the failure of flood plain management schemes (Kunreuther et al., 1978). The confluence of these traditions (often in joint projects) has produced research that is applied and interdisciplinary.

29.2. A DECISION THEORETIC FRAMEWORK

29.2.1. Background

The four steps to good decision making given previously say both a great deal and far too little. For the erstwhile maker of decisions, they prescribe a more elaborate and deliberate mode of operation than most people are accustomed to. However, without further specification, it is unclear how those steps are to be accomplished. For example, how does one identify, in advance, all pertinent courses of action? For the erstwhile describer of decisions, these four steps point to a very large set of considerations that can affect an individual's decision-making processes and, hence, might need to be addressed in a description of those processes. Further specification is needed to reduce this set to those that do actually affect decisions.

The many proposals for accomplishing this further specification can be seen in the legions of prescriptive and descriptive models of decision making, claiming to show, respectively, how decision making should be and actually is undertaken (Edwards, Lindman, & Savage, 1963; Feather, 1982; Fishburn, 1982; Keeney & Raiffa, 1976; Raiffa, 1968). In order to have a consistent means of describing these methods and strategies of decision making, we will introduce a set of formalisms adopted from decision theory. Although it has limitations (which are discussed later), variations on this perspective underlie most theories regarding individuals' active responses to environmental hazards. Indeed, we believe that it is not only possible but profitable to describe diverse approaches with a common conceptual scheme. Doing so would put the study of environmental decision making in the position of economics, where reference to such a scheme has facilitated comparing theories and evaluating empirical evidence. It can also show (1) what parameters must be specified if a study is to be interpreted unambiguously, (2) when seemingly diverse effects are actually special cases of more general phenomena, (3) when a common label (e.g., confirmation bias) has inadvertently been applied to diverse phenomena (Fischhoff & Beyth-Marom, 1983).

29.2.2. Basic Model

A central organizing device for decision theory is the *decision tree*. In its simplest form, it describes a series of possible *actions* (which the decision maker might take) and possible *outcomes* (which may arise from each action). As an example, Figure 29.1 shows a decision tree for a common decision concerning an environmental hazard, whether to drive and, if so, whether to use a seat belt. The square represents a *decision node* offering these three options. For the sake of simplicity, we will assume that "not driving" is not a feasible alternative and neglect its evaluation.

In decision making under conditions of *certainty,* the choice of an action completely determines which outcomes (or consequences) will arise. In such cases, the attractiveness of the outcomes determines the attractiveness of the actions. In decision making under *uncertainty,* one cannot be certain what outcomes will arise. Rather, somewhat unpredictable *events* intervene. In the driving example, the key event is either having or not having an accident. Its outcome depends, in turn, on what action was taken previously regarding seat belts. As a result, when uncertainty is present, one must consider the entire action–event–outcome sequence. In this decision tree, the same *event node* follows both actions; however, that need not be (e.g., the key event for the "do not drive" option might be "get mugged on the way to the bus").

Once the decision-making problem has been structured, its parameters can be estimated. These are the *attractiveness* of the various sequences and the *likelihood* of each occurring. Some suggestive values are given in Figure 29.1. On this trip, for this driver, the probability of an accident is set at 10^{-5}.

The same probability is used regardless of whether the driver is belted, insofar as there is no evidence that wearing seat belts makes drivers more (or less) reckless (Slovic & Fischhoff, 1982). The extreme right-hand column of Figure 29.1 gives numerical evaluations for the (un)attractiveness of these different outcomes. For this driver, arriving safely is a positive outcome, which is somewhat more positive if it has been accomplished without having worn an uncomfortable seat belt. An accident is, of course, negative. How negative obviously depends on how bad the accident is. In this simple tree, all possible accidents are lumped together, forcing the driver to consider intuitively the kinds of accidents associated with each action–event path, their relative likelihood, and aversiveness. These particular numbers might reflect thinking such as: "All accidents are grief. However, with seat belts, more accidents lead to no injuries at all. Also, seat belts reduce head injuries, which I am particularly afraid of." How such numbers might be derived, what metric properties they could have, and when such explicit numerical values are needed are discussed later.

29.2.3. Use of the Model

This commonplace example illustrates the potential usefulness of the decision theoretic framework. For a decision maker, any model provides a way of organizing thoughts about the question. Indeed, just knowing that such a way exists may encourage people to make decisions more deliberatively. This particular

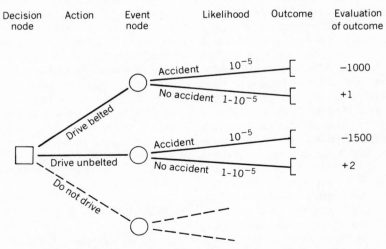

Figure 29.1 Decision tree for using a seat belt on a single auto trip.

framework focuses attention on a small set of well-defined concerns that can be isolated for separate consideration. Thus when new information comes in (e.g., through reading accident statistics or viewing an accident), or when values change (e.g., through a change in social position or viewing an accident), then refining the model to incorporate these new perceptions is straightforward. At times, the model can not only organize thinking but also strongly direct action. Clear recommendations arise when decision makers accept the model as describing their problem, know the values of the model's parameters, and have a firm decision rule for integrating the model's pieces. When these strict conditions are only partly fulfilled, the model can direct action through the judicious use of *sensitivity analysis,* whereby the decision maker identifies the best course of action for different possible representations of the decision-making problem. These different representations are created by varying the estimates of the model's parameters across the range of reasonable possibilities. If variations in a particular parameter (e.g., the exact probability of accident) have little effect on the choice of option, then the decision is *insensitive* to that parameter. Therefore, little additional effort need be invested in obtaining more precise estimates. For some decisions, even very imprecise estimates of all parameters will prove adequate. Where this is not the case, the procedures of *value-of-information analysis* can clarify what resources to invest in further analysis or the acquisition of better information (Raiffa, 1968).

For the researcher attempting to describe decision-making behavior, there is a continuum of philosophies regarding the decision theoretic approach. At one extreme, the *optimizing* approach assumes that people act as if they are using well-articulated decision-making models, while equipped with accurate perceptions of the likelihood and consequences of different action–event sequences. The researchers' task is to uncover that model. This is the approach adopted by most economists, who assume that people always act in an optimal (or rational) way. The conceptual difficulty with this philosophy is that, with sufficient ingenuity, any decision can be described as being in the decision maker's best interest.

In order to avoid the untestable (metatheoretical) assumption that all decisions are optimal, some investigators try to describe behavior as *suboptimal,* by relaxing various assumptions of the optimizing approach. For example, one might assume that drivers perceive highway risks correctly but use improper decision rules (e.g., ignoring some factors) which the investigator must uncover. Or one can assume that people use a proper decision rule but misperceive the facts or incompletely assess their own or their organization's values.

The *nonoptimizing* philosophy holds that people's decision-making procedures cannot be described as moderate deviations from optimality. Rather, they follow qualitatively different procedures, which need to be described in their own terms. What models of optimality can do is establish the magnitude of people's suboptimality. That magnitude shows how much intervention is needed to make people optimal or to protect them from the consequences of suboptimality. Some advocates of the nonoptimizing perspective hold that however people make decisions must be right for them and cannot be improved on. If the optimality of the decision theory model is accepted, then the nonoptimizing perspective implies that strong medicine, in the form of education or decision aids, is needed if people are to choose the best options for themselves by themselves. The suboptimizing perspective leads naturally to the search for ways to help people to overcome their weaknesses and exploit their strengths (e.g., by displaying risk information more cogently). By contrast, the optimizing approach flatters people — at the price of being unable to help them (because they are, by definition, doing fine). Many debates over environmental policy can be traced to the differences between these philosophies, with the optimizing approach advocating reliance on individual decision making in the marketplace, and the others acknowledging imperfections in it.

Discrepancies between the decisions that laypeople reach and the decisions that experts would make in their stead are not always signs of lay suboptimality. At times, experts perceive the problem wrongly; at times, they just perceive the problem differently. The decision theoretic model provides a way to describe different people's perceptions that allows one to diagnose the precise sources of disagreements. In environmental disputes, such diagnosis can itself have salutary effects. It may, for example, heighten mutual respect by showing that public discomfort with expert decisions reflects terminological differences or legitimate conflicts of interest rather than just public ignorance (Fischhoff, Slovic, & Lichtenstein, 1983). Or it may show how decisions on different levels of society interact, as with those made by traffic safety officials and individual drivers. Good descriptions can help the parties anticipate and understand one another's actions. Good descriptions of different parties' perspectives can also help resolve environmental conflicts by identifying key issues, revealing overlooked alternatives, and showing areas of agreement (Chen, 1980; Hammond & Adelman, 1976).

The following sections consider the techniques available for describing and improving these different aspects of decision-making processes.

29.3. DEFINING THE DECISION PROBLEM

Like other formalisms, decision theory requires a certain precision of expression. Also like other formalisms, it can justify that precision by pointing to the confusion that can arise with imprecision. Whether one's goal is to describe, advise, debate, or manipulate others, it is essential to know what decision problem they are addressing. Often, decisions that seem unreasonable in the context of one problem are readily defended in the context of another. Thus for example, nuclear power may be much more attractive when the only alternative is high-sulphur coal than when the option set includes radical energy conservation and a crash research and development program for renewables. Similarly, nuclear power may be much more attractive when *risk* is defined as "expected annual fatalities" than when extra weight is given to losses of life from catastrophic accidents. Its attractiveness may also vary with the time period over which costs, risks, and benefits are aggregated. Thus both parties might be right when proponents of nuclear power accuse its opponents of stupidly ignoring benefits and opponents accuse proponents of venally ignoring risks. However, empirical investigation may also show that both parties are acting in good faith and on the basis of good information—but solving different problems. In that case, conflict can be reduced by reaching a consensual problem definition. Although a formidable task, that is still easier than changing the parties' technical competence or moral stature (Bickerstaffe & Pearce, 1980).

It is uncommon for individuals to articulate their problem definitions in the detail required by decision theory. Even in public discussions, the focus is on specific issues of facts and values rather than on how to frame the discussion. Perhaps for these reasons, this is the least developed aspect of behavioral decision theory. Nonetheless, even the incomplete methods that are available can greatly reduce one's excessive freedom to interpret how others perceive their problems.

29.3.1. Terms

The first step in capturing how people view their environment is understanding the terms that they use to describe it. For familiar decisions, such as the seat belt example, clear consensual definitions are readily available. Most people agree about what *seat belt, usage,* and *discomfort* mean. If they make different usage decisions, it probably reflects differences in how they evaluate the risks. One possibly important exception is differences in the lay definition of *accident.* For example, some may think of running off a bridge (and being trapped by a seat belt), whereas others think of running into a bridge (and being saved by a seat belt). Thus different intuitive definitions could lead to different decisions. With less familiar risky decisions, definitional problems often impede coping with environmental issues. Without a precise language, individuals cannot get a consistent fix on the problems or communicate their concerns to others. Incoherence is common with environmental issues, in part, because the field "just grew," as different disciplines and interest groups were drawn to a diverse set of novel problems. Each of these groups has adapted old terms or concocted new ones to deal with the unique features of risk problems. This process is not, however, far enough along for the items to be thoroughly understood, for usage differences to be resolved, or for the experts' terms to penetrate everyday language.

Three recurrent terminological difficulties and the methods for uncovering them are described next.

Opacity

A frustrating, but readily treated, difficulty arises when one party uses terms that another does not understand. The common scripts for this conflict involve experts tossing jargon at a helpless public and the public responding in the imprecise vernacular. Such miscommunication occurs in many domains. What may be unique to environmental decisions is how long it takes to be detected. One can ask a physician or plumber to clarify an unfamiliar term, and they can detect a puzzled look. However, direct interchanges between the public and environmental experts are rare. Thus the public can only guess what the experts mean, and the experts can only guess what the public understands. Erroneous guesses may be discovered only when they lead to consequential mistakes or misstatements. All too often, the injury caused by such mishaps is compounded by the insults leveled against the public for not having understood and against the experts for not having told.

The great truth of cultural anthropology is that people underestimate by how much they fail to understand one another. As a result, researchers' intuitive assessments of the clarity of their messages are no more to be trusted than are the assessments of technical experts. The most direct procedure to measure understanding is to ask people if they understand terms. For example, Behrend (1981) found that many people still admit to being puzzled by the term *inflation*. This procedure is likely to exaggerate understanding to the extent that respondents feel that they should say "yes" or erroneously think that they do understand a term simply because they have devised a conceivable interpretation. Even if its estimate of understanding is accurate, the procedure gives no direct clues to the source of confusion or to its remedy.

A more intensive procedure has respondents endorse one of a set of possible definitions, which allows estimates of the rate and kinds of misunderstanding. The accuracy of that rate estimate will depend on the appropriateness of the alternative definitions used as distractors. In a study using this approach, Murphy, Lichtenstein, Fischhoff, and Winkler (1980) found a high degree of misunderstanding in lay interpretations of probabilistic precipitation forecasts. Contrary to the claims of many meteorologists, the confusion concerned the event being predicted rather than the numerical probability assigned to it. Respondents were equally likely to interpret a "70% chance of rain" as "rain 70% of the time," "rain over 70% of the area," and "70% chance of some measurable rain" (the official definition).

More intensive (and more expensive) still is having respondents actively use the term in question. For example, it might have been interesting to have observers of Three Mile Island describe the potential "explosion" reported in the news. How many thought that they understood it to be of the thermonuclear type? Geographers have used this technique effectively in studying responses to natural hazards (Burton et al., 1978), finding, for example, that "100-year flood" is often (mis)interpreted as "occurring at 100-year intervals." Scientists had inadvertently reduced public vigilance by describing disasters as "100-year floods" (thus ensuring a century of hydrological tranquility).

Even more ambitious are attempts to capture respondents' entire frame of reference regarding their environment; this is what anthropologists call "indigenous technical knowledge" (Brokensha, Warren, & Werner, 1980). Through a combination of in-depth interviews and field observations, they have often discovered striking discrepancies between the world views of native peoples and outside experts hoping to help them. Although used primarily to improve technology transfer to developing countries, these procedures could help workers put occupational hazards in context or laypeople relate dietary risks to other activities (Kjelling & Larsson, 1981; Tait, 1982). Where world views are extremely different, even careful term-by-term clarification of jargon may not ensure understanding.

Ethnocentrism requires two ethnic centers. Laypeople, too, may be unable to make themselves understood, despite having consistent and personally well-defined ways of referring to things. Physicians and auto mechanics are two groups of technical experts who often seem to understand us, only for us to learn later that we have failed to communicate.

Nonconsensual Usage

Another hard-to-detect terminology problem arises when different groups use the same term for different things. Confusion of this sort can be found at the heart of environmental risk management, with the definition of *risk*. Each discipline involved has evolved its own ways of measuring risks. For some, it means the total number of deaths (e.g., Zentner, 1979); for others, deaths per person exposed or per hour of exposure (e.g., Starr, 1969; Wilson, 1979); for others, it is loss of life expectancy due to exposure to the technology (e.g., Cohen & Lee, 1979; Reissland & Harries, 1979); for still others, it is the loss of the ability to work (e.g., Inhaber, 1979).

Unwitting use of different definitions can lead to controversy as well as confusion because the relative riskiness of different jobs, avocations, technologies, or diseases may depend on which definition is adopted. For example, hazards producing accidental deaths become relatively "riskier" if one counts the total days lost rather than weighing all deaths equally. Different conclusions regarding, say, the greatest risks confronting society may reflect differing definitions but be attributed to differences in judgment or intelligence. Choosing the proper definition for environmental decisions is a political/ethical question. Ensuring communication is a technical question that can be informed by descriptive research.

Although the techniques for diagnosing opacity can be useful here, they are fairly optimistic regarding people's ability to articulate their intuitive definitions. An alternative approach is to discern how people actually use a term, as opposed to what they say that they mean by it. For example, Fischhoff, Slovic, Lichtenstein, Read, and Combs (1978) and Slovic and colleagues (1979) had subjects judge the "risk of death for the average U.S. citizen" for each of 30 hazardous activities and technologies. Risk was deliberately not defined further. Other respondents drawn from the same population judged these technologies on other aspects of risk, including (1) the fatalities produced in a typical year, (2) catastrophic potential, and (3) various qualitative aspects of risk, hypothesized by commentators to affect lay risk perceptions (e.g., voluntariness, familiarity, and controllability). Subjects were drawn from these populations of citizens and from practicing risks analysts in the United States.

Correlations among mean responses showed that for the experts "risk" judgments resembled statistical estimates of average-year fatalities. Apparently the experts both viewed "risk" in those terms and held estimates close to those in the literature. Lay subjects' judgments of average-year fatalities were strongly correlated with the statistical estimates, meaning that the statistic was meaningful to them. However, their "risk" judgments were different. These differences were, in turn, strongly correlated with judgments of catastrophic potential. Thus they either gave extra weight to lives lost in catastrophic accidents or felt that average-year fatalities poorly captured the risks of technologies with catastrophic potential. Further investigations (described later) suggest the latter interpretation.

Unanalyzed Usage

Opaque or idiosyncratic terms may bump against other individuals who will question their usage. For vague (or illogical) definitions, life might be smoother, but more dangerous, because challenges are less likely to occur or to be diagnostic. Emerging fields such as environmental decision making must improvise some vocabulary in order to begin work at all. In time, some of these initial usages will require shaping or abandonment. When people use unclear terms, it frustrates their own efforts to make consistent decisions and investigators' efforts to describe their decisions consistently. Although there is no systematic way to discover the limits of terms, a mixture of empirical and conceptual analysis may speed the process. The following examples show possible ways to challenge even widely accepted terms of environmental management.

ACCEPTABLE RISK

The holy grail for hazard managers is the "acceptable level of risk," indicating how safe a technology must be before society should leave it alone. The literature is rife with proposals and counterproposals for what that level is (e.g., Atomic Industrial Forum, 1976, 1981; Comar, 1979; Farmer, 1967; Morgan, 1969; Rowe, 1977; U.S. Nuclear Regulatory Commission, 1981). The lack of consensus partly reflects the conflicting political perspectives of those making these proposals. However, analysis shows that consensus among even like-thinking people is frustrated by the vagaries of the term (Fischhoff, Lichtenstein, Slovic, Derby, & Keeney, 1981). From a decision-making perspective, it makes no sense to speak about acceptable risks. One adopts (or accepts) options, not risks. That option may entail some level of risk, but there is no way in which that risk can be separated from its other features. As a result, one may accept an option with a relatively high level of risk, if it has sufficiently high benefits. Similarly, one may abandon that option (and its risks) if a better option comes along offering, say, much greater safety at little extra cost.

For people to agree about the acceptability of a particular risk, they must have similar values and similar perceptions of available options. That is, they must make similar decisions. Calling the risk associated with an accepted option "acceptable" obscures the logic of their decision and may confer undue legitimacy to those risks, which are but one aspect of the technology. Such ascriptions are, of course, comforting to the promoters of technologies. It is probably neither surprising nor diabolical that people think less hard about terms that produce desired conclusions.

INFORMED CONSENT

Those who create risks such as employers, physicians, and scientists often hope to obtain informed consent from those exposed to them. Yet there is often uncertainty about whether it has been obtained. Here, too, observation of difficulties and logical analysis suggest an ill-fitting concept. Despite its apparent concern for those exposed to risk, *informed consent* reflects the perspective of the exposer. From the risk bearers' point of view, the critical issue is identifying the optimal course of action. Whether that adoption entitles the risk creator to some special moral or legal status is irrelevant (except insofar as it gives some strategic bargaining advantage). When the problem is cast as ensuring that potential risk bearers optimize their choices, one finds a clearly indicated set of procedures to follow (Fischhoff, 1985).

OBJECTIVE

Scientists involved in environmental debates often describe their work as "objective" and that of lay dissenters as "subjective." Here, too, imprecision produces confusion. Objectivity is a goal of good science, rather than a characteristic of its product. One strives to perform and report research in such a way that anyone following the same path would reach the same conclusion. Yet there is an element of subjectivity in all science, expressed in fundamental assumptions regarding its methods and their application. In addition, the need to guide action forces environmental scientists to make judgments going far beyond what could be rigorously defended by empirical evidence or what would be made in science conducted for science's sake. A better description of public-expert disagreements would be as conflicts between two sets of (inevitably subjective) judgments.

EXPERT

A bearer of the label *expert* should know all that is known about a topic. That is not the same as knowing all that could be or needs to be known. Environmental issues vary in novelty and complexity, and with them varies the definitiveness of available knowledge. One cannot know as much about the risks of recombinant DNA research as about those of home appliances or automobiles. When used uncritically, the term *expert* may imply absolute rather than just relative understanding.

We believe that the analysis of terms is an important area for social scientists' contributions to decision making. Being able to identify and sharpen alternative definitions does not, of course, guarantee being able to use them. Scientific groups might be persuaded to use some consensual term or at least to be explicit about their nonconsensual terms. Laypeople cannot, however, be told how to think or be asked to articulate their intuitive definitions. One can hope, though, that consistent use by scientists (and science journalists) will create a societal definition.

29.3.2. Decision Structure

The experts in eliciting decision problem structures are professional decision analysts and counselors

(Brown, Kahr, & Peterson, 1974; Janis, 1982; Keeney, 1982; Raiffa, 1968). One measure of the difficulty of problem structuring is experienced analysts' insistence that clients invest a substantial amount of time to discussing what the problem is. Even though these clients have pondered the problem intensively, they may not know how to think about it. Thus the analyst's initial task is eliciting the various inconsistent, incomplete, and tentative structures that their clients have contemplated (Keeney, 1977). The next job is to merge these sets of possible options, consequences, and uncertainties into a single representation that is best for the client. Sensitivity analysis is a key procedure for this activity. It can, for example, identify consequences that are sufficiently similar for all options that they can be ignored. However, analysts claim that, at the end of the day, interpretation is an art, with the ultimate criterion being their clients' feeling of satisfaction (Fischhoff, 1980; Phillips, 1982).

The generality of analysts' conclusions may be understood by considering the special features of the problems gaining their attention. One is that the problems are unique, meaning that the client has not had the opportunity to evolve a suitable representation through trial-and-error experience. As discussed later, decision making is most difficult when people must think their way through to a solution. The uniqueness of many environmental problems means that decision describers must expect unstable problem representations and that decision counselors have a contribution to make.

A second feature of the problems being analyzed is their importance to the clients. Although important decisions need not be outstanding in the quantity, complexity, or ambiguity of their options, consequences, or sources of uncertainty, they do draw a lot of attention. Worrying itself may tend to produce complex, uncertain structures, thereby reducing the chances of simple, unconflicted decisions.

Choosing the optimal level of complexity is part of the problem of deciding when to decide, as opposed to learning, ruminating, or procrastinating more (Corbin, 1980). The antithesis of paralyzing complexity is abandoning any semblance of analytical decision making in favor of simple rules such as "safety first," "look before you leap," or "nothing ventured, nothing gained." Although such rules are easily described, they short-circuit the decision-making process, leaving few clues to the structure that prompted them or how they were derived from it—if they were derived and not just produced associatively. This leaves a meager account for the decision describer and an im-

poverished basis for the decision aider having to identify a best structure.

Options

It is difficult to study simultaneously how people
structure a problem and how they integrate its pieces
in selecting a course of action. Interest in action has
focused experimental researchers' attention on situations in which subjects receive problems with
explicitly specified structures. The relatively few lab
studies of option selection have concentrated on the
completeness of option sets. For example, Fischhoff,
Slovic, and Lichtenstein (1978) had people assess the
percentage of car-starting failures that fall into each
major category in Figure 29.2, including "all other
problems." Because each diagnosis prompts a particular response, it represents both a hypothesis
regarding what might have happened to the car and
an action option. Both novices and professional
mechanics proved to be very insensitive to the list's
completeness. Eliminating major systems, such as
battery and fuel, effected small increases in the percentage of no-starts attributed to "all other problems." Although such obvious omissions might have
been easily detected and prompted skepticism regarding the entire representation, the dominant cognitive process seems to have been "out of sight, out
of mind." In other ways, subjects' evaluations were
more resilient to manipulations of the representation. For example, merely mentioning a system produced judgments of its likelihood of involvement
that were similar to those evoked by presenting it
in full detail. On the other hand, when a system
was split into subsystems, the combined importance
of the subsystems was greater than that for the
system as a whole.

In a more open-ended procedure, Gettys, Manning, Mehle, and Fisher (1980) had subjects list all
possible causes of various problems. These subject-
generated sets lacked important items but were regarded as complete (again, for experts as well as lay
subjects). A related study (Gettys, Manning, &
Casey, 1981), which developed a method for evaluating the "opportunity loss" of omitting specific options, found that omissions were serious as well as
numerous. Pitz, Sachs, and Heerboth (1980) found
similar deficiencies in response to problems such as
coping with a recalcitrant roommate. Their only success in improving the generation process was giving
subjects an explicit list of objectives as a prompt.

In considering the results of lab studies such as
these, a natural concern is whether participants
thought as creatively about options as they would

have in real-life situations. A review of attempts to
eliminate judgmental deficiencies (Fischhoff, 1982)
suggests that robust, well-designed experimental
tasks can generate considerable intrinsic motivation:
The problems seem real to subjects, even though the
need to solve them is artificial. When payment is offered for performance, it has typically had little effect
(unless the incentives evoked strategic behavior).
Moreover, similar patterns have been found in field
studies, particularly of responses to the threats of
natural hazards (Burton et al., 1978).

The impoverished action sets shown in these
studies include flood plain residents' ignorance of
seemingly obvious ways to reduce the risk of flood
damage (Kunreuther et al., 1978; White, 1974). Although these responses are very real, their usefulness as evidence is still imperfect. Such observations
may not capture the options that were considered
and rejected or the early options that were gradually
shaped into more satisfactory form. Even those options that were accepted may not reflect deliberative
choices. For example, people may have flood insurance because it came with their mortgage or because their insurance agent bought it on their behalf.
Pre- and postcrisis interviews can reduce these uncertainties about problem structure. These results
suggest that decision aiders cannot rely on the possibilities that spontaneously occur to the clients.
With a well-defined repetitive problem, prior research
may provide a definitive set, as Beach, Townes,
Campbell, and Keating (1976) did with birth-planning
possibilities (and Janis, 1982, and associates have for
several problems). For novel situations, a logical
scheme such as that in Figure 29.3, may help generate options. It describes hazards as a causal chain
leading from human needs to physical consequences.
Each link offers some opportunity for intervention,
hence an action option.

Once created, a definitive list of options might be
used in several ways for descriptive purposes. One is
to structure interviews, providing prompts to jog subjects' memories. A second, rooted in the optimizing
assumption, is to assume that people have considered all reasonable options, if only to dismiss them.
A third is to assume that the active list of options
was produced by systematic degrading of the definitive list. For example, social pressure or advertise-
ment (Tait, 1981) may emphasize some options
(e.g., Chemical X vs. Chemical Y) over others (e.g.,
integrated pest control); uncertainty may rule out options calling for immediate or irreversible action (Corbin, 1980); the scheduling of public decisions may
force a choice between accepting or rejecting a

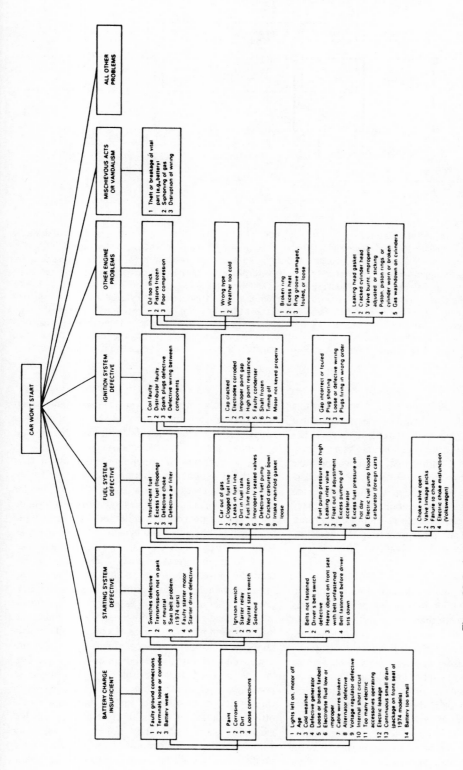

Figure 29.2. A possible fault tree for discovering why a car won't start. (*Source:* "Fault Trees: Sensitivity of Estimated Failure Probabilities to Problem Representation" by B. Fischhoff, P. Slovic, & S. Lichtenstein, 1978, *Journal of Experimental Psychology: Human Perception and Performance 4*, p. 331. Copyright 1978 by American Psychological Association. Reprinted by permission.)

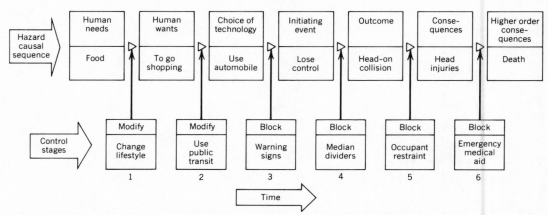

Figure 29.3. Illustration of the causal chain of hazard evolution. The top line indicates seven stages of hazard developments, from the earliest (left) to the final stage (right). These stages are expressed generically in the top of each box and in terms of a sample motor-vehicle accident in the bottom. The stages are linked by causal pathways denoted by triangles. Six control stages are linked to pathways between hazard states by vertical arrows. Each is described generically as well as by specific control actions. Thus Control State 2 would read: "You can modify technology choice by substituting public transit for automobile use and thus block the further evolution of the motor-vehicle accident sequence arising out of automobile use." The time dimension refers to the ordering of a specific hazard sequence; it does not necessarily indicate the time scale of managerial action. Thus from a managerial point of view, the occurrence of certain hazard consequences may trigger control actions that affect events earlier in the hazard sequence. (*Source*: "Target: Highway Risks" by T. Bick, C. Hohenemser, & R. Kates, 1979, *Environment, 21*, p. 9. Copyright 1979 by C. Hohenemser. Reprinted by permission of Heldref Publications.)

technology (e.g., "go" or "no-go" with nuclear power) as opposed to a choice between alternative technologies (e.g., different sources of energy). Referring to Figure 29.3, perhaps people concentrate on avoiding accidents, rather than on mitigating their consequences, or tend to ignore the more fundamental "upstream" changes (those to the left). Once excluded from active consideration, options are likely to fade away entirely, as facts relevant to them are neither generated nor incorporated in the decision-making process (Wright & Barbour, 1977).

Consequences

Although the consequence selection story is similar to that for option selection in many respects (hence is amenable to similar methods of study), there is one significant difference: The consequences deemed important are never as visible as the option eventually chosen. Ways to make consequences more observable include encouraging people to think aloud as they go (Payne, 1980; Svenson, 1979), seeing what consequences are mentioned when people reflect on past decisions (Aschenbrenner, Jaus, & Villani, 1980; Montgomery, 1983), and observing what consequences appear in advertisements and debates. As with options, the identification process is complicated when

decisions evolve over time, which impairs memory and allows consequences to move in and out of people's consciousness. These methods are, of course, limited by people's power of introspection and candor.

As a substitute or supplement, one may try to infer the consequences that people care about from the decisions that they take. A statistical method for such inferences is *revealed preference analysis*. A large set of similar decisions is collected for which all options can be characterized by a set of consequences (e.g., security, salary, location, etc., in a job decision). Multiple regression analysis is used to predict (actually postdict) the decisions from the consequences. Significant regression coefficients are interpreted as showing that the associated consequence affected those decisions. Because the magnitude of its coefficient may be taken as an estimate of a consequence's relative importance, these procedures are discussed further in the section on value assessment. We note here only that a variable may have a negligible regression coefficient not only if it is ignored but also if the set of options does not vary in that respect or if other consequences are highly correlated with it. For example, price is obviously important to students when considering apartments. It may not, however, predict choices if all considered apartments have similar prices or if the regression equation includes correlated variables (e.g., size, location) that divide the variance due to "quality" (of which price is one reflection).

As with options, some descriptive and prescriptive insights may come from creating definitive sets of consequences. One famous effort was Murray's (1938) identification of 43 basic human needs, with the most famous being the second—the need for achievement (and the most intriguing being the first, the need for abasement.) A comprehensive and consistent way to structure all decisions would be to characterize options in terms of how well they satisfy each need. As with definitive option lists, Murray's list could be degraded systematically to reflect substantive hypotheses regarding how these decisions are or should be made. One description principle is memory failure, leading to the neglect of consequences not experienced recently. A second is imagination failure, leading to the neglect of unfamiliar consequences. For example, those who have not been flooded out do not even consider some of a flood's effects on their lives (Kunreuther et al., 1978). Other omissions are domain-specific. For example, many decisions to develop technologies neglect their impact on the availability of capital for other projects (Fay, 1975); economists' recommendations for environmental decisions entirely neglect consequences that cannot be assigned a market value (Fischhoff et al., 1981); legal constraints often prevent regulatory bodies from considering the distributional effects of their decisions. Of course, officially inappropriate consequences can still affect decisions. For example, a company may tell managers to maximize profits but reward them for maximizing growth—a goal they cannot acknowledge explicitly. Reading the reward structure of people's institutions is an obvious key to the consequences that they consider.

Many environmental decisions pose a conflict between the official and psychological legitimacy of consequences, in the form of outcomes that are important to people but lack legal standing. For example, the U.S. Nuclear Regulatory Commission was challenged to consider the "psychological stress" caused by starting up the undamaged reactor at Three Mile Island. Although an appeals court concluded that the commission's enabling legislation only mentioned physical impacts, the issue does not seem closed. If one cannot argue that concern itself is a significant consequence or that people should be compensated for the loss of time and energy that could be devoted to something else (e.g., leisure, financial planning, improving profesional skills), then the issue may hinge on psychologists' assessments of the physiological effects accompanying chronic stress (Campbell, 1983;

Elliot & Eisdorfer, 1982). Such stress may not only precipitate problems of its own but also increase susceptibility to others. Thus environmental concern may hasten the end of a marriage by giving one more thing to fight about and less energy with which to look for solutions (Baum, Gatchel, & Schaeffer, 1983; Kasl, Chisholm, & Eskenazi, 1981). Such secondary consequences may be ignored, despite their significance, because they are too diffuse to be detected (a few more broken marriages, a few more cases of child abuse). Failing such demonstrations, the only legitimate costs of concern might be the protective actions taken by people to achieve an adequate level of safety (e.g., moving houses, extra medical examinations [Huff & Clark, 1978]). These are part of the technology's *externalized costs* (those borne by nonbeneficiaries).[1] If concern did have standing, then one would have to consider whether people's degree of concern is justified by the "facts" of the matter. The next section considers both the accuracy of laypeople's risk perceptions and the appropriateness of those perceptions' translation into a level of concern.

Uncertainties

As the seat belt example (Figure 29.1) showed, a problem structure must include sources of uncertainty, showing the events whose occurrence or nonoccurrence will determine the outcome (e.g., an accident). Assessing the magnitude of uncertainty raises many general issues, which are discussed in the section of fact assessment. Identifying the events whose uncertainty must be assessed is, however, much more situation-specific. Potentially important events are as diverse as environmental hazards and coping responses. As a result, it is reasonable to assume that people have equivalent difficulty spontaneously generating full sets of events. It is also possible to gain general guidance from schemes such as Figure 29.3, each transition in which represents an uncertain event.

The magnitude of uncertainty is often reduced to a probability or other summary statistic. However, people also want to know about the nature of the uncertainty. For example, there may be a special aversion to events whose probability is poorly understood (Slovic, Lichtenstein & Fischhoff, 1984). In such cases, a premium might be paid to compensate for the greater difficulty of planning and the added public concern caused by lack of expert understanding.

Much speculation has been devoted to these qualitative features of risk (e.g., Cole & Withey, 1982; Green & Brown, 1981; Lowrance, 1976; Slovic, Fischhoff, & Lichtenstein, 1980; Vlek & Stallen,

1981), with the set of proposed determinants of concern running to several dozen. This is an unwieldy number for a descriptive theory of risk perception, a prescriptive guide to risky decisions, or a scheme for predicting responses to new hazards or hazard reduction schemes. As a result, various empirical studies have attempted both to check these speculations and to reduce the number of considerations with a data-reduction technique such as factor analysis or multidimensional scaling. Most have followed (and elaborated on) a correlational scheme offered by Fischhoff, Slovic, Lichtenstein, Read, and Combs (1978). In it, members of a liberal civic organization rated environmental risks on many hypothesized aspects of risk. Factor analysis reduced the mean ratings of 30 hazards on nine aspects to two dimensions accounting for 78% of the variance. Similar patterns were found with students, members of a conservative civic organization, and (unlike the definition of *risk*) with technical risk assessors. Figure 29.4 shows the factor scores for 30 hazards within the common factor space for these four groups.

Hazards at the high end of the vertical factor (e.g., food coloring, pesticides) tended to be new, unknown, involuntary, and delayed in their effects. High (right-hand) scores on the horizontal factor (e.g., nuclear power, commercial aviation) meant consequences seen as certain to be fatal, often for large numbers of people, should something go wrong. The vertical factor was labeled *unknown risk* and the horizontal factor *dread risk*. They may be seen as capturing the cognitive and emotional bases of people's concern, respectively.

Other studies employing variants on this "psychometric paradigm" include Brown & Green (1980), Gardner, Tiemann, Gould, DeLuca, Doob, & Stolwijk (1982), Green (1980), Hohenemser, Kates, & Slovic (1983), Johnson & Tversky (1983), Lindell & Earle (1983), Renn (1981), Slovic, Fischhoff, & Lichtenstein (1985), Vlek & Stallen (1981), von Vinterfeldt, John, & Borcherding (1981). These studies have yielded results that are similar in many respects. For example, despite changes in elicitation mode, scaling techniques, items rated, and subject population, two or three dimensions have proven adequate. Where a third dimension emerges, it typically refers to the absolute number of lives exposed to the threat in present or future generations; *catastrophic potential* seems like a suitable label. The position of particular technologies in this space proves to be highly robust. Moreover, that position is correlated strongly with various risk attitudes, including the desired stringency of regulation.

Such analyses of mean responses are most suitable for predicting aggregate responses to hazards. Working in The Netherlands, Vlek & Stallen (1980) found substantial individual differences in the weighing of dimensions despite having an aggregate two-dimensional representation similar to that in Figure 29.4. These correlational analyses assume that carefully decomposing risk into component characteristics will evoke the most thoughtful responses. However, other features of people's perceptions may emerge in wholistic judgments such as the overall similarity of paired hazards. These could be analyzed by multidimensional scaling techniques to produce alternative dimensional representations or by feature-oriented methods to produce tree representations such as that in Figure 29.5. In such a figure (Tversky & Sattath, 1979), risks are the terminal nodes of the tree, and the distance between any pair of risks is given by the length of the horizontal parts of the shortest path that joins them; the vertical part is only a graphical convenience. A tree representation can be interpreted in terms of common and unique features. Figure 29.5 exhibits a distinct hierarchy of clusters that Johnson and Tversky (1983) call hazards, transportation accidents, violent acts, technological disasters, and diseases.[2] Such a comparative response mode might be particularly suited for describing decisions involving competing technologies. On the other hand, they might be influenced by irrelevant semantic features of the stimuli. For example, the risks of nuclear and non-nuclear electric power might be judged similar because both produce power, even though their other consequences are very different.

29.4. VALUE ASSESSMENT

Defining a decision problem creates a set of vectors, each representing an option, with its entries being the different possible consequences. Determining how much of each consequence each option will produce is a question of fact assessment, as treated in the following section. *Value assessment,* the topic of the present section, involves determining the attractiveness or aversiveness of consequences of that magnitude. In reality, these assessments cannot be separated so tidily. The consequences that people consider important shape their search for options and for facts; conversely, the importance of consequences depends on their ability to discriminate among available options.

In the absence of uncertainty, Figure 29.1's choice becomes a trade-off between the consequences:

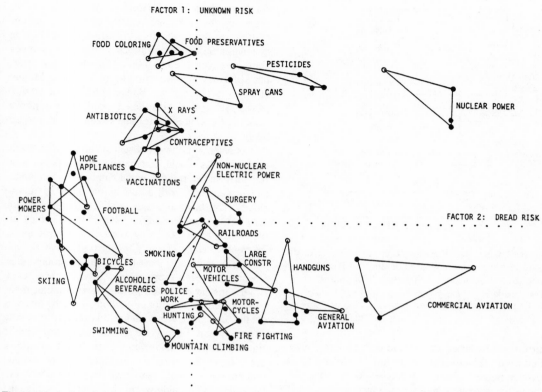

Figure 29.4. Location of 30 hazards within the two-factor space obtained from League of Women Voters, student, Active Club and expert groups. Connected lines join or enclose the loci of four group points for each hazard. Open circles represent data from the expert group. Unattached points represent groups that fall within the triangle created by the other three groups. (*Source*: "Characterizing Perceived Risk" by P. Slovic, B. Fischhoff, & S. Lichtenstein. In R. Kates, C. Hohenemser, and J. X. Kasperson (Eds.), *Perilous Progress: Managing the Hazards of Technology*, p. 103. Copyright 1985. Reprinted by permission of Westview Press.)

Does the reduced injury severity associated with seat belt usage compensate for the increased discomfort? The answer is obviously "yes." Once the uncertainties are considered, however, more precise evaluations are needed. Is the injury reduction sufficiently attractive to compensate for the unlikelihood of its being "enjoyed?"

More precise trade-offs may also be needed even in the absence of uncertainty. Figure 29.6 shows a set of consequences that might be considered in a deliberative national decision about energy systems. Although these outcomes are uncertainties for the individuals exposed to these technologies, they are virtual certainties at the national level. No one knows exactly who will be killed in coal or uranium mining, but there will be some deaths (just as the minute individual probabilities of auto accidents accumulate to the large death tolls seen by safety officials). Good

statistics might give a good guess at the expected consequences. Unless this (factual) assessment of effect magnitude fortuitously showed one system to be at least as good as all others in all respects, some difficult quantitative (value) trade-offs are needed. These trade-offs force questions such as: "How many additional expected deaths would an increase of 20% in net economic benefits justify?" The precision required in the answer depends on the sensitivity of the decision. There is, however, no way of avoiding some quantitative trade-offs, whether the decision maker is the secretary of energy or a citizen formulating a letter to the secretary.

The two families of techniques for assessing trade-offs are *expressed preferences* and *revealed preferences*. The former asks people directly about their values. It includes such familiar procedures as attitude research and such esoteric ones as reference

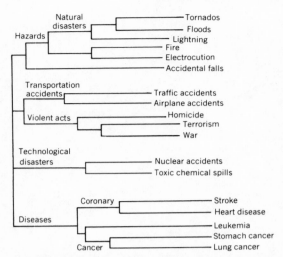

Figure 29.5. Tree representation of causes of death. (*Source:* "Affection Generalization and the Perception of Risk" by E.J. Johnson & A. Tversky, 1983, *Journal of Personality and Social Psychology, 45,* p. 22. Copyright 1983 by A. Tversky. Reprinted by permission.)

lotteries. The latter attempts to infer the preferences that prompted observed behavior. The following discussion presents these two families, contrasting their respective strengths and weaknesses.

29.4.1. Expressed Preferences

Surveys

If you want to know what people like and dislike, just ask them. The most prominent way of asking for values, and arguably the most prominent technique for studying human behavior, is survey research. In the United States alone, somewhere between $1 and $6 billion is earned annually by asking people questions on issues interesting those capable of sponsoring investigations (National Academy of Sciences, 1982).

In order to cope with the enormous diversity of questions that clients might bring up, survey researchers have evolved a highly sophisticated set of general techniques (e.g., Payne, 1952). They aim to render any question suitable for inclusion in a standard survey: one with a representative sample of respondents questioned individually in a noninteractive format, producing responses suitable for immediate data analysis. Special care is taken to avoid influencing respondents in any way, for example, by hints from the interviewer or biases in question wording.

Because of their political and economic importance, environmental issues have prompted many

surveys. Much of this work is proprietary, being sponsored by politicians plotting campaigns, by embattled corporations testing advertising messages, or by environmental organizations polling their membership. However, the open literature alone is substantial. In two separate surveys of surveys, Melber (1983) and Thomas and Baillie (1982) reported dozens of studies of attitudes toward nuclear power alone, in the United States and Great Britain, respectively.

Conscientious survey research can produce highly robust results. Public opinions on nuclear power have regularly shown roughly equal numbers of opponents and proponents, with a substantial block of "undecided." This balance seems relatively impervious not only to the details of methodology, but also to external events, responding only modestly and temporarily to events such as Three Mile Island (Thomas & Baillie, 1982). Public attitudes toward the environment as a whole are even more stable. For 10 years, most Americans have favored strong governmental measures for environmental protection—despite substantial fluctuations in attitudes toward other government interventions (Borelli, 1982; *BusinessWeek*, 1983; Harris, 1980). Considering the variety of questions used, these response patterns might be too robust, reflecting inadequate sensitivity to changes in wording and in the outside world. Because full-scale surveys are so expensive, direct comparisons of alternative wordings are relatively rare (Schuman & Presser, 1979). The consumer of survey research must, therefore, read the questions asked with a clinical eye and speculate about how respondents interpreted them.

One common interpretative ambiguity arises with popularity poll questions such as: "Do you support nuclear power?" Such questions can be straightforward when both the alternatives and the choice context are clear (e.g., Candidates X and Y in one particular election). They are less clear when the alternatives are less clear (e.g., "Who else is running besides X?") or there are alternative contexts (e.g., "I'd like Candidate X to win this election, but Y will so discredit his party if elected that it might be better in the long run to have him elected now"). With a question like "Do you favor X?", the respondent must infer the context, and the reader of the results must guess what context was inferred by most respondents. "Do you favor nuclear power?" is such a vague question. Providing a reasoned reply requires respondents to fill in missing details in order to create a complete problem definition. Specifying the relevant consequences means answering questions such as "Should I answer out of national interest or self interest? If the former, should I consider future or only present generations?" Specifying the set of options means considering the alternatives to nuclear power. Is this set meant to include conservation or solar power (after intensive federal investment)? One way to answer incompletely specified questions is to respond associatively, giving a gut-level feeling about nuclear power. Although such visceral opinions may predict some behavior, such as the trust evoked by nuclear industry statements, they should not be mistaken for reasoned ones. It would be unwise to use them to predict the results of a detailed national debate. It would be unfair to "derive" from them what opinions people should have (and to fault people for any lack of consistency). It would be dishonest to use them to justify specific claims about what the public wants.

A second way for respondents to address ambiguous questions is to flesh out the question by specifying the missing elements of the decision problem structure. In some cases, most subjects may do this similarly. For example, if the interview comes during a well-publicized national debate that frames the question in one way (should the United States go coal or nuclear?), then interpreters need only divine that consensual frame. However, if subjects complete the structure idiosyncratically, then they are effectively answering different questions, despite receiving the same wording.

These two possibilities produce different accounts of the stability in public opinion regarding nuclear power. If people are responding viscerally, then the stability means that their basic associations are unchanged, perhaps because information about the technology has come in such scattered bits over the years. If subjects do create more complete problem definitions, then the stability means consistency in both these definitions and their underlying beliefs. Conceivably, many proponents and opponents of nuclear power view its risks and benefits similarly. However, the former interpret the question as "should we get additional power via coal or nuclear?," whereas the latter interpret it as "do we need the additional power nuclear brings?"

The obvious solution to interpretative tangles is specifying the problem definition more precisely in the first place. Two potential difficulties confront this approach: (1) If the problem is complex (i.e., has many options or consequences), a full description may not be grasped by respondents on first reading; and (2) if the questioner views the problem differently than the respondent, then the answer may be confused.

Decision Analysis

These difficulties are ones that decision analysts would cite as justification for their own craft: helping

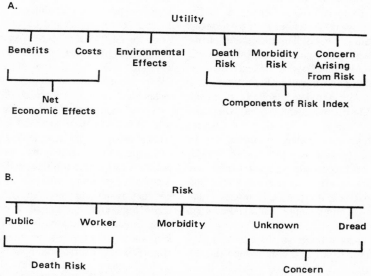

Figure 29.6. Possible dimensions of consequence in evaluating energy technologies, (a) for decision making, (b) for creating an index of risk. (*Source*: "Defining Risk" by B. Fischhoff, S. Watson, & C. Hope, 1984, *Policy Sciences, 8*, p. 129. Copyright 1984. Reprinted by permission.)

people formulate decision problems. The exercise of that craft requires extensive interaction with clients, a sort of contact that is anathema to survey research, with its emphasis on impassively stimulating subjects with questions and recording the response emitted. The leading principle of decision analysts' questioning is decomposition, reducing complex problems to more manageable parts, each of which can be contemplated separately. Most attempts to ask precise questions about value trade-offs represent special cases of these modeling methods, whether or not they are rooted in decision theory.

The theoretical basis for asking well-formulated questions about the relative importance of different consequences is found in multiattribute utility theory (MAUT). It provides ways to evaluate the elements of the consequence vectors associated with decision options. In principle, one rates the attractiveness of the different possible attribute vectors. Doing so automatically ranks any conceivable outcome, once it has been mapped into the evaluative space. Thus this strategy separates general value issues from the evaluation of specific outcomes. However, as the number of consequences or possible values becomes large (e.g., when they are continuous), evaluating all possible consequence vectors becomes arduous or impossible. In such cases, MAUT attempts to reduce the problem's size responsibly, by making simplifying assumptions regarding the structure of the consequence space. The possible assumptions have been lucidly discussed by several sources (e.g., Edwards, 1977; Fishburn, 1982; Keeney & Raiffa, 1976; Starr & Zeleny, 1977). Rather than try to recap these developments, we will illustrate some of the basic issues through an example. Specifically, we will elaborate on the question of how to evaluate the riskiness of energy sources (begun in Fig. 29.6a). If a decision problem considered risk alone (e.g., focusing research on the riskiest technologies), then this evaluation could dictate the decision. Of course, many risky decisions are not about risks alone but involve other certain costs as well as benefits. In such cases, focusing on risk isolates a subset of consequences that are relatively commensurable and separable. Analogous exercises might produce indices of nonrisk costs and benefits that could be compared with these risks.

Our example looks at the risks of six technologies designed to increase the supply or reduce the demand for electricity. The relative risks of these technologies has been the topic of lively and acrimonious debate, at least part of which reflects inadequate definitions of *risk* (e.g., Holdren, 1979; Inhaber, 1979; U.K. Department of Energy, 1979). It

has taken new importance with a U.S. Nuclear Regulatory Commission (1983) decision to set the allowable risk of nuclear power as similar to that of competing means of generating electricity (Fischhoff, 1983). Further details can be found in Fischhoff, Watson, and Hope (1984).

The first step in multiattribute evaluation is selecting relevant attributes. Figure 29.6b presents a set of five. The second step is specifying their meaning. The first two attributes will be defined in terms of the number of deaths caused per Gigawatt year (GWyr) of electricity generated or saved. Illness and injury (morbidity) might be measured in person days of incapacity per GWyr. The two concern attributes are defined in terms of the technology's location on the risk dimensions in Figure 29.4.

This definition is already controversial in several respects. It includes attributes that are not readily measured physical or physiological effects, whereas it ignores environmental and gene pool damage. Separating public from occupational deaths allows a different weight to be placed upon each (Derr, Goble, Kasperson, & Kates, 1983). The operationalization of the first two attributes ignores the age of those killed and how they die, thereby placing no premium on young or painful deaths.

The next step is to evaluate the different possible outcomes on each attribute. A convenient method is to assign 0 and 100 to the two most extreme outcomes possible and intermediate values to intermediate possibilities so as to create an interval scale. That is, equivalent scale differences (e.g., from 10 to 20 and 75 to 85) should be of equal significance. Here we let 0 deaths per GWyr be assigned 0, although a higher value might be used if some deaths were inevitable. At the other extreme, 10 deaths per GWyr seems like the worst tolerable toll from a technology, meriting a score of 100.

The obvious way of assigning intermediate values is to let 1 death equal 10 on the scale, 2 deaths equal 20, and so on, as in Figure 29.7, Curve 1. This translation means that all lives are equal, and a death is a death, whether it is the first or the fifth or the ninth. A competing argument (Curve 3) holds that the first life lost is an enormous watershed, making the technology lethal and the society that accepts it callous. Subsequent deaths have increasingly little effect, either on society's functioning or on its moral stature. The converse argument (Curve 2) holds that society must create some risks. Its institutions can accommodate some losses; however, it cannot absorb very large accidents. An energy technology that is expected to kill 10 people per GWyr on the average probably does that by, say, killing 1000 once in

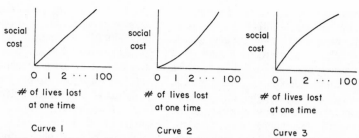

Figure 29.7. The impact of catastrophic events. Subjects were asked to rate their agreement with the principles embodied in each of the preceding three proposals. (*Source:* "Modeling the Societal Impact of Fatal Accidents" by P. Slovic, S. Lichtenstein, & B. Fischhoff. Copyright 1984, The Institute of Management Sciences, *Management Science*, Vol. 30, No. 4, April 1984, pp. 464–474, The Institute of Management Sciences, 290 Westminister Street, Providence, RI 02903.)

every 100 GWyr—an intolerable possibility. The choice of a function is an ethical one, which can be guided by facts regarding the consequences of various accidents. We will use the linear function of Curve 1. Similar logic leads to a linear function on Attribute 3 with 0 and 100 representing 0 and 60,000 person-days of incapacity per GWyr. As mentioned, scores on the two concern attributes followed the factor scores of Figure 29.4.

The next step is weighting the attributes, another value question with several incompatible answers. Table 29.1 shows four possible sets of importance weights, reflecting different moral philosophies. Each indicates how much of an increase on one attribute would just compensate for a given decrease on another. For example, if one were weighted .30 and another .15, then an increase from 30 to 50 on the former would be "canceled" by a decrease from 75 to 35.

The final step is estimating the magnitude of the consequences on each attribute. Having done so, the overall value of an option is the weighted sum of its consequence scores. For example, the risk from coal using Set A's weights might be .33(80) + .33(30) + .33(20) = 42.9. Standardizing the scores to range from 0 to 100 and the weights to sum to 1.0 makes it possible to compare scores across technologies and across weighting schemes. Using one set of consequence estimates, Fischhoff and colleagues (1984) found great differences in the relative riskiness of these technologies depending on the definition used. The fixed set of consequence estimates meant that these differences in riskiness reflected differences in values, not facts.

The purpose of this example is to show the steps involved in value assessment, rather than to provide definitive evaluations. Fuller details on its assumptions appear in Fischhoff and colleagues (1984). One of these assumptions is *pairwise preference indepen-*

dence of the attributes, meaning that trade-offs between two attributes do not depend on the levels of the other attributes; a second assumption is that the attributes are *compensatory,* meaning that being better in one respect can compensate (at least somewhat) for being inferior in another.

Assessing Trade-Offs

Three methods for deriving trade-offs were implied in the preceding discussion. One is *reasoning from principles:* Respondents state moral or ethical principles that the weights should embody. For example, public

Table 29.1. Four Possible Sets of Weights for Five Risk Attributes[a]

Attributes	A	B	C	D
1. Public deaths	0.33	0.40	0.20	0.08
2. Occupational deaths	0.33	0.20	0.05	0.04
3. Morbidity	0.33	0.20	0.05	0.40
4. Unknown risk	0	0.10	0.30	0.24
5. Dread risk	0	0.10	0.40	0.24
Sum of weights	1	1	1	1

Source: Fischhoff, Watson, and Hope, 1984.

[a]The first set rejects anything but readily measured physiological effects; treats a death as a death, whether it befalls a worker or a member of the public; views a life as equal to 6000 person-days of incapacity. Set B reflects a belief that concern is a legitimate consequence, that public deaths should be twice as important as worker deaths (perhaps because of the elements of choice and compensation in the worker's risk), and that a worker death should (still) be treated as equivalent to the loss of 6000 person-days. Set C increases the importance ratio for public to occupational deaths and assigns major significance to concern. The specific weights imply a willingness to trade off 10 public deaths per GWyr to move from a technology causing extreme dread to one that is about average, perhaps feeling that the toll from concern-generated stress is large or that even minor accidents in dreaded technologies can cause very costly social and economic disruptions. The D weights represent paramount concern with the suffering of the living, whether through injury or anxiety, rather than with the number of deaths.

and worker deaths have equal value, and concern is subordinate to physical losses. Although such principles can constrain weights, they usually cannot specify them entirely. Greater precision is provided by the second method: *direct estimation,* in the form of numbers summing to 1.0. This procedure has the advantage of asking for and getting exactly what the modeler needs and will use as an expression of the respondents' values. If respondents are uncomfortable with such numbers, then obvious variants include physically distributing 100 chips or eliciting unconstrained numbers over the categories, which the analyst will normalize. Care is needed to make the response mode compatible with the respondents' normal way of thinking about the problem and to avoid response biases such as leveling the assignments to different categories (Poulton, 1979, 1982).

The third approach requires *pairwise comparisons* of the form "Attribute A is X times more important than Attribute B." These numerical assessments could be preceded by qualitative judgments such as: Which is more important? Is that a clear preference? Estimates may be improved by consistency checks, first on the qualitative preferences, then on the numerical ratios. Such checks cannot be made with either the (more intensive) direct estimation method or the (less intensive) principles method. Inconsistencies may reflect problems with the underlying values or problems with expressing them in the required response mode. In the former case, discussion may resolve the inconsistencies. In the latter case, either the respondent should be trained in the response mode, or the mode should be changed to fit the respondent (perhaps sacrificing some formal purity in the process).

All three procedures compare the attributes with one another, which can lead to rather esoteric comparisons (e.g., days lost vs. concern due to uncertainty). One possible compromise is to compare each separately with a *common standard* such as money.[3] The following section considers using marketplace prices to evaluate consequences. Here we consider asking people to assign monetary values directly. Most economists avoid such questioning, assuming that respondents will misrepresent their values if there is any strategic advantage to doing so. Nonetheless, some economists have pioneered the use of bidding techniques to evaluate nonmarketable consequences such as changes in air clarity or scenery (Brookshire, Ives, & Schulze, 1976; Schulze, D'Arge, & Brookshire, 1981). In a typical exercise, respondents are asked if they would pay $1, $2...in additional park entrance fees to avoid having an ugly

power plant on the opposite shore of their favorite lakeside campground. The offers increase in dollar units until respondents say "no" and then decrease in $0.25 units until they say "yes." The values are constrained by respondents' candor, their ability to pay, and their willingness to pay personally to prevent degradation of a resource belonging to all. Strategic behavior seems relatively unimportant. However, responses have proven sensitive to supposedly irrelevant aspects of the elicitation procedure such as the payment vehicle (e.g., entrance fees vs. taxes) and the numbers offered (Gregory, in press).

A controversial topic in many environmental decisions is evaluating potential losses of human life relative to other consequences. Although people dislike the idea of comparing life with mundane consequences, some values are implicit in any life-threatening decision. The weights in the example assigned relative values directly. Other procedures are also possible. Although no one has suggested that people bid for others' lives, Howard (1978) has proposed having people bid to save their own lives. According to this argument, although people's lives are invaluable to them, they will take risks for money and, indeed, often do so. The price that individuals accept as compensation for a fractional increase in the risk of dying can then be extrapolated over a whole population.

29.4.2. Revealed Preferences

The byword of revealed preference approaches to measuring values is that actions speak louder than words: If you want to know what something is worth to people, see what they will pay for it. Specifically, look for an actual decision requiring a trade-off between two (or more) consequences and work backward to deduce how that trade-off was made. The strength of these approaches is looking at real-life behavior, which should encourage serious, candid responses. Their weakness is the tenuousness of the assumptions needed to infer values from behavior. These include assumptions about both the psychology of the decision makers and the sociology of the world. The key psychological assumption of most methods is that people are highly sophisticated decision makers. The sociological assumptions vary with method, as will be seen in the following three examples.

Direct Market Values
The basic tenet of mainstream Western economics is that freely traded goods reveal their true value in marketplace prices. Thus if you want to know what

canned peas are worth to U.S. consumers, look at the prices on the shelves of representative supermarkets (or, better, at their checkout counters). Such inferences require assumptions about the market and the actors within it. The former must be free of any restraint of trade either deliberate (e.g., collusion, monopoly) or inadvertent (e.g., firms independently deciding to sell very similar goods). The latter must know all pertinent properties of all available options, understand their own best interests, and unerringly select the optimal alternative. Threats to pricing peas include (1) a gentleperson's agreement among pea manufacturers or distributors to keep prices up or to use peas as a loss leader, (2) consumer ignorance regarding the nutritional values of competing products, (3) an advertising-induced artificial desire for peas, and (4) failing to decide, in favor of buying what one has always bought (or what is most conveniently displayed). Whether (or how often or how extremely) these violations of perfect market assumptions occur is an empirical question. When environmental consequences are not traded, economists may search for surrogate values. For example, the value of a viewpoint may be sought in people's expenditures for using and maintaining it (e.g., travel, lodging costs, entrance fees, taxes).

All of these procedures are threatened by imperfections in the market. For example, insurance premiums may not reflect the value of risk protection because consumers have incomplete information, because the insurance policies have confused them, because companies have coordinated their prices, or because premiums pay for company profits and inefficiency, as well as for protection.

Inferred Trade-offs

Even when they are traded freely, environmental amenities often have many effects, making it difficult to infer the value of any one consequence. For example, people seldom just accept money in return for an increased chance to die, but they might accept money and risk as part of a job promising fulfillment, advancement, and the like. For the market to provide insight, the role of specific consequences must be discerned.

The usual technique for revealing these embedded preferences is correlational analyses of decisions in which the consequence of interest may have played a consistent role. For the value of life risks, most analyses have focused on employment decisions (Graham, Shakow, & Cyr, 1983; Thaler & Rosen, 1976; Viscusi, 1983). Under the assumption that workers have knowingly and voluntarily accepted

their jobs, their pay can be reviewed to see how much more is paid for riskier jobs. In multiple regression terms, pay is the dependent variable, and risk is one predictor whose regression coefficient reflects how risk changes with pay. The other predictors would be other job characteristics that might affect pay (required experience, comfort, predominant sex of employees).

Unfortunately for the procedure, no theory guides the choice of variables. Without constraints, it may be impossible to disprove the hypothesis that workers are compensated for risks. Some set of predictors may always be found that gives risk's regression coefficient the correct sign (showing that pay increases with risk). Furthermore, with correlated predictors, the coefficient of each depends on the others. Therefore, the absolute magnitude of the risk coefficient or even its sign may be unreliable.[4]

Nonmarket Goods

In the absence of perfect markets, economists would hesitate to infer anything about values from observed decisions. For example, electricity prices and risks are determined by oligopolistic companies and government regulations. Rather than ignore these decisions, some investigators have generalized revealed preference analysis, by assuming that society's institutions take up where the market leaves off and manage to bring all technologies to an acceptable form.

The most prominent of these analyses is shown in Figure 29.8 (from Starr, 1969, 1972). It is described as showing that society has worked so as to make risk levels roughly proportional to the third power of the benefits; however, this relationship is achieved separately for voluntary and involuntary risks, with the latter being 1000 times safer at any given level of benefit. According to Starr, people want these same values to guide future decisions, in the sense that a technology is acceptable if it produces less risk than do other technologies producing comparable benefits. His claim is controversial in many respects. It assumes that society's mechanisms have functioned well (which seems unlikely given the desire for stricter environmental protection). It assumes that society's tastes are unchanging. It assumes constancy in the opportunities to achieve safety at a price. It also makes debatable technical assumptions about the measurement of risks and benefits (Otway & Cohen, 1975).

Figure 29.8 shows one scientist's perception of risks and benefits. Fischhoff, Slovic, Lichtenstein, Read, and Combs (1978) solicited laypeople's risk

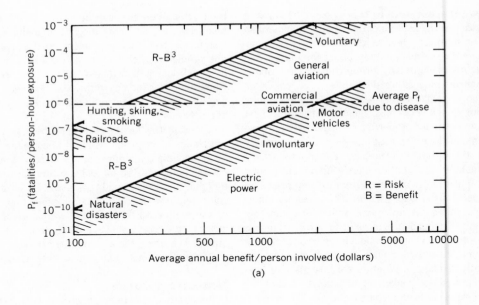

(a)

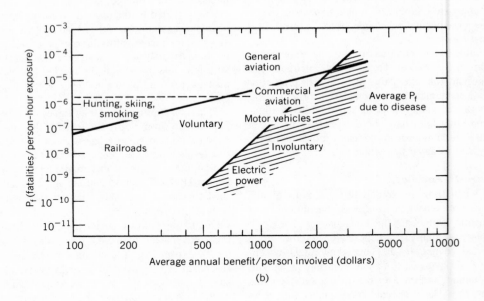

(b)

Figure 29.8. Relationship between statistically measured risk of death and economic benefit (1) as studied by Starr (1969, 1972) and (2) as reanalyzed by Otway and Cohen (1975). In both figures, risk is measured by fatalities per person per hour of exposure. Benefit reflects either the average amount of money spent on an activity by an individual participant or the average contribution an activity makes to a participant's annual income. In (a) the best-fitting lines were drawn by eye with error bands to indicate their approximate nature. In (b) regression procedures were used after deleting natural disasters from the category of involuntary risks. (*Sources*: Reprinted from (a) "Perspective on Benefit-Risk Decision Making," 1972, with permission of the National Academy of Sciences, Washington DC; (b) "Revealed Preferences: Comments on the Starr Benefit-Risk Relationships" by H. Otway and J. Cohen, 1975, International Institute of Applied Systems Analysis. Reprinted by permission.)

and benefit judgments for 30 technologies and found a modest *negative* correlation ($r = -.20$). Thus these subjects did not perceive that society had managed to get more benefit from riskier technologies. When asked what the risk levels should be, they wanted less risk in 40% of the cases, accepted current risks in 50%, and would tolerate more risk in 10%. Overall, their judgments of acceptable risk were positively related to their benefit estimates ($r = +.50$). Thus they agreed with Starr that society should function so as to allow more risk from more beneficial technologies; however, they doubted that it had done so already.

Subjects were willing to tolerate more risks with voluntary hazards than with equally beneficial involuntary ones, again confirming a Starr speculation in the desired world but not the real one. However, they also endorsed such double standards with several other qualitative aspects of risk, such as the perceived immediacy and controllability of its effects. Although this is to be expected, given the intercorrelations between these aspects (Figure 29.4), it leaves the effective element unclear. The same double standard would represent a different social policy if justified on the grounds of voluntariness, immediacy, controllability, ignorance, or equity.

29.4.3. Do People Have Values to Express?

The preceding discussion of methods presented a litany of possible problems in applying each technique and interpreting its results. Some reflect limits of the measurement techniques. But others reflect problems with the values that the methods intend to capture.

Determining the relative desirability of different consequences would seem to be the last redoubt of unaided intuition. Who knows better than an individual what he or she prefers? With simple, familiar events that people have experienced directly, it may be reasonable to assume that they have well-articulated opinions. But that may not be the case with environmental decisions involving such novel consequences as those following from CO_2-induced climatic change, nuclear meltdowns, or genetic engineering. In such situations, values may be incoherent, not sufficiently thought out. We may be unfamiliar with the terms used in such debates (e.g., social discount rates, minuscule probabilities, megadeaths). We may have contradictory values (e.g., a strong aversion to catastrophic losses of life but an awareness that we are no more moved by a plane crash with 500 fatalities than by one with 300). We may occupy different roles in life (parents, workers, children) that produce clear-cut but inconsistent values. We may vacillate between incompatible but strongly held positions (e.g., freedom of speech is inviolate, but it should be denied to authoritarian movements). We may not even know how to begin thinking about some issues (e.g., the appropriate trade-off between the benefits of dyeing one's hair and a minute risk of cancer 20 years from now). Our view may change so much over time (say, as we near the hour of decision or of experiencing the consequence) that we are disoriented as to what we really believe. We may not know, on a gut level, what it means to suffer the pain of cancer or to bear the responsibility for storing wastes for many generations.

When people do not know what they want, the way a question is posed may significantly affect the values expressed, or apparently expressed, in the responses it elicits. As a result, scientists, politicians, merchants, and the media can represent issues in such ways as to induce random error (by confusing respondents), systematic errors (by hinting at the "correct" response), or unduly extreme judgments (by suggesting clarity and coherence of opinion that are not warranted). In such cases, the method shapes the message. If elicited values are used to guide policy, they may lead to decisions not in the decision maker's best interests, to action when caution is desirable (or the opposite), or to obfuscation of poorly formulated views that need careful development and clarification.

The study of lability has focused on people's sensitivity to manipulations that models of rational decision making hold to be irrelevant. Three examples might give the flavor of the research: (1) people judge the risks of technologies to be more acceptable after assessing their risks than after assessing their benefits (see Fischhoff, Slovic, Lichtenstein, Read, & Combs, 1978; von Winterfeldt et al., 1981); (2) the relative attractiveness of gambles depends on whether people are asked how attractive each is or how much they would pay to play it (Slovic & Lichtenstein, 1983); and (3) insurance becomes much less attractive when the premium is described as a sure loss (Fischhoff, Slovic, & Lichtenstein, 1980). Fuller accounts may be found in Birch and Schmid (1980), Fischhoff and colleagues (1980), Hershey, Kunreuther, and Schoemaker (1982), Hogarth (1982), Kahneman and Tversky (1979), and Tversky and Kahneman (1981).

Judgments are sensitive to elicitation procedures because formulating a response always involves an inferential process. When neither habit nor tradition dictates our position on an issue, we must decide which of our basic values to invoke, how to apply them, and what weight to give to each. In the absence of an articulated response, it is natural to seek hints from the questioner for what to say. Table 29.2 summarizes the elicitor's opportunities. Looking at the first as an example, by raising a question, the elicitor may cast doubt on values that were previously unquestioned (e.g., the sanctity of marriage, the environment, private control of the means of production).

Wherever incoherence is possible, the elicitor must actively look for such trouble. That pursuit of discrepancies may not be satisfied by even such laudable practices as asking related questions in the same response mode and testing the answers for transitivity. Such consistency may just reflect respondents' success in devising a stylized strategy for coping with the task. When two seemingly equivalent response modes do evoke inconsistent responses, then four interpretations are possible, with different implications for describing and aiding decisions:

1. Only one of the responses is valid. The other response could be invalidated on the basis of any design detail that could justify a charge of methodological malpractice (Payne, 1952).

2. Both responses are valid because the questions are really different, despite superficial similarities. In this view, respondents can not only answer all questions but perceive all nuances of formulation. In order to interpret these responses, the investigator must be equally sensitive.

3. The differences are real but not meaningful. Rather, both response modes are hard to use and produce noisy responses. Solutions include averaging the responses, recalibrating the responses, or devising a better method.

4. The respondent has no values on the overall topic. The different questions have elicited real but incomplete responses. Here the elicitor must first evoke the full set of alternative perspectives and then help respondents integrate them. Doing so may require reactive questions (suggesting different possible perspectives), interactive interviewers (helping respondents to think through the issues), and protracted elicitation (allowing respondents time to ruminate).

The fact that we (the experimenters) have good questions is no guarantee that they (the respondents) have good answers. If we hope to study values on complex, novel issues, then we may have to help respondents worry about the questions that concern us. Uncertainty about desires may complicate decision making much more than does uncertainty about possibilities (March, 1978).

29.5. BELIEF ASSESSMENT

Describing or aiding decision making requires an understanding of what people believe, what facts they need, and what facts are available. As a result, investigators must consider not only psychology but also the information environment within which environmental decisions take place. It establishes what people need to know, what they can know, and what opportunities they have to develop and test their cognitive skills. Making such assessments requires investigators to have some substantive expertise on the pertinent scientific issues, although, paradoxically, they can learn too much. Mastering the dominant scientific perspective on a problem may render one incapable of empathizing with laypeople or looking critically at the experts.

Table 29.2. Ways an Elicitor May Affect a Respondent's Judgments of Value

Defining the issue	Changing the respondent's perspective
Is there a problem?	Altering the salience of perspectives
What options and consequences are relevant?	Altering the importance of perspectives
How should options and consequences be labeled.	Choosing the time of inquiry
How should values be measured?	Changing confidence in expressed values
Should the problem be decomposed?	Changing the apparent degree of coherence
	Changing the respondent
	Disrupting existing perspectives
	Creating perspectives
	Deepening perspectives

Source: B. Fischhoff, P. Slovic, and S. Lichtenstein, 1980.

29.5.1. The Informational Environment

What Needs to Be Known

Laypeople (including politicians) cannot master all scientific knowledge on all topics that interest them. Nor need they. They only need to know enough to distinguish among the available options. Establishing the needed degree of precision requires an explicit decision-making model. In the seat belt example, if one's decision would be the same for any plausible estimate of the accident rate, then the decision is insensitive to that variable, and current information is adequate. The precision required depends on the specific problem. For example, individual drivers' decisions may be much less sensitive than those of safety officials (for whom each shift of $.000X$ in accident probability translates into Y additional deaths nationwide). This problem specificity means that it is hard to determine how much general knowledge people should have. The frequency of being caught ill-prepared is one practical indicator, however, not an infallible guide. Given the costs of acquiring information, it is inefficient to try to know everything. The appropriate aspiration is getting the best return on one's investment in learning. *Value-of-information analysis* (Raiffa, 1968) shows how to weigh the cost of possible information items, the expected contribution of each to uncertainty reduction, and the impact of that reduction on the expected values of pending decisions.

What Constitute Fair Tests of People's Knowledge?

At first blush, assessing the public's risk perceptions seems straightforward. Just ask questions like: What is the probability of a reactor core meltdown? How many people die annually from asbestos-related diseases? How does wearing a seat belt affect your probability of living through the year? Differences between these responses and the best available technical estimates show the respondent's ignorance.

Methodologically, this strategy is threatened by people's problems with quantitative estimation, as reflected in the sensitivity of their responses to formally irrelevant aspects of question formulation (discussed later). Substantively, this strategy is threatened by the frequent irrelevance of quantitative estimates to decision making. Some decisions only require an ordering of events by likelihood or systems by riskiness. For others, only the change in risk level matters. When choosing the configuration of a technology or coping with an incident (e.g., Three

Mile Island), statistics are less important than a qualitative understanding of how the system works (e.g., Gricar & Baratta, 1983). In still other cases, knowing about the technology is less important than understanding the social institutions managing it.

What Can Laypeople Know?

When pertinent discrepancies emerge between lay and expert views, they may be attributed to failure to learn or inability to learn. The former seems like the more useful default assumption. Not only is it respectful but it encourages a creative search for correctable sources of ignorance (and ways to enhance people's abilities to make environmental decisions).

One generic barrier to lay understanding is inaccessibility of expert knowledge. The experts may not disseminate their knowledge. Or their dissemination may be biased to create a particular impression. Or its message may be garbled by scientifically untutored journalists.

A second generic barrier is that the process of science may give misleading cues about its substance. For example, the attention paid to a topic might be taken as indicating its importance. Yet researchers often go where the contracts, limelight, blue-ribbon panel, or juicy controversies are (e.g., the saccharin debate). When scientists argue in public, the listeners might think that one expert is as good as any other or that "my guess is as good as theirs." Laypeople may be baffled by the veil of qualifications that responsible scientists often cast over their work. Two-fisted debators (eager to make definitive statements) may prove more persuasive than two-handed scientists (saying "on the one hand X, but on the other hand Y," in an effort to achieve balance).

In each of these cases, the misunderstanding is excusable, in the sense that it need not reflect poorly on the intelligence of the public or its ability to govern itself. Such a public needs to be helped, not replaced. There is nothing in this analysis, however, to justify replacing or supplementing the experts' view with lay perceptions.

For laypeople to disagree reasonably with experts, they need some independent source of knowledge. One possible source is their overview on scientific debates. Laypeople may see the full range of expert opinions and hesitations, immune to the temptations or pressures felt by the actual debators. Laypeople may also be free of the unquestioned assumptions that every discipline adopts in order to go about its business. They may also see how many confident scientific beliefs have eventually been rejected (Frankel, 1974). Finally, laypeople's experiences sometimes reveal information that has escaped the experts (Brokensha et al., 1980). To take three examples.

1. The Berger Inquiry discovered that natives of the Far North knew things about ice-pack movement and sea-bed scouring that were unknown to the planners of a proposed MacKenzie Valley Pipeline (Gamble, 1978).

2. The designers of technical systems often miss problems that their operators know well (Seminara & Parsons, 1982; Sheridan, 1980).

3. Toxicologists may avoid hard-to-measure behavioral effects (e.g., dizzyness, tension) apparent to those experiencing them. In such cases, lay risk perceptions should influence the experts' risk estimates.

What Can Experts Know?

Although real and often overlooked, cases in which laypeople know more than the ranking technical experts are probably rare. However, accepting that experts know the most does not mean that they know all. There is an essential role of judgment in experts' production of knowledge that bounds what laypeople or decision makers can know.

Fortunately, the most fearsome events in nature are infrequent. By design, hazards of human origin are constrained to have a low probability of leading to disaster. For decision-making purposes, however, it is necessary to know just how low that low probability is. Unfortunately, quantitative assessment of very small probabilities is often very difficult (Fairley, 1977; Sampson & Smith, 1982).

At times, a historical record provides frequency estimates such as the U.S. Geological Survey's 75 years of data regarding earthquake probability or Iceland's millennium of ice-pack movement observations showing the past probability of extremely cold years (Ingram, Underhill, & Wigley, 1978). The absence of a full-scale meltdown in 500 to 1000 reactor years of nuclear power plant operation sets some bounds on the probability of future meltdowns (Weinberg, 1979). However large these historical records, extrapolation from them requires judgment. Artificial reservoirs may promote earthquakes in some rock formations, rendering historical earthquake data suspect. Increased atmospheric carbon dioxide concentrations may amplify or moderate yearly temperature fluctuations. Changes in design, staffing, and regulation may render the next 1000 reactor years appreciably different from their predecessors. Indeed, any attempt to learn from experience renders

that experience less relevant for predicting future performance.

Where historical records are unavailable or irrelevant, one must rely on conjecture. The more sophisticated conjectures are based on models such as fault trees (U.S. Nuclear Regulatory Commission, 1981), which provide a logical structuring of events leading to an accident. If sufficiently detailed, a fault tree will reach a level of specificity for which one may have direct experience (e.g., the operation of individual valves). The probability of system failure is determined by combining the probabilities of the necessary component failures (Green & Bourne, 1972). Figure 29.2 was a very simple model. Figure 29.9 adds the temporal dimension, showing the sequences of events leading to the rupture of a pressure tank.

The first step in such analyses is enumerating all major pathways to disaster. As discussed earlier, people have difficulty ensuring completeness or assessing incompleteness. Table 29.3 suggests some problems that threaten formal risk analyses.

The second step is estimating the model's parameters (e.g., the probability of installing the wrong tank), using statistics where available and judgment where not. As mentioned, judgment is still needed to extrapolate historical data to particular applications (considering maintenance procedures, employee training, etc.). Finally, one must estimate the definitiveness of the analysis, which means, in part, reflecting on the quality of one's own judgment.

Understanding the cognitive processes involved in experts' judgments is a task with both applied and basic implications (Fischhoff, in press). It can reveal how much credence to afford expert analyses as well as whether the training of experts changes *how* they think (in addition to changing what they know).

29.5.2. Assessing Facts

Given the variety of risk information, there is unlikely to be any general answer to the question "how well do people understand risks?" As a result, investigators have sought general patterns of information processing, which may or may not produce accurate perceptions. The following four case studies show some of the methods for studying these processes.

Estimating Risk Frequency

In order to acquit themselves in "straightforward" tests of their risk perceptions, people must not only have the required knowledge but also be able to express it in the terms of the summary statistics required by the investigator.

Table 29.3. Some Problems in Structuring Risk Assessments

Failure to consider the ways in which human errors can affect technological systems.
  Example: Owing to inadequate training and control room design, operators at Three Mile Island repeatedly misdiagnosed the problems of the reactor and took inappropriate actions (Sheridan, 1980; U. S. Government, 1979).

Overconfidence in curent scientific knowledge.
  Example: DDT came into widespread and uncontrolled use before scientists had even considered the possibility of the side effects that today make it look like a mixed blessing (Dunlap, 1978).

Failure to appreciate how technological systems function as a whole.
  Example: The DC-10 failed in several early flights because its designers had not realized that decompression of the cargo compartment would destroy vital control systems (Hohenemser, 1975).

Slowness in detecting chronic, cumulative effects.
  Example: Although accidents to coal miners have long been recognized as one cost of operating fossil-fueled plants, the effects of acid rains on ecosystems were slow to be discovered (Rosencranz & Wetstone, 1980).

Failure to anticipate human response to safety measures.
  Example: The partial protection afforded by dams and levees gives people a false sense of security and promotes development of the floodplain. Thus although floods are rarer, damage per flood is so much greater that the average yearly loss in dollars is larger than before the dams were built (Burton, Kates, & White, 1978).

Failure to anticipate common-mode failures, which simultaneously afflict systems that are designed to be independent.
  Example: Because electrical cables controlling the multiple safety systems of the reactor at Browns Ferry, Alabama, were not spatially separated, all five emergency core-cooling systems were damaged by a single fire (Jennergren & Keeney, in press; U.S. Government, 1975).

Source: B. Fischhoff, S. Lichtenstein, P. Slovic, B. Derby, & R. Keeney, 1981.

One way to prevent awkward response modes from producing a distorted picture of beliefs is to treat as meaningful only those patterns that emerge with several response modes. For example Lichtenstein, Slovic, Fischhoff, Layman, and Combs (1978) had people use several methods to estimate the frequency of 41 causes of death. One had subjects choose the more frequent cause of death in each of 106 randomly created pairs and then estimate how many times more deaths it caused. The consistency of choices was analyzed by looking at the transitivity of "triads" involving all pairs of three items (e.g., A and B, B and C, C and A). The consistency of quantitative estimates was analyzed by looking at the ratios of triads (e.g., did $A/B \times B/C = A/C$?). In both respects, considerable consistency was found, suggesting that respondents had fairly coherent subjective fatality scales. The second method had subjects directly estimate absolute annual fatality rates. Pretests revealed enormous variability in these estimates, partially due to differing beliefs about the overall U.S. population and its death rate. In order to anchor their responses, subjects in two different groups received the number of deaths from either electrocution (1000 per year) or motor vehicle accidents (50,000 per year). Figure 29.10 shows responses from the electrocution group. The second group's ordering was similar, as was the ordering inferred from the paired comparison methods. Thus

multiple methods showed a robust ordinal scale of subjective frequencies.

The robustness of this ordering allows analysis of individual causes within it. The subjective ordering of some causes of death differed consistently from their statistical ordering. The overestimated causes of death proved to be particularly vivid ones—a hypothesis that was borne out by a series of supplementary studies showing that that ordering was related both to subjects' personal experience with the different events and to the attention devoted to them by the news media (Combs & Slovic, 1979). This pattern can be attributed to reliance on the "availability heuristic" (Tversky & Kahneman, 1973), according to which one judges an event's likelihood by the ease with which examples of it come to mind. Although useful, this rule will bias responses when experience itself is biased. These subjects may have tracked their own informational environment very well but failed to see how it was unrepresentative. These bias-inducing processes seemed so natural that subjects were unable to overcome them even when told about availability.

These quantitative estimates proved problematic in other ways as well. Subjects receiving the higher anchor (50,000) gave estimates that were higher by a factor of 2 to 5 than those from subjects receiving the lower anchor (1000). A psychophysical explanation of this effect is that the magnitude of the presented

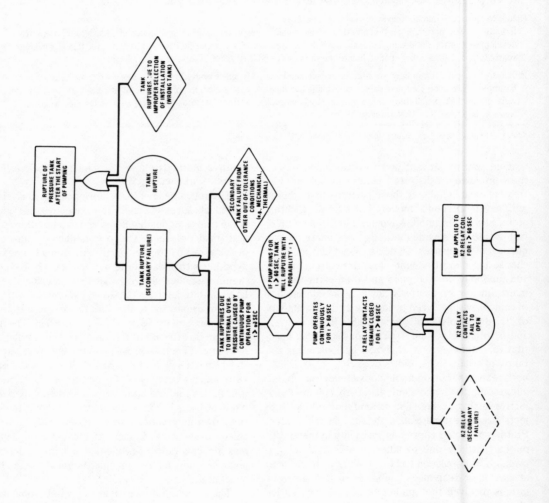

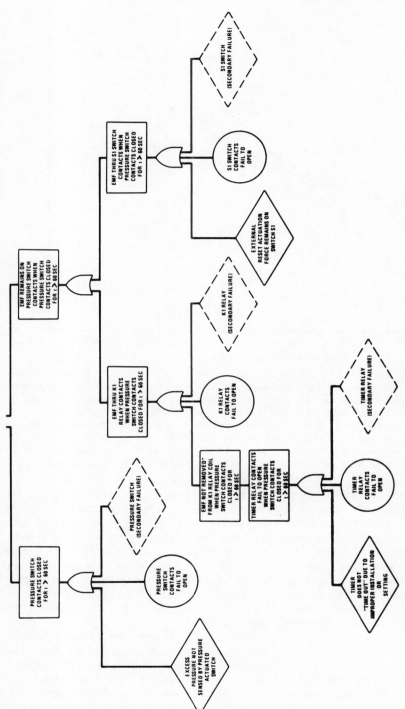

Figure 29.9. Fault tree for the rupture of the pressure tank in a nuclear power plant at the start of pumping. The curved arrowhead is an OR-gate joining events, any one of which could allow the sequence to continue. The symbol resembling an arched doorway is an AND-gate joining necessary events. (*Source:* U.S. Nuclear Regulatory Commission, 1981.)

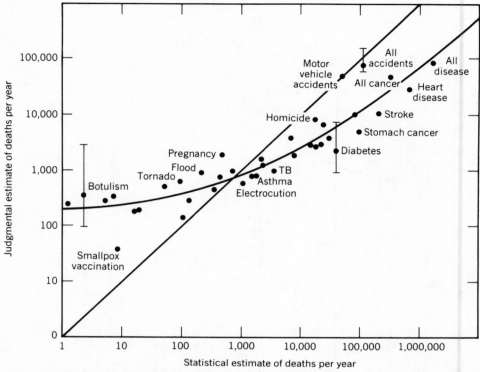

Figure 29.10. Relationship between judged frequency and the actual number of deaths per year for 41 causes of death. Respondents were told that about 50,000 people per year die from motor vehicle accidents. If judged and actual frequencies were equal, the data would fall on the straight line. The points and the curve fitted to them represent the averaged responses of a large number of laypeople. Although people were approximately accurate, their judgments showed some systematic distortions. To give an idea of the degree of agreement among subjects, vertical bars are drawn to depict the 25th and 75th percentile of individual judgments for botulism, diabetes, and all accidents. Fifty percent of all judgments fall between these limits. The ranges of responses for the other 37 causes of death were similar. (*Source*: "Rating the Risks" by P. Slovic, B. Fischhoff, & S. Lichtenstein, 1979, *Environment, 21*, p. 15. Copyright 1979. Reprinted by permission.)

number drew subjects' responses toward it (Poulton, 1982; Svenson & Åkesson, 1966, 1967; Tversky & Kahneman, 1974). Anchoring may also account for the flatness of the best-fit curve in Figure 29.10 (relative to the statistical estimates). Subjects' estimates fell too close to their own mean response and to the one estimate given to them. Although flattening could have followed from averaging estimates, it was found in the responses of individual subjects here and in other risk perception studies (Stallen & Tomas, 1981; von Winterfeldt et al., 1981).

Parameter Estimates

Death frequency is but one of the parameters appearing in environmental decisions. Where such an elaborate multimethod procedure is impractical, a single "best" procedure is needed. When there is a definitive evaluative standard, any procedure producing consistent estimates is adequate, insofar as a correc-

tion factor can be applied for any systematic bias. For example, Kidd (1970) found that standard methods for eliciting chief engineers' estimates of the time needed to return damaged power stations to services were too small by a factor of 2. The U.K. Central Electricity Generating Board could adjust all estimates to create a more realistic appraisal of power availability (assuming that the engineers did not discover the scheme and start to second-guess headquarters).

Often, though, no evaluative standard is available. For example, the criterion event may be distant (e.g., for estimates of the cancer rate 30 years hence), under study (e.g., the cause of disease X), or unobservable (e.g., subconscious thoughts). If no surrogate criterion can be found, then the judgment procedure itself must be examined. One of the most robust results of experimental psychology is that unless respondents are highly familiar with the response mode and stimuli used, then their judgments will be sensitive to the precise way in which the elicitation is conducted. Different judgments may be attached to the same physical stimulus (e.g., how loud is this tone?) as a function of whether it follows increasingly intense or weak alternatives, whether the alternative set is homogeneous or diverse, and whether the respondent makes one or many judgments. Even with the same presentation, different judgments might be obtained with numerical and comparative (ordinal) response modes, with instructions stressing speed or accuracy, with a bounded or an unbounded response set, and with verbal or numerical response labels (Fischhoff et al., 1980, and references within). The impact of anchors on frequency estimates is just one such effect.

Perhaps the most detailed documentation of such biases is in Poulton's (1968, 1977, 1979) secondary analyses of psychophysical experiments. In an initial statement (1968), he identified six laws governing the effects of elicitation procedure on the judgmental value assigned to a given physical stimulus. Poulton (1982) offers a flow chart (Figure 29.11) predicting the effects associated with procedure changes. Thus estimates obtained with one (possibly inferior) procedure can be adjusted to what would have been obtained with another.

These comparisons do not necessarily identify the procedure with the greatest fidelity to people's true beliefs. For example, Table 29.4 shows lay judgments of lethality elicited with four response modes. However the question was asked, the same underly-

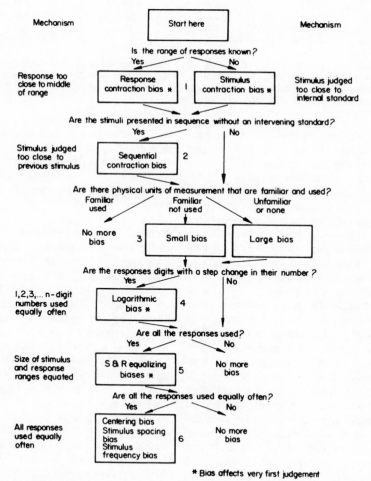

Figure 29.11. Flow chart for evaluation of experimental results where human judgments are used. (This figure is taken from a paper by E.C. Poulton and appeared in *Applied Ergonomics*, vol. 13, p. 33, published by Butterworth Scientific Limited, Surrey, United Kingdom. Copyright 1982 by Butterworth Scientific Limited. Reprinted by permission.)

Table 29.4. Lethality Judgments with Different Response Modes: Geometric Means[a]

Condition	Death Rate per 100,000 Afflicted				
	Estimate Lethality Rate	Estimate Number Died	Estimate Survival Rate	Estimate Number Survived	Actual Lethality Rate
Influenza	393	6	26	511	1
Mumps	44	114	19	4	12
Asthma	155	12	14	599	33
Venereal disease	91	63	8	111	50
High blood pressure	535	89	17	538	76
Bronchitis	162	19	43	2,111	85
Pregnancy	67	24	13	787	250
Diabetes	487	101	52	5,666	800
Tuberculosis	852	1,783	188	8,520	1,535
Automobile accidents	6,195	3,272	31	6,813	2,500
Strokes	11,011	4,648	181	24,758	11,765
Heart attacks	13,011	3,666	131	27,477	16,250
Cancer	10,889	10,475	160	21,749	37,500

Source: Fischhoff & MacGregor, 1983.

[a]The four experimental groups were given the following instructions: (1) Estimate lethality rate: For each 100,000 people afflicted, how many die? (2) Estimate number died: X people were afflicted; how many died? (3) Estimate survival rate: For each person who died, how many were afflicted but survived? (4) Estimate number survived: Y people died; how many were afflicted but did not die? Responses to questions (2), (3), and (4) were converted to deaths per 100,000 to facilitate comparisons.

ing subjective ordering emerged; yet there were large differences in the absolute estimates, ranging up to two orders of magnitude in some cases.

Which method best captures subjects' true beliefs? The survival rate estimates seem to be outliers, but who is to say that people do not intuitively underestimate lethality (as survival rate estimates suggest)? One supplementary technique for assessing the compatibility of response mode with subjects' mental representation of this information is asking them to judge which response mode was most natural. Here the two modes focusing on death were clear favorites. A second method considers people's ability to process information presented in each mode. Subjects first make estimates in one mode, then receive the correct answer in that mode, and, some time later, are asked unexpectedly to remember the correct answers. Here subjects seldom remembered the answers exactly, so that their memories could be treated as indicating their current beliefs. All groups were more accurate, with the greatest change in the survival rate group. Apparently, these subjects could absorb information in that mode, even though they had difficulty using it. A third method requires subjects to make estimates in two response modes, convert them into one anothers' units and then try to resolve the discrepan-

cies. If subjects access different knowledge with the different response modes, then the reconciliation could produce better estimates than either response mode by itself. It might be considered a settlement negotiated between a subject's two minds on the question.

Probability Assessment

In order to use judgments, one needs to know how good they are. Accurate assessments may prompt swift, confident action, whereas uncertain ones may prompt caution and hedging. An obvious way to learn about accuracy is to ask people how confident they are in their own opinions. One quantitative form of such assessments is probabilistic predictions of future events such as "I am .XX confident that A will happen." The closer .XX is to 0 or to 1, the more knowledgeable the predictor feels. A second form is confidence intervals such as "I am .98 confident that the true value of A lies between G and H." The more confident the expert is, the closer G and H will be to one another.

It is hard to evaluate a single expression of confidence; after all, unlikely events do happen. However, they should not happen often. Thus over a set of predictions, probable events generally should occur and improbable ones should not. If XX% of the events assigned a probability of *.XX* occur, then an individual is said to be *well-calibrated*. Figure 29.12 shows the probabilistic predictions of U.S. Weather Service forecasters. They are remarkably well-calibrated.

The secret of these forecasters' success is unclear. Possibly confidence assessment is a learned skill, acquired because forecasters have excellent conditions for learning: a large number of structurally similar trials, prompt feedback, a clear-cut criterion event (rain, no rain), and well-organized base-rate information. Figure 29.13 shows more typical results, drawn from studies in which subjects assessed the probability that their answers to various questions were correct. Although knowledge is related to confidence here (i.e., percentage correct increases with assessed probability of being correct), the calibration curve is flat. Whereas confidence assessments have a range of .5 (.5 to 1.0), the corresponding proportions of correct answers have a range of about .3. The location of the curve depends on subjects' overall knowledge level; when they know more, the curves are higher. Having a performance standard makes recalibration of these judgments possible. However, one would need some estimate of a specific task's difficulty. The one universally appropriate adjustment is discounting expressions of certitude. When people say that they are 1.00 confident, they are typically wrong 10 to 25% of the time (Lichtenstein, Fischhoff, & Phillips, 1982).

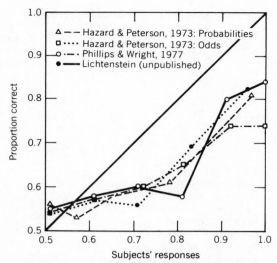

Figure 29.13. Calibration for half-range, general knowledge items. (*Source:* "Calibration of Probabilities: State of the Art" by S. Lichtenstein, B. Fischhoff, & L. D. Phillips, 1977. In H. Jungermann & F. deZeeuw (Eds.), *Decision-making and Change in Human Affairs.* Amsterdam: D. Reidel, p. 292. Reprinted by permission.)

Like other judgmental difficulties, miscalibration has been the focus of many attempts at debiasing. Table 29.5 summarizes the research literature in terms of a general scheme for bias-reduction efforts. Because investigators typically use tasks of medium difficulty, insensitivity typically expresses itself in overconfidence. Hence the table describes attempts to eliminate overconfidence. Ineffective manipulations include raising the reward for good performance, selecting questions from the respondents' area of expertise, varying instructions, changing response mode, and warning about bias. Effective manipulations include training with personalized feedback (Lichtenstein & Fischhoff, 1980) and forcing respondents to list reasons why their responses might be incorrect (Koriat, Lichtenstein, & Fischhoff, 1980). This was not just a requirement to work hard but to work hard in a particular, focused manner that seemed to bring to people's attention facts that they knew but would otherwise have neglected.[5]

Personal Risks

In order to cope with the risks in their personal lives, people need more than just societal statistics. They need to know their own risk relative to that of society's average citizen. Two interrelated difficulties threaten such estimates. One is the tendency to neglect background (or base rate) information and over-

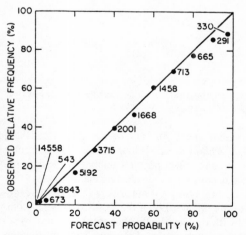

Figure 29.12. Calibration data for precipitation forecasts. The number of forecasts is shown for each point. (From "Can Weather Forecasters Formulate Reliable Probability Forecasts of Precipitation and Temperature" by A. H. Murphy and R. C. Winkler, 1977, *National Weather Digest, 2,* p. 5. Copyright 1977 by National Weather Association. Reprinted by permission.)

Table 29.5. Debiasing Methods and Experience

| | Number of Studies Reporting Manipulations That Were | | | |
| | At Least Partially Successful | | Unsuccessful | |
Strategies	Hindsight	Over-Confidence	Hindsight	Over-Confidence
Faulty tasks				
Unfair tasks				
Raise stakes	—	—	1	2
Clarify instructions/stimuli	—	—	1	5
Discourage second guessing	—	—	1	2
Use better response modes	—	1	1	8
Ask fewer questions	—	—	4	1
Misunderstood tasks				
Demonstrate alternative goal	—	—	5	1
Demonstrate semantic disagreement	—	—	—	3
Demonstrate impossibility of task	—	—	—	1
Faulty judges				
Perfectible individuals				
Warn of problem	—	—	—	1
Describe problem	—	—	1	1
Provide personalized feedback	—	1	—	—
Train extensively	—	9	—	—
Incorrigible Individuals				
Recalibrate their responses	—	—	—	3
Mismatch between judges and task				
Restructuring				
Make knowledge explicit	—	—	—	1
Search for discrepant information	1	1	—	—
Decompose problem	—	—	2	—
Offer alternative formulations	—	—	2	—
Education				
Rely on substantive experts	—	7	6	7
Educate from childhood	—	—	—	2

Source: Adapted from Fischhoff (1982). Manipulations that have yet to be subjected to empirical test or for which the evidence is unclear have been excluded from this task. Fischhoff (1982) identified the individual studies represented in the frequency counts.

emphasize individuating information, describing the particular case (Kahneman & Tversky, 1972). The second is the tendency for that (overemphasized) individuating information to exaggerate one's own abilities (e.g., Larwood & Whittaker, 1977; Svenson, 1981). Such systematic misestimation of a particular parameter can lead to incautious decisions when one relies on one's own (exaggerated) competence or to overly cautious ones if a premium is paid to protect against others' lack of skill.

The neglect of base-rate information seems to reflect a general problem with integrating different kinds of information. When asked to combine two kinds of information, people seem to defer to the one that seems most relevant or specific (Bar-Hillel, 1980; Fischhoff & Bar-Hillel, 1984). This particular bias seems to reflect people's ability to find some relevance in almost any individuating information.

It is, therefore, not surprising that people exaggerate the uniqueness of their own situations, compared with the population base rate. One way to account for the direction of the bias is by reliance on the representativeness heuristic (Kahneman & Tversky, 1972) which, in this case, would lead to a low perceived accident probability for drivers who look safe. Perceiving oneself as safer than average in a skill like driving could then result from an overly flattering self-image or from an accurate self-image compared with an unduly harsh image of other drivers (Svenson, 1981). A second account has drivers reviewing their own driving record but then misinterpreting the results. Drivers who have never had a (serious) accident may not realize how large a sample of experience is needed to estimate such low probability events accurately. Exaggerating the informativeness of small data sets has been called "belief in the law of small numbers" (Tversky & Kahneman, 1971). Drivers who have had accidents may feel, in hindsight, that these accidents were entirely predictable; hence they will be avoided in the future.

29.6. INTEGRATION—REACHING A DECISION

The final stage in the decision-making process is deciding, integrating the various facts and values in order to identify the most favorable course of action. Prescriptively, decision theory offers a variety of "appropriate" computational rules. Most descriptive theories attempt to characterize actual decisions as embodying or systematically deviating from this ideal. There are, however, some competing descriptive theories that reject even the basic assumption that decision making follows an analytical procedure. They provide a point of departure for a concluding section that considers the strengths and limitations of the decision theory perspective underlying this essay.

29.6.1. Analytical Decision Rules

Balance Sheet
Analytical decision rule refers to any procedure that systematically combines a set of components in order to evaluate the overall attractiveness of alternative actions. One archetype is the following rule that can be traced to, among other persons, Benjamin Franklin: List the reasons favoring a course of action (i.e., the good consequences that might come of it) and the reasons against it. Undertake it if and only if the good reasons outnumber the bad ones. Although this method is more systematic than many actual decisions, its limitations show the need for decision theory's more complex methods (Janis, 1982).

One obvious limitation is that the balance sheet method considers only one action. Even if an option has a positive balance sheet, other alternatives (including, perhaps, "do nothing") may be even more attractive. Alternative vacation plans should be such a set of options, for which it would be suboptimal to select the first option found to have more good than bad. A second limitation is treating all reasons equally. There are often many good reasons for an act such as buying a burglar alarm (or insurance protection or natural foods) and only one bad one—cost. If all reasons were weighted equally, then one would always buy. In some such cases, the balance sheet can be saved by sneaking weights into it, by using several reasons to express important consequences, or by deleting minor reasons. Finally, the balance sheet method ignores uncertainty, a key component of most environmental decisions. For example, it would treat certain discomfort with a seat belt and the improbability of an accident as one good and one bad reason, respectively.

Expectancy
Decision theory overcomes these limitations by offering rules that compare options, make trade-offs, and incorporate uncertainty. Its primary method is *expectancy rules*, which weight consequences by both their relative importance and their probability of occurrence (Feather, 1982). Following Edwards (1954, 1961), these rules can be characterized by how they interpret the values assigned to the uncertainties and consequences. The most general form is the Subjective Expected Utility (SEU) model, which treats probabilities as being subjective and consequences as being evaluated in terms of *utility*, a generalized measure of desirability. The *S*, for "subjective," is dropped if probabilities are considered to be "objective" (i.e., based on frequency counts). The *U*, for "utility," becomes a *V*, for "value," if an absolute standard of worth, like dollars, is used.

Applied to the seat belt example, the expectancy principle calculates the attractiveness of "drive belted" as $10^{-5} \times (-1000) + (1-10^{-5}) \times (+1) = +.99$, much less than the expected worth of "drive not belted" $(= +1.98)$. Used descriptively, the expectancy rule predicts that someone whose view of the problem was captured by Figure 29.1 would drive beltless. Used prescriptively, the rule advises such individuals to drive beltless; that is the decision in their best interests. The expectancy rule expresses a long-term perspective, showing how to achieve the highest return on repeated decisions. Although there are strong reasons why an individual would want to follow the same rule in unique decisions (Savage, 1954), the expectancy perspective might still be more appealing to safety officials, who must consider many driving decisions, than to individual drivers, who confront them one at a time.

Falsification

If people follow the expectancy rule, then they should use something like sensitivity analysis to test the robustness of their preferences. The theory shows that many decisions with continuous response options (e.g., invest $X), are fairly insensitive to changes in their parameters (von Winterfeldt & Edwards, 1982). This result simplifies decision making because one pays a small price for imprecision (assuming that one's problem definition is appropriate). It also simplifies predicting the choices of people relying on expectancy because the investigator needs only a rough idea of their perceptions. However, it complicates inferring those perceptions from choices because many different sets of beliefs and values could lead to the same conclusion.

Nor can the choices alone reveal whether people have, in fact, used an expectancy rule. With sufficient ingenuity, one can find some problem definition and set of parameters estimates such that the chosen option maximizes expected utility. Any difficulties in predicting choices can be attributed to the investigators' failure to capture the decision maker's perceptions rather than to the decision maker's failure to use the expectancy rule. Some of the more imaginative excuses involve *transaction costs,* which hold that people manage decision-making processes so as to optimize the effort spent as well as the utility enjoyed. Thus selection of suboptimal alternatives can be attributed to effort-saving simplifications (Fischhoff, Goitein, & Shapiro, 1982; Hogarth, 1981; March, 1978).

One way to avoid such ad hoc treatment of discrepant results is to insist that the descriptive system be consistent over a set of related decisions. That is, one should find a set of beliefs and values that would predict the outcome of many decisions, when combined according to the SEU rule. Even this strategy is complicated by the ability of additive linear models (of which SEU is one) to predict summary judgments generated by rather different rules.

Configural Judgment

Evidence for the power of linear rules comes from studies of clinical judgment, such as is exercised by a radiologist who sorts X rays of ulcers into "benign" and "malignant," by a personnel officer who evaluates job candidates, or by a crisis center counselor who considers the stability of callers threatening suicide. When the same cues characterize many similar decisions, it is possible to model a judge's decision-making policy statistically. Two decades of such policy-capturing studies showed that simple linear models, using a weighted sum of the cues, did an excellent job of postdicting judges' decisions, despite the judges' claim that they were using much more complicated strategies (Goldberg, 1968, 1970; Slovic & Lichtenstein, 1971).

A common complication is "configural" judgment, in which the diagnostic meaning of one cue depends on the meaning of other cues (e.g., "that tone of voice makes me think 'not suicidal' unless the call comes at midday"). In a SEU (or MAUT) context, configurality is equivalent to having the weight assigned to a consequence depend upon the values of the other consequences (e.g., "My aversion to a given physical risk increases greatly if it is accompanied by a financial risk that will affect my ability to recuperate").

Part of this discrepancy between these models of cognitive processes and the clinicians' own descriptions reflected failures of introspection. For example, clinicians might know that they sometimes use complex integrative rules, without realizing that their rule was too variable to allow any consistent pattern to emerge. Another part of the discrepancy reflected the power of improperly specified linear models to predict decisions generated by diverse procedures (Dawes, 1979). Because such models can replicate the input–output relations without any guarantee of fidelity to the underlying processes, there is an inherent indeterminacy in such modeling procedures.

Full Specification

An alternative to seeing whether some expectancy rule can be found to predict observed choices is to identify every parameter of the decision makers' model and then see if it predicts the resulting action. An example of such detailed work is found in Kunreuther and colleagues (1978). Despite years of building flood control projects, flood losses (in constant dollars) continue to rise. Apparently, the dam and levee builders failed to anticipate residents' reduced sensitivity to flood dangers. As a result, floodplains are overbuilt, leaving that much more in the path of the inevitable big, rare floods (Palm, 1981; White, 1974). The official United States response was the National Flood Insurance Program, which assumed that floodplain residents are fully informed users of the SEU model. Even though the federal government greatly subsidized premiums, supposedly making policies very attractive from an SEU perspective, few people bought them. The official explanation of the failure was that residents expected a government bailout in the event of flood. However, a field survey found that floodplain residents expected no help.

That survey also elicited residents' subjective estimates of the parameters of their personal insurance decision problem (e.g., probability of flooding, likely damage, insurance premium, deductible). Those estimates were different than those held by technical experts. For example, residents who had not experienced floods considerably underestimated the damages. Such misperceptions could rescue the expectancy rule, if applying the rule to those erroneous estimates would predict residents' decisions. However, no such relationship was observed. Rather, the main determinants of these decisions seemed to be social rather than intellectual variables, for example, whether neighbors had bought the insurance or whether it was pushed by insurance agents.

Other Analytical Rules

A third strategy for testing the model is devising stylized decision problems with explicitly specified parameters for which the model predicts specific behavior. Many investigators have used this strategy and have elicited a complex mixture of SEU and non-SEU behaviors. Kahneman and Tversky (1979; Tversky & Kahneman, 1981) have proposed an alternative analytical framework to account for these examples. Called "prospect theory," it predicts, among other things, that people apply a weighting function to their subjective probabilities before using them in decisions. In particular, they attach extra importance to very high probabilities, which is equivalent to giving extra weight to the consequences to which such probabilities are attached. The theory also predicts powerful changes in preferences following from seemingly irrelevant ways in which problems are presented (or *framed*).

29.6.2. Contingent Approaches

Description without Prescription

The doggedness with which expectancy models have been pursued is partly due to their reasonableness. Presumably, people try to make decisions in a way that makes sense to them. What could make more sense than the expectancy principle, which considers all consequences, weights them by their importance, and discounts them according to their improbability? It should, therefore, be possible to describe behavior as the decision maker's best attempt to use the expectancy principle. In this light, problems such as neglecting options or misassessing probabilities represent *suboptimality*, whereas failure to use the expectancy principle represents *irrationality*.

Before accepting the charge of irrationality, it is worth asking whether the expectancy rule really suits all situations. One possibly sustainable objection is that the rule's additive character allows good and bad consequences to compensate for one another. One noncompensatory rule, the *conjunctive*, requires an option to score higher than a fixed criterion for each consequence if it is to be considered at all. For example, a vacation apartment must be reasonably priced, available, sunny, *and* quiet, or else be rejected. The disjunctive rule accepts any option passing a fixed criterion on any one attribute. For example, one might accept an investment opportunity if it were a good speculation, tax shelter, or inflation hedge, even if it rated poorly on the other dimensions. Investment portfolios often include varied items chosen by the same disjunctive rule. Choice theory offers a variety of other occasionally observed noncompensatory rules (Coombs, Dawes, & Tversky, 1970). The appeal of noncompensatory strategies may be seen in Lichtenstein, Slovic, and Zink's (1969) unsuccessful attempt to convince people to abandon them in favor of expected value.

In such cases, it is sometimes possible to rescue the expectancy rule with a fancy model, such as a highly configural utility function. Perhaps a more productive strategy is to acknowledge that people can use a variety of decision-making rules and focus on identifying the conditions governing rule choice. Such *contingent decision making* (Beach & Mitchell, 1978; Payne, 1982) can include, but is not restricted to, analytical rules. For the dogged advocate of SEU, these alternative rules are "irrational." However, the pejorative connotations of that word may obscure the fact that they still represent deliberative choices of action.

Pseudoanalytical Procedures

Explicit analytical decision rules of any type can make life easier, even when they do not identify optimal choices. They show the logic of decisions to others; they allow review of one's own decisions; they show how to incorporate new information or changes in taste. The price they exact is requiring decision makers to contemplate and express the logic of their decisions in advance. For important (e.g., risky) decisions, it may be difficult even to admit that trade-offs need to be made, much less specify them in advance.

One way to avoid the hard questions without sacrificing the comforts of analytical rules is to try different ways of viewing a problem until one is found for which a single rule points to a relatively conflict-free choice. This process has been termed the *search for a dominance structure* (Montgomery, 1983; Montgomery & Svenson, 1982). The search may include "editing" operations such as eliminating consequences on which the seemingly best option rates poorly ("I shouldn't really consider that in this decision"), tinkering with the utilities and probabilities ("maybe an accident isn't all that likely—or all that bad"), or trying different decisions rules. The expectancy rule's flexibility makes it ideal for this role, although its computationally complex character and explicit acknowledgment of trade-offs may discourage some.

Discovering these rules requires a very different kind of research methodology than is used in the policy-capturing studies described earlier. Rather than trying to fit a single model to a large set of decisions, workers in this vein treat decisions individually and attempt to trace the process by which they are derived (Payne, 1982; Svenson, 1979).

Satisficing

Noting the large cognitive investment involved in using analytical rules, Simon (1957) proposed that decision makers often do not want or need to identify the best option. Rather, they look for an option that will *satisfy* their needs. Having found it, they stop their search and evaluation processes. If options are considered sequentially, then the accepted (satisfactory) option may be inferior to ones that have yet to be considered. In such cases, decision makers might be upset to see better options come along, or they might avoid such unpleasant surprises by preventing additional options from being created or coming to light.

Satisficing may be particularly attractive when one's preferences are poorly articulated, meaning that one cannot reliably make fine discriminations among options. Like the search for dominance, satisficing achieves efficient decisions in the short run at the price of the opportunity to sharpen one's preferences through looking for the best option.

Quick Rule-Based Decision Making

An attractive feature of the search for dominance is that it provides a readily enunciated justification for its outcome. A degenerate route to the same end is looking immediately for a decisive "rule of thumb," perhaps something as simple (or even flip) as "haste makes waste," "safety first," or "those who hesitate are lost." Although they may provide useful summaries, simple rules hardly provide insight. For example, their content can rarely withstand serious criticism (e.g., safety first at any price?). Even their application can be ambiguous, with a single rule potentially justifying several options. Often the set of adages contains contradictory items such as the first and third items in the preceding list.

Experience

Single rules are attractive, in part, because it is hard to think through the use of analytic decision rules. Repeated and reversible decisions open the middle path of trial-and-error learning, which can allow one to create better options, clarify one's preferences, or comprehend the system. "Trial-and-error decision making" (or "muddling through" [Lindblom, 1959]) can, however, be a high-sounding label for covering up errant or ad hoc decision making. To take it seriously, the minimal conditions for learning must exist—prompt, noticed feedback.

Social Support

A somewhat different kind of experience underlies another set of popular all-purpose, nonanalytic decision rules: "Do as I've always done," "do what we've always done," and "do what others are doing." These represent reliance on habit, tradition, and consensus, respectively. It would be foolish to ignore such experience or to rely on it too heavily—unless one is assured that past decision makers were well informed and shared similar values. The same hesitations and possibilities apply to copying contemporaries' decisions. However, even when colleagues are not more knowledgeable, they may be used as a sort of peripheral processor, helping one to think through problems too complex to keep in mind. A potentially useful way to rely on others is to single out an individual or two to consult about a particular topic. Thus one may have a personal expert for purchasing insurance, avoiding criminal assault, and responding to emergencies. These experts are valued for tracking a particular issue, not for generalized decision-making ability. They may have just as much difficulty with analytical thinking. They may also have a vested interest in the question. For example, it may be necessary (and advisable) to buy some unneeded insurance in order to secure the advice of an agent who stays up on those issues. In addition to exacting a price, interaction with others may generate additional consequences such as "go against *X*'s advice," or additional options such as "work together to change the situation." Yet people who take responsibility for their actions must make decisions, if only to let certain others decide for them.

29.7. CONCLUSION

Our concern has been how people cope actively with environmental hazards. That coping may include using a seat belt, maintaining exhaust emission controls, buying insurance, or joining a protest group. Whenever people select such courses of action, they are making a decision. The focal tasks for researchers are, then, understanding how people make such decisions and helping them do better.

As a basis for both tasks, we have proposed the most general form of decision theory's conception of decision making. In it, decisions are deliberative choices among alternative actions. These choices should be sensitive to the magnitude and likelihood of the consequences that may follow from them. The prescriptive and descriptive use of the model go hand in hand. Some description is needed to identify what problem people are trying to solve; some prescription is needed to help them see it more clearly.

The theoretical position adopted here is that most behavior can be productively described in terms of deviations from an idealized version of an individual's decision problem. Hence much of the discussion concerns systematic deviations from optimality and the methods used to study them. Where deviations can be identified, the opportunity exists for reducing them. However, before attributing suboptimality to people, it is important to establish what their decision problem was. Thus investigators must seek a delicate balance between giving people too much and too little credit for decision-making prowess.

One distinguishing feature of this perspective is its strong cognitive bias. Decisions are made in individuals' minds. They may consult with others before making their decisions. They may have their perception of the facts colored by emotion. They may be misled (e.g., by advertising) regarding what their own values are. They may have an unrealistic view of the ease of achieving their goals. All such problems are seen as sources of discrepancies between people's mental model of a situation and the optimal model that they would hold if they saw things as richly and veridically as possible.

Acknowledgment

This study was supported by the Swedish Energy Research and Development Commission, the Swedish Research Council for Research in the Humanities and Social Sciences, and by grants from the National Science Foundation to Decision Research, a Branch of Perceptronics. We wish to thank Gordon Goodman and Lars Kristoferson for interesting discussions and important ideas concerning the problems treated in the report. We also want to thank Kerstin Meyerhoffer, Rocio Klingsell, Cecelia Hagen, and Nancy Collins for their patient deciphering of the drafts and typing of the material.

NOTES

1. An interesting version of such costs is those associated with political action (e.g., lobbying zoning commissions, passing petitions). These might be viewed as a normal function of a healthy society or as another indication of the extent of externalities.

2. Figure 29.5 cannot be directly compared with Figure 29.4 because they contain different items. Particularly significant might be the addition of natural hazards to those of human origin. People might respond differently to things that other people do to them and those done by nature.

3. As a curiosity, we note an attempt by the American National Standards Institute (1967) to evaluate different injuries in terms of workdays lost. In their schemes, the consequences range from 15 days (loss of first digit of smaller finger of nondominant hand) to 6000 days (loss of life).

4. Variants of this procedure are very popular in applied psychology, where they are used to assess the contribution of various factors to productivity, compensation, motivation, or satisfaction. It is ironic that risk seldom appears as a predictor in these studies (Feather, 1982). Perhaps risk is fairly uniform or negligible in all jobs considered; perhaps employees are unaware of the risk to which they are exposed; perhaps they know but are insensitive to those risks; perhaps it is the investigators who are insensitive.

5. The second column summarizes the result of applying these procedures to eliminating another judgmental bias, the tendency to exaggerate in hindsight what one could have known in foresight. It reveals a similar pattern: with the bias responding to task restructuring but not to methodological manipulations such as clarifying instructions or exhortation to work harder.

REFERENCES

American National Standard Institute. (1967) *ANS Method of recording and measuring work injury experience.* ANSI Z16.1-1967. New York: Author.

Aschenbrenner, K.M., Jaus, D., & Villani, C. (1980). Hierarchical goal structuring and pupils' job choices: Testing a decision aid in the field. *Acta Psychologica, 45,* 35–49.

Atomic Industrial Forum. (1976). *Committee on Reactor Licensing and Safety Statement on Licensing Reform.* New York: Author.

Bar-Hillel, M. (1980). The base-rate fallacy in probability judgments. *Acta Psychologica, 44,* 211–233.

Baum, A., Gatchell, R.J. , & Schaeffer, M.A. (1983). Emotional, behavioral and physiological effects of chronic stress at Three Mile Island. *Journal of Consulting and Clinical Psychology, 51,* 565–572.

Beach, L.R., & Mitchell, T.R. (1978). A contingency model for the selection of decision strategies. *Academy of Management Review, 3,* 439–449.

Beach, L.R., Townes, B.D., Campbell, F.L., & Keating, G.W. (1976). Developing and testing a decision aid for birth planning decisions. *Organizational Behavior and Human Performance, 15,* 99–116.

Behrend, H. (1981). Research into public attitudes and the attitudes of the public to inflation. *Managerial and Decision Economics, 2,* 1–8.

Bick, T., Hohenemser, C., & Kates, R. (1979). Target: Highway risks. *Environment, 21,* 7–15, 29–38.

Bickerstaffe, J., & Pearce, D. (1980). Can there be a consensus on nuclear power? *Social Studies of Science, 10,* 309–344.

Birch, A.L., & Schmid, A.A. (1980). Public opinion surveys as guides to public policy and spending. *Social Indicators Research, 7,* 299–311.

Borelli, P. (1982, Winter). Shoot the messenger: Lou Harris. *Amicus,* pp. 25–30.

Bowonder, B. (1980). Environmental risk management in the third world. *International Journal of Environmental Studies,* pp. 1–9.

Brokensha, D.W., Warren, D.M., & Werner, O. (1980). *Indigenous knowledge: Systems and development.* Lanham, MD: University Press of America.

Brookshire, D.S., Ives, B.C., & Schulze, W.D. (1976). The valuation of aesthetic preferences. *Journal of Environmental Economics and Management, 3,* 325–346.

Brown, R.A., & Green, C.H. (1980). Precepts of safety assessments. *Journal of the Operational Research Society, 11,* 563–571.

Brown, R.V., Kahr, A.S., & Peterson, C. (1974). *Decision analysis for the manager.* New York: Holt, Rinehart & Winston.

Burton, I., Kates, R.W., & White, G.F. (1978). *The environment as hazard.* New York: Oxford University Press.

A call for tougher—not weaker—anti-pollution laws. (1983, January 27). *BusinessWeek,* p. 82.

Campbell, J.M. (1983). Ambient stressors. *Environment and Behavior, 15,* 355–380.

Chen, K. (1980). *Value oriented societal decision analysis.* Ann Arbor: University of Michigan.

Cohen, B., & Lee, I. (1979). A catalog of risks. *Health Physics, 36,* 707–722.

Cole, G., & Withey, S. (1982). Perspectives in risk perceptions. *Risk Analysis, 1,* 143–163.

Comar, C.L. (1979). Risk: A pragmatic de minimus approach. *Science, 203,* 319.

Combs, B., & Slovic, P. (1979). Newspaper coverage of causes of death. *Journalism Quarterly, 56,* 837–843, 849.

Coombs, C.H., & Avrunin, G. (1977). Single-peaked functions and the theory of preference. *Psychological Review, 84,* 216–230.

Coombs, C.H., Dawes, R.M., & Tversky, A. (1970). *Mathematical psychology: An elementary introduction.* Englewood Cliffs, NJ: Prentice-Hall.

Corbin, R. (1980). Decisions that might not get made. In T. Wallsten (Ed.), *Cognitive processes in choice and decision behavior.* Hillsdale, NJ: Erlbaum.

Dawes, R.M. (1979). The robust beauty of improper linear models in decision making. *American Psychologist, 34,* 571–582.

Derr, P., Goble, R., Kasperson, R.E., & Kates, R.W. (1983). Responding to the double standard of worker/ public protection. *Environment, 25*(6), 6–11, 35–36.

Dunlap, T.R. (1979). Science as a guide in regulating technology: The case of DDT in the United States. *Social Studies of Science, 8,* 265–285.

Edwards, W. (1954). A theory of decision making. *Psychological Bulletin, 51,* 380–417.

Edwards, W. (1961). Behavioral decision theory. *Annual Review of Psychology, 12,* 473–498.

Edwards, W. (1977). How to use multiattribute utility measurement for social decision making. *IEEE Transactions on Systems, Man, and Cybernetics, SMC-7,* 326–340.

Edwards, W., Lindman, H., & Savage, L.J. (1963). Bayesian statistical inference for psychological research. *Psychological Review, 70,* 193–242.

Eiser, J.R., & van der Pligt, J. (1979). Beliefs and values in the nuclear debate. *Journal of Applied Social Psychology, 9,* 524–536.

Elliot, G.R., & Eisdorfer, C. (1982). *Stress and human health.* New York: Springer.

Fairley, W.B. (1977). Evaluating the "small" probability of a catastrophic accident from the marine transportation of liquefied natural gas. In W.B. Fairley & F. Mosteller (Eds.), *Statistics and public policy.* Reading, MA: Addison-Wesley.

Farmer, F.R. (1967). Siting criteria—A new approach. *Containment and siting of nuclear plants* (pp. 303–318). Vienna, Austria: International Atomic Energy Agency.

Fay, A.J. (1975, September). *A public interest point of view.* Paper presented at the Risk-Benefit Methodology and Application Conference, Asilomar, CA.

Feather, N.T. (1982). *Expectations and actions.* Hillsdale, NJ: Erlbaum.

Fischhoff, B. (1980). Clinical decision analysis. *Operations Research, 28,* 28–43.

Fischhoff, B. (1982). Debiasing. In D. Kahneman, P. Slovic, & A. Tversky (Eds.), *Judgment under uncertainty: Heuristics and biases.* New York: Cambridge University Press.

Fischhoff, B. (1983). "Acceptable risk": The case of nuclear power. *Journal of Policy Analysis and Management, 2,* 559–575.

Fischhoff, B. (1985). Cognitive and institutional barriers to "informed consent." In M. Gibson (Ed.), *Risk, consent, and air.* Totowa, NJ: Rowman & Allenheld.

Fischhoff, B. (in press). Judgmental aspects of risk analysis. In *Handbook of risk analysis,* National Science Foundation for Office of Management and Budget. New York: Plenum.

Fischhoff, B., & Bar-Hillel, M. (1984). Diagnosticity and the base-rate effect. *Memory and Cognition, 12,* 402–410.

Fischhoff, B., & Beyth-Marom, R. (1983). Hypothesis evaluation from a Bayesian perspective. *Psychological Review, 90,* 239–260.

Fischhoff, B., Goitein, B., & Shapira, Z. (1982). The experienced utility of expected utility approaches. In N. Feather (Ed.), *Expectancy, incentive and action.* Hillsdale, NJ: Erlbaum.

Fischhoff, B., Lichtenstein, S., Slovic, P., Derby, S.L., & Keeney R.L. (1981). *Acceptable risk.* New York: Cambridge University Press.

Fischhoff, B., & MacGregor, D. (1983). Judged lethality. *Risk Analysis, 3,* 229–236.

Fischhoff, B., Slovic, P., & Lichtenstein, S. (1978). Fault trees: Sensitivity of estimated failure probabilities to problem representation. *Journal of Experimental Psychology: Human Perception and Performance, 4,* 330–344.

Fischhoff, B., Slovic, P., & Lichtenstein, S. (1980). Knowing what you want: Measuring labile values. In T. Wallsten (Ed.), *Cognitive processes in choice and decision behavior.* Hillsdale, NJ: Erlbaum.

Fischhoff, B., Slovic, P., & Lichtenstein, S. (1983). The "public" vs. the "experts": Perceived vs. actual disagreements about the risks of nuclear power. In V. Covello, G. Flamm, J. Rodericks, & R. Tardiff (Eds.), *Analysis of actual vs. perceived risks.* New York: Plenum.

Fischhoff, B., Slovic, P., Lichtenstein, S., Read, S., & Combs, B. (1978). How safe is safe enough? A psychometric study of attitudes towards technological risks and benefits. *Policy Sciences, 8,* 127–152.

Fischhoff, B., Watson, S., & Hope, C. (1984). Defining risk. *Policy Analysis, 17,* 123–139.

Fishburn, P.C. (1982). *Foundations of expected utility theory.* Dordrecht, Netherlands: Reidel.

Frankel, C. (1974). The rights of nature. In C. Schelling, J. Voss, & L. Tribe, *When values conflict.* Cambridge, MA: Ballinger.

Gamble, D.J. (1978). The Berger inquiry: An impact assessment process. *Science, 199,* 946–951.

Gardner, G.T., Tiemann, A.R., Gould, L.C., DeLuca, D.R., Doob, L.W., & Stolwijk, A.J. (1982). Risk and benefit perceptions, acceptability judgments, and self-reported actions toward nuclear power. *Journal of Social Psychology, 116,* 179–197.

Gettys, C.F., Manning, C.A., & Casey, J.T. (1981). *An evaluation of human act generation performance* (Rep. No. TR 15-8-81). Norman: University of Oklahoma, Decision Processes Laboratory.

Gettys, C.F., Manning, C.A., Mehle, T., & Fisher, S. (1980). *Hypothesis generation: A final report of three years of research* (Rep. No. TR 15-10-80). Norman: University of Oklahoma, Decision Processes Laboratory.

Goldberg, L.R. (1968). Simple models or simple processes? Some research on clinical judgments. *American Psychologist, 23,* 483–496.

Goldberg, L.R. (1970). Man vs. model of man: A rationale, plus some evidence, for a method of improving on clinical inferences. *Psychological Bulletin, 73,* 422–432.

Graham, J., Shakow, D.M., & Cyr, C. (1983). Risk compensation—In theory and practice. *Environment, 25*(1), 14–20, 39–40.

Green, A.E., & Bourne, A.J. (1972). *Reliability technology.* New York: Wiley-Interscience.

Green, C.H. (1980). Risk: Attitudes and beliefs. In D.V. Canter (Ed.), *Behaviour in fires.* Chichester, England: Wiley.

Green, C.H., & Brown, R.A. (1981). *The perception and acceptability of risk.* Dundee, Scotland: Duncan of Jordanstone School of Architecture.

Gregory, R. (in press). Interpreting measures of economic value: Evidence from contingent valuation and experimental studies. *Journal of Environmental Economics and Management.*

Gricar, B.G., & Baratta, A.J. (1983). Bridging the information gap at Three Mile Island: Radiation and monitoring by citizens. *Journal of Applied Behavioral Science, 19,* 35–49.

Hammond, K.R., & Adelman, L. (1976). Science, values and human judgment. *Science, 194,* 389–396.

Harris, L. (1980). *Risk in a complex society.* Public opinion survey conducted for Marsh and McLennan Companies, Inc.

Hershey, J.C., Kunreuther, H.C., & Schoemaker, P.J.H. (1982). Sources of bias in assessment procedures for utility functions. *Management Science, 28,* 936–954.

Hogarth, R.M. (1981). Beyond discrete biases: Functional and dysfunctional aspects of judgmental heuristics. *Psychological Bulletin, 90,* 197–217.

Hogarth, R.M. (Ed.). (1982). *New directions for methodology of social and behavioral science: The framing of questions and the consistency of response.* San Francisco: Jossey-Bass.

Hohenemser, C., Kates, R.W., & Slovic, P. (1983). The nature of technological hazard. *Science, 220,* 378–384.

Hohenemser, K.H. (1975). The failsafe risk. *Environment, 17*(1), 6–10.

Holdren, J. (1979). Energy: Calculating the risks. *Science, 204,* 564–568.

Howard, R.A. (1978). Life and death decision analysis. *Proceedings of the Second Lawrence Symposium on Systems and Decision Sciences,* pp. 271–277.

Huff, J.O., & Clark, W.A.V. (1978). Cumulative stress and cumulative inertia: A behavioral model of the decision to move. *Environment and Planning A, 10,* 1101–1119.

Ingram, M.J., Underhill, D.J., & Wigley, T.M.L. (1978). Historical climatology. *Nature, 276,* 329–334.

Inhaber, H. (1979). Risk with energy from conventional and nonconventional sources. *Science, 203,* 718–723.

Janis, I.L. (Ed.). (1982). *Counseling on personal decisions.* New Haven: Yale University Press.

Jennergren, L.P., & Keeney, R.L. (in press). Risk assessment. In *Handbook of applied systems analysis.* Laxenburg, Austria: International Institute of Applied Systems Analysis.

John, R.S., von Winterfeldt, D., & Edwards, W. (1983). The quality and acceptability of MAU performed by computer and analysis. In P.C. Humphreys, O. Svenson, & A. Vari (Eds.), *Analyzing and aiding decisions.* Amsterdam: North Holland.

Johnson, E.J., & Tversky, A. (1983). Affect generalization and the perception of risk. *Journal of Personality and Social Psychology, 45,* 20–31.

Kahneman, D., & Tversky, A. (1972). Subjective probability: A judgment of representativeness. *Cognitive Psychology, 3,* 430–454.

Kahneman, D., & Tversky, A. (1979). Intuitive predictions: Biases and corrective procedures. *TIMS Studies in Management Science, 12,* 313–327.

Kasl, S.V., Chisholm, R.F., & Eskenazi, B. (1981). The impact of the accident at Three Mile Island on the behavior and well being of nuclear workers. *American Journal of Public Health, 71,* 472–495.

Kates, R.W. (1978). *Risk assessment of environmental hazard.* Chichester, England: Wiley.

Keeney, R.L. (1977). The art of assessing multiattribute utility functions. *Organizational Behavior and Human Performance, 19,* 267–310.

Keeney, R.L. (1982). Decision analysis: An overview. *Operations Research, 30,* 803–838.

Keeney, R.L., & Raiffa, H. (1976). *Decisions with multiple objectives: Preferences and value tradeoffs.* New York: Wiley.

Kidd, S.B. (1970). The utilization of subjective probabilities in production planning. *Acta Psychologica, 34,* 338–347.

Kjelling, U., & Larsson, T.J. (1981). Investigating accidents and reducing risks—a dynamic approach. *Journal of Occupational Accidents, 3,* 129–140.

Koriat, A., Lichtenstein, S., & Fischhoff, B. (1980). Reasons for confidence. *Journal of Experimental Psychology: Human Learning and Memory, 6,* 107–118.

Kunreuther, H., Ginsberg, R., Miller, L., Sagi, P., Slovic, P., Borkan, B., & Katz, N. (1978). *Disaster insurance protection: Public policy lessons.* New York: Wiley.

Larwood, L., & Whittaker, W. (1977). Managerial myopia: Self-serving biases in organizational planning. *Journal of Applied Psychology, 62,* 194–198.

Lichtenstein, S., & Fischhoff, B. (1980). Training for calibration. *Organizational Behavior and Human Performance, 26,* 149–171.

Lichtenstein, S., Fischhoff, B., & Phillips, L.D. (1982). Calibration of probabilities: State of the art to 1980. In D. Kahneman, P. Slovic, & A. Tversky (Eds.), *Judgment under uncertainty: Heuristics and biases.* New York: Cambridge University Press.

Lichtenstein, S., Slovic, P., Fischhoff, B., Layman, M., & Combs, B. (1978). Judged frequency of lethal events. *Journal of Experimental Psychology: Human Learning and Memory, 4,* 551–578.

Lichtenstein, S., Slovic, P., & Zink, D. (1969). Effect of instruction in expected value on optimality of gambling decisions. *Journal of Experimental Psychology, 79,* 236–240.

Lindblom, C.E. (1959). The science of muddling through. *Public Administration Review, 19,* 79–99.

Lindell, M.K., & Earle, T.C. (1983). How close is close enough: Public perceptions of the risks of industrial facilities. *Risk Analysis, 3,* 245–254.

Lowrance, W.W. (1976). *Of acceptable risk.* Los Altos, CA: Kaufmann.

March, J.G. (1978). Bounded rationality, ambiguity, and the engineering of choice. *Bell Journal of Economics, 9,* 587–608.

Melber, B.D. (1983). Supply versus demand energy alternatives: Public attitudes toward resource conservation. In W.D. Conn (Ed.), *Energy and material resources.* Boulder, CO: Westview.

Mileti, D.S. (1980). Human adjustment to the risk of environmental extremes. *Sociology and Social Research, 64,* 327–347.

Montgomery, H. (1983). Decision rules and the search for a dominance structure: Towards a process model of decision making. In P. Humphreys, O. Svenson, & A. Vari (Eds.), *Analyzing and aiding decision processes.* Amsterdam, Netherlands: North Holland.

Montgomery, H., & Svenson, O. (1982). *A think aloud study of dominance structuring in decision processes*

(Rep. No. 2), Stockholm, Sweden: University of Stockholm, Department of Psychology, Cognition and Decision Research Unit.

Morgan, K.Z. (1969). Present status of recommendations of the International Commission on Radiological Protection. In A.M.F. Duhamel (Ed.), *Health physics*. New York: Pergamon.

Murphy, A.H., Lichtenstein, S., Fischhoff, B., & Winkler, R.L. (1980). Misinterpretations of precipitation probability forecasts. *Bulletin of the American Meteorological Society, 61,* 695–701.

Murphy, A.H., & Winkler, R.C. (1977). Can weather forecasters formulate reliable probability forecasts of precipitation and temperature? *National Weather Digest, 2*(2), 2–9.

Murray, H.A. (1938). *Explorations in personality.* New York: Oxford University Press.

National Academy of Sciences. (1982). *Survey measure of subjective phenomena.* Washington, DC: Author.

Otway, H., & Cohen, J. (1975). *Revealed preferences: Comments on the Starr benefit-risk relationships* (Research Memorandum No. 75-5). Laxenburg, Austria: International Institute for Applied Systems Analysis.

Otway, H., & Fishbein, M. (1976). *The determinants of attitude formation: An application to nuclear power* (Research Memorandum No. 76-80). Laxenburg, Austria: International Institute for Applied Systems Analysis.

Palm, R.I. (1981). Public response to earthquake hazard information. *Annals of the Association of American Geographers, 71,* 389–399.

Payne, J.W. (1980). Information processing theory: Some concepts applied to decision research. In T. Wallsten (Ed.), *Cognitive processes in choice and decision behavior.* Hillsdale, NJ: Erlbaum.

Payne, J.W. (1982). Contingent decision behavior. *Psychological Bulletin, 92,* 382–401.

Payne, S.L. (1952). *The art of asking questions.* Princeton, NJ: Princeton University Press.

Phillips, L.D. (1982). Requisite decision modeling: A case study. *Journal of Operations Research Society, 33,* 303–311.

Pitz, G.F., & Sachs, N.J. (1984). Judgment and decision: Theory and application. *Annual Review of Psychology, 35,* 139–163.

Pitz, G.F., Sachs, N.J., & Heerboth, J. (1980). Procedures for eliciting choices in the analysis of individual decisions. *Organizational Behavior and Human Performance, 26,* 396–408.

Pokorny, E. (1982). *Public attitudes toward energy production.* Cambridge: MA: Cambridge Reports.

Pollatsek, A., & Tversky, A. (1970). A theory of risk. *Journal of Mathematical Psychology, 7,* 540–553.

Poulton, E.C. (1968). The new psychophysics: Six models for magnitude estimation. *Psychological Bulletin, 69,* 1–19.

Poulton, E.C. (1977). Quantitative subjective assessments are almost always biased, sometimes completely misleading. *British Journal of Psychology, 68,* 409–425.

Poulton, E.C. (1979). Models for biases in judging sensory magnitude. *Psychological Bulletin, 68,* 779–803.

Poulton, E.C. (1982). Biases in quantitative judgments. *Applied Ergonomics, 13,* 31–42.

Prescott-Clarke, P. (1982). *Public attitudes towards industrial work-related and other risks.* London: SCPR.

Raiffa, H. (1968). *Decision analysis.* Reading, MA: Addison-Wesley.

Reissland, J., & Harries, V. (1979). A scale for measuring risks. *New Scientist, 83,* 809–811.

Renn, O. (1981, June). *Man, technology, and risk: A study on intuitive risk assessment and attitudes towards nuclear power* (Report Jul-Spez 115), Julich, West Germany: Nuclear Research Center.

Rosencranz, A., & Wetstone, G.S. (1980). Acid precipitation: National and international responses. *Environment, 22*(5), 6–20, 40–41.

Rowe, W.D. (1977). *An anatomy of risk.* New York: Wiley.

Sampson, A.R., & Smith, R.L. (1982). Assessing risks through the determination of rare event probabilities. *Operation Research, 30,* 839–866.

Savage, L.J. (1954). *The foundations of statistics.* New York: Wiley.

Schulze, W.D., D'Arge, R.C., & Brookshire, D.S. (1981). Valuing environmental commodities: Some recent experiments. *Land Economics, 57,* 151–169.

Schuman, H., & Presser, S. (1979). The assignment of "no opinion" in attitude surveys. In K.F. Schuessler (Ed.), *Sociological methodology.* San Francisco: Jossey-Bass.

Seminara, J.L., & Parsons, S.O. (1982). Nuclear power plant maintainability. *Applied Ergonomics, 13,* 177–189.

Sheridan, T.B. (1980). Human error in nuclear power plants. *Technology Review, 82*(4), 23–33.

Simon, H.A. (1957). *Models of man: Social and rational.* New York: Wiley.

Slovic, P., & Fischhoff, B. (1982). Targeting risks: Comments on Wilde's "Theory of Risk Homeostasis." *Risk Analysis, 2,* 231–238.

Slovic, P., Fischhoff, B., & Lichtenstein, S. (1977). Behavioral decision theory. *Annual Review of Psychology, 28,* 1–39.

Slovic, P., Fischhoff, B., & Lichtenstein, S. (1979). Rating the risks. *Environment, 21*(3), 14–20, 36–39.

Slovic, P., Fischhoff, B., & Lichtenstein, S. (1980). Facts and fears: Understanding perceived risk. In R. Schwing & W.A. Albers Jr. (Eds.), *Societal risk assessment: How safe is safe enough?* New York: Plenum.

Slovic, P., Fischhoff, B., & Lichtenstein, S. (1985). Characterizing perceived risk. In R.W. Kates & C. Hohenemser (Eds.), *Perilous progress: Managing the hazards of technology.* Boulder, CO: Westview.

Slovic, P., Kunreuther, H., & White, G.F. (1974). Decision processes, rationality and adjustment to natural hazards. In G.F. White (Ed.), *Natural hazards, local, national and global*. New York: Oxford University Press.

Slovic, P., & Lichtenstein, S. (1971). Comparison of Bayesian and regression approaches to the study of information processing in judgment. *Organizational Behavior and Human Performance, 6*, 649–744.

Slovic, P., & Lichtenstein, S. (1983). Preference reversals: A broader perspective. *American Economic Review, 73*, 596–605.

Slovic, P., Lichtenstein, S., & Fischhoff, B. (1984). Modeling the societal impact of multiple-fatality accidents. *Management Science, 30*, 464–474.

Stallen, P.J.M., & Tomas, A. (1981). *Psychological aspects of risk: The assessment of the real and control.* Presented at the International School of Technology, Erice, Sicily, Italy.

Starr, C. (1969). Social benefit versus technological risk. *Science, 165*, 1232–1238.

Starr, C. (1972). Benefit-cost studies in sociotechnical systems. In *Perspective on benefit-risk decision making.* Washington, DC: National Academy of Engineering, Committee on Public Engineering Policy.

Starr, M.K., & Zeleny, M. (Eds.). (1977). *Multiple criteria decision making.* Amsterdam, Netherlands: North Holland.

Svenson, O. (1979). Process descriptions of decision making. *Organizational Behavior and Human Performance, 23*, 86–112.

Svenson, O. (1981). Are we all less risky and more skillful than our fellow drivers? *Acta Psychologica, 47*, 143–148.

Svenson, O., & Akesson, C.A. (1966). *On a relation between functional and multiple estimates in ratio scaling* (Psychology Lab Rep. No. 220). Stockholm, Sweden: University of Stockholm.

Svenson, O., & Akesson, C.A. (1967). *A further note on fractional and multiple estimates in ratio scaling* (Psychology Lab Rep. No. 224). Stockholm, Sweden: University of Stockholm.

Tait, E.J. (1981). The flow of pesticides. In T. O'Riordan & R.K. Turner (Eds.), *Process in resource management and environmental planning.* Chichester, England: Wiley.

Tait, E.J. (1982). *Pest control decision making and brassica crops.* Milton Keynes, England: Open University.

Thaler, R., & Rosen, S. (1976). The value of saving a life: Evidence from the labor market. In N. Terleckyj (Ed.), *Household production and consumption.* New York: Columbia University Press.

Thomas, K., & Baillie, P. (1982). *Public attitudes to the risks, costs, and benefits of nuclear power.* London: Social Science Research Council.

Toda, M. (1976). The decision process: A perspective. *International Journal of General Systems, 3*, 79–88.

Tversky, A., & Kahneman, D. (1971). The belief in the "law of small numbers." *Psychological Bulletin, 76*, 105–110.

Tversky, A., & Kahneman, D. (1973). Availability: A heuristic for judging frequency and probability. *Cognitive Psychology, 4*, 207–232.

Tversky, A., & Kahneman, D. (1974). Judgment under uncertainty: Heuristics and biases. *Science, 185*, 1124–1131.

Tversky, A., & Kahneman, D. (1981). The framing of decisions and the psychology of choice. *Science, 211*, 453–458.

Tversky, A., & Sattath, S. (1979). Preference trees. *Psychological Review, 86*, 542–573.

United Kingdom Department of Energy. (1979). *Energy technologies for the United Kingdom* (Vols. 1 & 2). London: Her Majesty's Stationery Office.

U.S. Government. (1975). *Teton Dam disaster.* Washington, DC: Committee on Government Operations.

U.S. Government. (1979). *Report of The President's Commission on The Accident at Three Mile Island.* Washington, DC: U.S. Government Printing Office.

U.S. Nuclear Regulatory Commission. (1981). *Fault tree handbook* (Report NUREG-0492). Washington, DC: Author.

U.S. Nuclear Regulatory Commission. (1983). *Safety goals for nuclear power plants: A discussion paper* (Report NUREG-0880). Washington, DC: Author.

Viscusi, W.K. (1983). *Risk by choice.* Cambridge, MA: Harvard University Press.

Vlek, C.A.J., & Stallen, P.J. (1980). Rational and personal aspects of risk. *Acta Psychologica, 45*, 273–300.

Vlek, C.A.J., & Stallen, P.J. (1981). Judging risk and benefits in the small and in the large. *Organizational Behavior and Human Performance, 28*, 235–271.

von Winterfeldt, D., & Edwards, W. (1982). Costs and payoffs in perceptual research. *Psychological Bulletin, 91*, 609–622.

von Winterfeldt, D., John, R.S., & Borcherding, K. (1981). Cognitive components of risk ratings. *Risk Analysis, 1*, 277–288.

Weinberg, A.M. (1979, Summer). Salvaging the atomic age. *Wilson Quarterly*, pp. 88–112.

White, G. (Ed.) (1974). *Natural hazards: Local, national and global.* New York: Oxford University Press.

Whyte, A.V.T. (1977). *Guidelines for field studies in environmental perception.* Paris: UNESCO.

Wilson, R. (1979). Analyzing the daily risks of life. *Technology Review, 81*(4), 40–46.

Wolfenstein, M. (1957). *Disasters.* Glencoe, IL: Free Press.

Wright, P.L., & Barbour, F. (1977). Phased decision strategies: Sequels to an initial screening. In M.K. Starr & M. Zeleny (Eds.), *Multiple criteria decision making.* Amsterdam, Netherlands: North Holland.

Zentner, R.D. (1979). Hazards in the chemical industry. *Chemical and Engineering News, 57*(45), 25–27, 30–34.

PART 5

INTERNATIONAL PERSPECTIVES ON ENVIRONMENTAL PSYCHOLOGY

Chapter 30

ENVIRONMENTAL PSYCHOLOGY IN AUSTRALIA

Ross Thorne, *School of Architecture, University of Sydney, Sydney, Australia*

Rob Hall, *School of Behavioral Sciences, Macquarie University, North Ryde, Australia*

30.1. AN OVERVIEW

Environmental psychology can be viewed as one way in which a culture formalizes the explanations it gives about the relationship between people and their physical environment. It follows that the task of writing about environmental psychology in any particular culture is one of describing the way in which the resident experts in that country see the relationship between people and their environment: describing the issues that give rise to research and reviewing both the results and applications of it.

To understand environmental psychology in Australia[1] requires, within the context of Australia's short history of white settlement, an understanding of both the general intellectual climate of the country and the relationship of the people to the land they settled.

We have two aims in this chapter. The first is to discuss the cultural and historical influences that have shaped both Australia's intellectual life and Australians' perception of their environment. The reason for focusing on the history of this relationship is, in turn, twofold. It helps in an understanding of the motivation for, and reception of, some types of research within the Australian community, and it has its own intrinsic interest as a study in environmental perception. The second goal for this chapter is to outline the main trends in contemporary Australian research, and we plan to do this in the context of describing the Australian institutions that direct and fund this research.

30.2. AUSTRALIAN ENVIRONMENTAL PSYCHOLOGY: THE MILIEU

When reviewing current environmental psychology in Australia, a country with a culture closely linked to the cultures of the United States and the United Kingdom, it is superficially tempting to see much similarity between Australian and overseas research. Indeed, much of the Australian output in environmental psychology *is* presented at U.S. or U.K. conferences, and Australians *do* look to publish their work in U.S. or U.K. journals.

Australia's population is about 15 million people, and thus it represents a small market for specialized books, and in turn, it can only support a small publishing industry devoted to Australian-written textbooks. One consequence of this necessary reliance by most academic disciplines on imported books (and in the past, on imported academics) is that both the United States and the United Kingdom have had an important influence in setting the agenda for Australian research. For example, it was not until 1982 that a text focusing on Australian conditions and using Australian examples (Hanley & Cooper, 1982) was available for use in tertiary courses concerned with a broad range of environment–behavior topics.

This phenomenon of external agenda setting has been further exaggerated by the fact that the Australian academic year starts in February or March, at the end of summer, which is 6 months out of phase with the European and North American year. Thus although the time-and-distance gap between Australia and the rest of the European world had narrowed from 6 months at the time of British colonization in 1788 to a single day by the 1950s, there remains for some Australian academics a sense of lagging an irreducible 6 months behind the cutting edge of overseas research and teaching. This feeling of being both behind and far away from the rest of the Western world has been a powerful influence in Australia's past cultural and intellectual life and has led Australians to give an often disproportionate respect to imported ideas.

Much of the current study of the person–environment relationship in general and environmental psychology in particular is indistinguishable from environmental psychology worldwide. There is the same fascinating spread of research topics, and often

there is the same disappointing sense of smallness that comes from empirical work focused on topics that are anchored to particular times or places, without much in the way of integrating linkage.

Although it is true that American and British research have been major contextual influences for the study and practice of environmental psychology in Australia, it would be a mistake to regard Australian environmental psychology as simply a clone of either. The particular research into person–environment interaction that has been conducted in Australia has often reflected the context provided by the physical nature of the Australian continent, its particular natural resources, and the people who make up its particular population.

Much of Australia's economic activity rests on the extraction of natural resources (such as timber, minerals, natural gas, and oil). As Darroch and Miller (1981) point out, there are many roles for the environmental psychologist to play in this context. For example, the exploitation of natural resources in a continent about 84% the size of the United States, with its small population concentrated on a fraction of the coastal fringe, has necessitated the development of "instant" towns to house the people employed on mining, or pipe-laying projects. These towns are in areas such as the hot, dry, Northwest of the continent, remote from the large population centers. Research incorporating user participation to develop suitable house designs for these areas has been sponsored by both government and industry (Brealey, 1972, 1980; Heath, 1976). Other studies have looked at the relationship between personality and ability to accept the particular environment these isolated towns present (e.g., Syme, Illingworth, Eaton, & Kantola, 1981; Veno, 1982).

However, from an Australian perspective, probably the most significant work conducted in the area of environmental psychology is concerned with analyzing the change in the relationship between white Australians and their natural environment over the relatively brief period since colonial settlement. This research has been the province of historians (e.g., Blainey, 1980; White, 1981) and will be briefly reviewed now to set the context for other environmental psychology research.

30.3. AUSTRALIAN ENVIRONMENTAL PSYCHOLOGY: THE HISTORICAL CONTEXT

The white culture in Australia is not yet 200 years old. The original settlers from England found themselves in a land where much of the knowledge they brought with them about the physical environment was rendered useless. The seasons, the landform, the flora and fauna, and the black residents were all strange to them. As a result, lives were lost, farming was often fraught with unpredicted difficulties, and attempts to explore and discover the nature of the continent were fraught with hazard.

These problems were not confined to the uneducated and unskilled members of a past generation. As Seddon (1981–1982) has pointed out, Australian research, even in recent times, has suffered because of a frequent "Eurocentric" approach to science on the part of the experts. In other words, empirical generalizations about the environment that were known to apply in the northern hemisphere were assumed to apply in Australia. This assumption was often incorrect.

In 1788, when the first white settlers were raising the British flag on Australian shores and congratulating themselves on surviving the hazardous trip to the new land, the aboriginal inhabitants were in a position to celebrate something like 45,000 years of successful occupation. The aborigines, it appears, had evolved a very workable environmental psychology (Thorne, 1980).

The new settlers, blinkered by the zeitgeist of Britain set about trying to transform both the land and its residents into something more acceptably "civilized." It has taken a large part of the past 200 years for the immigrant population of Australia to come to terms with its physical environment. And it is only now that a significant number of white Australians are becoming aware that the aborigines their forebears tried so hard to "civilize" had a complex culture that incorporated a detailed understanding of the physical environment.

30.3.1. The White Perspective

It seems paradoxical that the "civilized" people invent to conquer and must continue to invent to overcome the results of their conquering. Thus much agricultural research is aimed at repairing what people have done to win land from forest and bush, and much medical research is aimed at repairing the damage of so-called civilized living. In a similar way, the discipline of environmental psychology has, for the most part, been motivated by a need to understand and correct the mismatch between so-called civilized people and their environment.

Australia is no different from any other developed country in this regard. However, if asked today, most Australians probably would claim a sensitive apprecia-

tion of their natural environment and much regard for sympathetic design in the built environment (Hall & Glaser, 1982). That these claims are both part of a national myth and ideas of relatively recent origin is not something that troubles the claimants.

Australia, like most countries where European settlement has occurred, has been widely regarded by the settlers and their descendants as a natural resource to be conquered, extracted, and exported. The same frontier attitudes that fought and won the American West seem to have been alive and well in Australia. The unfamiliar land and climate of Australia presented a formidable opponent, and it could never be claimed that the settlers had a harmonious relationship with it. In Blainey's words, "nature in the eyes of most Australians to 1900 remained an enemy" (Blainey, 1980, p. 360).

The original settlers in Australia came from two broad strata of eighteenth-century British society. First, there were the convicts, ex-convicts, and their Australian-born "currency" children. They were anti-church (Grocott, 1980), racist toward the aborigines (Broome, 1982) and, later, toward Chinese, Italians, or other visibly non-British arrivals (White, 1981). They were, by and large, ex-city dwellers with no knowledge of land husbandry.

The second group consisted of military and government officials, free settlers, and influential members of the church. It is clear that, although some of these people saw Australia as a land of opportunity, the majority found it poor compensation for their exile.

To both of these social groups, the Australian landscape appeared untidy — with a dreary sameness about it. They were surrounded by a strange, aberrant world.

> Nearly every immigrant arrived with strong north European preferences in landscape, sunlight, colour, temperature, and vegetation.... These preferences lived on through the songs and hymns the migrants carried here, the poems and paintings, and in the names they placed on the map. The preferences were subtly passed on to generations of Australian-borne children thus impeding their acclimatization. (Blainey, 1980, p. 360)

Prior to the arrival of the European settlers, the aborigines had used fire to promote the growth of grasses and reduce the undergrowth and thus develop grazing land for kangaroos. Their main achievement was "to develop Australia as a giant sheep run, ready for take-over" (Seddon, 1983, p. 12). The white settlers treated this landscape with a mixture of fear and scorn (Bolton, 1981). They perceived the land as being unused and ready for the taking and began to farm as they had farmed in Britain. They continued the process of land clearing for pasture and crops so industriously that two-thirds of Australia's forests have disappeared, and the resulting landscape of grassland with occasional clumps of eucalypts to shade the cattle or sheep is now thought to be a typically Australian scene.

Apart from a strip of land 200 to 300 miles wide stretching around the eastern half of the continent's perimeter and a small area in the southwestern corner, the remaining 90% of the continent is arid or semiarid. Despite the availability of appropriate technical advice from the state departments of agriculture (formed prior to 1900 in each state), much of the fragile environment has been overgrazed and over-cropped. The land has been mishandled in many ways. Thus loss of soil through erosion, dust storms, and salination has been all too common, and, from the evidence of satellite photos, arable land is still disappearing at an alarming rate. In addition to the usual desires for power and profit, this mishandling has been the result of a widespread misperception of the landscape.

Wherever possible, the early settlers tried to re-shape the land to resemble Britain: They planted European flora and introduced European fauna, and an Acclimatization Society was formed in order to import European game birds and animals. The rabbit, introduced in 1859 by an ex-yeoman who yearned to sport like the English gentry, found no natural predators and reached plague proportions. By 1880, sheep properties had to be abandoned to the rabbits that were moving north at the rate of 100 km per year. Domestic dogs, cats, pigs, donkeys, horses, and goats were imported, which led to large feral populations of each group. Imported camels and Indonesian water buffalo became so prolific that, in recent decades, a small but viable industry to export camels to the Middle East developed.

Cattle and sheep were taken into low-rainfall areas where their hooves compressed the topsoil and there was little regrowth of the grass cover. Sheep were allowed to graze on plants that naturally controlled the soil salinity. When the plants were consumed, increased soil salinity prevented grassland from developing. At the same time as the exotic animals were being introduced, the native macropods and marsupials were being slaughtered. Some of the smaller species soon became extinct. Koalas and platypus were still being hunted for skins in some areas until the 1920s.

30.3.2. The Black Perspective

In some parts of Australia, notably Tasmania, the aboriginal people fared no better than the koalas and platypus, and their population was decimated. For much of the period of European settlement in Australia, the aborigines were widely regarded as "clean slates," ready for a Christian education and initiation into what was ethnocentrically regarded as a "superior" white culture. The settlers were (and often still are) disappointed when the aborigines failed to grasp the opportunity they were offered.

> Their system of socialism is as great a bar to progress as their superstition, as it hinders any improvement or rightful ownership. The healthy competition so essential to the progress of any nation is conspicuous by its absence. (Unnamed missionary from Mapoon quoted by Roberts, 1981, p. 43)

It is only in the last 10 years that archaeological, anthropological, and archival research has been collected together to produce a reasonably clear general picture of the tribal aborigines who inhabited Australia at the time of settlement and of their fate under white domination (e.g., Blainey, 1975; Broome, 1982; Roberts, 1981).

The aborigines seem to have been in Australia for at least 45,000 years. At the time of European settlement, they occupied most of the continent, which was divided into hundreds of "fluid republics" (Blainey, 1975). In each area, the aborigines had developed their own language, adapted their diet to the particular environment, and had developed different artifacts such as musical instruments. A common thread, however, that was shared by all aboriginal groups was their relationship to the land (Jones, 1985).

People of European culture often find the aboriginal religion and its basis in the physical landscape difficult to comprehend. In the Australia of the 1980s, this leads to difficulties when, for example, mining companies and British justice clash with aborigines and tribal law over the reality of "sacred sites" that are located where commercially valuable minerals have been discovered.

The aboriginal religion made the human being subservient to the landforms and creatures that filled the environment. Each aborigine was allied to a totem such as an animal, reptile, bird, tree, or rock outcrop. A person then became responsible for protecting the history and sacred sites associated with their totem being, and for passing on this sacred knowledge to future generations (Broome, 1982).

Their religion, their own piece of tribal land, and their history were one.

> We see all things natural as a part of us. All the things on Earth we see as part human. This is told through the idea of "dreaming." By dreaming we mean the belief that long ago, these creatures started human society. These creatures, these great creatures are just as much alive today as they were in the beginning. They are everlasting and will never die. They are always part of the land and nature as we are. Our connection to all things natural is spiritual. (Silas Roberts, cited in Fox, 1982, p. 14)

Because their own piece of tribal land held all their history and education, the aborigines were not interested in "expansionist policies" as other land had no meaning for them. They did, however, consider that tribes from distant parts were inferior—a fact that the British exploited when using aborigines as part of the government police force (Broome, 1982).

The aborigines had come to terms with the Australian continent and, in places where European explorers perished from thirst or malnutrition, could find adequate water and enjoyed a diet rich in nutrition and variety.

The new settlers progressively dispossessed the black inhabitants from the more fertile regions and introduced them to new diseases, genocide, and bureaucratic government. Some of these early settlers did view the aborigines sympathetically (e.g., Tench, 1793/1961), and from time to time some bemoaned the treatment they received under white government (e.g., Bennett, 1867). Nevertheless, unlike the Indians of North America and the Maoris of New Zealand, the aborigines received no consideration under law as a "civilized" people. To the early British and other European settlers and to many of their descendants in the 1980s, the aboriginal groups had no recognizable form of government, no religion, and did no work. As Roberts (1981) notes, the aborigines have for the most part been treated as "child people of the human race."

30.4. CURRENT AUSTRALIAN VIEWS

In the preceding sections of this chapter we have sketched the details of the relatively recent white settlement of a continent, largely unknown to Europeans until the eighteenth century, and in which the environment was thought to be strange and unpredictable. Everything was perceived as being wrong: the inhabitants, the evergreen vegetation, and the na-

tive animals. Because of this, "there was no limit to the willingness of the nineteenth-century settlers to improve on the Creator's arrangements" (Bolton, 1981, p. 88). Less than 200 years ago the relationship between the typical settler and the Australian environment was tantamount to war. In some circles this attitude has moderated to rape:

> One must view with dismay...support of what any person (capable of reasoning for himself) must understand is the Number One enemy of civilisation, and hence Australia.
>
> The main danger today resides in the environmentalist movement. I am not referring to the great number of well-intentioned people who, out of sheer ignorance, don't realise the damage they are doing to Australia. I am referring to those subversives who, for personal gain or a lust for power, are desirous of breaking down what is left of our "free enterprise" system entirely; these latter people, whose numbers are swelled by a great mass of unwashed, unspanked, dole-bludging[2] drop-outs, are threatening the lives and fortunes of the Australian community as it has never been threatened before. (Lang Hancock, mining magnate, in *The Australian*, Letters to the Editor, 10 April 1978)

Given the historical background outlined previously, it may seem paradoxical that there were movements for the conservation of the natural bushland as early as 1880. In Australia, there *has* been a growing interest in the preservation of the natural environment since the early days of European settlement. Until the late 1800s, this interest was represented by "eccentric" individuals; in the late 1900s, it is represented by large and often politically powerful groups. In common with other developed countries (see e.g., Cotgrove, 1982), there is still, however, the tension between those who want to use resources and those who want to conserve them.

30.4.1. Attitudes Toward the Environment

The work of historians like Blainey and White has provided a fascinating view of the changing relationship between people and their physical (and social) environment in Australia. A concern with understanding the way the contemporary but mythical "average Australian" sees the present environment is shared by a number of researchers in Australia. Some studies have been within the "social indicator" tradition, treating the physical environment as one of a number of determinants of people's "quality of life." These social indicator studies have taken a more or less broad view, ranging from attempts to gauge Australians' "priorities, satisfactions, and well-being" (Headey & Wearing, 1981) or to establish a quality of life index (Jones, 1981), to more focused studies about the degree of social disadvantage in Sydney suburbs (Vinson & Homel, 1975).

Other studies have been more concerned with developing attitude scales relating to environmental issues (e.g., Ray, 1975, 1980) or studying the dimensionality of sets of items across cultures (e.g., Brebner, Rump, & Delin, 1976). Ray developed a Likert scale he called an "Australian Environmentalism Scale." This scale was normed on a number of urban samples and subsequently on a national sample, using a postal questionnaire.

Ray (1980) used the scale to see whether people living in a rural environment that was part of a rapidly developing open-cut coal-mining area differed from the general sample in their environmental attitudes. The results showed no differences between the samples on which the scale was normed and the mining sample. This result probably says more about the insensitivity of generalized attitude scales than it does about the actual populations involved.

Some work has put more emphasis on the problem of determining the criteria for validity of attitude and belief measures in the environmental context. This work has often been within the policy-capturing mould. For example, Schwartz and Syme (1982) adapted earlier work from the decision-making literature to produce a technique for modeling people's evaluation of complex projects and to provide criteria by which the success of the modeling could be assessed. The substantive topic they were concerned with was the development of nuclear power in Australia.

The studies discussed up to here have not been explicitly concerned with either the variety of points of view that Australians might have about environmental issues, or, with the exception of the Brebner and colleagues (1976) study, with a comparison of their points of view with those held by people in other countries. A study by Hall and Glaser (1982) looked at these questions. The study was a national, postal survey of Australians conducted in parallel with similar studies in the United States, the United Kingdom, and the German Federal Republic (Milbrath, 1981). A substantially similar questionnaire was used in each country.

Hall and Glaser regarded four issues that were dealt with in the questionnaire as being central to the whole range of issues being studied. These four issues were (1) whether or not there are environmental problems, (2) whether, if there are, the solution to them will come from a "technological fix" or a change in life-style, (3) whether the respondents felt able to influence affairs in their own communities, and (4) whether the respondents were for or against direct action (such as street demonstrations). The sample was segmented using cluster analysis applied to the questions dealing with these four issues.

The analysis led to the conclusion that the sample was comprised of people with one of four points-of-view. Those who saw our hope being in better technology and scientific development (the "scientists") were 21% of the sample. A change of life-style as the only hope was the view of 49% of the sample (the "humanists"), whereas 13% saw life-style change as the short-term need with technology as the long-term salvation. The remaining 17% of the sample took a "safe" middle position on all issues.

A comparison of the Australian data with the American revealed that the Australian scientist group had a profile very similar to the total American sample on most issues in the questionnaire. The profile for the *total* Australian sample was influenced by the large proportion of humanists and was different from the overall American pattern. Thus it appears as if the population of Australia (to the extent that it was represented by the sample gathered in the Hall and Glaser study) gives greater lip service to the need for a conservative approach to the environment. This is a radical change from the recorded opinions of the recent past.

30.5. SPONSORS OF RESEARCH

Although the polling of public opinion tells us something about "informal" environmental psychology in Australia, we need to look to large institutions, both government and private, to discover the extent to which the concerns of environmental psychology have become legitimized.

30.5.1. Funding

In an education system where universities are only part of the range of tertiary institutions, they have rather jealously pressed their case for being the rightful, preeminent homes of research. Traditionally, the expenditure on research and experimental development in Australia by organizations concerned with higher education has exceeded that by industry. In 1981–1982 for example, the educational expenditure was 31% of the national total, whereas the industrial expenditure was 21% and the government expenditure was 46% (A.B.S., April 1984). Since the establishment of colleges of advanced education in 1979, the universities have had major rivals for a share of research funding.

In 1973, the Australian federal government assumed responsibility for funding universities when the then-Labor government decided to abolish student fees. Thus most research in Australia is funded, directly or indirectly, by state or federal governments. Hence most formalized environmental psychology is government funded and is conducted as university research or as part of the activity of government or semigovernment departments.

By far the largest single research organization in Australia is the Commonwealth Scientific and Industrial Research Organisation (CSIRO). The work of the CSIRO is currently organized as five institutes: Animal and Food Resources, Biological Resources, Earth Resources, Industrial Technology, and Physical Sciences. It is claimed that "in no other country is there such an all-embracing research establishment" (Coogan, 1981, p. 81). Environmental psychology is, however, only a small fragment of the CSIRO's research output and is mostly in the areas of building design (e.g., Finigham, 1980) and resource management (e.g. Syme, Kantola, & Thomas, 1980).

A small percentage of research expenditure (in 1981-1982 the figure was 1% of the total) was accounted for by nonprofit organizations (which may still be subsidized by government funds). The Australian Institute of Urban Studies, for example, occasionally sponsors environmental psychology research.

30.5.2. Educational Institutions

In the universities, environmental psychology, in the narrower sense of being a recognized part of the academic discipline of psychology, has not been embraced with enthusiasm by the traditional departments of psychology. Although some departments, which are typically in the newer universities and colleges, have given support to the area, in the main, enthusiasm has been limited to individual faculty members.

The real-world, multivariate, problem-solving orientation that has made much of environmental psychology a refreshing change from the confines of some of the traditional areas in psychology carries with it the risk that environmental psychology can become a mere catalog of specific findings. What Darroch and Miller (1981) called the "quick and cute" studies in social psychology may be replaced by the "butterfly collections," of environmental psychology.

30.6. INTERDISCIPLINARY LINKS

What is needed, in Australia and elsewhere, are the links between researchers and between disciplines that extend beyond the limits of a particular study and can provide a forum in which broader questions can be addressed. From his survey of environment–behavior research around the world, Saarinen (1982) has concluded that Australia shares with countries like Turkey and the U.S.S.R. a stage of development in environment–behavior studies where researchers, isolated by distance or language, are becoming aware of one another's activities and are establishing links to share information. The first symposium on environmental psychology conducted under the auspices of the Australian Psychological Society was held as recently as 1981. (The Australian Psychological Association, it can be noted, was, until 1966, an overseas branch of the British society.)

In Australia, current research into, and application of, environmental psychology (using the term to refer to the full range of relevant environment–behavior issues, rather than any formalized province within the discipline of psychology), has been conducted, in the main, by four groups of people. These groups are (1) psychologists (and some sociologists), (2) architects (and some town planners), (3) geographers, and (4) engineers and others involved in ergonomics/human factors work or in environmental impact assessment.

The division of people into these groups is based on an analysis of the degree of cross-referencing that has taken place in the literature associated with them. Such a classification is, of course, a gross oversimplification of reality, and an injustice to those workers whose catholic tastes in research lead them to cover a wide range of issues and literature. Nevertheless, the classification has sufficient truth to warrant its use.

Until now, there has been minimal intergroup communication. Sometimes this has been because the groups are not sure what to say to each other and attempts at communication have faltered (e.g., Purcell & Heath, 1982). Sometimes it has been simply that some of the groups are not aware of the others' interest in the area. The latter seems to be the case with psychologists and geographers. However, the fact that the 1983 congress of the Australian and New Zealand Association for the Advancement of Science (ANZAAS) featured, among the many interdisciplinary symposia, a symposium entitled "The Impact of Environment–Behavior Research on Housing Policy," presented jointly by the divisions of psychology, geography, and environmental studies, may be a sign of the good times to come.

Some professional organizations (e.g., the Ergonomic Society of Australia and New Zealand and the Royal Australian Institute of Architects) have always promoted some contact between people working in a wide range of disciplines. However, a more deliberate and ultimately more wide-ranging attempt to link workers in the environment–behavior area is represented by the *People and the Man-Made Environment* newsletter that began circulating in 1981 and became the regional *People and Physical Environment Research* newsletter in June 1983. Informal groupings of individuals drawn together by an interest in the interdisciplinary focus of environmental psychology have been instrumental in providing a forum for both discussion and research. In 1972, Thorne, an architect who had been carrying out research with members of Glasgow's University of Strathclyde Building Performance Research Unit (Canter & Thorne, 1972) joined with three psychologists to form the Sydney-based Architectural Psychology Research Unit (Hall, Metcalfe, Purcell, & Thorne, 1972). The activities of this group in conducting research and organizing courses for members of the design professions, together with courses at Sydney University organized by Canter (from Strathclyde) and Moore (from Wisconsin-Milwaukee) provided an initial focus for regional conferences.

In 1980, the conference entitled "People and the Man-Made Environment" (Thorne & Arden, 1980) was held in Sydney. The success of this conference led the Australian and New Zealand Architectural Science Association (ANZAScA) to organize a related conference in 1981 (Szokolay, 1981). A widening of interest led, in turn, to a third conference held in New Zealand, with the amended title "People and Physical Environment Research" (Joiner, Brimilcombe, Daish, Gray, & Kernohan, 1983). One aim of the conference organizers was to inaugurate a southwestern Pacific regional, interdisciplinary environmental organization. This aim was achieved and the People and Physical Environment Research (PAPER) organization was born on June 11, 1983 with an objective of sponsoring a biennial conference, the last being held in Melbourne (Dovey, Downton, & Missingham, 1985) with the next planned for June 1987 in Perth, Western Australia.

30.6.1. Interdisciplinary Education

In 1969, Amos Rapaport began a series of courses in human–environment studies within the School of Architecture at the University of Sydney. Programs with a similar focus quickly became part of the course structure in most Australian and New Zealand faculties of architecture. However, the initial impetus quickly leveled off and declined in some cases.

A UNESCO conference, Man in the Biosphere, held in Australia in 1970 was one of the major precipitating factors that led to the establishment of multidisciplinary programs of "environmental studies" in many Australian universities and colleges. The first of these was a master's degree program offered at Monash University in 1973 (Ealey, 1982). Other universities began somewhat similar programs at about the same time or very soon afterward. These "centers" for environmental studies differ in emphasis in that some are oriented toward teaching, whereas others are oriented more toward research.

The environmental studies programs are, in the main, offered at postgraduate level and are designed around a set of core subjects from the physical and biological sciences. In some programs, environmental psychology is part of the core group of subjects, but in most it is one of the elective courses. In some universities and colleges, the geography faculty has had a strong interest in human geography, and these departments (notably at the Universities of New England and Macquarie) have made significant contributions to environmental psychology (e.g., Aplin, 1983, 1984; Payne & Pigram, 1973; Walmsley, 1982).

In Australia, at the present time, there are no postgraduate programs in environmental psychology of the type offered, for example, by some American and British universities. Hence, although there are master's and doctoral degree students working on aspects of environmental psychology in Australia, these students are found affiliated with almost any discipline and work in relative isolation.

30.7. ENVIRONMENTAL PSYCHOLOGY: DIRECTIONS OF CURRENT ACTIVITY

This chapter is not the place to produce an exhaustive review of the research that could be described as environmental psychology in Australia. Instead, we will merely outline some of the areas in which there is considerable current research activity in Australia, and we will conclude by suggesting some of the tasks that environmental psychology might profitably perform in the Australian context.

30.7.1. Environmental Impact Assessment

Closely following the example set by the National Environmental Protection Act in the United States, the

Australian government passed a similar act in 1974, differing from the American model mainly in details of procedure (see Fowler, 1982). However, this act only applies to projects involving the commonwealth government. State government legislation, which varies markedly from state to state and reflects the political attitudes of the party in power, determines the role to be played by impact assessment studies in most significant projects in Australia. As a result of these government initiatives (or lack of them), environmental psychology can be found making a meager contribution to environmental evaluation, amid the weight of biological, chemical, and engineering data.

Typically, even where the social impact of a development would appear to be potentially great, the analysis of "social impact" in the Environmental Impact Statement (EIS) is not well done, reflecting both the "hard" scientists' distrust of "soft" data, and the psychologists' failure to provide a relevant methodology. Fortunately, there are at least some exceptions to this gloomy state of affairs (e.g., Lynch, Spence, Pearson, & Consultants, 1976).

30.7.2. Landscape Evaluation

Some state forestry authorities (notably the Forests Department of Western Australia and the Forests Commission of Victoria) have supported substantial programs concerned, in particular, with assessing the perceptual character of landscapes (Herbert, 1983; Williamson & Chalmers, 1982). Landscape perception has also been of interest to researchers not directly affiliated with forestry authorities (e.g., Correy, 1981; Hawkins, 1983; Purcell & Lamb, 1984). Some researchers (e.g., Walmsley, 1982) have followed the "mental maps" tradition of Gould and White (1974) and have related personality variables to perceptions of the "macrolandscape," that is, at the regional level.

As a result of the widespread interest in landscape evaluation apparent among researchers, a program entitled "Landscape Planning and Management Workshops" was begun in 1980 (Williamson & Bishop, 1981). The first 2-day workshop brought together people from both academic, government, and private organizations. One of the private organizations was the National Trust of Australia, which is concerned with the protection of Australia's natural and manmade heritage. The National Trust representative at the workshop probably summarized the direction of landscape research in Australia as a whole when she said, describing changes in the trust's landscape evaluation criteria:

> The over-riding need to establish the significance of an area through the use of quantifiable, bio-physical data that was prevalent in the late 60's [and] early 70's seems to have lessened and we are now more aware of the importance of recognising the more subtle landscape values (i.e., aesthetic and cultural) which require sensitive interpretation. (Johnston, 1981, p. 6)

Much of the published research to date has been inspired by the work of Ervin Zube, Kenneth Craik, and Rachel and Steven Kaplan. It has been heavily reliant on the use of multivariate statistics to model observer's judgments, and, whereas some of the studies (e.g., Williamson, 1983) have made significant contributions to our knowledge of methods and techniques, there is still the fundamental problem of the appropriate "grain size" of a scene (Garner, 1974) to use for analysis. It is hoped that future research will address this problem more adequately and thus leave the reader with less of a feeling that the obvious has been ground small in the mill of analysis.

30.7.3. The Built Landscape

The built landscape has been analyzed at many levels, from the visually perceived detail of elevator foyers (Hall, Purcell, Thorne, & Metcalfe, 1976) through the perception of whole buildings (Purcell, 1984a) to the total impact of suburban (King, 1981), isolated small-town (Gribbin & Brealey, 1980) and "alternative" rural community (Munro-Clark, 1986) living. Attention has been given to studying the way in which people integrate design information into their cognitive structure (Lawrence, 1981, 1982; Mueller, 1981) and to the way in which they use this information in making choices about preferred residential environments (McKenzie, 1982).

Pearce has been particularly interested in people's images of cities. In a series of studies (Pearce, 1977; Pearce & Cairney, 1980; Pearce, Innes, O'Driscoll, & Morse, 1981), he examined people's perception of a number of cities and looked at the relationship between features recalled and variables such as amount of time spent in the city. This interest in perception of place has been extended into a series of studies focused on understanding the experience of being a tourist (Pearce, 1982).

Other researchers have used city or town characteristics as a variable in studies of social behavior. Amato (1980, 1981), for example, conducted comparisons of friendliness and helping behavior across countries and across population densities. Cairney and Brebner (1980) examined the effect of the imageability of the pattern of road closures in two towns and on people's satisfaction with the local authorities' road closure policy.

30.7.4. Climate and Other Environmental Stressors

The interaction of the built and natural environments and their joint impact on people has been studied at levels ranging from the office work place to cyclonic devastation. In a series of studies (Purcell, 1984b; Purcell & Thorne, 1977; Purcell, Hall, Thorne, & Metcalfe, 1973; Thorne & Purcell, 1976) the detrimental impact of steady-state climate and office noise on workers was studied. With a similar focus, a series of studies from the Brain-Behaviour Research Institute at La Trobe University has looked at hormonal indicators of stress in a wide range of physical and social work environments (Bartley, 1981).

At the level of whole buildings and their place in the cityscape, Aynsley (1980) has looked at the way in which the bulk, shape, and texture of the city form can produce wind effects that make parts of the city uncomfortable and at times dangerous for the pedestrian. De Gruchy and Hansford (1979) explored the "defensible space" concept (Newman, 1972) in a study of crime and architecture in four commercial areas of Brisbane.

At the macrolevel of climatic impact are the cyclones, droughts, floods, and bushfires that occasionally ravage parts of Australia. A number of researchers have looked at the impact of these events on people (e.g., Oliver, 1980; Payne & Pigram, 1973). More moderate climatic effects have been the focus for a series of studies by Auliciems, who on the one hand attempted to produce a model of thermal perception and a classification scheme for thermal stress assessment in Australia, and on the other attempted to relate personality and mood to climatic variables (1972, 1978, 1979, 1981; Auliciems & Kalma, 1979; Auliciems & Parlow, 1975).

30.7.5. Interaction of the Social and Built Environments

Although many of the studies mentioned under other headings in this chapter have an interest in the interaction between the social and the built environments, there are some studies where the nature of the interaction itself is a central concern in the investigation. For example, Bennett, Booker, Hewson, and Holliday (1983) studied the interaction of physical and psychological factors that affected the birth experience of a first child. Their study compared the experiences of women giving birth in a range of phys-

ical, social, and "medical" environments and looked at the interplay between these three classes of variables. A similar concern to understand the relative impact of social and physical variables motivated the design of the "Australia and New Zealand Haemodialysis Study" (Cairns, 1984). This research incorporates scales to measure the dialysis patient's "social climate" (Moos & Moos, 1976), desired locus of control, and perception of the environments in which the process of dialysis placed them.

Other work (e.g., Forgas, 1981), began as part of the mainstream of social psychology, looked at the problem of understanding the "natural units" of social behavior so that the interaction between the physical and social environments could be observed more meaningfully. This type of study raises the whole issue of appropriate methodologies for environment–behavior research.

In the main, the issue of social-physical interaction is one that has not been well handled in Australian environmental psychology to this point. Most of the research has been motivated by a demand for "usable information" and has been conducted in either the experimental or the positivist large-scale survey mould. Hence questions such as what an environment "means" to people have been explored through either the "thin" coverage of a large survey or by inference when experimental results are being interpreted. It is hoped that one trend that will develop in Australian research is a greater appreciation of the role that well-grounded qualitative methodology can play in the study of the environment–behavior interaction. (See Morgan, 1983, for a particularly clear statement of the role of research methods in constructing knowledge.)

30.8. FUTURE DIRECTIONS

The two areas where environmental psychology seems most likely to play a role at the policy level in Australia today are housing/urban land use and energy/resource use.

30.8.1. Housing and Land Use

In Australia, the earliest comprehensive report on slums and urban problems was in 1859 (Jevons, cited by Kelly, 1978). In line with the deterministic view that a poor standard of housing led to behavioral depravity, there was an emphasis on developing the suburbs and moving the population away from the crowded city centers. By the early part of this century, state governments had passed enforceable regulations for minimum subdivision sizes for land and minimum construction standards for dwellings. Over time, the regulations, combined with the aspiration of each family to own a detached house on a block of land (typically between 6 to 10 thousand sq ft in area) led to sprawling suburbs. The city of Sydney with its attendant suburbs, for example, now occupies an area more extensive than Greater London; yet the population is about one-third the number.

Of course, the deterministic model of the environment–behavior relationship was as invalid in Australia as anywhere else in the world, and social problems were discovered in the suburbs (e.g., King & Wyllie, 1981a, 1981b, 1982). Occasionally, the question has been raised as to whether the proliferation of the suburban sprawl was not ill-conceived and undesirable. However, the "right" to have a house and land of one's own has become such a strong part of the Australian dream that state governments do all they can to avoid the electoral wrath of would-be home owners, who are frustrated by high interest rates or high prices.

The case for a more flexible pattern of urban consolidation has been argued by the Australian Institute of Urban Studies (AIUS, 1982), and a large amount of current research into housing is aimed at understanding whether or not policies of urban/suburban development different from those currently followed would be more appropriate for Australian cities (e.g., Cardew, 1970, 1980; Gorrie, 1975; Gribbin & Brealey, 1980; Harrison, 1970; Halkett, 1976).

Although owning one's own home is the popular dream, a large number of Australians must rely on public housing for shelter. Indeed, the New South Wales Housing Commission, for example, provides accommodation for over half a million people, making it comparable in size of operation with the public housing authorities in, say, the State of New York that has a population about four times that of New South Wales.

A number of postoccupancy studies of public housing have been conducted. Some of these (e.g., DeMaria, 1973; Sutton & Richmond, 1974; Turnbull, Thorne, Anderson, Weiderman, & Butterfield, 1983) have been concerned with either looking at occupant satisfaction in high-rise dwellings and medium density housing (Johnson, 1983), or with investigating the hypothesis that high-rise dwellings are associated with medical and psychological problems. A number of broader based studies have looked at the difficulties associated with housing developments that lack amenities or in which the population is largely one that has been transferred from inner city locations (e.g., Brennan, 1973; Finch, 1968). Some studies of preoccupancy dwelling design for public housing have also

been sponsored by public housing authorities in Australia (Burrows, 1978; Girardi, 1978; Lewis, 1978).

In general, building evaluation or postoccupancy evaluation is only in an embryonic form in Australia. Among the factors contributing to this state of affairs are (1) lack of interest among designers (in a recent survey only 10% of architects claimed that they revisit their buildings to gather performance information, and when they did, they did so on an ad hoc basis and without a systematic methodology) (Law, 1981), (2) the stringent libel laws in Australia can inhibit researchers, other than the architect or client, from publishing a critical evaluation of a building if it is designed by a private architect, and (3) surveys of user satisfaction have failed to gather data that could be translated into action and thus provide little incentive for the designer to look to evaluation studies for guidance.

As Seddon (1983) pointed out:

> The design professions have played a miniscule part in the shaping of the Australian environment.... A very small proportion of the buildings other than those of the city centres in Australia are designed by architects, and landscape architecture is a fledgling profession in Australia, in contrast with its status in Europe, Japan, and the Americas. (p. 11)

Given this state of affairs and the dominant role of government in funding research in general the lead for both pre-and postoccupancy studies of buildings in Australia has come from federal and state government initiatives. The Federal Department of Housing and Construction has followed the New Zealand government model for postoccupancy evaluation of the buildings for which it is responsible (see Daish, Gray, Kernohan, & Joiner, 1983). The state government of New South Wales has established the Hosplan organization to evaluate recently completed state hospitals in order to provide guidelines for new building design programs.

The history of housing for aboriginal Australians highlights other problems. It appears that, despite the considerable sums of public money expended, "success" has largely eluded the white politicians and administrators. Housing for aborigines has been, in the main, a poorer version of white housing (Belling, 1980; Drakakis-Smith, 1981; Lovejoy, 1973). The authorities responsible for producing this housing have, by and large, failed to understand the nature of aboriginal culture and society (George & Clark, 1980; Hepple, 1979). Unfortunately, examples of a satisfying blend of aboriginal culture and white aspiration for that culture are rare. However, there are some (e.g., Bryant, 1981), and attempts to develop a more sensitive approach to aboriginal housing needs are reflected in the establishment of the Aboriginal Data Archive in the Department of Architecture at the University of Queensland (Memmott, 1981) and in the interest some white researchers have in understanding the topic (e.g., Hamilton, 1976, Reser, 1977, 1981).

30.8.2. Energy and Resource Use

Australia is a dry continent, and although the actions of some urban Australians who use water with gusto might suggest otherwise, there has always been some appreciation of the need for water conservation. Driven less by the extremes of climate than many other countries and buffered to some extent from the full impact of the first steep rises in oil prices, Australians have not been sensitive, however, to the need for resource conservation on a broad front.

In recent years, rising energy costs and reports of resource depletion have begun to change community and institutional attitudes and, in common with other countries, Australia has seen an increase in research aimed at both developing a less resource-hungry lifestyle and designing a built environment that is less wasteful of resources.

At the University of Western Australia and the CSIRO Division of Groundwater Research, for example, there has been a concerted study of demand management in relation to water. Winkler has been a leading exponent of applying behavioral technology to resource management (Winkler, 1982, 1983; Winkler, Syme, & Thomas, 1979). Kantola (1983), Syme (1983), and Thomas (1983) have examined the role of attitudes, media messages, and economic variables on water demand.

Government departments and instrumentalities in Australia have begun to fund research in this area for specific studies of conservation-related behavior. For example, in 1980 the National Research, Development and Demonstration Council released funds to the Royal Australian Institute of Architects (New South Wales chapter) for a study of strategies for encouraging energy conservation in buildings (Hayes & Angel, 1981).

Australians are congregated in an urban society on the fringe of a fragile environment. Although a sentimental appreciation of "the bush" and the "outback" have been absorbed into the popular mythology of most Australian-born citizens, there is little real understanding of the natural environment and its ecology. One of the major tasks confronting environmental psychology in Australia is to develop ways in which the problems of distance and time scale can be removed so that the politicians, the industrialists, and the general population can gain a clear perception of the environment that must support all of our activities.

Hayes and Angel (1981) made the point in the preface to their report that in Australia "the goal of energy conservation was clear, but the path was unknown." A similar comment could be made about Australian environmental psychology. We know that, if it is to be more than yet another arbitrary subdivision of knowledge and more than just another reason for conferences, newsletters, and trivial studies, environmental psychology must make a real contribution to the quality of life in Australia. The goal is clear, the path is not.

NOTES

1. Although there are some similarities between the forces that shaped the cultures of Australia and nearby New Zealand, the differences in history, landscape, and indigenous people make it difficult to discuss both countries in the same chapter and still maintain a coherent approach. For this reason, we will do no more than mention some of the more recent developments in New Zealand.

2. *Dole-bludging* is a derogatory term for unemployed people who live on social security payments (the dole) while making no serious attempt to find work.

REFERENCES

Amato, P.R. (1980). City size, sidewalk density, and friendliness toward strangers. *Journal of Social Psychology.* *111*(1), 151–152.

Amato, P.R. (1981). Urban-rural differences in helping: Behavior in Australia and the United States. *Journal of Social Psychology, 114*(2), 289–290.

Aplin, G. (1983, February). *Man and the environment in eighteenth century Sydney.* Paper presented to the Institute of Australian Geographers Conference, Melbourne.

Aplin, G. (1984, February). *Sydney landscapes: 1788–1825.* Paper presented to the Institute of Australian Geographers Conference, Sydney.

Auliciems, A. (1972). Classroom performance as a function of thermal comfort. *International Journal of Biometeorology, 16*(3), 233–246.

Auliciems, A. (1978). Mood dependency on low intensity atmospheric variability. *International Journal of Biometeorology, 22*(1), 20–32.

Auliciems, A. (1979). *Spatial, temporal, and human dimensions of air pollution in Brisbane.* St Lucia, Queensland, Australia: University of Queensland, Department of Geography.

Auliciems, A. (1981). Towards a psycho-physiological model of thermal perception. *International Journal of Biometeorology, 25*(2), 109–122.

Auliciems, A., & Kalma, J.D. (1979). A climatic classification of human thermal stress in Australia. *Journal of Applied Meteorology, 18*, 616–626.

Auliciems, A., & Parlow, J. (1975). Thermal comfort and personality. *Building Services Engineer, 43*, 94–97.

Australian Bureau of Statistics. (1984, February). *Research and experimental development: All sector summary, Australia, 1981-82* (Report No. 8112.0). Canberra, Australia: Author.

Australian Institute of Urban Studies. *Urban consolidation and Adelaide* (Occasional paper). Canberra, Australia: Author.

Aynsley, R.M. (1980). Airflow: Its effect on the environment and thermal comfort. In R. Thorne & S. Arden (Eds.), *People and the man-made environment* (pp. 77–98). Sydney: University of Sydney, Architecture Department.

Bartley, H.L. (Ed.) (1981). *Work effectiveness: Proceedings of a symposium held at Latrobe University.* Melbourne: Latrobe University, Brain Behaviour Research Unit.

Belling, W. (1980, December). Aboriginal housing in Latrobe Valley: Depressing and degrading. *Shelter.* Australia, 2–3.

Bennett, A., Booker, E., Hewson, D., & Holliday, S. (1983). *Factors affecting the physical and psychological experience of normal childbirth.* Sydney: Commonwealth Department of Health.

Bennett, S. (1867). *The history of Australian discovery and colonisation.* Sydney: Hanson and Bennett.

Blainey, G. (1975). *Triumph of the Nomads: A history of ancient Australia.* South Melbourne: Macmillan.

Blainey, G. (1980). *A land half won.* (revised edition, 1982). South Melbourne: Macmillan (revised edition, 1982).

Bolton, G. (1981). *Spoils and spoilers: Australians make their environment 1788-1980.* Sydney: Allen and Unwin.

Brealey, T.B. (1972). *Living in remote communities in tropical Australia: Exploratory study* (Rep. No. TB27.1).Highett, Victoria, Australia: Commonwealth Scientific and Industrial Research Organization, Division of Building Research.

Brealey, T.B. (1980). Popular myths and folklaw concerning planning in new mining towns in Australia. *Man-Environment Systems, 10*, 146–152.

Brebner, J., Rump, E.E., & Delin, P. (1976). A cross-cultural replication of attitudes to the physical environment. *International Journal of Psychology, 11*(2), 111–118.

Brennan, T. (1973). *New community: Problems and policies.* Sydney: Angus and Robertson.

Broome, R. (1982). *Aboriginal Australians.* North Sydney, New South Wales, Australia: Allen and Unwin.

Bryant, J.J. (1981). *The Robinvale aboriginal and islander community: Transition to independence* (Working paper No. 31). Clayton, Victoria, Australia: Monash University, Department of Geography.

Burrows, T. (1978). *New homes for Old: An analysis of resident satisfaction with the Midland Renewal Project* (unpublished internal rep.). East Perth: State Housing Commission of Western Australia.

Cairney, P., & Brebner, J. (1980). A tale of two cities: The relationship between knowledge and attitude to road closures in two south Australian local government areas. *Man Environment Systems, 10*, 131–138.

Cairns, D. (1984). *The Australia and New Zealand haemodialysis study.* Unpublished manuscript, North Ryde, New South Wales, Australia: Macquarie University.

Canter, D. & Thorne, R. (1972). Attitudes to housing: A cross-cultural comparison. *Environment and Behavior, 4*, 3–32.

Cardew, R.V. (1970). *Flats: A study of occupants and locations.* Sydney: University of Sydney, I.B. Fell Research Centre.

Cardew, R.V. (1980). Flats in Sydney: The thirty percent solution. In J. Roe (Ed.), *Twentieth century Sydney: Studies in urban and social history.* Sydney: Hale and Iremonger.

Coogan, C.K. (1981). CSIRO—An opportunity for the scientific industry (pp. 81–88). Melbourne: Australian Scientific Industry Association.

Correy, A. (1981). The landscape of Botany Bay: A visual assessment method. In D. Williamson & I. Bishop (Eds.), *Abstracts from the Proceedings of the Landscape Planning and Management Workshop: Melbourne 1980.* Melbourne: University of Melbourne, Centre for Environmental Studies & Forests Commission, Forest Environment and Recreation Branch, Victoria.

Cotgrove, S. (1982). *Catastrophe or cornucopia: The environment, politics, and the future.* Chichester, England: Wiley.

Daish, J., Gray, J., Kernohan, D., & Joiner, D. (1983). The management of a POE program. In D. Joiner, G. Brilicombe, J. Daish, J. Gray, & D. Kernohan (Eds.), *Conference on people and physical environment research.* Wellington North, New Zealand: New Zealand Ministry of Works and Development.

Darroch, R.K., & Miller, M. (1981). Environmental psychology: Coming and going. *Australian Psychologist, 16*(2), 155–171.

De Gruchy, F.G., & Hansford, G.J. (1979, November). *Crime and architecture in Brisbane: A pilot study of break and entry and vandalism and the architectural environment in four Brisbane commercial sub-centres* (Final Rep.). Canberra, Australia: Australian Institute of Criminology, Research Council.

DeMaria, W. (1973, March). Health and high-rise living: A study of interaction patterns in home units. *Hospital and Health Care and Administration, 3*, 13–16.

Dovey, K., Downton, P., & Missingham, G. (Eds.). (1985). *Place and placemaking: Proceedings of the PAPER 85*

Conference. Melbourne: Royal Melbourne Institute of Technology, Faculty of Architecture and Building.

Drakakis-Smith, D (1981, May). Aboriginal access to housing in Alice Springs. *Australian Geographer, 15,* 214–221.

Ealey, E.H.M. (1982, October). *An overview of environmental education and teacher training in Australia.* Paper presented at the Man-Environment Impact Conference, Ontario, Canada.

Finch, B. (1968). *Life and metropolitan location.* Sydney: I.B. Fell Research Centre.

Finighan, W.R. (1980). Some empirical observations on the role of privacy in the residential environment. *Man-Environment Systems, 10,* 153–159.

Forgas, J.P. (1981). The perception of social episodes: Categorical and dimensional representations in two different milieus. In A. Furnham & M. Argyle (Eds.), *The psychology of social situations.* New York: Pergamon.

Fowler, R.J. (1982). *Environmental impact assessment planning and pollution measures in Australia: An analysis of Australian environmental impact assessment procedures and their relationship with land-use planning and pollution controls.* Canberra, Australia: Australian Government Publishing Service.

Fox, A.M. (1982, Summer). KAKADU—Man and landscape. *Heritage Australia, 1*(2), 12–17.

Garner, W.R. (1974). *The processing of information and structure.* Hillsdale, NJ: Erlbaum.

George, K., & Clark, M. (1980). Aboriginal housing: Translating ideals into reality at Wilcannia, N.S.W. In R. Thorne & S. Arden (Eds.), *People and the man-made environment.* Sydney: University of Sydney, Architecture Department.

Girardi, J.P. (1978). *A user evaluation of housing trust sale houses.* Adelaide, Australia: South Australian Housing Trust.

Gorrie, G. (1975). *Housing needs related to lifestyle and life cycle: Notes on issues related to social mix.* Canberra, Australia: Commonwealth Department of Environment, Housing, and Community Development, Environment Policy Division.

Gould, P. & White, R. (1984). *Mental maps.* London: Penguin.

Gribbin, C.C., & Brealey, T.B. (1980). Social and psychological well-being and physical planning in new towns: How closely are they related? *Man-Environment Systems, 10,* 139–145.

Grocott, A.M. (1980). *Convicts, clergymen and churches: Attitudes of convicts and ex-convicts towards the churches and clergy of New South Wales from 1788 to 1851.* Sydney: Sydney University Press.

Halkett, I.P.B. (1976). *The quarter-acre block: The use of suburban gardens* (Report No. 59). Canberra, Australia: Australian Institute of Urban Studies.

Hall, R., Metcalfe, J., Purcell, T., & Thorne, R. (Eds.). (1972). *Social sciences in environmental design: A series of eleven papers presented at the Royal Australian Institute of Architects, N.S.W.* Sydney: University of Sydney, Architectural Psyhcology Research University.

Hall, R., Purcell, A.T., Thorne, R., & Metcalfe, J. (1976). Multi-dimensional scaling analysis of interior designed spaces. *Environment and Behavior, 8*(4), 595–610.

Hall, R.M., & Glaser, S. (1982, May). *The environment we want and the environment we anticipate.* Paper presented at the 52nd Australian & New Zealand Association for the Advancement of Science Congress, Sydney.

Hamilton, P. (1976). *Aboriginal housing bibliography.* Unpublished manuscript, lodged as microfiche at Architecture Library, University of Sydney, Sydney.

Hanley, W., & Cooper, M. (1982). *Man and the Australian environment.* Sydney: McGraw-Hill.

Harrison, P. (1970, July). Measuring urban sprawl. In N. Clark (Ed.), *Analysis of urban development, Proceedings of the Tewksbury Symposium* (pp. 3.3–3.6). Parkville, Victoria, Australia: University of Melbourne.

Hawkins, K. (1983, May). *Perception of Ambience: "Off-site" perceptions of the atmosphere of a setting. A study of the "ambience" of a forest setting.* Paper presented as the 53rd Australian & New Zealand Association for the Advancement of Science Congress, Perth.

Hayes, R.V., & Angel, J.S. (1981, March). *Social, legal and economic strategies to encourage energy conservation in buildings* (Report No. 66). Sydney: Macquarie University, Centre for Environmental and Urban Studies.

Headey, B., & Wearing, A.J. (1981). *Australians' priorities, satisfactions and well-being* (Monograph in Public Policy Studies No. 4). Melbourne: University of Melbourne, Department of Community Welfare Services.

Hepple, M. (Ed.). (1979). *A black reality: Aboriginal camps and housing in remote Australia.* Canberra, Australia: Australian Institute of Aboriginal Studies.

Herbert, E. (1983, May). *Application of landscape assessment procedures in the Darling Range.* Paper presented at 53d. Australian & New Zealand Association for the Advancement of Science Congress, Perth, Australia.

Johnson, P.A. (1983). User feedback and evaluation of some medium density housing in Sydney. In B. Judd & J. Dean (Eds.), *Medium density housing in Australia.* Canberra, Australia: Royal Australian Institute of Architects Education Division.

Johnston, C. (1981). The role of the national trust in landscape assessment. In D. Williamson & I. Bishop (Eds.), *Abstracts from the Proceedings of the Landscape Planning and Management Workshop: Melbourne 1980.* Melbourne: University of Melbourne, Centre for Environmental Studies, & Forests Commission, Forest Environment and Recreation Branch, Victoria.

Joiner, D., Brimilcombe, G., Daish, J., Gray, J., & Kernohan, D. (1983). *Conference on people and physical environment research.* Wellington North, New Zealand: New Zealand Ministry of Works and Development.

Jones, D. (1981). *Quality of life index: Australia 1981* (Unpublished rep.). Crows Nest, New South Wales, Australia: Communications Research Services.

Jones, R. (1985). Ordering the landscape. In I. Donaldson & T. Donaldson (Eds.), *Seeing the first Australians*. North Sydney: Allen and Unwin, 181–209.

Kantola, S.J. (1983, May). *An evaluation of media campaigns as a demand management tool*. Paper presented at 53d. Australian & New Zealand Association for the Advancement of Science Congress, Perth, Australia.

Kelly, M. (1978). Picturesque and pestilential 1860–1900 (citing an unpublished manuscript by W.S. Jevons). *Nineteenth-century Sydney: Essays in urban history*. Sydney University Press.

King, J.R., & Wyllie, A.G.J. (1981a). *Young families in high income suburbs* (Bulletin No. 3). Sydney: University of Sydney, Community Research Centre.

King, J.R., & Wyllie, A.G.J. (1981b). *Part 1. Young families in a multi-cultural suburb—Fairfield. Part 2. Young Families in public and private housing—Campbelltown* (Bulletin 4/5, 2 vols.). Sydney: University of Sydney, Community Research Centre.

King, J.R., & Wyllie, A.G.J. (1982). *Family care study: Young families in the West—An overview*. Sydney: University of Sydney, Community Research Centre.

King, R.J. (1981). *Melbourne housing study: Interim report*. Melbourne: Ministry of Housing, Melbourne and Metropolitan Board of Works, & Master Builders Association of Victoria.

Law, N.M. (1981, April). *A review of some approaches to post-occupancy evaluation of buildings* (Tech. Record No. 466). Chatswood, New South Wales, Australia: Commonwealth Scientific and Industrial Research Organization Experimental Building Research Station.

Lawrence, R. (1981). The optimization of habitat. *Open House, 6*(3), 35–43.

Lawrence, R. (1982). A psychological-spatial approach for architectural design and research. *Journal of Environmental Psychology, 2*, 37–51.

Lewis, E. (1978). *Consumer satisfaction with housing design: Assessment of Merredin and South Headland and prototype dwellings* (Unpublished internal rep. in 2 vols.). East Perth: State Housing Commission of Western Australia.

Lovejoy, F. (1973, January). Second-class housing for second-class citizens: Transitional housing for aborigines. *Beacon*. p. 1.

Lynch, Spence, Pearson and Consultants. (1976). *Parameters of a river: A prospectus for rehabilitation of Parramatta River* (Commissioned rep.). Sydney: National Trust of Australia (N.S.W.).

McKenzie, W.M. (1982, May). *Human limitations in environmental decision-making: Decision-aiding*. Paper presented at the 52nd Australian and New Zealand Association for the Advancement of Science Congress, Sydney.

Memmott, P. (1981). *Description of consultancy services on aboriginal projects*. St. Lucia, Queensland, Australia: University of Queensland, Department of Architecture.

Milbrath, L.W. (1981). General report: U.S. component of a comparative study of environmental beliefs and values. (Occasional Paper). Buffalo: State University of New York, Environmental Studies Center.

Moos, R, & Moos, B. (1976). A typology of family social environments. *Family Process, 15*, 357–371.

Morgan, G. (1983). Exploring choice: Reframing the process of evaluation. In G. Morgan (Ed.), *Beyond method: Strategies for social research*. Beverly Hills, CA: Sage.

Mueller, W.S. (1981). Translation of user requirements into house designs: A multi-dimensional scaling analysis. *Journal of Environmental Psychology, 1*, 97–116.

Munro-Clark, M. (1986). *Communes in rural Australia*. Sydney: Hale and Iremonger.

Newman, O. (1972). *Defensible space: People and design in the violent city*. London: Architectural Press.

Oliver, J. (Ed.), (1980). *Response to disaster*. Townsville, Queensland, Australia: James Cook University Press.

Payne, R.J., & Pigram, J.J.J. (1973). *Modelling human responses to natural hazards: A theoretical investigation* (Occasional Paper No. 3). Geography Society of New South Wales, Sydney.

Pearce, P.L. (1977). Mental souvenirs: A study of tourists and their city maps. *Australian Journal of Psychology, 29*(3), 203–210.

Pearce, P.L. (1982). *The social psychology of tourist behavior*. Oxford, England: Pergamon.

Pearce, P.L., & Cairney, P. (1980). Recognising city scenes: A test of Milgram's formula. *International Journal of Psychology, 15*(2), 95–103.

Pearce, P.L., Innes, J.M., O'Driscoll, M.P., & Morse, S.J. (1981). Stereotyped images of Australian cities. *Australian Journal of Psychology, 33*(1), 29–39.

Purcell, A.T. (1984a). Esthetics, measurement and control. *Ekistics, 307*, 379–387.

Purcell, A.T. (1984b). *The thermal environment and level of arousal: Field studies on office workers*. Sydney: University of Sydney, Architecture Department.

Purcell, A.T., Hall, R., Thorne, R., & Metcalfe, J. (1973). Models of man and environmental standards for tall buildings. *Proceedings of the Australian and New Zealand Conference on the Planning and Design of Tall Buildings*. Bethlehem, PA: Le High University.

Purcell, A.T., & Lamb, R.J. (1984, July–August). Landscape perception: An examination and empirical investigation of two central issues in the area. *Journal of Environmental Management, 19*, 31–63.

Purcell, A.T., & Thorne, R. (1977). An alternative method for assessing the psychological effects of noise in the field. *Journal of Sound and Vibration, 55*(4), 533–544.

Purcell, T., & Heath, T. (1982). Two Communities: Is there

a common focus for designer-researcher collaboration? In P. Bart, A. Chen, & G. Francescato (Eds.), *Knowledge for Design: Proceedings of the Thirteenth International Conference of the Environmental Design Research Association*. College Park, MD: Environmental Design Research Association.

Ray, J.J. (1975). Measuring environmental attitudes. *Australian and New Zealand Journal of Sociology, 11*(2), 70–71.

Ray, J.J. (1980). Does living near a coal mine change your attitude to the environment? A case study of the Hunter Valley. *Australian and New Zealand Journal of Sociobiology, 16*(3), 110–111.

Reser, J.P. (1977). What is a decent house: An examination of some cultural assumptions. *The Aboriginal Health Worker, 1*, 50–60.

Reser, J.P. (1981). Symbols and dwellings: The symbolic importance of indigenous Australian dwellings. In P. Oliver (Ed.), *Shelter in Asia and Australasia*. London: Barrie and Jenkins.

Roberts, J. (1981). *Massacres to mining: The colonisation of aboriginal Australia*. Blackburn, Victoria, Australia: Dove.

Saarinen, T.F., Sell, J.L., & Husband, E. (in press). Environmental perception: International efforts. *Progress in Human Geography*.

Schwartz, S., & Syme, G.J. (1982). Criteria-based measures of beliefs and attitudes towards nuclear development. *Australian Psychologist, 17*(1), 47–62.

Seddon, G. (1981–82, December/January). Eurocentrism and Australian science: Some examples. *Search, 12*(12), 446–450.

Seddon, G. (1983). The man-modified environment. In J. McLaren (Ed.). *A nation apart: Essays in honour of Andrew Fabinyi*. Sydney: Longmans Chesire.

Sutton, A.J., & Richmond, D.T. (1974). *Walk-up or high-rise?: Residents views on public housing*. Sydney: Housing Commission of New South Wales.

Syme, G.J. (1983, May). *The family as a firm: Consumer behaviour-approaches to household resource consumption*. Paper presented at 53rd Australian & New Zealand Association for the Advancement of Science Congress, Perth, Australia.

Syme, G.J., Illingworth, D.J., Eaton, E., & Kantola, S.J. (1981). Identification of early leavers from a remote mining community. *Population and Environment: Behavioral and Social Issues, 4*(3), 147–155.

Syme, G.J., Kantola, S.J., & Thomas, J.F. (1980). Water resources and the quarter-acre block. In R. Thorne & S. Arden (Eds.), *People and the man-made environment*. Sydney: University of Sydney, Department of Architecture.

Szokolay, C. (Ed.). (1981). *Understanding the built environment: Proceedings of the Australian and New Zealand Architectural Science Association 1981 Canberra Confer-*

ence. Brisbane, Australia: University of Queensland, Department of Architecture.

Thomas, J.F. (1983, May). *Economics and psychology: Interdisciplinary complementarities and conflicts*. Paper presented at 53rd Australian & New Zealand Association for the Advancement of Science Congress, Perth, Australia.

Thorne, A. (1980). The arrival of man in Australia. In A. Sherratt (Ed.), *The Cambridge encyclopedia of archeology*. Cambridge, England: Cambridge University Press.

Thorne, R., & Arden, S. (Eds.). (1980). *People and the man-made environment*. Sydney: University of Sydney, Department of Architecture.

Thorne, R., & Purcell, A.T. (1976). Environmental effects on subjective perception of level of arousal and human body temperature rhythm. *International Journal of Biometeorology, 20*(4), 318–324.

Tench, W. (1961). *Sydney's First Four Years*. Sydney: Angus and Robertson. (Original work published 1793, as *A complete account of the settlement at Port Jackson*.)

Turnbull, J.A.B., Thorne, R., Anderson, J., Weiderman, S., & Butterfield, D. (1983). *An evaluation of the interaction between elderly residents in high-rise flat accommodation in Sydney, Australia*. In D. Joiner, G. Brimilcombe, J. Daish, J. Gray, & D. Kernohan (Eds.). *Conference on people and physical environment research*. Wellington North, New Zealand: New Zealand Ministry of Works.

Veno, A. (1982, May). *Mine towns in Australia's North-West: Options for operations and quality of life*. Paper presented at the 52nd Australian and New Zealand Association for the Advancement of Science Congress, Sydney, Australia.

Vinson, T., & Homel, R. (1975, June). *Indicators of community well-being: Problems and services* (Discussion Paper). Queanbeyan, New South Wales, Australia: Australian Government Social Welfare Commission.

Walmsley, D.J. (1982). Personality and regional preference structures: A study of introversion-extraversion. *Professional Geographer, 34*(3), 279–288.

White, R. (1981). *Inventing Australia: Images and identity 1788–1980*. Sydney: Allen and Unwin.

Williamson, D. (1983, May). *Landscape management in Victorian forests*. Paper presented at the 53rd Australian and New Zealand Association for the Advancement of Science Congress, Perth, Australia.

Williamson, D., & Bishop, I. (Eds.). (1981). *Abstracts from the proceedings of the landscape planning and management workshop: Melbourne 1980*. Melbourne: University of Melbourne, Centre for Environmental Studies & Forests Commission, Forest Environment and Recreation Branch, Victoria.

Williamson, D., & Chalmers, J.A. (1982, November). *Perceptions of forest scenic quality in Northeast Victoria* (Landscape Management Series: Tech. Rep. of Research Phases I & II). Melbourne: Forests Commission, Victoria.

Winkler, R. (1982). Water conservation. In E.S. Geller, R.A. Winett, & P.B. Everett (Eds.), *Preserving the environment: New strategies for behavior change*. New York: Pergamon.

Winkler, R. (1983, May). *Behavioural approaches to water conservation*. Paper presented at the 53rd Australian & New Zealand Association for the Advancement of Science Congress, Perth, Australia.

Winkler, R., Syme, G.J., & Thomas, J.F. (1979). Social factors and water consumption. In *Hydrology and water resources symposium*. Perth: Australian Institute of Engineers.

Chapter 31

ENVIRONMENTAL PSYCHOLOGY IN JAPAN

Genichi Hagino, *Department of Psychology, Komazawa University, Tokyo, Japan*

Mamoru Mochizuki, *International College of Commerce and Economics, Tokyo, Japan*

Takiji Yamamoto, *Hiroshima University, Hiroshima, Japan*

31.1. THE PHILOSOPHICAL AND CULTURAL BACKGROUND OF JAPANESE ENVIRONMENTAL PSYCHOLOGY

31.1.1. Traditional Japanese Attitudes Toward Nature

An examination of the attitudes held by the Japanese toward nature should include a look at the geography, the folk history, the history, and the religion of the people in order to show just how strong the influence of nature was in shaping the thinking of the Japanese.

Japan has less land area than the State of California. Its islands lie in a temperate zone stretching from the northeast to the southwest. Sixty-seven percent of Japan is mountainous; 9% is volcanic; 11% is plateau; and 13% is composed of plain ice terrain.

The ancient Japanese had a great collection of creation myths and legends. The surviving legends were written up in the *Kojiki* [Ancient Chronicles of Japan] by Yasumaro Ono who compiled them by command of the Emperor Genmei in the eighth century. The first of three volumes of the *Kojiki* tells of husband and wife deities who created a land that was poetically named "the country in the midst of luxuriant reed plains." The daughter of this couple was Amaterasuoumikami, the Sun Goddess. She was very important historically because she was said to have been a direct ancestor of the legendary Emperor Jimmu, the founder of a line of 124 generations of emperors who ruled Japan over the course of more than 2600 years (true historical records have traced the Imperial Family back only to the fifth century). Throughout history, emperors were not always considered godlike, but the present emperor was revered as a god in human form until the end of World War II.

The word *god* in Japanese is translated as "Kami," but the word *Kami* does not correspond to the omnipresent or omnipotent concept held of "god" in many of the other world religions. *Kami* has a myriad of connotations and can denote formal objects of worship, ancestors, heroes, the ancestors of the Japanese, and a host of folk deities as well. The characteristics of the Kami and their worship can be roughly summarized as follows.

They are usually related to nature or natural phenomena. They were thought to have resided in heaven during some periods but on earth during other times. When they descended to earth, they were thought to have taken the form of high mountains or other impressive natural objects. During their visits to earth, the Kami were thought to visit shrines (particularly the ancestor Kami), and people prayed for a visitation or for protection in times of need or during ceremonial occasions. Natural objects were generally used in worship or celebration, and the altars of Shinto shrines were decorated with fruits, vegetables, and rice cakes. During times of celebration such as the New Year, the entrances to houses are decorated with pine boughs or wreaths in order to entice the Kami to visit individual homes.

Shinto stresses a strong distinction between purity and impurity, and in order to purify oneself a person goes to holy places that are often deep in forests or on mountains. In such settings, it is possible to experience the sublimity of nature and restrengthen one's faith.

Through Shinto and the native folk religions people were taught to believe that they were born in a special country created by the Kami and that they lived their lives under the divine protection of the Kami and the emperor. They were also taught to believe that the Japanese "race" was one family bound together in spirit. The community, as a vital organ in the nation, was a place for common beliefs where people worked together, held festivals, prayed for abundant harvests and catches, and for their success in business ventures. In the case of war, the first thing to be done by the community was to hold services to pray for victory.

Even though Shinto holds a central position in the "religious life" of the Japanese, two other important faiths that also stress the importance of nature—Buddhism and Zen Buddhism—played and still play a role in the lives of the Japanese.

Taoistic and Confucianistic thought also gained inroads into Japan where they existed in harmony with the native Shinto religion. Elements of these four belief systems formed the so-called Japanese philosophy, although it must be stated that this philosophy was actually a distillation of the most practical aspects of these belief systems.

The loyalty that many Japanese felt toward the emperor during World War II had its roots not only in Shinto but also in the other faiths. For example, the Confucian rules that stressed respect for the behavioral principles of "benevolence" and "fidelity" toward one's lord reinforced servitude to the emperor. And the Buddhistic belief in an afterlife of paradise for those who continued to do good in their lives also reinforced those who believed that serving the emperor well would assure them a place in Heaven.

31.1.2. The Japanese Living Environment and the Japanese Life-style: Historical Influences, Disasters, the Japanese House

Historical Influences

The major prehistoric periods in Japan are known as the Jomon and Yayoi periods. The Jomon period is thought to have begun around 7000 or 8000 B.C. This was followed by the Yayoi period. In the Jomon period, dwellings were dugouts, and the people appear to have lived a nomadic life: gathering, fishing, and hunting. Near the end of the Jomon period, people began to cultivate rice plants, but it was not until the Yayoi period when people began intensive wet-field, or paddy, cultivation.

There were both natural and political reasons for the spread of paddy cultivation. The Japanese climate was warm enough and wet enough, and rulers and landowners who controlled water supplies encouraged it because they could demand a share of the peasants' harvests. Because paddy field agriculture is highly influenced by weather conditions, rainy and dry seasons, temperature, and so forth, people were forced to perform certain tasks during certain seasons and this, combined with the great amount of labor required for paddy farming, necessitated cooperation among members of the different families in the communities.

These conditions led to the consciousness of a communal society whose spirit of living together, farming together, and facing uncontrollable fates together was different from the ethos of hunting societies. In the latter, one's livelihood depended on courageous invasions of neighboring tribes among whom an enterprising, competitive, and egotistical spirit was easily fostered.

The unpredictability of the weather necessitated a more sensitive observation of nature by Japanese farmers; therefore the early Japanese farmers were sensitive to changes in the weather and in ecological cycles. A type of lunar calendar was known to have been in use in Old Japan, and this recorded such days as the days that divided the seasons, the day on which snow turns into rain, the days certain insects appeared, and many other important and instructive dates. This calendar was used as a rough standard for making decisions on agricultural matters, but the final decisions were left up to careful observation. Keen observation and sensitivity to nature manifested itself in the traditional Japanese poetry forms—*haiku* and *tanka*. Haiku is in fact so filled with seasonal words and natural descriptions that without such words it simply would not be haiku.

Disasters

Because of the hard work required to maintain paddy fields, the Japanese people have traditionally been hard working. But no matter how hard working a society is, its members just cannot completely protect themselves against floods, fires, earthquakes, or typhoons. The Japanese topography makes floods a rather frequent danger because the distance between mountain ranges and populated plains is short. Steep slopes may cause sudden, dangerous flooding in many areas. Earthquakes, also common to Japan, result in fires that can envelop whole cities and cause incredible destruction. In the great Kanto earthquake of 1923 with its 8.2 magnitude on the Richter scale, shock and the fires it triggered claimed 100,000 lives with injuries estimated between 100,000 and 200,000. It would be difficult to predict whether or not a disaster of the magnitude of the great Kanto earthquake would occur again, but in looking at the cyclical pattern of earthquakes in Japan, another large one could well occur in the near future.

Fires alone were and, to some extent, still are a great danger in crowded Japan. The density of wooden houses made them so common in Tokyo during the Edo period (feudal era from the seventeenth to nineteenth century) that great fires were ironically called the "pride of Tokyo." Nowadays, however, there are considerably fewer fires occurring in Tokyo than in New York or London. One reason for this difference is that Japanese houses have very thin partitions between rooms; fires are thus more quickly noticed by relatives or neighbors, and they can be put out before they spread. Another reason is the excellent fire prevention resources and education. In Japan, fire prevention ordinances are normally very strict and well enforced.

In looking back at the many natural and man-made disasters facing the Japanese, it is not surprising that they prepare themselves to meet them: One way is through savings. The Japanese have the second largest amount of savings in the world after the Swiss.

The Japanese House

To better understand the Japanese life-style, it is necessary to examine the Japanese house. After paddy field cultivation began, people in warm regions often lived in communally built raised cottages. These afforded protection against floods, vermin, and high heat. Building materials used in house construction were almost exclusively wood. In colder regions, the houses were surrounded by earthen walls. Walls became a feature of homes in warm and cold regions, and materials were varied, to include wood and stone. Walls were built for several reasons, among them defense and privacy, but another common reason for building walls was (and still is) for status purposes.

Another interesting feature of Japanese homes is the *amado*. In places where hot weather and rain storms were most frequent, amado (large wooden shutters) came into use. Amado represent one example of how Japanese houses were designed to be as open as possible. Amado were made in several partitions and constructed so that they could slide across a rail to surround and protect the house during storms and at night. When the weather was good, however, they could be pushed back into built-in compartments, opening up almost the whole house.

The floors of ancient Japanese houses were built on supports like river houses in Southeast Asia, and until the fourteenth century, the floors of most Japanese homes were made from bamboo. After that time, thick wooden floors replaced the bamboo ones. Nowadays, the most refined examples of wooden floor and flooring technique can be found in temples and castles.

Sometime after the development of wooden flooring, *tatami* came into use. Tatami are thick rice-straw mats covered with woven rushes, and they are still used in most Japanese homes. The function of tatami is rather different from that of flooring; for example, teacups are often placed before guests directly on the tatami. Naturally, many rules came into existence regarding a "tatami etiquette." For example, no shoes or sandals were allowed on the tatami, and people were very careful to keep their feet clean. People even sleep on tatami but not directly on the mat itself. A type of bedding known as *futon* is taken out of closets where it is carefully stored and placed on the tatami, thus saving much space that a bed would take up.

The size of Japanese rooms is measured in tatami units. One tatami unit is 1.8 m x .9 m. The largest room in a standard Japanese house is rarely larger than 10 tatami; the living room is 6 tatami, the room housing the traditional Buddhist altar is 4.5 or 6 tatami, and guest rooms or tea rooms, although very rare, are 10 and 4.5 tatami, respectively.

Fusuma are a type of sliding partition used in Japanese homes. They are usually made from paper and framed in wood. When the fusuma are opened or removed, adjoining rooms can be converted into one large open room. Thus, the fusuma can create enough space for many different living requirements. In wealthier homes, fusuma were often decorated with panoramic paintings. The beauty of such paintings lies in the fact that varied artistic effects can be produced in rooms by opening or closing them.

Since World War II, great changes have occurred in Japanese housing. Many of the traditional furnishings and rooms are disappearing; the privately owned tea room is a thing of the past, and decorated alcoves (*tokonoma*) are disappearing in the constant battle for space. With this change in the house also came drastic changes in the life-style of the people. The guest room is no longer a part of the house, and guests, even close friends, are seldom invited over for a meal. It has become the custom to take guests, clients, and friends out to dinner or to a bar for entertainment.

Some of the reasons for these changes and some other changes are as follows. Just after World War II, the Japanese were faced with a terrible housing shortage. The destruction of war and the resultant fires left most houses in ruins. The postwar recovery further concentrated industry in the big cities and increased the concentration of administration buildings, companies, and educational facilities. This, of course, attracted more and more people and made the situation even worse. In order to cope with this rush to the cities, many high-rise housing complexes had to be built rapidly. These were in great contrast to the traditional one- or two-story houses of the recent past. After the construction of these buildings, Japan's economy and education began to improve, and furniture, including western furniture, appliances, and bookshelves were bought and utilized in the narrow apartments. People were virtually crowded out of their homes by material progress.

While all this expansion was going on, not enough thought was given to land management or city and road planning. Things were so bad that plans to relocate the capital of Japan to another city were seriously considered. One result today of this inadequate planning is the unbelievably high cost of real estate. For an ordinary salaried worker, a house is only a dream. Another result is the terrible crowding in the transportation systems. These problems have no short-range solutions.

Because there is little room for relaxation in such places as Tokyo, most of the residents of the big cities look forward to returning to their hometowns to relax during the traditional vacation seasons of Bon (a Buddhist summer festival) and Shogatsu, the New Year's vacation (lasting less than a week for most people). During these periods, already crowded transportation facilities are strained to the limit.

A considerable amount of overtime work, overtime socialization, weekend work, and commuting time is required of Japanese men. Whereas in the past families farmed and labored together, in recent years fathers are not able to devote much time to their families. This plus an increase in the number of working wives has contributed to a rise in family problems. One solution to these problems is a truly free weekend for Japanese workers, but other solutions are sorely needed before the collapse of the family becomes a reality.

31.1.3. The Japanese Natural Environment and the Arts

The major art form that survived from the Jomon and Yayoi periods was pottery. Because few cave drawings or other art forms remained after centuries of earthquakes, volcanic eruptions, and fires, little is known about these periods. Most of these ceramics were used to store foodstuffs or as implements of worship, but some clay figures were buried with the dead in place of mass live burials after the death of a great ruler. Decorative pottery was influenced over the years by Korea and China, and Japanese pottery is known all over the world for its beauty and simplicity.

After Buddhism was introduced in the fifth and sixth centuries by way of China and Korea, envoys and students were sent to China, and these pioneers enriched the Japanese arts by bringing back with them images of the Lord Buddha and illustrated scrolls containing the Sutras. These scrolls became a major art form in Japan. They were read from right to left and contained both scripture that was written on the lower half of the paper and illustrations that were drawn on the upper half. These scrolls were modified over the years into two other art forms—the *kakejiku* that were widened and hung vertically (usually as an alcove decoration) and the *hengaku* that were shortened, framed, and hung on the wall close to the ceiling.

Scrolls are a good example of one of the main differences between Western and Eastern art in that the display of Eastern art is not as conspicuous. Even if people owned a number of beautiful picture scrolls, they seldom displayed more than a few. Also scrolls and other forms of pictorial art are traditionally rotated as the seasons change, and their main themes are "retired" and "quiet" landscapes painted to depict depth and silence. The place in the Japanese home where scrolls are usually displayed is the alcove or *tokonoma*. Traditionally, the tokonoma was a Buddhist concept, but most people do not associate the tokonoma with religion. Now it is a place to house a kakejiku, a piece of pottery and a flower arrangement, or a bonsai. The shadowing in the tokonoma helped to heighten the landscape perspectives of the kakejiku, and the tokonoma room offered a place of serenity for quiet meditation and in which guests and family could relax.

Because the scriptures on the original scrolls were drawn in Chinese characters, calligraphy also became a major art form in Japan. The Chinese characters, depending on the style in which they were drawn, were thought to harmonize with landscape and natural drawings. Thus, Chinese and Japanese art were often fusions of scenery and calligraphy.

Another very interesting Japanese artform is *byobu*. These are decorative folding screens, approximately 2 m tall, and they normally consist of two, four, or six wood framed panels. Byobu were often illustrated with seasonal panoramic scenes, and the finer ones were coated in gold leaf before being illustrated. Byobu were used both for decoration and for partitioning rooms. Their primary motifs were flowers, birds, moonlight, and wind. They were not made to be displayed like flat one-dimensional paintings. The panels were arranged in a zigzag fashion making the whole structure self-supporting. Because of their flexibility, they could be used to change the curvature of a room, and even in less spacious places they could be folded inward a little more to be admired. When displayed in the right places during the proper seasons, byobu were a true source of pride to their owners. If one stood on the narrow porches of the old samurai homes with the sliding doors opened, one could see the garden on one side and a byobu with its characteristic landscape scenery on the other side as one walked slowly from one end of the porch to another. Thus a dynamic effect was produced.

Even though these seemingly large byobu would appear to take up a lot of space, the distance effects produced by the folds in them actually made a room look more spacious.

Wall paintings similar to byobu illustrations were popular among high-ranking samurai, but these were not portable like byobu and were mostly destroyed in castle fires. A smaller type of byobu was in use in Old Japan as well. These were known as *makura byobu*, or pillow byobu. They were placed at the head of the bedding behind the pillow. A noted byobu artist, Korin Ogata, painted makura byobu so that if a person woke up in the morning and looked at the byobu he or she would feel as if he or she were looking at a real bamboo grove at a distance from his or her open window.

With all of the pictorial art Japan has to offer, we note that nature itself is an art form in Japan. *Ikebana* or Japanese flower arrangement expresses the simple natural beauty of the four seasons, and without it the tokonoma just is not complete.

Sometimes, bonsai take the place of flower arrangements as a decoration. Bonsai are the living images of large natural trees, and they reflect the Asian fascination with miniaturization and models.

Japanese gardens are a man-made attempt to portray nature in a restricted space by the artistic arrangement of plants and stones. While meditating on their gardens, people can become absorbed in them, even to the point of projecting their feelings into them. Gardens offer the serenity of a brief return to living nature from the hectic life that most Japanese have to face.

This return-to-nature concept was greatly influenced by the Eastern philosophies of Buddhism and Zen. In Japan, this influence was strongly reflected in temple architecture, Zen gardens, and Japanese paintings. But nature is in short supply in Japan today, and the housing shortage has brought about a virtual end to privately owned gardens. The tokonoma is also disappearing and with it the kakejiku. Recently, framed oil paintings have gained popularity among apartment dwellers, and, of course, there is no room for a byobu. But the Japanese arts are not extinct, and many Japanese people, who still strongly desire a home and garden of their own, place bonsai on their porches and display *ikebana* (flower arrangement) on their coffee tables.

31.2. THE HISTORY OF JAPANESE ENVIRONMENTAL PSYCHOLOGY

31.2.1. The Psychology of Climate (Fudo)

There are various opinions among scholars concerning the origins of Japanese environmental psychology; however, one work is commonly acclaimed as being of great importance in stimulating environmentally oriented studies. It is the book called *Fudo*, which can be translated roughly as "climate." It was written by the renowned philosopher, Watsuji (1935). The definition of *fudo* is essential in understanding his theories. It has a deeper meaning than the English "climate" or "environment." The meaning of the word *fudo* includes "the natural environment of a given land, its climate, its weather, the geological and productive nature of its soil, its topographic and scenic features." Watsuji maintained that fudo should not simply be defined as something objective, which is located outside of people and which only affects them in a one-sided way. The definition of fudo should also include a deep and intentional relationship of the person with the environment. Through this relationship, we understand the fudo and as well, as Watsuji says, "find ourselves—ourselves as an element in the mutual relationship—in climate." Fudo includes in its meaning the historical and cultural accumulation of human experiences. Watsuji insisted that fudo does not exist apart from history nor history apart from fudo. Using a three-part classification—monsoon (Southeast Asia), desert (Arabia and Mongolia) and meadow (Parts of Europe)—he studied the relationship between fudo and history, fudo and culture, and fudo and people.

In order to clarify Watsuji's position, we can compare his rather Asian attempts to define the relation between environment and man with the European attitude toward nature.

The European attitude was one that subdued nature and used it for one's benefit and comfort. The elements were considered like objects that were completely separate from humans. The Asian way of understanding nature was, however, different. Nature was something to be held in awe, something to be respected, and something to live in harmony with and become one with. Watsuji, steeped in this philosophy of life, wrote about humans and fudo as an entity. For

his time, he produced a unique and meaningful theory of climate. In essence, he tried to explain that the relationship between humans and fudo was a self-apprehensive experience. After World War II, Watsuji's thought influenced such disciplines as anthropology, history, and other humanities.

Studies on the relationship between climate and human behavior were enhanced by Hasegawa (1953) and Imai (1973). Hasegawa wrote on the effect of climate on people, the relationship between climate and cultural activity and adaptation to climate. Imai studied the effects of climatic conditions (such as weather and the seasons) on human behavior, social structure, and national character.

In a similar vein, Umesao (1951) expressed the idea that humans and environment were one system. He believed that considering person and environment as separate was the problem and that to think of environment as a fixed stage with various backdrops and a person as an actor on such a stage was a great misunderstanding of reality. The question of defining the environment and of whether person and environment are regarded as separate entities or parts of one system is of marked theoretical significance for contemporary environmental psychology (see discussion by Altman and Rogoff, this volume, Chapter 41).

As an extra note on original Japanese theory, one recent outstanding work has appeared in an English translation. It is concerned with a neglected area of study—the mental landscape. The book's title is *The Visual and Spatial Structure of Landscape*, and it deals with the various ways the Japanese people internalize landscapes. The author, Higuchi (1983), approaches the problem of what an ideal landscape is and classifies the landscapes of Japan into seven types of home places, studying them in historical and modern perspectives.

Environment is said to have a considerable effect on shaping personality. During the 1960s and 1970s, a number of studies on Japanese personality appeared. Minami's (1953) *A Psychology of the Japanese People* was representative of this type of work. It was followed by studies by Sera (1963), Tanaka (1964), Yoda and Tsukishima (1970), Sofue (1976), and Miyagi (1972). The 1970s also saw a flood of books, reports, articles, and surveys on Japanese national consciousness.

Summary

In summary, previous sections discussed the influences that geography, climate, and history have had on the Japanese way of thinking and behavior. It is also interesting to speculate on what influences geography, climate, history, and culture have had on present-day environmental psychology. We must keep in mind that pure Japanese cultural elements are very difficult to isolate. Japan's history and culture have been greatly influenced by other Asian cultures and by Western culture. Japan is a cultural melting pot. The following example will serve to illustrate this point.

When a young Japanese couple marries, the ceremony can be held at a Shinto shrine, a Buddhist temple, or a Christian church. Usually, however, it is held in a high-rise hotel that houses a wedding hall and has its own miniature Shinto shrine. The wedding consists of various Shinto and Western elements all blended into one ceremony with the participants considering the whole process to be perfectly natural. As shown in the previous example, the Japanese have blended multiple cultures, and the same is true in the formation of environmental psychology in Japan.

However, a few elements of Japanese culture, many of them based on natural, geographical, and historical phenomena, can be seen as either indirectly or directly influencing studies by Japanese environmental psychologists. An obvious geographical influence is the prevalence of natural disasters. The Japanese have become an earthquake-conscious people, and numerous studies have been done on earthquakes and disasters. Various natural and historical phenomena have influenced Japanese housing, and the Japanese are thought by many to have a special spatial perception concerning housing. The natural beauty of the Japanese landscape has greatly dominated the arts of Japan in painting, sculpture, and architecture. Landscape perception and the arts have been the focus of a number of recent studies. The rapid modernization and urbanization of Japan has greatly influenced Japanese culture by way of changes in housing, human relations, and the personality formation of Japanese children. For example, the "community consciousness" of the Japanese has been greatly altered. Depopulation of rural areas has also been a concern of researchers, but more work is necessary in this area.

31.2.2. Advances in Japanese Environmental Psychology

A wide range of earlier Japanese studies related to environmental psychological topics have been done in various fields. However, studies specifically entitled as environmental psychological studies did not appear in Japan until the 1960s: for example, those by Kobayashi (1961), Akiyama (1967), and Ohyama and

Inui (1969). One reason for the growth of environmental psychology in Japan was the wave of international academic influence from abroad. Another was the growth of environmental problems facing Japan such as overpopulation, rising traffic deaths, and increases of all sorts of pollution. A glimpse of the dominant trends in Japan is evident in Table 31.1. It lists the major books on environmental psychology published since 1961. It shows a rapid development of interest in the field during the 1970s. During this period, Canter and Inui's (1972) book served to add momentum to the field and stimulated new research. Since its publication, numerous original and translated books have appeared with environmental psychology in their titles: Iritani (1974), Soma and Sako (1976), Soma (1979a, 1979b), Mochizuki and Ohyama (1979), and Inui, Osada, Watanabe, and Akiyama (1982). A number of translations of fundamental works are Proshansky, Ittelson, and Rivlin (1970), Ittelson, Proshansky, Rivlin, and Winkel (1974). Specialized books have also appeared, and paper presentations are also increasing.

Table 31.2 gives a list of symposiums that were given on environmental psychology at various annual psychological congresses in Japan. In looking at Table 31.2, we can see two trends. In the 1960s, the major topics of discussion were traffic safety, human engineering, family problems, personality formation, and adolescent maladjustment. In the 1970s, however, the major topics centered around more fundamental problems of environmental psychology. According to the number of paper presentations at the Japanese Psychological Association, since 1980 there has been a significant increase in articles related to environmental problems, community change, panic, and evacuation.

In the latter half of the 1970s, environmental psychology has become a much more active field. In 1980, the first Japan–U.S. Seminar of Interactive Processes between Human Behavior and the Environment was held in Tokyo. This seminar was, in a way, a turning point for environmental psychology in Japan. During the discussions at the seminar, the need for more interdisciplinary and international cooperation was expressed (Hagino & Ittelson, 1981). To help answer these needs, the Man–Environment Research Association (MERA) was formed in 1982. At this charter meeting, Mochizuki spoke on special problems in Japanese environmental psychology and Wapner discussed trends and issues in environmental psychology. The Man–Environment Research Association has a membership of 60 persons representing various fields. The International

Table 31.1. Trends of Research in Japanese Environmental Psychology

	Books and Translated Books	
	General	Special
1961	*An Introduction to Architectural Psychology* (S. Kobayashi)	
1964		(T) *Big School, Small School* (R. G. Barker & P. V. Gump)
1966		(T) *ªThe Silent Language* (E. T. Hall)
1967	*Design and Psychology* (S. Akiyama)	
1968		(T) *The Image of the City* (K. Lynch)
1969	*Psychology for Architects* (T. Ohyama & M. Inui)	
1970		(T) *The Hidden Dimension* (E. T. Hall)
1971		(T) *Image and Environment* (R. M. Downs & D. Stea)
1972	*What Is Environmental Psychology?* (D. Canter & M. Inui)	(T) *Personal Space* (R. Sommer)
1974	*An Introduction to Environmental Psychology* (T. Iritani) (T) *Environmental Psychology* (Vol 1–6) (H. M. Proshansky, W. H. Ittleson, & L. G. Rivlin	*Aggregate Housing, Housing Districts* (N. Suzuki)
1975	*Urban Environment and Dwelling Psychology* (M. Yoshida)	(T) *Living in Cities* (C. Mercer)
1976	*Environmental Psychology* (I. Soma & T. Sako)	(T) *Public Places and Private Spaces* (A. Mehrabian)
1977	(T) *An Introduction to Environmental Psychology* (W. H. Ittelson, H. M. Proshansky, L. G. Rivlin, & G. H. Winkel)	
1979	*Environmental Psychology* (M. Mochizuki & Ohyama, T.)	(T) *The Human Context* (R. H. Moos)
1980		*Interaction Processes between Human Behavior and Environment* (G. Hagino & W. Ittelson)
1982		(T) *The Psychology of Place* (D. Canter)

ª(T) = Translated book.

Association of Traffic and Safety Sciences (IATSS) promotes research related to environmental psychology. It sponsored a symposium on man and the high-speed society. At this meeting, Wapner spoke on the analysis of transactions of persons in a high-speed society, and Brown discussed the effect of speed stress on decision making. A special Man and Space Symposium was held also under IATSS sponsorship. Some of the papers given dealt with problems such as public space in cities, organization of space in high-density societies, interrelationships between high density and space–time patterns, and urban and transportation planning (Suzuki, 1983).

In Japan at the present time, the majority of pa-

Table 31.2. Symposiums on Environmental Psychology at Annual Meetings of Psychology in Japan

	Title of Symposium (Association)[a]
1948	Problems of Environment (JPA)
1956	The Countermeasure of Traffic Accidents (JAAP)
1959	Traffic Safety Problems (JAAP)
1960	Relations between Culture and Personality (JPA)
1962	Japanese Family and Personality Formation (JSSP)
1963	Car Driving and Ergonomics (JAAP)
1964	Maladjustment Problems of Early Adolescents Residing in Highrise Apartments (JAAP)
	Traffic Psychology Problems and Pedestrians (JAAP)
1967	Public Forum on Traffic Problems (JAAP)
1971	Person and Environment (JAAP)
1973	Psychological Effects of Aircraft Noise (JAAP)
1974	The Problems on Environment Psychology (JPA)
1976	The Effects of Community Population Changes on Social Behaviors (JSSP)
1978	Environment Cognition in Person–Environment Systems (JPA)
	Fundamental Problems of Community Psychology (JPA)
1981	Present Status and Future of Environmental Psychology (JPA)
1982	Disaster and Panic (JPA)
	Environmental Factors and Behavior (JPA)

[a]JPA = Japanese Psychological Association.
JAAP = Japanese Association of Applied Psychology.
JSSP = Japanese Society for Social Psychology.

pers are given at various specialized annual meetings and symposia such as the annual meetings of the Architectural Institute of Japan, The Japanese Psychological Association, The Japan Ergonomics Research Society, and others. A list of associations in Japan related to environmental psychology is shown in Table 31.3.

31.3. THE PRESENT STATE OF JAPANESE ENVIRONMENTAL PSYCHOLOGY

31.3.1. Disaster Research

Japan's geographical position makes it the target for an unusually high occurrence of natural disasters. In order to help in easing some of the problems associated with disasters, a number of studies have been carried out.

Evacuation during disasters is a particularly important problem for high-density societies, and much Japanese research focuses on this problem. The classification of evacuation behavior during fires and behavior patterns occurring during such evacuations (The Disaster Behavior Study Group, 1978; Kobayashi & Horiuchi, 1974a, 1974b) are examples of this type of research. Evacuation models have been considered in studying the problems of occupants' recognition of fire and their psychological state. Research on simulated disaster situations has increased.

The influence of earthquakes on human behavior has been investigated by numerous researchers (Kuroda, 1969; Ohta & Ohashi, 1979; Ohashi & Ohta, 1980; Omi, Nakamura, Shida, & Kamemura, 1982). Questionnaires and interviews have been designed to measure human response during and after large earthquakes. These have shown a remarkable correlation of human response to seismic intensity.

Numerous studies have been done on earthquake-related panic. Four days after the Izuoshima Kinkai earthquake, residents were cautioned that aftershocks were a possibility. This notice became more and more exaggerated as it passed from mouth to mouth, and soon rumors of a great impending earth-

Table 31.3. Associations in Japan Related to Environmental Psychology

Name of Association	Office	Journal
The Japanese Psychological Association	37-13-802, Hongo 4 chome Bunkyo-ku, Tokyo, 113 JAPAN	*The Japanese Journal of Psychology* (Abstract in English)
Architectural Institute of Japan	5-26-20, Shiba, Minato-ku Tokyo, 108 JAPAN	*Transaction of the Architectural Institute of Japan* (Abstract in English)
Japan Ergonomics Research Society	c/o Kyowa Bank Ikebukuro Shiten Kotsu Igaku Kenkyusho 1-9-3, Higashi Ikebukuro Toshima-ku, Tokyo, 170 JAPAN	*The Japanese Journal of Ergonomics* (Abstract in English)
The Japanese Group Dynamics Association	Institute for Group Dynamics Nishinippon Shinbun Kaikan 14F 4-11 chome, Tenjin, Chuo-ku Fukuoka-shi, 810 JAPAN	*The Japanese Journal of Experimental Social Psychology* (Abstract in English)
The Japanese Association of Educational Psychology	c/o Faculty of Education University of Tokyo 7-3-1, Hongo, Bunkyo-ku Tokyo, 113 JAPAN	*The Japanese Journal of Educational Psychology* (Abstract in English)
International Association of Traffic and Safety Sciences	6-20, 2-chome, Yaesu, Chuo-ku Tokyo, 104 JAPAN	*IATTS Review* (Abstract in English) *IATTS Research* (In English)
The Japan Association of Applied Psychology	c/o Department of Psychology College of Humanities and Science Nihon University 3-25-40, Sakurajosui, Setagaya-ku Tokyo, 156 JAPAN	*The Japanese Journal of Applied Psychology*
The Research Institute of Environmental Medicine, Nagoya University	Furo-cho, Chikusa-ku Nagoya, 464 JAPAN	*Annual Report of the Research Institute of Environmental Medicine, Nagoya University*
Tokyo Metropolitan Research Institute for Environmental Protection	2-7-1, Yuraku-cho, Chiyoda-yu Tokyo, 100 JAPAN	*Annual Report of the Tokyo Metropolitan Research Institute for Environmental Protection*
The Japanese Society of Social Psychology	c/o Department of Psychology Tokyo Institute of Technology 2-12-1, Ohokayama, Meguro-ku Tokyo, 152 JAPAN	*The Japanese Annals of Social Psychology*
Man–Environment Research Association	c/o Department of Psychology Faculty of Literature Waseda University 1-24-1, Toyama, Shinjuku-ku Tokyo, 612 JAPAN	

quake spread. The results of a questionnaire showed that in this situation, 20,000 people left their homes in search of a safer place; 110,000 people hurriedly stocked up on canned food provisions, and 70,000 people stopped what they were doing and rushed home (Abe, 1982).

The necessity of proper training in order to cope with earthquakes is illustrated in an article by Abe (1982). In Urakawa, Hokkaido, the emergency training for earthquakes was so effective that in spite of the high magnitude (7.3 on the Richter scale) of the quake and the fact that the great majority of the 6000 households were using heaters or gas stoves, no serious outbreak of fire was reported. Abe explained this in terms of housewives' appropriate responses, that is, following a "courselike" pattern of turning off gas and heaters. Ongoing cross-cultural research by Archae of the Georgia Institute of Technology and Kobayashi of Kyoto University on earthquake-related behavior seems promising.

A classic study on disaster-related panic is Kubo's (1952) study of behavior patterns during and after the Hiroshima atomic bomb.

31.3.2. Environmental Cognition Studies

In order to move freely in the environment, we must carefully perceive and understand it. It is necessary to orient ourselves by knowing which direction to take, how far away our goal is, which is the best route, and what landmarks are available. A number of environmental exploration studies were carried out in the 1970s (Ishii & Yamamoto, 1977; Yamamoto & Ishii, 1977; Yamamoto, Ishii, & Asakawa, 1978).

Ontogenetic and microgenetic studies of spatial cognition comparing sighted and blind persons has been carried out by Yamamoto (1981). The psychological distance map, as described by Wapner (1978), was used by Kogawa, Fujiwara, Inoue, Ishii, and Fukuda (1983) in an environmental organization study during the critical transition of college freshmen from home town to a university. The development of image map types in elementary-school children was studied by Tani (1980). Kamino and Mikami (1973) reexamined Shemyakin's developmental hypothesis using adult subjects. An extensive review of cognitive map studies was compiled by Sako (1981), and orientation studies have been done by giving subjects only written and map explanations and having them explore new environments (Ohyama, 1978). Studies done on small-scale and large-scale distance estimation have been carried out using multiple dimensional scaling (Asakawa, 1978).

Because architects have an actual problem in mind that they have to solve, architectural research is of a more concrete nature than is psychological research. When designing a structure, architects must precisely conceptualize actual architectural space from diagrams. Takahashi and Hatsumi (1978, 1979a) approached this problem by studying the effects of training students to conceptualize from two-dimensional diagrams to three-dimensional space and to reproduce two-dimensional diagrams from three-dimensional space. In later studies, he examined the psychological effects of ceiling height on room width

(Takahashi & Hatsumi, 1979b). Takahashi (1981) characterized the concept of space in the Japanese house as follows:

> In occidental architecture, space is enclosed by a thick vertical wall. In Japanese architecture, we have a horizontal margin of space composed by floormats and wooden thresholds. Sensation of space is reinforced by slender columns situated solely in four corners. We lack the solid wall of Western architecture. Our rooms are only visually separated from adjacent ones by light sliding panels.

It is necessary to harmonize the traditional concept of the Japanese house with contemporary architecture.

31.3.3. Design and Psychological Factors

In postwar Japan, design studies came to be more and more influenced by psychology. According a historical review by Hotta, Kawasaki, Morita, and Iwai (1973), there have been three levels of studies on the relations of psychology to design: (a) research that only investigated certain psychological factors such as attitude and so forth; (b) studies in which designers used psychological information and techniques; and (c) research in which actual psychological data were gathered, feedback was given, and the results influenced the actual design. In the field of city design, when we examine the papers presented at the annual meeting of the Architectural Institute of Japan, roughly three major types of studies can be distinguished: (1) Research on city residents' need for space and attitudes and opinions about space (the great majority of papers that deal with psychological factors come under this classification); (2) Papers dealing with human relations in different types of space (environments); research on high-rise public housing; and (3) Research on the cognition of cities.

As for architectural studies, even as early as the immediate postwar era, many Japanese architects understood the necessity of conducting psychological-type studies before designing habitats. However, during the early postwar period, there was neither time nor financial support for such studies. The result was that houses were constructed only for the most basic human needs. Recently, studies have been done on the human side, including studies on "atmosphere," spatial cognition, and architectural image. Notable studies have been done at the interface of architecture and psychology by Inui (1982); among his works are studies on the effect of windows on spaciousness.

Because ergonomics is important in helping to design products for safety and ease of use, it has a close connection with environmental psychology. In Japan, considerable work has been done in ergonomics: for example, visual perception and color (Iiyama, 1974; Kansaku, 1968; Takagi, 1968), rail and automobile accidents (Higuchi, 1980; Ikeda, 1980; Yamauchi, 1981), noise estimation and noise pollution (Kitamura, 1970; Namba, 1979), and studies in special environments such as undersea (Hori, 1969), atomic energy (Takeda, 1981) and outer space (Nakayama, 1980; Saiki, 1980; Yajima, 1980).

31.3.4. Other Topics: Crowding, Pollution, and Community Change

Crowding

The population of Japan in 1982 was 117,060,000 people, making an overall density of 314 people per square kilometer. In densely populated areas, however, this rises to 6982 people. Density problems in Tokyo, for example, are so bad that the occupation of "hip pusher" was created. This is a person who is hired to help to cram people into already packed commuter trains.

Interest is growing in studying crowding. Honma (1979) compiled a review of crowding research, and Nakanishi conducted a 1981 study on crowding perception using computer simulation. With crowding conditions as bad as they are, it would seem that Japanese people would be accustomed to crowding, but a study by Iwata (1974) showed that Japanese people in Hawaii were more sensitive to crowding than Caucasians or Pacific Islanders. Thus, the psychological and cultural factors behind crowding are more complex than may have been thought.

An early study of "seat occupancy behavior" on streetcars showed a relation between occupancy and place of entrance (Kinoshita, 1958). The author also explained that aged people and women generally occupied seats close to entrances, whereas the middle-range seats were occupied by young men. Another experiment was conducted by filling a small room to uncomfortable levels with students. Afterward the actual physical density was compared to the feelings of crowding (Tanaka & Inoue, 1976). In two studies by Iwata (1978, 1979), crowding questionnaires were given to students to examine the influence of subjective factors such as personal attributes on crowding perception.

A future problem facing researchers doing crowding studies is the need for development of field-survey methods and experimental studies. Personal distance and personal space studies are, of course,

related to the crowding phenomena, and Japanese researchers have conducted a number of studies on such topics (Aono, 1979).

Japanese people seldom touch other people or embrace one another on meeting. This cultural trait may be of interest to future cross-cultural researchers. In an architectural study on a problem related to the touching phenomenon, Takahashi, Nishide, Takahashi, and Hirata (1978) showed that patterns of space occupancy differed according to group size, group purpose, and group qualities, that is conformity and cohesiveness and personal space.

Pollution

Pollution is, of course, a major problem in Japan. Air pollution in large cities and water pollution of lakes, rivers, and the sea are still serious. Heavy metal pollution has resulted in death and disability. Noise pollution from construction is serious, and people living in areas close to the *shinkansen* bullet train and near airports are troubled by numerous physical and psychological problems.

Japanese environmental psychologists have not expended nearly enough effort in dealing with these problems, but there are a few studies on pollution and related problems. Some of these are by Asai, Kimura, and Takizawa (1971), Hori (1973), and Sei (1977).

Community Change

Industrialization and modernization have brought great changes to the Japanese countryside. When large apartment complexes and industries reach out to the suburbs or even into the sea (as in the case of land reclamation projects), changes occur in dwellers' attitudes toward their daily life and toward their community. The "bed town" phenomenon has come into being because many suburban dwellers live so far away from their homes that after commuting, their homes are little more than places to sleep. Surveys on community attitudes in bed towns have been made by Komazaki and Okamura (1978). Also a serious problem facing small towns is the large migration of young people to the large cities. Ogawa and Fukada (1976) did a study of the life consciousness of young people in these depopulated areas.

31.4. PROBLEMS AND PERSPECTIVES OF FUTURE JAPANESE ENVIRONMENTAL PSYCHOLOGY

As previously mentioned, Japan's development of environmental psychology as a field was influenced by two major factors. One was the academic influence from principally Europe and America, and the other was stimulation from the Japanese public for action against pollution. But the contribution of psychologists to these environmental problems has largely been through such methods as questionnaires and simple interviews. More significant contributions are necessary to cope with the problems.

Psychologists generally use the experimental method, and the great majority of psychologists are hesitant to approach environmental problems due to their complex nature and large number of variables.

Many architects have realized the importance of human factors in man–environment relationships, and to some extent this stimulated psychologists into giving more consideration to these problems. Because psychologists have systematic knowledge of human factors, they should certainly take a greater role in future environmental psychological studies.

Great problems face environmental psychology as a discipline in Japan. At the present time, there are almost no course offerings at the graduate or undergraduate level. One of the major reasons for this deficit is that the Japanese university system is rather rigid and not open to curriculum change. However, lectures and seminars in certain areas of environmental psychology are offered under the headings of social psychology and other fields. And although interest and activity are increasing and articles are appearing in various journals, there is still not an independent journal for dealing solely with environmental psychology.

Environmental psychology is a young and developing interdisciplinary science: It could be compared to something like a new country made up of immigrants who speak different languages and do things in many different ways. For example, the definition of *environment* is still a problem. If we look at how the word is used in various studies, we can conceptualize room environment, school environment, community environment, and even outer space as different *environments*. It is thus extremely important to make concepts such as these more standardized and clearer to help break down the barriers between fields. Another problem is the lack of overall structure and fixed content. If one compares various environmental psychology textbooks, this problem is apparent. There are almost as many methodologies as there are researchers, causing troublesome communication problems. To overcome the traditional limitations of the past and build a more holistic and integrated methodology, it is necessary to try new approaches such as ecological, phenomenological, and multidimensional ones. It is perhaps too early to expect a unified theory from

environmental psychology, but while researchers are working on solutions to practical problems, it is important for them not to forget the need for basic models and to upgrade general theory.

Along with working with the international community, it is also important to develop studies related to Japanese problems and conduct original research that may later be of benefit to both Japan and other countries. Japanese researchers are familiar with British and American studies, but there is still a paucity of information from the rest of Europe and other countries. Due to language problems, the flow of information from Japan to other countries is still poor. It is necessary to build on our individual cross-cultural contacts and expand them.

A whole host of important tasks faces future environmental psychologists in Japan. How can they ease the conflict between rapid industrialization and traditional Japanese culture? Japanese environmental psychologists will have to answer such questions as the following: How do we design habitats to better house our elderly and keep them in touch with other people? How do we design environments for our elderly where they can continue to do useful and confidence-building work? How do we design educational and relaxing playgrounds in a very small area? Because future Japanese citizens will be faced with the radical transition from a workaholic culture to one with more leisure, how do we design environments to meet the increasing demands for productive leisure? Other questions that need to be addressed are: How can the handicapped be aided? How can we plan for safer evacuation procedures? How can environmental psychology help people who must suddenly move to a radically different culture and environment?

Changes in Japanese socialization patterns due to industrialization present challenging topics for research, such as over- and undermanning and the effect of modernization on crime. In other words, the final task of environmental psychology is to keep its focus on social and ethical problems and to help in controlling the negative factors associated with industrialization and mechanization—to keep human progress in balance with material and mechanical progress.

Acknowledgments

The authors are deeply indebted to Takashi Takahashi of The Architecture Department of Tokyo University and to Masami Kobayashi of Kyoto University's architecture department for help with data collection. We are particularly grateful to: Joe Hicks, Michihisa Arima,

Hirofumi Minami, and Wataru Inoue of Hiroshima University's psychology department for advice and invaluable editorial assistance. We also thank Seymour Wapner of Clark University and Shinji Ishii of Hiroshima University for their encouragement throughout this project.

REFERENCES

Abe, K. (1982). *Introduction to disaster psychology.* Tokyo: Science Publishing.

Akiyama, S. (1967). *Design and psychology.* Tokyo: Kajima Institute Publishing.

Aono, A. (1979). A developmental study of personal distance. *Japanese Journal of Experimental Social Psychology, 19,* 97–105.

Asai, M., Kimura, S., & Takizawa, K. (1971). A socio-clinical study on cognition of environmental destruction [Summary]. *Proceedings of the 35th Annual Convention of the Japanese Psychological Association, 35,* 703–704.

Asakawa, K. (1978). A developmental study of spatial cognition. *Reports of the Doctoral Course of Hiroshima University, 4,* 165–168.

Barker, R.G., & Gump, P.V. (1982). *Big school, small school* (N. Ando, Ed. & Trans.). Tokyo: Shinyosha Publishing. (Original work published 1964)

Canter, D. (1982). *The psychology of place* (N. Miyata & S. Uchida, Trans.). Tokyo: Shokokusha Publishing. (Original work published 1977)

Canter, D., & Inui, M. (Eds.). (1972). *What is environment psychology?* Tokyo: Shokokusha Publishing.

The Disaster Behavior Study Group (1978). Psychological analysis of evacuation behavior during the Sakata fire. (Research Report). Tokyo: Author.

Downs, R.M., & Stea, D. *Image and environment: Cognitive mapping and spatial behavior* (T. Soda, A. Hayashi, S. Funo, & F. Oka, Trans.). Tokyo: Kajima Publishing. (Original work published 1973)

Hagino, G., & Ittelson, W.H. (Eds.). (1981). *Interaction processes between human behavior and environment.* Tokyo: Bunsei Printing.

Hall, E.T. (1966). *The silent language* (M. Kunihiro, Y. Nagai, & M. Saito, Trans.). Tokyo: Nanundo Publishing. (Original work published 1959)

Hall, E.T. (1970). *The hidden dimension* (T. Hidaka & N. Sato, Trans.). Tokyo: Misuzu Shobo Publishing. (Original work published 1966)

Hasegawa, M. (1953). Human ecology. In Japanese Applied Psychological Association (Ed.), *Series in psychology* (Vol. 8). Tokyo: Nakayama Shoten Publishing Co.

Higuchi, K. (1980). Driving vision for automobiles. *Japanese Journal of Ergonomics, 16,* 229–236.

Higuchi, T. (1983). *The visual and spatial structure of landscapes.* (C. Terry, Trans.). Cambridge, MA: MIT Press. (Original work published 1975)

Honma, M. (1979). Modern trends in crowding research. *Japanese Journal of Experimental Social Psychology, 19,* 81–90.

Hori, M. (1969). Human engineering in undersea activities. *Japanese Journal of Ergonomics, 5,* 226–232.

Hori, H. (1973). The relationship between consciousness of, and knowledge about pollution. *Annual Report of the Tokyo Metropolitan Research Institute for Environmental Protection, 4,* 292–297.

Hotta, A., Kawasaki, K., Morita, O., & Iwai, K. (1973). Design and psychological factors. *Kogei-news, 41,* 44–51.

Iiyama, Y. (1974). Man-machine simulation studies on train operation. *Japanese Journal of Ergonomics, 17,* 238–259.

Ikeda, T. (1980). Analysis and prevention of railway accidents. *Japanese Journal of Ergonomics, 16,* 101–106.

Imai, S. (1973). Natural environment and human behavior. *Japanese Psychological Review, 16,* 231–244.

Inui, M. (1982). The effect of windows on the subjective evaluation of spaciousness. *Japanese Psychological Review, 25,* 3–17.

Inui, M., Osada, Y., Watanabe, H., & Akiyama, T. (1982). *Environmental psychology.* Tokyo: Shokokusha Publishing.

Iritani, T. (1974). *An introduction to environmental psychology.* Tokyo: Japan Broadcast Publishing.

Ishii, S., & Yamamoto, T. (1977). A microgenetic developmental study on the cognition of an unfamiliar environment, Part II. *Bulletin of the Faculty of the Education, Hiroshima University, Part 1, 26,* 347–354.

Ittelson, W.H., Proshansky, H.M., Rivlin, L.G., & Winkel, G.H. (Eds.). (1977). *An introduction to environmental psychology* (K. Mochizuki, Ed. & Trans.). Tokyo: Shokokusha Publishing. (Original work published 1974).

Iwata, O. (1974). A comparative study on the perception of crowding. *Bulletin of the Shikoku Women's University, 16,* 25–34.

Iwata, O. (1978). Some personal attributes and spatial factors in the perception of crowding. *Japanese Psychological Research, 20,* 1–6.

Iwata, O. (1979). Selected personality traits as determinants of the perception of crowding. *Japanese Psychological Research, 21,* 1–9.

Kamino, K., & Mikami, T. (1973). A study of spatial cognition in the Umeda underground mall. *Transactions of the Architectural Institute of Japan, 206,* 57–63.

Kansaku, H. (1968). Color in visual display. *Japanese Journal of Ergonomics, 4,* 7–16.

Kitamura, O. (1970). Effects of noise from aircraft in flight. *Japanese Journal of Ergonomics, 6,* 235–240.

Kinoshita, T. (1958). A study of crowding: An analysis of commuters' seat occupancy behavior in street cars [Summary]. *Proceedings of the 22nd Annual Convention of Japanese Psychological Association, 22,* 312–313.

Kobayashi, M., & Horiuchi, S. (1974a). Analysis of occupant behavior in an office building during fire, Part 1: Extraction of behavior patterns. *Transactions of the Architectural Institute of Japan, 284*, 137–142.

Kobayashi, M., & Horiuchi, S. (1974b). Analysis of occupant behavior in an office building during fire, Part 2: Classification of behaviors. *Transactions of the Architectural Institute of Japan, 284*, 119–126.

Kobayashi, S. (1961). *An introduction to architectural psychology.* Tokyo: Shokokusha Publishing.

Kogawa, M., Fujiwara, T., Inoue, W., Ishii, S., & Fukuda, H. (1983). A microgenetic developmental study of interpersonal cognition during transition to a new environment. *Japanese Journal of Psychology, 53*, 330–336.

Komazaki, T., & Okamura, K. (1978). A survey on the life consciousness and dwelling condition on Bed-towns [Summary]. *Proceedings of the 42nd Annual Convention of Japanese Psychological Association, 42*, 1276–1279.

Kubo, Y. (1952). A study of A-Bomb sufferers' behavior in Hiroshima: A socio-psychological research on A-Bomb and A-Energy (1). *Japanese Journal of Psychology, 22*, 27–34.

Kuroda, M. (1969). Patterns of human behavior: With respect to the Niigata earthquake. *Japanese Journal of Ergonomics, 5*, 164–174.

Lynch, K. (1968). *The image of the city* (K. Tange & R. Tomita, Trans.). Tokyo: Iwanami Publishing. (Original work published 1960)

Mehrabian, A. (1981). *Public places and private spaces* (T. Iwashita & H. Morikawa, Trans.). Tokyo: Kawashima Publishing. (Original work published 1976)

Mercer, C. (1979). *Living in cities* (Y. Nagata, Trans.). Tokyo: Shinyosha Publishing. (Original work published 1975)

Minami, H. (1953). *A psychology of the Japanese people.* Tokyo: Iwanami Publishing.

Miyagi, O. (1972). *Who are the Japanese?* Tokyo: Asahi Shinbun Publishing.

Mochizuki, M., & Ohyama, T. (Eds.). (1979). *Environmental psychology.* Tokyo: Asakura Publishing.

Moos, R.H. (1979). *The human context: Environmental determinants of behavior* (M. Mochizuki, Ed. & Trans.). Tokyo: Asakura Publishing. (Original work published 1976).

Nakanishi, H. (1981). A study of crowding perception using computer simulation [Summary]. *Proceedings of the 45th Annual Convention of Japanese Psychological Association, 45*, 787.

Nakayama, H. (1980). Some physiological aspects of prolonged exposure to hyperbaric environment. *Japanese Journal of Ergonomics, 16*, 57–62.

Namba, S. (1979). On the psychological effects of noise. *Japanese Journal of Ergonomics, 22*, 182–199.

Ogawa, K., & Fukada, H. (1976). Life consciousness of young people in depopulated areas: U-turn probability of young people having left their home village to live in urban areas. *Bulletin of the Faculty of Education, Hiroshima University, Part 1, 25*, 197–206.

Ohashi, H., & Ohta, Y. (1980). Field survey on human response during and after a large earthquake, Part II: Collection of data by interview method and its tentative analysis. *Earthquake, 33* (2), 199–214.

Ohta, Y., & Ohashi, H. (1979). Field survey on human response during and after a large earthquake, Part I: Collection of data by questionnaire method and its tentative analysis. *Earthquake, 32* (2), 399–413.

Ohyama, T. (1978). The formation of spatial representation by the walking behavior. *Annual Report of Psychology Department at Rikyo University, 21*, 64–70.

Ohyama, T., & Inui, M. (1969). *Psychology for architects.* Tokyo: Shokokusha Publishing.

Omi, T., Nakamura, A., Shida, M., & Kamemura, Y. (1982). Study on human-behavior during the Miyagioki earthquake, 1978, Part II: Analysis correlating the factors of actors. *Transactions of the Architectural Institute of Japan, 314*, 154–165.

Proshansky, H.M., Ittelson, W.H., & Rivlin, L.G. (Eds.). (1974–75). *Environmental psychology: Man and his physical setting* (6 Vols., S. Akiyama, S. Imai, K. Hirota, K. Ohara, T. Iritani, T. Funatsu, Eds. & Trans.). Tokyo: Seishin Shobo Publishing. (Original work published 1970)

Saiki, H. (1980). Environmental physiology for space life. *Japanese Journal of Ergonomics, 16*, 45–52.

Sako, T. (1981). Cognitive maps. *Annual Review of Japanese Child Psychology, 20*, 241–262.

Sei, T. (1977). A social psychological study on the adjustment process of adults and socio-cultural change: Attitude towards nuclear energy sources [Summary]. *Proceedings of the 41st Annual Convention of Japanese Psychological Association, 41*, 1136.

Sera, M. (1963). *The Japanese personality.* Tokyo: Kinokuniya Publishing.

Sofue, T. (1976). *Culture and personality.* Tokyo: Kobundo Publishing.

Soma, I. (Ed.). (1979a). *Design and environment.* Tokyo: Waseda University Press.

Soma, I. (Ed.). (1979b). *Education and environment.* Tokyo: Waseda University Press.

Soma, I., & Sako, T. (1976). *Environmental psychology.* Tokyo: Fukumura Publishing.

Sommer, R. (1972). *Personal space: The behavioral basis of design* (S. Akiyama, Trans.). Tokyo: Kajima Publishing. (Original work published 1969)

Suzuki, Y. (1983). A report on the IATSS symposium on traffic science 1982 "Man and Space." *International Association of Traffic and Safety Sciences Research, 7*, 38–44.

Suzuki, N., Kurihara, K., & Tago, S. (1974). *Architectural planning 5: Aggregate housing, housing districts.* Tokyo: Maruzen Publishing.

Takagi, K. (1968). Visual perception and visual display. *Japanese Journal of Ergonomics, 4,* 2–6.

Takahashi, T., & Hatsumi, M. (1978). A study on the characteristics of spatial cognition [Summary]. *Proceedings of the Annual Convention of the Architectural Institute of Japan,* 695–696.

Takahashi, T., & Hatsumi, M. (1979a). A study on the characteristics of spatial cognition. *Proceedings of the Annual Convention of the Architectural Institute of Japan,* 695–696.

Takahashi, T., & Hatsumi, M. (1979b). A fundamental study of dimensional perception: Psychological effects of ceiling height on room width. *Proceedings of the Annual Convention of the Architectural Institute of Japan,* 697–698.

Takahashi, T., Nishide, K., Takahashi, K., & Hirata, K. (1978). A study on space occupancy patterns by groups. *Proceedings of the Annual Convention of the Architectural Institute of Japan,* 647–650.

Takeda, A. (1981). On human error and the nuclear power plant as a man-machine system. *Japanese Journal of Ergonomics, 17,* 157–160.

Tanaka, K. (1964). *Social attitude of the Japanese.* Tokyo: Seishin Shobo Publishing.

Tanaka, K., & Inoue, T. (1976). An experimental study of crowding [Summary]. *Proceedings of the 40th Annual Convention of the Japanese Psychological Association, 40,* 1227–1228.

Tani, N. (1980). A transformation of image maps from route-map type to survey-map type. *Japanese Journal of Educational Psychology, 28,* 19–28.

Umesao, T. (1951). Environment. In Shisonokagaku Study Group (Ed.), *Handbook of human science.* Tokyo: Kawadeshoboshinsha Publishing.

Wapner, S. (1978). Some critical person-environment transitions. *Hiroshima Forum for Psychology, 5,* 3–20.

Watsuji, T. (1961). *Climate-philosophical study* (G. Bownas, Trans.). Tokyo: Printing Bureau, Japanese Government, 1961. (Original work published 1935)

Yajima, K. (1980). Health care system of Japanese payload specialist. *Japanese Journal of Ergonomics, 16,* 53–56.

Yamamoto, T. (1981). The microgenetic development of environment cognition. In G. Hagino & W. Ittelson (Eds.), *Interaction processes between human behavior and environment* (pp. 211–220). Tokyo: Bunsei.

Yamamoto, T., & Ishii, S. (1977). A microgenetic developmental study on the cognition of an unfamiliar environment, Part I. *The Bulletin of the Faculty of Education, Hiroshima University, Part 1, 26,* 339–345.

Yamamoto, T., Ishii, S., & Asakawa, K. (1978). A microgenetic developmental study on the cognition of an unfamiliar environment (3). *The Bulletin of the Faculty of the Education, Hiroshima University, Part 1, 27,* 161–167.

Yamauchi, K. (1981). Human error and its prevention of train operation. *Japanese Journal of Ergonomics, 17,* 161–165.

Yoda, A., & Tsukishima, K. (Eds.). (1970). *The Japanese personality.* Tokyo: Asakura Publishing.

Yoshida, M. (1975). *Urban environment and dwelling psychology.* Tokyo: Shokokusha Publishing.

Chapter 32

THE STUDY OF PEOPLE–ENVIRONMENT RELATIONS IN FRANCE

Denise Jodelet, *Ecole des Hautes Etudes en Sciences Sociales, Laboratoire de Psychologie Sociale, Paris, France*

32.1. INTRODUCTION

In his introduction to the very first survey on the environmental field, published in the 1973 *Annual Review of Psychology*, Craik ascribed the expansion of this field during the previous decade in part to "its lively and thoroughgoing multidisciplinary character." Yet he chose to call the study of people–environment relations "environmental psychology," which he considered "to be useful as an inclusive, theoretically neutral term."

Any attempt to highlight the salient features of the field in France would encounter a similar situation: rapid development since the 1960s and a multidisciplinary nature. The latter is actually a problem in itself, for the study of people–environment relations draws on all of the human and social sciences. The scope of the field extends above and beyond the bounds of psychology per se and is certainly not totally encompassed by the term *environmental psychology*. It calls for a broader approach justified by the historical growth of the field and by the way of looking at the interactions between individuals and groups, taken as producers and users, and their environments.

Environmental studies began in France as early as

the late 1950s, but they were carried out mostly in psychology's neighboring sciences. Purely psychological research appeared more recently and later than in the rest of Europe or in the United States, as has been pointed out by Levy-Leboyer who stressed (1976) the extension of a branch of applied research on the environment to which psychologists could devote themselves using their own methods and concepts. Nevertheless, restricting environmental studies to the latter would be tantamount to painting a deceitful portrait of French research, because it would omit empirical and theoretical trends that for 20 years now have been used to examine the myriad facets of people–environment relations.

These trends present a double specificity as, from the onset, the main thrust of scientific policy in the environmental field strove to promote a multidisciplinary approach strongly encouraged by research-supporting institutions.

On the one hand, research has always been characterized by a comprehensive perspective. The environment is not merely defined in material and spatial terms. Its social and political dimensions are also taken into account in the study of its determining factors, significance, as well as the effects and reactions it entails. Regarding groups and individuals examined in relation to their environments, they are most often defined in social or cultural terms or as social agents through their interaction with space. Even in the psychological domain, subjects are frequently studied not only in their biopsychological dimensions but also from the point of view of their group membership, their social localization and practice, and the related needs, values, and beliefs they express regarding the context of everyday life.

On the other hand, the specialized literature, though bearing on studies of a more sociological kind, reveals a focusing on the individual aspects of environmental problems, a concern with psychosociological, if not psychological, dimensions, and psychologically relevant material. So one can say that environmental psychology as such emerged at the very beginning of environmental research. Moreover, the themes and problems contained in the latter overlap with the major pursuits in environmental psychology as defined in other countries. The difference has more to do with emphasis than with content.

This chapter will therefore propose an overview of the current trends in environmental research that incorporate different psychological and social disciplines because they give an insight on the life of individuals and groups in their environments. The following will be successively examined: (1) the intellectual and institutional framework of the field, giving a view of the main historical, political, philosophical, and cultural underpinnings of research and of the scientific operating of the field; (2) the environment-related subjects in French university research and education, with an examination of the topics being studied; (3) the branches of environmental research, focusing on the evolution of the domain from the point of view of the relative importance of disciplines and writings concerned by environmental problems; (4) the major trends in environmental research with an attempt to broach, in their conceptual unity and their specific approaches and methodologies, the most important research groups with respect to the bulk or the originality of their production. Research areas that are starting to grow and where the number of researchers is still limited will be mentioned before the conclusion.

32.2. THE INTELLECTUAL AND INSTITUTIONAL FRAMEWORK OF THE ENVIRONMENTAL FIELD

The fabric of environmental research in France is made up of scientific, cultural, institutional, and political factors, all of which are closely linked. This is certainly true, given science's ties with social problems and society's requirements in an intellectual context that is characterized by the expansion of the human sciences and the will to provide an all-encompassing conceptual framework for the study of humans and society.

At the scientific and cultural levels, attention must be drawn to some of the more specific features of France's intellectual community as it influences research trends.

32.2.1. Links and Gaps between French and Other Countries' Research Trends

Evidence that French research relates to that developed in other countries is given by reviews and introductory books on environmental problems which begun to appear in the early 1970s (Fischer, 1981; Gaillard, Quan Schneider, Sodre, Vidal, 1971; Gruska & Mazerat, 1975; Lecuyer, 1975, 1976a, 1976b). These publications show that research stemmed either from questions raised in theoretical analyses within a given field of study (especially social psychology) or from prevailing models in the international scientific community of people–environment relations from the individual, small group, or larger social unit point of view. In this respect, American scientists have unquestionably exercised a major influence on the fields of psychology, sociology, and cultural anthropology in France.

This influence is manifest in the social sciences at the problematic level (particularly about urban and technological growth and organization). As regards environmental psychology, in the strictest sense of the term, the connection is more extensive: It bears on the definition of research areas, the theoretical constructs, and the methodologies. Levy-Leboyer (1980) outlines these filiations in four specific domains: (1) perception and assessment of built and natural environment, (2) effect of environmental characteristics and stress on behavior, (3) personal space, and (4) defense and improvement of the environment by public and state agencies. She shows how French research interfaces with that done overseas by (1) highlighting reciprocal influence and dynamic interaction between people and their environments, the interrelations between physical and social features of the environment; and (2) adopting a molar, holistic perspective to study the various material aspects of the environment as well as the subject's involvement in reaction to and action on it.

However, this literature has revealed differences and discrepancies between research in France and elsewhere. First of all, France has lagged behind other countries in certain respects. This was mainly due to the fact that social problems arose at a later date than in other countries. For instance, I am speaking about industrial and urban-growth-related problems that came to researchers' attention during the 1960s or those linked to safety, violence, or vandalism that have just begun to be studied (Ackerman, Dulong, & Jeudy, 1983).

Second, there is a slight advance, in France, as to the examination of social fallout of environmental policies and a greater concern about public opinion as regards the detrimental effects of technological and scientific progress on the quality of life. This is due, in part, to the emergence of protest movements following the 1968 uprising that defended identity values related to territorial belonging (i.e., grass roots movements) and demanded a larger responsibility of people on life contexts and conditions (participationist movements). These movements opposed the risks that nuclear development imposes on nature and humans (antinuclear movements). This climate and the diffusion of trends of thougbht favoring the reinstatement of convivial, community, and traditional ways of life, combining a modernism *à la Illich*

and resurgences of the rural sensitiveness of the *France profonde*, have strongly contributed to the sudden eruption in the 1970s of a political trend, the so-called ecological party, or green party. This party's influence was not negligible. It caused an evident effect on the public that administrative and scientific authorities had to take in account. Thus a ministry dedicated to environment, local and regional polls of people affected by environmental changes, and even new research areas, as for instance, the creation of an ad hoc committee within the Cultural Affairs Ministry in order to protect ethnological patrimony have emerged.

Finally, French scientists have tried to get away from the assumptions of Anglo-Saxon models, which they criticize both from theoretical and ideological points of view. Such is the case, for example, for research on personal space (Lecuyer, 1976a) that seems contestable both conceptually (inaccuracy and contradiction in the notion's definition that lead to operational insufficiencies) and ideologically (to avoid considering social relations, studies only retain limited aspects of personal space, neglecting especially social context and communication that are always linked to spatial context). The same applies to trends in urban sociology that, as shown in Castells's criticism (1975), have neither proper theoretical object nor specific concrete object. The author relies on an examination of the concept of *urban culture*, which is stigmatized as "mythical," and on the theoretical weakness of approaches focusing on social integration to culture produced by capitalistic industrialization. The author also relies on the mistaken character of a conception of space–society relationships explaining social structure by the ecological system.

32.2.2. Specificities of the French Intellectual Framework

This distance has had a twofold impact: Scientists either turn away from fields of investigation, which explains the lack of research on certain environmental issues, or they try to discover original angles of attack based on specifically French trends. These original features spring from two main currents.

On the one hand, there is the desire to preserve ties with European scientific and intellectual traditions. Due to these historical ties, scientists refer extensively to European thinkers such as Durkheim and his conception of industrialization's role on types of social solidarity and his theory of the interdependence between social consciousness and social organization. They also refer to Weber who extends the approach of cities, including a political typology of their establishment (princely, patrician, plebeian cities) and an economic typology of their functioning (consummation or production types of cities). Also Heidegger is quoted. He gives a phenomenological formulation of relation to housing and explores what *to dwell* means.

As is made evident by a survey of the main research trends in France (see Section 32.4), this imprinting gives studies a sociological flavor, even those not in the social science area. Thus fields of study are chosen preferably among settings where collective activities and ways of life occur (factories, work places, housing projects, road networks, areas of vacation-time "transhumance") and where power relationships and group conflicts (companies, schools, town councils, etc.) are expressed. Moreover, more attention is paid to small groups and larger social units than to individuals. The predominance of studies of representations and value systems in the explanation of responses to environmental constraints must also be linked to these social philosophies' influence. Besides, one car observe a strong impact of phenomenology. It leads to a trend where attention paid to lived experiences of those who occupy and use environments, and examination of mental and symbolic mediations in the way people cope with built and natural environments prevail on the sole consideration of the physical aspects and effects of the latter.

This enables one to understand another tendency encountered among numerous researchers who turn to authors such as Bachelard (1964)[1], Eco (1972), Durand (1963), Levi-Strauss's anthropological data (1955), and Barthes (1964) and Greimas's (1976) semiology in order to highlight the role of symbolic and significant processes in individuals and groups' relations to space. This kind of preoccupation contributed to interesting methodological progresses in analyzing meanings of the material organization of environmental designs (illustrations are given in Section 32.4).

On the other hand, there is a tendency to rely on intellectual movements that act as a beacon "enlightening" thought on humankind and society. This includes the need to become affiliated with *maitrespenseurs* and typically Parisian parochialism that thrives on critique. Thus various sociological, psychosociological, and psychological approaches bear the stamp of Structuralism, Marxism, Freudianism and of new philosophies such as those of Baudrillard (1960) and Lyotard (1973).

These influences which are often the mere effects of fashion, are sometimes seen only in bibliographical references or terminological borrowing. They also have led, in models and methods, to heuristical outcomes, some of which deserve mention. For instance, the approach dealing with the environment as a place where fantasies articulated to the Freudian opposition between "the inside" and "the outside," are projected. In the same line, regarding the analysis of the subject's investment of space, approaches questioning the relevance of the notion of *need* in favor of terms judged more appropriate: *"desire"* and *"demand,"* borrowed from the psychoanalytical theory of Lacan (1966). Marxism, too, has produced such effects. At times it has only oriented attention toward the role of the economic dimension in environmental planning and dwelling (Godart & Pendaries, 1978); at times it allowed the formulation of hypotheses on "toposociology" (i.e., reproduction in built environment of production relationships through housing assignations that differ according to social classes on a geographical, material, functional, and qualitative point of view [dormitory developments, segregation of low-income people on the fringes of cities, etc.]). Marxism has also stimulated a whole series of research, concentrating on social conflicts about urban planning, transportation, and the like, or striving to demonstrate how production and use of space are determined by the location of social actors within social structure. Another approach of the social conflict literature has received a remarkable impetus based on "actionalist" sociology (Touraine, 1981).

Another influential work is that of Foucault (1977) with its reference to Bentham's "panopticum" model highlighting space distribution as a means of social control. It is well known that Bentham conceived, in 1796, an architectural device that is a way to establish disciplinary relations by a geometrical design of buildings. Suitable for factories, jails, schools, and so on, it allows the staff located in a central tower to control the activities of anybody in any part of the building surrounding the tower. For Foucault, this spatial device was more than a utopia, the "imaginary intensity" of which fostered actual or planned variations during two centuries. This model has served as the pattern of a power mechanism, showing how discipline is enforced throughout the social body in order to optimize social yield and manufacture useful individuals.

Last, the contribution of new scientific trends such as chronobiology, ethology, health and illness study have opened original research tracks. For instance, there are studies on temporal modalities of adaptation to environmental changes (Reineberg, 1979) and on morbidity factors due to space. New scientific trends have also favored methodologies centered on fastidious observation of space appropriation and use by children and adults (Montagné, 1980).

The confluence of these historical, political, philosophical, and scientific elements shaped French research in an original way. One can note the emphasis on unconscious determinations (of an emotional, cultural, ideological order) and tacit dimensions of relation to the environment that are studied with open methodologies (nonstructured interviews, projective tests, semantical analysis of discourses) and observations of ethological and ethnological types. One can note, too, the effort to highlight historical and sociological characteristics that modulate, on the part of individuals and groups, reactions to space (social representations, cultural values, etc.), and, on the part of material structures, the effects of physical features of the environment (semantics of spatial arrangements). We may take into account also the major concern with social movements that has led to innovative methodologies.

32.2.3. Institutional and Political Framework

These specific characteristics were reinforced by the institutional and political aspects of research. The environment is one of the scientific fields with the closest and most fruitful ties between social requirements and research. Problems raised both by private and government decision makers regarding space distribution and use have stimulated research and spawned interdisciplinary approaches. Evidence for this interdisciplinary approach is abundant. Some research teams have developed their programs in a multidisciplinary perspective, uniting sociology and semiology in their studies of cities' images or the various social meanings of the home. They also include psychoanalytical, economic, and sociological analyses of people's living experience in their homes. The interdisciplinary approach is also reflected in studies that, in order to broach specific environmental questions, take into account conclusions reached in other scientific fields. It is most interesting, in this respect, to read the bibliographical and documentary works[2] drawn up by departments of the various ministries that, in varying capacities and under different names, are in charge of environmental affairs (e.g., Ministère de l'Environnement et du Cadre de Vie, Ministère de l'Equipement et du Logement,

etc.). This literature includes the entire gamut of scientific output in the social sciences and psychology. Although the bulk of this scientific investigation had been requested by government bodies and public or semipublic institutions in charge of promoting research, the bibliographies published by or available at documentation centers are not restricted to this category and include all of the literature on general and specific environmental issues. With respect to the contents of this material, the number of identical quotations and cross-references is striking and testifies to similar views and approaches and to the interdisciplinary nature of the field. One could almost go so far as to state that in France, the environment is the scientific field allowing the best flow of information among disciplines as well as their mutual recognition. As a forum of reconciliation, if not yet one of concurrent scientific ventures, the environment has gradually given rise to a specific culture. The aforementioned trends shaped this culture, but it also bears the mark of other influences.

Government agencies' requests define the main orientations of research. Because these agencies provide funds, the focal points they propose for research strongly influence its structure. As noted earlier, social and political elements also shape the nature of research. Public opinion's growing awareness of environmental protection and ideas disseminated by ecology movements have highlighted a series of problems on which research is being carried out, ranging from the study of social movements (Coing, 1966; Durand & Harff, 1977; Mehl, 1975) to measuring anxiety and sensitivity vis-à-vis dangers threatening the environment (Chiva, Jodelet, Moscovici, Pujol, & Scipion, 1983).

Ideological influences had already been felt in the aftermath of the social upheavals of 1968 that deeply questioned our consumer society and state control, seriously disrupted architect's colleges and urbanism institutes, and called for a redefinition of responsibilities in the city planning sector. This resulted in an antiestablishment type ·of scientific output oriented toward user protection, the analysis of urban strife, and innovation in space utilization and building. One of the most interesting spinoffs of this trend has been the feedback to financing institutions provided by symposia that questioned the manifold aspects of government policy. In addition, this critical attitude was reinforced by ideas borrowed from ecological ideologies that have defined new types of social behaviors and new ways of relating to one's environment. These factors also explain the plethora of literary output of many thinkers and technocrats who have written on the general theme of the environment (e.g., Cayrol, 1968; Frémont, 1976; d'Iribarné, 1975; Jeannière & Antoine, 1970; La Rochefoucauld, 1971; Roche, 1970; Rougerie, 1975).

The environment, a topic that public opinion and all those involved in social development (administrators, directors, technocrats, politicians, journalists, scientists, etc.) are becoming more and more acutely aware of, is growing apace as a field of academic study in French universities. The following discussion will be devoted to this theme.

32.3. ENVIRONMENT-RELATED SUBJECTS IN FRENCH UNIVERSITY RESEARCH AND EDUCATION

Data on environment-related university programs was gleaned from the Centre de Documentation Sciences Humaines of the Centre National de la Recherche Scientifique. That department supplied a list of social and human science research centers and programs in French universities and institutes of higher learning affiliated with the French Ministry of Education. This list is a regularly updated data base that we searched for topics such as psychology, environment, and regional planning in order to cover the field in its historical perspective and to assess the relative importance of each discipline.[3]

In France, universities are public higher education institutes. There are 68 state universities distributed throughout France, according to an administrative division into 23 academies. Moreover, seven institutes of higher learning specialized in the social and human sciences have been selected for mention here: Conservatoire National des Arts et Métiers, Collège de France, Ecole des Hautes Etudes en Sciences Sociales, Ecole Normale Supérieure, Ecole Pratique des Hautes Etudes, Fondation Nationale des Sciences Politiques, and Maison des Sciences de l'Homme. All of the preceding have educators and researchers working either in university departments or in laboratories and research centers. Researchers at the Centre National de la Recherche Scientifique (CNRS) are appointed to these various institutes. There are also research groups, including educators and CNRS researchers, with a semipublic status (a 1901 act association, i.e., a state-approved, nonprofit association).

Our survey was carried out on a total of 75 universities and higher education institutes. It shows that environmental concerns are indeed a dominant theme both in research and education: 62 institutes

in the survey consider the environment as an object of scientific study. Moreover, the topic is broached in a multifaceted fashion by these institutes as is testified by 214 research centers and departments that study the environment in specific perspectives.

Out of these 214 programs, 12% have a predominantly psychological or psychosociological approach, including the following main themes: development, socialization, education; differential psychology[4]; perception, representation of space; ways of using space; social relations, types of social behaviors and life-styles; ergonomics, work, communication, organization; economic psychology; human ecoethology; health; tourism, transportation; and images and attitudes vis-à-vis environmental problems.

Eighteen percent apply a sociological, sociohistorical, and ethnological perspective to the following issues: behavior, needs, requests for housing; the history and social structure of cities; sociocultural space and urban growth; urban and rural sociology; community ethnology; health, work, pollution; daily living and deviance; urban groups, social movements, urban strife; and regional environments, ecosystem/society relations, and so forth.

Thirty-one percent of these programs study city and country planning from the legal, economic, and political standpoints. This research thrives especially in universities in the French provinces with a strong regional identity and deals with the following topics: public and international law (bearing on natural resources, pollution, sea, regional planning and natural, rural, urban environments, building and urbanism); economics (macroeconomics, regional economical planning and development; administrative management by regional and local authorities; political life; territorial decentralization); regional problems and planning (of health, energy conservation, urban change, employment and work systems, leisure, tourism and transportation).

Twenty-six percent of these programs are devoted to human geography: urban, rural, and industrial geography; demography; geography of regional space (local and regional planning, industrial and tertiary sector decentralization, communication, transportation, telecommunications, tourism).

Thirteen percent are involved in physical geography and ecology: the geophysical study of natural milieus; ecotoxicology; industrial and commercial hygiene; pollution; biogeography; geomorphology; physical and human geography of regions, and the like.

This list reflects the historical development of environment-related topics. As early as the pre-World

War II era, public authorities began giving top priority to city and regional planning. In the wake of World War II, especially with the coming to power of the Vème République, environmental planning became first and foremost a political issue related to economic growth and later to decentralization policies. Research in the geographical, political, economic, legal, and administrative fields was spurred on by local and central authorities as well as by private and public interests.

However, the emphasis placed on environmental problems in other disciplines must also be noted: Out of the 62 universities and institutes of higher learning that are developing curricula on the environment, 25 are carrying out their research in psychology or social science departments and laboratories. The latter account for 30% of all research and education institutes surveyed. This state of affairs confirms the increasing involvement of the social sciences in universities in the environmental field.

Moreover, this involvement is partly due to social requirements and pressure and government incentives aimed at promoting interdisciplinary research in order to support and highlight planners' decisions, as has already been mentioned. By virtue of such policies, both the social sciences and psychology are more deeply involved in the processes of research and consultation than it would appear, judging only by university curricula.

32.4. BRANCHES OF ENVIRONMENTAL RESEARCH

Two features testify to the presence of the human sciences in the environmental field: the literature published since the late 1950s and the scientific exchanges held at national or international levels.

32.4.1. Publications on Environmental Issues

The literature on environmental issues includes published articles and books and mimeographed research and symposium reports that were studied in order to establish the relative importance of each discipline and the various trends within the field, and to determine the evolution of the environmental field's structure throughout time.

In order to draw up a list of publications, we used resources provided by university libraries, by the library of the Ecole d'Architecture, and the documen-

tation centers of the Ministry of the Environment and the Ministry of Urbanism and Housing. We also carried out surveys on specialized study groups and the documentation centers of institutions providing financial support to scientific research. Previously published reviews and bibliographical lists established by public and private organizations were also taken into account. We divided our work into two consecutive steps. The first step involved identifying all publication titles referring to individual, group, community/natural and built environment relations. Second, these documents were examined and chosen according to their correlations with main currents in international research. The references of general works were also selected in view of their impact on the orientation of research, as is reflected by the publications and their bibliographies.

Our first list includes 820 publications covering the period between the late 1950s and 1981. This list allows us to paint a life-size portrait of the evolution of the people–environment relations approach, which was the object of this particular section. In addition, 450 publications were analyzed to identify the major trends and results in various fields of research. These will be presented in the following sections.

The growth of environmental research is reflected by the number of publications on the aforementioned list: Up to 1969, there were 373 references (books, articles, presentations, research documents) that were counted; from 1970 to 1979, the number rose to 655, and then reached the total of 820 at the end of 1981.

The 450 publications selected for the bibliographical analysis can be found in Table 32.1 where they have been classified according to their dates of publication. Furthermore, texts were divided into four categories—general, philosophical and scientific, sociological, or psychological—in order to show the relative importance of the various approaches to environmental issues and to specify research trends and their transformation.

General works make up a relatively large share of the literature, and they testify to public concern regarding the environment. In addition to the works of philosophers and thinkers whose powerful influence has left its mark on social scientists' views, there are also publications dealing with the environment in broad, general terms that are written by politicians, technocrats, writers, journalists, and the like. The philosophical texts that are more widely represented than the general ones in the 1960s (12 vs. 2%) and the first half of the 1970s (5 vs. 4%) tend to disappear in favor of the latter in the course of recent

Table 32.1. Temporal Distribution of Topics and Disciplines as Reflected in French Bibliograpic Citations of People–Environment Research.

Types of Texts	1960–1969	1970–1974	1975–1979	1980–1981
	Percentage			
General	2	4	18	18
Philosophical	12	6	1	0
Social Sciences	39	56	42	36
Psychology	47	34	39	46
Total References	53-100%	107-100%	238-100%	52-100%

years (1975–1979 = 1 vs. 18%; 1980 = 0 vs. 18%). Nevertheless, the authors of philosophical works continue to be quoted by research scholars, whereas the prevalence of general texts demonstrates a tendency toward the development of global and humanist reflections on the basis of the results of various research and of the themes that these deal with. This development certainly reflects a mode of thinking that is characteristically French, in the sense that fondness for general ideas is more prevalent than attention paid to empirical data, above all when issues of vital importance are concerned.

Scientific texts were classified according to their various disciplines into the social sciences, on the one hand, and psychology, on the other. The social sciences essentially include sociology (urban, rural, political, economic), ethnology, anthropology, and semiology. The psychology category is made up of research in the psychological field as a whole (general, developmental, social, environmental, ergonomic, pathological), psychiatry, and psychoanalysis.

The equal or greater proportion of social sciences works, as compared to psychological ones, clearly demonstrates a tendency that is characteristic of the field. The variation in volume of these texts, during the course of the periods surveyed, sheds light on the comeback of true psychological studies after a marked decline that they suffered at the beginning of the second decade.

This situation is due both to intrinsic and extrinsic factors of scientific development that responds either to theoretical questions raised in the scientific field or to social demands voiced in a given ideological and social context. Among the intrinsic factors, two elements may account for the evolution in psychological output over the past 20 years. During this period,

the peaks observed in booming psychological research actually correspond to two theoretical developments. On the one hand, in the late 1960s, spurred on by psychology's own momentum, behaviorist and experimental trends emerged rapidly in French research that, often following in the footsteps of its main American counterparts, dealt with the environment as it related to perception, cognition, small groups, and communication. On the other hand, during the second half of the 1970s, the growth of applied psychology and data on trends in environmental psychology in other countries gave a new impetus to psychological research in France. At the same time, after 1968, the inclusion of psychoanalysis in higher education curricula, the greater emphasis placed on symbolic processes in explaining behavior, and the influence of Marxist trends further extended the field of interdisciplinary research—in which psychology does indeed have a role to play—and modified some of the approaches of environmental psychology.

In the social sciences as well, structuralist and Marxist trends gradually widened and transformed the scope of environmental research. Interdisciplinary ventures promoted by the public authorities led the social sciences and psychology to converge. The following sections will provide concrete examples of this process.

32.4.2. Scientific Exchanges

Scientific meetings are the other indicator of the growing involvement of French researchers in the environmental field. First of all in quantitative terms, both the number of scientific meetings held at a national level and the number of international symposia held in France are increasing rapidly. In the 1960–

1969 period there were 2; in the 1970–1979 period there were 13; and in the 1980–1981 period, there were 7. Similarly, international symposia that mushroomed from 1970 onward have included more and more French participants[5]. Second, in qualitative terms, national symposia began to be held on a regular basis as of 1965. Changes in their topics reflect major trends in research over the past few years.

Up to 1975, research was mainly oriented toward the environment's functional aspects (e.g., identifying human requirements as regards noise level; the physiological and psychological impacts of their thermal environment on humans) and the consequences of urban development from the psychological and social points of view (urbanites and ruralists faced with "urban revolution"; pathology and mental health in cities; coordination between scientists, planners, and decision makers in order to prevent detrimental aspects of cities).

From 1975 onward, a greater emphasis was placed on environment practices, the microsocial reactions to environmental development, and the significant aspects of space. For example, under the topic of housing, marginality, and spatial segregation, one studies the following: localization of social marginals, immigrants, elderly and young people; growth and changes in type of housing (especially in suburbs) and their segregative effect on the inhabitants' life and culture. Under the topic of urban ecology, one studies urbanites' needs and requirements, the public's involvement and action with respect to green areas, types of housing, new types of sociability and so forth. Under the topic of urban planning and social control, one studies such themes as technocratic power versus social movements, and normalization, deviance, and conflicts. Finally, under the rubric of symbolic systems of urban environment, one focuses on mental imagery, representation, and semiotics of the environment.

32.4.3. Reviews of the French Literature on Environment

Another indicator of the focal points of scientific research is to be found in the general bibliographies and reviews published by various organizations. In addition to the publications mentioned at the beginning of this chapter that deal extensively with American trends in research, some of these works highlight trends emerging in the early 1970s. The French research in these bibliographies and reviews deal with the following topics: the psychological, social, and esthetic dimensions of housing complexes; physiolog-

ical, psychological, and pathological consequences of built environments marked by cost-effectiveness considerations; responses to noise conditions and the impact of the sonic boom on people and animals that seems to be more psychological than physiological; the differential psychology of people's surroundings and the structure of related needs; and the living experience of people in individual houses.

Two analytical reports on the research being carried out in the environmental field shed new light on its historical development and the various factors involved. The first one was published in 1971 (Gaillard et al.) and places French research within current trends in human and social science research. At that time, French research was devoted primarily to the following areas: studies on housing, inhabitants, and the living experience in the home; people–space relations (e.g., the perception, orientation, and symbolic system of space, and its organization and design, urban pathology; urban politics; and theoretical models of the city and urban phenomena.

The second report, published in 1975 (Gruska & Mazerat), covered 109 pieces of research dealing with environment-related representations, attitudes, aspirations, and interactions. This analytical report shows that the emphasis bears more on the environment's impact on the individual or social actor than on the latter's influence on the environment. Regarding the former, 38% of the research focused on the individual, 45% on small groups, and 16% on larger groups. Sixteen percent of the studies on people's impact on the environment were centered on the individual, 22% on small groups, and 62% on larger groups.

Moreover, the types of environments studied were predominantly large-scale ones: cities, villages, regions, and countries (over 40%), which were followed by districts and neighborhoods seen as meeting places (15%), housing as a place of private appropriation (12%), and last, proximical space and the body. According to the authors of this report, the preponderance of studies devoted to small groups' influence on the environment is due to social pressure to solve specific problems and to methodological considerations that involve analyzing representative samples of environment users. The predominance of studies on society's impact on the environment stems from the role of planning and development.

Both of these reports illustrate the trends that we found in our quantitative examination of the published literature.

However, this mapping of the environmental field reflects even more strikingly the dominant traits of social demands than it does the vitality of the scientific field. In order to fully grasp the latter, the theoretical and methodological trends of the past 20 years must be examined.

32.5. MAJOR TRENDS IN ENVIRONMENTAL RESEARCH

Throughout the growth and history of environmental research, researchers' interest has crystallized around specific approaches or fields of study. This, together with the fact that research is conducted within highly distinct institutional structures and often under the impulse of pioneering personalities in the scientific field, leads to specialization and the emergence of quasi-schools of thought. We shall successively examine current trends in psychology, psychosociology, and sociology, anthropology, and semiology.

32.5.1. Trends in Psychology

It must first be emphasized that research in psychology is heir to diverse theoretical approaches and relies on various methodological techniques (surveys, observation, experimentation) (Bresson & Chombart de Lauwe, 1974). These were influenced by the studies of Piaget and colleagues (1964), by phenomenology, by theories of perception and cognition (Huteau, 1975), small groups, communication and social control on the one hand, and by the various psychoanalytical schools of thought (e.g., Kaufmann, 1976; Marc, 1972; Mitscherlich, 1971) on the other hand. Last, some orientations in research stemmed directly from environmental psychological models and fields of study.

The most representative example of the latter is the research trend headed by C. Levy-Leboyer (1960, 1962, 1976a, 1976b, 1977, 1978) on the psychological dimension of people–environment relations in a differential perspective. Two main orientations have appeared.

One deals with the needs that must be met by the environment. Six needs were suggested, following a factorial analysis of correspondences: (1) security and safety requirements; (2) an evaluation of the environment's intrinsic and functional qualities; (3) an assessment of the latter in terms of social status or professional criteria; (4) belonging to society, a need for dependency or autonomy vis-à-vis the community; (5) orientation of social life toward the family or toward the outside world; and (6) the need to be active, to be involved, to participate.

These results were established for individuals and were confirmed by the responses of various sociodemographic groups. Age, sex, sociocultural level, social origin, and marital status all modulate the relative degree of the aforementioned needs. There is evidence that the environment's molar elements either inhibit or support and reinforce physiological, psychological, and behavioral needs.

Moreover, the importance of the need for security and safety has led researchers to seek the nature of its reinforcement within people's personalities or in their past environmental experience. The latter is not involved in the need for security and safety. However, anxiety-ridden people (as defined by the Cattel test) see the environment as something threatening and consequently seek social support, whereas they are less sensitive to comfort than nonanxious people.

The other orientation of research deals with responses to environmental stress. A study on noise showing a low correlation between expressed inconveniences and physical measurements of noise levels has isolated psychological factors accounting for distorted perception, such as attitudes and feelings vis-à-vis the environment, a comparison between real and expected noise levels, and the criteria used in assessing noise (level of danger, usefulness, pleasure).

These comprehensive data shed new light on the results of many studies carried out both in laboratories and in the natural milieu on noise, the perception of noise, its impact on diurnal activities, and sleep. (François, 1977; Laverrière, 1973; Metz & Muzet, 1975; Olivier-Martin, Scheiber, & Muzet, 1972). All of these studies have highlighted the discrepancy between physiological measurements of noise's effects and its psychological assessment.

A human ethnoecological trend stems from the research carried out by the psychiatrist Sivadon (1965, 1974a) who established a correlation between the structure of the human body and the structure of the environment: The body's spatial relations constitute the simplest aspect of situations, the internalization and integration of which are part and parcel of the human personality's temporal dimension. This approach advocates viewing the personality in spatial terms and including the spatial context in therapy. The study of psychopathological personalities highlights the specific qualitative nature of time. Each form of psychopathology creates a proper temporality expressing its singularity. Thus time appears as a human construction not entirely reducible to its spatial markers (watches, plannings, etc.). This chronogenesis has to do with peoples' forms of life, work, and pleasure. Sivadon distinguishes between this experiential time and a "chronic time" made of space and time. The latter implies the structuring of temporal dimensions of persons' experience and action within spatial patterns. This leads to an approach of human activity and work in terms of "temporal topology" and an explanation of social and work disturbances by time illnesses. Moreover, this approach has already been applied in hospital architecture and could be relevant in urbanism for the safeguard of mental health.

Headed by another psychiatrist, Leroy, this trend also draws upon other disciplines (psychoanalysis, psychology, psychiatry, physiology, sociology, etc.) in order to study the relations that exist between one's body, one's own self-image, the image one has of others, one's marking and use of the environment, on the one hand, and the structure, representation, and experience of the environment, on the other hand. Studies by Leroy (1977) and Leroy, Bedos, and Berthelot (1982) using various methodologies reveal, among other data:

1. As regards people–housing relations, "outside" constraints, that is, those pertaining to the city as a place of communication and movement, dominate the "inside" constraints of the home: The assessment of one's home depends on the environment. In high-rise buildings, identical time organization, space use and way of life, for all tenants, have four consequences: a homogeneous representation of life surroundings, an impoverishment of group relations, and the elaboration of a poor self-image by individuals that in turn entails aggressiveness and a lack of interest in the home.

2. As regards city nuisances, population density and overpopulation appear to be less important than the turnover of residents, thus stressing the extent of "migration" phenomena. Moreover, there are no universal optima to forecast the comfort requirements of society so as to counter nuisances and establish standards of tolerance. The study of human functional needs must include the problems of relationship between wants and needs; space gives shape to wants expressed as needs (Burlen, 1970). Consequently, one can only define the specific demands and requirements of given personality types and subgroups. Moreover, these requirements are linked to sociocultural elements within a given culture.

3. The imaginary structuring of space and its role both in structuring the ego and in determining relations of psychological and social adaptation, as intensively highlighted by psychoanalysis (Favez-Boutonnier, 1962; Sami Ali, 1974), has led to considering "stimuli situations" created by the individual, in the context of studies on the perception and use of the environment. The environment is not a neutral element. It bears the brunt of emotional projections and symbolic indicators that guide the selecting of information and appropriation behavior. This was confirmed by a research program carried out on the staff and the patients of a psychiatric institution, dealing with the representation of space and the way by which people, creating a private space by the positioning of their personal objects in the room they occupy, tend to constitute "pericorporal" spaces, that is, areas strongly linked to their body identity.

Yet a third trend of psychological research is characterized by the use of the experimental method, both in laboratories and in fieldwork. Three main lines of research have emerged. The oldest one, which belongs to the file of the psychosociology of space, deals with the effects of spatial distribution on communication. The studies bear on such matters as the attention paid to speakers in a group, according to their seat at a V-shaped table (Levy-Leboyer, 1960, 1962); the climate of interaction and communication and leadership in a problem-solving situation at a round or square table (Lecuyer, 1983–1984); the effect of visibility (discussions among people placed in rows or circles) on risk taking and extremism of attitudes (Moscovici & Lecuyer, 1972) and on the style of verbal expression in a conversation between two persons placed in various positions, one opposite the other (face to face, back to back, separated by a screen, etc.) (Moscovici & Plon, 1966); the importance of nonverbal behavior as a mediator of the influence of spatial distribution (Rime & Leyens, 1974); and interpersonal distances (Desportes & Lesieur, 1971).

The second line of research examines the impact of the environment on behavior through social codes (Fourcade, Lesieur, & Pages, 1976; Pages, Fourcade, & Gafsou, 1974). For example, a series of experiments in natural settings study the effect of normative constraints on the way children of different age groups behave. They compare how the children, placed in different contexts such as a restricting one (a classroom) and a free one (adventure playground), select postural media (a straight chair, a chaise lounge, a mattress). The results show the greater submission to standard ways of using each type of space by the older children. According to other experiments with children and adults, the influence of one's spatial surroundings is modulated by the conforming or opposing behavior of others vis-à-vis environmental pressures.

Finally, some researchers apply the experimental method on observing spatial behavior in the natural environment dealing with the following: under- and over-subjective estimation of urban space according to the spatial elements' dimension and to the previous personal experience of the environment (Battro & Ellis, 1972); the representation of the inhabited environment and the facilitation of expression planning requirements in front of a model, rather than a plan (Gottesdiener, 1976); and Parisian taxidrivers' representation of the urban environment that structures streets into a hierarchically organized network system (Pailhous, 1970). Some studies have led to ergonomics of the built environment (Grandjean, 1970; Sperandio, 1974, 1976a) from the physiological point of view (Scherrer, 1967) as well as the psychological point of view (Delahousse, 1976; Monod, Rohr, Wisner, 1976; Pavard & Berthoz, 1976; Sperandio, 1976b; Tapia, 1978). One may also mention studies of work stations in factories and offices (Alexandre & Barde, 1981; Monod, Rohr, & Wisner, 1973; Poirier & Beaugendre, 1978) of institutional environments, of public squares, cultural institutes, and public buildings (De Brigode, 1966; Mathieu & Muret, 1975; Maurice, 1974; Palmade, 1971; Sivadon, 1974b).

32.5.2. The Psychosociological Trend

Some psychosociological research is being carried out in concrete contexts taking into account the representations, attitudes, needs, aspirations, and behaviors of people identified by their social ties with and their fitting into specific spatial fields.

This type of research, due to the objects it studies, the contextualization of them into real social milieus and environments and the methods involved, usually falls into the sociology category of bibliographies and reviews. And yet researchers in this field are recognized psychosociologists who stand assertively at the interface between psychology and sociology and deal with social psychological problems. Consequently, we would prefer to present them apart from either psychology or sociology in order to respect their specificity. There are several research groups belonging to this school of thought.

The first one belongs to a trend that opened up the path of environmental investigation and surveys, initiated in the late 1950s by P.H. and M.J. Chombart de Lauwe and the Social Ethnology and Psychology Center. The approach of this research team relies on sociology (Halbwacks), ethnology (Mauss) as well as psychology (Sivadon, Wallon). At the beginning, the work was oriented by the words and deeds of Le Corbusier. Architectural trends at the time were functionalistic, and therefore aimed at meeting people's spatial needs. Identifying and comparing

human needs in various types of housing and urban developments, the experimental observation of social life, the search for satisfaction thresholds, and the like made it possible to better tailor space and the environment to family and social relationships (P.H. & M.J. Chombart de Lauwe et al., 1959). This allowed optimal living areas to be defined that would be most likely to minimize family life disruptions, lead to fewer disorders in children, and counter the so-called landing neurosis, that is, a psychological disturbance that, due to insufficient soundproofing and a lack of privacy, prevents all relations between neighbors. Later this research group looked at society–environment interactions as the crucial locus for social change. The environment is studied on different scales—the home, the neighborhood, the village, the city, the region—in order to assess the processes whereby social relations are structured. The main features of these processes lie in the shaping and transforming of collective representations; in the mechanisms of social marking, of exclusion, of marginalization; in the questioning of the rules of social organization and ways of social control and the exercise of power by means of innovative initiatives, social movements, and the appearance of new lifestyles in periurban and rural areas (P.H. Chombart de Lauwe, et al., 1976; P.H. Chombart de Lauwe, 1982, 1983).

A noteworthy development in this trend, in which M.J. Chombart de Lauwe (1979) has been very active, deals with child research as a specific field of inquiry. Because socialization and personality formation processes occur in and through interaction with the milieu, the environment is specified as a socialization framework as compared to other socialization realms (M.J. Chombart de Lauwe and Associates, 1976).

Thus the various living milieus are analyzed (housing, meeting areas, schools, etc.) from the standpoint of their impact on the satisfaction of needs and the harmonious development of children, the definition of which is compared to developers' conceptions (Bresson & Bresson, 1980). In this respect, areas of study include pedagogy on environmental issues and attempts to decompartmentalize day-care centers and schools for very young children (Lurçat, 1976; Mesmin, 1971; Perrinjaquet, 1980).

An original line of research from the theoretical and methodological points of view, which is more oriented toward the experience of living in the home, can be found in the work of Lugassy (1970), Palmade (1971, 1977), and Palmade, Lugassy, and Couchard (1970) who combine a clinical approach with a sociological approach. On the one hand, clinical techniques including numerous projective tests and nonstructured interviews are used in order to determine an individual's emotional investment in his or her home and environment on the basis of his or her past history. On the other hand, standardized data collection instruments used on a large scale make it possible to define the objective framework within which the practices, representations, and ideologies of the living experience in the home develop. These results are analyzed in a Marxist and psychoanalytic frame of reference.

At the University of Strasbourg, a large team of researchers led by A. Moles are studying people–environment relations. Moles and Rohmer (1964) have adopted a phenomenological position opposite the environment and they see space as a territory having a hold on people and as a place of anchorage, a field of freedoms enclosed, to a greater or lesser degree, by barriers. Starting from the self-centered position of the individual, they have highlighted the important role played by distance in a person's relations with others and the outside world. A similar perspective can be found in the work of Fischer (1980) who, considering people's place of work as a medium for psychologically and socially significant activities, is involved in setting up a theory on companies, based on the space concept.

Korosec-Serfaty and the Psychology of Space Study Group (1974, 1976, 1982) define various public areas in terms of their shape and their social nature in order to determine their shared and differring functions and practices. Focusing more specifically on public squares and their relation to other urban public areas, she has developed a pragmatics of space that runs counter to the hypothesis according to which urban practices are determined by the morphology of the area. She has postulated that subterritories are created by users' practices as an expression of their personalities and social identities.

Last, a group of psychosociologists working in the field of social representations that was first mapped by Moscovici (Farr & Moscovici, 1984) uses this corresponding conceptual model to highlight the cognitive and symbolic processes underlying spatial conducts and representations as well as stances vis-à-vis environmental problems. In the University of Aix-en-Provence, the model is used to deal with various questions of regional planning, ranging from the study of the habits of people traveling by car or by train to the analysis of the social dynamics that develops in tourist resorts during the summer months (Abric & Morin, in press; Morin, 1984a, 1984b).

At the Ecole Pratique des Hautes Etudes' Social Psychology Laboratory, research is being carried out on the representations of road safety (Barjonet, 1980) and the sociospatial representations of the city (Jodelet, 1982). Two lines of research are being carried out in the political sphere: (1) the impact of the representation of participation on the general public's involvement in community activities (Jodelet, Ohana, & Scipion, 1978; Jodelet, in press) and (2) the awareness and expectations of the French face to face with environmental issues (Chiva, Jodelet, Moscovici, Pujol, & Scipion, 1983).

32.5.3. The Sociological Trend

Sociological works make up a considerable share of the literature on the environment. They have benefited most from and responded most to government incentives, thereby becoming one of the most solid areas of research in sociology (Godelier, 1982). In this area of research, the studies refer to many authors: European sociologists from Durkheim and Weber to Morin (1967), American urban sociologists, historicist and structuralist Marxists, and the "actionalist" Touraine. Moreover, this area of research also bears relevance to environmental psychology inasmuch as it takes into account the agents of space-related social practices, the meanings involved in people–environment relations, and social responses to environmental planning policies (Reichert & Remond, 1980). It also borrows heavily from the methodologies of social psychology.

Social research commenced at a relatively early date right after World War II (one of the first urban studies dates back to 1950). It first focused on housing, due to problems of rebuilding and urban growth: describing life in slums and shantytowns and housing projects and seeing whether new housing met the needs and aspirations of dwellers (Besson, 1970; Chamboredon & Lemaitre, 1970; Cherki, 1973; Clerc, 1967; Freyssenet, Regazzola, & Retel, 1971; Huguet, 1972; Solignac, 1966). Then research developed in several major directions.

There is a culturalist orientation to which belong the studies carried out by Raymond and Haumont (1966) and the Institut de Sociologie Urbaine (Haumont, 1968, 1972). The working hypothesis of this group is that a given social and cultural type correlates with a given way of living in the home and a given spatial type of dwelling. According to this view, housing is the crystallization of a cultural model, the expression of social customs: Space is given meaning by practices that are closely related to social structure.

The interaction between spatial models and cultural models has been highlighted by a specific methodology. The semantical analysis of nonstructured interviews of people on their perceptions and feelings vis-à-vis their closest environment is used to find constants in their statements on space and objects. By virtue of this semantical analysis, the meanings attributed to the various elements of the environment may be grasped, and it becomes possible to understand how meaning circulates among them to establish the symbolism of housing. Three levels of symbolization have been advanced: appropriation of space, socialization, and ideology.

The individual attributions of space that appear in the marking of areas reflect the standards and values of the community. What has been culturally learned is manifest through behavior concerning space. A comparison between the psychological and social meanings attributed to various types of housing (town houses, detached houses, apartment buildings) shows that, regardless of the type of housing and the characteristics of the habitat, environment is organized according to shared cultural models that involve the following: sociability, privacy, family relations, and sexuality. In particular, the public/private opposition elicits environmental strategies in order to control social relations.

Other results highlight ties between housing design and ideological elements. The detached house is thought to be a means of establishing a cultural model of French ideology. It is thought that for executives, the place of residence is a way of expressing a specific life-style and is an element in recuperating the *work strength*, to use a Marxist term. Other studies have considered mobility in the urban environment and the learning and strategies of movement.

The Marxist orientation (Biolat, 1973; Lojkine, 1977) can be found in numerous studies that either apply it directly to the approach of environmental problems, draw on some of its analyses, or adopt some of its concepts. This orientation holds that work and reproduction relations in society determine the way in which life-styles fit into the environment. From the onset, this line of research purported to adopt a critical stance opposing city planning and technocratic ideology. As such, it has had an impact on the perspectives chosen by researchers rather than on practical developments. But inasmuch as it reintroduced into urban analyses the study of the contradictions between environmental planning and the requirements of those who live in that environment, it has indeed generated interesting research on groups/environment relations and groups/environmental policies relations. Several theoretical currents have emerged.

In the late 1960s and beginning of the 1970s, the historicist Marxism of Lefebvre (1968, 1970, 1974) revealed the importance of the urban phenomenon, a qualitative phenomenon linked to the quantitative growth of production. Urban society is viewed as the direction and end of industrialization. The urban phenomenon is characterized by the two following aspects: (1) the dialectics of centrality that highlight the political significance of having access to or being excluded from the center; and (2) contradictions between the socially produced environment and social practices. Lefebvre established the theoretical unity of physical space, mental space, and social space and was the first to attempt an analysis of "spatialization." Each mode of production includes among its elements an environment. For each mode of production exists a specific and proper structure of the environment. Due to the relation between the production of things and the production of space, the environment is not a neutral object. Both political and strategic, the environment constitutes a new scientific object: Knowledge must be used to change urban life-styles. Lefebvre's reflection has strongly marked research as is testified by the presence of themes such as the spatialization of social relations, toposociology, centrality, and urban strife in many studies (Debout, 1975; Kopp, 1975; Ledrut, 1968; Ragon, 1975).

Castells (1973, 1975), who has adopted a Marxist-structuralist viewpoint, is critical of the theoretical and empirical axes of environmental research. He has delineated the scope of urban sociology in terms of urbanization processes, urban ideology, urban structure, planning, action groups, and lodging claims.

The urban structure concept, defined by five related elements—production, consumption, exchange, management, and symbolic system—is a framework whereby concrete situations characterized by political practices and the emergence and effectiveness of specific subcultures can be studied. According to this view, the central object of urban research is the link between the urban environment and social milieus. New types of social conflicts linked to the collective organization of ways of living foster the blossoming of innovative and change-provoking groups. Studies dealing with the various facets of social life in the environment are considered close to this perspective (Caul-Futy & Louis, 1978; Charon, 1974; Mehl, 1975).

The systemic perspective that relates representations and behavior to systems of political, economic, social, and other activities has been adopted in various studies (Gaudin, 1979) not the least of which is the "actionalist" trend led by Touraine (1969). At first, the latter's research dealt mainly with the sociological study of urban politics that raises the question of local authority and people's involvement. According to Touraine, the city is not a consumer object for its inhabitants but is constituted by collective action. There is no specific set of urban problems per se, but rather sets of problems linked to institutions and groups. The question, then, is to discover how groups become involved and begin to interact as well as their ensuing impact on the environment's future. Later, Touraine (1981) and Touraine, Hegedus, Dubet, and Wieviorka (1983) studied social movements as such and the types of behaviors witnessed in these movements. Touraine devised an original methodology to study collective actions and conduct considered not as a response to a given situation but as a calling into question of it. As illustrated by research on ecology and antinuclear movements, this method is based on the intervention in real groups of participants involved in a common action. The sociologist, who considers group members as the bearers of meaning of their own action, stimulates self-analysis so as to increase their awareness, setting aside ideological and political pressure. He or she may suggest hypotheses regarding the highest level that the action under consideration may reach, and he or she uses the group's reactions as criteria testing the relevance of his or her hypotheses.

This shift in the emphasis placed on environmental issues is characteristic of the general evolution of sociological approaches. Research in the 1960s dealt primarily with the changes in social life linked to urban evolution (Cherki, 1973; Coing, 1966; Kopp, 1975). Later on, greater attention was paid to the production system of built space and the interplay of powers and the social control expressed therein (Claval, 1970; Coing & Meunier, 1980; Falque, 1978; Fourquet & Murard, 1976; Roux, 1975). At present, the main focus of environmental sociological research is on public involvement and the role of social movements (Charon, 1974; Mollet & Coit, 1981).

32.5.4. The Anthropological Trend

C. Lévi-Strauss's analysis of spatial symbolism in Bororo Villages (1961) had a considerable impact on French ethnologists and sociologists.

Since then, cultural anthropology has addressed

environmental questions, a tendency further reinforced by the expansion of ethnology and ethnohistory of French and European societies, thereby sharing research areas with rural sociology.

Research on rural phenomena (Courgeau, 1972; Rambaud, 1969; Vincienne, 1972; Picon, 1978) was long restricted to questions of country planning. But it has gradually begun to include environmental questions linked to the quality of the "landscape," (Rimbert, 1973) human behavior toward the latter, and the values attributed to it by rural people and tourists. Two viewpoints have emerged: one supporting the view that the symbolic system of space is a tool whereby attitudes and values can be grasped, whereas others feel that spatial representations and their symbolic systems can be inferred from rural people's behaviors. Other studies discard the notion of the "neutrality" of the scenery that is considered as belonging specifically to a given economy, philosophy, and culture. It is thus viewed as a human-made social space, both an object and stake of social relations; as the sparring grounds of social policies and structures marked by the dialectics of cohesion and violence, freedom and equality, the public and private sectors, work, and taxation.

Moreover, research discusses the symbolic marking of homes that makes it possible to reproduce or create ingroup and intergroup relations by a concrete representation in space (Bourdieu, 1970).

Ethnological research has also been devoted to the problems of individuals belonging to specific cultural and social units and their relation to their environment. Chiva (1970, 1980) analyzed the psychological reactions, perception of risk, and innovation in communities with a nuclear power plant in the vicinity.

The problem of migration drew attention to the processes of "urban socialization" and modes of "urban sociability." Barbichon (1973, 1982, in press) studied the learning of mobility in a new environment and the greater or lesser integration of dominant standards and life-styles by rural and urban migrants. He also examined the way in which different social groups use the same space and how a given group relates to its own specific space.

Anthropologists' consideration of the urban phenomenon spawned a new field of research called urban anthropology (Althabe, 1977; Augoyard, 1979; Pelletier, 1975). Borrowing its methods from ethnography and the Chicago school of sociology, it deals with phenomena occurring in microsocial environments (a building, stairways, etc.) and in small groups (families, tenants' associations, youth clubs, etc.). These studies are characterized by (1) the immersion of the researcher in the milieu he or she is studying; (2) grasping social relations that occur in complex situations of coexistence; (3) examining the way in which individuals step into the social field belonging to their living space, without breaking down the units under study or isolating the protagonists, thereby placing them in preestablished categories; and (4) not separating the place of residence from the place of work so as to observe and understand the inner workings of people's daily living experiences and environmental representations. Comparative studies carried out in various housing complexes have revealed that in places of residence, social hierarchies can be disregarded, and an image of one's social status can be created. Moreover, data on groups and associations contradict the postulates of sociologists who consider them to be a single, unanimous response to city planners.

32.5.5. The Semiological Trend

Linguistic (Jacobson, Saussure) and semiological (Barthes, Hjelmslev, Greimas) models have been used to explain the symbolic and significant nature of space and cities above and beyond their material nature or practical purposes. This movement began in the late 1960s and has continued to grow both as a complementary approach to urban image analysis and as a branch of research applied to urbanism and architecture. Several viewpoints have emerged.

One viewpoint considers the urban areas as a nonverbal system of significant elements whose structure is related to other cultural systems of significant elements and symbolic meanings.

Thus the city is treated in its architectural device, as a written text. It is branded by the transition from slowly changing closed systems (in archaic, ancient, and medieval cultures), rife with political, religious, and social significance, to fast-changing open systems that are "hyposignificant" because they are limited to their economic functions of producing and consuming (in modern society). This loss in meanings borne by built-up space has two consequences: (1) the creation in the collective unconscious of a compensatory urban mental imagery; and (2) the city's contamination by the linguistic system (Choay, 1965, 1972; Sansot, 1972; Sansot, Strohl, Torgue, & Verdillon, 1978).

Another trend relates the interpretation of urban devices and the cities to the use one makes of them. Cities have no independent life or significance on their own, outside the one given by their inhabitants. The production of space meaning is seen as related to the user observing it and fitting into it (Bertrand, 1978; Renier, 1982). Differing interpretations are due to several variables: (1) from the user's point of view, his or her emotional state and material conditions and the nature of his or her pathways; from the city's standpoint, its auditory, olfactory, and visual messages. The meanings people attribute to the city are predominantly evidenced by two means: studying patterns of the paths they follow in their everyday life or for occupational and leisure reasons; analyzing the structure of their discourses concerning the town.

The semantical analysis of space itself is differential: It defines elements of space characterized by distinctive traits (a long/short, narrow/wide street) whose spatial distribution conveys different messages. This is a systemic analysis that ascribes the meaning of a given element to its relation to other loci and establishes a distinction between the element's context-related static significance and its dynamic significance related to circuit patterns where it is embedded. Moreover, there is scientific evidence that perception of the city is structured by semantic dimensions that are selected by our culture. Here again, reference is made to the concept of urban mental imagery that is seen as a reserve of cultural archetypes we draw on to interpret the city. This urban mental imagery derives from users' actual interaction with the city and from their personal history (Fauque, 1973, 1975; Gouvion & Van De Mert, 1974).

According to yet another trend, the significance of space stems from this mental imagery and is social in nature. Some researchers make a distinction between a real relation to space based on actual use and interaction and a symbolic one of appropriation (Ledrut, 1973; Ostrowetsky, 1983). Others believe that the ways in which space is used may engender meanings far different from those initially programmed by city planners (Barreau, Godart, Sachs, Lenco, Leroy, & Perelman, 1975; De Certeau, 1980).

In spite of the difficulties encountered in devising a theoretical framework directly applicable to space, positive results have been obtained by virtue of semiological hypotheses and analytical instruments. Researchers as a whole consider this semiological approach to be extremely relevant for the upgrading of our urban environment. It improves the layout of cities by eliminating relations of elements considered to be detrimental to urbanites. It improves architectural training and practice by providing better analytical tools and more sensitive know-how. It promotes awareness of urban reality and defines the urbanist's field of study. And it develops new urban systems or transitional systems tailored to the public's needs.

English-speaking readers can glean additional information on some of the aforementioned orientations in the *Proceedings of the 3rd Conference of International Architectural Psychology, Strasbourg, 1976* (Korosec-Serfaty, 1976).

32.6. FURTHER FIELDS OF RESEARCH AND FUTURE PROSPECTS

The major trends outlined previously do not cover the entire field of scientific output in France. Other studies are being carried out on specific topics such as environmental perception and image (Ekambi-Schmidt, 1972; Neboit, 1974) or other, not numerous researches that may open up scientific investigation in the future: the aesthetics of everyday life (Bernard, 1986; Bernard & Gottesdiener, 1979; Le Men, 1966; Matoré, 1976; Segaud, 1982), environmental pathologies, the study of natural disasters, the use and development of the natural environment, tourism, and institutional environments (Barreau et al., 1975; Clément, 1971; Dreyfus & Pigeat, 1971; De Freudis, 1975; Morin, 1984b).

On the basis of the way in which French research functions today and its triple dependency on state directives, on arising social problems, and on the development of theoretical perspectives, we may try to set forth some of its possible future developments.

On the one hand, among the trends examined previously, certain programs, especially in experimental and applied psychology, will be continued in order to delve more deeply into given sets of problems or to glean additional information on specific topics. In the social field, research on social strife and movements is still very much alive, although there has been a slight shift in emphasis, and more studies are now devoted to the concrete modalities that encourage and facilitate the general public's becoming involved in controlling the environment they live in (Beaunez & Kohn, 1975; Bidou, 1979; Mollet & Coit, 1981; Vergnes, Kling, & Gueant, 1975).

On the other hand, recent calls for research projects by the state have oriented research toward studying delineated spatial units (urban areas, districts); scientific research should provide local officials with useful instruments of knowledge and intervention. New ideas have emerged that will no doubt spur research on to the domain of applied studies: for example, the idea of experimenting in the field and the new concept of innovative research, that is, research focused on the potential consequences, developments, and changes of people–environment relationships. It is hoped that these will allow researchers to discover and test means of (1) controlling and mastering the development of an "urban civilization" that French mentality, bearing until this very day the stamp of its rural origin, continues to resist and fear; (2) improving housing so as to better integrate new types of behaviors, new aspirations expressed by the public, and the constraints or new possibilities of modern technology; and (3) developing or redesigning public areas and places of work. Consequently, it is likely that approaches of an anthropological or social engineering type will develop in the future in a multidisciplinary perspective.

Last, but not least, new problems have come to researchers' attention. The growing use of computers and new means of telecommunications calls for studies on the learning of new ways of communicating in our environment and on the ensuing changes in behavior and mental structures. Problems relating to environment policies, such as pollution, energy conservation, protecting our heritage and the environment, and so forth are ever increasingly mobilizing public opinion, echoing the social and psychological reactions that they induce (Sachs, 1980; Verdes-Leroux, 1974). The recent upsurge of social violence has begun to arrest the attention of researchers bent on discovering the psychosocial dynamics that govern criminal acts or the motivations and representations underlying the responses of the people involved. In particular, researchers are interested in the spontaneous formation of individual or collective systems of self-defense. There is also a concern with environmental risks and the role of information campaigns on security-related behaviors.

Furthermore, the request for interdisciplinary research is voiced as strongly as ever, converging with the wishes expressed by scientists themselves. Long-term research programs will involve either the study of identical themes in different locations or different themes in the same area. This had led to the creation of interdisciplinary teams working jointly in the framework of "observatories" that allow them to approach a single territorial unit from several scientific viewpoints. This tendency echoes the expectations expressed throughout France's many regions and is supported by the French government's recent decentralization policies.

Consequently, research is likely to develop in the future in different regions, embracing environmental issues in a holistic and multidisciplinary perspective. Thus environmental psychology will be able to place its models, its methods, and its own set of original problems—still not very well known, even today—in concrete social fields.

Acknowledgments

My deepest gratitude goes to Alain Pujol for his intelligent and efficient contribution to this chapter; to Francis Chalanset, Geneviève Coudin, Jocelyne Ohana, and Christine Roland-Levy who helped with the documentary research, and to Patricia Hunter who translated this text into English.

NOTES

1. The work of Bachelard is currently being translated by the Dallas Institute of Humanities. The first book to appear (1984) is *Water and Dreams*.

2. Due to space limitation, I have been obliged to restrict the bibliography. So general documentary studies and the detailed list of symposia held in France have been omitted. Complementary information is available on request at Laboratoire de Psychologie Sociale—Ecole des Hautes Etudes en Sciences Sociales—44 rue de la Tour, 75716, Paris. The same is true for other bibliographical references.

3. This method was both time-saving and exhaustive because research and education are closely linked in the French university system. An additional survey was carried out on university departments not included on the list under research, but these did shed light on the subject.

4. The term *differential* is used in France to characterize psychological studies that aim to describe and explain differences of behavior observed between groups of subjects or between individuals belonging to a same group by biological factors (sex, age, heredity) or social factors (occupational or cultural membership, social milieu, etc.).

5. At these meetings and conferences on architectural psychology and the psychology of space, which were organized in various European countries, not a single French researcher attended the first conference held in England (Strathclyde, 1970); 3 participated in the second conference held in Sweden (Lund, 1973), and there were 21 French researchers at the third conference held in France (Strasbourg, 1976). French attendance increased at symposia focusing on specific topics such as the meeting of French-speaking psychologists to discuss: From corporal space to ecological space, the European meeting on people's living environment, and the symposium entitled Towards a Social Psychology of the Environment, all of which were held in 1977 and 1981.

REFERENCES

Abric, J.C., Morin, M. (in press). Social representations and the environment: Studies on urban and interurban travel. In D. Jodelet & P. Stringer (Eds), *Towards a social psychology of the environment*. London: Cambridge University Press.

Ackerman, W., Dulong, R., & Jeudy, H.P. (1983). *Imaginaires de l'insécurité, Paris: Librairé des Méridiens.*

Alexandre, A., & Barde, J.P. (1981). Le temps du bruit ou le temps de travail. *Futuribles 2000, 45,* 3–32.

Althabe, G. (1977). Le quotidien en procès. *Dialectiques, 21,* 67–77.

Augoyard, J.F. (1979). *Pas à pas, essai sur le cheminement quotidien en milieu urbain.* Paris: Seuil.

Bachelard, G. (1964)., *Poétique de l'espace.* Paris: Presses Universitaires de France.

Barbichon, G. (1973). Appropriation urbaine du milieu rural à des fins de loisirs. *Etudes Rurales, 49–50,* 97–105.

Barbichon, G. (1982). *Espace et sociabilité urbaine.* Paris: Centre d'Ethnologie Française.

Barbichon, G. (in press). Culture and spatial organisation of sociability. In D. Jodelet & P. Stringer (Eds), *Towards a social psychology of the environment.* London: Cambridge University Press.

Barjonet, P.E. (1980). L'influence sociale et les représentations des causes de l'accident de la route. *Le Travail Humain, 43,* 243–253.

Barreau, J., Godart, O., Sachs, I., Lenco, M., Leroy, C., & Perelman, R. (1975). *Environnement et qualité de la vie.* Paris: Le Prat.

Barthes, R. (1964), Elements de semiologie. *Communications, 4*(1), 91–135.

Battro, A.M. & Ellis, E.J. (1972). L'estimation subjective de l'espace urbain, *L'Année Psychologique, 1,* 39–52.

Baudrillard, J. (1960). *Le système des objets.* Paris: Gallimard.

Beaunez, R., & Kohn, F. (1975). *La démocratie locale, un préalable: l'information dans la cité.* Paris: Les Editions Ouvrières.

Bernard, Y. (1984). Dimensions subjectives de la perception du paysage. *Acts of the Colloquium man-environment qualitative aspects.* Barcelona, Spain: University of Barcelona.

Bernard, Y., & Gottesdiener, H. (1979). Les espaces architecturaux. In R. Francès (Ed.), *Psychologie de l'art et de l'esthétique.* Paris: Presses Universitaires de France.

et de l'esthétique. Paris: Presses Universitaires de France.

Bertrand, M.J. (1978). *Pratique de la ville*. Paris: Masson.

Besson, J.F. (1970). *L'intégration urbaine*. Paris: Presses Universitaires de France.

Bidou, D. (1979). Formes et structures de la participation des usagers. *Transport, Environnement, Circulation, 36*, 21–24.

Biolat, G. (1973). *Marxisme et environnement*. Paris: Editions Sociales.

Bourdieu, P. (1970). The Berber House or the world reversed. *Social Sciences Information, 9* (2), 151–170.

Bresson, F., & Chombart de Lauwe, P.H. (1974). *De l'espace corporel à l'espace écologique*. Paris: Presses Universitaires de France.

Bresson, T., & Bresson, J.M. (1980). *Les espaces de jeux et l'enfant*. Paris: Editions du Moniteur.

Burlen, C. (1970). La réalisation spatiale du désir et l'image spatialisée du besoin. Paris: Cahiers du RAUC.

Castells, M. (1973). *Les luttes urbaines et le pouvoir politique*. Paris: Maspero.

Castells, M. (1975). *La question urbaine*. Paris: Maspero.

Caul-Futy, L., & Louis, M. (1978). *Ca bouge dans les quartiers*. Paris: Editions Syros.

Cayrol, J. (1968). *De l'espace humain*. Paris: Seuil.

Chamboredon, J.C., & Lemaitre, M. (1970). Proximité spatiale et distance sociale. Les grands ensembles et leur peuplement. *Revue Française de Sociologie, 11*(1), 3–33.

Charon, J.M. (1974). L'animation urbaine ou comment désamorcer les mouvements sociaux urbains. *Espaces et Sociétés, 12*, 135–155.

Cherki, E. (1973). Le mouvement d'occupation des maisons vides en France. *Espaces et Sociétés, 9*, 63–91.

Chiva, I. (1970). Imagination collective et inconnu. In J. Pouillon & P. Marcendo (Eds.), *Echanges et communications*. Paris: Mouton.

Chiva, I. (1980). Perception du risque autour de quelques centrales nucléaires. *Colloque sur les risques sanitaires des différentes énergies*. Paris: Editions Gedim.

Chiva, I., Jodelet, D., Moscovici, S., Pujol, A., Scipion, C. (1983). *La sensibilité des français aux problèmes d'environnement*. Paris: Ministère de l'environnement.

Choay, F. (1965). *L'urbanisme, utopies et réalités*. Paris: Seuil.

Choay, F. (1972). *Sémiologie et urbanisme: Le sens de la ville*. Paris: Seuil.

Chombart de Lauwe, M.J. (1979). Espaces d'enfants. *Futuribles, 25*, 72–87.

Chombart de Lauwe, M.J., Bonnin, P., Perrot, M., & Soudiere, M. (1976). *Enfant en-jeu: Les pratiques des enfants durant leur temps libre, en fonction des types d'environnement et des idéologies*. Paris: Editions du Centre National de la Recherche Scientifique.

Chombart de Lauwe, P.H. (1982). *La fin des villes: Mythes ou réalités*. Paris: Calmann-Lévy.

Chombart de Lauwe, P.H. (1983). Oppression, subversion and self-expression in daily life. *International Social Science Journal, 96*, 353–365.

Chombart de Lauwe, P.H., Chombart de Lauwe, M.J., Jenny, J., Couvreur, L., Labat, P., & Dubois-Taine, D. (1959). *Famille et habitation*. Paris: Editions du Centre National de la Recherche Scientifique.

Chombart de Lauwe, P.H., Losonczi, A., Bolivar, T., & Nowskowski, S. (1976). *Transformations de l'environnement, des aspirations et des valeurs*. Paris: Editions du Centre National de la Recherche Scientifique.

Claval, P. (1970). *Espace et pouvoir*. Paris: Presses Universitaires de France.

Clément, J.F. (1971). Etude sociologique d'un tremblement de terre. *Cahiers Internationaux de Sociologie, 50*, 95–126.

Clerc, P. (1967). *Grands ensembles, banlieues nouvelles. Enquête démographique et psychosociologique*. Paris: Presses Universitaires de France.

Coing, A. (1966). *Rénovation urbaine et changement social*. Paris: Editions Ouvrières.

Coing, H., & Meunier, C. (1980). *Insécurité urbaine ? Une arme pour le pouvoir*. Paris: Anthropos.

Collot, C. (1980). Les personnes agées face aux opérations de restauration et de rénovation immobilière. *Gérontologie, 33*, 14–17.

Courgeau, D. (1972). Les réseaux de relations entre personnes. Etude d'un milieu rural. *La Population, 4–5*, 641–683.

Craik, K. (1973). Environmental Psychology. *Annual Review of Psychology, 24*, 403–422.

Debout, S. (1975). La ville de transition. *Espaces et Sociétés, 15*, 45–62.

De Brigode, G. (1966). *L'architecture scolaire*. Paris: Presses Universitaires de France.

De Certeau, M. (1980). *L'invention du quotidien*. Paris: Union Générale d'Editions.

De Freudis, F. (1975). La biologie de la solitude. *La Recherche, 55* (6), 344–356.

Delahousse, A. (1976). Sur le rôle psychologique de la complexité architecturale. *Travail Humain, 39* (2), 249–260.

Desportes, J.P., & Lesieur, L. (1971). La maximisation des distances inter-individuelles, étude en situation naturelle d'un comportement d'évitement de la présence d'autrui. *Bulletin de Psychologie, 25*, 312–314.

Dreyfus, C., & Pigeat, J.P. (1971). *Des maladies de l'environnement*. Paris: Denoël.

Durand, G. (1963). *Les structures anthropologiques de l'imaginaire*. Paris: Presses Universitaires de France.

Durand, M., & Harff, Y. (1977). *La qualité de la vie, mouvement écologique, movement ouvrier*. Paris: Mouton.

Eco, U. (1972). *La structure absente*. Paris: Mercure de France.

Ekambi-Schmidt, J. (1972). *La perception de l'habiter*. Paris: Editions Universitaires.

Falque, M. (1978). Environnement et contrôle social de l'espace: Analyse et propositions. *Futuribles, 18*, 713–732.

Farr, R., & Moscovici, S. (1984). *Social representations*. London: Cambridge University Press.

Fauque, R. (1973). Pour une nouvelle approche sémiologique de la ville. *Espaces et Sociétés, 9*, 15–27.

Fauque, R. (1975). Perception de la ville et imaginaire urbain. *Espaces et Sociétés, 16*, 63–76.

Favez-Boutonnier, J. (1962). *L'homme et son milieu*. Paris: Centre de Documentation Universitaire.

Fischer, G.N. (1980). *Espace industriel et liberté; L'autogestion clandestine*. Paris: Presses Universitaires de France.

Fischer, G.N. (1981). *La psychosociologie de l'espace*. Paris: Presses Universitaires de France.

Foucault, M. (1977). *Discipline and Punish*. New York: Pantheon.

Fourcade, G., Lesieur, L., & Pages, R. (1976). L'induction des postures: Supports spatiaux et emprise psychosociale. *Travail Humain, 39*. 261–272.

Fourquet, F., & Murard, L. (1976). *Les équipements du pouvoir: Villes, territoires et équipements collectifs*. Paris: Union Générale d'Editions.

François, G. (1977). *Gêne due aux bruits des avions pour les riverains des aérodromes*. Paris: Institut Français d'Opinion Publique.

Frémont, A. (1976). *La région, espace vécu*. Paris: Presses Universitaires de France.

Freyssenet, M., Regazzola, T., & Retel, S. (1971). *Ségrégation spatiale et déplacements sociaux dans l'agglomération parisienne de 1954 à 1968*. Paris: Copedith.

Gaillard, C., Sodre, O., Vidal, M., & Quan-Schneider, G., (1971). *Sciences humaines et environnement. Orientations bibliographiques*. Paris: Institut de l'Environnement.

Gaudin, J.P. (1979). *L'aménagement de la société: Politiques, savoirs, représentations sociales, la production de l'espace aux 19ème et 20ème siècles*. Paris: Anthropos.

Godart, F., & Pendaries, J.R. (1978). Rapports de propriété du logement et pratiques de l'espace résidentiel. *Espaces et Sociétés, 24–27*, 39–53.

Godelier, M. (1982). *Les sciences de l'homme et de la société en France*. Paris: La Documentation Française.

Gottesdiener, H. (1976). Difficulté de représentation de l'espace habité et méthode de simulation par maquette grandeur nature. *Travail Humain, 39* (7), 43–51.

Gouvion, C., & Van De Mert, F. (1974). *Le symbolisme des rues et des cités*. Paris: Berg International.

Grandjean, E. (1970). Ergonomie et architecture. *Ergonomics, 13* (3), 385–389.

Greimas, A.J. (1976). *Semiotique et sciences sociales*. Paris: Seuil.

Gruska, A., & Mazerat, B. (1975). *Inventaire des travaux et centres de recherche portant sur les représentations, attitudes, aspirations et pratiques des individus et des groupes relatives à l'espace, au cadre de vie et à l'environnement*. Paris: Laboratoire d'Eco–ethologie.

Haumont, A. (1972). L'image de la campagne chez les citadins. *Métropolis, 2* (2), 51–53.

Haumont, N. (1968). Habitat et modèle culturel. *Revue Française de Sociologie, 9*, 180–190.

Haumont, N. (1972). *Habitat et pratiques de l'espace. Etude des relations entre l'intérieur et l'extérieur du logement*. Paris: Institut de Sociologie Urbaine.

Huguet, M. (1972). *Les femmes dans les grands ensembles*. Paris: Editions du Centre National de la Recherche Scientifique.

Huteau, M. (1975). Un style cognitif: La dépendance-indépendance à l'égard du champ. *Année Psychologique, 75*, 197–262.

d'Iribarné, P. (1975). *Le gaspillage et le désir: De la voiture au vélo*. Paris: Fayard.

Jeannière, A., & Antoine, P. (1970). *Espace mobile, temps incertain. Nouveau milieu urbain, nouveau mode de vie*. Paris: Aubier Montaigne.

Jodelet, D. (1982). Les représentations socio-spatiales de la ville. In P.H. Derycke (Ed.), *Conception de l'espace*. Nanterre: Université Paris X–Nanterre.

Jodelet, D., Ohana, J., & Scipion, C. (1978). *Etude de la communication et de la participation dans une ville de moyenne importance*. Paris: EHESS-INA-CNRS.

Jodelet, D. (in press). Social representations of participation and related public's behavior in urban policies. In D. Jodelet & P. Stringer (Eds), *Towards a social psychology of the environment*. London: Cambridge University Press.

Kaufmann, P. (1976). *L'expérience émotionnelle de l'espace*. Paris: Vrin.

Kopp, A. (1975). Changer la vie, changer la ville. *De la vie nouvelle aux problèmes urbains*. Paris: Union Générale d'Editions.

Korosec-Serfaty, P. (1974). Fonctions et pratiques des espaces urbains. Psychosociologie des places publiques. *Neuf, 51*, 2–15.

Korosec-Serfaty, P. (1976) (Ed.). Appropriation de l'espace. *Proceedings of the 3rd International Architectural Psychology, Strasbourg, 1976*. Louvain-la-Neuve, Belgium: CIACO.

Korosec-Serfaty, P. (1982). *The main square*, Hassleholm, Sweden: ARIS.

La Rochefoucauld, B. de. (1971). *L'homme dans la ville à la conquête de sa liberté*. Paris: Dunod.

Laverrière. H. (1973). Vérités méconnues sur le bruit. *Santé Mentale, 4*, 27–30.

Lecuyer, H. (1975). Psychosociologie de l'espace—I. Disposition spatiale et communication en groupe. *Année Psychologique, 75*, 549–573.

Lecuyer, H. (1976a). Psychosociologie de l'espace—II. Rapports spatiaux interpersonnels et la notion d'espace personnel. *Année Psychologique, 76*, 563–596.

Lecuyer, H. (1976b). Adaptation de l'homme à l'espace, adaptation de l'espace à l'homme. *Travail Humain, 39* (2), 195–206.

Lecuyer, R. (1973). Space dimensions, the climate of discussion and group decisions. *European Journal of Social Psychology, 5* (2), 103–108.

Ledrut, R. (1968). *L'espace social de la ville*. Paris: Anthropos.

Ledrut, R. (1973). *Les images de la ville*. Paris: Anthropos.

Lefebvre, H. (1968). *Le droit à la ville* Paris: Anthropos.

Lefebvre, H. (1970). *La révolution urbaine*. Paris: Gallimard.

Lefebvre. H. (1974). *La production de l'espace*. Paris: Anthropos.

Le Men, J. (1966). *L'espace figuratif et les structures de la personnalité*. Paris: Presses Universitaires de France.

Leroy, C. (1977). Etude critique de la réponse humaine aux constructions en tour. *Actualités Psychiatriques Françaises, 1*, 43–46.

Leroy, C., Bedos, F., & Berthelot, C. (1972). Approche de l'utilisation de l'espace d'une chambre par l'étude du réseau des objets chez les malades mentaux. *L'Information Psychiatrique, 48* (4), 377–392.

Levi-Strauss, C. (1955). *Tristes tropiques*. Paris: Plon. (English translation: *A World on the Wane*. London: Hutchinson, 1961).

Levy-Leboyer, C. (1960). Etude méthodologique des tests de groupe. I—Place des participants et comportement observé. *Travail Humain, 23*, 163–171.

Levy-Leboyer, C. (1962). Etude méthodologique des tests de groupe. II—Composition du groupe et comportement individuel. *Travail Humain, 25*, 72–92.

Levy-Leboyer, C. (1976b). La psychologie de l'environnement. Recherches actuelles aux Etats-Unis. *Revue de Psychologie Appliquée, 4*, 609–616.

Levy-Leboyer, C. (1980). *Psychologie et environnement* (Psychology and environment). Paris: Presses Universitaires de France (English translation, London: 1982).

Levy-Leboyer, C., & Moser, G. (1976a). Que signifient les gênes exprimées? Enquête sur les bruits dans les logements. *Sondages, 38* (2), 7–22.

Levy-Leboyer, C., Vedrenne, B., & Veyssiere, M. (1977). Psychologie différentielle des gênes dues au bruit dans une situation constante. *Psychologie Française, 22* (1–2), 69–80.

Levy-Leboyer, C., & Veyssiere, M. (1978). Psychologie différentielle d'un groupe restreint. *Revue de Psychologie Appliquée, 28*, 247–260.

Lojkine, J. (1977). *Le marxisme, l'Etat et la question urbaine*. Paris: Presses Universitaires de France.

Lugassy, F. (1970). *La relation habitat, forêt. Significations et fonctions des espaces boisés*. Paris: Publication de la Recherche Urbaine.

Lurçat, L. (1976). *L'enfant et l'espace. Le rôle du corps*. Paris: Presses Universitaires de France.

Lyotard, J.F. (1973). *Des dispositifs pulsionnels*. Paris: Christian Bourgois.

Marc, O. (1972). *Psychanalyse de la maison*. Paris: Seuil.

Mathieu, M., & Muret, J.P. (1975). Signalisation urbaine. *Urbanisme, 149*, 52–57.

Matore, G. (1976). *L'espace humain: L'expression de l'espace dans la vie, la pensée et l'art contemporain*. Paris: Nizet.

Maurice, M. (1974). Travail, mode de vie et espaces sociaux. *Espaces et Sociétés, 12*, 111–120.

Mehl, O. (1975). Les luttes des résidents dans les grands ensembles. *Sociologie du Travail, 4*, 351–371.

Mesmin, G. (1971). *L'enfant, l'architecture et l'espace. De l'architecture du mépris à l'espace du bonheur*. Paris: Casteneau.

Metz, N. & Muzet, A. (1975). *Interaction du bruit et de la chaleur sur le sommeil*. Paris: Editions du Centre National de la Recherche Scientifique.

Mitscherlich, A. (1971). *Psychanalyse et urbanisme*. Paris: Gallimard.

Moles, A., & Rohmer, E. (1964). *Psychologie de l'espace*. Paris: Casterman.

Mollet, A., & Coit, K., (1981). La participation des habitants à la conception et à la gestion du cadre bâti. Participation ou lutte urbaine? *Economie et Humanisme, 260*, 51–73.

Monod, H., Rohr, D., & Wisner, A. (1973). *La conception ergonomique des bâtiments industriels*. Paris: Editions Revue de Métrologie.

Montagné, H. (1980). *Enfant et communication*. Paris: Stock.

Morin, E. (1967). *Commune en France. La métamorphose de Plodermet*. Paris: Fayard.

Morin, M. (1984a). Socio-psychological approaches to vacation and mobility in tourists sites. *Annals of Tourism Research, 11*, 113–127.

Morin, M. (1984b). Représentations locales et évaluation du cadre de vie urbain. *Bulletin de Psychologie, 37*, 822–832.

Moscovici, S., & Lecuyer, R. (1972). Studies on group decisions: Social space, patterns of communication and group consensus. *European Journal of Social Psychology. 2* (3), 221–244.

Moscovici, S., & Plon, M. (1966). Les situations colloques, observations théoriques et expérimentales. *Bulletin de Psychologie, 19,* 707–722.

Neboit, M. (1974). Perception, anticipation et conduite automobile. *Travail Humain, 37* (1), 53–72.

Olivier-Martin, N., Scheiber, J.P., & Muzet, A. (1972–73). Réponses à un questionnaire sur le sommeil nocturne et un questionnaire sur la forme diurne au cours d'une expérience de perturbations de sommeil par quatre types de bruits d'avion. *Bulletin de Psychologie, 26,* 972–994.

Ostrowetsky, S. (1983). *L'imaginaire bâtisseur. Les villes nouvelles françaises.* Paris: Librairie des Méridiens.

Pages, R., Fourcade, G., & Gafsou, S. (1974). La psychosociologie écologique: Applications validatrices ou analyse des mécanismes. *Psychosociologie et Espace,* Cahier pédagogique no. 1. Paris: Institut de l'Environnement.

Pailhous, J. (1970). *La représentation de l'espace urbain, l'exemple du chauffeur de taxi.* Paris: Presses Universitaires de France.

Palmade, J. (1971). Le psychologue et l'urbanisme. In *Le psychologue dans la société.* Paris: Editions Sociales Francaises.

Palmade, J. (1977). *Système symbolique et idéologique de l'habiter.* Paris: Centre Scientifique et Technique du Bâtiment.

Palmade, J., Lugassy, F., & Couchard, F. (1970). *La dialectique du logement et de son environnement; étude exploratoire. Contribution à une psychosociologie de l'espace urbain.* Paris: Copedith.

Pavard, B., & Berthoz, A. (1976). Perception du mouvement et orientation spatiale. *Travail Humain, 39* (2), 207–226.

Pelletier, F. (1975). Quartier et communication sociale; Perspective pour une anthropologie urbaine. *Espaces et Sociétés, 15,* 71–79.

Perrinjaquet, R. (1980). *The child in his surroundings and environment. Documentary guidance and experimental realizations in France.* Paris: Ministère de l'Environnement et du Cadre de Vie.

Piaget, J., Vinh Bang, & Greco, P. (1964). *L'épistémologie de l'espace.* Paris: Presses Universitaires de France.

Picon, B. (1978). *L'espace et le temps en Camargue.* LeParadou: Actes sud.

Poirier, J.L., & Beaugendre, J. (1978). Dégradation de la performance humaine sous vibrations mécaniques. *Médecine Aéronautique Spatiale. Médecine Subaquatique, 17,* 32–35.

Ragon, M. (1975). *L'homme et les villes.* Paris: Albin Michel.

Rambaud, P. (1969). *Société rurale et urbanisation.* Paris: Seuil.

Raymond, H., & Hautmont, N. (1966). *L'habitat pavillonaire.* Paris: Institut de Sociologie Urbaine.

Reichert, H., & Remond, J.D. (1980). *Analyse sociale de la ville.* Paris: Masson.

Reineberg, A. (1979). *L'homme malade de son temps.* Paris: Stock.

Renier, A. (1982). *Espaces, représentations et sémiotique de l'architecture.* Paris: La Villette.

Rimbert, S. (1973). Approche des paysages. *L'espace géographique, 2* (3), 233–241.

Rime, B., & Leyens, J.P. (1974). L'effet de facteurs écologiques et de signaux non verbaux sur les structures affectives dans les petits groupes. *Année Psychologique, 74,* 487–500.

Roche, M. (1970). *Vivre avec l'automobile.* Paris: Dunod.

Roux, J.M. (1975). Concentration urbaine, rationalité et pouvoir. *Métropolis, 2* (5), 21–30.

Rougerie, G. (1975). *Les cadres de vie.* Paris: Presses Universitaires de France.

Sachs, I. (1980). *Stratégies de l'éco-développement.* Paris: Economie et Humanités.

Sami Ali. (1974). *L'espace imaginaire.* Paris: Gallimard.

Sansot, P. (1972). *La poétique de la ville.* Paris: Klincksieck.

Sansot, P., Strohl, H., Torgue, H., & Verdillon, C. (1978). *L'espace et son double. De la résidence secondaire aux autres formes secondaires de la vie sociale.* Paris: Editions du Champ Urbain.

Scherrer, J. (1967). *Physiologie du travail.* Paris: Masson.

Sivadon, P. (1965). L'espace vécu: Incidence thérapeutiques. *L'Evolution Psychiatrique, 30,* 477–499.

Sivadon, P. (1974a). Aménagement architectural et hygiène mentale des grandes administrations. *Santé Mentale, 2,* 31–33.

Sivadon, P. (1974b). La pathologie de la civilisation et de la vie urbaine. *Médecine Praticienne, 4,* 79–85.

Solignac, P. (1966). La fatigue physique et nerveuse dans les grands ensembles. *Cité et Techniques, 33,* 27–35.

Sperandio, J.E. (1974). Collaboration de l'ergonome à l'aménagement de la salle de surveillance du centre culturel Beaubourg. In *Congrés SELF.* Brussels.

Sperandio, J.E. (1976a). De l'espace plan à l'espace mobile aérien. Comparaison expérimentale entre deux supports d'informations spatio-temporelles. *Travail Humain, 39* (1), 134–154.

Sperandio, J.E. (1976b). L'ergonomie du cadre bâti. *Travail Humain, 39* (2), 227–248.

Tapia, C. (1978). Environnement et odeur. *Revue Internationale de Psychologie Appliquée, 27* (1), 39–51.

Touraine, A. (1969). *La société post-industrielle.* Paris: Dehoël.

Touraine, A. (1979). *Le regard et la voix.* Paris: Seuil. (English translation: *The eye and the voice.* New York: Cambridge University Press, 1981).

Touraine, A., Hegedus, Z., Dubet, F., & Wieviorka, M. (1980). *La prophétie anti-nucléaire.* Paris: Seuil. (English translation: *Anti-nuclear protest*. New York: Cambridge University Press. 1983.)

Verdes-Leroux, J. (1974). Sur l'habiter des classes populaires. Quelques cas de résistance à l'idéologie dominante, *Perspectives Psychiatriques, 2* (46), 105–113.

Vergnes, B., Kling, P., & Gueant, M. (1975). *Du terrain pour l'aventure...Pratique anti-autoritaire de l'animation des loisirs en milieu urbain* Paris: Maspero.

Vincienne, M. (1972). *Du village à la ville. Le système de mobilité des agriculteurs*. Paris: Mouton.

Chapter 33

ENVIRONMENTAL PSYCHOLOGY IN GERMANY

Lenelis Kruse, *Psychology Department, Fern University, Hagen. Federal Republic of Germany*

Carl F. Graumann, *Psychology Institute, University of Heidelberg, Heidelberg, Federal Republic of Germany*

33.1. THE CULTURAL, HISTORICAL, AND PHILOSOPHICAL BACKGROUND[1]

33.1.1. Environmental or Ecological Psychology?

The practice of science, like any other cultural activity, is not only made possible, facilitated, or inhibited according to the general social and cultural climate of a given society; it is also, in theory and research, an effort to answer the questions and challenges of a society at a given time. Although we hold that this is true for all science, we shall restrict the thesis of cross-cultural variation in scientific theorizing and research to the social and behavioral sciences of which we consider environmental psychology to be a part. To report on and to discuss a branch of science in a given country demands a brief introduction into the cultural, historical, and philosophical background that, as a rule, is different in different countries (and epochs).

It is a fact that in North America *environmental psychology* is the comprehensive term for the field of study dealt with in this *Handbook*, whereas psychologists in Germany prefer the term *ecological psychology* (briefly, *ecopsychology*) as the more comprehensive or basic term for environmental psychology, which sometimes is used as the term for a more technological branch or correlate of ecopsychology (cf. Kaminski, 1976, 1978a, 1985). This difference is not due to a different verbal usage. On the contrary, a psychology of the environment had officially been introduced into the system of psychology in 1924 (Hellpach, 1924; cf. later text), whereas the term *ecological psychology* dates only from the 1970s. That the new field was baptized *ecological* rather than *environmental* psychology was due to a decision that, in turn, is intelligible for the outsider only when we look back at the historical background.[2]

33.1.2. The Roots of Ecological Psychology

Historiographers of science have become wary of fixing dates for the beginning of a field of research or of a discipline, and they are equally sceptical of so-called predecessors. Because ecological psychology did not begin in any given year but over a long period of time, from the turn of the century to the 1960s, we will have to deal with its roots in the nineteenth and twentieth centuries.

We shall distinguish between roots (1) in biological ecology; (2) in meteorobiology; (3) *Kulturkritik* and urban studies; and (4) phenomenology.

Biological Ecology

Ernst Haeckel (1834–1919), a biologist and philosopher, who is perhaps best known for his biogenetic law, established ecology as a branch of biology in his "general morphology of organisms" (Haeckel, 1866) as the study of the relationships of organisms and the outer world, from which developed the two branches of the ecological study of single organisms or species of organisms (autoecology) and—more important for the future social ecology—the study of different natural communities (biocenoses) in their habitat. Because there was an immediate transfer of these early Haeckelian categories to the human ecology of the Chicago school (Park, Burgess, & McKenzie, 1925; cf. Hawley, 1950) and to the subsequent social ecology (Mukerjee, 1940), we shall merely keep in mind that ecology had become an established branch of biology when, at the turn of the century, *Umwelt* was introduced as a technical term into the life sciences.

Here another linguistic note is required. Occasionally, in contemporary literature, the German word *Umwelt,* for which the average dictionary gives *environment* as the equivalent, remains untranslated (cf. Goffman, 1972, mainly the chapter "The *Umwelt*"; cf. Harré, 1979, pp. 193–196; also the entries *Umwelt* in English & English [1958] and in Harré & Lamb [1983]). This is, of course, not explainable by reference to a typically or allegedly typical German phenomenon but to a specific usage. *Umwelt* is "the circumscribed portion of the environment that is meaningful and effective for a given species and that

changes its significance in accordance with the mood operative at a given moment" (English & English, 1958, p. 568). In other words, *Umwelt* is not environment but "environment-as-experienced-and-acted-upon" (Graumann, in Harré & Lamb, 1983b, p. 647).

Basically, in this sense, *Umwelt* was introduced as a theoretical construct into biology by Jacob von Uexküll (1864–1944) when he first contrasted *Umwelt* and *Innenwelt,* the surrounding and the inner world of an organism or species (von Uexküll, 1909, 1957). While developing a theoretical biology (von Uexküll, 1920, 1973) in opposition to mechanistic conceptions of life, von Uexküll made *Umwelt* more than the mere sum of surrounding conditions or influences. *Umwelt* was theoretically construed as the counterpart to, and complement of, a subject-organism, together constituting a dynamic whole. This whole was described as a "functional circuit" *(Funktionskreis)* (Figure 33.1).

The structure and functioning of an organism is matched by the structure and functioning of its object. To the structure of a sense organ there corresponds a sense quality of the object that has (sensory) cue function for the organism. Equally true, the organism's effector organ is matched by motor cues that the object provides (for this organism). Subject and object are thus corresponding elements of one functional circuit. This means, on the one hand, that one and the same object will have different sensory as well as motor cues for different species; on the other hand it means that, biologically seen, there is no objective environment with "affordances" for any organism that may identify and use them. There are only species-specific *Umwelten* of differential meanings.

The meaning (or semiotic) character of Uexküll's *Umwelt* was theoretically so important that he developed a "theory of meaning" of his own (von Uexküll, 1940). Uexküll, the man who had fought anthropomorphism in animal psychology, established subjectivity in biology. Nevertheless, he was far from being a phenomenologist, nor could he ever sympathize with behaviorism. Still the psychologist whose conception of the relationship between organism and environment comes closest to Uexküll's subjective biology is Tolman (1958) in his theory of sign-gestalten. His strictly behavioral definitions of objects in terms of the behaving organism as *discriminanda, manipulanda,* and *means-end expectation,* depending on the prevailing behavior and the structure of the organisms, are close relatives to Uexküll's sensory and motor cues of objects. Uexküll's work gave the German word *Umwelt* (which had

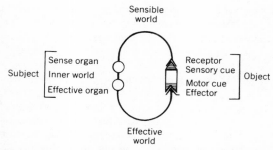

Figure 33.1. The inner world and *Umwelt* components of the "functional circuit" (after J. von Uexküll, 1922, p. 269).

been in general use since around 1800) this precise subjective meaning, which was taken up by social scientists inside and outside Germany. When psychology overcame its first elementaristic stage and came to theorize in terms of *Gestalten* and other wholes, a rapprochement between Uexküll's conception of *Umwelt* and molar structural theory in psychology was due (see the later section). In a general sense, ecology came to refer to analyses of individuals and groups in their natural habitats, mainly to the interactions and interrelationships between individuals or groups and their meaningful surrounds, that is, their *Umwelten*.

Meteorobiology

That weather and climate, different landscapes, like the mountains or the wide open spaces, have their differential impact on people's experiences and behaviors, that they elate or depress their moods, and so forth, has been part of the common stock of popular knowledge for a long time. Again, it was in the nineteenth century that attempts were made to transform such lore into science. More and more biological/physiological processes and states were studied with respect to their (often periodical or cyclic) dependence on meteorobiological, climatic, geographical, or even cosmic factors.

Psychological questions became inevitable. Does the annual cycle influence creativity, crime, suicide? Is emotionality susceptible to sudden changes in atmospheric pressure? Does the frequency of rape rise with air temperature? It was questions like these, first asked by nonpsychologists, that led to the conception of a "geopsychology" at the beginning of this century (Hellpach, 1911).

Kulturkritik and Urban Studies

When the process of civilization became marked by the dual feature of industrialization and urbanization toward the end of the last century, an essential part of the concomitant critique of civilization *(Kulturkritik)* concentrated on the big cities and on urban life. The public attitude toward cities has always been ambivalent, which is still reflected in contemporary urban studies (cf. Fischer, 1976; Pfeil, 1972). Cities were not only places to find freedom, individualism, art, political power, and novelties; they were, in an inverse perspective, also seen as places of anonymity, isolation, artificiality, deviance, *décadence,* and disease. But were those praises and accusations valid? Was all this urban reality or mainly prejudice? Empirical, first of all statistical, studies of urban phenomena took a very long time to corroborate or contradict the (basically moral) discourse about city life. Besides epidemiology it was mainly sociology, whose history is closely related with urban phenomena (Pfeil, 1972), where a nonevaluative approach to city life was tried. Partly under the influence of French scholars like Comte and Durkheim, who had shown the way to an empirical solution of sociological problems, it was Simmel (1903), Sombart (1907), and Thurnwald (1904) to whom we owe the first studies of urban sociology in Germany. Many of the phenomena dealt with in those studies were regarded as social psychological problems, at least as far as the individual experience of the new type of the urbanite or metropolitan person was concerned; psychology, the new science, though academically older than sociology, was challenged to take over.

Phenomenology: Philosophy of the Life-World

When the first sociological treatises on the city were published, phenomenology was only beginning to be what much later could become a metatheoretical framework for the study of person–environment relationships. But there was, from the beginning, the key concept of *intentionality* that brought the person-as-subject and his or her personal world (or *Umwelt*) inextricably together. Skipping the history of the concept (and of the phenomenological movement, cf. Spiegelberg, 1972), we mean by *intentionality* that in experience and behavior, in consciousness and action, we are related or referring to something that we posit as existing independently.

The whole of our intentional objects at a given time (but strictly within the limits of being meant or intended) is what phenomenologically may be called *Umwelt,* our intentional environment. The central idea is then, that for a human being or person to exist is to be situated in a *life world;* Husserl's term for the immediately experienced reality of our everyday activities and our natural (i.e., prescientific) attitude (Husserl, 1970; Schütz, 1962). To the degree that phenomenology (mainly Schütz's) is the philosophy of the total sphere of individual daily experiences (of persons, objects, and events), it is apt to become an optimal metatheory for any psychology that focuses on the person–environment relationship rather than on individuals and "their" behavior or experience (cf. Graumann, 1983a).[3]

There are other fields of research and practice that have contributed to the emergence of modern ecological psychology as, for example, geography, ethology, anthropology, systems theory, and—last not least—planning and architecture. But they are less historical roots than contemporary impacts. They deserve mentioning when we try to describe the most recent development. Before we do that, we note that there have been studies in environmental psychology since the beginning of this century that, in their own way, prepared the ground for present research.

33.1.3. Early Beginnings of Environmental Psychology

Just as the preceding one, this paragraph will have to be selective and biased: selective in focusing on the most important contributions and biased in emphasizing those approaches that for the English and American reader will be less familiar. Before we concentrate on urban psychology and geopsychology, we should discuss the first systematic and programmatic conception of environmental psychology in 1924.

Hellpach's Program of Environmental Psychology in 1924

Soon after World War I, one of the most ambitious enterprises of scientific publishing was launched, Abderhalden's huge *Handbook of Biological Methods,* several volumes of which were reserved for psychology, pure and applied. "Pure psychology" consisted of three books, two of which presented methods of individual psychology; the third volume was titled *Psychologie der Umwelt* [Environmental psychology] and edited by Hellpach (1924). It is safe to assume that Hellpach (1877–1955) became the editor because by then he was already known as an expert on natural influences on mental life. Besides, Hellpach was a liberal politician who held high offices in the government of the state of Baden; for example, he was Minister of Education from 1922 to 1925 and State President in 1924 and 1925. Later he even ran for president of the German *Reich,* but failed.

As the subject matter of the new branch of pure psychology, Hellpach (1924, p.110) regards "the mind as it is dependent upon its factual environment." The *Umwelt,* in turn, "as far as it has effects on human mental life," may be conceptualized in three "circles":

1. Humans are surrounded by nature, that is, soil, air, light, weather, woods, mountains, plains, rivers and lakes, and so on. These *geopsychological* facts (1924, p. 110) may have two kinds of effects on the human mind, either as immediate, sensory impressions or as tonic influences that affect the organism and, thereby, mental states.[4]

2. Humans are further "surrounded" by fellow humans. They are part of a community. The effects originating in other people are called *social psychological* facts. The ensemble of these facts is social *Umwelt.*

3. Finally, there is a "world" that has been made by humans in cooperation with their fellow humans, the world of books, laws, states, buildings, institutions of all kinds, that altogether have effects on our mental life. This circle, the objectivation of social life, is the world of *cultural psychological* and historical facts: *Umwelt,* then, impresses and influences us as natural, social, and cultural (historical) environments. Later (Hellpach, 1977, p. 5) the cultural branch of environmental psychology was specified as *tectopsychology,* that is, the study of all effects from "room and furniture, house and hall, street and place, road and vehicle."

Instead of discussing the various methods (mainly observation, statistics, and experiment) Hellpach presented in 1924, it is more instructive to see whether and how this programmatic system was realized. In a certain analogy to Wundt's monumental life work, we can state that it was mainly Hellpach himself who did it by means of research monographs and textbooks, some of which were widely read. They cover the three branches of environmental psychology, geo-, socio- and tectopsychology of which we will consider the first and the last, whereas social psychology, in the modern view, is not a part of environmental psychology. But as we shall see later, there is a growing awareness that social psychology is in need of "more ecology."

Geopsychology

The first treatise on geopsychological phenomena was published by Hellpach (1911) under that title. The book is presently in its eighth edition and still selling under the title *Geopsyche.* Translations were made into French, Dutch, and Spanish. An American edition had been planned but, according to Hellpach, it became victim to the declaration of war in 1941. The four major parts (and chapters) of geopsychology are the impressions and influences on experience and behavior of weather, climate, soil, and landscape. Because Hellpach was a very thorough and systematic man, almost no geopsychological factor, be it on the macro-, the meso-, or the microlevel, escaped his attention and system. So we find anything from the unsettled problem of possible effects of periodic sunspot activity, the lunar and the menstrual cycle, to the more "earthly" effects of colors and shapes of landscapes; from the effects of extreme environments such as the tropics and the arctic, to the influences of artificial climates of cities and the microclimate of our beds. Because Hellpach was also a very critical man who believed in final proofs by empirical, possibly experimental, methods, a considerable part of his geopsychology remained programmatic—up to this day.

Because the scientific community in Germany (and Europe) has been served with the latest in geopsychology for almost half a century by Hellpach himself, we have here at least one case of continuous tradition in environmental psychology, and there were and are others working in this field.

Urban Psychology

The other case, also largely represented by Hellpach, is urban psychology. What today we have come to call the typical stimulus overload of urban experience and its variants of information/attention/decisional/communication overload (Deutsch, 1970; Milgram, 1970; Saegert, 1976) is usually traced back via Wirth's theory of urbanism (Wirth, 1938, 1970) to Simmel's notions of the "intensification of nervous stimulation" and of the "heightened awareness" of the metropolitan (Simmel, 1903/1970, p. 778). Whereas Simmel's notions, owing to his prominent status in sociology and to translations of some of his publications, became internationally known, it went almost unnoticed that, also in agreement with the *Zeitgeist,* Hellpach in 1902 had introduced the term *Reizsamkeit,* that is, "heightened stimulability," to characterize the city dweller's proneness to overstimulation, the normal state of what popularly and clinically is called "nervousness" (Hellpach, 1902).

In his later analysis of the urban experience (Hellpach, 1939), this typical mental state of the urbanite is explained by a permanent "sociophysical constraint." The nature of this constraint is described in terms of the typically urban phenomena of crowds, crowding, haste, and continuous change. They are socio*physical* facts because they refer to the dense physical togetherness of inhabitants of large cities,

crowded in tight spaces, hurrying along without taking notice of one another (1939, p. 69). The crowded situation is not restricted to streets and places but is found in shops, department stores, railway stations, post offices, banks, streetcars, subways, and buses: "Like human beings their vehicles crowd and hurry along" (1939, p. 69). Masses, crowding, haste, and constant change also characterize urban dwelling: innumerable and large blocks of housing projects, highrise buildings, hundreds of anonymous co-tenants, frequently changing subtenants and night lodgers.

The permanent hurry in which metropolitans seem to be is not, Hellpach insists, just a "bad habit" or mere pretense: "Haste is an essential characteristic of metropolitan existence" (1939, p. 69). For, in order to come to grips with the many affairs they have to deal with, urbanites have to cope with frequent as well as quick changes. This having to deal with things speedily tends to generalize into other areas where speed is not required or even out of place, as in the realm of leisure. But "tempo" in all walks of life has become second nature for the inhabitants of large cities.

A necessary correlate of the speed of urban life is *vigilance,* the second characteristic of the typical urbanite. The higher the speed and the quicker the change the more important it becomes for the urbanite to be ready for sudden changes—opportunities or accidents. Hellpach (1939, p. 70) holds that the perceptual style of the city dweller has become different from a country dweller's: Acute observation, quick apprehension, and processing without delay have replaced deep processing and long-term retention. Both speed and vigilance are concomitants of the urbanite's "stimulability" due to the sociophysical constraints of city life.

Another feature of urban experience Hellpach labeled *social alienation.* Ever-changing impressions and situations will not result in familiarity, neither of things nor of persons. Metropolitans never get to know the thousands whom they pass every day. Their contacts are functional and superficial. Nodding acquaintances and anonymity are the rule; familiarity as well as enmity are exceptions. It is ultimately the interactions of the crowd, the tightness of place, the need for quick changes requiring alertness, from which follows alienation with respect to persons and things (Hellpach, 1939, p. 74). The tension resulting from these conflicting factors is stated in a formula meant to summarize the social psychology of living in cities: "sensory vigilance with emotional indifference" (1939, p. 74).

Even if leveling seems to be inevitable in large crowds of people, Hellpach warns us against the stereotype of mass life in cities. "Subjectivism" alias individualism is facilitated in the metropolitan milieu to a degree that no small town or village would tolerate. Again, the "liberating" effect of the urban environment is ambivalent: Freedom means both independence and isolation.

It is true that many of Hellpach's statements about the urban experience may have been premature generalizations from observation or from the critical discussion of theories of the city. But it is equally true that since the turn of the century we have had sociopsychological descriptions and interpretations of living in cities that, in principle, have not been rejected but rephrased, refined, and, partly, corroborated by subsequent empirical research.

Although there has been more continuity in geopsychology than in urban psychology, Hellpach was not the only psychologist to be interested in urban problems. There is at least one other student of the urban life space who deserves mentioning—Martha Muchow. She had become a student of Stern's in Hamburg before World War I. Later she joined his staff in 1920. After the dismissal of Stern and Werner by the Nazis in 1933 and the subsequent disbanding of the psychological institute, she committed suicide (Schoggen, 1985a, 1985b; Wohlwill, 1983; Zinnecker, 1980).

Her and her brother's study of the life space of the urban child (Muchow & Muchow, 1935) is the earliest research monograph in ecological child psychology. Although Lewin, before his emigration to the United States in 1933, had already published his conception of the "psychological life space" (Lewin, 1935) as well as his early field theoretical ideas about the environment as a field of forces (1931), Muchow's concept of *Lebensraum* (life space) owes its existence and its theoretical core to Stern and Uexküll (Muchow & Muchow, 1935, p. 10). Stern's "personal world," for which the major dimensions are "personal space" and "personal time" (cf. Stern, 1938), may be regarded as the "personalistic" equivalent of Uexküll's subjective and specific *Umwelt*.[5] Werner, Stern's junior colleague at Hamburg and one of Muchow's mentors, had succeeded in combining these conceptions for the purpose of developmental psychology (Werner, 1957), and for a long time Muchow's study remained Werner's (only) model for an ecologically oriented investigation in child psychology. Because Wohlwill only recently has made the American public familiar with Muchow's study (Wohlwill, 1983), it will suffice to refer to the three research perspectives that Muchow used to structure the life space of the children of Hamburg-Barmbeck: (1) The "space in which the child lives" was identified by individually filled and completed maps of Barmbeck; (2) the "space which the child experiences" by means of a mixture of interview/questionnaire, essay, and graphic methods; and (3) the "space which the child lives,"[6] that is, the actual behavioral space of children of different schools and ages (3–14 years), required observational methods. One of the major findings is that "lived space" (3) is much more child-specific than "experienced space" (2) or the more "cognitive" space (1) of the first study.

Muchow also did other ecological studies, for example, a geopsychological one on the effects of the maritime climate, especially of the beach, on children's mental life (Muchow, 1926, 1929). However, with regard to the evaluation of an ecologically oriented psychology (not only of development), Muchow's life-space study is the more important pioneering piece of work. She left it unpublished when she discovered that there was no more personal space for her to live in. For the rest, there was no continuity in urban psychological research until after World War II.

Psychotechnik *and Applied Psychology*

Very briefly we should point to the fact that there has been one other, relatively continuous, tradition that still today contributes to environmental psychology in the broadest sense, namely that part of applied psychology that deals with the diagnosis and optimization of the relationship between people and various professional environments: *Psychotechnik*. The term, originally introduced by Stern (1903), was defined most broadly by Münsterberg (1914)[7] as the science of the practical applications of psychology in the service of "cultural tasks" (education, health, law, art, economy, science) but was later narrowed to what today is treated under the title of *ergonomics*, mainly the systematic analysis and optimization of person–machine systems or of work in general. Because the work environment on which *Psychotechnik* focused was a special case of people–environment relations, it is legitimate and consensually acknowledged to consider this branch of applied psychology a precursor to modern environmental psychology.

33.2. CONTEMPORARY ECOLOGICAL PSYCHOLOGY

33.2.1. Incentives for a New Beginning

It would be a task of its own, though not in the framework of this *Handbook*, to describe and assess the reestablishment of psychology in postwar Germany. Because this has not yet been done satisfactorily, we must restrict ourselves to singling out a few impulses and trends that, in our opinion, led to the emergence of modern ecological psychology in Germany. Of the incentives for a new psychology of the environment, we shall briefly discuss four, two of which come from outside psychology: (1) effects of the postwar reconstruction of German cities; (2) the growth of environmental concern; (3) the growing uneasiness about the "ecological validity" of a predominantly experimental psychology; and (4) the advent of environmental psychology in the United States.

Architecture and Planning: Negative Aftereffects of Postwar Reconstruction

The most visible effect of World War II on what remained of Germany was the destruction of the cities. Because a considerable part of the population was literally homeless (one-quarter of all prewar dwellings had been destroyed), one of the first requirements in the years after 1945 and, mainly, after the foundation of the Federal Republic of Germany in 1949 was the massive reconstruction of cities and industries. It is now a historical fact that the concentrated effort of a whole nation, which was substantially aided by some of its former enemies and new allies, above all the United States, has economically been very successful. The irrational term *economic miracle* refers to this success. Within a surprisingly short time, the housing emergency *(Wohnungsnot)* was allayed. That millions could be housed again, including the poorest and more than eight million refugees from the eastern provinces, was made possible by huge subsidized housing projects *(sozialer Wohnungsbau)* in practically all German cities. These were frequently at their peripheries, thus giving birth to new suburban areas and satellite towns. Planners and architects competed for the most modern/esthetic, "functional," "human," and economic solutions—and for the corresponding prizes, awards, and honoraria. It was only after years of occupancy that the shortcomings of the quick and sometimes bold planning and the equally quick and sometimes negligent building of the new structures became evident in public. The new towns, suburbs, and satellite towns were criticized as inhuman, inimical to children and the aged, isolating housewives, stimulating vandalism and crime, and so forth. The pride in the building part of the "economic miracle" turned sour. But what was more important is that physical objects like buildings, blocks, streets, squares, means of transportation, which had always "surrounded" us, were gradually discovered as *Umwelt*. They were discovered as allegedly determining, but at least as constraining, inhibiting, or facilitating human modes of experience, of patterns of behavior and, mainly, of communication. For the first time, the psychology and psychopathology of planning and architecture became publicly recognized. In the beginning it was, of course, journalists, writers, and politicians (of the opposition) who articulated the criticisms and many a naive theory of architectural determinism.

One of the first psychologists who effectively bewailed the "inhospitality of our cities" was Mitscherlich (1965), a psychoanalyst and social psychologist. After the publication of his widely read pamphlet, interactions between planners, architects, and social and behavioral scientists became less exotic than before, although not normal. But, as a rule, psychologists who were confronted with questions about, and claims for, psychological prerequisites—or even norms—for building apartment houses for families having many children, homes for the aged, and so forth were at a loss for rational answers. They had not been trained to give them. In some universities, it was the students of architecture who felt the need to know more about psychology and sociology and demanded that these disciplines become part of their curricula. Sociology, because of a stronger tradition in urban sociology, was better prepared to step in than was psychology. Consequently, it was social psychologists, trained in both disciplines, who in the beginning dared to enter the new, that is, neglected field (Irle, 1960).

The Growth of Environmental Concern

Another reverse side of the relatively steep curve of growth in urbanization and industrialization, including the concomitant motorization, was and is the shrinking reserves of space in land and water and of energy. Years before the phrase *limits to growth* (Meadows, Meadows, Zahn, & Milling, 1972) became a catchword and a topic of heated discussions, an awareness was growing that *growth,* so far a term of definitely positive connotation, has its drawbacks and side effects. This change of consciousness was not a continuous process, but social representation developed by leaps and bounds whenever "the environment" got into the news. There had always been noise and pollution, mainly in high-density and industrial areas like the Ruhr, but they were accepted as the inevitable costs of economic growth and affluence. It was only the unprecedented sharp increase in industrial, traffic, and aircraft noise and in air and water pollution, accompanied by a series of disasters, blown up by mass media, that brought the environment-as-problem in focus.

The environment, which had always been "there," changed from ground to figure. Stress, a favorite catchword of the era of reconstruction, adopted the meaning of environmental stress. This "discovery" of the environment as stressor in the 1960s brought forth psychological questions that challenged psychology but for which, in most cases, psychology was unprepared.

The Growth of Methodological Concern within Psychology

The third current that contributed in a very specific way to the emergence of ecological psychology in Germany originated in the discipline itself. If we describe it as a growing concern over a methodological bias that favors laboratory experimentation and tends to disregard or, at least, belittle problems of ecological validity, one may argue that this has been an almost universal concern: "Crisis" articles filled many professional journals in most (Western) countries. Yet in two important respects the situation in postwar Germany was different.[8]

After 1933, the country had not only been deprived of a strong group of excellent psychologists who were forced to leave Germany, it was also cut off from the international exchange of persons and ideas, which had been very strong until 1933. One of the effects was that psychology in Germany was hardly influenced by what may briefly be called the behaviorist and operationist movement (between the 1930s and the 1950s). One is tempted to say "on the contrary": After the exodus of the emigrants a metatheoretical orientation prevailed that was marked by holism, emotionalism, even substantialism,[9] with a preference for characterology[10] (cf. Wellek, 1954) and for methods of *Geisteswissenschaft* rather than science (a forerunner of what some today call *humanistic psychology* [Graumann, 1981]).

When this kind of psychology was carried over into the postwar period by psychologists who could retain their academic positions after 1945, the counterreaction of the younger generation was a shift to the most hard-minded kind of neobehaviorism then available and to an overemphasis on quantitative methods. The idea was to make up for the years of isolation as quickly and thoroughly as possible. It is then not surprising that this belated and impetuous "honeymoon" was followed by qualms of various kinds. Since the 1960s we have had a whole literature of psychological self-criticism, partly associated with and stimulated by the student movement. One of the new or newly proclaimed goals then was to make psychology better prepared to cope with the essen-

tial problems of our social and physical environments. It was to make psychology better prepared in theory and methods. "Molar" instead of "molecular" behavior, complex and natural instead of artificially simplified lab situations, and representative instead of systematic designs (Brunswik, 1947) were solicited. The general quest for more meaningfulness pointed to a socially and ecologically enriched psychology.

The Advent of American Environmental Psychology

All these trends, currents, and undercurrents became reinforced, channeled, and multiplied by the reception of "the emerging discipline of environmental psychology" in America, as Wohlwill (1970) introduced it in the *American Psychologist*. Those psychologists, of course, who had already been interested in ecological problems had been familiar with earlier American contributions as, for example, Bailey, Branch, and Taylor (1961), Barker (1963, 1965, 1968), Barker and Wright (1955), Sommer (1967, 1969) as well as with British and American "architectural psychology" (Bailey et al., 1961; Lynch, 1960; Taylor, Bailey, & Branch, 1967). But, as historiographers of science would have predicted, it was only with the institutionalizing acts of publishing a specialized journal, namely *Environment and Behavior* in 1969, a comprehensive reader (Proshansky, Ittelson, & Rivlin, 1970), and a critical review (Craik, 1970) that a broader reception set in.

33.2.2. The "Foundation"

If one takes similar institutional criteria to mark the beginning of modern ecological psychology in Germany, 1974 would be the year. According to Kaminski's English review of environmental psychology in Germany (Kaminski, 1978a) from which we will take much information, the year 1974 was marked by two facts: the first doctoral thesis in the new field was published (Kruse, 1974). In her thesis, the author presented the early research work of American environmental psychology and criticizing its lack of theoretical foundation, she made use of phenomenological conceptions of the life-world and of lived space, with a view to developing key concepts for a theory of what was then still called man-environment interaction.[11] The major event of the year was, that at the occasion of the biennial conference of the German Psychological Association (Deutsche Gesellschaft für Psychologie), *Umweltpsychologie* appeared on the agenda for the first time. Kaminski had been asked to organize a symposium as well as a paper session dealing with basic conceptual and methodological issues as well as applied topics (cf. Kaminski, 1976, 1985).

The symposium not only took the occasion to commemorate the fiftieth anniversary of Hellpach's introduction of "environmental psychology" (Graumann, 1976). It was also then that the suggestion was made to reserve the term *Umweltpsychologie* for the psychological investigation of environmental problems such as noise, pollution, energy consumption, and the like and to use the term *ecological psychology* for the more fundamental analyses of people–environment interactions. Although the idea to distinguish between a more comprehensive and basic ecopsychology and a more technological subdiscipline of *Umweltpsychologie* has not found general agreement, it has been widely accepted in Germany not to establish and cultivate a new psychological ecodiscipline but to *penetrate all fields of psychology with the ecological viewpoint,* that is, to pay closer attention to those stimulus, sample, and procedural parameters that control the (ecological) representativeness (validity) of our findings (cf. Graumann, 1978). This, of course, does not only demand greater concern for natural or everyday settings, natural groups, and field or nonreactive methods. It also requires a theoretical orientation that, from the beginning, focuses on potential person–environment interactions rather than on the traditional individual homo psychologicus—a pledge that will take resolution, energy, and time to redeem (cf. also Mogel, 1984).

After this first official meeting of a group of scholars who stated their interest in problems of the spatial and material, the natural and human-made environment as basis, moderator, or object of human experience and behavior, it did not take very long until ecological psychology became "institutionalized" and part of the general environmental research enterprise that in the beginning had been almost exclusively dominated by natural science approaches (cf. Deutsche Forschungsgemeinschaft (DFG), 1976).

Prepared by means of several workshops and special symposia (cf. Eckensberger, 1976b; Graumann, 1978; Kaminski, 1975a), a special research program was established by the DFG (German Science Foundation) in 1978. In its first 5-year period of funding, 19 different research projects, which will be described later, were granted. The program has in the meantime been extended. Besides, the research group also organized several symposia and workshops on different subjects, most of them with guests from neighboring fields, some of them with in-

ternational experts for the various topics. After a first general discussion about "psychological aspects of environmental research" (cf. Kaminski, 1975a), other meetings took place in which representatives from various subdisciplines of psychology outlined ecological perspectives for their specific fields, thus arguing for an ecological enrichment of psychology as a whole (Graumann, 1978). Methodological issues of ecopsychology were topics of another series of workshops focusing on field methods (1979), methods of simulation (1982), including a planning game on housing for the aged (1980), and techniques of evaluation (1983). Centering on conceptual problems, psychologists discussed "ecosystems" with biologists and geographers (Eckensberger, 1976a; Eckensberger & Burgard, 1977). One of the workshops dealt with the concept of "behavior setting," its theoretical and methodological implications, and further developments (Kaminski, 1986; Saup, 1983).

Parallel with and rather independent of these "founding" activities, the advancement of ecopsychology in Germany was promoted by the ecological initiative taken by developmental psychologists. The discussion of "ecological factors in human development" was carried over from the United States and from international conferences (cf. e.g., Thomae & Endo, 1974) into Europe. This discussion continued at the Third Biennial Conference of the International Society for the Study of Behavioral Development in Guilford, England, in 1975 (cf. McGurk, 1977). In 1976, a symposium was organized at the conference of the Deutsche Gesellschaft für Psychologie on environmental and development psychology (Walter, 1977), which was then followed by other workshops and conferences (cf. Walter & Oerter, 1979). A number of publications, paper collections as well as literature reviews and position statements, reflect the broad spectrum of approaches in this field (Eckensberger, 1979; Thomae & Endo, 1974; Trudewind, 1978; Walter, 1975, 1977, 1980, 1981; Walter & Oerter, 1979).

The great variety of topics and methodological and conceptual approaches could also be demonstrated for ecopsychological research in general, when a first survey of ongoing research in the mid-1970s was published (Kruse, 1975a).

The following paragraphs intend to present some of this variety (cf. also Kruse, 1975b). We cannot and do not plan to give a complete review of research but rather to expand on the topics from the preceding paragraphs. We confess bias and selectivity.

Reviewing the topics that were shown to contribute to the development of modern ecopsychology, we shall first discuss ecopsychological research on urban problems — an area so widely defined that it will encompass the majority of research topics. We shall then refer to the growth of environmental concern and the research on those environmental problems that people are concerned about. It will become apparent that, except for problems of noise, the social science perspective on typical environmental problems, which are so extensively addressed in American research, for example, energy consumption and saving or problems of littering, recycling, and so forth, have not resulted in substantial research in Germany.

A third paragraph will address "ecological perspectives" in traditional fields of psychology with a major stress on the ecological movement in developmental psychology, most of which may be subsumed under the rubric *Sozialökologie*.

33.2.3. Research Areas

Architecture and Planning

As we pointed out before, the rapid and massive reconstruction of cities destroyed in World War II, the planning of new towns and satellite towns, and the quick planning and construction of thousands of houses and apartments brought about many problems, first for the inhabitants, finally for planners and architects. The "crisis of urban society," which was characteristic of the late 1960s, was to a large degree a crisis of urban planning and housing. This situation opened the opportunity for critique, for recommendations, for improvement, and for integrative efforts of those disciplines that dealt with environmental planning and design, on the one hand, and those that focused on the behavior and experience of users, their housing needs and satisfactions, their environmental perceptions and cognitions, their locomotions and communicative networks, and the like, on the other hand. There were, of course, a few psychologists, and psychoanalysts in particular, who raised their voices and objected to the "inhospitality of our cities" (Mitscherlich, 1965), criticized the ideologies of city planners (Berndt, 1968) and modern "functional" architecture in general (Berndt, Lorenzer, & Horn, 1968), and spoke up again and again in lectures, (architectural) journal articles and expert statements arguing for humane cities and housing (Mitscherlich, 1971). But, these exceptions notwithstanding, it was mainly sociologists who responded to the urban crisis, developed "new" theories of urban life (e.g., Bahrdt, 1961, 1968), began empirical studies of various urban and housing problems such as problems of

high-rise buildings (Herlyn, 1970), new towns, and suburbs (Becker & Keim, 1977; Dorsch, 1972; Heil, 1971; Schwonke & Herlyn, 1967; Weeber, 1971; Zapf, Heil, & Rudolph, 1969; cf. Deutsche UNESCO-Kommission, 1978). A closer cooperation between sociology and urban planning was pleaded for (Siebel, 1967; Schmidt-Relenberg, 1968; Zinn, 1970), and first outlines were given for an architectural sociology (cf. Thurn, 1972) and a sociology for architects (Feldhusen, 1975; cf. also Pieper, 1979).

In sociology, these approaches were advanced roughly a decade before psychologists entered the discussion with planners and architects Franke (1967), Harloff (1973), Kaminski (1973b, 1975b, 1979b), Kruse (1974), Dirlewanger, Geisler, and Magnano-Lampugnani (1977), Geisler (1977, 1978), Molt and von Rosenstiel (1978), Graumann (1979), and Fischer (1981a, 1981b).

One of the first psychologists working in the field, which was later recognized as architectural psychology, was Franke, in Nuremberg. He and his research group directed their attention primarily to residential areas and the way these were experienced by inhabitants, visitors, planning experts, and local government officials. Publications germane here include Franke (1969), Franke and Bortz (1972), Bortz (1972), Franke and Hoffmann (1974), Franke (1974), Franke and Rothgang (1975), Franke (1976), Klockhaus (1975), Tiedtke (1980), and Bauer (1981). The method preferred is a specifically adapted semantic differential that they also succeeded in making popular among architects and planners (cf. Franke, 1969, 1974; Markelin & Trieb, 1974; Trieb, 1974). The Nuremberg group has recently extended this approach to studies of landscapes, their aesthetic and recreational value, and the impact of change (cf. Bauer, Franke, & Gätschenberger, 1979a, 1979b). Providing methods for the improvement of citizens' participation in the planning process is another goal of this group (cf. Franke & Hoffmann, 1978). A recent DFG research project worked toward this goal by optimizing planning documents. One of the findings was that laypeople were superior to municipal experts with respect to the prediction from planning documents when these were easy to grasp (Franke, Bauer, & Kühlmann, 1982, 1983).

When sociologists and psychologists began to plead for a social and behavioral analysis of the built environment, of urban design and architecture (Fischer, 1981a, 1981b; Franke, 1974; Geisler, 1977; Graumann, 1979; Kaminski, 1973b, 1975b, 1979b; Mühlich, Zinn, Kröning, & Mühlich-Klinger, 1978; Zinn, 1970), of the world of things (e.g., Boesch,

1971, 1976, 1978, 1980, 1983; Graumann, 1974; Joerges, 1977, 1981; Linde, 1972), of technology and technological change (Joerges, 1981; Jungermann, 1982a, 1982b; Kruse, 1981a), they found assistance from some of the more progressive architects and planners (e.g., Dirlewanger, Geisler, Joedicke, & Magnano-Lampugnani, 1975; Durth, 1977; Garbrecht, 1976, 1981; Heidemann, 1972; Joedicke, 1977; Joedicke, Dirlewanger, Geisler, & Knoerzer, 1974; Joedicke, Dirlewanger, Markelin, Trieb, Geisler, & Magnano-Lampugnani, 1975; Trieb, 1974), landscape architects (e.g., Nohl, 1974, 1975, 1980), and human geographers (e.g., Höllhuber, 1979), but also criticism (e.g., Joerges, 1977).

It is worth mentioning, however, that the first evidence of a cooperative effort of psychology and planning (regional science) was an investigation by Heidemann and Stapf (1969) who studied time and activity budgets, home ranges, and social networks of urban housewives in a North German city (cf. also Stapf & Heidemann, 1971; Heidemann, 1972).

When urban sociologists began to analyze and to study problems of urban sprawl and of living in postwar cities, they often made use of psychological conceptualizations but only sometimes explicitly. Their empirical approach was, however, still sociological rather than psychological. One of the major issues was the concept of *neighborhood*. Implied was the question of whether and how neighborhoods can be planned, an issue that has attracted much attention as well as critique (cf. Hamm, 1973; Klages, 1958; Lorenzer, 1968; Pfeil, 1963). Neighborhood variables and relations are still of interest as empirical problems of urban sociology (e.g., Bahr & Gronemeyer, 1977; Becker & Keim, 1977; Jeggle, 1978; Kalwitzki, 1983; Keim, 1979; Kromrey, 1981; Miller, 1985; Schubert, 1977; Strohmeier, 1983; Vierecke, 1972). It was only recently that social and developmental and clinical psychologists "discovered" the impact of neighborhoods, sociotopes, and other milieus — defined in both objective and subjective terms (Kommer & Röhrle, 1983; Walter, 1981).

A further topic related to the neighborhood issue is place relatedness, or spatial identity. From the mid-1960s on (Treinen, 1965), it has remained a central topic for a number of studies. These include Schwonke and Herlyn (1967), Lenz-Romeiss (1970), Becker and Keim (1972), and Bodzenta, Speiser, and Thum (1981). All these studies were sociological. It was only after Proshansky (1978) introduced his term *place identity* that social psychologists broadened the scope of these studies. A DFG research project conducted by Graumann and Schneider (cf. Graumann &

Schneider [in preparation]; Graumann, Schneider, & Kany, 1981; Kany & Schneider, 1985; Schneider, 1986; Schneider & Weimer, 1981) investigated the relationship between the psychological identity of, and citizen's identifications with, urban areas. Loss of place identity as a result of change of place (moving) is seen as a critical life event by Fischer and Fischer (1981) and Fischer (1982), whereas Hormuth (1983, 1984) (in a DFG project at the psychological institute of the University of Heidelberg) tried to find out how a change of place affects one's self-concept. Furthermore, the hypothesis has been tested that there are people who make use of a change of place in order to modify their self-conception.

Several other studies have examined change of place, residential choice, or relocation (Harloff, 1973; Höllhuber, 1977, 1982; Klockhaus in a DFG project in the psychological institute, University of Erlangen-Nuremberg). Höllhuber, whose field was human geography, studied the influence of mental maps on the choice of a residential area. Klockhaus was only partly successful in finding a "fit" between residential satisfaction of people and specific personality variables, such as stages in the life cycle or personal well-being (cf. also Klockhaus & Habermann-Morbey, 1982).

A related area is the *cognition, perception,* or more generally, the *experience* of housing areas, neighborhoods, and cityscapes, down to architectural features of facades. In addition to the numerous research studies done by the Nuremberg group, Waterhouse (1972) studied the effects of physical alterations of urban areas in Berlin on attitudes and values as related to other personal variables. Sauter (1983) was interested in the impact of optical and acoustical factors on the evaluation of residential areas. Schneider (1981), of the Heidelberg group, compared data from verbal and nonverbal methods differentiating between urban objects of high and low semantic load (residential areas vs. facades).

Also in Heidelberg, Oster (1982), comparing cab drivers with nonprofessional motorists, investigated interference effects in driver's spatial orientation while using city plans. Prepared by early structuralist (Doelle, 1913) and later information-theoretical analyses (Bense, 1968, 1969), students of semiotics turned to urban structures as to their semiotic, "syntactic," symbolic character (Becker & Keim, 1972; Krampen, 1979, 1981a, 1981b, 1981c; Maderthaner, 1978; Schwarz & Werbik, 1971). Housing and residential satisfactions were topics of studies by Lantermann (1974) who concentrated on solidarity and social balance and by Pawlik (1976a) who observed effects of participatory planning. In an action-theoretical framework, Kasper and Krewer (1982) studied objective, in relation to subjective, indicators of quality of life. Psychologists also became engaged in housing experiments (alternative housing, solar architecture, living with plants) (Franke, 1982; Kaminski, 1982; Krampen, 1981b, 1981c; Weichardt, 1981).

Special housing and residential needs have been studied with respect to children and adolescents (Baumann & Zinn, 1973; Zinn, 1981); older people (Balkes, Barton, Orzech & Lager, 1983; Lantermann, 1976; Reimann, 1983; Saup, 1984a, 1984b; Schmitz-Scherzer, Plagemann, & Kühn, 1976); the physically disabled (Bürk & Strehlke, 1982; Day, 1981a, 1982; Fischer, 1986); long-term inpatients (Welter, 1976, 1978); vagrants (Geisler, 1981; Krebs, 1971).

The school is another environment serving special "users," (cf. e.g. Fatke, 1977; Karmann, 1985; Kraft, 1977). Psychological aspects of modern school design (open-plan school) have been studied by Schmittmann as part of an extensive research project of the Institut für Schulbau at the University of Stuttgart (König & Schmittmann, 1976; Schmittmann, 1977, 1981).

Relatively little research has been done so far in the field of apartment living, furniture style, and arrangement (cf. however, Silbermann, 1963; Peel, 1980, 1982; Thoma, 1980).

The street as environment has been studied from various perspectives. Molt and his group at Augsburg University used a modification of Barker's behavior setting approach to typify city streets (Molt, Golk, & Patschá, 1981, 1983). Other projects were concerned with aspects of security (Erke, 1975; Erke & Zimolong, 1978; Schenk & Schmidt, 1972), especially of children (Flade, 1981b, 1981c; Günther & Limbourg, 1976; Limbourg, 1976) and of older people (Mathey, Thomae, & Knorr, 1976). Finally, means of transportation and traveling (Held, 1982; Held, Verron, & von Rosenstiel, 1981; Molt, 1981), traffic noise (Kastka, 1976, 1981a, 1981b, 1981c; Knall & Schuemer, 1981; Schuemer & Schuemer-Kohrs, 1983a, 1983b), and traffic calming became objects of study (cf. Molt et al., 1981). As a major mode of inner-city locomotion, walking has been studied extensively by Garbrecht (1981). A social psychology of space and locomotion was presented by Kruse and Graumann (1978).

The space relatedness of social problems has been of interest to a wide range of social and environmental sciences (cf. e.g., Beorchia & Engels, 1983;

Herlyn, 1980; Hubbertz, 1979; Kommer & Röhrle, 1983; Vaskovics, 1982). The problem of criminal behavior and vandalism in urban settings has been dealt with in a series of ecopsychological studies. These include Bundeskriminalamt (1979); Flade (1981a, 1983a, 1983b, 1984), Keim (1981), Koch (1986), Meier (1985), and Rolinski (1980). The school as a preferred target of vandalism is the topic of a research project by Klockhaus and Habermann-Morbey (1984, 1985, 1986), whereas A. Mummendey and her group at Münster University take the school setting as a vantage point for the study of aggression (Bornewasser, Mummendey, Linneweber, & Loeschper, 1982; Loeschper, Mummendey, Linneweber, & Bornewasser, 1984; Mummendey, Linneweber, & Loeschper, 1984; Mummendey, Loeschper, Linneweber, & Bornewasser, 1984).

Spaces for outdoor recreation, particularly play areas for children, have also been addressed as important facets of urban life. Here we find user analyses, mostly of children in various types of play areas and recreational environments (Bierhoff, 1974; Bierhoff, Schmitz-Scherzer, Kranzhoff, & Alexa, 1977; Höltershinken, Hilker, Janssen, Kork, & Schulz, 1971; Otterstädt, 1962; Schmitz-Scherzer & Bierhoff, 1972; Schmitz-Scherzer, Bierhoff, Lustig, & Güth, 1974; Seidel, 1975), a more general social psychology of leisure time activities in recreational environments (Nohl, 1980; Schmitz-Scherzer, 1974, 1977; Winter, 1980a, 1980b, 1983) as well as applied research for the improvement of the design of recreational environments (Nohl, 1974, 1975, 1980). The vantage point, originating in landscape architecture, has been the so-called need for environmental complexity and variation (cf. also Fischer & Wiedl, 1973, 1979, 1981), which Nohl tried to convert into planning recommendations for outdoor spaces. Except for such aspects of leisure research and of landscape modification by land reform, referred to previously (Bauer et al., 1979a), the natural environment, which was Hellpach's favorite geopsychological topic, is only gradually attracting ecopsychological interest (cf. Kruse, 1983b; Spada, May, & Opwis, 1983).

Environmental Problems and Concern

Whereas environmental problems have increased in number and impact since the 1960s and although this development has been accompanied by an intensification of environmental concern, the number of pertinent psychological studies has lagged behind. Still, the major types of environmental problems have gradually been subjected to psychological research but actually only to the degree in which they have been "impressions" rather than mere "influences" to use Hellpach's (1977) traditional distinction between what comes to our awareness through the senses and what merely affects our "physiology." So noise has become the foremost research topic, as it always had been of industrial psychological interest, for example in *Psychotechnik* (cf. Guski & Rohrmann, 1981; Rohrmann, 1984a; Schick, 1979, 1981; Schick & Walcher, 1984, for an overview). The impact of road traffic and railway noise (Kastka, 1976; Kastka & Buchta, 1977; Knall & Schuemer, 1981; Mohler, Schuemer, Knall, & Schuemer-Kohrs (in press); Schuemer & Schuemer-Kohrs, 1983, 1984) as well as aircraft noise (Rohrmann, Finke, Guski, Schuemer, & Schuemer-Kohrs, 1978) has been extensively studied in both natural and experimental settings. In experiments on effects of traffic noise on learning and other "regulatory activities," Schönpflug and his Berlin group succeeded in increasing the ecological validity of their experimental data by using realistic simulations of work places (Mündelein & Schönpflug, 1984; Schönpflug & Schulz, 1979; Schulz, 1981). The theoretically and methodologically interesting relationship between noise and loudness has been approached under the category of annoyance (Kastka, 1981a, 1984, 1985; Rohrmann, 1984b; for measurement problems also see Hawel, 1967; Rohrmann, 1981). The relation between production of and annoyance by noise was examined by Day (1981b, 1984). Applications of such basic research may paradigmatically be taken from studies of subjective and objective effects of noise barriers (Kastka, 1981b, 1981c).

Another type of environmental pollution that in high-density and industrial areas usually occurs and is studied together with noise is odor (cf. Kastka, 1978, 1982). Very often annoying noise and odor are considered to be environmental stressors. We cannot enter into a critical discussion of the very broad stress category that permits the most diverse phenomena to be subsumed as "stressful." But we have to refer to one of the major stress phenomena: crowding. The many problems of density and crowding, topics almost overresearched in the United States, have only recently begun to attract the attention of German psychologists. A first review of the field was presented by Kruse in 1975 (1975a). Schultz-Gambard (1979, 1983, 1985) did empirical research, reviewed theoretical models, and offered suggestions for application. He has also started a research project on the impact of naturally occurring density situations in a university hall. A conceptual and empirical investigation of crowding was done by

Friedrichs (1979), Meier (1985), Streufert, Nogami, and Streufert (1980; cf. also Streufert & Nogami, 1979). In a past study, Six, Martin, and Pecher (1983) used a simulation technique for the analysis of intercultural differences between German and American experiences of crowding, replicating and extending a study by Arkkelin and Veitch (1978).

Although crowds and crowding are so closely intertwined in everyday urban experience, theory and research have strangely enough kept them apart. The former has traditionally been dealt with in social (collective) psychology, whereas problems of crowding were studied from an ecological viewpoint. Recently, however, the neglected relationship has been analyzed by Kruse (in press), and crowding is being accepted as an authentic topic in social psychology textbooks (Graumann & Kruse, 1984; Kruse, 1983a; Schultz-Gambard, 1983, 1985).

Another environmental problem, which only recently has been anchored in psychology, is energy shortage (cf. Bergius, 1982, 1984; Bergius, Engemann et al., 1982; Strümpel, 1978). Alternative energy technologies as well as nuclear power plants have become objects of attitude research (Hoffmann, Kattmann, Lucht, & Spada, 1975; Spada, Hoffmann, & Lucht-Wraage, 1977; Spada & Lucht-Wraage, 1980). Topics from natural hazard research, combined with findings from the field of decision making, have been applied to the study of risky technologies and risk acceptance (Jungermann, 1982a, 1986; Jungermann, Pfaffenberger, Schäfer, & Wild, 1986; Rohrmann & Borcherding, 1985; Winterfeldt, John, & Borcherding, 1981).

It will probably take some time before the behavioral science perspective on environmental problems will gain wider public recognition. A 1-year radio university course, *Mensch und Umwelt* (Funkkolleg, 1983), was almost exclusively concerned with natural science, technical, and political aspects of the people–environment relationship.

There is a growing literature about social science perspectives on environmental protection (Fietkau, 1981; Kaminski, 1973b; Kruse, 1983b; Mielke, 1985; Nöldner, 1984), environmental concern (Amelang, Tepe, Vagt, & Wendt, 1977; Fietkau, 1984; Fietkau & Kessel, 1981a; Fietkau, Kessel, & Tischler, 1982; Fietkau, Watts, Hassebrauck, & Tischler, 1980; Kley & Fietkau, 1979; Winter, 1981), and environmental learning and education (Bolscho, Eulefeld, & Seybold, 1980; Eulefeld, 1981; Eulefeld, Frey, & Haft, 1981; Fietkau & Kessel, 1981b; Lehmann, 1981; Minsel & Bente, 1981). The International Institute of Environment and Society in Berlin has conducted an international environment survey in Berlin, Bath, and Buffalo (Fietkau et al., 1980). Besides many local citizens' initiatives, there is a strong ecological (or environmental) movement politically active (the "Greens") for the protection of the environment, encouraging citizens to be more active in the defense of *Umwelt*. This activity has in itself become a social science topic (cf. Andritzki & Wahl-Terlinden, 1978; Beer, 1982; Buse, Nelles, & Oppermann, 1978; Fietkau & Hübner, 1978; Prester, Rohrmann, & Schellhammer, in press; Rammstedt, 1981; Rohrmann, 1983).

How environmental knowledge is acquired has become the object of a DFG-sponsored project by Spada and associates (1983). The related question of ecological thinking and problem solving has been taken up by Dörner (1975, 1982, 1983; Dörner, Kreuzig, Reither, & Stäudel, 1983).

Ecological Perspectives in Psychology

As indicated at the beginning of this chapter, environmental psychology in Germany was not only the result of psychology being confronted with and challenged by environmental problems. It was also, in a very basic sense, the outcome of a theoretical reorientation after the postwar wave of behaviorism had ebbed away. A lot of theorizing and modeling in ecological psychology is very closely related to the gradual and still ongoing transition from theories of behavior to theories of action. Traditionally, action has been the more comprehensive term for the active and interactive relationship of subjects with their social and material reality and was mainly used in philosophy and sociology. It used to be contrasted with the more impoverished S-R theoretical term behavior because action is goal-directed, meaningful, and systemic. As such, it is, in principle, the more appropriate concept for the complexities of everyday activities in natural settings, whereas *behavior* appears to be the adequate term for the highly restricted activities of organisms in lab settings. An exception may, however, be seen in naturalistic studies of behavior, for example, of spatial behavior (cf. Ahrens, 1969, with field vs. lab method). So, from the very first theoretical reflections and discussions, action theory became a kind of leitmotiv among ecopsychologists. Scholars who have written on this subject include Kaminski (1973a, 1978a, 1978b, 1983), Boesch (1971, 1976, 1978, 1980, 1983), Fuhrer (1983, 1984), Kruse (1986b), Lantermann (1980), Oerter (1979), and Winter (1983). Kaminski's theoretical thinking about an ecological action theory, even though originating from the area of problem solv-

ing, is closely but critically linked to Barker's notion of a "stream of behavior" and "behavior setting" (e.g., Kaminski, 1986). For structural as well as pragmatic reasons, models of action were related to, and partly derived from, models of problem solving. The obvious pragmatic reason is that much behavior in natural settings is of the problem-solving kind.

The association between problem-solving and action models has been facilitated by the elaboration of modern problem-solving models. It was mainly Dörner and his associates who, by means of ingenious simulation techniques, succeeded in bringing experimental problem-solving very close to everyday reality, thus increasing the ecological validity of his findings in a significant way (Dörner, 1975, 1982, 1983; Dörner, Kreuzig, Reither, & Stäudel, 1983). In order to solve problems, subjects in his experiments had to understand the systematic character of an environment, for example, its ecological balance, or they were bound to fail. In the same vein, Spada and his group analyzed the manner in which subjects acquired knowledge about ecological systems (Opwis & May, 1985; Spada, May, & Opwis, 1983; Spada & Opwis, 1985).

The more active emphasis put on the person in theories of action (as contrasted with the notion of a stimulus-controlled organism) also brought together models of action and of interaction. The latter had been discussed in the long-drawn-out person–situation controversy (cf. Buse & Pawlik, 1984; Lantermann, 1978, 1980; Pawlik, 1978; Pawlik & Buse, 1982, 1985).

A kindred, more comprehensive, but less formalized approach to the person–environment interaction is to be found in phenomenological psychology. It is the emphasis on the bodily nature of the subject, who is intentionally related to material, social, and historical environments, which suggests a metatheoretical framework for ecopsychological problems (Fischer, 1979; Graumann, 1974; Graumann & Schneider, in preparation; Kruse, 1974; Schneider, 1985, 1986). Efforts have been made to recover socially meaningful objects and spaces for a largely interpersonal but "immaterial" social psychology (Kruse, 1978; in press; Kruse & Graumann, 1978). A paradigm for this endeavor is the study of privacy (Kruse, 1980). Proceeding from rather unstructured methods such as in-depth interviews to more structured approaches such as multidimensional scaling and Rep Grid techniques, Kruse attempted to analyze personal constructs of privacy of individuals who differ, for example, as to state of life cycle, to housing conditions, and to professional status.

In the research areas of life-span development and socialization, the ecological perspective was adopted early, but it found different conceptualizations. As a pioneer for an ecologically oriented developmental psychology, Bronfenbrenner (1976) found a positive and lasting reception, resulting, for example, in a German contribution to the international research project on ecology of human development. Even before, Coerper, Hagen, and Thomae (1954) had directed a large government-sponsored longitudinal study of the German "postwar child," in which psychologists, pediatricians, and sociologists cooperated in order to discover the German postwar setting's possible (detrimental) effects on children's physical and mental health.

Today the notion of ecological orientation or perspective is common in developmental psychology, but it is also a heterogeneous conception. The different meanings of ecology were discussed by Eckensberger (1978, 1979), Trudewind (1975), Walter (1975, 1977, 1980, 1981), Walter and Oerter (1979), and Wohlwill (1981). The variety of meanings comes from the fact that sometimes the emphasis is placed on the social rather than the physical, on the objective rather than the subjective or experiential environment. Mainly in the study of socialization the emphasis is sometimes more sociological than psychological. It may, however, be possible to distinguish between three conceptions:

1. In a more traditional sense, developmental psychologists study the impact of social milieu factors on child development but "enriched" by physical objects (toys, child-rearing devices, etc.) (Wendt, Ewert, & Ewert, 1971). Based on taxonomies of family and school environments, Trudewind (1975; Trudewind & Husarek, 1979) studied the differential effects of specific environmental conditions on single variables, for example, learning and achievement motivation.

2. In a more modern sense, life-span developmental psychologists conceive of environment as the totality of social and physical forces acting on the development of an individual at a given stage. It is mainly the "social ecology" of the family (in different social strata, under different economic conditions, with different parental styles, attitudes, and "family climates"), (cf. Lüscher, Fisch, & Pape, 1985; Lukesch & Schneewind, 1978; Schneewind & Engfer, 1979; Schneewind, Beckmann, & Engfer, 1983) and of the school ("school climate") (Dreesmann, 1982) and the university (Dippelhofer-Stiem, 1983) that was to account for various forms of socialization.

The life-span scope of the new psychology of development requires differential analyses of age-specific environments, for example, for adolescents (Baacke, 1976; Hübner-Funk & Müller, 1981; Thomae & Endo, 1974) and for the aged (Lehr, 1976, 1979; Lehr & Olbrich, 1976; Tews, 1977; Thomae, 1976).

3. In its broadest sense, "social ecology" refers to the life spaces of individuals, as originally used by Muchow: the streets, blocks, and neighborhoods that contribute to "street socialization" (Zinnecker, 1980; Projektgruppe Jugendbüro, 1975, 1981; cf. also Walter, 1981). Another, more sociological conceptualization and a different methodological approach is found under the category *sociotope*. The term was coined in accordance with the original biotope that refers to a region uniform in environmental conditions and in its population for which it is the habitat. As contrasted with the more phenomenological "life-world" or "life space," the sociotope is objectively defined by statistics and census data (Bargel, Kuthe, & Mundt, 1977; Bargel, Fauser, & Mundt, 1981; Mundt, 1980).

It is mainly this expansion of environmental units into "regional" ones that attracts the interest of applied psychologists in the fields of counseling, intervention, and education (Fischer, 1978; Fischer & Wiedl, 1979; Kaminski, 1979a; Kaminski & Fleischer, 1984; Schultz-Gambard, 1978), and mental health (Fischer & Stephan, 1983; Heim, 1978; Kaminski, 1978c; Kommer & Röhrle, 1983; Schultz-Gambard, 1983). For some of these authors, ecological psychology blends with, or comprises, community psychology (Kommer & Röhrle, 1983). Also the first environmental psychology conference in Austria (cf. Janig, Löschenkohl, Schofnegger, Süssenbacher, 1982) focused on the application of psychological knowledge to coping with environmental problems.

Although in many developmental and clinical studies the use of the term *ecological* does not necessarily indicate conceptual and methodological clarity, for others the environmental problems or the ecological challenge has meant a methodological task, mainly about the development of so-called field methods (Brandstätter, 1977; Kaminski & Bellows, 1982; Pawlik & Buse, 1982, 1984) and the compatibility and comparability of experimental and field data (Mündelein & Schönpflug, 1984; Pawlik, 1976a; Schönpflug & Schulz, 1979). Considering the traditional sociocultural conception of *Umwelt* in German psychology, the impact of cross-cultural methodology is not surprising (Eckensberger, 1976a; Eckensberger & Kornadt, 1977).

33.3. PROSPECTS FOR THE ECOLOGICAL PERSPECTIVE IN GERMAN PSYCHOLOGY

If the authors of this review have been somewhat successful, then the present situation of environmental psychology in Germany should, seen from a distance, not be too much different from the international scene. Under closer scrutiny, however, differences should be seen that are due to a different history. Also, if it is true that to understand the present better one should know the past, then the same should be true for the future, only more so.

Because we were invited by the editors of this *Handbook* to conclude the review with a "prospective appraisal of future developments," given one's country's "unique cultural and theoretical orientation," we felt we should emphasize whatever is unique or culture-specific in an otherwise international and transcultural enterprise. That is why we were elaborate in the specific, but were restrictive in the common contributions to environmental psychology.

We also believe that we have brought forward what is necessary and justifiable for a prospective appraisal, namely an account of what has been going on and is being planned in this field of research. Borrowing two terms from linguistics, we would venture two kinds of prospective appraisal: (1) on the surface structure and (2) in the deep structures—an analogy that also assumes that the latter is considerably more speculative than the former. Accepting this risk, we would dare to propose that on both levels the evolution of an ecologically oriented psychology will make further progress. On the surface level there is, first of all, the steadily increasing stock of research within and outside the DFG- and government-sponsored projects. There have been, however, for some time, cuts in the various research budgets, as is true everywhere, but the readiness to sponsor is there and the attitude, in general, is positive. Three major publications are available or in press that should help in the establishment of ecopsychology: (1) a 6000-item documentation of international literature in environmental psychology (Kruse & Arlt, 1984); (2) an encyclopedic dictionary of key concepts in environmental psychology (Graumann, Kruse, & Lantermann, in preparation); and (3) a two-volume *Handbook of Ecological Psychology*, within the new *Encyclopedia of Psychology*. The first volume, to be edited by Kruse, addresses the more general and basic aspects of ecopsychology (as outlined at the beginning of this chapter), whereas the second volume, edited by Kaminski, deals with specific environments and their users as well as environmental stress and strain.

Because curricula in ecopsychology have been firmly established at some German universities (cf. Kaminski, 1978a), prospects for the field in terms of research, teaching, and training should be called "good." Not so good, however, is "the market"; openings for ecologically trained psychologists are still scarce, as one would expect a few years after the field's institutionalization. It is almost impossible to predict the development of what, by analogy, we have called the "deep structure." Here we again have to refer to the basic theoretical interest of some German psychologists who, in the 1970s, set about reorienting psychological research toward greater ecological representativeness. We have called this the "ecological perspective," a viewpoint that may benefit all fields of psychological research and, ultimately, may enrich psychology as a whole. To be better able to describe and to account for experience and behavior in terms of person–environment relationships or interactions has so far turned out to be a goal worth pursuing. We expect that the historically attested "subversive" nature of "ecology" gathers and maintains its stimulating force in Germany—and elsewhere. At present, one gets the impression that two major technological developments that are gradually changing both the environment and people's awareness of their *Umwelt* find increasing interest among psychologists. One is the ever-increasing armament that, although meant to better defend the country, paradoxically renders everybody's immediate environment more vulnerable, attackable, dangerous. For psychologists, this means a growing concern with risk perception, awareness of threat, and a new quality of environmental stress. The second type is the near omnipresence of computers and the invasion by new and more media. To the degree that our environment becomes more "electronic," it becomes more informational. Mainly, the home environment is changing in two opposite directions: (1) toward more interaction with more home or personal computers; and (2) toward more consumption with video, cable, and satellite TV bringing more entertainment for everybody. Both developments have their own social and psychological problems.

NOTES

1. Because we understand that in this *Handbook* there are no special reports on environmental research in the German Democratic Republic (GDR), Austria, and Switzerland,

we have tried to include such relevant publications from German-speaking countries as those that came to our attention. It may be that ecopsychological research in the GDR is underrepresented in our survey because whatever there is comes under categories from industrial psychology or ergonomics, which are only partly incorporated in our review.

Understanding that this *Handbook* will be mostly read by Americans or English-speaking readers, the authors of a chapter on environmental psychology in Germany are confronted with a specific, although familiar, problem. References to German publications are inevitable but not very helpful to those who do not read this language. Because this is the rule rather than the exception, we have tried to refer to English translations or original English publications of German authors wherever possible. The reader should, however, be cautioned with respect to the time lag between the original or first German communication of an idea and its later English version, which very often was due to the compulsory emigration of German psychologists when Hitler seized power in Germany and, 5 years later, in Austria. Because it is the editorial policy of this *Handbook* to introduce the reader to the historical and philosophical underpinnings of contemporary theories and research, the authors will have to refer to German literature, mainly of the first three decades of this century, the English versions of which—and that means accessibility to the American reader—came only very much later, and may, in the notorious cases of German emigrants in the 1930s, have become part and parcel of the American tradition in the interim.

2. We have, for example, *Ökologische Psychologie* (briefly, *Ökopsychologie*) in the internal terminology of the Deutsche Forschungsgemeinschaft (West Germany's national science foundation); also *Psychologische Ökologie* (psychological ecology). This mere verbal difference is *not* related to the distinction made by Brunswik between *psychological ecology* and *ecological psychology,* his two branches of environmental psychology (Brunswik, 1943). *Environmental psychology* is consistently translated by *Umweltpsychologie.*

3. One other feature of phenomenology, its insistence on the bodily nature of the subject of all intentional acts, has been explicated in a phenomenology of space (cf. Bollnow, 1963; Kruse, 1974). For the impact on the psychology of spatial experience and behavior, the American reader is referred to Straus (1966), Spiegelberg (1972), and van den Berg (1955).

4. The reader may be reminded of Koffka's distinction between geographical and behavioral environment (Koffka, 1935), with behavior occurring in the latter only. But for Hellpach, there is one nature only, yet with two different types of impacts on the organism: by means of *impressions* (another word for immediate experience) and of *influences* that cause physiological changes in the organism that, in turn, may be experienced.

5. While William Stern was chairman of the Psychological Institute of Hamburg University, Jacob von Uexküll had a very modest Institute for Environmental Research (since 1926). According to Stern, there was a lively exchange and communication between both institutions.

6. The transitive use of "live" *(leben)* is set off from *erleben* ("experience") in agreement with Stern's personalistic psychology (Stern, 1938) and with the phenomenological conception of "lived space" (von Durkheim, 1932).

7. Münsterberg wrote this first German textbook of *Psychotechnik* when he was already professor at Harvard.

8. For a limited account of the situation of psychology in the 1960s, see Graumann (1972).

9. Substantialism in psychology is a doctrine that behind all mental phenomena there is a mind substance.

10. Characterology was a European branch of the psychology of personality emphasizing character theory and diagnosis.

11. Now, in accordance with the new nonsexist regulations, one usually uses *person–environment.*

REFERENCES

Ahrens, H.J. (1969). Zur Systematik von Sitzplatzwahlen. *Psychologische Beiträge, 11,* 349–367.

Amelang, M., Tepe, K., Vagt, G., & Wendt, W. (1977). Mitteilung über einige Schritte der Entwicklung einer Skala zum Umweltbewußtsein. *Diagnostica, 23,* 86–88.

Andritzki, W., & Wahl-Terlinden, U. (1978). *Mitwirkung von Bürgerinitiativen an der Umweltpolitik.* Berlin: Umweltbundesamt, Bericht.

Arbeitsgruppe Umwelt-Taxonomie. (1973–74). *Bildungschancen und Umwelt* (2 Vols.). Braunschweig, F.R.G.: Westermann.

Arkkelin, D., & Veitch, R. (1978). The effect of number, interpersonal distance, sex, and acquaintance level on affective responses of males and females. Paper presented at the annual convention of the Midwestern Psychological Association, Chicago.

Atteslander, P., & Hamm, B. (Eds.). (1974). *Materialien zur Siedlungssoziologie.* Cologne, F.R.G.: Kiepenheuer & Witsch.

Baacke, D. (1976). Der ökologische Ansatz. In D. Baacke (Ed.), *Die 13-bis 16 Jährigen* (pp. 32–39). Munich: Urban & Schwarzenberg.

Bahr, H.F., & Gronemeyer, R. (Eds.). (1977). *Nachbarschaft im Neubaublock.* Weinheim, F.R.G.: Beltz.

Bahrdt, H.P. (1961). *Die moderne Großstadt. Soziologische Überlegungen zum Städtebau.* Reinbek, F.R.G.: Rowohlt.

Bahrdt, H.P. (1968). *Humaner Städtebau.* Hamburg, F.R.G.: Wegner.

Bailey, R., Branch, C.H.H., & Taylor, C.W. (1961). *Architectural psychology and psychiatry. An exploratory national research conference.* Salt Lake City: University of Utah.

Baltes, M.M., Barton, E.M., Orzech, M.J., & Lago, D. (1983). Die Mikroökologie von Bewohnern und Personal: Eine Behavior-Mapping-Studie im Altenheim. *Zeitschrift für Gerontologie, 16,* 18–26.

Bargel, T., Fauser, R., & Mundt, J.W. (1981). Soziale und räumliche Bedingungen der Sozialisation von Kindern in verschiedenen Soziotopen. Ergebnisse einer Befragung von Eltern in Landgemeinden und Stadtvierteln Nordhessens. In H. Walter (Ed.), *Region und Sozialisation* (Vol. 1, pp. 186–260). Stuttgart, F.R.G.: Frommann-Holtzboog.

Bargel, T., Kuthe, M., & Mundt, J.W. (1977). Zur Bestimmung sozialisationsrelevanter Areale (Soziotope). Modelle, Verfahren und Probleme. In Hoffmann-Nowotny, H.J. (Ed.), *Politisches Klima und Planung* (Soziale Indikatoren, Vol. 4, pp. 119–154). Frankfurt, F.R.G.: Campus.

Barker, R. (1963). On the nature of environment. *Journal of Social Issues, 19,* 17–38.

Barker, R. (1965). Explorations in ecological psychology. *American Psychologist, 20,* 1–14.

Barker, R. (1968). *Ecological psychology.* Stanford, CA: Stanford University Press.

Barker, R., & Wright, H.F. (1955). *Midwest and its children. The psychological ecology of an American town.* New York: Row & Peterson.

Bauer, F. (1981). *Sequenzeffekte in der umweltpsychologischen Forschung. Ein Beitrag zur Erklärung kontextbedingter Beurteilungseffekte.* Freiburg, F.R.G.: Hochschulverlag.

Bauer, F., Franke, J., & Gätschenberger, K. (1979a). Flurbereinigung und Erholungslandschaft — Empirische Studie zur Wirkung der Flurbereinigung auf den Erholungswert einer Landschaft. *Schriftenreihe des Bundesministers für Ernährung, Landwirtschaft und Forsten.* Heft 68. Reihe B: Flurbereinigung. Münster-Hiltrup, F.R.G: Landwirtschaftsverlag.

Bauer, F., Franke, J., & Gätschenberger, K. (1979b). Zur Messung der Erlebniswirkung von Landschaften. *Natur und Landschaft, 54,* 236–240.

Baumann, R., & Zinn, H. (1973). *Kindgerechte Wohnungen für Familien.* Bern, Switzerland: Eidgenössisches Büro für Wohnungsbau.

Becker, H., & Keim, D. (1972). *Wahrnehmung in der städtischen Umwelt. Möglicher Impuls für kollektives Handeln.* Berlin: Kiepert.

Becker, H., & Keim, D. (Eds.). (1977). *Gropiusstadt: Soziale Verhältnisse am Stadtrand. Soziologische Untersuchung einer Berliner Grobsiedlung.* Stuttgart, F.R.G.: Kohlhammer.

Beer, W. (1982). *Ökologische Aktiont und ökologisches Lernen.* Opladen, F.R.G.: Westdeutscher Verlag.

Bense, M. (1968). Semiotik und Urbanismus. *Archt, 3,* 23–25.

Bense, M. (1969). *Einführung in die informationstheoretische Ästhetik.* Reinbek, F.R.G.: Rowohlt.

Beorchia, D., & Engels, R. (1983). Psychische Gesundheit und Wohnumwelt. Ergebnisse einer empirischen Untersuchung in zwei Wiesbadener Wohngebieten. In D. Kommer & B. Röhrle (Eds.), *Ökologie und Lebensla-*

gen. Gemeindepsychologische (Perspektiven 3, pp. 91–96). Tübingen, F.R.G.: Deutsche Gesellschaft für Verhaltenstherapie.

Bergius, R. (1984). Sozialwissenschaftliche Forschungen zum Energieproblem der Wirtschaft. *Psychologische Rundschau, 35,* 185–197.

Bergius, R. (1982). Untersuchungen zum Energiekonsum als Aufgabe der Sozialpsychologie. In F. Seeger & U. Stadler (Eds.), *Die gesellschaftliche Verantwortung des Psychologen II* (pp. 72–82). Darmstadt, F.R.G.: Steinkopff.

Bergius, R., & Engemann, A. (1982). Sozialpsychologisches Verhaltensmodell: Modellentwicklung und Modelluntersuchungen zum Entscheidungsverhalten von Individuen und Gruppen in Fragen der Energiepolitik. *Research Report about a project funded by the Volkswagen Foundation.*

Berndt, H. (1968). *Das Gesellschaftsbild bei Stadtplanern.* Frankfurt: Suhrkamp.

Berndt, H., Lorenzer, A., & Horn, K. (1968). *Architektur als Ideologie.* Frankfurt: Suhrkamp.

Bierhoff, H.W. (1974). *Spielplätze und ihre Besucher.* Darmstadt, F.R.G.: Steinkopff.

Bierhoff, H.W., Schmitz-Scherzer, R., Kranzhoff, E., & Alexa, M. (1977). Spiel im Freien. Zur Erfassung der Umwelt des Kindes. In R. Schmitz-Scherzer (Ed.), *Aktuelle Beiträge zur Freizeitforschung* (pp. 102–115). Darmstadt, F.R.G.: Steinkopff.

Bodzenta, E., Speiser, J., & Thum, K. (1981). *Wo sind Großstädter daheim? Studien über Bindungen an das Wohnviertel mit einem Beitrag von R. Richter.* Vienna: Böhlan.

Boesch, E. (1971). *Zwischen zwei Wirklichkeiten. Prolegomena zu einer ökologischen Psychologie.* Bern, Switzerland: Huber.

Boesch, E. (1976). *Psychopathologie des Alltags.* Bern, Switzerland: Huber.

Boesch, E. (1978). Kultur und Biotop. In C.F. Graumann (Ed.), *Ökologische Perspektiven in der Psychologie* (pp. 11–32). Bern, Switzerland: Huber.

Boesch, E. (1980). *Kultur und Handlung.* Bern, Switzerland: Huber.

Boesch, E. (1983). *Das Magische und das Schöne. Zur Symbolik von Objekten und Handlungen.* Stuttgart, F.R.G.: Frommann-Holzboog.

Bollnow, O. (1971). *Mensch und Raum* (2nd ed.). Stuttgart, F.R.G.: Kohlhammer.

Bolscho, D., Eulefeld, G., & Seybold, H. (1980). *Umwelterziehung. Neue Aufgaben für die Schule.* Munich: Urban & Schwarzenberg.

Bornewasser, M., Mummendey, A., Linneweber, V., & Loeschper, G. (1982). Aggressive behaviour as social interaction. *School Psychology International, 3,* 157–160.

Bortz, J. (1972). Beiträge zur Anwendung der Psychologie auf den Städtebau II. Erkundungsexperiment zur Beziehung zwischen Fassadengestaltung und ihrer Wirkung auf den Betrachter. *Zeitschrift für Experimentelle und Angewandte Psychologie, 19,* 226–281.

Brandstätter, H. (1977). Wohlbefinden und Unbehagen. Entwurf eines Verfahrens zur Messung situationsabhängiger Stimmung. In W.H. Tack (Ed.), *Bericht vom 30. Kongreß der DGfPs in Regensburg 1976* (Vol. 2, pp. 60–62). Göttingen, F.R.G.: Hogrefe.

Bronfenbrenner, U. (1976). *Ökologische Sozialisationsforschung.* Stuttgart, F.R.G.: Klett.

Brunswik, E. (1943). Organismic achievement and environmental probability. *Psychological Review, 50,* 255–272.

Brunswik, E. (1947). *Systematic and representative design of psychological experiments.* Berkeley: University of California Press.

Bundeskriminalamt (Ed.). (1979). *Städtebau und Kriminalität* [Urban Planning and Crime]. Wiesbaden, F.R.G.: Bundeskriminalamt.

Bürk, S., & Strehlke, S. (1982). *Umwelt und Körperbehinderung—Unterschiede im Erleben, Verhalten und Urteil zwischen Rollstuhlabhängigen und Nichtbehinderten in ihrer städtischen Umwelt.* Unpublished diploma thesis, University of Heidelberg, Heidelberg, F.R.G.

Buse, L., & Pawlik, K. (1984). Inter-Setting-Korrelationen und Setting-Persönlichkeits-Wechselwirkungen: Ergebnisse einer Felduntersuchung zur Konsistenz von Verhalten und Erleben. *Zeitschrift für Sozialpsychologie, 15,* 44–59.

Buse, M., Nelles, W., & Opperman, R. (1978). *Determinante politischer Partizipation—Theorieansatz und empirische Überprüfung am Beispiel der Stadtsanierung Andernach,* Meisenheim am Glan, Germany: Hain.

Coerper, C., Hagen, W., & Thomae, H. (Eds.). (1954). *Deutsche Nachkriegskinder.* Stuttgart, F.R.G.: Thieme.

Craik, K. (1970). Environmental Psychology. In K. Craik, B. Kleinmuntz, R. Rosnow, R. Rosenthal, J.A. Cheyne, & R.H. Walters (Eds.), *New Directions in Psychology* (Vol. 4, pp. 1–121). New York: Holt, Rinehart & Winston.

Day, P. (1981a). Ökopsychologische Aspekte des Lebens mit Behinderten. *Blätter der Wohlfahrtspflege, 12,* 312–314.

Day, P. (1981b). Zur Psychologie der Lärmerzeugungs-, Unterlassungshandlung. In A. Schick (Ed.), *Akustik zwischen Physik und Psychologie* (pp. 214–221). Stuttgart, F.R.G.: Klett-Cotta.

Day, P. (1982). Beiträge der Ökopsychologie zur Bau- und Betriebsplanung eines Wohnheims für körperbehinderte Schüler. In U. Hensle (Ed.), *Einführung in die Arbeit mit Behinderten* (2nd ed., pp. 336–369). Heidelberg, F.R.G.: Quelle & Meyer.

Day, P. (1984). Zur Bewusstheit von Lärmerzeugungshandlungen. In A. Schick & K.P. Walcher (Eds.), *Beiträge zu einer Bedeutungslehre des Schalls* (pp. 27–38). Bern, Switzerland: Lang.

Deutsch, K.W. (1970). On social communication and the metropolis. In R. Gutman & D. Popenoe (Eds.), *Neighborhood, city, and metropolis: An integrated reader in urban sociology* (pp. 430–438). New York: Random House.

Deutsche Forschungsgemeinschaft; Senatsausschuß für Umweltforschung. (1976). *Beiträge zur Umweltforschung.* Bopphardt, F.R.G.: Bolt.

Deutsche UNESCO-Kommission (Ed.). (1978). *Stadtökologie.* Cologne: Verlag Dokumentation Saur KG.

Dippelhofer-Stiem, B. (1983). *Hochschule als Umwelt. Probleme der Konzeptualisierung, Komponenten des methodischen Zugangs und ausgewählte empirische Befunde.* Weinheim, F.R.G.: Beltz.

Dirlewanger, H., Geisler, E., Joedicke, J., & Magnano-Lampugnani, V. (1975). Der Einfluß der Umgebung beim Erleben von Architektur. *Bauen & Wohnen, 9,* 369–372.

Dirlewanger, H., Geisler, E., Magnano-Lampugnani, V. (1977). Architectur ohne Willkür. *Bild der Wissenschaft, 12,* 103–115.

Doelle, E.A. (1913). Reflexionen zur fundamentalen Duplexität der Umwelt. *Archiv für Fundamentalwissenschaften, 1,* 44–77.

Dörner, C.D. (1975). Wie die Menschen eine Welt verbessern wollten...und sie dabei zerstörten. *Bild der Wissenschaft, 12,* 48–53.

Dörner, D. (1982). The ecological conditions of thinking. In D.R. Griffin (Ed.), *Animal mind-human mind* (Dahlem Conferences 1982, pp. 95–112). Berlin: Springer-Verlag.

Dörner, D. (1983). Heuristic and cognition in complex systems. In R. Groner, M. Groner, & W.F. Bischof (Eds.), *Methods of heuristics* (pp. 89–107). Hillsdale, NJ: Erlbaum.

Dörner, D., Kreuzig, H., Reither, F., & Stäudel, T. (Eds.). (1983). *Lohhausen. Vom Umgang mit Unbestimmtheit und Komplexität.* Bern, Switzerland: Huber.

Dorsch, P. (1972). *Eine neue Heimat in Perlach. Das Einleben als Kommunikationsprozeß.* Munich: Callwey.

Durth, W. (1977). *Die Inszenierung der Alltagswelt. Zur Kritik der Stadtgestaltung.* Braunschweig, F.R.G.: Vieweg.

Eckensberger, L.H. (1976a). Der Beitrag kulturvergleichender Forschung zur Fragestellung der Umweltpsychologie. In G. Kaminski (Ed.), *Umweltpsychologie* (pp. 73–98). Stuttgart, F.R.G.: Klett.

Eckensberger, L.H. (1976b). Bericht über das DFG-Kolloquium, Ökosysteme in interdisziplinärer Sicht'. Schloß Reisensburg 17–19.6.1976. *Psychologische Rundschau, 27,* 295–296.

Eckensberger, L. (1978). Die Grenzen des ökologischen Ansatzes in der Psychologe. In C.F. Graumann (Ed.), *Ökologische Perspektiven in der Psychologie* (pp. 49–76). Bern, Switzerland: Huber.

Eckensberger, L.H. (1979). Die ökologische Perspektive in

der Entwicklungspsychologie: Herausforderung oder Bedrohung? In H. Walter & R. Oerter (Eds.), *Ökologie und Entwicklung* (pp. 264–281). Donauwörth, F.R.G.: Ludwig Auer.

Eckensberger, L.H., & Burgard, P. (1977). *Ökosysteme in interdisziplinärer Sicht.* (Rep. No. 49). Saarbrücken, F.R.G: Universität des Saarlandes, Arbeiten der Fachrichtung Psychologie.

Eckensberger, L.H., & Kornadt, H.J. (1977). The mutual relevance of the cross-cultural and the ecological perspective in psychology. In H. McGurk (Ed.), *Ecological factors in human development* (pp. 219–227). Amsterdam: North-Holland.

English, H.B., & English, A.C. (1958). *A comprehensive dictionary of psychology and psychoanalytical terms.* New York: Longsman Green.

Erke, H. (1975). Psychologische Untersuchungen zum Überquerverhalten der Fußgänger in Abhängigkeit von Farb-und Formmerkmalen von Kraftfahrzeugen. *Zeitschrift für Verkehrssicherheit, 21,* 173–182.

Erke, R., & Zimolong, B. (1978). *Verkehrskonflikte im Innerortsbereich.* Cologne, F.R.G.: Bundesminster für Verkehr und Bundesanstalt für Straßenwesen.

Eulefeld, G. (1981). Veränderung des Umweltbewußtseins. Eine Aufgabe der Schule? In H.J. Fietkau & H. Kessel (Eds.), *Umweltlernen. Veränderungen des Umweltbewußtseins* (pp. 187–220). Königstein (Ts.), F.R.G.: Hain.

Eulefeld, G., Frey, K., & Haft, H. (1981). *Ökologie und Umwelterziehung.* Stuttgart, F.R.G.: Kohlhammer.

Fatke, R. (1977). *Schulumwelt und Schülerverhalten.* Munich: Piper.

Feldhusen, G. (1975). *Soziologie für Architekten.* Stuttgart, F.R.G.: Deutsche Verlags-Anstalt.

Fietkau, H.J. (1984). *Bedingungen ökologischen Handelns.* Weinheim, F.R.G.: Beltz.

Fietkau, H.J. (1981). Umweltpsychologie und Umweltkrise. In H.J. Fietkau & D. Görlitz (Eds.), *Umwelt und Alltag in der Psychologie* (pp. 113–135). Weinheim, F.R.G.: Beltz.

Fietkau, H.J., & Görlitz, D. (Eds.). (1981). *Umwelt und Alltag in der Psychologie.* Weinheim, F.R.G.: Beltz.

Fietkau, H.J., & Hübner, H.J. (1978). *Bürgerengagement in Umweltschutz-Bürgerinitiativen.* Berlin: International Institute for Environment and Society.

Fietkau, H.J., & Kessel, H. (1981a). Beiträge aus den Sozialwissenschaften. In H.J. Fietkau & H. Kessel (Eds.), *Umweltlernen. Veränderungsmöglichkeiten des Umweltbewußtseins* (pp. 15–51). Königstein (Ts.), F.R.G.: Hain.

Fietkau, H.J., & Kessel, H. (Eds.). (1981b). *Umweltlernen. Veränderungsmöglichkeiten des Umweltbewußtseins.* Königstein (Ts.), F.R.G.: Hain.

Fietkau, H.J., Kessel, H., & Tischler, W. (1982). *Umwelt im Spiegel der öffentlichen Meinung.* Frankfurt: Campus.

Fietkau, H.J., Watts, N., Hassebrauck, M., & Tischler, W. (1980). *Umweltbewußtsein im internationalen Vergleich. Das "International Environment Survey." Methodische Entwicklung und Ergebnisse. Berlin, Bath und Buffalo 1979* (Project Report). Berlin: International Institute for Environment and Society.

Fischer, C.S. (1976). *The urban experience.* New York: Harcourt, Brace, Jovanovich.

Fischer, M. (1978). Ökologische Bedingungen für Verhaltensauffälligkeiten in der Schule. In J. Lohmann & B. Minsel (Eds.), *Störungen im Schulalltag* (pp. 157–181). Munich: Urban & Schwarzenberg.

Fischer, M. (1979). Phänomenologische Analysen der Person-Umwelt-Beziehung. In S.H. Filipp (Ed.), *Selbstkonzept-Forschung. Probleme, Befunde, Perspektiven* (pp. 47–73). Stuttgart, F.R.G.: Klett-Cotta.

Fischer, M. (1981a). Mensch und physische Umwelt. Eine Beziehungsanalyse aus der Sicht der Ökopsychologie. *Jahrbuch für Regionalwissenschaft, 2,* 63–87.

Fischer, M. (1981b). Möglichkeiten und Probleme einer Bestimmung von Zielen und Maßnahmen der Stadtplanung aus der Sicht der Psychologie. In H. Haase & W. Molt (Eds.), *Handbuch der Angewandten Psychologie: Vol. 3. Markt und Umwelt* (pp. 410–431). Landsberg am Lech, F.R.G.: Modern Industrie.

Fischer, M. (1982). Wohnortwechsel als psychischer Anpassungsprozeß. In H. Janig, E. Löschenkohl, J. Schofnegger, & G. Süssenbacher (Eds.), *Umweltpsychologie. Bewältigung neuer und veränderter Umwelten* (pp. 293–299). Vienna: Literas.

Fischer, M. (1986). Die Gestaltung des Lebensraumes Behinderter aus ökopsychologischer Sicht. In K.H. Wiedl (Ed.). *Rehabilitationspsychologie* (pp. 117–137). Stuttgart, F.R.G.: Kohlhammer.

Fischer, M., & Fischer, U. (1981). Wohnortwechsel und Verlust der Ortsidentität als nicht-normative Lebenskrisen. In S.H. Filipp (Ed.), *Kritische Lebensereignisse* (pp. 139–153). Munich: Urban & Schwarzenberg.

Fischer, M., & Stephan, E. (1983). Zur Analyse und Evaluation von Therapiesituationen aus ökopsychologischer Perspektive. In D. Kommer & B. Röhrle (Eds.), *Ökologie und Lebenslagen. Gemeindepsychologische Perspektiven 3* (pp. 43–52). Tübingen, F.R.G.: Deutsche Gesellschaft für Verhaltenstherapie.

Fischer, M., & Wiedl, K.H. (1973). Variationsmotivation. *Psychologische Beiträge, 15,* 478–521.

Fischer, M., & Wiedl, K.H. (1979). Umweltplanung als pädagogisch-psychologische Intervention. Grundvoraussetzungen, Ansatzpunkte und Prinzipien. In J. Brandstätter, G. Reinert, & K.A. Schneewind (Eds.), *Probleme und Perspektiven der Pädagogischen Psychologie* (pp. 445–464). Stuttgart, F.R.G.: Klett-Cotta.

Fischer, M., & Wiedl, K.H. (1981). Variationsmotivation. Empirische und theoretische Beiträge zur Weiterentwicklung eines persönlichkeitspsychologischen Konstrukts. In H.G. Voss & H. Keller (Eds.), *Neugierforschung* (pp. 109–143). Weinheim, F.R.G.: Beltz.

Flade, A. (1981a). Theorien und Erkenntnisse über bauliche Faktoren und Kriminalität. In Institut Wohnen und Umwelt (Ed.), *Wohnungspolitik am Ende?* (pp. 257–272). Opladen, F.R.G.: Westdeutscher Verlag.

Flade, A. (1981b). Umweltpsychologie und Verkehrsplanung. In H. Haase & W. Molt (Eds.), *Handbuch der Angewandten Psychologie, Vol. 3. Markt und Umwelt* (pp. 432–445). Landsberg am Lech, F.R.G.: Moderne Industrie.

Flade, A. (1981c). Objektive und subjektive Verkehrssicherheit von Kindern. *Zeitschrift für Verkehrssicherheit, 27,* 4–7.

Flade, A. (1983a). Die Jugendkriminalität in einer Gemeinde aus ökopsychologischer Perspektive. In D. Kommer & B. Röhrle (Eds.), *Ökologie und Lebenslage. Gemeindepsychologische Perspektiven 3* (pp. 86–90). Tübingen, F.R.G.: Deutsche Gesellschaft für Verhaltenstherapie.

Flade, A. (1983b). Jugendkriminalität in einer Neubausiedlung. *Monatsschrift für Kriminologie und Strafrechtsreform, 66,* 197–206.

Flade, A. (1984). *Jugendkriminalität in Neubausiedlungen. Eine empirische Untersuchung.* Weinheim, F.R.G.: Beltz.

Franke, J. (1967). Das Problem einer Anwendung der Psychologie auf die Umweltgestaltung—Eine Betrachtung zum Verhältnis zwischen Psychologie und Praxis. *Psychologische Rundschau, 18,* 155–168.

Franke, J. (1969). Zum Erleben der Wohnumgebung. *Stadtbauwelt, 24,* 292–295.

Franke, J. (1974). Stadtgestalt als Wissenschaft. In A. Markelin & M. Trieb (Eds.), *Mensch und Stadtgestalt* (pp. 70–78). Stuttgart, F.R.G.: Deutsche Verlags-Anstalt, Deutsche Gesellschaft für Verhaltenstherapie.

Franke, J. (1976). Die Erlebniswirkung von Wohnumgebung—Ein empirischer Ansatz der ökologischen Psychologie. In G. Kaminski (Ed.), *Umweltpsychologie* (pp. 134–143). Stuttgart, F.R.G.: Klett.

Franke, J. (1982). Erlebniswirkung der Natur in der Solararchitektur. In LOG ID (Ed.), *Mensch und Pflanze. Beiträge zum Projekt LOG ID Leben mit Pflanzen* (pp. 12–14). Karlsruhe, F.R.G.: Müller.

Franke, J., Bauer, F., & Kühlmann, T. (1982). Stadtplanung und Bürgerbeteiligung—Die Kompetenz der Laien. *Forschung, Mitteilungen der DFG, 4,* 22–24.

Franke, J., Bauer, F., & Kühlmann, T. (1983). Zur Prognostizierbarkeit der Eindruckswirkung von Wohnquartieren. *Landschaft Stadt, 15,* 72–79.

Franke, J., & Bortz, J. (1972). Beiträge zur Anwendung der Psychologie auf den Städtebau. I. Vorüberlegungen zur Beziehung zwischen Siedlungsgestaltung und Erleben der Wohnumgebung. *Zeitschrift für Experimentelle und Angewandte Psychologie, 19,* 76–108.

Franke, J., & Hoffmann, K. (1974). Beiträge zur Anwendung der Psychologie auf den Städtebau. III. Allgemeine Strukturkomponenten des Images von Siedlungsgebieten. *Zeitschrift für Experimentelle und Angewandte Psychologie, 21,* 181–225.

Franke, J., & Hoffmann, K. (1978). Informationsinstrumente zur Berücksichtigung der Bürgerurteile in der Planungsphase—Zur Prognose von Bewohnerreaktionen in geplanten Wohngebieten. In F. Böltken, J. Franke, K. Hoffmann, & M. Pfaff (Eds.), *Lebensqualität in neuen Städten— Planungskonzeption und Bürgerurteile* (pp. 40–90). Göttingen, F.R.G.: Vandenhoeck & Ruprecht.

Franke, J., & Rothgang, G.W. (1975). Beiträge zur Anwendung der Psychologie auf den Städtebau. IV. Zusammenhänge zwischen baulichen Merkmalen und dem Image von Siedlungsgebieten. *Zeitschrift für Experimentelle und Angewandte Psychologie, 22,* 181–225.

Friedrichs, J. (1979). Mensch und Umwelt aus der Sicht des Soziologen. In Bundeskriminalamt (Ed.), *Städtebau und Kriminalität.* Wiesbaden, F.R.G.: Bundeskriminalamt.

Fuhrer, U. (1983). Überlegungen zur Ökologisierung handlungs-psychologischer Theoriebildung. In L. Montada, K. Reusser, & G. Steiner (Eds.), *Kognition und Handeln* (pp. 54–63). Stuttgart, F.R.G.: Klett.

Fuhrer, U. (1984). *Mehrfachhandeln in dynamischen Umfeldern.* Göttingen, F.R.G.: Hogrefe.

Funkkolleg. (1983). Mensch und Umwelt. In T. Dahlhoff, H. Bick, K. Hansmeyer, & G. Olschowy (Eds.) Frankfurt: Fischer.

Garbrecht, D. (1976). Räume, Verhalten und Stadtgestaltung. *Baumeister, 73,* 1002–1008, 1012.

Garbrecht, D. (1981). *Gehen. Plädoyer für das Leben in der Stadt.* Weinheim, F.R.G.: Beltz.

Geisler, E. (1977). Psychologische Beiträge für die Bauplanung. *Architekturpsychologische Aspekte innovativen Bauens* (pp. 59–67). Stuttgart, F.R.G.: Krämer.

Geisler, E. (1978). *Psychologie für Architekten.* Stuttgart, F.R.G.: Deutsche Verlags-Anstalt.

Geisler, E. (1981). Bedürfnisanalyse und Planung. Fallbeispiel: Heim für Nichtseßhafte. In H. Haase & W. Molt (Eds.), *Handbuch der Angewandten Psychologie. Vol. 3: Markt & Umwelt.* Landsberg am Lech, F.R.G.: Moderne Industrie, 342–359.

Goffman, E. (1972). *Relations in public: Microstudies of the public order.* New York: Harper & Row.

Graumann, C.F. (1972). The state of psychology. *International Journal of Psychology, 7,* 123–134, 199–204.

Graumann, C.F. (1974). Psychology and the world of things. *Journal of Phenomenological Psychology, 4,* 389–404.

Graumann, C.F. (1976). Die ökologische Fragestellung—50 Jahre nach Hellpachs, 'Psychologie der Umwelt'. In G. Kaminski (Ed.), *Umweltpsychologie* (pp. 21–25). Stuttgart, F.R.G.: Klett.

Graumann, C.F. (Ed.). (1978). *Ökologische Perspektiven in der Psychologie*. Bern, Switzerland: Huber.

Graumann, C.F. (1979). Planung für den Alltag in sozialpsychologischer Perspektive. In G. Lammers (Ed.),*Aktivitätsmuster für die Stadtplanung* (pp. 337–350). Seminarberichte des Instituts für Städtebau und Landesplanung; Technical University, Karlsruhe.

Graumann, C.F. (1981). Psychology: Humanistic or human? In J.R. Royce & L.P. Mos (Eds.), *Humanistic psychology* (pp. 3–18). New York: Plenum.

Graumann, C.F. (1983a). Phenomenology. In R. Harré & R. Lamb (Eds.), *Encyclopedic dictionary of psychology* (pp. 470–472). Oxford, England: Blackwell.

Graumann, C.F. (1983b). Umwelt. In R. Harré & R. Lamb (Eds.), *Encyclopedic dictionary of psychology* (p. 647). Oxford, England: Blackwell.

Graumann, C.F., & Kruse, L. (1984). Masses, foules et densité. In S. Moscovici (Ed.), *Psychologie sociale* (pp. 513–538). Paris: Presses Universitaires de France.

Graumann, C.F., & Schneider, G. (in press). *Städtische Umwelt. Identität und Identifikation*. Munich: Urban & Schwarzenberg.

Graumann, C.F., Schneider, G., & Kany, W. (1981). Projektbericht: Umweltrepräsentation und umweltbezogenes Selbstverständnis. (Am Beispiel der Stadt). *ZUMA-Nachrichten 25–50*.

Günther, R., & Limbourg, M. (1976). Dimensionen der Verkehrswelt von Kindern. *Unfall-und Sicherheitsforschung Straßenverkehr, Heft 4*. Cologne, F.R.G..

Guski, R., & Rohrmann, B. (1981). Psychological aspects of environmental noise. *Zeitschrift für Umweltpolitik, 2,* 183–212.

Haeckel, E. (1866). *Generelle Morphologie der Organismen* (2 Vols.). Berlin: Reimer.

Hamm, B. (1973). *Betrifft: Nachbarschaft* Gütersloh, F.R.G.: Bertelsmann.

Harloff, H.J. (1973). Psychologische und soziologische Aspekte der Wohnsanierung. *Kölner Zeitschrift für Soziologie und Sozialpsychologie, 25,* 75–90.

Harré, R. (1979). *Social being—A theory for social psychology*. Oxford, England: Blackwell.

Harré, R., & Lamb, R. (Eds.). (1983). *Encyclopedic dictionary of psychology*. Oxford, England: Blackwell.

Hawel, W. (1967). Untersuchungen eines Bezugssystems für die psychologische Schallbewertung. *Arbeitswissenschaft, 6,* 50–53.

Hawley, A.H. (1950). *Human ecology: A theory of community structure*. New York: Ronald.

Heidemann, C. (1972). Städtebauliche Determinanten der Aktionsbereiche von Hausfrauen. *Hauswirtschaft und Wissenschaft, 20,* 22–27.

Heidemann, C., & Stapf, K.H. (1969). *Die Hausfrau in ihrer städtischen Umwelt. Eine empirische Studie zur urbanen Ökologie am Beispiel Braunschweigs* (Vol. 4). Braunschweig, F.R.G.: Veröffentlichungsreihe des Instituts für Stadtbauwesen.

Heil, K. (1971). *Kommunikation und Entfremdung. Menschen am Stadtrand—Legende und Wirklichkeit*. Stuttgart, F.R.G.: Krämer.

Heim, E. (Ed.). (1978). *Milieu-Therapie. Erlernen sozialer Verhaltensmuster in der psychiatrischen Klinik*. Bern, Switzerland: Huber.

Held, M. (1982). *Verkehrsmittelwahl der Verbraucher. Beitrag einer kognitiven Motivationstheorie zur Erklärung der Nutzung alternativer Verkehrsmittel*. Berlin: Duncker & Humblot.

Held, M., Verron, H., & von Rosenstiel, L. (1981). Verkehrsmittelwahl. In H. Haase & W. Molt (Eds.), *Handbuch der Angewandten Psychologie: Vol. 3. Markt & Umwelt* (pp. 386–409). Landsberg am Lech, F.R.G.: Verlag Moderne Industrie.

Hellpach, W. (1902). *Nervosität und Kultur*. Berlin: Räde.

Hellpach, W. (1924). Psychologie der Umwelt. In E. Abderhalden (Ed.), *Handbuch der biologischen Arbeitsmethoden*. Abt. VI. Methoden der experimentellen Psychologie. Teil C, Heft 3. Berlin: Urban & Schwarzenberg.

Hellpach, W. (1939). *Mensch und Volk der Großstadt*. Stuttgart, Germany: Enke.

Hellpach, W. (1977). *Die geopsychischen Erscheinungen: Wetter, Klima und Landschaft in ihrem Einfluß auf das Seelenleben*. Engelmann, Leipzig, 1911. 8th and last edition under the title "Geopsyche." Stuttgart, F.R.G.: Enke.

Herlyn, U. (1970). *Wohnen im Hochhaus*. Stuttgart, F.R.G.: Krämer.

Herlyn, U. (Ed.). (1980). *Großstadtstrukturen und ungleiche Lebensbedingungen in der Bundesrepublik*. Frankfurt: Campus.

Hoffmann, L., Kattmann, U., Lucht, H., & Spada, H. (1975). Materialien zum Unterrichtsversuch: Kernkraftwerke in der Einstellung von Jugendlichen. *IPN Arbeitsbericht* (No. 15). Kiel, F.R.G.: Institut fürdie Pädagogik der Naturwissenschaften.

Höllhuber, D. (1977). Mental Maps und innerstädtische Wohnstandortswahl. In G. Lammers (Ed.), *Verhalten in der Stadt* (pp. 275–305). Karlsruhe, F.R.G.: Seminarberichte des Instituts für Städtebau und Landesplanung.

Höllhuber, D. (1979). *Plädoyer für eine sozialpsychologisch fundierte Humangeographie*. (Habilitationsschrift) Erlangen, F.R.G.

Höllhuber, D. (1982). *Innerstädtische Umzüge in Karlsruhe. Plädoyer für eine sozialpsychologisch fundierte Humangeographie*. Erlangen, F.R.G.: Palm & Enke.

Höltershinken, D., Hilker, K., Janßen, K., Kork, H., & Schulz, A. (1971). Feldstudien öffentlicher Kinderspielplätze. *Schule und Psychologie, 18,* 200–215.

Hormuth, S. (1983). Veränderungen des Ortes und des Selbst. In G. Lüer (Ed.). *Bericht vom 33. Kongreß der Deutschen Gesellschaft für Psychologie* (pp. 634–639). Mainz 1982. Göttingen, F.R.G.: Hogrefe.

Hormuth, S. (1984). Transitions in commitments to roles and self concept change: Relocation as a paradigm. In V. Allen & E. van de Vliert (Eds.), *Role transitions: Explorations and explanations* (pp. 109–124). New York: Plenum.

Hubbertz, K.P. (1979). Wohnen und psychische Störungen. *Mitteilungen der Deutschen Gesellschaft für Verhaltenstherapie,* (2), 283–302.

Hübner-Funk, S., & Müller, H.U. (1981). Hauptschüler vor dem Eintritt in die Arbeitswelt. Eine vergleichende sozialökologische Studie aus bayrischen Stadtgebieten. In H. Walter (Ed.), *Region und Sozialisation* (Vol.2, pp. 137–187). Stuttgart, F.R.G.: Frommann-Holzboog.

Husserl, E. (1970). *The crisis of the European sciences and transcendental phenomenology* (David Carr, Trans.). Evanston, IL: Northwestern University Press.

Irle, M. (1960). Gemeindesoziologische Untersuchungen zur Ballung Stuttgart. *Mitteilungen aus dem Institut für Raumforschung,* Heft 42. Bad Godesberg, F.R.G.: Bundesanstalt für Landeskunde und Raumforschung.

Janig, H., Löschenkohl, E., Schofnegger, J., & Süssenbacher, G. (Eds.). (1982). Umweltpsychologie. Bewältigung neuer und veränderter Umwelten. *Bericht 23. Kongreß der Berufsverbände österreichischer Psychologen.* Vienna: Literas.

Jeggle, U. (1978). *Leben auf dem Dorf. Zur Sozialgeschichte des Dorfes und zur Sozialpsychologie seiner Bewohner.* Opladen, F.R.G.: Westdeutscher Verlag.

Joedicke, J. (Ed.). (1977). *Architekturpsychologische Aspekte innovativen Bauens.* Stuttgart, F.R.G.: Krämer.

Joedicke, J., Dirlewanger, H., Geisler, E., & Knoerzer, J. (1974). Entwerfen mit Hilfe empirischer Gestaltkriterien. *Bauen & Wohnen,* 385–388.

Joedicke, J., Dirlewanger, H., Geisler, E., & Magnano-Lampugnani, V. (1975). Baumerkmale und Nutzerreaktionen als Gestaltungshilfe im architektonischen Bauprozeß. In J. Joedicke (Ed.) Architekturpsychologische Forslump. *Psychologie und Bauen* (pp. 31–60). Stuttgart, F.R.G.: Krämer.

Joerges, B. (1977). *Gebaute Umwelt und Verhalten.* Baden-Baden, F.R.G.: Nomos.

Joerges, B. (1981). Zur Soziologie und Sozialpsychologie des alltäglichen technischen Wandels. In G. Ropohl (Ed.), *Interdisziplinäre Technikforschung* (Schriftenreihe Angewandte Innovationsforschung, Vol. 3, pp. 137–151). Berlin: Schmidt.

Jungermann, H. (1986). Die öffentliche Diskussion Technologischer Mega-Themen: Eine Herausforderung für Experten und Bürger. In H. Jungermann, W. Pfaffenberger, G.F. Schäfer, & W. Wild (Eds.), *Die Analyse der Sozialverträglichkeit für Technologiepolitik: Perspektiven und Interpretationen* (pp. 92–101). Munich: High Tech-Verlag.

Jungermann, H. (1982a). Zur Wahrnehmung und Akzeptierung von Risiko bei Großtechnologien. *Psychologische Rundschau, 33,* 1–21.

Jungermann, H., Pfaffenberger, W., Schäfer, G.F., & Wild, W. (Eds.). (1986). *Die Analyse der Sozialverträglichkeit für Technologiepolitik: Perspektiven und Interpretationen.* Munich: High Tech-Verlag.

Kalwitzki, K.P. (1983). *Ökologische Psychologie und Stadtentwicklung.* Mühlheim, F.R.G.: Westarp.

Kaminski, G. (1985). Zehn Jahre Ökopsychologie. In D. Albert (Ed.), *Bericht über den 34. Kongreß der Deutschen Gesellschaft für Psychologie in Wien 1984* (pp. 837–840). Göttingen, F.R.G.: Hogrefe.

Kaminski, G. (1973a). Bewegungshandlungen als Bewältigungd von Mehrfachaufgaben. *Sportwissenschaft, 3,* 233–250.

Kaminski, G. (1973b). Umweltschutz aus der Sicht der Psychologie. *Umschau in Wissenschaft und Technik, 73,* 240–242.

Kaminski, G. (1975a). Bericht über das Kolloquium 'Psychologische Aspekte der Umweltforschung' Februar 1975 in Bad Godesberg. *Psychologische Rundschau, 26,* 243–244.

Kaminski, G. (1975b). Einführung in den Problemkreis Psychologie und Bauen aus der Sicht des Psychologen. In J. Joedicke (Ed.), *Architekturpsychologische Forschung. Psychologie und Bauen* (pp. 6–30). Stuttgart, F.R.G.: Krämer.

Kaminski, G. (Ed.). (1976). *Umweltpsychologie.* Stuttgart, F.R.G.: Klett.

Kaminski, G. (1978a). Behavior and Environment: Ökologische Fragestellung in der Allgemeinen Psychologie. In C.F. Graumann (Ed.), *Ökologische Perspektiven in der Psychologie* (pp. 83–97). Bern, Switzerland: Huber.

Kaminski, G. (1978b). Environmental Psychology. *German Journal of Psychology, 2,* 225–239.

Kaminski, G. (1978c). Ökopsychologie und Klinische Psychologie. In U. Baumann, K.H. Berbalk, & G. Seidenstücker (Eds.), *Klinische Psychologie. Trends in Forschung und Praxis* (Vol. 1, pp. 32–73). Bern, Switzerland: Huber.

Kaminski, G. (1979a). Ökologische Perspektiven in pädagogisch-psychologischer Theoriebildung und deren Konsequenzen. In J. Brandstätter, G. Reinert, & K.A. Schneewind (Eds.), *Pädagogische Psychologie: Probleme und Perspektiven* (pp. 105–129). Stuttgart, F.R.G.: Klett.

Kaminski, G. (1979b). Stadt als Lebensraum in der Sicht der Psychologie. In: Bundesgemeinschaft der Architektenkammer (Ed.), *Die Stadt als Lebensraum* (pp. 101–108). Bonn.

Kaminski, G. (1982). Leben mit grüner Solararchitektur in psychologischer Perspektive. In LOG ID (Ed.), *Mensch und Pflanze. Beiträge Projekt LOG ID: Leben mit Pflanzen* (pp. 40–43). Karlsruhe, F.R.G.: Müller.

Kaminski, G. (1983). Probleme einer ökopsychologischen Handlungstheorie. In L. Montada, K. Reussser, & G. Steiner (Eds.), *Aebli-Gedenkband: 'Kognition und Handeln'* (pp. 35–53). Stuttgart, F.R.G.: Klett.

Kaminski, G. (1986). *Ordnung und Variabilität im Alltagsgeschehen*. Göttingen, F.R.G.: Hogrefe.

Kaminski, G., & Bellows, S. (1982). Feldforschung in der ökologischen Psychologie. In J.L. Patry (Ed.), *Feldforschung. Methoden und Probleme sozialwissenschaftlicher Forschung unter natürlichen Bedingungen* (pp. 87–116). Bern, Switzerland: Huber.

Kaminski, G., & Fleischer, F. (1984). Ökologische Psychologie: Ökopsychologische Untersuchung und Beratung (pp. 329–358). In H.A. Hartmann & R. Haubl (Eds.), *Psychologische Begutachtung*. Munich: Urban & Schwarzenberg.

Kany, W., & Schneider, G. (1985). *Ein linguistisch fundiertes inhaltsanalytisches System zur Erfassung des redferentiellen und prädikativen Gehalts verbaler Daten*. Bericht aus dem Psychologischen Institut der Universität Heidelberg (Research report No. 42).

Karmann, P. (1985). *Die Wahrnehmung von baulich- räumlicher Umwelt bei Kindern. Eine Untersuchung zum Vorstellungsbild des Klassenzimmers*. Frankfurt: Lang.

Kasper, L., & Krewer, B. (1982). *Die handlungstheoretische ekonstruktion von Mensch-Umwelt-Beziehungen am eispiel subjektiver erlebter Umweltgüte junger und lter Menschen in der Stadt Saarbrücken*. Unpublished Diploma Thesis, F.R.G.: University of Saarbrücken.

Kastka, J. (1976). Untersuchungen zur Belästigungswirkung der Umweltbedingungen Verkehrslärm und Industriegerüche. In G. Kaminski (Ed.), *Umweltpsychologie* (pp. 187–223). Stuttgart, F.R.G.: Klett.

Kastka, J. (1978). Zur inhaltlichen Bedeutung von Geruchsbelästigung und ihrer Bewertung. In K. Aurand (Ed.), *Organische Verunreinigungen in der Umwelt. Erkennen, Bewerten, Vermindern* (pp. 483–497). Berlin: Schmidt.

Kastka, J. (1981a). Psychologische Indikatoren der Verkehrslärmbelästigung. In A. Schick (Ed.), *Akustik zwischen Physik und Psychologie* (pp. 68–86). Stuttgart, F.R.G.: Klett-Cotta.

Kastka, J. (1981b). Untersuchungen zur subjektiven Wirksamkeit von Maßnahmen gegen Verkehrslärm und deren Moderation durch nichtakustische Faktoren. In H. Haase & W. Molt (Eds.), *Handbuch der Angewandten Psychologie: Vol. 3. Markt & Umwelt* (pp. 468–485). Landsberg am Lech, F.R.G.: Moderne Industrie.

Kastka, J. (1981c). Zum Einfluß verkehrsberuhigender Maßnahmen auf Lärmbelastung und Lärmbelästigung. *Zeitschrift für Lärmbekämpfung, 28*, 25–30.

Kastka, J. (1982). Erfassung und Bewertung von Gerüchen und ihrer Belästigungswirkung. In *Minderung von Geruchsstoff-Emissionen aus stationären Anlagen. Tagung Wiesbaden 1981. VDI-Berichte 46.*

Kastka, J. (1984). Zum Beitrag kausal-attributiver Konzepte bei der Analyse von Umweltgeräuschbelastung und Belästigungsreaktion. In A. Schick & K.P. Walcher (Eds.), *Beiträge zu einer Bedeutungslehre des Schalls* (pp. 337–356). Bern, Switzerland: Lang.

Kastka, J. (1985). Untersuchungen zu einem kognitiven Modell der Verarbeitung von aversiven akustischen Umweltreizen. In D. Alter (Ed.), *Bericht über den 34. Kongreß der Deutschen Gesellschaft für Psychologie in Wein 1984* (pp. 854–857). Göttingen, F.R.G.: Hogrefe.

Kastka, J., & Buchta, E. (1977). Zum Inhalt der Belästigungsreaktion auf Straßenverkehrslärm. *Kampf dem Lärm, 24*, 158–166.

Keim, K.D. (1979). *Milieu in der Stadt. Ein Konzept zur Analyse älterer Wohnquartiere*. Stuttgart, F.R.G.: Kohlhammer.

Keim, K.D. (1981). *Stadt und Gewalt. Problemstruktur—Fallstudien—Vorschläge*. Berlin: Deutsches Institut für Urbanistik.

Klages, H. (1968). *Der Nachbarschaftsgedanke und die nachbarliche Wirklichkeit in der Großstadt* (2nd ed.). Wiesbaden, F.R.G.: Westdeutscher Verlag.

Kley, J., & Fteikau, H.J. (1979). Verhaltenswirksame Variablen des Umweltbewußtseins. *Psychologie und Praxis, 23*, 13–22.

Klockhaus, R. (1975). *Einstellung zur Wohnumgebung. Empirische Studie an zwei Wohnarealen in Nürnberg-Langwasser*. Göttingen, F.R.G.: Hogrefe.

Klockhaus, R., & Habermann-Morbey, B. (1986). *Psychologie des Schulvandalismus*. Göttingen, F.R.G.: Hogrefe.

Klockhaus, R., & Habermann-Morbey, B. (1982). Entwicklung und Testung theoretisch begründeter Instrumente zur Erhebung von Wohnumgebungszufriedenheit. *Zeitschrift für Sozialpsychologie, 13*, 79–87.

Klockhaus, R., & Habermann-Morbey, B. (1984). Sachzerstörungen an Schulen und schulische Umwelt. *Zeitschrift für Entwicklungspsychologie und Pädagogische Psychologie, 16*, 47–56.

Klockhaus, R., & Habermann-Morbey, B. (1985). Zerstörerisches Verhalten Jugendlicher und räumliche Umweltmerkmale. In D. Albert (Ed.), *Bericht über den 34. Kongreß der Deutschen Gesellschaft für Psychologie in Wien 1984* (pp. 846–849). Göttingen, F.R.G.: Hogrefe.

Klockhaus, R., & Habermann-Morbey, B. (1986). *Psychologie des Schulvandalismus*. Göttingen, F.R.G.: Hogrefe.

Knall, V., & Schuemer, R. (1981). Reaktionen auf Straßenund Schienenverkehrslärm in städtischen und ländlichen Regionen. In A. Schick (Ed.), *Akustik zwischen Physik und Psychologie* (pp. 20–26). Stuttgart, F.R.G.: Klett-Cotta.

Koch, J.J. (1986). Vandalismus—Sozial—und umweltpsychologische Aspekte destruktiven Verhaltens. *Gruppendynamik, 17*, 65–82.

König, H., & Schmittmann, R. (1976). *Zur Ökologie der Schule. Eine ökopsychologische Untersuchung zum Einfluß von Schulbauten auf Lehr- und Lernprozesse*. Munich: Dokumentation.

Koffka, K. (1935). *Principles of Gestalt psychology*. New York: Harcourt, Brace & World.

Kommer, D., & Röhrle, B. (Eds.). (1983). *Ökologie und Lebenslagen* (Gemeindepsychologische Perspektiven 3). Tübingen, F.R.G.: Deutsche Gesellschaft für Verhaltenstherapie.

Kraft, P. (1977). *Der Schulhof als Ort sozialen Verhaltens.* Braunschweig, F.R.G.: Westermann.

Krampen, M. (1979). *Meaning in the urban environment.* London: Pion.

Krampen, M. (1981a). Advances in Visual Semiotics. *Semiotica, 36,* 339–359.

Krampen, M. (1981b). Grüne Archen. *Zeitschrift für Semiotik, 3,* 371–378.

Krampen, M. (1981c). Phytosemiotics. *Semiotica, 36,* 187–200.

Krebs, D. (1971). *Anwendung der Stress-Theorie in einer Felduntersuchung an Obdachlosen.* Unpublished doctoral dissertation, F.R.G.: University of Mannheim.

Kromrey, H. (1981). *Die gebaute Umwelt. Wohngebietsplanung im Bewohnerurteil.* Opladen, F.R.G.: Leske & Budrich.

Kruse, L. (1974). *Räumliche Umwelt. Die Phänomenologie des räumlichen Verhaltens als Beitrag zu einer psychologischen Umwelttheorie.* Berlin: de Gruyter.

Kruse, L. (1975a). Crowding. Dichte und Enge aus sozialpsychologischer Sicht. *Zeitschrift für Sozialpsychologie, 6,* 2–30.

Kruse, L. (1975b). Umfrage: Umweltpsychologische Forschung im deutschsprachigen Raum. *Zeitschrift für Sozialpsychologie, 6,* 364–382.

Kruse, L. (1978). Ökologische Fragestellungen in der Sozialpsychologie. In C.F. Graumann (Ed.), *Ökologische Perspektiven in der Psychologie* (pp. 171–190). Bern, Switzerland: Huber.

Kruse, L. (1980). *Privatheit als Problem und Gegenstand der Psychologie.* Bern, Switzerland: Huber.

Kruse, L. (1981). Psychologische Aspekte des technischen Fortschritts. In G. Ropohl (Ed.), *Interdisziplinäre Technikforschung* (Schriftenreihe Angewandte Innovationsforschung, Vol. 3, pp. 71–81). Berlin: Schmidt.

Kruse, L. (1983a). Crowding. In D. Frey & S. Greif (Eds.), *Sozialpsychologie. Ein Handbuch in Schlüsselbegriffen* (pp. 32–39). Munich: Urban & Schwarzenberg.

Kruse, L. (1983b). Katastrophe und Erholung—Die Natur in der umweltpsychologischen Forschung. In G. Großklaus & E. Oldemeyer (Eds.), *Verlorene Natur* (pp. 121–135). Karlsruhe, F.R.G.: von Loeper Verlag.

Kruse, L. (1986a). Conceptions of crowds and crowding. In C.F. Graumann & S. Moscovici (Eds.), *Changing conceptions of crowd mind and behavior* (pp. 117–142). New York: Springer-Verlag.

Kruse, L. (1986b). Drechbücher für Verhaltensschauplätze oder "Skripts für Settings." In G. Kaminski (Eds.), *Ordnung und Variabilität im Alltagsgeschehen* (pp. 135–153). Göttingen, F.R.G.: Hogrefe.

Kruse, L. (in press). Overcoming a dematerialized social psychology. In D. Jodelet & P. Stringer (Eds.), *Toward a social psychology of the environment.* Cambridge, England: Cambridge University Press.

Kruse, L., & Arlt, R. (Eds.). *Environment and behavior. An international and multidisciplinary bibliography (1970–1981)* (2 Vols.). Munich: Saur Verlag.

Kruse, L., & Graumann, C.F. (1978). Sozialpsychologie des Raumes und der Bewegung. In K. Hammerich & M. Klein (Eds.), *Materialien zur Soziologie des Alltags* (Sonderheft 20 der Kölner Zeitschrift für Soziologie und Sozialpsychologie, pp. 177–219). Opladen, F.R.G.: Westdeutscher Verlag.

Kruse, L., Graumann, C.F., & Lantermann, E.D. (Eds.). (in press). *Ökopsychologie. Ein Handbuch in Schlüsselbegriffen.* Munich: Urban & Schwarzenberg.

Lantermann, E.D. (1974). *Solidarität und Wohnen.* Darmstadt, F.R.G.: Steinkopff.

Lantermann, E.D. (1976). Eine Theorie der Umwelt-Kompetenz: Architektonische und soziale Implikationen für eine Altenheim-Planung. *Zeitschrift für Gerontologie, 9,* 433–443.

Lantermann, E.D. (1978). Situation x Person: Interindividuelle Differenzen des Verhaltens als Folge und Ursache ideosynkratischer Konstruktion von Situationen. In C.F. Graumann (Ed.), *Ökologische Perspektiven in der Psychologie* (pp. 143–160). Bern, Switzerland: Huber.

Lantermann, E.D. (1980). *Interaktionen. Person, Situation und Handlung.* Munich: Urban & Schwarzenberg.

Lehmann, J. (Ed.). (1981). *Hochschulcurriculum Umwelt.* Cologne, F.R.G.: Aulis Verlag & Deubner.

Lehr, U. (1976). Altern als soziales und ökologisches Schicksal. In M. Blohmke & U. Keil (Eds.), *Sozialpathologie: Epidemiologie in der Forschung* (pp. 63–70). Stuttgart, F.R.G.: Gentner.

Lehr, U. (1979). *Psychologie des Alterns.* Heidelberg, F.R.G.: Quelle & Meyer.

Lehr, U., & Olbrich, E. (1976). Ecological correlates of adjustment to aging. In H. Thomae (Ed.), *Patterns of aging* (pp. 81–92). Basel, Switzerland: Karger.

Lenz-Romeiβ, F. (1970). *Die Stadt—Heimat oder Durchgangsstation?* Munich: Callwey.

Lewin, K. (1931). Environmental forces in child behavior and development. In C. Murchinson (Ed.), *Handbook of child psychology* (pp. 94–127). Worcester, MA: Clark University Press.

Lewin, K. (1935). The psychological situation of reward and punishment. In *Dynamic Theory of Personality* (pp. 114–170). New York: McGraw-Hill.

Limbourg, M. (1976). Das Verhalten von 4–9 jährigen Kindern bei der Straβenüberquerung. *Zeitschrift für Experimentelle und Angewandte Psychologie, 23,* 666–677.

Linde, H. (1972). *Sachdominanz in Sozialstrukturen.* Tübingen, F.R.G.: Mohr-Siebeck.

Loeschper, G., Mummendey, A., Linneweber, V., & Bornewasser, M. (1984). The judgment of behaviour as aggressive and sanctionable. *European Journal of Social Psychology, 14*, 391–404.

Lorenzer, A. (1968). Städtebau: Funktionalismus und Sozialmontage? Zur sozialpsychologischen Funktion der Architektur. In H. Berndt, A. Lorenzer, & K. Horn (Eds.), *Architektur als Ideologie* (pp. 51–104). Frankfurt: Suhrkamp.

Lukesch, H., & Schneewind, K.A. (1978). Themen und Probleme der familiären Sozialisationsforschung. In K.A. Schneewind & H. Lukesch (Eds.), *Familiäre Sozialisation* (pp. 9–23). Stuttgart, F.R.G.: Klett-Cotta.

Lüscher, K., Fisch, R., & Pape, T. (1985). Die Ökologie von Familien. *Zeitschrift für Soziologie, 14*, 13–27.

Lynch, K. (1960). *The image of the city.* Cambridge, MA: MIT Press.

Maderthaner, R. (1978). Komplexität und Monotonie aus architekturpsychologischer Sicht. *Der Aufbau. Fachschrift für Planen, Bauen, Wohnen und Umweltschutz, 32*, 257–262.

Markelin, A., & Trieb, M. (Eds.). (1974). *Mensch und Stadtgestalt.* Stuttgart, F.R.G.: Deutsche Verlags Anstalt.

Mathey, F.J., Thomae, L.H., & Knorr, D. (1976). Verhaltensweisen älterer Fußgänger im Straßenverkehr. *Aktuelle Gerontologie, 6*, 567–572.

McGurk, H. (Ed.). (1977). *Ecological factors in human development.* Amsterdam: North-Holland.

Meadows, D., Meadows, D., Zahn, E., & Milling, P. (1972). *The limits to growth.* New York: Universe.

Meier, U. (1985). *Kriminalität in Neubausiedlungen.* Frankfurt: Lang.

Mielke, R. (1985). Eine Untersuchung zum Umweltschutz-Verhalten (Wegwerf-Verhalten): Einstellung, Einstellungs-Verfügbarkeit und soziale Normen als Verhaltensprädiktoren. *Zeitschrift für Sozialpsychologie, 16*, 196–205.

Milgram, S. (1970). The experience of living in cities. *Science, 167*, 1461–1468.

Miller, R. (1985). Wohnsituation und Umweltwahrnehmung—Eine empirische Analyse von drei Hochhausarealen. In D. Albert (Ed.), *Bericht über den 34. Kongreß der Deutschen Gesellschaft für Psychologie in Wien 1984* (pp. 849–851). Göttingen, F.R.G.: Hogrefe.

Minsel, W.R., & Bente, G. (1981). Pädagogik und Verhaltensmodifikation als Strategie zur Veränderung des Umweltbewußtseins. In H.J. Fietkau & H. Kessel (Eds.), *Umweltlernen. Veränderungsmöglichkeiten des Umweltbewußtseins* (pp. 149–186). Königstein (Ts.) F.R.G.: Hain.

Mitscherlich, A. (1965). *Die Unwirtlichkeit unserer Städte. Anstiftung zum Unfrieden.* Frankfurt: Suhrkamp.

Mitscherlich, A. (1971). *Thesen zur Stadt dur Zukunft.* Frankfurt: Suhrkamp.

Mogel, H. (1984). *Ökopsychologie. Eine Einführung.* Stuttgart, F.R.G.: Kohlhammer.

Möhler, U., Schuemer, R., Knall, V., & Schuemer-Kohrs, A. (1986). *Vergleich der Lästigkeit von Schienen- und Straßenverkehrslärm.* Zeitschrift für Lärmbekämpfung, *33*, 132–142.

Molt, W. (1981). Traffic as an economic and psychological problem. In W. Molt, H.A. Hartmann, & P. Stringer (Eds.), *Advances in economic psychology.* Heidelberg, F.R.G.: Meyn.

Molt, W., Golle, P., & Patscha, J. (1983). *Typisierung von Straßen im Innerortsbereich nach dem Nutzerverhalten* (Forschungsauftrag Bundesanstalt für Straßenwesen, Research Rep.). Augsburger Arbeiten zur ökologischen und ökonomischen Psychologie, 4.8, Augsburg.

Molt, W., & von Rosenstiel, L. (1978). *Bedarfsdeckung oder Bedürfnissteuerung— Anwendungsmöglichkeiten verhaltenstheoretischer Konzepte für die Planung—am Beispiel der Verkehrsplanung.* Berlin: Duncker & Humblot.

Molt, W., von Winnig, H.H., & Beyrle, H. (1981). Erprobung und Bewertung eines neuen Gestaltungskonzepts von Innerortsstraßen. In H. Haase & W. Molt (Eds.), *Handbuch der Angewandten Psychologie: Vol. 3. Markt & Umwelt.* Landsberg am Lech, F.R.G.: Moderne Industrie.

Muchow, M. (1926). Psychologische Untersuchungen über die Wirkung des Seeklimas auf Schulkinder. *Zeitschrift für Pädagogische Psychologie, 27*, 18–31.

Muchow, M. (1929). *Psychologische Probleme der frühen Erziehung.* Erfurt, F.R.G.: Stenger.

Muchow, M., & Muchow, H.H. (1980). Der Lebensraum des Großstadtkindes. *Päd. extra* (2nd ed.). Bensheim, F.R.G. (Original work published 1935).

Mühlich, E., Zinn, H., Kröning, W., & Mühlich-Klinger, J. (1978). *Zusammenhang von gebauter Umwelt und sozialem Verhalten im Wohn- und Umweltbereich.* Schriftenreihe "Städtebauliche Forschung" des Bundesministeriums für Raumordnung, Bauwesen und Städtebau (Vol. 03.062). Bonn: Bad Godesberg.

Mukerjee, R. (1940). *Man and his habitation: A study in social ecology.* London: Longmans, Green.

Mummendey, A., Linneweber, V., & Loeschper, G. (1984). Aggression: From act to interaction. In A. Mummendey (Ed.), *Social psychology of aggression* (pp. 69–106). Berlin: Springer-Verlag.

Mummendey, A., Loeschper, G., Linneweber, V., & Bornewasser, M. (1984). Social-consensual conceptions concerning the progress of aggressive interactions. *European Journal of Social Psychology, 14*, 379–389.

Mündelein, H., & Schönpflug, W. (1984). Ökologische Validierung eines simulierten Büroarbeitsplatzes mit Hilfe des Fragebogens zur Arbeitsanalyse (FAA). Ein Beitrag zum Verhältnis von Labor und Feldforschung. *Psychologie und Praxis, 28*, 2–100.

Mundt, J.W. (1980). *Vorschulkinder und ihre Umwelt.* Weinheim, F.R.G.: Beltz.

Münsterberg, H. (1914). *Grundzüge der Psychotechnik.* Leipzig, F.R.G.: Barth.

Nohl, W. (1974). Ansätze zu einer umweltpsychologischen Freiraumforschung. *Beiheft zu Landschaft + Stadt.* Stuttgart, F.R.G.: Ulmer.

Nohl, W. (1975). Zur Ermittlung planungsrelevanter Bedürfnisse—dargestellt am Beispiel städtischer Freiräume. *Natur und Landschaft, 50,* 228–236.

Nohl, W. (1980). *Freiraumarchitektur und Emanzipation. Theoretische Überlegungen und empirische Studien zur Bedürftigkeit der Freiraumbenutzer als Grundlage einer emanzipatorisch orientierten Freiraumarbeit.* Frankfurt: Lang.

Nöldner, W. (1984). *Psychologie und Umweltprobleme.* Unpublished doctoral dissertation. Regensburg, F.R.G.: University of Regensburg.

Oerter, R. (1979). Ein ökologisches Modelle kognitiver Sozialisation. In H. Walter & R. Oerter (Eds.), *Ökologie und Entwicklung* (pp. 57–70). Donauwörth, F.R.G.: Ludwig Auer.

Opwis, K., & May, R. (1985). *Determinanten der Risikoakzeptanz bei Umweltproblemen* (Research Rep. No. 21). Freiburg, F.R.G.: Psychological Institute, University of Freiburg.

Oster, M. (1982). *Mögliche Interferenzen bei der Orientierung anhand von Stadtplänen.* Unpublished diploma thesis, F.R.G.: University of Heidelberg.

Otterstädt, H. (1962). Untersuchungen über den Spielraum von Vorortkindern einer mittleren Stadt. *Psychologische Rundschau, 13,* 275–287.

Park, R.E., Burgess, E.W., & McKenzie, R.D. (1925). *The city.* Chicago: University of Chicago Press.

Pawlik, K. (1976a). Ökologische Validität: Ein Beispiel aus der Kulturvergleichsforschung. In G. Kaminski (Ed.), *Umweltpsychologie* (pp. 59–72). Stuttgart, F.R.G.: Klett.

Pawlik, K. (1976b). Wohnmodell Hamburg-Steilshoop. Ergebnisse einer wissenschaftlichen Begleituntersuchung. *Archiv für Kommunalwissenschaften, 15,* 249–261.

Pawlik, K. (1978). Umwelt und Persönlichkeit: Zum Verhältnis von Ökologischer und Differentieller Psychologie. In C.F. Graumann (Ed.), *Ökologische Perspektiven in der Psychologie* (pp. 112–134). Bern, Switzerland: Huber.

Pawlik, K., & Buse, L. (1982). Rechnergestützte Verhaltensregistrierung im Feld: Beschreibung und erste psychometrische Überprüfung einer neuen Erhebungsmethode. *Zeitschrift für Differentielle und Diagnostische Psychologie, 3,* 101–118.

Pawlik, K., & Buse, L. (1985). Verhalten in situ: Felduntersuchungen zur Umwelt-Verhaltens-Kovariation an männlichen Jugendlichen. In D. Albert (Ed.), *Bericht über den 34. Kongreß der Deutschen Gesellschaft für Psychologie in Wien 1984* (pp. 843–846). Göttingen, F.R.G.: Hogrefe.

Peel, R. (1980). *Die Wahrnehmung von Wohnzimmern und ihrer Bewohner.* Unpublished doctoral dissertation, Heidelberg, F.R.G.: University of Heidelberg.

Peel, R. (1982). Wer wohnt wo? Zur Psychologie des Wohnzimmers. *Psychologie heute, 9,* 20–29.

Pfeil, E. (1963). Zur Kritik der Nachbarschaftsidee. *Archiv für Kommunalwissenschaften, 2,* 39–54.

Pfeil, E. (1972). *Großstadtforschung: Entwicklung und gegenwärtiger Stand* (2nd ed.). Hanover, F.R.G.: Jänecke.

Pieper, R. (1979). *Soziologie im Städtebau. Eine Einführung für Architekten, Stadtplaner und Sozialwissenschaftler.* Stuttgart, F.R.G.: Enke.

Prester, G., Rohrmann, B., & Schellhammer, E. (in press). Environmental evaluations and participation activities—A social-psychological field study. *Journal of Applied Social Psychology.*

Projektgruppe Jugendbüro und Haptschülerarbeit. (1975). *Die Lebenswelt von Hauptschülern. Ergebnisse einer Untersuchung.* Munich: Juventa.

Projektgruppe Jugendbüro (J. Behnken & J. Zinnecker). (1981). Grundschule im Wohnquartier: Erkundungen zu einer regional versteckten Klassenschule. In H. Walter (Ed.), *Region und Sozialisation* (Vol. 1, 261–287). Stuttgart, F.R.G.: Frommann-Holzboog.

Proshansky, H. (1978). The city and self-identity. *Environment and Behavior, 10,* 147–169.

Proshansky, H., Ittelson, W., & Rivlin, L. (Eds.). (1970). *Environmental psychology. Man and his physical setting.* New York: Holt, Rinehart & Winston.

Rammstedt, O. (1981). Verändern soziale Bewegungen das Umweltbewußtsein? In H.J. Fietkau & H. Kessel (Eds.), *Umweltlernen. Veränderungsmöglichkeiten des Umweltbewußtseins* (pp. 117–148). Königstein (Ts.), F.R.G.: Hain.

Reimann, H. (1983). Wohnverhältnisse und Wohnbedürfnisse älterer Menschen. In H. Reimann & H. Reimann (Eds.), *Das Alter* (pp. 97–118). Stuttgart, F.R.G.: Enke.

Rohrmann, B. (1981). Psychometrische Befunde zum Begriff Belästigung. In A. Schick (Ed.), *Akustik zwischen Physik und Psychologie* (pp. 94–99). Stuttgart, F.R.G.: Klett-Cotta.

Rohrmann, B. (1983). Psychologische Determinanten des Protests gegen belästigende Umweltstressoren. In G. Lüer (Ed.), *Bericht über den 33. Kongreß der Deutschen Gesellschaft für Psychologie, Mainz 1982* (pp. 911–915). Göttingen, F.R.G.: Hogrefe.

Rohrmann, B. (1984a). Psychologische Kriterien der 'Erheblichkeit' von Belästigungen. In A. Schick & K.P. Walcher (Eds.), *Beiträge zu einer Bedeutungslehre des Schalls* (pp. 139–149). Bern, Switzerland: Lang.

Rohrmann, B. (1984b). *Psychologische Forschung und umweltpsychologische Entscheidungen: Das Beispiel Lärm.* Opladen, Germany: Westdeutscher Verlag.

Rohrmann, B., & Borcherding, K. (1985). Die Bewertung von Umweltstressoren unter Risiko-Aspekten. In D. Albert (Ed.), *Bericht über den 34. Kongreβ der Deutschen Gesellschaft für Psychologie in Wien 1984* (pp. 851–854). Göttingen, F.R.G.: Hogrefe.

Rohrmann, B., Finke, H.O., Guski, R., Schuemer, R., & Schuemer-Kohrs, A. (1978). *Fluglärm und seine Wirkung auf den Menschen.* Bern, Switzerland: Huber.

Rolinski, K. (1980). *Wohnhausarchitektur und Kriminalität.* Wiesbaden, F.R.G.: Bundeskriminalamt.

Saegert, S. (1976). Stress-Inducing and Stress-Reducing Qualities of Environment. In H.M. Proshansky, W.H. Ittelson, & L.C. Rivlin (Eds.), *Environmental psychology: People and their physical settings* (2nd ed., pp. 218–223). New York: Holt, Rinehart & Winston.

Saup, W. (1983). Barkers Behavior Setting-Konzept und seine Weiterentwicklung. *Psychologische Rundschau, 34,* 134–170.

Saup, W. (1984a). Streβ und Streβbewältigung bei der Heimübersiedlung älterer Menschen. *Zeitschrift für Gerontologie, 17,* 198–204.

Saup, W. (1984b). *Übersiedlung ins Altenheim. Belastende Umweltbedingungen in Altenheimen und Bewältigungsreaktionen von Altenheimbewohnern.* Weinheim, F.R.G.: Beltz.

Sauter, G. (1983). *Untersuchung über das Zusammenwirken optischer und akustischer Eindrücke bei der Beurteilung von Wohnumgebungen.* Unpublished diploma thesis, University of Saarbrücken, F.R.G..

Schenk, S., & Schmidt, G. (1972). Psychologische Analyse einer auffälligen Verteilung von Straβenbahnunfällen in einer Groβstadt. *Probleme und Ergebnisse der Psychologie, 40,* 49–68.

Schick, A. (1979). *Schallwirkung aus psychologischer Sicht.* Stuttgart, F.R.G.: Klett.

Schick, A. (Ed.). (1981). *Akustik zwischen Physik und Psychologie.* Stuttgart, F.R.G.: Klett-Cotta.

Schick, A., & Walcher, K.P. (Eds.). (1983). *Beiträge zu einer Bedeutungslehre des Schalls.* Bern, Switzerland: Lang.

Schmidt-Relenberg, N. (1968). *Soziologie und Städtebau.* Stuttgart, F.R.G.: Krämer.

Schmittmann, R. (1977). Zur Arbeitsplatzsituation der Lehrer im Zusammenhang mit der baulichen Organisation und Gestaltung der Lehrerarbeits- und Aufenthaltsbereiche. In Institut für Schulbau (Ed.), *Untersuchungen zur Qualität gebauter Schulumwelt* (pp. 131–163). Villingen-Schwenningen, F.R.G.: Neckar.

Schmittmann, R. (1981). Handlungstheoretische Analyse und Planung. Fallbeispiel: Die Groβraumschule. In H. Haase & W. Molt (Eds.), *Handbuch der Angewandten Psychologie: Vol. 3. Markt & Umwelt* (pp. 260–379). Landsberg am Lech, F.R.G.: Moderne Industrie.

Schmitz-Scherzer, R. (1974). *Sozialpsychologie der Freizeit.* Stuttgart, F.R.G.: Kohlhammer.

Schmitz-Scherzer, R. (Ed.). (1977). *Aktuelle Beiträge zur Freizeitforschung.* Darmstadt, F.R.G.: Steinkopff.

Schmitz-Scherzer, R., & Bierhoff, H.W. (1972). *Benutzeranalysen von Freizeitanlagen.* Düsseldorf, F.R.G.: Deutsche Gesellschaft für Freizeit.

Schmitz-Scherzer, R., Bierhoff, H.W., Lustig, A., & Güth, K. (1974). Besucherfrequenzen von Spielplätzen. *Zeitschrift für Entwicklungspsychologie und Pädagogische Psychologie, 4,* 51–59.

Schmitz-Scherzer, R., Plagemann, K., & Kühn, D. (1976). Ökologische Aspekte des Lebens in Altenheimen aus der Sicht des Personals. *Aktuelle Gerontologie, 6,* 561–565.

Schneewind, K.A., Beckmann, M., & Engfer, A. (1983). *Eltern und Kinder. Umwelteinflüsse auf das familiäre Verhalten.* Stuttgart, F.R.G.: Kohlhammer.

Schneewind, K.A., & Engfer, A. (1979). Ökologische Perspektiven der familiären Sozialisation. In H. Walter & R. Oerter (Eds.), *Ökologie und Entwicklung* (pp. 247–261). Donauwörth, F.R.G.: Ludwig Auer.

Schneider, G. (1981). *Ein Vergleich verbaler und nonverbaler Verfahren zur Erfassung kognitiver Strukturen in der Umweltpsychologie im Rahmen der Kelly-Grid- und MDS-Methodologie.* Unpublished diploma thesis, Heidelberg, F.R.G.: University of Heidelberg.

Schneider, G. (1985). Qualitativität als methodologisches Desiderat der Umweltpsychologie. In G. Jüttemann (Ed.), *Qualitative Forschung in der Psychologie* (pp. 297–323). Weinheim, F.R.G.: Beltz.

Schneider, G. (in press). Psychological identity of and identification with urban neighborhoods. In D. Frick (Ed.), *Quality of urban life: Social, psychological, and physical conditions.* Berlin: de Gruyter.

Schneider, G., & Weimer, E. (1981). *Aspekte der Kategorisierung städtischer Umwelt. Eine empirische Untersuchung* (Rep. No. 25). Heidelberg, F.R.G.: Universität Heidelberg, Bericht aus dem Psychologischen Institut.

Schoggen, P. (1985). Martha Muchow: Precursor to ecological psychology. *Human Development, 28,* 213–216.

Schönpflug, W., & Schulz, P. (1979). Lärmwirkungen bei Tätigkeiten mit komplexer Informationsverarbeitung (Research Rep.). Berlin: Umweltbundesamt.

Schubert, H.A. (1977). *Nachbarschaft, Entfremdung und Protest. Welche Chancen haben Gemeinschaftsinitiativen in der Groβstadt?* Freiburg, F.R.G.: Alber.

Schuemer, R., & Schuemer-Kohrs, A. (1983). The influence of some nonacoustical factors on reactions to road and railway traffic noise. *Proceedings of Internoise, 83,* 935–938.

Schuemer, R., & Schuemer-Kohrs, A. (1984). Zum Einfluβ auβer-akustischer Faktoren ("Moderatoren") auf die Reaktionen auf Verkehrslärm. In A. Schick & K.P. Walcher (Eds.), *Beiträge zu einer Bedeutungslehre des Schalls* (pp. 87–98). Bern, Switzerland: Lang.

Schultz-Gambard, J. (1978). Umweltpsychologische Aspekte frühkindlicher und vorschulischer Sozialisation. In R. Dollase (Ed.), *Handbuch der Früh- und Vorschulpädagogik* (pp. 27–54). Düsseldorf, F.R.G.: Schwann.

Schultz-Gambard, J. (1979). Social Determinants of Crowding. In W.A. LeComte & M.R. Gürkaynak (Eds.), *Human Consequences of Crowding*. New York: Plenum.

Schultz-Gambard, J. (1983). Crowding: Dichte und Engeals Gegenstand angewandter sozialpsychologischer Forschung. In J. Haisch (Ed.), *Angewandte Sozialpsychologie* (pp. 171–193). Bern, Switzerland: Huber.

Schultz-Gambard, J. (1985). Crowding: Sozialpsychologische Erklärungen der Wirkung von Dichte und Enge. In D. Frey & M. Irle (Eds.), *Theorien der Sozialpsychologie* (Vol. 3, pp. 175–208). Bern, Switzerland: Huber.

Schulz, P. (1981). Die Beeinträchtigung von Lernprozessen durch Verkehrslärm bei unterschiedlich leistungsfähigen Personen. In A. Schick (Ed.), *Akustik zwischen Physik und Psychologie* (pp. 188–192). Stuttgart, F.R.G.: Klett-Cotta.

Schutz, A. (1962–66). *Collected papers* (Vols. 1–3). The Hague, Netherlands: Nijhoff.

Schwarz, H., & Werbik, H. (1971). Eine experimentelle Untersuchung über den Einfluß der syntaktischen Information der Anordnung von Baukörpern entlang der Straße auf Stimmungen des Betrachters. *Zeitschrift für Experimentelle und Angewandte Psychologie, 18,* 499–511.

Schwonke, M., & Herylyn, U. (1967). *Wolfsburg. Soziologische Analyse einer jungen Industriestadt.* Stuttgart, F.R.G.: Krämer.

Seidel, G. (1975). Spielplatzausstattung und Gerätebenutzung. *Zeitschrift für Pädagogik, 21,* 399–401.

Siebel, W. (1967). Zur Zusammenarbeit zwischen Architekten und Soziologen. *Argument, 9,* 287–299.

Silbermann, A. (1963). *Vom Wohnen der Deutschen. Eine soziologische Studie über das Wohnerlebnis.* Opladen, F.R.G.: Westdeutscher Verlag.

Simmel, G. (1970). The metropolis and mental life. In R. Gutman & D. Popenoe (Eds.), *Neighborhood, city and metropolis: An integrated reader in urban sociology* (pp. 777–787). New York: Random House. (Original work published 1903).

Six, B., Martin, P., & Pecher, M. (1983). A cultural comparison of perceived crowding and discomfort: The United States and West Germany. *Journal of Psychology, 114,* 63–67.

Sombart, W. (1907). Der Begriff der Stadt und das Wesen der Städtebildung. *Archiv für Sozialwissenschaft und Sozialpolitik, 25,* 1–9.

Sommer, R. (1967). Small Group Ecology. *Psychological Bulletin, 67,* 145–152.

Sommer, R. (1969). *Personal space. The behavioral basis of design.* Englewood Cliffs, NJ: Prentice-Hall.

Spada, H., Benda, H. von Erke, H. et al. (1979). Psychologische Ökologie. In L.H. Eckensberger (Ed.), *Bericht über den 31. Kongreß der DGfPs in Mannheim 1978* (Vol. 1, pp. 471–491). Göttingen, F.R.G.: Hogrefe.

Spada, H., Hoffmann, L., & Lucht-Wraage, H. (1977). Student attitudes toward nuclear power plants and problems of energy supply. A classroom experiment in the field of environmental psychology. *Studies in Educational Evaluation, 3,* 109–128.

Spada, H., & Lucht-Wraage, H. (1980). A paper-and-pencil situation test to assess attitudes: An analysis of reactions to open-end items based on the model of Rasch. In L.J.Th. van der Kamp, W.F. Langerak, & D.N.M. de Gruijter (Eds.), *Psychometrics for educational design* (pp. 277–289). New York: Wiley.

Spada, H., May, R., & Opwis, K. (1983). *Wissensaufbau und Handlungsbewertung bei ökologischen Problemen.* (Research Rep.). Freiburg, F.R.G.: University of Freiburg, Psychological Institute.

Spada, H., & Opwis, K. (1985). Die Allmende-Klemme: Eine umweltpsychologische Konfliktsituation mit ökologischen und sozialen Komponenten. In D. Albert (Ed.), *Bericht über den 34. Kongreß der Deutschen Gesellschaft für Psychologie in Wien 1984* (pp. 840–843). Göttingen, F.R.G.: Hogrefe.

Spiegelberg, H. (1960). *The phenomenological movement: A historical introduction* (Vols. 1–2). The Hague, Netherlands: Nijhoff.

Spiegelberg, H. (1972). *Phenomenology in psychology and psychiatry.* Evanston, IL: Northwestern University Press.

Stapf, K.H., & Heidemann, C. (1971). Das Tätigkeitsfeld von Hausfrauen. Zeitbudget und Tagesablauf. *Hauswirtschaft und Wissenschaft, 19,* 125–129.

Stern, W. (1903). Angewandte Psychologie. In *Beiträge zur Psychologie der Aussage* (Vol. 1, pp. 1–45). Leipzig, F.R.G.: Barth.

Stern, W. (1938). *General psychology from the personalistic standpoint.* New York: Macmillan.

Straus, E. (1966). *Phenomenological psychology: Selected papers.* New York: Basic Books.

Streufert, S., & Nogami, G.Y. (1979). *Der Mensch im beengten Raum.* Darmstadt, F.R.G.: Steinkopff.

Streufert, S., Nogami, G.Y., & Streufert, S. (1980). Crowding and incongruity adaptation. In J. Sarason & C. Spielberger (Eds.), *Stress and anxiety* (Vol. 7, pp. 185–202). Washington, DC: Hemisphere.

Strohmeier, K.P. (1983). *Quartier und soziale Netzwerke. Grundlagen einer sozialen Ökologie der Familie.* Frankfurt: Campus.

Strümpel, B. (1978). Sozialwissenschaftliche Aspekte einer alternativen Energiepolitik. *Zeitschrift für Umweltpolitik, 1,* 95–112.

Taylor, C.W., Bailey, R., & Branch, C.H.H. (Eds.). (1967). *Second National Conference on Architectural Psychology.* Salt Lake City: University of Utah.

Tews, U. (1977). Sozialökologische Einflußfaktoren auf das Verhalten alter Menschen. *Zeitschrift für Gerontologie, 10,* 322–342.

Thoma, A. (1980). *Die Beurteilung architektonischer Innenräume in Abhängigkeit von Proportion und Funktion.* Unpublished diploma thesis, University of Heidelberg, F.R.G.

Thomae, H. (1976). Ökologische Aspekte der Gerontologie. *Zeitschrift für Gerontologie, 9,* 407–410.

Thomae, H., & Endo, T. (Eds.). (1974). *The adolescent and his environment. Contributions to an Ecology of Teen-Age Behavior.* Basel, F.R.G.: Karger.

Thurn, H.P. (1972). Architektursoziologie. Zur Situation einer Forschungsrichtung. *Kölner Zeitschrift für Soziologie und Sozialpsychologie, 24,* 301–341.

Thurnwald, R. (1904). Stadt und Land im Lebensprozeß der Rasse. *Archiv für Rassen: und Gesellschaftsbiologie, 1,* 718–735.

Tiedtke, R. (1980). Beiträge zur Anwendung der Psychologie auf den Städtebau. V. Erkundungsuntersuchung zur Beziehung zwischen Wahrnehmung und Image der gebauten Umwelt. *Zeitschrift für Experimentelle und Angewandte Psychologie, 27,* 295–325.

Tolman, E.C. (1958). Gestalt and Sign-Gestalt. In *Behavior and psychological man* (pp. 77–93). Berkeley: University of California Press. (Original work published 1933).

Treinen, H. (1965). Symbolische Ortsbezogenheit. *Kölner Zeitschrift für Soziologie und Sozialpsychologie, 17,* 73–97, 254–297.

Trieb, M. (1974). *Stadtgestaltung—Theorie und Praxis.* Düsseldorf, F.R.G.: Bertelsmann.

Trudewind, C. (1975). *Häusliche Umwelt und Motiventwicklung.* Göttingen, F.R.G.: Hogrefe.

Trudewind, C. (1978). Probleme einer ökologischen Orientierung in der Entwicklungspsychologie. In C.F. Graumann (Ed.), *Ökologische Perspektiven in der Psychologie* (pp. 33–38). Bern, Switzerland: Huber.

Trudewind, C., & Husarek, B. Mutter-Kind-Interaktion bei der Hausaufgabenanfertigung und die Leistungsmotiventwicklung im Grundschulalter—Analyse einer ökologischen Schlüsselsituation. In H. Walter & R. Oerter (Eds.), *Ökologie und Entwicklung* (pp. 229–246). Donauwörth, F.R.G.: Ludwig Auer.

Van den Berg, J.H. (1955). *A phenomenological approach to psychiatry.* Springfield, IL: Thomas.

Vaskovics, L.A. (Ed.). (1982). *Raumbezogenheit sozialer Probleme.* Wiesbaden, F.R.G.: Westdeutscher Verlag.

Vierecke, K.D. (1972). *Nachbarschaft. Ein Beitrag zur Stadtsoziologie.* Cologne, F.R.G.: Bachem.

von Dürckheim, K. (1932). Untersuchungen zum gelebten Raum. *Neue Psychologische Studien, 6,* 383–480.

von Uexküll, J. (1921). *Umwelt und Innenwelt der Tiere* (2nd ed.). Berlin: Springer.

von Uexküll, J. (1922). Wie sehen wir die Natur und wie sieht sie sich selber? *Die Naturwissenschaft, 10,* 265–271, 296–301, 316–322.

von Uexküll, J. (1940). Bedeutungslehre. In A. Meyer-Abich (Ed.), *Bios* (Vol. 10). Leipzig, F.R.G.: Barth.

von Uexküll, J. (1957). A stroll through the worlds of animals and man (with G. Kriszat). In C.H. Schiller (Ed.), *Instinctive behavior* (pp. 5–80). New York: International Universities Press.

von Uexküll, J. (1973). *Theoretische Biologie.* Frankfurt: Suhrkamp. (Original work published 1920).

Walter, H. (Ed.). (1975). *Sozialisationsforschung: Vol. 3. Sozialökologie—Neue Wege in der Sozialisationsforschung.* Stuttgart, F.R.G.: Frommann-Holzboog.

Walter, H. (1977). Umweltpsychologie und Entwicklungspsychologie. In W.H. Tack (Ed.), *Bericht über den 30. Kongreß der DGfPs 1966* (Vol. 1, pp. 205–215). Göttingen, F.R.G.: Hogrefe.

Walter, H. (1980). Ökologische Ansätze in der Sozialisationsforschung. Eine Problemskizze. In K. Hurrelmann & D. Ulich (Eds.), *Handbuch der Sozialisationsforschung* (pp. 285–298). Weinheim, F.R.G.: Beltz.

Walter, H. (Ed.). (1981). *Region und Sozialisation* (Vols. 1–2). Stuttgart, F.R.G.: Frommann-Holzboog.

Walter, H., & Oerter, R. (Eds.). (1979). *Ökologie und Entwicklung.* Donauwörth, F.R.G.: Ludwig Auer.

Waterhouse, A. (1972). *Die Reaktion der Bewohner auf die äußere Veränderung der Städte.* Berlin: de Gruyter.

Weeber, R. (1971). *Eine neue Wohnumwelt.* Stuttgart, F.R.G.: Krämer.

Weichardt, H. (Ed.). (1981). *Grüne Solararchitektur.* Karlsruhe, Germany: Müller.

Wellek, A. (1954). *Die genetische Ganzheitspsychologie.* Munich: Beck.

Welter, R. (1976). Experimentelle Milieuveränderungen auf einer Bettenstation für Langzeitkranke. *Bauwelt, 67,* 1430–1433.

Welter, R. (1978). *Adaptives Bauen für Langzeitpatienten. Eine explorative Studie über Zusammenhänge zwischen horizontalen Bedingungen auf Bettenstationen in Krankenhäusern und territorialem Verhalten von Langzeitpatienten.* Unpublished doctoral dissertation, Zurich: Technical University of Zurich.

Wendt, H.W., Ewert, O., & Ewert, U. (1971). Die vorsprachliche Umwelt des Kindes aus einiger Entfernung betrachtet. Kinderpflegeartikel, Konfession und Risikoverhalten. *Archiv für Psychologie, 123,* 17–34.

Werner, H. (1957). *Comparative psychology of mental development* (rev. ed.). New York: International Universities Press.

Winter, G. (1980a). Freizeitverhalten und Umwelt. In Deutsche Gesellschaft für Freizeit (Ed.), *Freizeit in*

Theorie und Forschung (pp. 137–149). Düsseldorf: Deutsche Gesellschaft für Freizeit.

Winter, G. (1980b). Einige theoretische Überlegungen zur Strukturierung der Mensch-Umwelt-Beziehung im Lebensbereich Freizeit. *Freizeitpädagogik, 3,* 83–103.

Winter, G. (1981). Umweltbewußtsein im Licht sozialpsychologischer Theorien. In H.J. Fietkau & H. Kessel (Eds.), *Umweltlernen. Veränderungen des Umweltbewußtseins* (pp. 53–116). Königstein (Ts.), F.R.G.: Hain.

Winter, G. (1983). Psychologische Beiträge zu einer Theorie der Freizeit. In F.G. Vahsen (Ed.), *Beiträge zur Theorie und Praxis der Freizeitpädagogik* (pp. 151–176). Hildesheim, F.R.G.: Turnier.

Winterfeldt, D., John, R.S., & Borcherding, K. (1981). Cognitive components of risk ratings. *Risk Analysis, 1,* 277–287.

Wirth, L. (1970). Urbanism as a way of life. In R. Gutman and D. Popenoe (Eds.), *Neighborhood, City, and Metropolis. An Integrated Reader in Urban Sociology* (pp. 54–69). New York: Random House. (Original work published 1938).

Wohlwill, J. (1970). The emerging discipline of environmental psychology. *American Psychologist, 23,* 303–312.

Wohlwill, J. (1981). Umweltfragen in der Entwicklungspsychologie: Eine kritische Betrachtung zur Repräsentanz und Validität. In H.J. Fietkau & D. Görlitz (Eds.), *Umwelt und Alltag in der Psychologie* (pp. 91–111). Weinheim, F.R.G.: Beltz.

Wohlwill, J. (1985a). Martha Muchow, 1892–1933: Her life, work, and contribution to developmental and ecological psychology. *Human Development, 28,* 198–200.

Wohlwill, J. (1985b). Martha Muchow and the life-space of the urban child. *Human Development, 28,* 200–209.

Zapf, K., Heil, C., & Rudolph, J. (1969). *Stadt am Stadtrand.* Frankfurt: Europäische Verlagsanstalt.

Zinn, H. (1970). *Beziehungen zwischen Raumgestaltung und Sozialleben.* (Schriftenreihe Wohnungsbau O9d). Bern, Switzerland: Eidgenössische Forschungskommission Wohnungsbau.

Zinn, H. (1981). Kinder und Jugendliche unter beengten Wohn-und Wohnumfeldbedingungen. In Institut Wohnen und Umwelt (Ed.), *Wohnungspolitik am Ende?* (pp. 243–256). Cologne/Opladen, F.R.G.: Westdeutscher Verlag.

Zinnecker, J. (1980). Recherchen zum Lebensraum des Großstadtkindes: Eine Reise in verschüttete Scheinwelten und Wissenschaftsstrukturen. In M. Muchow & H.H. Muchow, *Der Lebensraum des Großstadtkindes* (2nd ed., pp. 10–52). Päd. extra. Bensheim.

Chapter **34**

ENVIRONMENTAL PSYCHOLOGY IN THE NETHERLANDS

Peter Stringer *and* André Kremer, *Department of Social Psychology, University of Nijmegen, The Netherlands*

34.1. INTRODUCTION

Environmental psychology in the Netherlands is relatively scarce. A crucial factor underlying its slow development has been the influence of certain norms and values on behavioral scientists in the postwar decades. There was a strong emphasis in social as well as in cognitive/experimental psychology, on the experimental approach, theory-development, and theoretically based research in laboratory settings. Problem-oriented or applied research, apart from that in certain traditional fields such as clinical or work psychology, was very rare and had a much lower status. Ample financial resources for "pure" research gave no stimulus for seeking grants outside the scientific sector. Only in the last decade has some measure of change occurred, with the government's call for more societally oriented research and with the pressure of decreasing funds for theoretical research. Until now, environmental psychology would have been seen as no more than a theoretically underdeveloped mongrel. (Perhaps it is still.)

For these reasons, we can locate the earliest steps in the field in the initiatives of individuals or in the stimulation provided by specific research contracts, rather than in disciplinary moves as such or in the policy of university psychology departments. Usually, there was no question of a conscious choice to specialize in environmental psychology. And after accidental beginnings, it is perhaps not surprising to find that individual pioneers abandoned the field. They felt themselves isolated in their departments and found it difficult to make any progress on their own. Even where a department (Department of Social and Organizational Psychology, University of Leiden) chose environmental psychology as a concentration point, it was changed with time into a focus on energy problems.

Prior to some 5 years ago, when a shift appeared in some places in the universities toward a greater concern with the substance of theoretical disciplines and a more conscious problem orientation, the only exception of note was to be found in the technological universities where the design disciplines began to express a need for a contribution from the social sciences. This was translated into the establishment of posts for social scientists, for teaching and research purposes; and in one institution (Technological University of Delft), a fully integrated approach by designers and behavioral scientists was sought. For the rest, one had to look to a few research institutions outside the universities that now and again carried out projects that could be viewed as environmental psychology.

34.2. SOME LANDMARKS IN THE EARLY DEVELOPMENT OF ENVIRONMENTAL PSYCHOLOGY IN THE NETHERLANDS

Against this background we can best begin by enumerating a number of landmarks in the field, as a means of tracing the gradual development of environmental psychological research in the 1960s and 1970s.

A very early beginning was provided by the sociologist de Jonge's (1962) studies of urban image which were carried out in the style of Kevin Lynch. This has been one of the few pieces of Dutch research in the area of environmental psychology to have been, at one time regularly, cited in international texts.

Wentholt's (1968) work on the inner city of Rotterdam was probably the first research to pay explicit attention to environmental psychological factors. The inner city was largely rebuilt after its wholesale destruction during World War II, and a department store financed research into inhabitants' reactions to the redevelopment. This question of how a new residential area is perceived, experienced, and used was to prove to be one of the principal themes of subsequent environmental research.

Van Dijk and Steffen's research in Delft between 1966 and 1970, on the experience of different room heights, represents the beginning of an attempt by social science to meet the needs of architecture. (Shortly before this, de Jonge had been recruited to

Delft to provide the same service). Behind the research initiative lay designers' disquiet over people's experience of and satisfaction with the currently dominant styles of architecture, which was large scale, high-rise, linear, and severe. Many Dutch architects (e.g., Hertzberger, van Eijck) were beginning to place an emphasis in their designs on "quality of life" (referred to in Dutch by *leefbaarheid* or "livability"). They felt inadequate, however, to deal with these problems themselves, and declared themselves open to contributions from social scientists.

In 1970, Ackermans completed a PhD thesis[1] on play behavior. The Dutch Institute for Preventive Medicine, where the researcher worked, for a decade facilitated research on sociomedical aspects of the design of residential areas, for example, on social isolation in tall buildings and child safety in the environment. Although Ackermans' research did not produce particularly striking results in itself, it represented the first of a series of observational studies of human behavior from a more or less ecological approach, in which the unity of behavior and environment played a central part. Most of this research has been carried out on child behavior, especially in the traffic environment; where adults are concerned, behavior measurements have nearly always been made by means of questionnaire.

The first major conference in the field, on perception of environmental quality, was organized in 1977 at the request of UNESCO in connection with their Man and the Biosphere program. Conference proceedings were published in *Urban Ecology* (Sanders, 1979). A particular attempt was made to relate perceptual processes at various levels of scale and to bring together research and practice.

A year earlier, a special issue of the *Dutch Journal of Psychology* (Nieuwenhuijse, 1978) was devoted to environmental psychology. This can be taken as representing more or less the first institutionalization of the field. The contents of the issue dealt with: effects of density on the level of children's motoric activity; the height/distance ratio as a predictor of perceived "spatial openness-enclosure" and emotional responses in normal and phobic subjects; the influence of wall color on the judgments of a space; and the evaluation of different types of street. It is striking that none of the authors of these articles is still working as an active researcher in environmental psychology. In part, this may be because the work represented classical, experimental research, rather than foreshadowing the subsequent development of the field toward a problem orientation.

In 1979, the first Dutch-language textbook on environmental psychology, *Psychologie van Bouwen en Wonen*, and to date the only one of its kind in the field, appeared. It set out to provide a survey, for designers primarily, of the possibilities of using insights from psychology for designing a livable environment (Smets, 1979).

In the same year, Ester (1979b) edited *Sociale Aspecten van het Milieuvraagstuk* [Social aspects of environmental issues]. This collection is social scientific, rather than specifically psychological, and treats the environment rather broadly. It includes general articles, with a rather limited research base, on environmental behavior and consciousness, resource consumption, noise annoyance, environmental calamities, nuclear energy risk, environmental policy, and environmental groups (Ester, 1979b).

34.3. CENTERS OF ENVIRONMENTAL RESEARCH

Another way of characterizing our field of interest is in terms of the major centers that are actively engaged in relevant research. The list that follows might not be treated as definitive by one or two individuals in the field, but it does cover the greater part of the group endeavors that have developed, in the 1970s in particular. A list of addresses of these centers is appended to this chapter, so that interested readers may make contact—for example, for the lists of publications that are often available.

The Center of Architectural Research at the Technological University of Delft is the most important center of environmental psychological research in the Netherlands. It engages both in contract research and fundamental research into relations between people and the built environment, especially at the microlevel. Both theory development and the solution of practical design and management problems are dealt with. In the center's early years, a more cognitive research approach was followed (e.g., mapping, experiential aspects of design); now there is more attention to the use of the built environment and postoccupancy evaluation. Fields of application include housing and the residential environment, buildings other than for housing, social facility provision, and the evaluation of health centers.

The Department of Housing Ecology (Ekologie van het wonen) at the Agricultural University of Wageningen attempts to integrate social scientific, and particularly microsociological, knowledge with insights into the design process. In the dialogue between user and creator, science is given a par-

ticipative and supporting role. In addition to the development of the necessary theoretical knowledge, this group devotes considerable attention to giving it concrete form. Extensive equipment is available for simulation work. The principle research themes are: residents' participation in the development and management of buildings; the position of exceptional groups in the housing market; communal and collective forms of residential provision; the use and experience of the residence and of the residential environment in urban and rural areas.

At the Technological University of Eindhoven, there is an interdepartmental work group—Built Environment, Design and Behavior—that draws on researchers from architecture and the social sciences. An environmental psychological focus has been chosen, though architects also make important substantive contributions to research themes and problems. A new research program, on environmental technology, is being developed, with a strong emphasis on the relation between interior design and social processes. Some recent research projects include: the effect of changes in the residential environment on children's play behavior; the use and evaluation of offices; and the recording and processing of behavioral science information by architects during the design process.

The Social Psychology Department at the University of Nijmegen has since 1980 had environmental psychology as one of its two major research themes. The focus is on the relation between social and psychological aspects of the built environment and, more particularly, on positive and negative aspects of the urban residential environment. Research is directed at gaining insight into the conditions under which the residential climate can be improved. There is a systematic attempt to interpret environmental psychology as a branch of applied social psychology. Recent research topics include: the residential experience in heavily industrialized, hazardous environments; feelings of personal security and insecurity in the residential environment; the significance of leisure behavior and its place in the urban environment; and sociopolitical participation in the residential environment.

At Tilburg University, there is a joint endeavor between the Department of Planning Sociology and a section of the Institute for Social Scientific Research that deals with housing and planning. This is a good example of primarily sociological research on environmental questions, which from time to time has some relevance for environmental psychology. At present, there are six major themes of research: functional change in urban areas; migration and mobility; housing density; the housing market and housing policy; housing for exceptional groups; and leisure time in the urban environment. Research projects with a more psychological component include: a comparative study of residents' images of their city in two medium-sized cities; the significance of the garden; and comfort and discomfort (*behagen en onbehagen*) in postwar neighborhoods.

The Dutch Institute for Preventive Health Care (NIPG) is a department of the National Institute for Applied Natural Science Research (TNO). Over the years, a number of projects have been carried out there that fall within the realm of environmental psychology. After the initial research of Ackermans, referred to above, on children's play behavior, several studies were done on the influence of the housing situation on sociomedical factors. Another theme has been research on children's traffic behavior, and, more particularly the relation between street design and traffic safety.

The Traffic Studies Center at the University of Groningen carries out research into various aspects of traffic behavior and traffic safety, primarily from a viewpoint of physiological and experimental psychology. Although environmental psychology is not used as a research framework, the use of techniques of behavioral observation and the attention given to physical design features in the environment make much of the research of relevance for our field. (This applies equally for other traffic research institutes, such as NIPG and Soesterberg that also fall under TNO). Important research themes are: behavior analysis and behavior change (e.g., evaluation of traffic education programs for preschool children); effects of medicines and drugs on traffic behavior; and mobility and travel demand.

The Institute for Environmental Issues (Free University, Amsterdam) and the Department of Social and Organizational Psychology at the University of Leiden can be taken as particular representatives of a rather different line of research— concentrating on a (social) psychological approach to energy and other environmental problems. The word *milieu* is used, to refer to the environment at a more global or ecological level than in the term *omgeving*, or "surroundings," which is used in the context of environmental psychology. The type of research that is conducted varies from the strongly policy oriented to the more fundamental. In the earlier years, a good deal of attention was given to environmental consciousness and attitudes. This was followed by modeling approaches to individual environmental behavior and

more recently to policy-supportive research and research into environmental policy options. The two groups have collaborative links.

The Institute for Environmental Hygiene and Health Technology (IMG) is also a branch of TNO. It carries out research into the relations between environmental factors and health and into possible ways of achieving an ecologically responsible living environment. Although the emphasis in most of the research lies on more technological aspects, more and more attention is being paid to experience of the environment. Recent themes of research are: experiences having to do with lighting conditions, noise, smell, and heating systems; risk perception; and problems of older inner cities. Noise is a particularly important topic, with much research on the noise annoyance caused by traffic, railways, airplanes, and industry. Evaluation research is carried out on the effects of noise-prevention provisions in dwellings.

34.4. THE RECENT STATE OF ENVIRONMENTAL (PSYCHOLOGICAL) RESEARCH

During the period of slow development in the 1960s and early 1970s, it was noticeable that research questions were dealt with primarily for their own sake— that is, as stimuli for scientific research. Only an incidental gesture would be made in the direction of society at large, with a pious hope that the sponsor could do something with the results. More recently, there has been a shift toward a clearer identification on the part of the researcher with a specific problem or target group, especially in the case of design-oriented research. For example, if research is done now on the influence of room height or color on psychological functioning, it is with a view to incorporating results in actual designs, rather than as an opportunity for fundamental research. The psychologist may even feel himself or herself to be in part a designer. Or again, whereas energy problems were initially treated as an interesting topic for attitude research, attention now is more often paid to the problem itself, from a specialist and interdisciplinary environmental perspective.

This shift from scientific researcher to problem solver can sometimes be so striking as to lead to a feeling of alienation from one's original discipline. The distance between the two approaches can also lead to the creation of separate traditions. Yet it is probably precisely because of this trend that Dutch university subfaculties of psychology have failed to invest, to any extent, in environmental psychology. The problem orientation still does not properly fit the dominant scientific norm, which is only very slowly and reluctantly admitting the implications of the decreasing resources and governmental pressures to which we referred before. This difference in values and goals between scientific norms and problem orientation may also be a reason for the small amount of (English language) international publications that we are able to refer to in this review.

To give an idea of some of the major substantive categories in that recent research which have more or less an environmental psychological emphasis, we have summarized in Table 34.1 some 300 projects that were under way during the 5-year period prior to our review. The numerical values should be taken only as approximate indicators of the relative attention given to what we have chosen to see as the more prominent categories. Some of the projects tabulated were at a preliminary stage, and some should perhaps be considered less as research than as commentary on a topic. There must be some double counting due to changes in the title and even content of research during its course. And a number of

projects, for example, on the evaluation of experimental housing, are essentially identical in purpose and design.

The last three main categories are much more extensively represented in research outside the field of environmental psychology. By contrast, there is probably an underrepresentation of research on the work environment. Its industrial sponsorship is associated with even less public availability than is usual for Dutch social scientific research.

The resources for the information in the table were of several kinds. In the course of a postal request for copies of reviews, reports, articles, and research notes relevant to environmental psychology, about 150 institutions and individuals were contacted. They received our list of contacts and were asked to add to it, if appropriate. In the end, some 60 contacts provided us with material that they believed would be useful in writing this chapter. This material consisted of research reports and news of ongoing research. Also, the usual Dutch sources for information on recent and ongoing studies were consulted. In addition, information was collected by personal visits to institutions, and interviews were conducted with

Table 34.1. Summary of Dutch Research Projects, 1978–1982

Category		
Architectural psychology		130
Perception and cognition (general)	23	
Perception of specific building types	10	
Visual evaluation, including landscape	13	
Experience of built environment (general)	39	
Residential satisfaction, evaluation	22	
Evaluation of alternative housing types	23	
Urban planning and design		67
City planning and design	24	
Citizen participation	20	
Urban behavior	23	
Environmental issues		46
Pollution, energy conservation, environmental awareness, and education	46	
Theory development		17
Sociologically oriented	9	
Environmental psychological	8	
Traffic		24
Traffic noise and health	19	
Other traffic research	5	
Risk perception, hazard, and associated decision processes		11
Recreation		9
Total		304

selected individuals and representatives of institutions. We should emphasize that our aim was, as far as possible, to allow contributors to the field to have a definite influence on the way in which it is represented here. This chapter is thus intended as a communal response rather than as a scholarly review.

The hesitancy with which we present the information in the table should not be read as natural reserve on our part, however, but as reflecting characteristics of the national field under discussion here. These make it extremely difficult to offer a comprehensive and useful inventory of Dutch environmental psychology. In the first place, it is striking that the majority of research to which we might wish to refer does not appear in publications, that is, in books or journals. It tends to be disseminated by way of "reports," which rather quickly can become unobtainable. Sometimes no more than 20 copies will have been produced. This characteristic is due in part, of course, to the small number of outlets for Dutch-language publication and to the extra work entailed by writing in a "world language"; but it is also due to a rather different attitude on the part of Dutch researchers to written communication and publication. Normative expectations about how much an academic should publish are certainly lower than in many other countries (and not only the United States). In the case of contract research, there seems to be a disinclination to distil the final report of the project into the form of scientific articles. In the research institutes, where much of this type of work is done, there is often very little time available for that sort of writing. The more applied a piece of research is, the less likely one is to find it in the libraries.

For these reasons, we have chosen, in the following sections, to give only limited examples of the projects in the table and of antecedent research. By no means is all of it published and very little is in a language other than Dutch. We assume that most Dutch references would be difficult for readers of this *Handbook* to read, even if they could find them, and that too long a list would be of dubious value. To compensate, we have given the addresses of the most important centers of environmental psychological research in an appendix.

Another important decision that we made was to attempt to draw a fairly sharp distinction between environmental psychology and environmental research centered in other disciplines and to concentrate on the former. This is a problematic issue. In part, it is forced on us by the fact that most of the more inter- and multidisciplinary research is done in research institutes, under contract, and is subject to the publication limitations referred to. The early growth of environmental psychology in the United States and the United Kingdom was very closely bound up with developments in architecture and human geography, for example. This connection has not been entirely absent in the Netherlands, but we believe that it has been of much smaller significance. The intense interdisciplinarity that is generally characteristic of French intellectual and academic life is certainly not to be found. In Dutch social science faculties, there tends to be a jealous distinction between the disciplines, so that collaboration is rare.

The number of people in the Netherlands who might wish to label themselves *environmental psychologists* is very small—certainly no more than 20. In comparison, the number of urban sociologists (*sociologen van bouwen en wonen*) is considerably larger. One would expect much of their research in Anglo-Saxon countries to be done by psychologists. In recent years, the Netherlands has had the highest proportional number of sociologists in the world. Sociology is represented in the universities by a broad range of specialized subdisciplines, many of which are applied, and social science research institutes or departments of research institutes tend to be dominated by sociologists. The emphasis in sociology lies in a combination of theory and application, which so far has not characterized psychological research. There status is given to experimental, analytic, and theoretically based work. For several reasons, then, environmental psychology, as such, faces strong institutional barriers.

Perhaps because of this, we have preferred to stay within the boundaries suggested by this *Handbook*'s title, as far as possible. The only exception, and it is not an inconsiderable one, is that we have included in the review research carried out by microsociologists, which we believe is virtually indistinguishable from social environmental psychology.

34.5. CONTRIBUTIONS OF ENVIRONMENTAL PSYCHOLOGY TO DESIGN PROBLEM SOLVING

Both from a quantitative and qualitative viewpoint, research to inform design problem solving is by far the most important component of Dutch environmental psychology. Of particular interest, on the positive side, is the exemplification of a trend toward problem solution that is developing widely in psychology.

More negatively, difficulties in the relationship between the different disciplines involved can also be viewed as having a general significance for applied fields.

The origins of this kind of work lay with the felt need of designers for a social scientific contribution to their activities. A specific motive cannot be adduced. It was probably a combination of the stage of development both of the social sciences, which at the end of the 1950s were at the beginning of a tempestuous period, and of architecture and urban design, where doubts were increasing about the possible inhumanity of large-scale building. Many designers were experiencing a new feeling of responsibility with regard to the social impact of their work.

In the architecture departments of Delft and Eindhoven, it certainly became a basic point of policy that the social aspects of designing should be given much more emphasis. Delft was the first place in which a social scientist was appointed, and this led ultimately to the creation there of the Center for Architectural Research. The role of social scientists, however, was one of support; there has never been talk of full integration. They contribute to teaching primarily through optional or subsidiary subjects and carry out research on questions that the designers hand out. The possibilities for developing specific, relevant psychological knowledge and theory are limited by this support role. Research and teaching must above all produce concrete, usable results for designers. In addition to restricting the psychologists' scope, this produces frustrations when results that were thought in principle to be usable are not actually put into practice. The problem is not really solved by the research groups having become self-supporting in their work.

Other aspects of the relationship between the two groups are their very different identities and ways of thinking and working. In the Netherlands, designers, and especially architects, form what is almost a caste; the separation both of the profession and the discipline is more marked than in other countries. A self-determining orientation makes them not only less susceptible to outside influences or to invitations to cooperate, but also strengthens the tendency to allow new styles continually to outstrip evaluation of the old. An education for continually creative and independent design contrasts strongly with the psychologist's socialization into a form of knowledge in which the world is conceived of as essentially static.

The two groups are aware of their own differences in style and in the focus of their interest. It is probably no surprise that architects appear as intuitive, synthesizers, adventurous, active, and creative; they are interested in morphology, spatiality, what is unique, the approximate and the implicit. Psychologists seem more analytical, systematic, cautious, precise, explicit, and verbal; and their interest is more in demythologizing architecture, in behavior, and in generalities. These differences were even apparent to us in the way in which they were expressed. In our interviews, the social scientist would generally look for the kernel of the question and attempt to generalize it to a more abstract level. By contrast, designers came out with an anecdote to illustrate various facets of the issue, not least whatever was exceptional. Designers' responses tended to be much longer than those of social scientists.

Differences in style of working can lead to the two groups being quite out of phase. Collaboration began, broadly speaking, with architects' doubts about prevailing norms for large-scale development and with worries that they produced an inhuman, uninhabitable environment. Social scientists responded by probing the effects of high- and low-rise building types and by measuring residential satisfaction. Meanwhile, new styles of building were emerging, with a greater variety of forms, on a smaller scale, and more "hospitable" (*herbergzaam*). These were criticized by some in the design world as being too middle class and "cosy" (it was termed the *nieuwe kneuterigheid*); and yet another phase in the evolution of style arrived. This new style stemmed from designers who wished to exercise more freedom in their design activities. They wanted to be more creative again. They became impatient with the encumbrance on their creative work of human factors and user participation. They now actually worked against the efforts of those social scientists who were still engaged with problems of human scale and people's experience of the built environment.

This type of difficulty is probably fundamental to the position of social scientists who would engage in applied research. A more conscious step in the direction of the problematic itself and its context is called for. New approaches and theory are necessary. Meanwhile, the younger researchers are pursuing a more independent path than did their predecessors of 15 years ago. Instead of waiting for questions from designers, with all the frustrations which that can entail, they are more likely to use insights from the subject matter itself, as they see it, to provide them with their starting point.

Against this background, a number of typical examples of research can be highlighted. Several dissertations that have been published give an idea of the range of the more productive academic work. A methodological study of different means of simulating the built environment, with particular attention to the "enthoscope" was done by Bouwman (1979). Danz (1981) conducted a field study in an apartment complex, on the relation between tenant mix, social contacts between neighbors, and well-being. Pennartz (1979) examined the social meaning of the built environment in terms particularly of privacy, "feeling at home," and "comfort." Reactions to different street images were the subject of Schellekens'(1976) research: On the basis of Berlyne's theoretical work, variations in arousal level were related to preferences for streets that differed in complexity and variety. Van Wagenberg (1982) completed his dissertation at SUNY/Stony Brook: It evaluated an educational program in participatory design (cf. also van Wagenberg, Krasner, & Krasner, 1981).

Berlyne's theory also formed a partial basis for one of a number of studies of satisfaction with the living environment. Driessen, Tazelaar, and Wippler (see Driessen & Beerenboom, 1983) developed a "subjective expected utility" model on the basis of his theory about preferences for complexity and a modified Maslow need hierarchy. Their attention to explicit theory is relatively rare in this area of research, as Tacken and de Kleijn (1979) also point out in their literature review. Driessen, Tazelaar, and Wippler's study was also unusual in its treatment of multiple aspects of a broadly conceived living environment, rather than just parts of it such as the street, dwelling, and so on. A study that responded directly to a rather dramatic feature of the Dutch environment was van Rijn's (1976–1977) research on residents' satisfaction in the North Sea Canal area in the Rijnmond, a very heavily developed industrial area with a high concentration of petrochemical installations. Although an extensive study, this was also typical of much work in this field, in being descriptive rather than addressing specific questions. It also had its (tenuous) theoretical base in a need hierarchy.

An earlier study of different methods of visual representation was done by Rongen (1973) in a comparison of maquettes, drawings, photographs, slides, and films. More recently, the same researcher and his colleagues (Rongen, Kiel, & Eckardt, 1979) have examined the way in which residents use degrees of freedom that have been designed into their dwellings.

A small cluster of researchers have concentrated on the case of children in the built environment, especially with regard to play behavior and traffic hazards. Reference has already been made to Ackermans' (1970) dissertation research, in which he conducted a descriptive and observational study of play behavior in different locations and made comparisons between an "experimental" and "standard" playground. Van Andel (1982) has a long-term research project on play spaces, with a strong socioecological orientation. Güttinger (1980) compared play behavior across comparable neighborhoods that provided different environments and found a microlevel of analysis of observations to be of importance for showing the influence of design details. Bleeker and Mulderij (1980; Mulderij & Bleeker, 1982) provide a discussion of much of the literature on children's play in the environment, together with suggestions for improving facilities. In a different tradition, Dijkink and Elbers (1981) have published work on children's development, in terms of Piagetian stages, of geographic representation.

It is not surprising that one finds research on landscape that may reflect a number of preconceptions about the Netherlands. For example, Boerwinkel (Boerwinkel & Broekhuizen-Bos, 1976) has looked at the image that the poplar and other sorts of tree have for the professional, in relation to the aesthetics and economics of landscape planning, and has examined (Boerwinkel, van Berkel, Klüppel, & Slijkerman, 1982) the use and evaluation of urban parks in Arnhem. Coeterier (1980) has conducted an exploratory and typological study of the experience, representation, and evaluation of landscape images in Gieten and Heiloo. Coeterier and Rijkes (1981), also with attention to landscape, looked at the relation between design and perception in the context of village expansion. The flat landscape that is a feature of much of the Netherlands provided the field for de Jonge's (1979) study of people's experience of nature and landscape. Hengeveld and de Vocht (1982) edited an international collection of papers on water in urban ecology, which included attention to social and psychological factors.

A somewhat more unusual focus has been on monuments, to which de Vocht (1978) has provided an introduction. Ganzenboom (1982–1983) has done an empirical study of people's experience of monuments, in Utrecht, their recognizability and the value attached to them. Although there were individual differences in reaction, with respect to knowledge level and education, it was suggested that monuments represent a less elitist cultural resource than, say, theaters or museums.

34.6. RESEARCH WITHIN URBAN DESIGN AND PLANNING[2]

This other major research category contains much that can be typified as especially Dutch—despite many of our informants' denial that there were specific Dutch currents or a relation between research topics and other aspects of Dutch culture. Certainly, research reports reveal that investigators rely on Anglo-American literature in designing their research. Nevertheless, we would suggest that many of the topics chosen do reflect certain cultural values. We have already referred to work in relation to the question of "human scale." Another example occurs in the context of urban renewal, which in the Netherlands is especially concerned with maintenance of the residential areas directly around the old city centers. In purpose and design, it has an essentially different character than similar research in other countries.

Although issues of crowding lay claim to be the prototypical concern for environmental psychology (cf. the chapter on the environment in almost any recent social psychology textbook) and although population density in the Netherlands is second only to that in Bangladesh, Dutch research has followed no such obvious path. Space allocation is certainly a problem—in housing, road construction, the siting of industry or airports—but it is typically treated as a political rather than a social (scientific) problem. This suggests that not only is crowding not experienced primarily as a density phenomenon, but also that research attention to it has cultural rather than physical antecedents. The Dutch language has no words of its own for "crowding" and "privacy."

However, many of the more central aspects of research on the perception and evaluation of the immediate residential environment incorporate implicitly a number of concepts that came particularly to the fore in the 1960s and 1970s and that reflect peculiar features of Dutch culture. This peculiarity can be seen partly in the difficulty of translating the relevant terms, though that in turn is due to some extent to the lack of agreement over their precise significance and to a failure to operationalize them specifically.

One of these terms is *herbergzaamheid* (perhaps "hospitableness"). It has been much used by Hertzberger, particularly in relation to his designs for office buildings. The cities of Groningen and Delft used it as the central criterion for inner-city development plans. The term suggests "being made to feel at home, to feel good in one's surroundings." A comparable term is *geborgenheid*, which conveys something like, but more than, "security." It suggests that there is a feeling of reassurance that can be a quality of the built environment. These two terms probably correspond to that ideal of environmental satisfaction, the comfort (*gezelligheid*) of the domestic hearth. The word *gezellig* is another difficult term to translate. The best indication is perhaps given by some combination of the nuances of "friendly," "easy," "personal," and "intimate." It is not restricted to the domestic context. A residential neighborhood can also be *gezellig*; many designs for new developments or renewal areas are based on an attempt at *gezelligheid*. However, although there have been research studies motivated by concepts like these, they have not led to a distinctive line of research, not least, of course, because they were not intended as research concepts. Even where the intention for a new line of research was present, as in the case of Grunfeld's (1970) concept *habitat* (the total lifespace, based on both spatial and social components of behavior), problems of operationalization have led to a deadend in research. Tacken and de Kleijn (1979) conclude their review of research on the residential experience with the remark that it is very disappointing that after so many years of housing research no agreement has yet been arrived at over the definition of concepts. Pennartz's (1979) research, already referred to, on the social significance of the built environment, directed particularly at the residential space of families, is an example of research of this kind. But more recently, any attempt to elaborate those concepts that would correspond to more specifically Dutch features has been replaced by a concern for new scientific paradigms such as the participatory and qualitative.

More promising perhaps is research that focuses on less abstract aspects of the Dutch residential environment. A nice example is the *woonerf*,[3] whereby a neighborhood's streets are changed in various ways to shelter them from traffic. This measure was first taken in the older quarters of cities to increase safety, but came to be valued for its general effect on the appearance of residential neighborhoods. It seemed to give an air of the desired "hospitableness." Various research projects have been carried out on traffic safety in the *woonerf* and on its aesthetic value as a place to live (e.g., de Jonge, 1981). Increases in safety have been difficult to demonstrate. But though people sometimes spoke critically of them as "parking lots," because of the large number of parked cars that stay behind in a *woonerf*, an increase in neighborhood attractiveness due to informal design characteristics was clearly demonstrated.

The regulatory role of government has also had its effect on environmental research. Although not uniquely Dutch, regulation sometimes goes further than one might expect. For example, in large cities one has to obtain permission to live in any particular house in order to maintain an appropriate relation between the size of dwellings and the number of occupants. (The full extent of government regulation generally is nicely illustrated in aviation legislation: The relevant law begins, "Flying is forbidden, unless an exemption is granted"). Considerable research on the housing market has accordingly been stimulated: for example, with a view to estimating future needs for a particular type of dwelling, or to evaluating satisfaction with various forms of experimental and alternative housing.

As far as the reported research is concerned, we could probably have cited some of our earlier references here, for example the work of Danz (1981). Within an appreciable range, levels of scale are ambiguous. This ambiguity is present, in particular, in much of the work done in research institutes that have a strong sociological component—for instance, the IVA. Examples are the dissertation by Stoppelenburg (1982) on prewar neighborhoods and Brouwer and Tacken's study of new suburbs (1977); and a report on the image of the city center in promoting residential satisfaction and social and emotional ties (Dekkers & Kuijstermans, 1983). The Institute of Applied Sociology at the University of Nijmegen is another example. In recent years, researchers there have done research on recreation, including sportfishing and the use of the bicycle for recreation, as well as a long series of evaluations of experimental housing developments (e.g., Pas & Kropman, 1977). At the University of Utrecht, the Department of Urban Sociology (Sociologie van bouwen en wonen) has pursued the same theme, as well as research on residents' participation in housing management and on neighborhood renewal.

One of the more psychologically substantial areas of research has been on aspects of migration; we may cite especially a dissertation study by Gall (1983). He examined the relations between well-being, need satisfaction, and personal control, elaborated in terms of the concept *attribution*, in the context of migration from a large city to a new town. Blaauw (Blaauw, 1982; Blaauw & Pastor, 1980) has done studies of the consequences for social contact of moving from old neighborhoods to new towns and of motivations for moving back into the inner city of Utrecht from the new suburbs. Social contact between neighbors (cf. Danz, 1981) appears again in a study by Staats (1980) (see also Knegtmans & Staats, 1982). It attempted to predict the satisfaction of inhabitants with the social life of their neighborhood, as well as testing a number of central propositions of Maslow's theory.

In this section, more than in the preceding one, we have experienced the procedural problems of review that we discussed earlier. Certainly, there is research being done on people and their urban environment. Much of it justifies itself with reference to social scientific concepts. But reference explicitly to what one would recognize as concepts, theories, or methods peculiar to the science of psychology is very much rarer. It is our impression that research at the macroscale of the built environment is much more likely to be done within a broadly sociological framework and even less likely to be published in a readily accessible form.

34.7. OTHER AREAS OF RESEARCH

We have already pointed out that traffic research and research on noise annoyance and abatement has been largely dominated by subfields of psychology other than environmental psychology. However, several dissertation topics have been of more immediate interest. Güttinger (1980) attempted to find an alternative to traffic accidents as an index of traffic unsafety, and centred his research on "conflicts" between traffic participants. He used his conflict observation technique in field studies of child pedestrians in urban neighborhoods. Van der Molen (van der Molen, 1983; van der Molen, Kerkof, & Jong, 1983; van der Molen, van den Herik, & van der Klauw, 1983) also used an observational methodology to study the road-crossing behavior of adults and children under different conditions. Rothengatter (1981, 1982) evaluated an experimental traffic education program for children. In the somewhat different tradition of "mental mapping" research, Janssen (1974) studied strategic route choice of city drivers and applied the results to a new system of district signposting.

Risk perception is a highly specific area of environmental psychology, and is unusual in the Netherlands in its close association with social psychology and in having firm theoretical roots. Stallen and Meertens (1979) examined the opinions of a large sample of scientists on nuclear energy. A more extensive survey was done by Vlek and Stallen (1980) in which a typology of risks of various kinds was developed. They also studied the judged advantages and acceptability of risky phenomena. More recent research by Midden, Daamen, and Verplanken (1983) combined a large-scale survey with an experimental study of attitudes toward different forms of energy generation, including attitudes toward the risk component. Kok (1983) studied the effect of temporal distance on risk perception. Stallen and Tomas (1983) have developed and tested a model of coping processes in the context of perceived risk in a mixed residential and petrochemical industrial area. Ongoing research includes work on perception of risk in relation to liquid petroleum gas and sulphur dioxide, and on the influence of the mass media on risk perception.

Despite the potential, environmental psychological aspects are not generally seen as an interesting component of leisure and recreation research, which is itself rather underdeveloped. In comparison with international trends, there is less interest in the Dutch research in sports and countryside experience than in urban studies. Existing research has an extremely restricted or nonexistent theoretical basis. Most studies are primarily policy oriented, under contract to central or local government, and have limited scope and generality. The question of whether recreation outside the city compensates for a less positive and natural urban environment was the explicit topic for a study by Katteler and Kropman (1975). The same authors (1977) examined relative preferences for extensive and intensive forms of leisure. Beckers, Aldershoff, ter Veer-Bos, and van 't Eind (1981) used a simulation game, among other techniques, to study the meaning of the residential environment as a field of leisure for housewives. In a series of studies (Coops, Kremer, & Mulder, 1978; Kremer & Veen, 1983; Mulder, 1981), the multifunctionality of city areas was found to be bimodally related to their attractiveness for leisure. Kremer and Veen (1983) also examined personal meanings and preferences for leisure in the residential environment.

We suggested earlier that research on environmental issues has a somewhat different role in a review of environmental psychology than the other topics, largely because of its attention to the environment as "milieu." It also represents, in the Netherlands, a more determinedly interdisciplinary context for environmental psychologists to work in—

a context, however, that tends to be dominated by biologists and biotechnologists. The research is heavily policy oriented. Typical concentration points are research on the effect of information and publicity campaigns on attitudes and behavior toward pollution and energy consumption and conservation. Edited collections by Ester (1979b), Ester and de Leeuw (1981), and Aiking, Ester, Hordijk, and van de Veen (1982) give a good idea of this kind of work, with regard especially to social scientific aspects, as does Ester's own work on attitudes and behavior (Ester, 1979a), environmental concern (Ester, 1981), and attitudes to nuclear power (van der Pligt, van der Linden, & Ester, 1982). Van Raaij (van de Maele-Vaernewijck, van Raaij, & Verhallen, 1980; van Raaij & Verhallen, 1980) has done research on consumer behavior in a glass recycling program and on household behavior and energy consumption. The work of Kok (Bosma & Kok, 1982; Kok, 1983) is typical of an approach that uses environmental issues (especially the energy crisis) as a context for traditional theoretical studies on, for example, attitudes and behavior. A rather new and developing area of research is environmental crime (cf. Hoefnagels, 1981).

34.8. CONCLUDING REMARKS

First, what can we say of the future of environmental psychology in the Netherlands? There are positive points to be made, but also a bleaker picture to paint. The main positive element is the growing scientific output of the field, even though it tends to be scattered over divergent research questions and not to have too much reference to environmental psychology as such. There is a growing number of dissertations in which environmental psychological topics are central to the research. The number of publications in international journals is growing, though the absolute total is still small. The development of research in the institutes, where work is done more from an applied than an academic orientation, is another feature that may lead the field to greater independence and strength. The changing scene in psychology as a whole, with pressure from a reduction in funds and the diminishing number of students, will also be positively influential in leading to a reevaluation of applied branches of psychology. Topics within environmental psychology having to do with, for example, social gerontology, traffic behavior, and the psychology of work can be expected to be in a healthier position than more traditional psychological topics. The growing number of new, professionally oriented specializations within Dutch psychology is an indication of this reorientation. It is to be hoped that environmental psychology will benefit from this development.

However, the bleak picture is easier to paint. In many respects and despite the Green party nearby in West Germany, much of the force of the environmental movement seems to have been expended. Peace, employment, health, and emancipation are more stirring themes. Environmental research will continue to be done, but only so long as policy makers wish to spend money on it. It will take place mainly outside the universities and tend to be highly specific and atheoretical. There will be a quick turnover of short-term contracts, with little incentive for reflection or wider publication. Environmental psychology, as such, will be limited to one or two of the specialist research programs within which all university research is now being regulated, and in a new bureaucratic system that promises to inhibit the risk and ambiguity of a continuously developing creative endeavor. It will increasingly be torn apart between artificially imposed poles of fundamental and applied goals. Disciplinary loyalty will be demanded by the university professors and a superficial multidisciplinarity by government contractors.

Second, what are our reflections on the writing of this chapter? Although we can speak about environmental psychology in the Netherlands, we would not wish to underwrite the parochial and patronizing notion of a peculiar Dutch version of that field. It is presumably the difficulty of language that prevents material from non-English-speaking countries being readily incorporated into the main substantive chapters of this *Handbook* or that leads generally to little reference to work from outside North America in most North American literature. (One does wonder, however, why Britain and Australia are also subject to this trend.) We would rather see environmental psychology constructed in the future as an integratable, international field.

A more fundamental doubt has to do with the way in which the scientific storytelling in this chapter may be read. We would wish to deter readers from allowing our glossed account of the "reality" behind the literature references to become naturalized. Our history and sociology is largely bogus. We relay impressions of the field given to us by others through correspondence and interview. What is interesting ultimately is not the account, as such, of environmental psychology in the Netherlands, but the way in which our informants and ourselves attempted to construct an acceptable account. This comment is by way of deconstructing it.

A final doubt has to do with an "invisible college," with "practice" and with "disciplines." The small size of the Netherlands, particular norms about publication, and our own choice to focus on environmental *psychology* have shown us how artificial the conventional academic review may be when it has a plethora of disciplinary literature to discuss. There is a need for institutionalized ways of discussing our field of interest so that the invisible college beyond publication, multidisciplinary compromises, and actual practice are given full respect. If we could start over again, we would try to do rather more of that. We shall be curious to see whether any other contributors to the *Handbook* had a similar urge.

APPENDIX

Addresses of Some Environmental Research Groups in the Netherlands

Center for Architectural Research
TH Delft
Berlageweg 1
2628 CR Delft

Department of Housing Ecology
Landbouwhogeschool Wageningen
Ritsema Bosweg 32a
6703 AZ Wageningen

Department of Behavioral Sciences
Social Psychology Section
W&MW, HG 9-29, TH Eindhoven
Postbus 513
5600 MB Eindhoven

Department of Social Psychology
Katholieke Universiteit Nijmegen
Psychologisch Laboratorium
Postbus 9104
6500 HE Nijmegen

Department of Planning Sociology/Housing Section, IVA
Katholieke Hogeschool Tilburg
Hogeschoollaan 225
5037 GC Tilburg

NIPG/TNO
Postbus 124
2300 AC Leiden

Traffic Research Centre
Rijksuniversiteit Groningen
Rijksstraatweg 76
9752 AK Haren (Gr.)

Institute for Environmental Issues (IVM)
Vrije Universiteit
Postbus 7161
1007 MC Amsterdam

Department of Social Psychology
Rijksuniversiteit Leiden
Hooigracht 15
2312 KM Leiden

IMG/TNO, Department of Sound, Light and Indoor
Climate
Postbus 214
2600 AE Delft

NOTES

1. This is a more momentous event than in Anglo-Saxon countries, for example. A *proefschrift* (literally a "test writing") may represent many years' work. It is often written while holding a university post. The proefschrift is regularly published in book form and is readily available to the academic public.

2. This field is often referred to as *bouwen en wonen*, literally "building and living." The term means more than most obvious English-language equivalents.

3. A *woonerf* is a pedestrianized "residential territory" where pedestrians have overall priority over cars, and cars may only proceed at a walking pace.

REFERENCES

Ackermans, E. (1970). *De woonomgeving als speelgelegenheid* [The vicinity of the home as a play area]. Groningen, Netherlands: Wolters-Noordhoff.

Aiking, H., Ester, P., Hordijk, L., & van de Veen, H.E. (1982). *Mozaiek van de milieuproblematiek* [A mosaic of environmental issues]. Amsterdam: Free University, IVM (Instituut voor Milieuvraagstukken).

Beckers, T., Aldershoff, D., ter Veer-Bos, M., & van 't Eind, A. (1980–81). *Huisvrouwen, uit of thuis: De recreatie van huisvrouwen in de woonomgeving* (2 Vols.) [Housewives at home and abroad: Housewives' recreation in the residential environment]. Wageningen, Netherlands: Agricultural University, Department of Sociology.

Blaauw, P.W. (1982). *Moving from old neighbourhoods to new towns: Consequences for social contacts.* Paper presented at the 10th World Congress of Sociology, Mexico City.

Blaauw, P.W., & Pastor, C. (1980). *Terug naar de grote stad* [Back to the city]. Utrecht, Netherlands: State University, Institute of Geography.

Bleeker, H., & Mulderij, K.J. (1980). *Kinderen buiten spel* [Children play out]. Meppel, Netherlands: Boom.

Boerwinkel, H.W.J., & Broekhuizen-Bos, G.E. (1976). Het image van populieren en andere boomsoorten bij gebruikers [Users' image of poplars and other species of tree]. *Nederlands Bosbouw Tijdschrift, 48*(10), 189–200.

Boerwinkel, H.W.J., van Berkel, H.P.M.M., Klüppel, J.E.J., & Slijkerman, A.J.M. (1982). *Rapport over de parken Sonsbeek, Zijpendaal en Gulden Bodem te Arnhem: Psychologisch en sociologisch onderzoek naar gebruik, beleving en waardering* [Report on the parks Sonsbeek, Zijpendaal and Gulden Bodem in Arnhem: A psychological and sociological study of use, experience and evaluation]. Wageningen, Netherlands: Agricultural University.

Bosma, S., & Kok, G.J. (1982). *Studies in attitude en gedrag 6: Isolatiegedrag, een onderzoek naar woningisolatie* [Studies in attitude and behaviour 6: A study on the insulation of houses]. Groningen, Netherlands: State University, Heijmans Bulletin.

Bouwman, M.J.A. (1979). *De waarde van het gebruik van de enthoskoop in relatie tot andere presentatietechnieken voor de gebouwde omgeving* [The value of the enthoscope in relation to other techniques for representing the built environment]. Wageningen, Netherlands: Agricultural University.

Brouwer, K., & Tacken, M. (1977). *Wonen in nieuwe stadsuitbreidingen* [Living in new suburban developments]. Delft, Netherlands: Technical University, Instituut voor Stedebouwkundig Onderzoek.

Coeterier, J.F. (1980). *Het landschapsbeeld in Gieten en Heiloo* [The image of the landscape in Gieten and Heiloo]. Wageningen, Netherlands: Agricultural University, de Dorschkamp.

Coeterier, J.F., & Rijkes, M. (1981). *Onderzoek naar het verband tussen ontwerp en perceptie van twee dorpsuitbreidingen* [A study of the relation between design and perception in two village developments]. Wageningen, Netherlands: Agricultural University, de Dorschkamp.

Coops, R.H., Kremer, A.A., & Mulder, W.A.M. (1978). *De belevingswaarde van de binnenstad van Arnhem* [Experiencing the inner city of Arnhem]. Groningen, Netherlands: State University, Department of Social Psychology.

Danz, M.J. (1981). *Buren: Een onderzoek naar de invloed van overeenkomsten en verschillen tussen buren op het welbevinden* [Neighbours: A study of the influence of similarities and differences between neighbours on well-being]. City University, Amsterdam.

De Jonge, D. (1962). Images of urban areas. *Journal of American Institute of Planners, 28,*266–276.

De Jonge, D. (1979). Verschillen in gebruik, beleving en waardering van het groen door diverse sociale categorien. In *Beleving en waardering van groen* [Differences in the use, experience and evaluation of greenery by different social categories. In *Experiencing and evaluating greenery*]. Delft, Netherlands: Technical University, Instituut voor Stedebouwkundig Onderzoek.

De Jonge, D. (1981). Waardering van woonerven [Evaluation of 'woonerven']. *Verkeerskunde, 32*(12).

Dekkers, H., & Kuijstermans, K. (1983). *Stad in beeld: Een verkennende studie naar de beeldvorming van twee steden* (2 Vols.) [Town image: An exploratory study of image formation in two cities]. Tilburg, Netherlands: Catholic University, Department of Sociology.

De Vocht, C.L.F.M. (1978). *Beleving van monumenten: Een verslag van bevindingen* [Experiencing monuments: A report of findings]. Nijmegen, Netherlands: Catholic University, Department of Sociology.

Dijkink, G., & Elbers, E. (1981). The development of geographic representation in children: Cognitive and affective aspects of model-building behavior. *Tijdschrift voor Economische en Sociale Geografie, 72*(1), 2–16.

Driessen, F.M.H.M., & Beerenboom, H.J.A. (1983). *De kwaliteit van het stedelijk leefmilieu: Bewoners en hun voorkeuren* [The quality of the urban living environment: Residents and their preferences]. Utrecht, Netherlands: State University, Department of Sociology.

Ester, P. (1979a). *Een sociologisch onderzoek naar attituden en gedragingen van de Nederlandse bevolking met betrekking tot het milieuvraagstuk* [A sociological study of the attitudes and behavior of the Dutch population with regard to the environmental question]. Amsterdam: Free University, Instituut voor Milieuvraagstukken.

Ester, P. (Ed.). (1979b). *Sociale aspecten van het milieuvraagstuk* [Social aspects of the environmental question]. Assen, Netherlands: van Gorcum.

Ester, P. (1981). Environmental concern in the Netherlands. In T. O'Riordan, & R.K. Turner (Eds.), *Progress in resource management and environmental planning*. Chichester, England: Wiley.

Ester, P., & de Leeuw, F.L. (Eds.). (1981). *Energie als maatschappelijk probleem* [Energy as a societal problem]. Assen, Netherlands: van Gorcum.

Gall, J.C. (1983). *Welbevinden, attributie en migratie* [Wellbeing, attribution and migration]. Leiden, Netherlands: State University.

Ganzenboom, H. (1982–83). *Beleving van monumenten* (2 Vols.) [The experience of monuments]. Utrecht, Netherlands: State University, Department of Sociology.

Grunfeld, F. (1970). *Habitat and habitation: A pilot study.* Alphen aan den Rijn, Netherlands: Samson.

Güttinger, V.A. (1980). *Met het oog op hun veiligheid: De ontwikkeling van een konfliktobservatietechniek ter beoordeling van de verkeersveiligheid van woongebieden voor kinderen* [With an eye on their safety: The development of a conflict observation-technique for evaluating the traffic safety of residential areas for children]. City University, Amsterdam.

Hengeveld, H., & de Vocht, C.L.F.M. (Eds.) (1982). Water in Urban Ecology. *Urban Ecology, 7*(3).

Hoefnagels, G.P. (1981). *Witte boorden-criminaliteit* [White collar criminality]. Assen, Netherlands: van Gorcum.

Janssen, W.H. (1974). "De strategie van de routekeuze" [Strategies of route-selection]. *TNO-projekt, 4,* 140–143. Apeldoorn, Netherlands: TNO, Organisatie voor toegepaste natuurwetenschappelijk onderzoek.

Katteler, H.A., & Kropman, J.A. (1975). *Openluchtrekreatie binnen en buiten de woonkern: Kompensatie of komplement* [Outdoor recreation inside and outside the residential core: Compensation or complement]. Nijmegen, Netherlands: Catholic University, Instituut voor Toegepaste Sociologie.

Katteler, H.A., & Kropman, J.A. (1977). *De voorkeur voor intensieve en extensieve openluchtrecreatie* [The preference for intensive or extensive outdoor recreation]. Nijmegen, Netherlands: Catholic University, Instituut voor Toegepaste Sociologie.

Knegtmans, J.J., & Staats, H.J.A.M. (1982). Sociale kontakten in de woonomgeving [Social contacts in the neighborhood]. *Gedrag, 10*(6), 424–439.

Kok, G.J. (1983). The further away, the less serious: Effect of temporal distance on perceived value and probability of a future event. *Psychological Reports, 52,* 531–535.

Kremer, A.A., & Veen, P. (1983). *De plaats en betekenis van stedelijke recreatie binnen het vrijetijdsgedrag* [The place and meaning of urban recreation and leisure]. Den Haag: Ministerie van Landbouw.

Midden, C.J.H., Daamen, D.D.L., & Verplanken, B. (1983). *De beleving van energierisico's: Een landelijk onderzoek naar veronderstellingen, attitudes, normen en gedragingen met betrekking tot het opwekken van elektriciteit met kolen, uraan en wind* [The experience of energy risks: A national study into assumptions, attitudes, norms and behaviour in respect of the production of electricity from coal, uranium and wind]. The Hague, Netherlands: Ministerie van Volkshuisvesting, Ruimteÿke Ordening en Milieubeheer.

Mulder, W.A.M. (1981). *Recreatie in de stadsrandzone van Breda* [Recreation in the vicinity of the city of Breda]. Heerenveen, Netherlands: Ingenieursburo Oranjewoud.

Mulderij, K.J., & Bleeker, H. (1982). *Suggesties ter verbetering van de woonomgeving voor kinderen* [Suggestions for the improvement of the residential environment for children]. Deventer, Netherlands: van Loghum-Slaterus.

Nieuwenhuijse, B. (Ed.). (1978). Omgevingspsychologie [Environmental Psychology]. Special issue, *Nederlands Tijdschrift voor de Psychologie, 33*(6), 349–421.

Pas, B., & Kropman, J.A. (1977). *Experimenteren in de woningbouw: Kasbah, Hengelo* [Experiments in house-building: Kasbah, Hengelo]. Nijmegen, Netherlands: Catholic University, Instituut voor Toegepaste Sociologie.

Pennartz, P.J.J. (1979). *Mensen en ruimte, een studie naar de sociale betekenis van de gebouwde omgeving* [People and space, a study of the social meaning of the built environment]. Wageningen, Netherlands: Agricultural University.

Rongen, M.J.T. (1973). *Visuele representaties: Hun toepasbaarheid in gedragsonderzoek en beoordeling van de gebouwde omgeving* [Visual representations: Their applicability in studies of behaviour and judgment of the built environment]. Rotterdam, Netherlands: Bouwcentrum.

Rongen, M.J.T., Kiel, R.G., & Eckardt, H.O. (1979). *Onbepaaldheid en vrijheid: Variatie in woningbouwprojekten* [Indeterminacy and freedom: Variations in housing projects]. Rotterdam, Netherlands: Bouwcentrum.

Rothengatter, J.A. (1981). *Traffic safety education for young children: An empirical approach*. Lisse, Netherlands: Swets.

Rothengatter, J.A. (1982). A behavioral approach to training pedestrian behavior of young children. *Ergonomics, 25*, 325–326.

Sanders, A.F. (Ed.) (1979). Special issue on perception and the environment. *Urban Ecology, 4*(2), 95–177.

Schellekens, H.M.C. (1976). *De straat: Een omgevingspsychologisch proefschrift* [The street: An environmental-psychological dissertation]. Eindhoven, Netherlands: Technical University.

Smets, G.F.M. (1979). *Psychologie van bouwen en wonen* [Psychology of building and living]. Deventer, Netherlands: van Loghum-Slaterus.

Staats, H.J.A.M. (1980). *Kontakten in de woonomgeving* [Contacts in the residential environment]. Leiden, Netherlands: State University, Department of Social Psychology.

Stallen, P.J.M., & Meertens, R.W. (1979). Beoordeling van risico's van kernenergie. In P. Ester (Ed.), *Sociale aspecten van het milieuvraagstuk* [Judgement of risks in nuclear energy. In P. Ester, Social aspects of the environmental question]. Assen, Netherlands: van Gorcum.

Stallen, P.J.M., & Tomas, A. (1983). Psychological risk: The assessment of threat and control. In P. Ricci, L. Sagan, & C. Wipple (Eds.), *Technological risk assessment*. The Hague, Netherlands: Sijthof.

Stoppelenburg, P.A. (1982). *Woonmilieu en woongedrag: Een evaluatieonderzoek onder bewoners van een aantal vooroorlogse woonwijken in Amsterdam* [Behavior and the residential environment: An evaluation among in-

habitants of several pre-war residential areas in Amsterdam]. Tilburg, Netherlands: Catholic University.

Tacken, M., & de Kleijn, J. (1979). *Beleving van woonsituaties* [Experiencing residential settings]. Delft, Netherlands: Technical University, Instituut voor Stedebouwkundig Onderzoek.

Van Andel, J.A. (1982). *Children's activities in neighbourhoods and playgrounds*. Paper presented at the 20th Congress on Applied Psychology, Edinburgh.

Van de Maele-Vaernewijck, M.C.L., van Raaij, W.F., & Verhallen, T.M.M. (1980). Energiegedrag in de woning: Literatuuroverzicht en gedragsmodel. In *Jaarboek van de Nederlandse Vereniging van Marktonderzoekers* [Energy behavior in the home: A literature review and behavioral model. In Yearbook of the Dutch Association of Market Researchers]. Nederlandse Vereniging van Marktonderzoekers.

Van der Molen, H.H. (1983). *Pedestrian ethology: Unobtrusive observations of child and adult road-crossing behaviour in the framework of a child pedestrian training programme*. Groningen, Netherlands: State University.

Van der Molen, H.H., Kerkhof, J.H., & Jong, A.M. (1983). Training observers to follow children and score their road-crossing behavior. *Ergonomics, 26*, 535–553.

Van der Molen, H.H., van den Herik, J., & van der Klauw, C.J. (1983). Pedestrian behaviour of children and accompanying parents during school journeys: An evaluation of a training programme. *British Journal of Educational Psychology, 5*, 152–168.

Van der Pligt, J., van der Linden, J., & Ester, P. (1982). Attitudes to nuclear energy: Beliefs, values and false consensus. *Journal of Environmental Psychology, 2*, 221–231.

Van Raaij, W.F., & Verhallen, T.M.M. (1980). Huishoudelijk gedrag en stookgasverbruik [Domestic behavior and gas use]. *Economisch Statistische Berichten, 65*, 8–13.

Van Rijn, H.T.U. (1976–1977). *Geïntegreerd milieu onderzoek: Een onderzoek naar de beleving van het ruimtelijk milieu in het Rijnmondgebied* [Integrated environmental research: A study of the experience of the spatial environment in the Rhine Delta area]. Rotterdam, Netherlands: Openbaar Lichaam Rijnmond.

Van Wagenberg, A.F. (1982). *Theory, methodology and studies on participatory environmental design in a middle school*. Unpublished doctoral dissertation, State University of New York, Stony Brook.

Van Wagenberg, A.F., Krasner, M., & Krasner, L. (1981). Children planning an ideal classroom: Environmental design in an elementary school. *Environment and Behavior, 13*(3), 349–359.

Vlek, C.A.J., & Stallen, P.J.M. (1980). Persoonlijke beoordeling van riskante activiteiten [Personal judgement of risky activities]. *Gedrag, 8*(6), 379–401.

Wentholt, R. (1968). *De binnenstadsbeleving en Rotterdam* [Experiencing the inner city and Rotterdam]. Rotterdam, Netherlands: Donker.

Chapter 35

ENVIRONMENTAL PSYCHOLOGY FROM A SWEDISH PERSPECTIVE

Rikard Küller, *Environmental Psychology Unit, Lund Institute of Technology, Lund, Sweden*

35.1 THE EMERGENCE OF ENVIRONMENTAL PSYCHOLOGY

The Scandinavian countries are often looked on as a unity, especially by the foreigner. It is true that Denmark, Finland, Iceland, Norway, and Sweden share much in terms of historical and cultural backgrounds. Also in modern times the development has been parallel in many respects, for example, in the introduction of modern housing and social welfare and a common labor market. However convenient it might be to consider these five countries as one cultural unit, this would not be entirely true. Even if the language is similar, except for Finnish, people from Stockholm will find it difficult to understand what is said in Copenhagen. There are also borderlines of an administrative or sometimes political kind, which act as barriers to mutual understanding.

As far as research is concerned, general policies as well as funding priorities might differ considerably, and as for the communication of scientific results, this is more likely to take place via international channels than through formal or informal Scandinavian contacts. Due to highly set standards about public health and welfare and similar external conditions, for example, the cold climate and the low population density, much direct cooperation has, however, occurred in fields like architectural design, indoor climatology research, and work safety legislation. The new journal, *Scandinavian Housing and Planning Research*, bears witness to this. But also the *Scandinavian Journal of Psychology*, and the *Scandinavian Journal of Work, Environment & Health*, among others, exemplify the cooperative efforts.

The first conference on environmental psychology in the Scandinavian countries was held at the University of Lund on January 31, 1967. In 1969, some of the delegates met again in order to formally establish the Swedish Committee for Architectural Psychology. Since then, there have been numerous conferences, some with Scandinavian and international participation. In this as in many other respects, the growth and development of environmental psychology in our corner of the world parallels what has been going on in Britain and North America (Arlock & Küller, 1973; Edberg, 1971; Edberg & Ericson, 1975; Hedborg, 1984; Hellquist & Thafvelin 1985; Küller, 1967, 1969, 1973; Sällström, 1981; Sorte, 1978; Wallinder, 1977).

Undoubtedly, the conferences have served the purpose of promoting environmental psychology research and application, but it is only fair to admit that much of what is today regarded as environmental psychology emerged as a natural development of academic psychology, sociology, and medicine. Therefore, a description of the history of environmental psychology must include not only the turbulence created by the union between planners and human scientists in the late 1960s and early 1970s but also the perhaps somewhat less conspicuous everyday work within the established institutions. But let us start by looking back much earlier than the 1960s to some events that might have indicated the arrival of environmental psychology.

Inspired by the ideas of functionalism and backed by the Swedish government, already in the 1940s, planners and social scientists started a large-scale program for the rehousing of the Swedish population. Among the pioneers were Åkerman (1941) and Boalt and Karlsson (1948–1949). Boalt later became the first professor of building function analysis in Sweden (e.g., Boalt, 1968a). She has made a great impact on housing research in Scandinavia and although retired, she is still active in research on housing for the elderly. One of her students, Cronberg, is now director of the Department of Housing at the Danish Building Research Institute (Cronberg, 1982). One of the first PhD theses to appear in this field carried the title *Family and Housing*. It was presented in 1955 by Holm, now director general of the National Board of Physical Planning and Building in Sweden. Also, one may refer to the early work carried out by Brochmann (1952) in Norway.

Another major event, this time related to architecture and aesthetics, was the presentation in 1954 of a PhD thesis entitled *The Language of Architecture* by the Swedish architect Hesselgren (1954a). His work, which was obviously influenced by the psychology of perception, inspired much of the aesthetic research in Scandinavia, and two of his students, Gärling at Umeå University and Sivik at Gothenburg University, are now associate professors of environmental psychology.

In the field of human factors, Ronge in 1948 produced his PhD thesis: *Ultraviolet Irradiation with Artificial Illumination. A Technical, Physiological, and Hygienic Study*. In this pioneering work, Ronge studied the impact of one specific environmental factor—ultraviolet light—on some constituents of the blood, physical fitness, and absenteeism. Ronge's approach may be recognized in the later work on indoor climatology by Löfstedt, Wyon, and others.

Then, in the 1960s several significant developments took place in close succession. Acking, who became the first professor of aesthetics at the newly opened Institute of Technology, in Lund, together with Edberg, Wallinder, and the present author, founded the Committee for Architectural Psychology mentioned before. Within the field of occupational research, the methodology branched out considerably and began to encompass an increasing number of complex environments. Influenced by the new theory of Selye, who introduced into biology and medicine the concept of nonspecific stress, the Laboratory for Clinical Stress Research was established in Stockholm.

It is not an exaggeration to say that what is today known as environmental psychology already at the end of the 1960s was well established in Sweden. In the other Scandinavian countries, the development of environmental psychology as a specific field has perhaps been somewhat less pronounced. However, two authors, both of them architects, had, and still have, a great impact on the psychology of architecture. In Denmark, Rasmussen published his book *Experiencing Architecture* in 1957 (in English, 1962). In this classic work, he treats in a poetic, yet systematic way, the various elements of the built environment as perceived by man. Ten years later, Norberg-Schulz, in Norway, in his book *Intentions in Architecture*, set out to integrate the perceptual and cognitive processes into a comprehensive theory of architecture (Norberg-Schulz, 1967, 1971).

I will now try to introduce, in a slightly more detailed way, some of the research, past and ongoing, within the various areas of environmental psychology. The perspective will be mostly Swedish. However, except for some specific areas where there seems to have been very little direct influence, reference will also be made to related work in the other Scandinavian countries. The field at hand may be subdivided in a number of ways. I have chosen to begin with some basic studies of environmental perception and cognition. Then I continue with research on major settings, that is, housing and urban design, landscape, and work and traffic environments. This includes a discussion of environmental stress and hazards, which may be regarded as an attempt to describe in a general way the net effects of several situational factors acting simultaneously. However, because the research on basic factors like light, noise, heat, and air pollution to a certain extent has led its own life, these areas receive their own account. There has also been a considerable amount of research aimed at special groups, that is, children and old or disabled persons. These groups are treated separately. I have also included one section on person–environment models and another on simulation. Finally, an attempt is made to look at what might lie ahead in our field of research.

The present synopsis is pragmatic more than anything else. In itself it gives a picture of the multitude of work carried out in numerous places by groups or individuals who not always refer to themselves as environmental psychologists. In an attempt to exclude major parts of medicine, social psychology, sociology, geography, and architecture, I have put forth two criteria in my definition of environmental psychology. First, the word *environment* has been taken to mean something substantial, like a building or neighborhood, or the various properties of a lighting condition. Second, the word *psychology* implies a certain depth of analysis either in terms of experience, behavior, or physiology. Even with these restrictions, my selection is far from inclusive. Unfortunately, space has not permitted that the material be placed into an international perspective. It is hoped that the topic-centered chapters in this book will provide such an outlook. For previous reviews in this area, one may refer to Gärling (1982) and Küller (1975b, 1979a). One may also refer to the following bibliographies: Ahlin (1983), Hellner, Johansson, & Wallroth (1983), Horelli (1982), Hovden, Paasche, Röe, & Sten (1977), M. Küller (1980) and Nummenmaa (1980).

35.2. THE STUDY OF MEANING IN ARCHITECTURE

In early Swedish studies, psychophysical scaling methods were used in order to assess architectural space (Gärling, 1969; Holmberg, Küller, & Tidblom, 1966; Küller, 1971). This approach was severely criticized by Sandström (1974). However, in a series of studies beginning in 1966, factor analysis of semantic ratings was employed in order to extract dimensions of architectural meaning. This work that was influenced by Osgood's book *The Measurement of Meaning* (1957) resulted in one of the first PhD theses in environmental psychology to appear in the Scandinavian countries (Küller, 1972, also 1975a,

1979b). Employing about 200 different scales with a wide range of environments and subjects, eight perceptual dimensions were identified that may be used to characterize the built environment. Thanks to numerous validation studies, it has been possible to incorporate these dimensions into a neuropsychological model of environmental interaction (refer to Figure 35.5 on page 1264).

Gärling, in 1970, employed semantic scales in a study on work environments at the Gustavsberg factory not far from Stockholm. In 1976, Gärling made a successful attempt to validate, by means of multidimensional scaling, the dimensions found by Küller. Kwok (1979) presented a cross-cultural replication on one population in London and another in Singapore with the same semantic scales.

The semantic approach has been employed not only in order to analyze architectural space. Sorte, in his PhD thesis (1982), analyzed the visual characteristics of building components like windows, roofs, and furniture. As might be expected, some of the dimensions pertaining to architectural space were valid for describing the components as well. However, some new and more specific dimensions also appeared. In order to explain preferences for various types of buildings and objects, Sorte carried his analysis one step further. By means of Q-factor analysis, he managed to identify several syndromes of dimensions common to objects in high- and low-preference groups. For an application on windows, see Olsson-Jonsson (1984).

Also, more specific areas like lighting, coloration, and the sonic environment have been analyzed by means of the semantic technique. Sivik had subjects judge color samples by means of semantic scales (Sivik 1969, 1974a, 1974b, 1974c, 1974d). In an investigation of blind persons, Acking, together with Janssens and Jonasson, employed a similar approach in order to compare various types of nonvisual perception. Four groups of subjects (recently blind, blind rehabilitated, normal blindfolded, and normal vision) were asked to assess different types of floor materials, either by touching them with their feet, the white stick, the hand, or for the normal group, visually. Amazingly enough, the factor structures for the four different groups were highly similar, irrespective of the way of assessment (Acking, 1976).

In her PhD thesis (1976), Westerman again employed magnitude estimations and pair comparisons in order to obtain aesthetic evaluations of building exteriors. The stimuli consisted of photographs of actual building facades as well as models, in which the degree of plasticity was varied. The number of surfaces and edges and the depth of the three-dimensional facade seemed to have a greater aesthetic impact than aspects like order and complexity. There seems to be a certain range of plasticity within which maximum pleasantness is perceived. In 1980, Westerman continued her research by comparing estimated beauty of building models varying in plasticity, proportions, and number of windows. The high shapes were generally thought of as office buildings and the low as industrial or school buildings, whereas the shapes of intermediate height were identified as apartment houses. Buildings of moderate height, high plasticity, and a fenestration of 25 to 40% were experienced to be the most pleasant.

An interesting way of studying the meaning of architecture was employed by Janssens in his PhD studies from 1976 to 1984. Subjects were shown a number of color slides representing different building exteriors; their task was to identify the functions of the buildings. Looking time and eye movements were recorded as well as the time required to identify each building. The subjects also had to motivate their interpretations and rate the pictures in a number of semantic variables, for example, pleasantness. Results indicated that windows and entrances were the most frequently looked at parts. Buildings that were hard to identify promoted a more intensive eye movement behavior (Figure 35.1). A straightforward connection between ease of identification and ratings of pleasantness had been hypothesized; however, no such relationship emerged in this work (Janssens, 1984).

Lynch's book, *The Image of the City* (1960) signaled the introduction of the cognitive approach into environmental psychology. This book quickly became a primer at the schools of architecture. In Gothenburg, at the Chalmers University of Technology, it inspired Wallinder and his co-workers, Branzell and Goude, to develop systems for spatial analysis and denotation (Branzell, 1976; Goude, 1967; Wallinder, 1967). Edberg, working at the Royal Institute of Technology, in Stockholm, carried out a systematic comparison of the methods of Cullen, Gehl, Lynch, and Thiel (Edberg 1975). Two psychologists, Biel and Torell (1979; also Biel, 1982a, 1982b), focused their interest on children's cognition. Other examples of the cognitive approach may be found in studies on blind persons' orientation by Acking (1976) and Gustafson and Månsson (1980). This work is reviewed later in the section on special groups.

For several years, basic research on environmental cognition has been carried out by Gärling and his co-workers, Böök, Lindberg, and Mäntylä, at the University of Umeå. Their work has centered on problems of orientation, memory for spatial layouts, and spatiotemporal sequences of everyday activities. They have, for instance, made a number of studies of the maintenance of orientation while subjects move around a place (Böök, 1981; Böök & Gärling, 1981). They also investigated the rate at which the spatial layout of real environments is learned in order for orientation to be achieved without effort. These studies include topics like the effects of familiarity, visual access, and orientation aids, when walking around in a building, and the problem of how people memorize their everyday physical environment (Gärling, Böök, & Lindberg 1982; Gärling, Lindberg, & Mäntylä, 1983). Recently, the group has proposed a theory of cognitive mapping for large-scale environments. The main assumption is that action plans, in order to be executed, necessitate the formation of travel plans, which in turn control the acquisition of information about the environment. The theory also makes assumptions about which properties of the environment are mapped, how the mapping is accomplished, how the information is internally represented, and how travel plans are formed and executed (Gärling, Böök, & Lindberg, 1984). One may also refer to the work carried out in Denmark by Christiansen, Flyvbjerg, Jenson-Butler, Jeppesen, and Sorensen (1978).

In Sweden, as elsewhere, attempts have been made to develop semiotics as used in the study of languages, into a theory of architectural semiotics (Wåhlin, 1984). Indeed, over the years many authors have had something important to say about meaning in architecture and the arts (Hesselgren 1979, 1985; Norberg-Schulz, 1980: Råberg, 1983; Sandström, 1983; Thiis-Evensen, 1982).

35.3 HOUSING AND URBAN DESIGN

The accelerated technical and economic development in the 1960s promoted urbanism and also led to the construction of huge suburban housing areas. This was especially the case in Sweden, where the government had instigated the so-called million dwellings program in order to meet the increasing demands on modern housing (G. Boalt, Holm, & Boalt, 1959). At the same time, postwar functionalism made many architects and urban designers more than willing to think big. The buildings of Le Corbusier attracted more interest than the writings of Hesselgren, Rasmussen, and Norberg-Schulz.

However, at the end of the 1960s, both psychologists and architects became more involved in the social aspects of housing (e.g., Andersson-Brolin & Lindén, 1974; Lindberg, 1971; Marek, Jystad, Dörum, & Brantenberg, 1971). In 1971, two books were published in Copenhagen that were to further this change of attitude. One of the books was written by the Danish architect, Jan Gehl. It described housing areas in a new way, arguing that "the life between the houses" is to a considerable degree influenced by physical planning. Gehl concluded:

> If a group of planners and architects had been asked to reduce the life between houses by physical means, it could hardly have been done more efficiently, although unintentionally, than in the industrialized countries of the post World War II period.

Gehl then gave a number of design suggestions in order to improve the quality of the life between the houses, with the emphasis on normal everyday activities like walking, standing, sitting, seeing, hearing, and talking.

The same year Ingrid Gehl, a psychologist and Jan's wife, published her book *Living Environment*, which was based on Maslow's theory of human motivation. She listed a number of human needs and then set out to analyze the built environment from this perspective, ending up with the following list: the need for contact, the need for isolation (today we would call it privacy), the need to experience, the need for activity, the need to play, the need of structuring one's environment, the need to identify oneself with the environment, and the aesthetic need. In the last section of the book, she discussed the specific needs of children, adolescents, adults, and older people (I. Gehl, 1971).

In Sweden the ethnologist Daun, in his book *Suburban Life* (1974), compared the cultural changes in Vårberg and Reimersholme, two Stockholm suburbs differing in character. By describing the various conditions of life and the resulting living patterns, he managed to give an understanding of community life that had been lacking in earlier research. The author, in his analysis, employed concepts like identity and difference between people, culturally, socially, and economically as a basis for contact seeking or alienation. He also proposed that when a great number of persons are brought together in one place without knowing each other, they will have to learn to ignore each other.

These books, by an architect, a psychologist, and an ethnologist stimulated the discussion of housing and urban design in the Scandinavian countries. Actually, many architects became amateur scientists and renounced their former interest in aesthetics. This antiaesthetic reaction, which was to last about 10 years, was probably not the original intention of the three writers.

The 1970s gave birth to a new strategy of housing design in the Scandinavian countries, which is summarized in the slogan *close and compact* (Nejst-Jensen, Kirstein, Ryding, & Vedel-Petersen, 1971). This was partly a reaction against the functionalistic thinking of the 1950s and 1960s. Also the increasing amount of environmental psychology research might well take its share of the credit. Architects, psychologists, and sociologists joined forces in promoting a new kind of thinking that placed action, perception, and participation foremost (Acking, 1974). Also the holistic outlook of the ethnological approach became increasingly familiar to the environmental researcher. Ingrid Gehl's conclusions were actually put to test in the construction of a housing area, Galgebakken, in the outskirts of Copenhagen where they formed part of the building program. The success of this project has recently been confirmed in a postevaluation carried out by Vedel-Petersen, Jensen, and Storgaard (1983). For the later work of Jan Gehl and Daun, please refer to Daun (1979) and Gehl (1980).

A number of authors have since made serious attempts at employing the methods and results of the social sciences in the study of architectural design. Torsson, in his thesis *The City as Space and Gestalt* (1974), set out to discuss how the city is perceived and used and how mental constructs are formed in order to enhance legibility and support orientation. Based on Barker's ecological psychology, Ås developed a technique of time–budget analysis that was then used in numerous studies of Norwegian housing areas (Ås, 1975, 1976). More recently, Cold Brantenberg (1981) carried out a psychological and aesthetic evaluation of a glassed-in street at the University Center at Dragvoll, Trondheim. The attempt to integrate social as well as aesthetic aspects was also well exemplified in a study of the main square, in Malmö, Sweden, carried out by guest researcher Korosec-Serfaty (1982). Another example was the study by Dalgard on mental health, neighborhood, and related social variables in Oslo (1980). In their book *Comfort in Housing* (1983), Marek and Hovden reported the results of an extensive evaluation study of a modern housing project in Trondheim. In Finland, there has also been an interest for urban and suburban life, its background, and consequences. In one study reported in 1981, Kortteinen studied the change in living habits that may occur as a result of moving from the countryside into a suburban neighborhood (also

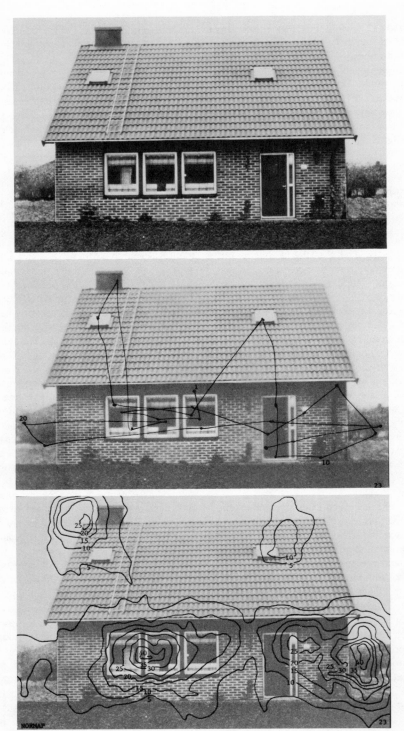

Figure 35.1. As can be seen on pages 1248 and 1249, two building facades (top) with typical individual eye scanning paths (middle) and 20 subjects' eye fixations plotted as isorithm charts (bottom) (see Janssens, 1984). (*Source:* By permission of Jan Janssens.)

Figure 35.1.(*Continued*)

refer to Aaltonen, Lahti, & Piha, 1978; Diderichsen, 1981; Ilstad, 1978; Järnegren, Liedholm, & Sandin, 1981; Nordström, 1982).

The new knowledge that resulted from studies like these has given rise to lively discussions and a reevaluation of design policies (Aura, 1982a, 1982b; Börjesson, Grytt, & Kjessel, 1979; Wikforss, 1981). Attempts at bringing the user into the planning process have been made by ambitious planners and architects. Influenced by the work of Alexander and the Gehls, Olivegren carried out a program for 12 one-family houses in Gothenburg (Olivegren, 1975). Methods enabling the users to participate in the planning and design of their housing environment were also developed at the beginning of the 1970s by Kukkonen at the Helsinki University of Technology (1983). This self-planning system was tested in several housing experiments in which families designed their individual homes and planned the common quarters together. An evaluation of these projects carried out by Horelli (1981) showed that the residents were extremely satisfied with the results of their own planning (cf., Kukkonen, Horelli, & Kemppinen 1981; for a study on housing and creativity, see Jarlöv, 1982).

The postmodernistic movement of the late 1970s and early 1980s may take credit for bringing back aesthetics as a legitimate aspect of architectural design. It is only to be hoped that the social interest nourished during the last decades will have left an impact strong enough to resist the sudden swings and whims of modern architecture. For further discussions on these issues, refer to the following reviews: Björnberg, Carlestam, Eriksson, & Lundahl (1975), Groth, Hansen, Christiansen, & Jörgensen (1975), Röed Helgesen (1979), Sanne et al. (1985), and *Svensk boendeforskning. En bibliografi.* (1974).

35.4. THE NORDIC LANDSCAPE

Except for a few densely populated urban regions with about a million inhabitants and some medium-sized regional centers, most parts of the Scandinavian countries are sparsely populated, leaving huge areas of cultivated landscape or wilderness for recreational purposes. Understandably, the study of the landscape as a human environment has attracted considerable interest among researchers in these countries, who have employed techniques like questionnaires, semantic ratings, and visual simulation. Already in 1974, Sorte presented the results from a semantic analysis of how people used Oslomarka, the natural recreational region surrounding Oslo

(Lind, Oraug, Skjervold Rosenfeld, & Östensen, (1974). Similar studies were made by, among others, Marek and co-workers in the Bergen region, and Koch, at the Danish Forest Experiment Station (Koch, 1978, 1980; Marek & Kvittingen, 1976).

Hultman (1981), at the University of Agricultural Sciences in Uppsala, examined the attitude toward the Swedish landscape as well as the differences between foresters and the general public. Differences appeared between the two forester groups, one working in the conservation section and the other in large forestry companies, and between both forester groups and the general public. Somewhat contrary to expectations, the conservation foresters seemed to deviate more than the other group from the general public. In another study by Kardell and Johansson (1982), a comparison was made between parents and children and their attitudes toward nature. It seems that foresters' parents were much more interested in natural environments than other parents and conveyed this interest to their children by bringing them into active contact with nature.

Due to the worldwide energy crisis, there has recently been an attempt to analyze the influence of wind energy conversion systems on the visual character of the landscape. The visual effects of single windpower units and group stations were studied by means of perception theory, field observations, visual simulation, and case studies. Nine areas on the island of Gotland were chosen for the localization of windpower stations 50 to 150 m high. For each of these areas, the positive and negative conditions for windpower development were described, including factors like land consumption, accident hazards, noise, visual influence, radio and television disturbances, collision hazards, and preservation interests due to natural historical and recreational values (Bergsjö, Nilsson, & Skärbäck, 1982; Engström & Pershagen, 1980).

An experimental study of landscape versus townscape was made by Ulrich while working as a guest researcher at the Environmental Psychology Laboratory, in Lund. He had his subjects view color slides of either nature with water, nature dominated by vegetation, or urban environments without water or vegetation. Measurements were taken of the effect of the slide presentations on EEG alfa amplitude, heart rate, and self-reported emotional states. Results revealed significant differences as a function of environment, which together indicated the two categories of nature views had more positive influences than the urban scenes. One salient finding was that water, and to a lesser extent vegetation views, held attention and interest more effectively than the urban scenes (Ulrich, 1981).

For other studies of the natural environment, one may refer to Feste and Oterholm (1973), Jörgensen (1976), Vanhalakka-Ruoho (1981), and Wallsten (1982). For a theoretical analysis of outdoor environment and recreation one may refer to Aldskogius (1977) and Marek, Bennett, and Kjöde (1983); also one may refer to the bibliography by Hultman (1976). There have also been numerous attempts to design for nature in residential areas [e.g., Open Space In Housing Areas (1972); Persson (1982); Seipel & Sohlberg (1982)]. However, it seems that psychological methods have rarely been brought into this process for purposes of analysis or postevaluation (Nordström, 1979).

35.5. STRESS AND THE WORK ENVIRONMENT

Leymann, at the National Board of Occupational Safety and Health, in his review of occupational research in Sweden, divides the development of occupational research into three time periods. In the 1940s and 1950s, this research was dominated by differential and experimental psychology. The worker and his individual work capacity were the main subjects of study. In the 1960s, social psychology predominated. In the wake of the North American human relations movement, interest in the study of the problems in work groups and in work supervision arose at the end of the 1960s. In the 1970s, research measures branched out considerably and began to encompass an increasing number of complex fields. The work environment in itself, people's degree of integration in it, their opportunities to exercise influence, their total situation in life with work as only one aspect, all became fields of research (Leymann, 1981).

During the last 10 years, the approach of occupational research has become very similar to that of environmental psychology (Lennerlöf, 1981). Current research fields within occupational research are, for instance, stress and accident research, physical and chemical loading factors, and research into work organization. As some of these topics are reported elsewhere in this chapter, only studies where the work environment was considered as a totality will be discussed here. Many studies of this kind have been undertaken in Sweden. Typical of this approach was, for instance, a study by Ekvall and Larsson concerning the effects of a profound change of the work environment at a Swedish factory. The study covered aspects of a technical, economical, administrative, social, psychological, and medical kind (Ekvall, 1979; Larsson, 1978).

Probably the experiment at the Volvo Kalmarverken has attracted more attention, internationally, than any other Scandinavian project concerned with the work environment (Figure 35.2). The aim of the project was expressed by the chairman, Gyllenhammar, in the following way:

In Kalmar, we must produce a factory which, without sacrificing efficiency and economic results, provides the possibility for the employees to work in groups, to communicate freely, to carry out job rotation, to vary their rate of work, to feel identification with the products, to feel responsibility for quality, and be in a position to influence their working environment (Agurén, Hansson, & Karlsson, 1976 pp. 5–6).

The experiences of this project were summarized by Agurén, Hansson, & Karlsson (1976); (also one may refer to the study of apartment factories by Henriksson & Lindqvist [1977] and Ranhagen [1980]; the study of technological change by Langaa Jensen & Möller [1984]; and the reviews by Häkkinen [1980] and Kirjonen [1980]).

Today, the concept of stress has become the theoretical basis in many studies of work environments. The study of stress has its roots not so much in psychology as in physiology. Going back to important discoveries within biology and medicine, the importance of the concept for environmental psychology emanates from the definition of stress as a generalized response to environmental factors. It is generally assumed that stress is a response to overload, resulting in a shift in body physiology like blood pressure, pulse rate, and the secretion of adrenalin, nor-adrenalin, and cortisol. In addition, there might be changes in perception, emotion, and behavior. However, this straightforward view on the relationship between overload and stress is now being replaced by more elaborate models where cognitive or motivational factors are assumed to mediate the stress reaction.

In an attempt to formulate a new psychosomatic theory, Ursin, at the University of Bergen, wrote:

The essential element in this new psychosomatic theory is that it is possible to specify the psychologic conditions which produce sustained activation. Activation depends on the individual perception of the stimulus situation, the available responses, and the

Figure 35.2. The design of the assembly halls at Volvo-Kalmarverken provides for individual control and social interaction. (*Source:* By courtesy of Volvo-Kalmarverken.)

previous experience with stimuli and responses. Processes identified as defence and coping are of decisive importance for the resulting activation, and hence the internal state of the organism. Activation is a multivariate process and should be studied as such. The individual variance is related to personality traits affecting both defence and coping mechanisms. This makes it possible to develop specific hypotheses in psychosomatic theory, identifying risk groups based on personality, somatic responses, and life situations. The activation process relates to pathology in two ways. Normal short-lasting activation may be too great a load for a diseased organ. The other aspect is that sustained, long-lasting activation may produce somatic changes (Ursin, 1980, p. 275; also Ursin & Ursin, 1979).

Initially, stress was mostly studied as a response to single environmental factors like noise. However, already in the 1960s, stress researchers began to look at more complex human situations. In 1972, Levi, at the Laboratory for Clinical Stress Research, in Stockholm, published his work on stress and distress in response to psychosocial stimuli. The author discussed existing evidence supporting the hypothesis that psychosocial stimuli can evoke disease and suggested that control of the psychosocial environment might reduce the disease (cf. also Levi, 1979).

In a paper on work stress related to social structures and processes, Levi, Frankenhaeuser, and Gardell (1981) listed the following four detrimental conditions:

Quantitative overload. Too much to do, excessive time pressure, or repetitious work flow in combination with one-sided job demands and superficial attention. This is, to a great extent, typical of mass-production technology and routine office work.

Qualitative underload. Too narrow and one-sided job content, lack of stimulus variation, no demands on creativity or problem solving, or low opportunities for social interaction. These jobs seem to become more common with automation and increased use of computers in both offices and manufacturing.

Lack of control. Especially in relation to pace of work and working methods.

Lack of social support. Inadequate social networks at home and with fellow workers.

Frankenhaeuser, in her work, has managed to unify an advanced psychophysiological model on one hand with a broad environmental outlook on the other. In a paper from 1981, she considered the quality-of-life concept from the point of view of harmony between fundamental human needs and environmental conditions. Emphasis was placed on coping and adaptation in workers exposed to conditions characterized by underload, overload, and lack of control. On the basis of empirical results, including physiological as well as psychological measurement, it is argued that a moderately varied flow of stimuli and events, opportunities to engage in psychologically meaningful work, and to exercise personal control over situational factors may be considered key components in the quality-of-life concept (cf. also Frankenhaeuser, 1979).

Various conditions related to work satisfaction have been discussed by Gardell. In a number of studies, the impact of factors like income level, type of payment, mechanization, job demand, and possibility of control were investigated. One major hypothesis confirmed by Gardell's studies is that people with hard repetitive and programmed work in industries and offices, because they have a low degree of control over their own work situation, run the risk of becoming passive (Gardell, 1976, 1980). The hypothesis of an interaction between job demand and control on one hand, and satisfaction and stress on the other, has been further elaborated by Karasek, a guest researcher in Stockholm, who compared national survey data from Sweden and the United States (Karasek, 1976).

As mentioned before, one of the most salient factors under study has been the worker's possibility to control his or her own working situation. For instance, in one study by Dalgard, a random sample of about 500 adults from Oslo were interviewed with respect to mental health, occupational experience, and a number of social variables. Special emphasis was placed on closeness of supervision at work. A rather strong correlation between mental health problems and degree of closeness of supervision was found. It was found that the stronger the external control at work, the higher the risk of mental health problems, even when controlling for a number of variables like age, education, income, type of work, and quality of neighborhood. The trend was particularly strong for younger, well-educated people doing nonmanual work (Dalgard, 1981).

Magnusson and co-workers at the University of Stockholm have approached stress in a somewhat different way. Comparing perception of, and reactions to, anxiety-provoking situations, these researchers have managed to identify several dimensions of stressful situations. In accordance with research on autonomic functions, in one study it was argued that the organization of behavioral reactions expressed by an individual in one threatening situation tends to be reproduced across different kinds of anxiety-provoking situations and over time. A self-report instrument was employed in which subjects rated their different psychic and somatic anxiety reactions for each of a set of anxiety-evoking situations. The inventory was administered twice over an interval of 6 months. The results provided support for the hypothesis of stable idiosyncratic organizations of reactions over different kinds of threatening situations and of stable reaction patterns over time. Finally, it was argued that the strength of the expressed reaction patterns was related to perceptual characteristics of the situations. The empirical results also supported this hypothesis (Stattin & Magnusson, 1980). In his interactional model of behavior, Magnusson has also tried to put the situational determinants of stress into an interactional perspective (Magnusson, 1981; Magnusson & Stattin, 1981; Magnusson, Stattin, & Iwawaki, 1982).

Based on the fundamental work of Frankenhaeuser, Levi, Gardell, and others, a number of applied studies have been carried out. Rissler and Elgerot, for instance, investigated the accommodation to work in an open-space office in three groups of insurance employees who had different work tasks. Difficulties of adjustment were clearly traceable to the type of work content and also were related to different coping reactions. Employees with routine and service tasks were physiologically mobilized during the months immediately after change of work environment, but their difficulties of adaptation were temporary. However, a group of employees with complex problem-solving tasks had considerable problems adjusting to the open space. They were troubled much more than the other groups by auditory and visual disturbances that interfered with efficient work completion. This group coped by maintaining a high physiological activation level at the cost of qualitative and quantitative performance deterioration. They also expressed more psychological and physiological disturbances after a day's work than the other groups. These symptoms were not alleviated even after 15-months' work in the open-space office. The results were interpreted in terms of lack of control over environmental disturbances (Rissler & Elgerot, 1980; cf. also Rissler, 1977).

Studies on environmental stress have also been carried out by the following authors: Borg (1978), Eide (1983), Johansson, Aronsson, & Lindström (1978), and Vikman (1982). In addition to studies of this more basic or theoretical kind, many specific work environments have been investigated, for instance, the clinical laboratory (Johansson, 1982), farm buildings (one may refer to Johannesson, 1982, for a list of publications), a North Sea oil platform (Tangenes, Marek, & Hellesöy, 1981), or the naval environment (Küller, 1980b; Werthén, 1976).

In environmental psychology, the study of social stress is often referred to in terms like *personal space*, *crowding*, or *human territoriality*. Some research of this kind has been carried out by Dahlman (1973), Rivano-Fischer (1984), Lundberg (1976), and T. Malmberg, who also published a comprehensive survey on the topic (T. Malmberg, 1980).

35.6. TRAFFIC AND OTHER ENVIRONMENTAL HAZARDS

The study of risk, actual or experienced, deserves its own place within environmental psychology research. Part of this research is devoted to specific environments, for example, the experience of risk on a North Sea platform (Marek, 1978, 1981; Marek, Tangenes, & Hellesöy, 1981); worker safety in farm buildings labor (Sundahl, 1980); and near accidents in greenhouses (Lundqvist, 1982). However, the single largest area of hazard research concerns the traffic environment.

At the National Swedish Road and Traffic Research Institute, in Linköping, Rumar has been engaged in improving the traffic environment in various ways. In a paper, he points out that most researchers have tried to establish the relative weight of vehicle, road, and human factors as causes in road accidents. The results clearly point to the human factor as the main cause. However, an analysis of the road traffic process and its development in a historical perspective indicates that the question and consequently also the answer are improper. It is normally not the failure of a component but the failure of a system interaction that causes accidents. Rumar concludes that the common denominator of human mistakes seems to be lack of adequate information from the road, the road environment, other road users, and the vehicle. Finally, the author tries to evaluate the possible effects of improvements like user selection, education, and training enforcement as well as various ways to adapt road design and delineation signs and signals, rules and laws, and vehicle dynamics to human characteristics and limitations (Rumar, 1982; cf. also Rumar, 1975).

Based on psychological considerations, research on the traffic environment has also been carried out by the Danish Council of Road Safety at Lyngby (Engel, Nygaard, Schiötz & Christgau, 1978; Iver-sen, 1981; Kromann, 1976; Nygaard et al., 1976; Nygaard & Schiötz, 1975). A number of factors have been investigated such as the effect of vegetation, behavior in unregulated crossroads, monotony on highways, and the traffic behavior of children. In Finland, the Road Safety Organization has promoted research on children's traffic behavior in order to increase the efficiency of the existing road safety teaching program (Nummenmaa, Ruuhilehto, & Syvänen, 1975; Nummenmaa & Syvänen, 1974). A monograph on driving behavior and training in an international perspective has been completed by Marek and Sten (1977), (also one may refer to Engfors & Fog, 1978; Gärling & Svensson, 1983, Gårder, Hydén, & Linderholm, 1979, Hydén 1977, Mashour, 1974, and Ståhl, 1984). It may be noted that in studies of traffic behavior, a rather specific technique of eye movement registration has been developed (Figure 35.3) (Larsson & Rumar, 1974; Nilsson, 1975; Nygaard, 1977).

35.7. THE IMPACT ON MAN OF LIGHT, COLOR, AND TEXTURE

Research on color, light, and texture has attracted Swedish researchers for many years. There is one name in particular that should be mentioned in this context—the physicist Johansson—who created the Natural Colour System. The system was later turned into a color atlas by Hesselgren and then was again modified by Hård (Hård, 1975; Hesselgren, 1952, 1954b; Johansson, 1952). The Natural Colour System has played a significant role in much of the color research in Sweden, but also, unfortunately, made this work somewhat less comprehensible to readers accustomed to more established systems like the Munsell (e.g., Hård, Sivik, & Svedmyr, 1983; Sivik & Hård, 1978).

By means of isosemantic mapping based on the Natural Colour System, Sivik was able to show that the affective value for a certain hue varies with its coloristic position. For instance, although blue is generally preferred to yellow, it is easy to find a specific yellow sample that is preferred to a blue one (Sivik, 1974a, 1974b, 1974c, 1974d). One of the most striking features of the results concerning preferences and color-mood associations is the consistency from one individual to another, from group to group, and even across cultures. However, in a study carried out both in Sweden and Greece, it was possible to demonstrate a certain influence of the cultural setting. The Greeks, for instance, regarded all colors as equally cultivated, whereas the Swedes judged the saturated colors as more vulgar than the unsaturated ones (Sivik, 1969).

There also exist a few studies where the appreciation of an environment was studied as a function of its colors. In spite of the general color preference order established by Eysenck and others, studies employing drawings of interiors as well as full-scale or model rooms showed that neither hue, lightness, or chroma will affect the perceived pleasantness of an interior space in any consistent way (Acking & Küller, 1972). One study indicated that the presence of color generally gave rise to positive evaluation, whereas the absence of color was considered to be negative (Sorte, personal communication).

Küller also demonstrated that the color and pattern of the visual environment not only has a profound effect on the EEG but also on pulse rate and on subjective emotions. The subjects were placed in two rooms, one gray and the other colorful, for periods of 3 hours. The alpha component of the EEG was attenuated in the colorful room, indicating higher arousal. The pulse rate was also slower in the color-

ful room, which is an agreement with the finding that intense attention might be accompanied by cardiac inhibition. Furthermore, subjects generally experienced a lack of emotional control in the colorful room (Küller, 1976, 1980a, 1983).

Influenced by the ideas of the Natural Colour System and also the work by James Gibson, Edberg (1977), in a series of experiments, developed what might be called a "natural texture system." Together with Eisler, he found that an observer seems to pay attention to three primary visual attributes of textures: texture strength, that is, the intensity of the texture experience; pattern of texture, that is, the regularity among the texture elements; and, finally, the form of the individual texture elements, for example, grainy-fibrous. Using these three dimensions, it was possible to establish a texture atlas similar to the ones used for color (Eisler & Edberg, 1982).

Pioneering lighting research in the Scandinavian countries is credited to people like Henningsen and Voltelen, in Copenhagen, and Pleijel, in Stockholm (Frandsen & Voltelen, 1978; Pleijel, 1954). The general policy of much of the research carried out since

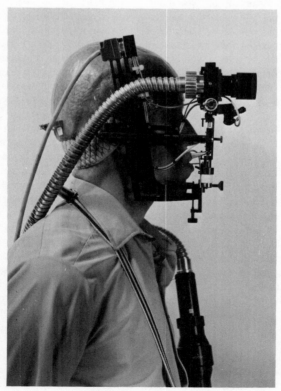

Figure 35.3. This eye movement camera was employed in studies of traffic behavior. (*Source:* By courtesy of Kåre Rumar).

then was expressed by one of Pleijel's former students, Liljefors, now professor of lighting design in Stockholm.

> Good lighting does not need more energy but better planning with respect for individual needs and for good perception of the environment. To solve this problem is more important for the lighting planner than the calculation of illumination values. (Liljefors, 1973, p. 68)

The fact that all existing artificial light sources deviate considerably from natural daylight raises the question whether artificial light might, in the long run, have detrimental effects on persons spending a large part of their life indoors. In 1974, Knave and colleagues investigated a large office landscape in which 22% of the personnel complained of bad lighting. The authors concluded that discomfort glare was the reason behind the complaints.

In an experiment carried out by Erikson and Küller, two offices at a large factory in central Sweden were supplied with different types of flourescent lighting (white and daylight type), and the health conditions of the personnel were studied from November until June. Measurements included subjective reports of emotions and well-being as well as analysis of the hormones melatonin and cortisol. Results indicated persons lacking natural daylight were adversely affected. Artificial illumination of the daylight type caused less eye strain. It also has an effect on the hormones more similar to that of natural daylight (Erikson & Küller, 1983; also see M. Küller, 1982, and the bibliography *Non-Visual Effects of Light and Colour*, by Küller, 1981).

In 1964, Holm, Pleijel, and Ronge presented an interdisciplinary study on sunshine in dwellings. This was followed in 1969 by a report by Löfberg on the lighting of classrooms (also Tikkanen, 1976). Wyon and Nilsson (1980) made extensive interviews with people working in windowless factories, offices, shops, and colleges, in the south and far north of Sweden. Windows were regarded as more essential the further north the work place was situated; job categories with less stimulating work regarded windows as more important; however, people working in windowless rooms were less positive to windows than people who could take them for granted. The reverse had been hypothesized. There may have been a degree of self-selection, but there is no doubt windows are of emotional importance, not only because they admit daylight but also because of the information they provide about the outside world. Another study showed that the "meaning" of lighting is differ-

ent for different groups of employees (Tangenes, Marek, & Hellesöy, 1981).

Concerning natural daylight, a research group at Tromsö, situated north of the polar circle in Norway, studied the relationship between sleeping difficulties, on the one hand, and the secretion of the hormones melatonin and cortisol, on the other. Disturbances in melatonin secretion clearly depend on light, and this work suggests it might also be the basis of some sleeping difficulties (Hansen, 1982; Weitzman, De Graaf, et al., 1975). The visual environment in road traffic was studied by Rumar (1980). Recently, a new problem area related to the visual indoor environment has been brought to attention. This concerns possible effects of visual display units, which are becoming an important part of many work environments (Bradley, 1981; Hedman & Briem, 1984; Johansson & Aronsson, 1979; Shahnavaz & Hedman, 1984).

35.8. THE AUDITIVE ENVIRONMENT

In comparison to visual factors, the auditive environment has received less attention from environmental researchers. In Stockholm, Gabrielsson and Sjögren for several years have carried out an analysis of perceived sound quality. Working mainly with loudspeakers, headphones, and hearing aids for the deaf, this group has managed to identify the following perceptual dimensions by means of multivariate technique: clearness, sharpness, brightness, fullness, sense of space, nearness, noisiness, and loudness (Gabrielsson, 1979, 1981; Gabrielsson & Sjögren, 1979).

By far, the largest part of the research on the auditive environment, however, deals with various effects of noise. Birgitta and Ulf Berglund and Lindvall, in Stockholm, have investigated the contribution of community noise to the perception of loudness, noisiness, and annoyance. Various types of noises have been investigated: aircraft noise under different flying conditions; traffic noise; and a number of other community noises. Besides specific scaling problems, the investigations have addressed themselves to the question of observers' abilities to differentiate among noises that are combined in a complex setting as well as their abilities to integrate various noises into a unified perception of loudness and annoyance (Berglund, Berglund, & Lindvall, 1975, 1980; also Ahlström, 1981). In one experiment, three community noises—pile driving, jackhammering, and street traffic—were combined pairwise at different sound levels. The observers judged total loudness of the combined noises as well as the loudness of each component noise when heard alone. Three models of annoyance summation for noise were tested, and all three fitted the data satisfactorily from a statistical point of view (Berglund, Berglund, Goldstein, & Lindvall, 1981).

A group at the University of Lund has studied the reaction to noise in relation to various personality characteristics. In a study carried out in the 1960s, housewives in one noisy and one quiet housing area were compared with respect to noise annoyance. At the same time, their personalities were assessed by means of psychological tests, among others, a defense mechanism test. Generally, there were more complaints in the noisy area than in the quiet area. However, some persons reported high annoyance from noise in the quiet area or very little annoyance in the noisy area. The clinical tests indicated these persons had a greater proportion of defense mechanisms than was to be expected by chance (Arvidsson, Johansson, Olsson, & Wigeman, 1965).

In a study from 1983, Johansson showed that children with high intelligence solved more items on a multiplication task in noisy than in quiet conditions. The reverse was found for children with low intelligence who were also more affected on a reading task. Wyon (1970) showed that classroom behavior and the performance of schoolwork were adversely affected by intermittent noise even at a level below that prevailing in the classroom. In other words, it is the disturbance and distraction caused by audible noise that affects people, rather than the dB level per se. In the previously mentioned study on a North Sea platform, it was found that the contribution of noise to the general satisfaction with the physical conditions at work is not unequivocal. It varies for different groups of employees depending on type of work and prevailing conditions (Tangenes, Marek, & Hellesöy, 1981; also Frankenhaeuser & Lundberg, 1977; Wyon, 1974).

An interesting study on the effects of traffic noise on sleep was reported in 1980 by Eberhardt and his colleagues. By means of a portable equipment they managed to monitor the physiological responses of the brain (EEG), the eyes (EOG), the heart (EKG), and the muscles (EMG) during the night in home environments situated along routes with heavy traffic. It was demonstrated that a sound insulation corresponding to a 10-dB reduction of the indoor noise level had a clearly positive effect on the individual's sleep pattern and that the type of improvement was related to the age of the subject. Also, there has been some research in the frequency range below what is normally perceived, so-called infrasound (Liszka, Danielsson, Söderberg, & Lindmark, 1978).

35.9. THE THERMAL INDOOR CLIMATE

Löfstedt, working at the University of Lund, and Fanger, at the Technical University of Denmark, in Lyngby, (Fanger, 1970; Löfstedt, 1966) pioneered the field of thermal comfort and human heat tolerance. Working mostly in Sweden but also in Denmark, Wyon has been the initiator of several psychological climate studies (e.g., Wyon, Asgeirsdottir, Kjerulf-Jensen, & Fanger, 1973; for a review, see Wyon, Hygge, & Löfberg, 1982). A typical study concerned the mental performance of subjects at different air temperatures (Wyon, Fanger, Olesen, & Pedersen, 1975). Thirty-two subjects performed sedentary work in a climate chamber. On one occasion, the subjects wore light, on the other, heavy clothing. During the exposures, the air temperature was continuously adjusted up or down at the subject's request so that he or she remained in thermal comfort. Measurements included skin temperature, performance, recognition, and cue utilization as well as subjective rating of effort, arousal, and fatigue. Results indicated male subjects maintain a higher skin temperature than females do. However, there were no differences between the air temperatures preferred by male and female subjects. Having worked for several years at the climate chambers of Löfstedt and Fanger, Wyon was instrumental in designing the advanced climate chambers at the Swedish Institute of Building Research in Gävle.

Working at Löfstedt's laboratory, Johansson (1975) presented his PhD thesis on mental and perceptual performance in heat. The effect of heat load on the thermoregulatory system and on performance appeared after a short period of exposure. In practiced numerical tasks, significant adverse effects of heat appeared, averaging 10%. These effects occurred independently of physiological and psychological strain, general intelligence, and personality. An inverted u-shaped relation between heat load, on the one hand, and cue utilization or attention, on the other, was found for all subjects independently of their individual characteristics.

Olesen, Fanger, Jensen, and Nielsen (1973) found that subjects introduced into a thermally assymetrical room selected that uniform environment that rendered them thermally neutral. Tangenes and colleagues (1981) concluded that experience of heat has to be differentiated from that of cold because they are likely to enter into different dimensions of evaluation. For instance, for the operator personnel on an oil platform, the evaluation of heat goes together with that of ventilation and humidity, whereas for drillers both heat and cold form important components of a common factor concerning ambient temperature and noise. Recently, a number of climate studies have been carried out in various environments (e.g., Lindholm & Lindholm, 1982).

With respect to factors other than cold and heat, Andersson, Frisk, Löfstedt, and Wyon (1975) presented a study on human response to dry, humidified, and intermittently humidified air in large office buildings. The authors concluded that artificial humidification is not generally needed in the Scandinavian countries if the room temperature can be prevented from rising above 22° C. Finally, it should be mentioned that an interaction has˙ been established between body temperature and level of illumination, on the one hand, and task difficulty, on the other. In a study by Löfberg and colleagues, it was found that increasing the level of illumination during moderate heat stress might even have a negative effect on tasks where visual concentration was less essential (Löfberg, Löfstedt, Nilsson, & Wyon, 1973).

35.10 AIR QUALITY, POLLUTION, AND RADIATION

The olfactory sense has traditionally been regarded as a rather exclusive research area. However, in the light of what is known today about the dangers of air pollution, olfactory research is getting increasingly more attention. For more than 10 years, the group in Stockholm consisting of the Berglunds, Lindvall, and co-workers have systematically tried to analyze industrial odors by means of human subjects. To quote Birgitta Berglund (1974, p. 35):

> Odour research on mixtures is a classical area of research. Little effort, however, has been devoted to the perception of odour mixtures in general and to malodorous air pollution in particular.... One of the main aims of the experimental work has therefore been to develop a mathematical model for perceptual odour interaction that is applicable to malodours. Such a model should predict the odour strength of the resultant effluent when process technology is changed, or when new filtering techniques are considered at the source.

Following this program, the research group has studied air quality in preschool and office buildings and a pulp mill and also tried to develop a psychophysical model for air quality (Berglund & Berglund, 1981; Berglund, Berglund, & Lindvall, 1973; Berg-

lund, Berglund, Lindvall, & Nicander-Bredberg, 1982; Berglund, Johansson, & Lindvall, 1981, 1982a, 1982b). The group has also developed a highly advanced laboratory for the study of air quality.

In Lund, Johansson (1976) carried out an experimental investigation where acute irritation effects and odor perception of tobacco smoke were studied for smokers and nonsmokers who were exposed three or four at a time in a climate chamber to different kinds of tobacco smoke. Results indicated irritation intensity increased more rapidly, odor intensity more slowly, than the smoke concentration. Irritation in the eyes grew more rapidly than nasal irritation. Nonsmokers were more distressed by odor than were smokers.

There has also been a number of studies on exposure to various organic solvents. Many of these studies have been carried out by means of epidemiological techniques. In one study by Knave and colleagues (1978), 30 jet-fuel-exposed workers and 30 nonexposed controls from a jet motor factory were examined with special reference to the nervous system by occupational hygiene physicians, psychiatrists, psychologists, and neurophysiologists. This investigation revealed differences between the exposed and nonexposed groups for incidence and prevalence of psychiatric symptoms, psychological tests with the load on attention and sensorimotor speed, and brain waves (EEG).

In another study by Elofsson and colleagues (1980), spray painters with long-term low-level exposure to organic solvents were examined and compared with two matched reference groups of nonexposed industrial workers. The aim of the study was to investigate the possible effects of the solvent exposure on health. The measurements included psychiatric interviews, psychometric tests, physiological examinations, and computer tomography of the brain. Significant differences between the exposed individuals and the reference group were found for psychiatric items indicative of a slight cerebral lesion. The psychometric tests revealed differences with respect to reaction time, manual dexterity, perceptual speed, and short-term memory. Differences were also found for the majority of the physiological parameters measuring peripheral nerve functions. Moreover, EEG and visually evoked responses showed some differences between the groups as did the results of the ophthalmologic examination and the computer tomography. The authors emphasized that the exposure levels were considerably lower than the valid threshold limit values in Sweden (cf. also Åstrand, 1978). There have also been some studies on the biological effects of light air ions and their relation to human stress (Knox 1982a, 1982b), of exposure to electric fields (Gamberale et al., 1978), and attitudes toward radioactive radiation (Sjöberg & Jansson, 1982).

35.11. CHILDREN'S ENVIRONMENT

At the beginning of the century, there was no need for special child environments except for schools. Children could play more or less everywhere. The streets were safe for walking and playing. Then the traffic situation, the construction of large housing areas, and the functional segregation of the cities drastically changed the children's outdoor environment. The debate became very intense in the end of the 1960s.

Sandels (1968) studied children in the traffic environment for several years. She pointed out that children experience and perceive the world around them differently than grown-ups. Children can only be trained to manage the traffic situation of today to a certain extent. According to Sandels, the only way to prevent children from getting injured or killed in traffic accidents is to adjust the traffic to the children, not the other way around. Research on causes of accidents among children and how to prevent them from happening has also been carried out by Bell and Westius (1979), Bäckström (1980), Flodström, Larsson, & Rehnström (1970), Gärling & Svensson (1983), Iversen (1981), Kromann (1976), Nummenmaa, Ruuhilehto & Syvänen (1975); Nummenmaa & Syvänen (1974), and Schioldborg (1974).

Already in the early 1970s, Ås and his collaborators investigated what children in a residential area in Oslo did when they were outdoors, where they did it, and with whom. The mothers were interviewed about their opinion of the area. The children's indoor activities were also studied (Ås, Lian, Thaule, & Selnaes, 1973; Lian, Thaule, & Selnaes, 1972; also Kolbenstvedt, 1975). Also in Finland, children's places for play and movement were examined at this time, and an attempt was made to bring together the developmental and environmental psychological viewpoints with the aid of the conception of conveying a play culture (Nummenmaa, Syvänen, & Weckroth, 1970; Rouhiainen & Nummenmaa, 1971; Setälä, 1972; Syvänen & Setälä, 1972; Takala, Alanen, Luolaja, & Pölkki, 1979; Vanhalakka-Ruoho, 1981). In Denmark, similar work was carried out by, among others, Morville (1969) and Christiansen, Flyvbjerg, Jenson-Butler, Jeppesen & Sorensen (1978).

In Sweden, Bengtsson (1974) worked to improve and enrich the outdoor environment in the city. He became internationally recognized for his ideas on children's environments and his plea for children's rights to play. Dahlén (1977), in his studies on children's physical environment, pointed out that when housing projects are planned, very little use is made of all the knowledge we actually have about children's use of their outdoor environment. He suggested one way to rectify this would be to let children participate in the planning of the physical environment. Ögren (1979) drew the same conclusions from her investigation of children's living situation in two housing areas. She found that if you want to know anything about a neighborhood, then ask the children (cf. also Höweler, 1973).

At the Stockholm Institute of Education, Björklid (1982), for her PhD thesis, studied two housing projects from the perspective of environmental and developmental psychology. The aims of the study were to obtain a broad picture of children's interactions with their outdoor environment and to provide a frequency description of children's play on those two projects. The study showed that it was mainly older preschool children and younger schoolboys who made use of the open spaces between the houses. The different designs of the play areas were reflected in the children's interaction with their environments insofar as activities were more varied on the more diverse and natural project than on the more artificial one. Björklid made two general recommendations: Set aside all open spaces between houses for play and provide playgrounds with play leaders (cf. also Björklid, 1980).

At the department of psychology, in Gothenburg, Biel and Torell (1979, 1982) studied children's cognition of their outdoor environment. In his PhD thesis, Biel found that children's knowledge of the large-scale environment can be classified into two categories—knowledge of environmental features and knowledge about spatial relations. He also found the home acts as a central reference point in the child's mental representation of the environment (Biel, 1979, 1982a, 1982b). Furthermore, he showed that given a distance comparison task, children succeed at the age of 6 to reconstruct with relative accuracy the area's landmarks. In their studies, Biel and Torell also found that children's outdoor activities and activity range correlated with the content and size of the sketch map, which was used as a manifestation of the relative amount of children's knowledge of their neighborhood.

Gaunt, at the National Swedish Institute for Building Research, asked the question: "What do children do when it rains?" She found that parents were rather restrictive about children's use of the living room and the kitchen; more so if they had many children. The most common place for children to spend their time at home was in their bedrooms. Practically no time was spent in the parents' bedroom. Schoolchildren were less restricted in their dwelling use than preschool children. Calm, quiet, sitting, "clean" activities and games were most common, whereas mobile, noisy, and messy ones were less common. Schoolchildren with a room of their own or access to an extra space (basement, hobby room, etc.) were found to be more active than children who shared a room and had no extra space. This difference in activity level was not found among the preschool children, probably due to the fact that young children are not able to fully make use of larger areas (Gaunt, 1977, 1979b).

In 1979, the Swedish Council for Building Research arranged a symposium on children and the built environment (Gaunt, 1979a). The council has also supported projects dealing with day-care centers. von Schéele (1979) studied day-care centers and neighborhoods and discussed their qualifications as good environments for children. In another day-care project, the main aims were to deformalize the area of contact between the family and the local authorities and to use the day-care center as a meeting point in the neighborhood. The thought was to open up the day-care centers for more people and to use them as multipurpose centers. There were eight day-care centers involved in the study—five around Stockholm (Colven, William-Olsson, & Cederquist, 1979) and three around Malmö (af Klercker & Cederquist, 1979).

Research in the Scandinavian countries also includes issues like the maladjustment of schoolchildren as a consequence of the family's moving (Vikman, 1982). For a study of Norwegian children's adjustment to their school and home environments, one may refer to Raundalen (1978) and to the Scandinavian report in the *Childhood City Newsletter* (1980).

35.12 ENVIRONMENTS FOR ELDERLY AND DISABLED PERSONS

Research on the aging person has a long tradition in the Scandinavian countries. As one of the first in the world, the Norwegian Institute of Gerontology was established in 1957 (Solem, Guntvedt, & Beverfelt,

1982). In Sweden, there is a well-established geriatric research mainly focusing on the diseases of old age (Svanborg, Djurfeldt, & Steen, 1980), but also the study of the normal aging processes has received considerable attention. The Institute of Gerontology in Jönköping was founded in 1970, and 4 years later the Center of Gerontology was established in Lund (Berg, 1980; Helander, 1972; B. Malmberg, 1980).

Of the Swedish population, today about 17% are retired, and the proportion is steadily increasing. Obviously, this change in age distribution will give rise to problems on all levels of the society (Statens Offentliga Utredningar, 1984). In order to study the consequences of the change in age distribution, a major research project entitled Old People and Society—Past, Present, and Future Aspects has been going on for several years (Odén, Svanborg, & Tornstam 1983; Tornstam, Svanborg, & Odén, 1982). In order to get an overall perspective on problems related to housing as well as an analysis of the elderly's needs from a psychological, medical, and sociogerontological viewpoint, a number of symposia have been arranged by the Committee for the Study of the Elderly's Problems and others during the last 10 years (e.g., Ström & Ottosson, 1983; Ström & Zotterman, 1975).

In 1976, Simovici investigated what might happen when people stop working after retirement. In his PhD study from 1981, Samuelsson presented unique data from a longitudinal study carried out on people, from the age of 67 until they reached the age of 76, living in a small community. Results from these and other studies showed that although placing, to some extent, special demands on the physical environment and social services, the elderly form a healthy, resourceful group, often until the age of 80. Then, gradually, the need for institutional care becomes a major issue.

Recently, problems related to the environment of old people have attained considerable attention. About 10% of the retired persons in Sweden today live in special housing. In two studies, Lindström and Åhlund (1982a, 1982b) studied and evaluated the environmental qualities of these residences and day centers for elderly persons. The work was based on a model developed by Powell Lawton, where the persons' competence is related to the demands placed on them by the environment (Svensson, 1984; Sundström, 1983). The emotional impact of the built environment on the elderly was studied at the Environmental Psychology Unit in Lund. Retired persons living in the countryside or in old city centers and modern housing areas were compared in terms of activity patterns, social interaction, and environmental preferences. The preliminary results indicate retired people in suburban high-rise areas feel more isolated and engage in less social interaction and recreational activities than people in central parts of the same town (Küller, 1984; also Watzke & Küller, 1986).

A few projects have been devoted to the question of how to activate elderly persons either by social intervention or designing a special environment. Arnetz (1983) divided the tenants at a service house into an experimental and a control group. The experimental group was interviewed about their interests and encouraged to carry out a program that would realize these interests. This was further supported by special training of the staff. Psychological and physiological measurements taken before the project, after 3 months, and after 6 months revealed considerable effects of the activation program. In the experimental group, the subjects became more happy and extroverted, less restless, and the generally submissive tone was replaced by a will to protest. In contrast to the controls, the experimental group increased in body weight and length and also gave indications of a more healthy metabolism and decrease in hormonal stress level (cf. also Andersson, 1984).

The purpose of a study reported by Küller and Mattsson (1986) was to redecorate the dining-room environment at a geriatric hospital in a way that agreed with the prior living conditions of the patients, most of whom suffered a mild confusion due to dementia. Based on informal interviews with the patients, the dining room was redecorated in a style reminiscent of a Swedish home from the 1930s or early 1940s (Figure 35.4). A special program was set up in order to evaluate the psychological and medical effects of the changed environment. There was an overall increase in social interest and conversation, and the patients also smiled more in the new environment. In the postinterview, the patients expressed a clear preference for the redecorated dining room, whereas the personnel seemed to be influenced by functional rather than aesthetic considerations.

A visiting researcher from the United States made an extensive comparison of old-age care in Sweden and Norway (Altman, 1982). The amount of research on the elderly that has been carried out in recent years, especially in Sweden, is quite extensive (e.g., Fagerberg, Kärnekall, Landell, & Liljeström, 1980; Hurtig, Paulsson, & Schulz, 1981; Lidmar-Reinius, 1984; Simovici, 1981; Ståhl, 1984; Vang, Gripenlöf, & Husberg, 1984). Still, Boalt and Åkerman in their recent bibliography (1984, p. 137) gave a word of warning: "An examination of research reports reveals that a theoretical approach and attempts at a professional discussion and analysis of the problems are frequently lacking."

One group of disabled that has received considerable interest from environmental psychology researchers are the blind. No doubt, one reason for this is the unique insight such studies might give into the nonvisual perceptual and cognitive processes. In 1976, Acking and co-workers made an extensive study of the perception of blind people by means of semantic ratings. It was shown that the blind use the same words to describe their nonvisual perception of various materials as do sighted people (Acking, Ohlsson, & Sjögren, 1976). Drawing on these and other basic results, Gustavsson and Månsson (1980) studied the orientation of blind persons in a number of buildings especially designed to supply nonvisual orientation clues.

The most extensive research in Sweden on blind persons' mobility has been carried out by Jansson and his associates in Uppsala. This group has, among other things, contributed to the development of various aids for the blind, including relief maps and tactile point stimulation. Their work has bearings on the design of the physical environment. Jansson's work is partly based upon the experimental and theoretical studies of event perception initiated by Johansson (Jansson, 1981, 1982; Johansson, von Hofsten, & Jansson, 1980). For other studies on blind persons' orientation, I refer the reader to Juurmaa & Suonio (1975). Finally, there has been some research on environments for mentally disabled persons (e.g., Hirvonen & Katajisto, 1976; Ojanen, 1975; Palmér, 1982; Setälä, Nummenmaa, Nupponen, Syvänen, & Weckroth, 1972).

35.13. PERSON–ENVIRONMENT MODELS

Few systematic attempts have been made at putting together the various facets of person–environment research into one comprehensive yet precise model. Not that there is any lack of models, but most of them focus on one central concept, like arousal, comfort, or cognitive competence and include only one or two environmental aspects. Still a number of instances have already been mentioned where models of a somewhat more inclusive kind have been employed. We refer the reader to the theory of cognition developed by Gärling and colleagues (1984); the studies on housing and urban design by Gehl (1971), and by Daun (1974); the work on stress and coping

Figure 35.4. A dining room at a geriatric hospital in Sweden before (top) and after redecoration (after Küller, Mattsson & Steen, 1985).

by Levi, Frankenhaeuser, and Gardell (1981); Karasek (1976); and Dalgard (1981); the studies of thermal indoor climate by Wyon and colleagues (1975); and of odor perception by Berglund and Berglund (1981).

Over the years, Marek has elaborated a model that may be used in order to articulate psychological problems in various types of environments (Marek, 1976, 1978; Marek & Hovden, 1983; Marek & Kvittingen, 1976). Together with Gump, Marek has also employed the framework of behavior settings developed by Roger Barker (Gump & Marek, 1970). Syvänen at Tampere University has constructed a model relating human activity to factors in the physical and social environments (Syvänen, 1981). From his perspective of cultural and economic geography, Hägerstrand, in Lund, has constructed a model that considers the individual's movements in terms of space and time (Hägerstrand, 1975).

A comprehensive model of person–environment interaction has also been developed by Küller (Fig. 35.5). According to this model, a person continually interacts with his or her physical and social environments. This influence is modified by the person's own activities and personal resources. The actual interaction proceeds in four steps, activation, orientation, evaluation, and control—what is called the "basic emotional process." All events that prevent this basic process from running smoothly will result in adjustment on behalf of the person, whereas strong or prolonged disturbances might lead to maladjustment. The model has been employed in studies of various kinds of environments, for example, theaters, ships, and housing for the elderly (Küller, 1976, 1977, 1979c, 1980a, 1980b, 1984).

It might be argued that conventional person–environment theory, with its independent and dependent variables, is about to become obsolete. Instead, there might be the need for a new kind of holistic and interactionistic theory, where there are no fixed relationships between humans and environments, but where the essentials instead have to be redefined in each new situation. Magnusson tried to find a remedy for this by elaborating an interactional model of behavior. He argued that the rapidly growing interest with respect to the person by situation interaction emphasizes the need for systematic studies of situational characteristics. One basic assumption in Magnusson's model is that individual behavior is more similar across situations that are perceived and interpreted as similar by the individual. Magnusson summarized his interactional paradigm for human development in the following words:

This general framework for the analysis of behavior makes the basic assumption that the thoughts, feelings, and actions of a person cannot be explained by taking into account person factors or situation factors alone; instead, the joint operation of the person-environment system must be considered in order to gain an adequate understanding. (Magnusson & Allen, 1983, p. 3; cf. also Magnusson, 1974; Magnusson & Ekehammar, 1978; Sjöberg, 1979; Thoresen & Öhman, forthcoming)

35.14. SIMULATION IN ENVIRONMENTAL RESEARCH

Environmental researchers have made abundant use of full-scale and model simulation techniques of various kinds. Pleijel, in Stockholm, and Voltelen, in Copenhagen, already in the 1940s and 1950s undertook attempts at simulating daylight. Pleijel's simulator consisted of an indirectly lit semispherical construction, whereas Voltelen used a small room completely covered with mirrors (Liljedahl & Löfberg, 1968). Korsmo, at Trondheim, in the 1960s built a laboratory where the walls consisted of drawers that could be drawn out, thus diminishing the width of the room. The fronts of the drawers were exchangeable and could be supplied with sheets with various three-dimensional patterns. At one end of the room, there was a screen supplied with fluorescent tubes of various colors. This laboratory was used mainly for perceptual studies. In another of Korsmo's laboratories, white-and-black pillows could be used in order to simulate functional relationships within the room. Hesselgren, in his studies, employed an experimental church where various screens could be moved around to form a small space within the larger space. Supplying the size of the small space with various kinds of illumination, this arrangement was used to assess the perception of enclosed space (Hesselgren, 1967).

At the Norwegian Building Institute in Oslo, Björkto, in the 1960s constructed a more advanced full-scale laboratory where proper walls, doors, and ceilings could be arranged in order to simulate a normal apartment for living (Björkto, 1968). The technically most advanced full-scale laboratory of its day, however, came into existence when the School of Architecture was built in Lund in 1965–1966. Under the leadership of Boalt, this laboratory was supplied with elements of all kinds, making possible the construction of large apartments, even in two stories, that had a natural look and could be supplied with running

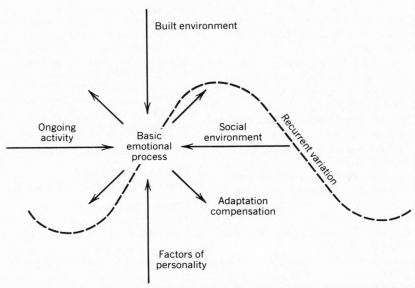

Figure 35.5. A model of person–environment interaction (after Küller 1976, 1984). According to this model human beings are partly affected by the physical environment and partly by the social network. In addition, they are influenced by the activities in which they engage. This influence, which varies in extent over time, is modified by their own personal resources, constitution, experience, and the like. Although the environment activates them in various ways, human beings at the same time endeavor to retain control over their situation. What the model indicates is, in part, that activation from various sources must be adjusted and adapted to the resources of the individual.

water, toilets, bathrooms, kitchens, and so forth. It was monitored by equipment for automatic still picture and, later, video recordings. The laboratory has been used for a variety of studies, among others, the simulation of a rehabilitation clinic of the university hospital (Åhlund, 1976; Boalt, 1968b; Dahlman, Sjölin, & Åhlund, 1971).

Concerning architectural aesthetics, other types of simulation have been employed. One example consists of large screens placed in a semicircle and furnished with wide-angle back projections. Built by Branzell at the Chalmers University of Technology, in Gothenburg, this simulator can be used for redrafting parts of an urban area. At the School of Technology, at Otnäs in Finland, Paasi is employing central-projection-type pictures with the extreme wide-angle of 360 × 210° on the inside of a spherical screen that extends all-around the subject (Paasi, 1978).

In the early 1970s, a simulator of the model-scope type was built in Lund by Acking and Küller. It consists of a mobile television camera with a relatoscope, that is, a pencil-shaped tube with a lense at one end, extending from the camera into the architectural model below. Sitting in front of his or her monitor, the subject has access to a foot pedal and a steering wheel by means of which he or she can

make a tour in the model. In order to evaluate what he or she sees, the subject is supplied with a semantic lever, that is, a manual seven-graded rating scale. By combination with an eye-movement recorder, the subject's point of fixation may also be registered. All the information, that is, the view from the model itself, the fixation spot, and the semantic rating can be continously recorded on tape. The group in Lund also made a systematic attempt at evaluating various kinds of visual simulations, among others, the one just described. The results indicated there are large random as well as systematic errors attached to the different kinds of visual simulations. However, presentations based on model-scope recordings in naturalistic models tend to give a more accurate result than the more conventional architectural presentations (Acking & Küller, 1973; Acking & Sorte, 1972; Acking, Ohlsson & Sjögren, 1976; Janssens & Küller, 1986). A model simulator also exists at the Tampere University of Technology in Finland.

The research on indoor climatology has encouraged the development of a completely different kind of simulation—the climate chamber. Pioneering this field in the Scandinavian countries were Löfstedt, who created several climate chambers for advanced human studies in Lund, and Fanger, working in

Copenhagen. Löfstedt's climate chambers were designed in order to study human heat tolerance through the systematic variation of temperature and humidity gradients. Recordings included physiological parameters like oxygen consumption and EKG as well as psychological measurements of mental performance and personality (Fanger, 1970; Löfstedt, 1966; cf. also Andersen & Lundqvist, 1970). In 1976, the Swedish Institute for Building Research established a new research center at Gävle, where two large climate chambers were built under the supervision of Wyon (Figure 35.6). These chambers are fully computerized and among the most modern in the world today (Wyon, 1975).

In the early 1970s, a chamber was constructed by Küller, in Lund, with the main purpose of studying physiological and psychological effects of light, color, and visual patterns. In addition to monitoring daylight, artificial illumination, and temperature, the walls are exchangeable in order to present different color schemes. Measurements include subjective evaluation, on-line analysis of EEG and EKG, and the sampling of various hormones (Küller, 1976, 1980a, 1983; Ulrich, 1981). Another type of simulation is exemplified by the laboratory for sensory and chemical analysis used by Berglund and Lindvall in their studies on indoor air quality. The outfit makes it possible to simulate, for example, various kinds of industrial pollution. There is also a mobile unit for field experiments, which may be used for "on-site" studies (Berglund, Johansson & Lindvall, 1981).

Today, in Sweden as elsewhere, computers are beginning to take over certain parts of the simulation by means of graphic displays on monitors or printouts. Undoubtedly, this development is at its very beginning. So far, the perceptual quality of the display has, in general, not been as good as the architectural simulation mentioned previously. However, for the purpose of studying traffic behavior, the Swedish Road and Traffic Research Institute in Linköping has developed a car-driving simulator that uses a computer-based graphical display of high quality. By means of this equipment, various aspects of the sensory input may be coordinated and presented to the "driver."

35.15. RETROSPECT AND PROSPECTS

As might be seen from the present review, environmental psychology in Sweden and the other Scandinavian countries constitutes a resourceful branch of scientific endeavor. Borrowing support from several adjacent fields, it is methodologically sophisticated; it tackles real-life problems; it has a wide, sometimes holistic, outlook; and it seems to realize the importance of theory construction. It is, however, also obvious that the study of environment–people relations is not a unified field and will probably never be so. There are innumerable methods, approaches, and theories. No attempt will be made to evaluate the success of the various projects described previously

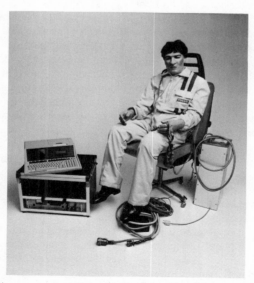

Figure 35.6. Subjective sensations are well predicted by this thermal manikin, which is used to measure heat flow from the body in complex thermal environments. (*Source:* By courtesy of David P. Wyon.)

or to assess the importance of the different problem areas. However, some personal comments might still be worth making.

The Nordic countries can be described as thoroughly industrialized consumer societies. The national economies are highly internationalized; industry is presently faced with problems of low utilization of its capacity. Per capita incomes are among the highest in the world, and personal incomes are comparatively evenly distributed. The rate of taxation is high due to a large public sector and large public income transfers (this is less pronounced, however, in Finland). In Sweden, expenditure on social welfare quadrupled from 1930 to 1945 and multiplied by more than six times between 1950 and 1975. The occupational rate is high for both men and women; part-time work is very common. Agricultural labor has been on the decrease for many years; in the 1960s industrial employment reached its peak (this occurred in Finland somewhat later), and the only sector showing recent growth is the service sector, notably the public service sector (Sanne, 1983).

As far as building is concerned, the massive housing program that began after World War II is now more or less completed. The focus has shifted toward renovation and rebuilding, in order to improve the quality of older dwellings and of the urban environment in general. There is also an interest in bringing the various life sectors of housing, work, services, and recreation closer together, in an attempt to make the environment more livable and counteract the negative effects of traffic and transportation.

The research on aesthetics and urban design has not been very successful as a basis for this. The study of architectural meaning by means of semantic methods in the 1960s and 1970s looked promising. The techniques could easily be applied in, for example, postoccupancy evaluation. But this is seldom done, except in projects where the original research groups themselves are involved. Architectural simulation is another sad example. The equipment works well and is not expensive to use. Still this type of simulation is used very little in real-world projects. Actually, it seems to be very hard to get this kind of methodology fed back into the planning process. The architects, planners, and politicians either are not aware of or not interested in it; or at least, it seems so. The application gap that Appleyard described in 1973 is still with us.

At the same time, the improvement of the work environment continues. Undoubtedly, the results from studies of environmental factors, like noise, have been successfully applied. The research has

made us aware of the numerous health hazards of the human-made environment. The main explanation is that the occupational sector in Sweden and the other Scandinavian countries has been strongly influenced by legislation as a result of various government and trade union initiatives. In Sweden, the Work Environment Act, from 1978, laid down the worker's right to physical and mental health. In addition to environmental effects on health and well-being, recently there has been an intense discussion of genetic damage in the long-term perspective. There has also been a growing concern about stress caused by the psychosocial environment.

However, legislation or political programs do not always lead to success. The socialist orientation of the Swedish government over several decades has no doubt promoted research on housing and social planning for special groups. The creation of housing areas that are safe enough to let small children play outdoors; the development of special facilities for old people; the adjustment of the environment for the physically disabled; the organization of space in a way that makes it comprehensible for blind persons — these have been regarded as important areas for research. Much has certainly been done, but most of the accumulated knowledge is still left unused. In some cases, society obviously cannot afford to do anything. In other cases, the existing planning principles are too well established to let themselves be reorganized. Still the research related to special groups is continuing to hold a strong position in Sweden.

The causes for success or failure are often to be found outside the scientific world itself. Real-life problems as formulated by politicians are all too often confused with scientific problems. Even when a problem can be properly formulated, it often takes too much time to solve by means of research. By the time the researcher has come up with a solution, the politicians might have lost their patience. The application gap becomes a time gap. As a consequence, the attempt to solve environmental problems directly by means of research has more or less failed.

At other times, the knowledge does not lend itself to application. Not because it is too theoretical but because of lack of a good theory. Kurt Lewin once said that there is nothing more practical than a good theory. Had I to pinpoint one shortcoming of person–environment research in Sweden and elsewhere, it would be the rather limited scope of most of its models and theories. Architects and builders generally assume that the environmental researcher has a sound basis in theory. This is certainly not true. Human factors, for instance, have generally been studied one or two at a time. Allegedly, in some cases the effects are bound to be rather specific, but often the situation is much more complicated, involving interactions between many environmental and individual factors at the same time. Still data are often treated by means of simplistic formulas reminiscent of the psychophysical laboratory 100 years ago. What might be needed is an overall change in the research approach from the single-factor experiment or even the unidisciplinary study toward the multifactor, interdisciplinary field study.

Another problem is that much of the basic work on perception, cognition, personality, and the like is loosely or not at all connected with environmental factors. Perhaps stress research is unique within our field in combining sound theoretical reasoning in physiology, psychology, and sociology with a powerful set of methods and an eye for real-world problems. Stress researchers actually seem to come to terms with a number of environmental problems. In most other areas, there is still a lack of models that would help us understand the complex cultural, social, psychological, and physiological issues that constitute person–environment research. But this kind of broad interdisciplinary approach also has its shortcomings. Who should, for instance, be responsible for the theory, the physicist, the physiologist, or the psychologist? Can there be a truly interdisciplinary theory, or does theory always have to remain within each separate discipline?

A problem that is perhaps more pertinent in person–environment research than in most other fields concerns the dissemination of knowledge. Unfortunately, a great portion of the research mentioned in this chapter is only published in a Scandinavian language. This is especially true within the fields of architecture, housing, and urban design, which are regarded by many as local businesses lacking international interest. This is sometimes the case not only for the output, in terms of reports, but also for the input, with quotations being restricted to work done by colleagues in one's own country. Naturally, for such a small part of the world as the Scandinavian countries constitute, this is a serious error. However, in sectors like stress research, the normal international publication policy is generally adhered to. One attempt to improve the situation is the recent introduction of the computer-based Swedish Environmental Research Index—SERIX.*

A problem that has not been touched on at all in this review concerns environmental education.

---

*SERIX, Swedish Environmental Research Index. Statens Naturvårdsverk, Box 1302, 171 25 Solna, Sweden.

Briefly, it can be said that the new knowledge that comes out of the studies described here only occasionally finds its way into the teaching in our high schools and universities. This is not the place to analyze the reasons for this. However, at present neither the authorities nor the universities themselves seem able to face up to their responsibilities in this matter. (For an attempt to introduce environmental education in primary schools in Norway, see Björndal & Lieberg, 1975.)

Finally, I have come to the question: "Who governs the research in Sweden?" It is generally assumed that the universities and independent research institutions serve as nourishing grounds for free research. Having worked at one of the major universities for nearly 20 years makes me accept this view without reservation. Scholars are amazingly free to initiate whatever research they fancy, as long as they can get the project funded. Their colleagues, the students, and the university board are likely to be in favor of most initiatives as long as these are ethically acceptable. Thus funding becomes a major issue. A scientist may receive a grant from:

Governmental research councils conducted by selected scientists.

Ministries, which are government-controlled bodies. Ministries finance research either through grants via delegations or institutes that allocate further funds.

The Bank of Sweden Tercentenary Fund, which is governed by members of parliament and scientists appointed by the parliament.

Independent funds such as the Swedish Work Environment Fund which has a board where representatives from the labour market are in a majority.

A large number of small funds of varying origin, often private donations (Leymann, 1981).

Concerning environmental psychology, in particular, the Swedish Council for Building Research has taken an enlightened and generous view from the beginning (Eriksson, 1975). More recently, the Swedish Work Environment Fund, the Delegation for Social Research, the Swedish Council for Research in the Humanities and Social Sciences, and several other organizations have shown their recognition of the field. The development in Sweden is currently characterized by a rapid growth in sectorial research, that is, applied research and development linked to different sectors of the society. This means various councils and agencies are making priorities based on important trends in society, political ideas, or international developments. Projects in line with those priorities are most likely to get funded. In addition to the research propositions regularly advanced by the government, the major funding organizations make their own project evaluations and long-term programs (*Byggsektorn 1990*, 1982; Mundebo, 1982; *Mänsklig arbetsmiljö*, 1984).

Basic research has by no means displayed the same growth. Due to the partial failure of applied environmental research, however, politicians and administrators have become more aware of the fact that breakthroughs in research are notoriously unpredictable phenomena. Voices are now heard saying that research must be allowed more freedom. It is too early to say whether this trend will change the pragmatic research policy that has dominated the scene for the last 15 years. Another interesting development is the new form of direct cooperation taking place between an increasing number of industrial concerns and the universities. In Lund, for instance, this has resulted in the recent construction of the research village called "Ideon." So far, none of this research has been within the person–environment sector. However, a development in that direction might be expected in the near future.

Acknowledgments

The writing of this chapter was made possible through a grant from the Swedish Council for Building Research. The author wishes to thank about 20 persons in Denmark, Finland, Norway, and Sweden who have read and commented on the manuscript.

REFERENCES

Aaltonen, J., Lahti, I.A., & Piha, J. (1978). Housing environment, family, and mental health. A clinical psychiatric perspective. *Social Review, 72*(4), 36–42.

Acking, C-A. (Ed.). (1974). *Bygg mänskligt*. Stockholm: Askild & Kärnekull.

Acking, C-A. (1976). *Hur miljön upplevs vid nedsatt synförmåga* (Rep. No. 31), Stockholm: Statens Råd för Byggnadsforskning.

Acking, C-A., & Küller, R. (1972). The perception of an interior as a function of its colour. *Ergonomics, 15*(6), 645–654.

Acking, C-A., & Küller, R. (1973). Presentation and judgement of planned environment and the hypothesis of arousal. In W.F.E. Preiser (Ed.), *Environmental design*

research. *Proceedings of the Fourth International EDRA Conference* (Vol. 1, pp. 72–83). Stroudsburg, PA: Dowden, Hutchinson & Ross.

Acking, C-A., Ohlsson, C., & Sjögren, U. (1976). *Environmental simulating methods and public communication* (Document No. 8). Stockholm: Swedish Council for Building Research.

Acking, C-A., & Sorte, G.J. (1972). *Metoder för presentation av planerad miljö* (Work report No. 2), Lund, Sweden: Lunds Tekniska Högskola, Formlära.

af Klercker, J., & Cederquist, B. (1979). Föränderbar fysisk miljö som pedagogiskt hjälpmedel. In L. Gaunt (Ed.). *Som man bygger får man barn.* (pp. 151–163) Notation 16. Gävle, Sweden: Statens Institut för Byggnodsforskning.

Agurén, S., Hansson, R., & Karlsson, K.G. (1976). *Volvo Kalmarverken. Erfarenheter av nya arbetsformer.* Stockholm: Rationaliseringsrådet, SAF & LO.

Ahlin, J. (Ed.) (1983). *Report from the Swedish-American Architectural Research Seminar in Stockholm 1982.* Stockholm: Royal Institute of Technology, School of Architecture.

Ahlström, R. (1981). *Differentiation of community sounds by means of emotional selfratings.* (Rep. No. 3), Stockholm: National Institute of Environmental Medicine.

Aldskogius, H. (1977). A conceptual framework and a Swedish case study of recreational behavior and environmental cognition. *Economic Geography, 53*(2), 163–183.

Altman, W.M. (1982). *Old age care in Sweden and Norway.* Thomas J. Watson Foundation.

Andersen, I., & Lundqvist, G.R. (1970). Design and performance of an environmental chamber. *International Journal of Biometeorology, 40*, 402–405.

Andersson, L. (1984). *Aging and loneliness. An interventional study of a group of elderly women.* Stockholm: Karolinska Institute, Department of Psychosocial Environmental Medicine.

Andersson, L-O., Frisk, P., Löfstedt, B., & Wyon, D.P. (1975). *Människans reaktioner för torr, fuktad och intermittent fuktad luft* (Rep. No. 63), Stockholm: Statens Råd för Byggnadsforskning.

Andersson-Brolin, L., & Lindén, A. (1974). *Var man känner sig hemma och vilka man kallar sina grannar* (Rep. No. 59), Stockholm: Statens Råd för Byggnadsforskning.

Appleyard, D. (1973). Professional priorities for environmental psychology. In R. Küller (Ed.), *Architectural Psychology. Proceedings of the Lund Conference 1973.* (pp. 85–111). Shtroudsburg, PA: Dowden, Hutchinson & Ross.

Arlock, M., & Küller, R. (Eds.). (1973). *Gruppen för arkitekturpsykologi. Symposium 1972.* Göteborg, Sweden: Chalmers Tekniska Högskola, Formlära.

Arnetz, B. (1983). *Psycho-physiological effects of social un-*

derstimulation in old age. Stockholm: Karolinska Institute, Laboratory for Clinical Stress Research.

Arvidsson, O., Johansson, C.R., Olsson, K., & Wigeman, H. (1965). Samhällsbuller. En sociologisk-psykologisk studie. *Nordisk Hygienisk Tidskrift, 45*(2), pp. 153–186.

Aura, S. (1982a). *Huomispäivän kaupunki. Arkkitehtuuripsykologisia havaintoja rakennetun ymparistön ja ihmisen vuorovaikutuksesta.* Helsinki, Finland: Rakennuskirja.

Aura, S. (1982b). *Studying the experience of the urban environment* (Rep. No. 74, pp. 1–8). Tampere, Finland: Tampere University of Technology, Department of Architecture.

Bell, R., & Westius, S. (1979). *Barn under två år. Samband mellan utveckling och olycksfall i hemmen* (Rep. No. 58). Stockholm: Statens Råd för Byggnadsforskning.

Bengtsson, A. (1974). *The child's right to play.* Sheffield, England: Tartan.

Berg, S. (1980). Psychological functioning in 70- and 75-year-old people. A study in an industrialized city. *Acta Psychiatrica Scandinavica, 62* (Suppl. 288).

Berglund, B. (1974). Quantitative and qualitative analysis of industrial odors with human observers. *Annals of the New York Academy of Sciences, 237*, 35–51.

Berglund, B., & Berglund, U. (1981). Human olfactory perception of environmental chemicals. In D.M. Norris (Ed.), *Perception of behavioral chemicals* (pp. 81–101). Amsterdam: Elsevier/North-Holland Biomedical.

Berglund, B., Berglund, U., Goldstein, M., & Lindvall, T. (1981). Loudness (or annoyance) summation of combined community noises. *Journal of the Acoustical Society of America, 70*(6), 1628–1634.

Berglund, B., Berglund, U., & Lindvall, T. (1973). Perceptual interaction of odors from a pulp mill. *Proceedings of the Third International Clean Air Congress, Düsseldorf 1973.* Düsseldorf, West Germany: VDI.

Berglund, B., Berglund, U., & Lindvall, T. (1975). A study of response criteria in populations exposed to aircraft noise. *Journal of Sound and Vibration, 41*(1), 33–39.

Berglund, B., Berglund, U., & Lindvall, T. (1980). Loudness separation of community noises. *ASHA Report, 10*, 349–354.

Berglund, B., Berglund, U., Lindvall, T., & Nicander-Bredberg, H. (1982). Olfactory and chemical characterization of indoor air. Towards a psychophysical model for air quality. *Environment International, 8*, 327–332.

Berglund, B., Johansson, I., & Lindvall, T. (1981). *Underlag för ventilationsnormer. Etapp II.* Stockholm: Stockholms Universitet, Psykologiska Institutionen.

Berglund, B., Johansson, I., & Lindvall, T. (1982a). The influence of ventilation on indoor/outdoor air contaminants in an office building. *Environment International, 8*, 395–399.

Berglund, B., Johansson, I., & Lindvall, T. (1982b). A longitudinal study of air contaminants in a newly built preschool. *Environment International, 8*, 111–115.

Bergsjö, A., Nilsson, K., & Skärbäck, E. (1982). *Vindkraft i landskapet* (Rep. No. 13). Stockholm: Nämnden för Energiproduktionsforskning.

Biel, A. (1979). Accuracy and stability in children's representation of the large-scale environment. *Göteborg Psychological Reports, 9*(2).

Biel, A. (1982a). Children's spatial knowledge of their home environment. *Göteborg Psychological Reports, 12*(10).

Biel, A. (1982b). Children's spatial representation of their neighbourhood. A step towards a general spatial competence. *Journal of Environmental Psychology, 2*(3), 193–200.

Biel, A., & Torell, G. (1979). The mapped environment. Cognitive aspects of children's drawings. *Man-Environment Systems, 9*(4 & 5), 187–194.

Biel, A., & Torell, G. (1982). Experience as a determinant of children's neighbourhood knowledge. *Göteborg Psychological Reports, 12*(9).

Björklid, P. (1980). *Ut och lek. Bostadsområdets utemiljö ur miljö- och utvecklingspsykologisk synvinkel* (Rep. No. 65), Stockholm: Statens Råd för Byggnadsforskning.

Björklid, P. (1982). *Children's outdoor environment.* Lund, Sweden: Liber.

Björkto, R. (1968). Den aktuelle situasjon i Norge. In C. Boalt (Ed.), *Byggnadsfunktionella Studier i Fullskalel aboratorium. Rapport fran Konferensen i Falsterbo 1967.* Lund, Sweden: Lunds Tekniska Högskola, Byggnads funktionslära.

Björnberg, U., Carlestam, G., Eriksson, R., & Lundahl, I. (1975). *Research on quality of life in urban settlements in Sweden.* (Rep. No. T3). Stockholm: Swedish Council for Building Research.

Björndal, B., & Lieberg, S. (1975). Environmental education in primary school. A presentation of a Norwegian curriculum development project. *Scandinavian Journal of Educational Research, 19*, 131–151.

Boalt, C. (1968a). *Boendestudier i fem bostadsområden i Stockholm* (Rep. No. 13). Stockholm: Statens Råd för Byggnadsforskning.

Boalt, C. (Ed.). (1968b). *Byggnadsfunktionella studier i fullskalelaboratorium. Rapport från konferensen i Falsterbo 1967.* Lund, Sweden: Lunds Tekniska Högskola, Byggnadsfunktionslära.

Boalt, C., & Karlsson, G. (1948–49). *Mor och barn från morgon till kväll* (Meddelande No. 2). Stockholm: Hemmens forskningsinstitut.

Boalt, C., & Åkerman, K. (1984). Research on the elderly and their life environment. In K. Lidmar-Reinius (Ed.), *The elderly and their environment. Research in Sweden.* Document No. 27. Stockholm: Swedish Council for Building Research.

Boalt, G., Holm, L., & Boalt, C. (1959). *Bostadssociologi.* Stockholm: Natur och Kultur.

Borg, G. (1978). Subjective effort in relation to physical performance and working capacity. In H.L. Pick, H.W. Leibowitz, J.E. Singer, A. Steinschneider, & H.W. Stevenson. (Eds.). *Psychology. From research to practice* (pp. 333–361). New York & London: Plenum.

Bradley, G. (1981). *Arbetsmiljö och terminaler.* Stockholm: Arbetarskyddsfonden.

Branzell, A. (1976). *Att notera rumsupplevelse* (Rep. No. T1). Stockholm: Statens Råd för Byggnadsforskning.

Brochmann, O. (1952). *Livsform og boligform.* Oslo, Norway: Johan Grundt Tanum.

Byggsektorn 1990. Behov av forskning och utveckling under 80-talet. (1982). (Rep. No. G13). Stockholm: Statens Råd för Byggnadsforskning.

Bäckström, K. (1980). Prevention of childhood accidents. A compulsory task for the society. *Childhood City Newsletter, 19,* 17–18.

Börjesson, B., Grytt, H., & Kjessel, B. (Eds.). (1979). *Brukarmedverkan. Om brukarmedverkan vid lokalplanering* (Rep. No. 146, del 1 & 2). Stockholm: Byggnadsstyrelsen.

Böök, A. (1981). *Maintenance of environmental orientation during locomotion.* Umeå, Sweden: University of Umeå, Department of Psychology.

Böök, A., & Gärling, T. (1981). Maintenance of orientation during locomotion in unfamiliar environments. *Journal of Experimental Psychology: Human Perception and Performance, 7,* 995–1006.

Childhood City Newsletter (1980). (No. 19). New York: City University of New York, Center for Humanities Graduate School.

Christiansen, E., Flyvbjerg, G., Jenson-Butler, C., Jeppesen, S., & Sorensen, P.T. (1978). *Mental maps of Danish school children* (Work Report No. 6). Aarhus, Denmark: Geografisk Institut.

Cold Brantenberg, B. (1981). *Forprosjekt til evaluering af den overdekte gaten på universitetssentret på Dragvoll.* Trondheim, Norway: Norges Tekniske Högskole. Selskapet for Industriell og Teknisk Forskning.

Colven, R., William-Olsson, I., & Cederquist, B. (1979). Sektoriseringsproblem vid planering av barnstugor. In L. Gaunt (Ed.). *Som man bygger får man barn.* (Notation 6). (pp. 139–150). Gävle, Sweden: Statens Institut för Byggnodsfarskning.

Cronberg, T. (Ed.). (1982). *Socialt bostadsbyggande och boendedemokrati i Norden* (NU-serien No. 10). Stockholm: Nordiska Rådet; & Copenhagen & Oslo: Nordisk Ministerråd.

Dahlén, U. (1977). *Småhusbarnen. En studie av barns uppväxtvillkor i en modern småhusstadsdel.* Lund, Sweden: Liber.

Dahlman, S. (1973). *Personal space in airport waiting lounges* (Rep. No. 4). Lund, Sweden: University of Lund, Building Function Analysis.

Dahlman, S., Sjölin, E., & Åhlund, O. (Eds.). (1971). *Di-*

mensionering och disponering av boenderum för rehabiliteringsklinik. Lund, Sweden: Lunds Tekniska Högskola. Byggnadsfunktionslära.

Dalgard, O.S. (1980). Mental health, neighbourhood and related social variables in Oslo. *Acta Psychiatrica Scandinavica, 62*(Suppl. 285), 298–304.

Dalgard, O.S. (1981). Occupational experience and mental health, with special reference to closeness of supervision. *Psychiatry and Social Science, 1,* 29–42.

Daun, Å. (1974). *Förortsliv. En etnologisk studie av kulturell förändring.* Stockholm: Prisma.

Daun, Å. (1979). Social and economic problems of Swedish housing environments. *Man-Environment Systems, 9*(4 & 5), 195–199.

Diderichsen, F. (1981). Omflyttning, boende och hälsa. *Socialmedicinsk Tidskrifts Skriftserie* (No. 45).

Eberhardt, J., Akselsson, R., Carlsson, L-E., & Redinge, C. (1980). *Trafikbullers inverkan på sömnen hos unga och äldre män.* Lund, Sweden: Lunds Universitet, Institutionen för Hygien.

Edberg, G. (Ed.). (1971). *Gruppen för miljö-psykologi. Symposium 1971.* Stockholm: Kungliga Tekniska Högskolan, Formlära.

Edberg, G. (1975). *Metoder för rumsanalys.* Stockholm: Kungliga Tekniska Högskolan, Formlära.

Edberg, G. (1977). *Systematisering av texturer. Texturers egenskaper* (Rep. No. 90). Stockholm: Statens Råd för Byggnadsforskning.

Edberg, G., & Ericson, M. (Eds.). (1975). *Gruppen för arkitektur och miljöpsykologi. Symposium 1974.* Stockholm: Kungliga Tekniska Högskolan, Formlära.

Eide, R. (1983). *Psychosocial factors and indices of health risks.* Bergen, Norway: University of Bergen, Institute of Somatic Psychology.

Eisler, H., & Edberg, G. (1982). The visual perception of texture. A psychological investigation of an architectural problem. In B. Wegener (Ed.), *Social attitudes and psychophysical measurement* (pp. 237–281). Hillsdale, NJ: Erlbaum.

Ekvall, G. (1979). *Tillfredsställelse med ny arbetsmiljö* (Rep. No. 133). Stockholm: Personal Administrativa Rådet.

Elofsson, S-A., Gamberale, F., Hindmarsh T., Iregren, A., Isaksson, A., Johnsson, I., Knave, B., Lydahl, E., Mindus, P., Persson, H.E., Philipson, B., Steby, M., Struwe, G., Söderman, E., Wennberg, A., Widén, L. (1980). Exposure to organic solvents. *Scandinavian Journal of Work Environment and Health, 6,* 239–273.

Engel, U., Nygaard, B., Schiötz, I., & Christgau, O. (1978). *Trafiksikkerhed og beplantning* (Notat. No. 1). Lyngby, Denmark: Rådet for Trafiksikkerhedsforskning.

Engfors, C., & Fog, H. (1978). *Motilitetsstudier. Upplevelseskillnader vid utomhusförflyttningar* (Rep. No. 90). Stockholm: Statens Råd för Byggnadsforskning.

Engström, S., & Pershagen, B. (1980). *Aesthetic factors and visual effects of large-scale WECS* (Rep. No. 20). Stockholm: National Swedish Board for Energy Source Development.

Erikson, C., & Küller, R. (1983). Non-visual effects of office lighting. *20th Session Amsterdam 1983* (Vol. 1, D602/1-4). Commission Internationale De L'Éclairage.

Ericksson, O. (1975). Man and Environment in the field of building research in Sweden. *Man-Environment Systems, 5*(3), 131–133.

Fagerberg, S., Kärnekull, K., Landell, N.E., & Liljeström, R. (1980). *Vi bor för att leva* (Rep. No. T11). Stockholm: Statens Råd för Byggnadsforskning.

Fanger, P.O. (1970). *Thermal comfort*. Copenhagen, Denmark: Danish Technical Press.

Feste, J., & Oterholm, A.I. (1973). *Landskapskaraktär*. As, Norway: Norges Landoukshögskole, Institutt for Landskapsarkitektur.

Flodström, E., Larsson, M., & Rehnström, L. (1970). *Barns trafikuppfattning som funktion av informationsmängd*. Uppsala, Sweden: Uppsala Universitet.

Frandsen, S., & Voltelen, M. (1978). *PH's eksempel*. Copenhagen, Denmark: Kunstakademiets Arkitektskole.

Frankenhaeuser, M. (1979). Psychoneuroendocrine approaches to the study of emotion as related to stress and coping. In H.E. Howe & R.A. Dienstbier (Eds.), *Nebraska Symposium on Motivation 1978* (pp. 123–161). Lincoln: University of Nebraska Press.

Frankenhaeuser, M. (1981). Coping with stress at work. *International Journal of Health Services, 11*(4), 491–510.

Frankenhaeuser, M., & Lundberg, U. (1977). The influence of cognitive set on performance and arousal under different noise loads. *Motivation and Emotion, 1*(2), 139–149.

Gabrielsson, A. (1979). Dimension analyses of perceived sound quality of sound-reproducing systems. *Scandinavian Journal of Psychology, 20*, 159–169.

Gabrielsson, A. (1981). *Problems and methods in judgement of perceived sound quality* (Rep. No. 103). Stockholm: Karolinska Institute, Department of Technical Audiology.

Gabrielsson, A., & Sjögren, H. (1979). Perceived sound quality of hearing aids. *Scandinavian Audiology, 8*, 159–169.

Gamberale, F., Knave, B., Bergström, S., Birke, E., Iregren, A., Kolmodin-Hedman, B., & Wennberg, A. (1978). Exposition för elektriska fält. *Arbete och Hälsa* (No. 10). Stockholm: Arbetarskyddsverket.

Gardell, B. (1976). *Arbetsinnehåll och livskvalitet*. Stockholm: Prisma.

Gardell, B. (1980). Arbetsmiljön i socialpsykologisk belysning. In M. Küller (Ed.). Humanekologi på social och biologisk grund. *Miljöpsykologiska monografier*, (No. 1). Lund, Sweden: Lunds Tekniska Högskola. Sektionen för Arkitektur.

Gaunt, L. (1977). *158 småbarns bostadsanvändning* (Meddelande 1). Gävle, Sweden: Statens Institut för Byggnadsforskning.

Gaunt, L. (Ed.). (1979a). *Som man bygger får man barn* (Notation 16). Gävle, Sweden: Statens Institut för Byggnadsforskning.

Gaunt, L. (1979b). *205 skolbarns bostadsanvändning* (Notation 7). Gävle, Sweden: Statens Institut för Byggnadsforskning.

Gehl, I. (1971). *Bo- miljö* (Rep. No. 71). Copenhagen, Denmark: Statens Byggeforskningsinstitut, Teknisk Forlag.

Gehl, J. (1971). *Livet mellem husene*. Copenhagen, Denmark: Arkitektens Forlag.

Gehl, J. (1980). The residential street environment. *Built Environment, 6*(1), 51–61.

Goude, G. (1967). En experimentell prövning av en metod för mätning av upplevelser i uterum. In *Upplevelse av uterum*. (Rep. No. 1). Göteborg, Sweden: Chalmers Tekniska Högskola, Formlära.

Groth, N.B., Hansen, K.E., Christiansen, U., & Jörgensen, H. (1975). *Research on quality of life in urban settlements in Denmark*. Hoersholm, Denmark: Danish Building Research Institute.

Gump, P.V., & Marek, J. (1970). Behavior settings, synomorphy, and environmental design. *Proceedings of the Interprofessional Council on Environmental Design, Maryland 1970*. New York: American Society of Civil Engineers.

Gustafson, M., & Månsson, K. (1980). *Byggnaders tillgänglighet för synskadade* (Rep. No. 93). Stockholm: Statens Råd för Byggnadsforskning.

Gårder, P., Hydén, C., & Linderholm, L. (1979). *Olika faktorers inverkan på rödgåendet i signalreglerade korsningar* (Bulletin No. 29). Lund, Sweden: Lunds Tekniska Högskola, Trafikteknik.

Gärling, T. (1969). Studies in visual perception of architectural spaces and rooms. *Scandinavian Journal of Psychology, 10*, 250–256.

Gärling, T. (1970). *Upplevelsen av en arbetsmiljös arkitekturala utformning. En undersökning med semantiska skalor*. Stockholm: Stockholms Universitet, Psykologiska Institutionen.

Gärling, T. (1976). A multidimensional scaling and semantic differential technique study of the perception of environmental settings. *Scandinavian Journal of Psychology, 17*, 323–332.

Gärling, T. (1982). Swedish Environmental Psychology. *Journal of Environmental Psychology, 2*(3), 233–251.

Gärling, T., Böök, A., & Lindberg, E. (1982). Adult's memory representations of the spatial properties of their everyday physical environment. In R. Cohen (Ed.), *The development of spatial cognition*. Hillsdale, NJ: Erlbaum.

Gärling, T., Böök, A., & Lindberg, E. (1984). Cognitive mapping of large-scale environments. The interrelationship of action plans, acquisition, and orientation. *Environment and Behavior, 16*(1), 3–34.

Gärling, T., Lindberg, E., & Mäntylä, T. (1983). Orientation in buildings. Effects of familiarity, visual access, and orientation aids. *Journal of Applied Psychology, 68*(1), 177–186.

Gärling, T., & Svensson, A. (1983). *Parental concern about children's traffic safety in residential areas. A conceptual analysis.* Umeå, Sweden: University of Umeå, Department of Psychology.

Hansen, T. (1982). Sövnforskning i den mörke årstid nord for polarsirkelen. In M. Küller (Ed.). Icke-visuella effekter av optisk stråjning. *Miljöpsykologiska Monografier* (No. 2). Lund, Sweden: Lunds Tekniska Högskola, Sektionen för Arkitektur.

Hedborg, J. (Ed.). (1984). *Arkitektur-och miljöpsykologiskt symposium 1982.* Göteborg, Sweden: Chalmers Tekniska Högskola, Formlära.

Hedman, L., & Briem, V. (1984). Short term changes in eye-strain of video users as a function of age. *Human Factors, 26*(3), 357–370.

Helander, J. (1972). *Gerontologi.* Stockholm: Almqvist & Wiksell.

Hellner, B., Johansson, A., & Wallroth, K. (1983). *Svensk miljöforskning. Projekt och rapportkatalog.* Stockholm: Statens Naturvårdsverk.

Hellquist, T. & Thafvelin, H. (Eds.) (1985). *Göra, veta, tala arkitektur. Gruppen för arkitekturens estetik och psykologi. Symposium 1984.* Lund, Sweden: Lunds Tekniska Högskola, Formlära.

Henriksson, J., & Lindqvist, S. (1977). *Lägenheter på verkstadsgolvet* (Rep. No. T14). Stockholm: Statens Råd för Byggnadsforskning.

Hesselgren, S. (1952). *Hesselgrens färgatlas.* Stockholm: Torsten Palmer.

Hesselgren, S. (1954a). *Arkitekturens uttrycksmedel.* Uppsala, Sweden: Almqvist & Wiksell.

Hesselgren, S. (1954b). *Subjective Color Standardization.* Stockholm: Almqvist & Wiksell.

Hesselgren, S. (1967). *Forskningsrapport beträffande arkitektural perception,* Sigtuna, Sweden.

Hesselgren, S. (1979). Emotional loading of environmental perception. A contribution to architectural psychology. In D. Soen (Ed.), *New trends in urban planning.* New York: Pergamon.

Hesselgren, S. (1985). *Om arkitektur. En arkitekturteori baserad på psykologisk forskning.* Lund, Sweden: Studentlitteratur.

Hirvonen, T., & Katajisto, K. (1976). *Kehitysvammaisten asumisopetus.* Unpublished licentiate thesis. Tampere, Finland: University of Tampere.

Holm, L. (1955). *Familj och bostad.* Stockholm: Hemmens Forskningsinstitut.

Holm, L, Pleijel, G., & Ronge, H. (1964). *Bostad och sol* (Rep. No. 100). Stockholm: Statens Råd för Byggnadsforskning.

Holmberg, L., Küller, R., & Tidblom, I. (1966). The perception of volume content of rectangular rooms as a function of the ratio between depth and width. *Psychological Research Bulletin, 6*(1).

Horelli, L. (1981). *Asuinympäristön ympäristöpsykologisesta arvioinnista.* Helsinki, Finland: Helsinki University, Department of Psychology.

Horelli, L. (1982). *Ympäristöpsyhologia.* Espoo, Finland: Weilin & Göös.

Hovden, J., Paasche, T., Röe, B., & Sten, T. (1977). *Det fysiske miljö og mennesket. Seminar ved NTH 1976.* Trondheim, Norway: Norges Tekniske Högskole.

Hultman, S.G. (1976). *Miljöupplevelse, landskap, skogsbruk. En kommenterad bibliografi.* Stockholm: Akogshögskolan, Avdelningen för Landskapsvård.

Hultman, S.G. (1981). Jägmästarns yrkesroll— På gott och ont. *Sveriges Skogsvårdsförbunds Tidskrift (No. 6).*

Hurtig, E., Paulsson, J., & Schulz, S. (1981). *En vill bo där en é känd. Varsam ombyggnad efter gamla människors behov* (Rep. No. T33). Stockholm: Staten Råd för Byggnadsforskning.

Hydén, C. (1977). *A traffic-conflicts technique for determining risk.* (Bulletin No. 15B). Lund, Sweden: Lund Institute of Technology, Department of Traffic Planning and Engineering.

Hård, A. (1975). NCS. A descriptive colour order and scaling system with application for environmental design. *Man-Environment Systems, 5*(3), 161–167.

Hård, A., Sivik, L., & Svedmyr, Å. (1983). *Belysning och färgseende II* (Färgrapport No. 23). Stockholm: Skandinaviska Färginstitutet.

Hägerstrand, T. (1975). Survival and arena. On the life-history of individuals in relation to their geographical environment. *Monadnock, 49,* 9–27.

Häkkinen, S. (1980). Industrial psychology at the Helsinki University of Technology. *Acta Psychologica Fennica, 7,* 83–88.

Höweler, M. (1973). *En studie av barn från låghus- och höghusområden* (Rep. No. 38). Lund, Sweden: Lunds Universitet, Pedagogiska Institutionen.

Ilstad, S. (1978). Why families move. A social psychological study of residential mobility in the city of Bodö, northern Norway. In W.E. Rogers & W.H. Ittelson (Eds.), *New directions in environmental research. Proceedings of the 9th annual conference of the Environmental Design Research Association,* (pp. 162–181), Tucson, AZ.

Iversen, L. (1981). *Börns udeförden i leg og trafik.* (Notation 6). Lyngby, Denmark: Rådet for Trafiksikkerhedsforskning.

Janssens, J. (1984). *Looking at buildings. Individual variations in the perception of building exteriors.* Lund, Sweden: Lund Institute of Technology, School of Architecture.

Janssens, J., & Küller, R. (1986). Utilizing an environmental simulation laboratory in Sweden.' In R.C. Smardon,

J.F. Palmer, & J.P. Felleman (Eds.), *Foundations for visual project analysis*. New York: Wiley.

Jansson, G. (1981). *Förflyttninghjälpmedel för synskadade*. Uppsala, Sweden: Uppsala Universitet, Psykologiska Institutionen.

Jansson, G. (1982). Tactile guidance of movement. Paper presented at the first world congress of the International Brain Research Organization, Lausanne, France.

Jarlöv, L. (1982). *Boende och skaparglädje*. Göteborg, Sweden: Chalmers Tekniska Högskola, Sektionen för Arkitektur.

Johannesson, M. (1982). *List of publications from 1971*. Lund, Sweden: Swedish University of Agricultural Sciences, Department of Farm Buildings.

Johansson, C.R. (1975). *Mental and perceptual performance in heat* (Document No. 4). Stockholm: National Swedish Institute for Building Research.

Johansson, C.R. (1976). Tobacco smoke in room air. An experimental investigation of odour perception and irritating effects. *Building Services Engineer, 43*, 254–262.

Johansson, C.R. (1982). Cytologassistenters arbetsmiljö. *Laboratoriet, 28*(2), 4–12.

Johansson, C.R. (1983). Effects of low intensity, continuous and intermittent noise on mental performance and writing pressure of children with different intelligence and personality characteristics. *Ergonomics, 26*(3), 275–288.

Johansson, G., & Aronsson, G. (1979). *Stressreaktioner vid arbete vid bildskärmsterminal* (Rep. No. 27). Stockholm: Stockholms Universitet, Psykologiska Institutionen.

Johansson, G., Aronsson, G., & Lindström, B.O. (1978). Social psychological and neuroendocrine stress reactions in highly mechanized work. *Ergonomics, 21*, 583–599.

Johansson, G., von Hofsten, C., & Jansson, G. (1980). Event perception. *Annual Review of Psychology, 31*, 27–63.

Johansson, T. (1952). *Färg. Den allmänna färglärans grunder*. Stockholm: Natur och Kultur.

Juurmaa, J., & Suonio, K. (1975). The role of audition and motion in the spatial orientation of the blind and the sighted. *Scandinavian Journal of Psychology, 16*, 209–216.

Järnegren, A., Liedholm, M., & Sandin, M. (1981). *Den byggda miljöns symbolvärden. Attityder till bevarande av industrialismens boendeformer* (Rep. No. 22). Stockholm: Statens Råd för Byggnadsforskning.

Jörgensen, J. (1976). *Perceptionsanalyse, eksperimenter i landskapsevaluering*. Aarhus, Denmark: Geografisk Institut.

Karasek, R. (1976). *The impact of the work environment on life outside the job*. Unpublished doctoral dissertation, Massachusetts Institute of Technology, Cambridge, MA.

Kardell, L., & Johansson, M-L. (1982). *Gislavedsborna och torvmarksdikning. En attitydstudie* (Rep. No. 26), Uppsala, Sweden: Sveriges Lantbruksuniversitet, Avdelningen för Landskapsvård.

Kirjonen, J. (1980). Six decades of occupational psychology. *Acta Psychologica Fennica, 7*, 22–35.

Knave, B., Anshelm Olsson, B., Elofsson, S., Gamberale, F., Isaksson, A., Mindus, P., Persson, H.E., Struwe, G., Wennberg, A., & Westerholm, P. (1978). Longterm exposure to jet fuel II. *Scandinavian Journal of Work Environment and Health, 4*, 19–45.

Knave, B., Ottosson, A., Werner, M., Bergqvist-Poppen, M., & Paasikivi, J. (1974). Belysningen i kontorslandskap. Risk för kontrastbländning vid höga belysningsstyrkor. *Nordisk Hygienisk Tidskrift, 55*, 116–128.

Knox, S.S. (1982a). *Biological effects of light air ions and their relation to human stress* (Rep. No. 1). Stockholm: National Institute of Environmental Medicine.

Knox, S.S. (1982b). *Light air ions and human psychophysiology*. (Rep. No. 7). Stockholm: National Institute of Environmental Medicine.

Koch, N.E. (1978). *Skovenes friluftsfunktion i Danmark. Del 1: Befolkningens anvendelse af landets skove*. Klampenborg, Denmark: Statens Forstlige Forsögsväsen.

Koch, N.E. (1980). *Skovens friluftsfunktion i Danmark. Del 2: Anvendelsen af skovene regionalt betragtet*. Klampenborg, Denmark: Statens Forstlige Forsögsväsen.

Kolbenstvedt, M. (1975). Töyenbarn forteller om sin bydel. *Barn og Bomiljö*. (No. 11). Oslo, Norway: Norsk Institutt for By- och Regionforskning.

Korosec-Serfaty, P. (1982). The main square. Functions and daily uses of Stortorget, Malmö. *ARIS. Nova Series* (No. 1). Lund, Sweden: Lund University Art Institute, Department of Contemporary Art and Environmental Studies.

Kortteinen, M. (1981). *Asumalähiö ja elämäntapojen muutos*. Helsinki, Finland: Helsinki University, Institution of Sociology.

Krohn, B., & Niinivaara, R. (1985). *Registrering av nordiska projekt inom handikappområdet*. Bromma, Sweden: Nordiska Nämnden för Handikappfrågor.

Kromann, O. (1976). *Effekten av färdselundervisning* (Notation 140). Lyngby, Denmark: Rådet for Trafiksikkerhedsforskning.

Kukkonen, H. (1983). *Design language for the selfplanning system*. Otaniemi, Finland: Helsinki University of Technology.

Kukkonen, H., Horelli, L., & Kemppinen, J. (1981). The self-planning system: A method for enabling residents to create their own housing environments. In T. O'Riordan & R.K. Turner (Eds.), *Progress in resource management and environmental planning* (Vol. 3). New York: Wiley.

Küller, M. (Ed.). (1980). Humanekologi på social och biologisk grund. *Miljöpsykologiska Monografier* (No. 1). Lund, Sweden: Lunds Tekniska Högskola, Sektionen för Arkitektur.

Küller, M. (Ed.). (1982). Icke-visuella effekter av optisk strålning. *Miljöpsykologiska Monografier* (No. 2). Lund, Sweden: Lunds Tekniska Högskola, Sektionen för Arkitektur.

Küller, R. (Ed.). (1967). *Rapport från konferensen 1967. Forskning inom samhällsplanering och miljögestaltning.* Lund, Sweden: Lunds Tekniska Högskola, Formlära.

Küller, R. (Ed.). (1969). *Anteckningar från symposium 1969.* Lund, Sweden: Lunds Tekniska Högskola, Formlära.

Küller, R. (1971). *Rumsperception.* Lund, Sweden: Lunds Tekniska Högskola, Formlära.

Küller, R. (1972). *A semantic model for describing perceived environment* (Document No. 12). Stockholm: National Swedish Institute for Building Research.

Küller, R. (Ed). (1973). *Architectural Psychology. Proceedings of the Lund Conference 1973.* Stroudsburg, PA: Dowden, Hutchinson & Ross.

Küller, R. (1975a). *Semantisk miljöbeskrivning.* Stockholm: Psykologiförlaget.

Küller, R. (Ed.). (1975b). Swedish Issue. *Man-Environment Systems, 5*(3), 129–200.

Küller, R. (1976). The use of space. Some physiological and philosophical aspects. In P. Korosec-Serfaty (Ed.), *Appropriation of space. Proceedings of the Strasbourg Conference 1976* (pp. 154–163). Louvain-la-Neuve, Belgium: CIACO.

Küller, R. (1977). Psycho-Physiological conditions in theatre construction. In J.F. Arnott, J. Chariau, H. Huesmann, T. Lawrenson, & T. Rainer, (Eds.), *Theatre Space.* München: Prestel.

Küller, R. (Ed.). (1979a). Scandinavian Issue. *Man-Environment Systems, 9*(4 & 5), 165–256.

Küller, R. (1979b). A semantic test for use in crosscultural studies. *Man-Environment Systems, 9*(4 & 5), 253–256.

Küller, R. (1979c). Social crowding and the complexity of the built environment. A theoretical and experimental framework. In M.R. Gürkaynak & W.A. LeCompte (Eds.), *Human consequences of crowding* (pp. 139–146). New York: Plenum.

Küller, R. (1980a). Architecture and emotions. In B. Mikellides (Ed.), *Architecture for People.* London: Studio Vista.

Küller, R. (1980b). Differing demands on interior space in naval environments. In J.G. Simon (Ed.), *Conflicting experiences of space. Proceedings of the 4th International Architectural Psychology Conference July 1979* (Vol. 2, pp. 645–654). Louvain-la-Neuve, Belgium: Catholic University of Louvain.

Küller, R. (1981). *Non-visual effects of light and colour. Annotated bibliography* (Document No. 15). Stockholm: Swedish Council for Building Research.

Küller, R. (1983). Ljus och färg påverkar hur vi mår. *Forskning och Framsteg, 1*, 35–39.

Küller, R. (1984). Environment and retirement. In E. Pol, J.

Muntanola, & M. Morales (Eds.), *Man-environment. Qualitative aspects. Proceedings of the 7th conference of the International Association for the Study of People and their Physical Surroundings* (pp. 254–263). Barcelona, Spain: Edicions Universitat de Barcelona.

Küller, R., & Mattsson, R. (1986). The dining room at a geriatric hospital. In M. Krampen (Ed.), *Environment and Human Action. Proceedings of the Eighth International Conference of the IAPS* (International Association for the Study of People and their Physical Surroundings), July 1984. West Berlin: Hoschschule der Künste.

Kwok, K. (1979). Semantic evaluation of perceived environment. A cross-cultural replication. *Man-Environment Systems, 9*(4 & 5), 243–249.

Langaa Jensen, P., & Möller, N. (1984). *Technological changes and the quality of working life.* Lyngby, Denmark: Danmarks Tekniske Höjskole. Institut for Arbejdsmiljö.

Larsson, L.E., & Rumar, K. (1974). *A versatile recorder of visual point of regard* (Rep. No. 162). Uppsala, Sweden: University of Uppsala, Department of Psychology.

Larsson, R-Å. (1978). *Bättre arbetsmiljö i samverkan.* Stockholm: Personal Administrativa Rådet.

Lennerlöf, L. (1981). *Arbetsmiljön ur psykologisk och sociologisk synvindel. En introduktion till beteendevetenskaplig arbetsmiljöforskning.* Stockholm: Liber.

Levi, L. (Ed.). (1972). Stress and distress in response to psychosocial stimuli. *Acta Medica Scandinavica,* (Suppl. 528) *191.*

Levi, L. (1979). Psychosocial factors in preventive medicine. In *Healthy people.* Washington DC: U.S. Department of Health, Education and Welfare.

Levi, L., Frankenhaeuser, M., & Gardell, B. (1981). Work stress related to social structures and processes. In G.R. Elliott & C. Eisdorfer (Eds.), *Research on stress and human health.* New York: Springer.

Leymann, H. (1981). Occupational research in Sweden. In E.N. Corlett & J. Richardson (Eds.), *Stress, work design, and productivity.* New York: Wiley.

Lian, R.V., Thaule, J., & Selnaes, G. (1972). *Barnas miljö i byen.* Oslo, Norway: Norges Byggforskningsinstitutt.

Lidmar-Reinius, K. (Ed.). (1984). *The elderly and their environment. Research in Sweden.* (Document No. 27). Stockholm: Swedish Council for Building Research.

Lie, I. (1981). Funksjonshemninger, miljö, tekniske hjelpemidler. *Tidskrift for Norsk Psykologforening, 18,* 173–177.

Liljedahl, S., & Löfberg, H.A. (1968). *Dagsljusmätningar i modell* (Byggforskningen Informerar No. 36). Stockholm: Statens Institut för Byggforskning.

Liljefors, A. (1973). Light planning with minimum energy consumption. The quality of light. In R. Küller (Ed.), *Architectural Psychology. Proceeding of the Lund Conference 1973,* (pp. 68–75). Stroudsburg, PA: Dowden, Hutchinson & Ross.

Lind, T., Oraug, J., Skjervold Rosenfeld, I., & Östensen, E. (1974). *Friluftsliv i Oslomarka.* Oslo, Norway: Norsk Institutt for By- og Regionforskning.

Lindberg, G. (Ed.). (1971). *Urbana processer. Studier i social ekologi.* Lund, Sweden: Gleerups.

Lindholm, E., & Lindholm, N. (1982). *Klimatkomfort i förarhytter* (Rep. No. 4). Stockholm: Statens Miljömedicinska Laboratorium.

Lindström, B., & Åhlund, O. (1982a). *Åldrande och boende. Att bo i det ordinära bostadsbeståndet* (Rep. No. 3). Lund, Sweden: Lunds Universitet, Byggnadsfunktionslära.

Lindström, B., & Åhlund, O. (1982b). *Åldrande och boende. Utvärderingsstudier av särskilda boendeformer för pensionärer. Del 1: Metodutveckling* (Rep. No. 4). Lund, Sweden: Lunds Universitet, Byggnadsfunktionslära.

Liszka, L., Danielsson, Å., Söderberg, L., & Lindmark, A. (1978). *En undersökning av långtidseffekter av ventilationsbuller på människor.* Stockholm: Arbetarskyddsstyrelsen.

Lundberg, U. (1976). Urban commuting. Crowdedness and catecholamine excretion. *Journal of Human Stress, 2,* 26–32.

Lundqvist, P. (1982). *Olyckstillbud i växthusodlingen* (Rep. No. 22). Lund, Sweden: Sveriges Lantbruksuniversitet, Institutionen för Lantbrukets Byggnadsteknik.

Löfberg, H.A. (1969). *Belysning i skolsalar* (Rep. No. 29). Stockholm: Statens Institut för Byggnadsforskning.

Löfberg, H.A., Löfstedt, B., Nilsson, I., & Wyon, D.P. (1973). The effect of heat and light on the mental performance of school children. Introduction to a climate chamber experiment. In R. Küller (Ed.). *Architectural Psychology. Proceedings of the Lund Conference 1973.* (pp. 64–67). Stroudsburg, PA: Dowden, Hutchinson & Ross.

Löfstedt, B. (1966). *Human heat tolerance.* Unpublished doctoral dissertation, Lund, Sweden: University of Lund.

Magnusson, D. (1974). The individual in the situation. *Studia Psychologica, 16*(2), 124–131.

Magnusson, D. (1981). Situational determinants of stress. An interactional perspective. *Reports from the Department of Psychology* (Suppl. 55). Stockholm: University of Stockholm.

Magnusson, D., & Allen, V.L. (1983). An interactional paradigm for human development. In D. Magnusson & V.L. Allen (Eds.), *Human development. An interactional perspective* (pp. 3–31). New York: Academic.

Magnusson, D., & Ekehammar, B. (1978). Similar situations—Similar behaviors? *Journal of Research in Personality, 12,* 41–48.

Magnusson, D., & Stattin, H. (1981). Methods for studying stressful situations. In H.W. Krohne & L. Laux (Eds.), *Achievement, stress, and anxiety* (pp. 317–331). Washington DC: Hemisphere.

Magnusson, D., Stattin, H., & Iwawaki, S. (1982). Cross-cultural comparisons of situational anxiety reactions. In C.D. Spielberger & R. Diaz-Guerrero (Eds.), *Cross-cultural anxiety* (Vol. 2, pp. 177–190). Washington DC: Hemisphere.

Malmberg, B. (1980). *Pensioneringsprocessen. En kunskapsöversikt* (Rep. No. 42). Jönköping, Sweden: Institutet för Gerontologi.

Malmberg, T. (1980). *Human territoriality.* Paris: Mouton.

Marek, J. (1976). *Metoder og strategi i boligforskningen.* Bergen, Norway: Universitetet i Bergen, Psykologisk Institutt.

Marek, J. (1978). System-orientierte Strategie in der Unfallforschung. In H. Kuderna (Ed.), *12. Tagung der Österreichischen Gesellschaft für Unfallchirurgie 1976. Hefte zur Unfallheilkunde* (Vol. 130). Berlin: Springer.

Marek, J. (1981). *Safety, experience of risk, and type of work.* Bergen, Norway: University of Bergen, Department of Social Psychology.

Marek, J., Bennett, R., & Kjöde, A. (1983). *Outdoor leisure pursuits. Opportunities and constraints.* Paper presented at the Congress of the International Geographical Union, Edinburgh, Scotland.

Marek, J., & Hovden, J. (1983). *Trivsel i boligblokk. Beboernes vurdering af et nytt boligfelt.* Oslo, Norway: Universitetsforlaget.

Marek, J., Jystad, R., Dörum, O-E., & Brantenberg, T. (1971). *Boligsituasjon og boligönsker. Trondheim kommunes boligundersökelse 1969–70* (Rep. No. 2). Trondheim, Norway: Norges Tekniske Högskole, Institutt for Psykologi og Socialforskning.

Marek, J., & Kvittingen, K.T. (1976). *Friluftsliv. Persepsjon og atferd.* Bergen, Norway: Universitetet i Bergen, Psykologisk Institutt.

Marek, J., & Sten, T. (1977). *Traffic environment and the driver.* Springfield, IL: Thomas.

Marek, J., Tangenes, B., & Hellesöy, O.H. (1981). *Experience of risk on a North Sea platform.* Bergen, Norway: Mobil Exploration Norway Inc.

Mashour, M. (1974). *Human factors in signalling systems. Specific application to railway signalling.* Stockholm: Almqvist & Wiksell; New York: Wiley.

Morville, J. (1969). *Borns brug af friarealer.* No. 10. Copenhagen, Denmark: SBI-byplanleagning.

Mundebo, I. (1982). *Byggnadsforskningen. En översyn och utvärdering.* Stockholm: Bostadsdepartementet.

Mänsklig arbetsmiljö. Angelägen beteendevetenskaplig arbetsmiljöforskning. (1984). (Rep. No. 4). Stockholm: Arbetarskyddsfonden.

Nejst Jensen, C., Kirstein, T., Ryding, E., & Vedel-Petersen, F. 1971. *Tät lav—en boligform. Bo—Miljöundersögelse i 11 bebyggelser.* (Rep. No. 76). Copenhagen, Denmark: Statens Byggeforskningsinstitut.

Nilsson, L.E. (1975). An eye movement apparatus. *Man-Environment Systems, 5*(3), 170.

Norberg-Schulz, C. (1967). *Intensjoner i arkitekturen*. Oslo, Norway: Universitetsforlaget.

Norberg-Schulz, C. (1971). *Existence, space and architecture. New concepts of architecture*. London: Studio Vista.

Norberg-Schulz, C. (1980). *Genius loci. Towards a phenomenology of architecture*. London: Academy Editions.

Nordström, M. (1979). *Gårdsförändringar. Ett sätt att förbättra boendemiljön?* (Meddelande 2). Gävle, Sweden: Statens Institut för Byggnadsforskning.

Nordström, M. (1982). *Sex differences in the experiences of the physical environment*. Paper presented at the International Interdisciplinary Congress on Women, Haifa, Israel.

Nummenmaa, T. (1980). Developmental, clinical, and environmental studies of the University of Tampere. *Acta Psychologica Fennica, 7*, 89–96.

Nummenmaa, T., Ruuhilehto, K., & Syvänen, M. (1975). Traffic education programme for preschool aged children and children starting school. *Reports from Liikenneturva*, No. 17.

Nummenmaa, T., & Syvänen, M. (1974). Teaching road safety to children in the age range 5–7 years. *Paedagogica Europaea, 9*, 151–161.

Nummenmaa, T., Syvänen, M., & Weckroth, J. (1970). *Lapsen leikki-ja liikkumatila kaupunkiympäristössä* (Rep. No. 50). Tampere, Finland: University of Tampere, Department of Psychology.

Nygaard, B. (1977). *Anvendelse af öjenbevögelses-registreringer i trafikken* (Notation 1). Lyngby, Denmark: Rådet for Trafiksikkerhedsforskning.

Nygaard, B., Buch, M., Christgau, O., Friis, A., Möller, J., & Schelling, A. (1976). *Oplevet farlighet i uregulerede villavejs kryds* (Notation 137). Lyngby, Denmark: Rådet for Trafiksikkerhedsforskning.

Nygaard, B., & Schiötz, I. (1975). *Monotoni på motorveje* (Notation 135). Lyngby, Denmark: Rådet for Trafiksikkerhedsforskning.

Odén, B., Svanborg, A., & Tornstam, L. (Eds.). (1983). *Äldre i samhället förr, nu och i framtiden. Del 2: Probleminventering*. Stockholm: Liber.

Ojanen, M. (1975). *Mielisairaalapotilaan ura. Sairaalaan tulon syyt, hoitoaikaan vaikuttavat tekijät ja yhteiskuntaan paluu* (Rep. No. 95). Tampere, Finland: University of Tampere, Department of Psychology.

Olesen, S., Fanger, P.O., Jensen, P.B., & Nielsen, O.J. (1973). Comfort limits for man exposed to asymmetric thermal radiation. In *Thermal comfort and moderate heat stress. Proceedings of the CIB Commission W45* (pp. 133–148). Her Majesty's Stationery Office, Great Britain: Department of the Environment, Building Research Establishment.

Olivegren, J. (1975). *Brukarplanering*. Göteborg, Sweden: Flack, Fågelvik, Nordström & Smas-gruppen.

Olsson-Jonsson, A. (1984). *Utbyte av fönster. Upplevelse av fasadförändringar* (Rep. No. 5). Lund, Sweden: Lunds Tekniska Högskola, Byggnadskonstruktionslära.

Open space in housing areas. Documentation of a colloquium (Rep. No. T15). (1972). Stockholm: National Swedish Institute for Building Research.

Paasi, J. (1978). *Menetelmä arkitehtonisen tilan havainnoimiseksi laboratorioolusuhteissa*. (Rep. No. A40). Otaniemi, Finland: Teknillinen korkeakoulu, Arkkitehtiosasto, Rakennussuunnittelun laitos.

Palmér, R. (1982). A longitudinal study of the social adjustment of mentally retarded adults in Sweden. *Uppsala Reports on Education*. Uppsala, Sweden: University of Uppsala, Department of Education.

Paulsson, J. (Ed.). (1981). *The built environment and the handicapped. Proceedings from a research colloquium in Gothenburg*. Stockholm: Swedish Council for Building Research.

Persson, B. (Ed.) (1982). *Stadens uterum*. Malmö, Sweden: Sveriges Trädgårds Anläggnings Förbund.

Pleijel, G. (1954). *The computation of natural radiation in architecture and town planning* (Meddelande No. 25). Stockholm: Statens Institut för Byggnadsforskning.

Ranhagen, U. (1980). *Förnyelse av industriell arbetmiljö* (Rep. No. T2). Stockholm: Statens Råd för Byggnadsforskning.

Rasmussen, S.E. (1957). *Om at opleve arkitektur*. Copenhagen, Denmark: Gads.

Rasmussen, S.E. (1962). *Experiencing architecture*. Cambridge, MA: MIT Press.

Raundalen, M. (1978). Barns trivsel i skole- og hjemmemiljö. In G.J. Sorte (Ed.). *Gruppen för arkitektur- och miljöpsykologi. Nordiskt Symposium 1978*. Lund, Sweden: Lunds Tekniska Högskola, Formlära.

Rissler, A. (1977). Stress reactions at work and after working during a period of quantitative overload. *Ergonomics, 20*, 13–16.

Rissler, A., & Elgerot, A. (1980). *Omställning till arbete i kontorslandskap* (Rep. No. 33). Stockholm: Stockholms Universitet, Psykologiska Institutionen.

Rivano-Fischer, M. (1984). Interactional space. Invasion as a function of the type of social interaction. *Psychological Research Bulletin, 26*(4).

Ronge, H. (1948). Ultraviolet irradiation with artificial illumination. A technical, physiological and hygienic study. *Acta Physiologica Scandinavica, 15*, (Suppl. 49).

Rouhiainen, S., & Nummenmaa, T. (1971). *Lasten Leikki-ja liikkumatila kaupunkiympäristössä. Havaintoja Forssan kaupungista*. (Rep. No. 82). Tampere, Finland: University of Tampere, Department of Psychology.

Rumar, K. (1975). Causes and prevention of night driving accidents. *Man-Environment Systems, 5*(3), 171–174.

Rumar, K. (1980). The visual environment in road traffic. *Proceedings 19th Session CIE, Kyoto 1979*. (Publication No. 50). Paris: Bureau Central de la Commission International De L'Éclairage.

Rumar, K. (1982). The human factor in road safety. *Australian Road Research Board Proceedings, 11*(1), 63–80.

Råberg, P.G. (1983). *Vår bild av den absoluta verkligheten* (Rapport No. 2). Umeå, Sweden: Umeå Universitet, Konstvetenskap.

Röed Helgesen, A. (1979). *Bomiljöforskning. Norske forskningsprojekter 1970–1978.* Oslo, Norway: Norsk Institutt for By- og Regionforskning.

Samuelsson, G. (1981). *Dagens pensionärer— Sekelskiftets barn. Åldrandeprocessen i ett individ- och samhällsperspektiv.* Lund, Sweden: Studentlitteratur.

Sandels, S. (1968). *Små barn i trafiken.* Stockholm: Läromedelsförlaget.

Sandström, C.I. (1974). Proposals to phenomenological approaches in determining architectural spaces. *Scandinavian Journal of Psychology, 15,* 81–88.

Sandström, S. (1983). *Se och uppleva.* Kristianstad, Sweden: Kalejdoskop.

Sanne, C. (1983). *Living people. Long term perspective for human settlements in the Nordic countries* (Document No. 10). Stockholm: Swedish Council for Building Research.

Sanne, C., Daun, Å., Gaunt, L., Werner, K., Hjärne, L., Küller, R., & Walldén, M. (1985). *Forskare om samhälle, välfärd och boende.* Stockholm: Statens Råd för Byggnadsforskning.

Scandinavian Housing and Planning Research. Stockholm: Almqvist & Wiksell.

Scandinavian Journal of Psychology. Stockholm: Almqvist & Wiksell.

Scandinavian Journal of Work, Environment and Health. Helsinki, Finland: Finnish Institute of Occupational Health.

Schioldborg, P. (1974). *Barn, trafik og trafikopläring. En analyse af Barnas Trafikklubb.* Oslo, Norway: Universitetet i Oslo, Psykologisk Institutt.

Seipel, L., & Sohlberg, A. (1982). *Att skapa och förstärka stadsrum med vegetation.* (Rep. No. 5). Alnarp: Stad och Land.

Setälä, M.L. (1972). *Leikki-ja elintilan laajeneminen 10-12 vuoden iässä* (Rep. No. 58). Tampere, Finland: University of Tampere, Department of Psychology.

Setälä, M.L., Nummenmaa, T., Nupponen, R., Syvänen, M., & Weckroth, J. (1972). *Asuntola ja keskuslaitos aikuisten kehitysvammaisten asuinympäristöinä* (Rep. No. 64). Tampere, Finland: University of Tampere, Department of Psychology.

Shahnavaz, H., & Hedman, L. (1984). Visual accommodation changes in VDU-operators related to environmental lighting and screen quality. *Ergonomics, 27*(10), 1071–1082.

Simovici, S. (1976). *Slut vid 60?* Stockholm: Pan/Norstedts.

Simovici, S. (1981). *Grannansvar och social gemenskap inom äldreomsorgen, en försöksverksamhet.* Stockholm: Norstedt.

Sivik, L. (1969). Colour connotations and perceptive variables. *Association Internationale de la Coleur. Color 69, Vol. 2,* 1064–1072.

Sivik. L. (1974a). Color meaning and perceptual color dimensions: A study of color samples. *Göteborg Psychological Reports, 4*(1).

Sivik, L. (1974b). Color meaning and perceptual color dimensions: A study of exterior colors. *Göteborg Psychological Reports, 4*(11).

Sivik, L. (1974c). Measuring the meaning of colors: Problems of semantic bipolarity. *Göteborg Psychological Reports, 4*(13).

Sivik, L. (1974d). Measuring the meaning of colors: Reliability and stability. *Göteborg Psychological Reports, 4*(12).

Sivik, L., & Hård, A. (1978). *Farg och varierande yttre betingelser* (Färgrapport No. 17). Stockholm: Skandinaviska Färginstitutet.

Sjöberg, L. (1979). Life situations and episodes as a basis for situational influence on action. *Göteborg Psychological Reports, 9*(4).

Sjöberg, L., & Jansson, B. (1982). *Boendes uppfattningar om och reaktioner på eventuell förekomst av strålning från radongas i bostaden.* Göteborg, Sweden: Göteborgs Universitet, Psykologiska Institutionen.

Solem, P.E., Guntvedt, O.H., & Beverfelt, E. (Eds.). (1982). *Norsk Gerontologisk Institutt 25 år.* Oslo, Norway: Norsk Gerontologisk Institutt.

Sorte, G.J. (Ed.). (1978). *Gruppen för arkitektur- och miljöpsykologi. Nordiskt Symposium 1978.* Lund, Sweden: Lunds Tekniska Högskola, Formlära.

Sorte, G.J. (1982). *Visuellt urskiljbara egenskaper hos föremål i den byggda miljön* (Rep. No. 5). Stockholm: Statens Råd för Byggnadsforskning.

Statens Offentliga Utredningar. Bo på egna villkor. Om att förbättra boendet för gamla, handikappade och långvarigt sjuka. (1984). (No. 78). Bostadsdepartementet. Stockholm: Liber.

Stattin, H., & Magnusson, D. (1980). Stability of perceptions of own reactions across a variety of anxiety-provoking situations. *Perceptual and Motor Skills, 51,* 959–967.

Ström, C., & Ottosson, D. (Eds.). (1983). *Åldrande och psykisk hälsa.* Stockholm: Liber.

Ström, C., & Zotterman, Y. (Eds.). (1975). *Boendeformer för pensionärer.* Stockholm: Liber.

Ståhl, A. (1984). *Public transportation for the elderly in Sweden.* Lund, Sweden: Lund Institute of Technology, Department of Traffic Planning and Engineering.

Sundahl, A-M. (1980). Accident prevention prescriptions for the Commission Internationale du Genie Rural. *Working session of the 2nd Technical Section of the CIGR 1980,* (Vol. 1, pp. 380–388). Winterthur, Switzerland: Tänikon.

Sundström, G. (1983). Caring for the aged in a welfare society. *Studies in Social Work* (No. 1). Stockholm.

Svanborg, A., Djurfeldt, H., & Steen, B. (Eds.) (1980). *Frisk eller sjuk på äldre dar. Rapport från populationsstudien "70-åringar i Göteborg"* (H 70) (Rep. No. 4). Stockholm: Delegationen för Social Forskning.

Svensk boendeforskning. En bibliografi. (1974) (Rep. No. 43). Stockholm: Statens Råd för Byggnadsforskning.

Svensson, T. (1984). Aging and environment. Institutional aspects. *Linköping Studies in Education* (No. 21). Linköping, Sweden.

Syvänen, M. (1981). *Ympäristöpsyhologia ja toimintamallien teoria* (Rep. No. 122). Tampere, Finland: University of Tampere, Department of Psychology.

Syvänen, M., & Setälä, M.L. (1972). *Maalaislapsen elinympäristö.* (Rep. No. 67). Tampere, Finland: University of Tampere, Department of Psychology.

Sällström, P. (Ed.). (1981). *Göra och veta vid miljögestaltningen. Rapport från arkitekturpsykologiskt symposium 1980.* Stockholm: Kungliga Tekniska Högskolan, Formlära.

Takala, M., Alanen, L., Luolaja, J., & Pölkki, P. (1979). *Perheen elämänlapa, vanhempien kasvatustietoisuus ja lapsen sosiaalinen kehitys* (Rep. No. 129). Jyväskylä, Finland: University of Jyväskylä, Department of Psychology.

Tangenes, B., Marek, J., & Hellesöy, O.H. (1981). *Work and physical environment on a North Sea platform.* Bergen, Norway: Mobil Exploration Norway Inc.

Thiis-Evensen, T. (1982). *Arkitekturens uttrycksformer.* Oslo, Norway: Universitetsforlaget.

Thoresen, C.E., & Öhman, A. (in press). The type A behavior pattern. A person-environment interaction perspective. In D. Magnusson, & A. Öhman (Eds.). *Psychopathology. An interactional perspective.* New York: Academic.

Tikkanen, K.T. (1976). A study of emotional reactions to light and colour in a school environment. *Lighting Research and Technology,* 8(1), 27–30.

Tornstam, L., Svanborg, A., & Odén, B. (Eds.). (1982). *Äldre i samhället. Förr, nu och i framtiden. Del 1. Teorier och forskningsansatser.* Stockholm: Liber.

Torsson, B. (1974). *Staden som rum och gestalt.* Stockholm: Kungliga Tekniska Högskolan, Sektionen för Arkitektur.

Ulrich, R.S. (1981). Natural versus urban scenes. Some psychophysiological effects. *Environment and Behavior,* 13(5), 523–556.

Ursin, H. (1980). Personality, activation and somatic health. In S. Levine & H. Ursin. (Eds.), *Coping and health* (pp. 259–279). New York: Plenum.

Ursin, H., & Ursin, R. (1979). Physiological indicators of mental workload. In N. Moray (Ed.), *Mental workload* (pp. 349–365). New York: Plenum.

Vang, K., Gripenlöf, M., & Husberg, L. (1984). *Äldreomsorg, en vårdform eller en boendeform. En studie om miljön vid 6 danska plejehjem* (Rep. No. 36). Stockholm: Statens Råd för Byggnadsforskning.

Vanhalakka-Ruoho, M. (1981). *Perhe ja urheileva lapsi* (Rep. No. 123). Tampere, Finland: University of Tampere, Department of Psychology.

Vedel-Petersen, F., Jensen, O., & Storgaard, J.P. (1983). *Galgebakken, en bomiljöundersögelse* (Rep. No. 145). Hörsholm, Denmark: Statens Byggeforskningsinstitut.

Vikman, J.P. (1982). Perheen muutto lapsen ongelmatilanteena. *Acta Universitatis Tamperensis,* Ser. A, *143.*

von Schéele, A. (1979). Barnmiljö—Barnreservat eller god miljö för alla. Om barns avskildhet på daghem i granskap. In L. Gaunt (Ed.). *Som man bygger får man barn* (pp. 117–130). (Notation 16). Gävle, Sweden: Statens Institut för Byggnadsforskning.

Wallinder, J. (1967). Försök med perceptionspsykologiska övningar i arkitektutbildningen. In *Upplevelse av uterum* (Rep. No. 1). Göteborg, Sweden: Chalmers Tekniska Högskola, Formlära.

Wallinder, J. (Ed.). (1977). *Gruppen för arkitektur och miljöpsykologi. Symposium 1976.* Göteborg, Sweden: Chalmers Tekniska Högskola, Formlära.

Wallsten, P. (1982). *Vad tål vildmarken? En studie av rekreativ bärförmåga* (Rep. No. 10). Alnarp, Sweden: Stad och Land.

Watzke, J.R., & Küller, R. (1986). The Conflict Situations Technique: A projective method for elderly persons. *Miljöpsykologiska Monografier* (Environmental Psychology Monographs No. 4). Lund, Sweden: Lund Institute of Technology, School of Architecture.

Weitzman, E.D., De Graaf, A.S., et al. (1975). Seasonal patterns of sleep stages and secretion of cortisol and growth hormone during 24 hour periods in northern Norway. *Acta Endocrinologica 78,* 65.

Werthén, H.E. (1976). *Sjömannen och hans yrke. En socialpsykologisk undersökning av trivsel och arbetsförhållanden på svenska handelsfartyg.* Göteborg, Sweden: Göteborgs Universitet, Psykologiska Institutionen.

Westerman, A. (1976). *Estetisk värdering av byggnadsexteriörer* (Skrift 16). Stockholm: Kungliga Tekniska Högskolan, Arkitektur.

Westerman, A. (1980). *Estetisk värdering av storlek och up prepning i byggnadsexteriörer* (Rep. No. 151). Stockholm: Statens Råd för Byggnadsforskning.

Wikforss, Ö. (1981). *Brukarmedverkan. Arbetsformer och uttrycksmedel vid brukarsamråd* (Rep. No. 146, pt. 3). Stockholm: Byggnadsstyrelsen.

Wyon, D.P. (1970). Studies of children under imposed noise and heat stress. *Ergonomics,* 13(5), 598–612.

Wyon, D.P. (1974). Noise in dwellings. *Build International,* 7, 1–15.

Wyon, D.P. (1975). Human-laboratoriet i Gävle. In *Årsbok 1975.* Gävle, Sweden: Statens Institut för Byggnadsforskning.

Wyon, D.P., Asgeirsdottir, T., Kjerulf-Jensen, P., & Fanger, P.O. (1973). The effects of ambient temperature swings on comfort, performance and behavior. *Proceedings of the CNRS International Symposium, Strasbourg 1973.*

Wyon, D.P., Fanger, P.O., Olesen, B.W., & Pedersen, C.J.K. (1975). The mental performance of subjects clothed for comfort at two different air temperatures. *Ergonomics*, *18*(4), 359–374.

Wyon, D.P., Hygge, S., & Löfberg, H.A. (1982). Interpersonal differences in environmental effects upon performance and behaviour. A review. In *Proceedings of the CIB W77 CIE (T.C. 3.3) workshop, Chester 1982.*

Wyon, D.P., & Nilsson, I. (1980). Human experience of windowless environments in factories, offices, shops and colleges in Sweden. In J. Krochmann (Ed.), *Proceedings of the Symposium on Daylight, CIE* (pp. 216–225). Berlin: Technische Universität, Institut für Lichttechnik.

Wåhlin, R. (1984). *Betydelseframtagning. Mot en bebyggelsesemiotisk teori.* Stockholm: Kungliga Tekniska Högskolan, Formlära.

Åhlund, O. (1976). *Full-scale plan laboratory Lund Institute of Technology* (Document No. 10). Stockholm: Swedish Council for Building Research.

Åkerman, B. (1941). *Familjen som växte ur sitt hem.* Stockholm: Lindbergs Tryckeri.

Ås, D. (1975). Observing environmental behavior. The behavior setting. In W. Michelsson (Ed.), *Behavioral research methods in environmental design.* Stroudsburg, PA: Dowden, Hutchinson & Ross.

Ås, D. (1976). Explorations with alternative methodologies for data on time use. *Society and Leisure, 8*(3).

Ås, D., Lian, R.V., Thaule, J., & Selnaes, G. (1973). *Barnas miljö i byen. En studie av bydelen Sandaker og Nordre Åsen i Oslo.* Oslo, Norway: Norges Byggforskningsinstitutt.

Åstrand, I. (Ed.). 1978. Exposition för xylen. *Arbete och Hälsa* (No. 3). Stockholm: Arbetarskyddsverket.

Ögren, K. (1979). Fråga barnen. Om barns liv i två bostads- områden i Orebro. In L. Gaunt (Ed.). *Som man bygger får man barn* (pp. 91–100). Notation 16. Gävle Sweden: Statens Institut för Byggnadsforskning.

Chapter 36

ENVIRONMENTAL PSYCHOLOGY IN THE UNITED KINGDOM

David Canter, *Department of Psychology, University of Surrey, Guildford, United Kingdom*

Ian Donald, *Division of Applied Psychology, University of Aston in Birmingham, United Kingdom*

36.1. INTRODUCTION

The roots of environmental psychology in England, Scotland, Wales, and Ireland are many. The disciplines that have contributed have also been varied, the contributions from academic psychology having been surpassed, at times, by those from human geography and urban sociology. Practicing planners and architects have also been instrumental, not only in motivating their academic colleagues in the social and design disciplines to explore environmental ques-

tions, but also in contributing to substantive developments in theory and methods. Neither has Britain's island location on the edge of continental Europe led to insularity in the growth of research and practice. The ready access to Europe (Amsterdam and Brussels, after all, are nearer to London than Glasgow or Belfast; Paris and Frankfurt are not much further away) has led to increasing interchange between British and continental researchers. The British Commonwealth has facilitated full and continuous contact with, for example, Australia and Canada.

The shared language and open communications with the United States has also meant that British researchers have not been ignorant of North American activities.

When this complexity of influences and concerns is added to the social, political, technological, and even artistic developments that have left a direct mark on British environmental psychology, it can be appreciated that no single chapter can ever give a full account. Any selection will inevitably have its biases, giving emphasis where others would not. For our selection, we have chosen to give a brief account of the historical antecedents of present-day British environmental psychology and then after a summary of the pioneering work in the 1960s and early 1970s to concentrate on published research from the mid-1970s onward. In the published literature to which we have referred, we have striven to draw on work from as many of the contributing disciplines as possible, but our own training and base within psychology has probably weighted our overview toward our parent discipline. In the spirit of all empirical research, we invite others to articulate and test their own accounts of British environmental psychology.

The early British psychologists such as Galton (1883), McDougall (1908), Myers (1911), Burt (1940), and Bartlett (1932) established a context that was not only firmly empirical but also drew heavily on increasingly sophisticated statistical procedures. However, this orientation was never, from its earliest days, a solely academic endeavor. Thus the second way in which the context was set by these founding fathers was by establishing the firm belief that scientific psychological investigations could have direct implications for policymakers. The third way in which they established principles that can be seen in present-day environmental psychology was in their eclectic approach to theory. In particular, they embraced frameworks that included both cognitive and behavioral components and recognized the value of understanding the objectives and intentions of individuals as well as their physiology.

One final aspect of the context they created is worth mentioning. This is the relative weakness of the interest in social psychological and sociological processes. Although the need for connections with sociology and anthropology were recognized by the founders of British psychology (especially McDougall), unlike their colleagues in France and Germany, they established a tradition that was probably more at home with statisticians and physiologists.

Hearnshaw (1964) and Thomson (1968) both give detailed accounts of early British psychology in which the origins of present-day environmental psychology can be perceived. We must omit any more detailed account of the first 100 years or so and move on to the initial emergence of environmental psychology as an identifiable area.

36.1.1. The Pioneers

By the early 1960s, besides developments in psychology, those in urban sociology, behavioral geography, and the environmental design disciplines had created a context in which British environmental psychology could grow. Canter (1975b) summarized these developments and emphasized the effect of the massive postwar rebuilding program, that had led some people in the design disciplines to appreciate the need for a more systematic social science input to their activities. The interplay between academic and applied social scientists and psychologists had indicated the feasibility of such input, although the social scientists had not yet recognized that they could learn from the design professionals. Within this context, a few individuals began to pioneer the new, and as yet unnamed, field of environmental psychology.

These pioneers include Langdon (1966), Lee (1954), McKennell (1963), and Wells (1964). They all shared a style and approach to their environmental researches that reflected the historical origins outlined. The methods they preferred were field surveys that owed much to the psychometric tradition of Galton and of the Victorian social reformers. Their work was consciously focused on policy implications, whether it was guidelines for office design or the optimum size of a neighborhood. Indeed, the subjects they selected related directly to concerns of the day—the great boom in office buildings, the development of airports, and the building of new towns. Yet their studies were conducted in the academic framework of hypothesis testing and theory development. Furthermore, the theoretical tradition within which they worked was clearly cognitive, putting emphasis on the conceptions and satisfaction of building users and city dwellers rather than their mere behavior. They all searched for fairly simple and direct relationships between physical variables and human responses to them while still placing emphasis on the need to understand individual variations.

All these early studies were responses to problems defined within a policy and design framework. It was architects and planners who shaped the questions that the psychologists were answering. For instance, the first major study dealing with questions of behavior and design had no psychologists or social scientists on the research team. This was the Nuffield study of hospital ward design that, as was unique then and is still rare now, proposed architectural designs were developed on the basis of a detailed analysis of the activities carried out in existing wards (Nuffield Provincial Hospital Trust, 1955).

In phrasing their questions for psychological and social research in the late 1960s, planners, and more especially architects, were influenced by the discussions on systematic design that had grown up in part as a response to the massive postwar building program and in part out of the ideals of the modern movement and LeCorbusier's "modulor." Manning (1965), the director of the Pilkington Research Unit, had been part of a group of architectural commentators who had criticized architectural practice for being "a system with no feedback." They had argued for the need to introduce "design methods" in architectural education and practice. The culmination of the variety of perspectives on this debate was brought together by Broadbent and Ward (1969).

Central to these considerations was a specific overt model of how design ought to proceed. This was usually expressed as variants on three broad stages—analysis, synthesis, and appraisal. This had been enshrined in the Royal Institute of British Architects' Plan of Work and in other civil service procedures for guiding building design, such as the Department of Health's CAPRICODE. From the psychologist's perspective, the important conclusion was drawn that the "appraisal" stage required an examination of the users' reactions to the building. Thus user evaluation was seen as a necessary component of systematic design. It was only a small step from this view to argue that psychologists were uniquely well placed to carry out studies of user satisfaction.

The term for the field at that stage was *architectural psychology*, and this was the title of the book edited by Canter (1970) that resulted from the conference held in 1969 at Dalandhui, on the shores of Gareloch outside Glasgow. Lee presented a paper at that conference with the provocative title "Do We Need Theory or Is Operational Research Enough?" Stringer, a psychologist on an educational research team at the Bartlett School of Architecture, also launched a crusade to introduce Kelly's personal construct theory into architecture as a broad framework for environmental research. A number of other contributors to this significant conference also raised questions about the most appropriate models for studying people in their physical context.

Most of the papers were heavily weighted to what would now be recognized as a "cognitive" perspective, which is perhaps best summarized by the rhetorical question in the title of Canter's contribution: "Should we treat building users as subjects or objects?" For although Canter argued that there was some value in looking at the "objective" behavior of building users, he sided with the dominant British tradition that the individual's own understanding and experience of an environment ought to be the primary concern of environmental psychologists.

The Dalandhui conference had been held under the auspices of the School of Architecture at Strathclyde University, in Glasgow. In that school, Markus had set up the Building Performance Research Unit (BPRU) in 1967 with the objective of developing systematic, empirical procedures for the evaluation of buildings. He argued that evaluation would become a more active component of the design process if standard tools for all aspects of evaluation were made available. With support from architectural practices and government funds, he brought together, besides a psychologist, a services engineer and an architect to form the core of the BPRU that also had a physicist and a quantity surveyor working with it for part of its duration.

As the book this team later published (BPRU, 1972) testifies, the interdisciplinary group were uncomfortable with a strictly technological role. They saw the need to define the nature of the interactions between people and buildings more closely and the need to provide design tools that would contribute directly to the practice of architecture.

The desire to build more effective models of the mechanisms underlying user evaluations also gave rise to other studies using simulations in the form of slides taken from scale models. The widely quoted work by Canter and Wools (1970) showed that aspects of building form such as ceiling angle and window size, could be linked directly to the meanings assigned to those rooms using semantic differential scales. Other studies of meaning in architecture followed in North America, Britain, and Australia.

36.1.2. Current Themes

In looking for milestones in the emergence of environmental psychology in the United Kingdom, the Dalhandui conference in 1969, the establishment of the environmental psychology program at the University of Surrey in 1972, and the seminar at the London School of Economics (LSE) in the same year on environmental perception are all of some significance. These milestones highlight the diverse institutional and professional contexts out of which the field grew. The Dalandhui conference had its support in a school of architecture, whereas the environmental psychology course is based entirely within a department of psychology, and the LSE seminar was led by geographers. Physicists, service engineers, sociologists, and planners had also all made a definite contribution in the early years of the field, and this multifarious set of influences can still be discerned in current activities.

Having ended our brief historical review in the early 1970s with the recognized existence of a highly diverse community of interest, it is appropriate to change our perspective from the historical past to the present, leaving the reader (or a more extended publication) to fill in the gaps between "now" and "then."

In reviewing current themes, then, it is inevitable that any division for the sake of clarity of presentation will obscure some important links and interactions. In their review of the field from a British perspective in 1975, Canter and Stringer chose to organize the material in terms of increasing scale and complexity, starting with the thermal and acoustic environment and concluding with studies of the natural environment and landscape. This has the distinct advantage of producing a book the first third of which is read by service engineers, the middle third by architects, and the final third by planners and geographers, with psychologists dipping into it to lift juicy theoretical morsels. Such a division of readership cannot be avoided entirely, but there do appear to be themes that are common to all substantive areas and discipline foci, that is, theory, methods, and applications to practice. We have therefore chosen this threeway division for our review here.

36.2. ENVIRONMENTAL PERCEPTION AND COGNITION

Sir Francis Galton had carried out studies of environmentally related images in the nineteenth century, and the sceptical empiricism of Hulme had also left a philosophical penchant in British psychology and geography for a concern with internal mental processes and experience. Furthermore, Bartlett's (1932) writing on memory schemata has always been an accepted part of British psychological thinking. So there is no surprise in the fact that in terms of

theory, one of the recurrent concerns has been to understand the processes involved in the formation of internal representations of the physical surroundings, (e.g., Canter, 1975a).

Since the late 1960s, a key aspect of these explorations has been the challenge of Lynch's early work (Lynch, 1960). His approach was taken as an impetus for theoretically richer and empirically more acceptable formations. For example, Sarré (1972) and Goodey, Duffett, Gold, and Spencer (1971) have questioned Lynch's typology of five spatial cognitive elements. Sarré found a need to add an additional category—function. Goodey and colleagues (1971) found the original five categories to be conceptually attractive but often inappropriate and proposed a more radical change than did Sarré. They found it difficult, for example, to distinguish whether certain features were "landmarks" or "nodes." As the original typology had no underlying theoretical justification (Gold, 1980), such modifications are acceptable if not inevitable. It is reasonable that different data sets require other classifications. However, it does (1) stress the need for precise theory and (2) demonstrates the increased complexity that has grown from the early attempts to understand environmental transactions.

Pocock (1975) proposed a tripartite classification. In a study of Durham, he divided the elements into point features (buildings), linear features (paths), and areas. Modifications of Pocock's classifications have been successfully used in a number of studies since (e.g., Murray & Spencer, 1979). Canter (1977b) took an even more radical stance. He reduced Lynch's categories to two in a quest for what might be thought of as Euclidean purity—locations and links between them. This scheme proved to be very fruitful in examining the growth of sketch maps over time. Lynch's concept of buildings as landmarks has also been challenged. The studies have shown size and prominence often to be of little importance. Goodey and colleagues (1971), in a study of Birmingham, found the post office tower (the tallest building in the city) rarely featured in people's mappings of the city. Similarly, Pocock (1975) found that only a small minority of respondents in his study made use of the two most prominent features in Durham, the cathedral and castle, when orienting themselves. These along with other findings have demonstrated that although such landmarks may be known, the significance or meaning they have are an important factor in their being included in such maps.

British researchers have also criticized early studies for the scant regard given to more than the visual sense. Auditory aspects of the environment, which are likely to be of considerable importance, have received little attention except when they reach the level of nuisance (Burgess, 1979). Also, as Gold (1980) and Canter (1977b) point out, the blind are capable of forming stable coherent spatial schemata.

The concept of neighborhood perception has also received more detailed consideration during the 1970s and 1980s that also showed that early studies were inadequate to various degrees. For example, in a major review of studies of neighborhood perception, Spencer (1973) concluded that the area was inconclusive mainly due to three factors: (1) diverse research aims, (2) a lack of standardized sampling procedures, and (3) small sample sizes. The criticisms made in the review are relevant to the pioneering work of Lee (1954, 1968).

Briefly, Lee asked people to draw a map of their neighborhood, "a concept they readily understood." Comparing the elements of the cognitive map or the person's "sociospatial schemata," as Lee called it, with those on a cartographical map, Lee calculated a "neighborhood quotient." He found each person had a unique schemata, but there was a tendency to norm formation in the size of these neighborhoods and the sharing of social and spatial experiences. However, Spencer (1973) encountered problems when applying Lee's methodology. In a study of working-class residents in Birmingham, he found his subjects had problems in grasping the concept of neighborhood. Additionally a marked variation in the resulting maps was found depending on the particular methodology used to uncover neighborhood delineation: whether graphical or verbal accounts were given. Canter (1977b) also reports great variation in the "neighborhood" definition as a function of how respondents are asked to indicate its extent; clearly not only are the emerging theories or concepts in environmental psychology open to question, but also, as one expects with a developing field, the methodology.

Spencer and Canter both argue that to attribute significance to the lines people drew to such an extent as to calculate a neighborhood quotient was inappropriate. As Gold (1980) later reiterated, Lee's method contained implicit assumptions that the houses and shops all had a significance and that neighborhoods are continuous. Spencer (1973) went on to argue that the study lacked phenomenological validity because of the procedure of asking people to respond by means of a format that was prepared by the researcher. The extent to which the person was able to respond was then a function of the degree to which they shared an understanding of the concepts with the researcher. The study of Lee's approach certainly emphasizes the theoretical significance of the particular methodologies employed.

It is worth, for a moment, considering how the methods and studies of environmental cognition and perception have been reviewed and criticized by a number of authors in recent years (e.g., Burgess, 1979; Pocock, 1979; Spencer & Dixon, 1983). Pocock (1979) classifies mental maps according to two principle methodologies. The respondent may (1) actually perform the cartography or (2) provide the information from which the map can be drawn by the researcher. In the latter case, for example, Gould and White (1968, 1974) obtained a residential preference map of the United Kingdom by asking people to rank or evaluate various places.

Distance estimations may also be used. A map may be constructed from a series of distance estimations and direction measurements. These studies have focused on the particular properties of distance estimation and orientation rather than on a cognized map per se. For example, Pocock (1972) produced a map of Dundee from the mean conceptualizations of a city based on these two parameters. The results showed the cognitive image of the city to be more circular than that of the actual city. His findings were remarkably similar to those reported by Canter (1977b) for Tokyo, which were also based on distance estimations.

There are a large number of examples of studies in which the cartography is performed by the respondent. These may be (1) structured, with a supplied outline (e.g., Canter, 1977b; Lee, 1954), or (2) unstructured with the respondent drawing a map from memory (e.g., Pocock & Hudson, 1978). The maps may then be presented in aggregate to give a summary map—a consensus or public image.

Mental maps only show conceptualizations at any point in time. However, as environmental knowledge is dynamic, it is also necessary to study change or growth over time. There are basically two approaches to the study of the dynamic aspects of environmental cognition (Pocock, 1979): (1) to use different samples from different age groups or (2) to conduct a longitudinal study of the same subject(s).

From a series of studies (e.g., Canter, 1977b; Pocock & Hudson, 1978) of the growth of cognitive representations, a general consensus has emerged that a progressive increase in detail occurs with an increase in integration and hierarchicization among map elements. Spencer and Weetman (1981) also demonstrated stylistic and sex differences. Overall maps of the city were drawn sequentially or spatially as a function of the individual's preferred style. The studies by Canter (1977b) and Wood and Beck (1976) have been criticized for being conducted over too short a time (Pocock, 1979). However, the more extended study conducted by Spencer and Weetman (1981) over a 3-month period did not reveal greatly differing results.

Mapping studies have also been criticized by Burgess (1979), Pocock (1979), and Spencer and Dixon (1983) for paying too little attention to the affective component of environmental cognition, despite lip service being given to it. In addition, Pocock (1976) showed considerable differences between, for example, a schoolchild who drew a map with home and school as domicentric and tourists' maps that focused on the city center.

In the first study to attempt to investigate the development of the affective urban image among prospective long-term residents of a city, Spencer and Dixon (1983) used Wood's (1973; Wood & Beck, 1976) mapping system, Environmental A, to produce, on a cartographical base, the affective qualities of a city image. They found that although individuals have more to relate about their feelings toward a city after 3 months, the content of the affective map is not greatly different from that produced after 1 week. However, considerable difference was found when these were compared with maps produced by people on their first visit to the city, which was probably due to the latter's stereotypical image of a northern English city. Additionally, the latter emphasized the factual, physical characteristics. The results also showed no difference between people of different "environmental sensitivity," sex, or mobility, although Murray and Spencer (1979) had found mobility to be a predictor of "cognitive" mapping style. The researchers concluded that Wood's methodology was fruitful and recommended that it be used in future empirical research into environmental perception, allowing affective, phenomenological considerations to be incorporated into the mainstream empirical tradition. This leads to the possibility of rectifying the criticism that phenomenal aspects of the urban experience are under-represented (Burgess, 1978; Smith, 1974).

Burgess (1978) has reviewed a number of studies of environmental cognition and image that have looked at the role of literature and the media in shaping people's stereotypes of particular regions. She found, for example, that the external image of the city she studied (Kingston-on-Hull) was stereotypical and reflected in media reports found around the country.

36.2.1. Environmental Cognition in Children

Considerable light has been thrown on the cognitive processes associated with effective use of the physical surroundings from studies carried out with children. These studies were conducted, predominantly in the United States by geographers (e.g., McCleary, Blaut, & Blaut, 1970) and later by psychologists (e.g., Neisser, 1976; Piche, 1977). A series of publications by Spencer and his associates in Sheffield have attempted to replicate and expand these early investigations. It is probably a criticism of the field that there were no reported replications or extensions of the important study by Blaut and Stea (1969) until Spencer some 14 years later, even though Canter had publicly advocated such replications (1977b).

Following the arguments of Blaut and Stea (1969), recent publications, reviewing the pertinent literature, have forcefully argued that children's cognitive abilities with regard to the environment have been underestimated, partly as a result of the use of inappropriate research methods (Catling, 1979; Spencer & Darvizeh, 1981a). Spencer and his colleagues have demonstrated that studies based on the ideas of Piaget (e.g., Piaget & Inhelder, 1967) have overestimated the limitations of children's cognitions and the influence of egocentricity (Spencer, Harrison, & Darvizeh, 1980; Spencer & Darvizeh, 1981a, 1981b).

Spencer and colleagues (1980), for example, provided evidence that the ability to recognize objects and geographical areas, which involves rotation, reduction, and abstraction, from aerial photographs is present in 3-year-olds even when they have not previously experienced such representations. They also provide some evidence that children can understand maps and the perceptual maps developed by Fisher (1973). One explanation proffered by the authors to explain this ability is the use of models, cars, trains, and the like by the children during play. Play gives them an understanding of the aerial view of certain objects that then provide cues regarding the others.

Additionally, the same authors (Spencer & Darvizeh, 1981b) have shown that 3- and 4-year-old children are good at route finding although they may be poor in their descriptions and representations of routes. Thus although children have much environmental knowledge, studies relying on graphic and verbal skills are likely to seriously underestimate the children's abilities. Spencer and Darvizeh (1983) in a cross-cultural study carried out in the United Kingdom and Iran have also given evidence to show that "expressive style" may differ from one culture to another, although the individual may have the same amount of information on which to draw. From their study, they conclude that as early as 3 years, children have become socialized into the manner of describing a route.

Looking toward possible future developments in the area, Spencer and Darvizeh (1981a) argue that studies should consider the potential and abilities of children in "real environments" rather than laboratory settings and should include children who have considerable freedom and range to move around their locality, as may be likely to be found in rural settings.

36.2.2. The Theory of Place

The explorations of environmental cognition provided a framework for the development of theoretical formulations about the nature of human transactions with the physical surroundings. The personal cognitive tradition that has already been frequently mentioned was at the core of this development. However, a number of researchers in both psychology and geography saw the need to integrate processes of internal representation to ways of exploring the physical environment per se. In doing this, they turned to the notion of *place* as a central concept. The concept of place has been evident in the writings of geographers since the early part of the present century. Herbertson, for example wrote that "the geographer is no more confined to materialistic consideration than the historian. There is a genius loci, as well as Zeitgest—a spirit of place as well as time" (1915, p. 153).

The comments of Herbertson reflect the principal interest of geographers' concerns with place—the phenomenological experience of place. Appleton (1975a), Lowenthal and Prince (1976), and P.F. Smith (1974), for example, emphasize individual experiences of places, feelings, and attitudes toward environments. Burgess (1978), in a review of much of the geographical contribution to place, states that:

> meaning of place incorporates the association of ideas and emotions evoked in the individual both from direct environmental experience of the place and from secondary information, (including) mass media, literature and social and cultural traditions. (p. 2)

However the objective aspects of the environment, incorporating for example the activities associated with various places, have also received some consideration:

Many places have special significances for individuals and larger groups of people. These significances may be denotative in the sense that a place may be classed as a location, or that landscapes may be classified according to their use or utility. Additionally, places may have connotative meanings in the sense that they have emotional metaphorical or symbolic value. Any consideration of the connotative meanings of places requires interpretation of the inherent qualities of places, the experiences people have with them, and at many different scales...sense of place may be determined by the individuals themselves rather than by its physical appearances. (Burgess, 1978, pp. 3–4)

The seeds, then, of a *theory* of place are found in many of the discussions of the behavioral geographers and studies of environmental perception. However, although they put great significance on the understanding that people have of their surroundings and the meanings assigned to given locations, as shown for example in the review of Pocock and Hudson (1978), it was the psychological recognition that these meanings give rise to a structuring of human cognitive processes that also contain distinct information about anticipated physical forms of places and associated activities, which laid the ground for a systematic theoretical perspective (Canter, 1977b). This has generated considerable subsequent academic (e.g., Groat, 1982) and applied research (cf. Canter, 1982b) as well as giving rise to a general model for evaluation (Canter, 1983c; Donald, 1985).

36.3. METHODS

36.3.1. New Data Collecting Methodologies

The early years of environmental psychology saw the development of few new methodologies, with the exception of "neighborhood" maps (cf. Lee, 1954), despite the unique demands of the emerging field. Rather, there was a tendency to transport data collection techniques from other areas of psychology such as the introuuction of repertory grids by Stringer (1970) from clinical psychology. However, more recently, there has been the development of new methodologies within environmental psychology, which eschew the laboratory and frequently seek phenomenological validity.

The development of methods has to some extent reflected differences in approach that exist between the United Kingdom and the United States. Researchers on both sides of the Atlantic have shared a common interest in approaches to environmental cognition. Yet possibly because of its closer links to the European traditions of, for example, Merleau-Ponty and Hegel, it is predominantly in the United Kingdom and mainland Europe that the phenomenological orientation and consideration of personal meanings (e.g., Brown & Sime, 1981) in the environmental context has been adopted. Conversely, it is possible to see a greater development of behavioral measures in America. For example, Proshansky, Ittelson, and Rivlin's (1976) collection of readings includes no methodologies for studying environmental meanings.

The movement toward understanding and consideration of personal meanings in environmental psychology is reflected by changes occurring in social psychology. Numerous books have been published that expound the view that personal accounts and meanings should be central aspects of any research endeavor (Antaki, 1981; Argyle, Furnham, & Graham, 1981; Brenner, 1980; Ginsburg, 1979; Harré & Secord, 1972), a number of which have been reviewed by Spencer (1981) in the context of environmental psychology. Such publications between them argue for a new paradigm in social psychology that follow trends in environmental psychology, bringing the two subdisciplines closer together. For example, the notion of social situations draws on much of the work conducted in place psychology (e.g., Canter, 1977b), and the psychology of situations has been readily embraced, with some reservations, by environmental psychologists (e.g., Canter, 1984b). The "new" social psychology also calls for field-based research (Ginsburg, 1979), which is arguably the hallmark of much British environmental psychology.

A number of methodologies have developed within environmental psychology. The first was a direct outgrowth of Kelly's (1955) Role Repertory Test, which has been fruitfully used in studies ranging from shopping centers (Stringer, 1974, 1976) to seaside resorts (Riley & Palmer, 1976). In the late 1970s, a number of environmental psychologists began to criticize the repertory grid on several grounds (Brown, Richardson, & Canter, 1976; Canter et al., 1976). Principally, it was seen as being too cumbersome and time-consuming, and its developments detracted from the original theoretical intentions of Kelly himself. Consequently, the procedure of the multiple sorting task has been developed (Brown et al., 1976; Canter, Brown, & Richardson, 1976; Canter, Brown, & Groat, 1985).

The sorting procedure, which may also simply provide a focus for an interview, involves the subject's sorting elements into categories according to some construct. As the elements may take several forms—written names of people, physical artifacts, buildings, activities, and the like—pictures may be used as they have the value of not relying on verbal ability, making them suitable for use with children. The analysis of the derived data may be made in a number of ways to explore individual differences, the interrelations of the elements or the concepts. Some of the most fruitful analyses thus far have been obtained by the application of nonmetric multidimensional scaling procedures (see Canter, 1985a) that are sensitive to qualitative differences.

New methods especially suited to environmental psychology have also been developed in a more directly architectural context. Peled (1975) has developed a phenomenologically based "location task." A generalized circular board is given to the subjects who then arrange particular elements of a given environment according to their own particular spatial ideal. Thus far, the majority of the research using this method is unpublished. However, it has considerable potential for use with both adults and children in environmental and clinical studies.

An approach, which has likewise had limited use but has great potential for the spatial analysis of buildings, has been developed by Hillier at the Bartlett School of Architecture (Hillier & Hanson, 1984). This approach uses a spatial algebra to analyze the layout of buildings and settlements revealing a "social logic" in many otherwise apparently haphazard configurations. It seems likely that the use of the "spatial syntax" method will increase with the recent publication of Hillier and Hanson's book. The method may prove powerful and influential, especially with architects, and could well be enhanced if used in conjunction with the methods of Peled and the multiple sorting task, which will add a stronger psychological perspective to its use.

36.3.2. New Forms of Data Specification and Analysis

As is evident from the preceding section on environmental perception and cognition, environmental and architectural psychology is a multivariate research area. In order to make work in this area more applied, systematic, and understandable, a number of researchers have adopted the metatheoretical framework of facet theory (Canter, 1985a; cf. Guttman, 1954). Guttman (1979, p. 1) summarizes the contribution of facet theory as providing "an effective approach for fruitful design of content, leading to appropriate data analysis techniques, and producing laws of human behaviour in a cumulative fashion. One by-product is the establishment of more solid bases for policy decisions."

Facet theory utilizes three major constituents of scientific activity: (1) formal definition of the variables being studied, (2) hypotheses of some specified relationship between the definition and an aspect of empirical observations, and (3) a rationale for the correspondence between 1 and 2. The definition is provided by the specification of the "facets" from which the variables are derived and the conceptual relationship they bear to each other. A "facet" is any way of categorizing observations in which the elements of the category scheme are mutually exclusive (Canter, 1982a).

The facet approach has been used to study a number of person–environment issues, for example, behavior in fires (Canter, 1980; 1985b), prison design and use (Canter, Ambrose, Brown, Comber, & Hirsch, 1980), hospital ward evaluation (Kenny & Canter, 1981), housing evaluation (Canter & Rees, 1982), office evaluation (Donald, 1983, 1985), energy conservation (Miles & Canter, 1976), architectural semiotics (Canter, 1977a), and several others.

One area which has proved most fruitful is that of place evaluation. Canter (1983c) has developed a facet model of place evaluation in the form of a "general mapping sentence." The use of the model has facilitated the resolution of a number of criticisms of building evaluation research (e.g., Canter, 1983c; Kenny, 1983) allowing research into a diverse range of places to be cumulative and comparable (Donald, 1985).

36.4. AREAS OF APPLICATION

36.4.1. Introduction

Although the theoretical developments of British environmental psychology, whether in geography or psychology, have been strongly cognitive in their orientation, this has not meant a lack of interest in human actions and behavior vis-à-vis the environment. Indeed, when areas of application are considered, it is apparent that a full range of instruments and problem areas have been tackled. It would seem that to theoreticians in Britain the critical conceptions that explain human behavior are looked for within internalized mental processes rather than environmental contingencies. As a consequence, in turning our attention to areas of application of envi-

ronmental psychology, we shall still see a focus on the interpretive and other cognitive processes that are relevant to people's interactions with their surroundings, but this focus is applied more directly to the actions that people perform in any specific setting.

To British researchers in environmental psychology, then, studies of specific settings have always been directed to the objectives and aspirations that people have for being in those settings. This means that the classification of settings for research is most effectively tied to the overall functions of these settings in daily life. We shall follow this framework by looking at a variety of settings, starting with the domestic and moving, by way of educational and office buildings, to the therapeutic context and on to transport and studies of the natural landscape.

The other way in which application has been organized has been in relation to major policy and central decision-making processes. Thus planning for noise reduction, energy conservation, and designing for effective building egress in emergencies have all been foci of research. These studies cut across settings but still place their emphasis on the understanding that individuals have of their context and draw the policy implications from that framework.

36.4.2. Homes and Housing

Studies of housing and homes have occurred at a number of levels from the use of single rooms to whole housing developments. They have also considered aspects from motivation for moving houses to the arrangement of furniture. Research carried out in the United Kingdom and by British environmental psychologists working in other countries has demonstrated interesting cross-cultural similarities in the arrangements of activities and rules in the use of space in the home across cultures.

Canter and Lee (1974) made a study of furniture arrangements in Japanese apartments. A content analysis of furniture and its arrangements revealed consistent patterns that ran contrary to the disorganized stereotypical conceptions of Japanese houses held in the West. Clearly demonstrated areas were evident for sleeping, cooking, reading, and the like. A study by Tagg (1974) in British houses revealed a remarkably similar structure. A past study by Canter and Rees (1982) of British houses identified a consistent, multifaceted structure of people's evaluations of their houses and neighborhood. The evaluation revealed distinct classifications of the elements of the environment. Three qualitatively differentiated aspects were revealed—social, service, and spatial components, thus suggesting people's houses and the proximate environment are experienced as consisting of three distinct yet related aspects.

The results of these studies show general "rules," which may well apply cross-culturally and at different levels of an environmental hierarchy. They provide a framework for people's classification and use of their houses and surrounding areas. In so doing, they provide a conceptual framework within which to locate studies made at different levels, for example, room and neighborhood.

A large-scale study has been sponsored and carried out by the government's Department of the Environment into "difficult-to-let estates" (Power, 1982, 1984)—housing developments that represent 5.5% of the British council housing stock. The "priority estates," as they are now termed, suffered a general malaise—high crime rates, asocial "unneighborly" behavior, physical degeneration, and vandalism. The priority estates projects scored a major success in overcoming these problems. Two key ingredients of the projects are tenants' involvement in and commitment to the improvement of the estate and the establishment of local estate-based management. Also included are connection with other agencies such as the police who reintroduced a local constable to patrol the area. The project's success in a number of areas is beyond the scope of the present chapter, but at least one point has importance for consideration by environmental psychologists. Lower crime rates, reductions in vandalism, indeed the opposite—a positive contribution to the physical condition of the estates was often the case—were all achieved without changes in the design and layout of the estates and dwellings.

These studies by Power are part of the wide criticism (e.g., Ellis, 1982a, 1982b; Hillier, 1973, 1983; Mawby, 1977) of the concept of defensible space (Newman, 1972) that captured the British popular imagination after it was featured in a BBC program. The deterministic notion that such asocial behavior as that found on these estates may be "designed away" is a gross and naive simplification. Improved quality in the "priority estates" was achieved by involving the residents in the estate and changing their attitudes, and by committed involvement of the "authorities" to them.

Differences between groups in terms of their evaluations and conceptualizations of homes and housing have also been studied. In the study cited before, Canter and Rees found differences in the structure of the evaluation of housing between husbands and wives. They differed in terms of the focus of their interaction with the environment. The differences in focus related directly to their activities. The relationship between the individual and the environment has been conceptualized by Canter (1977b) in terms of environmental role. Using this concept, Canter and Walker (1980) analyzed the differences in housing conceptualizations held by various "provider" groups (e.g., caretakers, architects, and administrators) and these groups and the users. The results revealed considerable differences in terms of the focus and degree of interaction that each has with the environment, clarifying their roles in relation to the environment and one another.

A number of studies and reports have considered the effects, usually the disadvantages, of living in high-rise blocks of apartments. Such dwellings have been said to increase physical and mental ill health (Fanning, 1967; Stewart, 1970). It is argued that the designs of such environments prevent contact with neighbors. The most-at-risk groups, the old or families with young children, have had their problems documented (e.g., Jephcott, 1971). The problems of providing adequate and appropriate play space for children have been highlighted. The Department of the Environment (1972), for example, stressed the need for children to be able to run back to a familiar person. This is not possible with the necessity of using elevators or stairs.

A study by Richman (1974) directly looked at the effects of housing on preschool children and their mothers. Richman interviewed 25 families from high-rise apartments, low-rise apartments, and houses. Each of the 75 families had at least two children, one 3 years old and another of less than 3 years. No significant differences were found between the three groups in the number of children with behavior problems (21% of the total) or in the number of mothers who were psychiatrically disturbed. However, in both of the groups living in high-rise or low-rise apartments there were more mothers complaining of depression and loneliness and significantly expressing more dissatisfaction with their housing and the lack of play space in particular.

A related but different approach to housing was taken by Burgess (1979). She plotted the changes in British architecture and planning and the ideologies of architects and planners that led to the construction of high-rise apartments in the 1960s. She argues for the inclusion of perception studies in planning as a way toward "place making." This accords well with Ellis's (1982a, 1982b) findings from a study of housing developments in London. Open-space areas on two different projects were studied from a phenomenological perspective. Ellis uses the term *activity scheme* (the conception of one or more activities as appropriate or inappropriate to a particular setting).

Ellis found that whether or not behavior of people of various kinds in different places were acceptable depended on the meanings attached to such places and what the residents saw as appropriate for the places. A consensus as to what was appropriate was achieved through negotiation among the residents. In reporting the study, Ellis reiterates the criticisms of Newman's deterministic approach.

36.4.3. Educational Environments

Although the differences in housing requirements have been brought about by changes in the structure of society, it seems unlikely that the nature of the home as such has changed dramatically over the last 100 years in Britain. By contrast, school design and educational philosophy have changed dramatically over the last century. The reasons for change are both technological, pedagogical, and epistemological. The improvements in lighting technology, the dominant factor in designs between the wars, has allowed an alternative to the once-common "finger plan." The typical plan today is a tight cluster of classrooms around a central assembly hall (Manning, 1967). Such designs complement the changes within educational practice, although this may have been more by accident than design (Manning, 1967).

The view of the learner has gone through two distinct stages, the first of which can be divided into three substages in which the learner has been seen as an empty organism, an active organism, and a social organism. All share the common paradigm: The pupil is seen as motivated by tension reduction and basic drives acting to reduce the "tensions" (Getzels, 1975). The teacher bestowed knowledge and was dominant, the pupil was passive. The design translated this into a form where the teacher occupied the "dominant" position in the room and the pupil remained static.

The preceding has given way, in theory, if not always in practice, to the second stage in which the child is seen as a "stimulus-seeking organism" (Getzels, 1975). The implication from such an approach is to provide an environment in which the pupil can explore, investigate, and thus learn. The environment deemed appropriate was the open-plan classroom—a large, open, and flexible space. Studies

have examined both the actual use of classrooms and the expectations that underlie the production of them. In a review of the politics of education and architectural design, Cooper (1981b) demonstrates that the schools have often been designed within the framework of architectural determinism. A particular design is believed to produce the appropriate teaching methods and space use.

The deterministic assumptions linking the use of school buildings to their design are, according to some authors (e.g., Bennet & Hyland, 1979), widespread. Indeed, there is little difficulty in finding publications that reveal deterministic beliefs especially about the direct effects of open-plan designs (e.g., Burnham, 1970; O'Connor, 1977). Empirical research, however, has not supported these views. Instead it has been consistently shown through case studies that there is no necessary relationship between open design and use (e.g., Arnold, 1976; Cooper, 1979; Evans, 1975; Jarvis, 1976; Spencer & Taylor, 1980). A number of surveys (e.g., Arkwright, Hewitt, Thorne, & Webb, 1975; Bennett et al., 1980; Strathclyde Regional Council, 1976) have supported the results of these case studies. As a result Bennett and Hyland (1979, p. 164) remarked that "the message seems unequivocal that open-plan schools are no guarantee of open teaching."

However, as Cooper (1981b) points out, this should not be taken to dismiss designs as unimportant as they do have both symbolic and functional utility. It is probably best to summarize the role of design by saying that it provides a *potential*; whether or not the potential is achieved depends on those using the buildings; it is not enough to provide a design without educating the educators in its use and rationale.

Cooper (1982d) provides a good example of the way in which open-plan schools may be "misused." His study showed how verbal directives from teachers are used to manipulate children's use of space, usually resulting in a static use. These directives impose particular definitions of educational order, transgressions of which may be punished by using space in a particular way.

A number of proponents of open planning and education (e.g., Bennett, 1976; Pearson, 1971) have claimed that open approaches lead to scholastic and personal improvements in the pupil. Research in the United States has frequently supported these claims (e.g., Bloom & Jacobson [1979] and Bennett [1976] provide a review of studies of open planning in the United States). However, past studies in the United Kingdom (Hendry & Matheson, 1979; Spencer &

Taylor, 1980) have failed to find support for scholastic improvement and some aspects of personal improvement. Hendry and Matheson (1979) found, in a comparison of open-plan and conventional Scottish primary schools, virtually no differences in intelligence, reading, or vocabulary. However, they did find differences in informal social interactions in the classroom.

Spencer and Taylor (1980), in a comparative study of open and less open schools, present a number of interesting findings. There were no significant differences in the number of friendships or the number of social isolates. (Pupils in open-plan schools did, however, have more friends from other classes). Overall, happiness was the same in both schools, though there was more alienation in the traditional school, but even this was still low. Both schools showed a similar degree of involvement in specified school activities. Further, the number of extraverts was the same for both schools, but the traditional school contained a significantly greater proportion of introverts. There was, however, greater pupil confidence in the open-plan school, and there also was a greater level of creativity in the open-plan school, but this was not statistically significant. The authors argued, therefore, that the open-plan school cannot by itself by expected to foster greater creativity, and the like: This stems from educational practices.

The teaching style in the schools was similar and not related to the design, whether open or otherwise. They thus concluded there is not disagreement between American and British studies but that the U.S. schools adopted an open education style of teaching that was not evident in the U.K. schools. This indicates that the essential element was the schools' educational philosophy and physical layout, not merely the physical layout on its own.

36.4.4 Use of Space in Schools and Playgrounds

Beyond the general relationship between school design and educational philosophy and approach, the school setting raises a number of specific questions about space use. The importance of this is revealed from a study by P.K. Smith (1974). He indicated that teachers lacked knowledge of how to use space, lacked motivation because of school organization, and lacked knowledge of the potential of the space available to them. In addition, he found many spaces unsuitable for activities, because they had inadequate facilities. Smith also discovered a discrepancy between the intended use of space as conceived by designers and the resultant use by teachers and pupils.

He thus argued for a new approach to design of general learning areas.

In order to understand the etiology of these problems, there has been an examination of the design process itself. In 1977, The Department of Education and Science agreed to a request from the School of Advanced Urban Studies of the University of Bristol to support research into the briefing process in school design. This was a consequence of a realization that "too often a dramatic and imaginative visual concept was not related to educational need or, conversely, an educationally interesting plan was not adequately reflected in the architectural quality of the built form" (Burns, 1979, p. 213).

The researchers used a sample of eight local education authorities and found that the design neither began with people and ended with building, nor were they a result of collaboration between administrator, educator, and architect as equal partners. Planning did not arise from an analysis of possible patterns of the activities of groups of varying sizes for varying periods of time, requiring spaces of differing areas, related to each other in specific ways. The designs usually began, in the early stages, as a sketch. As the initial sketch could not be changed to any significant degree, the possibility of incorporating alternative ideas, conceptualizations, and innovations was thus considerably constrained. One consequent recommendation was therefore that the concept of a *brief* should be replaced by a "briefing *process*" (Burns, 1979).

For a good design, the following four points were suggested:

1. It should be recognized that there is a need for collaboration between administrators, educators, and architects as *equal* partners.
2. More than lip service should be given to the fundamentals of fitness for purpose, value for money, character and style, general appearance, and match with setting.
3. The design should satisfy the requirements of educators, administrators, and architects alike: "A building is not a beautiful shell and neither is it a functional shed."
4. Good practice is not confined to the design process itself; elected members, parents, and the general public should be involved. The briefing of those who use the building is an important part of good procedure.

Having looked at the problems inherent in the design process, it is likely that future research will examine the other issue—the teachers' understanding of space use and the reasons for the particular designs.

36.4.5. Offices

Whereas educational settings have evolved over a century, office building in Britain developed very rapidly in the 1960s as the work force changed from a manufacturing emphasis to a service and commercial management emphasis. This development coincides with the early years of environmental psychology in Britain. It is probably because of this historical coincidence that research into office environments played a central role in the genesis of environmental psychology (e.g., Canter, 1969, 1972b; Langdon, 1966; Manning, 1965, Wells, 1965). The initial interest, however, has not been sustained in the United Kingdom, although it has grown on the other side of the Atlantic, despite the increasing number of people spending large proportions of their lives in such environments. The research that does exist has nonetheless been diverse (Canter, 1983a). However, there are some common themes that link it to that of educational and institutional environments.

In the early years of office research, psychologists concentrated on obtaining the optimum working conditions in a rather mechanical way, in that the worker was viewed as a machine that merely required the appropriate operating conditions to achieve optimum functioning. The rationale behind such research and the early design of offices lay in the supremely positivistic theories of Taylor (discussed fully by Schein, 1965). Given the context of "scientific management" principles, it was highly unlikely that the early environmental psychologists should adopt any other approach. In later years, the Taylorist views gave way to more humanistic approaches. It is not possible to discuss here whether, as Clegg and Dunkerly (1980) argue, such approaches also miss the point of the nature of human functioning in organizations. What is important, as the symbolic interactionists in sociology would remind us, is that the new approach was real in its consequences, especially with regard to design and environmental psychologists.

First, design, with the introduction of *burolandschaft*, emphasized the social role of groups and individuals in the office. From this, the focus shifted to the study of the individual as a part of an organic whole with interplaying connections and roles in the organization. Studies then addressed issues such as design and organizational structure (e.g., Duffy, 1974a, 1974b).

Additionally, problems with privacy and distraction that resulted from too much attention being paid to the organization/environment "fit," although ignoring the individual, led to many studies of open-plan offices (e.g., Canter, 1972b; Donald, 1983; Ellis & Duffy, 1980; Hedge, 1982). Despite the evidence for the negative effects of open planning, including possible health hazards for employees (Canter & Donald, 1983b), it is still a popular approach to office design. There may be a number of reasons for this, including real estate and tax advantages, but one important feature emphasized by Lipman, Cooper, Harris, and Tranter (1978) is the opportunity it provides for the control of the work force.

The future of the office is perhaps one area that, due to the advent of computer technology, will be an area of increasing interest (e.g., ORBIT, 1983). The influence of information technology has considerable implications for both organizational structure and office design. These issues may become paramount in the area. But, as with so many areas of environmental psychology today, another direction lies in a more phenomenological approach to older issues such as lighting (Ellis, 1986). The movement toward an understanding of meanings attributed to the environment is a feature we will see again in the following sections.

36.4.6. Total Institutions and Therapeutic Environments

Evaluation of total institutions and therapeutic environments, which are not mutually exclusive categories, share a common theme—the relationship between society's conceptualizations of the "visitors" (the term *inmates* is becoming increasingly inappropriate) to such environments, the therapeutic process, and the design and administration of those settings. The environments are provided for individuals who are considered socially, psychologically, or physically deviant from the general population.

Early studies of therapeutic environments, especially in the United States, tended to concentrate on the effects of the manipulation of various elements, for example, seating arrangements and observed behavior. Although such studies are still being carried out, increasing emphasis in the United Kingdom is on the models of the various disabilities and how these are reflected, contradicted, or supported by design. A clear evidence of this change is given by Canter and Canter's (1979) review.

The initial custodial model, which demanded a separation of the "deviant" from society at large and was reflected by the monolithic institutions, has gradually been usurped. The medical model then came to the fore, with the emphasis on problems seen in terms of "disease." The result has been designs that are inappropriate for many disabilities (cf. Richer, 1979). The prosthetic model whereby the environment "supports" the individual has been criticized as often being counterproductive, as is shown by Wolff's (1979) evaluation of a playground for partially sighted children.

Gunzburg and Gunzburg (1979) have argued for therapeutic environments that are as normal as possible to aid a return to normal life. However, such a model may be rather optimistic (Canter & Canter, 1979), and environments should be enhanced to meet the various needs (Wolff, 1979). The final model is one of individual growth where the environment allows people to grow to their full potential (Canter & Canter, 1979). Such changes in the function of the environment are closely linked to changing views of policymakers, psychologists, and psychiatrists (e.g., Clare, 1976). However, as was also clearly the case in educational establishments, the way in which the environment is used can reveal underlying contradictions between overt statements and the use of the environment (Canter & Canter, 1979; Tyerman & Spencer, 1980). Tyerman and Spencer have indeed shown how official goals may be negated by misuse of environmental designs, producing the opposite effect to that desired.

A similar movement has been shown with regard to "criminals" and penal institutions. In the only large-scale systematic psychological study of prison design and use in the United Kingdom Canter et al. (1980) revealed the relationship between various designs—related to models of the criminal—and the dimensions used by prisoners and prison staff to classify various institutions. In a similar vein, Tyerman and Canter (1983) considered the organizational variables used to differentiate hostels by alcoholics.

Besides the physical form of these institutions, there has been consideration of the location of residential care in the community from the perspective of the resident (e.g., Felce, 1982). However, the reverse side of the coin is now also being considered. Burnett and Moon (1983), for example, report a study into the effects of community-based residential facilities on the neighborhood. Like other areas of environmental psychology, the preceding research is showing a greater level of sophistication and a rejection of simplistic, deterministic studies of the person–environment relationship.

36.4.7. Psychological Aspects of Transportation

Although transport is not a setting in the same sense as a school or a hospital, many aspects of the design and use of transportation are similar to those found in other major institutions, with the additional consequence that transport systems have for all other aspects of urban life. However, in this context, it can be seen that the research moves more toward the implications for regional and national policy than the studies discussed so far. By focusing on transport as a related set of environmental psychology problems, we also are able to demonstrate the links between studies that may often seem peripheral or academic.

Studies of transportation have been made by workers in a number of disciplines, including planning, economics, and political science. Such studies, although relevant, are on the periphery of the interests of environmental psychologists; we therefore limit our review to those studies made by environmental psychologists, behavioral geographers, and to a more limited extent, planners. A number of reviews of the other perspectives exist, and many provide a useful source of reference (e.g., Cresswell, 1977; Rothenberg & Heggie, 1974; Stringer & Wenzel, 1976).

The consideration of the psychological aspects of transport fall into three broad areas of concern: (1) the study of transport as a disrupting or disturbing element in the environment; (2) the problems associated with the use of particular forms of transport or transport systems; and (3) the psychological consequences of using a particular mode of transport. Studies of transport as a negative element in the environment have primarily concentrated on those who may be termed *bystanders*. The primary area of study has been transport as a pollutant—usually noise or air pollution. Studies of noise have primarily been made in relation to aircraft noise (e.g., McKennell, 1963, MIL Research Ltd, 1971; Robinson, Bowsher, & Copeland, 1963) and road traffic noise (e.g., Flindell, 1979; Griffiths & Delauzun, 1977; Griffiths & Langdon, 1968; Griffiths, Langdon, & Swan, 1980; Langdon, 1976; Lawson & Walters, 1974). The effects of noise from various transport sources on sleep have also been considered and reviewed by a number of authors (e.g., Dobbs, 1972; Langdon & Buller, 1977). A number of studies have direct policy implications, and it is some of those we will consider here.

An important study in relation to policy implications was made by Griffiths and colleagues (1980). They discovered that the subjective rating of noise remained relatively constant despite noise attenuation and falls in objective noise levels. Griffiths and his colleagues argued that such results could be accounted for by the phenomena of perceptual constancy. Support for these findings is available (Wilkinson, 1980; Wilkinson & Cambell, 1984). Wilkinson and his colleagues report that subjective evaluations of sleep remain similar after attenuation of noise by, for example, double glazing. However, when Wilkinson's data were combined with those from three other European studies (Wilkinson, 1980), which had been conducted in conjunction with his own, a significant difference in subjective ratings of sleep before and after attenuation was found.

Results of studies on subjective ratings of sleep quality in relation to noise should be treated with caution, but the indications are clear. Further results from the study by Wilkinson shed some light on the area. The study also considered "objective" physiological measures; the most important in terms of sleep quality was the effect of noise on fourth-stage (delta) sleep. Here attenuation (by approximately 10 dBA) of noise was associated with a significant increase in delta activity, suggesting an improvement in the quality of sleep as a result of noise attenuation. Thus although subjective measures tend to show little effect resulting from attenuation of noise, there may be improvements in certain physiological states. However, as subjective responses to environmental pollutants such as noise do lead to stress, they certainly cannot be discounted.

Lawson and Walters (1974) have taken the debate more directly into the area of policy and class politics arguing that the present level at which noise is considered acceptable may be too high and should be reduced by 2dBA. They also noted in their study of a new urban motorway in Birmingham that residents ceased complaining about noise levels. They argue that this may possibly be because they see themselves as powerless to remove or influence the source. The residents were all working-class. Lawson and Walters note the stoicism of the working-class to such environmental intrusions compared to the more vocal resistance of the middle classes. They further warn of the possibility of advantage being taken of this by policymakers who may prefer to route highways through working-class areas to avoid resistance from influential persons in the middle-class areas. It is worth noting, in terms of the historical context of policy, that such policy was pursued during the nineteenth century in relation to the routing of railway lines.

Work by O'Cathain (1976) has indicated that there is scope for much more effective research on the psychological effects of transport for planning. In an attempt to consider noise more directly in relation to planning and architectural design, O'Cathain related traffic noise to housing configuration and density. He showed that by taking into account layout geometry, orientation, and proximity to highways designs this could greatly reduce noise problems produced by transportation routes.

The issue of social severance produced by major roads has also been considered (Lee & Tagg, 1976). Social severance is considered, by Lee and Tagg, to be a complex social response to the presence of a physical barrier. Measures of social severance are made at cognitive, perceptual, and instrumental levels. Their major finding was that major urban roads acted as both cognitive and behavioral barriers, in effect, distorting people's sociospatial schemata. However, there was also significant accommodation to the barrier with people "shifting" their neighborhoods back and allowing them to expand away from the road.

It is difficult to see solutions to such problems. However, if the routes of new roads run along the path of already existing barriers, as has been done in the case of the M6 in Birmingham that runs on pillars along the path of an existing canal, its impact will be likely to be less significant.

In considering problems associated with the use of various modes of transport or transport systems, one aspect that has received attention is wayfinding. With regard to maps, Arnheim (1964) has noted the highly successful form of the London underground map that he attributes to the reduction of detail except for the pertinent topological properties of stops and interconnections. The use of maps by the blind has also been investigated (e.g., James & Swain, 1975; Leonard & Newman, 1970), revealing considerable ability to use tactual maps effectively and so enhance people's knowledge of a city and allow the blind to use various forms of public transport. The role and use of signposts has also been considered (Agabani, 1975; Canter, 1984c; Canter & Donald, 1983). Such studies are largely unpublished, small-scale, and relatively limited. However, they do indicate possible theoretical models that have implications for navigation of the urban and building labyrinths.

The policy of segregation of traffic and people in

residential areas has been questioned, and a number of attempts have been made to integrate the car and pedestrian by the use of "shared space" (Baker, Thompson, & Bowers, 1983). In an attempt to reduce the subordination of pedestrians and reduce the bleak, hard residential landscapes, the designers, rather than segregate traffic, aimed at stricter control of vehicle speed by, for example, narrow carriageways, cul-de-sacs, and the use of materials and textures more associated with pedestrian areas. Use was also made of shared pedestrian/vehicle access ways.

The results were frequently not as predicted. Although residents found the townscape more pleasing aesthetically and the small cul-de-sac units better socially, they perceived the "road" as being more dangerous. There were numerous examples of traffic exceeding safe levels, in the context of the new design. Designers had thought, for example, that high corners and narrow "roads" would lead to a reduction in speed. However, their deterministic assumptions proved inadequate; young motorists saw the environment as a challenge and consequently drove at unsafe speeds. The design, although criticized, is thought by Baker and colleagues to be potentially useful with certain additions, for example, ramps to reduce motorists' speed.

The international concern regarding the levels of lead in the atmosphere as a result of road traffic has stimulated research in the United Kingdom. One area of focus has been the Gravelly Hill interchange in Birmingham. A working party on lead pollution around this area was set up in 1974. Their report, published in 1978, concluded that although respiration of airborne lead appeared not to be a general problem and that although there was no evidence of general risk to schoolchildren from exposure to lead, there was evidence of a problem among preschool children. It was found that a relatively high proportion of children from the inner city areas showed raised blood-level concentrations. In only one case could this be attributed to, for example, lead in paint.

The more direct impact of traffic on pedestrians through accidents is a related area of concern. Chapman, Wade, and Foot (1982) have brought together a number of studies relating to this theme and have shown clearly the wide range of contributions that the psychological perspective can make to this area. Curiously, the large international problem of road accidents generally has been rather neglected by environmental psychologists in Britain, possibly because the research field has been rather monopolized by applied psychologists at the government's road research laboratory.

As an area of study, then, transportation brings together many differing issues. Perhaps even more than with other areas of research, there is a need here for environmental psychologists to understand the concepts and principles on which designers base their decisions. There is also a need for a closer examination of how people-at-large decide about their transport mode choice. Stringer and Wenzel (1976) have made a start on this topic, but there are clearly complex interactions between the private decisions of individual members of the public, drawing on their own internal representations of what is available, and the public decisions of the planners and transport engineers.

36.4.8. Landscape Assessment

In moving from transport to the natural environment, there is a distinct change in tone and gear. We leave behind issues relating directly to design decision making and move more directly into the realm of national policy. Intriguingly, in doing this, some of the general theoretical concerns reviewed at the beginning of this chapter reemerge as important foci for research activity.

Research into the natural environment has been predominantly the domain of geographers and planners (Gold, 1980). For example, the most active school of environmental psychology in the United Kingdom at the University of Surrey produced very few research theses on the topic in over 15 years of research activity. Landscape assessment has been tied to and characterized by the demands of government policy since the National Parks and Countryside Act of 1949. This made it obligatory for local authorities to evaluate the aesthetic quality of landscape for the purposes of protection and improvement—an obligation that has resulted in attempts to evaluate aspects of the landscape in simple statistical terms in order to allow trade-offs with other features such as motorway developments (Penning-Rowsell, 1981). However, over a period of almost 20 years, there has been an increase in the complexity of the attempt to assess the natural environment that to some extent parallels the building evaluation work of psychologists.

Gold (1980) has classified approaches to the landscape in terms of landscape evaluation and landscape assessment. Penning-Rowsell (1981), in a review of the relevant literature, proposes three chronologically ordered approaches: (1) intuitive evaluation (1967 to 1971), (2) statistical approaches (1971 to 1976), and (3) landscape preference approaches (1973 to the present). The former two accord with Gold's evaluation category, the latter with his assessment classification.

The intuitive method (e.g., Clark, 1968; Fines, 1968; Linton, 1968) was based on extensive field studies, took a "broad brush" approach, and classified landscape tracts according to the intuitive judgments of planners (Penning-Rowsell, 1981). Criticisms that such an approach was too subjective, biased toward the opinions of professionals (Penning-Rowsell, 1974), and resulted in a plethora of methods and assumptions depending on the orientation of each particular planning department resulted in a call for a more systematic approach. The resultant approach was to measure, weigh, and combine landscape elements into indexes of landscape quality (Penning-Rowsell, 1981). Such methods were enthusiastically endorsed by planning departments who found the mathematical methods more acceptable; they thought the more mechanical approach had greater objectivity and validity and thus was more scientific.

Statistically more sophisticated approaches (e.g., Coventry-Solihull-Warwickshire Sub-Regional Planning Study Group, 1971) later developed under governmental pressure to devise definite evaluating techniques that would allow noncontroversial decision making. Under this approach, the subjective elements that would be incapable of future prediction were separated out and reduced to a minimum (Penning-Rowsell, 1981).

Along with this development was the increasing use of secondary data sources, for example, photographs. Such data sources were a response to criticism that field studies were too subjective, expensive, and unreliable. Although secondary data sources did show high correlations with the "original" sources, facilitated the use of factor analysis to explore fundamental dimensions, and allowed the exclusion of distracting elements (e.g., Clamp, 1975, 1976), a number of criticisms of the approach in general were made. Penning-Rowsell and Searle (1977) argued that there was too much focus on statistical issues and the use of professional observers. Turner (1977) regarded the narrowness of purely visual assessment to be a drawback. Gold (1980) criticized the approach for being too elemental. It was also claimed that the true qualities of the landscape may be somewhat different to the sum of its parts (Duf-

field & Coppock, 1975). Indeed, the approach was seen as departing little from the intuitive methods (Penning-Rowsell & Searle, 1977).

The ensuing landscape preferences approaches were pioneered in the United States, probably as a result of much input from social psychologists (e.g., Craik, 1972). The aim of these approaches was to consider the landscape in *totality* (e.g., Dunn, 1976; Penning-Rowsell, Gullett, Searle, & Witham, 1977) and to "understand the forces determining the attractions of valued landscapes, dispensing with surrogates for landscape value in the form either of checklists produced by intuition or of predictive regression equations" (Penning-Rowsell, 1981, p. 31).

The majority of studies used photographs to elicit reactions to scenic attractiveness but *not* to predict landscape value. Free response questionnaires were used instead of rating scales and semantic differentials in order to account for the full complexity of the phenomena, and preferences were assessed directly by local residents and users (e.g., Penning-Rowsell, 1980). Additionally, it was found that use associations dominated perceptions, as would be expected from psychological conceptions of the environment (e.g., Canter, 1977b), and that pure aesthetic judgments were rare (Dunn, 1976; Penning-Rowsell, 1980).

Although criticisms have inevitably been made of this approach (e.g., see Penning-Rowsell, 1981), it provides the most fruitful approach to date, in terms of results and potential (Gold, 1980). However, other criticisms, which are more fundamental, remain. The most overriding was the development of a theory for the domain (Gold, 1980). Attempts that have been made have proved inadequate (e.g., Appleton, 1975a). The positivist tradition of planning and geography has resulted in an emphasis on measurement. Progress requires not further development in measurement but a refinement of the questions concerning the nature and dimensions of landscape (Penning-Rowsell, 1981). It is worth comparing these statements with those made by psychologists in relation to the evaluation of the built environment that has been subjected to similar criticisms especially in relation to the emphasis on measuring instruments and a lack of theory development.

36.4.9. Building Evaluation

Building evaluation in the United Kingdom began with the early studies by the Pilkington Research Unit (e.g., Manning, 1965) and later the BPRU (1972). The feature characterizing these studies and setting them apart from those collected previously is the emphasis they gave to evaluating the environment as a whole. Rather than seeing the environment as being made of unrelated elements, the BPRU stressed the importance of conceptualizing the environment as a unit made up of interacting and interdependent parts.

In 1972, the BPRU developed a model of person–environment interaction and evaluation. In producing the model, the BPRU were also attempting to produce an "all-purpose" generalized instrument for evaluation, an aim paralleled in the field of landscaped assessment. There were additional features of this early work that are still present today. First, the users' assessment formed the cornerstone, usually by dutifully filling out questionnaires, of evaluations. Something that only appeared after in landscape assessment, but it was a factor realized as essential in later years. A second important feature of evaluation research was, and still is, the notion of feedback. The idea was discussed earlier—that evaluation be fed into the design process in order to change future analysis and synthesis of designs. This feature has two implications: Evaluation research is pragmatic in that evaluation is worthwhile even if there is not a theoretical base and that such research is, if nothing else, applied.

In considering the notion of "feedback" (or possibly more accurately "feed forward"), a curious distinction between the development of landscape assessment and building evaluation emerges. As we saw earlier, landscape assessment, for the large part, came about as a response to policymakers requesting details about the value people put on various aspects of the landscape in order to make decisions with regard to future plans. Assessment is used in the feed-forward mode. Building evaluations, on the other hand, tend to be in response to a request to evaluate a building that has already been completed and typically has not "worked." The results may then be fed back in improving the design or forward into future designs. As the client tends to have one building in which considerable capital has been invested, evaluation research tends to fulfill a "feedback" role. The pragmatism of evaluation research has led to problems similar to those found in landscape assessment. As mentioned earlier, a number of authors have criticized evaluation research on the grounds that it is atheoretical. From this stems the additional criticisms that it is also noncomparative and noncumulative. Although landscape assessment has suffered the same drawback, commentators have been more vocal in addressing building evaluation.

In an attempt to answer this fundamental criticism, Canter and his colleagues have conducted a number of studies in various settings with the aim of developing a facet model of evaluation (e.g., Canter, 1983c; Canter & Rees, 1982; Donald, 1983, 1985; Kenny & Canter, 1981). Rather than concentrating on the instruments of evaluation or the process of evaluation research, they have had as their focus the structure of the users' conceptualizations of setting. As a result, it has been possible to develop the instrumentation and produce a template for evaluations that is applicable across a number of settings.

The model has been criticized for lacking phenomenological validity (Donald & Hedge, 1984); however, the nature of the model is such that such a validity could be achieved within its existing framework. Finally, and linking to the separately developing area of landscape assessment, it is possible that the model developed in the field of building evaluation may be applicable to the area of landscape assessment.

36.4.10. The Acoustic Environment

In considering transportation, we had occasion to review some of the related research on noise. However, over many years, there has been an active research involvement in many other facets of the psychological aspects of the acoustic environment. Research into environmental noise changes slowly, and to date it is rather similar to that found in earlier reviews (e.g., Walters, 1975). However, there are notable criticisms and trends within the field that are likely to be influential for future development in the area. It is mainly on these we will concentrate.

Noise effects in the work environment have always been central to research in this area. Comprehensive reviews have been given by Broadbent (1978, 1981), and Davies and Jones (1981) of the harmful physical effects. Early research concentrated on direct relationships between noise and productivity or task performance; such research continues (e.g., Fisher, 1983a, 1983b; Smith, 1983a, 1983b). However, even at this level, awareness of some of the more subtle complexities in the noise–performance relationship are being noted (e.g., Broadbent, 1983). Additionally, the wide implications of high levels of noise at work on people's behavior in other situations (see Jones & Chapman, 1979, for a review), including leisure (Jones, Chapman, & Auburn, 1981), are under increased investigation. Thus the perspective of noise research at work is broadening considerably.

Also abroad in the area is a greater consideration of epistemological assumptions and methodological inadequacies. In 1974, two highly respected researchers, McIntyre and Griffiths, stated:

> In the field of…environmental psychophysics, there are normally clear and direct effects on human beings…which enable the researcher to escape from philosophical discussions about the existence or nonexistence of architectural determinism. (McIntyre & Griffiths, 1974, p. 14)

In 1981, Jones et al. argue the following:

> The person is seen as an agent: not a passive respondent to environmental stimuli, but one who acts to create change in the environment through the construction of goals and the performance of intentional behaviour. We suggest that noise can interfere with various conscious intentions either by virtue of its physical properties…or psychological properties. (p. 44)

They are not alone in this approach. Workers in the area of noise and performance have also shown recent movements in this direction (e.g., Broadbent, 1981; Rabbitt, 1979). Thus the foundations of one of the bastions of architectural determinism are beginning to crumble or at least shake a little.

The adequacy of techniques for investigating subjective responses to noise and the relationship between personality and noise annoyance have also come under increased scrutiny. Griffiths and colleagues (1980) argued that, in the area of traffic noise, a number of ad hoc questionnaire techniques had been used that had not been adequately assessed in terms of either reliability or validity; neglect of the issue was a significant contributor to the controversy over idiographic data. The results of this research concurred with earlier studies by Griffiths and Delauzun (1977) and Bradley and Jonah (1979), demonstrating support for their argument. Griffiths and colleagues thus concluded that in view of such low test–retest correlations and reliability, attempts to intercorrelate dissatisfaction with noise and, for example, personality are premature and that further progress in the assessment of dissatisfaction requires the development of more reliable scales (Griffiths & Delauzun, 1977). Such a scale may go some way to answer the criticism made later by Langdon and Griffiths (1982) that it has not been possible to compare studies of subjective situations where different scales are used.

Such criticism has brought into question previous studies of noise and personality (e.g., Anderson & Robinson, 1972; Hockey, 1972). Indeed the notion of a bimodal distribution of noise sensitivity (Bryan & Tempest, 1973) has been directly challenged by a systematic study by Griffiths and Delauzun (1977).

A number of intriguing and important findings have been made in recent research. For example, the effect of pessimism about one's likely performance on tasks in noisy situations (Fisher, 1983b) or the role of "perceptual constancy" in the subjective experience of noise (Griffiths et al., 1980) that was discussed in relation to traffic noise has considerable implication for the government policy of allocating grants to insulate against noise. The phenomenon of perceptual constancy would suggest that insulation may be ineffective and that the noise source needs to be tackled—a more expensive and far-reaching prospect. Other social consequences of noise have been researched and reviewed (Jones et al., 1981); space constraints preclude a repetition of such reviews.

Recent years have then seen a challenging of earlier simple notions of the person–noise relationship (widening the gap between psychological and ergonomic studies of noise) and the method used to study it and in so doing have witnessed trends paralleled in many other areas of environmental psychology discussed in this chapter.

36.4.11. Behavioral Aspects of Energy Conservation

One area of research initiated almost entirely in response to public concern and the shaping of government policy has been the study of energy use. Since the so-called energy crisis of the early 1970s, the British government has pursued an energy conservation policy. The policy has taken several forms, including the use of various technologies and campaigns such as the "Save It" campaign. Some unexpected consequences have followed from the former; behavioral and perceptual issues from the latter.

The government has encouraged the appointment of "energy managers," within nondomestic environments, with a responsibility for regulating energy consumption. The preferred method has been the introduction of energy management systems—microprocessor-based products that lead to the centralization and automation of fuel consumption (Cooper, 1981a, 1982b). However, research has shown such policy to have unexpected political consequences. The installation of such systems has resulted in a redistribution of power with a removal of the freedom of individuals to alter their own immediate environment and an extension of the loci of managerial control, thus reinforcing the social relations that exist between managers and those who occupy their buildings (Cooper, 1982b).

The government has adopted a strategy for domestic energy conservation through "economic individualism" (Cooper, 1982a). Occupants are economically stimulated to take conservation measures, partly through the action of the price mechanism but also by publicity. They are also informed and advised of measures and techniques for saving energy. Having been motivated and informed, individuals can then help themselves (Cooper, 1981a; Gaskell & Ellis, 1982). A number of studies have examined some of the assumptions underlying the present policy, demonstrating that the area is rather more complex than seems to be realized by the policymakers. For example, Miles and Canter (1976) showed that different universities took very different actions with regard to energy saving, and a follow-up some years later revealed that some were now doing less than at the height of the "crisis."

Gaskell and Ellis (1982) have applied the concept of feedback and "energy literacy" to an understanding of energy conservation behavior. In order to conserve energy, they argue, it is necessary for the individual to have knowledge about how energy is consumed and how it may be conserved. Without such knowledge, even strong motivation—economic or otherwise—to conserve will not be effectively realized. The policy of giving specific suggestions as to how to reduce energy consumption during the British government's "Save It" campaign led to increased energy literacy (Gaskell & Ellis, 1982) and was largely responsible for its success (Phillips & Nelson, 1976). The impact of the British campaign has been contrasted with those in North America that have had minimal impact (Olsen & Goodnight, 1977) using general publicity that did not aim at increased energy literacy, even though they did raise motivation and willingness to conserve.

Ellis and Gaskell have proposed that the literate energy consumer should be conceptualized as an information processor engaged in operating a complex system (Ellis & Gaskell, 1978). The individual is seen as actively engaged in making sense of the world, making plans of action and monitoring the results through feedback. They are thus adopting a perspective taken by Annett (1969) in his consideration of feedback and task performance. The results of the two studies by Gaskell and Ellis suggest that learning from feedback occurs but only in relation to major energy-consuming devices, heating, cooking, and the like. They also argue the importance of goal setting

based on knowledge of the potential benefits in terms of savings, which provides the motivation to save. Economic benefits as a motivational factor are, however, not always the most salient or important perceived reasons for conserving energy. A study by Cooper (1983), for example, showed schoolteachers, who had been given responsibility for promoting energy conservation among children, viewed energy conservation in moral rather than economic terms.

Research by Tong and Griffiths (1982) made use of a "trade-off" methodology where trade-offs between energy-conserving goods and other consumer goods provided a measure of the "value" of energy conservation. The results of their study show that consumers drawn from a sample of middle-income earners place a higher subjective value on goods that conserve energy than on other goods of equivalent price. The authors also echo the sentiments of Gaskell and Ellis (1982), stating that "this research endorses proposals for services that break consumer inertia by offering more detailed, individual advice" (p. 14).

Energy conservation research is, it is probably true to say, in its early stages being held back by reliance on technological innovations, inadequate conceptualizations of comfort (reviewed by Cooper, 1982c), and naive models of economic activity. It has, however, begun, and there is likely to be an increase in research and particularly research sponsored by public bodies. Some evidence of this is already available with the Hertford County Council financing research at Portsmouth Polytechnic, the Economical and Social Research Council sponsoring work at the London School of Economics, and the South Eastern Gas Board sponsoring work at Surrey University.

36.4.12. Fire Behavior Research

One final area of policy-related research is worthy of mention because it serves to illustrate the overlap between a number of theoretical and practical issues. This is the study of human behavior in buildings on fire and other emergency situations. Research into behavior in fires (Canter, 1980, 1985b) pose a number of problems. The information source most widely available is newspaper reports. These are notoriously inaccurate and sensationalistic promoting a stereotypical image of behavior. In order to obtain a more "objective" understanding of what actually occurs during fires, the researchers here made considerable use of personal accounts, statements, and official records. A similar approach of using statements has also been adopted by Poyner into the relationship between crime and the environment (e.g., Poyner, 1980, 1983).

Taking this approach to research a number of intriguing findings has emerged. Little evidence was found, for example, to support the folk concept of "panic" (Sime, 1980). People, it was discovered, acted in a rational manner in the particular context in which they found themselves. The major condition leading to supposedly irrational "panic" behavior was a lack of information. Many procedures such as hiding from people the actual state of affairs which is aimed at reduction of "panic," contribute to this lack of information.

Thus the confusion in the early stages of fires, which can be so dangerous, can be traced to ambiguous warnings and lack of clear instructions. The work has thus led to the development of new types of alarm and warning systems (Tong & Canter, 1985). The study of the internal models of what is happening in the environment can thus be seen to have a strong relevance even in these extreme cases. But the importance of role has also been clearly shown (Canter, 1980). People in fires tend to act according to their existing role in the organization. This has implications for training and education.

36.4.13. The Utilization of Research in Design

Although we have emphasized the policy and design *orientation* of British research, limited *application* of social science research to design has been a concern of British architects and environmental social scientists since the 1960s. One area that has been a primary focus in the type and presentation of the information that may be used by designers.

The integration of specialist inputs into architectural education has been sought since the early 1970s. However, a study by Cardona, Aparicis, Powell, Thompson, Weaver, and Carden (1981) revealed that few schools of architecture show full integration of the specialist subjects such as social science into the courses. The final portfolios of architectural students often reveal the limited extent to which an understanding has made its way through to students' design skills (Lera, Cooper, & Powell, 1983). Two problems have been identified: (1) the wrong information is being taught; and (2) the information is being taught in the wrong way.

Lera and colleagues (1983) argue that specialists, who have little knowledge of how "their" information can be assimilated into design, put an emphasis on teaching "know-that" rather than "know-how" that fails to give the potential designer the appropriate skills. Second, the use of lectures fails to promote an exploration of ideas as well as fragmenting the education into subdisciplines that leads to inappropriate compartmentalization of thinking. Studies of practicing designers have been made by a number of authors. Goodey and Matthew (1971), in a study commissioned by the Building Research Establishment (BRE), looked at the sources of information consulted by designers. They concluded that it was usually information that was brief, clear, and well-illustrated that was used.

In another study commissioned by the BRE, Mackinder and Marvin (1982) looked at the interaction between the designers and the information. One of their findings was that there was an unwillingness on the part of designers to consult written data and a preference for relying on experience. When other information was used, this was technical information rather than general design references. Designers preferred trade association literature as it was clearer and better illustrated. The results thus supported those of the earlier study by Goodey and Matthews.

Ever since Canter's book (1972a), *Psychology for Architects*, there has been concern expressed by those psychologists who work directly with designers that material should be presented in a way that is directly appropriate for designers. In yet another BRE-sponsored study, Lera (1982) found that design was guided by the designers' own preferences or a reliance on the brief and technical references. Other sources included published precedents, previous experience, stereotypes, imagery, self-imposed goals, and rules of thumb. The preceding studies emphasized the quantity and quality of information. Three studies have emphasized different aspects.

In the first of these studies, Asprino, Broadbent, and Powell (1981) compared the information consulted by architectural students and practicing designers when producing school designs. The students consulted sources that included literature on child psychology, educational philosophy, and teaching methods. The practicing architects, however, considered "needs" in rather general terms and aimed at producing an adequate external enclosure for effective environmental control. They made no attempt to consult information related to education. Thus even if the information were available, it would *not* have been utilized.

Similar findings resulted from a study by Powell and Nichols (1981). One of the concerns of the designers was energy conservation. They found that designers were not interested in professional development (education) due to a lack of financial and personal incentives and that any reading of related literature was casual. Cooper and Crisp (1983) also found predispositions on the part of designers to utilize only certain sources such as personal experience.

Thus content and presentation of information is only part of the problem. The predispositions and belief systems of designers may have an overriding effect. Thus if material is relevant and collected within more appropriate philosophical frameworks (i.e., nonpositivist) as proposed by various people (e.g., Ellis, 1983b; Ellis & Duffy, 1982), it may still not be consulted. One consequence of focusing on the information is to direct attention away from the social, economic, and political context in which designers operate (Lera et al., 1983). The preferences, prejudices, and beliefs of the designer need to be considered. Ellis (1983a), for example, has pointed to institutional problems in the design professions that prevent the utilization of social science research. For example, the Royal Institute of British Architects' (RIBA) Code of Practice makes the inclusion of such studies optional and thereby creates problems of financing such studies.

36.5. FUTURE PROSPECTS

Social and technological changes and needs must influence a field as applied in its orientation as ours. These changes will always have implications for the physical surroundings, the way they are used, managed, and experienced. Thus in looking to the future of British environmental psychology, the most likely changes are those that will be linked by social and technological developments. Indeed, these new developments can already be perceived in their early stages at present. The most obvious technological development is that relating to microcomputers and information technology. Cheap and powerful computing power has already transformed many places of work, both industrial and commercial, and it is finding its way into schools and hospitals and most other settings. The use of microcomputers for recreation and the unbiquitous "home computer" are both already accepted as virtually inevitable.

It is clear that the environmental design implications of these developments are very great. Offices,

in particular, designed in the 1960s to maximize daylighting and to facilitate open planning, provide a very poor context for visual display units, networked computers, and the coming generation of bleeping, talking word processors (Ellis, forthcoming). The issues of space utilization, role differentiation in space use, and flexible planning that are central to earlier studies in schools and offices take on different, and possibly more critical, dimensions when combined with microcomputing capability.

But there is another aspect of these developments in which environmental psychologists can and are making a contribution. This is in the design and development of the computing systems themselves (Canter, 1984a). Here the skills of the human factors specialists can be fruitfully complemented by the more global perspective of the environmental psychologist. The tools of observation and questioning and the techniques of field research that it has been necessary to develop in order to study schools or to evaluate the landscape may well find a place in the study of new, complex computing systems, with relatively little modification.

The wave of technological change that is much discussed as following on information technology is that growing out of the technological applications of biology. These developments are especially likely in relation to food and its processing and distribution. So far environmental psychologists have spared little time for food distribution and consumption (with the notable exception of Sommer, 1980). But as the food technologies begin to change important aspects of our styles of life, then it is possible that their environmental implications will lead to psychological attention.

A third development that has already generated much research and is the focus of a special issue of the *Journal of Environmental Psychology* for 1985 is the management and perception of industrial risk. All the changes in technology bring with them potential risks and hazards, but a combination of the scale of technologies has drawn the attention of the public and policymakers alike to the importance of studying how to manage and control these risks and to the need to study what people see the perceived risks as actually being.

The area of risk management has very great potential as one of international significance, to which many research disciplines are now contributing, most especially because of its technical and conceptual links to the central concern of the modern world—the risk of nuclear war. Most commentators accept that the other problems the world faces such as lack of food and lack of space could be solved if the horrific spending on weapons of mass destruction could be reduced. However, this expenditure is a direct reflection of the risks perceived by decision shapers and the people who elect or support them. There are already indications that studies of the management and perception of the risks from, say, nuclear-powered generators and from nuclear weapons are beginning to overlap (Thompson, 1985).

On a more optimistic front, the developments in mass technologies and the affluence they are affording to some sections of the world are opening up many new possibilities for leisure and tourism. Stringer and Pearce (1984) have brought together a number of the British studies in this area, and it is clear from them that there are enough intellectual and instrumental attractions to this field of research to ensure that it will continue to grow. As Canter (1983b) has pointed out, the selling of tourism requires an understanding of the internal representations people have of the places they visit. Such an understanding can be greatly helped by the developments in the theories of environmental psychology discussed in the opening sections of this chapter.

The growth in international travel has also been paralleled by increasing contact between countries and the growth of international contacts. This is occurring both at the national level through the growth of organizations such as the European Economic Community (EEC) and can be seen in the contact between individuals. For example, we have had occasion throughout this chapter to refer to the growth of the phenomenological perspective in British environmental psychology. This is undoubtedly, in part, a product of the increasing contact between researchers in Britain and those in the rest of Europe. The embracing of social actions theory (Canter, 1984b; and cf. Spencer, 1981) by environmental psychologists is another instance of European cross-fertilization.

As environmental psychology in Britain approaches the last decade of the twentieth century, it is possible to see a potential turning point of great significance. Government reduction of funding and pressure on higher education may stifle the field just as it is beginning to establish its capabilities. Researchers themselves may move toward the more negative issues of the day—warmongering and the ignorance that breeds it. Or they may grasp the opportunities that are emerging, becoming lotus-eating leisure researchers begging at Mammon's table.

It seems likely that all these possibilities will come to pass. The only question is whether environmental psychology will continue to exist as a distinct entity in Britain in the future as recognizably as it has in the past.

REFERENCES

Agabani, F. (1975). *Way-finding behaviour.* Unpublished master's thesis, University of Surrey, Guildford.

Anderson, C.M.B., & Robinson, D.W. (1972). *The effects of interruption rate on the annoyance of an intermittent noise* (Report No. AC53). National Physical Laboratories Acoustics. London, England.

Annett, J. (1969). *Feedback and Human Behavior.* Harmondsworth, England: Penguin.

Antaki, C. (Ed.). (1981). *The psychology of ordinary explanations of social behaviour.* London: Academic.

Appleton, J.H. (1975a). *The experience of landscape.* New York: Wiley.

Appleton, J.H. (1975b). Landscape evaluation: The theoretical vacuum. *Transactions of the Institute of British Geographers, 66,* 120–123.

Argyle, M., Furnham, A., & Graham, J.A. (1981). *Social situations.* Cambridge, England: Cambridge University.

Arkwright, D., Hewitt, M., Thorne, K., & Webb, W. (1975). *Survey of open-plan schools in Derbyshire.* Derbyshire Local Education Authority. Derby, England.

Arnheim, R. (1964). *Art and visual perception.* Berkeley: University of California Press.

Arnold, R. (1976). *The effects of a change in school buildings on a school community.* Unpublished doctoral dissertation, University of Wales.

Asprino, A., Broadbent, G., & Powell, J. (1981). A critical examination of design failures in buildings and their relation to design processes. In R. Jacques & J. Powell (Eds.), *Design: Science: Method.* Guildford, England: Westbury.

Baker, I., Thomson, J.C. & Bowers, P.H. (1983, March–April). The use of shared space in residential areas. *Housing Review,* 46–49.

Bartlett, F.C. (1932). *Remembering.* Cambridge, England: Cambridge University Press.

Bennett, S.N. (1976). *Teaching styles and pupil progress.* London: Open Books.

Bennett, N., Andreae, J., Hegarty, P., & Wade, B. (1980). *Open-plan schools: Teaching, curriculum, design.* Slough: National Foundation for Educational Research.

Bennett, N., & Hyland, T. (1979). Open plan—Open education? *British Educational Research Journal, 5,* 159–166.

Blaut, J.M., McCleary, G.S., & Blaut, A.S. (1970). Environmental mapping in young children. *Environment and Behavior, 2*, 335–349.

Blaut, J.M., & Stea, D. (1969). *Place learning* (Place Perception Research Report No. 4), Worcester, MA: Clark University.

Blaut, J.M., McCleary, G.S., & Blaut, A.S. (1970). Environmental mapping in young children. *Environment and Behavior, 2*, 335–349.

Bloom, L.J., & Jacobson, L.S. (1979). Psychological and behavioural functioning of first grade children in open and traditional school settings. *Child Study Journal, 9*, 121–131.

Bradley, J.S., & Jonah, B.A. (1979). The effects of site selected variables on human response to traffic noise. Part I: Type of Housing by Traffic Noise Level. *Journal of Sound and Vibration, 66*, 589–604.

Brenner, M. (1980). *The structure of social action.* Oxford, England: Blackwell.

Broadbent, D.E. (1978). The current state of noise research: A reply by Poulton. *Psychology Bulletin, 85*, 1052–1067.

Broadbent, D.E. (1981). The effects of moderate levels of noise on human performance. In J. Tobias & E. Schubert (Eds.), *Hearing research and theory.* New York: Academic.

Broadbent, D.E. (1983). The relation between task parameters and allocation of effort in noise. *Architectural Psychology Newsletter, 13*, 3–4.

Broadbent, G., & Ward, A. (Eds.). (1969). *Design methods in architecture.* London: Lund Humphries.

Brown, J., Richardson, H., & Canter, D. (1976). Instead of grids. *Psychology and Psychotherapy Association FORUM, 3*(4), 2–5.

Brown, J.M., & Sime, J.D. (1981). A methodology for accounts. In M. Brenner (Ed.), *Social method and social life.* London: Academic.

Bryan, M.E., & Tempest, W. (1973). Are our noise laws adequate? *Applied Acoustics, 6*, 219–232.

Building Performance Research Unit. (1972). *Building performance.* London: Applied Science Publishers.

Burgess, J. (1978). *Image and identity* (Occasional Papers in Geography No. 23). Hull, England: University of Hull Publishers.

Burgess, J.A. (1979). Place making: The contribution of environmental perception studies in planning. *Geography, 64*, 317–326.

Burnett, A., & Moon, G. (1983). The effects of community based residential facilities on the neighbourhood: A case study of hostels for homeless single men in Portsmouth. *Architectural Psychology Newsletter, 13*, 4–6.

Burnham, B. (1970). *A day in the life: Case studies of pupils in open plan schools.* Aurura, Ontario, Canada: York County Board of Education.

Burns, P.M. (1979). The weaknesses in current school design. *Education, 154*, 213–215.

Burt, C. (1940). *The factors of the mind.* London: London University Press.

Canter, D. (1969). *The psychological implications of office size.* Unpublished doctoral dissertation, University of Liverpool, Liverpool.

Canter, D. (Ed.). (1970). *Architectural psychology.* London: Royal Institute of British Architects.

Canter, D. (1972a). *Psychology for architects.* London: Applied Science.

Canter, D. (1972b, October). Reactions to open-plan offices. *Built Environment,* pp. 465–467.

Canter, D. (1975a). *Behavioural maps or cognitive maps?* Paper presented to the International Society for the Study of Behavioural Development Conference, University of Surrey, Guildford.

Canter, D. (1975b). An introduction to environmental psychology. In D. Canter & P. Stringer (Eds.), *Environmental interactions.* London: Surrey University Press.

Canter, D. (1977a). *Is there a mapping sentence for architectural semiotics?* EDRA 8. Proceedings of 8th International Conference of the Environmental Design and Research Association, Priorities for Environmental Design Research, Washington, DC: EDRA.

Canter, D. (1977b). *The psychology of place.* London: Architectural Press.

Canter, D. (Ed.). (1980). *Fires and human behaviour.* Chichester, England: Wiley.

Canter, D. (1982a). Facet approach to applied research. *Perceptual and Motor Skills, 55*, 143–154.

Canter, D. (1982b). Psychology and environmental design. In S. Canter, & D. Canter (Eds.), *Psychology in practice: Perceptives on professional psychology* (pp. 289–311). Chichester, England: Wiley.

Canter, D. (1983a). The physical context of work. In D.J. Oborne & M.M. Gruneberg (Eds.), *Physical environment at work.* Chichester, England: Wiley.

Canter, D. (1983b). Psychology and tourism management. *Tourism Management* (pp. 193–195). London: Butterworth.

Canter, D. (1983c). The purposive evaluation of places: A facet approach. *Environment and Behavior, 15*(6), 659–698.

Canter, D. (1984a, August). From knobs and dials to knowledge. *Design,* pp. 31–33.

Canter, D. (1984b). Putting situations in their place. In A. Furnham (Ed.), *Social behaviour in context.* London: Allyn and Bacon.

Canter, D. (1984c). Way-finding and signposting: penance or prosthesis? In R. Easterby & H. Zwaga, (Eds.), *Information design: The design and evaluation of signs and printed material.* Chichester, England: Wiley.

Canter, D. (Ed.). (1985a). *Facet theory: Approaches to social research*. New York: Springer-Verlag.

Canter, D. (1985b). *Studies of human behaviour in fires*. London: Her Majesty's Stationary Office.

Canter, D., Ambrose, I., Brown, J., Comber, M., & Hirsch, A. (1980). *Prison design and use study* (Final Report). University of Surrey, Department of Psychology, Guildford.

Canter, D., Brown, J., & Groat, L. (1985). A multiple sorting procedure for studying conceptual systems. In M., Brenner, J. Brown, & D. Canter, (Eds.), *The research interview: Uses and aproaches*. London: Academic.

Canter, D., Brown, J., & Richardson, H. (1976). *Constructs without tears: Is there life beyond the grid?* Paper presented to the British Psychological Society Annual Conference, Exeter, England.

Canter, D., & Canter, S. (Eds.). (1979). *Designing for therapeutic environments: A review of research*. Chichester, England: Wiley.

Canter, D., & Donald, I. (1983a). *Sign-posting at the University of Surrey*. University of Surrey, Department of Psychology, Guildford.

Canter, D., & Donald, I. (1983b). *The psychological and health aspects of open-plan offices: A review* (Report to British Petroleum). University of Surrey, Guildford.

Canter, D., & Lee, K.H. (1974). A non-reactive study of room usage in modern Japanese apartments. In D. Canter, & T. Lee (Eds.), *Psychology and the built environment*. London: Architectural Press.

Canter, D., & Rees, K. (1982). A multivariate model of housing satisfaction. *International Review of Applied Psychology, 31*, 185–208.

Canter, D., & Stringer, P. (Eds.). (1975). *Environmental interactions*. London: Surrey University Press.

Canter, D., & Walker, E. (1980). Environmental role and conceptualisations of housing. *Journal of Arechitectural Research, 7*, 30–35.

Canter, D., & Wools, R. (1970). A technique for the subjective appraisal of buildings. *Building Science, 5*, 187–198.

Cardona-Aparicis, C., Powell, J., Thompson, M., Weaver, M.J., & Carden, J. (1981). An introductory essay concerning the integration of special subject disciplines into architectural education. In R. Jacques & J. Powell (Eds.), *Design: Science: Method*. Guildford, England: Westbury.

Catling, S. (1979). Maps and cognitive maps: The young child's perception. *Geography, 64*, 228–296.

Chapman, A.J., Wade, F.M., & Foot, H.C. (Eds.). (1982). *Pedestrian accidents*. Chichester, England: Wiley.

Clamp, P. (1975). A study in the evaluation of landscape and the impact of roads. *Landscape Research, 1* (11), 6–7.

Clamp, P. (1976). Evaluating English landscapes—Some recent developments. *Environment and Planning, A, 8*, 79–92.

Clare, A. (1976). *Psychiatry in dissent: Controversial issues in thought and practice*. London: Tavistock.

Clark, S.B.K. (1968). Landscape survey and analysis on a national basis. *Planning Outlook, 4*, 15–29.

Clegg, S., & Dunkerly, D. (1980). *Organization class and control*. London: Routledge and Kegan Paul.

Cooper, I. (1979, July 17). *Design and use of primary school buildings: An examination of government-endorsed advice*. Paper presented at the International Conference on Environmental Psychology, University of Surrey, Guildford.

Cooper, I. (1981a). *Energy conservation in Britain: Technical problem or social issue*. (Martin Centre Working Paper). University of Cambridge, Department of Architecture.

Cooper, I. (1981b). The politics of education and architectural design: The instructive example of British primary education. *British Educational Research Journal, 7*, 125–136.

Cooper, I. (1982a). Comfort theory and practice: Barriers to the conservation of energy by building occupants. *Applied Energy, 11*, 243–288.

Cooper, I. (1982b). Energy conservation in buildings: Part 2—A commentary on British government thinking. *Applied Energy, 10*(1), 1–45.

Cooper, I. (1982c, July 20–23). *Energy conservation in non-domestic premises: The politics of technological innovation*. Paper presented at the Design Research Conference on Design Policy, Royal College of Art, London.

Cooper, I. (1982d). The maintenance of order and use of space in primary school buildings. *British Journal of Sociology of Education, 3*, 267–279.

Cooper, I. (1983). *Lay views of energy conservation in Britain: The significant case of primary school teachers* (Martin Centre Working Paper). Cambridge, England: University of Cambridge, Department of Architecture.

Cooper, I., & Crisp, V. (1983). *Barriers to the exploitation of daylighting in building design UK experience*. Paper presented to the Phoenix International Daylighting Conference USA, Phoenix.

Coventry-Solihull-Warwickshire Sub-Regional Planning Study Group (1971). *A strategy for the sub-region* (Supplementary Report No. 5) "Countryside," Coventry, England: Author.

Craik, K.H. (1972). Psychological factors in landscape appraisal. *Environment and Behavior, 4*, 255–266.

Cresswell, R. (Ed.). (1977). *Passenger transport and the environment*. London: Hill.

Davies, D.R., & Jones, D.M. (1981). Hearing and noise. In W.T. Singleton (Ed.), *The body at work: Biological ergonomics*. Cambridge, England: Cambridge University Press.

Department of the Environment. (1972). *The estate outside the dwelling: Reactions of residents to aspects of housing layout*. London: Her Majesty's Stationery Office.

Dobbs, M.E. (1972). Behavioral responses to auditory stimulation during sleep. *Journal of Sound and Vibration, 20,* 467–476.

Donald, I.J. (1983). *The multivariate structure of office evaluation.* Unpublished master's thesis, University of Surrey, Guildford.

Donald, I.J. (1985). The cylindrex of place evaluation. In D. Canter (Ed.), *Facet theory: Approaches to social research.* New York: Springer-Verlag.

Donald, I.J., & Hedge, A. (1984, July, 25–29). Office evaluation: Sterile research on a fertile topic. Paper presented to IAPS 8, 8th International Conference on Environment and Human Action, West Berlin.

Duffield, B.S., & Coppock, J.T. (1975). The delineation of recreational landscapes: The role of a computer-based information system. *Transactions of the Institute of British Geographers, 66,* 141–148.

Duffy, F. (1974a). Office design and organisations: 1. Theoretical Basis. *Environment and Planning B, 1,* 105–118.

Duffy, F. (1974b). Office design and organisations: 2. The testing of a hypothetical model. *Environment and Planning B, 1,* 217–235.

Dunn, M.C. (1976). Landscape with photographs: Testing the preference approach to landscape evaluation. *Journal of Environmental Management, 4,* 15–26.

Ellis, P. (1982a). The phenomenology of defensible space. In P. Stringer (Ed.), *Confronting social issues: Applications of social psychology* (Vol. 1). London: Academic.

Ellis, P. (1982b). Shared outdoor space and shared meaning. *International Review of Applied Psychology, 31,* 209–222.

Ellis, P. (1983a, June). Institutional problems with design research in Britain. Paper to PAPER (People and Physical Environment Research Association) Conference, Wellington, New Zealand.

Ellis, P. (1983b, September 1–3). *Making buildings work: Should designers get involved in politics?* Paper given a the Conference on Designing for Building Utilisation, Portsmouth Polytechnic, Portsmouth.

Ellis, P. (1986). Functional, aesthetic and symbolic aspects of office lighting. In J.D. Wineman (Ed.), *Behavioural issues in office design.* New York: van Nostrand Reinhold.

Ellis, P., & Duffy, F. (1980, May). Lost office landscapes. *Management Today,* r47 FF.

Ellis, P., & Duffy, F. (1982). Design research in practice: Can it be scientific as well as respectable? Paper presented at the 7th International Association for the Study of People and their Physical Surroundings Conference, Barcelona, Spain.

Ellis, P., & Gaskell, G. (1978). *A review of social research on the individual energy consumer.* London: London School of Economics. Department of Social Psychology.

Evans, K. (1975). *Spatial relations in an infant school.* Unpublished doctoral dissertation, University of London.

Fanning, D.M. (1967). Families in flats. *British Medical Journal, 4,* 382.

Felce, D. (1982). The planning and evaluation of community based residences for severely and profoundly handicapped people. *Proceedings of NICHD Conference on the Impact of residential environments on retarded persons and thehir caregivers,* University of Washington, 1982. Baltimore, MD: University Park Press.

Fines, K.D. (1968). Landscape evaluation: A research project in East Sussex. *Regional Studies, 2,* 41–55.

Fisher, G. (1973). *The perceptual cartography project* (Report No. HR 848/1). London: Social Science Research Council.

Fisher, S. (1983a). Memory and search in loud noise. *Canadian Journal of Psychology, 37,* 439–449.

Fisher, S. (1983b). Pessimistic noise effects: The perception of reaction times in noise. *Canadian Journal of Psychology, 37,* 258–271.

Flindell, I.M. (1979). A combined laboratory and field study of traffic noise. *Proceedings of the Institute of Acoustics Spring Meeting,* Southampton, England.

Galton, F. (1883). *Inquiries into human faculties and its development.* Oxford, England: Oxford University Press.

Gaskell, P., & Ellis, P. (1982). Energy conservation: A psychological perspective on a multidisciplinary phenomenon. In P. Stringer (Ed.), *Confronting social issues: Applications of social psychology* (Vol. 1). London: Academic.

Getzels, J. (1975). Images of the classroom and visions of the learner. In T. David & B. Wright (Eds.), *Learning environments.* Chicago: University of Chicago Press.

Ginsburg, G.P. (Ed.). (1979). *Emerging strategies in social psychological research.* New York: Wiley.

Gold, J. (1980). *An introduction to behavioural geography.* Oxford, England: Oxford University Press.

Goodey, B., Duffett, A., Gold, J.R., & Spencer, D. (1971). *The city scene: An exploration into the image of central Birmingham as seen by area residents* (Research memorandum No. 10), University of Birmingham, Birmingham, England: Centre for Urban and Regional Studies.

Goodey, J., & Matthew, K. (1971). *Architects and information* (Research Paper No. 1). University of York, York, Institute of Advanced Architectural Studies.

Gould, P.R., & White, R. (1968). The mental maps of British school leavers. *Regional Studies, 2,* 161–182.

Gould, P.R., & White, R. (1974). *Mental maps.* Harmondsworth, England: Penguin.

Griffiths, I.D., & Delauzun, F.R. (1977). Individual differences in sensitivity to traffic noise: an empirical study. *Journal of Sound and Vibration, 55,* 93–107.

Griffiths, I.D., & Langdon, F.J. (1968). Subjective responses to road traffic noise. *Journal of Sound and Vibration, 8*, 16–32.

Griffiths, I.D., Langdon, F.J., & Swan, M.A. (1980). Subjective effects of traffic noise exposure: Reliability and seasonal effects. *Journal of Sound and Vibration, 71*, 227–240.

Groat, L. (1982). Meaning in post-modern architecture: An examination using the multiple sorting task. *Journal of Environmental Psychology, 2*, 3–22.

Gunzburg, H.C., & Gunzburg, A.L. (1979). "Normal" environment with a plus for mentally retarded children. In D. Canter & S. Canter (Eds.), *Designing for therapeutic environments: A review of research*. Chichester, England: Wiley.

Guttman, L. (1954). A new approach to factor analysis: The radex. In P.F. Lazarfeld (Ed.), *Mathematical thinking in the social sciences*. New York: Free Press.

Guttman, L. (1979, October). *New developments in integrating test design and analysis*. Paper presented to the 40th International Conference on Testing Problems on the Educational Testing Service. New York.

Harré, R., & Secord, P.F. (1972). *The explanation of social behaviour*. Oxford, England: Blackwell.

Hearnshaw, L.S. (1964). *A short history of British psychology, 1840–1940*. London: Methuen.

Hedge, A. (1982). The open-plan office: A systematic investigation of employee reactions to their environment. *Environment and Behavior, 14*, 519–542.

Hendry, L.B., & Matheson, P. (1979). Teachers and pupils in open-plan and conventional classrooms. *Scottish Educational Review, 11*, 107–117.

Herbertson, A.J. (1915). Regional environment, heredity and consciouisness. *Geographical Teacher, 8*, 147–153.

Hillier, B. (1973, November). In defence of space. *Royal Institute of British Architects, 80*, 539–544.

Hillier, B. (1983, November 30). Space syntax: A different urban perspective. *Architects Journal*, pp. 47–63.

Hillier, B., & Hanson, J. (1984). *The social logic of space*. Cambridge, England: Cambridge University Press.

Hockey, G.R.J. (1972). Effects of noise on human efficiency and some individual differences. *Journal of Sound and Vibration, 20*, 299–304.

James, G., & Swain, R. (1975, May). Learning bus routes using a tactual map. *New Outlook for the Blind*, 212–217.

Jarvis, C. (1976). *The organisation of space and space-use in the open-plan school*. Paper presented at the Sociology of Education Graduate Association Conference, Middlesex Polytechnic, London.

Jephcott, P. (1971). *Homes in high flats*. University of Glasgow, Department of Social and Economic Studies. Occasional Papers, No. 13, Edinburgh: Oliver and Boyd.

Jones, D.M., & Chapman, A.J. (1979). Stress after hours. In C. Makay & T. Cox (Eds.), *Responses to stress: Occupational aspects*. London: International Publishing Corp.

Jones, D.M., Chapman, A.J., & Auburn, T.C. (1981). Noise in the environment: A social perspective. *Journal of Environmental Psychology, 1*, 43–59.

Kelly, G.A. (1955). *The psychology of personal constructs* (Vols. 1–2). New York: Norton.

Kenny, C. (1983). *A multivariate model of hospital ward evaluation*. Unpublished doctoral dissertation, University of Surrey, Guildford.

Kenny, C., & Canter, D. (1981). A facet structure for nurses' evaluations of ward designs. *Journal of Occupational Psychology, 54*, 93–108.

Langdon, J. (1966). *Modern offices: A user survey*. London: Her Majesty's Stationery Office.

Langdon, F.J. (1976). Noise nuisance caused by road traffic in residential areas: Part 1. *Journal of Sound and Vibration, 47*, 243–263.

Langdon, F.J., & Buller, I.B. (1977). Road traffic noise and disturbance to sleep. *Journal of Sound and Vibration, 50*, 13–28.

Langdon, F.J., & Griffiths, I.D. (1982). Subjective effects of traffic noise exposure, II: Comparisons of noise indices, response scales, and the effects of changes in noise levels. *Journal of Sound and Vibration, 83*, 171–180.

Lawson, B.R., & Walters, D. (1974). The effects of a new motorway on an established residential area. In D. Canter & T. Lee (Eds.), *Psychology and the built environment*. London: Architectural Press.

Lee, T.R. (1954). *A study of neighbourhood*. Unpublished doctoral dissertation, University of Cambridge, Cambridge, England.

Lee, T.R. (1968). Urban neighbourhood as a socio-spatial schema. *Human Relations, 21*, 241–267.

Lee, T.R., & Tagg, S. (1976). The social severance effects of major urban roads. In P. Stringer & H. Wenzel (Eds.), *Transportation planning for a better environment*. London: Plenum.

Lera, S. (1982, May 28). At the point of decision. *Building*, 47–48.

Lera, S., Cooper, I., & Powell, J. (1983, September 1–3). *Designers and information*. Paper presented at Conference on Designing for Building Utilisation. Portsmouth Polytechnic, Portsmouth, England.

Leonard, J.A., & Newman, R.C. (1970). Three types of 'maps' for blind travel. *Ergonomics, 13*, 165–179.

Linton, P.L. (1968). The assessment of scenery as a natural resource. *Scottish Geographical Magazine, 84*, 219–238.

Lipman, A., Cooper, I., Harris, R., & Tranter, R. (1978). Power, a neglected concept in office design. *Journal of Architectural Research, 6*, 28–37.

Lowenthal, D., & Prince, H.C. (1976). Transcendental experience. In S. Wapner, S.B. Cohen, and B. Kaplan

(Eds.), *Experiencing the environment*. London: Plenum.

Lynch, K. (1960). *The image of the city*. Cambridge, MA: MIT Press.

Mackinder, M., & Marvin, H. (1982). *Design decision making in architectural practice* (Information Papper 11/82). Building Research Establishment.

Manning, P. (Ed.). (1965). *Office design: A study of environment*. Liverpool, England: University of Liverpool, Department of Building Science.

Manning, P. (Ed.). (1967). *The primary school: An environment for education*. Liverpool, England: Liverpool University, Department of Building Science, Pilkington Research Unit.

Mawby, R.I. (1977). Defensible space: A theoretical and empirical appraisal. *Urban Studies, 14*, 169–179.

McDougall, W. (1908). *Introduction to social psychology*. London: Methuen.

McIntyre, D.A., & Griffiths, I.D. (1974). The thermal environment: Buildings and people. In D. Canter & T. Lee (Eds.). *Psychology and the built environment*. London: Architectural Press.

McKennell, A.C. (1963). *Aircraft noise annoyance around London (Heathrow) Airport, government social survey, SS337*. London: Her Majesty's Stationery Office.

Miles, H., & Canter, D. (1976). *Energy conservation in British Universities*. University of Surrey, Guildford.

MIL Research Ltd. (1971). *Second survey of aircraft noise annoyance around London (Heathrow) Airport*. London: Her Majesty's Stationery Office.

Murray, D., & Spencer, C. (1979). Individual differences in the drawing of cognitive maps: The effects of geographical mobility, strength of mental imagery and basic graphic ability. *Transactions of the Institute of British Geographers, N.S.4*, 385–391.

Myers, C.S. (1911). *Text book of experimental psychology*. Cambridge, England: Cambridge University Press.

Neisser, U. (1976). *Cognition and reality: Principles and implications of cognitive psychology*. San Francisco: Freeman.

Newman, O. (1972). *Defensible space*. New York: Macmillan.

Nuffield Provincial Hospital Trust (1955). *Studies in the function and design of hospitals*. London: Oxford University Press.

O'Cathain, C. (1976). Motor traffic noise and housing. In P. Stringer & H. Wenzel (Eds.), *Transportation planning for a better environment*. London: Plenum.

O'Connor, M. (1977). *Your child's primary school*. London: Pan Original.

Olsen, M.E., & Goodnight, J.A. (1977). *Social aspects of energy conservation* (Study Module 18, Final Report). Northwest Energy Policy Project, Seattle.

ORBIT *Information Technology and Office Design Orbit Report*. London: Duffy, Eley, Giffone, and Worthington.

Pearson, E. (1971). *Trends in school design*. London: Macmillan.

Peled, A. (1975). *The spaciality of situations*. Unpublished doctoral dissertation, University of Strathclyde, Glasgow.

Penning-Rowsell, E.C. (1974). Landscape evaluation for development plans. *Journal of the Royal Town Planning Institute, 60*, 930–934.

Penning-Rowsell, E.C. (1980). The social value of English landscapes. In G.H. Elsner & R.C. Smardon (Eds.), *Our national landscape: A conference on applied techniques for analysis and management of the visual resource* (Report No. PSW-35). Berkeley, California: U.S. Forest Service.

Penning-Rowsell, E.C. (1981). Fluctuating fortunes in gauging landscape value. *Progress in Human Geography, 5*, 25–41.

Penning-Rowsell, E.C., Gullett, G.H., Searle, G.H., & Witham, S.A. (1977). *Public evaluation of landscape quality* (Report No. 13). London: Middlesex Polytechnic Planning Research Group.

Penning-Rowsell, E.C., & Searle, G.H. (1977). The 'Manchester' landscape evaluation method: A critical appraisal. *Landscape Research, 2*, 6–11.

Phillips, N., & Nelson, E. (1976). Energy savings in private households—An integrated research programme. *Journal of the Market Research Society, 18*(4), 180–200.

Piaget, J., & Inhelder, B. (1967). *The child's conceptions of space*. London: Routledge.

Piche, D. (1977). *The geographical understanding of children aged 5–8 years*. Unpublished doctoral dissertation, London School of Economics, London.

Pocock, D.C.D. (1972). Perspective and urban perception. *Architectural Psychology Newsletter, 2*, 1–6.

Pocock, D.C.D. (1975). *Durham: Images of a cathedral city* [Occasional Publication (New Series) 6]. Durham, England: University of Durham, Department of Geography.

Pocock, D.C.D. (1976). Some characteristics ot mental maps: An empirical study. *Transactions of the Institute of British Geographers, N.S.1*, 493–512.

Pocock, D.C.D. (1979). The contribution of mental maps in perception studies. *Geography, 64*, 279–287.

Pocock, D.C.D., & Hudson, R. (1978). *Images of the urban environment*. London: Macmillan.

Powell, J., & Nichols, T. (1981). The utilisation of technical information in the design of buildings. In E. Gibb *Transfer and Exploitation of Scientific and Technical Information*. EEC Document, G.E.C.

Power, A. (1982). *Priority estates project 1982. Improving problem council estates: A summary of aims and progress*. London: Department of the Environment.

Power, A. (1984). *Local housing management: A priority estates project survey*. London: Department of the Environment.

Poyner, B. (1980). *A study of street attacks and their environmental settings*. London: Tavistock Institute of Human Relations.

Poyner, B. (1983). *Design against crime: Beyond defensible space*. Kent, England: Butterworth.

Proshansky, H., Ittelson, W., & Rivlin, L. (Eds.). (1976). *Environmental psychology: People and their physical settings* (2nd ed.). New York: Holt, Rinehart & Winston.

Rabbitt, P.M.A. (1979). Current paradigms and models in human information processing. In V. Hamilton & D.M. Warburton (Eds.), *Human stress and cognition* (pp. 115–140). Chichester, England: Wiley.

Richer, J. (1979). Physical environments for autistic children—Four case studies. In D. Canter & S. Canter (Eds.), *Designing for therapeutic environments: A review of research*. Chichester, England: Wiley.

Richman, N. (1974). The effects of housing on pre-school children and their mothers. *Developmental Medicine and Child Neurology, 16*, 53–58.

Riley, S., & Palmer, J. (1976). Of attitudes and latitudes: A repertory grid study of perceptions of seaside resorts. In P. Slater (Ed.), *The measurement of interpersonal space by grid technique* (Vol. 1). Chichester, England: Wiley.

Robinson, D.W., Bowsher, J.M., & Copeland, W.C. (1963). On judging the noise from aircraft in flight. *Acustica, 13*, 324–336.

Rothenberg, J.G., & Heggie, I.G. (Eds.). (1974). *Transport and the urban environment*. London: Macmillan.

Sarré, P.V. (1972). Perception: Unit 16. In *New Trends in Geography* (pp. 10–43). Milton Keynes: Open University.

Schein, E.H. (1965). *Organisational Psychology*. Englewood Cliffs, NJ: Prentice-Hall.

Sime, J.D. (1980). The concept of panic. In D. Canter (Ed.), *Fires and human behaviour*. Chichester, England: Wiley.

Smith, A.P. (1983a). The effects of noise and memory load on a running memory task. *British Journal of Psychology, 74*, 439–445.

Smith, A.P. (1983b). The effects of noise and time on task on recall of order information. *British Journal of Psychology, 74*, 83–89.

Smith, P.F. (1974). *The dynamics of urbanism*. London: Hutchinson.

Smith, P.K. (1974). *The design of learning spaces*. London: Council for Educational Technology.

Sommer, R. (1980). *Farmers markets of America: A renaissance*. Santa Barbara, CA: Capra.

Spencer, C. (1981). The new social psychology and its relation to environmental psychology. *Journal of Environmental Psychology, 1*, 329–336.

Spencer, C., & Darvizeh, Z. (1981a). The case for developing a cognitive environmental psychology that does not underestimate the abilities of young children. *Journal of Environmental Psychology, 1*, 21–31.

Spencer, C., & Darvizeh, Z. (1981b). Young children's descriptions of their local environment. *Environmental Education and Information, 1*, 275–284.

Spencer, C., & Darvizeh, Z. (1983). Young children's place-descriptions, maps and route finding: A comparison of nursery school children in Iran and Britain. *International Journal of Early Childhood, 15*, 26–31.

Spencer, C., & Dixon, J. (1983). Mapping the development of feelings about the city: A longitudinal study of new residents' affective maps. *Transactions of the Institute of British Geographers, N.S.8*, 373–383.

Spencer, C., Harrison, N., & Darvizeh, Z. (1980). The development of iconic mapping ability in young children. *International Journal of Early Childhood, 12*, 57–64.

Spencer, C., & Taylor, K. (1980). Further observations on pupils in open-plan and conventional classrooms. *Scottish Educational Review, 12*, 108–112.

Spencer, C., & Weetman, M. (1981). The microgenesis of cognitive maps: A longitudinal study of new residents of an urban area. *Transactions of the Institute of British Geographers, N.S.6*, 375–384.

Spencer, D. (1973). *An evaluation of cognitive mapping in neighbourhood perception* (Research memorandum No. 23). Birmingham, England: University of Birmingham, Centre for Urban and Regional Studies.

Spencer, D. (1981). The new social psychology and its relation to environment psychology. *Journal of Environmental Psychology 1*(4), 329–336.

Stewart, W.F.R. (1970). *Children in flats: A family study*. London: National Society for the Prevention of Cruelty to Children.

Strathclyde Regional Council (1976) *Primary School Building Report*. Author, Glasgow, Scotland: Department of Education.

Stringer, P. (1970). Architecture, psychology, the game's the same. In D.V. Canter (Ed.), *Architectural psychology*. London: Royal Institute of British Architects.

Stringer, P. (1974). Individual differences in the construing of shopping centre redevelopment proposals. In D. Canter & T. Lee (Eds.), *Environmental psychology—Psychology and the built environment*. London: Architectural Press.

Stringer, P. (1976). Repertory grids in the study of environmental perception. In P. Slater (Ed.), *The measurement of interpersonal space by grid technique* (Vol. 1). Chichester, England: Wiley.

Stringer, P., & Pearce, P.L. (1984). Towards a symbiosis of social psychology and tourism studies. *Annuls of tourism research* (Vol. 11, pt. 1), 5–17.

Stringer, P., & Wenzel, H. (Eds.). (1976). *Transportation planning for a better environment*. London: Plenum.

Tagg, S.K. (1974). The subjective meanings of rooms:

Some analyses and investigations. In D. Canter, & T. Lee (Eds.), *Psychology and the built environment*. London: Architectural Press.

Thompson, J. (1985). *Psychological aspects of nuclear war*. Chichester, England: Wiley.

Thomson, R. (1968). *The Pelican history of psychology*. Harmondsworth, England: Penguin.

Tong, D., & Canter, D. (1985). Informative warnings: In situ evaluations of fire alarms. *Fire Safety Journal, 9*, pp. 267–279.

Tong, D.A., & Griffiths, I.D. (1982, September 26–29). *The subjective economics of energy conserving goods: A heuristic investigation*. Paper presented at the International Conference on Consumer Behaviour and Energy Policy, Noordwijkerhout, Netherlands.

Turner, T.H.D. (1977). Landscape evaluation. *Town and Country Planning, 45*, 282–293.

Tyerman, C., & Canter, D. (1983). A taxonomy of small hostels for alcoholics. *Drug and Alcohol Dependence, 11*, 225–231.

Tyerman, C., & Spencer, C. (1980). Normalised physical environment for the mentally handicapped, and its effects on patterns of activity, social relations and self-help skills. *British Journal of Mental Subnormality, 26*, 47–54.

Walters, D. (1975). The acoustic environment. In D. Canter & P. Stringer (Eds.), *Environmental interaction*. London: Surrey University Press.

Wells, B.W.P. (1964). *Office design and the office worker*. Unpublished doctoral dissertation, University of Liverpool, Liverpool, England.

Wells, B.W.P. (1965). Subjective responses to the lighting installation in a modern office building and their design implications. *Building Science, 1*, 51–68.

Wilkinson, R.T. (1980). Effects of traffic noise upon sleep in the home: Subjective report, EEG and performance the next day. In W.P. Koella (Ed.), *Sleep 1980: Fifth European Congress of Sleep Research*. Basel, West Germany: Karger.

Wilkinson, R.T., & Cambell, K.B. (1984). Effects of traffic noise on quality of sleep: Assessment by EEG, subjective report or performance the next day. *Journal of the Acoustic Society of America, 75*, 468–475.

Wolff, P. (1979). The adventure playground as a therapeutic environment. In D. Canter & S. Canter (Eds.), *Designing for therapeutic environments: A review of research*. Chichester, England: Wiley.

Wood, D. (1973). *I don't want to but I will—The genesis of geographic knowledge: A real time development study of adolescent images of novel environments*. Worcester, MA: Clark University, Cartographic Laboratory.

Wood, D., & Beck, R. (1976). Talking with Environmental A, an experimental mapping language. In G.T. Moore & R.G. Golledge (Eds.), *Environmental Knowing*. Stroudsburg, PA: Dowden, Hutchinson & Ross.

Chapter 37

ENVIRONMENTAL PSYCHOLOGY IN THE SOVIET UNION

Toomas Niit, *Department of Sociology, Institute of History, Tallinn, Estonia, U.S.S.R.*

Mati Heidmets *and* **Jüri Kruusvall,** *Environmental Psychology Research Unit, Tallinn Pedagogic Institute, Tallinn, Estonia, U.S.S.R.*

37.1. GENERAL FEATURES OF THE RESEARCH

37.1.1. Development of the Environmental Psychological Approach

At the end of the 1960s and the beginning of the 1970s several problems connected with natural and human environments caught the attention of the Soviet people. It was understood that the human-made environment and the extent of its detachment from nature have considerable influences (both positive and negative) on social life—that the principle "the newer (more artificial) the better" is not always valid everywhere. According to Gvishiani,

> The question nowadays is not only "what does the scientific and technical revolution give to mankind," [but also] how it transforms and influences its culture, way of life, interaction patterns, and relations with nature. In these matters, it is not possible to

be limited to prophesies and utopian opinions only. The primary task of humankind is not only to predict the development and consequences of the scientific and technical revolutions but also to control and direct them. (Gvishiani, 1976, p. 23)

The first treatments of people's relations with human-made environments were mostly philosophical or popular in their nature, delineating the problems and calling for more thorough research in this field (Tonev, 1970; Yanitsky, 1967). Prompted by widespread environmental issues within Soviet Society, the first scientific studies were written and published in this field. Interest emerged simultaneously among several professional groups—architects, city planners, and environmental designers. As their general interest in human beings, culture, and social processes increased, several empirical studies in this area were carried out. Kartashova, Timyashevskaya, Savchenko, Rouge, Kogan, Kaganov, and others were pioneers in this field.

Another professional group was social and behavioral scientists whose interest concentrated on social and psychological problems of human–environment relations. Yanitsky, Baranov, Yankova, and Travin were perhaps the best-known names in this tradition. At the beginning of the 1970s, the first group of environmental psychologists began to form at the sociological laboratory of Tartu State University, which was the basis for the research unit (Kruusvall, Heidmets, Niit, Raudsepp) that exists at the present time at Tallinn Pedagogic Institute. Still another group of researchers emphasizes geographical perspectives on people–environment relations (Barbash, Kostinsky, Raitviir).

The previously mentioned approaches differed from one another in terminology, problem areas, and methods. Recently, the architectural, geographical, and social-psychological trends have, to a certain extent, converged, but even at the present time they exist as separate theoretical entities.

As environmental research in the Soviet Union stems from several different sources, the range of problems studied is very wide. Therefore, we can only conventionally use the label *environmental psychology* (we could speak about environmental sociology, environmental culturology, environmental semiotics, etc.). Although the label *environmental psychology* is used mostly by the psychological researchers (the other schools use labels like: *architectural social problems, psychological basis for environmental design, sociogeography,* etc.), we use it to embrace the whole research area.

Before analyzing the different trends of Soviet environmental psychology more thoroughly, we will introduce some principles of the Soviet philosophical tradition that have influenced the conceptualization of environmental problems in this country.

37.1.2. Philosophical Background

The dialectical materialistic world view determines several approaches that have profoundly influenced environmental studies in the Soviet Union. The most important are the historical-developmental approach to social events, the dialectical treatment of developmental process, and interpreting phenomena in their social context. What do all these approaches mean for environmental psychology?

The historical approach to human–environment relations has as its focus that the existing forms of these relations are the result of a certain developmental process. We can understand social functions and the inner logic of certain environmental phenomena (as, for instance, privacy, crowding, territoriality, etc.) only by analyzing their *development* and historical changes at different stages of social organization of the society. The types of relations between persons and environments are not everlasting and unchanging; environmental phenomena without temporal perspective have only form but lack (social) content. A prerequisite of the dialectical approach to development process is recognizing contradiction as the main determiner of development. For psychology (including environmental psychology), the dialectical contradictions between individuals and social processes, between the independence of an individual and his or her dependence on society, are the essential ones (see Abulkhanova, 1973, pp. 192–194). The dialectical nature of their relation is based on the antagonism of both polar entities and their simultaneous unity--one cannot exist without the other; their mutual "struggle" is the basis for their development.

Physical objects do not appear in these processes as independent units but are included in the general process of social development, being, as a rule, means of action for social subjects. Thus the physical environment is a component of social development, and changes in the physical environment can be understood only in their social context. This is the method of taking the social context into account in environmental psychology. The determining factor, in the end, is the social environment—humans and their places in the social system. It is important to know how persons are connected with the social system because "society is not simply a social environment; a person is an organic part of it, connected into social relations through his or her actions. The qualities of person as a subject of action develop by functioning in this system" (Lomov, 1981, p. 7).

37.1.3. Psychological Viewpoint: Environmental Psychology as an Extension of Traditional Psychology

What is environmental psychology as compared to traditional Soviet psychology? During the whole course of its existence, the research areas of psychology have widened. Beside the person as its main object of investigation, all spheres connected with human activity, step by step, have come to be embraced under its research umbrella.

Environmental psychology is another extension of psychological science. It makes an attempt to determine the role of the physical environment in human behavior and relations. As an attempt to systematize things and phenomena more and more in an objective direction, it is obvious that there is a need for environmental psychology. It does not matter whether we call it *environmental psychology* or give to it some other label; psychology becomes more and more environmental. Therefore, environmental psychology is nothing extraordinary; it is just another stage in the development of psychological thought.

We could point out two new features in the *conceptualizations of humans* that environmental psychology has advanced. First is the acknowledgment of the importance of the physical environment in psychological research. Environmental psychology is often defined as investigation of relations between humans and the physical environment. This definition seems to be only partly correct. In fact, the physical environment, as such, very rarely relates directly with human activity. Its influence and "activities" are, as a rule, socially mediated. Thus it is not reasonable to abstract the physical environment from the rest of the environment and declare it to be the only object of interest in environmental psychology. It is more appropriate to treat environmental psychology as a school of thought trying to unite influences coming from the physical environment with other environmental components and analyzing the transactions of persons and their environment as a whole.

As the last developments show just the previously mentioned tendency, the second new trend could be the general orientation to the "integral molar environment"—that is, human behaviors and relations are treated together with all the environmental components, with environment as an integral *system*.

The main problems of contemporary environmental psychology arise from the previously mentioned two features. First, how can we include the "newly discovered" physical environment in the system of psychological knowledge? What is the role of the physical environment in human activities and rela-

tions? Second, how may we use this orientation to the "integral environment"? What does this "integral whole" consist of? How do human beings function in this environment?

Environmental psychology, with its aim to integrate, fits well into the traditional picture of Soviet psychology, some principles of which can be transferred directly to environmental psychology studies. Generally speaking, Soviet psychology is first and foremost the *psychology of action*. Human beings are treated as active subjects whose psychological and social qualities are determined, in the first place, by external, object-related activities. Activity is the main link that connects the person (in his or her historical development as well as in his or her ontogenesis) to the surrounding world. Such activity changes the environment and transforms persons. "What man has become is the result of his activity, the level of development of tools he uses, and his social organization" (Leontyev, 1975, p. 22). Several postulates of the theory of action have also determined the development of Soviet environmental psychology. We could mention the following.

First is the unity of humans and their environment, their inseparableness: They are bound together by action. "Unity of such antagonistic sources as subject and object is based on action...Subject and object are components of an integral system, only within the boundaries of which they can be treated in their completeness" (Davydov, Zinchenko, and Talyzina, 1982, p. 62). Thus the "environmental nature" of a subject is one of the main postulates of action theory.

Second is the primary role of object-related activity in the development of humans. The essential form of activity for the theory of action is external activity, activity directed toward environmental objects. Only in the course of such activity do the inner mental processes take shape, that is, the external becomes internal. "The internalization does not mean that external activities are transferred into an existing internal level of consciousness. In the course of this process, the inner level is formed" (Leontyev, 1975, p. 98). Hence, there is the utmost importance of "environmental activity" in the process of human beings' development, in the formation of their minds. It is possible to understand cognitive processes (memory, imagery, etc.) and their logic only by analyzing external activities because these are in accordance with them.

Third, we have action as mediator of environmental influence. In the context of this theory, the direct relation of human/physical environment is not valid. The physical environment can influence humans only through action or social relations. It is a component of actions or relations and, it directs, restricts, or organizes them.

Therefore, the psychological trend in Soviet environmental psychology, based on the theory of action, proceeds first and foremost from the person. It investigates environmental problems through the prism of human activities and relations. On the other hand, for the "environmental trend," the human-made environment and the problems of its creation and design are of the utmost importance.

37.1.4. Environmental Viewpoint: Looking for the Meaning and Social Functions of the Human-Made Environment

Although the theory of action as a starting point is similar more or less for all the representatives of the psychological trend, the situation among the representatives of the "environmental viewpoint" (i.e., architects, geographers, environmental designers, etc.) is much more complicated.

We can point out four main trends in this field. One is trying to find out the "social requirements" of architecture. The representatives of this group — mostly architects — try to find out the wishes and needs concerning apartment planning, the location of service establishments, and the like among different groups of the population by using statistical data analysis and interviewing. They make proposals based on the results of their research for improving architectural planning (e.g., Rouge, 1983; Rubanenko & Kartashova, 1982). Some purely sociological studies about city life, human-made environment, and the like have been carried out in this field (e.g., Baranov, 1981; Travin, 1979; Yankova, 1979).

Second is searching for the meaning and sociocultural functions of architectural environment. This kind of research is also carried out mostly by architects. The aim of such research is either to analyze the problems of architectural semiotics (Kaganov, in press; Rappaport, 1981) or to deal with the human-made environment in a culturological context (Glazychev, 1982; Kogan, 1982). The representatives of this trend often use the term *environmental approach*.

Third is looking for the psychological basis of designing things. This trend is based mostly on perception psychology and ergonomics. Its aim is the optimization of the world of things, according to the laws of psychology and ergonomics (Han-Magomedov, 1982). Some general theoretical conceptions have been also formed in this field (Zelenov, 1980).

Fourth is the socio-geographical trend. Geographers try to connect the geographical approach with social science approaches. As the result of this, there are several studies about dividing urban territories into zones and about the perception of these zones by the inhabitants (Barbash, 1981). Some research has been carried out in the field of settlement typology and different regional ways of life (Raitviir, 1979).

All the previously mentioned trends depend greatly on the "basic sciences" (theory of architecture, geography, etc.). They find expression in the terminology and in the researchers' "environment-centered" way of thinking. Therefore, the best results in Soviet environmental psychology have been achieved with the collaboration of psychologists/sociologists and architects/planners — when "person-centered" and "environment-centered" approaches have been combined. In the next sections, we will devote our main attention to these kinds of studies.

37.1.5. Organizational Activities

At the present time, there may be about 200 to 300 researchers whose work can be considered to be environmental psychology. At the same time, there are probably no more than 10 people who call themselves environmental psychologists. Based on one major conference in Lohusalu, Estonia, in 1983, at least 40% of interested people are architects and city planners; 15% are psychologists; another 15% are sociologists; and 10% are geographers. The remainder consist of philosophers, educators, economists, and art historians (A similar analysis of a conference in Lohusalu, in 1981, has been presented by Saarinen [1982]). The range of research institutions, where problems of environmental psychology are dealt with, is wide. The previously mentioned conference had participants from 20 cities, including such faraway places as Dushanbe, Lvov, Baku, Kiev, Novosibirsk, Tashkent, Sverdlovsk, Moscow, Leningrad, Simpheropol, Tbilisi, and Tallinn.

In most cases, there are single researchers working at various institutions. The centers where the number of interested people is larger are the Central Research Institute of Theory and History of Architecture, in Moscow (Glazychev, Rappaport, Zabelshansky, etc.), the Research Institute of Theory, History, and Perspectives of Soviet Architecture, in Kiev (Marder, Zinchenko, etc.), the Department of Architecture at Lvov Polytechnic Institute (Durmanov, Bevz, Krivoruchko), the Central Research and Experimental Planning Institute of Residential Buildings (Kartashova, Orlov, Koloskov, Albanov, Ovsyannikov, etc.), the All-Union Research Institute of Industrial Design (VNIITE), in Moscow (Kaganov and others), and its branches, the Institute of Geography of the U.S.S.R. Academy of Sciences (Barbash, Kostinsky, and others), the Institute of Socioeconomic Studies of the U.S.S.R. Academy of Sciences, in Leningrad (Travin, Rzhevskaya, and others), and the previously mentioned Environmental Psychology Research Unit at Tallinn Pedagogic Institute.

Information about the studies being done and information exchange is limited due to the absence of both newsletters and organization that could bind the researchers together. The distances between research centers are large (e.g., it is 12,000 km from Tallinn to Vladivostok). The only way to be informed about what is going on is to attend various conferences and symposia. We could mention the conference entitled "The Development of Ergonomics in the System of Design," in Borzhomi, Georgia, in 1979 (*Abstracts* 1979), the symposium entitled "Typology of the World of Things," at Gorki, in 1980 (Zelenov, 1980), three conferences — "Man and Environment: Psychological Aspects" and "Psychology and Architecture" — at Lohusalu, Estonia, in 1981 and 1983, and "The Sociopsychological Basis of Environmental Design" at Loksa, Estonia in 1985 (Niit, Heidmets, & Kruusvall, 1981, 1983a, 1985), the seminar entitled "Social Problems and Architecture of Mass Residential Construction," in 1982 in Moscow (Kartashova & Kanayeva, 1985), the conference entitled "The Results of Applied Sociological Research of the City and Residential Buildings" (cf. Kutyryov, 1986), in Novosibirsk, in 1983, and the conference entitled "The Ergonomic and Psychological Problems of Designing Environments for Human Activities at Industrial Enterprises" at Telavi, Georgia, in 1983 (Bigvava, 1983). The social geographers, design theorists, and others have also begun to organize their own conferences.

University courses in environmental psychology are not widespread in the Soviet Union. The authors of the present review teach such courses in Estonia to the psychologists at Tartu State University and to interior designers at the Estonian State Institute of Art. Usually, the social-behavioral science knowledge of architects is restricted to courses in ergonomics; the few exceptions known to us are the courses Social Aspects of Residential Design at Moscow Institute of Architecture (Kartashova) and Sociology of Residential and Public Buildings at Byelorussian Polytechnic Institute (cf. Hachatryants, 1983).

37.2. THEORETICAL APPROACHES

37.2.1. Introduction

Both Marxist epistemology as well as the experience of practical research show that the study of human behavior without taking the qualities of the environment where a person lives into account does not give authentic results. Therefore, as a rule, most disciplines dealing with human beings (including psychology) advance sooner or later to the environmental viewpoint, trying to approach the human being in his or her "wholeness." Human beings are surrounded by an outer world that exists independently from them and forms their environment. Humans' behavior can be influenced by environmental processes that take place in the near as well as distant surroundings (a person may not even be aware of these processes). A person's perception of the environment and his or her subjective attitude toward it have also developed in interaction with the environment and are objective to their character.

Different researchers pay attention to different aspects of the human–environment relations. That accounts for differences in the way the environment is viewed as an object of investigation. The different interpretations of the environment were important themes of discussion at both Lohusalu conferences (see Niit, Heidmets, & Kruusvall, 1981, 1983a).

The following approaches can be distinguished: (1) Some authors take, as the basis, the ways of organizing the environment proceeding from the person (subject) (person-centered theories); and (2) another group of authors tries to model the structure of the environment and the influence of the environment on human beings (environmental theories).

Two person-centered approaches to environment can be distinguished. First, the environment is treated as a person's subjective, integral, and continuous perceptual image of one's surroundings, where separate objects are not distinguished. A person perceives his or her surroundings in accordance with his or her environmental state (that cannot be described objectively) in a way that is characteristic to that person alone and that often determines one's behavior in different places.

Second, the environment is divided into parts, according to their different entrances into the activity of the subject. A person controls different spheres of the environment to different degrees and identifies oneself with them (e.g., the degree of personalization). Different subjects have different structures of environmental control. The basis of these differences is human interaction, and this environment is influenced by a person's own actions as well as by wider social processes.

Three types of environmental approaches can be distinguished. First, the environment is multistructural, and therefore, it is only natural to divide it into parts and types, which proceed from different disciplines dealing with human beings and which have different research aims. Every such differentiated part of the environment (e.g., psychological, geographical, juridical) has its specific features. A person's activities in different parts of the environment and the interrelations between those parts cannot be compared. To achieve a complete picture of a person's relations with the environment as a whole, it is necessary to collect data from as many spheres as possible.

Second, the environment is an integral system, and the relations of its separate parts with a person (as an integral being) can be measured on the same scale. General laws exist that characterize the relations between humans and their environment. The influence of the environment as a whole on a human being depends on whether the qualities of different parts of the environment are in mutual accord or disaccord. The term *environment* can be used in theoretical approaches and in interpreting the research results, but it cannot be used in empirical studies because it has no operational content.

Third, there is a trend, proceeding from traditional environmental psychology and dealing with the influence of different sociophysical environments (e.g., behavior settings) on humans' actions.

These approaches are not mutually exclusive; rather, they are definitions of the environment that various groups of researchers rely on in their studies. Several such conceptions were presented in the proceedings of the Lohusalu conferences (cf. Niit, Heidmets, Kruusvall, 1981, pp. 13–74; Niit, Heidmets, & Kruusvall, 1983a, Vol. 1, pp. 14–173). Usually they are fragmented or situation- (environment-) specific; there are very few elaborated models.

Next we present several examples of theoretical approaches. The conceptualizations of Heidmets and Mihhailov are examples of the subject-centered approach. Kruusvall discusses the relations between different parts of the environment and their influence on the way of life of the subject (an example of the second type of approach mentioned previously). Savchenko's model represents a paradigmatic approach to architectural environment, and Niit tries to connect different levels of analysis and concepts in dealing with human–environment relations. Whereas the first models are explanatory, the last two are methodological schemes for research.

37.2.2. Approaches to the Environment Emanating from the Subject

Several researchers have conceptualized the environment emanating from the subject. In this case, the environment consists of the objects and phenomena of the outer world that are objectively connected with the subject's everyday activities (Heidmets, 1983a, p. 61; Kaganov, 1983, p. 49).

The most important features of this approach are the following:

1. The observation unit can only be the "subject–environment" system; none of the two poles can be fully treated independently (Heidmets, 1983b, p. 47).

2. It is not correct to observe the subject and the environment as being mutually influential but at the same time separate units. The environment is connected with the subject's functioning and is an inseparable part of every subject (Abzianidze & Dzhorbenadze, 1983, p. 57).

3. The development of the subject takes place through "occupying" the environment (Kaganov, 1983, p. 49). In the process of this development, the subject "builds" himself or herself into the outer world of objects, ideas, and people (Heidmets, 1983b, p. 65), whereas the structure and qualities of this world determine the future qualities of this subject (Mihhailov, 1983, p. 46).

Let us have a closer look at two theoretical conceptions, emanating from the previously mentioned viewpoints. Heidmets, (1980, 1983b) in his model of "environmental subject," proceeds from the historical development of society and the changes in relations between the subject and the environment that have taken place in the course of their development. Following the individual's historical development into an autonomous subject, we can point out three kinds of changes in his or her relations with the outer world: (1) development of *control* over a certain part of the environment by the person; (2) *separating* the controlled part of the environment *socially*, that is, limiting the influence of other subjects in this environment; and (3) *identification* with the controlled/separated environment, the feeling its being of one's "own."

Hence, humans' formation as subjects occurs with the help of the environment; in the course of this process a part of the environment becomes one's "own" for a person objectively because he or she controls and separates it—as well as subjectively—he or she perceives it as valuable and essential, as a part of oneself. Historically, the first objects through which humans realized their subjectiveness were evidently their own bodies and activities. This controlled sphere extended to the nearest environment (home, domestic objects), and later on it developed still further.

The development of human dwellings serves as a good example of how every historically "new" subject needs his or her own environment (his or her own object of control). That is why the primary commune dwelling has, in the course of historical development, become differentiated into the numerous dwellings of nuclear families (for more detailed information, see Heidmets, 1983b, pp. 48–51).

Therefore, every subject is inevitably an "environmental phenomenon" (in addition to an individual, a group, or an organization can also be subjects), but it is necessary for their existence as subjects to incorporate into themselves a certain number of objects from the outer world through which they can realize their subjectiveness. These objects may be either physical (things, places), intellectual (thoughts, ideas), or social (people, other subjects) in their character. Proceeding from the previously mentioned division of objects into three classes, we can depict "the environmental subject" schematically as shown in Figure 37.1.

In Figure 37.1 the disrupted boundary marks the identification border between the subject and the world—inside the boundary are objects perceived as one's "own"; outside is the "strange" world.

Such an "extension" of the subject into the environment seems to be one of the driving needs in social life. At the same time, "the incorporated environments" are the main arena where relations between subjects and changes in these relations are determined.

What could such an approach to a subject give to environmental psychology? Theoretically, it enables one to observe the components of the environment functioning in an integral system that is determined by the activities of a social subject and his or her social relations. Therefore, we have not got two different realities (an environment that influences human beings and a human being who changes the environment) but an integral system where we can speak about transaction not between subject and environment but between different subjects. Practically, proceeding from the subject gives a basis for understanding the spatial structure of existing human-made environments and their tendencies toward change [cf. Heidmets, 1983b, pp. 51–65]).

The main idea of Mihhailov (1983) is also the merging of the subject and the environment. He observes this process against the background of humans' relations with the city environment. The basic quality of a city environment, according to him, is marginality. It finds expression in the antagonism between *street* and *yard*, the first of which represents the open, communicative pole of city, the other, the closed pole that helps the subject to develop. In the present-day city, the street has begun to dominate over the yard. The street as a borderline determines the marginality of the city environment. The marginal state of the environment also conditions the marginal subject: In the case of the city, it is expressed in "the state of intertwinement of the subject and environment, which has the structure of street/yard" (Mihhailov, 1983, p. 48). Here is a field for environmental researchers and architects—to take counteraction against the marginalization of subjects by creating a "nonmarginal" environment.

37.2.3. Environment as an Integrated Whole

According to Kruusvall's (1980) model, the environment that surrounds humans consists of four self-regulating parts (natural, activity, social, and cultural environments), the interrelations of which find realization at three different levels (humans, immediate environment, metaenvironment).

As a *living being*, humans belong to the *natural environment* where interactions between different species and populations are regulated by narrower and wider ecosystems and life activities are influenced by topography, soil, climate, water conditions, and the like. People who act together, the instruments they use for their activities, and their interrelations in the course of these actions (the division of labor, instruments, and distribution of products) form the *activity environment* where humans are (depending on their freedom of activity) *subjects* of activity. Regulation in an activity environment takes place according to laws of economy; the metaenvironment is determined by the prevailing social mode of production. The *social environment* determines humans'

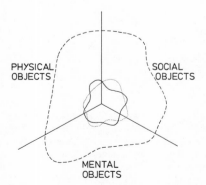

Figure 37.1. A model of an "environmental subject", _____ boundary of separation, ... boundary of control, - - - - - - - - - - - - - boundary of identification.

stable group relations, gives to each member of a group social status and roles and regulates interrelations between large social groups—classes. Society as a social metaenvironment is based on the organizational structure of the institutions of social control. A human being as a *personality* is opposed to the social environment. This personality develops through positions and roles acquired in the course of life into a permanent complex of interactional traits. The *cultural environment* fixes and passes on modes of action and behavior, systems of values, models of objects, social institutions, and the like that are accepted by a certain group of people (society). The structure of the cultural environment is formed by cultural complexes that may be connected with the activity environment (agro culture, car culture, trade culture, etc.), with a social group (class, family, etc.), or with a certain population group (nation, culture of a certain village, etc.). Humans as *individuals* follow cultural standards selectively, adding new features to them that proceed from their personal experience.

Dispositional interrelations between those different environments are important from the viewpoint of the integrity of the environment (see Figure 37.2). Thus the stability of the natural environment is a necessary precondition for the development of a cultural environment; the stability of a cultural environment is a precondition for the development of a social environment; the stability of a social environment is a precondition for the development of an activity environment, the stability of which is, in turn, important for the development of certain aspects of the natural environment. The developmental processes in some part of the environment inevitably cause changes in other parts of the environment (causal relations). The development of an activity environment causes a disruption in the stability of the social environment (which will be solved by the changes in the latter). The development of the social environment disrupts the stability of the cultural environment (which is solved by cultural change). This development, in turn, brings a disruption of the stability of the natural environment (which is solved by the transformation of natural environments). Such changes resulting from, for example, pollution or the depletion of resources cause instability of the activity environment (which is solved by changing the activity environment in accordance with the changed natural conditions).

Studying the influence of the intermediate environment on human beings, the processes forming this environment, that is, causal influence proceeding from the metaenvironment, must also be taken

into account. In this case, *correspondence* (or *contradictions*) of those four environments is essential. Contradictions in the metaenvironment will be reflected, sooner or later, in people's behavior and will change their way of life accordingly. A contradictory way of life is characterized by low productivity (e.g., few children in the family, few activities at home, low productivity of labor, etc.) as well as "social cocooning" (e.g., individualism and closed groups).

Kruusvall emphasizes that an important quality of interrelations between a human and the environment is their *mediated* interaction (perception, overt action, etc.). The parts of humans (or an activity group) that process information (human brain, the leader of a group, computer's memory, etc.) are always isolated from the direct influences of the environment. Information arrives there and departs from there by (sensory, effectory, communicative, etc.) channels, the information-transmitting capacity of which is limited. Therefore, humans (like any other living beings) perceive the environment as undetermined to a certain extent. Their activity toward the environment always means the

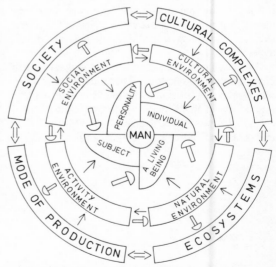

Figure 37.2. Dispositional and determinative (causal) relations between environments. ——————▶ denotes the causal direction for solving contradictions in the environment; and ⟨══════ denotes dispositional relations between environments. (Adapted from "The Determination of Family's Way of Life in an Urban Environment," by J. Kruusvall, 1980. In H. Mikkin (Ed.), *Man, Environment, Interaction.* Copyright 1980 by Tallinn Pedagogic Institute.)Adapted by permission.

transition of the environment to a more determined (stable) state.

In the natural environment, a living being can survive only by occupying a certain space (in phylogenesis it is characterized by more and more closed metabolism in one organism; control of nest and of a certain territory by outspacing other individuals and species, etc.); in an activity environment, a subject realizes oneself through means of action and space that are at one's disposal. In the social environment, the development of personality is connected with opportunities to control and direct other people's activities. In the cultural environment, every individual creates a subculture with its original features. Therefore, phenomena connected with the personalization of space belong to the sphere of the social environment because they do not outspace other people from a certain part of space entirely but control and determine their behavior in this space. Kruusvall (1983a, 1983c) has shown that control over behavior often means stimulating certain ways of behavior among other people. Therefore, the influence of the social environment can be treated as generating a complementary behavioral engagement, the task of which is to determine people's position with regard to each other.

The results of activity depend on the state of people as well as on the state of the environment. When we associate the "number" of changes that have taken place in the environment during a certain period of time with the "number" of people's reactions to those changes, we get the indicator of the *degree of man's dependence on the environment* (DDE) (Kruusvall, 1978, 1981a). At the given level of information processing, the composite DDE can be considered a constant. As means for operating in one part of the environment are often taken from another, different part of the environment, we can presume that DDE also travels from one part of the environment to another. A decrease of humans' dependence on the natural environment calls forth their greater dependence on the activity environment (on means of action, other people, etc.). A decrease of humans' dependence on the activity environment is often achieved at the cost of greater dependence on the social environment, and so on. This capacity of the social environment to generate a complementary behavioral engagement can be used as an example of the increase of DDE.

37.2.4. Methodological Approaches

Savchenko (1981, in press) argues that every study of spatiotemporal relations in architecture is based on some a priori paradigm of knowledge. He has identified six different paradigms, which are the different cognitive projections of the unitary spatiotemporal continuum. One of these paradigms is *inborn* knowledge. Architecture here is the embodiment of an architectural idea. The spatial language for this idea consists of architectural universals (above, below, vertical, center, etc.). The space of universals is topological, and time in such space is eternity. The invariant universals transmit the essence of architecture everlastingly through its metamorphoses.

The opposite to architecture as an idea is architecture as a thing. This is an *experiential* (empirical) paradigm—the world of particular spatial goals and resources. Such space has no metrics; it is governed by the paths of maximal spatial efficiency (usefulness). Time in such space is drifting, accelerating and decelerating as the gradient of spatial behavior. The drifting of time proceeds here through the succession of spatial objects, and several independent times can drift in such space simultaneously.

These two paradigms define the *existence* dimension of architectural space-time. On the dimension of *content*, we can oppose ritual and figurative space.

Ritual space is characteristic for the paradigm of symbolic knowledge. Architecture here appears as an institution, a phenomenon of culture. Space consists of locuses with symbolic meaning; its purpose is to maintain the existing order. Time in such space is cyclical, a ritual that usually has a complex organization from introduction to finale.

On the other hand is the *apprehensive* paradigm, the space of which is figurative space. This kind of space is filled with cubes, cylinders, cones, and the like, the interaction of which creates the spatial situation. The forms of meanings and the meanings of forms transform into each other, and the architectural synonyms come into being. When ritual space maintains the tradition, figurative space brings novelty into spatial culture. Time in this paradigm consists of insights, apprehensions of spatial truths, and is therefore a sequence of peaks of apprehension, between which nothing happens.

On the third dimension—*definability*—we can distinguish between the space organ and metric space. The space organ is characteristic for the paradigm of *intuitive* knowledge. Architecture here is an extension of a subject; architecture-as-environment is given only to the subject included in it. *Own* is opposed to *alien* in this paradigm, and the boundaries of "one's own space" are fluctuating constantly, depending on the activity of the subject. It is the tremor of architectural time—"eternal present," constant activity, and sensitivity— that corresponds to such space.

The opposite to this paradigm is *positive* knowledge. Architecture stands out as object in this paradigm, and the space is homogenous and metrical, without a preferential point of reference. Every particular object is measurable, with discrete boundaries, that is, it is definable. Usually this definition is expressed in a number. Time in such space is a directed time arrow.

Thus we can deal with architectural environment from at least six different paradigmatic perspectives, and any architectural construction can be presented through the prism of any given paradigm. The subject is included in this model in a rather obscure and undefinable manner. In one case, he or she is an ideal observer (positive knowledge); in another, a creator designer (apprehensive knowledge).

Niit (in press) has tried to interpret the psychological content of this model and has compared it with the classification scheme of Stokols (1978). Kruusvall (1983c) analyzed the properties of environment that are engaging humans, using these paradigms as a starting point.

Niit (1983b, 1983c; Niit & Lehtsaar, 1984) has proposed a scheme for analyzing human–environment relations on the level of a social unit (group, family, community, etc.). In every sociophysical system, it is possible to differentiate for analytic purposes at least three realities--activity, relations, and various characteristics of place (cf. Figure 37.3). A system characterized by those three facets both takes into account and, in the course of its functioning, generates sociocultural norms. At the level of the social unit, these are interpreted as something given, and they probably influence activities and relations as well as places.

Activity is the reality where the influence of both place (size, number of people, etc.) and relations (role and status relations) finds its expression. At the level of the social unit, we are interested in the complex pattern of transactions between place, activities, and relations. But during the analysis, we may, and probably have to, differentiate the main directions and components of these transactions (see arrows on Figure 37.3): The parameters of place may support or constrain some activities; at the same time, the functioning social unit changes several parameters of this place in the course of its activities. The relations between the participants create the conditions for some kind of activity or set limits for it, but these relations also change during this activity. It is hard to find direct influences between places and relations (if we try to avoid falling into architectural determinism); probably activities function here as mediating links. Thus place and relations are the relatively stable components of the system, whereas activity is the dynamic one. Nevertheless, this activity in a particular place is characterized by considerable regularity and stability, which at the

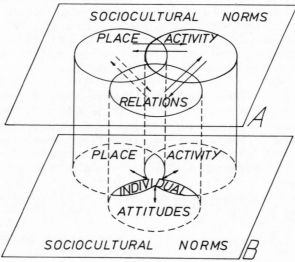

Figure 37.3. A scheme for analyzing human–environment relationships (A) the level of the social unit; and (B) the level of the individual. (From "Privacy Preferences of Family Members," by T. Niit and T. Lehtsaar, 1983. In H. Mikkin (Ed.), *Problems in Practical Psychology*, 1983. Copyright 1983 by Tallinn Pedagogic Institute. Reprinted by permission.)

group level could be called "the behavioral way of life." Such a way of life could be characterized both quantitatively (frequency of various activities, variety of activities, etc.) and qualitatively (see Niit, 1983c).

Depending on the specifics of place, there may be more or less significant parameters and dimensions for describing the functioning of the system. During such an analysis, we have to descend to the level of the individual to incorporate his or her attitudes that arise in the course of the functioning of some social unit into the complex picture. When, at the level of the social unit, the individual is a component of the sociophysical system, at the level of the individual, the analysis is possible only when confronting him or her with the environment. At this level we have to deal with attitudes instead of relations (see Figure 37.3.), either toward place (e.g., place identity), other people (emotional relations), one's own activity, or the activity of others. At this level, the individual is constrained by parameters of place, the activity of others, and their attitudes and, trying to balance these, he or she seeks a niche "to build himself or herself into the environment." At the same time, the individual connects in himself or herself activities, attitudes, and, through his or her physical existence, the parameters of place.

Thus the processes and phenomena that we have examined are partly overlapping and partly different at the different levels of analyses, but, from the viewpoint of environmental design, we should not restrict ourselves to the level of the individual only as much of environmental psychology has done until now. At the level of the social unit, there is no need to use the term *environment* at all. At the level of the individual, the environment consists of several realities, with which the individual confronts himself or herself.

37.3. EMPIRICAL STUDIES

37.3.1. Introduction

In this part of our review, we will try to describe the empirical studies carried out in the Soviet Union that in our opinion fall under the label *environmental psychology*. We have not discussed the studies about the influence of ambient environmental conditions (noise, temperature, light, etc.) or ergonomical studies in which humans are conceptualized mainly as anatomical biological beings.

To classify the studies is rather difficult, having their diversity and the differences in conceptual start-

ing points in mind. Therefore, we have organized these studies in the same way as did the editors of this *Handbook*: Some studies will be reviewed from the *processual* viewpoint; the others will be classified on the basis of *environments* under study. The processual approach will be represented by sections on environmental perception and cognition and human spatial behavior. From different environments, we will deal with studies on home and dwelling, work environments, recreational environments, and city and neighborhood space. Such a division will also be quite adequate to show the main trends of empirical research in the Soviet Union.

At the present time, very few empirical studies stem directly from the major theoretical approaches presented previously. The main problem seems to be that these approaches are too recent and still too poorly operationalized. The empirical studies presented here usually have their own fragmentary concepts and hypotheses that they try to prove. We hope that the consolidation of the direction of research and contacts between researchers will reduce the gap between general theorizing and empirical studies in the years to come.

Some of the following studies have been described in more detail in our two recent reviews (Niit, Kruusvall, & Heidmets, 1981; Niit, Heidmets, & Kruusvall, 1983b). In the present review, we have tried to include as much as possible the studies that are available in English.

37.3.2. Environmental Perception and Cognition

The perception of architecture was a field of considerable interest among the Soviet architects and psychologists in the 1920s and 1930s, long before anybody spoke about environmental psychology (for details, see Niit, Kruusvall, & Heidmets, 1981, pp. 163–164). In these years, the influence of form, light, color, or texture on the perception of architectural objects was studied. In the 1950–1960 decade the locuses of interest were differences in the perception of proportions, distances, and so on in drawings and reality (Feodorov & Koroyev, 1961), and perception of scale in architecture (Kirillova, 1960).

In the 1970s, the first influences of Western theories and approaches can be noted. Several monographs were published dealing with quantitative measures as a criterion of beauty in architecture (Azgaldov, 1978), perception of architecture from the viewpoint of information theory and semiotics (Seredyuk, 1979), the informative-emotional potential of architecture (Strautmanis, 1978), and characteristic features of perception of the city environment (Belyayeva, 1977).

Two essential features characterize almost all studies concerned with perception of the architectural environment carried out by architects: (1) Architecture is "empty"—it is treated as distinct from human relations, and persons acquire the role of outside spectators; and (2) the objects are examined mostly from the outside. One of the few investigators who treats architecture not merely as an object of perception but also as a situation for satisfaction of human needs is Tkachikov (1980). According to him, a human being perceives architecture in the course of functional process (i.e., activity). In the course of the same functional process, a human being acquires needs and attitudes as well, which in turn influence environmental perception.

Several past studies have touched on more specific problems of the perception of architecture. Marder (1981) has discussed the role of the architectural image in environmental perception, and Negai (1981) and Tregubov (1981) have dealt with the psychophysiological basis of perceiving proportion and scale. From the phenomenological point of view, problems of environmental perception have been discussed by Rappaport (1981), who distinguishes four categories of perceptual experience—point, figure, thing, and concept—and analyzes the relations between them. Shmelyov (1983) has discussed the phenomenology of the golden section in architecture and has proposed an improved canonical system called "duplex-modulor." And Ibragimbekova (1983) has presented some evidence from the studies of perception of architecture that stress the role of the vertical as a psychological universal in architecture.

Küller's (1979) semantic scale for describing perceived molar environment has been translated into Estonian, and Käärik (1983) has used it to compare the perception of churches from various cultures and styles in Estonia and Georgia.

Very few studies have been devoted to environmental cognition. Apart from the early studies of Shemyakin (1962), which seem to be well known to English readers, the only experiments known to us are by Sokolov (1971) and Raudsepp (1981). Sokolov examined the possibilities of using collective cognitive maps in city planning and demonstrated the role of functional buildings (shops, cinemas, etc.) for orientation in new districts with monotonous architecture. Raudsepp has studied high-school students' images of Tallinn. She demonstrated the interrelationship between the use of various map elements and the active, as opposed to the passive, mode of movement about the city, emphasizing the role of activity in the development of mental images of large-scale environments.

A few names can be also mentioned in connection with research on the effects of color environment on humans. Kitayev-Smyk (1981) has shown in his experiments that subjects in stress conditions suffering from kinetosis (feeling sick, heaviness in abdomen, etc.) feel themselves much worse in yellow, orange, or brown environments or during bright illumination. During the first days of these experiments, the subjects preferred poorly illuminated rooms in shades of blue. Ponomaryova (1981) has been interested in the ways in which changes in children's color preferences vary with age. According to her studies, younger children form color pairs from contrasting colors but with an increase in age, children seem to prefer shades of closer hues (see also Ponomaryova, in press). Relying on her studies, she gives proposals for designing school interiors.

37.3.3. Human Spatial Behavior

Human spatial behavior is a field of research that has almost without exception belonged to psychologists and psychiatrists. The number of studies has not been large, but the researchers have been interested in all the conceptualizations proposed to describe the use of space—personal and group space, crowding, territoriality and personalization of space, and privacy.

Both projective methods as well as observation in natural or experimental conditions have been used to study personal space. Duke and Nowicki's (1972) CID scale has been used in several studies. Ruse (1976) demonstrated that normal subjects had significantly lower preferred interaction distance than did mentally ill subjects. The results of Solozhenkin (1980) show that the imaginary intruders into personal space can be divided into three large groups according to the preferred distance: relatives, acquaintances, and strangers. Pulver and Tammiste (1983) used the stop-distance method alongside the projective method. They point out a rather high correlation ($r = .62$) between the results obtained by different methods and significant sex differences in spatial behavior. Ojala (1980) has studied interaction distances from the developmental point of view, measuring the preferred distance of children between 7 and 12. The results show that personal space increases with age, showing a tendency toward stabilization at the age of 12. Again, significant sex differences were observed (for a more detailed description of some of the previously mentioned studies, see Niit, Kruusvall, & Heidmets, 1981, pp. 165–166).

In recent years, some studies of group space and the permeability of its boundaries have been carried out. Visamaa (1982) demonstrated the influence of a group's sex composition, member's age, and the activity and interpersonal distance on the size of group space and its permeability. A similar study was done by Siilsalu (1983) who added a cross-cultural comparison. The permeability of a group's space in its own and in a strange culture was measured both in Estonia and Georgia, and significant cross-cultural differences were demonstrated.

From the studies dealing with territoriality, the work of Solozhenkin, Shilin, Sirota, and Ivashchenko (1981) could be mentioned. They observed the development of territoriality in a children's ward. They show the different roles of institutional and interpersonal control in the use of different territories within the ward and state that the failure to take into account the peculiarities of human territorial behavior in designing wards may lead to chronic stress among the patients.

Kitayev-Smyk (in press) has described the development of territoriality during the prolonged stay in a small cabin, when people are influenced by environmental stressors (the cabin is revolving, etc.) at the same time. He described the territories with different levels of personalization and the different reactions on intrusion into them.

Heidmets (1977) has shown that the more precisely the personal territories of family members are fixed at home, the more positively the other family members are evaluated and the more joint activity can be found in the family. This opportunity of personalization of space is of especially great importance for adolescents (8–14 years) who have, in this case, remarkably more positive attitudes toward *home*. One of the few empirical studies about the means of environmental personalization was carried out by Kordon (1981), who used the iconographic method to study the personalization of rooms in dormitories. It was shown that in men's rooms the desire for personalization was more intense than in women's rooms. It was also found that the forms of personalization depended on one's sphere of activity and socioeconomic status.

There are only a few studies on privacy that have been conducted in the Soviet Union. Niit and Lehtsaar (1984) developed a privacy preference scale in Estonian, which consists of 45 statements. According to Altman's (1975) privacy conception, these statements include both wishes to be left alone as well as seeking contacts with others. Until now, the privacy preferences of 200 mothers, fathers, and teenage children from city families have been analyzed (Niit & Lehtsaar, 1984). The factor analysis of the results shows that the concept of privacy includes at least 7 to 8 interpretable dimensions. The data also demonstrate significant differences in the privacy preferences of parents and children (see also Kobolt, 1983).

Parktal (1982) has analyzed the relationships between real and preferred privacy during various domestic activities, using the data of the Environmental Psychology Research Unit at Tallinn Pedagogic Institute about city homes.

We are not aware of experimental laboratory studies about the influence of population density on human behavior. Nevertheless, residential density has been a significant variable in the studies of homes and dormitories. Therefore, we shall review them in the corresponding section.

37.3.4. Home Environments

One of the first empirical studies about home environment was carried out from 1970 to 1974 in the Laboratory of Sociology at Tartu State University as a work grant from the All-Union Institute of Industrial Design, in Moscow. The methodology used was in many ways a basis for the more recent studies by the Environmental Psychology Research Unit in Tallinn. One of the central concepts of the previously mentioned research project (cf. Kruusvall, 1979) was *activity*. All the main activities of the family members at home as well as outside the home were taken under observation. Every activity can be observed as a conventional "act of production"; the environment of this activity consists of the subject of activity, the means of activity (objects, instruments, activity space), the product of activity, and the process of activity (which characterizes the change of the components of the environment where activity takes place in time).

When family members perform certain activities for themselves (prepare meals or sew their dresses themselves, etc.), they are subjects of action. When they use services of other people who are not members of their family (e.g., a relative, an acquaintance, a friend, a private entrepreneur, a state service enterpriser, etc.), the subject is not the family member but the one who does the work. All the steps taken by family members to get a certain thing done (but not the service itself) are, in this case, considered to be the activities of family members. The environment of every activity can be characterized by nine parameters that are summarized in Table 37.1. Every activity of the family was measured with the help of the previously mentioned parameters. The standardized interview consisted of 1600 single items. Two thousand families from the different types of settlements (from village to city) and representing very different types of dwellings were chosen in Estonia.

As a result of computer analysis, eight different types of domestic lives were distinguished. Two types of parameters had greater power of differentiation: social distance of services (domestic, nondomestic, private or public) from the consumer's home and the degree of mechanization of domestic activities. The first of them differentiates mainly urban families, the second, rural families.

Since 1974, the Environmental Psychology Research Unit has continued to study the domestic way of life with funding from the Central Research and Experimental Planning Institute of Residential Buildings. The way of life of families in new residential districts in standard apartments was investigated. The first stage of interviewing and survey research was carried out in 4 cities of the Soviet Union, the second stage in 12 cities, and at the present time (third stage), 10 more cities have been taken under investigation.

In every city, 1 new residential district was chosen where 200 families (representing 16 different family types), living in apartments with a different number of rooms (1-, 2-, 3-, and 4-room apartments) were interviewed using the directed choice of respondents. With a standardized interview (more than 600 single items), relations between a family's domestic and nondomestic activities, the spatial organization of the domestic family activities, the number of members in domestic activity groups, lack of space, and personalization of space at home were studied (see Kruusvall & Heidmets, 1979).

The choice of respondents enabled the researchers to find out regional and cultural differences in the domestic way of life of habitants of new residential districts as well as differences that arose from variations in apartment planning and number of rooms, differences in demographic profiles of families, and the like. The main result of the study is to make apparent the necessity of differentiated planning of city dwellings and working out practical advice for it. The study shows that the number of activities performed outside the home is greater (compared to domestic activities) in the Ukrainian and Baltic cities, average in the Russian cities, and smaller in the cities of the southern republics. Only spending leisure time at home is in correlation with apartment conditions (the number of family members and the number of rooms in an apartment). Leisure time was less often spent in small apartments. Other activities depended on the development of the level of services but, to a greater extent, on the established way of life of the family.

The research has produced interesting results about social organization of domestic activities and their relations with apartment conditions (Kruusvall, 1981b).

1. The number of rooms in apartments influences activities performed separately—the greater the number of rooms, the greater the number of activities performed separately.

2. Apartment planning influences the number of activities performed together. In apartments with bigger and isolated rooms, the number of activities performed together is greater than in apartments with smaller and unisolated rooms. This conclusion confirms the well-known fact in environmental psychology that, for performing activities together successfully, there must be a certain possibility for the members of a group to isolate themselves from the others from time to time. At the same time, Kruusvall (1980) has shown that the personal division of rooms in larger apartments is influenced not only by the need for privacy. The domination of personal division of rooms over functional division can be taken as an indication of domination of purely social (often conflicting) human relations over activity relations in family.

3. Comparing the cities of the Soviet Union, it was found that there are more activities performed together in the cities of the southern regions. Activities performed separately are more common in the cities of the western regions and in the big cities, where urbanization has greater influence on the way of life. (Additional information on this research project can be found in Kruusvall, 1981b, 1983b; Lauristin, Kruusvall, & Raitviir, 1975).

The researchers have different opinions about which spatial organization in houses and in the vicinity would enhance the contacts between inhabitants. Some authors (Ovsyannikova, 1983; Taut, 1983) see the solution in joint leisure and interaction because up to 60% of city inhabitants have to spend the greater part of their spare time at home, but the apartments often do not offer enough space or opportunities. Other authors maintain that contacts between families develop through helping and cooperation in household activities (Kanayeva, 1983). At the

Table 37.1. A System of Parameters for the Description of Environment (adapted from Kruusvall, 1979).

Parameters of environment	Subject (caterer)	Means of activity			Product	Process
		Instrument	Object	Place		
Distance of subject from environment	Social distance from consumer	—	—	Distance of place of activity from home	Distance from final product	Duration of activity
Degree of organization	Organizational structure	Degree of mechanization	Degree of preparedness	Degree of separatedness	Degree of integrity	Frequency of activity
Degree of multifunctionality	Degree of specialization	Degree of universality		Degree of multifunctionality	Quantity of different products	Number of different functions
Degree of substitutability	Existence of different service possibilities	Possibility of replacement with means of different kinds			Replaceability of the product	Replaceability of the mode of action
Degree of ordinariness or originality	Distribution of different services	Distribution of the utilized means in the environment			Originality of the product	Distribution of mode of action
Degree of outdatedness	Degree of lagging behind compared to latest developments	Physical and moral outdatedness			Moral outdatedness of product	Moral outdatedness of mode of action
Material value	Material status	Value (price) of means			Value of product	Complexity of action
Quality	Social status	Sociocultural value of means			Quality of product	Attractiveness of the activity
Orientation of subject toward environment	Desirable service-worker	Preferred means of action			Desired product	Desirable activity

Source: Adapted from Kruusvall (1979).

same time, the surveys show that in the cities of the western and central regions of the U.S.S.R., 40 to 60% of city inhabitants do not maintain contacts with neighbors; the remaining part interacts with only one or two neighbors (Heidmets, 1983b; Yankova, 1979). To enhance the contacts between neighbors, the housing of families correlating with each other sociopsychologically into one apartment block has been suggested, or the opportunity to design the inside and outside space by the inhabitants of the housing block has been proposed.

The construction of high-rise buildings (5 to 25

floors) is today the main way for relieving the housing shortage in the cities. At the same time, the studies show that only about 30% of citizens wish to live in these buildings. Seventy percent of the inhabitants in new city districts want to live on the second to the fourth floors; the same proportion do not want to live on the ground floor (Kartashova, 1983). The advantages of low-rise buildings in satisfying housing needs have been stressed by several authors—the possibility to build auxiliary rooms, have a private entrance and yard, and the like (Preem, 1981; Sidorov, 1983). Real perspectives for low-rise housing are apparent in the suburbs and in countryside settlements, where until now cheap high-rise buildings were also constructed under economic pressure (Raig, 1983).

In studying the functional use of space in apartments, the changes in spatial needs during the various stages of a family's life cycle (childless period, family with small children, family with adolescents, etc.) have been stressed. This calls for greater flexibility in the distribution of apartments (so that the family could get a suitable apartment for every stage of the life cycle [Orlov, 1981]) as well as for greater polyfunctionality of rooms in apartments (rooms have different functions at various stages of the life-cycle [Smotrikovsky, 1983]).

In connection with the "Family and Apartment" project, Niit studied 200 families in the new living districts of Tallinn and Tartu (Estonia) in 1981. The emphasis of this study was on the sociopsychological aspects of families' ways of life (family relations, privacy needs of family members, etc.) (Niit, 1983c). The main difference of this project from the analogous studies is that the mother, father, and a teenage child were interviewed in each family. This enabled the analysis to be conducted on the level of the social unit and allowed Niit to describe the interrelationships between family relations, activity patterns, and various parameters of home more precisely. The first publications on this project have appeared (Niit & Lehtsaar, 1984).

As was mentioned previously, various studies have looked upon residential density as a significant variable in housing research. We shall present some examples here. Valdma (1983) demonstrated in a study of teenagers that in the homes with high residential density, family members were more reserved, spent less spare time out of the home, and that an authoritarian atmosphere prevailed in these homes. She has also shown that under similar conditions of density, teenagers with deviant behavior have significantly higher privacy needs compared with the control group.

Niit and Kuivits (1983) studied the interrelationships between the behavior and intelligence and residential density of 6-year-old children. They found that at homes with higher residential density the children were behaviorally more passive, were rarely leaders in games, and had lower scores on Raven's intelligence test.

Toomsalu (1983) carried out the only environmental psychology study in university dormitories known to us. Among various relationships, she showed the mediating role of activity in the perception of crowding and the interrelationships of feeling crowded with evaluations given to the self and others.

37.3.5. Work Environments

Work and the work environment have been objects of investigation in the Soviet Union for a long time. Nevertheless, only a very small portion of these studies can be considered to be environmental psychological in nature. Usually, when researchers speak about work environment, they have only the social environment in their minds (for studies of the social psychological climate, see Shorokhova & Zotova, 1979 and Parygin, 1981, as examples), or attention is centered on humans as anatomical, physiological and/or information-processing beings, with the goal being to optimize the interaction between humans and machines or tools (for the ergonomic approach, see Zinchenko & Munipov, 1979). In the final example, humans as social beings often get lost in the studies. Niit (1983a, pp. 23–25) has tried to describe the interrelations of environmental psychology and other traditional sciences studying humans in their working environment. Therefore, only these studies will be described here that have an obvious environmental psychological orientation.

Niit (1983a), relying on the data of a representative survey of an Estonian working population, showed that the more variation there is in a person's work and the more opportunities for interaction he or she has, the more active he or she is, both in work and nonwork activities. He proposed a hypothesis that persons can be characterized by some level of general social activeness, which can be considered to be a function of sociophysical environment. If choice and free decision in activities that occupy major parts of a person's time are limited, the level of social activeness may decrease, and a stereotype of passivity may be generalized to other situations and activities.

Concerning larger studies, a research project carried out by the Environmental Psychology Research Unit of Tallinn Pedagogic Institute in 1980–1981 could be mentioned. This project tried to find psychological foundations for the spatial organization of administrative buildings (for the description of method and some results, see Heidmets & Niit, 1983a). The results show that differences in real and preferred locations of activities are remarkable. Workrooms are, in fact, overloaded with every kind of nonwork activity. Many employees prefer therefore to do quiet work elsewhere (in the libraries or at home in the evenings). Taking into account the wishes and preferences of the employees, it was possible to construct an ideal model for the spatial structure of activities in an administrative building, which could be a starting point for design (Heidmets & Niit, 1983a, p. 92).

Some studies that deal with risk in work and the subjective assessment of dangers by the employee could also be considered to fall under the label of *environmental psychology* (for a review, see Kotik, 1981). For example, Kotik (1980) has demonstrated the interrelationships between dangerousness, emotionalism, and uncertainty of a task.

The interest in studies using an environmental approach is growing. A recent indication of it is a conference held in Georgia entitled "The Ergonomic and Psychological Problems of Designing Environments of Human Activities at Industrial Enterprises" (Bigvava, 1983).

37.3.6. Cultural and Recreational Institutions

Several studies carried out in the area of cultural and recreational institutions are concerned with the so-called Soviet club (community center). This is an institution integrating the majority of cultural life in a certain district (city, region, village). It brings together hobby groups; dancing parties, disco nights, cinema and theater performances, and concerts take place at these centers. Several environmental psychological studies have tried to answer the question: "What should a suitable environment for such a polyfunctional institution be?" In the period from 1976 to 1978, a research project about dancing-party visitors was carried out in Tallinn and Tartu by studying the preferences and wishes concerning space division and interior design in clubs. The results of this research showed that the intensity of using different rooms was very different. The "open" parts of rooms parts of rooms (the well-lighted and exposed central parts of the bigger rooms) were relatively empty. Visitors who came alone seemed to prefer these parts. Groups, on the other hand, preferred more closed and separated rooms for communicating (corners, corridors, lobbies, niches). Based on this study, we may draw a conclusion about the aims of going to dancing parties. The most important of these seems to be self-exposure with the aim of making contacts and for group interaction. Dancing is only a ritualized means to an end, which is well accepted by society (Kruusvall, Heidmets, & Kilgas, 1979, pp. 100–117).

The problems of a particular club were studied in Tallinn in 1979 and 1980 (Kruusvall, Heidmets, & Toomla, 1980). In this research project, the space usage of the club staff and visitors and their wishes and proposals about the organization of club work were analyzed.

A third research project in this area carried out by environmental psychologists at Tallinn Pedagogic Institute dealt with problems of club activities of elderly people in Tallinn and in Pskov (RSFSR) (Heidmets & Kruusvall, 1980). Different forms of common activities among the elderly and ways of supplying them with suitable environments for these activities were analyzed in this study.

In all these research projects, a combined methodology was used, that is, interviewing combined with observations (fixation of actual behavior). Now the same group continues work at investigating "natural clubs." In the course of this study, spontaneous leisure groups (societies) were described (the so-called yard societies, fans at sports events, etc.). The contents of their activities and the environment where their gatherings took place were analyzed (Heidmets & Niit, 1984).

Some other cultural and recreational institutions were studied also. In research about cinemas (Heidmets & Kruusvall, 1979; Heidmets & Niit, 1983b; Niit, 1980), the main attention was focused on lobbies and their equipment. According to the data collected in several cities of the Soviet Union, there is a certain contingent of people who use cinema lobbies as places where they can spend their leisure time, and they come there nearly an hour before the performance. According to the wishes of moviegoers, a number of proposals were made to improve the spatial conditions in movie lobbies (Niit & Heidmets, 1984). Some research has been carried out concerning theaters (Belyak, Nozdrachov, & Rodionov, 1983).

Some interesting proposals were made by Allakhverdov and Belyak (1983) for the environmental design of a scientific conference. According to them, every scientific conference has three different aims— symbolic, conceptual, and pragmatic—and achieving each of them depends on organizing the environment.

Several authors have analyzed the natural environment adjusted for recreation. Lepik (1981), studying the visitors of a nature preserve in Estonia—the

Lahemaa National Park—concluded that the majority of the visitors had an orientation for passive observation and the enjoyment of nature. Activities that call for some intellectual effort (e.g., investigating animals' behavior, collecting plants) and that give a more complete picture of the natural environment are popular only with a small number of visitors. The history of development of Soviet parks has been analyzed by Lapshin and Shklyayev (1983). They showed that parks with the sociopedagogical functions of the early days of the Soviet state have gone through transformations, and today the park is a place for interacting, especially within small groups.

Attractions as a substantial component of entertainment parks were studied by Levinson (1984), who elaborated a "theory of attractions," verifying some of its aspects in an empirical study about Gorky Park in Moscow. From the results, we note that very rarely are the attractions and entertainments visited by the whole family—only 5% of groups in the park were "complete families" (i.e., consisted of mother, father, and one or more children).

Trushinsh, from Latvia (1983), has offered a new unit—the "recreon"—for measuring the recreational potential of the natural environment. It depends on the attractiveness of the environment (compared to the standard) and the time spent in this environment. Using this criterion, the author has studied very different objects (botanical gardens, mountains, parks, etc.) from the viewpoint of their recreational potential.

37.3.7. City and Neighborhood Space

Many studies on city and urbanization have been published in the Soviet Union (see, e.g., Akhiezer, Nochevik, Yanitsky, & Moskvin, 1980; Kogan, 1982; Medvedkov, & Kantsebovskaya, 1979). Most of them have backgrounds in sociology, geography, or city planning, and the city as a whole is the object of investigation. The empirical data in these studies are presented rather selectively, to support theoretical conceptions. In this section, we will review studies that deal with the microlevel. The purpose of the studies is to create more acceptable city space psychologically and culturally. The studies with a psychological background also contain much theoretical material. Some examples are Iodo and Kolantai (in press) who conceptualized the image of the city as a congruent set of ordered "cosmos" and "chaos," with implications for city planning; Mihhailov (1983) who conceptualized the city using the street/yard dichotomy; or Stepanov (1983) who differentiated three types of environments (A-, E-, and M-environments) in the city. An E-environment is an objectively existing setting whose parameters can be measured. An A-environment is an anthropocentric, cultural space with meaning. Most important in such a space is what is popular. An M-environment is a conceptual environment where images of the city are loaded with personal meanings.

The studies on microlevel can be conventionally divided into two groups: (1) investigations of the psychological aspect of the functioning of city centers; and (2) studies where the object of investigation is a living district or neighborhood space.

In the present case centers may be both city centers, as well as squares, transport centers or trade centers of living districts. Essential is the concentration of some kind of activity. Kaganov (1975) characterizes a city center as the most diverse city territory both behaviorally and environmentally, which is public, functionally saturated, and where usually the city's past, present, and future are "coded." In the same study, he shows that in the historical center of Leningrad (Nevsky Prospect) the behavioral diversity is more than a hundred times greater than in the new districts (64,000 bits and 580 bits per hectare, respectively).

Kaganov (1981) has also studied the attitude of city dwellers toward various environmental elements from which the city center is made up. In the center of Leningrad, the favorite places appear to be streets and street corners (33%) and parks, squares, and gardens (19%). Usually a place becomes a favorite due to traditions or its "historic soul"; the existence of shops and services is not essential.

Borisevich (1981) considers the main function of city centers to be the model (prescription and influencing behavior) and the generation of the new (goods, impressions, information). While passing from outer parts of a city center to its heart, behavioral changes also take place. The number of reasons which bring people to the center, the number of concrete activities and the time spent in the center increases.

The Environmental Psychology Research Unit at Tallinn Pedagogic Institute carried out three investigations dealing with the problems of centers, getting information regarding the functioning of various centers. This information would enable it to design better functioning centers at the city and district level.

In the first study the behavioral patterns in two (old and new) centers of Tallinn as well as in Tartu were compared. The results show that in old centers with their human-scale architecture and closed space more social interaction takes place and the interacting groups are larger. Fewer single persons were also present in old centers. The major factor constraining interaction in new centers was traffic. The ratings on semantic differential scales also demonstrated that the old centers are preferred to new ones (cf. Heidmets, Kruusvall, & Kilgas, 1979).

In another study four different centers in Tallinn were investigated: the city center, transport center, and the centers of the old and new districts. The results show that different centers clearly have different behavioral structures. The old center is used more frequently on work days and during the daytime. The new district is more intensively used during weekends and evenings. The behavioral pattern in the city center differs sharply from the pattern in the surrounding area. The activity structure depends mainly on the contingent and specific needs of its users. The sociocultural meaning of the center is also of great importance (cf. Heidmets, Niit, & Kruusvall, 1979).

In the third study (Heidmets & Kruusvall, 1980), the activity structure of centers at various levels was investigated both in Tallinn and in Moscow. The study showed that the centers form a certain hierarchy for every citizen from the public territory near his or her residence to the city center. Each level has a specific activity structure. It was found that the contradiction between environment and activity is the sharpest in centers near one's residence. The main problem is the discrepancy between *social* conditions created by the environment (exposure, density of people, control over territory) and needs called forth by the activity itself. Public and open, uncontrollable and used by everybody, the territory is not really suitable for many activities. The solution is seen in creating a number of common miniterritories or minicenters characterized by group or collective (but not public) usage and control, which would differ in the number of users (family, neighbors, etc.) and form a smooth gradation on the dimension "private—public."

The last study brings us to investigations concerned with planning of neighborhood space. Several studies look at this space as a place for interaction and as a basis for community development. Taut (1981, 1983) has studied the problems of interaction in the neighborhoods of new Uzbek cities where interaction with neighbors traditionally occupies a considerable part of leisure time. She also suggests that at least two types of common territories should be designed in the neighborhoods—the so-called common for neighbors (a yard for the inhabitants from

one to two houses), and the other a recreation area (for inhabitants of a housing block). According to Taut (1981), a spatial organization has to be found to encourage the use of the territory by only a restricted contingent of people, the common territory must be visible from the apartments, and it should be used by a limited number of people (400 to 600 for the neighborhood and not more than 2000 for the recreation territory).

Pavlovskaya (1983) studied the means of personalization and self-expression in yards. She maintains that a hierarchy of territories with different user categories exists in most yards of multistorey buildings, which symbolizes archetypes and world order for the inhabitants. The role of environmental design to support such division of neighborhood space is emphasized in her work.

Giorgadze and Abzianidze (1983) conducted an ethnographic study of traditional city yards in Georgia. They emphasized the theatrical nature of connected inner yards with balconies around them and the functional properties of these yards. They proposed analogous contemporary design solutions.

Grebenshchikova (1983) studied the perception of dangerousness and safety in neighborhood areas of Kaluga (RSFSR). Her data showed that 54% of the residents feared walking in the streets in the evening. She proposed design solutions that would enhance the safety of the neighborhoods. Many of her ideas resembled the "defensible space" concept of Newman (1973).

Certain geographic studies are concerned with the perception of neighborhood and neighborhood preferences. For example, Barbash (1983) analyzing the advertisments of apartment exchanges in Moscow shows that the central districts lost their popularity as living places. She stresses the role of city transportation as a major determinant of preferences (additional information on some of the studies described can be found in Niit, Kruusvall, & Heidmets, 1981, pp. 170–173).

37.4. PERSPECTIVES ON ENVIRONMENTAL PSYCHOLOGY

The past decade was a period of emergence and development in Soviet environmental psychology. At present it has become an independent research trend with a characteristic set of problems and a group of interested researchers. The future development of environmental psychology depends on its ability to help solve practical environmental problems. To increase the practical efficiency of environmental psychology, the following problem must be solved beforehand: First adequate theoretical conceptions for the research domain of environmental psychology must be worked out. The existing models could be a basis for it, but in their present state they need to be worked on, in some cases verifying, and especially, binding them with each other. Theoretical clearance is indispensable especially for empirical work. The abundance of hypothetical starting points, definitions, and ways of interpreting the data at the present moment makes the generalization and application of the results of research work very complicated.

And second, there is a need to organize research. Hitherto, research has been based on the enthusiasm of individual researchers or on the interest (in narrow problems) of some institutions. It is clear that the solution of wider environmental problems presupposes the existence of long-term complex research programs. Up to now only one such research program has been carried out—namely, the previously mentioned "Family and Apartment" project.

The two previously mentioned trends of action will probably become the leading trends in Soviet environmental psychology during the next decade. In addition to the solution of these "inner" problems of environmental psychology, the interdisciplinary coordination with researchers from other disciplines is clearly needed in the near future. Here ecologists and specialists in wildlife preservation, regional and city planners, as well as managers and organizers of cultural and social life could be mentioned as prospective representatives for closer contacts. What will be especially essential for the development of environmental psychology will be demarcating more precisely its role and perspectives within mainstream psychological thought.

The research on housing will probably remain the most active domain in the Soviet Union in the next decade. The role of studies on work environment is certainly increasing, although office automation and computerization is still on a rather primitive level in the Soviet Union. We have mentioned some studies carried out in connection with the space programs (cf. Kitayev-Smyk, 1981, in press). The role of environmental and psychological research in this area is increasing, but much of it may not reach a wide audience. Several blank spots still exist in Soviet environmental psychology. Little research has been carried out on psychological aspects of ecologically relevant behavior, environmental assessment, the perception of hazards, and so on—or it has been published in sources that have not yet reached our attention due to disciplinary specialization and communication bar-

riers. Several key philosophical concepts await operationalization in the next decade as well.

The exciting period of discovering a new field is over. Now environmental psychology must prove (to itself and also to others) its value and usefulness.

Acknowledgments

We would like to thank Maarika Saarna and the editors of this Handbook for help in preparing the English version of this chapter, and Hille Kalmus, Kadi Liik, Airi Maripuu, and Maaris Raudsepp for various kinds of technical help. We are also grateful to a number of our colleagues in the Soviet Union who have sent to us their publications and thus made the writing of this review possible.

REFERENCES

Abstracts of papers from the All-Union Conference 'The Development of Ergonomics in the System of Design'. (1979). Borzhomi, U.S.S.R.: State Committee of Science and Technology.

Abulkhanova, K.A. (1973). *About the subject of mental activity.* Moscow: Nauka.

Abzianidze, S.G., & Dzhorbenadze, R.S. (1983). On the spatial dimensions of personality. In T. Niit, M. Heidmets, & J. Kruusvall (Eds.), *Psychology and architecture* (vol. 1, pp. 57–60). Tallinn, U.S.S.R.: Estonian Branch of the Soviet Psychological Society & Tallinn Pedagogic Institute. (pp. 57–60).

Allakhverdov, V.I., & Belyak, N.V. (1983). Organization of environment and planning of activities of participants at a scientific conference. In T. Niit, M. Heidmets, & J. Kruusvall (Eds.), *Psychology and architecture* (vol.1, pp. 200–203) Tallinn, U.S.S.R.: Estonian Branch of the Soviet Psychological Society & Tallinn Pedagogic Institute. (pp. 200–203).

Altman, I. (1975). *The environment and social behavior: Privacy, personal space, territory, crowding.* Monterey, CA: Brooks/Cole.

Akhiezer, A.S., Nochevnik, M.N., Yanitsky, O.N., & Moskvin, L.B. (Eds.). (1980). *Some problems of urbanization and city planning (socio-economical aspects).* Moscow: U.S.S.R. Academy of Sciences, Institute of the International Labor Movement.

Azgaldov, G.G. (1978). *Quantitative measures and problems of architectural beauty.* Moscow: Stroiizdat.

Baranov, A.V. (1981). *Socio-demographical development of a great city.* Moscow: Finances & Statistics.

Barbash, N.B. (1981). The knowledge of city territory as an indicator of population's attitude to various elements of city environment. In T. Niit, M. Heidmets, & J. Kruusvall, (Eds.) *Man and environment: Psychological as-*

pects, (p. 189). Abstracts of a conference held in Lohusalu (Estonia) January 20–22. Tallinn, U.S.S.R.: Estonian Branch of the Soviet Psychological Society.

Barbash, N.B. (1983). Selectiveness of population's attitudes toward the city environment. In T. Niit, M. Heidmets, & J. Kruusvall (Eds.), *Psychology and architecture* (vol. 1, pp. 55–58). Tallinn, U.S.S.R.: Estonian Branch of the Soviet Psychological Society & Tallinn Pedagogic Institute.

Belyak, N.V., Nodrachov, V.D., & Rodionov, V.D. (1983). Problems of organizing man-environment interactions and the theatre. In T. Niit, M. Heidmets, & J. Kruusvall (Eds.), *Psychology and architecture* (vol. 1, pp. 67–70). Tallinn, U.S.S.R.: Estonian Branch of the Soviet Psychological Society & Tallinn Pedagogic Institute.

Belyayeva, Y.L. (1977). *Architectural-spatial environment of the city as the object of visual perception.* Moscow: Stroiizdat.

Bigvava, Z.I. (Ed.) (1983). *Abstracts of papers from the All-Union Conference on 'The Ergonomical and Psychological Problems of Designing Environments for Human Activities at Industrial Enterprises'.* Tbilisi, U.S.S.R.: Georgian Branch of All-Union Research Institute for Industrial Design.

Borisevich, Y.A. (1981). City center and its role in the activities of its inhabitants (using Leningrad as an example). In T. Niit, Heidmets, & Kruusvall, (eds.) *Man and environment: Psychological aspects,* (pp. 177–180) Abstracts of a conference held in Lohusalu (Estonia) January 20–22. Tallinn, U.S.S.R. Estonian Branch of the Soviet Psychological Society.

Duke, M.P., & Nowicki, S. (1972). A new measure and social-learning model for interpersonal distance. *Journal of Experimental Research in Personality,* 6, 119–132.

Davydov, V.V., Zinchenko, V.P., & Talyzina, N.F. (1982). Problems of activity in A.N. Leontyev's works. *Voprosy Psikhologii,* 4, 61–66.

Feodorov, M.V., & Koroyev, Y.M. (1961). *Spatial composition in project and in nature.* Moscow: Gosstroiizdat.

Giorgadze, G.K., & Abzianidze, S.G. (1983). Regional specifics of everyday life as a factor in designing residential environments. In T. Niit, M. Heidmets, & J. Kruusvall (Eds.) *Psychology and architecture* (Vol. 2, pp. 170–175). Tallinn, U.S.S.R. Estonian Branch of the Soviet Psychological Society.

Glazychev, V.L. (Ed.). (1982). *Problems of designing the city environment.* Moscow: Central Research Institute of Theory and History of Architecture.

Grebenshchikova, L.H. (1983). The feeling of social protectedness as a parameter of the socialist way of life and its meaning in designing of housing blocks. In Niit, M. Heidmets, & J. Kruusvall (Eds.), *Psychology and architecture* (Vol. 2, pp. 164–165). Tallinn, U.S.S.R.: Estonian Branch of the Soviet Psychological Society & Tallinn Pedagogic Institute.

Gvishiani, D.M. (1976). The interaction of scientific-technical revolution and social progress. *Voprosy filosofii,* no. 11, 16–30.

Hachatryants, K.K. (1983). *The basis for social typology of residential buildings.* Minsk, U.S.S.R.: Belorussian Polytechnic Institute.

Han-Magomedov, S.O. (Ed.). (1982). *Scientific-technical progress and the problems of man-made environment.* Moscow: All-Union Research Institute for Industrial Design.

Heidmets, M. (1977). Spatial regulation of human interaction: Some current problems. In *Studies in Psychology VI. Acta et Comm. Univ. Tartuensis 429* (pp. 72–84). Tartu, U.S.S.R.: Tartu State University.

Heidmets, M. (1980). The socio-psychological problems of housing (personalization of environment). In H. Mikkin (Ed.), *Man, environment, interaction* (pp. 26–49). Tallinn, U.S.S.R.: Tallinn Pedagogic Institute.

Heidmets, M. (1983a). Subject, environment, and boundaries between them. In T. Niit, M. Heidmets, & J. Krusvall, (Eds.) (Vol. 1, pp. 61–63). *Psychology and Architecture.* Tallinn, U.S.S.R.: Estonian Branch of the Soviet Psychological Society & Tallinn Pedagogic Institute.

Heidmets, M. (1983b). Subject and environment. In H. Liimets, T. Niit, & M. Heidmets (Eds.), *Man in sociophysical environment* (pp. 38–66). Tallinn, U.S.S.R.: Estonian Branch of the Soviet Psychological Society and Tallinn Pedagogic Institute.

Heidmets, M., & Kruusvall, J. (1979). *Psychological problems of spatial organization of cinema buildings* (Interim Report, Grant 78/9). Tallinn, U.S.S.R.: Tallinn Pedagogic Institute.

Heidmets, M., & Kruusvall, J. (1980). *Studies on the psychological problems of spatial organization of club buildings and city centers* (Final Report, Grant 78/6). Tallinn, U.S.S.R.: Tallinn Pedagogic Institute.

Heidmets, M., Kruusvall, J., & Kilgas, R. (1979). Human interaction in public squares. In P. Tulviste (Ed.), *Man, environment, space* (pp. 82–99). Tartu, U.S.S.R.: Tartu State University.

Heidmets, M., & Niit, T. (1983a). An activity analysis of office environments: Reality and preferences. In *Problems of Perception and Social Interaction. Acta et Comm. Univ. Tartuensis 638, Studies in Psychology* (pp. 86–94). Tartu, U.S.S.R.: Tartu State University.

Heidmets, M., & Niit, T. (1983b). *An investigation and proposals for optimization of spatial parameters in cinema buildings* (Final Report, Grant 82/9). Tallinn, U.S.S.R.: Tallinn Pedagogic Institute.

Heidmets, M., & Niit, T. (1984). Group forms of leisure: Results of a comparative analysis. In H. Mikkin (Ed.), *Problems in practical psychology* (pp. 106–123). Tallinn, U.S.S.R.: Tallinn Pedagogic Institute.

Ibragimbekova, R.F. (1983). Emotional reaction to spatial axes in the perception of architecture. In T. Niit, M. Heidments, & Krusvall, J. (Eds.) (Vol. 1, pp. 170–173). *Psychology and Architecture.* Tallinn, U.S.S.R.: Estonian Branch of the Soviet Psychological Society & Tallinn Pedagogic Institute.

Iodo, I.A., & Kolontai, A.N. (in press). Aspects of cognitive activity as the basis for designing city environment. unpublished manuscript.

Käärik, H. (1983). *Basic dimensions of environmental perception* (Põhi-dimensioonid keskkonna tajumisel). Graduation thesis, Tartu State University, Tartu, U.S.S.R.

Kaganov, G.Z. (1975). City in the city: Social and planning aspects of the development of city centers. *Stroitelstvo i Arkhitektura Leningrada, 4,* 15–18.

Kaganov, G.Z. (1981). The perception of spatial environment by the inhabitants of a historical city (using the center of Leningrad as an example). In T. Niit, M. Heidmets, & J. Kruusvall, (Eds.) *Man and Environment: Psychological Aspects* Abstracts of a conference held in Lohusalu (Estonia) January 20–22. Tallinn, U.S.S.R. Estonian Branch of the Soviet Psychological Society. (pp. 173–176).

Kaganov, G.Z. (1983). On the parameterization of environment. In T. Niit, M. Heidments & J. Krusvall (Eds.) *Psychology and Architecture.* Tallin, U.S.S.R.: Estonian Branch of the Soviet Psychological Society & Tallinn Pedagogic Institute. (Vol. 1, pp. 49–52).

Kaganov, G.Z. (in press). Environmental behavior: Genres and styles. *Man-Environment Systems.*

Kanayeva, I.N. (1983). The psychological prognostication in designing socio-spatial systems. In T. Niit, M. Heidmets & J. Krusvall (Eds.) *Psychology and Architecture.* Tallinn, U.S.S.R.: Estonian Branch of the Soviet Psychological Society & Tallinn Pedagogic Institute. (Vol. 2, pp. 147–151).

Kartashova, K.K. (1983). The reflection of inhabitants' preferences in the development of residential buildings. In T. Niit, M. Heidmets & J. Krusvall (Eds.) *Psychology and Architecture.* Tallinn, U.S.S.R.: Estonian Branch of the Soviet Psychological Society & Tallinn Pedagogic Institute. (Vol. 2, pp. 136–139).

Kartashova, K.K, & Kanayeva, I.N. (Eds.). (1985). *Social problems of architecture of residential construction.* Moscow: Union of Architects of the USSR.

Kirillova, L.I. (1960). *Scale in architecture.* Moscow: Gosstroiizdat.

Kitayev-Smyk, L.A. (1981). Problems of color space optimization in stressful conditions. In T. Niit, M. Heidmets, & J. Kruusvall (Eds.) *Man and Environment: Psychological Aspects* Abstracts of a conference held in Lohusalu (Estonia) January 20–22. Tallinn, U.S.S.R.: Estonian Branch of the Soviet Psychological Society (p. 128).

Kitayev-Smyk, L.A. (in press). Proxemic studies in stress conditions. *Man-Environment Systems.*

Kobolt, N. (1983). *Privacy preferences of family members* (Perekonnaliikmete privaatsuseelistused). Graduation thesis, Tartu State University, Tartu, U.S.S.R.

Kogan, L.B. (Ed.). (1982). *Socio-cultural functions of the city and the spatial environment.* Moscow: Stroiizdat.

Kordon, S.I. (1981). An empirical investigation of semiotic means of separating the space 'for oneself'. In T. Niit, M. Heidmets, & J. Kruusvall (Eds.) (1981) *Man and Environment: Psychological Aspects* Abstracts of a conference held in Lohusalu (Estonia) January 20–22. Tallinn, U.S.S.R.: Estonian Branch of the Soviet Psychological Society. (pp. 111–114).

Kotik, M.A. (1980). On the influence of dangerousness on the conception of task uncertainty. In *Problems of Cognitive Psychology. Acta et Comm. Univ. Tartuensis 522, Studies in Psychology VIII* (pp. 3–21). Tartu, U.S.S.R.: Tartu State University.

Kotik, M.A. (1981). *Psychology and safety.* Tallinn, U.S.S.R.: Valgus.

Kruusvall, J. (1978). General problems of transaction between man and environment. In T. Frey (Ed.), *Problems of contemporary ecology* (Vol. 2, pp. 63–65). Tartu, U.S.S.R.: Academy of Sciences of the Estonian SSR.

Kruusvall, J. (1979). Principles for creating a system of parameters for the comparative study of human activities in urban and rural environments. In T.E. Kuznetsova et al. (Eds.), *Problems of the countryside and the city. Proceedings of an All-Union Seminar* (Vol. 1). Tallinn & Tartu, U.S.S.R.: Academy of Sciences of the Estonian SSR.

Kruusvall, J. (1980). Determination of family's way of life in the urban environment. In H. Mikkin (Ed.), *Man, environment, interaction* (pp. 50–89). Tallinn, U.S.S.R.: Tallinn Pedagogic Institute.

Kruusvall, J. (1981a). The dependence of the subject from environment. In T. Niit, M. Heidmets, & J. Kruusvall (Eds.) (1981) *Man and Environment: Psychological Aspects* Abstracts of a conference held in Lohusalu (Estonia) January 20–22. Tallinn, U.S.S.R.: Estonian Branch of the Soviet Psychological Society. (pp. 44–46).

Kruusvall, J. (1981b). *An elaboration of complex indices for describing the way of life of children, adults and elderly in new living districts* (Final Report, Grant 80/15). Tallinn, U.S.S.R.: Tallinn Pedagogic Institute.

Kruusvall, J. (1983a). Engagement and organization. In H. Liimets, T. Niit, & M. Heidmets (Eds.), *Man in the sociophysical environment* (pp. 69–98). Tallinn, U.S.S.R.: Estonian Branch of the Soviet Psychological Society & Tallinn Pedagogic Institute.

Kruusvall, J. (1983b). At home and out of home. In Niit, M.

Heidmets, & J. Kruusvall (Eds.) (1983a) *Psychology and Architecture* (Vol. 2, pp. 133–135). Tallinn, U.S.S.R.: Estonian Branch of the Soviet Psychological Society and Tallinn Pedagogic Institute.

Kruusvall, J. (1983c). Engagement and organization. In E.M. Vernik (Ed.), *Psychological conditions of social interaction.* (pp. 17–46). Tallinn, U.S.S.R.: Tallinn Pedagogic Institute.

Kruusvall, J., & Heidmets, M. (1979). Family and apartment in a new living district. In P. Tulviste (Ed.) *Man, environment, space* (pp. 43–81). Tartu, U.S.S.R.: Tartu State University.

Kruusvall, J., Heidmets, M., & Kilgas, R. (1979). Psychological problems of spatial organization of community centers. In *Man, environment, space* (pp. 100–117). Tartu, U.S.S.R.: Tartu State University.

Kruusvall, J., Heidmets, M., & Toomla, H. (1980). *The accordance of spatial conditions, organizational and cultural activities to the needs of administration, group members and visitors in J. Tomp Cultural Palace* (Grant No. 9013003). Tallinn, U.S.S.R.: Estonian Rural Planning Institute.

Küller, R. (1979). A semantic test for use in cross-cultural studies. *Man-Environment Systems, 9*(4–5), 253–256.

Kutyryov, B.P. (Ed.). (1986). *Results of applied sociological studies of the city and residential environments (1970–1980).* Novosibirsk, U.S.S.R.

Lapshin, V., & Shklyaev, N. (1983). The functionality of city parks and its environmental embodiment. In T. Niit, M. Heidmets, & J. Kruusvall (Eds.) (1983a) *Psychology and Architecture* (2 vols.). Tallinn, U.S.S.R.: Estonian Branch of the Soviet Psychological Society and Tallinn Pedagogic Institute (Vol. 2, pp. 71–73).

Lauristin, M., Kruusvall, J., & Raitviir, T. (1975). Regional sociological study of the way of life (experience of sociologists at Tartu University). In A.N. Alekeseyer & O.I. Shkaratan (Eds.), *Planning the social development of cities* (Book 2, pp. 154–175). Moscow: Institute of Sociological Studies of the USSR Academy of Sciences & Soviet Sociological Association.

Leontyev, A.N. (1975). *Activity. consciousness. personality.* Moscow: Politizdat.

Lepik, J. (1981). The psychological aspect of maintenance of recreational woods. In T. Niit, M. Heidmets, & J. Kruusvall (Eds.) (1981) *Man and Environment: Psychological Aspects* (Abstracts of a conference held in Lohusalu (Estonia) January 20–22. Tallinn, U.S.S.R.: Estonian Branch of the Soviet Psychological Society (pp. 219–222).

Levinson, A. (1984). *Comparative analysis of attractions-related behavior in various environments.* Unpublished manuscript.

Lomov, B.F. (1981). The problem of activity in psychology. *Psikhologicheskii Zhurnal, 2*(5), 3–32.

Marder, A.P. (1981) Architectural image as a factor in envi-ronmental perception. In T. Niit, M. Heidmets & J. Kruusvall (Eds.), *Man and environment: Psychological aspects* (pp. 95–98). Tallinn, U.S.S.R.: Estonian Branch of the Soviet Psychological Society.

Medvedkov, Y.V. & Kantsebovskaya, I.V. (Eds.). (1979). *Geographical studies of city environment.* Moscow: U.S.S.R. Academy of Sciences Institute of Geography.

Mihhailov, D.R. (1983). The analysis of intertwinement of subject and environment. In T. Niit, M. Heidmets & J. Kruusvall (Eds.), *Psychology and architecture* (Vol. 1, pp. 44–48). Tallinn, U.S.S.R.: Estonian Branch of the Soviet Psychological Society & Tallinn Pedagogic Institute.

Negai, G.A. (1981). Psychophysiology of perception and informational analysis of proportionality in architecture. In T. Niit, M. Heidmets & J. Kruusvall, (Eds.), *Man and environment: Psychological aspects* (p. 104). Tallinn, U.S.S.R.: Estonian Branch of the Soviet Psychological Society.

Newman, O. (1973). *Defensible space,* New York: Collier.

Niit, T. (1980). *Psychological problems f spatial organization of cinema buildings* (Final Report, Grant 78/9). Tallinn, U.S.S.R.: Tallinn Pedagogic Institute.

Niit, T. (1983a). Work environment, work content, and human social activity. In H. Liimets, T. Niit & M. Heidmets (Eds.), *Man in sociophysical environment* (pp. 23–37). Tallinn, U.S.S.R.: Estonian Branch of the Soviet Psychological Society & Tallinn Pedagogic Institute.

Niit, T. (1983b). Some prerequisites for understanding the behavior of people in the sociophysical enviroment. In T. Niit, M. Heidmets & J. Kruusvall (Eds.), *Psychology and architecture* (Vol. 2, pp. 98–101). Tallinn, U.S.S.R.: Estonian Branch of the Soviet Psychological Society & Tallinn Pedagogic Institute.

Niit, T. (1983c). Activity patterns of the family and the experience of home. In *Problems of Perception and Social Interaction. Acta et Comm. Univ. Tartuensis 638, Studies in Psychology* (pp. 79–85). Tartu, U.S.S.R.: Tartu State University.

Niit, T. (in press). Comments on Savchenko's paper. *Man-Environment Systems.*

Niit, T., & Heidmets, M. (1984). Psychological problems of designing cinemas. In H. Mikkin (Ed.), *Problems in practical psychology* (pp. 133–148). Tallinn, U.S.S.R.: Tallinn Pedagogic Institute.

Niit, T., Heidmets, M., & Kruusvall, J. (Eds.). (1981). *Man and environment: Psychological aspects.* Abstracts of a Conference Held in Lohusalu (Estonia), January 20-22, 1981. Tallinn, U.S.S.R.: Estonian Branch of the Soviet Psychology Society.

Niit, T., Heidmets, M., & Kruusvall, J. (Eds.). (1983a). *Psychology and architecture* (2 Vols). Tallinn, U.S.S.R.: Estonian Branch of the Soviet Psychological Society & Tallinn Pedagogic Institute.

Niit, T., Heidmets, M., & Kruusvall, J. (1983b). Environmental psychology in Estonia. Unpublished manuscript.

Niit, T., Heidmets, M. & Kruusvall, J. (Eds.) (1985) *The sociopsychological basis of environmental design*. Tallinn, U.S.S.R.: Estonian Branch of the Soviet Psychological Society & Tallinn Pedagogic Institute.

Niit, T., Kruusvall, J., & Heidmets, M. (1981). Environmental psychology in the Soviet Union. *Journal of Environmental Psychology, 1*(2), 157–177.

Niit, T., & Kuivits, M. (1983). Residential density and the children. In T. Niit, M. Heidmets, & J. Kruusvall, (Eds.) *Man and environment: Psychological aspects*. (Abstracts of a conference held in Lohusalu (Estonia) January 20–22. Tallinn, U.S.S.R.: Estonian Branch of the Soviet Psychological Society (Vol. 2, pp. 186–189).

Niit, T., & Lehtsaar, T. (1984). Privacy preferences of family members. In H. Mikkin (Ed.), *Problems in practical psychology* (pp. 124–132). Tallinn, U.S.S.R.: Tallinn Pedagogic Institute.

Ojala, H. (1980). *Personal space of man and factors influencing it* Graduation thesis, Tartu State University, Tartu, U.S.S.R.

Orlov, P.B. (1981). The provision of residential space at the various stages of development of family structure in new cities. In T. Niit, M. Heidmets, & J. Kruusvall, (Eds.) *Man and environment: Psychological aspects* (Abstracts of a conference held in Lohusalu (Estonia) January 20–22). Tallinn, U.S.S.R.: Estonian Branch of the Soviet Psychological Society. (pp. 135–138).

Ovsyannikova, N.V. (1983). Interaction of parameters activity-environment as shown on an example of investigation and architectural solution of environment for leisure in the apartment. In T. Niit, M. Heidmets, & J. Kruusvall (Eds.) *Psychology and Architecture* (2 vols.) Tallinn, U.S.S.R.: Estonian Branch of the Soviet Psychological Society & Tallinn Pedagogic Institute. (Vol. 2, pp. 128–132).

Parktal, A. (1982). *Privacy aspirations and possibilities for satisfying them during various domestic activities* Graduation Thesis, Tartu State University, Tartu, U.S.S.R.

Parygin, B.D. (1981). *Social-psychological climate of the collective*. Leningrad: Nauka.

Pavlovskaya, Y.E. (1983). Socio-psychological aspects of designing spatial environment of neighborhood territories. In T. Niit, M. Heidmets, & J. Kruusvall (Eds.) 1983a *Psychology and Architecture* (2 vols.) Tallinn, U.S.S.R.: Estonian Branch of the Soviet Psychological Society & Tallinn Pedagogic Institute. (Vol. 2, pp. 66–169).

Ponomaryova, Y.S. (1981). A study of color preferences in children as a basis for designing color climate of the school. In T. Niit, M. Heidmets & J. Kruusvall, (Eds.) (1981) *Man and environment: Psychological aspects* Abstracts of a conference held in Lohusalu (Estonia) January 20–22. Tallinn, U.S.S.R.: Estonian Branch of the Soviet Psychological Society 1981, p. 129.

Ponomaryova, Y.S. (in press). Color—Man— Environment. *Man-Environment System*.

Preem, M. (1981). Some aspects of residential selection and improving the spatial solutions of multi-apartment houses. In T. Niit, M. Heidmets, & J. Kruusvall, (Eds.) *Man and environment: Psychological aspects* Abstracts of a conference held in Lohusalu (Estonia) January 20–22. Tallinn, U.S.S.R.: Estonian Branch of the Soviet Psychological Society (pp. 147–149).

Pulver, A., & Tammiste, S. (1983). Investigation of personal space with behavioral and simulated measures. In *Problems of Perception and Social Interaction. Acta et Comm. Univ. Tartuensis, 638, Studies in Psychology* (pp. 95–105). Tartu, U.S.S.R.: Tartu State University.

Raig, I.H. (1983). The use of home-plots by population and settlement and residence types. In T. Niit, M. Heidmets, & J. Kruusvall (Eds.) 1983a *Psychology and Architecture* (2 vols.) Tallinn, U.S.S.R.: Estonian Branch of the Soviet Psychological Society & Tallinn Pedagogic Institute. (Vol. 1., pp. 194–196).

Raitviir, T. (1979). *A socio-geographic investigation of way of life and its elements (using Estonian SSR as an example)*. Tallinn, U.S.S.R.: Tallinn Polytechnic Institute.

Rappaport, A.G. (1981). Categories of perceptual experience. In T. Niit, M. Heidmets, & J. Kruusvall, (Eds.)(1981) *Man and Environment: Psychological Aspects* (Abstracts of a conference held in Lohusalu (Estonia) January 20-22. Tallinn, U.S.S.R.: Estonian Branch of the Soviet Psychological Society (pp. 85–86).

Raudsepp, M. (1981). *Image of environment (cognitive maps) and the factors influencing its development* Graduation Thesis, Tartu State University, Tartu, U.S.S.R.

Rouge, V. (1983). Personality and the residential environment. In T. Niit, M. Heidmets, & J. Kruusvall (Eds.) 1983a *Psychology and Architecture* (2 vols.) Tallinn, U.S.S.R.: Estonian Branch of the Soviet Psychological Society & Tallinn Pedagogic Institute. (Vol. 2, pp. 107–113).

Rubanenko, B.D., & Kartashova, K.K. (Eds.). (1982). *Future homes*. Moscow: Stroiizdat.

Ruse, M. (1976). About the effect of age, sex and acquaintance on the interaction distance of normal people and psychiatric patients. In *Perception and social interaction* (pp. 59–65). Tartu, U.S.S.R.: Tartu State University.

Saarinen, T.F. (1982). Review of 'Man and Environment: Psychological Aspects'. In T. Niit, M. Heidmets, & J. Kruusvall (Eds.), *Environment and Behavior, 14*(5), 611–613.

Savchenko, M.R. (1981). Six kinds of architectural space-time. In T. Niit, M. Heidmets, & J. Kruusvall, (Eds.)(1981) *Man and Environment: Psychological Aspects* (Abstracts of a conference held in Lohusalu (Estonia) January 20–22. Tallinn, U.S.S.R.: Estonian Branch of the Soviet Psychological Society (pp. 47–49).

Savchenko, M.R. (in press). The architectural space-time: Universals, paradigms, types. *Man-Environment Systems*.

Seredyuk, I.I. (1979). *Perception of architectural environment*. Lvov, U.S.S.R.: Vishcha Shkola.

Shemyakin, F.N. (1962). Orientation in space. In B.G. Ananyev *et al.* (Eds.), *Psychological science in the U.S.S.R.* (Vol. 1). Washington, DC: Office of Technical Services.

Shmelyov, I.P. (1983). The phenomenon of structural harmony in the environment. In T. Niit, M. Heidmets, & J. Kruusvall (Eds.) (1983a) *Psychology and Architecture* (2 vols.) Tallinn, U.S.S.R.: Estonian Branch of the Soviet Psychological Society & Tallinn Pedagogic Institute. (Vol. 1, pp. 176–180).

Shorokhova, Y.V. & Zotova, O.I. (Eds.). (1979). *Social-psychological climate of the collective: Theory and methods of study.* Moscow: Nauka.

Sidorov, V.A. (1983). About planning of low-rise housing for big families in the city. In T. Niit, M. Heidmets, J. Kruusvall, (Eds.) (1983a) *Psychology and Architecture* (2 vols.) Tallinn, U.S.S.R.: Estonian Branch of the Soviet Psychological Society & Tallinn Pedagogic Institute. (pp. 160–163).

Siilsalu, A. (1983). *The permeability of group space in different cultures* Graduation Thesis, Tartu State University, Tartu, U.S.S.R.

Smotrikovsky, V.I. (1983). An empirical investigation of city families' household activities. In T. Niit, M. Heidmets, & J. Kruusvall (Eds.) (1983a) *Psychology and Architecture* (2 vols.) Tallinn, U.S.S.R.: Estonian Branch of the Soviet Psychological Society & Tallinn Pedagogic Institute. (pp. 121–124).

Sokolov, S.I. (1971). Psychological aspects of the perception of the city. In B.S. Meilakh (Ed.), *Art perception*, (pp. 309–324). Moscow: Nauka.

Solzhenkin, V.V. (1980). Distance in interpersonal interaction. In E.D. Shukurov (Ed.) *Social interaction in the light of reflection theory* (pp. 61–69). Frunze, U.S.S.R.: Ilim.

Solzhenkin, V.V., Shilin, V.A., Sirota, N.A., & Ivashchenko, V.V. (1981). Factors of social regulation of behavior and parameters of man-made environments mediating the territorial behavior of teenagers. In T. Niit, M. Heidmets & J. Kruusvall, (Eds.) (1981) *Man and environment: Psychological aspects*. Abstracts of a conference held in Lohusalu (Estonia), January 20–22, 1981. Tallinn, U.S.S.R.: Estonian Branch of the Soviet Psychological Society. (pp. 115–119).

Stepanov, A.V. (1983). Trinity of the concept 'City environment.' In T. Niit, M. Heidmets, & J. Kruusvall (Eds.) (1983a) *Psychology and Architecture* (2 vols.). Tallinn, U.S.S.R.: Estonian Branch of the Soviet Psychological Society & Tallinn Pedagogic Institute (pp. 15–18).

Stokols, D. (1978). Environmental psychology. *Annual Review of Psychology, 29*, 253–295.

Strautmanis, I.A. (1978). *Informative-emotional potential of architecture*. Moscow: Stroiizdat.

Taut, M.P. (1981). Some problems of designing spatial-architectural environments for supporting leisure and social interaction behavior in the cities of Central Asia (social-psychological aspects). In T. Niit, M. Heidmets, & J. Kruusvall, (Eds.)(1981) *Man and environment: Psychological aspects*. Abstracts of a conference held in Lohusalu (Estonia), January 20–22. Tallinn, U.S.S.R.: Estonian Branch of the Soviet Psychological Society (pp. 194–197).

Taut, M.P. (1983). A study of neighborhood contacts with implications for design of residential environments in the cities of Central Asia. In T. Niit, M. Heidmets, & J. Kruusvall (Eds.) (1983a) *Psychology and Architecture* (2 vols.) Tallinn, U.S.S.R.: Estonian Branch of the Soviet Psychological Society & Tallinn Pedagogic Institute. (Vol. 2, pp. 176–181).

Tkachikov, I.N. (1980). *Architectural psychology*. Kiev, U.S.S.R.: Society 'Znanie' of the Ukrainian SSR.

Tonev, L. (1970). Sociological problems of city planning. *Arkhitektura SSSR, 11*, 58–59.

Toomsalu, S. (1983). *On dormitory ecology* Graduation Thesis, Tartu State University, Tartu, U.S.S.R.

Travin, I.I. (1979). *Man-made environment and the socialist way of life*. Leningrad: Nauka.

Tregubov, V. (1981). Psychophysiological peculiarities in the sensation of scale of architectural environments. In T. Niit, M. Heidmets, & J. Kruusvall, (Eds.)(1981) *Man and environment: Psychological aspects*. Abstracts of a conference held in Lohusalu (Estonia), January 20–22. Tallinn, U.S.S.R.: Estonian Branch of the Soviet Psychological Society (p. 103).

Trushinsh, Y.K. (1983). Recreon—a unit for measuring the quality of recreational environments. In T. Niit, M. Heidmets, & J. Kruusvall (Eds.) (1983a) *Psychology and Architecture* (2 vols.) Tallinn, U.S.S.R.: Estonian Branch of the Soviet Psychological Society & Tallinn Pedagogic Institute. (Vol. 2, pp. 82–84).

Valdma, E. (1983). Teenagers' deviant behavior and the sociophysical environment at their homes. In T. Niit, M. Heidmet & J. Kruusvall (Eds.)(1983a) *Psychology and Architecture* (2 vols.) Tallinn, U.S.S.R.P Estonian Branch of the Soviet Psychological Society & Tallinn Pedagogic Institute. (Vol. 2, pp. 194–197).

Visamaa, S. (1982). *Personal space and group space: The development of conceptions about human spatial behavior* Graduation Thesis, Tartu State University, Tartu, U.S.S.R.

Yanitsky, O. (1967). Empirical sociological research in city planning. *Arkhitektura SSSR, 2*, 18–24.

Yankova, Z.A. (1979). *The urban family*. Moscow: Nauka.

Zelenov, L.A. (Ed.). (1980). *Man and the world of things* [Symposium Abstracts]. Gorki, U.S.S.R.: Council of Scientific-Technical Societies.

Zinchenko, V.P., & Munipov, V.M. (1979). *Fundamentals of ergonomics*. Moscow: Moscow State University.

Chapter 38

ENVIRONMENTAL PSYCHOLOGY FROM A LATIN AMERICAN PERSPECTIVE

Euclides Sánchez, Esther Wiesenfeld, *and* **Karen Cronick,** *School and Institute of Psychology, Central University of Venezuela, Caracas, Venezuela.*

An examination of environmental psychology in its Latin America expression is not an easy task. Latin America covers more than 20 million km², contains over 20 countries, and is varied in geography, economic systems, and political characteristics. The scientific activity of these countries is correspondingly varied. This heterogeneity, in the case of environmental psychology, is found in the different levels of development that have been achieved in the field as well as other individual expressions that are characteristic of each country. Thus, although in some countries the discipline seems to be practiced by individual psychologists on their own initiative, in others they enjoy institutional support in teaching as well as in research and in the application of research to the resolution of practical problems.

Because of the immensity of the area, it was deemed necessary to limit the present analysis to those countries in which the authors were aware of activity in environmental psychology. Even taking into consideration this limitation, the task has been complex. One reason for the difficulties is that work that is done in the field is often not published. When work is published, the journals used are distributed only locally and at times are nonspecialized, sometimes even totally unrelated to traditional professional interests. Also, because the field is new, much work is not yet finished, and it was decided that these projects and research efforts should be included because they are an indication of the vigor of present Latin American interest in the area. Often within a given area, there are researchers actively engaged in work that is unknown even to the other psychologists who are also active in similar research in the same country.

To obtain the information for this review, psychologists who were known to be interested in environmental themes were interviewed in their own countries (Brazil, Colombia, Mexico, and Venezuela), and available literature was examined. In addition, work from Argentina and the Dominican Republic was reviewed.

We are sure that the number of researchers working in environmental psychology is larger than those we have been able to consider. Nevertheless, our conclusions must be understood to be based on those activities we have been able to detect, and our sample is limited to those countries mentioned previously.

Also we would like to make clear that the term *environmental psychology* is not the only one used to describe work in the area of environment and behavior in the countries we have visited. For example, in Brazil the term *social psychology* is used to describe research in the field, whereas in Colombia one finds *psychology of housing*, and in Mexico *ecological psychology* is sometimes used.

In this chapter we will limit ourselves to the use of the term *environmental psychology*, and we will identify teaching, research, and applied activities in which the psychological dimension is particularly emphasized in the consideration of the interactions between humans and their environments.

We have organized our analysis in the following way: First, we consider the Latin American context as a background against which this new science is growing and taking form. Then we consider in a general way the effect of the social background on the thinking of the social scientists. Third, we briefly review the development of the discipline of environmental psychology in Latin America. Fourth, we review Latin American research and applied work. Finally, we offer a brief section of final conclusions.

38.1. SOCIAL BACKGROUND AND HISTORY

38.1.1. Science and Society: Their Relation

In any scientific endeavor, but above all in the social sciences, the idea of "pure science" or the creation of a unique, true, and disinterested body of knowledge that is unrelated to the society that nurtured it

is unrealistic. Scientists depend on their society for training, funds, and motivation in the choice of themes for study.

One must take into consideration the meaning of a given social situation in its historical context because the attention of social scientists is drawn to problems in terms of this meaning. For example, crowding in the factories of nineteenth-century Europe and North America or around the mines of Potosí, Bolivia, has a different meaning than the same physical fact in twentieth-century metropolitan life. This meaning is given by a combination of social utility and social consciousness.

In consequence, in reviewing the development of the new science of environmental psychology in a particular geographical area, we feel that we must consider this development in terms of its social context. This concern takes two modes of thinking; the first is to be able to understand the problems that are being studied in Latin America, and the second is to analyze these choices and the methods that are being employed in trying to understand the phenomena behind them.

38.1.2. General Historical Overview

Historically, Latin America has one overriding characteristic that colors all the others. This characteristic is dependence. The subsistence economy of a great part of Latin America and the precolombian irrigation-based empires were converted to an economy of the production of raw materials and the mining of precious metals with the arrival of the Europeans. The Spanish introduced monetary exchange, animal husbandry, and the monoexploitation of nonessential luxury agrarian interests such as cacao, sugar, and coffee. In the beginning, all of the economy was dominated by Spanish interests, and all the benefits were returned to Europe. After independence, the economic structures remained very much the same, with other European and North American interests becoming the dominating forces. Inside the continent, cities founded by the Spanish and the Portuguese, dominated the countryside. The Indian and later the black slave communities were controlled by the Spanish and Portuguese conquistadores, and the cities were the points of departure for the goods that went to Europe. The contradiction between the cities and the countryside became more and more accentuated with time. In many areas, there were civil wars that largely were a result of this contradiction. Venezuela, Argentina, Colombia, Brazil, and Mexico were all scenes of civil wars or localized uprisings that partly incorporated the tension between the interests of a centralized versus a decentralized conception of national interests.

Also present in these uprisings were the "artisan rebellions" (Cueva, 1979, p. 55). For example, in 1847, artisans from Bogotá, ruined by foreign manufactured products, began to participate in political agitation. In 1853, they attempted to obtain import taxes, but this attempt was defeated by the import interests that controlled the congress. They began violent street demonstrations, and in 1854, under General José María Melo, they obtained power in a coup d'état. The Colombian liberals and conservatives, together with the foreign interests in importation then formed an entente. Some months later, the experiment ended with the physical annihilation of a number of its participants.

The contrasts between the interests of the capital and of the countryside have been the subject of literary and scholarly reflection. For example, da Cunha (1975) and later Vargas Llosa (1981) described the population of the *Sertao* an "archaic and rebellious" culture in Brazil.[1] Rulfo (1953), in Mexico, described the terrible aftermath of the infighting between the conflicting armed groups in the last part of the Mexican Revolution. And in Colombia, the last part of the conservative–liberal wars has been described by García Márquez (1970) in *One Hundred Years of Solitude*.

The prosperity of the cities was largely dependent on the ups and downs of the export economies that they were involved in. Manaos, for example, became a flourishing city when natural rubber was a prime export product, but when artificial rubber was developed during World War II, this city became a sudden ghost town. Another example is Caracas, which grew suddenly after the petroleum industry took on importance in the late 1930s and later expanded again with the increase in petroleum exportation after 1959.

Industry began to attract people from the provinces to the capitals in the last century. However, nonindustrial jobs were more important in many areas. Construction, financed by petroleum prosperity, was a chief attraction in Caracas for many years. In other areas, for example, in Rio de Janeiro, people came to the cities because of the difficulties of surviving in the countryside and because of the myth of prosperity in the city.

The poverty of the rural areas has several causes. Although agricultural products like coffee, sugar, and bananas continue to be important export products, in many Latin American countries, food is imported. This has been true since the days of the colonies. In Brazil, for example, the importation of food represented one-fifth of all importations in the nineteenth-century (Cueva, 1979). At the present time, Venezuela imports grains and meat, among other products, because local production is either not sufficient or does not reach the consumers.

All over Latin America, shack towns called *favelas*, *barriadas*, *barrios*, or *ranchitos* house the majority of urban dwellers. The spectacle of extreme wealth, contrasted with extreme poverty, is commonplace. We will return to this phenomenon later in our discussion.

38.1.3. General Environmental Expressions of Social and Economic Conditions

From this background of domination and social inequality comes a difficult social reality. De Morais (1981) talks about the fear of the urban dweller: fear of being attacked by a thief in the streets, fear of being caught between the police and their adversaries in a police action, fear of losing one's job, or fear of arriving late for work because of endless traffic snarls. Furthermore, the cities are decorated with sumptuous buildings such as Bancomer in Mexico City or The Black Cube in Caracas. Huge sculptures in Caracas are part of elaborate urban renewal projects, whereas nearby, people live in precarious conditions on the mountainsides and under bridges.

Outside the cities, there are also contradictions that influence the lives of the people. León (1981), in his book *Ecology and Environment in Venezuela*, mentioned what he calls "monumental engineering" in which huge structures produce modifications in the environment that are not always beneficial. He mentions the Guri Dam and the proposed bridge to the Island of Margarita. Another modification that has been the subject of criticism in a documentary movie is the effect of the changes produced in Caño Mánamo. Parts of the waterways in the delta of the Orinoco River were modified to deepen one canal for the passage of large boats. This change produced ecological changes in the surroundings that have been responsible for economic tragedies and even the loss of life of the inhabitants of the region. The effects of the Mexican oil spills as well as the regional social influence of "petroleum towns" on the fishing and shrimp industries of the area are well known. And the deforestation that has resulted from the cutting of trees for lumber and from the unsupervised clearing of farmland is common throughout Latin America.

38.2. THE EFFECT OF SOCIAL BACKGROUND ON THE THINKING OF SOCIAL SCIENTISTS

38.2.1. Environmental Problems

These historical and social conditions affect the scientific development of the social sciences. When one asks the professionals who are working in environmental psychology what the major environmental problems are, the answers are varied. In Colombia, both rural and urban problems are mentioned. Among the rural problems are the cutting of trees at the sources of the rivers, the contamination of the soil, the water, and the atmosphere, and the possession of the land by a minority of the population. The urban problems are seen as sonic contamination, indiscriminate urbanization for the purpose of economic gain rather than for the benefit of those who will live in the new areas, and the increasing density of the population of the cities. In Brazil and in Venezuela, the answers are largely in terms of urban problems, although deforestation and rural contamination were also mentioned. The urban problems are seen as housing, transport problems, urban violence, and pollution. Another problem was seen to be the existence of the poverty populations with their problems of poor sanitation. The Mexicans cited urban problems, largely the ones associated with the capital city: crowding, traffic and transport, housing deficiencies, and stress caused by the large cities, the problems caused by rural migrations to the cities, and the insufficient communication between the planners and the architects, on the one hand, and those who understand the problems, on the other.

The emphasis given to urban problems is, perhaps, another example of the domination of the cities over the countryside. The conditions that cause the great migrations to the cities are barely mentioned. In Latin America, the indigenous groups that still attempt to maintain their cultures are disappearing quickly, in part due to the same problems of dependence that were mentioned earlier. Instead, traffic problems constitute, together with urban crowding, the major concern, even though the proportion of the population with cars is relatively small in comparison with Europe and North America. The automobile industry does not even represent an authentic regional economic interest because the vehicles that are produced are usually only assembled locally, whereas the design, the technology, and the basic economic control remain outside the area.

Even urban crowding is the result of a social process that originates elsewhere. Barkin and Downing (1980) discuss the Mexican rural process of recent years, and some of what they describe is true for many of the Latin American experiences.

> The producers...of the basic elements for the [local] diet were punished.... Without being given financial resources and technical aid, the producers stayed behind; some survived and others abandoned their farms to become day workers, peones, and displaced persons, underemployed, and without possibilities of contributing productively or participating in the general modernization of the country. (p. 252)

These people often end up in the cities. Nolasco (1980) has described their arrival in the cities.

> Since there is no space in the city for them the "marginals" create their own urban habitat, the lost city, and there they construct their houses as a family business....The migrants...don't find work in industry and in services in the same proportion that they solicit it. There is open unemployment and above all underemployment, and an enormous range of antisocial occupations and socially unnecessary occupations....They employ themselves in thieveries...begging...garbage combing....[They become] windowshield washers and street vendors of articles such as chewing gum,...and in-season fruits. (pp. 128–130)

38.2.2. Organizations that Are Concerned with Environmental Problems

The organizations that have voiced concern about these problems are varied. In Brazil, church organizations, trade unions, and professional and ecological organizations maintain publications, denounce abuses, and carry out consciousness-raising campaigns. In Colombia, there are university-based organizations and governmental entities that inform the public and maintain environmental education campaigns as well as establish norms and supervise their compliance. In Mexico, both public and private organizations disseminate information and maintain campaigns. The new Secretariate for Urban Development and Ecology is evidence of the importance that is officially given to environmental issues in Mexico. The universities are especially active in this sense, both through their own programs and through the participation of university professionals in governmental activities. There are a number of popular, spontaneous organizations, and one finds active newspaper coverage of environmental issues. Also in

Venezuela, there is a ministry-level governmental agency, the Ministry of the Environment and Renewable Resources as well as certain environmental awareness programs connected with the Ministry of Education. Both of these institutions reveal the official activist stance of the government. Other governmental agencies offer seminars, and there are private foundations that carry on campaigns for the betterment of the surroundings. The universities and university-associated centers and research institutions, which are mostly official, maintain research on the physical aspects of the environment and offer seminars. There is also a large number of popular action groups and community movements in Venezuela that carry on campaigns and denounce abuses.

38.2.3.　The Effects of Environmental Activities

In general, the effect of all these activities is complicated by at least two regional phenomena. The first is in Colombia where some of the people who work in environmental psychology feel that there is a tendency to separate ideological considerations from ecological ones and to prefer one of these viewpoints over the other instead of integrating them into a component solution to problems. For example, in the middle class, a problem can be seen as one of land management and rational farming procedures, whereas among the lower classes the same problem is viewed as one of a need for a more equitable distribution of land.

Second, sometimes there is a tendency to focus attention on problems that have been identified in environments outside Latin America instead of using the information obtained outside to come to terms with the problems that are affecting the area. One of the reasons for paying more attention to the problems from other areas is the fact that research is more developed in Europe and North America.

The image of the efforts of the groups interested in environmental issues is still one of impotence, in spite of the clear manifestations of popular and official concern. This is due in part to a complicated network of conflicts of interests between those who are concerned about the conditions that are being created and those who are benefiting from these conditions in some way. There are, however, isolated success stories such as in the case in Brazil where construction of a new international airport was stopped because of the pressure brought to bear by ecological groups. In Mexico, there is a growing consciousness of the need for environmental activities,

which in terms of the field of environmental psychology, is partly due to the aggressive, dedicated attempts of the people in the field to make their point. They are actively soliciting new forums such as in the case of a series of "popular audiences" that were held by the government of the Federal District that were attended by representatives of the newly developing graduate department of environmental psychology at the National Autonomous University of Mexico (UNAM). Nevertheless, the successes of environmental activities are limited. Industry in Mexico City continues to pollute the air despite numerous protests and warnings. In Venezuela, the grass and forest fires that are due in part to careless behavior on the part of the citizens have not been controlled, even in the national parks. Other problems such as the contamination of the major waterways and lakes, industrial air contamination, and the destruction of the fish and fauna are seldom investigated after disasters happen, nor are they remedied.

38.3.　THE DEVELOPMENT OF THE DISCIPLINE OF ENVIRONMENTAL PSYCHOLOGY IN LATIN AMERICA

38.3.1.　Recent History

The development of environmental psychology as a separate discipline in Latin America began in the 1970s. The degree of development is uneven in the countries studied, with Mexico being the one with the most activity and structure in the field; Mexico is followed by Venezuela. The process of this development was also found to be different from one country to another because the universities perform an activating role in Mexico and Venezuela, whereas in Brazil and Colombia academic interests have responded to activities previously initiated in the community.

In Brazil, interest first developed in institutions that are professionally somewhat distant from psychology such as the Technological Research Institute (IPT) that began to study user satisfaction in public housing projects and also in the interest of architects. One psychologist who was interviewed began to teach psychology to architects, at their invitation, in the architecture department of the University of São Paulo. Also there were psychologists who became interested in environmental issues as a result of community organization projects. These community organizers use environmental themes as a nucleus around which community consciousness is aroused and maintained. The first formal university undergraduate course to include environmental psychology was given by Susana Prado, from 1973 to 1978, in the University of São Paulo in the Faculty of Architecture and Urbanism. In the Pontifical Catholic University of São Paulo, there are courses in social psychology at the masters level that now include themes from environmental psychology and undergraduate courses called habitational psychology and housing problems in which María do Carmen Guedes has played an important role. Also in Brazil, there is research done on housing questions in thesis projects at the universities. The Technological Research Institute, which is a governmental institution that offers consulting to private concerns that are responsible for the financing of services they solicit and also the Regional and Urban Planning Institute (URPLAN) which is a private center, carry on research in environmental psychology. The federal government neither gives research grants nor trains professionals in the area. The Technological Research Institute has one interesting project being developed that consists of a design for housing to be used in the Amazon region. The houses will be built of wood that is indigenous to the area. The role of the psychologists in this project is fourfold: (1) identification of traditional wooden construction systems in the region, (2) identification of traditional spatial arrangements in housing, (3) consulting on technological and architectural solutions to the problems raised in 1 and 2, and finally (4) evaluation of a prototype of these houses in the Amazon area.

In Colombia, the development of the field has been somewhat similar to that of Brazil. In general, the professionals working on environmental problems began with the physical, ecological, and community problems they experienced and later developed their ties to the more specifically psychological approaches to these problems. Interest developed from their work with ecologically oriented groups, work with poverty and community organizations, and work with architectural concerns. From 1977 to 1978, Gerardo Marín taught a course in environmental psychology in the Andes University (ULA), in Bogotá; this course was the result of the personal interest of this educator, however, and ended when he left the university. He inspired thesis work that has grown together with other research in the field, both in Bogotá and Cali. Work in applied environmental psychology began with programs in environmental education and work such as that of de los Ríos (1984) that consisted of an evaluation of the area around Cali using cognitive maps. The work was publicized and became instrumental in a later political decision not to urbanize the hills around the city because the researcher found that the hills, as they are, represent important points of reference for the inhabitants of the area. At present, other applications involving psychologists consist of evaluations of deterioration and the establishing of norms.

Even before 1970 there was interest in the relation between the environment and psychology in Mexico. Some professionals link the development of this interest to the national census at that time. A number of researchers had been concerned about the environmental effects of contamination, overpopulation, and other problems. One source that gave a name to this environmental–behavioral connection was the work of Proshansky, Ittelson, and Rivlin that came to prominence in Mexico at this time. It has now been translated into Spanish (1978). Héctor Capello organized the first course given on the theme, whereas Emilio Ribes and Efraín Galván were among the first researchers to explore the relation between environment and behavior. In 1981, Serafín Mercado and Javier Urbina invited a number of people who had been interested in the discipline to participate in regular seminars that became known informally as the Friends of Environmental Psychology. The idea of developing a graduate department of environmental psychology at UNAM grew out of Javier Urbina's original idea of offering specialization courses. This graduate program is now in the final stages of preparation. The curriculum planners wrote to a number of researchers in the field (Stokols, Canter, and Proshansky, among others) and to other places where interest was known to be. Also they distributed questionnaires among local governmental and other centers that might be the future employers of their graduates, to ask what abilities would be considered desirable in an environmental psychologist. Out of these contacts came the tentative plan to locate the students in public offices while they study to provide work experience, economic help, and institutional contacts with the realities of Mexico's needs in a very direct and experiential way. The plan is to begin offering preparatory classes to "level" the students by June or July of 1987. Formal classes should begin by September of that year.

There is a plan to begin to publish a series of anthologies with the editorial offices of UNAM and of the Metropolitan Autonomous University (UAM). At present, Javier Urbina is the regional representative for the International Association for Applied Psychology. The forming graduate school at UNAM already receives, either directly or on microfilm, 22 international journals related to environmental psychology.

In Venezuela, in the early 1970s, interest developed in several architecture faculties and in the School of Psychology at the Central University of Venezuela (UCV) when research was done on space perception, human behavior in open and closed spaces, and other variables such as littering. David Canter, of the University of Surrey, offered a course in the faculty of architecture in the University of Zulia in 1975, which crystallized the developing interest in the field. That same year, themes from environmental psychology were included in an applied social psychology course at the UCV. In 1977, environmental psychology was offered as a seminar in the masters program in social psychology and as an elective course at the University of Zulia. In 1979, a research unit was formed at the Psychology Institute, a center connected with the UCV, with Euclides Sánchez and Esther Wiesenfeld. At present, the theme is included as an optional, one-semester course in the undergraduate social psychology specialization at the UCV. This same course, in 1980, was offered in the faculty of architecture. It now consists of joint field projects shared between the psychology and architecture students, in which the psychology students study the social and psychological variables relevant to the design of actual architectural projects and apply theoretical concepts from environmental psychology to the development of these designs. Also environmental psychology is taught at an undergraduate level at the Simón Bolívar University in Caracas.

The two main tendencies that can be seen in the development of environmental psychology in Latin America are (1) for the work to begin academically and then spread to the community through applications as in the case of Mexico and Venezuela, and (2) for the field to grow organically from the need to use psychological concepts in the solution of environmental problems as in Brazil and Colombia. These two tendencies may relate to the amount of exposure that the psychologists who were involved in these experiences had with outside literature and contacts. Nevertheless, as will be seen later, there is no difference in Brazilian-Colombian and the Mexican-Venezuelan research efforts, proportionally speaking, regarding the amount of work that is dedicated to academic or applied themes, although there is more theoretically focused research (as opposed to pragmatic, experimental, or testing efforts) in Mexico than in the other countries. The main difference in these two groups seems to be one of volume of work and organization in the structures for teaching and research.

Also, as will be seen later, there is a tendency to produce socially oriented focuses such as community organization in all of the countries studied. This coincidence is especially interesting because of the different influences that the academic orientations have had. One researcher told of the experience of having been asked by his students where to find the environmental variables that they should study. This researcher led his students to the window and pointed to a popular neighborhood that could be seen clearly from that academic vantage point. "There," he said, "is where you will find what to study."

38.3.2. Teaching and Educational Tendencies

In this section, we refer especially to teaching and educational tendencies in the countries reviewed. It was found that in Venezuela and Mexico, there is more teaching structure than either in Brazil or Colombia. In Colombia, environmental psychology as well as housing psychology have been taught at the Andes University. In Cali, there is no structured course given. In Brazil, in the Faculty of Architecture and Urbanism of the University of São Paulo, there used to be a design course that included certain aspects of environmental psychology such as interpersonal distance, but this course was discontinued. At the present time, there is a course being given at the Pontifical University of São Paulo in the Psychology Department, the purpose of which is to increase awareness of the role of the environment at the undergraduate level.

In Venezuela, courses are given in the field at three different universities, the Central University of Venezuela, the Simón Bolívar University, and the University of Zulia. In both the Simón Bolívar and Zulia universities, one course is given. In the Simón Bolívar University, the course is given to the undergraduate students of engineering, science, and architecture. In the University of Zulia, the course is given to architecture students. At the Central University, there is one undergraduate elective course given to psychology students, and also there is a graduate seminar on contemporary Venezuelan life that includes a section dedicated to environmental psychology.

In Mexico, there is considerable teaching activity. The original course given in ecological psychology continues at an undergraduate level at the National Autonomous University of Mexico. In addition, there is a seminar course in supervised research that is given by the environmental psychologists. At the Metropolitan Autonomous University, the urban question in social psychology, environmental psychology, and the psychology of poverty and the poverty of psychology have been offered. At the University of

San Luis Potosí, environmental design was once given. Also in Mexico, there is the beginning of a graduate program dedicated to environmental psychology, which has already been discussed in Section 38.1.2. This program will have a duration of 2 to 2-1/2 years and will offer a master's degree in environmental psychology.

The main purpose of these courses is to develop awareness and specific skills. They are still largely dependent on the individual personalities of the professionals who created them as can be seen by the fact that when the creator of a course goes on to other activities or leaves the institution, the course also ends. The graudate department at the National Autonomous University of Mexico is an exception to this rule because environmental psychology has become much more institutionalized at this university. This graduate department is designed to produce professionals in the field capable of doing research and of working on the resolution of practical problems in applied practice outside the university.

In addition, there is the intended result of encouraging an interdisciplinary approach to environmental problems in all of the countries studied.

It is worth mentioning, finally, that a difficulty that was felt by educators in all of the countries visited was that of the lack of a Spanish or Portuguese bibliography. We know of the following texts that have appeared in local languages: Canter (1974, 1978), Dominguez (1982), Heimstra and McFarling (1979), Lee (1981), Llorens, Canter, Stringer, Sommer, and Lee (1973), Moles and Rohmer (1972), Proshansky, Ittelson, and Rivlin (1978), and Sommer (1974). Most of these texts were originally written in English, but sources that have originated in Latin America are also beginning to appear.

38.4. RESEARCH AND APPLIED WORK

38.4.1. Research

Research in environmental psychology began fairly recently. One can date this beginning at the start of the 1970s, but it is at the end of the decade that there was a more lively development in the field. Because of this recent acceleration of research, at the present time there are a number of studies being carried out in the countries reviewed for this chapter. It was therefore considered necessary to include these efforts in our review in order to offer a complete insight into what is being done in Latin America.

Due to the relative frequency of the various types of work being done and because we feel that these frequencies are significant in terms of the special characteristics of Latin America, we have classified the studies according to the type of research being done in empirical and nonempirical projects.

Empirical Work

This work will be considered in terms of the theme of the research and in terms of its theoretical and methodological strategy.

RESEARCH THEMES
Empirical research in Latin America is done on themes that reflect the varied interests of the people who carry them out. These interests run from the analysis of certain microenvironments such as one's living room to the cognitive representation of macroenvironments, such as the city. Also considered are techniques for measuring processes such as the satisfaction that people feel with their surroundings. These themes will be considered in terms of the following categories: (1) the impact of the environment on the individual and (2) the psychological processes that influence the interaction between the person and his or her environment. In addition, this empirical research will be considered in terms of Stokols' (1978) "modes of human–environment transaction."

THE IMPACT OF THE ENVIRONMENT ON THE INDIVIDUAL. In Latin America, there is considerable concern for the problem of the impact of the environment. Of a total of 71 research reports, 47 were addressed to the influence of human-made environments and to environmental "stressors" on the individual, both on a cognitive and on a behavioral level. Of the settings studied, housing ($N = 21$) and educational buildings ($N = 7$) were the ones that most attracted research attention.

HOUSING. In the Technological Research Institute (IPT) in São Paulo, Brazil, in the section called Analysis, Projects, and Rationalization of Construction, there have been several studies designed to determine the level of satisfaction on the part of the users of low-income housing. In one of these studies, which was coordinated by Rosenbaum (1981), it was found that although the inhabitants of these dwellings evaluated the materials and the technical comfort of their surroundings unfavorably, they expressed global satisfaction with where they lived in comparison with the shacks (*favelas*) where they had to live before. In another project, directed by Attadia da Motta (n.d.), similar results were obtained. These results show that residential satisfaction for these people who live in conditions associated with low income is primarily due to their ownership of the dwelling and with its objective economic worth, rather than with its physical characteristics.

In Colombia, Escallón, Gutierrez, and Salas (1976) attempted to identify the behaviors of residents who live in the areas of Bogotá associated with low socioeconomic levels, in which high density and poor public services are common. They found that there is a relation between high density and aggressive behavior, and also that certain activities, which in other residential environments are carried out inside the residences, are accomplished in the roadways. An example of these activities is children's playing. De Angulo, Escobedo, Pabón, and Peña (1979) observed the relationship between high residential density, the sensitivity of subjects of low socioeconomic level to the experience of crowding and interpersonal distance. They found that those subjects who lived in conditions of high density were more sensitive to crowding and maintained greater interpersonal space in the different environments studied. Camacho, Prado, and Salcedo (1976) analyzed the relation between the physical characteristics of multifamily housing and the kinds of delinquent behaviors that developed. The results showed that the height and the location of the buildings significantly influenced the incidence of such kinds of delinquencies as thievery, assault, vandalism, and injurious behavior. Other factors such as certain cultural determinants that influence which populations move into, or are moved into, these areas of high delinquency were not mentioned.

In Mexico, Ribes, Galván, and Villanueva (1973) registered the "density of use" of different areas of residences, finding that the frequency of use of a given area is not related to its size. Similar work has been done by Galván and colleagues (1976). Other authors are evaluating the role of housing in several kinds of behaviors such as aggressiveness (Montero y López, 1983a; Virgen, 1983).

In Venezuela, the impact of housing has been studied in terms of vandalism (Montero, 1976, 1979), spatial behavior and spatial evaluation (Hernández, 1979), neighbor relations (Castro, Guerrero, & Hernández, 1979; Curtis, García, & Naveda, 1978), residential satisfaction (Anca, Fandiño, & Monasterios, 1984; Sánchez, 1983; Sánchez & Wiesenfeld, 1983a), the achieving of privacy (Salgado, 1985), and the perception of crowding (Wiesenfeld, 1984; Wiesenfeld & Sánchez, 1983). In all of these studies, significant associations have been found between the housing characteristics and the psychological aspects that were considered.

Educational environments. In relation to educational environments, Leite de Oliveira (1979), in Brazil, described a night school, based on Barker's ecological theory, considering the students' demographic data, their scholastic achievement, their attitudes toward the school, and the opportunities that the school offered them for extracurricular participation. He found that participation in general was less satisfactory in the night school than in a corresponding day school, although it was not clear from the report of this work what role was played by each of the variables studied. The role of the environment as an independent variable, especially, was not clear in the research report.

In Mexico, Galván and Hernández (1972) studied the influence of the physical characteristics of the classroom in terms of the amount of attention that was given to each area by the teachers; Sánchez (1981) related the amount of space in a preschool environment and the cooperative behavior of the classmates, controlling for the interpersonal attraction that was preexistent among them; and Urbina (1981) found, also in a preschool setting, that the frequency of certain behaviors was a function of the arrangement in the classrooms.

In Venezuela, the relation between building design, user attitudes, and spatial use have been explored (Sánchez, Cano, & Hug, 1979). It was found that the people who use these educational installations tended to feel uncomfortable in the absence of windows and in the presence of artificial light and temperature. In other research efforts, the influence of the interior design of educational facilities on academic achievement (Díaz, Alarcon, and Romero, 1981) was analyzed as was the satisfaction and the participation of students in the classroom (Suárez, 1984). In both of these studies, the influence of the interior environment of the classroom was confirmed.

Macroenvironments. In Colombia, de los Ríos, Tafur, and Arango (1983) identified (1) the areas in the center of Cali in which people sensed more stress and (2) the causes of this stress in these areas. In Mexico, Reid and Aguilar (1983) described the psychological impact of an urban development project in which a centralized food depot for the city of Mexico was moved from one community to another within the city. In Venezuela, Rúa, Serbin and Muñoz (1983) analyzed migration patterns, behaviors, life-styles, and satisfaction with the city environment. Lobo and Verdes (1984) have been studying the effect of tourist development on the life-style of the inhabitants who live in an area in which a traditional culture is maintained.

Other environments. The influence of other environments also has been studied, although to a lesser degree. In Colombia, the effect of the density and the distribution of furniture in a workshop on task completion was studied (Vega, Finkelman, & Bernal, 1978). In another report, the influence of changes made in an institutional setting was evaluated in terms of the interaction of children with cerebral paralysis (Lehoueq & Barrera, 1982). In Mexico, Ortega (n.d.) manipulated density in a work situation, a pharmaceutical laboratory. She found a positive relation between density and satisfaction with the physical environment. Also in Mexico, Arredondo and Doke (1971) measured behaviors in a sample of children in park settings; Botero, Correa, and Franceschi (1975) examined the effects of spatial manipulation in a library; and Montero y López (1983b) is evaluating the role of psychological and environmental factors in the anxiety of the institutionalized elderly. In Venezuela, Sánchez (1976) registered pedestrian behavior in children in terms of the physical characteristics of the roadway; and La Scalea and De Pablos (1985) have measured the degree of satisfaction of university educators with their place of work, in terms of the physical characteristics of the offices.

In all of these reports, a relation was found between the physical characteristics of the institutions and the psychological states and the behaviors of the subjects.

Specific environmental stressors. The environmental stressors that have been studied are noise, contamination, and density. In Argentina, Murat, Romera, Serra, and Fuchs (1979) made an experimental study of the aftereffects of being subjected to prolonged noise. They divided the subjects according to whether or not they were exposed to the noise. These researchers found that, although at first an adaptation occurs to the noise in the experimental subjects, with time there was more variation in achievement behavior in the experimental group than in the control group.

In Colombia, Arroyo and Castro (1977) explored attitudes regarding contamination in a sample of subjects from Bogotá who were divided into three groups according to their cultural level (office work-

ers, university students, and professionals). Although there were no differences found in the three groups in what they were prepared to do for improving environmental conditions or in their emotional reactions with respect to the environment and problems of contamination, there were differences in what they reported that they were actually doing about these issues and on the amount of knowledge they had about them. Mejías and Torres (1976) showed that the kind of vehicle, the sex of the driver, and his or her age were related to (1) the amount of information he or she had about the secondary effects of traffic noise and (2) his or her attitudes about this problem. Gutierrez de Gómez (1980) demonstrated that diminishing noise level in an industrial setting also diminished the rate of accidents and absenteeism, but it did not increase work productivity.

In Mexico, Mercado (1982a) found that noise affected cognitive processes in exposed subjects in the completion of complex cognitive tasks, and de la Torre, González, and Perez Grovas (1982) examined the opinions and attitudes about contamination in a sample of university laborers.

Morakis, Daza, and Fuentes (1979), in Venezuela, found that the frequency of competitive behavior is greater than cooperative behavior in high-density conditions.

A methodological contribution to the study of the impact of stressors is the Noise Related Attitude Scale developed by Romera and Bonet (n.d.) in Argentina. This scale employs Thurstone's successive intervals method.

THE PSYCHOLOGICAL PROCESSES THAT INFLUENCE THE INTERACTION BETWEEN HUMANS AND THEIR ENVIRONMENT. In this group of studies, cognitive processes and other intraindividual characteristics are considered as independent variables in the transactions between humans and their environment. In the first section of studies of this group, certain psychological variables of the future users of housing that might aid in the decision-making processes are considered in the design procedure of the residences. In the second section, the study of psychological variables that are related to the design of educational buildings is considered. In the third group, there are similar studies that have been carried out in settings other than housing and educational ones, and finally, in the fourth section, the development of procedures that promotes the direct participation of the future users in housing design is considered. This last section differs from the first in that, in the first section, intrapersonal variables are considered, whereas in the second, the chief interest of the researcher is the development of a participative methodology.

Intrapersonal variables and housing. In the Technological Research Institute, in São Paulo, Brazil (1982), the reasons for which families from low-income groups are motivated to change their place of residence were investigated, together with the choices these families made in deciding on their new homes. It was found that the reasons they gave were related to their real possibilities, which shows that the awareness of their possibilities was an antecedent to their later decisions. The major wish is to have one's own home, and those who do own their homes do not tend to change them even though these houses do not satisfy their needs. Lemza (1980) studied the social representations of the conditions of popular housing and of neighborhood relations in urban settings in an effort to clarify what lies behind urban ideology. She found that psychological and situational factors in the social structure influence the production of these social representations. Also, Almeida (1985) examined social representations in housing, but, in this case, in a middle-class setting.

Intrapersonal variables and educational buildings. In Venezuela, Sánchez and colleagues (1983) determined children's needs in order to advise the designers of a preschool center in an economically depressed neighborhood, and Wiesenfeld and colleagues (1983) interviewed university students who were the future users of a university campus that was to be built in order to find out their preferences for lawn and park areas around the buildings.

The psychological variables related to other settings. Lemza and Liebesny (1973), in Brazil, and later Rodríguez, Salvato, and Witzke (1984), in Venezuela, have studied such psychological variables as attitudes toward the subway systems ("metros") in their cities; in Colombia, there are three reports of work on the cognitive representation of the city in adults (de los Ríos, 1983, 1984; Granada, 1983). And in both Mexico and in Venezuela there has been work done on children's cognitive representations of their cities (Alvarez, Russo, Russo, & Ramirez, 1982; Méndez, 1985). The role of certain psychological aspects of drivers in the consumption of gasoline has been investigated in the Dominican Republic (Martínez, 1983; Silvestre, 1982); and finally, beliefs about the behavior of throwing away garbage have been considered in Venezuela (Luces, 1983).

In Mexico, in two very interesting reports,

Domínguez (1982) and Reid and Aguilar (1983) induced social changes that had implications for the residents of (1) a children's home in the first report and (2) a community in the second report. In each case, the changes were intended to produce cognitive modifications in the subjects of these settings that would then be instrumental in motivating the subjects to act on their physical environments. Both of these projects will be discussed in the conclusions of this chapter.

Procedures that promote the participation of the future users of housing. Das Gracas (1981), in Brazil, explored the attitudes of the designers of housing projects toward the participation of the future users in the design process. She found that the designers felt threatened by the interference of the future residents, on the one hand, and, on the other, they tended to devalue them. In addition, the designers expressed the belief that participation was impossible because the public authorities in charge of these constructions were too authoritarian. The author concluded that there are serious difficulties in the establishment of cooperative mechanisms between the architects and the future residents.

These difficulties would not be important if there were some degree of coincidence between what the residents and the architects feel to be important in housing. Nevertheless, Liebesny (1984) compared these attitudes in a low-rent population and found that there were discrepancies between them and that the idea of participation was undesirable for the designers.

Fenley (1982), of the Technological Research Institute, considered the problem of how to establish communication mechanisms between the technical interests in the construction of housing and the satisfaction of the future user's needs. She carried out a project designed to gather information about problems of low-income residents and to determine ways of overcoming them. In this project she developed mock-up models as instruments for permitting interaction between the residents and the architects. These interactions showed that the residents clearly perceived the precarious nature of their living conditions. Nevertheless, they usually attempted to solve their problems individually. Group attempts at problem solving usually took the form of soliciting solutions from public officials or other people who were considered to be responsible for solving the problems. Community variables that affected the attitudes were found to be (1) the degree of consolidation in the community, (2) the political orientation of the community, and (3) the kinds of housing there. The mock-up models were found to be effective in determining community needs, even though there were some difficulties in interpreting the results.

In a similar study, also carried out by the Technological Research Institute, Fenley (n.d.) investigated users' needs in order to develop a construction system using locally found wood in the Amazon region, particularly in Manaos. After having collected the information, Fenley designed a prototype house.

In Colombia, Ungar and Salas (1983) studied the significance of housing for people who were participating in programs of self-building in order to assure that the structures would satisfy their needs.

In Mexico, Mercado and colleagues (1983) are carrying out a project designed to determine the minimum requirements acceptable for lower-class housing projects that will permit the government to take decisions about housing design. As a part of this project, Mercado (1983a) is developing a Scale of Inhabitability.

In Venezuela, González (1984) developed a simulation technique to determine housing needs.

LATIN AMERICAN EMPIRICAL STUDIES CLASSIFIED IN TERMS OF STOKOLS' (1978) "MODES OF HUMAN–ENVIRONMENT TRANSACTION"

The authors have considered that Stokols' classification system, because it refers to the nature of people's interaction with their environment in a general sense that goes across specific environmental settings, might be useful in understanding what is being accomplished in this area. Stokols' system of modes of transaction is based on the interaction of two dimensions: (1) the cognitive versus the behavioral dimension that refers to the nature of the variables that are studied; and (2) the active versus the reactive dimension that refers to the degree of participation of the subject in determining the results of the study. These two dimensions combine to produce four modes of transaction: (1) the interpretative that includes cognitive representation of the spatial environment and personality variables, (2) the operative, which includes the experimental analysis of ecologically relevant behavior, (3) the evaluative, which includes environmental attitudes and assessments, and finally (4) the responsive, which includes the impact of the environment and ecological psychology (see Table 38.1).

According to this system, we see in the table that the majority of empirical work in Latin America ($N = 44$) is "reactive" in both the cognitive and behavioral forms of transaction. In the first, the cognitive, are

found the evaluative studies; that is, those studies that take into consideration the attitudes of the subjects toward their environments. These environments included housing situations, educational and institutional settings, and places of work. In this evaluative category, there are 13 classifiable reports, and it is the third most populated category of our analysis. The second, the "responsive mode," is the most frequently used, with 27 research reports. In this category, the reactions of the subjects to environmental impact are considered. The responses studied included attention, achievement, cooperation, aggression, drug use, vandalism, and behavior on the roadway. There were four studies that explored both modes, the evaluative as well as the responsive, which were not classified with the others in the table.

The rest of the research was distributed in the "interpretive" and "operative" modes. In the interpretive ($N = 15$), the work that considered cognitive representations of housing, educational institutions, and cities is found. In the operative mode ($N = 8$) are the studies that include the actions by which people can modify in some way their housing situation. Two studies combine the evaluative and the interpretive modes, and these were not classified with the others.

THEORETICAL AND METHODOLOGICAL APPROACHES

There were a number of different theoretical and methodological approaches. Among the theoretical approaches were behaviorism, general cognitive approaches, and social representations of reality. The different methodologies included laboratory experiments, field experiments, and field studies.

In both theoretical and methodological respects, tendencies were observed. Regarding theory, there was frequent use of the principles associated with perception theories and cognition; attitude studies and the attribution to causality (derived from social learning theory) were prominent.

Although usually the focus has been on single paradigms in psychology, one can find some studies that combine paradigms in their approach to a problem. Examples of work that has shown a combination of theoretical approaches are found in a curious coincidence of two research efforts, one in Mexico and one in Venezuela (Alvarez et al., 1982; Méndez, 1985). In these two efforts, children's drawings or cognitive maps were analyzed for their themes as well as for their use of color and other drawing elements. In Mexico, this research is continuing and will include a consideration of the cognitive maturity

Table 38.1. Stokols' "Modes of Human—Environment Transaction": Latin American Examples and Frequencies.

Phase of Transaction	Forms of Transaction	
	Cognitive	Behavioral
Active	Interpretive	Operative
	Cognitive representation of the spatial environment	Environmental analysis of ecologically relevant behavior
	(Examples: Cognitive representation of the city in adults and children; space perception as a function of environmental exposure).	(Examples: The effects of attitude change and locus of control on fuel consumption; litter control program in a university campus).
	Personality and the Environment	Human Spatial Behavior
	(Example: Relationship between locus of control, residential density, and crowding perception).	(Examples: Coping mechanisms for privacy achievement in different socioeconomic populations; children's use of their preschool setting).
	$N = 15$	$N = 8$
Reactive	Evaluative	Responsive
	Environmental attitudes	Impact of the physical envirnoment
	(Examples: Users' attitudes toward public transportation; beliefs associated to litter behavior).	(Examples: Effects of density on group cohesion, cooperation; relation between type of housing and delinquent behavior).
	Environmental Assessment	Ecological Psychology
	(Examples: Evaluation of educational environments and of different public housing developments; users' satisfaction with their faculty office).	(Examples: The behavioral ecology of a night school setting; participation as a result of classroom redesign).
	$N = 13$	$N = 27$

Source: Adapted from Stokols 1978.

of the children in terms of Piaget's system of genetic epistemology—a variable that is included also in Méndez's work. The Mexican results, which have been organized into a slide presentation, reveal that the children, whose natural environment is Mexico City, include largely skyless representations of big buildings, traffic, smog, and urban violence. In terms of methodology, field studies are common, both experimental and ex post facto; the latter are the more important. The most frequent techniques used for data collection were interviews, questionnaires, and observation. Less frequent were cognitive maps, simulation, and behavioral maps.

There is a large amount of work that deals with collective transactions with the environment (Castro, Guerrero, & Hernández, 1978; Domínguez, 1982; Fenley, n.d., 1982; González Pozo, 1983; Reid & Aguilar, 1983; Sánchez, 1981; Santi, Silva, & Colemenares, 1978; Wiesenfeld, 1980). In addition, there are several attempts at community organization

that have not been included in this review as research efforts because their use of psychological variables was marginal to the central activity, which was more clearly sociological or architectural. One example (Coreno Rodríguez, personal communication, 1980) of these marginally related activities is a community organization project near Acapulco, Mexico. In this project, a group of "squatters" were threatened with the removal of their community because of their alleged contamination of the bay by untreated refuse water. The Self-Government Section of the School of Architecture at UNAM investigated the situation and (1) found that natural filtering was eliminating the alleged contamination, and then (2) began to organize the community to resist removal and to improve their physical surroundings through a project of autoconstruction. The psychologist's role in the project was to help with the organizing through group interventions and through the obtainment of attitudinal data.

Nonempirical Work

Nonempirical studies that are carried out in Latin America, and particularly in Mexico, are (1) reviews and analyses of professional literature, (2) suggestions for the use of concepts and methods from environmental psychology in environmental modifications, and (3) the formulation of theoretical models for the study of environmental problems.

In the first group, the reviews of the literature, the authors consider the role of stressors such as noise (García Bustos, 1978; Zapata, 1977, in Colombia; Covarrubias, 1982; Mercado & Virgen, 1982; Mercado, 1982b, in Mexico); contamination (Restrepo, 1977, in Colombia); urban stimulation (Ribes & Bijou, 1972, in Mexico); crowding (Montero y López, 1983; Santoyo, 1982, in Mexico; Wiesenfeld, 1985, in Venezuela); the importance of environmental education (Orozco, 1980; Uribe, 1978, 1980); the need for an interdisciplinary attack on environmental problems (Covarrubias, 1979, 1982; González Pozo, 1982, 1983; in Mexico), and the theoretical aspects of environmental psychology (Aguilar, 1983; Covarrubias, 1983; Covarrubias & Mercado, 1980; Ortega, 1982; Sanchez et al., 1982; Urbina & Ortega, 1982, in Mexico).

Also in Mexico, recommendations have been made to use the concepts from environmental psychology to produce changes in the environment in hospitals (Santillan, 1980; Urbina, 1980) and to study social problems (Montero y López, 1982). Peniche (1982) has suggested directions for research in the labor environment.

Also there have been models that have been developed to guide research on such problems as crowding (Montero y López, 1981, in Mexico; Wiesenfeld, 1986, in Venezuela); urban perception viewed through information theory (Covarrubias, 1979, in Mexico); and environmental problems (Santoyo, Montero, & López de Rivera, 1983, in Mexico).

Two examples of theoretical models (Covarrubias, 1979; Wiesenfeld, 1986) are the following. Covarrubias has developed a model that relates the complexity of an environment to the individual's cognitive and affective reactions to it. This model proposes a curvilinear reaction to environmental complexity in which both highly complex and highly monotonous environments produce stress. Wiesenfeld (1986) has developed a model in which the relation between external locus of control, long-term exposure to high residential density, and crowding perception are included. The coping mechanisms that people use in terms of this relation and the costs of these mechanisms are considered independently of the mechanisms' success or failure.

38.4.2. Applications

Governmental and private interests in Latin America sometimes accuse the social sciences of not contributing to national development, that is, of finding ways of increasing agriculture, of increasing workers' efficiency, of producing inexpensive housing, and of organizing transportation efficiency. On the other hand, academic representatives complain that their work receives little attention. Environmental psychology, however, is beginning to be recognized for its value in the application of academic expertise to these issues. In some places, there have already been applications. For example, in Colombia, garbage control (Salas & Correa, 1983) has been applied, as well as the formulation of protection norms (de los Ríos, 1983) and environmental restoration (Campos, 1978; Santi, Silva, & Colmenares, 1978). In Brazil, Mexico, and Venezuela there has been work done on housing design (Fenley, 1982; González, 1984; Mercado et al., 1983). In Venezuela, the design of university offices has been facilitated (Wiesenfeld, 1980). In addition, in Venezuela, comparative evaluations have been made of the subjective judgments of the inhabitants of several cities on their life-styles and their quality of life. (Granell, Rúa, Pitaluga, Serbin, & Muñoz, 1980; Rúa, 1981, 1982). These evaluations demonstrate the need for subjective as well as objective assessments of living conditions, in addition to the need to take into account the aspirations of the people in contrast to their objective physical conditions.

38.5. FINAL CONSIDERATIONS AND CONCLUSIONS

Rather than formulating formal and specific conclusions based on the information about Latin America that we have been able to present, we feel that it would be more appropriate to discuss, in a general way, the tendencies and points of interest that have appeared as a result of our analysis. One reason for our caution is the necessarily incomplete state of our data due to the semipublic nature of the work that is done in the area. We have justified its use in this incomplete state because we feel that we have been able to sense a growing interest, an original and creative tendency, that in many ways is a distinctly Latin American expression. We feel that this tendency should not only be encouraged but should also be examined and analyzed by all of the practitioners of environmental psychology in Latin America because, in this way, all of the separate efforts that have been detected can become part of a conscious and critical design, whereas other aspects such as a certain lack of rigor which is sometimes found and a tendency to repeat uncritically what is done elsewhere, can be reformulated.

Of interest are three manifestations of the relation between the social context of Latin America and the research characteristics that have been examined. The first case is a continuation of the cities' domination over the surrounding countryside. The interests of the researchers tend to concentrate on the urban context, with its problems of housing and contamination, leaving aside important questions such as the special characteristics and difficulties of the remaining indigenous groups, the farming communities, and rural problems like grass and forest fires, floods, and deforestation. These problems all have strong behavioral and psychological components that require urgent attention. These components range from the often-bureaucratic and paternalistic behaviors on the part of the authorities charged with the problems to the anarchic and egocentric behavior of farmers, rural developers, and squatters who clear land, destroy rivers, and ignore the local ecological characteristics of the areas they manipulate. The work in Brazil on the part of the Institute of Technological Research, in which houses were developed for the Amazon area using local woods, is an exception to the urbanized focus. More of this style of facing and offering localized solutions to rural problems is necessary.

Until now, ways of dealing with the indigenous communities have remained outside the sphere of environmental psychology and have ranged from the creating of a "reserve" in the Mato Grosso area of Brazil where these groups can continue to use their traditional life-styles, within the limitations imposed by their reduced numbers, to the tendency to absorb these groups into the day worker populations as is happening in the southeastern part of Venezuela. In between these two solutions are the rural indigenous communities that one finds in Colombia and Mexico that live in impoverished conditions and that maintain their languages and traditions at the cost of not participating in the general economic and cultural life of their countries. Environmental psychology, with its combination of a behavioral and a cognitive-affective focus, together with the inclusion of aspects from the physical and external cultural surroundings, is in a unique position to be able to understand the

dynamics of these problems and to suggest solutions.

Another problem that requires attention and that is not strictly urban is the need for work on the conservation of energy (the use of solar energy and the "saving" of water, electricity, and fuels). In the Dominican Republic, Silvestre (1982) and Martínez (1983) have done work on the problem, but these were the only efforts we found on this theme.

The second manifestation of the relation between the social context and research is found in the special responses that have developed to certain urban problems such as the need for community organization. In Mexico, for example, two research groups working separately have used a different kind of environmental manipulation. Reid (1982) and Reid and Aguilar (1983) introduced information into the communities they were working with, and this introduction took the form of an independent variable. The project is not yet finished, but considering the amount of information that is available to a community as an environmental variable that can be manipulated, it is an interesting innovation. In this case, the information consisted of pamphlets and other written tracts that described in everyday language the legal property and other rights of the citizens of the area. The purpose of this modification is to observe the community's reactions.

Another example of this kind of community work (Domínguez et al., 1979), which also includes a strong flavor of social advocacy, is a self-government system that was established in a home for abandoned children in Mexico City. In this effort, modification techniques from the behaviorist orientation were used to induce the boys to cooperate in a system that had far-reaching consequences for them. They made several changes in their social environment such as in the way their meals were served, and, also, the physical aspects of the grounds and building were improved because the boys began to help in maintaining the grounds. Certain signs of deterioration such as cracks in the doors which had been opened before with a kick, disappeared because of a new respect that they began to feel for their environment. This example shows how research with a combination of behavioral modification and community organization can have strong ties to environmental research and at the same time be socially relevant.

In contrast with these two examples that stress the active role of the subjects in controlling their environment is the preponderance of work that is classified as "reactive" in Stokols' system. These reactive efforts are largely directed toward understanding the impact of a noxious environment on the subjects studied. They tend to be descriptive. These efforts are valuable in obtaining a precise knowledge of what is the result of many undesirable present conditions. Nonetheless, the authors of this chapter hope that in the future there will be a tendency to move toward a more active conception of human beings that includes an understanding of their cognitive and affective interactions with the environment. Many of the findings from evaluative and responsive studies can be incorporated in work that not only diagnoses problems and supplies passive solutions but uses the subjects in the solutions of their own design, based on a true understanding of the issues involved.

Two of the present authors, Sánchez and Wiesenfeld (1983b), have done some preliminary applied work on social technology that includes the conscious use of the findings of social psychology in the resolution of social problems. As yet, these efforts have not been developed in terms of their possible environmental applications.

The third manifestation of the relation between the social context and research characteristics is the concern that researchers have shown with housing issues. This theme has been mentioned repeatedly in this chapter because of its enormous importance. At this point, we consider it important to emphasize a few final aspects of environmental psychology's present role and future possibilities in terms of this problem. At the present time, the studies are often interdisciplinary attempts at combining architecture or sociology with environmental psychology. These professional combinations are not casual but rather are considered to be attempts to combine knowledge and techniques and were often cited by the practitioners as an important aspect of what was being accomplished.

The variety of different focuses on the problem of housing is worth mentioning. Although almost all of the work is directed at the problem of housing in the lower socioeconomic levels of the populations of the countries studied, the approaches ran from the Brazilian attempt (Liebesny, 1983) to find out why the architects and the future residents of popular housing are unable to work together in order to satisfy more of the users' needs—to the Mexican (Mercado, 1983b) attempt to find the minimum requirements for popular housing projects, a study that has the nickname "the VW of housing."

In summary, research and teaching tend to coincide with the general theoretical tendencies in the field in the international literature in that there is often use of cognitively oriented theoretical approaches and also the methodology tends to use the techniques found in social psychology. There is some use of simulation and often more specialized methods, but, as yet, methodology is conservative. It is supposed that, as new problems are faced, new techniques will be developed to handle them.

There tends to be more awareness of the international literature than there is of what is being done by Latin American colleagues, even in the same country. One reason for this lack of communication is the lack of a Latin American publication or newsletter that could permit local Spanish language distribution of environmental efforts. There was a conference in Mexico in 1985 on environmental themes, but conferences require travel funds that are difficult to obtain in this region. Some sort of international, systematic Latin American communication modus operandi is now a prime necessity.

A final observation is in order about the emphasis that has been made in the chapter on the coincidence of the cultural context and environmental psychology in Latin America. We do not want to propose an entirely applied approach, nor one in which all research is directed toward the immediate resolution of a specific practical problem. Nonetheless, we feel that this particular branch of psychology maintains an intimate tie with the culture in which it arises because a large part of people's environment is made by them. We would like to see the thoughtful development of an interchange between theoretical development, empirical research, and the ecological, cultural, economic, and political backgrounds in which the research is accomplished. In this respect, we agree with Stea's (1979) proposition in which he suggested a transcultural development of environmental psychology. At the present time, theoretical work is often untested, and empirical work often has tenuous ties with a particular theoretical backing. An integration is necessary.

Acknowledgments

The following people were interviewed in the process of data research for this chapter. We would like to thank them for their attention and cooperation. In Venezuela, Virginia Diaz, Rosalba Alarcon, Oswaldo Romero, Jose Rúa, and Eduardo Habach; in Colombia, Henry Granada, Carlos Araujo, Hernan de los Ríos, from Cali; and Miguel Salas, from Bogotá; in Brazil, Paulo de Gusmao, Aroldo Rodriguez, and Bernard Rangé, from Rio de Janeiro; Silvia T. Lane, Maria do Carmen Guedes, Susana Prado, Sergio Avanani, Caio Fabio Attadia da Motta, Sheila Regina de Al-

meida, *Alberto Abíb Andery, Elisabeth Helena Fenley Lemza, Bronia Liebesny, and Yudith Rosenbaum, from Sao Paulo; in Mexico, Javier Urbina Soria, Patricia Ortega Andeane, Serafín Mercado, Maria Enedina Montero y López Lena, Anne Cecilia Reid, Reyna César, German Alvarez, C.J. Covarrubias, Victor Coreno Rodriguez, Benjamín Domínguez Trejo, Efraín Galvan, Miguel Angel Miron, Irene Ruiz, Miguel Angel Aguilar, and Adrian Virgen.*

We would also like to thank our editors, Irwin Altman and Dan Stokols for their valuable comments on the original manuscript of this chapter. Many of their suggestions have been included in our work.

Funding for the research for this chapter was provided by the Faculty of Humanities and Education and by the Institute of Psychology of the Central University of Venezuela.

NOTE

1. *Archaic* and *rebellious* are the adjectives used by Darcy Ribeiro in his book *Los Brasileños, Teoría del Brazil,* 1975.

REFERENCES

Aguilar, M. (1983). *Percepción y representación del medio ambiente físico y social: Algunas reflexiones.* Unpublished manuscript, Universidad Autónoma de México, México, D.F., México.

Almeida, S. (1985). *O lugar de morar: Sua representacao por moradores de apartamento.* Unpublished manuscript. Pontifica Universidade Católica, São Paulo, Brazil.

Alvarez, G., Russo, S., & Ramirez, A. (1982, April-May). De como perciben los niños la ciudad. *Comunidad Conacyt, 8,* (84–86, 136–137).

Anca, R., Fandiño, F., & Monasterios, E. (1985). *Evaluación sociopsicológica de viviendas de crecimiento progresivo vertical.* Unpublished manuscript, Universidad Central de Venezuela, Escuela de Psicología, Caracas, Venezuela.

Arrendondo, V., & Doke, L. (1971). *Medición de la conducta en parques infantiles recreativos de la comunidad.* Paper presented at the first Latin American Meeting of Applied Behavioral Analysis, México, D.F., México.

Arroyo, M.E., & Castro, M.C. (1977). *Actitudes y conocimientos sobre la contaminación ambiental.* Unpublished manuscript, Universidad Javeriana, Facultad de Psicología, Bogotá, Colombia.

Attadia de Mota, C. (Undated). *Nivel de satisfacao de moradores de conjuntos habitacionais de grande São Paulo.* São Paulo, Brazil: Instituto de Pesquisas Tecnológicas.

Barkin, D., & Downing, T. (1980). El Estado y la penetración del sistema urbano en el campo mexicano. In I. Restrepo (Ed.). *Conflicto entre ciudad y campo en América Latina.* México, D.F., Mexico: Editorial Nueva Imagen.

Botero, M., Correa, E., & Franceschi, M. (1975). *Efectos de la manipulación de condiciones del espacio físico e instrucciones en al repertorio de los usuarios de una biblioteca.* Unpublished manuscript, Universidad Nacional Autonoma de México, México, D.F., México.

Camacho, C.A., Prado, A., & Salcedo, C. (1976). *Algunas características de la vivienda urbana y su relación con un tipo específico de conductas delictivas.* Unpublished manuscript, Universidad Javeriana, Facultad de Psicología, Bogotá, Colombia.

Campos, T. (1978). *La dinámica de grupos en el desarrollo comunal: Un estudio psicosocial del barrio "La Luz."* Unpublished manuscript, Universidad Central de Venezuela, Escuela de Psicología, Caracas, Venezuela.

Canter, D. (1974). *Psicología en el diseño ambiental.* México, D.F., México. Editorial Concepto.

Canter, D. (1978). *Interacción ambiental.* Madrid, Spain: Nuevo Urbanismo.

Castro, L., Guerrero, R., & Hernandez, D. (1978). *Estudio exploratorio sobre la influencia de la densidad residencial y el nivel socioeconómico en la cohesión de grupo vecinal.* Unpublished manuscript, Universidad Central de Venezuela, Escuela de Psicología, Caracas, Venezuela.

Coreno-Rodríguez, V. (1980). (Verbal report of a project).

Covarrubias, C. (1979). Análisis informacional de la arquitectura. *Cuadernos de Comunicación, 47,* 23–45.

Covarrubias, C. (1982, April–May). Impacto emocional de la ciudad. *Comunidad Conacyt, 7*(136–137), 93–103.

Covarrubias, C. (1983). Teorías, paradigmas y psicología ambiental. *Revista Autogobierno.* Universidad Nacional Autónoma de México, Facultad de Arquitectura, México, D.F., México.

Covarrubias, C. & Mercado, S. (1980, August). Psicología ambiental: El ambiente, los significados del uso, la comunicación y el cerco artificial. *Comunidad Conacyt. 6*(116), 80–88.

Cueva, A. (1979). *El desarrollo del capitalismo en América Latina.* México, D.F., México: Editorial Siglo XXI editores.

Curtis, I., Garcia, B., & Naveda, E. (1978). *Influencia del diseño arquitectónico de las viviendas multifamiliares sobre las relaciones vecinales.* Unpublished manuscript, Universidad Central de Venezuela, Escuela de Psicología, Caracas, Venezuela.

Da Cunha, E. (1975). Os Sertaoes 1911 Río de Janeiro. In D. Ribeiro (Ed.). *Los Brasileños, teoría del Brasil* (p. 197). México, D.F., México: Siglo XXI.

Das Gracas, N. (1981). *Planejadores e participaeao da popolacao no planejamento habitacional: Percepcao, atitudes e relacoes de poder*. Unpublished manuscript, Universidade do São Paulo, São Paulo, Brazil.

De Angulo, O.L., Escobedo, M., Pabon, Z., & Peña, T. (1979). *Influencia de la densidad social de la vivienda en la sensibilidad de la experiencia de hacinamiento y en la distancia interpersonal*. Unpublished manuscript, Universidad Javeriana, Facultad de Psicología, Bogotá, Colombia.

De La Torre, A., González, M., & Pérez Grovas, S. (1982, September–October). Encuesta: Y tu cómo contaminas? *Secuencias, 2*(1), 5.

De Los Ríos, H. (1984). La psicología social aplicada. Ejemplo de experiencias en la Universidad del Valle. *Boletin de AVEPSO, 7*(1), 17–22.

De Los Ríos, M. (1983). *Mapa cognoscitivo en vendedores ambulantes*. Unpublished manuscript, Universidad del Valle, Departamento de Psicología, Cali, Colombia.

De Los Ríos, H., Tafur, F., & Arango, M. (1983). *El centro urbano de Cali como desencadenante de stress psicológico*. Unpublished manuscript, Universidad del Valle, Departamento de Psicología, Cali, Colombia.

De Morais, R. (1981). *O que violenca urbana*. São Paulo, Brazil: Brasilense.

Díaz, V., Alarcon, R., & Romero, O. (1981). *Modificaciones ambientales, actitudes hacia el taller y rendimiento académico*. Mérida, Venezuela: Universidad de los Andes, Facultad de Arquitectura, Departamento de Diseño.

Domínguez, B. (1982). *Psicología ecológica*. México, D.F., México: Universidad Autónoma de México.

Domínguez, B. et. al. (1979). Sistemas de autogobierno con poblaciones marginales en instituciones de custodia. In S.W. Bijou y G. Becerra (Eds.), *Modificación de conductas. Aplicaciones sociales*. México, D.F., México: Trillas.

Escallon, A.M., Gutierrez, A., & Salas, M. (1976). *Estudio exploratorio sobre los efectos del medio ambiente marginal en el comportamiento humano*. Unpublished manuscript, Universidad de los Andes, Departamento de Psicología, Bogotá, Colombia.

Fenley, E.Z. (1982). *Populaco de baixa rende. Problema habitacional e participacao: Um estudo psico-social*. São Paulo, Brazil: Universidade de São Paulo, Instituto de Psicología.

Fenley, E.Z. (Undated). *Sistema constructivo en madera para uso en la región amazónica*. São Paulo, Brazil: Instituto de Pesquisas Tecnológicas.

Gálvan, E., & Hernandez, G. (1972). *La atención de maestras y disposición física del salón de clases*. Unpublished manuscript, Universidad Nacional Autónoma de México, México, D.F., México.

Gálvan, E. et al (1976). Mapas conductuales: Una posible aportación al estudio ecológico humano. In *El análisis de la conducta: Investigación y aplicaciones. Memorias de 2° Congreso Mexicano*. México, D.F., México: Trillas.

García Bustos, C. (1978). El ruido en el trabajo. *Contaminación Ambiental, 2*(3), 8–18.

García Márquez, G. (1970). *One hundred years of solitude*. New York: Avon.

González, R. (1984). *La simulación: Su aplicación a viviendas de interés social*. Unpublished manuscript, Universidad Central de Venezuela, Escuela de Psicología, Caracas, Venezuela.

González Pozo, A. (1982). Investigaciones en autoconstrucción. *Entorno, 1*(1), 1–2.

González Pozo, A. (1983). Entorno y asentamientos humanos. Su pertenencia en la teoría de la arquitectura. Paper presented at the seminar on *Nuevos Enfoques en la Teoría de la Arquitectura*. Universidad Autónoma Metropolitana, Azcapotzalco, México, D.F., México.

Granada, H. (1983). *Percepción del espacio en función del habitat donde se permanece*. Cali, Colombia: Universidad del Valle, Centro de Acción Ecológica.

Granell, E., Rúa, J., Pitaluga, C., Serbin, A., & Muñoz, C. (1980). *Estado preliminar del impacto socio-económico DCMA*. Caracas, Venezuela: Universidad Simón Bolívar, Departamento de Ciencias y Tecnología del Comportamiento.

Gutierrez De Gómez, T. (1980). *Efectos de la disminución del ruido industrial en la productividad. Ausentismo y accidentabilidad en un grupo de trabajadores*. Unpublished manuscript, Bogotá, Colombia: Universidad de Los Andes, Departamento de Psicología.

Heimstra, N., & McFarling, L. (1979). *Psicología ambiental*. México, D.F., México: Manual.

Hernandez, O. (1979). *La solución integrada del ambiente social y de trabajo en viviendas urbanas de bajo costo*. Unpublished manuscript, Universidad Central de Venezuela, Facultad de Arquitectura, Caracas, Venezuela.

La Scalea, L., & De Pablos, Y. (1985). *Evaluación de oficinas de profesores universitarios*. Unpublished manuscript, Universidad Central de Venezuela, Escuela de Psicología, Caracas, Venezuela.

Lee, T.L. (1981). *Psicología y medio ambiente*. Barcelona, Spain: Ceac.

Lehoucq, K., & Barrera, F. (1982). *Análisis de los efectos de una manipulación ambiental sobre la interacción de niños con parálisis cerebral*. Unpublished manuscript, Universidad de los Andes, Departamento de Psicología, Bogotá, Colombia.

Leite de Olivera, F. (1979). *Um estudo sobre a ecologia de escola noturna*. São Paulo, Brazil: Pontifica Universidade Católica.

Lemza, E. (1980). *Relacoes pessoais no ambiente urbano: Um estudo de um conjunto habitacional popular*. São Paulo, Brazil: Pontifica Universidade Católica.

Lemza, F.E., & Liebesny, B. (1973). *Um estudo de atitudes de usuarios de Transportes Colectivos*. Unpublished manuscript. Cametro, São Paulo, Brazil.

León, J.B. (1981). *Ecología y ambiente en Venezuela*. Caracas, Venezuela: Equinoccio Ariel, Seix Barral.

Liebesny, B. (1984). *Um estudo sobre expectativas habitacionais*. Unpublished manuscript, Pontifica Universidade Católica, São Paulo, Brazil.

Llorens, T., Canter, D., Stringer, P., Sommer, R., & Lee, T.R. (1973). *Hacia una psicología de la arquitectura: Teoría y métodos*. Barcelona, Spain: Publicaciones del Colegio Oficial de Arquitectos de Cataluña y Baleares.

Lobo, E., & Verdes, P. (1984). *Percepción del barloventeño del efecto Caracas*. Unpublished manuscript, Universidad Central de Venezuela, Caracas, Venezuela.

López, J. (1978). *Las ciencias y el dilema de América Latina. Dependencia o liberación*. México, D.F., México: Siglo XXI.

Luces, M. (1983). *Un estudio exploratorio sobre creencias asociadas a la conducta de botar basura*. Unpublished manuscript, Universidad Central de Venezuela, Escuela de Trabajo Social, Caracas, Venezuela.

Martínez, A. (1983). *Cambio de actitudes y el efecto de la persuación, la expectativa y la externalidad sobre el ahorro de combustible*. Unpublished manuscript, Universidad Nacional Pedro Henríquez Ureña, Departamento de Psicología y Orientación, Santo Domingo, Dominican Republic.

Mejías, M., & Torres, P. (1976). *Información y actitudes hacia el ruido automotor en conductores bogotanos*. Unpublished manuscript, Universidad Javeriana, Facultad de Psicología, Bogotá, Colombia.

Mendez, M. (1985). *Representación mental de la ciudad en niños*. Unpublished manuscript, Universidad Central de Venezuela, Escuela de Psicología, Caracas, Venezuela.

Mercado, S. (1982a, November 24–25). El ruido en la industria. Implicaciones para la seguridad y la salud. Paper presented at the seminar on *La Salud en el Trabajo*. México, D.F., México.

Mercado, S. (1982b). Angustia en decibeles: Ruidos, ruidos, ruidos. *Comunidad Conacyt, 8*, (136–137), 114–119.

Mercado, S. (1983a). *Evaluación habitacional*. Unpublished manuscript, México: Universidad Nacional Autónoma de México.

Mercado, S. (1983b). *Percepción en la Arquitectura*. Paper presented at the seminar on *Nuevos Enfoques de la teoría en la Arquitectura*. Universidad Autónoma Metropolitana, Azcapotzalco, México, D.F., México.

Mercado, S., & Virgen, A. (1982). *El ruido y sus efectos sobre la conducta humana*. Paper presented at the 3rd Congreso Mexicano de Psicología, México, D.F., México.

Mercado, S., et al. (1983). *El Volkswagen de la vivienda*. Unpublished manuscript, Universidad Nacional Autónoma de México, División de Postgrado de Arquitectura, México, D.F., México.

Moles, A., & Rohmer, E. (1972). *Psicología del espacio*. Madrid, Spain, Ricardo Aguilera.

Montero, M. (1976). Estudio psico social de la propiedad *Psicología, 3*(2), 229–235.

Montero, M. (1979). Relación entre tipo de vivienda, deterioro y clase social percibida. *Psicología, 7*(2–3), 125–132.

Montero y López, M.E. (1981). *Psicología ecológica: Una perspectiva constructivista para un fenómeno específico*. Unpublished manuscript, Universidad Nacional Autónoma de México, México, D.F., México.

Montero y López, M.E. (1982). *Psicología ecológica: Una alternativa de estudio para problemas sociales. Sus posibilidades de aplicación en México*. Paper presented at the 3rd Congreso Mexicano de Psicología. México, D.F., México.

Montero y López, M.E. (1983a). *Evaluación de la calidad de la vivienda en Tlatelalco*. Unpublished manuscript, Unidad Habitacional Monoalco, Tlatelalco, México.

Montero y López, M.E. (1983b). *Evaluación de ajuste psicoambiental en los ancianos*. Unpublished manuscript, Instituto Nacional de Sonectud y Asilos Particulares, México.

Montero y López, M.E. (1983c). *El hacinamiento en las ciudades grandes. Algunos de sus efectos psicológicos*. Paper presented at the conference on Consulta Popular. Desarrollo Urbano y Vivienda. México, D.F., México.

Morakis, A., Daza, B., & Fuentes, G. (1979). *Efectos de la densidad espacial sobre la conoducta cooperativa*. Unpublished manuscript, Universidad Central de Venezuela, Escuela de Psicología, Caracas, Venezuela.

Murat, F., Romera, A.M., Serra, E.C., & Fuchs, G. (1979). After effects of exposure to a high intensity noise. *Acústica, 42*(4), 270–273.

Nolasco, M. (1980). El sistema urbano de los paises subdesarrollados: El caso de Coatzaejaleos. Minatilán. In I. Restrepo (Ed.), *Entre ciudad y campo en América Latina*. México, D.F., México: Nueva Imagen.

Orozco, Y. (1980). Papel de la comunicación en la educación ambiental. *Educación Ambiental, 4*(7), 50–55.

Ortega, P. (1982). Psicología ambiental. *Comunidad Conacyt, 7*(136–137).

Ortega, P. (undated). *Efectos de dos situaciones de densidad sobre la ejecución de una tarea grupal y la percepción de características ambientales en un escenario laboral de México*. Unpublished manuscript, Universidad Nacional Autónoma de México, Facultad de Psicología, México, D.F., México.

Peniche, C. (1982). *Perspectivas de Investigación sobre Condiciones y Medio Ambiente de Trabajo*. Paper presented at a seminar on La salud en el trabajo. México, D.F., México.

Proshansky, H., Ittelson, W.H., & Rivilin, L.G. (1978). *Psicología ambiental. El hombre y su entorno físico*. México, D.F., México: Trillas.

Reid, A. (1982, September–October). El deterioro ambiental y la Nueva Central de Abastos. *Secuencia*, 1(5).

Reid, A., & Aguilar, M. (1983). *Impactos psicosociales del desarrollo económico a nivel urbano. Caso: Central de Abastos*. Unpublished manuscript, Universidad Autónoma de México, México, D.F., México.

Restrepo, M. (1977). Contaminación, temores y personalidad. *Contaminación Ambiental*, 1(1).

Ribeiro, D. (1975). *Los Brasileños: Teoría del Brasil*. México, D.F., México: Siglo XXI.

Ribes, E., & Bijou, S. (1972). *Modificación de conducta, problemas y extensiones*. México, D.F., México: Trillas.

Ribes, E., Galvan, E., & Villanueva, L. (1973). *Estudio piloto de evaluación conductual de interiores de vivienda*. Unpublished manuscript, Instituto para el Fondo Nacional de la Vivienda para los Trabajadores, México.

Rodríguez, O., Salvato, M., & Witzke, M.E. (1984). *Creencias y actitudes hacia las normas para el uso del metro de Caracas*. Unpublished manuscript, Universidad Central de Venezuela, Escuela de Psicología, Caracas, Venezuela.

Romera, M., & Bonet, Y.M. (Undated). Construcción de una escala de actitudes hacia el ruido. *Interdisciplinaria*, 2(1), 69–87.

Rosenbaum, Y. (1981). *Acompanhamento e avaliacao de desempenho e ocupacao das unidades evolutivas construídas com alvenario de tijolos macicos em blocos. Nazado de Solo Cemiento*. São Paulo, Brazil: Instituto de Pesquisas Tecnológicas, Guaianazes.

Rúa, J. (1981). Hacia una estrategia para el estudio de la satisfacción. *Psicología*, 8(4), 307–326.

Rúa, J. (1982). Satisfacción ambiental y satisfacción con la vida entre grupos de estudiantes universitarios. *Psicología*, 9(1), 161–194.

Rúa, J., Muñoz, C., & Serbin, A. (1983). La evaluación de la calidad de la vida. *Boletín de AVEPSO*, 4(3), 10–17.

Rúa, J., Serbin, A., & Muñoz, C. (1983). *Estudio del impacto psico-social del proyecto DSMA*. Caracas, Venezuela: Universidad Simón Bolívar, Departamento de Ciencia y Tecnología del Comportamiento.

Rulfo, J. (1953). *El llano en llamas*. Barcelona, Spain: Planeta.

Salas, M., & Correa, H. (1983). *Programa de control de basura en el campo de la universidad de los Andes*. Unpublished manuscript, Universidad de los Andes, Departamento de Psicología, Bogotá, Colombia.

Salgado, A. (1985). *El significado y la obtención de privacidad en la vivienda en madres de bajo nivel socioeconómico*. Unpublished manuscript, Universidad Central de Venezuela, Escuela de Psicología, Caracas, Venezuela.

Sánchez, E. (1976). Exposición al tráfico. Un estudio exploratorio. *Psicología*, 3(1), 3–7.

Sánchez, E. (1986). *Evaluación de viviendas unifamiliares de interés social*. Unpublished manuscript, Universidad Central de Venezuela, Escuela de Psicología, Caracas, Venezuela.

Sánchez, E, Cano, R., & Hug, L. (1979). *Psicología ambiental. Estudio de una edificación educativa*. Unpublished manuscript, Universidad Central de Venezuela, Escuela de Psicología, Caracas, Venezuela.

Sánchez, E., Wiesenfeld, E., Ceballos, L., Sanabria, A., Espina, J., Patiño, M. (1983). *El uso del espacio en preescolares: En estudio de necesidades*. Unpublished manuscript, Universidad Central de Venezuela, Escuela de Psicología, Caracas, Venezuela.

Sánchez, E., & Wiesenfeld, E. (1983a). *Evaluación de viviendas multifamiliares de interés social*. Unpublished manuscript, Universidad Central de Venezuela, Escuela de Psicología, Caracas, Venezuela.

Sánchez, E., & Wiesenfeld, E. (1983b). Psicología social aplicada a la participación. Una metodología general. *Boletín de AVEPSO*, 6(3), 20–27.

Sánchez, M. (1981). Efectos del espacio, los recursos y las relaciones afectivas sobre las conductas de intervención social. *Revista de la Asociación Latinoamericana de Psicología Social*, 1(2), 241–242.

Sánchez, V., et al. (1982). *Glosario de términos sobre el medio ambiente*. México, D.F., México: El Colegio de México.

Santi, B., Silva, I, & Colmenares, F. (1978). *Desarrollo comunal en la urbanización urdaneta de Catia, Caracas: Organización de un grupo de vecinos contra el deterioro ambiental mediante la aplicación de tecnología psicosocial*. Unpublished manuscript, Universidad Central de Venezuela, Escuela de Psicología, Caracas, Venezuela.

Santillan, C. (1980). *Consideraciones para una propuesta de modificación institucional en un hospital psiquiátrico*. Paper presented at the 3rd Congreso Mexicano de Psicología Clínica. Guadalajara, Mexico.

Santoyo, C. (1982, April–May). Hacinamiento: Peligrosa ruptura con el medio ambiente. *Comunidad Conacyt*. 7(136–137), 127–129.

Santoyo, C., Montero y Lopez, M.E., Rivera, M. (1983). *Un modelo para la investigación de algunos problemas ambientales en México*. Unpublished manuscript, Universidad Nacional Autónoma de México, México, D.F., México.

Silvestre, E. (1982, September). *Efecto de la persuación y la externalidad sobre el ahorro de combustible*. Santo Domingo, Dominican Republic: Comisión Nacional de Política Energética, Secretaría Ejecutiva.

Sommer, R. (1974). *Espacio y comportamiento individual*. Madrid, Spain: Nuevo Urbanismo.

Stea, D. (1979). *Toward a cross-cultural environmental psychology*. Paper presented at the 18th Interamerican Congress of Psychology. Lima, Peru.

Stokols, D. (1978). Environmental Psychology. *Annual Review of Psychology*, 29, 253–259.

Súarez, A. (1984). *Influencia del diseño del aula de clase sobre la satisfacción y participación de los alumnos.* Unpublished manuscript. Universidad Central de Venezuela, Escuela de Psicología, Caracas, Venezuela.

Technological Research Institute. (1982). *Analise do processo de decisao habitacional de familias de baixa renda do município de São Paulo.* São Paulo, Brazil.

Ungar, B., & Salas, M. (1983). *Significado de la vivienda en usuarios de programas de autoconstrucción.* Bogotá, Colombia: Universidad de los Andes, Departamento de Ciencias Políticas, Departamento de Psicología.

Urbina, J. (1980). *Psicología ambiental: Algunos conceptos y su aplicación en hospitales psiquiátricos.* Paper presented at the 3rd Congreso Mexicano de Psicología Clínica, Guadalajara, Mexico.

Urbina, J. (1981). *Investigación experimental de algunos factores ambientales de los centros de desarrollo infantil y su influencia en las interacciones sociales y el involucramiento en actividades académicas.* Unpublished manuscript, Universidad Nacional Autónoma de México, México.

Urbina, J. & Ortega, P. (1982, April–May). No lloremos mañana los errores de hoy. *Comunidad Conacyt, 7*(136–137, 130–134).

Uribe, A. (1979). Ideas generales sobre la educación ambiental. *Contaminación Ambiental, 3*(5), 4–11.

Uribe, A. (1980). La educación ambiental en los niveles de bajos índices cronológicos. *Contaminación Ambiental, 4*(7), 5–12.

Vargas Llosa, M. (1981). *La guerra del fin del mundo.* Barcelona, Spain: Seix Barral.

Vega, N., Finkelman, F., & Bernal, R. (1978). *Efectos Comportamentales del rediseño ambiental de un taller en una institución para menores en la ciudad de Bogotá.*

Unpublished manuscript, Universidad de los Andes, Departamento de Psicología, Bogotá, Colombia.

Virgen, A. (1983). *El efecto de los conglomerados habitacionales sobre características de personalidad tales como la agresividad.* México, D.F., México: Universidad Nacional Autónoma de México.

Wiesenfeld, E. (1980). *La tecnología psicosocial aplicada a la participación del usuario en el diseño de un instituto universitario.* Unpublished manuscript, Universidad Central de Venezuela, Instituto de Psicología, Caracas, Venezuela.

Wiesenfeld, E. (1984). *Relación entre densidad residencial, locus de control y percepción de aglomeración en la vivienda.* Unpublished master's thesis, Universidad Central de Venezuela, Caracas, Venezuela.

Wiesenfeld, E. (1985). El impacto de la densidad, análisis y modelos para su estudio. *Boletín de AVEPSO, 8*(2), 23–32.

Wiesenfeld, E. (1986). Modelos de aglomeración: Análisis y proposiciones para un nuevo modelo. In Instituto de Psicología (Ed.), *Contribuciones recientes a la psicología en Venezuela* (Vol. 2). Caracas, Venezuela: Universidad Central de Venezuela.

Wiesenfeld, E., & Sánchez, E. (1983). *Creencias y actitudes hacia la aglomeración en el hogar.* Unpublished manuscript, Universidad Central de Venezuela, Instituto de Psicología, Caracas, Venezuela.

Wiesenfeld, E., Sánchez, E., Oropeza, A., Barraneo, M., Alcala, R., González, R. (1983). *La representación cognitiva de diseño de una edificación universitaria.* Unpublished manuscript, Universidad Central de Venezuela, Escuela de Psicología, Caracas, Venezuela.

Zapata, J. (1977). El ruido como forma de contaminación. *Contaminación Ambiental. 1*(2), 34–37.

Chapter 39

ENVIRONMENT AND BEHAVIOR RESEARCH IN NORTH AMERICA: HISTORY, DEVELOPMENTS, AND UNRESOLVED ISSUES

Gary T. Moore, *Center for Architecture and Urban Planning Research, University of Wisconsin Milwaukee, Milwaukee, Wisconsin*

39.1. INTRODUCTION

The purpose of this chapter is to offer an overview of the environment and behavior field in North America. The multidisciplinary field of environment, behavior, and design issues has been variously called *environmental psychology, environmental design research*, or *environment and behavior*. The term *environment and behavior* is gaining common currency as it broadly refers to the multidisciplinary field of research and practice encompassing the rest. Environment and behavior is the study of the mutual relations between the sociophysical environment at all scales and human behavior at all levels of analysis, and the utilization of knowledge thus gained in improving the quality of life through better informed environmental policy, planning, and design. Environment and behavior research focuses on the interdependence of physical environmental systems and human systems and explicitly includes both environmental and human factors. It also includes studies of the political-economic context of research and studies of environmental intervention—the processes of research and research translation and application.

The task of this chapter is not without difficulty, and the hazards are many. Most geographic definitions of North America include Mexico and Central America, but as there is a separate chapter on Latin America (Sánchez, Wisenfeld, and Moore, Chapter 38, this volume), no attempt will be made to review here work emanating from Central America. The field in the United States and Canada has had a relatively long history, beginning in the early 1950s. Any attempt to overview its 30-year history to date must necessarily be superficial. A rough estimate would put the number of people involved at 2500 (the membership lists of the two largest groups, Division 34 of the American Psychological Association and the Environmental Design Research Association, number 1800, though there is of course some overlap). For the 2500 or so members of the field, there are 2501 conceptualizations of the field. This is only one of them.

An important aspect of the environment and behavior field in North America is its emerging multidisciplinary (or transdisciplinary) character. Although aspects of the field have been influenced by the theoretical interests of the social and behavioral sciences, most particularly psychology, other parts of the field have been influenced by the pragmatic concerns of the environmental design and planning professions, especially architecture. The chapter will review environment–behavior research that goes beyond a strictly environmental psychology perspective. Although general themes from environmental psychology will be presented as a delimited area, the chapter will be more wide ranging and will provide a picture of the whole environment–behavior field as it has evolved in North America. This is no simple task. The many contributing subdisciplines make the outlines of the field hard to discern, and the portrayal thereof not without controversy.

Consistent with the general tone of this volume, my inclination is to view environment and behavior as a multifaceted reality that can be understood from several different perspectives. There is no one, true, integrated history and no one set of agreed-on current emphases or future directions. We should not feel compelled to try to describe the field as if there were, and I will not. Rather, the field will be viewed from a number of different perspectives, keeping open the possibility that some recurrent themes, issues, or unifying principles might emerge. In this review, the field will be described from the following perspectives, and these will provide the structure to the chapter: (1) cultural and historical origins including the pioneers, dissidents, and the mainstream; (2) organizational and institutional infrastructure; (3) theoretical orientations and philosophical underpinnings; (4) mainstreams of recent research and the directions from which the concerns emerged—theory, methods, substantive issues, and applications; and (5) future directions.

39.2. CULTURAL AND HISTORICAL ORIGINS OF ENVIRONMENT AND BEHAVIOR IN NORTH AMERICA

39.2.1. Contextual Environmental Problems

Critical world problems are not unique to the 1980s. People have always been faced with wars, famines, natural disasters, and disease. Overarching social, political, and environmental conditions that face the world today have provided the context for the environment and behavior field. These issues include limitations in global resources, the continued deterioration of the environment, dramatic social changes brought about by rapid technological development, and the volatile and changing nature of political and economic systems for the allocation of resources.

The dramatic social and cultural changes affecting every aspect of North American life influence the environment–behavior relationship and are a major modifying factor in that relationship. With the dramatic changes now affecting cultures, subcultures, and lifestyles, the existing physical environment is no longer able to satisfy its users in the same way as before. For example, women are no longer exclusively staying at home and taking care of the house and children but are demanding their rightful place in society as equal partners with men in the work force and in meaningful decision making.

Present industrial work places are not operating under the same assumptions and conditions about worker productivity they once were. How we determine environmental quality and people's satisfaction with that quality is being affected by the rapid changes that the continent is undergoing. It has been important to recognize these changes for their impacts on the definition of problems to study and also to understand the process of cultural change as a factor mediating the environment–behavior relationship.

The political–economic context of today's culture must be understood if applications of environment–behavior research are to be effective in solving environmental problems. This context provides design professionals and environmental policymakers the conditions and constraints for any attempt to improve the quality of the environment.

39.2.2. Environment and Behavior as an Integrated Field: From Research to Practice

Many designations for the field have been used in North America—*environment and behavior, environment–behavior studies, man–environment studies, environmental psychology, architectural psychology, environmental perception,* and *environmental sociology.* Environment and behavior research encompasses each of these but with some differences. Many of these designations have developed within the context of one or another traditional or parent field. As illustrated in Figure 39.1, the truly interdisciplinary nature of the field and the dialectic between environment and behavior have meant that two designations—*environment and behavior* and *environment–behavior studies* have taken precedence over all others.[1]

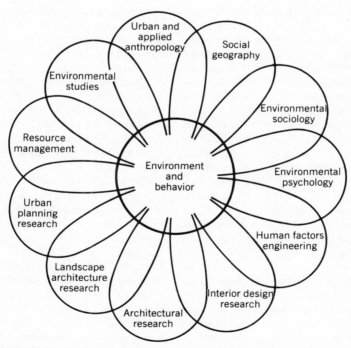

Figure 39.1. The field of environment and behavior—the confluence of several contributing subdisciplines from the social sciences and the environmental professions. (*Source:* Moore, Tuttle, & Howell, *Environmental Design Research Directions,* 1985. All illustrations by the author. Used with permission of Praeger Publishers.)

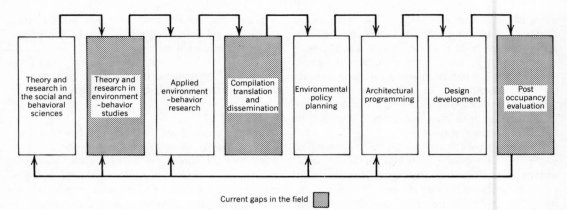

Current gaps in the field ▨

Figure 39.2. The gamut of environment–behavior research and applications. (*Source:* Based on Moore, 1979c.)

Earlier designations implied pure research endeavors without attention to the amelioration of environmental problems or the application of knowledge to the environmental professions. As illustrated in Figure 39.2, the field of environment and behavior is concerned with the entire gamut of research and practice—from basic research and the construction of explanatory theories to the utilization of research for the solution of environmental problems in both the natural and built environments.

Many of the questions addressed in the field are influenced jointly by considerations of theory and of practical application. One of the two heartlands of environment and behavior is represented by the second box from the left in Figure 39.2—*theory and basic research* in environment–behavior studies, the mainstream of the research side of the field. This work is derived from, and in turn contributes to, basic theory in the social and behavioral sciences. A prime example is the work of the ecological psychologists, both articulating a perspective on environment–behavior phenomena and contributing to the infrastructure of psychology as a discipline (e.g., the work of Barker & Wright, 1955; Barker & Gump, 1964; Wicker, 1979; Willems, 1977).

Another body of empirical work has focused on *applied research* in particular settings important to the quality of the environment. This line of work, represented in the next box to the right, is influenced by the environmental professions and contributes to the solution of environmental problems *and* to the more general corpus of theory and research in the field. Prime examples are the work of Appleyard (e.g., his 1981 book, *Livable Streets*) and of his long-time associate and mentor, Kevin Lynch (e.g., the 1960 classic *The Image of the City*). These have been di-

rected to understanding environmental issues faced daily by the public and by landscape architects, urban designers, and urban planners, issues of the planning and design of the urban fabric of our cities (see also Hack, 1984).

Yet another heartland of environment and behavior in North America is the arena of *environmental problem-solving* via the various environmental professions. Although not represented in the association structures and scientific literature until recently, this has been a major thrust of the field since its inception (e.g., the early work of Ittelson and his colleagues on the effects of psychiatric ward design [Ittelson, Proshansky, & Rivlin, 1970] and the formation of the Environmental Design Research Association in 1968 comprised of applied researchers from the professions and the social sciences). It is represented by three boxes on the right side of Figure 39.2—*environmental policy planning, facility programming*, and *design development*—the range of professional activities whereby environmental policy is set and design is realized. At their best, these professional activities are derived from the latest research, including environment and behavior research. Prime examples of policy development at the building scale are the work of Archea, Margulis, and Ventre at the U.S. National Bureau of Standards (Archea, 1977; Archea & Margulis, 1979; Margulis, 1977; Ventre, 1975, 1982). Examples of facility programming include the anthologies of programming methods in Sanoff (1977), Preiser (1978), and Palmer (1981). In design, process models have been advocated by Conway (1973), Zeisel (1975, 1981), and Villecco and Brill (1981), and an empirical assessment of the impact of research on design has been given by Reizenstein (1975).

Between environment–behavior theory and the

environmental professions is a box representing the *compilation, translation, and dissemination* of research findings to the professions. The American Planning Association maintains a research office charged with the compilation, translation, and dissemination of research-based information to the planning field. The U.S. Army Corps of Engineers and the American Institute of Architects has created a series of planning and design guides in order to increase social science input into architectural practice (see American Institute of Architects, 1982; Moore, Cohen & McGinty, 1979; Zeisel, Epp, & Demos, 1978; Zeisel, Welsh, Epp, & Demos, 1984). This link represents both a feed-forward of information, and equally importantly, a feed-back of questions needing research resolution.

On the far right side of Figure 39.2 is a box representing *environmental* or *postoccupancy evaluation* — the evaluation of environments in use to determine lessons for future planning and design and to answer questions needing further research resolution (see the collections of evaluation methods and case studies in Friedman, Zimring, & Zube, 1978; Moore, 1982; Reizenstein & Zimring, 1980; Zube, 1980a).

Environment and behavior in North America is characterized by all of these concerns, most especially the concerns of the social sciences for basic research and theory construction and the concerns of the environmental professions for readily applicable research findings to environmental problems. This dual nature of the field is not without tension, as has been evident in a number of the *Proceedings* of the Environmental Design Research Association (1969, etc.).

39.2.3. A Historical Sketch: Stages of Development

Research on questions of environment and behavior can be traced to the turn of the century. The American geographer F.P. Gulliver published on orientation in children in 1908, and the American scientist C.C. Trowbridge published on "imaginary maps" in 1913. An even earlier piece of research was that of the French missionary Pierre Lafitau (cited in Claparède, 1943), who recorded the ability of the North American Iroquois to find their way in dense, unmarked regions.

The field may be characterized as following orthogenetic principles of development (Werner, 1949): (1) a global exploratory stage; (2) the period of systematic differentiation and isolated research; and (3) the emergence of the field as an integrated entity.[2]

Global Exploration during the Late 1940s and Early 1950s

The first period of environment and behavior research in North America can be characterized as the period of exploration by intellectual dissidents within the social sciences (now seen as forerunners, once as dissidents). A number of groundbreaking studies were published in the late 1940s and early 1950s that had their ardent but small group of followers. The work of the sociologist Walter Firey (1945) on the symbolism of cities led later to the work of Anselm Strauss and his students on imagery of the city (Strauss, 1961). This work can be traced back to the 1850s to the lectures of Horace Greeley on people's images of cities and how this influenced urban behavior (Strauss, 1968). A radical view in sociology with few followers, this view is now well accepted (Pipkin, LeGory, & Blau, 1983).

In geography, the work of Wright in the late 1940s explored ground for others to follow (Wright, 1947). Parting with physicalistic and environmental deterministic colleagues, Wright studied *terrae incognitae* or *geosophy* — geographical knowledge in all its forms and how people's conceptions of their geographical environment affect spatial behavior. Until the early 1960s, despite Wright's prestige in the field, geography was content to explore the nature of the environment as if this exploration could be divorced from those experiencing and imaging the structure of that environment (see Lowenthal, 1961; Saarinen, Seamon, & Sell, 1984).

In psychology, the work of Edward C. Tolman in the late 1940s on cognitive maps in animals and humans (Tolman, 1948; also Tolman, 1932; Tolman & Brunswik, 1935) and Festinger, Schachter, and Back's (1950) study of the development of informal social groups as a function of design factors are often cited as early forerunners of environment–behavior research. Other studies did exist, for example, the famous Hawthorne study (Roethlishberger & Dickson, 1939), but these latter did not affect environment and behavior in any significant way. Prior to that time, the primary concern of psychologists was on the processes of behavior, treating environment as an undifferentiated whole and most often ignoring the products of behavior. Festinger, Schachter, and Back (1950), in conducting a conventional social psychological study of group behavior, found that the layout of the physical environment had a marked influence on behavior. Their study is cited extensively as a starting point for the study of the influences of the designed environment on human behavior, though it was a one-off study that waited many years for its successor or its recognition.

In the environmental professions, the period of exploration by the dissidents did not come until the beginning of the 1960s. Kevin Lynch's *The Image of the City* (1960) challenged urban designers and planners to consider the role of legibility and imagability in design and planning and to study qualities of the physical environment that lead to greater recognition, memory, and recall. Lynch and his followers argued that the categories of design be based not on artistic and historic categories but on the ways in which everyday users of the environment see, think about, and react to the environment (Appleyard, 1969).

No evidence has come forth that these scholars were aware of each other's work during the period of the late 1940s, 1950s, and into the beginning of the 1960s, or saw their work as part of a more general move toward a comprehensive, integrated field.

Systematic Differentiated Research during the Mid- and Late-1950s

A series of well-known studies was initiated during the mid- and late-1950s that have continued to have a marked impact on the field. They constitute what appears to be the second stage of development of the field.

Among the early bodies of systematic research were the studies started in 1947 by Barker and his colleagues at the Midwest Psychological Field Station in Topeka, Kansas. As detailed in Bechtel (n.d.), the field station was set up to study the effects of the total environment on child development (Barker & Wright, 1951). Early studies looked at small-town behavior in the United States in comparison to England (Barker & Wright, 1955) and at schools (Barker & Gump, 1964). Barker and his associates laid out a new method for the study of behavior in the ecological environment based on systematic observation, behavior specimens, and settings. The Psychological Field Station closed in 1972, but a series of studies emanated from these beginnings by Barker, his colleagues, and his students (Barker & Associates, 1978; Barker & Schoggin, 1973; Bechtel, 1977; Wicker & Kirmeyer, 1976; Willems, 1977; cf. Wicker, 1979).

The landscape naturalist, Jackson, had a profound influence on the field (Jackson, 1951–1968; cf. Zube, 1970). Jackson's roots can be traced to the influence of Sauer and the Berkeley school of historical geography, who long advocated looking at the landscape in terms of different cultural appraisals (Gold, 1980).

Jackson was a careful observer of the American landscape—both natural and human made—and many scholars in the field credit their beginnings to his writings. His journal, *Landscape*, provided a forum for discussion and debate among many people from different disciplines. The first published papers of Rapoport (1964–1965) and Stea (1967) were actively sought out by Jackson and published in *Landscape*. The earlier paper by Tuan (1961) on "topophilia" was published in *Landscape* and led to his book by the same title.

The first anthropologist to begin systematic writings that were later incorporated into the field was E.T. Hall. His influence stemmed from two widely read books, *The Silent Language* (1959) and *The Hidden Dimension* (1966), which are still on the shelves of many university bookstores. Hall demonstrated the power of spatial distances as a "silent language" affecting behavior and showed how they are culturally relative. He developed the concept of *proxemics*, which has come to be associated with the study of spatial behavior and distances between people. Of the four major categories of spatial distance among humans, personal space and territoriality have been subject to the most extensive research, books, and reviews (Altman & Vinsel, 1977; Hayduk, 1983).

In Canada, Humphrey Osmond (1957), a research psychiatrist, published a paper on psychiatric ward design wherein the concepts of *sociofugal space* (the organization of space that encourages small–group interaction) and *sociopetal space* (discourages social interaction) were first articulated and demonstrated. Working together with Osmond, Kyo Izumi (1957) translated these concepts into a new mental hospital design. Also in Saskatchewan, Robert Sommer, a social psychologist working as a postdoctoral fellow with Osmond, completed a study of territoriality in humans (Sommer & Ross, 1958). He went on to study a number of dimensions of personal space, published collectively in his now classic *Personal Space: The Behavioral Basis of Design* (1969).

In the United States, Ittelson, Proshansky, Rosenblatt, and Rivlin began a research program in the late 1950s on the influence of ward design on patients in mental hospitals. A grant was awarded by the U.S. National Institute of Mental Health (NIMH) in 1958, and led to the first report from this group, "Some Factors Influencing the Design and Function of Psychiatric Facilities" (Ittelson, 1961; see Ittelson, Proshansky, & Rivlin, 1970). One of the early programs of systematic research on environment–behavior phenomena, it also led to the formation of the most enduring program in interdisciplinary "environmental psychology" and the first textbook (Ittelson, Proshansky, Rivlin, & Winkel, 1974).

At much the same time, White and his colleagues in geography initiated a program of research at the University of Chicago (White, 1945, 1961; cf. Gold, 1980). White was influential in the development of behavioral geography and in starting the broader environment–behavior field in relation to resource management. A prominent product of that school, Kates, has since extended this work into human-made hazards, risk assessment, and human relationality (Fischoff, Hohenemser, Kasperson, & Kates, 1978; Hohenemser, Kasperson, & Kates, 1977; Kates, 1978) that can be traced back to his dissertation (1962, 1967; cf. Mitchel, 1984).

Meanwhile, from the professional side, the Research Committee of the American Institute of Architects (AIA) submitted a proposal to the National Science Foundation (NSF) in 1956 to host a conference on the relationship of the physical, biological, and social sciences to the problems of "optimum created environments for human activities" (Magenau, 1959, cited in Bechtel, n.d.). The conference was held in 1959 at the University of Michigan. The AIA Convention in Cleveland in 1958 had a seminar on research that foreshadowed it, including representatives from architecture, civil engineering, urban planning, environmental health, psychology, and sociology. It produced an agenda for sociobiological research in architecture. Influenced by these stirrings, Miller, an architect, and Wheeler, a psychologist, began what may be the first collaboration of an architect with a social scientist in 1958. This resulted in a series of dormitories built for the University of Indiana (later evaluated and documented by Wener, 1982).

The eighth group to be mentioned is that of Alexander, his students and followers. Though Alexander began his work later than the others, his historical place is assured by his own contributions, bringing people together who later contributed to the infrastructure of the field, and by the influence of his colleagues and students. Alexander's Notes on the Synthesis of Form (1964) led to a revolution in systematic design methods (see the Design Methods Group Newsletter and its successor journal, Design Theories and Methods). Alexander's writings have been translated widely, and he is considered by some to be the most influential writer on architectural theory and research in the past 25 years (see Alexander, Ishikawa, & Silverstein, 1977).

The "field" did not have a comprehensive integrated conception by the beginning of the 1960s, but important programs of research had begun and continued, including research by the same investigating teams and by leaders and their students and followers spreading out over the continent.

Emergence as an Integrated Field

During the 1960s and 1970s, the field emerged as one of the fastest growing areas of both psychological and architectural research and witnessed major contributions from a variety of other disciplines from human factors to urban anthropology, interior design to public administration. Classic works published during that time include the architect and anthropologist Rapoport's (1969) book on the relation of culture to house form, the series of bibliographic volumes edited by architect Larson (1965) on schools, sociologist Gans's (1962) study of the life space, housing, and neighborhoods of immigrant groups, social psychologist Altman's studies of the ecology of isolated groups (Altman & Haythorn, 1967), and the psychologist Stea's (1969) studies of cognitive mapping.

Collective interest among psychologists, geographers, sociologists, and architects became evident with the publication of the first directory of Behavior and Environmental Design (Studer & Stea, 1965; most recently updated by White, 1984) and the first special issue of a journal devoted to this new area, the Journal of Social Issues, "Man's Response to the Physical Environment" (Kates & Wohlwill, 1966; cf. Craik, n.d.). The results include widespread research activity in universities, industry, government, and the professions and the beginning of the application of findings in government policymaking and professional practice.

As an expression of these developments, a group was called together by the present author at the Massachusetts Institute of Technology after the 1968 international conference of the Design Methods Group, also organized by the present author. Representatives from both the Design Methods Group and the Architectural Psychology Newsletter formed a new integrative, scholarly, and professional association, the Environmental Design Research Association (EDRA), in June, 1968. EDRA held its first annual conference in 1969 and published the first annual Proceedings the same year. It is the oldest and largest organization in the world devoted to environment–behavior studies and applications. The major research journal in the field, Environment and Behavior, began in 1969 and has been published in cooperation with EDRA since 1980. The American Psychological Association formed a Task Force on Environment and

Behavior in 1974 and began a joint Division of Population and Environmental Psychology in 1976.

Since then the field has developed coherent statements of definition and purpose that are agreed on by members hailing from different parent disciplines (e.g., Zeisel, from sociology, 1975; Stokols, from psychology, 1977a; and Villecco & Brill, 1981, and Moore, Tuttle, & Howell, 1985, from environment, behavior, and design).

39.2.4. The Utility of Environment–Behavior Research

Environment and behavior research is an emergent discipline old enough to have produced results and impacts in North America. A few examples will be given.

Based on research done in the 1960s at the National Bureau of Standards on human performance in office buildings, we know that the ratio of personnel to capital costs in major corporations is about 30:1 (Villecco & Brill, 1981). First-year costs are 2:1 between salaries and new construction, but over a 25-year life cycle of a building, capital costs drop to less than 3% of total costs. If there is a causal relationship between the design of office environments and the productivity of office workers, the economics of environment–behavior research and of behaviorally supportive design are very attractive (Brill, 1982). This causal relationship has been demonstrated. The Harris Organization showed that the office environment is important for job satisfaction (41% of a national sample) (Harris & Associates, 1978). Other studies have shown that job satisfaction affects productivity (by lowering absentee rates, turnover, and grievance actions—Brill, 1982; Sundstrom, Kastenbaum, & Konar-Goldband, 1978; Villecco & Brill, 1981). Studies that led to these findings were conducted for major U.S. corporations (Steelcase, Monsanto, IBM, Kodak, Port of New York Authority, Exxon, and the U.S. General Services Administration) and are currently being applied to the redesign of existing offices and to design guidelines for new offices (see Sundstrom, Chapter 19, this volume).

An early study that had a major impact on environmental policy was Schorr's *Slums and Social Insecurity* (1963) that probed housing from various angles to see how it related to the lives of the poor. Schorr argued, with evidence from the social sciences, that housing affects the perception of one's self, stress, and health. He found that a wide range of architectural, political, and social decisions about housing—like providing choice, identity, and diversity—have explicit consequences for security or insecurity. A series of policy recommendations for reducing poverty in the United States led, in part, to the formation of the U.S. Department of Housing and Urban Development, which was chartered to give cabinet status to efforts to provide housing, development, and open space for all Americans.

Vandalism and crime have been increasing problems in public schools, transportation systems, recreational facilities, and public spaces in the United States, costing public schools alone about $220 million in 1975 (National School Public Relations Association, 1975) and an estimated $377 million in 1981 (Brill, 1982). Applied environment–behavior research looked at this issue, finding five environmental design factors related to low incidence of school vandalism: (1) aesthetic quality; (2) good maintenance; (3) natural surveillance; (4) location in areas of diversified and high activity; and (5) in areas of high illumination (Allen, 1978; Pablant & Baxter, 1975). A series of design guidelines for reducing school vandalism (Zeisel, 1976) was published by Educational Facilities Laboratories and the American Association of School Administrators for use in the nation's schools.

Newman (1976) described vandalism as a factor in the cycle of disintegration of public housing in the United States. Newman's studies, published widely in the popular press including *Newsweek*, *Time*, *Intellectual Digest*, and the *New York Times*, argued that four factors can contribute to the reduction of vandalism in housing: (1) natural surveillance, or what Jacobs earlier called "eyes on the street" (Jacobs, 1961); (2) well-defined territories; (3) image; and (4) proximity to safe zones (Newman, 1971, 1973, 1976, 1980). Though there is ample criticism of the methods and findings (see Fisher, Bell, & Baum, 1984), many housing projects around the country have been affected by these findings, as was the Crime Prevention through Environmental Design Program developed by the U.S. Law Enforcement Assistance Administration. It is safe to say that most urban design and architectural students in the country routinely—if blindly—apply these four design principles.

Research in environment–behavior issues have also had impacts on policy, planning, and design in natural environments, including parks and forests. As Pitt and Zube note (Chapter 27, this volume), increased demands for use of natural environments for both commodity and noncommodity interests has frequently shifted managers and planners from a primary focus on natural resources to a focus on the users of the resources, their values, and conflicts among them. Research findings have influenced timber harvest practices so as to reduce aesthetic impacts, stimulated programs for coping with deviant behavior in campgrounds, picnic areas, and other natural settings, and contributed to revisions of management schemes to accommodate the varying motivations of users to reduce potential conflicts among them.

Legislative bodies, regulatory and enforcement agencies, and the courts have shown an increasing concern for the environmental aspects of consumer safety. The U.S. Consumer Protection Safety Commission (1975) identified stairs and children's playgrounds among the top 10 causes of consumer accidents. The National Bureau of Standards and the National Park and Recreation Association were asked to conduct research on the causes of these accidents and to recommend new planning and design standards. The single greatest cause of accidents was found to be the type of surface under play equipment (with 59% of all injuries caused by falls directly to a hard surface (Rutherford, 1978; U.S. Consumer Product Safety Commission, 1975). These and other findings have been translated into a set of national recommendations for playground safety issued by the U.S. Consumer Product Safety Commission (1981), impacting school, recreation, and county playgrounds across the country.

One of the most powerful demonstrations of the impacts of environment–behavior research on new planning and design standards is the revision of the American National Standards Institute (ANSI) standards on access to buildings for the visually and physically handicapped. A state-of-the-art literature search was followed by field and laboratory research and simulation of potential economic consequences of various regulatory changes (Steinfeld, 1979). This research led to new ANSI Standard A117.7 (American National Standards Institute, 1979) that received accolades from *Progressive Architecture* in the 1978 awards program and has been implemented in most states.

39.3. ORGANIZATIONAL AND INSTITUTIONAL INFRASTRUCTURE

39.3.1. Conferences, Newsletters, and Journals

In 1967, Richard Meier gave a talk at Berkeley in which he recounted the benchmarks in the development of a discipline. This section will outline some of the benchmarks in our field.

The first conferences were sponsored by the AIA. The research committee of the AIA organized a research seminar as part of their 1958 annual convention in Cleveland, and organized, under NSF sponsorship, the first conference focused on the relationships of the social sciences to the environmental professions, held in 1959 at the University of Michigan. Meanwhile, at the University of Utah, under the guidance of Roger Bailey from architecture and Calvin Taylor from psychology and sponsorship from the U.S. National Institute of Mental Health, two national conferences were held in 1961 and 1966 that brought together for the first time many people who are now recognized as leaders in the field. Informal proceedings were produced on Taylor's well-known yellow pulp paper, a few faded copies of which can still be found (Bailey, Branch, & Taylor, 1961; Taylor, Bailey, & Branch, 1967).

Formed in 1966 at the end of a conference at the University of Waterloo, in Canada by myself and others, the Design Methods Group held its first conference in June 1968 at the Massachusetts Institute of Technology. Dissatisfaction with planning and design methods divorced from the content of architectural psychology led to a series of annual conferences sponsored by the newly formed Environmental Design Research Association (about which more will be said later). The first of these was held in 1969 at the University of North Carolina and has been held annually since.

Parallel to the emergence of conferences were newsletters devoted to work in progress. The first were the *Design Methods Group Newsletter* from Berkeley (Moore, 1966), and the *Architectural Psychology Newsletter* from the University of Utah (Archea, 1967). When Archea and company moved to the new program at Pennsylvania State University in 1969, the *Architectural Psychology Newsletter* was combined with Esser's similar efforts to create the news journal *Man–Environment Systems* (Archea & Esser, 1969). The *DMG Newsletter* was picked up by Sage Publications and led to the development of the journal *Design Methods and Theories*, also in 1969.

At the same time, a group led by psychologist Joachim Wohlwill and geographer Robert Kates, both at Clark University, compiled the first special issue of a journal devoted to research on environment and behavior—"Man's Response to the Physical Environment" in the *Journal of Social Issues* (Kates & Wohlwill, 1966; see Wohlwill, in press).

Meanwhile, on the other coast, there were stirrings led by Gary Winkel and Philip Thiel at the University of Washington, joined later by Francis Ventre at UCLA, that led in March of 1969 to the first issue of *Environment and Behavior*, published by Sage Publications (Winkel, 1969). With the emergence of *Environment and Behavior*, regular and systematic communication of research was available to the field.

Other journals appeared during this time, some continuing and some appearing only for a few years. *Design and Environment* began publication in 1969 to communicate research results to practitioners. In 1971, the *Journal of Architectural Research* appeared. After a few successful years, it succumbed to low readership and financial difficulties, then reemerged under new sponsorship as the *Journal of Architectural and Planning Research* (Seidel, 1983). *Nonverbal Behavior and Environmental Psychology* met the same difficulties. Other journals appeared that publish some environment–behavior research—*Human Ecology* (Vayda, 1973) and *Population and Environment* (Thompson & Taylor, 1978). Journals in traditional fields now also publish environment–behavior articles. An international effort has led to publication of the *Journal of Environmental Psychology* (Canter & Craik, 1981b). Presently, there are two main journals in the field: the *Journal of Environmental Psychology*, contributed to by research psychologists and other social scientists; and the interdisciplinary *Environment and Behavior*.

Having recounted these "benchmarks" of the discipline, it must be noted that the lack of an agreed-on name for the discipline seems to be a sign of the lack of complete integration of the field and commitment to one set of principles and goals.

39.3.2. Organizations

The Environmental Design Research Association (EDRA) was founded in June of 1968 immediately after the Design Methods Group Conference (DMG) at MIT. The reason for EDRA's formation was a general feeling at the end of that conference that the two most visible areas of new research related to environmental design and planning—namely architectural psychology and design methods—should be combined, not separated. A group of 27 people formed EDRA, including John Archea, Gerald Davis, Charles Rusch, Henry Sanoff, David Stea, and Raymond Studer from architectural psychology, and Thomas Heath, Alan Hershdorfer, Christopher Jones, Richard Krauss, Marvin Manheim, Thomas Maver, William Porter, and myself, from design methodology (White, 1984). EDRA hosted its first conferences at Chapel

Hill, North Carolina, and Pittsburgh, Pennsylvania, devoted to the combination of architectural psychology and design methodology (Archea & Eastman, 1970; Sanoff & Cohn, 1970). By 1972, the two groups split, with DMG going its own way separate from EDRA due to differences in methodological orientations and organizational objectives.

Although EDRA began as a loosely organized group of environmental professionals and behavioral scientists, it has emerged to become the major international organization devoted to improving the quality of the physical environment through research and research utilization in design. The organization continues to hold annual conferences and publish *Proceedings*; these volumes serve as an archive of recent research in the field. Since 1969, EDRA has published a quarterly newsletter, *Design Research News*, which has taken the place of the former newsletters. EDRA has a number of standing committees focused on research, practice, education, information dissemination, interdisciplinary relations, and international outreach, and several research networks focused on child–environment research, environmental cognition, environment and aging, handicapped and the environment, housing, interiors, women's issues, participation, and postoccupancy evaluation (White, 1984). In addition to publishing the *Proceedings* and *Design Research News*, EDRA also collaborates in the publication of the two major journals in the field and has initiated a major publishing agreement for a series of research reviews—*Advances in Environment, Behavior, and Design*—published by Plenum Press.

In the early years, EDRA's membership was made up primarily of architects and psychologists. The organization has continued to grow and to diversify. Now numbering over 900 people, EDRA's membership is composed of four groups—psychologists (30%), architects (30%), other environmental professionals (interior designers, landscape architects, planners, urban designers, 25%), and other social scientists (geographers, sociologists, human/social ecologists, anthropologists, 15%; compiled from White, 1984). Although EDRA has attempted to be an international organization and has always had strong representations from European, Asian, and Australasian countries, it has remained a primarily North American association in terms of membership (27 countries are represented, but 77% of the members are from the United States, 10% from Canada, 1% from Mexico and Central America, and only the remaining 12% are not from North America; compiled from White, 1984).

39.3.3. Textbooks, Annual Reviews, and Book Series

Another benchmark of the emergence and stability of a discipline is the appearance of the first textbooks, annual reviews, and series of books. This has occurred, starting with the publication in 1970 of Proshansky, Ittelson, and Rivlin's reader, *Environmental Psychology*, and the first comprehensive review article in *New Directions in Psychology* (Craik, 1970b).

A series of texts are now on the market, beginning with the Proshansky and colleagues reader (1970, 2nd ed., 1976) and their follow-up textbook (Ittelson, Proshansky, Rivlin, & Winkel, 1974). In psychology, the major texts on environment and behavior are those by Heimstra and McFarling (1974, 2nd ed., 1978), Bell, Fisher, and Loomis (1978; excellent 2nd ed. by Fisher, Bell, & Baum, 1984), and Holahan (1982). All are titled *Environmental Psychology*. These texts are closely aligned with psychology as the parent discipline but make efforts to embrace the interdisciplinary nature of the broader environment and behavior field. Each of the following topics is covered by at least three of these texts: environmental perception, cognition, and attitudes; privacy, personal space, and territoriality; crowding; stress; built environment; urban environments; research methods; and theory—but for the most part they summarize traditional psychological investigations focusing on intrapersonal processes.

A contrast with this picture emerges when looking at the environment and behavior texts used in sociology and geography. The four major texts are the sociologist Michelson's *Man and his Urban Environment* (1970; 2nd ed., 1976), the geographer Saarinen's *Environmental Planning: Perception and Behavior* (1976), the Canadian geographer Porteous's *Environment and Behavior* (1977), and, most recently, Gold's *An Introduction to Behavioral Geography* (1980). Although treating some of the same topics as the environmental psychology texts, these volumes also treat life-style and life-cycle analyses, housing and neighborhoods, natural environments, regional analysis, decision making, and implications for urban policy planning.

These textbooks are complemented by a series of annual reviews. Starting with Craik's (1970b) review in *New Directions in Psychology*, they continued in the *Annual Review of Psychology* (Craik, 1973; Holahan, 1986; Russell & Ward, 1982; Stokols, 1978b), in the *Annual Review of Sociology* (Dunlap & Catton, 1979), and in *Progress in Human Geography* (Gold & Goodey, 1983, 1984; Saarinen & Sell, 1980, 1981). There are no official annual reviews in the environmental professions; somewhat equivalent reviews have appeared as invited chapters in edited volumes in *Architectural Research* (e.g., Moore, 1979a, 1984).

A number of series of research monographs and books are devoted to the publication of research in the field. The first, and the one to which the field in North America owes an inestimable debt, is the Community Development Series under the guidance of Hutchinson for many years at Dowden, Hutchinson & Ross. Over 25 books were published in this series in the 1970s. Other monograph series include Advances in Environmental Psychology from Erlbaum (Baum & Singer, 1981), Environment and Behavior from Brooks/Cole and now Cambridge University Press (e.g., Zeisel, 1981), Human Behavior and Environment (Altman & Wohlwill, 1976), and the latest series, Advances in Environment, Behavior, and Design from Plenum Press (Zube & Moore, Vol. 1, 1987, Vol. 2, in press). Judging from these developments, environment–behavior studies and applications have established themselves as viable branches of the social sciences and the environmental professions, and as the beginnings of a multidisciplinary field of its own.

39.3.4. Personnel and Sponsors

The members of the field and the sponsors for research have come from a multitude of directions in North America. There are about 2500 people actively involved in the field in North America, in research or in direct applications. Of these, 90% are working in the United States, about 10% in Canada, and a handful in Mexico and Central America (estimated from the membership list of EDRA). It is not known how many people received their training in different fields, but again, based on the EDRA membership, about 30% received the major portion of their education in psychology, 30% in architecture, 25% in the other environmental professions (interior design, landscape architecture, urban planning, and urban design), and 15% in the other social sciences (sociology, geography, anthropology, and human factors). The majority of those trained in the social sciences hold PhD degrees, whereas those from the environmental professions hold professional master's degrees. Until very recently, few received degrees in environment–behavior studies. The first wave entered after establishing careers in one of the "parent" disciplines. Others were students and had to bootleg their training in departments that were at best benignly inclined toward the new field. The second wave is now entering the field from training in programs devoted to environment and behavior (Moore & Templer, 1984).

There are no accurate figures on the major sources of support for research in the field, but until recently, the major sources of support were various agencies of the governments of the United States and Canada (Schluntz, 1984). A shift is now being experienced in both countries away from federal support to more private, nongovernmental support (private foundations and industry). Transition is slow and not without difficulties. There is grave danger in the pressure to abandon basic research and theory in favor of shorter term and more agency- or industry-serving interests (see Moynihan, 1980; Muller, 1980).

39.3.5. Educational Programs

Important developments occurred during the early and mid-1960s in educational programs at the graduate and undergraduate levels. The first formal courses in environment–behavior studies were taught by Stea and Studer at Brown University and the Rhode Island School of Design and by Proshansky and Ittelson at Brooklyn College and the City University of New York in the early 1960s.

The earliest formal program was an interdisciplinary architectural psychology program started in 1964 at the University of Utah under the direction of Bailey and Taylor (Bailey, 1967). Funded by a 5-year National Institute of Mental Health development grant, it ended in 1969. A graduate specialization in environmental psychology at the City University of New York was initiated in 1968 by Ittelson and Proshansky. Now over 15 years old, it was awarded a special commendation by EDRA for graduate education in the field. The "man"–environment relations graduate program begun in 1969 at Pennsylvania State University under the leadership of Studer has recently been eliminated due to an internal reorganization within the university that reflected what may be a fundamental incompatibility of an environmentally oriented program within a strongly articulated human-services mission college.

Another early cooperative effort contributed many researchers to the field from the psychology and geography departments at Clark University under the leadership initially of Kates, Wohlwill, Stea and, more recently, Wapner. This cooperative effort emerged in the late 1960s just after the publication of Kates and Wohlwill's (1966) *Journal of Social Issues*, supported in large part by an NSF training grant. A special issue of the *Journal of Environmental Psychology* (Craik, n.d.) is being devoted to this period. Other sustained programs include the social ecology program at the University of California, Irvine, the environmental psychology program at Cornell University, and the environment–behavior studies program at the University of Wisconsin, Milwaukee.

Four surveys have been made of graduate programs in environment and behavior in North America (White, 1979, 1984, for psychology departments; Hassid, 1972, and Moore, 1984, for architectural departments). As of 1986, 24 universities had formal programs leading to the PhD degree focusing on environment and behavior with an additional 14 universities having programs terminating at the master's level.

Of the 24 PhD programs, 3 are in Canada and 21 in the United States, 8 are housed in psychology departments (Arizona, Arizona State, British Columbia, City University of New York, Claremont, Colorado State, Rutgers, and Utah), 6 in architecture departments (Berkeley, Georgia Tech, Michigan, Montreal, UCLA, and Wisconsin, Milwaukee), 4 in sociology departments (Kansas, Michigan State, Rutgers, and Washington State), 3 in geography departments (Nebraska, Santa Barbara, and Toronto), 2 in natural resource departments (Arizona and Michigan), and 1 in an interdisciplinary unit (social ecology at Irvine). Three other interdisciplinary programs lead to master's degrees (environmental design at Calgary, design and environmental analysis at Cornell, and environmental studies at York).

The fact that programs in environment and behavior are housed in many different departments and colleges (predominantly still psychology and design departments, which are in totally different colleges with different persuasions) and the difficulty that some have had in sustaining their curriculum and independence of research reflect the difficulties that interdisciplinary social science/environmentally oriented programs experience and the related more general problem of finding suitable academic structures for environment and behavior.

Nevertheless, the multidisciplinary environment and behavior field as a whole has evolved a relatively stable organizational and institutional infrastructure in North America. Conferences have been held on an annual basis since the late 1960s, newsletters have been published as long, two journals have devoted 100% of their coverage to the field since approximately 1970 with another three devoting approximately 50% coverage, a national/international organization has existed since 1968, and other associations have had speciality groups since the mid-1970s. A wide assortment of textbooks and readers are on the market, some of which have gone into second editions and multiple printings; annual reviews are written in various subareas of the field; and book series have been launched by major publishers. Finally, a number of universities continue to prepare additional researchers and practitioners for the field.

39.4. THEORETICAL DEVELOPMENTS AND PHILOSOPHICAL UNDERPINNINGS OF ENVIRONMENT–BEHAVIOR RESEARCH

39.4.1. Dimensions of Theoretical Development: Formality, Scope, Units of Analysis, and the Locus of Control of Behavior

There are significant differences in the use of the word *theory* in science. At one extreme, it describes general orientations to research. At the other extreme, it characterizes a systematic constellation of concepts, variables, and mechanisms used for the interpretation and explanation of particular phenomena.

Research in the early period—the 1950s to about 1970—was atheoretical. It was not until the third meeting of EDRA (EDRA 3, Los Angeles, 1972) that a symposium was devoted specifically to theoretical issues in one domain of environment–behavior research—environmental cognition (Moore, 1972). The following year (EDRA 4, Blacksburg, Virginia, 1973), there were two sessions devoted to the comparison of different theories (Altman, 1973b; Chase 1973). Since then, many advances have been made in environment–behavior theory (Archea, 1975; Rapoport, 1973; Stokols, 1977b, 1983).

The field of environment and behavior in North America is in a preparadigmatic stage. There is no agreement on a major unifying theoretical perspective. The study of behavior in designed settings has typically proceeded from a general ecological orientation, borrowing parts of the ecological theory of Barker and his students (Barker, 1968). Although this general *perspective* is shared by many, it has not been embraced—nor has any other theoretical orientation—as an underlying world view, paradigm, or explanatory theory for the field as a whole. The early history of environment and behavior has been far from cumulative. The conceptions of our forerunners

have seldom been built on, tested, extended, refined, or consolidated into a cumulative product.

There is no one perspective from which to view theories of environment and behavior. In this chapter, we will examine four dimensions of theoretical development in North America. First, we examine the ontological status of theories or *form*— from general orientations to specific explanatory theories. Second, we look at the *scope* of theories—do they attempt to account for all phenomena in the field as a whole or for specific subareas of the field? Third and fourth, we look at the *units of analysis* and the locus of *control of behavior*.

39.4.2. Form and Scope: General Orientations, Explanatory Theories, and Theories of the Middle Range

A first way to view environment–behavior theories is in terms of the type—or *form*—of the theory. There have been four different types of theoretical development: theoretical orientations, frameworks, conceptual models, and explanatory theories.

Theoretical orientations are broad conceptual approaches to a subject matter. They are heuristics in that they orient an investigator to look at phenomena in particular ways and to identify new and interesting lines of investigation. A well-known example in environment–behavior research is the cultural orientation of Rapoport (e.g., 1969, 1976b, 1977, 1979, 1982). Rapoport has conceptualized major portions of data in the field in cultural and cross-cultural terms. His work has led to the notions of the cultural influences on building form (Rapoport, 1969), complexity and ambiguity in environmental design (Rapoport & Kantor, 1967), subjective and cultural definitions of crowding (Rapoport, 1975), cultural variability in physiological responses to the environment (Rapoport & Watson, 1972), and a cross-cultural viewpoint on environmental cognition (Rapoport, 1976a), among other topics. It has not been Rapoport's primary interest to develop and test an explanatory theory of each of these phenomena but to point to a new direction for theoretical and empirical development.

Frameworks array the relations among existing findings. A framework goes beyond an orientation by providing a systematic organization to data. An example is Craik's organization of data on environmental preferences and attitudes in terms of observers, environmental displays, response formats, and media of presentation (Craik, 1968). Subsequent work using this framework has led to the conceptualization and measurement of environmental dispositions (Craik, 1975, 1976) and the development and utilization of personality inventories to predict peoples' use and modification of the physical environment (Bunting & Semple, 1979; Marshall, 1974; McKechnie, 1974).

Conceptual models articulate the dynamic mechanisms among organized bodies of findings; they are theoretical simulations of events in the real world. Models predict future events given certain parameters but do not necessarily explain those events. Examples of conceptual models in environment–behavior research are Altman's (1975) model of the mechanisms regulating privacy and environmental adaptation to crowding and Marans's (1976; Marans & Spreckelmeyer, 1981) model for residential environmental quality.

Explanatory theories are explicit, systematic, and testable sets of assumptions and constructs linking and explaining aspects of behavior in relation to characteristics of environments. They attempt to explain why a set of phenomena behave as they do; they join empirical facts on a more abstract and general level and account for, or explain, publicly observable data.

Where theoretical statements did exist in the early history of the field in North America, they were broad and philosophical (Archea, 1975). Theories have now become more focused, more specific, more limited to a specific set of data, and more explicitly explanatory. Emerging theories have sought to explain specific bodies of observable data through the positing of nonobservable but explicit explanatory structures. Although general orientations, frameworks, and models continue to be important to the field, explanatory theories are on the ascendency in North America as the field moves toward greater maturity.

There are several functions of explanatory theories: (1) theories summarize large amounts of data; (2) they help us to understand and explain observable data; (3) they permit—with appropriate caution—generalization to new settings, user groups, and phenomena; (4) they permit prediction of relationships over time (not to be confused with explanation); (5) they suggest new lines of research and new relationships between concepts; and (6) they aid in application to practical environmental problems.

Another way to view theories has to do with the *scope* of the theory—how wide a swath does the theory cut through the field? A distinction has been drawn between big *T* and little *t* theories (Downs, 1976; likely based on Merton, 1957). Big *T* theories are coherent, explicit, and account for a wide range of data across several substantive subareas of a field.

The prime example in environment and behavior research is the ecological theory of Barker and his colleagues (Barker, 1968; Wicker, 1979; see Smith, 1977). Little *t* theories are also coherent and explicit but do not attempt to stretch beyond the substantive area for which they were developed. Little *t* theories account for limited bodies of data (e.g., the location theory of Alonso, 1964).

A third possibility is what the sociologist Merton (1948, 1957) called "theories of the middle range—those theories intermediate to the minor working hypotheses developed in abundance during the day-to-day routines of research, and the all-inclusive speculations comprising a master conceptual scheme" (Merton, 1957, pp. 5–6). Most of the theories dealt with in the next section are theories of the middle range.

39.4.3. Units of Analysis and the Control of Behavior: From Person-Based to Transaction-Based Theories

A common method for ordering the field has been to divide it into research subareas of substantive empirical issues (Craik, 1977; Rapoport, 1973; Stokols, 1977a). This is useful as a framework but is most often not a framework of theories (even when termed *competing paradigms*).

Some reviewers have suggested philosophical dimensions along which theories can be viewed. In an earlier chapter, Moore and Golledge (1976, chapter 1) noted three fundamentally different ways in which the relationship between environment and behavior has been conceptualized—empiricism and environmental determinism, rationalism and nativism, and interactionism and constructivism (defined later). Stokols (1977b) saw the major theories as being of two types—the ecological theories of collective processes by which groups adapt to the environment and the environmental psychological theories focusing upon intrapersonal processes like perception, cognition, and learning. Fisher and colleagues (1984) presented theories of environment and behavior without reference to a systematic framework. Gold and Goodey (1983, 1984) noted a growing schism between positivist empiricist theories and humanist phenomenological theories, with radical dialectical materialist views being a third vertex. Catton and Dunlap (1978a, 1978b, 1980) referred to the human exceptionalism group of theories, which are anthropocentric, optimistic, and unecological, being replaced by what they initially called a new environmental paradigm and later the new ecological paradigm that stresses the interdependence of culture, technology, purposive human behavior, and a social ecology (see especially Table 1 in Catton & Dunlap, 1980). Cutting through all these distinctions, Smith (1977) maintained that the only theoretically focused approach to environment and behavior that has been pursued far enough to allow us to take stock of its accomplishments is the behavior-setting theory of Barker and his colleagues, which he characterized as being essentially an empiricist theory.

In the discussion that follows, I will attempt to develop a framework for the theories being most actively pursued in North America. The framework is generated by two fundamental considerations in the construction of any theory—the units of analysis selected[3] and the presuppositions taken for granted about the locus of control of behavior.

The units of analysis underlying a theory are the basic atoms or building blocks on which the theory is constructed. Thus, as we shall see, person-centered theories assume that the single individual is an indivisible atom, with group behavior being explained in terms of the coming together of individuals in space. Conversely, social group-based theories assume that social rules and norms are central and that individual behavior is to be explained in terms of group behavior. In each class of theories to be discussed, the approach is based on the unit of analysis thought by the theorist to be central to the environment–behavior nexus: the person, the social group, the environmental situation, culture, and so forth.

When focusing on a particular unit of analysis, a theory also tends to place emphasis on that unit's ability to determine or control behavior. Cultural theories posit that the cultural unit is the most logical unit of first analysis and that culture is a major determinant of behavior, and so on for the other positions. In this way, it may be that all theories in environment and behavior are in some sense "deterministic," not in the empiricist or environmental determinist sense, but rather in the sense that all theories seem to posit some cause–effect relations, either between culture and behavior, the structure of environmental situations and behavior, phenomenological experience and behavior, and the like. The point is that the analysis of units cannot be separated from discussion of the locus of control of behavior for the dominant theoretical basis for the control of behavior has tended to be within the unit of analysis.[4]

Person-Based Theories

The dominant unit of analysis in this group of theories is the person. In Altman's (1975) privacy theory and Craik's (1976) personality theory and use of the Environmental Response Inventory (McKechnie, 1970, 1974), the starting point for empirical research and for the construction of theory is the individual.

Altman's (1975) theory is concerned with privacy as a central regulatory process by which a person makes him or herself accessible to others. Although the environment is viewed as shaped by the individual's personal space and territorial behaviors and as influencing the actual level of achieved privacy, the driving force behind environmental adaptation is the individual's desired level of privacy and ability to manipulate the privacy regulating mechanisms in order to obtain that desired level. Through these mechanisms, Altman's theory stresses the individual as the unit of analysis and as the dominant shaper of behavior.

A similar set of assumptions underlies the personality theory of Craik and his colleagues (Craik, 1976; McKechnie, 1974) who argue that the assessment of personality dispositions can predict a range of environmental behaviors and outcomes. A key to this theory is its method of operationalization. Craik and McKechnie developed the Environmental Response Inventory, a 184-item inventory to assess 8 environmental dispositions that were defined as individual variations in enduring styles of relating to the everyday physical environment. A further development is the anticipation of being able to predict a wide range of environmental behaviors as a function of environmental dispositions, such as adjustment to migration, judgments of environmental quality, outdoor recreational activities, housing choices, adjustment to natural hazards, and environmental policy orientations (Craik, 1976, Table 2).

Social Group Theories

In social group-based theories, the focal point is the social group as the unit of analysis and the determinant of social and individual behavior. Rather than assuming groups are formed from collections of individuals, it is assumed that individuals take on characteristics by virtue of their membership in primary or secondary groups and that individual behavior in the environment is a function of social rules and norms of the group.

One of the early progenitors of this point of view in environment and behavior was Buttimer (1972, 1974) who argued that to understand residential behavior, it is necessary to understand the nature of the norms, membership, and reference groups of people, or what she called their "social space." In a later paper, Buttimer (1976a) argued for the necessity of studying the dialectical tension between social reference systems and spatial reference systems as they jointly affect the person–place interaction.

Social-group-based theories have also been advanced by sociologists and social geographers. One is the people–place model put forth by Gerson and Gerson (1976) and pursued empirically by Duncan and Duncan (1976). Gerson and Gerson (1976) pointed out the social context of place perspectives. The components of social perspectives were argued to be temporal (pace, rhythm), monetary (the degree that economics has penetrated social organization), sentimental (emotional tone and image), and ideological (institutional or group image). These social group perspectives shape the individual's conception of the place and his or her conduct in it.

Another clear statement for the social-group basis of environmental behavior is a theoretical paper by Altman (1977). Although eschewing the presentation of a hypothetical-deductive theory in this paper, Altman presented an argument for a perspective on environment–behavior research that would emphasize the social unit as the basic element of study. He gave, as examples, intact social units such as couples, teams, and families and argued in this paper for the centrality of these concepts to understanding environmental aggression, territoriality, and performance.

Empiricist Theories

The emphasis within this group of theories is on the environment—most often the strictly physical environment— treated as a complex of factors that affect behavior in a causal way. This group of theories is most often and most appropriately referred to as *environmental deterministic* or *empiricist* in the philosophical sense (not to be confused with empirical in the methodological sense).

The philosophy of empiricism contends that behavior is under the control of the environment. Reality, in this view, can only be contained in sensation; knowledge of reality is built up from a succession of sensations impressed on a tabula rasa. Empiricism argues that there is but one source of knowledge— sensation—and one source of behavior—the objectively defined external environment. The view is based on two additional assumptions. The first is that the content of behavior can be analyzed into basic elements, or atoms. Second, mind and experience, indeed all of behavior, are an empty slate, without preimpressions, images, innate patterns of behavior, or any other manifestations prior to experience. Actions or events are then assumed to be situationally determined by the elements of the environment.

In Barker's (1968) theory, the unit of analysis, and the assumed controller of behavior, is the behavior setting. The behavior setting is more than just elements of the physical environment; it also includes the social and temporal environment, the existing pattern of behavior, social rules associated with the setting, and the time locus of the setting, but the emphasis within this theory has been argued to be clearly on the physical determinants of behavior (Smith, 1977; Winett, in press).

Considerable research has followed from the environmental determinist position. Much of the work reviewed in Craik (1970b), collected in the early Proshansky and colleagues reader (1970) and in textbooks (Bell et al., 1978; Fisher et al., 1984; Heimstra & McFarling, 1978; Holahan, 1982) has followed explicitly, or, more often, implicitly from the environmental deterministic model. Fisher and colleagues (1984), for example, devote large sections to the causal effects of noise, temperature, air pollution, and wind on behavior and to what they call "molding behavior to fit the environment."

The empiricist view in environment and behavior can be traced to Wohlwill's (1966) theoretical statement about behavior as a function of external stimulus properties of the environment. Wohlwill extended this view to migrants adapting to new environments (Wohlwill & Kohn, 1973, 1976) whereas others have taken it to the study of undersea habitats (Helmreich, 1974), home environment satisfaction (Steidl, 1972), and university halls (Moos, 1973), among others. Moos (1973) labeled his approach a "functional" or "reinforcement analysis" of environments. Other prominent examples include the work of Golledge and his students, who have investigated how a "learned model of a city" is built up through "perception of those elements that have a high probability of occurrence in the immediate environment" (Golledge & Zannaras, 1973, pp. 112–113; cf. Golledge, 1979, 1981; Golledge & Couclelis, 1984; Zannaras, 1976). The most extreme versions of this view have been advanced by Studer (1967, 1969, 1973), who advocated the manipulation of behavior by designed changes in the environment, in Everett's (1981) reinforcement theory of transit behavior, and in Geller's (1980) application of behavior analysis to litter control, but little other work has emanated from this extreme behaviorist position (cf. Geller, Chapter 11, this volume; Winett, in press).

Mediational Theories

A fourth group of theories are mediational theories. This is the class of theories that postulate any one of a number of intervening or mediating variables between the environment and behavior, most often stress, perception, or cognition. Mediational theories are atomistic in that they assume an independence between variables and between observer and observed. They are often a variation on a stimulus-response model in that they assume a passive organism and that behavioral outcomes are a causal function of independent situational variables, albeit mediated by intrapersonal, social, or cultural mediators.

An early progenitor of this view in psychology, who has had an enormous albeit indirect impact on the field of environment and behavior, was Tolman (1932, 1948). In Tolman's theory, some form of covert representation—expectancies and cognitive maps—were assumed to mediate between stimuli and overt behavior. These mediational responses were said to "represent" the object or situation confronting the organism.

A number of contemporary mediational theories have been advanced in environment and behavior. For example, the environmental stress approaches to understanding environment–behavior interactions are mediational theories in that stress is considered a mediating variable (Baum, Singer, & Baum, 1981; Evans, 1983; Lazarus & Cohen, 1977). The role of stress in environment and behavior involves a number of important cognitive mediating components (e.g., cognitive appraisal of an aversive event like crowding, primary appraisal, secondary appraisal, and various coping strategies (Baum et al., 1981; Holahan, 1978; Lazarus, 1966). A specific example is Baum and Greenberg's (1975) work, showing that the expectation of crowding affects one's perception of space and that the anticipation of crowding affects spatial behavior in group situations.

Another body of work representing mediational theories is environment perception, cognition, and meaning. Starting with groundbreaking books like the economist Boulding's *The Image* (1956), the urban planner Lynch's *The Image of the City* (1960), and the sociologist Strauss' *Images of the American City* (1961), this research has assumed that in order to understand environment and behavior it is necessary to understand the perceptions people have of their environment, the images they form of it, and the meanings they ascribe to it. This mediational point of view is especially clear in the work of White, Burton, Kates, and their colleagues (e.g., Burton, Kates, & White, 1968; Kates, 1967; White, 1945, 1975) who did a series of studies on the role of expectations and how people's beliefs about natural hazards affect their subsequent behavior. Hart and Moore's (1973) cogni-

tive-developmental theory also started from this point of view and postulated that the child's behavior in space is in part a function of his or her cognitive representations of those spaces. The most recent environmental cognitive theory has been put forth by Kaplan and Kaplan (1982; Kaplan, 1983). They argue that environmental behavior is a function of the actions a person is trying to carry out, the informational patterns of the environment, the person's perception and knowledge of the situation, and internal reflection (Kaplan, 1983; cf. also Garling & Golledge, in press).

Research on environmental *perception* (in the strict sense of the word) is also mediational in character, for example, the research of Appleyard, Lynch, and Myer (1964) on environmental perception from roadways and of Hayward and Franklin (1974) on the perceived openness or closure of architectural spaces. At the other extreme of the perceptual-conceptual continuum are the theories of environmental meaning and symbolism (e.g., Bonta, 1979; Groat & Canter, 1979; Rapoport, 1982; cf. Groat, 1981, for a critical review).

The various mediational theories place a different status on the notion of mediational variables "representing" the object or situation confronting the organism. Mediational variables can be of two primary types—either simply a shorthand for the objective fact of stimulus-response connections (e.g., the stress literature where it is not necessarily assumed that the person is cognitively aware of stress) or an explicit ideational process (e.g., the environmental cognition literature where it is assumed that the person has experiential thoughts, images, and plans for action that mediate the impacts of environmental situations).

Mediational theories, furthermore, can be linear and noninteractive, assuming that the physical environment affects behavior through mediators (a variant on empiricist theories, e.g., Tolman's "cognitive learning" theory), or nonlinear interactional theories, assuming that the interaction of person *and* environmental variables affect behavior through mediators (see the section on interactional theories).

Cultural Theories

Whereas the previously mentioned theories have for the most part been explanatory theories of the middle range, culturally based theories are more of a general orientation or heuristic, a way of seeing environment–behavior phenomena in cross-cultural perspective. As Altman, Rapoport, and Wohlwill (1980) say, "There has often been a neglect of the crucial role of cultural variables as important determinants and mediators of the interaction between people and environments" (p. 2).

The general point of view has been best expressed by Rapoport (e.g., 1969, 1977, 1979, 1982). In one paper, Rapoport (1976a) juxtaposes a culturally based theory of environmental cognition against what he calls the psychological theory of environmental cognition. The psychological approach suggests that representations result from an interaction between internal organismic factors and external environmental demands. A culturally based theory, on the other hand, accepts the mediating role of representation but adds that organismic, physical environmental, and cultural factors interact to form cognitive representations and that cognitive processes are also concerned with understanding how people make the world meaningful through ascribing symbolism to environmental events and settings. Choices with regard to ideal or even satisfactory environmental designs are also culturally specific and reflect certain culturally based ideal images and schemata (Rapoport, 1980).

Past theoretical statements have been Berry's (1980) theory of individual behavior in its ecological and cultural contexts, Aiello and Thompson's (1980) analysis of cross-cultural differences in how people actively use space and shape the environment in order to regulate social interaction and proxemics, and Sorensen and White's (1980) cross-cultural analysis of natural hazards and human adjustment (see also Altman & Chemers, 1980; Altman, Rapoport, & Wohlwill, 1980).

Phenomenological Theories

Phenomenologically based theories focus on experience in its own terms before and unencumbered by cognitive categories or extrinsic structures and phenomena as they are experienced by people. As its major proponent in our field has said: "Phenomenology is a science of beginnings.... Phenomenologists work to separate themselves from all preconceptions, prejudices, and commonsense notions and to see the phenomenon as it is in itself" (Seamon, 1982, p. 119).

Phenomenology strives to make genuine contact with dimensions of environmental experience and thereby to secure qualitative descriptions by which to provide a base for "authentic" conceptual portrayals of the various dimensions of the environment–behavior nexus.

Phenomenology is often juxtaposed against various forms of positivism, various other forms of envi-

ronmental determinism, and even mediational and transactional theories. Phenomenology tends to distrust the validity of a priori theories. From a phenomenological perspective, behavior is not to be explained but understood, not to be predicted but described.

Although phenomenology eschews the subdivision of holistic experience into atomistic parts, Seamon (1980) was able to group environmental experience into three components—movement, rest, and encounter—and three processes—noticing, body habit and routine, and human attachment to place. These characteristics of environmental experience underlie and perhaps explain other manifest aspects of environmental behavior. The underlying presupposition is that these components and processes determine how people interact with space. The body subject and subcortical routines are suggested as the explanatory constructs determining, or at least influencing, spatial behavior.

The impact of phenomenology in North America has yet to be felt to the degree of its potential. Seamon (1982) suggests that for the environment and behavior researcher, existential phenomenology is the most relevant, especially the ethnomethodology of Garfinkel (1967) and the psychological research of the Duquesne school (Giorgi, 1971). In environment and behavior, there are several proponents, including Lowenthal (1961), Relph (1970, 1976, 1981), Tuan (1971, 1974, 1977), Buttimer (1974, 1976b; Buttimer & Seamon, 1980), and most recently and ardently, Seamon (1980, 1982, 1983, 1984b; Seamon & Mugerauer, 1985; cf. Seamon, in press).

Structuralistic Theories

In one of the early statements of the structuralistic point of view in North America, Archea (1975) argued that the relationship between events interacts to account for the events. The focus of structuralism is the exploration of the world to find systematic patterns that are general to all examples of a similar kind (Lévi-Strauss, 1966; Piaget, 1970b). The pattern or underlying structure of events can be used to explain any particular observable event. Structures frame behavior in the environment. As behavior is in the form of structures, knowledge of it is embodied in taxonomies (Archea, 1975; Hillier & Leaman, 1973).

The unit of analysis is the structure—elements and their relations. Some structuralists (e.g., Turner, 1983) suggest that alternative readings of a situation can lead to the attribution of more than one structure to the set of phenomena—a type of transactional structuralism. Some hold that structures are in the environment and are paralleled or isomorphic to the structures of mind (e.g., the gestaltists); others hold that structures are in the mind, a neo-Kantian epistemology (e.g., Lévi-Strauss, 1966); and still others say that structures arise through adaptation and the interaction of organism, mind, and environment—a genetic epistemology (e.g., Piaget, 1970a). Although there are these differences in the origins of behavior and the "location" of structures, the underlying assumptions appear to be that the most salient unit of analysis is the structures of behavior and/or of environment and that these structures interact to account for observable behavioral events.

Examples of actual studies developed from a structuralist position are hard to find in North America; the tendency to date has been to argue the position but show little supporting evidence. The case might be made that Hall's taxonomy of interpersonal distances and their role in determining cross-cultural communication (Hall, 1966) is a structural analysis, as is Lynch's (1960) analysis of the role of cognized edges, paths, nodes, and districts in urban orientation and wayfinding. The search for patterns in the development of environmental cognition (the development through egocentric, partially coordinated fixed-point and fixed-route, and coordinated survey-type representations of space) is also an example of a structural approach to environment and behavior (Hart & Moore, 1973; Moore, 1976). Other examples include Glassie's (1975) analysis of folk housing, Stiny's (1981; Stiny & Mitchell, 1978) work on shape grammars, Bonta's (1979) work on expressive systems and a taxonomy of signs, and Krampen's (1979) work started in Canada on the use of set theory to show how people understand buildings in terms of classifications of building types followed by a classification of architectural styles (see also Groat, 1981). These later proponents of structuralism in environment and behavior have been focusing on questions of meaning and symbolism, whereas other questions about the environment–behavior relationship that could be analyzed in structural terms stand waiting.

Interactional and Transactional Theories

The last two groups of theories to be considered are those that are either interactional or transactional in nature. Although the interactional theories resemble the mediational theories, the transactional theories are very different.

Interactional and transactional positions are indebted to the nineteenth-century German philosopher Kant and subsequent neo-Kantians (see Bochenski, 1966; Hendle's introduction to Cassirer, 1953, vol. 1; Kaplan, 1967; Moore & Golledge, 1976, chapter 1). They are an attempt to synthesize the sometimes polarized nativist and environmental determinist positions. Kant argued a position different from either rationalism or empiricism. He started with a fundamental distinction between the matter or content of knowledge (that which corresponds to sensation) and the form of knowledge (that which causes the matter to be arranged in a certain order). Reminiscent of empiricism, the matter of knowledge is given through experience, but reminiscent of rationalism, its form is given a priori. Knowledge of the world is the result of a synthesis that the subject "constructs out of the formless stuff of experience" (Bochenski, 1966, p. 4). Kant argued that the form of knowledge is not influenced by the environment: It is constant and universal and that instead of knowledge ever representing exactly what is real, what we take to be real is a product of the act of knowing— that is, a construction of thought.

Neo-Kantian theories of knowledge such as those of philosophers like Cassirer (1953–1957) and psychologists like Claparede (1943), Werner (1948), and Piaget (1970a, 1975) accepted the interactive contention that, far from being only a function of the mind, an empirical reality exists independent of mind, but this reality can only be grasped through the effort of particular minds. The subject actively enters into a creative interaction with the environment, and the result is a construction of the object by the subject.

This constructivist position on epistemology is related to interactional and transactional theories in environment and behavior. Transactions between the organism and the environment are mediated by cognitive representations of the environment constructed by an active organism through an interaction between inner organismic factors and external situational factors (Moore & Golledge, 1976; Wapner, 1981, Chapter 41, this volume). Behavior, then, is understood in the context of the total organism-in-environment situation (see Lewin, 1946) and as a function of ongoing transactions between the two (Dewey & Bentley, 1949; Heft, 1981; Mead, 1934; Tibbetts, 1972; Von Uexkull, 1957; Werner & Kaplan, 1963; Whorf, 1956). Far from being passive recipients of external forces moving them to conform to the demands of the external stimulus situation and far from being driven simply by biological factors and inherited patterns of response, in this view persons are conceived of as active organisms adapting to the world in response to both internal and external demands. Behavior is more than a function simply of biological factors or environmental factors, and more than a summation of these two; behavior is an interaction of biological, personality, social, situational, and cultural factors, each in the context of the other and each defined in the context of the ongoing transaction between person and environment.

There are important—though subtle and slippery—distinctions between interactional and transactional theories. Many investigators embrace one or the other but not both.

Lewin (1946) proposed that behavior is a function of the total situation and of the interaction of persons and environments, his now famous equation $B = f(P, E)$. Nahemow and Lawton (1973) specified this interdependence further by viewing persons as a set of competencies and the environment as a set of demand characteristics or environmental press. Behavior was seen as a function of the interaction of personal competencies and environmental press. This theory has led to a rich set of deductions ripe for test (see Lawton, 1975). Lawton (1980) also argued that the classic Lewinian equation should be extended to read $B = f(P, E, P \times E)$, where $P \times E$ is the interaction between the two elements in addition to and independent of either the person or the objective environment. It is clear in this formulation, as in the other interactional theories, that the environment and the person are defined "objectively," independently of each other, that is, interactionalism accepts the dualism between person and environment while arguing that behavioral outcomes are a function of inner organismic variables, external socioenvironmental variables, and the interaction of the two (Moore, 1976; Stokols, 1981b; Stokols & Shumaker, 1981). Although most interactional theories are also mediational, that is, the person × environment interaction is exemplified by internal representations of the external environment (e.g., Lawton, 1975; Moore, in press), it is also logically possible to have a nonmediational interactionalism, a type of interactional behaviorism, though no concrete exemplars come immediately to mind.

In transactional theories, person and environment are defined dependently on each other, that is, in the context of each other and of the person–environment events that join the two in space and time (this is also a phenomenological perspective). As mentioned earlier, transactional theories assume an active organism and a construction of thought (neither of which is necessary for nonmediational interactional theories, but both of which are necessary for mediational interactional theories). But the critical compo-

nent is the nondualism assumption that behavior is to be understood as the interaction of variables in the context of ongoing person–environment transactions that define the variables. For example, Altman (1981) has argued the position that "environment and behavior are an integral or *transactional* unity, such that behavior and environment mutually define one another, and that, indeed, one cannot understand a phenomenon without studying environment and behavior as a *single* unit of analysis" (p. 5).

Another recent proponent has been Wapner (1981, Chapter 41, this volume). He has suggested a number of additional assumptions of transactionalism in environment and behavior, some of which on examination do not appear to be necessary components of transactionalism. Among the other defining characteristics of transactionalism are holism, the organismic world hypothesis of Pepper (1942; versus atomism), teleological or dynamic means–ends analysis (versus mechanistic), spatiotemporality (versus treating each separately), diacronic, longitudinal, or frame sequence analysis (versus synchronic or cross-sectional analysis), and multiple intentionality (versus, in the extreme, S-R behaviorism). Other theoretical propositions, like structural part–whole analyses, levels of organization, and the orthogenetic principle that structures and levels of organization of structures are developmentally orderable (Werner, 1948), although interesting and powerful additions in Wapner and his colleagues' work, are not necessary components of transactionalism. Just as mediationalism can be attached or not attached to interactionalism, these three theoretical assumptions can be attached or not attached to a transactional, or, for that matter, an interactional theory. Altman's (1981) writings, for example, do not include structural or organizational-developmental assumptions in his transactionalism, whereas Wapner's (1981; Chapter 41, this volume) do. Both Altman and Wapner have exemplified transactionalism by a series of demonstration studies (e.g., Kaplan, Wapner, & Cohen, 1976; Wapner, 1981; Wapner, Kaplan, & Cohen, 1973; Wapner, Chapter 41, this volume).

Other researchers and practitioners who have followed from the interactional and transactional positions are legion. It might be said that in the absence of any other explicitly stated position, theoreticians have followed implicitly from an interactional position by virtue of the nature of studying environment–behavior interactions. Other proponents of interactional theories include Kaplan's (1983) work on information processing and information patterning in environmental cognition, Loo's (1977) work on crowding, Bronfenbrenner's (1977) analysis of the ecology of human development, the congruence models of human–environment interaction (e.g., Carp & Carp, 1984; Kahana, 1975; Kahana, Liang, & Felton, 1980), Hart and Moore's (1973; Moore, 1979b) work on the development of environmental cognition, and Stokols's (1981b; Stokols & Shumaker, 1981) theory of group × place interactions. Other proponents of the transactional theory in addition to Altman (1981) and Wapner (Chapter 41, this volume), include Ittelson's (1970) theory of environmental perception and Pick's (1976) commentary on environmental cognition.

39.5. MAINSTREAMS AND DEVELOPMENTS IN RECENT RESEARCH

39.5.1. The Ebb and Flow of Content Areas: Changing Emphases and Orientations

It is not possible in these few pages, and perhaps not even desirable, to review the mainstreams of environment–behavior research over the past 25 years in North America. This task is left to the collection of chapters elsewhere in this *Handbook*.

There have been a number of reviews of portions of the field from different disciplinary orientations, especially from the vantage point of psychology, but also from geography, sociology, anthropology, and architecture. Interestingly, the first reviews all appeared in 1970 in the *American Psychologist* (Wohlwill, 1970), *New Directions in Psychology* (Craik, 1970b), *Architecture in Australia* (Rapoport, 1970), and the *International Social Science Journal* (Kates, 1970).

Other reviews have been written since for the *Annual Review of Psychology* (Craik, 1973; Holahan, 1986; Russell & Ward, 1982; Stokols, 1978b), *International Journal of Psychology* (Craik, 1977), *Resources in Environment and Behavior* (Proshansky & Altman, 1979), *Journal of Environmental Psychology* (Canter & Craik, 1981a), *G. Stanley Hall Lecture Series* (Stokols, 1981a), *Progress in Human Geography* (Gold & Goodey, 1983, 1984; Saarinen & Sell, 1980, 1981), *American Sociologist* (Gutman, 1975), *Annual Review of Sociology* (Baldassare, 1978; Dunlap & Catton, 1979), *Sociological Inquiry* (Dunlap & Catton, 1983), *Proceedings of the Environmental Design Research Association* (Ross & Campbell, 1978),

World Anthropology (Rapoport, 1976b), and *Architectural Research* (Moore, 1984). Still other treatments are given in the textbooks reviewed earlier. These reviews help us to determine if the field is dying (Taylor, 1980) or if it is a blueprint for the future of psychology (Sommer, 1980), a new environmental paradigm for sociology (Catton & Dunlap, 1978a), a renaissance in geography (Bowden, 1980), and/or a new ecological perspective for architecture (Moore, 1984).

Similarity of Beginnings – The Global Undifferentiated Stage

I will take as my point of departure the comprehensive review by Craik (1970b). The perspective was primarily from geography and psychology, though many studies were included from sociology and architecture. Accomplishments were cited on the built and urban environments, the geographic and natural environments, comprehension of the everyday physical environment, and environmental experience and cognition.

Within the built environment tradition, topics focused on behavior in architectural spaces (Appleyard, 1969; Cooper, 1972; Good, Siegel, & Bay, 1965; Thiel, 1961; Van der Ryn, 1967). Related to this was interest in ways to make the design process more amenable to a behavioral orientation (Alexander, 1964; Halprin, 1965; Moore, 1970; Studer, 1966). A large body of work was devoted to the spatial properties of human behavior including studies of behavior settings (Barker & Gump, 1964; Barker & Wright, 1955), social interaction in space, or proxemics (Hall, 1959, 1963, 1966), and privacy, personal space, and small-group ecology (Sommer, 1959, 1966, 1967, 1969). Some work focused on environmental characteristics as independent variables (Festinger, Schacter, & Back, 1950; Maslow & Mintz, 1956; Mintz, 1956; Srivastava & Good, 1968; Wilner, Walkley, Pinkerton, & Tayback, 1962). Case studies had looked at specific settings — psychiatric wards, nurseries, university dormitories, libraries, and public housing (Esser, Chamberlain, Chapple, & Kline, 1965; Shure, 1963) — though only these few setting types had been studied by 1970.

Research on geographic and natural environments looked at the ecology of natural hazards (Burton, 1961; Burton & Kates, 1964; Kates, 1967; Saarinen, 1966; White, 1945, 1961), people's influence on the physical environment (Thomas, 1956), and geosophy, the study of geographical knowledge (Kates, 1967; Lowenthal, 1964, 1967; Lowenthal & Prince, 1964 1965; Sonnenfeld, 1967; Wright, 1947, 1966).

A third major area of research was on the comprehension of the everyday physical environment, including research on the effects of different media of presentation (Weiss & Boutourline's 1962 study of the Seattle World's Fair), different response formats (Kasmar, 1970), environmental dimensionality and assessment (Appleyard, Lynch, & Myer, 1964; Halprin, 1965; Thiel, 1961), and environmental preferences, attitudes, and dispositions (Craik, 1970a, 1976; McKechnie, 1970).

Finally, Craik devoted a section of the review to environmental experience and cognition (Appleyard, 1969; Lynch, 1960; Stea, 1969).

In the same year, Wohlwill (1970) portrayed the emerging field of environmental psychology as dealing primarily with three of these topics: spatial behavior including proxemics and affective and attitudinal responses to the environment (Rapoport & Kantor, 1967; Wohlwill, 1968); approach and avoidance responses to environmental stimuli (Gould, 1967; Shafer, 1969; Stea, 1967); and stress or adaptation as a function of prolonged exposure (Gunderson, 1968; Sonnenfeld, 1966; Wohlwill, 1966).

In only slight contrast, Rapoport (1970), an anthropologist/architect, conceptualized the emerging field as dealing with questions of spatial behavior including proxemics, personal space, and territoriality, environmental preferences, environmental perception, and environmental cognition. Rather than interpreting these phenomena in individualistic, psychological terms, he saw them in group, cultural, and cross-cultural terms.

Yet a fourth view of the field was represented in the same year by the geographer Kates (1970). His conception was in terms of perceptual illusions (Segall, Campbell, & Herskovits, 1966), images of the city and environmental cognition (Lynch, 1960), attitudes toward landscapes (Lowenthal & Prince, 1965; Tuan, 1968), and responses to natural hazards (Burton, Kates, & White, 1968).

We see from these early reviews a similarity in basic ways of conceptualizing the field. Despite differences in disciplinary backgrounds (psychology, architecture, anthropology, geography), each saw the field in North America circa 1970 in much the same way. The field as seen by different people bore a striking resemblance—it really did look like the same field. Each reviewer went to some pains to suggest the unity of the field, though, with the exception of Craik (who had 122 pages); each also stated that he was dealing only with certain aspects of the field (environmental psychology, "man"–environment studies in architecture, and human perception of the environment).

Divergences Over Time—Differentiation and Articulation

During the middle and late 1970s and into the 1980s, the field in North America has gone through a period of rapid development but has begun to become internally differentiated and articulated in terms of the types of questions addressed.

In environmental psychology, subsequent reviews by Craik (1973, 1977), Canter and Craik (1981a), Proshansky and Altman (1979), Russell and Ward (1982), and Stokols (1978b, 1981a) all documented continuing vigor in the following six areas: ecological psychology, behavior settings, and behavioral ecology (Wicker, 1976; Willems, 1977); human spatial behavior including privacy, personal space, density, and crowding (Altman, 1975; Loo, 1979; Stokols, 1972, 1978a); architectural spaces including educational, residential, and institutional environments (Cooper, 1972; Weinstein, 1979); environmental assessment (Craik & Zube, 1976); environmental attitudes, personality, and the environment (Craik, 1976; McKechnie, 1974); and environmental cognition, including some work on environmental perception and meaning (Downs & Stea, 1973; Evans, 1980; Hart & Moore, 1973; Moore & Golledge, 1976).

On the other hand, a number of new areas of study emerged during the 1970s and early 1980s. One was the study of adaptation and environmental stress. Developing from work on privacy and crowding, this area focuses on the factors leading to stress and the effects of environmentally influenced stress on performance (Cohen, Glass, & Singer, 1973; Glass & Singer, 1972; Milgram, 1970; Stokols, 1979). Other emerging research includes operant analyses of environmental behavior (Everett, 1981, on transportation behavior; Geller, 1980, on littering; and Cone & Hayes, 1980, on other environmental behaviors); environmental simulation (Appleyard & Craik, 1978); the temporal context of behavior (Cohen, Krantz, Evans, & Stokols, 1981; Lynch, 1972; Michelson, 1980; Rowles, 1978; Wolfsy, Rierdan, & Wapner, 1979); and an increased interest in applications to environmental policy, planning, and design (DiMento, 1981; Kantrowitz & Seidel, 1985; Zeisel, 1981; Zube, 1980a, 1980b; cf. Schneekloth, in press).

These developments suggested to some reviewers that the field has its core in psychology and has a coherent theoretical framework for the psychological analysis of environment–behavior phenomena. Some reviewers also acknowledge strengths from other disciplines and recognize the interdisciplinary and applied nature of the field (Canter & Craik, 1981). Environmental psychology has been going through an intense period of defining its own topics in psychological terms and borrowing from well-established areas of psychological theorizing and methods.

Meanwhile, in sociology and geography, the picture is quite different. In environmental sociology, the initial characterization of areas of research indicated a division between those sociologists interested in urban built environments (Baldassare, 1978; Gutman, 1975; Michelson, 1970; Zeisel, 1975) and those interested in natural and rural environments (Catton & Dunlap, 1978a; Dunlap & Catton, 1979, 1983; Heberlein, 1972). The major emphases during the 1970s and early 1980s are eight, only three of which overlap with psychology.

In the area of built environments, research focuses on social group behavior in the designed or planned environment including buildings, housing, neighborhoods, cities, and suburbs (Gans, 1968; Gutman, 1972; Loring, 1956); life-style, life cycle, and social class analyses of the environment (Michelson, 1980); the effects of the environment on society and of society on the environment (Catton & Dunlap, 1978a); and applications to environmental programming, design, and planning processes (Gutman, 1975; Zeisel, 1975).

From the natural environmental side, research focuses on the natural environment at all scales, including geographic regions and global ecosystems (Dunlap & Catton, 1979, 1983); natural and technological hazards (Quarantelli, 1979; White, 1967; White & Haas, 1975); and outdoor recreation, wildland, and resource management (Catton, 1971, 1978; Dunlap & Catton, 1979; Heberlein, 1972; Heberlein & Shelby, 1977; cf. Buttel, Murdock, Leiseritz, & Hamm, in press).

The range of interests of the environmental sociologists and the environmental psychologists overlap only partially, primarily in the area of social behavior and the designed environment. But even here the differences are noticeable—the sociologists tending to focus on group behavior, and the psychologists tending to focus on individual behavior and internal psychological processes.

As we move to social and behavioral geography and to environmental "perception" in geography, the picture of the field changes again. There is, in geography, a fairly sharp distinction between those who use the term *environmental perception* and those who more generally call themselves *behavioral geographers*. The former look at questions of environmental attitudes, preferences, and images, while the latter look at a wide range of geographical behavioral questions from an analytical and quantitative perspective (see discussions in Golledge, 1979, 1981a; Golledge & Couclelis, 1984).

A series of reviews in *Progress in Human Geography* (Gold & Goodey, 1983, 1984; Saarinen & Sell, 1980, 1981; see also Golledge, 1981a) characterizes the contributions of geographers to the field in terms of seven areas. The largest area is that of natural hazards (Burton, Kates, & White, 1968), which, along with research on residential mobility, are perhaps the only areas of research studied among psychologists, sociologists, and geographers. Other areas include the spatial distribution of behavior of various population aggregates like children, older people, women, and the physically and mentally handicapped (Donnelly, 1980; Golledge, 1981b; Hart, 1979, 1981; Hart & Perez, 1980; Rowles, 1978); environmental cognition, images, attitudes, meaning, and symbolism (Downs, 1981; Moore & Golledge, 1976); sense of place and environmental experience (Buttimer, 1979; Buttimer & Seamon, 1980; Lewis, 1979; Rowles, 1981; Seamon, 1980); consumer behavior (Cox & Golledge, 1969; Golledge & Rushton, 1975); planning and environmental problems including resource conservation (Morrison, 1980); and national and international concerns about human–environmental problems like acid rain and the possible occurrence of a nuclear winter on the quality of life (O'Riordan, 1980; Saarinen & Gibson, 1980). During this period, there has been little overlap with either environmental sociology or with environmental psychology except in the area of environmental cognition (see general commentaries in Golledge, 1979, 1981a; see also Garling & Golledge, in press).

From the point of view of anthropology (Rapoport, 1980), the field is seen in terms of culture and environmental design, the variety of culture–environment relations, culture-specific environments, and a range of more specific behaviors from a cultural perspective, including spatial organization, the interpretation of places, the relation of places to cognitive categories, and the effect of design on traditional cultures.

Finally, from the point of view of architecture, the field includes research on a wide range of the built environments from social and behavioral vantage points, research on traditional sociobehavioral issues, and research on user groups, the impact of the designed environment on them, and how they adapt to and change the built environment (cf. reviews in Moore, 1979a, 1984).

We thus see that by the beginning of the 1980s the field was well differentiated along disciplinary lines. The environmental psychologists were interested primarily in questions of intraorganismic processes (attitudes, privacy, cognition, stress) and, to a lesser extent, individual spatial behavior in mesoscale environments (behavioral ecology, interior settings), whereas the environmental sociologists were interested in social phenomena in urban built environments (life-style, housing, and neighborhoods) and society–environment relations in large-scale natural environments (global ecosystems, natural hazards); the social geographers were interested in the spatial distribution of different populations (children, elderly) and experience and cognition of place (environmental cognition, sense of place); and the urban cultural anthropologists were interested in culture and the environment (cultural perspective on spatial organization, culture-specific environments). From the applied side, research architects were interested during this same period of time in research on user groups and a range of sociobehavioral issues in built environments.

Disciplinarity or Transdisciplinarity

It does not appear that the field was conceptually integrated by the mid-1980s. Although some might claim there was a reappearance of a consolidated perspective in the early 1980s, it is not generally the case for the field as a whole, though it may be for certain subdisciplines like environmental psychology or each of the two halves of environmental sociology.

Reviewers from different disciplines (Dunlap & Catton, 1979; Gold & Goodey, 1983; Stokols, 1981a) have, however, cited the scientific and applied accomplishments of their subdisciplines. The first is the incorporation of physical environmental variables into traditional social science theories and areas of study. Stokols (1981a) suggested that one of the important scientific contributions of environmental psychology has involved the extension of existing theories to include physical environmental variables. Gold and Goodey (1983) added that a fuller understanding of environmental "perception" and of the processes that inform environmental decision making has influenced the underlying behavioral assumptions of geographical spatial theory.

The second accomplishment is the application of existing social science theories and methodologies to research on human–environmental problems. There is evidence of this view in the social sciences themselves (e.g., work on transportation behavior [Altman, Wohlwill, & Everett, 1981] and housing for the elderly [Lawton, 1975], among others). There is also evidence in the applied environmental professions, where the primary form of research has been the application of existing social science theories and methods to environmental issues (e.g., Appleyard, 1981; Rapoport, 1977; Zeisel, 1975; Zube, 1980b; cf. Moore et al., 1985).

A third accomplishment is the application of research findings to the amelioration of environmental problems through environmental policy, planning, and design. This portion of the field has been characterized not as applied research but as research applications (Villecco & Brill, 1981). Examples of successful research applications include the legions of planning and design guides based on translations of research to environmental and community problem solving (Clipson & Wehrer, 1974; Cohen & Moore, 1977; Moore et al., 1979; Zeisel et al., 1978, 1984) and evidence in the professional press of using research in actual design projects (Villecco, 1983). Researchers approaching the field from the viewpoints of applied research and research applications have also been heavily involved in the development of research agendas on behalf of federal agencies (Lagorio, 1976; Moore et al., 1985; Snyder, 1982; Villecco & Brill, 1981).

My own view is that there is still a fourth accomplishment that has *begun* to emerge in embryonic form—an emergent, integrated, multidisciplinary perspective. Although each of the characterizations outlined previously offer a perspective on one or another important aspect of the field, they do not exhaust the possibilities nor the reality of the present situation. The field has developed a number of newly emergent concepts. Proshansky (1972) identified the concept of ecological behavior settings (Barker, 1968) and the use of behavioral mapping (Ittelson, Rivlin, & Proshansky, 1976) among others. Stokols (1978b, 1981a) further identified the concepts of boundary regulation process (Altman, 1975), social climate (Moos, 1976; Moos & Lemke, 1980), the distinction between fundamental and macrospatial cognition (Hart & Moore, 1973), and the new techniques of behavior setting analysis (Barker & Schoggen, 1973) and urban simulation (Appleyard & Craik, 1978). We can add to these the environmental attitudes approach to natural hazards (Burton, Kates, & White, 1968), the concepts of environmental roles and lifestyles (Michelson, 1980), and the phenomenology of place (Seamon, 1980, 1982), among others.

In summary, in large part this overview has been an attempt to look at the field in both differentiated and integrative terms to assess to what degree it is a multidiscipline of overlapping interests or a transdiscipline of emerging common concerns and approaches. The truth seems to lie somewhere in between, with major portions of the field withdrawing into their own parent disciplines and developing new environmental or behavioral perspectives for traditional areas of concern, whereas a few attempts have been made in the direction of integration.

39.5.2. A Multidimensional Framework[5]

An attempt has been made to articulate an underlying transdisciplinary framework that could help structure research in the field (Moore, 1979a; Moore et al., 1985). Earlier frameworks have been suggested by Craik (1968), Altman (1973a), Zeisel (1975), and Villecco and Brill (1981). The framework suggested here builds from those earlier statements.

A framework describes the conceptual organization or structure of a field. Frameworks are not theories. They do not attempt to explain the phenomena discovered in the field. They highlight the structural connections between features of the field. But, like theories, frameworks are not right or wrong, just more or less useful to the degree that they present a structure that is descriptive of, and useful to, the field. And, like theories, they are evolutionary, building from earlier statements and setting the stage for their own demise as a more inclusive, more veridical, and more useful framework is created.

The framework presented here consists of four components: (1) a conceptualization of environment–behavior questions in terms of places, user groups, sociobehavioral phenomena, and time; (2) the role of theory in elucidating the relations among these dimensions; (3) the cyclical, iterative process of environment–behavior research and applications; and (4) the context of cultural and environmental factors acting on the field that impel it forward and constrain it in its development.

Environment–behavior research deals with particular types of places or environmental settings at all scales of the environment (interiors, housing, health care facilities, the work place, factories, neighborhoods, landscapes, regions, etc.); with particular groups of environmental users (intact groups, aggregates, or workers, or groups defined in terms of life-styles or stages in the life cycle—the people who inhabit, work in, or visit the settings under consideration); and the social and behavioral phenomena at all levels of analysis—from physiological to cultural—involved in the interaction of people with environments. Environment and behavior is concerned with these three dimensions and with the dynamic mechanisms of interaction over time.

Any one of these dimensions may be the prime focus for a program of research (see Figure 39.3). Research on crowding or environmental cognition is focused primarily on the sociobehavioral dimension (Evans, 1980; Stokols, 1972). Research on housing or environmental resources is focused on place types (Craik & Zube, 1976; Michelson, 1977). Research on older people, children, or the handicapped is a focus on environmental user group issues (Howell, 1980; Steinfeld, 1979; Weinstein, 1979). And investigations of environmental adaptation and coming to terms with a new environment are examples of research focused on the time dimension (Wapner, 1981).

Although research on sociobehavioral processes examined, for the most part, these intraorganismic processes in isolation, research on user groups and on place types has tended to emphasize a cross-dimensional focus: children and housing (Cooper, 1975); older people and housing (Lawton, 1980); older people and environmental cognition (Regnier, 1981); territorial behavior in a range of different settings (Taylor, 1978, 1980), and so on. One view is that this may be in reaction to much of the prior research done on intraorganismic processes in isolation, with no differentiation among user groups and especially none among physical environmental factors.

Some research has begun to look at three dimensions simultaneously—the interaction of social environmental and physical environmental factors on behavior—(Moore, in press a; Stokols, 1981b). Research could look at all four dimensions simultaneously, for example, by asking how choice behavior is affected by different hospital environments for different types of people and how it evolves over the course of shorter versus longer stays in hospitals. Any question in our field is inherently a question involving all four of these dimensions—a question involving behaviors specific to a particular user group in a particular setting evolving over time.

The second major component of the framework is the development and test of explanatory theory. The dimensions of people, place, behavior, and time are linked by a set of assumptions, accepted principles, and constructs devised to explain the nature of a specified set of phenomena. The development and test of integrative, explanatory theories of different environment and behavior phenomena is one of the most pressing needs for the field (see Figure 39.4).

The third aspect of this framework is the notion that research and application, although contributing to each other, are distinct conceptually and are cyclical (Villecco & Brill, 1981). Research involves the systematic analysis of phenomena under conditions allowing facts, laws, and theories to arise. *Design*, used in the broadest sense, is the application of the knowledge thus gained to the solution of real-world problems in the everyday physical environment. Both design practice and scientific research have their own system and rules and at their best share a common commitment to a body of knowledge (Zeisel, 1981).

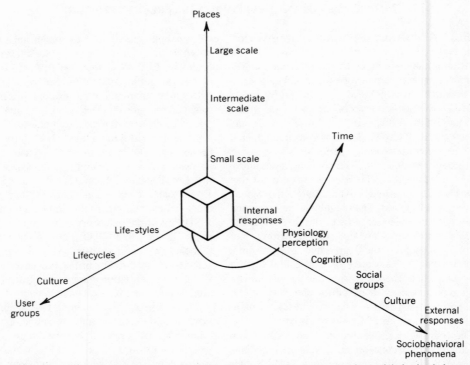

Figure 39.3. Four dimensions of analysis for environment–behavior research: places, people, sociobehavioral phenomena, and time.

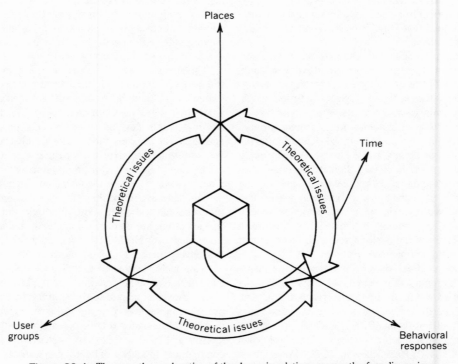

Figure 39.4. Theory—the explanation of the dynamic relations among the four dimensions.

As shown in Figure 39.5, the cycle of environment–behavior research and applications consists of (1) environmental policy planning (including problem identification, policy formulation, goals and objectives, program alternatives, and plan implementation [Zube, 1980a]); (2) environmental design (programming, schematic design, design development, construction documents, and supervision [Palmer, 1981]); (3) environmental evaluation (defining the questions, research design, data collection, and data analysis [Bechtel, n.d.; Friedman et al., 1978]); and (4) research (basic research, applied research, and research applications [Zeisel, 1981]).

Virtually any environment–behavior topic can be researched that relates people to environments and changes in the quality of life as a result of environment–behavior interactions. Traditional design practice, planning practice, and the process of public policymaking involve the informal or tacit application of knowledge, information, and research results (Caplan, 1977; Caplan, Morrison, & Stembaugh, 1975; see Figure 39.5).

Surrounding these three components, and especially the inner dimensions of places, people, and sociobehavioral phenomena, are a number of contextual factors involving issues of environmental deterioration, depletion of natural resources, and enhancing the quality of life. These issues set the agenda for the field, as they define the most critical issues facing our environment and therefore our field. As well as contributing to the infrastructure of science itself, environment–behavior research has been devoted to the creation of knowledge on which to base public and private actions for resolving environmental issues (see Figure 39.6).

39.5.3. Developments in Recent Research

Up to the mid-1970s, contributions to the literature were organized primarily along the lines of traditional behavioral science categories like privacy, personal space, environmental cognition, attitudes, and preferences (see, e.g., the EDRA *Proceedings*, 1969 on). A review based on research published in the EDRA *Proceedings* (Ross & Campbell, 1978) noted a shift to most research being organized around place types by the end of the decade. This section will briefly highlight some recent developments in empirical research organized in terms of the framework.

Research on Place Issues
The emergence of research organized in terms of different environmental settings addresses the applied side of the field and may provide an integrative approach. For practicing professionals in environmental

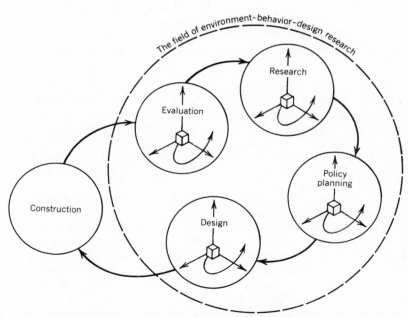

Figure 39.5 The cyclical and iterative nature of environment—behavior design research—research and the application of knowledge to environmental policy, planning, design, and education.

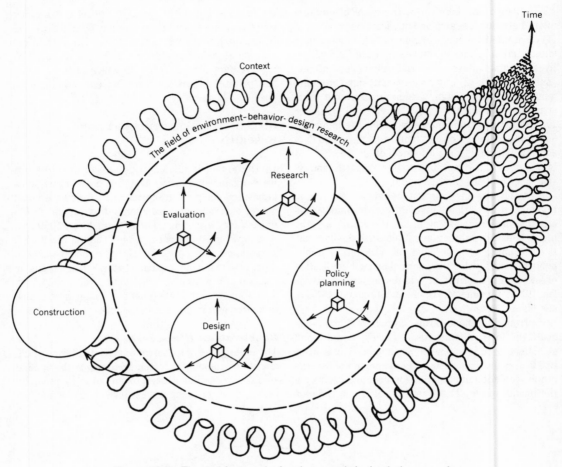

Figure 39.6. The total framework of environment–behavior design research.

design, evaluation, and management whose work is organized in terms of place types (interiors, building types, or urban and regional areas), research that is organized by place is most convenient for finding relevant behavioral information, for analyzing critical environment–behavior dependencies, and for generalizing information to professional practice. Research organized in terms of places can also serve a conceptual function for integrating a number of behavioral and design issues in a way that highlights the fundamental relationships between people, their environment, and responses to environment.

Place-type research falls into three categories of scale from the scale of regions, through the intermediate scale of buildings, to the scale of interiors, products, and materials (cf. Saarinen, 1976). The divisions between scales may seem arbitrary, but they are the same general categories used in the professions applying environment–behavior research to en-

vironmental decision making. Larger scale spaces are typically the province of resource managers, urban planners, landscape architects, urban designers, and civil engineers. The intermediate scale is the home range of architects, building designers, and consulting engineers. And the smallest scale issues fall within the purview of interior designers, product designers, graphic designers, and architects dealing with building subsystems and materials.

These scales of the environment are nested, one within the other. Rather than being separate places with firm boundaries, the concept of a nested hierarchy of place types may allow research across scales. Overall satisfaction (or other measures of behavioral response) may be seen in terms of the relative contributions of variables identified at the large, intermediate, and small-scale levels.

Natural environments have attracted considerable interest in the past 20 years. The growing public awareness of environmental issues is evident in the significant increase in outdoor camping and recreational activities, the popularity of ecology, preservation, and conservation movements, the number of books and journals published on the subject of outdoor life, and the rising membership in clubs and organizations that center on environmental concerns. A number of nations are passing environmental legislation for the protection of the natural landscapes. These concerns have been recognized by the developing nations as well. Worldwide attention has been focused on the issues of environmental protection, preservation, and conservation, through world conferences on the environment, United Nations committees, international treaties, and environmental conservation organizations (Zube, 1980b). However, attitudes and values toward the natural landscape often treat it as another resource for human exploitation, whether for exploitation of natural resources for production or preservation of outdoor scenic landscapes for recreational use. The result is that most of the natural environment is currently in the process of becoming planned, designed, and managed for human use.

Environment–behavior research has looked at these issues. Zube, Brush, and Fabos (1975) studied values associated with landscape settings (Riley, in press), human responses to the visual landscape, and models and applications that have been developed for rural and landscape planning and management (see Buttel et al., in press). The aesthetic assessment of landscapes has also become a topic of significant interest for policy and decision making (Craik & Zube, 1976; see Knopf, Chapter 20, and Pitt & Zube, Chapter 27, this volume).

Urban areas are being seen as human a well as physical systems (see Francis, in press). The study of cities has focused on the interaction of the people with the physical environment in light of new social conditions, emerging economic constraints, and technological changes (Hack, 1984; Michelson, 1980).

Concern for worker productivity and reindustrialization and the growing percentage of office workers in the employment sector have led to a body of research on the interrelationship between the human, economic, and physical aspects of the work place. A series of studies on offices was conducted by Brill and his associates (Brill, 1982; Sundstrom, Kastenbaum, & Konar-Goldband, 1978; cf. Gaskie, 1980; Villecco & Brill, 1981). Starting from a critical assessment of earlier studies on office environments (Sundstrom et al., 1978), Brill and his associates conceptualized the relationship between worker satisfaction, worker productivity, and attributes of the office environment, and have shown a number of impacts that design has on satisfaction and productivity (see also Sundstrom, Chapter 19, this volume).

Housing continues to be over 60% of all construction activity in the United States by volume. Cooper's (1975) study of planned housing continues to be cited as a prime example of housing studies (see also Cooper, 1972). Research conducted at the University of Illinois (Francescato, Weidemann, Anderson, & Chenoweth, 1977; Weidemann, Anderson, Butterfield, & O'Donnell, 1982) is the type of methodologically sophisticated studies needed in the field (see also Tognoli, Chapter 17, this volume).

Environment–behavior research has also dealt with relationships at the microscale, the smallest and most immediate level of human–environment interaction—those physical elements that we all touch, see, and use daily. Human factors started with a concern for designing hardware to fit people, but research interests have broadened. Early studies were Kira's (1966) on bathrooms and Clipson and Wehrer's (1974) on cardiac care units. Subsequent work has looked at practical aspects of anthropometric fit and has quantified physical reactions to sensory stimuli in the luminous, sonic, and thermal environments (Bennett, 1977; Kleeman, 1981).

Health, human safety, and security have emerged as important microscale research issues. Research has been conducted on the toxic effects of building materials and systems, accidents in different types of environments, and planning and design for safety and security (see Levin & Duhl, 1984).

Research on User Group Issues

Research on *user group* issues (as it has come to be known) is actually of three types—research on individual differences like gender differences; research on aggregates of people brought together by a particular function, like children and teachers in child care centers; and research on intact primary or secondary groups, like families and religious groups (Michelson, in press).

The traditional environment–behavior classification of people into "user groups" such as children, elderly, or handicapped may have created an insular approach to each issue. A more useful conceptualization may be to see the interrelationship of all these groups within a larger economic, political, and social framework (Moore et al., 1985). Such an approach acknowledges design topics relevant to each group, integrates their various environmental requirements, and is more holistic as it reintegrates people into their life situations. For instance, the understanding of children and elderly in the environment can be enhanced greatly by seeing both user groups as part of a developmental cycle over the life span.

A large portion of what is usually considered the "average" population in North America has experienced profound changes in social and political-economic structures within the last 10 to 20 years. These changes have led to changes in life-styles. Divorce, the changing role of women, and inflation are just some of the causes that have affected life-styles. Environment and behavior have begun to give attention to defining different life-styles and conducting research on the relationships between life-style and the environment (Hayden, 1981; Michelson, 1976).

The changing role of women in society is having great impact on cultures across the world and continues to be a vital concern for the future. Current research in the area of changing environmental roles of women, men, and the family have been conducted by Hayden (1976, 1981) and Saegert (1980; Saegert & Winkel, 1980), among others. Some anthologies on the topic include Stimpson, Dixler, Nelson, and Yatrakis (1980) on women in the city, Rosaldo and Lamphere (1974) on women and society, and Wekerle, Peterson, and Morley (1980) on spaces for women. These volumes and a major review chapter (Peterson, in press) outline the major issues and report the latest research and research needs on changing gender roles and the environment.

As people develop, age, and pass through the life cycle, behavioral patterns, dependence, and vulnerability to the environment shift dramatically. People do not remain in any one stage very long. Although this seems rather obvious, it is frequently forgotten when policy, planning, and design decisions are made. In recent years a certain amount of research has been devoted to various stages of the life cycle, for example, the special needs of children and the elderly. Other stages in the life cycle, like adolescence and the middle-age years, have been relatively neglected.

The major collections of work on children and the environment are by Altman and Wohlwill (1978) and Weinstein and David (in press). Some of this research has been translated into planning and design guidance (Moore et al., 1979). Although research in this area has been expanding rapidly (see reviews by Gump, 1975; Weinstein, 1979; Wohlwill & Heft, Chapter 9, this volume), questions have been raised about the reliability and validity of much of it (Moore, 1982; Weinstein, 1979). At a methodological level, questions revolve around the use of case study research designs, inadequate calibration of measurement instruments, and problems of small samples and external validity.

The fastest growing sector of the North American population is people over 70 years of age. Previous assumptions about the numbers of older people in the world and meeting their needs are no longer applicable. Due to higher standards of living, including better health care and changes in life-styles, people are simply living longer than before. Environment–behavior research has begun to look at the environmental conditions associated with prolonging productive, useful, and meaningful life experiences (Altman, Lawton, & Wohlwill, 1984; Lawton, 1980; Moos & Lemke, 1980; cf. Carp, 1966, Chapter 10, this volume). Research on older people and the environment has also begun to find applications, most recently in the award-winning work of Zeisel and his colleagues (1978, 1984).

Groups that are the most highly impacted by their environment and have the least amount of control relative to day-to-day functioning include institutionalized people, those who are mentally or physically impaired, and handicapped people who are living in the mainstream of society subject to environmental and physical barriers in their daily lives. Environments generally are not designed to support the needs of these user groups. Starts have been made in research and application of research on populations highly impacted by the environment. The research of Steinfeld and his associates (Steinfeld, 1979) has contributed to the development of revised standards addressing barrier-free design (see ANSI A117.1, 1979). The award-winning work of Farbstein and Wener (1979, 1982) on correctional environments has also had an eye to new policy and design guidelines (see also the chapter by Zimring, Reizenstein & Michelson, Chapter 24, this volume).

Large portions of the urban United States and Canada are made up of suburbs, single-family housing, commercial strips, and shopping malls stretched across the landscape. Design professionals and researchers alike have often ignored these environments as unworthy of study. The suburban landscape is seen as the result of middle-class, unsophisticated design awareness. Its design and study are often left to the discretion of developers, contractors, real estate salespeople, and finance companies. The situation is changing. One of the leading researchers in the area of ordinary people and the physical environment is Gans, including his work on "urban villagers" (1962), Levittown (1967), and popular culture (1974).

Research on Sociobehavioral Issues

A major focus of empirical research in the field has been behavioral and sociocultural responses to environments. The first 10 annual EDRA *Proceedings*, for example, were clustered around such topics as environmental perception, cognition, privacy, crowding, and personal space. This reflected the contributions of researchers trained primarily in the social and behavioral sciences with highly differentiated conceptual systems for studying individual and group behaviors. Although the field of environment–behavior studies is experiencing a shift toward issues organized by place, settings, and types of environments, a number of social and behavioral issues continue to receive considerable attention.

Human "behavior" in the broadest definition of the word can be conceptualized in terms of levels of analysis from inner, organismic responses to external, sociocultural responses. Within these two basic levels further classifications can be made between physiological and psychological responses, individual and social behavior, and sociocultural responses of organizations and society. Work has proceeded at all levels. Review of the literature has identified approximately 20 major areas of research within these categories (Moore et al., 1985). They will not be repeated, but a few emerging areas will be highlighted.

Some research has been conducted on physiological response to the environment (see Weiss & Baum, in press). Starting with the work on noise (Farr, 1972), showing that noise exceeding certain levels contributes to nervous tension and anxiety and exacerbates effects of other illnesses, a body of research has looked at other effects of noise from a stress perspective (Cohen et al., 1973; Glass & Singer, 1972; Stokols, 1979; cf. Evans, 1983; Evans & Cohen, Chapter 15, this volume). Other research has begun to investigate physiological and health responses to indoor air quality, pollution, and building materials (Levin & Duhl, 1984).

Studies of internal psychological responses to the environment have focused on issues of human perception, cognition, meaning, symbolism, and affect, among others. These responses have no directly observable, objective measures. The measures of internal psychological processes are less quantifiable because they deal with more subjective aspects of human experience. In the past, there was considerable research on environmental cognition (see reviews in Downs & Stea, 1973; Evans, 1980; Moore & Golledge, 1976; Moore, 1979b; cf. Golledge, Chapter 5, this volume and Garling & Golledge, in press). The study of meaning and symbolic interpretation has gained significant interest in the research and design community (Bonta, 1979; Jencks, 1981; Rapoport, 1977; see Groat, 1981). Unfortunately, little research has been done that teases out the specific relations

between perceptions, images, or meanings and subsequent spatial behavior.

A range of research has been conducted in the area of social behavior and the built environment, including the social life of small urban places (Whyte, 1980), sociology of neighborhoods (Jacobs, 1961; Michelson, 1980; Saarinen, 1976), and social aspects of city life (Duhl, 1963; Gans, 1968; Michelson, 1980; Milgram, 1970; Saarinen, 1976).

The third level of external human behavioral responses to the environment deals with those aspects of culture that form the larger backdrop of human interaction with the environment. This includes latent and manifest cultural norms, rules, and attitudes that affect human behavior individually or as a group, and it includes such concepts as family structure, status, and the social organizational hierarchy of roles and class structure, group identity, and culturally defined group behaviors. For examples of work on some of these relationships, see Stea (1982), Rapoport (1977), and Altman et al. (1980).

39.6. EMERGING ISSUES, CHALLENGES, AND DIRECTIONS

39.6.1. Issues and Challenges

North American research on environment and behavior has continued in the 1980s to enlighten us to the complexities and subtleties of the environment–behavior transaction and to lead to scientific advances and applied contributions. Emerging issues and challenges still remain for the field.

Applied and Fundamental Interests
Since the beginning, the field has had both pure and applied interests. Although many would argue that these distinctions are arbitrary and not useful, there is a continuum of work that has focused on fundamental questions about human phenomena to that which has focused on environmental interventions. Rather than distinguishing basic *from* applied research, it is now possible to see the field in terms of this continuum of research, including both fundamental and professional contributions. A hallmark of the field may be the dialectic tension between apparent opposites. The best research may be that which contributes simultaneously to theory and to application. In addition to seeing applications as research translations, a model is emerging of action research (Sommer, 1980; Weisman, 1983). Both action research and the evaluation of participatory processes of planning and design (Stea, 1982) are signaling a diminution of

the prior boundaries and conceptual distinctions between basic and applied research and between research and practice (Perez-Gomez, 1983; see Schneekloth, in press).

Developing Conceptualizations of the Environment

A few years ago, Canter and Craik (1981a) noted the distressing lack of vigorous conceptual discourse. Proponents of even modest new conceptual formulations, they suggested, were seldom greeted with informed commentary or close critical appraisal, or worse, they were greeted with an alternative conceptual scheme that failed to engage the earlier in any substantive way. A number of theoretical perspectives and explanatory theories are now emerging and are turning the corner on that commentary.

Canter and Craik also recognized that the conceptions of environments held by leading practicing architects, urban designers, landscape architects, and other environmental professionals are far from fully examined, and the situation has not changed in the intervening years. There are few studies that take as their point of departure the insights gained about the nature of environment by intuitive practitioners with a lifetime of experience. Although there has been some interest in the examination of literary texts as a source of understanding aspects of the environment–behavior nexus (Seamon, 1976, 1984a; Tuan, 1976), little has been done to explore the insights that could be gained from other secondary sources like designers' diaries and published writings.

Search for Appropriate Units of Analysis

Since the beginning of the field, there has been lively debate about the most appropriate units of analysis (Craik, 1970a, 1971). This debate has centered on appropriate units of analysis on the behavioral side of the equation (Altman, 1977; Dunlap & Catton, 1979).

A more pressing need may be for appropriate units of analysis on the environmental side (e.g., attempts at defining a taxonomy of environments and environmental variables; Frederickson, 1974; Lazarus & Launier, 1978; Moos, 1973, 1974, 1976; Pervin, 1978; Price, 1974; Wohlwill & Kohn, 1976). A second task for the field would be to specify structural relationships between articulated and agreed-on attributes of environments and critical behavioral outcomes.

There appear to be three levels of analysis that are necessary. The first deals with spatial scales of the environment. A complete taxonomy will, by necessity, have to deal with all spatial scales—micro-,

meso-, and macro-(Saarinen, 1976). The second level is the development of a taxonomy of types of environments—a taxonomy of settings (in architecture this is known as a "building type analysis"). These taxonomies might be based on biological analogies and may need to be developed within a formal geometry allowing comparison and manipulation (Mitchell, 1977; Stiny, 1981). The third level of analysis is the definition of the characteristics or variables of settings that have noticeable relationships with behavioral outcomes and the quality of life.

The classification of environments—by scales, taxonomies, and dimensions—is similar to the levels of environmental influence discussed by Bronfenbrenner (1977) and can have profound effects on the field as a whole. With a clear system of organization, research can more easily focus on the environmental determinants or correlates of the quality of life. Concepts like complexity, incongruity, salience, congruence, and unity can also be more easily studied as intervening concepts between objective dimensions of the environment and behavioral outcomes.

Array of Response Formats

A methodological issue of continuing centrality to the field is the development of ways to characterize people's responses to environments (Craik, 1968, 1970a; Mandel, 1984). A more fundamental look at the issue of response formats is to question what are the fundamental outcomes in which we should be interested—productivity, successful aging, independence, individual locus of control, quality of life (Gutman, 1981; Villecco & Brill, 1981; cf. Moore et al., 1985)?

Methodological Rigor

Russell and Ward's (1982) review concluded with a call for more methodological rigor, or, as they said, opposing the view that a young field must settle for data less than rigorously gathered. There are few textbooks that do not have a chapter on research methods (e.g., Mandel, 1984, in Fisher et al., 1984), and there are texts devoted entirely to advances in quantitative and qualitative methods of research design, data gathering, and analysis (Michelson, 1975; Zeisel, 1981; see Zube & Moore, in press). Two of the greatest advances have been the adoption of quasi-experimental field methods (Cook & Campbell, 1979) to a wide range of issues, thus allowing near-experimental control consistent with ecological validity (see also Marans & Ahrentzen, in press; Moore, in press b) and the renewed, serious treatment given to qualitative methods of research and analysis (Low, in press).

Environmental Meaning and Symbolism, the Role of History, and the Sense of Place

Three of the central debates in architecture in the mid-1980s have been the ability of the environment to convey meaning and the role of history and contextualism in the design of quality environments. By no means is there agreement on these issues (compare Bonta, 1979; Groat, 1981; Jencks, 1981; Rapoport 1982). There has been, however, scant empirical research on these issues (see Baldassare, 1978; Dunlap & Catton, 1983; Meinig, 1979).

Cross-Cultural Studies

A strong interest has arisen in cross-cultural comparisons of environment–behavior phenomena and the concept of culture-specific design (Rapoport, 1979). This has been fueled by concerns for the development in the Third World on their own terms rather than blindly exporting North American technology and attitudes and by the great number of Third World students presently taking advanced degrees in environment and behavior. The upsurge in interest has been witnessed by empirical studies (Burton, 1980; Huber, 1979; Quarantelli, 1979) but also in reviews (Altman & Chemers, 1980; Baldassare, 1978) and in collected volumes (Altman et al., 1980; Altman & Chemers, 1980).

The Humanistic Upsurge

In parts of the field, there has been a strong humanistic upsurge, which has been seen as part of a larger philosophical and social science movement that questions the basic contentions of positivistic social science (Bunting & Guelke, 1979; see reviews in Gold & Goodey, 1983; Saarinen & Sell, 1980). Much of this criticism has been directed at behavioral geographers (e.g., Golledge, 1979) even though, ironically, their own beginning was in reaction to the simplistic, nonhumanistic assumptions about people used in much of quantitative urban geography. The humanistic upsurge has erupted into a major split between the phenomenologists (Seamon, 1982, 1984b), the environmental determinists (Golledge & Couclelis, 1984), and the Marxists (Cosgrove, 1978), though there are now valiant attempts at reasoned discourse on all sides of the issue (Saarinen, Seamon, & Sell, 1984; Franck, in press).

Environmental Effects on Society and of Societies on the Environment

Another emerging issue that provides a challenge for the field is to understand the mutual effects of the environment on society and of different societies on the environment. Catton and Dunlap (1978a) see this issue as emanating from what they called the "new environmental paradigm" (1978a) and later the "new ecological paradigm" (Catton & Dunlap, 1980). The new ecological paradigm suggests that researchers can no longer afford to ignore the environment in their investigations of the role and effects of different societies (Schnaiberg, 1975). It posits four basic assumptions:

1. Although humans have exceptional characteristics (culture, technology), they remain one among many species that are interdependently involved in the global ecosystem.

2. Human affairs are influenced not only by social and cultural factors but also by intricate linkages of cause, effect, and feedback in the web of nature; thus purposive human actions have many unintended consequences.

3. Humans live in and are dependent on a finite biophysical environment that imposes potent physical and biological restraints on human affairs.

4. Although the inventiveness of humans and the powers derived therefrom may seem for a while to extend carrying capacity limits, ecological laws cannot be repealed (Catton & Dunlap, 1980, p. 34).

New questions have arisen from this "paradigm," among them the environmental context of social stratification, an ecological analysis of the recent decline in the standard of living, the relation of the material environment to the stratification system, analysis of the role of the work place in the "culture of poverty," and the effects on the sociophysical environment on economic growth (Buttel, 1978; Catton & Dunlap, 1978a, 1978b; Dunlap & Catton, 1983).

Environmentalism and the Environmental Movement

Although the late 1960s and the 1970s were the heyday of the environmental movement in North America, researchers have continued to focus on a number of issues including the origins of the movement, memberships of environmental organizations, reasons for affiliation and participation, attitudes toward environmental problems, and the future of environmentalism (see Dunlap & Catton, 1979; Heberlein, 1972 for reviews). Public support for environmental protection remained strong through the end of the 1970s, despite its earlier peak, and membership in environmental organizations continued to increase. But despite substantial efforts by environmentalists, government interest has waned, and observers warn that ecological problems are more serious now than before the rise of the environmental movement a decade ago (Dunlap & Catton, 1979). The gravity of the situation in North America suggests the necessity of renewed efforts in understanding environmental attitudes, how they evolve and change, and to study issues of contemporary social concern such as pollution, poverty, and welfare, the "carrying capacity" of different environments, the problems associated with allocation of scarce environmental resources, how government and the private sector might be influenced, and how research may have more direct input into public planning and policy (Buttel et al., in press).

Concern with the City and Regional Scales and with Public Policymaking

While much of the early work in the field was directed toward the building scale and toward design implications, recent work has begun to address city and regional scales and the utilization of research in public policy formulation and environmental planning. At the regional level, research has addressed visual landscape assessment, wildlife maintenance, water quality, noise, air quality, litter control, public participation in the planning for parks, forests, and desert areas, preservation of archaeological and historic sites, strip mining, anticipated developments, boom towns, water conservation, and appropriate technology in resource conservation (see reviews in Dunlap & Catton, 1979; Saarinen & Sell, 1980). At the metropolitan level, research has proceeded apace on questions about streets, community parks, public squares, housing, imagery of built form, and the planning and development of new cities (see review in Gold & Goodey, 1983).

Environment–behavior research information may be utilized in all aspects of policymaking, physical planning, and design that are concerned with both the physical environment (at all scales) and its relationship to human behavior (at all levels). Many aspects of environmental policy planning have been of concern to environment–behavior research (e.g., Cooper, 1972). Because of the applied and action orientation of much of the field in North America, the role of knowledge and uses of scientific information in environmental decision making is seen as very important (Ventre, 1982). The role of knowledge in public policy formation has been studied extensively in the fields of policy analysis, planning, and public adminis-

tration (see Caplan, 1977; Caplan et al., 1975; Weiss, 1977; Weiss & Barton, 1979; Wilensky, 1976).

Instrumental utilization suggests that ideas are instruments applied in decision making as guides for action; their validity is determined by the success of the action. The main purpose of instrumental utilization is legitimizing or motivating decision making interest. There are many reasons why instrumental utilization has not been enormously effective in national policy formulation, including the frail character of the knowledge that social science research (and environment–behavior research) produce, the lack of clarification of policy choices, the implicit values embodied in social science research not being congruent with decision makers, the nature of the decision-making process, researchers' lack of knowledge about how decisions are made (Ventre, 1975; in press), and the mistaken assumption that there are identifiable actors who "make the decisions" (Weiss, 1977).

A number of characteristics of successful utilization of research have been identified (Caplan et al., 1975):

1. Decision makers are oriented to and appreciate the scientific aspects of policy issues.
2. The ethical and scientific values of policymakers are oriented toward a sense of social direction and responsibility.
3. The policy issue is well defined and requires research knowledge.
4. The research findings are not counterintuitive and have politically feasible action implications.
5. The policymakers and researchers are linked by information specialists capable of translating scientific findings and coupling those findings to the policy goals and objectives of the decision makers or decision-making agency.

A different approach to the utilization of research based on the notion of the reflective practitioner has been taken recently by Schneekloth (in press).

39.6.2. Directions for the Future

In addition to the previously mentioned emerging issues and challenges, there are other directions for future development in the field. Several agendas have been written, mostly sponsored by federal agencies, that attempt to outline the range of empirical issues needing attention (Villecco & Brill, 1981, sponsored by the U.S. National Endowment for the Arts; Snyder, 1982, 1984, sponsored by the National Science Foundation; American Institute of Architects Research Council, 1984, sponsored by the American Institute of Architects; and Moore et al., 1985, sponsored by the National Endowment for the Arts and EDRA). No attempt will be made to review their suggestions here; the reader is directed to these sources.

A number of broader conceptual issues also face the field, the resolution of which may hold promise for illuminating a general theory of environment–behavior design relations. The remainder of this chapter will discuss some of these issues.

Assessment of Different Research Designs for the Study of Environment–Behavior Research

Since the 1970s (Proshansky, 1972), the field has had a commitment to studies of behavior in situ, that is, in everyday environmental settings. This has called for greater reliance on field research methods, including systematic observation and focused interviews, than on laboratory research methods and experimental designs. Yet the scientific training of most members of the field has been in the social and behavioral sciences (the largest number in psychology), where quantitative and experimental methods are stressed. The result has been criticism on both sides. Those with rigorous training criticize studies from the qualitative side as being open to massive problems of internal and external validity. Those with applied interests criticize studies from the quantitative side as addressing those variables that, although they may be measured precisely, are inconsequential to the everyday environment. A resolution has been arising recently in the form of adopting several of the quasi-experimental research designs of Campbell and his colleagues (Campbell & Stanley, 1966; Cook & Campbell, 1979; cf. Patterson, 1977; Marans & Ahrentzen, in press). Meanwhile, some scholars and commentators believe that the field needs more research from scholarly, historical, ethnographic, and participatory directions (Rapoport, 1977; Stea, 1982; cf. Low, in press). It is unlikely that any one approach is unilaterally "better" than any other. The field would greatly benefit by an in-depth analysis of the pros and cons of all these different approaches to environment–behavior research.

Refinement of the Definitions of Environmental Quality and the Quality of Life

Environmental quality and its role in the quality of life is the heartland of environment and behavior. With changes in political and economic structures, the focus of quality has shifted from the well-being of consumers to the efficiency of the production process. Continued research attention needs to be given to the issue of defining the quality of life, environmental quality, and the relations between them. What are to be the critical variables by which the quality of the environment is to be judged? What aspects of human functioning are most related to the quality of life? And how is the quality of the designed environment related to the quality of life?

Conceptual Issues of Place

There are a number of research questions that apply to places at any scale and thus help to describe the nature and experience of place in general. The term *place* is a particularly rich one as it has geographical, architectural, and social connotations. A few researchers study "place" and placeness as a phenomenological experience (Buttimer & Seamon, 1980; Jackson, 1951–1968, 1972; Lowenthal, 1961; Relph, 1976; Rowles, 1978; Seamon, 1984c; Tuan, 1977).

A basic question is what makes space into place? What characteristics of the environment, of group activity, human experience, and cognition comprise the essence of place? A task for environment–behavior design research is to study place from the perspective of the various users, how places are organized and used within a given culture, and the character of particular types of archetypal places: the home, the work place, the place of public assembly, the place of sacredness, the place of entertainment and relaxation, the place of learning, the place for being born, and the place of dying.

Places offer us insights into the historical character of a society. Research into the origin and evolution of places can be long and difficult, handicapped by the comparative newness of the topics. But knowledge of the origins of place is essential to understanding the nature of human relationship with the environment at all levels. The web of interrelationships between behavior and the environment becomes more complex as the social, political, and economic growth of a place is investigated (Clay, 1973; Jackson, 1972). The significance in such an area of investigation is not simply backtracking to describe history of particular places but rather a historical perspective and theory on the nature and development of place.

The management of place can affect its use significantly. As the quality of place is somewhat fragile, management may destroy place. Conversely, the sensitive management of the environment can effectively lead to the possibilities of its being used and interpreted as place. The relations between management and place are even less understood than the history of place (Lynch, 1972, 1976).

Places affected by change need examination in the light of rapid social and technological change and the impacts on inhabitants. High rates of technological change can affect the character of reused existing urban buildings, transportation and communication systems, the building industry, and the people within them. Recent economic and social changes have made it necessary to adapt existing environments for different uses—adaptive reuses. Basic research is needed to identify which aspects of place are critical to achieve a successful behavioral fit with new uses.

The Continued Development and Testing of Theories of the Middle Range

The development—and the testing—of explanatory theories of environment and behavior continues to be important for at least six reasons: (1) the development and articulation of theory advances the field as a whole; (2) theory will help to make sense of disparate findings and to reveal inconsistencies and gaps in our knowledge; (3) theory advances us from the description of phenomena to their explanation in larger conceptual terms; (4) theory suggests new lines of inquiry, new approaches, and new ways of conceptualizing old problems; (5) theory aids in the application of research to environmental problem solving; and (6) theory aids in teaching environment–behavior design studies, especially at the graduate level.

It has been suggested that environment–behavior research is in a preparadigmatic stage (Stokols, 1977a) and that there are the beginnings of multiple competing paradigms (Craik, 1977). Merton (1957) cautioned against the overreliance on grand theories, which he termed "all-inclusive speculations." What is needed is a shift in emphasis both from grand theories and from the ad hoc, often atheoretical collection of data on single phenomena to the development and testing of theories of the middle range.

It is also important that attention be given to moving from general theoretical orientations through frameworks and models to specific explanatory theories that can explain the different domains of the multiple interactions between physical environments and human behavior. Since the early work of Lewin in the 1930s and Barker in the 1950s, behavior in real environments has been seen as a joint product of personal forces and situational factors involving social rules and sociocultural definitions of the environment. Theory must account for the mechanisms linking these personal and situational factors.

Different Scales of Analysis

Theory should address and account for data at different scales of the physical environment. Theory should imbed conceptualizations in the larger context of the social, cultural, economic, and political environments. Environment and behavior research historically has focused on intrapersonal processes and mesoscale environments—privacy, cognition, buildings, public open spaces. This is an artifact of the origins of the field and because its membership is largely from psychology and architecture. However, environment and behavior research pertains to all levels of the environment. Theories need to respond to all three scales: macro-, meso-, and micro-. At the macroscale, theory needs to account for group behavior within large-scale environments (urban areas, landscapes, communities, cities, geographic regions); at the mesoscale, for individual and group behavior within intermediate-scale environments (buildings, urban open spaces); and at the microscale, for individual behavior and environmental units (ambient light, noise, stimulus complexity, materials). These three scales must receive equal emphasis in consideration of the overall environment–behavior relationship.

Different Levels of Behavior

The multidisciplinary character of environment–behavior research and application implies that theory should be able to deal with all levels of *behavior* in the broadest sense of the word. Elaborating on the dictum of Lewin (1946) that behavior is a joint product of personal and situational forces, Stokols (1977a) proposed a profile of the environment and behavior field as composed of "intrapersonal process" (physiological and psychological processes) and "environmental dimensions" (physical, social, and cultural). Theory should be able to account for data across levels of analysis, for physiological responses (e.g., fatigue, arousal), psychological responses (perception, cognition), individual behavioral responses (territorial behavior, privacy regulation), social group responses (small-group dynamics, proxemics), and sociocultural responses (neighboring, cultural values).

Emergent Conceptual Ideas

In one of the early papers in the field, Proshansky (1972) called for the development of emergent concepts and methods uniquely suited for describing, explaining, and studying environment–behavior phenomena and applications. Recent reviews (Russell & Ward, 1982; Stokols, 1978b) identified a number of concepts that pertain specifically to environment–

behavior interactions. Stokols (1978b) suggested that the field has moved beyond simple application of established social science theories and concepts to the formation of new concepts and models pertaining to specifically environment–behavior phenomena. For continued conceptual development, the field needs to look for more powerful and useful conceptualizations from intellectual parent disciplines in both the social sciences and the environmental professions. And yet there is a question as to how far one can take social science theories that are intended to account primarily for person variables and intrapersonal processes. Perhaps more fundamentally, we need to understand the integrity of environment–behavior transactions in their own terms.

The Utilization of Environment–Behavior Research in Environmental Problem Solving

It has not gone unrecognized in this chapter that the study of environment and behavior in North America, although it is a scientific discipline, is also problem centered and applied. While pursuing interesting lines of inquiry that promise to lead to more fundamental knowledge about environment–behavior transactions, the field is also concerned with the very real questions of making the physical environment a better place in which to live. A central set of issues in the field, therefore, relates to the processes by which knowledge may be utilized in societal problems at all scales, that is, ways to increase the effective application of and practice with environment–behavior research in all the professions charged with the planning and design of our environment (cf. Schneekloth, in press).

This intent can be achieved in three ways. First, research on process issues may be able to increase the knowledge that actors involved in environmental planning, design, and building fields have of themselves, of their actions, of the criteria for their decisions, and of the factors that mitigate, influence, and impinge on their decisions. Second, process research may help to improve the effectiveness of the design and environmental planning decision-making process and institutions. And, third, process research may affect institutional and individual processes in such a way that they may be more receptive to information generated by the field.

Resolution of the Theoretically Focused View and the Problem-Centered View of the Field

Many conferences have had as their theme some aspect of "bridging the gap" between research and re-

search utilization. Smith (1977) discussed the issue in conceptual terms. On the one hand, various psychologists and other social and behavioral scientists have attempted to establish a conceptual framework that would give proper attention to the environmental contexts of behavior. Although developing elaborate conceptual and methodological schemes, these traditions have paid considerably more attention to the internal organismic locus of behavior than to the environmental—and especially the physical environmental—context. The theories, methods, and results, although conceptually interesting, are difficult if not impossible for environmental professionals to understand and use.

On the other hand, there are problem-centered approaches contributing through research and application to the development of a more humanly advantageous physical environment. Various research architects and other environmental professionals have attempted to erect systems that would utilize environment–behavior data in the service of environmental interventions, most notable among them Alexander, his students, and associates (e.g., 1964). But, although developing operational systems for utilizing research information, these approaches have been, for the most part atheoretical and have not contributed to the conceptual development of the field.

The challenge now is to conduct research, both basic and applied, that contributes equally to understanding fundamental environment–behavior phenomena, to the development and articulation of theory, and to the solution of environmental problems.

Acknowledgments

My deep appreciation to my colleagues and students at the University of Wisconsin, Milwaukee and to my colleagues elsewhere for sharpening and extending many of these thoughts on earlier drafts. These include Sherry Ahrentzen, Irwin Altman, Robert Bechtel, Michael Brill, Riley Dunlap, Reginald Golledge, Byung-Ho Min, Monica Paciuk, Amos Rapoport, Thomas Saarinen, Daniel Stokols, Kathleen Stumpf, Vehbi Tosun, Paul Tuttle, Francis Ventre, Joachim Wohlwill, and Ervin Zube; I am grateful to Bonny Celine for excellent editorial assistance, and to Annabelle Sherba, Janet Tibbetts, and the SARUP staff for flawlessly wordprocessing the manuscript.

NOTES

1. A past review of environmental psychology (Russell & Ward, 1982) defined it as that branch of psychology "con-

cerned with providing a systematic account of the relationship between person and environment." Russell and Ward's definition sees environmental psychology as being analogous to what they considered to be developmental psychology, that is, a unified perspective on strictly psychological processes. (It may be disputed that this is the intention of developmental psychology; see the variety of multidisciplinary contributions in the major journal, *Child Development*.) The authors differentiated *environmental psychology* from *ecological psychology, human ecology, ecocultural psychology,* and *behavioral geography* but stopped short of equating environmental psychology with any or all of these other fields and with what they called "the larger field of environment and behavior." Rather, they defined environmental psychology as "the area of *overlap* between the two *larger* disciplines, psychology and environment and behavior." This may be the first time that other disciplines have defined themselves in terms of the larger field of environment and behavior — a sure sign of the emergence of the field (see also Bowden, 1984).

2. For other views of the history of the field, see Carson (1965), Rapoport (1970), Archea (1975), Zeisel (1975), Saarinen (1976), Proshansky and O'Hanlon (1977), Stokols (1977a), Dunlap and Catton (1979), Proshansky and Altman (1979), Bowden (1980), and Bechtel (n.d.). As pointed out by White (1979) in her introduction to the Proshansky and Altman review, the authors of most of these histories have chosen to focus on particular portions of the multidisciplinary field and not on the broader field of environment and behavior. The reader is directed to the chapters by Barker, Wapner, Proshansky, and Sommer in this *Handbook* that also contain historical background regarding the field. Although mostly complementary with present treatment, they place differing emphasis on different historical issues.

3. The ideas on units of analysis were developed in collaboration with Kathleen Stumpf and were first presented in an unpublished doctoral seminar paper, "Organization for the Content Area of Theories" (March, 1984).

4. Since writing this portion of the chapter, I have seen Altman and Rogoff's chapter on world views in environmental psychology based on Pepper's (1942) world hypotheses. That chapter takes a broader view, categorizing theories into four types, whereas the present chapter sees them as being of eight more specific types. It is possible to nest my eight types into their four world views, an exercise that has already been found to be valuable in our own doctoral proseminar (Spring, 1985).

5. Portions of this section are drawn from material prepared by the author for Moore, Tuttle, and Howell, *Environmental Design Research Directions* (New York: Praeger, 1985) and are used by permission.

REFERENCES

Ahrentzen, S., & Evans, G.W. (1984). Distraction, privacy, and classroom design. *Environment and Behavior, 16,* 437–454.

Aiello, J.R., & Thompson, D.E. (1980). Personal space, crowding, and spatial behavior in a cultural context. In I. Altman, A. Rapoport, & J.F. Wohlwill (Eds.), *Environment and Culture.* New York: Plenum.

Alexander, C.W.J. (1964). *Notes on the synthesis of form.* Cambridge, MA: Harvard University Press.

Alexander, C.W.J., Ishikawa, S., & Silverstein, M. (1977). *A pattern language.* New York: Oxford University Press.

Allen, V.L. (1978). On convergent methodology: An aesthetic theory of school vandalism. In L. Van Ryzin (Ed.), *Research methods in behavior-environment studies.* Madison: University of Wisconsin, Institute for Environmental Studies.

Alonso, W. (1964). The historic and structural theories of urban form: The implications for urban renewal. *Land Economics, 40,* 227–231.

Altman, I. (1973a). Some perspectives on the study of man-environment phenomena. *Representative Research in Social Psychology, 4,* 109–186.

Altman, I. (Chair). (1973b). Theory of man-environment relations. In W.F.E. Preiser (Ed.), *Environmental design research* (Vol. 2). Stroudsburg, PA: Dowden, Hutchinson & Ross.

Altman, I. (1975). *Environment and social behavior.* Monterey, CA: Brooks/Cole.

Altman, I. (1977). Research on environment and behavior: A personal statement of strategy. In D. Stokols (Ed.), *Perspectives on environment and behavior.* New York: Plenum.

Altman, I. (1981). Reflections on environmental psychology. *Human Environments, 2,* 5–7.

Altman, I., & Chemers, M. (1980). Cultural aspects of environment-behavior relationships. In H. Triandis & R. Brislin (Eds.), *Handbook of cross-cultural psychology* (Vol. 5). Boston: Allyn & Bacon.

Altman, I., & Haythorn, W. (1967). Ecology of isolated groups. Behavioral Science, *12,* 169–182.

Altman, I., Lawton, M.P., & Wohlwill, J.F. (Eds.). (1984). *Elderly people and the environment.* New York: Plenum.

Altman, I., Rapoport, A., & Wohlwill, J.F. (Eds.). (1980). *Environment and culture.* New York: Plenum.

Altman, I., & Vinsel, A.M. (1977). Personal space: An analysis of E.T. Hall's proxemics framework. In I. Altman & J.F. Wohlwill (Eds.), *Human behavior and environment* (Vol. 1). New York: Plenum.

Altman, I., & Wohlwill, J.F. (Eds.). (1976). *Human behavior and environment.* New York: Plenum.

Altman, I., & Wohlwill, J.F. (Eds.). (1978). *Children and the environment.* New York: Plenum.

Altman, I., Wohlwill, J.F., & Everitt, P.B. (Eds.). (1981). *Transportation and behavior.* New York: Plenum.

American Institute of Architects. (1982) *Direction '80s.* Washington, DC: Author.

American Institute of Architects Research Council. (1984). *Architectural Research Priorities, 1984.* Washington, DC: American Institute of Architects.

American National Standards Institute. (1979). *Standards for Barrier-Free Design* (ANSI A117.1). Washington, DC: Author.

Appleyard, D. (1969). Why buildings are known. *Environment and Behavior, 1,* 131–156.

Appleyard, D. (1981). *Livable streets.* Berkeley: University of California Press.

Appleyard, D., & Craik, K.H. (1978). The Berkeley Environmental Simulation Laboratory and its research programme. *International Review of Applied Psychology, 27,* 53–55.

Appleyard, D., Lynch, K., & Myer, J.R. (1964). *The view from the road.* Cambridge, MA: MIT Press.

Archea, J. (Ed.). (1967–69). *Architectural Psychology Newsletter.* Salt Lake City: University of Utah, Architectural Psychology Program.

Archea, J. (1975). Establishing an interdisciplinary commitment. In B. Honikman (Ed.), *Responding to social change.* Stroudsburg, PA: Dowden, Hutchinson, & Ross.

Archea, J. (1977). Behavioral science impact to environmental policy: Applications to stairs. In P. Suedfield, J.A. Russell, L.M. Ward, F. Sziegeti, & G. Davis (Eds.), *The behavioral basis of design* (Vol. 2). Stroudsburg, PA: Dowden, Hutchinson, & Ross.

Archea, J., & Eastman, C.H. (Eds.). (1970). *Proceedings of the 2nd Annual Environmental Design Research Association Conference.* Stroudsburg, PA: Dowden, Hutchinson, & Ross.

Archea, J. & Esser, A.H. (1969). *Man-environment systems.* Orangeburg, NY: Association for the Study of Man-Environment Relations.

Archea, J., & Margulis, S.T. (1979). Environmental research inputs to policy and design programs: The case of preparation for involuntary relocation of the institutionalized elderly. In T.O. Byerts, S.C. Howell, & L.A. Pastalan (Eds.), *The environmental context of aging.* New York: Garland.

Bailey, R. (1967). Training and research in architectural psychology. In C.W. Taylor, R. Bailey, & C.H.H. Branch (Eds.), *Second National Conference on Architectural Psychology.* Salt Lake City: University of Utah.

Bailey, R., Branch, C.H.H., & Taylor, C.W. (Eds.). (1961). *Architectural psychology and psychiatry.* Salt Lake City: University of Utah.

Baldassare, M. (1978). Human spatial behavior. *Annual Review of Sociology, 4,* 29–56.

Baltes, P.B., Reese, H.W., & Nesselroade, J.R. (1977). *Life-span developmental psychology.* Monterey, CA: Brooks/Cole.

Barker, R.G. (1963). On the nature of the environment. *Journal of Social Issues, 19,* 17–38.

Barker, R.G. (1965). Explorations in ecological psychology. *American Psychologist, 20,* 1–14.

Barker, R.G., (1968). *Ecological psychology.* Stanford, CA: Stanford University Press.

Barker, R.G., & Associates. (1978). *Habitats, environments, and human behavior.* San Francisco: Jossey-Bass.

Barker, R.G., & Gump, P.V. (1964). *Big school, small school.* Stanford, CA: Stanford University Press.

Barker, R.G., & Schoggen, P. (1973). *Qualities of community life.* San Francisco: Jossey-Bass.

Barker, R.G., & Wright, H.F. (1951). *One boy's day.* New York: Row Peterson.

Barker, R.G., & Wright, H.F. (1955). *Midwest and its children.* New York: Row Peterson.

Barnett, J. (1974). *Urban design as public policy.* New York: Architectural Record Books.

Baum, A., & Greenberg, C.I. (1975). Waiting for a crowd: The behavioral and perceptual effects of anticipated crowding. *Journal of Personality and Social Psychology, 32,* 667–671.

Baum, A., & Singer, J.E. (Eds.). (1981). *Advances in environmental psychology.* Hillsdale, NJ: Erlbaum.

Baum, A., Singer, J.E., & Baum, C.S. (1981). Stress and the environment. *Journal of Social Issues, 37,* 4–35.

Bechtel, R.B. (1977). *Enclosing behavior.* Stroudsburg, PA: Dowden, Hutchinson, & Ross.

Bechtel, R.B. (in preparation). *The history and promise of environment-behavior research.* Unpublished manuscript, University of Arizona, Department of Psychology, Tucson.

Bechtel, R.B. (undated). *What are post-occupancy evaluations?: A laymen's guide to the POE for housing* (Final Report). Tucson, AZ: U.S. Department of Housing and Urban Development, Environmental Research and Development Foundation.

Bell, P.A., Fisher, J.D., & Loomis, R.J. (1978). *Environmental psychology.* Philadelphia: Saunders.

Bennett, C. (1977). *Spaces for people.* Englewood Cliffs, NJ: Prentice-Hall.

Berry, J.W. (1980). Cultural ecology and individual behavior. In I. Altman, A. Rapoport, & J.F. Wohlwill (Eds.), *Environment and culture.* New York: Plenum.

Bochenski, I.M. (1966). *Contemporary European philosophy.* Berkeley: University of California Press.

Bonta, J.P. (1979). *Architecture and its interpretation.* New York: Rizzoli.

Boulding, K. (1956). *The image.* Ann Arbor: University of Michigan Press.

Bowden, M.J. (1980). Cognitive renaissance in American geography: The intellectual history of a movement. *Organon, 14,* 199–204.

Bowden, M.J. (1984). Environmental perception in geography: A commentary. In T.F. Saarinen, D. Seamon, &

J.L. Sell (Eds.), *Environmental perception and behavior* (Research Paper No. 209). Chicago: University of Chicago, Department of Geography.

Brill, M. (1982). *Do buildings really matter?* New York: Academy for Educational Development, Educational Facilities Laboratories.

Bronfenbrenner, U. (1977). The ecology of human development in retrospect and prospect. In H. McGurk (Ed.), *Ecological factors in human development.* New York: North Holland.

Bunting, T.E., & Guelke, L. (1979). Behavioral and perception geography: A critical appraisal. *Annals of the Association of American Geographers, 69,* 448–474.

Bunting, T.E., & Semple, T.M.L. (1979). The development of an environmental response inventory for children. In A.D. Seidel & S. Danford (Eds.), *Environmental design.* Washington, DC: Environmental Design Research Association.

Burton, I. (1961). Invasion and escape on the little Calumet. In G.F. White (Ed.), *Papers on flood problems* (Research Paper No. 70). Chicago: University of Chicago, Department of Geography.

Burton, I. (1980). Perception of the environment. *International Geographical Union Bulletin, 31,* 67–70.

Burton, I., & Kates, R.W. (1964). The perception of natural hazards in resource management. *Natural Resources Journal, 3,* 412–441.

Burton, I., Kates, R.W., & White, G.F. (1968). *The human ecology of extreme geophysical events* (Natural Hazard Research Working Paper No. 1). Toronto, Canada: University of Toronto, Department of Geography.

Buttel, F.H. (1978). Environmental sociology: A new paradigm? *American Sociologist, 13,* 252–256.

Buttel, F.H., Murdock, S.H., Leiseritz, F.L., & Hamm, R.R. (in press). Rural environments. In E.H. Zube & G.T. Moore (Eds.), *Advances in environment, behavior, and design* (Vol. 1). New York: Plenum.

Buttimer, A. (1972). Social space and the planning of residential areas. *Environment and Behavior, 4,* 279–318.

Buttimer, A. (1974). *Values in geography* (Resource Paper No. 24). Washington, DC: Association of American Geographers, Commission on College Geography.

Buttimer, A. (1976a). Exploring the social dimension of environmental knowing: A commentary. In G.T. Moore & R.G. Golledge (Eds.), *Environmental knowing.* Stroudsburg, PA: Dowden, Hutchinson, & Ross.

Buttimer, A. (1976b). Grasping the dynamism of lifeworld. *Annals of the Association of American Geographers, 66,* 277–292.

Buttimer, A. (1979). Insiders, outsiders, and the geography of regional life. In A. Kuklinski, O. Kultalahti, & B. Koskiah (Eds.), *Regional dynamics of socioeconomic change.* Tampere, Finland: Finn.

Buttimer, A. & Seamon, D. (Eds.). (1980). *The human experience of space and place.* London: Croom Helm.

Campbell, D.T. (1957). Factors relevant to the validity of experiments in field settings. *Psychological Bulletin, 54,* 297–312.

Campbell, D.T., & Stanley, J.C. (1966). *Experimental and quasi-experimental designs for research.* Chicago: Rand McNally.

Canter, D.V., & Craik, K.H. (1981a). Environmental psychology. *Journal of Environmental Psychology, 1,* 1–11.

Canter, D.V., & Craik, K.H. (1981b). (Eds.). *Journal of Environmental Psychology.* London: Academic.

Caplan, N. (1977). A minimal set of conditions necessary for the utilization of social science knowledge in policy formulation at the national level. In C.H. Weiss (Ed.), *Using social research in public policy making.* Lexington, MA: Lexington.

Caplan, N., Morrison, A., & Stembaugh, R. (1975). *The use of social science knowledge in policy decisions at the national level.* Ann Arbor: University of Michigan, Institute for Social Research.

Carp, F.M. (1966). *A future for the aged.* Austin: University of Texas Press.

Carp, F.M., & Carp, A. (1984). A complementary/congruence model of well-being or mental health for the community elderly. In I. Altman, M.P. Lawton, & J.F. Wohlwill (Eds.), *Elderly people and the environment.* New York: Plenum.

Carson, D.H. (1965). The interactions of man and his environment. In C.T. Warson (Ed.), *School environments research* (Vol. 2). Ann Arbor: University of Michigan, College of Architecture and Design.

Cassirer, E. (1953–57). *The philosophy of symbolic forms* (3 Vols.). New Haven, CT: Yale University Press.

Catton, W.R., Jr. (1971). The wildland recreation boom and sociology. *Pacific Sociological Review, 14,* 339–359.

Catton, W.R., Jr. (1978). Carrying capacity, overshoot, and the quality of life. In J.M. Yinger & S.J. Cutler (Eds.), *Major social issues.* New York: Free Press.

Catton, W.R., & Dunlap, R.E. (1978a). Environmental sociology: A new paradigm. *American Sociologist, 13,* 41–49.

Catton, W.R., & Dunlap, R.E. (1978b). Paradigms, theories, and the primacy of the HEP-NEP distinction. *American Sociologist, 13,* 256–259.

Catton, W.R., & Dunlap, R.E. (1980). A new ecological paradigm for post-exhuberant sociology. *American Behavioral Scientist, 24,* 15–47.

Chase, R.A. (Chair). (1973). Theoretical issues in man-environment relations. In W.F.E. Preiser (Ed.), *Environmental design research* (Vol. 1). Stroudsburg, PA: Dowden, Hutchinson, & Ross.

Claparede, E. (1943). L'orientation lointaine [Distance orientation] (J. Wapner, Trans.). *Nouveau traite de psychologie* (Vol. 8). Paris: Presses Universitaire de France.

Clay, G. (1973). *Close-up.* New York: Praeger.

Clipson, C., & Wehrer, J. (1974). *Planning for cardiac care.* Ann Arbor, MI: Health Administration Press.

Cohen, S., Glass, D.C., & Singer, J.E. (1973). Apartment noise, auditory discrimination, and reading ability in children. *Journal of Experimental Social Psychology, 9,* 407–422.

Cohen, S., Krantz, D.S., Evans, E., & Stokols, D. (1981). Cardiovascular and behavioral effects of community noise. *American Scientist, 69,* 528–535.

Cohen, U., & Moore, G.T. (1977). The organization and communication of behaviorally-based research information. In L. van Ryzin (Ed.), *Behavior-environment research methods.* Madison: University of Wisconsin, Institute for Environmental Studies.

Cone, J., & Hayes, S. (1980). *Environmental problems/Behavioral solutions.* Monterey, CA: Brooks/Cole.

Conway, D. (1973). *Social science and design.* Washington, DC: American Institute of Architects.

Cook, T.D., & Campbell, D.T. (1979). *Quasi-experimentation.* Chicago: Rand McNally.

Cooper, C.C. (1971). St. Francis Square: Attitudes of its residents. *American Institute of Architects Journal, 53,* 22–27.

Cooper, C.C. (1972). Resident dissatisfaction in multi-family housing. In W.M. Smith (Ed.), *Behavior, design, and policy aspects of human habitats.* Green Bay: University of Wisconsin-Green Bay Press.

Cooper, C.C. (1975). *Easter Hill Village.* New York: Free Press.

Cosgrove, D. (1978). Place, landscape, and the dialectics of cultural geography. *Canadian Geographer, 22,* 66–72.

Cox, K.R., & Golledge, R.G. (Eds.). (1969). *Behavioral problems in geography.* Evanston, IL: Northwestern University Press.

Cox, K.R., & Golledge, R.G. (Eds.). (1981). *Behavioral problems in geography revisited.* London: Methuen.

Craik, K.H. (1968). The comprehension of the everyday physical environment. *Journal of the American Institute of Planners, 34,* 27–37.

Craik, K.H. (Chair). (1970a). Environmental dispositions and preferences. In J. Archea & C.M. Eastman (Eds.), *Proceedings of 2nd Annual Environmental Design Research Association Conference.* Stroudsburg, PA: Dowden, Hutchinson, & Ross.

Craik, K.H. (1970b). Environmental psychology. In K.H. Craik, B. Kleinmuntz, R.L. Rosnow, R. Rosenthal, J.A. Cheyne, & R.H. Walters (Eds.), *New directions in psychology* (Vol. 4). New York: Holt, Rinehart and Winston.

Craik, K.H. (1971). The assessment of places. In P. McReynold (Ed.), *Advances in psychological assessment* (Vol. 2). Palo Alto, CA: Science and Behavior Books.

Craik, K.H. (1973). Environmental psychology. *Annual Review of Psychology, 24,* 403–422.

Craik, K.H. (1975). Individual variations in landscape description. In E.H. Zube, R.O. Brush, & J.G. Fabos (Eds.), *Landscape assessment.* Stroudsburg, PA: Dowden, Hutchinson, & Ross.

Craik, K.H. (1976). The personality research paradigm in environmental psychology. In S. Wapner, S.B. Cohen, & B. Kaplan (Eds.), *Experiencing the environment.* New York: Plenum.

Craik, K.H. (1977). Multiple scientific paradigms in environmental psychology. *International Journal of Psychology, 12,* 147–157.

Craik, K.H. (Ed.). (in press). The Clark period of 1970–72. *Journal of Environmental Psychology.*

Craik, K.H., & Zube, E.H. (Eds.). (1976). *Perceiving environmental quality.* New York: Plenum.

Daniel, T.C., & Boster, R.S. (1976). *Measuring landscape esthetics* (Paper No. RM-167). Washington, DC: U.S. Department of Agriculture, Forest Service.

Design Research News. (1969). Washington, DC: Environmental Design Research Association.

Dewey, J., & Bently, A.F. (1949). *Knowing and the known.* Boston: Beacon.

Di Mento, J.F. (1981). Making usable information of environmental stressors: Opportunities for the research and policy communities. *Journal of Social Issues, 37,* 172–204.

Donnelly, D. (1980). The child in the environment. *Built Environment, 6,* 62–67.

Downs, R.M. (1976). Personal constructs of personal construct theory. In G.T. Moore & R.G. Golledge (Eds.), *Environmental knowing.* Stroudsburg, PA: Dowden, Hutchinson, & Ross.

Downs, R.M. (1981). Maps and mapping metaphors for spatial representation. In L. Liben, A.H. Patterson, & N. Newcombe (Eds.), *Spatial representation and behavior across the life span.* New York: Academic.

Downs, R.M., & Stea, D. (Eds.). (1973). *Image and environment.* Chicago: Aldine.

Duhl, L.J. (Ed.). (1963). *The urban condition.* New York: Clarion.

Duncan, J.S., & Duncan, N.G. (1976). Social worlds, status passage, and environmental perspectives. In G.T. Moore & R.G. Golledge (Eds.), *Environmental knowing.* Stroudsburg, PA: Dowden, Hutchinson, & Ross.

Dunlap, R.E. (1980). Paradigmatic change in social sciences: From human exceptionalism to an ecological paradigm. *American Behavioral Scientist, 24,* 5–14.

Dunlap, R.E., & Catton, W.R. (1979). Environmental sociology. *Annual Review of Sociology, 5,* 243–273.

Dunlap, R.E., & Catton, W.R. (1983). What environmental sociologists have in common (whether concerned with "built" or "natural" environments). *Sociological Inquiry, 53,* 113–135.

Environment and Behavior. (1969). Beverly Hills, CA: Sage.

Environmental Design Research Association Proceedings. (1969). Washington, DC: Environmental Design Research Association.

Esser, A.H., Chamberlain, A.S., Chapple, E.D., & Kline, N.S. (1965). Territoriality of patients on a research ward. In J. Wortis (Ed.), *Recent advances in biological psychiatry* (Vol. 7). New York: Plenum.

Evans, G.W. (1980). Environmental cognition. *Psychological Bulletin, 88,* 259–287.

Evans, G.W. (Ed.). (1983). *Environmental stress.* New York: Cambridge University Press.

Evans, G.W., Jacobs, S.V., & Frager, N.B. (1982). Behavioral responses to air pollution. In A. Baum & J. Singer (Eds.), *Advances in environmental psychology.* Hillsdale, NJ: Erlbaum.

Everett, P.B. (1981). Reinforcement theory strategies for modifying transit ridership. In I. Altman, J.F. Wohlwill, & P.B. Everett (Eds.), *Transportation and behavior.* New York: Plenum.

Farbstein, J., & Wener, R.E. (1979). *Evaluation of correctional environments.* San Luis Obispo, CA: Farbstein/Williams.

Farbstein, J., & Wener, R.E. (1982). Evaluation of correctional environments. *Environment and Behavior, 14,* 671–694.

Farr, L.E. (1972). Medical consequences of environmental home noises. In R. Gutman (Ed.), *People and buildings.* New York: Basic Books.

Festinger, L., Schacter, S., & Back, K.W. (1950). *Social pressures in informal groups.* Stanford, CA: Stanford University Press.

Firey, W. (1945). Sentiment and symbolism as ecological variables. *American Sociological Review, 10,* 140–148.

Fischoff, B., Hohenemser, C., Kasperson, R.E., & Kates, R.W. (1978, September). Handling hazards. *Environment, 20,* 16–20, 32–37.

Fisher, J.D., Bell, P.A., & Baum, A. (1984). *Environmental psychology* (2nd ed.). New York: Holt, Rinehart & Winston.

Francescato, G., Weidemann, S., Anderson, J.R., & Chenoweth, R. (1977). *Residents' satisfaction in HUD-assisted housing.* Washington, DC: U.S. Government Printing Office.

Francis, M. (in press). Urban open spaces. In E.H. Zube & G.T. Moore (Eds.), *Advances in environment, behavior, and design* (Vol. 1). New York: Plenum.

Franck, K.S. (in press). A comparative analysis of theories in environment-behavior studies and in design. In E.H. Zube & G.T. Moore (Eds.), *Advances in environment, behavior, and design* (Vol. 1). New York: Plenum.

Frederickson, N. (1974). Toward a taxonomy of situations. In R.H. Moos & P.M. Insel (Eds.), *Issues in social ecology.* Palo Alto, CA: National Press.

Friedmann, A., Zimring, C., & Zube, E. (Eds.). (1978). *Environmental design evaluation.* New York: Plenum.

Gans, H.J. (1962). *The urban villagers.* New York: Free Press.

Gans. H.J. (1967). *The Levittowners.* New York: Random House.

Gans, H.J. (1968). *People and plans.* New York: Basic Books.

Gans, H.J. (1974). *Popular culture and high culture.* New York: Basic Books.

Garfinkel, H. (1967). *Studies in ethnomethodology.* Englewood Cliffs, NJ: Prentice-Hall.

Garling, T., & Golledge, R.G. (in press). Environmental perception and cognition. In E.H. Zube & G.T. Moore (Eds.), *Advances in environment, behavior, and design* (Vol. 1). New York: Plenum.

Gaskie, M.F. (1980, August). Toward workability of the workplace. *Architectural Record, 168,* 70–75.

Geller, E.S. (1980). Applications of behavior analysis for litter control. In D. Glenwik & L. Jason (Eds.), *Behavioral community psychology.* New York: Praeger.

Geller, E.S. (1987). Environmental psychology and applied behavioral analysis. In D. Stokols & I. Altman (Eds.), *Handbook of environmental psychology.* New York: Wiley.

Gerson, E.M., & Gerson, M.S. (1976). The social framework of place perspectives. In G.T. Moore & R.G. Golledge (Eds.), *Environmental knowing.* Stroudsburg, PA: Dowden, Hutchinson, & Ross.

Giorgi, A. (1971). Phenomenology and experimental psychology. In A. Giorgi, W. Fischer, & R. von Eckartsberg (Eds.), *Duquesne studies in phenomenological psychology* (Vol. 1). Pittsburgh, PA: Duquesne University Press.

Glaser, B.G., & Strauss, A.L. (1971). *The discovery of grounded theory.* Chicago: Aldine.

Glass, D.C., & Singer, J.E. (1972). *Urban stress.* New York: Academic.

Glassie, H. (1975). *Folk housing in middle Virginia.* Knoxville: University of Tennessee Press.

Goffman, E. (1959). *The presentation of self in everyday life.* New York: Doubleday/Anchor.

Gold, J.R. (1980). *An introduction to behavioural geography.* London: Oxford University Press.

Gold, J.R., & Goodey, B. (1983). Behavioural and perceptual geography. *Progress in Human Geography, 7,* 578–586.

Gold, J.R., & Goodey, B. (1984). Behavioural and perceptual geography: Criticisms and response. *Progress in Human Geography, 8,* 544–550.

Golledge, R.G. (1976). Methods and methodological issues in environmental cognition research. In G.T. Moore & R.G. Golledge (Eds.), *Environmental knowing.* Stroudsburg, PA: Dowden, Hutchinson, & Ross.

Golledge, R.G. (1979). Reality, process, and the dialectical relation between man and environment. In S. Gale &

G. Olsson (Eds.), *Philosophy in geography.* Dordrecht, Netherlands: Reidel.

Golledge, R.G. (1981a). Misconceptions, misrepresentations, and misinterpretations of behavioral approaches in human geography. *Environment and Planning A, 13,* 1325–1344.

Golledge, R.G. (1981b). The spatial competence of selected mentally retarded populations. In H.L. Pick & L.P. Acredolo (Eds.), *Spatial orientation.* Hillsdale, NJ: Erlbaum.

Golledge, R.G., Brown, L.A., & Williamson, F. (1972). Behavioral approaches in geography: An overview. *Australian Geographic, 12,* 57–79.

Golledge, R.G., & Couclelis, H. (1984). Positivist philosophy and research on human spatial behavior. In T.F. Saarinen, D. Seamon, & J.L. Sell (Eds.), *Environmental perception and behavior* (Research Paper No. 209). Chicago: University of Chicago, Department of Geography.

Golledge, R.G., & Rushton, G. (1975). *Spatial choice and spatial preference.* Colombus: Ohio State University Press.

Golledge, R.G., & Zannaras, G. (1973). Cognitive approaches to the analysis of human spatial behavior. In W.H. Ittelson (Ed.), *Environmental cognition.* New York: Seminar Press.

Good, L.R., Siegel, S.M., & Bay, A.P. (1965). *Therapy by design.* Springfield, IL: Thomas.

Gould, P.R. (1967). Structuring information on spatio-temporal preferences. *Journal of Regional Science, 7,* 259–274.

Groat, L.P. (1981). Meaning in architecture: New directions and sources. *Journal of Environmental Psychology, 1,* 73–83.

Groat, L.P., & Canter, D. (1979, December). Does postmodernism communicate? *Progressive Architecture, 60,* 84–87.

Gulliver, F.P. (1908). Orientation of maps. *Journal of Geography, 7,* 55–58.

Gump, P.V. (1975). *Ecological psychology and children.* Chicago: University of Chicago Press.

Gunderson, E.K.E. (1968). Mental health problems in Antarctica. *Archives of Environmental Health, 17,* 558–564.

Gutman, R. (Ed.). (1972). *People and buildings.* New York: Basic Books.

Gutman, R. (1975). Architecture and sociology. *American Sociologist, 10,* 219–228.

Gutman, R. (1981, May). *New strategies for the building community.* Paper presented at the Urban Design Educator's Symposium, San Juan, Puerto Rico.

Hack, G. (1984). Research for urban design. In J.C. Snyder (Ed.), *Architectural research.* New York: Van Nostrand Reinhold.

Hall, E.T. (1959). *The silent language.* Garden City, NY: Anchor/Doubleday.

Hall, E.T. (1963). A system for the notation of proxemic behavior. *American Anthropologist, 65,* 1003–1027.

Hall, E.T. (1966). *The hidden dimension.* Garden City, NY: Anchor/Doubleday.

Halprin, L. (1965). Motation. *Progressive Architecture, 46,* 126–133.

Harris, L., & Associates. (1978). *The Steelcase national study of office environments: Do they work?* Grand Rapids, MI: Steelcase.

Hart, R.A. (1979). *Children's experience of place.* New York: Irvington.

Hart, R.A. (1981). Children's representation of landscape: Lessons and questions from a field study. In L. Liben, A.H. Patterson, & N. Newcombe (Eds.), *Spatial representation and behavior across the life span.* New York: Academic.

Hart, R.A., & Chawla, L. (1981). The development of children's concern for the environment. *Zeitschrift fur Umweltpolitik, 4,* 271–294.

Hart, R.A., & Moore, G.T. (1973). The development of spatial cognition: A review. In R.M. Downs, & D. Stea (Eds.), *Image and environment.* Chicago: Aldine.

Hart, R.A., & Perez, C. (1980). Beyond playgrounds: Children's access to resources. In P. Wilkinson (Ed.), *Innovation in play environments.* London: Croom-Helm.

Hassid, S. (1972). Status and trends in dissertation content and program for doctoral studies in architecture. In W.J. Mitchell (Ed.), *Environmental design.* Los Angeles: University of California, School of Architecture and Urban Planning.

Hayden, D. (1976). *Seven American utopias.* Cambridge, MA: MIT Press.

Hayden, D. (1981). *The grand domestic revolution.* Cambridge, MA: MIT Press.

Hayduk, L.A. (1983). Personal space: Where we now stand. *Psychological Bulletin, 94,* 293–335.

Hayward, S.C., & Franklin, S.S. (1974). Perceived openness-enclosure of architectural spaces. *Environment and Behavior, 6,* 37–52.

Heberlein, T.A. (1972). The land ethic realized: Some social psychological explanations for changing environmental attitudes. *Journal of Social Issues, 28,* 79–87.

Heberlein, T.A., & Shelby, B. (1977). Carrying capacity, values, and the satisfaction model. *Journal of Leisure Research, 9,* 142–148.

Heft, H. (1981). An examination of the constructivist and Gibsonian approaches to environmental psychology. *Population and Environment, 4,* 227–245.

Heimstra, N.W., & McFarling, L.H. (1978). *Environmental psychology* (2nd ed.). Monterey, CA: Brooks/Cole.

Helmreich, R. (1974). Evaluation of environments: Behavioral observations in an undersea habitat. In J. Lang, C. Burnette, W. Moleski, & D. Vachon (Eds.),

Designing for human behavior. Stroudsburg, PA: Dowden, Hutchinson, & Ross.

Hillier, B., & Leaman, A. (1973). The man-environment paradigm and its paradoxes. *Architectural Design, 8,* 507–511.

Hohenemser, C., Kasperson, R.E., & Kates, R.W. (1977, April). The distrust of nuclear power. *Science, 196,* 5–34.

Holahan, C.J. (1978). *Environment and behavior.* New York: Plenum.

Holahan, C.J. (1982). *Environmental psychology.* New York: Random House.

Holahan, C.J. (1986). Environmental psychology. *Annual Review of Psychology, 37.*

Howell, S.C. (1980). *Designing for aging.* Cambridge, MA: MIT Press.

Huber, P.B. (1979). Anggor floods: Reflections on ethnogeography and mental maps. *Geographical Review, 69,* 127–139.

Humphrey, C.R., Bradshaw, D.A., & Krout, J.A. (1978). The process of adaptation among suburban highway neighbors. *Sociology and Social Research, 62,* 246–266.

Ittelson, W.H. (1961). *Some factors influencing the design and function of psychiatric facilities* (Progress Report). Brooklyn, NY: Brooklyn College, Department of Psychology.

Ittelson, W.H. (1970). Perception of the large-scale environment. *Transactions of the New York Academy of Sciences* (Series II), *32,* 807–815.

Ittelson, W.H., & Cantril, H. (1960). *Perception.* Garden City, NY: Doubleday.

Ittelson, W.H., Proshansky, H.M., & Rivlin, L.G. (1970). Bedroom size and social interaction of the psychiatric ward. *Environment and Behavior, 2,* 255–270.

Ittelson, W.H., Proshansky, H.M., Rivlin, L.G., & Winkel, G.H. (1974). *An introduction to environmental psychology.* New York: Holt, Rinehart and Winston.

Ittelson, W.H., Rivlin, L.G., & Proshansky, H.M. (1976). The use of behavioral maps in environmental psychology. In H.M. Proshansky, W.H. Ittelson, & L.G. Rivlin (Eds.), *Environmental psychology.* New York: Holt, Rinehart and Winston.

Izumi, K. (1957). An analysis for the design of hospitals quarters for the neuropsychiatric patient. *Mental Hospitals, 8,* 31–32.

Jackson, J.B. (Ed.). (1951–68). *Landscape* (Vols. 1–18).

Jackson, J.B. (1972). *American space.* New York: Norton.

Jacobs, J. (1961). *The death and life of great American cities.* New York: Random House.

Jencks, C. (1981). *The language of post-modern architecture* (rev. ed.). New York: Rizzoli.

Jenkins, T.H. (1978). *Social factors and environmental design.* Monticello, IL: Council of Planning Librarians.

Kahana, E. (1975). A congruence model of person-environ-

ment interaction. In P.G. Windley, T.O. Byerts, & E.G. Ernst (Eds.), *Theoretical developments in environments for aging.* Washington, DC: Gerontological Society.

Kahana, E., Liang, J., & Felton, B.J. (1980). Alternative models of person-environment fit. *Journal of Gerontology, 35,* 584–595.

Kantrowitz, M., & Seidel, A.D. (Eds.). (1985). Applications of E & B research. *Environment and Behavior, 17*(1).

Kaplan, B. (1967). Meditations on genesis. *Human Development, 10,* 65–87.

Kaplan, B., Wapner, S., & Cohen, S.B. (1976). Exploratory applications of the organismic-developmental approach to the transactions of the men-in-environments. In S. Wapner, S.B. Cohen, & B. Kaplan (Eds.), *Experiencing the environment.* New York: Plenum.

Kaplan, S. (1983). A model of person-environment compatibility. *Environment and Behavior, 15,* 311–332.

Kaplan, S. & Kaplan, R. (1982). *Cognition and environment.* New York: Praeger.

Kasmar, J. (1970). The development of a useful lexicon of environmental descriptors. *Environment and Behavior, 2,* 135–169.

Kates, R.W. (1962). *Hazard and choice perception in flood plain management,* (Research Paper No. 78). Chicago: University of Chicago, Department of Geography.

Kates, R.W. (1967). The perception of storm hazard on the shores of megalopolis. In D. Lowenthal (Ed.), *Environmental perception and behavior* (Research Paper No. 109). Chicago: University of Chicago, Department of Geography.

Kates, R.W. (1970). Human perception of the environment. *International Social Science Journal, 22,* 648–660.

Kates, R.W. (1978). *Risk assessment of environmental hazard.* New York: Wiley.

Kates, R.W., & Wohlwill, J.F. (Eds.). (1966). Man's response to the physical environment. *Journal of Social Issues, 22*(1).

Kira, S. (1966). *The bathroom.* New York: Viking.

Klausner, S.Z. (1971). *On man in his environment.* San Francisco: Jossey-Bass.

Kleeman, W. (1981). *The challenge of interior design.* Boston: CBI Publishing.

Krampen, M. (1979). *Meaning in the urban environment.* London: Pion.

Lagorio, H.J. (1976). *Environmental design research.* Washington, DC: National Science Foundation.

Larson, C.T. (Ed.). (1965). *School environments research* (3 vols.). Ann Arbor: University of Michigan, College of Architecture and Design.

Lawton, M.P. (1975). Competence, environmental press, and the adaptation of older people. In P.G. Windley, T.O. Byerts, & F.G. Ernst (Eds.), *Theory development in environment and aging.* Washington, DC: Gerontological Society.

Lawton, M.P. (1977). The impact of the environment on aging and behavior. In J.E. Birren & K.W. Schaie (Eds.), *Handbook of the psychology of aging*. New York: Van Nostrand Reinhold.

Lawton, M.P. (1980). *Environment and aging*. Monterey, CA: Brooks/Cole.

Lazarus, R.S. (1966). *Psychological stress and the coping process*. New York: McGraw-Hill.

Lazarus, R.S., & Cohen, J.B. (1977). Environmental stress. In I. Altman & J.F. Wohlwill (Eds.), *Human behavior and environment* (Vol. 2). New York: Plenum.

Lazarus, R.S., & Launier, R. (1978). Stress related transactions between person and environment. In L.A. Pervin & M. Lewis (Eds.), *Perspectives in interactional psychology*. New York: Plenum.

Levin, H., & Duhl, L.J. (1984). Architectural research and the impact of buildings on health. In J.C. Snyder (Ed.), *Architectural research*. New York: Van Nostrand Reinhold.

Levi-Strauss, C. (1966). *The savage mind*. Chicago: University of Chicago Press.

Lewin, K. (1946). Behavior and development as a function of the total situation. In L. Carmichael (Ed.), *Manual of child psychology*. New York: Wiley.

Lewis, P. (1979). Defining a sense of place. In P.W. Prenshaw & J.R. McKee (Eds.), *The American land*. New York: Smithsonian Exposition Books.

Liben, L.S., Patterson, A.H., & Newcombe, N. (Eds.). (1981). *Spatial representation and behavior across the life span*. New York: Academic.

Loo, C. (1977). Beyond the effects of crowding: Situational and individual differences. In D. Stokols (Ed.), *Perspectives on environment and behavior*. New York: Plenum.

Loo, C. (1979). A factor-analytic approach to the study of spatial density effects on preschoolers. *Population, 2*, 47–68.

Loring, W.C. (1956). Housing characteristics and social disorganization. *Social Problems, 3*, 160–168.

Low, S.M. (in press). Developments in research design, data collection, and analysis: Qualitative methods. In E.H. Zube & G.T. Moore (Eds.), *Advances in environment, behavior, and design* (Vol. 1). New York: Plenum.

Lowenthal, D. (1961). Geography, experience, and imagination: Toward a geographical epistemology. *Annals of the Association of American Geographers, 51*, 241–260.

Lowenthal, D. (1964). Images of nature in America. *Columbia University Forum, 7*, 34–40.

Lowenthal, D. (Ed.). (1967). *Environmental perception and behavior* (Research Paper No. 109). Chicago: University of Chicago, Department of Geography.

Lowenthal, D. (1968). The American scene. *Geographical Review, 58*, 61–88.

Lowenthal, D. (1979). Environmental perception: Preserving the past. *Progress in Human Geography, 3*, 549–559.

Lowenthal, D., & Prince, H.C. (1964). The English landscape. *Geographical Review, 54*, 309–346.

Lowenthal, D., & Prince, H.C. (1965). English landscape tastes. *Geographical Review, 55*, 186–222.

Lynch, K. (1960). *The image of the city*. Cambridge, MA: MIT Press.

Lynch, K. (1972). *What time is this place?* Cambridge, MA: MIT Press.

Lynch, K. (1976). *Managing the sense of a region*. Cambridge, MA: MIT Press.

Magenau, E. (Ed.). (1959). *Research for architecture*. Washington, DC: American Institute of Architects.

Mandel, D.R. (1984). Methodological approaches to environmental psychology. In J.D. Fisher, P.A. Bell, & A. Baum (Eds.), *Environmental psychology* (2nd ed.). New York: Holt, Rinehart and Winston.

Marans, R.W. (1976). Perceived quality of residential environments; Some methodological issues. In K.H. Craik & E.H. Zube (Eds.), *Perceiving environmental quality*. New York: Plenum.

Marans, R.W., & Ahrentzen, S. (in press). Developments in research design, data collection, and analysis: Quantitative methods. In E.H. Zube & G.T. Moore (Eds.), *Advances in environment, behavior, and design* (Vol. 1). New York: Plenum.

Marans, R.W., & Spreckelmeyer, K.F. (1981). *Evaluating built environments*. Ann Arbor, MI: University of Michigan, Institute for Social Research.

Margulis, S.T. (1977). How environmental research may affect the technical provisions and enforcement of regulations. In P. Cooke (Ed.), *Research and innovation in the building regulatory process*. Washington, DC: National Bureau of Standards.

Marshall, N.J. (1974). Dimensions of privacy preferences. *Multivariate Behavior Research, 9*, 255–272.

Maslow, A.H., & Mintz, N.L. (1956). Effects of esthetic surroundings: I. Initial effects of three esthetic conditions upon perceiving "energy" and "well being" in faces. *Journal of Psychology, 41*, 247–254.

McKechnie, G.E. (1970). Measuring environmental dispositions with the environmental response inventory. In J. Archea & C.M. Eastman (Eds.), *Proceedings of the 2nd Annual Environmental Design Research Association Conference*. Stroudsburg, PA: Dowden, Hutchinson, & Ross.

McKechnie, G.E. (1974). *Manual for the environmental response inventory*. Palo Alto, CA: Consulting Psychologists Press.

Mead, G.H. (1934). *Mind, self, and society*. Chicago: University of Chicago Press.

Meinig, D.W. (Ed.). (1979). *The interpretation of ordinary landscapes*. New York: Oxford University Press.

Merton, R.K. (1948). The position of sociological theory. *American Sociological Review, 13*, 164–168.

Merton, R.K. (1957). Theories of the middle range. *Social*

theory and social structure (rev. ed.). New York: Free Press.

Michelson, W. (Ed.). (1975). *Environmental design research methods*. Stroudsburg, PA: Dowden, Hutchinson, & Ross.

Michelson, W. (1976). *Man and his urban environment* (rev. ed.). Reading, MA: Addison-Wesley.

Michelson, W. (1977). *Environmental choice, human behavior, and residential satisfaction*. New York: Oxford University Press.

Michelson, W. (1980). Spatial and temporal dimensions of child care. *Signs, 5*, 242–247.

Michelson, W. (in press). Groups, aggregates, and the environment. In E.H. Zube & G.T. Moore (Eds.), *Advances in environment, behavior, and design* (Vol. 1). New York: Plenum.

Milgram, S. (1970). The experience of living in cities. *Science, 67*, 1461–1468.

Mintz, N.L. (1956). Effects of esthetic surroundings: II. Prolonged and repeated experience in a "beautiful" and an "ugly" room. *Journal of Psychology, 41*, 459–466.

Mitchell, J.K. (1984). Hazard perception studies: Convergent concerns and divergent approaches during the past decade. In T.F. Saarinen, D. Seamon, & J.S. Sell (Eds.), *Environmental perception and behavior* (Research Paper No. 209). Chicago: University of Chicago, Department of Geography.

Mitchell, W.J. (1977). *Computer-aided architectural design*. New York: Petrocelli/Charter.

Moore, G.T. (Ed.). (1966–68). *Design Methods Group Newsletter*. Beverly Hills, CA: Sage.

Moore, G.T. (Ed.). (1970). *Emerging methods in environmental design and planning*. Cambridge, MA: MIT Press.

Moore, G.T. (Chair). (1972). Symposium on conceptual issues in environmental cognition research. In W.J. Mitchell (Ed.), *Environmental design* (Vol. 2). Los Angeles: University of California, School of Architecture and Urban Planning.

Moore, G.T. (1976). Theory and research as the development of environmental knowing. In G.T. Moore & R.G. Golledge (Eds.), *Environmental knowing*. Stroudsburg, PA: Dowden, Hutchinson, & Ross.

Moore, G.T. (1979a). Environment-behavior studies. In J.C. Snyder & A.J. Catanese (Eds.), *Introduction to architecture*. New York: McGraw-Hill.

Moore, G.T. (1979b). Knowing about environmental knowing: The current state of theory and research on environmental cognition. *Environment and Behavior, 11*, 33–70.

Moore, G.T. (Ed.). (1982). Applied architectural research: Post-occupancy evaluation of buildings. *Environment and Behavior, 14*(6).

Moore, G.T. (1984). New directions for environment-behavior research in architecture. In J.C. Snyder (Ed.), *Architectural research*. New York: Van Nostrand Reinhold.

Moore, G.T. (1985). The state-of-the-art in play environment research and applications. In J. Frost & S. Sunderlein (Eds.), *When children play*. Wheaton, MD: Association of Childhood Education International.

Moore, G.T. (in press a). Cognitive development and the physical environment in child care centers. In C.S. Weinstein & T.G. David (Eds.), *Spaces for children*. New York: Plenum.

Moore, G.T. (in press b). Effects of the spatial definition of behavior settings on children's behavior: A quasi-experimental field study. *Journal of Environmental Psychology, 6*.

Moore, G.T., Cohen, U., & McGinty, T. (1979–1981). *Planning and design guidelines: Child care centers and outdoor play environments* (7 vols.). Milwaukee: University of Wisconsin-Milwaukee, Center for Architecture and Urban Planning Research.

Moore, G.T., & Golledge, R.G. (Eds.). (1976). *Environmental knowing*. Stroudsburg, PA: Dowden, Hutchinson, & Ross.

Moore, G.T., & Templer, J.A. (Eds.). (1984). *Doctoral education for architectural research*. Washington, DC: Architectural Research Centers Consortium.

Moore, G.T., Tuttle, D.P., & Howell, S.C. (1985). *Environmental design research directions*. New York: Praeger.

Moos, R.H. (1973). Conceptualizations of human environments. *American Psychologist, 28*, 652–665.

Moos, R.H. (1974). Systems for the assessment and classification of human environments: An overview. In R.H. Moos & P.M. Insel (Eds.), *Issues in social ecology*. Palo Alto, CA: National Press.

Moos, R.H. (1976). *The human context*. New York: Wiley.

Moos, R.H., & Lemke, S. (1980). Assessing the physical and architectural features of sheltered care settings. *Journal of Gerontology, 35*, 571–583.

Morrison, D.E. (1980). The soft cutting edge of environmentalism: Why and how the appropriate technology notion is changing the movement. *Natural Resources Journal, 20*.

Moynihan, D.P. (1980). State vs. academe. *Harpers, 261*(1567), 31–40.

Muller, R.A. (1980). Innovation and scientific funding. *Science, 209*, 880–883.

Nahemow, L., & Lawton, M. (1973). Toward an ecological theory of adaptation and aging. In W.F.E. Preiser (Ed.), *Environmental design research* (Vol. 1). Stroudsburg, PA: Dowden, Hutchinson, & Ross.

National School Public Relations Association. (1975). *Violence and vandalism*. Washington, DC: Author.

Newman, O. (1971). *Architectural design for crime prevention*. Washington, DC: U.S. Government Printing Office.

Newman, O. (1973). *Defensible space.* New York: Macmillan.

Newman, O. (1976). *Design guidelines for creating defensible space.* Washington, DC: U.S. Government Printing Office.

Newman, O. (1980). *Community of interest.* New York: Anchor/Doubleday.

O'Riordan, T. (1980). Environmental issues. *Progress in Human Geography, 4,* 417–432.

Osmond, H. (1957). Function as a basis of psychiatric ward design. *Mental Hospital, 8,* 23–29.

Pablant, P., & Baxter, J.C. (1975). Environmental correlates of school vandalism. *Journal of the American Institute of Planners, 41,* 270–279.

Palmer, M. (1981). *The architect's guide to facility programming.* Washington, DC: American Institute of Architects and Architectural Record Books.

Patterson, A.H. (1977). Methodological developments in environment-behavior research. In D. Stokols (Ed.), *Perspectives on environment and behavior.* New York: Plenum.

Pepper, S.C. (1942). *World hypotheses.* Berkeley: University of California Press.

Perez-Gomez, A. (1983). *Architecture and the crisis of modern science.* Cambridge, MA: MIT Press.

Pervin, L.A. (1978). Definitions, measurements, and classifications of stimuli, situations, and environments. *Human Ecology, 6,* 71–105.

Peterson, K.B. (in press). Gender issues in the home and urban environments. In E.H. Zube & G.T. Moore (Eds.), *Advances in environment, behavior, and design* (Vol. 1). New York: Plenum.

Piaget, J. (1970a). *Genetic epistemology.* New York: Norton.

Piaget, J. (1970b). *Structuralism.* New York: Basic Books.

Piaget, J. (1975). *The development of thought.* New York: Viking.

Pick, H.L. (1976). Transactional-constructivist approach to environmental knowing. In G.T. Moore, R.G. Golledge (Eds.), *Environmental knowing.* Stroudsburg, PA: Dowden, Hutchinson, & Ross.

Pipkin, J.S., LaGory, M.E., & Blau, J.R. (Eds.). (1983). *Remaking the city.* Albany: State University of New York Press.

Porteous, J.D. (1977). *Environment and behavior.* Reading, MA: Addison-Wesley.

Preiser, W.F.E. (Ed.). (1978). *Facility programming.* Stroudsburg, PA: Dowden, Hutchinson, & Ross.

Price, R.H. (1974). The taxonomic classification of behavior and situations and the problem of behavior-environment congruence. *Human Relations, 27,* 567–585.

Proceedings of the Annual Environmental Design Research Association Conferences. (1969). Washington, DC: Environmental Design Research Association.

Proshansky, H.M. (1972). Methodology in environmental psychology: Problems and issues. *Human Factors, 14,* 451–460.

Proshansky, H.M., & Altman, I. (1979). Overview of the field. In W.P. White (Ed.), *Resources in environment and behavior.* Washington, DC: American Psychological Association.

Proshansky, H.M., Ittelson, W.H., & Rivlin, L.G. (Eds.). (1970). *Environmental psychology.* New York: Holt, Rinehart & Winston.

Proshansky, H.M., & O'Hanlon, T. (1977). Environmental psychology: Origins and development. In D. Stokols (Ed.), *Perspectives on environment and behavior.* New York: Plenum.

Quarantelli, E.L. (1979). Some needed cultural studies of emergency time disaster behavior: A first step. *Disasters, 3,* 307–314.

Rapoport, A. (1964–65). The architecture of Isphahan. *Landscape, 14*(2), 4–11.

Rapoport, A. (1969). *House form and culture.* Englewood Cliffs, NJ: Prentice-Hall.

Rapoport, A. (1970, April). Man-environment studies: A review. *Architecture in Australia, 59,* 257–264.

Rapoport, A. (1973). An approach to the construction of man-environment theory. In W.F.E. Preiser (Ed.), *Environment design research* (Vol. 2). Stroudsburg, PA: Dowden, Hutchinson, & Ross.

Rapoport, A. (1975). Toward a redefinition of density. *Environment and Behavior, 7,* 133–158.

Rapoport, A. (1976a). Environmental cognition in cross-cultural perspective. In G.T. Moore & R.G. Golledge (Eds.), *Environmental knowing.* Stroudsburg, PA: Dowden, Hutchinson, & Ross.

Rapoport, A. (1976b). *The mutual interaction of people and the built environment: World anthropology.* The Hague, Netherlands: Mouton.

Rapoport, A. (1977). *Human aspects of urban form.* New York: Pergamon.

Rapoport, A. (1979). Cultural origins of architecture. In J.C. Snyder & A.J. Catanese (Eds.), *Introduction to architecture.* New York: McGraw-Hill.

Rapoport, A. (1980). Cross-cultural aspects of environmental design. In I. Altman, A. Rapoport, & J.F. Wohlwill (Eds.), *Environment and culture.* New York: Plenum.

Rapoport, A. (1982). *The meaning of the built environment.* Beverly Hills, CA: Sage.

Rapoport, A., & Kantor, R.E. (1967). Complexity and ambiguity in environmental design. *Journal of the American Institute of Planners, 33,* 210–221.

Rapoport, A., & Watson, N.J. (1972). Cultural variability in physical standards. In R. Gutman (Ed.), *People and buildings.* New York: Basic Books.

Regnier, V. (1981). Neighborhood images and use: A case study. In M.P. Lawton & S.L. Hosen (Eds.), *Community housing choices for older Americans.* New York: Springer.

Reizenstein, J.E. (1975). Linking social research and design. *Journal of Architectural Research*, 4(3), 26–38.

Reizenstein, J.E., & Zimring, C.M. (Eds.). (1980). Evaluating occupied environments. *Environment and Behavior*, 12(4).

Relph, E.C. (1970). An inquiry into the relations between phenomenology and geography. *Canadian Geographer*, 14, 193–201.

Relph, E. (1976). *Place and placelessness*. London: Pion.

Relph, E. (1981). *Rational landscapes and humanistic geography*. London: Croom Helm.

Riley, R.B. (in press). Vernacular landscapes. In E.H. Zube & G.T. Moore (Eds.), *Advances in environment, behavior, and design* (Vol. 1). New York: Plenum.

Roethlishberger, F., & Dickson, W. (1939). *Management and the worker*. Cambridge, MA: Harvard University Press.

Rosaldo, M.Z., & Lamphere, L. (1974). *Women, culture, and society*. Stanford, CA: Stanford University Press.

Rosow, I. (1961). The social effects of the physical environment. *Journal of the American Institute Planners*, 27, 127–133.

Ross, R.P., & Campbell, D.E. (1978). A review of the EDRA Proceedings. In W.E. Rogers & W.H. Ittelson (Eds.), *New directions in environmental design research*. Washington, DC: Environmental Design Research Association.

Rowles, G.D. (1978). *Prisoners of space?* Boulder, CO: Westview.

Rowles, G.D. (1981). Geographical perspectives on human development. *Human Development*, 24, 67–76.

Russell, J.A., & Ward, L.M. (1982). Environmental psychology. *Annual Review of Psychology*, 33, 651–688.

Rutherford, G.W. (1978). *Hazard analysis*. Washington, DC: U.S. Consumer Product Safety Commission, Bureau of Epidemiology, Directorate for Hazard Identification and Analysis.

Saarinen, T.F. (1966). *Perceptions of the drought hazard on the Great Plains* (Research Paper No. 106). Chicago: University of Chicago, Department of Geography.

Saarinen, T.F. (1976). *Environmental planning*. Boston: Houghton Mifflin.

Saarinen, T.F., & Gibson, L.J. (1980). Change in public perception of environmental quality indices: A Tucson example. *Geographical Perspectives*, 46, 13–23.

Saarinen, T.F., Seamon, D., & Sell, J.L. (Eds.). (1984). *Environmental perception and behavior* (Research Paper No. 209). Chicago: University of Chicago, Department of Geography.

Saarinen, T.F., & Sell, J.L. (1980). Environmental perception. *Progress in Human Geography*, 4, 525–548.

Saarinen, T.F., & Sell, J.L. (1981). Environmental perception. *Progress in Human Geography*, 5, 525–547.

Saegert, S. (1980). Masculine cities and feminine suburbs: Polarized ideas, contradictory realities. *Signs*, 5, 596–611.

Saegert, S., & Winkel, G.H. (1980). The house: A critical problem for changing sex roles. In G.R. Wekerle, R. Peterson, & D. Morely (Eds.), *New space for women*. Boulder, CO: Westview.

Sanoff, H. (1977). *Methods of architectural programming*. Stroudsburg, PA: Dowden, Hutchinson, & Ross.

Sanoff, H., & Cohen, S. (Eds.). (1970). *Proceedings of the 1st Annual Environmental Design Research Association Conference*. Stroudsburg, PA: Dowden, Hutchinson, & Ross.

Schluntz, R.L. (1984). An overview of sponsored research in schools of architecture. In J.C. Snyder (Ed.), *Architectural research*. New York: Van Nostrand Reinhold.

Schnaiberg, A. (1975). Social synthesis of the societal-environmental dialectic: The role of distributional impacts. *Social Science Quarterly*, 56, 5–10.

Schneekloth, L.H. (in press). Advances in practice in environment, behavior, and design. In E.H. Zube & G.T. Moore (Eds.), *Advances in environment, behavior, and design* (Vol. 1). New York: Plenum.

Schorr, A.L. (1963). *Slums and social insecurity*. Washington, DC: U.S. Government Printing Office.

Seamon, D. (1976). Phenomenological investigation of imaginative literature. In G.T. Moore & R.G. Golledge (Eds.), *Environmental knowing*. Stroudsburg, PA: Dowden, Hutchinson, & Ross.

Seamon, D. (1980). *A geography of the lifeworld*. London: Croom/Helm.

Seamon, D. (1982). The phenomenological contribution to environmental psychology. *Journal of Environmental Psychology*, 2, 119–140.

Seamon, D. (1983). Response to Sixsmith's comments on the phenomenological contribution. *Journal of Environmental Psychology*, 3, 199–201.

Seamon, D. (1984a). Heidegger's notion of dwelling and one concrete interpretation as indicated by Hassan Fathy's *Architecture for the poor*. *Geoscience and Man*, 24, 43–53.

Seamon, D. (1984b). Philosophical direction in behavioral geography with an emphasis on the phenomenological contribution. In T.F. Saarinen, D. Seamon, & J.C. Sell (Eds.), *Environmental perception and behavior* (Research Paper No. 209). Chicago: University of Chicago, Department of Geography.

Seamon, D. (1984c). Toward a phenomenology of place and place-making: Interpreting landscape, life-world and aesthetics. *Oz*, 6, 6–9.

Seamon, D. (in press). Phenomenological theories in environment and behavior. In E.H. Zube, & G.T. Moore (Eds.), *Advances in environment, behavior, and design* (Vol. 1). New York: Plenum.

Seamon, D. & Mugerauer, R. (Eds.). (1985). *Dwelling,*

place, and environment. Dordrecht, Netherlands: Martines Nijhoff.

Segall, M.H., Campbell, D.T., & Herskovits, M.J. (1966). *The influence of culture on visual perception.* Indianapolis, IN: Bobbs–Merrill.

Seidel, A.D. (Ed.). (1983). *Journal of Architecture and Planning Research.* New York: Elsevier.

Shafer, E.L., Jr. (1969). Perception of natural environments. *Environment and Behavior, 1,* 71–82.

Shure, M.B. (1963). Psychological ecology of a nursery school. *Child Development, 34,* 979–992.

Smith, M.B. (1977). Some problems of strategy in environmental psychology. In D. Stokols (Ed.), *Perspectives on environment and behavior.* New York: Plenum.

Snyder, J.C. (Ed.). (1982). *An agenda for architectural research 1982.* Washington, DC: Architectural Research Centers Consortium.

Snyder, J.C. (Ed.). (1984). *Architectural Research.* New York: Van Nostrand Reinhold.

Sommer, R. (1959). Studies in personal space. *Sociometry, 22,* 247–260.

Sommer, R. (1966). The ecology of privacy. *Library Quarterly, 36,* 234–238.

Sommer, R. (1967). Small group ecology. *Psychological Bulletin, 67,* 145–152.

Sommer, R. (1969). *Personal space.* Engelwood Cliffs, NJ: Prentice-Hall.

Sommer, R. (1980). Environmental psychology: A blueprint for the future. *American Psychological Association Monitor, 11,* 3–47.

Sommer, R., & Ross, H. (1958). Social interaction on a geriatrics ward. *International Journal of Social Psychiatry, 4,* 128–133.

Sonnenfeld, J. (1966). Variable values in space landscape: An inquiry into the nature of environmental necessity. *Journal of Social Issues, 22,* 71–82.

Sonnenfeld, J. (1967). Environmental perception and adaptation level in the Arctic. In D. Lowenthal (Ed.), *Environmental perception and behavior* (Research Paper No. 109). Chicago: University of Chicago, Department of Geography.

Sorenson, J.H., & White, G.F. (1980). Natural hazards: A cross-cultural perspective. In I. Altman, A. Rapoport, & J.F. Wohlwill (Eds.), *Environment and culture.* New York: Plenum.

Srivastava, R.K., & Good, L.R. (1968). *Patterns of group interaction in three architecturally different psychiatric treatment environments.* Topeka, KS: Environmental Research Foundation.

Stea, D. (1967). Reasons for our moving. *Landscape, 17,* 27–28.

Stea, D. (1969). The measurement of mental maps: An experimental model for studying conceptual spaces. In K.R. Cox & R.G. Golledge (Eds.), *Behavioral problems in geography* (No. 17). Evanston, IL: Northwestern University Studies in Geography.

Stea, D. (1982). Cross-cultural environmental modeling. In J.C. Baird & A.D. Lutkus (Eds.), *Mind child architecture.* Hanover, NH: University Press of New England.

Steidl, R.E. (1972). Difficult factors in homemaking tasks: Implications for environmental design. *Human Factors, 14,* 471–482.

Steinfeld, E. (1979). *Access to the built environment* (7 Vols.). Washington, DC: U.S. Government Printing Office.

Stimpson, C.R., Dixler, E., Nelson, M.J., & Yatrakis, K.B. (Eds.). (1980). *Women and the American city.* Chicago: University of Chicago Press.

Stiny, G. (1981). Introduction to shape and shape grammars. *Environment and Planning B, 8,* 393–404.

Stiny, G., & Mitchell, W.J. (1978). The Palladian grammar. *Environment and Planning B, 5,* 5–18.

Stokols, D. (1972). A social psychological model of human crowding phenomena. *Journal of the American Institute of Planners, 38,* 72–83.

Stokols, D. (1977a). Origins and directions of environment-behavior research. In D. Stokols (Ed.), *Perspectives on environment and behavior.* New York: Plenum.

Stokols, D. (Ed.). (1977b). *Perspectives on environment and behavior.* New York: Plenum.

Stokols, D. (1978a). Environmental psychology. *Annual Review of Psychology, 29,* 253–296.

Stokols, D. (1978b). A typology of crowding experiences. In A. Baum & Y. Epstein (Eds.), *Human response to crowding.* Hillsdale, NJ: Erlbaum.

Stokols, D. (1979). A congruence analysis of human stress. In I.G. Sarason & C.D. Speilberger (Eds.), *Stress and anxiety.* Washington, DC: Hemisphere.

Stokols, D. (1981a). Environmental psychology: A coming of age. In M.A. Kraut (Ed.), *G. Stanley Hall Lecture Series* (Vol. 2). Washington, DC: American Psychological Association.

Stokols, D. (1981b). Group × place transactions: Some neglected issues in psychological research on settings. In D. Magnussen (Ed.), *Toward a psychology of situations.* Hillsdale, NJ: Erlbaum.

Stokols, D. (Ed.). (1983). Theories of environment and behavior: New directions. *Environment and Behavior, 15*(3).

Stokols, D., & Shumaker, S.H. (1981). People in places: A transactional view of settings. In J.H. Harvey (Ed.), *Cognition, social behavior, and the environment.* Hillsdale, NJ: Erlbaum.

Strauss, A.L. (1961). *Images of the American city.* New York: Free Press.

Strauss, A.L. (Ed.). (1968). *The American city.* Chicago: Aldine.

Studer, R.G. (1966). On environmental programming. *Architectural Association Journal, 81,* 290–296.

Studer, R.G. (1967). Behavior manipulation in designed environments. *Connection, 5*, 7–13.

Studer, R.G. (1969). The dynamics of behavior contingent physical symptoms. In G. Broadbent & A. Ward (Eds.), *Design methods in architecture*. London: Lund Humphries.

Studer, R.G. (1973). Man-environment relations: Discovery or design? In W.F.E. Preiser (Ed.), *Environmental design research* (Vol. 2). Stroudsburg, PA: Dowden, Hutchinson, & Ross.

Studer, R.G., & Stea, D. (1965). *Directory of behavior and environmental design*. Providence, RI: Brown University.

Stumpf, K.R. (1984, March). *Organization for the context area of theories*. Unpublished seminar paper, Department of Architecture, University of Wisconsin, Milwaukee.

Sundstrom, E., Kastenbaum, D., & Konar-Goldband, E. (1978). *Physical office environments, employee satisfaction, and job performance* (Final Report). Buffalo, NY: American Institute of Architects Research Corporation, Buffalo Organization for Social and Technological Innovation.

Taylor, C.W., Bailey, R., & Branch, C.H.H. (Eds.). (1967). *Second National Conference on Architectural Psychology*. Salt Lake City: University of Utah.

Taylor, R.B. (1978). Human territoriality: A review and model for future research. *Cornell Journal of Social Relations, 13*, 125–151.

Taylor, R.B. (1980). Is environmental psychology dying? *Population and Environmental Psychology Newsletter, 7*, 14–15.

Thiel, P. (1961). A sequence-experience notation for architectural and urban space. *Town Planning Review, 32*, 33–52.

Thomas, W.L., Jr. (Ed.). (1956). *Man's role in changing the face of the earth*. Chicago: University of Chicago Press.

Thompson, V.D., & Taylor, R.B. (1978). *Population and environment*. New York: Human Sciences Press.

Tibbetts, P. (1972). The transactional theory of human knowledge and action: Notes toward a "behavioral ecology." *Man-Environment Systems, 2*(1), 37–59.

Tolman, E.C. (1932). *Purposive behavior in animals and men*. New York: Appleton-Century-Crofts.

Tolman, E.C. (1948). Cognitive maps in rats and men. *Psychological Review, 55*, 189–208.

Tolman, E.C., & Brunswik, E. (1935). The organism and the causal texture of the environment. *Psychological Review, 42*, 43–77.

Trowbridge, C.C. (1913). On fundamental methods of orientation and "imaginary maps." *Science, 88*, 888–896.

Tuan, Y.F. (1961). Topophilia. *Landscape, 11*, 29–32.

Tuan, Y.F. (1968). Discrepancies between environmental attitudes and behavior: Examples from Europe and China. *Canadian Geographer, 12*, 176–191.

Tuan, Y.F. (1971). Geography, phenomenology, and the study of human nature. *Canadian Geographer, 25*, 181–192.

Tuan, Y.F. (1974). *Topophilia*. Englewood Cliffs, NJ: Prentice-Hall.

Tuan, Y.F. (1976). Literature, experience, and environmental knowing. In G.T. Moore & R.G. Golledge (Eds.), *Environmental knowing*. Stroudsburg, PA: Dowden, Hutchinson, & Ross.

Tuan, Y.F. (1977). *Space and place*. Minneapolis: University of Minnesota Press.

Turner, S. (1983). Studying organization through Levi-Strauss's structuralism. In G. Morgan (Ed.), *Beyond method*. Beverly Hills, CA: Sage.

U.S. Consumer Product Safety Commission. (1975). *Hazard analysis of injuries relating to playground equipment*. Washington, DC: U.S. Consumer Product Safety Commission.

U.S. Consumer Product Safety Commission. (1981). *A handbook for public playground safety* (2 Vols.). Washington, DC: U.S. Government Printing Office.

Van der Ryn, S. (1967). A case study of dormitory living. In C.W. Taylor, R. Bailey, and C.H.H. Branch (Eds.), *Second National Conference on Architectural Psychology*. Salt Lake City: University of Utah.

Vayda, A.P. (1973). *Human ecology*. New York: Plenum.

Ventre, F.T. (1975). Transforming environmental research into regulatory policy. In B. Honikman (Ed.), *Responding to social change*. Stroudsburg, PA: Dowden, Hutchinson, & Ross.

Ventre, F.T. (1982). Building in eclipse: Architecture in secession. *Progressive Architecture, 62*, 58–61.

Ventre, F.T. (in press). The policy environment for environment-behavior research. In E.H. Zube & G.T. Moore (Eds.), *Advances in environment, behavior, and design* (Vol. 2). New York: Plenum.

Villecco, M. (1983, October). Housing designed for special needs. *Architecture*, pp. 50–56.

Villecco, M., & Brill, M. (1981). *Environmental design/research*. Washington, DC: National Endowment for the Arts.

Von Vexkull, J. (1957). A stroll through the worlds of animals and men: A picture book of invisible worlds. In C.H. Schiller (Ed.), *Instinctive behavior*. New York: International Universities Press.

Wapner, S. (1981). Transactions of persons-in-environments: Some critical transitions. *Journal of Environmental Psychology, 1*, 223–239.

Wapner, S., Kaplan, B., & Cohen, S.B. (1973). An organismic-developmental perspective for understanding the transactions of men and environments. *Environment and Behavior, 5*, 255–289.

Weidemann, S., Anderson, J.R., Butterfield, D.I., & O'Donnell, P.M. (1982). Residents' perception of satisfaction and safety: A basis for change in multifamily housing. *Environment and Behavior, 14*, 615–724.

Weinstein, C.S. (1979). The physical environment of the school: A review of the research. *Review of Educational Research, 49*, 577–610.

Weinstein, C.S., & David, T.G. (Eds.). (in press). *Spaces for children*. New York: Plenum.

Weisman, G.D. (1983). Environmental programming and action research. *Environment and Behavior, 15*, 381–408.

Weiss, C.H. (Ed.). (1977). *Using social research in public policy making*. Lexington, MA: Lexington.

Weiss, C.H., & Barton, A.H. (Eds.). (1979). *Making bureaucracies work*. Beverly Hills, CA: Sage.

Weiss, L., & Baum, L.S. (in press). Physiological aspects of environment-behavior relationships. In E.H. Zube & G.T. Moore (Eds.), *Advances in environment, behavior, and design* (Vol. 1). New York: Plenum.

Weiss, R., & Boutourline, S. (1962). *Fairs, exhibits, pavilions and their audiences*. New York: IBM Corporation.

Wekerle, R., Peterson, R., & Morley, D. (Eds.). (1980). *New space for women*. Boulder, CO: Westview.

Wener, R.E. (1982). Post-occupancy evaluation success stories. Unpublished manuscript, Polytechnic Institute of New York, Department of Psychology, Brooklyn, NY.

Werner, H. (1948). *The comparative psychology of mental development* (rev. ed.). New York: International Universities Press.

Werner, H., & Kaplan, B. (1963). *Symbol formation*. New York: Wiley.

White, G.F. (1945). *Human adjustment to floods* (Research Paper No. 29). Chicago: University of Chicago, Department of Geography.

White, G.F. (Ed.). (1961). *Papers on flood problems* (Research Paper No. 70). Chicago: University of Chicago, Department of Geography.

White, G.F., & Haas, J.E. (1975). *Assessment of research on natural hazards*. Cambridge, MA: MIT Press.

White, W., Jr. (1967). The historical roots of our ecological crisis. *Science, 155*, 1203–1207.

White, W.P. (Ed.). (1975). *Design Research News*. Washington, DC: Environmental Design Research Association.

White, W.P. (Ed.). (1979). *Resources in environment and behavior*. Washington, DC: American Psychological Association.

White, W.P. (Ed.). (1984). *Environmental design research association membership handbook*. Washington, DC: Environmental Design Research Association.

Whorf, B.L. (1956). *Language, thought, and reality*. Cambridge, MA: MIT Press.

Whyte, W.H. (1980). *The social life of small urban spaces*. Washington, DC: Conservation Foundation.

Wicker, A.W. (1972). Processes which mediate behavior-environment congruence. *Behavioral Science, 17*, 265–277.

Wicker, A.W. (1979). *An introduction to ecological psychology*. Monterey, CA: Brooks/Cole.

Wicker, A.W., & Kirmeyer, S.L. (1976). From church to laboratory to national park. In S. Wapner, S.B. Cohen, & B. Kaplan (Eds.), *Experiencing the environment*. New York: Plenum.

Wilensky, H.L. (1976). *Organizational intelligence*. New York: Basic Books.

Willems, E.P. (1977). Behavioral ecology. In D. Stokols (Ed.), *Perspectives on environment and behavior*. New York: Plenum.

Wilner, D.M., Walkley, R.P., Pinkerton, T.C., & Tayback, M. (1962). *The housing environment and family life*. Baltimore, MD: Johns Hopkins University Press.

Winett, R.A. (in press). Empiricist-positivist theories of environment and behavior: New directions for multilevel frameworks. In E.H. Zube & G.T. Moore (Eds.), *Advances in environment, behavior, and design* (Vol. 1). New York: Plenum.

Winkel, G.H. (Ed.). (1969). *Environment and behavior*. Beverly Hills, CA: Sage.

Wohlwill, J.F. (1966). The physical environment: A problem for a psychology of stimulation. *Journal of Social Issues, 22*, 29–38.

Wohlwill, J.F. (1968). Amount of stimulus exploration and preference as differential functions of stimulus complexity. *Perception and Psychophysics, 4*, 307–312.

Wohlwill, J.F. (1970). The emerging discipline of environmental psychology. *American Psychologist, 25*, 303–312.

Wohlwill, J.F. (1980). The confluence of environmental and developmental psychology: Signpost for an ecology of development? *Human Development, 23*, 354–358.

Wohlwill, J.F. (1984). Psychology and the environmental disciplines. In M.H. Bornstein (Ed.), *Psychology and its allied disciplines* (Vol. 2). Hillsdale, NJ: Erlbaum.

Wohlwill, J.F. (in press). The origins of environment and behavior at Clark: Recollections from pre- and neonatal life. *Journal of Environmental Psychology*.

Wohlwill, J.F., & Carson, D.H. (Eds.). (1972). *Environment and the social sciences*. Washington, DC: American Psychological Association.

Wohlwill, J.F., & Kohn, I. (1973). The environment as experienced by the migrant: An adaptation level view. *Representative Research in Social Psychology, 4*, 135–164.

Wohlwill, J.F., & Kohn, I. (1976). Dimensionalizing the environmental manifold. In S. Wapner, B. Kaplan, & S.B. Cohen (Eds.), *Experiencing the environment*. New York: Plenum.

Wolfsy, E., Rierdan, J., & Wapner, S. (1979). Planning to move: Effects on representing the currently inhabited environment. *Environment and Behavior, 11*, 3–32.

Wright, J.K. (1947). Terrae incognitae: The place of imagination in geography. *Annuals of the Association of American Geographers, 37,* 1–15.

Wright, J.K. (1966). *Human nature in geography.* Cambridge, MA: Harvard University Press.

Zannaras, G. (1976). The relation between cognitive structure and urban form. In G.T. Moore & R.G. Golledge (Eds.), *Environmental knowing.* Stroudsburg, PA: Dowden, Hutchinson, & Ross.

Zeisel, J. (1975). *Sociology and architectural design.* New York: Russell Sage Foundation.

Zeisel, J. (1976). *Stopping school property damage.* Arlington, VA: American Association of School Administrators.

Zeisel, J. (1981). *Inquiry by design.* Monterey, CA: Brooks/Cole.

Zeisel, J., Epp, G., & Demos, S. (1978). *Low-rise housing for older people.* Washington, DC: U.S. Government Printing Office.

Zeisel, J., Welsh, P., Epp, G., & Demos, S. (1984). *Midrise housing for older people.* Washington, DC: U.S. Government Printing Office.

Zube, E.H. (Ed.). (1970). *Landscapes: Selected writings of J.B. Jackson.* Amherst: University of Massachusetts Press.

Zube, E.H. (1980a). *Environmental evaluation.* Monterey, CA: Brooks/Cole.

Zube, E.H. (Ed). (1980b). *Social sciences, interdisciplinary research, and the U.S. Man and the Biosphere Program.* Washington, DC: U.S. Department of State, Man and the Biosphere Secretariat.

Zube, E.H., Brush, R.O., Fabos, J.G. (Eds.). (1975). *Landscape assessment.* Stroudsburg, PA: Dowden, Hutchinson, & Ross.

Zube, E.H., & Moore, G.T. (Eds.). (in press). *Advances in environment, behavior, and design* (3 Vols.). New York: Plenum.

PART 6

ENVIRONMENTAL PSYCHOLOGY: PROSPECTS FOR THE FUTURE

Chapter 40

PROSPECTING IN ENVIRONMENTAL PSYCHOLOGY: OSKALOOSA REVISITED

Roger G. Barker, *University of Kansas, Lawrence, Kansas*

Thirty-five years ago, Herbert F. Wright and I established the Midwest Psychological Field Station in Oskaloosa, Kansas, to undertake research in an area of science now known as environmental psychology; parallel research was carried out later in Leyburn, North Yorkshire, England. The goals of the Station were to discover and describe the everyday living conditions and behavior of the children of the town and to investigate their relationships. We had some success in these efforts in spite of unexpected difficulties, and we also made some surprising discoveries. Detailed reports of the projects have been made elsewhere and will not be reviewed here;[1] rather, I shall devote this chapter to difficulties and discoveries that are relevant to present-day environmental psychology.

40.1. THE ENVIRONMENTAL PSYCHOLOGY OF A NEW SCIENCE

Wright and I had both been students of Kurt Lewin, and his teachings should have forewarned us about the hazards to come in our venture into new territory. According to Lewin, a new psychological situation is one where (1) the paths (the actions) leading to goals are not known; (2) the valence of each action is simultaneously positive and negative; and (3) the perceptual field is unstable (Lewin, 1936b). Each of these properties has its inevitable consequences for behavior; in our case, we should have expected (1) progress toward our goals would not be parsimonious; false steps and lucky breaks would occur; (2) there would be conflict, tension, alertness, and vacillation with respect to particular procedures; (3) and research plans would change on the basis of seemingly minor observations and experiences.

These theories have very practical implications for the new discipline of environmental psychology; the name of the game for much of it in the near future is *discovery* research, that is, exploring and prospecting a new field of inquiry. According to the theories, this means that the design and methods of much of its research cannot be spelled out in detail. Unfortunately, however, funding agencies and evaluation panels usually place great emphasis upon details of tried-and-true methods and established concepts and theories. This effectively eliminates discovery research from consideration. Urgent efforts are required, therefore, to make clear the difference between discovery research and what we may call *verification* research, that is, projects that replicate, test, correct, refine, and elaborate previous developments and discoveries. In these cases, the methodological and theoretical directions that have proven to be effective and ineffective are usually well established, and it is important for panel members to know if the applicant is profiting from the earlier trials and errors. But requiring such procedural details for discovery research is not only futile but contraindicated. They are futile because tried-and-true methods and concepts are not tried and true in new situations, and they are contraindicated if they are seen by the applicant to be unavoidable window dressing or, more unfortunately, if they are taken seriously. In the latter case, the research will begin in old ruts, and time and energy will be wasted in escaping from them.

Entirely different criteria from those suitable for verification research are required for discovery research. Apparently, little thought has been given to them, and appropriate guides have not been formulated. In consequence, review panels are likely to measure all projects by the well-known standards for verification research. In a recent case that has come to my attention, panel members were directed to consider six criteria: (1) relation of findings to significant social issues; (2) familiarity of the applicant with details of previous research; (3) clear, complete, and precise description of the design and methodology of the research; (4) usefulness of the expected product for administrators, practitioners, and researchers; (5) qualification of the applicant; and (6) reasonableness of cost estimates. The project to which these criteria were to be applied was a pioneer investigation from the perspective of environmental psychology of an institution that had been the locus of much inconclusive research by psychiatrists, sociologists, psychologists, anthropologists, and other professionals. To my mind, the crucial criterion among those prescribed was (5) — qualification of the applicant. The project was rejected but not on the basis of the applicant's qualifications.

Standards for evaluating discovery research should be as clearly formulated as those for verification research. A step toward a set of criteria has been made by Wicker (1985). Here, then, is a task for environmental psychology — to restructure the environments (the panel meetings) where research applications are evaluated by introducing two scoreboards: one when the game is verification research and one when it is discovery research.

Fortunately for Wright and me, review panel meetings in the 1940s were, themselves, frequently new situations for the participants, so lucky hits (and false steps) were more common than they are today. Furthermore, my knowledge of the makeup of some early panels suggests that the members were more likely to be entrepreneurs of science with more experience and appreciation of new beginnings than today's more bureaucratized members. For whatever reason, lucky hit or brilliant insight, the good news that our project was approved gave us, we thought, a free-wheeling opportunity.

40.2. UNLEARNING THE 1940s

In fact, we were not free. We were saddled with the zeitgeist of the psychology in which we had been trained, and this came almost exclusively from laboratories and clinics. We wished to discover what environments Oskaloosa dealt to its 100 children (in its streets, dentists' offices, stores, vacant lots, churches, scout troops, and so forth), to describe how these environments treated children and the children's responses. Laboratory experiments, and clinical procedures were of no help and much hindrance; there was much we had to unlearn.

Among the 1940 canons of psychological research we had to discard were these:

1. Human behavior is solely a property of individual persons; generalizations require statistical aggregation of a particular behavior attribute across designated persons.

2. A subject's behavior is best studied by interrupting, probing, and rearranging it in accordance with the investigators' concerns via experiments, tests, questionnaires, and interviews.

3. Behavior can be observed most adequately by focusing on delimited segments or aspects of it and by restricting observer descriptions to predefined dimensions.

4. The physical-social environment of human behavior is largely unstructured, probabilistic, and passive; persons organize it according to the programming they carry within themselves; the black box brings order out of chaos via an integrated sensory-perceptual-cognitive-motivational-motor system that is the key to an understanding of whatever order, stability, and predictability there is in human behavior.

5. The environment of human behavior has a spacial locus and extent.

6. Collecting data without theoretical guides is futile.

On the contrary we discovered the following:

1. Human behavior occurs in an extraindividual as well as an individual form; environmental units such as grocery stores generate a characteristic pattern of behavior independently of the particular persons involved, and the characteristics and amount of the behaviors can be determined en bloc without reference to particular persons.

2. Experimental and clinical intrusions remove from scientific scrutiny one of behavior's most fundamental attributes; they destroy its natural (investigator-free) structure.

3. Narrative accounts in the language of Shakespeare and the street can be excellent symbolic representations of the spontaneous, ongoing behavior of persons.

4. Much of the order, stability, and predictability of human behavior comes from the ecological environment: from the structured, homeostatic, coercive behavior settings that people inhabit.

5. The environment of human behavior has a spacial locus, but time is also an important dimension of its extent.

6. Theories can blind as well as guide; the best preventative for this kind of blindness is data: data gathered without benefit of theories (as far as possible) on expeditions and at field stations far removed from laboratories, clinics, and think tanks. One or more of these hangups from the 1940s haunted many of our ventures and will be considered further in connection with them.

40.3. MOTHER LODES E∈ AND Eψ

Wearing 1940s blinders, the only way we knew to proceed was to describe the everyday behavior and situations of individual children. This effort was rewarding in ways we did not anticipate; it led via a number of minor discoveries to a major one: to two orthogonal veins of rich ore in the region of environmental psychology.

We immediately ran into a technical problem and later into problems of theory. At the very beginning, we were confronted with the surprising fact that after almost 100 years, scientific psychology could provide us with no procedures, concepts, or technical language for describing its phenomena as they occur intact outside laboratories, clinics, and testing and interview situations where the subject rather than the investigator calls the shots. It was as if botanists had no way of describing plants in the field except after taking them to the laboratory and cutting them into parts of the investigator's design. However, by starting from zero we had the advantage (and disadvantage) of a new situation with enhanced alertness, flexibility, and possibly, lucky breaks. For whatever reason, our studies of the stream of individual behavior led us to some important discoveries: (1) Narrative accounts in the language of laymen provide excellent coded descriptions of ongoing behavior; (2) environmental psychology is a schizoid discipline encompassing two incommensurable sciences—one concerned with the ecological environment, E∈, and one with the psychological environment, Eψ; (3) the E∈ initiates, organizes, terminates, and gives stability to much human behavior.

Video techniques were not available 35 years ago, but if they had been they would have delayed us from facing the real problems: to determine the structure and content of the stream of individual behavior and situation, to describe the parts, and to invent ways of representing them and their attributes. So we resorted to narrative accounts in literary language. To our surprise, these turned out to be no expedient; in fact we found that narrative accounts are an excellent system of symbols for representing the ongoing behavior and situation of a person. For one thing, the structure of a narration (the successive words, clauses, sentences) is isomorphic with the structure of the behavior stream, with the succession of events in a person's day (movements and short and long actions). Because of this isomorphism, a narrative record, itself, displays in some degree the behavior structure that is directly perceived by the observer. We called these narrative accounts *specimen records*, and we count them the first lucky strike in our prospecting venture. Subsequent research has shown them to have practical as well as research uses (Willems & Halstead, 1978).

After the records were made, the problem remained of identifying and describing the parts with precision and reliability. We sought units of the behavior stream that occurred without input from us as scientists. Textbooks were of no help; they did not tell us how to identify the behavioral analog of cells, organs, and somatic systems, if there were such. There were some theories (actone, action, reflex) but no operations for identifying them in drugstores and school classes. On the other hand, there were an endless number of behavior tesserae, pieces of the behavior stream selected or created by investigators: one-minute segments, answers to questions, discriminations between stimuli, repetitions of nonsense syllables, solutions of problems—all prescribed by investigators. But these were of no help to us; they destroyed what we were searching for—investigator-free units.

It is no great mystery why psychology has dealt mainly with behavior tesserae rather than with its intact structure. From the beginning, scientific psychology has been primarily concerned with the processes underlying behavior: with how we perceive, with learning mechanisms, with the black box arrangement for reading. Manipulation of the environment and the person are essential in this research; test holes must be sunk without regard for the surface structures. Although no mystery, it is nonetheless unfortunate that psychology has paid so little attention to a primary datum of the science—the undisturbed landscape of behavior. This was a pioneering opportunity for us, and it remains one for environmental psychology.

Specimen records enabled us to identify a number of investigator-free units; two of them were of great importance for our prospecting efforts. They brought us to a fork in the trail. We did not appreciate at first the significance of this bifurcation and proceeded on the assumption that the two branches were alternate routes to the hoped-for, rich, unitary mother lode of environmental psychology. But we were wrong. We discovered after much scouting, during which we were often confused and discouraged, that one path led to the ecological environment, $E\epsilon$, namely to the parts of the surround that are independent of a person's psychological system but that, nevertheless, affect the system and, therefore, affect behavior; and that the other path led to the psychological environment, to $E\psi$: the surround that is part of a person's psychological system with direct effects on behavior. We discovered, too, that these environments are the material of two sciences that have nothing in common; the concepts and laws of the $E\epsilon$ are as different from those of the $E\psi$ as the laws of gravity that are implicated in a child's pencil's lodging in a crack are different from the laws of perception that make it difficult to find the pencil. This confronted us with the realization that environmental psychology is not a univocal science, but, rather, at the present time, an empirical technology. Here are the behavior units that led us to this conclusion.

40.3.1. Behavior Episodes

Taking tips from the structure of specimen records and from Lewin's theory of molar actions, we identified a basic unit that we called a behavior episode (Barker & Wright, 1955; Wright, 1967). Behavior episodes are goal-directed actions; they are identified independently of their content. For example, the day of 8-year-old Mary Ennis contained 969 of these molar actions in its 14 hours and 27 minutes; they included "brushing hair," "hunting for pencil," and "watching teacher scold Shirley" (Barker, Wright, Schoggen, & Barker, 1978). We believe that behavior episodes are structurally similar within the stream of behavior to cells within organisms. Like cells, they have interior parts and they form the interiors of more inclusive behavior structures. Behavior episodes have many attributes; they are long and short, continuous and interrupted, overlapping and nonoverlapping, social and nonsocial; and in the social episodes, behavior toward associates may be submissive, dominating, nurturant, aggressive, resisting, avoiding, and so forth.

We discovered that some behavior episodes are initiated, monitored, and terminated by the $E\epsilon$ and some by $E\psi$ (Barker, et al., 1961; Schoggen, 1963). The episode "writing in copybook" from the specimen record of Clifford Mathews, 8 years old, in the behavior setting Lower Juniors Academic Class of the Leyburn Primary School, is an example of the former (Barker, et al. 1961). The episode occurred when forces from the $E\epsilon$ acted on Clifford via Miss Culver, the teacher; she instigated the episode "Children, it is time to get out your copybooks"; she monitored it; and she terminated it after 23 minutes "That's enough writing." This is an $E\epsilon$ episode; the causal regress receded into the $E\epsilon$ from Miss Culver to the established program of the encompassing Lower Juniors Academic Class (one remove), to the headmaster of the primary school (two removes), to the curriculum committee of the County Education Authority that created the program (three removes). The regress beyond Miss Culver was unknown to Clifford. Writing in the copybook was mandated by the $E\epsilon$. Overlapping with it were short episodes initiated, monitored, and terminated within Clifford's $E\psi$. There was, for example, the behavior episode "watching Miss Culver deal with Philip Butley" ("Clifford watched Miss Culver as she went towards the back of the room and spoke earnestly to Philip Butley. She tapped him smartly on the head saying he had to settle down and be quiet"). Other episodes from the $E\psi$ were "wiping nose," "resting, stretching, and playing with pencil." These are $E\psi$ episodes; they are autonomous to Clifford, P, and his psychological environment, that is, to his immediate perceptions, cognitions, motivations, and motor processes: to his psychological system, $PE\psi$.

It is important to understand that $PE\psi$ is involved in both $E\epsilon$ and $E\psi$ episodes. In both cases, behavior is determined by the psychological system, $B = f(PE\psi)$; but for $E\epsilon$ episodes, the psychological system is momentarily subordinate to control by systems of the ecological environment, $PE\psi = fE\epsilon$. This is not the case for $E\psi$ episodes, $PE\psi = fE\epsilon$. The former was the case when Miss Culver, in accordance with the program of the setting Lower Juniors Academic Class, as established by the curriculum committee, instigated the episode "writing in copybook," monitored it, and terminated it. The latter was the case for Clifford in the episodes "watching Miss Culver deal with Philip Butley" and "wiping nose, resting, stretching, and playing with pencil." These were autonomous actions by Clifford.

We were committed to psychological explanations of the behavior of Oskaloosa's children and were greatly surprised to discover the importance of the ecological environment in determining their behavior: to find, for example, that 45% of their episodes were initiated and 17% terminated by the $E\epsilon$; for English children in Leyburn, Yorkshire, the influence of the $E\epsilon$ was even greater; 62% of their episodes were initiated and 25% terminated by the $E\epsilon$ (Schoggen, Barker, & Barker, 1978).

40.3.2. Behavior Objects

The succession of behavior episodes in a person's day involves a variety of objects, both human and nonhuman. Mary Ennis, in the examples given before, transacted behavior with her own hair, with a pencil, with the teacher, and with Shirley. These are behavior objects (Barker & Wright, 1955). There were 571 different objects and 1882 transactions with objects in Mary's day; for example: 33 different foods (including two radishes) were the objects of 2% of Mary's object transactions, 97 different people (including 11 adult females and 4 adult males) were the objects of 33% of her transactions, 7 animals (including one worm) were the objects of 2% of Mary's transactions, and 23 playthings (including 3 dolls) were the objects of 5% of Mary's object transactions (Barker et al., 1978).

Behavior objects are observable points of intersection between a person's $E\epsilon$ and $E\psi$; they are the routes by which the relation $PE\psi = f(E\epsilon)$ occurs. In Lewin's terms, they are parts of the "foreign hull" of the $E\psi$ (Lewin, 1936a), and in Brunswik's terms, they are distal objects of the environment-organism-environment arc (Brunswik, 1955). There were unnumbered objects in Mary's surround, but only a few—the behavior objects—were also a part of her personal, psychological environment, $E\psi$. These objects had different properties in the two environments. Within Mary's $E\psi$, the pencil had the properties of usefulness (for writing a riddle for her mother) and lostness; within her $E\epsilon$, it had the properties of weight and shape, both of which were implicated in its being lodged in a crack.

Both the $E\epsilon$ and the $E\psi$ extend away from their intersection at behavior objects and encompass other objects and relations that are not revealed by the specimen records. The significance of behavior objects in the context of a person's psychological system is a psychological problem that we did not explore. Their place in the ecological environment is a problem for environmental psychology that we did investigate further.

Behavior objects differ in the amounts and routes of their impact on behavior. Some are passive, bringing no forces from the ecological environment. Mary's pencil, lodged in the crack, applied no pressure on her to search for it. The drive to do this came solely from Mary. It was an autonomous action. Other behavior objects are intrusive and act via the person's soma. An example is the slippery slide on the school playground that impelled Mary downward without effort on her part. Mary decided to play on the slippery slide (an $E\psi$ episode) and when she "let go" at the top, she put herself in charge of the ecological forces deriving from her body, gravity, and the slope. During this process, Mary's $E\psi$ was changed but not via psychological mechanisms. Other examples are a banana skin that sends a person sprawling and a sheriff who manacles a prisoner. Still other behavior objects bring ecological forces to bear on people via psychological mechanisms. P. Schoggen (1963, pp. 42–69) called these forces environmental force units. Mary's dog was such a behavior object. He initiated the episode "patting pet dog" by nuzzling Mary until she interrupted playing in the sand and patted him and rubbed his ears. He maintained her action by gently nudging her when her stroking declined in vigor, and he withdrew when Mary had done enough. Miss Culver was also such a behavior object in Clifford's episode "writing in copybook," but there was an important difference: Miss Culver was a component of the larger environmental entity, Lower Juniors Academic Class; she was its agent and subject to its program. Mary's dog on the other hand was independent, subject to no superordinate unit of the environment.

Behavior objects present a serious problem for environmental psychology. All varieties are sources of influence on behavior: by merely being present for person–object transactions, by altering the person's physical position or functioning without involving psychological mechanisms, and by establishing a linkage between ecological and psychological systems. The problem is this: The occurrence of a dog, a slippery slide, a pencil, a teacher, and so forth at the boundary of a person's psychological and ecological environments is beyond the science of psychology. It is in the realms of history, technology, economics, politics, and other disciplines. This does not present a problem for psychology (without the modifier environmental) that operates solely within psychological systems. But the intention of environmental psychology is precisely to bring the ecological environment (space, furniture, the weather, buildings, towns) into the science. This is, perhaps, clearer if we consider a similar problem for physics. If physics attempted to incorporate psychological phenomena into its laws and theories; if, for example, it attempted to derive not only the direction and strength of the force acting on Mary on the slippery slide but also whether she would "let go" at the top, physics would be in trouble, for gravity and motives are incommensurate phenomena. The physicist can only make a probabilistic estimate of the likelihood that Mary will climb the slide and deliver herself to the physical forces operating there, and the psychologist can only make a probabilistic, empirical estimate of the likelihood that there will be a slippery slide for Mary to climb (Barker, 1968).

Links between incommensurate systems are common. The gasoline pump, hose, and nozzle of a service station connect mechanical systems (engines) that operate in accordance with the laws of physics, chemistry, and electricity and a business system (the station) that operates in accordance with industrial, economic, and political rules and laws. The nature of the input from the latter system such as the octane level and lead content of the gasoline affects the operation of the engine as much as Miss Culver's input affected Clifford's behavior. The pump–hose–nozzle apparatus at the boundary of the engine is the equivalent of a behavior object, of Miss Culver, at the boundary of Clifford's psychological system. And from this object there is a long regress of influences into the industrial-economic-political environment via the station, the supplier, the oil company, and government agencies.

It is useful to distinguish between two parts of the ecological environment. The immediate $E\epsilon$ consists of behavior objects at the boundary of the psychological system and entities located no more than one remove from the psychological system of the person. The immediate $E\epsilon$ of Clifford's episode "writing in copybook" embraces Miss Culver and the established program of the setting Lower Juniors Academic Class (laid out in official, daily schedules and lesson plans). The remote $E\epsilon$ includes all other $E\epsilon$ entities, the headmaster and curriculum committee in Clifford's case. This distinction is important because the immediate $E\epsilon$ can be precisely identified, its bounds determined, and its extent measured. It is coextensive with the circumjacent behavior setting considered later. The remote $E\epsilon$ often extends without limit into the spatial-temporal surround.

After reaching the fork in the trail and realizing the significance of the difference between the $E\psi$ branch and the $E\epsilon$ branch, we devoted most of our effort to exploring the latter branch, while recognizing the importance of both to the new discipline.

40.4. PLACE-SPECIFIC BEHAVIOR

As people move from one place to another, their behavior changes accordingly. Behavior that occurs in one place would be out of place elsewhere. This place-specificity of behavior is the fundamental fact of environmental psychology…[it] requires an explanation. (Russell & Ward, 1982, p. 652)

Place-specificity was, indeed, a "fundamental fact" of behavior in Oskaloosa. We identified 884 places in the public areas of the town with distinctive patterns of behavior. In the beginning, we had no difficulty in accounting for this feature of the town. We saw the Sunflower Cafe as a place where Tom, Dick, and Helen went when they were hungry for food, drink, or companionship, and we saw the Presbyterian Church Annual Meeting and the Second Grade Music Class as places where other needs of particular persons were satisfied. The equation $B = f(PE\psi)$ appeared to account very well for the relationship between places and the behavior of people gathered in them. Similarity and restricted range of personal attributes (P) and opportunities ($E\psi$) seemed to explain the similarity of behavior across persons inhabiting places. Our firm allegiance to our roots in psychology prevented us from understanding what the town told us daily: that psychology is not enough, that the $E\epsilon$ is the source of the specificity of behavior to many places. We finally discovered that the $E\epsilon$ operates in two ways in these places: by selecting appropriate persons to inhabit places and by regulating behavior in places.

The $E\epsilon$ selects the inhabitants of places in two ways: by press-gangs and by gatekeepers. Almost every issue of the local paper reported press-gang activity; for example:

Courthouse News—District Court...State of Kansas vs. NG (Name Given), criminal damage to property...ordered to pay restitution of $200, fined $100, sentenced to 90 days in jail, ordered to pay court cost of $40.

Translated, this brief news item meant that NG was delivered to the County Jail by a chain of influences (messages and actions) within the $E\epsilon$ involving the state criminal code, the district judge, the sheriff, and the County Jail. The press-gang of messages and actions searched for, captured, and lodged NG in the jail. As for NG's *behavior*, it was undoubtedly directed away from the jail, but NG's *movement* was toward and into the jail. The forces of NG's psychological system ($P_{NG}E\psi$) were overpowered by those of the $E\epsilon$. Assembling people in places by means of press-gangs is not unusual in Oskaloosa. In fact, they operate in connection with approximately one-third of the public places of the town. This includes most places connected with the schools and government agencies. Thus, for example, if 7-year-old Ben Hutchings is not present at the Second Grade Music Class, this information is delivered to the second grade teacher who searches the homeroom and adjacent halls for him, and if unsuccessful informs the school principal who makes wider inquiries, finally informing Ben's

parents, who if unaware of his whereabouts, institute a still wider search, and if necessary alert the sheriff. Although Ben often told his parents he hated the Music Class and sought by all legitimate ways to absent himself, he was usually present by order of the second grade teacher and performed the activities without enthusiasm under the alert eye of the music teacher. A difference between Jail and Music Class is that prisoners are assembled by press-gang actions, whereas this is true for only a few pupils. For many pupils, $B = f(PE\psi)$ accounts for their presence and their enthusiastic participation. The press-gang (teacher, principal, parents, sheriff) is a backup system for Second Grade Music Class.

The $E\epsilon$ also selects the inhabitants of places by functioning as gatekeeper, admitting only persons with the appropriate attributes. Criteria for admission are often specified by a charter, constitution, papers of incorporation, or bylaws prepared over long periods of time in distant places, documents that are alien to the $E\psi$ of most aspiring inhabitants. In the case of the Presbyterian Church Annual Meeting, for example, the *Book of Order* of the Presbyterian Church (U.S.) requires that only church members vote. This requirement is implemented by an elected committee (Presbyterian Church Session Meeting) that examines candidates and accepts into membership those who have made a profession of faith in Christ and have been baptized. Their names are placed on a list of persons who may vote in the Annual Meeting. The Session Meeting is the gatekeeper in this case; it assures that $B = f(PE\psi)$ has a very limited range of variation within the Presbyterian Church Annual Meeting. It is a fail-safe way of separating the sheep from the goats. Gatekeepers that enforce entrance tests originating in the $E\epsilon$ are common in Oskaloosa; they determine who enters the meetings of most social, fraternal, service, and commercial organizations. The common financial entrance fee is an important selection device; people on welfare do not congregate in the Sunflower Cafe or Rotary Club meeting.

It is important to understand that press-gangs and gatekeepers operate within the $E\epsilon$; $E\psi$ is involved in the incarceration, admittance, or rejection of a person only at the final stage when the $E\epsilon$ introduces behavior objects (manacles, a teacher, session members, and so forth) at the boundary of the person's $E\psi$. It is also important to understand that the processes within the $E\epsilon$ operate without regard for particular persons. The Kansas criminal code is not directed at NG or any other person; it is directed at criminal acts; and the Presbyterian entrance requirements were not targeted to particular persons but to beliefs. Most forces of the $E\epsilon$ are person blind.

The $E\epsilon$ contributes to the place specificity of behavior not only by selecting appropriate people but by regulating the behavior that occurs in places. We turn to this after considering the next problem.

40.5. WHAT IS A PLACE?

The place specificity of behavior in Oskaloosa was impressive. The differential distinctiveness of the behavior of second graders in Music Class, Playground, and Cafeteria was so obvious that we considered using a sample of such geographical areas as sites for observing child behavior in the town. But before we were underway, we discovered that distinctive behavior was not so closely anchored to particular locations as at first appeared. The high school auditorium was sometimes the place for basketball game behavior, sometimes for junior class dance behavior, sometimes for PTA-carnival behavior, and so forth. And, on the contrary, the same behavior occurred in different places: the Home Extension Unit Meeting took place according to a rota in the members' homes. Although there was much clear-cut place-specific behavior in Oskaloosa (swimming only in the swimming pool, banking only in the bank), it was also true that in many cases a perceived place was not a unit of the geographical environment; frequently it was identified in space–time terms. The "meeting place" of the Independent Baptist Church Worship Service with its unique pattern of behavior, was the public room of the Building and Loan Office from 11 A.M. to noon each Sunday and only at this time. The space–time identification of places introduces manifest difficulties for explaining the connection between behavior and places. Although it is possible to conceive that some geographical places such as a dentist's office with its room arrangement and equipment might produce dentist office behavior, it is difficult to imagine how Oskaloosa's city room could produce congregate-meals behavior between 11:30 A.M. and 1:30 P.M. and conference-on-road-safety behavior at 3 P.M. Something more than geography and time seemed to be involved in the distinctive, bounded patterns of behavior that were so prominent in Oskaloosa.

These observations and experiences were important in starting us on the trail to behavior settings. The nature of behavior settings has been presented

elsewhere and will not be reviewed here (Barker, 1968). In brief, they are hybrid ecobehavioral phenomena; they are bounded standing patterns of human and nonhuman activity with integrated systems of forces and controls that maintain their activities at semistable equilibria; the parts and processes of behavior settings have high degrees of internal interdependence in consequence of which they are discrete units—they are entities within the ecological environment. I shall not retravel the trail to behavior settings here but shall turn to the relevance of this particular kind of place for environmental psychology. I shall do this by means of an example, the Vista Cafe, of Leyburn.

40.6. THE EXTRAINDIVIDUAL BEHAVIOR OF BEHAVIOR SETTINGS

Three attributes of the setting Vista Cafe and of all behavior settings must be emphasized. First, the Vista Cafe is an entity of the ecological environment; it has a life of its own, existing independently of particular persons. This is fundamental and is often dramatically demonstrated. In Oskaloosa, for example, the human components of Second Grade Academic Class sometimes change completely between terms, yet at the beginning of the new year the Second Grade, with essentially the same pattern of behavior, continues as vigorously as ever with a different teacher, different pupils, and in 1 year, a different site (a new school building). There are other phenomena in the Oskaloosa region that display these same characteristics. The occasional tornado has no fixed position; its component raindrops, hail, and debris continually change, yet at every moment it displays the distinctive pattern of activity called a funnel cloud. Perhaps tornadoes tell us something about the sources of the persisting, distinctive patterns of behavior in the wandering Home Extension Unit Meeting, in the reconstituted Second Grade Academic Class, and in the more common behavior patterns that are demonstrably place specific because they have not been observed to move, such as the Vista Cafe.

The second important feature of the Vista Cafe, and of all behavior settings, is that it behaves—it generates extraindividual behavior. The essence of the Cafe is its ongoing program of actions; these actions are place–time specific; they pertain to the securing, preparing, serving, consuming, and buying and selling of food and drink. For this, human inhabitants (patrons, cooks, waiters, and so forth) and nonhuman fixtures (stoves, tables, food blenders, and so forth) are essential en masse, but particular persons and fixtures are not essential. Cooking is required, but Joe, the cook, and Aga #19765E, the stove, are not; replacements are available. Eating and drinking are fundamental, but there are alternatives to Don, a diner, and to the plate from which he eats. Paying is vital to the program but there are stand-ins for Helen (customer), for Joyce (cashier), and another 10-pound note is as good as the proffered note #783B6795F. The fact that Joe, Don, Helen, and Joyce, and their compeers, and the stove, plate, and 10-pound note are here today and gone tomorrow while the Vista Cafe continues (it was founded in 1897) means that its place-specific activity is determined by an extraindividual something (like the forces of a tornado?) that outlasts the component parts. The actions of the inhabitants of the Vista Cafe and of its fixtures are, therefore, extraindividual actions generated by the Cafe.

The third feature of behavior settings to be emphasized is implicit in the second, but it deserves special attention. Extraindividual, place–time-specific actions that are imposed on the components by the program of the setting are actions that maintain the setting; they are setting-maintenance actions. Inhabitants that do not carry out these maintenance actions properly (cleaning tables, beating eggs) are instructed, reprimanded, or discharged; inadequate fixtures (tables, blenders) are repaired or discarded.

The distinctive pattern of activity known as the Vista Cafe is made up of a variety of maintenance actions, but they are not the only actions occurring in the Cafe; there are also individual actions. These actions are not determined by the Vista Cafe, and they are not essential to its occurrence. They are produced by the inhabitants and fixtures pari passu with their maintenance actions. The food blenders of the Cafe not only stir and whip food, the blades also vibrate, and the bearings heat. The vibration and heating derive from the blenders, from the balance of their blades, and from the friction of their bearings. Similarly, the hostess not only welcomes and seats patrons according to the rather precisely programmed rigamarole of the setting, ending with "have a nice meal," but she is also Madge Metcalf who walks with a limp and makes friends as she escorts the guests. The limp and the friendliness are not programmed by the Vista Cafe; they derive from attributes of Madge herself, from her injured ankle, and her friendly disposition that are among many other of Madge's attributes as a person with distinctive motives, perceptions, cognitions, and capacities.

The directly observed programs and standing patterns of behavior settings are phenotypic manifestations of their genotype: a theoretical construct in terms of which many of their aspects can be explained. However, the sine qua non of behavior settings is this: They are not neutral places where people congregate for their own purposes; they are superordinate, self-regulating, dynamic entities that manipulate the behavior of their human components toward an equilibrium state for the setting. This can be seen without intervening concepts and theories in a particular behavior setting outcrop, namely in settings where the number of human components is less than the number the program of the setting calls for. Consider the Vista Cafe when it was short of staff—when it had two cooks instead of the three prescribed by the program, when one waitress substituted for the ill hostess, and another was on jury duty. During this period, the whole standing pattern was altered: The remaining staff was busier than usual meeting the demands of the undiminished clientele; the service was slower; the menu was shorter; the lunch hour was longer for patrons; the fewer waiters received more frequent and stronger inputs from the greater number of more restless patrons per waiter; the remaining cooks prepared a greater number and more varied servings under greater pressure from waiters trying to deal with complaining patrons and competing waiters; and patrons waited to be seated by the amateur hostess and be served by the overworked staff. It required no theoretical insight for the waiters, cooks, and patrons of the Vista Cafe to directly experience the manipulative power of this settings and to understand that it was not a neutral place for satisfying work and pleasant dining.

A more extreme example of the power of a behavior setting over its inhabitants is found in meetings of Oskaloosa's Women's Bridge Club II. Here eight human components are required by the program of the setting. If a single member is absent, a substitute must be found, so there is much urgent consultation before the meeting to assure a full house. An eight-member bridge club is always in a precarious state; every member is a key person. This is also true of the undermanned Vista Cafe; each remaining staff member is more crucial than formerly to its survival. In general, the importance to a behavior setting of its inhabitants, the strength of its claim over them, and the vigor of their maintenance actions are directly related to its precariousness.

We first became aware of the importance and generality of the relationship between the number of human components and the behavior of behavior settings when we observed that the people of Oskaloosa were busier in its public habitat than the people of Leyburn. We later found that, in fact, Oskaloosa's public habitat generates 25% more behavior per town inhabitant than Leyburn's (Barker & Schoggen, 1973). Oskaloosa's 830 inhabitants are active in the public sector of the town for 3 hours and 44 minutes per day on the average, and Leyburn's 1310 inhabitants are active for 2 hours and 58 minutes. This finding was impressive in view of the similarity of the towns' behavior settings and the small difference in their extents. We wondered why the people of Oskaloosa spend 46 minutes more per day in the public part of the town than the people of Leyburn. We were aided in finding the answer by discovering that there are 63% as many inhabitants in Oskaloosa to maintain 95% as much habitat, two-thirds as many per unit of habitat. Oskaloosa's settings are more precarious than Leyburn's.

Consider the fate of identical twins separated at birth and reared in Oskaloosa and Leyburn. Oskaloosa, with its shorter roster of persons available to maintain its more precarious settings, would invite, urge, select, elect, summon, commission, order its twin to attend concerts, play on teams, chair meetings, clerk in stores, sing in choirs, go to church, serve on a jury, and so forth more frequently and more urgently than Leyburn would call on its twin. If the twins were in the normal range of receptivity to environmental inputs, Oskaloosa's public habitat would exact more behavior from its twin than Leyburn's public habitat.

The consequences of what we have called the undermanning of behavior settings demonstrates the dynamic, purposeful, coercive nature of the ecological environment with respect to people when they are components of behavior settings. The Vista Cafe under these crisis conditions in an $E\epsilon$ outcrop that displays to the naked eye (1) a behavior setting behaving and (2) the inhabitants behaving "Vista Cafewise."

Our early understanding of behavior settings was guided by our observations of the Vista Cafe and other settings and by the naive psychology taught us by the inhabitants of Oskaloosa and Leyburn. Thereafter, three publications were important to our increasing comprehension of behavior settings: *An Introduction to Cybernetics* (Ashby, 1956), "Thing and Medium" (Heider, 1959), and "Analyses of the Concepts Whole, Differentiation, and Unity" (Lewin,

1941). These theoretical treatises provided bases for accepting behavior settings as fundamental units of the ecological environment: Ashby's by showing that relationships among the parts of machines (inhabitants) and between the parts and the machine (behavior setting) are common to many sciences and can be handled with precision; Heider's by revealing fundamental properties of elements (inhabitants) and patterns of elements (behavior settings); and Lewin's by providing the theoretical basis for defining and identifying dynamic wholes (behavior settings).

40.7. RESEARCH WITHOUT SUBJECTS

Methodological problems arose in connection with out efforts to identify the kinds and measure the amounts of extraindividual behaviors produced by the public habitats of Oskaloosa and Leyburn. Our backgrounds in psychology disposed us to select samples of subjects from each public setting, secure the requisite data for each subject by observations, questionnaires, and interviews, and compute measures of central tendency and variation within and across settings. However, even in the planning stage, it became obvious that this was an impossible task. Minimal samples within Oskaloosa's 884 and Leyburn's 758 behavior settings would have required fieldwork far beyond our resources. But more important, our growing understanding of behavior settings showed us that such data, if they could have been obtained, would have been irrelevant to our concern for the behavioral attributes of behavior settings. This is true because the significance of an action by a particular person as a behavior-setting component is determined by the setting in which it occurs. This holds for the parts of all bounded dynamic systems. The strength of a beam is determined by its place in a structure; the meaning of a word depends on the utterance to which it contributes; the significance of a "strike" for a baseball game will differ if it is a Strike 1 or Strike 3 for the batter or "third out" for the side; and it will end the game (the setting) if it is "Strike 3 and third out at the bottom of the ninth."

In all of these cases, it is the momentary properties of the superordinate entity vis-á-vis the parts that determine the significance of the parts. One would learn more about the strength of the beam in situ from the plans and specifications of the structure than from tests of the beam in isolation, about the meaning of the word from the thought expressed by the utterance than from a dictionary, and about the import of the strike from its place in the program (rules and regulations) of the game than from an analysis of the player's action. The meanings of all of these maintenance actions are determined by what they maintain. In the case of behavior settings, the program tells what this is.

An engine is an informative analog of a behavior setting in these respects. If one knows the specifications of an engine and the sequence of events built into it, one knows much about what the component parts do when it operates normally. No investigation is required. In the case of an internal combustion engine of a particular type, one knows as it hums smoothly along that the spark plugs are sparking, the crankshaft is rotating, and the fuel vapors are exploding. Similarly, if one knows the program of a cafe, one knows what its component parts are doing when it is in operation: The cooks are cooking, the lights are lighting, and the customers are eating and drinking. The engine in operation is the essential condition for the spark plugs to spark, the crankshaft to rotate, and the vapors to explode; spark plugs do not spark on a dealer's shelf. And it is only when a cafe is in operation that its cooks cook, its lights light, and its customers eat and drink. Cooks do not cook in a post office. It is knowledge of the program that enables us to describe the behavior of behavior settings (their extraindividual, setting-maintaining, $E\epsilon$ actions) without recruiting subjects.

I shall explicate the nature and sources of data obtained without subjects by referring again to the behavior setting Women's Bridge Club II Meeting. Here is its program: The Club meets monthly, with one exception in December, from 7:30 P.M. to 11:30 P.M.; there are always eight players; the hostess greets members, provides a place, equipment, and refreshments; the members play cards according to the official rules for contract bridge; they converse and have refreshments. Although not inscribed in bylaws or a constitution, informants agree that these are facts of the Club's life that are known and accepted by the members.

The basic measure of the amount of extraindividual behavior produced by a behavior setting is person-hours per year (P-H). P-$H = o \times d \times i$ where o = number of occurrences per year, d = average duration of occurrences in hours, and i = average number of inhabitants per occurrence. The values of o, d, and i for the Women's Bridge Club II are provided by the program: $o = 11$ (meets monthly with one exception); $d = 4$ (meets from 7:30 to 11:30 P.M.); and $i = 8$ (there are always eight players). The P-H produced by the Club is, therefore, $11 \times 4 \times 8 = 352$.

The P-H generated by a behavior setting can be partitioned among its classes of inhabitants. In our studies, we have grouped inhabitants by sex, age, social class, and race. Informants identified the members of the Club; sex, age, and race were secured from official census records, and social class was judged by fieldworkers on the basis of the community associations with the members. The output of the Club by classes was:

Class	P–H
Females	352
Aged adults (65 + years)	308
Adults (18–64 years)	44
Social Class I	264
Social Class II	88
White	352

These are measures of the extent to which Women's Bridge Club II made use of various classes of the town's inhabitants; there was no output via males, adolescents, children, Social Class III, or blacks.

The standing pattern of the Club has many discriminable features. The physical milieu had a temperature of 68–73°F; it was 15 × 20 ft in area, and eight ft high; the refreshments were sherbet, cake, coffee, candy, and nuts; and there were unnumbered other physical features. The behavioral side of the Club had many attributes, too: card playing, conversing, eating, manipulating, thinking, and so forth. These attributes differed greatly in prominence; therefore we devised scales for rating those attributes in which we were interested as (1) primary (attribute pervades the entire standing behavior of the setting); (2) secondary (attribute present but not ubiquitous); and (3) attribute absent. The program of the Club identified its primary behavior attributes as follows: recreation (playing cards, conversing), social interaction (greeting, conversing, competing, cooperating), manipulation (handling cards and utensils). It produced 352 P-H of behavior with each of these attributes. Field observations disclosed the occurrence of some secondary behavior attributes: nutrition (eating and drinking), talking, thinking, affective behavior (overt emotional expression), aesthetics (looking at and commenting on beautiful things), personal appearance (exhibiting self via grooming, clothing, and adornments). The Club did not produce behavior with other attributes with which we were concerned; there was no education (formal teaching and learning), religion (worshiping behavior), business (exchanging goods, services, or privileges for money), physical health (health-promoting behavior), professional activities (paid performances), or gross motor actions (use of large muscles).

Women's Bridge Club II demonstrates the availability of data for environmental research without subjects in the usual sense. A basic source is the written or unwritten program of the behavior setting. The frequencies, schedules, and durations of behavior settings are posted on the doors of establishments and on bulletin boards, and they are announced in newspapers, bulletins, and posters. The number and categories of inhabitants of many settings are recorded in precise form in school, Sunday school, and organization records. These data for less formal settings (commercial, sport, social) can be obtained by fieldworkers attending settings and counting inhabitants. Attribute ratings are made on the basis of direct observation, evidence from informants, and programs and minutes of meetings. There are many opportunities to cross-check field data; behavior settings are relatively permanent (recurring) and can be observed and assessed repeatedly by different fieldworkers; they are known to numbers of informants who provide independent reports. Behavior settings within the public habitat are open to public scrutiny; indeed, their programs, structures, and components are common knowledge. An important part of the socialization of children and immigrants is learning about community behavior settings.

It should be noted that the extraindividual behavior of a behavior setting and its standing pattern of human activity are parts of the $E\epsilon$ the setting provides its inhabitants. The hostess of the Vista Cafe escorts guests in an $E\epsilon$ of cooks cooking, waiters serving, patrons dining. Indeed, Madge Metcalf is friendly and walks with a limp in the $E\epsilon$ of her own actions as hostess. The methods we have considered here inform us only about the behavior setting component, hostess; they tell us nothing about Madge Metcalf who is friendly and walks with a limp. For that, the methods of individual psychology are required.

40.8. INDIVIDUAL BEHAVIOR IN BEHAVIOR SETTINGS

I return briefly to the $E\psi$ lode that runs through the territory of environmental psychology. It occurs pari passu with the $E\epsilon$ lode of extraindividual, setting-maintaining behavior we have been considering and consists of individual, person-satisfying behavior that is not mandated by the setting in which it occurs. Such were Madge Metcalf's friendliness as she, as hostess, prescriptively escorted patrons of Vista Cafe, and Clifford Mathews's furtive watching of Miss Culver as he obediently carried on the writing-in-copybook program of Lower Juniors Academic Class. Other examples are self-reports by high school students of experiences in school settings: "I enjoyed being in the Junior Class Play." "It [the parade] gave me recognition." "I worked hard [on a committee]" (Gump & Friesen, 1964).

Research in this vein makes use of the well-established methods of individual psychology, with each inhabitant of a behavior setting treated as a subject. This vein was worked extensively; of particular importance were studies in the behavior settings of large and small schools (Gump & Friesen, 1964; Wicker, 1968; Willems, 1964), of large and small churches (Wicker, 1969), and of Oskaloosa and Leyburn (Barker & Barker, 1978; Schoggen, Barker, & Barker, 1963). The methods and results of the school and church studies have been reviewed in detail by Wicker (1979). Important discoveries about the effects of behavior settings and of positions within them on individual behavior issued from this research. It was found, for example, that experiences of satisfaction and responsibility are more frequent and intense (1) for the inhabitants of undermanned than optimally manned behavior settings and (2) for inhabitants in more powerful than less powerful positions within settings. The first finding appears to be due to the fact that a greater proportion of the inhabitants of relatively undermanned behavior settings are in positions of power; they are key people. But the greatest significance of these results in the present context is the evidence they provide that behavior settings are, indeed, powerful, dynamic entities of the $E\epsilon$.

40.9. HABITAT SIZE: AT HAND AND HANDY

Prospectors want to know the size of their strikes. We wanted to know the size of the Vista Cafe, the Second Grade Music Class, the Worship Services of Oskaloosa and Leyburn, and others. We first investigated this problem with reference to the public habitats of the towns (Barker & Schoggen, 1973). These habitats consist of the behavior settings located within the borders of the towns and outside the homes; they are the extrahome places where people satisfy personal needs (engage in individual actions), fulfill obligations (carry out setting-maintenance actions), and submit to confinement (imposed by press-gangs). They cover all public parts of the towns; there are no interstitial areas. It seemed, therefore, that the number of such settings near in time and place (*at hand*, according to Webster) and conveniently accessible (*handy*, according to Webster) would be a measure of the extents of these important places.

There was much evidence that the inhabitants of the towns agreed with the proposition that habitat size is positively related to the number of settings that are at hand and handy. Both towns were generally perceived as being "closed down" on Sunday, when, in fact, there were only about 25% as many public settings as on other days. Common comments were "there's nothing to do here on Sunday" (few places for individual actions) and "Sunday is the only day I can do my own thing" (escape from imposed setting-maintenance actions). Leyburn was known to be greatly reduced in size on Wednesday afternoons— officially designated as "early closing day." Most business and government settings closed their doors at 1 P.M. On the other hand, Leyburn's public habitat was greatly enlarged on Fridays—Market Day. Many settings occurred mainly on this day (e.g., market stalls, Magistrates Court, coffee mornings, auction sales). Market Day was seen as a very busy day in Leyburn. The people of the towns endorsed this naive theory of the size of their public habitats.

Methodologically, the theory was attractive; it appeared to entail only counting settings. In the year 1964, there were 884 behavior settings in Oskaloosa and 758 in Leyburn. Accordingly, by the theory, Oskaloosa's public habitat was larger than Leyburn's by 17%. However, we later discovered that Oskaloosa's greater number of behavior settings occurred on fewer days during the year. The mean number of settings per day was 146 in Oskaloosa and 178 in Leyburn. By the day, then, Oskaloosa was smaller than Leyburn—18% smaller. Still other data revealed that Oskaloosa's fewer settings per day continued for more hours; therefore the mean number of behavior settings per hour was 32.6 in Oskaloosa and 37.2 in Leyburn. We were baffled. How could Oskaloosa be larger than Leyburn by the year and smaller by the day and hour? Was there no univocal difference?

We found a solution when we turned from the frequency of behavior settings within temporal intervals to other temporal aspects of settings and behavior. Both behavior settings and the molar actions that

occur in them are flexible in duration and intermittent in occurrence; they are adjustable in these respects, so that temporal structures can be imposed on them. Many actions are shortened, lengthened, and interrupted (to be completed later) to fit behavior setting requirements. The behavior episode "getting the mail at the Post Office" is completed quickly at the end of the day when the setting "Post Office closes in 10 minutes" is known, whereas, the same episode may consume half an hour earlier in the day. If the Library closes before the episode "finding the date of the destruction of Pompeii" is completed, the action can usually be interrupted and finished the next day. Many behavior settings are similarly responsive. The behavior setting Leyburn Parish Council Meeting will be as short as 30 minutes if there is little business and brief discussion (few and short actions), and it will continue for hours if there is much business and protracted discussion (many and long actions). Many behavior settings exist intermittently; some recur on a regular schedule (Ellson's Drugstore ceases to operate at 6 P.M. and resumes at 8 A.M. the next day); others recur irregularly (Oskaloosa's Fire Station is activated only when there is a fire).

In general, actions and settings within the towns are adjusted to the temporal structures imposed on them from the remote ecological environment. Local time in both towns is divided into arbitrary units by intruding calendars, clocks, almanacs, radio signals, and so forth that establish the times of the noon siren, the official lunch hour, the monthly telephone bill, the weekly wage, the monthly salary, the hour-long church service, the 2-week vacation, the 4 to 5 P.M. "Sesame Street" TV program. Our observations indicated that the durations of actions within the towns were, in general, in accord with these imposed structures and that they were distributed with approximately equal frequency around three modal durations: (1) brief actions, those requiring less than an hour, such as eating a meal at the Vista Cafe, singing a song in the Second Grade Music Class, and getting a prescription filled at Ellson's Drugstore; (2) middling long actions requiring more than an hour and less than a day for completion, for example, repairing a refrigerator in the Vista Cafe, preparing the lesson for Home Extension Unit Meeting, and stocking the shelves of Ellson's Drugstore; (3) long actions continuing for more than a day and less than a year: redecorating Vista Cafe, planning and practicing the Second Grade Concert, and finding and appointing a new teacher for Second Grade Music Class. For brief actions, the public habitat of the towns consisted of 33 behavior settings on the average in Oskaloosa and

37 in Leyburn. These were the numbers of settings at hand and handy for action that were completed within an hour of their initiation; for longer actions that were usually completed within the day, the town's public habitats were much larger, amounting to 146 settings in Oskaloosa and 178 in Leyburn. And for still longer actions that might require a year for completion, there were 884 settings in Oskaloosa and 758 in Leyburn.

To the degree that actions occur with equal frequency within the three time intervals, a general measure of habitat extent must weight the three corresponding habitat sizes equally. The technical question of how to give equal weight to Oskaloosa's 884 settings per year, 146 settings per day, and 33 settings per hour was accomplished by transforming these measures of habitat extent into percents of corresponding measures of a "standard town," a town whose dimensions were the mean number of settings for each time interval in Oskaloosa and Leyburn on two occasions a decade apart. The dimensions of the standard town, which we have called an *urb*, were 680.5 settings per year, 151.0 per day, and 34.1 per hour. Relative to these dimensions, Oskaloosa's dimensions in 1963–1964 were 1.30, 0.97, and 0.96, respectively, with a mean of 1.07. Oskaloosa's public habitat was, therefore, 1.07 urbs in extent or 107 *centiurbs* (cu); Leyburn's habitat was 113 cu in extent.

Using this method, the extents of many parts of the towns' habitats can be determined: For example, Leyburn's Vista Cafe was 2.2 cu and Oskaloosa's Second Grade Music Class was 0.36 cu in extent; there were five churches in Oskaloosa and three in Leyburn, but the extent of the worship services were almost identical, 1.55 and 1.54 cu, in Oskaloosa and Leyburn, respectively. Aesthetic activities were prominent in 5.3 and 8.0 centiurbs of habitat; children were prohibited from entering 15.0 and 19.0 centiurbs of habitat; national and state (counties in England) authorities controlled 8.5 and 35.7 centiurbs of habitat; and eating and drinking were prominent in 7.4 and 18.6 centiurbs of habitat.

The absence of a spacial dimension in the urb measure of habitat size may be surprising at first, but a review of the nature of behavior settings and of the theory of habitat size in terms of the nearness and accessibility of settings makes it clear why this is the case. The spacial extent of a behavior setting is one of its attributes, along with the number and characteristics of its human and nonhuman components; these are all determined by the setting, by the homeostatic mechanisms that maintain it at a semistable

level. In fact, space is one of the most easily adjusted attributes of a behavior setting; therefore it is generally true that a setting that is at hand and handy, whether it be a 9 ft^2 Telephone Kiosk or a 20,000 ft^2 Supermarket, has the requisite spacial extent for its operating level. Emergencies do arise, of course; unprecedented surges of inhabitants sometimes overwhelm available space. When this occurs, the setting is inaccessible (it is too small) for those at the end of the line. But there are a number of ways of quickly enlarging a setting, and two of them involve altering its time dimension. First, the duration of the setting may be extended. When it became clear that the Presbyterian Church Annual Dinner would be overcrowded with patrons, serving was begun earlier and continued longer than scheduled. Second, the setting may be repeated. Leyburn's Dramatic Society Play was repeated on the following day to accommodate an overflow audience. These ways of increasing the size of the dinner and the play were much easier than enlarging the dining room and theater. But time cannot always substitute for space. Some behavior settings have time-limited programs and/or programs that cannot be repeated. In these cases, only an increase in the spacial extent of a setting can increase its accessibility and hence its size. A game and a stage show are interesting in this respect. A championship football game cannot be reenacted, and its duration is fixed by its program of operation, but a stage show can have an indefinite run. So we have stadia for 100,000 spectators and theaters for audiences of 1,000.

Changes in the spacial extents of behavior settings do regularly occur, however, Some of these are quickly accomplished. When the sanctuary of the Presbyterian Church is filled with worshipers, the movable rear walls are raised, adding the lecture room for late arrivals. Other changes occur slowly in response to gradual changes in the operating level of settings. When technological and economic changes in the remote environment reduced the farm implement business in Oskaloosa, the behavior setting Lesters's Farm Center was left with large unoccupied display and shop areas. In its efforts to maintain itself, the setting reduced its space stepwise, first turning over the front display area to another setting, then partitioning off part of the shop area. During the same period, business increased for the setting Auto Parts Store (more older cars were in use requiring repairs); when the shelves and the area for customers became too crowded, an addition was constructed.

The dynamic, homeostatic nature of behavior settings insures that in the long run all of their essential attributes (parts, processes, dimensions) are harmonious; therefore mismatches between the space and the number of inhabitants are temporary and rare.

40.10. UNFINISHED BUSINESS

Twenty-five years of prospecting at the Midwest Psychological Field Station produced a larger agenda of "difficulties and discoveries that are relevant to present day environmental psychology" than can be considered here. So, in order to bring a degree of closure to this report I shall end with brief statements about items which must be laid on the table.

40.10.1. Item: Variety, Stability, and Coercive Power of Behavior Settings

Behavior settings differ greatly in the variety and stability of their standing patterns and in the strength of their maintenance forces. It is easily observed that Oskaloosa's behavior setting City Park has more varied behavior at particular times, less stable behavior over extended periods, and weaker coercive forces than the setting Dr. Sterne's Dental Office. In spite of this, the structural-dynamic properties of these settings are identical. The examples cited earlier in this chapter (Second Grade Music Class, Vista Cafe, Women's Bridge Club II, and so forth) appear to fall toward the less varied, more stable, and more coercive ends of the distributions in Oskaloosa and Leyburn. In a complete record of our work, such properties of settings would be entered as important problems calling for investigation, including developing methods of measuring the variables and relating them to inhabitant behavior. Measures of a community's or an institution's behavior settings on these variables would reveal aspects of the quality of life it provides the inhabitants.

40.10.2. Item: Power of People

My informal observations tell me that laypersons and professionals who deal with people on a face-to-face basis often view behavior settings with misgivings. This appears to occur to the degree that settings are perceived to dominate people and thereby diminish their freedom of action. Our research may have contributed to this view by concentrating on people as components of superordinate behavior settings rather than as persons who create, alter, and choose them, where people have the ultimate power.

Nevertheless, our investigation of behavior settings may have been fortunate, for it is possible to effectively deal with settings only to the degree that knowledge of their operation is available. With this knowledge, people can, in fact, add the power of behavior settings to their own by creating, altering, and choosing settings with desirable consequences for themselves as human components. The whole story of behavior settings is this: People are creatures of the behavior settings they create, alter, and choose.

So creating, altering, and choosing behavior settings are of the greatest practical importance, and psychology is the basic relevant science. It is relevant to teaching the technology of behavior settings and the psychology of their human components to those who create, alter, and choose them. It is also relevant to teaching the human components themselves about the settings they inhabit and how to cope with them. In all of these tasks, the teacher must be an expert in both psychology and behavior-setting technology.

This is not the place to present details of the applied psychology of behavior settings, but it may be appropriate to mention one general principle: Behavior-setting experts and those who actually create, alter, and choose them must be outsiders, that is, people who are not yet creatures of the settings they will deal with. Settings are obviously created and chosen by outsiders; it is also true that they can be altered in fundamental ways only when people are outside the power fields of the settings to be changed. Miss Culver could not do much to improve the setting Lower Juniors Academic Class while she and the pupils were engaged by the program underway. To do this, she would have to disengage herself from the setting, act as an independent behavior-setting technician (preferably with the advice of an expert), make new lesson plans, secure new materials, and so forth. This is true, too, for other entities of the ecological environment. A person cannot significantly modify an automobile while driving it; that is, while being a part of the vehicle-in-operation. To do this, the person must cease being a part of the functioning machine and become an engineer or mechanic who views and works on the vehicle from outside free from constraints imposed by the machine in operation. Here is an important task for psychology: to provide expertise for persons desiring to create, alter, and choose behavior settings and for persons who are subordinate setting components.

In this connection, one notes that whereas the psychological systems of aircraft pilots, typists, automobile drivers, and so forth are involved in the operation of machines, making psychological expertise important for the design of machines and the selection and training of operators, psychological expertise is even more important in dealing with behavior settings where (contrary to machines) some of the parts, the human components, also require psychological know-how. Wicker, Chapter 16, this volume, deals with these issues.

40.10.3. Item: Harmony, Interference, and Incompatibility within Behavior Settings

The inhabitants of behavior settings are simultaneously under pressure to engage in component actions by the setting, $E\epsilon$, and in personal actions by their own psychological systems, $E\psi$. Some of these dual pressures converge and lead to harmonious actions. Madge Metcalf, as hostess of the Vista Cafe, officially welcomed and escorted the guests; at the same time as friendly Madge Metcalf, she engaged in genial interaction with them. These actions were mutually supportive and harmonious. Other setting and personal pressures diverge and issue in actions that are mutually interfering. In his diary, Samuel Pepys reports many activities within particular behavior settings. He has this to say on December 3, 1665 (Latham & Mathews, 1972, p. 316):

> "Up and to church" [a behavior setting] where I hear "a good sermon by Mr. Plumes" [setting actions by Pepys and Mr. Plumes]; and enjoyed the "sight, by chance, and very near my fat brown beauty of the parish" [personal action of Pepys].

Undoubtedly gazing at and appreciating his brown beauty interfered with Pepys's attention to the sermon, and vice versa, but the two were not completely incompatible. Still other setting and personal pressures are so opposed they produce incompatible behavior. This occurred in the case of Madge Metcalf when, as hostess, the pressure on her to welcome and escort guests was opposed and bested by the personal counterpressure to remain immobile with her painful ankle. In fact, the Vista Cafe ejected Madge as a component until the disruptive personal pressure was removed by medical treatment.

We did not investigate the relative occurrence of convergence, divergence, and opposition within behavior settings, but two general observations suggest that convergence is common. When there is a high degree of convergence, both the setting and the inhabitants benefit, and the setting survives. An inhabitant's reaction to a behavior setting that prevents actions that bring satisfaction to him or her as

a person is to try to leave the setting. And a setting's response to an inhabitant who balks at actions essential to its maintenance is to seek to eject the person. Human components are essential to the continuation of behavior settings; therefore there must be an essential minimum person-setting harmony within the settings that do survive, as most do; 61% of the settings of both Oskaloosa and Leyburn survived for a decade (Barker & Schoggen, 1973, p. 58).

It is our observation that the power of behavior settings over inhabitants is not often experienced by the inhabitants. This oversight easily occurs when personal and setting pressures coincide; it is dramatically illustrated by experiences of river boatmen. Nathan Rabin, in his account of his one-man voyage down the Mississippi River, describes one section of the river as follows:

> The boat streamed with the river....for a mile and a half the water has the immaculate polish of new silver. There wasn't a scratch on it....the river looked absolutely still. But the great silent power of the river environment was made immediately apparent by the appearance of tows making their way up the chute.....They crept painfully....their screws thrashing against the glacial hill of water. (Rabin, 1981, p. 304)

In this case, the physical force of the river, $E\epsilon$, coincided completely with Rabin's own psychological force, $E\psi$, his intense desire to make it through the chute below Island No. 8. The water and Rabin moved synchronously, so from his perspective vis-á-vis the surrounding water, there was no movement, no forces were operating. The ecobehavioral forces of behavior settings will be equally obscure when personal needs and setting pressures coincide. But occasionally, the equivalent of an upstream tow occurs: The second grader who "misbehaves," the guest of the bridge club who does not play by the rules, the member of the congregation who argues with the preacher, and the choir member who sings loudly in a monotone are examples. They all act against the current (the program) of their settings, and unlike the upstream tow that finally made it around Island No. 8, they are sooner or later "taken care of." Mechanisms for dealing with these problems are parts of the programs of some settings: Game officials call fouls, and bench players and bouncers remove troublemakers from dances; parliamentarians rule motions out of order.

Although there is undoubtedly a high degree of convergence between setting forces and personal forces within behavior settings, there is also a constant tension and fluctuation in the relative degree and loci of the converging, diverging, and opposing forces. As a result, behavior settings and their human components continually change, and some of the changes become permanent with settings, persons, or both being permanently modified. For many members of the Home Extension Unit, the requirement (setting pressure) that each member take her turn in "giving the lesson" is a source of anxiety and resistance (personal pressure) during its preparation, but members report terminal and continuing satisfaction in a job well done. A number of studies have discovered that behavior settings that make demands on their inhabitants often have more favorable consequences for the inhabitants than do settings that make few demands (Gump & Friesen, 1964; Wicker, 1968). Only further research will disclose how generally true this is.

The problem of identifying settings whose imposed actions have favorable effects on the psychological systems and behavior of the inhabitants is one of great practical significance because many ameliorative social programs operate by way of behavior settings (in schools, correctional institutions, vacation areas, etc.) on the assumption that setting maintenance actions and the conditions behind them will not only alter present behavior but also the inhabitant's psychological systems and enduring behavior.

40.10.4. Item: Qualities of Environments

Much of our prospecting was devoted to the development of methods for identifying and assaying the behavior settings of institutions and communities. In the course of this rather technical work, it became apparent to us that we were, in effect, learning how to assess the qualities of environments. A number of particular discoveries and limited insights contributed to this wider understanding.

A surprising early discovery was that the behavior settings located outside the homes of Oskaloosa and Leyburn blanketed the public regions; persons outside their homes were always inhabitants of behavior settings; there were no interstitial areas. Another discovery was that each behavior setting had many attributes that varied greatly in degree across a town's whole roster of settings: The environments of the towns were not homogeneous. Different persons and classes of persons frequently inhabited different environments within a town. Oskaloosa adolescents spent 54% as much time in behavior settings with activities and fixtures of religious significance as was expected on the basis of their total involvement in

the town, whereas the town's aged spent three times the expected time in these settings. In Leyburn, on the other hand, adolescents spent twice as much time as expected and the aged 4% less time than expected in religious settings (Barker & Schoggen, 1973, p. 391).

The different attributes of behavior settings are due mainly to their different programs, but their differential accessibility is influential, too. Kings Arms Pub, in Leyburn, did not admit 12-year-olds, but Secondary Modern School English Class required their attendance—a requirement that was enforced by the area attendance officer. And there is differential permeability with respect to physical conditions: District Court Session in Oskaloosa was insulated from the outside temperature and sound, and certain pollutants were removed from the air as it entered the setting, but the ambient temperature, sound, and air quality flowed freely through Bethel's Service Station.

The method we developed—the behavior setting survey—is an inventory of a town's (or an institution's) ecological environment in terms of behavior settings; it emphasizes the behavioral rather than the physical attributes of settings, and it omits data on the distinctive behavior of individual inhabitants. Inhabitants of behavior settings engage simultaneously in extraindividual behavior as components of settings and in individual behavior as distinctive persons. These coupled but incommensurable behaviors require different methods and different theories. Psychology has methods and theories for dealing with the inhabitants of behavior settings as distinctive persons but not with them as behavior-setting components who, with their behavior, are parts of the environment. So behavior settings are something of an enigma to psychology; it is relevant to only a part of the behavior occurring in behavior settings. An example will give substance to these abstract statements.

In the behavior setting Lower Juniors Music Program, the singing pupils, the sounding instruments, the directing teacher, the shaped and sized room, the listening audience, the music scores, and so forth create a musical environment to which John Smith, a 7-year-old pupil, both contributes and responds. His strike-the-triangle action is determined by and is a part of this musical environment—$E\epsilon$. His way of striking (energetically as he grimaces at his neighbor) is determined by and is an expression of John Smith's distinctive psychological system, $PE\psi$. The latter is a function of John's perceptions, social sensitivity, aggressiveness, energy levels, and so forth with which psychology can deal. But his strike-the-triangle action is determined by the superordinate behavior setting that incorporates and organizes a multiplicity of both human and nonhuman entities, conditions, and processes (including John Smith, the triangle, the action). Psychology has no concepts and theories for dealing with it. No amount of information about John Smith would account for the strike-the-triangle action; indeed, John is expendable; another pupil, even a machine, could take his place. The action would occur, and the setting would operate as smoothly as before. To comprehend it, overarching and behavior–milieu concepts and theories are required.

The paradoxical position of people in behavior settings presents methodological as well as theoretical problems to psychology. Psychology has methods for dealing with John Smith, with the teacher, and with audience members as individual subjects via observations, interviews, and questionnaires. They are the sole and sufficient source of information about their own psychological environments, about how they respond to Lower Juniors Music Program. But they are unsatisfactory sources of information about the setting within which their psychological environments are formed. Inhabitants have limited perspectives and biased perceptions of the unitary settings within which they are engaged. Activities that are specialized and demanding command their attention. So psychology's old reliable data source, individual subjects, are adequate for only a part of the behavior occurring in behavior settings. As with the tasks of creating, altering, and choosing behavior settings, that of assaying their behavioral, physical, and dynamic properties is one for outsiders: The behavior setting survey, which does not make use of subjects, is one approach to it.

40.11. NEW BUSINESS, OLD BUSINESS

Veteran prospectors often hedge their bets by staking new claims while working on old ones. We followed this prudent policy by continuing research on the original lode we staked, $E\psi$, while laying claim to and exploring the new one, $E\epsilon$. And now there are still newer claims.

After we discovered behavior settings and began to understand their importance for human behavior and for evaluating environments, we had a bright vision of their place in the behavior sciences. We even dreamed that the behavior setting survey would become a standard "instrument" for assessing the attributes of environments on a par with tests of the

traits of persons. But it has not happened, and now we understand why. Most of the journals that reviewed our publications were concerned primarily with the behavior of individual persons; they inevitably found our methods and theories difficult to incorporate into their procedures and ways of thinking. Few notices were severely critical, and many were hopefully intrigued, but there were few buyers until Karl Fox, an economist and student of social indicators and social accounts, wandered into the corner of environmental psychology where we were prospecting.

It happened in this way, a way that points to the fragility of connections across the behavioral sciences. At the invitation of an agency of the Methodist Church, Louise Barker and I attended a conference on research in the small community with special reference to the place of churches within it. This occurred on October 24–25, 1966. Five other social scientists and seven church administrators were present. Among the social scientists was Karl Fox, distinguished professor of economics at Iowa State University. We gave a paper entitled "The Churches of Midwest, Kansas, and Yoredale, Yorkshire: Their Contribution to the Environments of the Towns" (Gore & Hodapp, 1967, pp. 159–185). It was based on behavior-setting survey data. Fox's paper, entitled "Metamorphosis in America: A New Synthesis of Rural and Urban Society" (Gore & Hodapp, 1967, pp. 62–104) reported changes over half a century in the size and shape of rural communities using data on transportation, road systems, trade areas, labor markets, and so forth. Looking at these papers now, I see similarities that escaped me at the time: Both deal with specific place–time regions; both describe their attributes quantitatively; one common set of attributes is the behavior of the inhabitants of the regions.

Karl Fox must have seen similarities at the time, for after our paper he immediately expressed his interest, but only briefly, perhaps 15 minutes, for the conference was ended. My memory of his comments is dim, but the fragments "behavior output," "measurement in terms of time," and "in line with economic theory" remain. So exit Fox from our domain for a number of years. When he returned via correspondence and publications, we found that he and his colleagues and students had turned to behavior settings with great energy. In this they had important advantages:

1. They were not constrained by reductionist assumptions that limit observations and thinking about

behavior to persons; they were able to deal theoretically and methodologically with behavior en bloc.

2. They knew about and had access to extensive regional and national data archives that can be interpreted in behavior-setting terms (government, industry, and social publications on occupations, organizations, retail trade, population, manufacturing, and so forth).

3. They were skilled in quantitative economic models into which they have been able to fit behavior-setting survey data. Our early vision of regional and national assessments of "everyday living conditions" has been revived by Karl Fox and his associates (Felson, 1979; Fox, 1969a, 1969b, 1974a, 1974b, 1977, 1980, 1983, 1985, 1986; Fox & Ghosh, 1980, 1981; Fox & van Moeseke, 1973).

When we turn to the oldest claim we staked in Oskaloosa, the outlook is not so bright. The original claim was the field station, itself. Wright and I believed the success of the field station as a research facility would be an important contribution to environmental psychology. Its 25 years of operation turned up findings that would appear to vindicate it in this respect, but there is little evidence that the idea has caught on. We look in vain for environmental psychology equivalents of a Hopkins Marine Station, a Wood's Hole, a Lick Observatory, a Natural History Research Preserve, or other facilities common to the biological, geological, and astronomical sciences for continuously observing the ceaseless changes in particular volcano, prairie, or sector of the heavens. The ecological environments of people also ceaselessly change, and their nature, the processes involved, and their sources can only be discovered by ceaselessly observing the changes for which established research stations in particular communities, businesses, schools, churches, and so forth are essential. We have made a pitch for field stations in a number of publications (Barker, 1969, pp. 31–43; Barker & Associates, 1978, pp. 43–48; Barker & Wright, 1955, pp. 12–19), and we have investigated environments in Oskaloosa and Leyburn (Barker & Schoggen, 1973). We believe these discussions and studies have demonstrated the value of field stations for environmental psychology.

NOTE

1. For systematic accounts of methods and theories see Barker and Wright (1955), Barker (1968), and Barker and Associates (1978); reports and interpretations of major empirical investigations will be found in Barker and Gump (1964) and Barker and Schoggen (1973); important journal articles includes Barker (1960, 1963, 1965); a complete chronological list of the Midwest Psychological Field Station publications and theses is given in Barker and Associates (1978).

REFERENCES

Ashby, W.R. (1956). *An introduction to cybernetics.* New York: Wiley.

Barker, R.G. (1960). Ecology and motivation. In M.R. Jones (Ed.), *Nebraska symposium on motivation.* Lincoln: Nebraska University Press.

Barker, R.G. (1963). On the nature of the environment. *Journal of Social Issues, 19,* 17–38.

Barker, R.G. (1965). Explorations in ecological psychology. *American Psychologist, 20,* 1–14.

Barker, R.G. (1968). *Ecological psychology.* Stanford, CA: Stanford University Press.

Barker, R.G. (1969). Wanted: An eco-behavioral science. In E.P. Willems & H.L. Raush (Eds.), *Naturalistic viewpoints in psychological research.* New York: Holt, Rinehart, & Winston.

Barker, R.G., & Associates (Eds.). (1978). *Habitats, environments, and human behavior.* San Francisco: Jossey-Bass.

Barker, R.G., & Barker, L.S. (1978). Social actions of American and English children and adults. In R.G. Barker & Associates (Eds.), *Habitats, environments, and human behavior,* (p. 99–120). San Francisco: Jossey-Bass.

Barker, R.G., & Gump, P.V. (1964). *Big school, small school.* Stanford, CA: Stanford University Press.

Barker, R.G., & Schoggen, P. (1973). *Qualities of community life.* San Francisco: Jossey-Bass.

Barker, R.G., & Wright, H.F. (1971). *Midwest and its children.* Hamden, CT: Archon. (Original work published 1955).

Barker, R.G., Wright, H.F., Schoggen, M.F., & Barker, L.S. (1978). Day in the life of Mary Ennis. In R.G. Barker & Associates (Eds.), *Habitats, environments, and human behavior* (pp. 51–98). San Francisco: Jossey-Bass.

Barker, R.G., Wright, H.F., Barker, L.S., & Schoggen, M. (1961). *Specimen records of American and English children.* (Deposited in Spencer Research Library, University of Kansas.)

Brunswik, E. (1955). The conceptual framework of psychology. *International encyclopedia of unified science* (Vol. 1, Pt. 2). Chicago: University of Chicago Press.

Felson, M. (1979). How should social indicators be collected, organized, and modeled? *Contemporary Sociology, 8,* 40–41.

Fox, K.A. (1969a). Operations research and complex social systems. In J.K. Sengupta & K.A. Fox (Eds.), *Economic analysis and operations research: Optimization techniques in quantitative economic models.* Amsterdam: North-Holland.

Fox, K.A. (1969b). Toward a policy model of world economic development with special attention to the agricultural sector. In E. Thorbecke (Ed.), *The role of agriculture in economic development.* New York: Columbia University Press.

Fox, K.A. (1974a). Combining economic and noneconomic objectives in development planning: Problems of concept and measurement. In W. Sellekaerts (Ed.), *Economic development and planning: Essays in honour of Jan Tinbergen.* London: Macmillan.

Fox, K.A. (1974b). *Social indicators and social theory: elements of an operational system.* New York: Wiley.

Fox, K.A. (1977, June). Measuring economic and social performance: New theory, new methods, new data. In *Lectures in agricultural economics: Bicentennial year lectures sponsored by the Economic Research Service.* Washington, DC: U.S. Department of Agriculture, Economic Research Service.

Fox, K.A. (1980). Philosophical implications of a system of social accounts based on Roger Barker's ecological psychology and a scalar measure of total income. *Philosophica, 25,* 33–54.

Fox, K.A. (1983). The eco-behavioral view of human societies and its implications for systems science. *International Journal of Systems Science, 14,* 895–914.

Fox, K.A. (1985). *Social system accounts: Linking social and economic indicators through tangible behavior settings.* Dordrecht, Holland: Reidel.

Fox, K.A. (1986). An eco-behavioral approach to social system accounting. In A.J. MacFadyen & H.W. MacFadyen (Eds.), *Economic psychology: Intersection in theory and practice.* Amsterdam: North-Holland.

Fox, K.A., & Ghosh, S.K. (1980). Social accounts for urban centered regions. *International Regional Science Review, 5,* 33–50.

Fox, K.A., & Ghosh, S.K. (1981). A behavior setting approach to social accounts combining concepts and data from ecological psychology, economics, and studies of time use. In F.T. Juster & K.C. Land (Eds.), *Social accounting systems: Essays on the state of the art.* New York: Academic.

Fox, K.A., & van Moeseke, P. (1973). Derivation and implications of a scalar measure of social income. In H.C. Box, H. Linnemann, & P. de Wolff (Eds.), *Economic structure and development: Essays in honour of Jan Tinbergen.* Amsterdam: North-Holland, New York: American Elsevier.

Gore, W.J., & Hodapp, L.C. (Eds.). (1967). *Change in the small community.* New York: Friendship Press.

Gump, P.V., & Friesen, W.V. (1964). Satisfactions derived from nonclass settings. In R.G. Barker & P.V. Gump (Eds.), *Big school, small school* (pp. 94–114). Stanford, CA: Stanford University Press.

Heider, F. (1959). Thing and medium. *Psychological Issues, 1*(3), 1–34.

Latham, R., & Mathews, W. (Eds.). (1972). *The diary of Samuel Pepys* (Vol. 6, 1665). London: Bell.

Lewin, K. (1936a). *Principles of topological psychology.* New York: McGraw-Hill.

Lewin, K. (1936b). Lectures on topological psychology, University of Iowa, 1936. Notes by author elaborated in Barker, 1953 (pp. 30–37).

Lewin, K. (1941). Analyses of the concepts of whole, differentiation, and unity. *University of Iowa studies in child welfare, 18*(1), 226–261. (Reprinted in K. Lewin, *Field theory and social science.* New York: Harper & Bros., 1951).

Rabin, J. (1981). *Old glory: An American voyage.* New York: Simon & Schuster.

Russell, J.A., & Ward, L.M. (1982). Environmental psychology. *Annual Review of Psychology, 33,* 651–688.

Schoggen, M.F., Barker, L.S., & Barker, R.G. (1963). Structure of the behavior of American and English children. In R.G. Barker (Ed.), *The stream of behavior* (pp. 160–168). New York: Appleton-Century-Crofts.

Schoggen, M.F., Barker, L.S., & Barker, R.G. (1978). Behavior episodes of American and English children. In R.G. Barker & Associates (Eds.), *Habitats, environments, and human behavior* (pp. 121–124). San Francisco: Jossey-Bass.

Schoggen, P. (1963). Environmental forces in the everyday lives of children. In R.G. Barker (Ed.), *The stream of behavior* (pp. 42–69). New York: Appleton-Century-Crofts.

Wicker, A.W. (1968). Undermanning, performances, and students' subjective experiences in behavior settings of large and small high schools. *Journal of Personality and Social Psychology, 10,* 255–261.

Wicker, A.W. (1969). Size of church membership and members' support of church behavior settings. *Journal of Personality and Social Psychology, 13,* 278–288.

Wicker, A.W. (1979). *An introduction to ecological psychology.* Monterey, CA: Brooks/Cole.

Wicker, A.W. (1985). Getting out of our conceptual ruts. *American Psychologist, 40,* 1094–1103.

Willems, E.P. (1964). Forces toward participation in behavior settings. In R.G. Barker & P.V. Gump (Eds.), *Big school, small school* (pp. 115–135). Stanford, CA: Stanford University Press.

Willems, E.P., & Halstead, L.S. (1978). An eco-behavioral approach to health status and health care. In R.G. Barker & Associates (Eds.), *Habitats, environments, and human behavior* (pp. 169–189). San Francisco: Jossey-Bass.

Wright, H.F. (1967). *Recording and analyzing child behavior.* New York: Harper & Row.

Chapter 41

A HOLISTIC, DEVELOPMENTAL, SYSTEMS-ORIENTED ENVIRONMENTAL PSYCHOLOGY: SOME BEGINNINGS

Seymour Wapner, *Department of Psychology, Clark University, Worcester, Massachusetts*

The need for a theoretical perspective that will serve to integrate the work of the pragmatically oriented professional (e.g., architect, designer) and the theoretically oriented social scientist (e.g., environmental psychologist) is being recognized increasingly (cf. Ittelson, 1981; Moore, Tuttle, & Howell, 1982; Wapner, 1982-83; Wohlwill, 1982).[1] In this essay, I will describe some central issues relevant to the goal of the shaping of such an overarching perspective. These issues—including the controversies over psychology adopting a "natural science" versus "human science" approach, the unit of analysis to be employed, the appropriateness of descriptive versus causal explanation, teleological versus mechanistic analysis, precision versus validity, and the like—will

be resolved in a manner deemed consonant with the perspective offered here, which is presumed to have the potential to be integrative. I will then characterize the basic principles and central assumptions of this approach that is labeled as *holistic, developmental,* and *systems oriented.* Finally, I will sketch some implications for research provided by this perspective and some plans for its further development.

41.1. NEED FOR AN OVERARCHING THEORETICAL ORIENTATION

Both practitioners in the environmental field and social scientists, within and outside of environmental psychology, have expressed discontent, which directs us to a number of central issues relevant to development of an overarching theoretical orientation. On the one hand, there is concern by practitioners and by social scientists about the inadequacy of research and theory in the field of environmental study: For example, as Altman (1976) noted, the maverick environmental psychologists rejected laboratory investigation and pressed for naturalistic studies, and the maverick environmental practitioners objected to the traditionalists' focus on aesthetics and pressed for taking into account the needs and behaviors of the user. On the other hand, consternation is expressed by "mainstream" psychologists from such diverse quarters as those who point to the limitations of the natural science model (Giorgi, 1970; Russell & Ward, 1982), to the importance of context (Bell, 1979; Endler & Magnusson, 1976; Mischel, 1968; Scarr, 1979; White & Siegel, 1984), and to the need for ecological studies (Barker, 1968; Bronfenbrenner, 1977, 1979a, 1979b). The issues to be described that relate to these and other concerns of the environmental practitioner and psychologist (see e.g., Altman, 1973; Ittelson, 1973, 1981; Wohlwill, 1982) serve two important goals: (1) the characterization of differences in perspective of the social scientist and of the environmental practitioner; and (2) the formulation of resolutions of these issues that define the requisites of a theoretical approach that might provide overarching, integrative functions.

41.2. SOME BASIC ISSUES

41.2.1. Natural versus Human Science

The general differences between environmental psychologists and environmental practitioners parallel differences between a basic, standard, natural science approach and an applied, humanistic approach. The differences between these perspectives are mirrored in the history of psychology itself. From the time of its earliest beginnings as a scientific discipline, psychology has been overtly and covertly torn by the oppositional perspectives of "natural science" and "human science." Building on the now questionable interpretation that Wundt (1912, 1916, 1961) founded psychology as a natural science some 100 years ago (cf. Blumenthal, 1975; Mischel, 1970; Rychlak, 1981), the large majority of psychologists, giving selective attention to Wundt's accomplishments in his experimental laboratory, increasingly adopted the natural science perspective and it became the dominant view of twentieth-century psychology. At the same time, a minority of

psychologists over the years pointed out the failings of a psychology shaped by the natural science perspective. As an alternative, they advocated changes in keeping with the human science perspective that were laid down in the middle of the nineteenth century by Wilhelm Dilthey and others (cf. Giorgi, 1970).

As commonly understood, the natural science perspective regards observable behavior as the appropriate subject matter of psychology; specifies its goals as the explanation of behavior in terms of functional, cause–effect relations; prefers an analytic mode of analysis that begins with elements or parts and assumes that the whole can be understood through addition of those elements; minimizes differences between studying animals and humans; and adopts scientific experimentation as the appropriate methodology. Scientific experimentation involves the study of isolated behaviors in a laboratory situation rather than in the complexity of their natural context, the formulation of hypotheses, the assessment of relations between independent and dependent variables with other factors held constant, the treatment of the experimenter as a confounding variable, the minimization of the experimenter's effect on the experiment, the minimization of the subject's awareness of the object of the experiment, and the use of random sampling and quantitative techniques to generalize from the sample studied to the population as a whole.

In contrast, as shown by Giorgi (1970) and others, the human science perspective regards human experience and the higher functions of human thought and action as the appropriate subject matter of psychology; specifies as its goal the understanding of experience or the explication of structural relationships, pattern, or organization that constitutes its meaning; prefers a synthetic mode of analysis that begins with the whole field of which they are parts; adopts the descriptive method where close, empirical analysis is made of what is given in human experience with the goal of explicating the structural relationships among the elements that constitute a phenomenon; seeks detailed analysis of limited numbers of cases that are presumably prototypic of larger classes of events; accepts experimenter bias that is part of the analysis; uses open-ended nonleading questions so that the subject can, implicitly or explicitly, choose his or her terminology and organization in structuring his or her experience; investigates prototypic cases naturalistically, in the complexity of the life situation; and carries out qualitative analysis through naturalistic observation, empirical, and phenomenological methods.

The differences between these two perspectives touch on a number of specific issues, now to be considered, that are relevant to the task—describing a perspective that may serve to integrate the work of the pragmatically oriented professional and the social scientist in the environmental fields—addressed by this essay.

41.2.2. Unit of Analysis and Transactionalism

What constitutes the unit of analysis in environmental psychology probably comprises the most central of current issues facing the field and its future. Its definition is at once a reflection of, and a determiner of, theoretical perspectives, of the formulation of research problems, methodologies, interpretations, and of the nature of potential applications. Its definition permits or excludes avenues of communication and commonality of research by practitioner and scientist. Altman (1976), especially, and others (Ittelson, 1973; Wapner, Kaplan, & Cohen, 1973; Wapner, 1978, 1980, 1981a, 1981b) have made this issue focal. Altman (1981), for example, refers to this issue of unit of analysis as part of "the emerging revolution in psychology" and states:

> Traditionally, the environment has been treated as a primary class of independent variables, and as being distinctively *separate* from behavior and thereby existing in its own right. Environmental factors have been considered to be important determiners of behavior, but they have been viewed as being separate, different and independent from psychological processes. (Altman, 1981, p. 5)

This separatist approach is taken, for example, by Wohlwill and his associates in their attempts to relate dimensions of *E* (environment) to *R* (response) (e.g., Wohlwill, 1973; Wohlwill & Kohn, 1976). The separatist approach is also taken by others who adopt a stimulus-response view that assumes the environment is an independent variable and behavior a dependent variable.

In a past *Annual Review of Psychology* chapter on environmental psychology, Russell and Ward (1982) question this partitive, causal view by emphasizing goal orientation and planning and by recognizing that "the environment is more than an antecedent to behavior; it affords opportunities for future action" (p. 154). Altman (1981) notes "that environment and behavior are an integral or *transactional* unity, such that behavior and environment mutually define one another, and that, indeed, one cannot literally understand a phenomenon without studying environment and behavior as a *single unit* of analysis" (p. 5). He also states that "this transactional view implies that environments cannot be dealt with independently of

the behaviors that occur within them. Thus this emerging point of view does not refer to the *inter*-action of people and environments but to *trans*-action of people and environments" (p. 7).

The transactional view was described almost four decades ago by Dewey and Bentley (1949), advanced by Ames (1951), Cantril (1950) and Ittelson and Cantril (1954), and elaborated systematically by Ittelson (1960, 1973, 1975, 1976, 1978). It is implied as well in the notion of "behavior setting" originated by Barker (1968) and his associates. The transactionalist view is also explicitly stated as an ingredient in the organismic-developmental theory by Wapner and associates (cf. Wapner, 1977, 1980, 1981a, 1981b). Furthermore, Stokols (1978) seems to adopt the transactional perspective when he states that "the focus of analysis generally is on the interrelations among people and their sociophysical milieu" (p. 254). A similar emphasis is implied when he calls attention to *"behavior–environment" congruence* as an increasingly important theoretical and environmental design tool, and when he speaks of the organism as active and reactive in its goal-directed activity to achieve optimal self-world states (cf. Stokols, 1979; Stokols & Shumaker, 1981). It is also to be noted that Zube, Sell, and Taylor (1982) have analyzed landscape perception, a problem clearly of interest to both the practitioner and environmental psychologist, from a transactionalist point of view.

As I see it, adoption of the transactionalist view by environmental practitioner and psychologist should provide a potential for a synergistic relation between both because it will make for recognition of commonality among problems, foster interdisciplinary cooperation, and promote the possibility of solutions that are satisfactory to both.

41.2.3. Holism versus Elementarism

The practitioner and the social scientist, as human beings who are prone to seek simplicity (cf. Rapoport, 1972), are both self-pressured to seek an elementaristic analysis and are thereby subject to its limitations. Such elementaristic, partitive analysis is exemplified (1) in treatment of the person-in-environment system as if each part, person, or environment exists in isolation; (2) in treatment of aspects of person functioning (cognitive, affective, and valuative processes) and within cognition (sensorimotor, perceptual, memory, imaginative thought, and symbolic processes) as if each part process exists in isolation; and (3) in treatment of aspects of the environment (physical, interpersonal, sociocultural) as if each facet exists in isolation.

Because of the differential emphasis by environmental practitioners and environmental psychologists on parts that are isolated or hypostatized, the potential common ground on which they might relate is not so readily available. A holistic view that emphasizes relativity of a unit or part to a larger whole seems to provide a greater opportunity for the interaction and intersection of research activities of environmental psychology and the practitioner. Hence, when the practitioner takes on the holistic attitude that the physical aspects of the environment do not exist independent of its interpersonal and sociocultural aspects, then his or her research questions may be broadened or made more amenable to considering the larger whole, that is, considering a larger range of the facets of the environment and of the person-in-environment system. For example, with a holistic approach, the American city planner is more likely to give attention to helping people solve their problems and realize their goals rather than being concerned only with buildings and the physical environment (cf. Gans, 1969). Similarly, a holistic approach should operate to mitigate the neglect of the physical environment attributed to the early human ecologists by Michelson (1976).

41.2.4. Explication versus Causal Explanation

Because a considerable amount of the practitioner's research is concerned with description or explication, in some scientifically oriented quarters the pressure to shape such studies into causally oriented research questions represents a point of tension between practitioner and social scientist. This issue of explication (description) versus causal explanation has already been touched on earlier in the discussion of the distinction between natural science and human science.

The central antagonism here seems to come from the degree of remoteness between the phenomena of everyday life and the theoretical constructs used to account for the phenomena (Bibace, Kaplan, & Wapner, 1969) and from the explicationists' view that the causal explanationists sacrificed relevance for rigor and focused on methodology and hypothetical, theoretical entities. Explication involves identifying the meaning of the phenomena studied, the phenomena's structure, or how the parts are organized in a subject's description of a situation.[2] Because explication makes focal the meaning of the phenomenon or what is to be explained, and causal explanation suggests directions for reexamination of phenomena, both of these approaches to understanding comple-

ment each other, and both should be fostered (cf. Bibace et al., 1969).

41.2.5. Teleological versus Mechanistic Analysis

Another point of controversy relevant to the tension between practitioner and social scientist concerns the preference of some social scientists for mechanistically oriented analyses over teleologically oriented approaches. Those who are mechanistically oriented object to a teleological formulation on the grounds that it implies that a consequence of behavior is treated as a cause. This does not hold if it is assumed that the goal is represented in disposition to act prior to appearance of the overt behavior. I believe that both causal and teleological analyses are necessary in analyzing person-in-environment system functioning because they answer different questions that contribute to understanding. A causal analysis seeks to answer what, under what conditions, does such and such take place ("how"); a teleological analysis explains "why" the behavior occurred in terms of the goal or end state toward which the system was directed (Bibace et al., 1969; Kaplan, 1967).

However, insistence on the admissability of teleological analysis opens the way for systematically including *planning* in the analysis of person-in-environment systems. The problem of planning is a crucial aspect of the work of practitioners in the environmental fields and represents an important, although until recently neglected, problem in psychology. That is, as described later, planning should be considered with respect to the general problem of the spatiotemporal character of daily life.

41.2.6. Spatiotemporality and Planning

Both the spatiotemporal features of ongoing behavior (events) and the correlated problems of planning are of crucial significance for the development of a perspective that attempts to satisfy the needs of both the environmental psychologist and the practitioner. This gap in treatment of events and planning touches on an area that is obviously of central concern, for example, for the city planner whether his or her objectives are buildings and the physical environment or the people who use the environment (Gans, 1969). It is also of central concern for the architect, independent of whether he or she is of the "architecture and design" variety or of the "landscape" variety.

Psychology has focused on spatiality and temporality as two separate entities.[3] Psychology has to some extent neglected to recognize that the everyday activity of the human being always involves ongoing events that by definition are characterized spatiotemporally and that it is only for purposes of analysis that spatial features and temporal features are abstracted from this primordial condition of the ongoing flow of experience.

A spatiotemporal analysis is implied by planning because it involves reference to a future course of action or a series of actions. A decade ago, when Wapner and Cirillo (1973) reviewed the literature on development of planning,[4] we concluded that this problem had not been explored extensively. We noted that Murray (1938, 1951, 1959) recognized this neglect by pointing to the need for analysis of *serials* or the long-term activities of individuals in keeping with plans and actions. He accounted for the paucity of work on this problem by recognizing that the cognitive psychologists' main concern was restricted to conditions, processes, or operations whereby the person comes to acquire objective knowledge and understanding about his or her physical environment. Miller, Galanter, and Pribram (1960) sharply and creatively focused on the relation between image and planning. In contrast to the cognitive psychologists who are concerned only with images (cognitive representation), Miller and colleagues' (1960) goal was to point the "way to map the cognitive representation into the appropriate pattern of activity" (p. 13). Accordingly, they defined a plan as "an hierarchical process in the organism that can control the order in which a sequence of operations is to be performed" (Miller et al., 1960, p. 16). They are not concerned with the problem of analyzing a plan "as the everyday activity of working out in advance a future course of action" (Wapner & Cirillo, 1973, p. 8).

Although earlier efforts on studying planning were sporadic,[5] there has been a burgeoning of psychological work on the problem of planning during the last few years in concert with large strides in advancing computers and work in artificial intelligence. Though the more recent interest in studying development of planning (cf. Forbes & Greenberg, 1982; Pea, 1982) and Schutz's (1951) earlier efforts on describing projects of action are clearly relevant to the theoretical problem of concern here, it seems most appropriate to turn to some other recent voices within environmental psychology proper who are also expressing the need for introducing spatiotemporal relations and planning. This is expressly the case in Russell and Ward's (1982) annual review of environmental psychology. For them these notions are so pervasive that

three steps serve as the organizing framework for their review, namely, (1) planning and the image, (2) travel, and (3) behavior-in-place. Another voice, that of Little (1983), builds on Murray's (1938, 1951, 1959) work in personality theory. Little makes a powerful case for the notion of "personal projects," which he believes is "a new unit of analysis for the study of personality in its social, physical and temporal context" (Little, 1983). He sketches four general steps in the development of personal projects: Stage 1—Inception; Stage 2—Planning; Stage 3—Action; and Stage 4—Termination. Four to six substages are further delineated within each of these, and a methodology for assessing structure and content of personal projects is described. This concept of "personal project" is considered a basis for linking personality and environmental psychology.

Related to Little's (1983) notion is the concept of "subjective life stage" proposed by Stokols (1982) and Stokols and Shumaker (1983). This is a contextual unit of analysis referring to the "spatially and temporally bounded phases of a person's life that are associated with particular goals and plans" (Stokols, 1982, p. 40). Each life stage is uniquely and subjectively characterized with respect to "personal projects," settings, routines, and life domains, including home, work, community, and recreation. Experientially defined intra- and interstage units of analysis are distinguished that incorporate spatial and temporal features and the relations between the life domains.

Another perspective on planning was described by Wapner and Cirillo (1973) and is synoptically characterized in the following quotation:

> Our own concern is with planning in the sense of plotting a future course of action....If one emphasizes not "methodical arrangement" but "prior formulation" in the definition of "plan," one is oriented not to methods of action in general but methods which include as an early step a certain type of *symbolic preparation*. A *preparatory action* (cf. Kotarbinski, 1965), in general, is some concrete act, such as striking a match, which makes a subsequent concrete act, such as lighting a fire, possible or easier. Preparatory actions may include acquiring appropriate materials, learning how to use them, etc. A plan is a symbolic preparatory action in that the planner conceives of, imagines a method independently of carrying out the concrete actions embodying that method. (Wapner & Cirillo, 1973, p. 13)

These and other efforts that introduce spatiotemporality and planning in the analysis of experience and transactions of persons-in-environments represent advances in conceptualization that may effectively contribute to an overarching theoretical perspective.[6]

41.2.7. Synchronic (Cross-Sectional, Single Frame) versus Diachronic (Longitudinal, Frame Sequence) Analysis

If one takes seriously the proposition that a spatio-temporal characterization of the living situation is primordial, then research problems of interest to both the practitioner and scientist necessarily encompass both diachronic (temporally changing relationships in and among environmental objects) and synchronic (an atemporal relationship between abstracted variables) analyses. For the practitioner, the unfolding of a project on city planning or the characterization of the standing patterns of behavior in a building complex quickly come to mind as examples respectively of diachronic and synchronic analyses. For the academician, such problems as the changing relations in transactions from the time of entry to the time of exit in a new environment and the comparisons of experience and transactions in a given environment are also respective comparisons that fit under the diachronic and synchronic categories, respectively. This kind of formal, organizational characterization of empirical studies alerts us to ask different questions and provides a common ground for categorization of the work of practitioners and scientists that features large differences in content.

41.2.8. Value-Free versus Action-Oriented Research

Research may be regarded as involving a value-free, objective examination of what exists—the position held by many a social scientist with a natural science view—or as being *directly* concerned with improving the lot of the human being—the position taken by the pragmatically oriented environmental professional with a human science orientation. This distinction requires resolution.

I believe that to serve the efforts of both the professionally oriented practitioner (e.g., architect, urban planner) and the academic scientist, an overarching theoretical perspective should accept and incorporate in inquiry a number of value assumptions. It should, for example, recognize that it is impossible to conduct value-free research; it should further reject the assumption that science is value free; and it should also accept the value that inquiry and praxis

are interrelated scientific goals. More concretely, an integrative perspective should be concerned with knowing about the nature of person-in-environment transactions so as to help people improve the quality of those transactions, to enable them to enrich their experience of the world in which they live, to change those environments that hamper their functioning, and to build environments that optimize the quality of their lives. With such goals, no exception can be taken. The question of the most effective means to those ends remains, for now, an open one.

41.2.9. Basic versus Applied Research

A related issue concerns the differences between basic and applied research. Some representatives of the natural science perspective assume that fundamental—basic, if you will—theoretical research can only be conducted under the restricted conditions of a laboratory and that research loses its theoretical potency once it moves to the setting of the everyday world in which we all live. That we do research on problems in the complexity of everyday life that have implications for everyday behavior as well as for private and public policy does not mean that such ecologically oriented research is not basic. On the contrary, it is basic in the sense that it contributes to understanding and theoretical conceptualization.[7] This issue seems best resolved for the practitioner and for academicians by eliminating the distinction between basic and applied, or, more positively, by accepting the proposition that basic research—research that leads to general understanding and clarification of conceptualization of a broad range of phenomena and questions—can appropriately be done on problems that immediately, as well as remotely, touch on human needs for which action may be readily required or taken. Moreover, if the academician, in the stages of formulating a problem and shaping a relevant methodology, followed the lead of the practitioner and took on an action-oriented concern that posed questions of praxis, it might bring us even closer to our long-term goals of finding ways to achieve more optimal relations between persons and the world in which they live.

41.2.10. Precision versus Validity

Another issue that is closely related to the dichotomy between basic and applied research separates the practitioner from the academic researcher.

This concerns the conflict that exists between precise analysis of highly limited, controlled phenomena in laboratory situations that are distant from the life situation and ethologically or clinically oriented closer-to-life situations whose complexity obviates the possibility of precision. This issue, it seems to me, can be resolved not by taking sides on either end of this polarity but rather by admitting as good science both kinds of studies and characterizing conditions when one or the other type of study is more appropriate.

Levels of Organization

The resolution to this issue resides in the recognition that organisms, environments as well as the ends toward which organisms are directed and the instrumentalities by which they achieve them may be described and arranged in a series of successively ordered levels of complexity with striking changes in patterns of organization (Wapner et al., 1973). Categorizing organismic-environment systems in this way builds on the *levels of organization* concept (von Bertalanffy, 1950, 1962, 1968; Feibleman, 1954; Herrick, 1949, 1956; Lazlow, 1969; Novikoff, 1945a, 1945b; Schneirla, 1949, 1957; Steward, 1951). In using this concept, we assume that physical-biological, psychological, and sociocultural subsystems are qualitatively different but related according to specifiable contingencies, that is, the levels of organizations are nested or in graduated order. Sociocultural functioning (e.g., living by governmental rules and regulations) requires or is contingent on psychological functioning (e.g., sensorimotor acting, perceiving, thinking, imagining, feeling, valuing) that, in turn, is contingent on physical-biological functioning (e.g., blood circulation).

Because the laws describing the levels differ qualitatively, a critical task is to characterize organism—environment system functioning at each of these levels. This requires "methods of research and analysis appropriate to the particular level" (Novikoff, 1945a, 1945b). Precise, controlled laboratory experimentation might appropriately be used with phenomena at lower levels of organization (i.e., biological systems) and more complex, less precise modes of analysis used when addressing person–environment relations at the sociocultural level of organization. Thus to encompass the needs of both the scientist and the practitioner, science must regard as admissible both controlled laboratory studies and ethologically or clinically oriented field studies appropriate to the problem addressed and the levels of organization or relations among levels of organization to which the analysis is directed. Moreover, such a stance will have integrative value for scientist and practitioner and thereby have a salubrious effect on each of their independent activities.

41.2.11. Means-Oriented versus Problem-Oriented Investigations

Despite Whyte's (1977), Michelson's (1975), and Zeisel's (1981) surveys, some have expressed the concern that environmental psychology is relatively restricted in the methods it employs; that the methods employed are restricted insofar as they have their origins in the disciplines of the particular investigator; and that a given technique—for example, a sketch map—sometimes shapes the problem rather than the problem and theory shaping the method.[8] We are grappling here with the fact that one's theoretical perspective has a powerful impact on problem formulation and methodology. For some, this is acknowledged and accepted (Allen, 1977; Wapner, 1981a; Winkel, 1977). For others, method should be free from the bonds of theory. Although this issue is perhaps not resolvable to everyone's satisfaction, it is wise to alert ourselves again that there is "no such thing" as pure objectivity; rather, we all start with a perspective. The issue comes down to one of developing self-recognition of our own perspective and then being able to make overt our hidden, covert assumptions, metaphors, and world views (Wapner, 1980).

New directions are needed. Allen (1977) suggested the use of convergent methodologies, that is, a diverse range of methods focusing on a single construct of theoretical interest. One difficulty, of course, is that differences in methods may be bound to differences in substantive aspects of conceptualization. In choosing methods, it is necessary to be careful lest concern for sophisticated methodology blind one from following the crucial dictum that method, means, or instrumentalities are subordinate to theoretical conceptualization, problems, and goals. Neither practitioner nor social scientist should attempt to take over a set of methods from the other without questioning their relevance to the problem. A rule that must appropriately hold for social scientist and practitioner alike is that the method must not dictate the nature of the problem; we must remain problem oriented and be creative in developing new methods to fit the requirements of the particular research problem to be solved (Maslow, 1946).[9]

41.2.12. Summary of Requisites for an Overarching Approach

Some recent reviews of the field of environmental psychology and design research (Moore et al., 1982; Russell and Ward, 1982; Villeco & Brill, 1981) have expressed opinions that show a remarkable convergence with my own stance on the issues just discussed. Villeco and Brill (1981) and Moore and colleagues (1983, 1985) point to the insufficiency and needs in theory and method. According to these two reviews, environment research design questions the traditional hypothesis-testing approach; it is showing a growing rejection of the simple cause–effect model of science; it is concerned with applied as well as basic research; it favors multiple, interdisciplinary, holistic methods; it admits qualitative as well as quantitative analysis at all levels of complexity; it recognizes the role of values in shaping research; and it is devoted explicitly to inquiry that is problem oriented, action oriented, and studies experience and action in real-life settings.

We find a parallel consonance of opinion in Russell and Ward's (1982) contribution to the *Annual Review of Psychology*. They view the organism as cognitively active, as goal directed, and as continuously involved in broadly conceived planned activity. Their conception of the environment as a complex of hierarchically experienced aspects focuses on person-environment relationships and on meaning and expectation. They include affective as well as cognitive part processes, and advocate analyzing psychological processes. However, they restrict the importance of development to ontogenesis, reject S-R approaches, and view the laboratory as less than ideal for studying many issues in environmental psychology. Finally, they focus on "thinking rather than data gathering" (Russell & Ward, 1982, p. 680).

Given the description of issues and modes of resolving them, we may now turn to the organismic-developmental systems approach that is presumed to have potential to serve as an overarching integrative perspective.[10]

41.3. THE ORGANISMIC-DEVELOPMENTAL SYSTEMS PERSPECTIVE

After describing synoptically the current formulation of this approach,[11] some of its implications for research will be sketched, and brief mention will be made of some plans for its further development.

The version of the theoretical approach presented here has changed and evolved in interaction with empirical study of research problems linked to environmental psychology (e.g., Kaplan et al., 1976; Wapner et al., 1973; Wapner, 1978, 1981a). The characterization presented is organized around a series of basic assumptions and procedural principles.

41.3.1. Basic Assumptions and Procedural Principles

Psychological Inquiry
From the organismic-developmental perspective, it is assumed that the purpose of psychological inquiry is to understand living organisms in their environments. Although the approach has applicability to all living organisms, here, despite the value of comparative animal study, the presentation is largely restricted to human beings.

Transactionalism
In keeping with the purpose of understanding living organisms in their environment, transactionalism is accepted. Transactionalism treats the person's "behavings, including his most advanced knowings, as activities not of himself alone, nor even as primarily his, but as processes of the full situation of organism-environment" (Dewey & Bentley, 1949, p. 104; also see Cantril, 1950; Ittelson, 1973.)

Person-in-Environment System Is the Unit to be Analyzed
Correlative with transactionalism is the assumption that the person-in-environment system is the unit to be analyzed.[12] This implies that every person is always inextricably embedded in some environment, that is, in some physical, chemical, biological, interpersonal, sociocultural context. It implies that the human being is part of a larger whole—the person-in-environment system. Accordingly, the treatment of the person and his or her environment as separable, independent parts, which influence one another, represents a partitive, elementaristic, and interactional analysis that is rejected.

Basic Components of the Person-in-Environment System
Person-in-environment system functioning is viewed as having both structural and dynamic components. Structural components are the person and his or her environment. Dynamic components are involved in the transactions of the person with his or her environment.[13] Central here are purposive transactions in

which an organism employs specifiable means to achieve some person-in-environment end state or a particular relation between the person and his or her environment.

Structural (Part–Whole) and Dynamic (Means–Ends) Analyses

Given these components of person-in-environment systems, we may analyze and compare them with one another in formal terms. In such a formal, comparative analysis, a system is treated as having a characteristic structure that is maintained or transformed by specifiable dynamic processes. Focusing on the characteristic structure of the system entails its analysis into more or less differentiated parts or subsystems that are more or less integrated with one another in specifiable ways. Focusing on the dynamics of the system entails the determination of the means by which a characteristic structure is achieved or maintained. The structural, or part–whole, analysis of a system and the dynamic, or means–ends, analysis of a system are two complementary aspects of the formal description of the system.

Teleological Directedness

The inclusion of dynamic components—means and ends—in the person-in-environment system is consonant with the proposition that transactions are regarded not simply as being random and chaotic but rather as being teleologically directed, that is, the person-in-environment system exhibits directed change from some initial state of functioning to some end state. Such change can vary widely in complexity, for example: (1) change from the person being initially located in one place to an end state in which the person is located in another place; or (2) change from the person living in a depressed, crime-laden city to the person living in a crime-free, exciting, growing community, and the like. The person-in-environment end state is assumed to be an ingredient in the initial person-in-environment state, for example, as a potential for particular transactions. The "means" brought into play may refer to structures used as instrumentalities (e.g., legs, an automobile, a building) or to the processes (e.g., walking, moving from one place to another, constructing a building) in which the instrumentalities play a role.

Planning

The concept of planning incorporated as part of the approach directly follows from the notion of teleological directedness. Planning is used here in the sense of plotting a future course of actions that move the person-in-environment system from some initial state of functioning to some end state. Such movement involves transactions (cognitive, affective, and evaluative experience, and action)[14] with the environment on the part of the person. Moreover, the formulation of a plan involves a set of acts that are preparatory for carrying out a more complex set of concrete actions. The person who formulates the preparatory plan may or may not carry out the concrete actions defined by the plan.

> To plan is sometimes used to mean to give visible form or representation to a method, especially graphically, as in "architect's plan." Our use of the term "plan" in the sense of formulating beforehand, or preparing symbolically, entails that the planner conceives of a method independently of carrying it out and so can represent the method independently of embodying it in action, e.g., by depicting it, diagramming it, playacting it and, most importantly, by describing the method verbally. For our purposes, then, a plan is a representation, verbal or otherwise, of a method of action being considered or adopted for the future. (Wapner & Cirillo, 1973, p. 27)

Structuring and Organizing

That the organism actively structures and transacts with the environment in terms of goals or ends that are achieved by a variety of means or instrumentalities is in keeping with the constructive emphasis of the perspective. Human beings are regarded as spontaneously active, striving agents capable of constructing and construing their environments in various ways and acting in terms of their own experience. They are active creators of the experienced environment in which they function. Wapner and colleagues (1973) have characterized such striving in terms of Kuntz's (1968) notion that the human organism, functioning at the sociocultural level, exhibits a "rage for order."

Multiple Intentionality

Closely linked to structuring and organizing is the capacity of the person to adopt different intentions or cognitive attitudes with respect to self/world relations and thereby experience different figure ground relationships with respect to the person-in-environment system of which he or she is a part. The experience of "object" or "figure" (as opposed to ground) holds not only for the various features of the environment (e.g., size, shape, and form of objects—things and people—"out there") but also for various features of the self (e.g., size and shape of my own body, or self-esteem, etc.), and for the relation between self and environment (e.g., feeling secure and comfortable in a given building).[15]

Environmental Objects

The variety of objects comprising the person-in-environment system is broadly defined to include the interpersonal (people) and the sociocultural (laws, codified rules, mores, etc.) domains as well as the physical domain (e.g., things, flora, places). The person and environment are complementary parts of a single system. Identifying the person pole as the experiencing subject raises the question of identifying his or her environment. A variety of terms have been used to describe the experienced environment ("behavioral environment"—Koffka, 1935; "umwelt," "phenomenal world," "selfworld"—von Uexkül, 1957; "psychological environment"—Lewin, 1935) and to distinguish it from the physical environment (e.g., Koffka's, 1935, distinction between the "behavioral" and the "geographic" environment). A crucial reason for distinguishing between these environments is that there is no one-to-one correspondence between them. A single perceptual experience may correspond to many different physical inputs (e.g., perceptual constancy), and a single physical input may correspond to more than one perceptual experience (e.g., ambiguous figures). Moreover, evidence can be adduced to show that the experienced environment, rather than the physical environment, is the effective environment within which an experiencing person functions. For example, despite physical indicators of the security of an environment such as patrolling police officers, an elderly person may not be willing to venture out of his or her apartment unless he or she experiences the neighborhood as safe. There is also evidence to show that the goals, plans, and tasks of the person have a significant effect on the way he or she experiences the environment (Apter, 1976; Wofsey, Rierdan, & Wapner, 1979).

Another important consideration relates to the inclusion of people as one class of objects in an environment structured by the experiencing person. The person who structures the environment is considered focal in the analysis of that person-in-environment system; in other words, that system is phenomenologically defined from the person's perspective. We may also analyze transactions from the vantage point of the people who comprise the environment of the original focal person. In that process, those people in turn become focal as analysis proceeds from their perspective. By considering a series of such analyses, each from the perspective of a different focal person, it is possible in effect to create a collage comprised of the multiple perspectives of person components of the system. Consider some examples. Though a child may be focal in the study of transition into nursery school, we may also look into the perspectives of teachers, of peers, or of others constituting the person component of the child's nursery school or home environment. In a study of retirement in which the retiree is the focal person, we also may be concerned with how members of the retiree's environment, for example, spouse, construe the retiree's experience (Hornstein & Wapner, 1984, 1985).

Transactions with Objects (Experience and Action)

Transactions with objects are assumed to take place in terms of cognition (objects as known through sensorimotor, perceptual, learning, memory, thinking, imagining, and symbolizing processes), affection (processes involved in feeling and emotional tone), and valuation (processes involving comparison with personal and collective standards, e.g., as in aesthetic evaluation). These processes and correlated aspects of experience are generally treated separately to simplify analysis even though they occur simultaneously in everyday life. Such independent analyses of these processes may result in losing the essence of the phenomena we seek to describe and analyze. An important task to be solved is one of developing units and modes of analysis that will preserve and reflect our everyday experience in all of its complexity. A step in this direction was made by Werner (1940) when he distinguished between *physiognomic* perception (though actually lifeless, things appear animate with affective qualities, e.g., a landscape appears gay, melancholy, or pensive) and *geometric-technical* perception (things are known according to their matter of fact qualities such as color, size, and shape).

Multiple Worlds

People are assumed to live in different, yet related experiential worlds (Schutz, 1971) or diverse spheres of activity such as the multiple worlds of family, of work, of school, of recreation, of community, and others. Taken more generally, this relationship can be described with respect to a given person's involvement in one or more person-in-environment systems, for example, home, school, work, and the like. Any one person, for example, a child, may be considered as central in each of these worlds, and the relationship among these worlds may be characterized in structural terms. This has been assessed in a study on retirement by use of a questionnaire that examines the structural relation between the individual's "work world" and other social worlds.[16] Individuals are characterized as having an "isolated" relation between work and other worlds (where worlds are separate), a "moderately integrated" relation (where worlds affect one another), or a "closely integrated" relation between these worlds (where worlds are interdependent) (Hornstein & Wapner, 1984, 1985).

Holistic Nature of Person-in-Environment Functioning

The perspective is principally rooted in the organismic world hypothesis (Pepper, 1942).[17] For this world view, the root metaphor is the living organism where a *holistic* unity or oneness is maintained transcending and integrating local or partial functions. In general, the person-in-environment system operates as a unified whole so that a disturbance in one part affects other parts of the totality. Part processes of person-in-environment system functioning are integrated in such a way that the system operates as a unified whole.

Levels of Organization

Processes or functions may be, as noted earlier, categorized in terms of levels of organization. Biological functioning (e.g., respiration), psychological functioning (e.g., perceiving, thinking, remembering), and sociocultural functioning (e.g., living by governmental rules and regulations) are respectively related in a contingency fashion, the latter requiring functioning at the prior levels and psychological functioning requiring biological functioning. The levels differ qualitatively, and functioning at one level is not reducible to functioning on a lower level.

When the levels-of-organization notion is considered with respect to the proposition that the person-in-environment system is the unit to be analyzed, then the person-in-environment system can be further differentiated. At the highest level of the organism–environment system functioning is the person, an acculturated human being who operates in a world governed by collective rules and is directed toward long-term values and norms that are achieved by conceptual systems, language, logic, science, and the like. The person–world system is contingent on its functioning at the agent–habitat level. Here the human operates in an environment, termed habitat, where social (people) and nonsocial (things) objects are present. Operating at this level, the human is referred to as agent and is directed toward episodic incentives such as finding food or a mate, avoiding danger by use of such instrumentalities as tools and mechanisms that enhance the senses and extend the

functions of the body parts. Operation at the agent–habitat level is contingent on operation at the respondent–ambience level. This involves reflex responsivity to the physical-chemical environment or ambience (e.g., temperature) by use of biological, inherited parts (e.g., metabolic rate). Thus sociocultural functioning on the person–world level is contingent on functioning at the agent–habitat level that in turn is contingent on functioning at the respondent–ambience level (Wapner et al., 1973).

The holistic assumption holds for functioning at different levels of organization. A person acts with respect to ambience, habitat, and world in relation to one and another. Responsivity at the respondent–ambience level may affect the higher levels, that is, the mode of transacting at the agent–habitat and/or the person–world levels. In contrast, perturbations to functioning at the higher level, the person–world level, may affect modes of transacting at the lower levels. (See Feibleman, 1954, for a discussion of relationships among levels.)

The holistic assumption also holds for functioning with a given level. Such part processes, identified earlier, as knowing (including, e.g., sensorimotor functioning, perceiving, thinking, learning, imagining, symbolizing), feeling, and valuing are contemporaneous and integrated in the normal functioning adult. The holistic assumption also bears on components of the person-in-environment system. The person, his or her environment, and the transactions among them involving means and ends are all interdependent.

Equilibration Tendencies

Person-in-environment systems are characterized as operating in a dynamic equilibrium or steady state. These ongoing person-in-environment states may be disturbed by a change in the person, in the environment, or in both. Such perturbations may make for dramatic qualitative changes in relations among system components (transactions, person, environment, ends and means). It is assumed that following a perturbation of the person-in-environment system, there is a tendency toward reestablishment of a new dynamic equilibrium or ongoing person-in-environment state directed toward accomplishing short-term and long-term goals (cf. Piaget, 1952, p. 256; 1971, p. 25).

Spatiotemporal Nature of Experience

As noted earlier, everyday life is characterized by the ongoing flow of events. That the person-in-environment system is in dynamic equilibrium implies that it is always undergoing change. If one considers the daily activities of the ordinary person over the course of an ordinary day, he or she is constantly carrying out various activities while moving from one place to another, namely bedroom, bathroom, kitchen, garage, automobile, city streets, office buildings, office, meeting room, restaurant, and is in contact with different people at different places, and so forth. Though this ongoing flow of events is continuous, it is usually structured into a succession of discrete units, for example, having breakfast, that are separated from preceding and subsequent units by temporal boundaries (Wapner & Lebensfeld-Schwartz, 1976). The abstraction from continuous spatiotemporal change may not merely be temporally bounded units independent of spatial objects (e.g., an event described with respect to its duration independent of changes in people and/or objects); rather, the abstraction can also be with respect to spatially bounded units independent of temporality (e.g., a building that represents a spatial figure abstracted from the flow of everyday spatiotemporal events).

Thus we may look at the person-in-environment system diachronically and conduct longitudinal or frame sequence studies, or we may look at the person-in-environment system synchronically and conduct cross-sectional or single-frame studies (Kaplan et al., 1976).

Orthogenetic Principle

Components of systems and relations among such components as well as part processes of person-in-environment systems are assumed to be *developmentally orderable* in terms of the orthogenetic principle (Kaplan, 1967; Werner, 1940, 1957). This principle defines development in terms of the degree of organization attained by a system. The more differentiated and hierarchically integrated a system is in terms of its parts, and of its means and ends, the more highly developed it is said to be.[18] As a formal definition of development, the orthogenetic principle is applicable both to a comparison of different person-in-environment systems and to the characterization of a single system in transition (Kaplan, 1966). If one system is more differentiated and hierarchically integrated than another, it is considered to be developmentally more advanced than the other. If a single system is increasing in differentiation and hierarchic integration, that person-in-environment system is seen as developing. If it is dedifferentiating and disintegrating, it is seen as regressing.

The orthogenetic principle is a formal, organizational definition of development. As such, it is applicable both to the comparison of different systems and

to the characterization of a single system in transition (cf. Kaplan, 1966). Thus the orthogenetic principle has been used to compare groups ordered with respect to age, to psychopathology, to stress, and the like. This principle, coupled with the concept of levels of organization (von Bertalanffy, 1950, 1962; Novikoff, 1945a, 1945b), has been used to conceptualize relations among cognitive processes—for example, sensorimotor action, perception, and conception—and the experienced relations between percepts (Wapner, 1969; Wapner, Cirillo, & Baker, 1969). Most recently, these concepts have been applied to the interrelations among cognition, affect, and value in the construal of, orientation in, and transactions with the complex, everyday environment including its physical, interpersonal, and sociocultural aspects (Kaplan et al., 1976; Wapner, 1981a; Wapner et al., 1973; Wapner, Cohen, & Kaplan, 1976; Wapner et al., 1983).

The organismic-developmental approach stipulates movement toward ideal person-in-environment relationships. It values as optimal development a differentiated and hierarchically integrated person-in-environment system with capacity for flexibility, freedom, self-mastery, and the capacity to shift from one mode of person-in-environment relationship to another as required by goals, by the demands of the situation, and by the instrumentalities available (Kaplan, 1966; Wapner et al., 1973; Wapner, Kaplan, & Ciottone, 1981).

In agreement with this formulation, the most developmentally advanced person-in-environment state is presumed to exist when the person controls his or her transactions by participating or by withdrawing, depending on current goals, long-term values, likes, and dislikes. There is neither general surrender nor opposition to the urgency and press of the environment (broadly conceived to include physical, interpersonal, and sociocultural dimensions). The person may develop control over and modulate his or her own natural scheduling with that of external demands, to move to high-quality completion of fewer goal-oriented activities, and to act in concert with internal and external temporal demands. It is assumed that with control over self and world, the adoption of stable (rather than labile), flexible (rather than rigid) person–world relations with means subordinated to ends moves persons toward optimal self–world dynamic equilibria. Such movement is assumed to involve (1) greater salience of positive affective states; (2) diminution of isolation, anonymity, helplessness, depersonalization, and entrapment; (3) coordination of long-term and short-term planning; and (4) optimal use of available instrumentalities to accomplish personal goals. In short, the developmental ideal involves movement toward an integrated unity of the person's overt and covert actions.[19]

To exemplify the orthogenetic principle, let us consider planning that, like other part processes of the person-in-environment system, has some features which also are developmentally orderable. This is the case for the

progressive differentiation of a method from concrete action. Three distinct ideal forms of action constituting a developmental sequence delineate this differentiation: (1) Fusion of method and concrete action instrumental to a goal; (2) Differentiation of concrete preparatory actions from actions immediately instrumental to goal; and (3) Differentiation of symbolic actions (planning) from other preparatory actions. There is a movement from merely acting in an attempt to achieve a goal, to getting ready for such actions concretely (motor set, finding an instrument, etc.), to getting ready for such actions conceptually by formulating a method ahead of time.

This differentiation of method from action may be further specified as ways (Burke, 1962) in which the growing distance of the person from his immediate milieu is evidenced: (1) Planning comes to have its own sub-goals, distinguishable from those of subsequent action—the plan should be formulated clearly and be communicable, planning itself should be carried out economically and efficiently, etc.; (2) Instrumentalities different from those of the planned action are developed for planning—models, diagrams, pencil and paper, planning conferences, etc.; (3) The scene in which planning goes on becomes distinguished from the subsequent scene of action— the props of action are no longer necessary, the conditions for action need not be present to envisage the action, etc.; and (4) The agents of planning become differentiated from the agents of action—the planning function may be carried out by people (planners) other than those realizing the plan. (Wapner & Cirillo, 1973, pp. 13–15)

Clearly, there is great variation in the degree of complexity of a plan and its relation to action. Specifically, there is both a hierarchy of plans and of actions. Some plans are

rather quite complex, subordinating simpler actions as means to their attainment (Schutz, 1951, 1971). For example, in planning to visit a foreign country (the action here is quite general and may be designated as taking a trip) one entertains a series of subordinate plans and one carries out a whole host of subordinate actions (getting one's passport, packing one's clothes) [cf. Gärling et al., 1984, 1985]. These are all infused with the terminal goal of the larger

scale project, but the scenes as construed within the attempts to attain subgoals have a certain autonomy with respect to each subgoal. For example, in planning a trip and beginning to undertake it, one regards one's clothes to be taken by projecting oneself into the environment in which one expects to be. Thus, in action, one is not locked into the present world of stimuli but considers and utilizes the present scene with respect to projected or alternative scenes. (Wapner et al., 1973, pp. 275–276).

Finally, I note that expectations regarding the character of future person-in-environment states are linked to planned actions, independent of whether or not they are actualized. Expectations can remain at a very general, diffuse level of wishful thinking, or they can be part of a general expectation regarding a person-in-environment state that may or may not be in keeping with or in conflict with actual concrete actions.

To concretize the way in which planning and expectations regarding the person-in-environment state have been approached, we may briefly review two studies that use developmental conceptualization in interpreting their findings. One study (Wofsey et al., 1979) shows how formulation of plans to leave the university at which one is currently a senior affects the manner of experiencing that university environment. One group of seniors had clearly articulated plans as to what they could do after graduation; the other group had no such plans. Both groups were asked to represent the university both verbally and pictorially. There was consonance between the findings for representations in both media. Relative to the group without plans for the future, the group with plans represented the university where they were still located in a more impersonal, more "objective," more psychologically distant (greater selfworld distancing) manner as measured by diverse criteria.

A second study (Apter, 1976) shows the relation between formulation of plans for leaving and how the individual handles discrepancies between expectation and actuality in terms that are developmentally orderable with respect to the orthogenetic principle. Planning groups were established as in the previous study. All subjects were asked how they acted or coped with the discrepancies between their expectations about the environment and their actual experiences in the environment. They were asked to recall, from their own recent experiences, incidents involving transactional conflict in the academic, administrative, domestic, and physical aspects of the environment.

Status of plans was related to modes of coping.

1. Dedifferentiated person-in-environment system state. — The senior without plans was hyper-invested in and identified with the present environment; he or she coped with transactional conflict (expectation vs. actuality) by accommodation, that is, where a student who expected the physical facilities (e.g., a washing machine) to work took no action, conforming outwardly to "fit in" with the environment.

2. Differentiated and isolated or in conflict person-in-environment system state. — The senior in the process of actively making plans was less invested in and more differentiated from the environment and coped with transactional conflict by nonconstructive ventilation and disengagement, that is, he or she coped with the interpersonal environment, namely a roommate who turns the room upside down to satisfy a weekly compulsion of washing and waxing its floor, by disengagement; he or she distanced himself or herself from the situation by mocking it. When another student was faced with dormitory washing machines that, contrary to his expectation, did not work, he kicked the machine and left in disgust (coping by expressing frustration, anger, disappointment — nonconstructive ventilation).

3. Differentiated and integrated person-in-environment system state. — The senior whose plans for the future were securely established handled transactional conflict by constructive assertion. For example, when a shower in a university apartment broke down, the student threatened not to pay the rent unless the shower was fixed by Wednesday. The shower was readily fixed. This is coping by planned action, with different alternatives to achieve a goal. The person was less dominated by emotions and engaged in an integrated self/environment relationship.

Conditions Making for Developmental Change

In addition to describing transactions (experience and action) of the focal agent and, in some instances of significant others of his or her environment, there is a further question of "how" or under what *conditions* developmental transformation is reversed, arrested, or advanced.[20] It is assumed, for example, that person-in-environment transactions experienced as critical involve developmental arrest or regression. What transpires concerning the course of change under such conditions will depend on the characteristics of the agent, of the environment, and their interrelationship. Consider some examples from Wapner and colleagues (1983):

A mother of a handicapped child who seeks to protect her child rather than challenge him or her maintains a set of demands differing from those of a young, change-oriented teacher who values increasing independence in children. In this way, the child is presented with contradictory demands from both the home and school worlds. Such contradictory demands may make for advancement or retardation, and this may vary, depending on the degree of conflict between the demands. Mild conflict may make for advancement, severe conflict for retardation (cf. Wapner, 1976). Considering differences in environment, what is the impact of nursery schools with varying degrees of structure in their programs? Further, considering interaction of agent and environment, does a child who is handicapped construe and transact differently and exhibit more marked developmental advance in a "mainstream" as compared with a "segregated" environment?

Given that for some children, the experience of transition to nursery school is conflicted and traumatic, what conditions can help in advancing social and cognitive developmental status of the child undergoing that transition? We know that in the development of a cognitive organization of the spatial features of a new environment the person utilizes an anchor point or home base (Schouela, Steinberg, Leveton, & Wapner, 1980). We know that in exploring a new environment a child will utilize his or her mother as anchor point (Ainsworth & Wittig, 1969; Rheingold & Eckerman, 1969, 1970). Will fostering the child's use of an anchor point (whether an actual or symbolic object) in the new environment help the child move closer to the developmental ideal of integrating the new world of school with the old world of home and in experiencing stability, comfort, and satisfaction in both? ... We have found that adaptation is more effective for residents of nursing homes who are permitted to bring personal objects with them than for those residents not permitted to do so (Schmitt, Redondo, & Wapner, 1977). ... [See Pastalan (1983) for a general discussion of relocation of the elderly, and Gutman and Herbert (1976) for effects of a preparation program for relocation.] Are there key people in the new environment [social anchor points], for example, kin or friends who will become instrumental in the development of the social network of the migrant, and then serve as anchor points or referents for establishing the migrant's social world? (Wapner et al., 1983, pp. 123–124)

Such questions concerning the conditions that make for developmental change can be asked with respect to any person-in-environment system. There is, of course, the open problem as to whether there are somewhat general conditions that make for developmental advance or regression. Does the utilization of anchor points (things and/or people, both symbolic and actual) generally make for developmental advance (or regression, e.g., overattachment) of the person-in-environment system state (Schouela et al., 1980)? Is perturbation and regression of the person-in-environment system a necessary condition for developmental advance (Wapner et al., 1983)? And, if so, to what degree does a simple request for the person to verbalize plans about actions to be taken to advance to a new, more ideal person-in-environment state, which is responded to, actually have such an effect (cf. Shapiro, Rierdan, & Wapner, 1973)?

41.3.2. Some Implications for Research

By presenting a few paradigmatic research problems in a diagrammatic or outline form that is consonant with some central figures of the approach, its mode of categorizing and of shaping research problems as well as its heuristic value for reinterpreting previous research and opening new research questions will become evident. This will be done with a few research areas, some where studies have already been carried out and others that are at an early planning stage.

Before attempting to diagram some person-in-environment systems and system changes that are examined in particular empirical studies, it is helpful to list (See Figure 41.1) some major properties of the person, the environment, and the relations between them that enter as relevant features of experience and action. Some high points of physical, interpersonal, and sociocultural features have been selected for presentation for both the person and the environment. The features of the person–environment relationships highlighted include those of temporality, spatiality, connectedness, focus, and planning. There are, of course, many other relationships that might be relevant. However, albeit limited, this listing may serve as a reference when posing research questions as well as developing diverse methodologies (interview questions, modeling techniques, questionnaires, observational categories, etc.) to assess transactions of persons-in-environments.

We shall outline a number of research problems to illustrate some of the ways in which the approach is actualized and how it has heuristic value for empirical inquiry.

Relocation of a Psychiatric Therapeutic Community

The first problem that concerns the relocation of a psychiatric therapeutic community is based on a study conducted some years ago (Demick, 1977; Demick & Wapner, 1980; Wapner, 1981a). The study

is outlined in Figure 41.2 that describes transactions of a group of patients diagnosed as chronic, undifferentiated schizophrenics and a group of patients diagnosed as antisocial personalities (data collected for staff members are omitted here) on four occasions: 3 to 4 weeks prior to relocation, 2 to 3 days prior to relocation; 2 to 3 days following relocation; and 3 to 4 weeks following relocation. In keeping with Figure 41.1, the transactions of the two groups of subjects are categorized in terms of experience of self (P), of environment (E), and of person-environment relations (P-E) and in terms of the physical, interpersonal, and sociocultural aspects of the environment and person–environment relations. It is noteworthy that (1) physical relocation of a psychiatric therapeutic community makes for profound changes in experience of self, of environment, and of self-environment relations; (2) these changes vary, depending on the nature of the pathology of the patient—the schizophrenic becomes more dedifferentiated with impending relocation, and the antisocial personality becomes more vigilant; (3) thus, with variation in parts—environment and person—of the person-in-environment system, there is impact on the entire system that 3 to 4 weeks following relocation is largely restored to a level of operation prior to relocation. Although this study illustrates the way in which the perspective shapes a problem, it should be noted that it was conducted a few years ago and has some striking omissions if viewed from the conceptualization of the organismic-developmental perspective presented here. One such omission concerns the presence and nature of the planning activity of the two patient groups. It would have been of interest and value to incorporate questions and analyses of answers to questions about the patients' plans for coping with the oncoming transition and to their expectations concerning the impact of relocation.

One could effectively seek answers to such research questions as the following:

For synchronic designs—what expectations are held by patient and staff regarding the nature of the experience of self, of environment, and of self-environment relations at the new location, including cognitive, affective, and valuative aspects of the anticipated experience? Have plans been formulated for coping with relocation? What is the nature of the plans? How are the plans related to modes of experience of self, environment, and self-environment relations with respect to cognitive, affective, and valuative processes? What preparations are made personally and by psychiatric institutions (with respect to physical and sociocultural aspects of the environment) to reduce vulnerability—stress associated with environmental transitions and relocations into and out of the hospital setting? Considering transitions more generally, what is the nature of the experience, feeling, and actions, taken separately at each stage of the hospitalization process (e.g., entrance into the hospital, hospitalization per se, and planning to leave the hospital)?

For diachronic designs—for patients and members of the staff (nurses, aides, physicians), what changes occur in expectations, plans, actuality, and the relations among them over the course of assessment

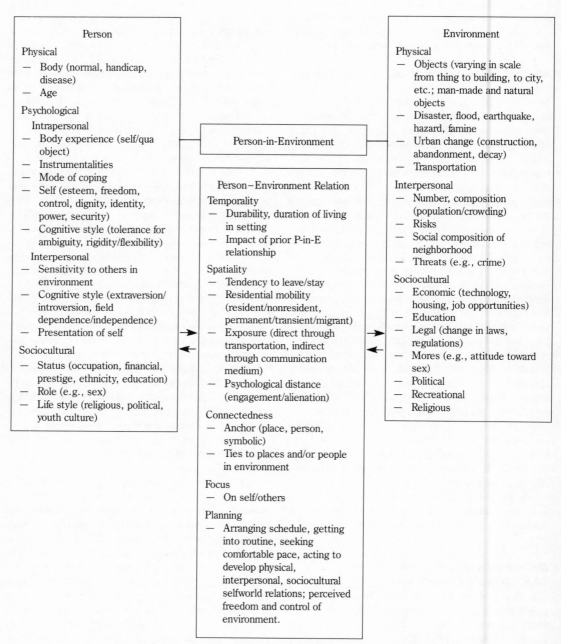

Figure 41.1. Some selected aspects of the Person-in-Environment System.

from some time in advance, say at some weeks prior to announcement of impending relocation, to some time after relocation? More generally, how are all phases of psychiatric hospitalization (pre-, during, posthospitalization) related with respect to transactions, expectations, planning? Do the changes in person-in-environment system states over the hospitalization sequence conform to the idealized developmental sequence? Is there evidence that following hospitalization, person-in-environment system states become less advanced and that with recovery the person-in-environment system state moves toward the end point postulated by the developmental ideal?

Radical Disruption (e.g., by Tornado, Earthquake) of the Person-in-Environment System

This second research problem differs from the first (relocation of a psychiatric community) in at least two ways: (1) the former was planned by the administrator of the setting, and therefore the change was anticipated for some time by patients and staff, whereas, the radical disruption is unanticipated except for a very brief time prior to impact; and (2) the former presentation is based on data collected in a well-defined study, whereas the work to be presented on radical disruptions provides descriptions that are unsystematic and are culled from a variety of diverse sources. One might regard the diagrammed presentation (See Figure 41.3) as an incomplete sketch of a research proposal that hopefully is worthy of more complete definition.

For convenience only, three system states are described, namely "disastrous event remove," "impact/system shock," and "postimpact."[21] Again, the diagrams at each stage give representative expectations of examples of transactions in terms of person, environment, and person–environment relations, including cognition, feelings, and evaluation. Included in each rectangle describing a system state is a dotted box containing plans. Plans are represented this way because they involve plotting future courses of action that are an ingredient in the "early" person-in-environment state as a potential for particular transactions that will move the person-in-environment system to a projected state with various characteristics.

Given this background, the remainder of Figure 41.3 is self-explanatory, showing some of the ways in which the research problem is conceptualized and the kind of research questions, both for synchronic and diachronic studies, that are shaped by the conceptualization. There are, of course, many other questions that derive from the conceptualization that are

not apparent in this incomplete diagram. For example, one may ask, what is the nature of the multiple worlds constituting the experiences of given person-in-environment systems. How are these worlds—for example, the world of family, of work, of recreation, of community—related structurally when the disastrous event is remote?[22] How is the structure changed, with respect to differentiation and hierarchic integration, at the time of occurrence and following the impact of system shock? Baum, Fleming, and Davidson's (1983) analysis suggests that the studies proposed might profit from systematically assessing differences between natural disasters and technological catastrophe, and so forth.

The Freshman's Year at College

The third study, which is diagrammed in Figure 41.4, is concerned with changes in self, environment, and self-environment relationships during the first half of the freshman year.[23] Again, it can be considered as a proposal rather than a completed research project. It samples the transactions of first-year students in the university environment during an early phase, at the end of the first month of residence and at the end of the first semester. The diagram in Figure 41.4 includes a plan describing a desirable, more optimal person-in-environment system state and the actions to be taken to achieve that state. A listing of actions taken in carrying out the plan follows, and, finally, a later phase of the person-in-environment system state. All of the expected transactions, including those in the plan, are categorized with respect to the person (self), the environment (physical, interpersonal, and sociocultural), and the person–environment relationships. A number of synchronic and diachronic research questions are listed.

Some Further Problems for Study

It is worthy of note that all of the paradigms presented have been simplified in many ways. One very important way in which the analysis has been simplified is by omitting individual differences in terms of processes, transactions, coping strategies, and so forth. Though we have pointed to differences between such diagnostic groups as schizophrenics and antisocial personality types, there are individual differences within these pathological groups and within normal groups that are of concern. Although the approach is nomothetic, it is ideographic as well. We are concerned with the modes of transacting and planning of various kinds of individuals who are obliged to cope with the stresses and strains of life in various settings, under various conditions, and at different times throughout the life cycle. Moreover, we

Before relocation

P-in-E SYSTEM STATE

T₁ (3–4 weeks prior to relocation)

P-in-E SYSTEM STATE
T$_1$ (3–4 weeks prior to relocation)

Transactions (experience and action)

P (Self): Overestimates head width reflecting lack of differentiation between self and world

E (Physical): Few elements on sketch map reflecting dedifferentiated, global environment

   (Interpersonal): Relatively few people entered on Psychological Distance Map reflecting dedifferentiation of interpersonal environment

   (Sociocultural): Little accurate knowledge of hospital rules reflecting dedifferentiation of sociocultural environment

P-E (Physical): Focus on self rather than on environment reflecting egocentricity

   (Interpersonal): Rated relationships with others as relatively transitory and superficial reflecting focus on self

   (Sociocultural): Strict adherence to hospital rules reflecting dedifferentiation of self from environment

---

P-in-E SYSTEM STATE
T$_2$ (2–3 days prior to relocation)

Transactions (experience and action)

P (Self): Increased overestimation of head width reflecting increased lack of differentiation of self and world with impending relocation

E (Physical): Even fewer elements on sketch map reflecting even greater dedifferentiation with impending relocation

   (Interpersonal): Even fewer people entered on Psychological Distance Map reflecting even greater dedifferentiation of interpersonal environment

   (Sociocultural): Even less knowledge of hospital rules reflecting even greater dedifferentiation of sociocultural environment

P-E (Physical): Greater focus on self reflecting increasing egocentricity (also withdrawal) with impending relocation

   (Interpersonal): Rated relationships with others as even more transitory and superficial with impending relocation

   (Sociocultural): Even stricter adherence to hospital rules reflecting even greater dedifferentiation of self from environment with impending relocation

(a)

P-in-E SYSTEM STATE
T$_1$ (3–4 weeks prior to relocation)

Transactions (experience and action)

P (Self): Overestimates head slightly like normals reflecting average degree of differentiation between self and world

E (Physical): Many elements on sketch maps reflecting differentiated environment

   (Interpersonal): More people entered on Psych Distance Maps reflecting differentiation of interpersonal environment

   (Sociocultural): Accurate knowledge of hospital rules reflecting differentiation of sociocultural environment

P-E (Physical): Focus on environment rather than self reflecting directedness to outside world and denial of illness

   (Interpersonal): Rated relationships with others as relatively permanent and intense reflecting focus on interpersonal environment.

   (Sociocultural): Felt rules inapplicable to self; tried to test limits reflecting focus on sociocultural environment

---

P-in-E SYSTEM STATE
T$_2$ (2–3 days prior to relocation)

Transactions (experience and action)

P (Self): Decreased overestimation of head width reflecting increasing hypervigilance with relocation

E (Physical): Even more elements on sketch maps reflecting hypervigilance with relocation

   (Interpersonal): Even more people on Psych Distance Maps

   (Sociocultural): Continued accurate knowledge of hospital rules reflecting differentiation of sociocultural environment with relocation

P-E (Physical): Greater focus on environment reflecting increasing directedness to outside world and denial of illness

   (Interpersonal): Rated relationships with others as even more permanent and intense with relocation

   (Sociocultural): Felt even stronger about rules applying to self; tests limits more with relocation

(b)

After relocation

P-in-E SYSTEM STATE	P-in-E SYSTEM STATE
T_3 (2–3 days following relocation)	T_4 (3–4 weeks following relocation)
Transactions (experience and action)	Transactions (experience and action)
P (Self): Same degree of overestimation of head width as at T_2	P (Self): Restoration of degree of overestimation of head width as at T_1
E (Physical): Same degree of dedifferentiation of environment as at T_2	E (Physical): Restoration of degree of dedifferentiation of environment as at T_1
(Interpersonal): Same degree of dedifferentiation of interpersonal environment as at T_2	(Interpersonal): Restoration of degree of dedifferentiation of interpersonal environment as at T_1
(Sociocultural): Same degree of dedifferentiation of sociocultural environment as at T_2	(Sociocultural): Restoration of degree of dedifferentiation of sociocultural environment as at T_1
P-E (Physical): Same degree of self-focus as at T_2	P-E (Physical): Restoration of degree of self-focus as at T_1
(Interpersonal): Same degree of permanence/intensity of relationships with others as at T_2	(Interpersonal): Restoration of degree of permanence/intensity of relationships with others as at T_1
(Sociocultural): Same degree of adherence to rules as at T_2	(Sociocultural): Restoration of degree of adherence to rules as at T_1

(a)

P-in-E SYSTEM STATE	P-in-E SYSTEM STATE
T_3 (2–3 days following relocation)	T_4 (3–4 weeks following relocation)
Transactions (experience and action)	Transactions (experience and action)
P (Self): Same degree of overestimation of head width as at T_2	P (Self): Same degree of overestimation of head width as at T_1
E (Physical): Same degree of hypervigilance as at T_2	E (Physical): Same degree of hypervigilance as at T_1
(Interpersonal): Same differentiation of interpersonal environment as at T_2	(Interpersonal): Same differentiation of interpersonal environment as at T_1
(Sociocultural): Same degree of differentiation of sociocultural environment as at T_1	(Sociocultural): Same degree of differentiation of sociocultural environment as at T_1
P-E (Physical): Same degree of focus on environment as at T_2	P-E (Physical): Restoration of degree of focus on environment as at T_1
(Interpersonal): Relationships rated as permanent and intense as at T_2	(Interpersonal): Restoration of same rating of relationships as at T_1
(Sociocultural): Same degree of adherence to rules as at T_2	(Sociocultural): Restoration of same degree of adherence to rules as at T_1

(b)

Figure 41.2. Anticipated relocation of Person-in-Environment System: Effects of relocation on members of a Psychiatric Therapeutic Community. (a) Person diagnosed as schizophrenic and (b) person diagnosed as antisocial personality.

are interested in identifying groupings of persons-in-environments so that it is possible to more readily match treatment and intervention to particular person-in-environment system states and thereby assist people selectively in better managing their life situations (see Hornstein & Wapner, 1984, 1985).[24]

A simple diagram (Figure 41.5), adapted from

Wapner and Ittelson (1981), schematizes the relation among person-in-environment system state, *perceived* environmental change, and environmental action, which is another problem briefly touched on here. This diagram, which treats an elderly person in a decaying urban environment, illustrates some other ways in which individual differences may be studied,

P-in-E System State

Disastrous Event Remote

P: I am not worried. Self-confident. (I know what to do in danger . . .)

E: Tornado struck 30 years ago; will not happen again; people will let us know.

P-E: It can't happen here; if it does the government has a good warning system.

PLANS:
"No plans for next few years."

P-in-E System State

Impact/System Shock

P: Panic; extreme emotional behavior; worrying about self; loss of self esteem, self-confidence; apathetic; demoralized; inactive, anxiety, grief, despair, fear, rage; helpless, uncertain, vulnerable, disorganized, sluggish thinking; regression, psychic numbing; denial of danger; death guilt; trying to be in control and watchful, vigilant

E: Destruction of places, people, way of life; misreading of events; wishful thinking about physical events; "Trees will never grow again;" people dazed, puttering around, others will take care of this; need for affection, support; "end of world"

P-E: "This is not happening to me"; dependence on others; loss of communality, connection relation to places, friends, relations; disorientation; isolation; alienation. Safety rules are realistic. The government will help.

Plans: Predispositions to act in relation to projected P-in-E System State

Ends: Projected P-in-E System State

Means: Action to be taken (covert or overt)

P: Feel secure, organized, and in control of self; capable of leadership and constructive activity.

P: Rapidly accept leadership; protector role; practice actions so that they are automatic; get in habit of checking weather warning system.

E: Safe for physical belongings and people; have appropriate warning system; caring neighbor and governmental support system in case of destruction; appropriate insurance laws; natural hazards (earthquake, tornado, etc.) do not happen; helpful neighbors.

E: Rebuild, if projected character guaranteed; otherwise move to location with those features.

P-E: Feel belongings, family, friends are safe from destruction; feel secure, comfortable in home and neighborhood. Feel government warning system and rules for disaster help are more than adequate.

P-E: Fight to obtain adequate warning system, new laws, adoption of preventative measures (e.g., earthquake-proof buildings); insist on all family members remaining vigilant about warnings and appropriate action.

Figure 41.3. An unanticipated powerful system shock to the P-in-E System: Involvement in a radical disruption by tornado, earthquake, and so on.

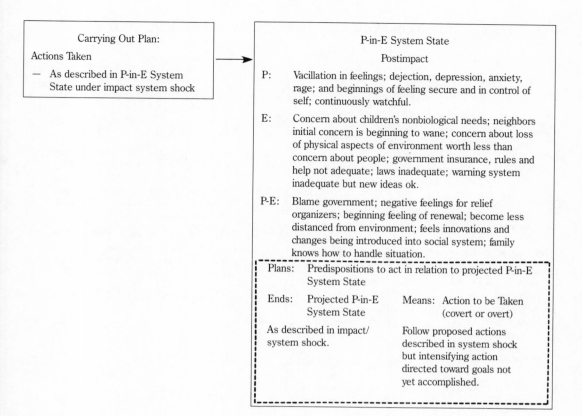

Some research questions:

Single Frame (synchronic)

— What is the nature of the experience, feeling and actions taken separately at each stage (disastrous event remote; impact; postimpact)? (This would involve a phenomenological, open-ended description followed by questions concerning feelings about self; physical, interpersonal, and sociocultural aspects of the environment; and self-world relations).
— What is the range of individual differences at each of the three stages of disaster?
— What preparations are made personally and by governmental agencies to reduce vulnerability to disastrous events?
— How do people judge likelihood of occurrence of a disastrous event? What is relation of likelihood of occurrence and preparedness?

Frame Sequence (diachronic)

— How are all phases of disaster (preshock; during shock; postshock) related with respect to experience and transactions?
— What relationships hold over time concerning experience of self, of environment (physical, interpersonal, sociocultural) and of self to environment? How do various members of one's interpersonal environment (neighbor, relation, support group) interact with focal person? What grouping of individual response can be established so that conditions of intervention can be shaped for individuals?
— Do the changes over the sequence in person–environment relations conform to the idealized developmental sequence? Is there evidence that following system shock person-in-environment system states become less advanced and that with recovery the person-in-environment system state moves toward the end point postulated by the developmental ideal?

Figure 41.3. *(Continued)*

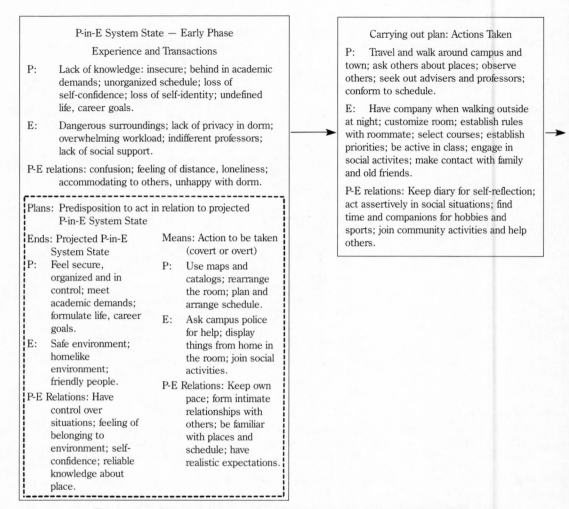

Figure 41.4. Phases of the transactions of freshmen during the first 6 months of college.

namely whether action is taken to cope by attempting to change the person (e.g., carry a gun), change the environment (e.g., board up the windows), or change the person-in-environment relationship (e.g., go to housing for the elderly) (see Wapner, 1983b).

Finally, another direction for study of individual differences involves characterizing the person-in-environment system states in developmental terms. As noted earlier and elsewhere (Wapner, 1980, 1981a; Wapner et al., 1983), one may characterize person-in-environment system states from less to more advanced developmentally in keeping with the orthogenetic principle: (1) Dedifferentiated self-world relationships, where the person changes readily in keeping with the environment or the environment changes in keeping with the person; (2) differentiated and isolated self-world relationships, where the person is withdrawn from or isolated from the environment, or differentiated and in conflict self-world relationships, where the person is in open conflict with the environment or erratically shifts from conformity to opposition with the environment; and (3) differentiated and integrated self-world relationships, where the person controls his or her relationship to the environment by participating or withdrawing from it depending on his or her long-term and short-term goals and plans of action.

Before closing this exemplification of research, let us consider another, more complicated, problem of interest. This problem involves another aspect of the

P-in-E System State — Late Phase

Experience and Transactions

P: Familiar with places and utilities; feel relaxed in dorm; confidence in course work; able to manage disturbances and unexpected events; acquire new knowledge and perspectives; have articulated life, career goals.

E: Streets feel safe; feel secure and at home; work schedule is routinized; feel academic opportunities attractive; feel faculty and administration supportive; have good friends.

P-E relations: Self-identity maintained in diverse situations; feel secure on campus; feel comfortable with people; act constructively on environment; flexible, using different modes of coping with environmental stress; utilize environmental resources for actualizing own goals; feel content with present life structure.

Plans: Predisposition to act in relation to projected in P-in-E System State

Ends: Projected P-in-E System State Means: Actions to be taken (covert or overt)

As described in Early Phase. Follow proposed actions described in early phase but intensifying action directed toward goals not yet accomplished.

Some research questions:

Single Frame (synchronic)

— How do college freshmen construe the college environment in terms of its physical, psychological, interpersonal, and sociocultural aspects?

— What is the nature or types of conflict that college freshmen have after being exposed to the college environment? What are the relationships between the nature of the conflict and the person's values, expectations, aspirations, etc.?

— What is the nature of the freshman's process of planning? What kind of experiences lead the freshman to engage in planning? What individual differences in planning occur, and how can they be characterized in terms of the level of structurization, articulation, flexibility, complexity, etc.?

Frame Sequence (diachronic)

— What relations are there between freshman's previous experience in his or her environment and his or her experience in college?

— How are plans carried out? What factors are related to the degree to which plans are actualized? How are such features of plans as the structure, degree of articulation, flexibility, etc., related to freshman's transactions in the college environment?

— How are the discrepancies between initial plans and actuality resolved? How are new plans formed based on transactions?

— What is the nature of the experience and transactional conflicts of freshmen who later drop out or transfer? How is the planning process related to dropping out or transferring?

Figure 41.4. *(Continued)*

relationship between experience of environmental change and initiation of environmental action (Wapner, 1983b; Wapner & Ittelson, 1981). Moreover, it is linked to the notion of levels of organization. In general, it concerns the question of the relationship between goals and instrumentalities governing action at the individual or interpersonal levels and the sociocultural-group level, which has been discussed by Wapner (1983b):

Since growth and recovery of older cities and of rapidly growing new cities are correlated with in-migration, out-migration and other population movements, differences among people varying in length of stay in a given community—e.g., long-term residents, newcomers, visitors, tourists, and migrants—might profitably be compared with respect to the relation between perceived environmental change and environmental action. In what ways are environmental change and action related on individual, group and societal levels? How are these levels of organization related with respect to the linkage between perceived environmental change and action? What processes determine whether policy on the governmental-societal level is or is not actualized on the individual and group levels? (Wapner, 1983b, p. 28)

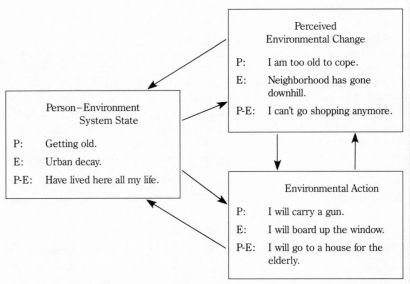

Figure 41.5. An unanticipated gradual deterioration of a Person-in-Environment System: The elderly person in a decaying urban environment (Adapted from Wapner & Ittelson, 1980).

Further, Wapner has stated that

instituting a change in environmental policy at the socio-cultural level depends on some form of group consensus process whereas instituting a change like an environmental move depends on individual psychological process (perceptual or more generally experience and action). The relationships can be supportive, antagonistic, substitutive (vicarious) between these two levels [see Figure 41.5]. Suppose we are dealingwith an environmental change of urban decay perceived by the person as "neighborhood gone down hill," which is coupled with the action of "boarding up the windows." The local government could provide such *supportive action* as greater police protection through increasing walking police patrols and neighborhood cruiser patrols. The local government could provide such *antagonistic action* as decreasing protection (not paying attention to poor neighborhoods), prohibiting boarding up windows, or indeed ignoring the situation. Or, the local government could provide such *vicarious or substitutive action* as alternative low-cost housing for the elderly from the affected neighborhood. It would be of interest to conduct research which would provide information under what conditions the relationship between action at the individual and the community level is supportive, antagonistic, or substitutive.

Many studies of policy decision-making to ameliorate environmental disaster, like nuclear accidents, have been restricted to the socio-cultural level. Pros-

criptive rules and laws are instituted but there is little work available on how awareness of such an accident is integrated into action on the individual level. [See Craik (1982) as the exception who is studying factors influencing individual and group perceptions of technological risk.] There is need for exactly that kind of study. It can directly serve to tell us how change at the policy level is actualized on the individual level and the various processes underlying such events. With knowledge of conditions which underlie the integration of experienced change and action, we will be better able to introduce prescriptions for actions as well as environment change which will effectively change people's behavior. This will require obtaining information concerning the individual's phenomenological experience and the process whereby he or she constructs his or her multiple worlds. Such information might profitably be sought rather than findings from large-scale surveys which characterize the "average" person's willingness to take or to refrain from action. It is possible that only a very restricted number of persons may experience what the "average" person experiences and only a very restricted number of persons may take the same action the "average" person takes. (Wapner, 1983b, pp. 21–22)

Taken more generally, the research problem areas exemplified concern the general question of analyzing (both synchronically and diachronically) relationships among operations of the person, the environment, and the person-in-environment system at the various levels of organization described earlier in this chapter, namely the person-in-environment operating at the person–world level, the agent–habitat level, and the respondent–ambient level.

This array of illustrations serves to concretize the manner in which the theoretical perspective shapes problems, methods of inquiry and, indeed, findings. The difficulties and successes in establishing methodologies and the nature of the findings obtained are linked to problem formulation and the theoretical approach. This interplay between conceptualization and empirical study is at the heart of the development of a perspective and underpins the very general plans of action for advancing the theoretical approach from its beginnings as described here to a more advanced, differentiated, and hierarchically integrated status.

41.3.3. Plans for Future Development

Our plans for advancing the approach from these small beginnings involve two obvious aspects. First, because of the powerful interpenetration of theory with empirical study, we shall explore many of the untouched research problems mentioned here as well as other related problems. Such empirical study will hopefully force articulation and refinement of conceptualization. Second, we shall try to advance the conceptual approach by reviewing, from our perspective, studies in the literature, especially those by practitioners in the environmental field. This will permit assessing whether a fit can be established between the conceptual approach described here and research that has been conducted in the environmental design field. The patterns of fit and misfit, I hope, will help advance the theoretical approach.

Another, more difficult direction for development involves moving the perspective from relative focus on the individual to applicability to larger scale organizational entities. Involvement in the day-to-day activities of designing a science building, a new housing project, or some other complex setting, for example, Appleyard's (1976) planning of a city, would force direct confrontation with the practical problems of professional planning practice. We believe that this kind of down-to-earth, concrete action, has, as has been so vividly described by Rand (1983), the potential to infuse "everyday life" complexity and large-scale relationships into the relatively abstract perspective proposed. We believe such involvement will serve to provide a significant creative function for future development of the perspective.

Acknowledgments

The author wishes to express his deep appreciation to I. Altman, R. Ciottone, J.A. Collazo, J. Demick, M.B. Franklin, G.A. Hornstein, H. Minami, A.M. Pacheco, M. Quirk, and D. Stokols for their constructive comments on an early version of this chapter.

NOTES

1. At the same time, it is acknowledged that some, like Broadbent (1980), believe that "scientific theory building itself, whilst applicable to the non-motivated physical environment, does not, and cannot, apply to human beings, except at the grossest physiological levels. The recognition of this fact will be a great liberation to architectural psychology, for instead of playing at being 'scientific' we shall be free to engage in other and rather more worthwhile pursuits" (Broadbent, 1980, p. 350). As we shall see, this conclusion, though appropriate in highlighting the importance of levels of organization (e.g., physiological vs. psychological) is complicated by whether one restricts science to natural science or leaves room for a human science orientation.

2. An example of one such approach—a variation of a phenomenological method described by Giorgi (1971, 1975) and Watkins (1977) employed in a study of retirement (Hornstein & Wapner, 1984, 1985)—aims to describe how subjects structure their experience of a life event. The procedure involves dividing a protocol, derived from a relatively unstructured interview, into meaning units, articulating the themes of each unit, tying them together into what is called a "situated structure" for a particular subject, developing a set of "typical structures" representing qualitatively different experiences, and then generating from the typical structures a "general structure" that describes the essential features of the given phenomena.

3. There are, of course, such obvious exceptions in psychology as the perceptual analysis of movement and speed and of causality (Johansson, 1950; Michotte, 1946) (for a review see Vernon, 1952). Exceptions in geography and sociology include Elliot and Clark's (1978) study of the spatial context of urban activities, Michelson's (1978, 1980) treatment of temporal activities in different contexts, and Newtson's (1973) and Barnes's (1981) attempts to identify choice points in behavior–environment interactions. These reports represent both a recognition of and attempts to analyze the spatiotemporal flow of experience.

4. The review presented here is in large part based on this analysis.

5. See Wapner and Cirillo (1973) for a review.

6. At the time of submission of this chapter, two relevant papers by Gärling, Böök and Lindberg (1984, 1985) came to my attention. These articles, featuring a spatiotem-

poral analysis linking action plans (e.g., travel plans) to acquisition and use of cognitive maps of large-scale everyday environments, speak to the growing recognition of the importance of spatiotemporality and planning in the analysis of person-in-environment transactions and represent a viable theoretical effort worthy of further exploration.

7. The correlated issue of policy implications is complex. For an analysis of this problem, see Kaplan, Wapner, Hornstein, Cohen, Pacheco, Redondo, and Ciottone (1978).

8. See, for example, the Report on the Conference on Behavior–Environment Research Method at the University of Wisconsin's Institute for Environment Studies (van Ryzin, 1977).

9. See Tolman and Brunswik (1935) for a more elaborate treatment of the complexities involved in means–ends analysis.

10. Other analyses that have bearing on integrating the interests and efforts of environmental practitioner and social scientist include Altman (1973, 1977, 1981); Archea (1975, 1982); Canter and Craik (1981); Cohen and Moore (1977); Craik (1977); Moore (1979); Proshansky (1976, 1980); Proshansky and Altman (1979); and Wener (1982). Two other directions for theory development may be singled out because they have elements linked to the stance taken in resolving issues presented and to the perspective to be described here. The first, suggested by Rand (1983), attempts to unite developmental theory and systems theory in examining environmental design and architecture. He reviews salient examples in the history of architecture and proposes an analysis of project planning based on a dialectic between romantic/intuitive and rational/deductive procedures. He uses comparative developmental theory to formulate a psychological view of systems analysis and create an anthropology of planning and public policy. Bridges between the environment practitioner and scientist can presumably be built by integrating developmental and systems theories through cogent examples that reflect the unique complexities of practical affairs. The second approach, suggested by Ittelson (1981), calls for a theory that should involve at least three components— *knowledge* about the environment and human behavior, a process orientation as suggested by *actions*, and *purpose* or goal orientation. The approach should address such issues as the relationship between knowing and doing, the role of purpose, of foresight, of conscious planning, and of technology as means directed toward some purpose. The approaches suggested by Rand (1983) and Ittelson (1981) introduce comparative developmental and systems theory concepts and include such notions as purpose, planning, directedness toward goals, action as well as relations between knowing and doing, which are an ingredient to the organismic-developmental systems approach offered here.

11. The current formulation of the organismic-developmental perspective has its origins in Heinz Werner's (1926, 1940) comparative developmental psychology (cf. Werner, 1978; Witkin, 1965) that he later termed the organismic-developmental approach (Werner, 1957; Werner & Kaplan, 1963). Werner's (1940) classic work, *Comparative Psychology of Mental Development*, described dimensions (global articulated, syncretic discrete, labile stable, rigid flexible) ranging from less advanced to more advanced; delineated three levels of mental functioning, namely sensorimotor affective, perceptual and conceptual; utilized a phenomenological and organismic approach to development; took opposition to elementarism; questioned the assumption that objects are made up of fixed static properties that are always experienced as external to self; and considered multiple phases of reality in describing aesthetic experience, dreams, fantasy, and the experiential world of both child and adult. Werner utilized these dimensions and ideas in analyzing various cognitive processes (time, space, number) and applied his developmental principles to ontogenesis, phylogenesis, psychopathology, ethnogenesis, and to the various levels of functioning and states of the normal adult. With Kaplan, Werner systematized the approach describing the orthogenetic principle and attributing to it the status of a heuristic law, that is, directing inquiry but not subject to empirical test (Kaplan, 1966, 1967; Werner & Kaplan, 1956). The organismic-developmental perspective was generally characterized as one that treats all psychological events as developmental processes (Werner, 1957). The perspective was brought to fruition in Werner and Kaplan's (1963) now classic work, *Symbol Formation*; it was utilized in a study of developmental changes in perception with age (Wapner & Werner, 1957) and linked with an organismic perceptual theory by Wapner, Cirillo, and Baker (1969). Inroads into problems of environment psychology were made by Wapner and colleagues (1973) and Kaplan et al. (1976). In a past volume (Wapner & Kaplan, 1983), colleagues and students of Werner build on his insights in approaching a variety of subject matters. For example, Kaplan (1983a, 1983b) and Cirillo and Kaplan (1983) integrate Wernerian conceptualization with that of Burke (1945, 1954, 1962, 1972) and advance an approach labeled *genetic dramatism* where the genetic or developmental aspect stresses the movement toward perfectionism in the human and the dramatistic aspect focuses on the means people utilize to achieve their ends. An analysis of critical person-in-environment transitions from the organismic-developmental perspective permits application of the perspective to problems of environmental psychology (Wapner, Ciottone, Hornstein, McNeil, & Pacheco, 1983).

12. A more general statement of the perspective treats all living organisms by referring to the organism-in-environment as the unit of analysis. Here, we shall, for simplicity and in keeping with our concern to address issues of the practitioner and social scientist, restrict our analysis to the human being.

13. Kaplan's (1966, 1967, 1983a, 1983b) creative use of Burke's (1962, 1972) "dramatistic" analysis of human action to elaborate organismic-developmental theory has influenced the formulation presented here.

14. Action is distinguished from a discrete set of responses by muscles (movement) or other effectors and is presumed to involve a set of organized activities in relation to some environmental object.

15. For a description of studies dealing with changes in space organization dependent on changes in the self–object cognitive set induced by instructions and environmental arrangement of subject and object, see Wapner (1969).

16. See Verbrugge (1983) and Stokols and Shumaker (1983) for studies on the relationship between multiple worlds (e.g., interconnections between home and work) and psychological and physical well-being.

17. Pepper (1942) describes other "relatively adequate" world hypotheses, that is, formism, mechanism, and contextualism. The perspective is partially linked, especially its developmental aspect, to *contextualism* that is close to the organismic position but is still distinguishable from it. For a critical treatment of the organismic-developmental viewpoint relevant to perspectivism, see Kaplan's (1974) review of the tension between its organismic and developmental aspects (see Altman & Rogoff, Chapter 1, this volume, for a general treatment of the world views proposed by Pepper, 1942).

18. Open systems are generally characterized as moving in the direction of differentiation and integration (e.g., von Bertalanffy, 1956, 1968; Katz & Kahn, 1978; Miller, 1978.)

19. Of direct relevance to the developmental ideal offered here is the concept of perceived freedom and perceived control that has appeared in the literature during the last decade. In reviewing this work, Barnes (1981) describes (1) the applied approach to these and parallel concepts by urban planners (e.g., Perin, 1970) and by environmental psychologists (e.g., Proshansky, Ittelson, & Rivlin, 1970a, 1970b; and Altman, 1973, 1976, 1981) as a criterion for the built environment; and (2) the research-oriented approach to these concepts by psychologists who studied these determinants and their consequences (e.g., Baron & Rodin, 1978; Seligman, 1975; Sherrod, 1974; Stockdale, 1979). Although many unsolved problems remain such as defining, distinguishing, and measuring these dimensions, enough progress has been made (e.g., Baron & Rodin, 1978; Bechtel, 1977; Canter, 1974; Moos, 1972) to suggest that the notions of perceived freedom and control are not only of theoretical value but are also methodologically manageable. From the perspective offered here, the concepts of perceived freedom and control must be conceived of, as well as measured, not as a personality characteristic abstracted from the environment context but as part of a person-in-environment system state, that is, as a personality disposition in relation to some physical, interpersonal, or sociocultural object.

20. A parallel question and some suggestions for solution is given by Stokols (1981) in his discussion of the "transformational potential" of setting. He notes "that psychology has paid too little attention to the ecological conditions under which generative thought, adaptive social behavior, and functional environmental change occur (Gergen, 1978)" (Stokols, 1981, p. 412). He also describes three categories of transformational constructs—two categories defining environmental conditions that prompt insight and imagination, one set with a mental image of the alternate environment present, and another without such an image present; there is a third category that is unintentional, unplanned, and serendipitous—and it has criteria for measurement that might distinguish between "generative" and "degenerative" environments.

21. There are, of course, many ways of dividing the sequence. Stoddard (1968) described nine different time models. In an earlier paper, Wapner (1983a) drew on the five stages described by Miletti, Drabek, and Haas (1975).

22. As mentioned earlier, an assessment technique for characterizing the structure of the individual's multiple worlds has been devised by Hornstein and Wapner (1984, 1985).

23. Many other studies have been conducted that are related to this problem, for example, the study by Schouela, Steinberg, Leveton, and Wapner (1980) that treated the development of the cognitive organization of the university environment during the freshman year.

24. Cf. Moore (1974).

REFERENCES

Ainsworth, M.D., & Wittig, B.A. (1969). Attachment and exploratory behavior of one-year-old children in a strange situation. In B.M. Foss (Ed.), *Determinants of infant behavior* (Vol. 4). London: Methuen.

Allen, V.L. (1977). On convergent methodology. In L. van Ryzin (Ed.), *Proceedings of the Wisconsin Conference on Research Methods in Behavior-Environment Studies*. Madison: University of Wisconsin Press.

Altman, I. (1973). Some perspectives on the study of man-environment phenomena. *Representative Research in Social Psychology, 4*, 109–126.

Altman, I. (1976). Environmental psychology and social psychology. *Personality and Social Psychology Bulletin, 2*, 96–113.

Altman, I. (1977). Research on environment and behavior: A personal statement of strategy. In D. Stokols (Ed.), *Perspectives on environment and behavior: Theory, research, and applications*. New York: Plenum.

Altman, I. (1981). Reflections on environmental psychology: 1981. *Human Environments, 2*, 5–7.

Ames, A., Jr. (1951). Visual perception and the rotating trapezoidal window. *Psychological Monographs, 65* (7). (Whole No. 324).

Appleyard, D. (1976). *Planning a pluralist city*. Cambridge, MA: MIT Press.

Apter, D. (1976). *Modes of coping with conflict in the presently inhabited environment as a function of variation in plans to move to a new environment.* Unpublished master's thesis, Clark University, Worcester, MA.

Archea, J. (1975). Establishing an interdisciplinary commitment. In B. Honikman (Ed.), *Responding to social change.* Stroudsberg, PA: Dowden, Hutchinson, & Ross.

Archea, J. (1982). Conceptual and methodological conflicts in applied interdisciplinary research on environment and aging. In M.P. Lawton, P.G. Windley, & T.O. Byerts (Eds.), *Aging and the environment: Theoretical approaches.* New York: Springer.

Barker, R.G. (1968). *Ecological psychology: Concepts and methods for studying the environment of human behavior.* Stanford, CA: Stanford University Press.

Barnes, R.D. (1981). Perceived freedom and control in the built environment. In J.H. Harvey (Ed.), *Cognition, social behavior and the environment.* Hillsdale, NJ: Erlbaum.

Baron, R.M., & Rodin, J. (1978). Personal control as a mediator of crowding. In A. Baum, J.E. Sinaer, & S. Valins (Eds.), *Advances in environmental psychology* (Vol. 1). Hillsdale, NJ: Erlbaum.

Baum, A., Fleming, R., & Davidson, L.M. (1983). Natural disaster and technological catastrophe. *Environment and Behavior, 15,* 259–272.

Bechtel, R. (1977). *Enclosing behavior.* Stroudsburg, PA: Dowden, Hutchinson, & Ross.

Bell, R.W. (1979). Parent, child and reciprocal influences. *American Psychologist, 34,* 821–826.

Bibace, R., Kaplan, B., & Wapner, S. (1969). The organismic-developmental perspective. Unpublished manuscript, Clark University, Worcester, MA.

Blumenthal, A.L. (1975). A reappraisal of Wilhelm Wundt. *American Psychologist, 30,* 1081–1088.

Broadbent, G. (1980). A semiotic programme for architectural psychology. In G. Broadbent, R. Bunt, & T. Llorens (Eds.), *Meaning and behavior in the built environment.* Chichester, England: Wiley.

Bronfenbrenner, U. (1977). Toward an experimental ecology of human development. *American Psychologist, 32,* 513–531.

Bronfenbrenner, U. (1979a). Contexts of child rearing: Problems and prospects. *American Psychologist, 34,* 844–850.

Bronfenbrenner, U. (1979b). *The ecology of human development.* Cambridge, MA: Harvard University Press.

Burke, K.W. (1945). *A grammar of motives.* New York: Prentice-Hall.

Burke, K.W. (1954). *Permanence and change* (2nd rev. ed.). Los Altos, CA: Hermes.

Burke, K.W. (1962). *A grammar of motives and a rhetoric of motives.* Cleveland, OH: Meridian, World.

Burke, K.W. (1972). *Dramatism and development.* Worcester, MA: Clark University Press.

Canter, D.V. (1974). *Psychology for architects.* London: Applied Science Publishers.

Canter, D.V., & Craik, K.H. (1981). Environmental psychology. *Journal of Environmental Psychology, 1,* 1–11.

Cantril, H. (1950). *The why of man's experience.* New York: Macmillan.

Cirillo, L., & Kaplan, B. (1983). Figurative action from the perspective of genetic-dramatism. In S. Wapner & B. Kaplan (Eds.), *Toward a holistic developmental psychology.* Hillsdale, NJ: Erlbaum.

Cohen, U., & Moore, G.T. (1977). The organization and communication of environment-behavior research information in architectural programming. In L. van Ryzin (Ed.), *Behavior-environment research methods* (Conference). Madison, WI: University of Wisconsin. Institute of Environmental Studies.

Craik, K.H. (1977). Multiple scientific paradigms in environment psychology. *International Journal of Psychology, 12,* 147–157.

Craik, K.H. (1982, January 8–9). Fundamental research issues in risk analysis: Perceptions of technologies and their societal contexts. Paper presented at the Principal Investigators' Conference on Fundamental Issues in Risk Analysis, National Science Foundation, Division of Policy Research and Analysis, Technology Assessment and Risk Analysis Program, Washington, DC.

Demick, J. (1977). *Effect of environmental relocation on members of a psychiatric therapeutic community.* Unpublished master's thesis, Clark University, Worcester, MA.

Demick, J., & Wapner, S. (1980). Effect of environmental relocation on members of a psychiatric therapeutic community. *Journal of Abnormal Psychology, 89,* 444–452.

Dewey, J., & Bentley, A.F. (1949). *Knowing and the known.* Boston: Beacon.

Elliot, D.H., & Clark, S. (1978). The spatial context of urban activities: Some theoretical, methodological and policy considerations. In W. Michelson (Ed.), *Public policy in temporal perspective.* The Hague, Netherlands: Mouton.

Endler, N.S., & Magnusson, D. (1954). Toward an interactional psychology of personality. *Psychological Bulletin, 83,* 956–974.

Feibleman, J.K. (1954). Theory of integrative levels. *British Journal of Philosophy of Science, 5,* 59–66.

Forbes, D., & Greenberg, M. (Eds.) (1982). *The development of planful behavior in children.* San Francisco: Jossey-Bass.

Gans, H.J. (1969). Planning for people, not buildings. *Environment and Planning, 1,* 33–46.

Gärling, T., Böök, A., & Lindberg, E. (1984). Cognitive mapping of large-scale environments, action plans, orientation, and their interrelationships. *Environment and Behavior, 16* (1), 3–34.

Gärling, T., Böök, A., & Lindberg, E. (1985). Adults' memory representations of the spatial properties of their everyday physical environment. In R. Cohen (Ed.), *The development of spatial cognition*. Hillsdale, NJ: Erlbaum.

Gergen, K.J. (1978). Toward generative theory. *Journal of Personality and Social Psychology, 36*, 1344–1360.

Giorgi, A. (1970). Towards phenomenologically based research in psychology. *Journal of Phenomenological Psychology, 1*, 75–98.

Giorgi, A. (1971). Phenomenology and experimental psychology I and II. In A. Giorgi, W.F. Fischer, & A. von Eckartsberg (Eds.), *Duquesne Studies in Phenomenological Psychology*, Vol. 1 (pp. 6–29). Pittsburgh, PA: Duquesne University Press.

Giorgi, A. (1975). Convergence and divergence in qualitative and quantitative methods in psychology. In A. Giorgi, W.F. Fischer & R. von Eckartsberg (Eds.), *Duquesne Studies in Phenomenological Psychology*, (Vol. 2). Pittsburgh, PA: Duquesne University Press.

Gutman, G.M., & Herbert, C.P. (1976). Mortality rates among relocated extended care patients. *Journal of Gerontology, 31*, 352–357.

Herrick, C.J. (1949). A biological survey of integrative levels. In R.W. Sellars, V.J. McGill, & M. Farber (Eds.), *Philosophy for the future*. New York: Macmillan.

Herrick, C.J. (1956). *The evolution of human nature*. Austin: University of Texas Press.

Hornstein, G.A., & Wapner, S. (1984). The experience of the retiree's social network during the transition to retirement. In C.M. Aanstoos (Ed.), *Exploring the Lived World. Readings in Phenomenological Psychology*. Carrollton, GA: West Georgia College Press.

Hornstein, G.A., & Wapner, S. (1985). Modes of experiencing and adapting to retirement. *International Journal of Aging & Human Development, 21* (4), 291–315.

Ittelson, W.H. (1960). *Visual space perception*. New York: Springer.

Ittelson, W.H. (1973). Environment perception and contemporary perceptual theory. In W.H. Ittelson (Ed.), *Environment and cognition*. New York: Seminar Press.

Ittelson, W.H. (1975). Notes on environmental change. In W.H. Ittelson, T. O'Hanlon, K.H. Franck, & C.T. Unseld (Eds.), *Toward a theory of environment, behavior and experience*. New York: City University of New York.

Ittelson, W.H. (1976). Environmental perception and contemporary perceptual theory. In H.M. Proshansky, W.H. Ittelson, & L.G. Rivlin (Eds.), *Environment psychology* (2nd ed.). New York: Holt, Rinehart & Winston.

Ittelson, W.H. (1978). Environmental perception and urban experience. *Environment and Behavior, 10*, 193–213.

Ittelson, W.H. (1981). Environmental psychology: Past accomplishments and future prospects. In G. Hagino, & W.H. Ittelson (Eds.), *Interaction processes between human behavior and environment: Proceedings of the Japan-United States Seminar. Tokyo, Japan, September, 1980* (pp. 233–241). Tokyo: Bunsei.

Ittelson, W.H., & Cantril, H. (1954). *Perception, a transactional approach*. New York: Doubleday.

Johansson, G. (1950). *Configurations in event perception*. Uppsala, Sweden: Almqvist & Wiksells.

Kaplan, B. (1966). The comparative developmental approach and its application to symbolization and language in psychopathology. In S. Arieti (Ed.), *American handbook of psychiatry* (Vol. 3). New York: Basic Books.

Kaplan, B. (1967). Meditations on genesis. *Human Development, 10*, 65–87.

Kaplan, B. (1974). Strife of systems: Rationality and irrationality in development. Paper presented at the Heinz Werner Lecture Series, Clark University, Worcester, MA.

Kaplan, B. (1983a). Genetic dramatism: Old wine in new bottles. In S. Wapner & B. Kaplan (Eds.), *Toward a holistic developmental psychology*. Hillsdale, NJ: Erlbaum.

Kaplan, B. (1983b). Reflections on culture and personality from the perspective of genetic dramatism. In S. Wapner & B. Kaplan (Eds.), *Toward a holistic developmental psychology*. Hillsdale, NJ: Erlbaum.

Kaplan, B., Wapner, S., & Cohen, S.B. (1976). Exploratory applications of the organismic-developmental approach to man-in-environment transactions. In S. Wapner, S.B. Cohen, & B. Kaplan (Eds.), *Experiencing the environment*. New York: Plenum.

Kaplan, B., Wapner, S., Hornstein, G.A., Cohen, S.B., Pacheco, A., Redondo, J.P., & Ciottone, R.A. (1978). *Systems analysis of critical transitions*. Symposium presented at the meeting of the American Psychological Association, Chicago, Illinois.

Katz, D., & Kahn, R.L. *The social psychology of organizations*. New York: Wiley.

Koffka, K. (1935). *Principles of Gestalt psychology*. New York: Harcourt Brace.

Kotarbinski, T. (1965). *Praxiology*. Oxford, England: Pergamon.

Kuntz, P.G. (1968). *The concept of order*. Seattle: University of Washington Press.

Laszlo, E. (1969). *System, structure and experience*. New York: Gordon and Breach Science.

Lewin, K. (1935). *A dynamic theory of personality*. New York: McGraw-Hill.

Little, B. (1983). Personal projects: A rationale and method for investigation. *Environment and Behavior, 15*, 273–309.

Maslow, A.H. (1946). Problem-centering versus means-centering in science. *Philosophy of Science, 13*, 326–341.

Michelson, W. (Ed.). (1975). *Behavioral research methods in environmental design*. Stroudsberg, PA: Dowden, Hutchinson, & Ross.

Michelson, W. (1976). *Man and his urban environment: A sociological approach.* Reading, MA: Addison-Wesley.

Michelson, W. (Ed.). (1978). *Public policy in temporal perspective.* The Hague, Netherlands: Mouton.

Michelson, W. (1980). Spatial and temporal dimensions of child care. *Journal of Women in Culture and Society, 5,* 242–247.

Michotte, A.E. (1946). *La perception de la causalité.* Louvain, Belgium: Institut Supérieur de Philosophie.

Miletti, D.S., Drabek, T.E., & Haas, J.E. (1975). *Human systems in extreme environments: A sociological perspective* (Program on Technology, Environment, and Man, Monograph No. 21). Boulder, CO: University of Colorado Press.

Miller, G.A., Galanter, E., & Pribram, K.H. (1960). *Plans and the structure of behavior.* New York: Holt, Rinehart & Winston.

Miller, J.G. (1978). *Living systems.* New York: McGraw-Hill.

Mischel, T. (1970). Wundt and the conceptual foundations of psychology. *Philosophical and Phenomenological Research, 31,* 1–26.

Mischel, W. (1968). *Personality and assessment.* New York: Wiley.

Moore, G.T. (1974). The development of environmental knowing: An overview of an interactional-constructivist theory and some data on Witkin Individual Development Variation. In D.V. Canter & T. Lee (Eds.), *Psychology and the built environment.* New York: Halstead.

Moore, G.T. (1979). Knowing about environmental knowing. *Environment and Behavior, 11,* 33–70.

Moore, G.T., Tuttle, D.P., & Howell, S.C. (1985). *Environmental design research directions for the future.* Washington, DC: Environmental Design Research Association.

Moos, R.H. (1972). Assessment of the psychosocial environments of community-oriented psychiatric treatment programs. *Journal of Abnormal Psychology, 79,* 9–18.

Murray, H.A. (1938). *Explorations in personality.* New York: Oxford University Press.

Murray, H.A. (1951). Some basic psychological assumptions and conceptions. *Dialectica, 51,* 266–292.

Murray, H.A. (1959). Preparation for a scaffold of a comprehensive system. In S. Koch (Ed.), *Psychology: A study of science* (Vol. 3). New York: McGraw-Hill.

Newtson, D. (1973). Attribution and the unit of perception of ongoing behavior. *Journal of Personality and Social Psychology, 28,* 28–38.

Novikoff, A.B. (1945a). The concept of integrative levels and biology. *Science, 101,* 209–215.

Novikoff, A.B. (1945b). Continuity and discontinuity in evolution. *Science, 102,* 405–406.

Pastalan, L.A. (1983). Environmental displacement: A literature reflecting old-person-environment transactions.

In G.D. Rowles (Ed.), *Aging and Milieu: Environmental perspectives on growing old.* New York: Academic.

Pea, R. (1982). What is planning development the development of? In D. Forbes & M. Greenberg (Eds.), *The development of planful behavior in children.* San Francisco: Jossey-Bass.

Pepper, S.C. (1942). *World hypotheses.* Berkeley: University of California Press.

Perin, C. (1970). *With man in mind: An interdisciplinary prospectus for environmental design.* Cambridge, MA: MIT Press.

Piaget, J. (1952). Autobiography. In E.G. Boring, H.S. Langfield, R.M. Yerkes, & H. Werner (Eds.), *A history of psychology in autobiography.* Worcester, MA: Clark University Press.

Piaget, J. (1971). *Biology and knowledge.* Chicago: University of Chicago Press.

Proshansky, H.M. (1976). Environmental psychology and the real world. *American Psychologist, 31,* 303–310.

Proshansky, H.M. (1980). Prospects and dilemmas of environment psychology. Paper presented at the Virginia Symposium on Environmental Psychology.

Proshansky, H., & Altman, I. (1979). Overview of the field. In W.P. White (Ed.), *Resources in environment and behavior.* Washington, DC: American Psychological Association.

Proshansky, H.M., Ittelson, W.H., & Rivlin, L.G. (1970a). Freedom of choice and behavior in a physical setting. In H.M. Proshansky, W.H. Ittelson, & L.G. Rivlin (Eds.), *Environmental psychology* (Vol. 1). New York: Holt, Rinehart & Winston.

Proshansky, H.M., Ittelson, W.H., & Rivlin, L.G. (1970b). The influence of the physical environment on behavior: Some basic assumptions. In H.M. Proshansky, W.H. Ittelson, & L.G. Rivlin (Eds.), *Environmental psychology* (Vol. 1). New York: Holt, Rinehart & Winston.

Rand, G. (1983). A developmental approach to systems theory. In S. Wapner & B. Kaplan (Eds.), *Toward a holistic developmental psychology.* Hillsdale, NJ: Erlbaum.

Rapoport, A. (1972). The search for simplicity. *Main Currents in Modern Thought, 28,* 79–84.

Rheingold, H.L., & Eckerman, C.O. (1969). The infant's free entry into a new environment. *Journal of Experimental Child Psychology, 8,* 271–283.

Rheingold, H.L., & Eckerman, C.O. (1970). The infant separates himself from the mother. *Science, 168,* 78–83.

Russell, J.A., & Ward, L.M. (1982). Environmental psychology. *Annual Review of Psychology, 33,* 651–658.

Rychlak, J.F. (1981). The case for a modest revolution in modern psychological science. In R.A. Kasschau & C.N. Cofer (Eds.), *Psychology's second century.* New York: Praeger.

Scarr, S. (1979). Psychology and children: Current research and practice. Introduction to the special issue. *American Psychologist, 34*, 809–811.

Schmitt, V., Redondo, J.P., & Wapner, S. (1977). The role of transitional objects in adult adaptation. Unpublished manuscript, Clark University, Worcester, MA.

Schneirla, T.C. (1949). Levels in the psychological capacities of animals. In R.W. Sellars, V.J. McGill, & M. Farber (Eds.), *Philosophy for the future*. New York: Macmillan.

Schneirla, T.C. (1957). The concept of development in comparative psychology. In D.B. Harris (Ed.), *The concept of development*. Minneapolis: University of Minnesota Press.

Schouela, D.A., Steinberg, L.M., Leveton, L.B., & Wapner, S. (1980). Development of the cognitive organization of an environment. *Canadian Journal of Behavioural Science, 12*, 1–16.

Schutz, A. (1951). Choosing among projects of action. *Philosophy and Phenomenological Research, 12*, 161–184.

Schutz, A. (1971). *Collected papers* (M. Natanson Ed.). The Hague, Netherlands: Nijhoff.

Seligman, M.E.P. (1975). *Helplessness: On depression, development, and death*. San Francisco: Freeman.

Shapiro, E., Rierdan, J., & Wapner, S. (1973). Effect of planning by children and adults on serial learning. Unpublished manuscript, Clark University, Worcester, MA.

Sherrod, D.R. (1974) Crowding, perceived control and behavioral aftereffects. *Journal of Applied Psychology, 4*, 171–186.

Steward, J.H. (1951). Levels of socio-cultural integration: An operational concept. *Southwestern Journal of Anthropology, 7*, 374–390.

Stockdale, J.E. (1979). Crowding: Determinants and effects. In L. Berkowitz (Ed.), *Advances in experimental social psychology* (Vol. 10). New York: Academic.

Stoddard, E.R. (1968). *Conceptual models of human behavior in disaster*. El Paso, TX: Texas Western.

Stokols, D. (1978). Environmental psychology. *Annual Review of Psychology, 29*, 253–295.

Stokols, D. (1979). A congruence analysis of human stress. In I.G. Sarason & C.D. Spielberger (Eds.), *Stress and anxiety*. (Vol. 6). Washington, DC: Hemisphere.

Stokols, D. (1981). Group x place transactions: Some neglected issues in psychological research on settings. In D. Magnusson (Ed.), *Toward a psychology of situations: An interactional perspective*. Hillsdale, NJ: Erlbaum.

Stokols, D. (1982). Environmental psychology: A coming of age. In A. Kraut (Ed.), *G. Stanley Hall Lecture Series* (Vol. 2). Washington, DC: American Psychological Association.

Stokols, D., & Shumaker, S.A. (1981). People in places: A transactional view of settings. In J. Harvey (Ed.), *Cognition, social behavior and the environment*. Hillsdale, NJ: Erlbaum.

Stokols, D., & Shumaker, S.A. (1983). The psychological context of residential mobility and well being. *Journal of Social Issues, 38*, 149–171.

Tolman, E.C., & Brunswik, E. (1935). The organism and the causal texture of the environment. *Psychological Review, 42*, 43–77.

van Ryzin, L. (Ed.). (1977). *Proceedings of the Wisconsin Conference on Research Methods in Behavior-Environment Studies*. Madison: University of Wisconsin Press.

Verbrugge, L.M. (1983). Multiple roles and physical health of women and men. *Journal of Health and Social Behavior, 24*, 16–30.

Vernon, M.D. (1952). *A further study of visual perception*. Cambridge, England: Cambridge University Press.

Villeco, M., & Brill, M. (1981). *Environmental design research: Concepts, methods and values*. Washington, DC: National Endowment for the Arts, Design Arts Program.

von Bertalanffy, L. (1950). An outline of general systems theory. *British Journal of Philosophy of Science, 1*, 139–164.

von Bertalanffy, L., (1956). A biologist looks at human nature. *Scientific Monthly, 82*, 33–41.

von Bertalanffy, L. (1962). *Modern theories of development*. New York: Harper Torch.

von Bertalanffy, L. (1968). *Organismic psychology and systems theory*. Worcester, MA: Clark University Press.

von Uexkül, J. (1957). A stroll through the world of animals and men. In C.H. Schiller (Ed.), *Instinctive behavior*. New York: International Universities Press.

Wapner, S. (1969). Organismic-developmental theory: Some applications to cognition. In P.H. Mussen, J. Langer, & M. Covington (Eds.), *Trends and issues in developmental psychology*. New York: Holt, Rinehart & Winston.

Wapner, S. (1976). Process and context in the conception of cognitive style. In S. Messick (Ed.), *Individuality in learning: Implications of cognitive styles and creativity for human development*, San Francisco: Jossey-Bass.

Wapner, S. (1977). Environmental transition: A research paradigm deriving from the organismic-developmental systems approach. In L. van Ryzin (Ed.), *Proceedings of the Wisconsin Conference on Research Methods in Behavior-Environment Studies*. Madison: University of Wisconsin Press.

Wapner, S. (1978). Some critical person-environment transitions. *Hiroshima Forum for Psychology, 5*, 3–20.

Wapner, S. (1980). Toward an analysis of transactions of persons-in-a-high-speed society. *Man and a high speed society. The IATSS (International Association of Traffic and Safety Science) Symposium on Traffic Science, 1980 Reports*. Tokyo: Kiyotsuga Nishikawa.

Wapner, S. (1981a). Transactions of persons-in-environ-ments: Some critical transitions. *Journal of Environmental Psychology, 1*, 223–239.

Wapner, S. (1981b). Transactions of persons-in-environ-ments: Some issues, problems and methods from the organismic-developmental viewpoint. In G. Hagino & W.H. Ittelson (Eds.), *Interaction processes between human behavior and environment. Proceedings of the Japan-United States Seminar, Tokyo, Japan, 1980.* Tokyo: Bunsei.

Wapner, S. (1982–83). Some trends and issues in environment psychology. *Hiroshima Forum, 9*, 47–59.

Wapner, S. (1983a). Living with radical disruptions of person-in-environment systems. *IATSS (International Association of Traffic and Safety Sciences) Review, 9* (2), 133–148. (In Japanese; English translation available from the author)

Wapner, S. (1983b, March 9–11). The experience of environmental change in relation to action. Paper presented at "Social Implications of Environmental Problems: A Mexico/United States Workshop," Rio Rico, Arizona.

Wapner, S., Ciottone, R.A., Hornstein, G.A., McNeil, O.V., & Pacheco, A.M. (1983). An examination of studies of critical transitions through the life cycle. In S. Wapner & B. Kaplan (Eds.), *Toward a holistic development psychology*. Hillsdale, NJ.: Erlbaum.

Wapner, S. & Cirillo L. (1973). *Development of planning* (Public Health Service Grant Application). Clark University, Worcester, MA.

Wapner, S., Cirillo, L., & Baker, A.H. (1969). Sensory-tonic theory: Toward a reformulation. *Archivia Di Psicologia Neurologia E. Psichiatria, 30*, 493–512.

Wapner, S., Cohen, S.B., & Kaplan, B. (Eds.) (1976). *Experiencing the environment*. New York: Plenum.

Wapner, S., & Ittelson, W.H. (1981). Environment perception and action. In G. Hagino & W.H. Ittelson (Eds.), *Interaction processes between human behavior and environment. Proceedings of the Japan-United States Seminar, Tokyo, Japan, September, 1980*. Tokyo: Bunsei.

Wapner, S., & Kaplan, B. (Eds.). (1983). *Toward a holistic developmental psychology*. Hillsdale, NJ: Erlbaum.

Wapner, S., Kaplan, B., & Ciottone, R. (1981). Self-world relationships in crucial environment transitions: Childhood and beyond. In L. Liben, A. Patterson, & N. Newcombe (Eds.) *Spatial representation and behavior across the life span*. New York: Academic.

Wapner, S., Kaplan, B., & Cohen, S.B. (1973). An organismic-developmental perspective for understanding transactions of men in environments. *Environment and Behavior, 5*, 255–289.

Wapner, S., & Lebensfeld-Schwartz, P. (1976). Toward a structural analysis of event experience. *Acta Psychologica, 41*, 397–401.

Wapner, S., & Werner, H. (1957). *Perceptual development*. Worcester, MA: Clark University Press.

Watkins, M. (1977). A phenomenological approach to organismic-developmental research. Unpublished manuscript, Clark University, Worcester, MA.

Wener, R.E. (1982, February). *Environment-behavior research "success stories."* Paper presented at a symposium on "Evaluating Occupied Environments," Georgia Institute of Technology, Atlanta.

Werner, H. (1926). *Einführungin die Entwicklungspsychologie* (4th ed.). Leipzig, East Germany: Barth. (Original work published 1926)

Werner, H. (1940). *Comparative psychology of mental development* (3rd ed.). New York: International Universities Press. (Original work published 1940)

Werner, H. (1957). The concept of development from a comparative and organismic point of view. In D. Harris (Ed.), *The concept of development*. Minneapolis: University of Minnesota Press.

Werner, H. (1978). *Developmental processes: Heinz Werner selected writings* (S.S. Barten & M.B. Franklin, Eds.). New York: International Universities Press.

Werner, H., & Kaplan, B. (1956). The developmental approach to cognition: Its relevance to the psychological interpretation of anthropological and ethnolinguistic data. *American Anthropologist, 58*, 866–880.

Werner, H., & Kaplan, B. (1963). *Symbol formation*. New York: Wiley.

White, S.H., & Siegel, A.W. (1984). Cognitive development in time and space. In B. Rogoff & J. Lave (Eds.), *Everyday cognition: Its development in social context*. Cambridge, MA: Harvard University Press.

Whyte, A.V.T. (1977). *Guidelines for field studies in environmental perception* (Man and the Biosphere Technical Notes No. 5). Paris: UNESCO.

Winkel, G.H. (1977). The role of ecological validity in environmental research. In L. van Ryzin (Ed.), *Proceedings of the Wisconsin Conference on Research Methods in Behavior-Environment Studies*. Madison: University of Wisconsin Press.

Witkin, H.A. (1965). Heinz Werner: 1890–1964. *Child development, 30*, 307–328.

Wofsey, E., Rierdan, J., & Wapner, S. (1979). Planning to move: Effects on representing the currently inhabited environment. *Environment and Behavior, 11*, 3–32.

Wohlwill, J.F. (1973). The environment is not in the head. In W.F. Preiser (Ed.), *Environmental design research: Vol. 2. Symposia and workshops*. Stroudsberg, PA: Dowden, Hutchinson, & Ross.

Wohlwill, J.F. (1982). Psychology and the environmental disciplines. In M. Bornstein (Ed.), *Psychology and its applied disciplines*. Hillsdale, NJ: Erlbaum.

Wohlwill, J.F., & Kohn, I. (1976). Dimensionalizing the environmental manifold. In S. Wapner, S.B. Cohen, & B. Kaplan (Eds.), *Experiencing the environment*. New York: Plenum.

Wundt, W. (1912). Principles of physiological psychology. In

B. Rand (Ed.), *The classical psychologists*. New York: Houghton Mifflin.

Wundt, W. (1916). *Elements of folk psychology*. New York: Macmillan.

Wundt, W. (1961). Contributions to the theory of perception. In T. Shipley (Ed.), *Classics in psychology*. New York: Philosophical Library.

Zeisel, J. (1981). *Inquiry by design*. Monterey, CA: Brooks/Cole.

Zube, E.H., Sell, J.L., & Taylor, J.G. (1982). Landscape perception: Research, application, theory. *Landscape Planning, 9*, 1–33.

Chapter 42

THE FIELD OF ENVIRONMENTAL PSYCHOLOGY: SECURING ITS FUTURE

Harold M. Proshansky, *Graduate School and University Center, City University of New York, New York*

42.1. INTRODUCTION

Environmental psychology is a fledgling behavioral science field that emerged swiftly in the early 1960s. For some 20 years it has revealed signs of growth in its theory, research, and influence and indeed has established a place for itself in psychology as well as in other scientific and professional fields. Given its short life, however, it does not measure up in these respects to the long-established subareas of psychology or to the other traditional human sciences. The critical question, however, is will it measure up in time in these ways? What is its future? Is it secure enough so that we can be reasonably certain that over the next few decades its productivity in research, theory, and problem solving will in fact keep pace with its original objectives? Perhaps what is more important, will the work maintain its unique conceptual point of view and the epistemological integrity that first spawned its development? As the title of this chapter suggests, I do not feel sanguine

about the future of the field of environmental psychology and indeed believe that steps can and must be taken to ensure its future. What these steps are will be the major concern of this chapter.

Before turning to this task, however, other questions must be answered. To begin with, there is the question of how I arrived at this less than optimistic view of the future of the field of environmental psychology. It was not, as some readers might expect, from any systematic review of the field as a scientific and social institution in which positive and negative "growth indicators" were established and measured. My prediction regarding the future of the field of environmental psychology was derived from a far more informal procedure, but one that I consider to be no less reliable. I responded to what I believe are a number of important indicators of the present viability of the field and that, in my judgment, do not portend a healthy future for it. For example, I asked myself how much, and more significantly, what kind of theory is being developed by researchers in environmental psychology. This and other criteria were considered in the light of the theoretical and empirical "accomplishments" of other behavioral science fields. Given the uncertainties inherent in making predictions and the relatively meager knowledge that we as social scientists have regarding the important growth indicators to be used in such predictions, this approach seemed as reasonable as any.

Taking this approach makes much sense, if one considers for a moment what I mean by the "future" of environmental psychology. My concern is not whether it will serve as an independent field, but rather how it will survive: whether it will indeed grow and develop to the point that a cumulative body of knowledge is established concerning the relationship between human behavior and experience and the properties of physical settings. The social institutional nature of all sciences or fields, including one as young as environmental psychology, ensures their survival regardless of their progress in achieving their scientific objectives. Thus my real concern is not whether environmental psychology will survive, but it is rather with the quality of that survival. I am concerned with whether its level of scientific accomplishments in the understanding and solving of person/physical setting problems will make that survival worthwhile.

Another question that should be answered before considering the future of environmental psychology concerns its past. How did the field begin, and what happened along the way in its two-decade history? I will not attempt a very detailed analysis of the origin and development of the field because not only has that been done (Proshansky & Altman, 1979; Proshansky & O'Hanlon, 1977), but there is no need for it in this analysis. What is necessary is a description of some of the factors that shaped the emergence and development of the field so that the reader can see how it began and where it got to, and indeed what it "delivered" and failed to deliver. Such an analysis will reveal the basis of my pessimism for its future and by implication the conditions necessary to strengthen the field of environmental psychology so that its future will be secured.

42.2. ENVIRONMENTAL PSYCHOLOGY: YESTERDAY AND TODAY

42.2.1. Yesterday: Some Background

It is difficult to pinpoint with any precision the exact period when the field of environmental psychology began to take root. There is evidence of relevant writing and research by psychologists, psychiatrists, and architecture and design specialists as early as the mid-1950s. Humphrey Osmond, the psychiatrist, had already published his work "Function as the Basis of Psychiatric Ward Design" by 1957, and Sommer and Ross's research on social interaction in a geriatrics ward followed soon after, coming into print by 1958. At roughly the same time, Ittelson, Proshansky, and Rosenblatt were working on an analytic framework for the study of factors influencing the design and functioning of psychiatric facilities (1960). And on the other side of the Atlantic, Kuper's study of the physical and social effects of adjacent new family homes on the residents of these homes was published as early as 1953.

These early studies, however, in no way heralded the emergence of the field of environmental psychology. Given the fact that concerns with person/physical environment relationships were virtually nonexistent in psychology and the other behavioral sciences, it had to be a convergence of influences occurring at the right time and under the right circumstances that set the stage for the birth of the field. There is much that suggests that it was the social and political upheavals of the 1960s that precipitated that birth. Although this seems a reasonable premise, I would add that the conditions underlying the upheavals of the 1960s began to occur and develop in the 1940s and 1950s. It is important for us to consider this period briefly in order to fully understand the "internal conditions" that set the stage for the emergence of environmental psychology during that period.

The end of World War II brought with it not only the sense of a new era of peace and democracy but an almost insatiable demand for places, spaces, goods, services, and technological equipment that was unparalleled in the history of Western society. To satisfy this demand, skilled technicians and highly trained professionals became the single greatest priority in postsecondary education. Although educational subsidies available to World War II veterans were in part responsible for the surging numbers of high school graduates who went on to college or professional/technical schools, the inexorable force behind this growth of students was the persistent market demand for technically and professionally trained personnel.

The behavioral sciences had acquitted themselves well during World War II. Experimental psychology in particular, with its "human factors" applications, had served the armed services and the war industries perfectly. Diagnostic testing for any number of purposes (e.g., psychiatric care, personnel placement, evaluation of training programs) had also been productive for the war effort. Finally, and perhaps what is most important, social psychology began to come into its own. Problems of individual motivation, intergroup conflicts, minority group prejudice, intellectual competence, personnel selection and placement, and group structure and process plagued the armed services and related civilian work forces during World War II (Hoveland, Lumsdaine, & Sheffield, 1949). Social and personality psychologists not only revealed some of the factors underlying these problems but also developed relatively successful programs for their resolution.

Following World War II, research in social psychology grew at an accelerated rate, particularly with reference to attitude change, small-group processes, and intergroup conflict. And it was during this same period that Lewin (1948) and his students Festinger, Schacter, and Back (1950) and Deutsch (1949) began to apply field theory conceptions to various social problems. At the root of Lewin's thinking was the view that social research could be theoretically meaningful as well as socially useful. It was assumed that in the very process of attempting to investigate and resolve such complex social problems as intergroup prejudice or war and peace, underlying conceptions and principles would emerge. Clearly, research of this kind had to occur in the real world, although the laboratory was not ruled out as the place to develop more embracing abstract and generalized theories.

At this same time, Hoveland and his associates (1949, 1951) were doing systematic research on social attitudes, particularly with respect to changing attitudes. The fertile ground out of which this research grew was studies undertaken during World War II that demonstrated the successful application of concept and principle to problems of attitude formation and change, particularly in enlisted men. But, for the sake of both accuracy and clarity, it is critical to point out a major difference between the research and application that went on during World War II and what followed in the research efforts of Lewin and Hoveland and their respective associates.

As Deutsch and Hornstein (1975) indicate, Lewin and the other field theorists barely left the laboratory. Relatively speaking—and this is evident if one reviews their research efforts over a two-decade period—they were primarily involved with doing experimental laboratory studies of social behavior and experience at both the individual and group levels of social function. In essence, they continued the tradition of social psychologists in their search for

generalized concepts and principles to explain complex social processes and functions in both the individual and the social group. "Action research," which as defined and advocated by Lewin meant attacking complex social problems in the natural ongoing contexts in which they occurred, became the exception rather than the rule among these field theorists.

Hoveland and his associates were not committed at all to action research, and so in their studies of social attitudes and social change the college laboratory was just the place they wanted to be. For them as well as Lewin and his associates, the college student was the focus of study whether at the individual or group level of investigation. This kind of social psychology simplified the real world not only by its almost exclusive concern with college students but also at times by assuming the existence of simplified and easy-to-measure indicators of social attitudes and social behavior.

This, then, in the briefest of descriptions is what happened to psychology and, in particular, the field of social psychology during World War II and in the two decades following. As we shall soon see, although it was an extremely productive period in which the field grew in almost every regard, problems began to develop regarding the validity of the assumptions involved in carrying out laboratory-experimental social psychological research. And it was these problems that served as the nexus of forces underlying the emergence of environmental psychology as a scientific field of inquiry.

42.2.2. Confluence of Forces

The primary assumption whose validity came into question was that the real world of social process and social relationships could be duplicated in the laboratory of the university. The challenge to this assumption came from an increasing awareness that the laboratory had its own world of actors, namely college student subjects and faculty member researchers, both of whom confounded attempts to duplicate reality. In this respect, each of these groups exerted influences on experimental findings that had little, if anything, to do with the problems being studied. It was, therefore, not only difficult to bring the real world into the university setting to do relevant research but just as difficult to suspend or "control" that other world of the university in its influence on this research (Orne, 1962; Rosenthal, 1966).

The reader should not assume that the strong commitment of social psychologists (and other specialists in psychology) to the laboratory-experimental approach was some whim or vested-interest concern of those who took the lead in the field. Clearly, the commitment was rooted in the belief that physical-natural science epistemology was the most appropriate if not the only model for the development of a cumulative body of knowledge in the behavioral sciences. What must be emphasized is that research psychologists were searching for general principles of behavior and experience inherent in complex psychological and social processes and often not directly with solutions to human problems. Thus the university experimental-laboratory setting was just the place with the means to get at such principles.

The laboratory-experimental model came into question for at least two other reasons besides the intrusion of the student–faculty university culture into attempts to duplicate the real world in social psychological research. First, not only did findings in relation to the same problem show, in many cases, little consistency, but as Katz (1972) pointed out, there was very little of what can best be called "scientific outcome." His now classic statement simply and directly states that

> of the thousands of experimental social psychological experiments in the past 20 years, the number that supplies new information to the cumulative body of knowledge is surprisingly small....The development of Experimental Psychology has been costly if the energy input is compared to the significant output. (Katz, 1972, p. 557)

Although Katz explains this poor scientific outcome as a problem in method and Proshansky (1976a) believes that epistemological and theoretical issues are the key, the fact remains that there has been almost no systematic cumulation of verifiable knowledge in social psychology to date. The sad reality that must be faced is that the vast quantities of data produced in relation to problems such as attitude formation and change, small-group dynamics, and cognitive dissonance have produced findings no better than the findings resulting from animal and human studies of 50 years ago.

But the next and even more telling problem that confronted experimental social psychology was, in a sense, its "failure" in the real world. During the period of the 1960s when the hope for a Great Society was at its peak, social psychologists both experimental and otherwise were asked to solve problems of school learning, poverty, intergroup and racial prejudice, and many others. Unfortunately, the pressing social issues of the day could not be thoughtfully approached based on existing social psychological research and theory. To some degree, it

can be said that for a time in the 1970s social psychology and other fields in the behavioral sciences lost their credibility in the eyes of social practitioners and government officials in the real world, not to mention among some of its own researchers and theorists.

It is small wonder, given the problems and difficulties that confronted the field of social psychology in the 1960s and early 1970s, that a malaise characterized the field at the end of this period (Berkowitz, 1970; Elms, 1975; Proshansky, 1976b; Smith, 1972). Put simply, some social psychologists became alienated from their academic training. There is no need to exaggerate this malaise by invoking any deep-seated interpretation of their alienation. The promise that social psychology held out immediately following World War II was becoming increasingly elusive and was leaving social psychologists frustrated, disappointed, and more and more skeptical about the particular epistemology that identified social psychology as a science. Of course, how this group of psychologists responded to their alienation is another story. As we shall see later, not all of those who moved into environmental psychology or more broadly stated, "environment and behavior," saw the solution to the problem of social psychology or psychology in general in the same way.

By itself, the malaise in social psychology during the late 1960s and early 1970s would not have led to the new field of environmental psychology. The malaise came about from and sensitized many social psychologists to other factors that cast doubt on the value of the scientific as well as the applied value of their research efforts. And it was this confluence of factors that both allowed and directed those who experienced the alienation to consider turning their attention to problems of physical settings and human behavior and experience. Perhaps the most conspicuous factor among these was the absence from social psychology of concept, theory, or research relevant to the day-to-day built environment of the individual. The built environment of urban and suburban (and even rural) life as it affected human experience was largely overlooked. Relevant social psychological issues such as crowding, place-identity, territoriality, personal space, environmental learning, and environmental competence were blatantly ignored.

The reasons were clear enough. The focus on general principles meant that a concern with rooms, streets, transportation, hospital wards, or other loci of the real world was unnecessary and could, in fact, be transcended. Furthermore, the laboratory setting, by definition, virtually excluded the physical settings of the real world except for some limited possibilities using simulation techniques.

What began to happen, however, was that a series of external factors began to exert considerable pressure on all fields of behavioral science. To begin with, in the midst of an unprecedented growth of urban and suburban settings, design professionals found themselves increasingly in need of answers to questions about physical settings and human needs, values, behaviors, and experiences. Thus architect planners such as Alexander (1964), Fitch (1965), Izumi (1965), and Lynch (1960) were poised and ready to act out new professional values in response to growing pressures from community leaders for more and more construction. No one knew better than they did what the issues were, because it was their thinking that challenged the traditional underlying assumptions being made about the needs, values, feelings, and conceptions of people in relation to the places that defined their day-to-day existence. However, not all of these professionals including architects, interior designers, town planners, and landscape architects responded to these needs in any serious way. Indeed, only a small number sought answers to questions of human needs and experience. Initially, it was this group of architect planners and perhaps a handful of others who recognized and faced the need for input from psychologists, sociologists, and other behavioral science specialists. It is interesting to note that Lynch's now classic *Image of the City* was already published by 1960 and therefore was being written as early as the late 1950s.

There was yet another powerful force for social change that helped bring about the emergence of the field of environmental psychology, and that was the urgency and the threat of the environmental crisis. Earth Day, in 1970, was merely the culmination of interest in environmental problems that were edging into consciousness beginning in the mid-1960s. Suddenly the sporadic and relatively ineffective protests of some environmental groups concerned with urban blight, the destruction of wilderness areas, and the increasing tinsellike neon-lighted culture of the American city gave way to a wave of public concern and protest. A threat to human sensibilities is one thing; a threat to human life is still another. Air pollution and food and water contamination, along with the hasty and reckless introduction of new chemical compounds, electronic devices, and other technical innovations, all carried with them the stark reality of the possibility of the loss of human life in very large numbers.

Less immediately threatening but far more difficult to come to grips with were matters of human dignity. There was a growing awareness that the quality of urban life went well beyond the question of human survival. A physical setting in which the individual's day-to-day existence robbed the individual of his or her right to realize his or her full capacity as a human being because of crowding, intense noise, physical inconvenience, and still other stressors clearly cast doubt on the value of technological and scientific progress. But, in turn, it did not seem that the question of human dignity could be answered by urban settings that were clean, efficient, and safe. There was the matter, for example, of increasing numbers of individuals being forced into smaller and smaller physical settings in which efficiency, speed, and uniformity assumed greater importance than individual variation, freedom of choice, and aesthetic expression.

A no less important force in the emergence of environmental psychology was the expression of the social upheaval of the 1960s on the college or university campus. For those social psychologists who felt alienated from their field of specialization, the campus uprisings that occurred undoubtedly provided some sense of justification for their alienation. While students expressed their outrage over the Vietnam War, the violation of civil rights of minority groups, and the inexorable and unyielding social ills of our society, a key issue that was closer to home for them was the precedence of research over teaching, which was made even more profound by the lack of relevance in both. What these students sought were courses, experiences, and even research endeavors that would give them a better understanding of the day-to-day political, social, and economic worlds in which they lived. They believed that through their active participation in these experiences with interventions aimed at change, a better existence could be achieved for all social groups.

It is easy to look back now and be critical of the open-ended influence that the concept of "relevance" had on the training programs taken by graduates and undergraduates in many of the person-oriented fields of psychology. Yet one should not ignore the very important positive aspects of this influence, including the long-needed reviews of these programs. As I have already suggested, the emphasis on "relevance" tended to legitimize the views of some psychologists already poised to turn their backs on the traditional scientific model that guided concept, theory, and problem formulation in their fields. But they were not the only ones affected. For many traditional laboratory social psychologists with some interest in physical settings, the possibility of studying major social problems in the real-life context in which they occurred no longer seemed threatening or an abandonment of the scientific method. Interest was particularly generated in regard to the physical settings of urban neighborhoods as well as the city as a whole. If crowding, urban decay, loss of privacy, and water and air pollution were not relevant, then what problems were?

By the middle 1960s so much was in place: the demand from government and community leaders for physical settings to be responsive to human needs, support for these demands and concerns by students and citizens alike, dissident social psychologists and other behavioral scientists ready to plunge into physical real-world problems in collaboration with equally eager design professionals, and university programs that showed signs of indeed supporting the necessary changes. Given this context, the flow of federal, state, and foundation funds to support physical setting research, to train graduate students for such research, and to develop programs for environmental change grew from a trickle to a swiftly flowing stream that was cresting by the early 1970s. Under these circumstances, the emergence and development of environmental psychology was inevitable.

42.2.3. Today: Where Are We?

I will attempt to answer the preceding question in very specific ways that will not at all involve a detailed description of what the field of environmental psychology looks like in 1983. For the latter purpose, I recommend some earlier accounts by Proshansky and Altman (1979), Proshansky and O'Hanlon (1977), and Stokols (1977), as well as some more recent historical presentations that will bring the reader right up to date (Russell & Ward, 1982; Wohlwill, 1983). Finally, Sommer, Chapter 43, this volume, has as a penetrating and comprehensive up-to-date account of the field recommended discussing its past, present, and future.

My concern here will be different. I will attempt to answer some critical questions through which I hope to reveal where the field is regarding its status and progress as a scientific field of inquiry. The first question focuses on what the field of environmental psychology turned out to be some 20 years after it first emerged. That is by no means a simple question. Its answer is difficult to trace because as interest peaked in the relationship between the physical environment and human experience, not only psychologists but a whole raft of academics and professionals showed interest in the issues. Sociologists,

geographers, economists, anthropologists, and, of course, those in the design and environmental management professions all brought a unique frame of reference for understanding problems of human interaction with the built environment. To put the matter boldly, from the very beginning it became apparent that because the turf known as the physical environment was not only complex but "belonged" to no one, it necessarily would turn out to be a multidisciplinary endeavor.

Can one refer to such a multidisciplinary endeavor as an "environmental psychology?" In one sense one cannot, because concerns with human experience and behavior from an analytical point of view are not confined to the discipline of psychology. What is distinctive for the fields of psychology is their emphasis on such experience and behavior at the *individual* level of analysis. Sociologists, anthropologists, and other behavioral scientists are no less concerned with behavior and experience, but for them it is the group, social organization, and still larger aggregates that represent the critical unit of analysis. Be this as it may, the whole range of problems and of scientific disciplines and professional groups responsible for the growth of interest in relating spaces and places to people's behavior, attitudes, and experiences has led to the designation of this broad problem area as "environment and behavior" (Epstein, 1976; White, 1979).

White (1979) points out that the "field" of environment and behavior does not exist in the same sense as the recognized fields of psychology such as social, personality, or child psychology, or even such specialized subareas as attitudes and attitude change. The distinguishing factor with respect to each of these fields is that psychologists are referring to an area of scientific inquiry with delineated boundaries of selected problems, methods, relevant concepts, theoretical formulations, and a corpus of research findings. Ostensibly for the broad multidisciplinary area of environment and behavior, such boundaries and the set of criteria that define them do not as yet exist.

What, then, is environmental psychology? It can be conceived of as one of the scientific fields belonging to the broader problem area of "environment and behavior" (Epstein, 1976). Furthermore, in terms of the number of psychologists involved and indeed the criteria for speaking of a "field" as indicated by White, there is little question that "environmental psychology" has emerged as an area of scientific specialization in the broader field of psychology.

Through the remainder of this discussion my focus will be on environmental psychology as it evolved from and in relation to the more established fields of psychology, particularly the field of social psychology. It is true that the field of environmental psychology can be identified in terms of the criteria noted by White (1979) but certainly with far less clarity, depth, and definition than is true of such fields as social, personality, child, or physiological psychology. Furthermore, as one reviews this new field in psychology, it becomes evident that within it, there are clearly fundamental differences in approach. In effect, there are "types" of environmental psychology, and the differences among them, at least in certain instances, are by no means trivial.

Based on the brief historical analysis of the field already presented, this should come as no surprise. Clearly psychologists, social or otherwise, reacting to external social pressures both in and off campuses would be expected to respond differently to these events depending on whether or not they were already alienated from their established field. And even among those who were alienated, some were disaffected by what was happening in their field in one way, and others were disaffected in still other ways. Thus, to take but one example, some social psychologists really had no quarrel with the concepts and methods of their field except that they felt that far more "field research" was necessary. As the promise of systematic field research faded from the activities of the disciples of Lewinian field theory, some of these disciples clearly became alienated and ready to leave the laboratory and "do battle" in the real world (Deutsch & Hornstein, 1975). For others, the alienation was of a more serious nature. Indeed, it was epistemological in character, and the move into environmental psychology was seen as an irreversible one in which "burning one's bridges behind one" was both deliberate and necessary.

That social psychologists played a significant role in the development of the field of environmental psychology is not surprising—even apart from issues of alienation or the influences of Lewin and his associates. A concern with social interaction, social process, and social structure requires some minimal awareness of if not interest in the physical settings in which all of this occurs. However, it literally took a social revolution to get the field of social psychology to pay attention to and consider the role of places and spaces in human behavior and experience.

What occurred because of the "revolution" was simple enough. The problem was perceived as one of omission and not commission. Issues either directly or indirectly relevant to person/physical-setting relationships became the focus of concern and were subjected to traditional psychological analysis and empirical study. Everything remained pretty much the same—except the nature of the problem. It was assumed that the laboratory-experimental approach was not only necessary but sufficient to establish fundamental cause-and-effect relationships between physical-setting variables and human behavior and experience. This can be seen in the work of Canter (1975), Kaplan (1977), Mehrabian and Russell (1974), and others. This outcome was neither unexpected nor unreasonable. The application, for example, of cognitive concepts and data to the problem of cognitive mapping or environmental meaning was a very appropriate response. These social psychologists were neither alienated from their field nor overly concerned with solving complex environmental problems.

Furthermore, some dimensions of established "environment and behavior" concepts such as personal space, privacy, crowding, and territoriality do, on the face of it, lend themselves to study in the laboratory using the existing methodology. Therefore, it should come as no surprise that some social psychologists were ready and simply did change the problem foci of their thinking and research but not the epistemology underlying it. As Epstein points out, these are

individuals who are more likely to be identified by others as environmental psychologists than to identify themselves as such...whose research topic is "environmental" but who adhere to the norms and research traditions of Social Psychology. (1976, 345–349)

In this category are environmental researchers such as Aiello (1975), Baum and Valins (1973), Baum, Harpin, and Valins (1975), and Freedman (1975).

It was suggested earlier that there were other social psychologists who were far less content with the traditional goals and approaches of social psychology. They were clearly dissatisfied, if not alienated from the field. They were not only disenchanted with the traditional experimental laboratory approach in social psychology and all that it implied but were even less enamored with the goals of social psychology. The search for basic principles was not merely viewed as futile; it was seen as quite inimical to a field that purported to be value oriented. For these social psychologists, the attraction to environmental issues was rooted in the relevance of these issues to the real world in which human behavior and experience takes place. Not only was it necessary for social psychological research to be relevant and meaningful to problems in the real world, but its applied orientation had to produce socially useful outcomes.

Epstein (1976), however, identifies still another group of dissident social psychologists. They tended to be senior researchers who were also dissatisfied and perhaps alienated from their fields. The root of their complaint was not the search for general principles but rather the traditional methodology employed in the attempt to achieve this goal. Pessimism and doubt among these social psychologists were focused on the experimental-laboratory paradigm with all of its attendant problems of distortions of reality, subject deception, demand characteristics, and so on. What attracted them to environmental problems was not so much their interest in these problems, as it was the desire to work with others sympathetic to their need to establish a new methodology for social psychologists that would indeed lead to research outcomes that would be (as Lewin, 1948, urged) theoretically meaningful and socially useful.

Perhaps the key distinction that can be made among social psychologists who were both impelled and attracted to environmental problems concerns the degree to which they were willing to give up on social psychology. Thus Altman (1976) and Proshansky (1976a) clearly differed over the value of the tenets and practices of social psychology for the inchoate and fledgling field of environmental psychology. Proshansky saw little value for environmental psychology in maintaining a theoretical and methodological relationship with social psychology; on the other hand, for Altman, there was much to be gained by environmental psychology drawing on concepts and data of social psychology. Altman believed that social psychology could learn much from environmental psychology concerning how to integrate physical setting research in the real world into the analysis and study of social process, social interaction, and social functions. In this respect, Epstein (1976) points out that "close contact with real world problems is a healthy antidote to abstract theory." I would agree, as I do with the view that out of such contact may come the formulation of *new* theoretical conceptions. Epstein concludes that this "approach is more meaningful than attempts to generalize from basic research studies to the solution of applied problems." Whether, in return, environmental psychology can benefit from the traditionally derived theoretical constructs and generalizations of social psychology, I

am not sure. But as the reader will see in the final section of this chapter, my position described previously on the relationship between social psychology and environmental psychology has clearly "softened."

42.2.4. Environmental Psychology Today: Some Properties

At this point in the discussion, it is important to describe in somewhat more detail the nature of environmental psychology today insofar as its approach to theory and method is concerned. I refer here to an environmental psychology that was developed by those social psychologists who turned away from the goals and methodological approaches of social psychology. These social psychologists were deeply committed to developing a discipline that was both value oriented and problem oriented. The purpose of research was to resolve complex environmental problems and thereby contribute to the well-being of individuals and the larger society in which they lived. Its methodology was to be rooted in the real world in which these problems occurred. Thus what became known as "contextual research" demanded that conceptions of environmental problems and possible solutions be drawn from the real settings in which they occurred and be directly connected to human experience within those settings.

An environmental psychology that was focused on the real world and directly concerned with solutions to complex environmental problems must by definition be interdisciplinary in character. Indeed, Lewin (1948) from the very first in his emphasis on "action research" knew that the kind of social psychology he was proposing had to involve research and conceptual linkages with the other behavioral sciences. That environmental psychology in the 1980s is interdisciplinary in its stated approach and orientation is undeniable. However, much of what occurs in environmental psychology in this respect is actually interdisciplinary awareness, association, and at times "cohabitation." There is little in these efforts that truly can be regarded as interdisciplinary integration of concepts and theory as a basis for empirical research that links together the various levels of societal organization (i.e., individuals, groups) involved in complex environmental problems. I will have more to say about this issue in the final section of this chapter.

For the environmental psychologist, the interdisciplinary approach has inherent in it the fundamental assumption that complex social and physical-setting problems are not caused by one or a few variables that can be isolated. Not only are there many such variables involved, but they interact with each other and indeed are themselves influenced by the very events to be "explained." Still another property of environmental psychology then is its focus on "systems analysis," that is, determining the pattern of mutually influencing characteristics of sociophysical settings. Some of these characteristics change as events external or internal to the setting change; and as a result still other changes in the properties of these settings occur. These changes may occur either rapidly or slowly, depending on the circumstances. For example, high unemployment in a community is likely to take longer to produce basic changes in the sociophysical properties of that community than, say, a natural or even person-made disaster (e.g., devastating flood or nuclear power plant explosion).

To engage in systems analysis of complex environmental problems in the ongoing day-to-day context in which they occur implies still another major property of environmental psychology as a field of scientific inquiry. Such contexts have both a space and place immediacy and a reality extending over time. What complicates systems analysis is that environmental problems or for that matter, all human behavior and experience are as much tied to changes in any given context over time as they are to the interplay of cultural, social, and psychological influences that occur at a given point in time. Time as well as space and place is a critical consideration and indeed must be treated as such in an approach that purports to study environmental problems in the naturalistic contexts in which they occur.

The kind of environmental psychology described here is by no means easy "to practice." It is one thing to establish the essential properties of an applied, problem-oriented, system-analytic research approach and still another to carry it out. If one asks how environmental psychology as a scientific field of inquiry was doing in 1983, the answer depends on how one defines *doing*. As an organized endeavor of research, publications, meetings, participants, teaching, professional organizations and policy development, it is not showing signs of real growth, but it is holding its own. This is to be expected given the growing and intense suspicion of behavioral science research engendered by the Reagan administration and the effects of the economic recession on university funding over the last 5 to 7 years. One consequence of these restraints on the behavioral sciences has been the return to an emphasis on traditional approaches in what is taught and how research is done

in many psychology departments across the nation. Cast against this background, environmental psychology has done far better than one might expect for a relatively new and inchoate scientific field.

Environmental psychologists seem neither dismayed nor discouraged. Although there has not been any real growth in the last 5 years in the number of undergraduate courses, specialized environmental programs at the doctoral level, nor a vast burgeoning of sponsored or voluntary research endeavors, volumes in environmental psychology continue to be published, new journals started, and conferences held. Thus Holohan's text, *Environmental Psychology,* was published in 1982. In 1979, Sarason and Spielberger devoted a good part of Volume 6 of their *Stress and Anxiety* series to environmental stress, and the International Congress of Applied Psychology was able to establish a section on environmental psychology under the leadership of Kenneth Craik. It is also important to note that both at the Central University of Venezuela and the University of Mexico, undergraduate and graduate programs in environmental psychology are in the process of being or have been established. Perhaps of even greater significance is the birth of a new journal in 1981, *The International Journal of Environmental Psychology,* a collaborative effort involving American and British environmental psychologists. Much more evidence can be given that although not developing by leaps and bounds, the field is holding its own. The crucial question then becomes how long can this go on? Will growth occur over time that is significant or will the field eventually fade away? These questions will be addressed in the final section of this chapter.

42.3. SECURING THE FUTURE

All sciences are social institutions. Like any other social institution, they are rooted in and express an array of political, social, and economic forces that shape their purposes, activities, and organizational structures. Thus scientists do research, publish, belong to relevant professional organizations, teach, serve as consultants, and above all identify with and protect the values and purposes of their particular scientific field. In all of this, of course, individual scientists derive satisfactions and rewards of recognition, prestige, income, power, material goods, and indeed still other personal, cultural, and social benefits. It is easy to see why sciences continue almost inexorably in their pursuit of a cumulative body of knowledge. Not unlike other social institutions, the sciences are organized to function and carry out their relevant activities in ways that protect and ensure their continued existence.

It is the very nature of a science as a social institution that makes its emergence, growth, and development possible in the first place. However, it is important to distinguish between the growth of a science as a social institution and its growth as an empirical and theoretically integrated cumulative body of knowledge. The growth of a science as a social institution cannot in any way by itself be used as a measure of its actual "scientific productivity." All of the institutional activities mentioned previously — research, university teaching, professional memberships, publications in journals and books, and so forth — are necessary but not sufficient for achieving such productivity. And there is no better scientific arena for demonstrating this view than the behavioral sciences.

The promise that the fields of sociology and psychology held for solving complex social problems and making a "better society" during the Johnson administration and thereafter was never realized. Yet the social and behavioral sciences continue to endure, and indeed the demand on them for solutions to society's problems continues to grow. Whether in the university, the community, or the government setting, the status and influence of the behavioral sciences are secure. Perhaps this is the case because alternative paths to providing answers to society's social problems are few and far between, and the behavioral sciences at least provide initial conceptions and tentative answers to some social problems. But what has truly made the "voice" of the behavioral and social sciences heard is their growth as social institutions during the last half century. They have grown in numbers of theorists and researchers, influence on government and foundation funding agencies, status and influence in the university, significance in relation to other social institutions (e.g., primary and secondary schools), the size and number of their professional organizations and, finally, in their financial resources and political strength.

If the behavioral sciences in general and psychology in particular have grown and flourished in this way, would not the same be true for environmental psychology? In its short history, it has indeed evolved at least some of the same social institutional properties as the other fields of psychology. As Sommer (Chapter 43, this volume) points out, not only do many person/physical setting problems remain unsolved, but other new ones are beginning to appear in the wake of new advances in technology (e.g., telecom-munication, nuclear power). Thus the demand for scientific fields to do something about environmental problems will intensify rather than abate. Yet with all that I have said about sciences as social institutions, the future of environmental psychology may still be in jeopardy. Its ability to endure and continue to develop as a social institution and, therefore, in its scientific achievements is cast in considerable doubt.

The reasons are clear enough. Environmental psychology not only has a relatively small number of researchers and university faculty who identify themselves as environmental psychologists, but it is scarcely represented as a field of specialization for undergraduates and graduate students in traditional departments of psychology. In effect, whatever its initial growth in the 1960s, it scarcely "took off" or "made it" in the 1970s. In part, its growth was "stunted" by a period of economic decline both generally and for universities in particular. Even now these conditions prevail such that government and foundation funding for training and research has declined considerably. Competition for funds has intensified among the traditional fields of psychology to the point that environmental psychology cannot compete. Finally, to compound the problem of its being a small fledgling field with little influence by way of numbers of researchers, university representation, or discipline status is the fact that environmental psychology views itself and is viewed by others as an interdisciplinary field.

Its interdisciplinary orientation to social/environmental problems means that its social institutional nature hardly rests on a clear and firm base of discipline, definition, and purpose. In effect, its stance is not simply nontraditional, but beyond that, its "fit" into the organizational structure of universities, government research and training programs, and in many instances even private research institutes is by no means a simple matter. We already know that in general, interdisciplinary fields in the behavioral sciences have not fared well in university and even foundation settings. The social institutional activities that serve to perpetuate a field of specialization also serve to prevent a change in purpose, image, or identity that would result from its interdisciplinary "blending" with other fields or sciences.

Is the future of environmental psychology doomed? I am not sure, but I am certain that its future is hardly secure. It is important to stress that the more traditional fields of psychology such as social, personality, and developmental are becoming increasingly interested in environmental problems. Environmental psychology, because of its nontraditional as well as interdisciplinary stance, will find itself increasingly unable to compete for the funding and organizational supports needed to give it its place in the sun. The field's future is clearly in peril unless it can strengthen its own social institutional resources by establishing in a convincing, coherent, and systematic fashion the precise nature of its approach as a scientific field of inquiry. This means examining in more detail and with greater precision the implications of its major defining properties that not only stamped it as an "alternative" approach but helped set it apart from other traditional fields of psychology. What I will attempt to demonstrate, however, is that there are implications to be drawn from the basic tenets of environmental psychology that draw it closer to more traditional fields of psychology rather than isolating it from these fields. This point of view has largely been ignored and is in direct contrast to the earlier isolationist position taken by this writer (Proshansky, 1976a).

In the remaining discussion, four major orientations of environmental psychology will be considered. In each instance, the underlying assumptions or implications of the orientation will be made explicit, particularly those that have been ignored or overlooked by researchers and theorists. Not only should this provide a more precise analysis of the approach of environmental psychology, but perhaps what is more important, it should also give us a clearer understanding of what environmental psychologists should be doing in their thinking and research in relation to other environmentally focused behavioral scientists and design professionals, (e.g., architects, etc.). Essentially, it is out of such self-conscious deliberate analysis in the thinking and research of environmental psychologists that the approach of the field and its institutional credibility will be strengthened.

42.3.1. Problem Oriented

The description of environmental psychology as a "problem-oriented" field has had and continues to have a very specific meaning for many environmental psychologists. In brief, the field lays claim to complex environmental problems that threaten the well-being and indeed, in some instances, the very existence of the members of our society. The problems are pervasive and touch almost all institutional settings of our society, that is, family households, schools, work places, hospital settings, recreation areas, means of transportation, and so on. They extend from such broad issues as urban decay and sub-

standard levels of day-to-day living to crowding in hospitals and noise pollution in public spaces and then to more focused issues such as restricted access for children in high-rise urban housing.

Such research, of course, is not only problem oriented but value oriented as well. Without denying the search for understanding through establishing a cumulative body of knowledge, the commitment to make a better world in which human potential and growth are fully realized is just as strong. Yet one must be careful not to view the problem–value orientation of environmental psychologists in itself as a unique aspect of their approach. Many environmental, social, and personality psychologists—and other specialists as well—see themselves as equally problem and value oriented while working in the university laboratory context. I am certain that Freedman (1975) who has studied the nature and effects of crowding in the university laboratory sees himself in just this fashion. What, then, is the difference?

The problem-oriented approach that I have just described has an *urgency* that requires that both an understanding and a solution to environmental problems be achieved as soon as possible. On the other hand, for those environmental, social, and personality psychologists who search for answers to these problems in the experimental laboratory, the direction or the objective is the same, but the path is longer and in a sense "detoured." Establishing general concepts and principles that indeed transcend both given situations and even the nature of classes of specific problems is the first priority of concern. Under these circumstances, the urgency to both understand and solve complex environmental problems is not only far less, but in a sense it is never experienced as "urgency" at all. The urgency and single determination that do occur are for the achievement of general abstract concepts and principles because it is at this level of theoretical integration that a cumulative body of scientific knowledge is to be established. Thus there is an urgency but not for the direct understanding and solution of complex environmental problems.

The focus of the environmental psychologist on this kind of approach has two obvious implications. The first is that problems must be defined and studied in the ongoing, real-life contexts in which they occur. The second is that to best understand and thereby solve environmental problems, concepts and principles must be evolved directly from the specific problems and physical settings being studied. In this regard, then, the integrity of such problems emerging from a complex of psychological and cultural forces cannot and should not be violated by the research process. Of course, the mere fact that environmental research is undertaken in the real world is by no means a guarantee that such violation will not occur. One can mold and carve real-life events to fit some a priori model developed for field research and thereby distort those events not unlike what occurs in the experimental laboratory setting.

The environmental psychologist's concern with solving complex environmental problems through his or her direct study in the real world does not mean that the concern with establishing a cumulative body of scientific knowledge has been forsaken or even that it is to play a secondary role in his or her efforts. What does underlie the approach is the firm belief that such knowledge can only be accumulated, whether for particular settings or more generally across settings, by means of both theories and a relevant methodology that are derived from this world. The crucial point to be made is that the environmental psychologist begins in the real world, with a limited focus, and neither desires to nor is concerned with a unified, general theory of physical-setting problems. If that is to occur, it can only be a long-range possibility. The search is for a cumulative body of knowledge, however limited it might be, that could provide an understanding and possible solutions to specific environmental problems.

Not all environmental psychologists who moved into the real world would necessarily subscribe to the approach that has been described here. But of the many who did, it can be said that to some degree between pronouncements and practice some of the underlying assumptions and implications of the approach have been overlooked if not ignored. To this extent, in my judgment, the approach is weakened, and indeed the future of the field in terms of developing a cumulative body of knowledge is far less certain.

Let me indicate then why the problem-oriented dimension of environmental psychology as I have discussed it is not being completely fulfilled. A commitment to study complex environmental problems "naturalistically" is not enough. I have often been critical of the emphasis on method and data at the expense of theory in the fields of social psychology and indeed other fields (1973, 1983). I would not level the same criticism at environmental psychology as it has developed in the last two decades. Theory has indeed characterized the thinking and research of Altman (1973), Baum and Epstein (1978), Saegert (1976), Stokols (1976), and still others; and I might add the willingness to formulate environmental problems in theoretical terms as a basis for doing research characterizes many younger environmental psychologists just coming into the field. What, then, is the problem? To state the problem, the reader must again be reminded of the nexus of the theoretical approach that must be taken, given the environmental psychologist's commitment to solving complex environmental problems in the real world without violating the integrity of these problems and the events out of which they grow. No matter how unstructured or innovative the nature of the methodology to be employed is, appropriate theoretical concepts and principles are prerequisite stepping stones. The search for solutions to complex environmental problems was never meant to move toward an inductive empiricism as the way to find these solutions. Indeed, just the opposite is the case.

To reject the laboratory-experimental model in favor of studying human problems in the actual context in which they occur is to deny the supremacy of method in building theory and a corpus of valid and useful scientific knowledge. If the "reality" of complex problems eluded the grasp of psychologists in the laboratory, then the attention to that reality in the real world can mean only one thing: However difficult or complex, those problems must determine the methodology to be employed in their study by environmental psychologists. Theory, then, is essential inasmuch as complex problems have to be defined, circumscribed, and made explicit.

But it is the nature of the theory that troubles me. I do not deny that in the humanistic specializations of psychology (e.g., social, personality, and others) there is an array of concepts and theories that can serve as a basis of analysis. However, great care is needed because the meaning and significance of some, if not many, of these formulations were evolved in the context of laboratory research and may require a methodology that produces distortions in the phenomena to be studied—even when transferred out of the laboratory into the real world. I am not suggesting that is true in all instances, but it is true in enough to cause concern. For example, the concept of attitude and its measurement is applied first to questions of environmental attitudes or more particularly with reference to specific settings and spaces and places in them (Kaplan, 1977). This leaves much to be desired in the light of the distortions introduced to attitude assessment by direct measurement techniques. This is but one example. What I would say generally is that in measuring environmental attitudes, analyzing privacy, or studying crowding, many of the concepts and analytic models reflect the approach of traditional social psychology. To some extent, this indeed may be necessary but not to the neglect of the theoretical empirical study of environmental problems in a naturalistic context so that both theory and data emerge out of the very nature of the phenomena themselves. So much of what environmental psychologists study involves a structuring and definition of both the events and how they are to be studied before the events are even dealt with. As we shall soon see, environmental psychologists are doing at least two different types of research. How, where, and why they do it tend to remain as problems.

If a problem orientation requires *relevant* and *reality-related* theory, then to some degree it must be concerned with generalizations of concept and principle. This implication seems almost to have been denied. The denial is tacitly expressed in the view that the study of environmental problems, because of their complexity involving events and processes of the psychological, social, organizational, and cultural levels of behavior and experience, cannot be and is not concerned with evolving general principles and concepts. One could conclude that the study of such problems requires a situation-specific approach in which problems are uniquely defined and concepts and generalizations limited in their application to the specific setting.

Although the challenge of doing ecological research that truly captures the setting-specific characteristics of a given environment is great, it should not preclude the possibilities of developing empirical generalizations or principles, if the concepts of "empirical generalization" and "principles" are not misunderstood. By and large, environmental psychologists do not reject a science that generalizes data and theory, but they do reject one that seeks universal and unifying principles to explain all environmental behavior and experience based on the model of the physical and natural sciences.

Thus what is fundamental in the approach of the environmental psychologist is the need to develop a generalizable body of data, concepts, and theory. The key question is how much generality of data and principle is possible at this stage in the field of environmental psychology. The answer is little, and to search for more, that is, universals is to belie the essential importance of studying complex environmental problems in the real world in which they are to be found. I will have more to say about this issue later in the chapter.

More immediately, there are two points to be made. First, so little systematic research on environmental problems has been done that it may well be too early to speak even of some limited generalizations of data and concepts, especially because the research that has been done varies in breadth, depth, and purpose. The second point is more important. There are commonalities across physical settings, environmental issues, individuals involved, and the problems that emerge. The fact is that if environmental psychologists increase their output of such research, with a sensitivity to issues of generality, there is little question that slowly but surely they can build a body of cumulative knowledge. Such knowledge will undoubtedly be limited, tentative, and indeed may have to be modified in the face of a changing society and/or a more productive science of environmental psychology; however, that should not serve as a deterrent in accumulating such knowledge.

To be problem oriented in the real world—as we shall soon see—means not only that environmental psychologists must have an interdisciplinary orientation but that they must be concerned with all levels of analysis. The focus on environmental problems as experienced by individuals in ongoing physical settings does not permit the luxury of casting aside particular levels of analysis. Thus in the move to the real world, the environmental psychologist did *not* reject the individual psychologist level of analysis. Nor did he or she reject the view that basic psychological structures and processes such as motivation, perception, emotion, and others and their organization into attitudes, values, personal identities, cognitive structures, and belief systems underlie more complex human phenomena having to do with social interaction and other social processes. What was rejected, of course, was the use of traditional laboratory-experimental methodology for the study and explanation of basic psychological structures and processes, and, in addition, the implicit if not explicit view of traditional psychology that these structures and processes *alone* were sufficient to explain all complex human, social, and environmental problems. To the environmental psychologist, the individual psychological level of analysis is necessary and even critical, but it is by no means sufficient. The empirical and conceptual input of behavioral scientists dealing with such complex problems at the level of groups, organizations, or the communities indeed contribute to understanding the reality of individual experience, and the latter in turn is equally important in understanding the environmental issues and problems at the level of groups, social organizations, and communities.

What needs to be stressed, however, is that the

environmental psychologist should not forget his or her commitment to the individual level of analysis, that is, to describing and explaining psychological structures, mechanisms, and processes that relate the person to his or her physical setting. I have in mind here such person/physical environment behaviors and processes as personal space, privacy, crowding, territoriality, cognitive mapping, environmental competence, place-identity, and others. To be sure, these types of investigations are being undertaken with some frequency, and in many respects they stand in contrast to the study of complex environmental problems in the real world—the very problems that attracted the environmental psychologist to this world in the first place.

In comparing the two types of investigations, it is important to note that the latter are setting specific and are therefore less capable of providing empirical or conceptual generalizations. In many instances, they clearly involve the study of groups, organizations, and other complex entities at more complex levels of analysis than the individual, requiring the input of concept and theory from relevant professionals aside from environmental researchers. The study of how, for example, lower class households in a given community manage personal privacy in these settings as compared to middle-class ones as a function of spatial area, size, design, and numbers of family members involves just such input—in addition to concepts and data at the level of individual functions.

The first type of study referred to previously, that is, those of environmental behaviors and processes that relate the person to his or her physical setting, involve a concern with these phenomena for their own sake. Not only are investigators searching for generality across situations, but their primary interest lies in how these mechanisms and processes emerge and subsequently influence the behavior and experience of the person in physical settings. The essential point to be made is that general findings along these dimensions in regard to person/environment relationships such as privacy, territoriality, place-identity, and others will only serve to make setting-specific research more meaningful.

It seems appropriate, indeed even necessary, to speak of the latter as Level II research in its focus on complex environmental problems involving more than the individual level of analysis. The former, of course, is clearly former Level I research with the emphasis on person/physical setting behaviors and processes at the individual level of analysis. What is being emphasized here is that whereas Level I research is never sufficient in the study of complex environmental problems, it is necessary. While new events and properties emerge in environmental problems at the level of groups, social organizations, and the community, these events and properties often, if not always, have their roots in Level-I conceptions (e.g., need for privacy, personal space, place-identity, etc.).

In stressing Level I research in this chapter, I do so not only because there is not enough of it but because so much of what has been reported fails to come to terms with the issues of theoretical development and integration. The lack of extended analytical conceptualization leaves different studies of privacy, personal space, and even crowding essentially unconnected with each other. Early studies by Sommer (1969) on territoriality in the library or Milgram's study of crowding in the city (1970) are useful Level-I investigations, but they are limited to some extent by their lack of theoretical development. Indeed, Sommer's work is essentially empirical. Yet there are problems with many, many other Level-I studies with the result that the possibility of cumulative knowledge building is almost nil. The major difficulty is that some environmental psychologists have drifted back, if not completely returned, to the laboratory-experimental paradigm. Even where there is no "experiment" involving the use of old established measurement techniques, subject instructions, and contrived situations, vestiges of the old approach, methodology, and more importantly, epistemology remain (Freedman, 1975). Oddly enough, one finds theories of crowding (Baum et al., 1975) and territoriality (Esser, 1971; Goffman, 1969) but little attempt to test these theories systematically.

To study the psychological bases of privacy, territoriality, or crowding requires no less a concern with doing research that preserves the integrity of these phenomena than the study of some complex environmental problem. Attempts to manipulate variables, contrive research settings, and fall back on "standard" research techniques (e.g., semantic differentials) will do no more for our understanding of these phenomena than early studies of group pressure, attitude change, or level of aspiration. In time, it may be possible to study particular aspects of personal space, privacy, territoriality, or environmental stress in the context of the experimental-laboratory model. I have no quarrel with this point of view if the attempt is not a premature one evolving out of expediency. That time has not come and may not for some time. In the meantime, psychologists have shown themselves capable of doing natural setting, nonexperimental research both in the university setting as well as outside of it in ways that have provided some meaningful data on social and environmental psychological processes.

42.3.2. Systems Oriented

From the very first, environmental psychologists, in their rejection of the laboratory-experimental paradigm, were also taking a decisive position with respect to its oversimplified and distorted view of cause-and-effect relationships in human behavior and experience. Cognizant of the wide range of forces underlying environmental problems, they could not in any sense be satisfied with a methodology that seeks to measure the effects of one or a few parameters while others are controlled. Such experimental manipulation is not only impossible in real-world settings, but it is directly antithetical to the environmental psychologist's approach.

How does the environmental psychologist view causality? As Epstein (1976) describes it, in systemlike terms. Whether dealing with the individual and his or her physical setting or a complex environmental problem involving individuals, groups, and organizations in a community context, behavior and experience at any level are determined by the patterning of sociocultural and psychological factors acting on each of these units of social integration.

One important implication follows from the systems orientation that many environmental psychologists choose to ignore, overlook, or simply cannot accept. As I indicated earlier, Level-I research is confined to the study of environmentally relevant psychological processes, structures, and behaviors in the individual (e.g., place-identity, personal space, privacy). The implication to be stressed is that the systems orientation is no less applicable to the individual level of analysis than it is to higher order levels of analysis required by complex environmental problems involving groups and organizations. However, one need only review some of the relevant literature (e.g., personal space, crowding, etc.), and it becomes evident that systems analysis at the individual level of research by and large does not occur. The major tendency seems to be one of relying on the familiar approach of the laboratory-experimental model and its focus on simple cause-and-effect relationships. The unknowns, complexities, and uncertainties of exploratory research in ongoing naturalistic settings dampens considerably the motivation of many environmental psychologists to engage in this kind of research.

Thus not only is a real-world context necessary for Level-I research, as I suggested earlier, but systems analysis is essential as well. Accounting for privacy, territoriality, cognitive mapping, crowding, place-identity in simplified one- or two-variable terms is no more valid than earlier social psychological research on small-group process, intergroup attitudes, or social conformity.

If Level-I research must involve a systemslike approach to causality, then it must necessarily be interdisciplinary in nature. Although the psychological level of analysis focuses on person/physical setting responses and processes, the theoretical and empirical input of social, personality, cognitive, and developmental psychologists is by definition necessary. The patterning of sociocultural and psychological factors underlying how individuals achieve privacy, for example, or develop place-identity can only be understood in relation to the data and theoretical conceptions generated by these fields.

That privacy conceptions and behaviors, for example, are normative in character is clearly the case, but how these are learned, what role personality, child development processes, and other factors play in the formation of these person/physical setting responses are important questions that must be answered in the attempt to understand them. If one examines research on human privacy, to take but one example, there is little if any evidence that concepts and theoretical principles from these other fields of specialization play a role in the formulation of problems in this research. An analysis of human privacy by Laufer, Proshansky, and Wolfe (1976) at least points in this direction in its description of various dimensions of human privacy.

Another major implication of a systems orientation, whether at Level-I or Level-II research in the context of an "undisturbed" real world setting is that such research will necessarily require a qualitative methodological approach. Certainly this must be the case at the beginning of such research where the initial and essential goal must be "to capture" the problem in all of its complexity. This means that observation and description as a means of formulating the problem and subsequently studying aspects of it are critical in this methodology. To be sure, such research is difficult, more time consuming, and less than conclusive at times. However, none of these considerations matter if our concern is with first defining and understanding complex environmental problems and not with meeting the requirements of the laboratory-experimental model implicitly, if not explicitly, required by journal publication policies and/or doctoral training requirements (Proshansky, 1976b).

Because psychology, like any other science, is a social institution, escape from its socializing effects is not simple. One does not shed the past just by turning one's back on the university laboratory and moving into the real world. What makes systems and problem-oriented research difficult for the traditional researcher is his or her preoccupation with data collection and quantification, on the one hand, and the overriding concern with establishing universal concepts and principles by means of highly abstract theoretical formulations, on the other. If problem must determine method, then theory in the form of concepts, organizing assumptions, and even tentative principles is critical in formulating Level-I and Level-II research problems. But it has to be the right kinds of concepts and theory.

The fact is that qualitative research of complex environmental settings is rendered far less difficult if the initial concern is with theoretical developments and formulations that establish the nature and direction of that research. I agree with Gergen (1973) that abstract theory in the search for universal principles does little for formulating complex human problems. Concepts and theory that stay closer to the events being studied are far more useful for the environmental psychologist. The environmental psychologist can and should be concerned with the generalization of data and theoretical concepts but not with the aim of establishing universal principles. Rather, his or her goal should be the development of a cumulative body of data relevant to limited periods of time and places and spaces, and therefore subject to change.

42.3.3. Interdisciplinary Orientation

Environmental psychology as I have defined it here — a systems approach to environmental problems in the real world — is necessarily an interdisciplinary field of inquiry. But the conception of "interdisciplinary approach" in this instance is by no means a simple one, particularly with respect to the interests of the environmental psychologist. It is important to note that, following World War II and for a period of some 15 years, conferences and programs on interdisciplinary research and training were prevalent, to say the least. The focus then was on the *behavioral science disciplines,* that is, the field of psychology in relation to sociology, political science, anthropology, economics, and even such fields as ecology and demography. There were great hopes expressed in relation to such complex community problems as mental health, intergroup conflict, and urban depersonalization.

By the late 1960s much of these efforts fell by the wayside within governmental and university settings by virtue of organizational, communication, and philosophical problems between and among the behavioral sciences that seemed insurmountable. Perhaps the more fundamental reasons were to be found in two other facts at that time: First, the demand for interdisciplinary collaboration among the behavioral sciences translated to a demand for applied solutions to complex human problems for which these sciences were not ready; and second, apart from superficial cooperation in dividing a research problem into the "areas that were relevant for two or more disciplines," the conceptual and theoretical integration among these disciplines had not as yet evolved. It would not be an exaggeration to say that each of these disciplines had enough theoretical and methodological difficulties in establishing a cumulative body of knowledge at that time so that it was much easier to talk about interdisciplinary analysis and research than to really engage in it.

However, it can be said categorically that the interdisciplinary orientation is crucial in securing the future of environmental psychology — past difficulties in interdisciplinary efforts notwithstanding. If such an effort is to succeed, however, I believe that there are three types of interdisciplinary cooperative endeavors that must be the focus of concern of the field of environmental psychology.

The first type I have already alluded to previously, and it involves the collaboration between psychology including environmental psychology and other fields within the behavioral sciences. The significance and critical importance for this kind of interdisciplinary integration and cooperation cannot be stressed too strongly. The fact is that so many of these problems addressed by investigators in a given discipline have not provided us with the understanding required both to advance theory or solve the problems on a practical level. In the last analysis, such understanding can only occur if from the very first the interrelationships between people as psychological and physical beings and the social, cultural, economic, and political groups and institutions that define their existence are expressed by corresponding theoretical and empirical concepts that guide our thinking and research.

To what extent have researchers in other behavioral sciences and environmental psychologists actively collaborated since the advent of the field of environmental psychology? Very little, and what collaborative interdisciplinary efforts have gone forward have produced very little, if any, theoretical integration. I strongly recommend a chapter by Wohlwill (1983) that reviews and evaluates interdisciplinary relationships between environmental psychology and other behavioral sciences, the design professions, geography, and other environmental disciplines. In the case of sociology and environmental psychology, for example, each has tended to work alone at its appropriate level of analysis with regard to such issues as crowding and urban life, but few attempts have been made to integrate their respective findings. The picture with respect to economics and environmental psychology is no better.

There is no need to continue to cite "bad news." Environmental psychology is no more interdisciplinary in its relationships to the other behavioral sciences than other fields of psychology have been in the past and are at present. Yet, in fairness, as Wohlwill's chapter reveals, the environmental psychologist does to some extent get involved with economists, sociologists, political scientists, and anthropologists but rarely in any systematic fashion. But can we expect more if within the field of psychology itself interdisciplinary collaboration is infrequent?

Inherent to the approach of environmental psychology is a second type of interdisciplinary collaboration that can be referred to as "interspecialization" collaboration. How individuals learn to use space, acquire privacy, identify themselves in relation to space, and control space are all matters — if we remain consistent with a systems orientation — that require the input of social psychologists, developmental psychologists, cognitive psychologists, and still others. This does occur in some instances, where environmental psychologists are colleagues with those in other fields in traditional departments of psychology, but given the small number of environmental psychologists and certainly their very limited representation in traditional departments of psychology, interspecialization collaboration still remains the exception rather than the rule. But then again, this is to a large extent true for these other relevant fields of psychology and not just environmental psychology.

In the real world, an "interdisciplinary approach" in environmental psychology can have only one meaning. In Level-II research, it means the formulation of theory and empirical research such that what emerges from these efforts are conceptual linkages between data and analytic principles whether they are derived at the individual level of analysis or at more complex levels of social organization. Actual research collaboration and/or systematic interdisciplinary conferences between environmental psychology and other behavioral sciences are instrumental to establishing such linkages, but they are not in and of themselves measures of advances in interdisciplinary efforts in the behavioral sciences.

In the case of Level-I research, although the level of analysis is the same, namely individual behavior and experience, conceptual linkages are sought between qualitatively different psychological processes, structures, and functions. That such linkages are crucial in Level-I research for environmental psychology, in relation particularly to the field of social psychology, is evident if one considers that there is no physical setting that is not also a social setting and that the reverse is also true. Nor can we ignore the fact that person/physical-setting interrelationships of privacy, personal space, crowding, and territoriality are inextricably rooted in the social and cultural dynamics of how individuals perceive, think, and feel about social contexts, the other people in them, and the activities that define them. In this respect, the interrelationships among the concepts and principles that define environmental psychology are not significantly different from those that define social psychology and perhaps some other subareas of psychology as well.

In response to a paper by Altman (1976) on what the relationship between social psychology and environmental psychology ought to be, I took an extreme position (Proshansky, 1976a). To put the matter simply, not only was environmental psychology to avoid the laboratory model like the plague, but existing concepts and principles in social psychology derived from this model were seen as useless. What was urged was almost a conceptually and theoretically autonomous environmental psychology insofar as social psychology (and other fields of psychology) were concerned.

On reflection, it is evident now that this position — at least from a theoretical point of view — is untenable and that, in effect, it must be abandoned. Given the systems orientation of environmental psychology, it makes no theoretical sense to throw out the baby with the bathwater. However limited the existing concepts and generalizations of social psychology due to the inherent problems with the laboratory-experimental model, its focus on social structure, social process, and social interaction is inextricably related to the problems and concepts of environmental psychology. I accept and take far more seriously Altman's view that social psychology and environmental psychology must nurture each other (1976). But how?

To begin with, environmental psychology must "inventory" the value of concepts and principles derived from social psychology's research, laboratory and otherwise. Some of what exists may be less than useful, but there are data and theory that at this point may help in our attempts to study privacy, crowding, territoriality, and other environmental conceptions in the real world. It is apparent, for example, that such social psychological issues as altruism, group pressures, role requirements, and relationships—and others—have direct implications for how individuals use their physical settings to both achieve and maintain privacy. The "nurturing" that each field must be involved in clearly must extend far beyond this first step to a real attempt at making conceptual linkages between social psychology concerns such as social interaction process, group structures and functions, social attitudes and values, and environmental psychology concerns such as privacy, territoriality, crowding, place-identity, personal space, and so on. At another level, one can expect to establish still other conceptual relationships between these latter environmental response systems and concepts and principles of learning social attitudes and social motivation.

The third kind of interdisciplinary relationship that must concern the environmental psychologist is that between his or her field and the design professions of architecture, interior design, landscape architecture, and others. Here again an important implication is overlooked, but before considering it, I must ask how much value there has been in this kind of collaboration since it emerged—at least in principle—some two decades ago. As Wohlwill (1983) notes, the results are by no means promising. The root problem has to do with fundamental differences in approach, purposes, and values of those in the design professions and environmental psychologists or other research psychologists. Altman (1973) has discussed in detail the problems of communication and collaboration between psychologists and designers and how their approaches to problem definition and problem solving varies.

It must be noted that from the very beginning those in the design professions who desired to and/or actually collaborated with environmental psychologists did so for a very practical purpose. It was to obtain answers to questions about people, attitudes, and behavior in relation to space that would both deepen and validate the assumptions underlying the efforts of the design professional. Whether the problem involved user needs regarding space or place or how users actually behaved in physical settings, the answers to these questions were sought in order to help to extend the range of factors entering into the decisions made in the design process. Certainly this is a level of interdisciplinary collaboration that has value, but more to the design professional than to the environmental psychologist. Not only were the answers being sought very difficult to provide, but the basic requirement that had to be met in order to answer them was being ignored. That argument was that the physical properties of behavior settings including not only basic characteristics of space but its organization, complexity, and aesthetic values had to be conceptually linked to the behavior and experience of the individual, groups of individuals, and even more complex social units. In effect, whether we seek to understand complex environmental problems or Level-I research conceptions such as human privacy, territoriality, or personal space, these "dimensions" of the person's physical world must be conceptually integrated into any analytic model for research and theory in environmental psychology that is to be developed. Little consideration, if any at all, has been given to this implication of the interdisciplinary orientation of environmental psychology as it relates to the design professions.

In outlining these three types of interdisciplinary collaboration, I do not wish to suggest that they are currently integral parts of environmental psychology, or that they are easy to achieve. Whether in actual research practice, interdisciplinary conferences, or the actual development of conceptual linkages, the obstacles are many, to say the least. At least one of those obstacles relates to the whole question of how traditional psychology deals with theory, and whether or not it is even ready to begin any serious interdisciplinary developments (Proshansky, 1976b).

42.3.4. Space over Time Orientation

The space-over-time orientation of environmental psychology has not received much attention. This may be because from a theoretical and systematic research point of view it presents more than a few difficulties. Thus the traditional psychologist in social psychology, personality, and other fields has eschewed the time dimension in considering the behavior and experience of individuals and groups. In part, of course, the search for universal principles of such basic psychological processes as perception, motivation, learning, and emotion not only seem to transcend place considerations but time as well. The laboratory-experimental model that is the core of the search for such principles kept considerations of time in abeyance of the social psychologist's concern with social interaction, social structure, and social process.

For environmental psychology, time as well as place is an essential consideration. To be concerned with complex environmental problems involving person/physical-setting relationships requires by definition a concomitant concern with the behaviors, processes, and events that define these relationships, not only at the moment but over extended periods of time. The direct concern with the day-to-day physical setting, behavior, and experiences of individuals requires that we recognize that they not only have a beginning and continuity but are often repetitive over time. And although there is evidence of "constancy," there is no less evidence of change. Indeed, physical places and spaces change over time. A systems orientation to environmental problems necessarily includes in the patterning of determinants underlying these problems events of the past as well as those of the present. Historical accounts of spaces and places are no less a dimension of a qualitative-descriptive methodology necessary in the study of physical settings than the observation of events that are going on in the present. If a problem and its properties must determine research methodology, then time must be included as a critical dimension in the methodology of environmental psychology.

The concept of the *life cycle*—so clearly of central importance in the fields of developmental psychology and personality—is a clear recognition that human behavior and experience must be described and explained at various time periods in a person's life, if for no other reason than that the manifest biological nature of the individual is easily observed as changing over time. Implicit in this concept is the assumption that the properties of any one stage are in part a function of and related to those that came before and that together these successive stages will influence those that have yet to emerge. What is clearly true of the behavior and experience of the person is no less true of environmental settings. The latter, too, have a "life cycle," but this view has hardly had much recognition from those in the design professions, let alone environmental psychologists.

Physical settings change over time, and these changes occur at two levels of analysis: They change in their physical properties because, not unlike the individuals who use them, they are subject to wear and tear, but they also change because the individuals who use them themselves change, whether in physical capacity, social role, or their attitudes, interests, and desires. A changed person in these respects often means changed ways of using relevant physical settings.

It can be said with certainty that questions of change in physical settings over time—for whatever reasons—have received only the barest attention in the systematic research of environmental psychologists. Yet, in part, environmental psychologists have moved in this direction and certainly have gone further than those in the design professions. Insofar as architecture and landscape architecture are concerned, attempts to observe and study planned structures once they emerge completed and used has been the rare exception rather than the rule. In the last decade or more, there has been a growing interest in postoccupancy research, that is, the study of space as it is being established but not being used as yet and then again after it is actively being used (Zimring & Reizenstein, 1980). Although not longitudinal studies in any real sense, such research does answer questions about what happens to space in its use over at least a short period of time and whether its desired purposes and usages are actually being realized once it is in use.

The life cycle of space and its change over time raises a very critical issue regarding individual behavior and experience in relation to the properties of physical settings. Both the traditional approach of psychology, including its laboratory-experimental model, has fostered a singular emphasis on the behavior and experience of the person as the dependent variables. Physical stimuli, outside events, and so on were the presumed causes of such behavior and experience. In its extreme, this can be found among design professionals whose approach is often a simple environmental determinism.

But what about the behavior and experience of the person or groups of people as agents of change or sources of influence with respect to what happens to physical settings? The "dependent variables" in longitudinal concerns with space must necessarily involve the space itself—its properties, uses, functions, and so on. If one reconsiders the systems orientation, that is, that there is a patterning of forces or influences that underline complex environmental problems, then it becomes clear that individual behavior and experience are events that are subject to change and are events that bring about change. There is only the dynamics of system change in which one part of the system induces changes in others and the latter in turn have still other consequences of change for the system. The environmental psychologist must be concerned as much with what individuals do to space and place as the obverse.

42.4. SOME FINAL COMMENTS

It should be evident from the previous discussion that the field of environmental psychology, as I have defined and analyzed its major properties, is still closely tied to the field of psychology. However problem oriented, interdisciplinary, and systems oriented, the nexus of its theoretical approach to complex environmental problems and person/physical-setting relationships, behaviors, processes, and structures is the behavior and experience of the person. If Level-I environmental processes and behavior underlie Level-II complex environmental problems, then clearly the former are rooted in basic psychological processes of perception, learning, thinking, emotion, and their organization into attitudes, self-structures, and so on. But I also suggested that psychological analysis at the level of the individual is not enough to explain events of greater complexity and at higher levels of human organization. To the extent that these are environmental problems defined solely at the level of groups, organizations, or communities with no concern with the individual's behavior and experiences, then indeed such field designations as environmental sociology of social ecology may be far more appropriate.

It is critical that the central role in psychology in its specialized field of environmental psychology not be misconstrued. I am not suggesting a return in any sense to the traditional laboratory-experimental approach. On the contrary, what the previous analysis makes evident is not simply that a systems orientation is needed to understand how change occurs. This orientation strongly implies that Level-I research whether in environmental psychology or in other related specializations cannot be concerned with establishing universal principles of psychological processes. General principles and concepts in both Level-I and Level-II research are clearly important whether created in data or theory. However, these must be principles and concepts closely tied to the phenomena being studied, and their generality is necessarily confined by historical-cultural considerations of time, place, and purpose. As these factors change, new concepts and principles need to replace those that exist. In this regard, Gergen's emphasis on the historical sociocultural context as a critical factor in evolving concepts and principles of social behavior, social process, and social structure (1973) is clearly a view that supports the kind of environmental psychology that I have proposed in this chapter.

Finally, I have also recommended an environmental psychology—again a point inherent in the systems approach to change—that focuses as much attention on how individuals influence, affect, or change physical settings by their behavior, social interactions, roles, and relationships as on how the latter are determined or modified by physical-setting properties. It is Wohlwill's view that just this focus would provide the means by which environmental psychology could make some meaningful and lasting interdisciplinary contacts with architects, interior designers, and other design professionals (1983).

What does all of this have to do with securing the future of environmental psychology? To the extent that environmental psychology can "stake out" its place and purpose in relation to the larger field of psychology, the other behavioral sciences, and the design professions—that is, put its house in order—it is more likely to have some impact on the difficult task of cumulating at least some scientific knowledge about physical settings in relation to human behavior and experience. If, as I firmly believe, nothing succeeds like success, then clearly such success can lead to a strengthening of the social institutional characteristics of the field.

However one might long for such success, it cannot occur at all until environmental psychology can strengthen itself as a social institution. From a very practical point of view, it can be said that environmental psychology needs to be in interdisciplinary relationships with other fields of psychology, not just to establish linking concepts, but because each side needs the other to extend and deepen its analysis of its own research problems. There is a critical role for environmental psychology to play in a traditional department of psychology to the extent that environmental psychology can demonstrate its significance for other fields of psychology, particularly because none of the latter bother with physical settings as a parameter in their own research even though they grudgingly admit to its importance. It is in this way that the social institutional strengths of environmental psychology will increase.

Furthermore, if environmental psychologists need and want to establish interdisciplinary associations and conduct research with those who have environmental interests in the other behavioral sciences, then the environmental psychology field in a traditional department of psychology can serve as the liaison between various other specialized but isolated fields in that department and other behavioral science fields. Here again the usefulness of the field of environmental psychology in this way can, to some degree, strengthen its properties as a social institution. But none of this can happen until environmental psychologists do in fact put their house in order so that they know what their field is, what its objectives are, and what it must do empirically and theoretically in relation to other fields of psychology, other behavioral sciences, and those disciplines we call the design professions.

Acknowledgments

I would like to express my deep appreciation to my research assistant, Abbe Fabian, for the care and concern that she gave in helping me write this chapter. I would also like to thank my colleagues in environmental psychology who in one way or another helped to pinpoint and enhance my thinking about the future of environmental psychology.

REFERENCES

Aiello, J.R., Epstein, Y.M., & Karlin, R.A. (1975). Effects of crowding on electrodermal activity. *Sociological Symposium, 14,* 43–57.

Alexander, C. (1964). *Notes on the synthesis of form.* Cambridge, MA: Harvard University Press.

Altman, I. (1973). Some perspectives on the study of man-environment phenomena. *Representative Research in Social Psychology, 4,* 109–126.

Altman, I. (1976). Environmental psychology and social psychology. *Personality and Social Psychology Bulletin. 2,* 96–113.

Baum, A., & Epstein, Y.M. (Eds.). (1978). *Human responses to crowding.* Hillsdale, NJ: Erlbaum.

Baum, A., Harpin, R.E., & Valins, S. (1975). The role of group phenomena in the experience of crowding. *Environment and Behavior, 7,* 185–198.

Baum, A., & Valins, S. (1973). Residential environments, group size, and crowding. *Proceedings, 81st Annual Convention, American Psychological Association, 8,* 211–212.

Berkowitz, L. (1970). Theoretical and research approaches in experimental and social psychology. In A.R. Gilgen (Ed.), *Contemporary scientific psychology.* New York: Academic.

Canter, D. (1975). *Environmental interaction.* London: Surrey University Press.

Deutsch, M. (1949). An experimental study of the effects of cooperation and competition upon group process. *Human Relations, 12,* 199–231.

Deutsch, M., & Hornstein, H.A. (1975). *Applying social psychology: Implications for research, practice and training.* Hillsdale, NJ: Erlbaum.

Elms, A.C. (1975). The crisis in confidence in social psychology. *American Psychologist, 30,* 967–976.

Epstein, Y.M. (1976). Comment on environmental psychology and social psychology. *Personality and Social Psychology Bulletin, 2,* 346–349.

Esser, A.H. (Ed.). (1971). *Behavior and environment: The use of space by animals and man.* New York: Plenum.

Festinger, L., Schacter, S., & Back, K. (1950). *Social pressures in informal groups.* New York: Harper.

Fitch, J.M. (1965). Experimental bases for aesthetic decisions. *Annals of the New York Academy of Sciences, 128,* 706–714.

Freedman, J.L. (1975). *Crowding and behavior.* New York: Viking.

Gergen, K.J. (1973). Social psychology as history. *Journal of Personality and Social Psychology, 26,* 309–320.

Goffman, E. (1969). *Strategic interaction.* Philadelphia: University of Pennsylvania Press.

Holohan, C.J. (1982). *Environmental psychology.* New York: Random House.

Hoveland, C.I. (1951). *Changes in attitudes through communication.* Presidential Address at the meeting of the Eastern Psychological Association, Brooklyn, New York.

Hoveland, C.I., Lumsdaine, A.A., & Sheffield, F.D. (1949). *Experiments on mass communication.* Princeton, NJ: Princeton University Press.

Ittleson, W.H., Proshansky, H.M., & Rosenblatt, D. (1960). *Some factors influencing the design and function of psychiatric facilities* (Progress Report). Brooklyn, NY: Brooklyn College.

Izumi, K. (1965, July–August). Psychosocial phenomena and building design. *Building Research, 4,* 9–11.

Kaplan, R. (1977). Patterns of environmental preference. *Environment and Behavior, 9,* 195–216.

Kaplan, S. (1978). The search for cognitive clarity. In S. Kaplan & R. Kaplan (Eds.), *Humanscape: Environments for people* (pp. 84–90). North Scituate, MA: Duxbury Press.

Katz, D. (1972). Some final considerations about experimentation in social psychology. In C.G. McClintock (Ed.), *Experimental social psychology.* New York: Holt, Rinehart & Winston.

Kuper, L. (1953). Neighbour on the hearth. In L. Kuper (Ed.), *Living in towns.* London: Cresset Press.

Laufer, R., Proshansky, H., & Wolfe, M. (1976). Some analytic dimensions of privacy. In H. Proshansky, W. Ittleson, & L. Rivlin (Eds.), *Environmental psychology* (2nd ed.). New York: Holt, Rinehart & Winston.

Lewin, K. (1948). *Resolving social conflicts: Selected papers on group dynamics.* New York: Harper & Row.

Lynch, K. (1960). *The image of the city.* Cambridge, MA: MIT Press.

Mehrabian, A., & Russell, J.A. (1974). *An approach to environmental psychology.* Cambridge, MA: MIT Press.

Milgram, S. (1970). The experience of living in cities. *Science, 167,* 1461–1468.

Orne, M.T. (1962). On the social psychology of the psychological experiment: With particular reference to demand characteristics and their implications. *American Psychologist, 17,* 776–783.

Osmond, H. (1957). Function as the basis of psychiatric ward design. *Mental Hospitals, 8,* 23–30.

Proshansky, H.M. (1973). Theoretical issues in environmental psychology. *Representative Research in Social Psychology, 4,* 93–109.

Proshansky, H.M. (1976a, Fall). Comment on environmental and social psychology. *Personality and Social Psychology Bulletin, 2,* 359–363.

Proshansky, H.M. (1976b). Environmental psychology and the real world. *American Psychologist, 4,* 303–310.

Proshansky, H.M. (1983). Prospects and dilemmas of environmental psychology. In N.R. Feimer & E.S. Geller (Eds.), *Environmental psychology; Directions and perspectives.* New York: Praeger.

Proshansky, H.M., & Altman, I. (1979). Overview of the field. In W. White (Ed.), *Resources in environment and behavior* (pp. 3–36). Washington, DC: American Psychological Association.

Proshansky, H.M., & O'Hanlon, T. (1977). Environmental psychology: Origins and development. In D. Stokols (Ed.), *Perspectives on environment and behavior: Theory, research, and application* (pp. 101, 129). New York: Plenum.

Rosenthal, R. (1966). *Experimental effects in experimental research.* New York: Appleton-Century-Crofts.

Russell, J.A., & Ward, L.M. (1982). Environmental psychology. *Annual Review of Psychology, 33,* 652–688.

Saegert, S. (1976). Stress inducing and reducing qualities of environments. In H.M. Proshansky, W.H. Ittleson, &

L.G. Rivlin (Eds.), *Environmental psychology: People and their physical settings* (pp. 218–224). New York: Holt, Rinehart & Winston.

Sarason, I.G., & Spielberger, D.C. (1979). *Stress and anxiety* (Vol. 6). New York: Halstead.

Smith, M.B. (1972). Is experimental social psychology advancing? *Journal of Experimental Social Psychology, 8,* 86–96.

Sommer, R. (1969). *Personal space: The behavioral analysis of design.* Englewood Cliffs, NJ: Prentice-Hall.

Sommer, R. (1987). Dreams, reality, and the future of environmental psychology. In D. Stokols & A. Altman (Eds.), *Handbook of environmental psychology* (pp. 1489–1511). New York: Wiley.

Sommer, R., & Ross, H. (1958). Social interaction on a geriatrics ward. *International Journal of Social Psychiatry, 4,* 128–133.

Stokols, D. (Ed.). (1976). *Psychological perspectives on environment and behavior: Conceptual and empirical trends.* New York: Plenum.

Stokols, D. (1977). Environmental psychology. *Annual Review of Psychology, 29,* 253–295.

White, W. (Ed.). (1979). *Resources in environment and behavior.* Washington, DC: American Psychological Association.

Wohlwill, J.F. (1983). Psychology and the environmental disciplines. In M. Bornstein (Ed.), *Psychology and its allied disciplines.* Hillsdale, NJ: Erlbaum.

Zimring, C.M., & Reizenstein, J.E. (1980). Post-occupancy evaluation: An overview. *Environment and Behavior, 12,* 429–450.

Chapter 43

DREAMS, REALITY, AND THE FUTURE OF ENVIRONMENTAL PSYCHOLOGY

Robert Sommer, *Department of Psychology, University of California, Davis, California*

43.1. ORIGINS OF A NEW FIELD

Environmental psychology arose at a particular period in Western history as a response to certain internal forces within the behavioral sciences and external forces in the larger society. The field was not the brainchild of a charismatic individual or group; rather it arose from the joint efforts of many individuals from diverse disciplines in many places. The field was accretive and operationally defined according to the interests and projects of its practitioners and researchers. Its existence preceded deliberate attempts to distill and define its essence. An understanding of its origins is necessary in order to comprehend its present condition and predict its future course. As Bevan (1982) reminds us: "No discipline or profession can thrive in these United States and remain indifferent to its social setting" (p. 1314).

Most contributors to this volume will concentrate on the present status of research and theory in some area. My task will be to search the past and present for guideposts into the future.

Environmental psychology arose as a self-conscious field of study in the 1960s, primarily in the United States and Canada. Its diffusion to other parts of the world came somewhat later. Its roots could be traced back to the writings of earlier theorists and researchers. Although these individuals did not identify themselves specifically as environmental psychologists, their ideas, theories, and concepts influenced the field. This group includes Roger Barker and his research on psychological ecology, Daniel Berlyne on environmental aesthetics, J.J. Gibson on landscape perception, Kurt Lewin on life space and action research, B.F. Skinner on operant conditioning, and E.B. Tolman on cognitive maps.

Various writers outside of psychology such as Jane Jacobs and Lewis Mumford from city planning, Richard Neutra from architecture, Erving Goffman from sociology, Edward Hall from anthropology, and Nikko Tinbergen and Heini Hediger from ethology called attention to the need for studying the connections between people and the environment.

Institutions, organizations, and scientific disciplines arise in response to certain pressures that shape their form and set their course and then develop an internal dynamic to fit the needs of the membership but all the time influenced by the ebb and flow of external pressures. A scientific discipline does not arise automatically because an issue is "out there" available for study. It would be possible to conceive of a new academic specialty called aquatic psychology that would deal with the relationship between people and the nautical environment of ships, shoreline, and water. Because more than three-quarters of the earth's surface consists of water and swimming and other water pastimes are ubiquitous human activities, this would seem to be a reasonable field of study. Yet I have never heard any proposals for developing a special training program in this area nor for establishing a separate journal or organization for people interested in human response to the aquatic environment. Neither the needs of practitioners nor of society have been of sufficient strength to produce this new field. Despite the importance of agriculture in the United States and the Third World, I do not know of any programs in agricultural psychology. There are research programs in rural mental health but not directly on the psychology of farming. To farmers, who they are and where they work are intertwined (Turkington, 1983).

The existence of a specialty area is not exclusively a matter of need or importance. In some cases it can be a single individual who doggedly pursues work on a given issue, publicizes it through articles and lectures, and eventually starts a training program and organization devoted to the topic. The availability of funds to study specific issues can help to institutionalize a new discipline or field of study. If grants for the psychological study of farming became available, a new specialty area would not lag far behind. The study of rural life by sociologists is well accepted, and there are many departments of rural sociology. Some of the most systematic studies of housing had been funded by the Federal Farm Home Administration (Grady, 1959).

The conditions necessary for a new discipline can be internal, external, or both. By internal is meant the needs of the members of an existing occupation or profession who perceive that existing organizations and institutions are not serving their needs, and who break away to establish a new organization. External forces can include a perception of need by policymakers, major institutions, and agencies who make available resources to start new programs. It will most often be the case that a new field is the product of a combination of internal and external forces rather than either one separately. At various stages in the evolution of a new field, the relative strengths of internal and external pressures will vary. Initially a field may arise largely in response to external pressures. Yet as the field is established and becomes institutionalized, its future course is set by the concerns and interests of the membership (internal forces). If the organization becomes totally self-serving and no longer meets the needs of the larger society, there will be conflict with external forces, a likely withdrawal of resources, and strong pressures for internal change.

43.2 INTELLECTUAL CLIMATE OF THE 1960s

The 1960s were a time of moral outrage, protest, flux, and uncertainty. The political historian Samuel Huntington (1982) likened the 1960s to three earlier periods of reform in American history, the Revolution, the Jacksonian era, and the Progressive era, all marked by pervasive discontent, moral indignation, criticism of authority, and the questioning of specialization. Traditional assumptions of the nature of society and the allocation of power and resources were challenged. Behavioral scientists had not predicted in advance the turbulence of that period and played little role in guiding it, although a few spent considerable time analyzing its significance and effects. On the debit side, there was tumult, controversy, superficiality, and antiintellectualism. On the positive side, there was a tremendous release of creative energies, of optimism, social experimentation, and expressed concern for the poor and neglected segments of society and the environment.

The swirling currents left untouched few institutions or nations. Not everything was changed or turned around, but all institutions and nations were affected to some degree, if only to define themselves more clearly in opposition to the demands for economic, social, and political justice. The origins of environmental psychology as a self-conscious field of study can be understood with reference to two intellectual movements of the period—the Human Rights Movement and the Environmental Movement. Activists demanded a widening of boundaries for professional responsibility. Prior to this time, it had been customary to examine professions from the standpoint of their effects on their membership and on the people directly served. The 1960s enlarged these responsibilities to include the general population and the environment. It became legitimate to ask what professionals were doing for the environment, for ethnic minorities and the poor, and for the struggle for economic justice in the Third World. The expansion in perceived responsibility was expressed in the aphorism that if you are not part of the solution, then you are part of the problem.

The demands for relevance to pressing political and social problems affected psychology and architecture, the two professions that had been most closely involved in the development of environmental psychology, in different ways. Prior to World War II, psychology had been a small esoteric specialty with little money or influence, whose roots lay in philosophy and physiology. This changed during World War II with the development of such applied areas as clinical, industrial, and organizational psychology. In these applied fields, many psychologists gained experience in working for social justice but had little exposure to issues connected with environmental quality. As a profession, however, psychology was ill-prepared for the 1960s' demand that it become relevant to the worldwide struggles for human justice and preservation of the environment.

Architecture had traditionally been a profession that served the wealthy and powerful by building monuments, castles, and cathedrals. At the end of World War II, its major clients were corporations, government, and wealthy individuals. The work of architects was largely irrelevant to the lives of most people whose housing was constructed without architects. Whatever activism existed within architecture had been directed to issues of environmental quality. Some architects as individuals and some local professional societies had been active in campaigns to preserve important landmarks. The profession was not prepared to respond to demands that it join in campaigns for social and economic justice. Environmental psychology presented the opportunity for both these professions to come together and deal *as professions* with the social concerns of the 1960s.

43.2.1. Human Rights Movement

World War II sounded the death knell for colonialism. In response to struggles for national liberation in the Third World, Western nations gradually relinquished control over their former colonies that became independent states. There were also struggles within nations for the removal of barriers limiting social, economic, and political equality of opportunity. In the United States, the early campaigns centered around political rights for blacks who, in southern states, were denied the right to vote, attend decent schools, live in desirable neighborhoods, and who were excluded from well-paying jobs. Within the next two decades, their struggle was joined by other ethnic minorities, the elderly, the handicapped, consumers, women, and other groups who believed that they were denied a fair share of resources and power. The quest for economic justice accompanied the struggle for political rights because those excluded from power tended to be among the economically most deprived segments of society. According to Camus (1960), what made this era different from the past is the way

the masses and their wretched condition have burst upon contemporary sensibilities. We know now that they exist, whereas we once had a tendency to forget them. And if we are more aware, it is not because our aristocracy, artistic or otherwise, has become better—no, have no fear—it is because the masses have become stronger and keep people from forgetting them. (p. 250)

The stirrings of protest were sparked by a recognition that poverty, malnutrition, substandard housing, disease, and unemployment were remediable conditions. Prior to this, there had been more or less an acceptance of a harsh existence for most peoples of the world. Technological advances and great affluence following World War II gave credence to the writings of earlier utopians who had maintained that a better world was possible not only for a chosen few but for all humankind. Improvement in the situation of the poor and oppressed was seen as improvement for all because privation, malnutrition, disease, and unemployment lead to political and social instability. Raising the standard of living of ethnic minorities or Third World nations would also provide a stable work force and markets for industrialized nations.

Social psychologists assisted the Civil Rights Movement in the United States as researchers documenting the effects of discrimination and prejudice. The early peak of such involvement was participation by distinguished social psychologists as expert witnesses in the lawsuit *Brown v. Board of Education* challenging the constitutionality of segregated schools. This was the first time that the U.S. Supreme Court took seriously the methods and findings of the behavioral sciences. Psychologists had also been active in efforts to integrate housing, labor unions, the military, and so forth. Activists within psychology had previously organized the Society for the Psychological Study of Social Issues, Division 9 of the American Psychological Association. These were mostly white male professionals of middle-class backgrounds with middle-class values who saw their role as providing information on pressing social issues that could be applied by government or private agencies. They were unprepared for the demand that psychology do more than define problems, write about issues, and propose solutions. To the 1960s' activists, psychology was seen as part of the problem-definition industry that seemed to stand in the way of solutions. The demand arose that psychologists join in efforts to ameliorate the discrimination and oppression that they had identified in their writings.

The Human Rights Movement also affected psychology in its demands for the ethical treatment of human subjects. Previously the rules for psychological experimentation had been vague and left largely to the discretion of individual investigators. Although there had not been the extreme danger to human life that had come to public notice in some biomedical experimentation, a number of studies such as those of Milgram (1964) on obedience raised important ethical issues regarding the responsibilities of researchers to those who participated in their experiments. The concern was most clearly felt toward those populations lacking power or ability to give informed consent, such as inmates of institutions and children. Ethical codes were constructed to provide for independent review of research upon human subjects. At the same time, animal welfare activists were calling for a review of confinement procedures and experimental methods used in animal research.

43.2.2. Ecology Movement

The single event that most served to catalyze interest in the environment was the publication in 1962 of Rachel Carson's *Silent Spring*. The book had a tremendous impact on the public, policymakers, and the scientific community. In exposing humankind's deliberate pollution of the environment through pesticides, the book drastically changed the prevailing optimistic faith in science and forced scientists and technicians alike to recognize and accept their awesome and inescapable social responsibilities (Iltis, 1966). Carson was both an experienced scientist and a sensitive writer who had attained financial independence through her earlier nature books and had been able to devote herself almost completely to studying the effects of pollution upon the environment. President John F. Kennedy was impressed with *Silent Spring* and called the book to the attention of policymakers and the general public. Within 2 years, Congress had passed the Wilderness Bill, the Land and Water Conservation Act, National Seashores, and Ozark River Bills, which are considered landmarks in American conservation (Iltis, 1966). The book changed the direction, goals, and methods of what had previously been known as the conservation movement and brought it together with a larger, more youthful constituency concerned with many facets of environmental quality. The earlier conservation movement had been dominated by middle-aged men and women, largely successful in their careers, dependent on wealthy donors for contributions, and accustomed to working in boardrooms and through formal organizations. The major emphasis was on protecting wilderness areas, natural landmarks, and wildlife. The members were birdwatchers, natural history buffs, and organized hunting and fishing enthusiasts desirous of protecting the wildlife habitat as a means of ensuring a continued supply of game and fish. The role of sporting enthusiasts in protecting the wildlife habitat in the early days of the conservation movement should be acknowledged.

The ecology movement that developed in the 1960s was more youthful, enthusiastic, and centered about the universities. Whereas the earlier conservation movement had been concerned with the natural environment and wilderness areas, the ecology movement expanded its mandate to include urban spaces, population control, and energy usage. Its campaigns combined direct action in the form of various types of nonviolent protest with grass-roots political organizing and lobbying efforts in state capitals and Washington, DC. Its success in helping create the Environmental Protection Agency (EPA), various strip mining and reclamation acts, park acquisition projects, and the National Environmental Policy Act (NEPA) inspired some writers to label the 1960s as *the environmental decade*.

Legislative activism went hand in hand with lifestyle issues. Following the slogan "Environmental Activism Starts at Home," campaigns were launched to deal with local sources of pollution, litter, and wasteful use of resources. Conservation became a way of life that would affect one's choice of housing, mode of transportation, attitudes toward different foods, types of packaging, and the like. There was renewed interest in small-scale farming, life in rural areas, appropriate technology, and in personal health and nutrition.

Environmental activists believed that they had to move quickly to translate the increased public interest into legislation and protective regulations. There was also recognition that there would soon be a counterreaction from entrenched forces responsible for creating and maintaining environmental problems. There was not time for research to develop precise measures of environmental quality. Passing legislation meant "guesstimating" standards and goals based on whatever sketchy information was available. On many environmental issues, laws preceded research. If this were not good science, it was at least sound politics considering the fickleness of the electorate.

At least in the beginning, the environmental movement did not call on psychologists for assistance. Although population control and energy conservation had behavioral aspects, there was scant precedent for psychologists to be involved in such issues. There was little research available, for example, on methods for persuading households to conserve resources or energy. In fact, there was a far greater marketing literature by psychologists on ways to induce consumers to increase their purchases.

The liaison between psychology and the ecology movement was initiated by a few psychologists concerned about environmental issues who asked themselves how they could participate in the ecology movement as researchers, teachers, and practitioners. They sought methods, concepts, and information from their own field that could be used in the search for environmental quality. There was also recognition that psychological research and theory could benefit from an enlarged understanding of environmental influences. The inability of most psychological theories to accurately predict behavior was attributed to the omission of situational variables.

The ecology movement at the time was a loose aggregation of organizations and individuals with varied goals and a shared dedication to environmental quality. Those who viewed the chief problem as unchecked population growth directed their efforts at family planning. Those concerned with the wildlife habitat organized to create and expand wilderness areas and protect endangered species. Civic groups lobbied to protect landmarks and buildings of historical and cultural significance. Rural residents were concerned with the spillover of people and problems from the city and the urbanization of prime agricultural land. City dwellers were becoming upset with increased air, noise, and water pollution. All groups were faced with the likelihood of future scarcity of nonrenewable resources. Even though the short-

range goals were disparate, these organizations saw their long-range goal as the improvement of environmental quality.

43.2.3. The State of Architecture

Architecture had grown tremendously in stature and importance in the period after World War II. A tremendous construction boom had taken place throughout the Western world. This was partly to replace buildings destroyed in the war but also to provide new housing, commercial, and industrial facilities during a period of economic expansion in which large amounts of capital became available and new materials and construction methods freed architects from many of the older constraints. It was technically possible to put up any type of building virtually anywhere in the world, providing one was willing to pay the cost. Architecture students in their studios spent time and serious discussion about cities on the moon, buildings on water, mile-high skyscrapers, and megabuildings enclosing entire communities. Energy was cheap and abundant. To make room for new buildings, old buildings were torn down, and available open space encroached on. Cities flowed out into the countryside creating the need for major highways, shopping centers, and an increased dependence on fossil fuels. Architecture schools across the country expanded in size and influence.

Despite the boom atmosphere and increased public visibility, all was not well within the architectural profession. Beneath the surface, there was unease and guilt. The architectural heritage of past centuries was fast disappearing and being replaced by faceless anonymous glass brick skyscrapers that few people liked and many resented. The clients for such projects tended to be anonymous corporate boards or government agencies. This led to occasional misfits between building form and the occupants who were not consulted during the design phase. Residential construction was taken over by developers, engineers, and banks. Few private homes, except those for the very wealthy, were designed by architects. Contact between architects and the public was becoming restricted to the boardroom and the country club. The awards system of the profession was dominated by the quest for novelty and self-expression. Architectural criticism supported a fine-arts approach that left little room for user opinion. The most flagrant manifestation of this disinterest in occupant response was the frequent tendency to give awards to new buildings prior to their being opened for use.

Architecture had become a private game played by

a small circle of designers, wealthy corporate, governmental, or individual clients, and architectural critics. The profession was ill-prepared to face the winds of change blowing in the 1960s. People with whom architects had previously had no professional contact such as the poor, ethnic minorities, the elderly, youth, and women were demanding to be heard. Neighborhood groups were starting to resist efforts to tear down graceful and historic buildings and develop every inch of available open space. Environmental activists pressed for legislation to protect landmarks, open space, and neighborhoods. All this confronted architects with new issues, new constituencies, and new adversaries.

There was rarely the opportunity to try out buildings on a trial basis, evaluate them, and make changes before they were actually constructed. This could be done with a model or mock-up but not a full-scale building. In almost all cases, the building itself became the test. Methods for accurately gauging occupant response to buildings were lacking. Little about human behavior was taught in schools of architecture, design, or landscape. In fairness to the professional schools of design and architecture, little systematic research on such issues had been conducted prior to the 1960s. All this created a need among design educators and practicing architects for valid and systematic information about human behavior. These pressures for information arose from questions asked by students, government agencies, and the general public.

Architecture lacked a research tradition that could provide answers, except in the areas of structures and materials, where research had largely been done by engineers or industry. The phrase *architectural research* lacked clear meaning even within the profession. Research was not a common or expected activity among practitioners or architectural faculty. There was no research journal of architecture, landscape architecture, or interior design. Most of the periodicals in the field were "glossies" with more pictures than solid information. There were few courses in architectural research that would enable design students to obtain necessary research skills. Thus the critical questions raised in the 1960s regarding the effects of the designed environment on people could not be answered by designers themselves, who lacked the necessary research skills and training. It was necessary for them to seek out other groups and individuals who might help provide some answers or at least techniques that the designers themselves could use to find answers. Given the fact that most of the questions concerned human response to the environ-

ment, it was logical that designers should approach behavioral scientists for assistance. This was a period when the behavioral sciences were seen as having the potential for finding systematic and valid information about human behavior. It was recognized that psychology, sociology, and anthropology were more youthful than the better established physical and biological sciences, but they had the potential for obtaining valid information.

Some individual architects had organized communities to save and restore buildings of historical, cultural, or architectural significance. This activism was later to translate into campaigns to preserve neighborhoods and open spaces against unwise and unplanned development. Architects were less directly involved in the larger social issues connected with the ecology movement such as population control, energy conservation, antipollution laws, and the like. Many practicing architects viewed such laws and regulations as unwarranted interference in their professional activities. The need for environmental impact statements, required by NEPA, was seen as a barrier to new construction. Although architecture as a profession remained largely aloof from the environmental movement, some architects as individuals were active. Architectural students in particular were heavily involved in campaigns for social justice. Their activism was confined largely to the universities but on occasion flowed out into the communities, leaving most of architectural practice largely untouched. Urban planning in particular was affected by certain aspects of the human rights movement, especially the demand that people should be consulted in decisions that would materially affect their lives.

Thus the first connection between the emerging field of environmental psychology and the environmental movement came directly through a shared interest in behavioral aspects of ecological problems. The second linkage came indirectly through the effects of the ecology movement on the design professions, and architecture in particular. This pressure caused design fields to look at the behavioral sciences for assistance in meeting many of the new questions that involved human rather than technical issues.

43.3 INTERNAL CRITICISM OF PSYCHOLOGY

Within the ranks of psychologists, disapproving comments were heard regarding the state of the field. Whereas outsiders were most critical of a perceived lack of usefulness of results, internal criticism was directed at the preoccupation with the experimental method to the exclusion of all other approaches, the effects of the laboratory situation on the participants and experimental outcomes, the narrowness of problems studied and populations tested, the disinterest in application within academic departments, and the neglect of environmental factors. These criticisms laid the basis for the development of an environmental psychology that was multimethod in its approach, undertook field as well as laboratory studies, and possessed a strong applied orientation.

Academic psychology entered the laboratory over a century ago and still has not emerged fully into the light. An entire psychology has been constructed around the study of the white rat and the college sophomore in the darkened basements of university buildings. Judge David Bazelon (1982), one of the strongest supporters of psychology in the judiciary, complained that social psychologists always seem to have one eye fixed on the physics laboratory, a tendency others have described as "physics envy." Bazelon added that the social scientist's image of the physical sciences was remarkably naive. It was the genius of Wilhelm Wundt (1862) to recognize that human response could be studied using experimental methods, providing that external variables could be controlled. This led to the establishment of the psychological laboratory as the testing ground for psychological truth. Studies undertaken in any other location were regarded as tentative and preexperimental because of the inability to control all relevant variables. Proshansky (1981) maintains that the experimental-laboratory model

> continues to dominate both directly and indirectly the approach of psychology as a field of scientific inquiry.... If we review any of the research findings of psychology, the sovereignty of an experimental-laboratory empiricism as an approach still reigns supreme as it continually reflects and echoes the view that method must determine problem and theory. (p. 8)

The hegemony of the laboratory-experimental method determined which types of problems were legitimate research issues and which were not. Those aspects of behavior that could not be brought into the laboratory became off limits to respectable psychologists. Such exclusion encouraged complex experimental designs manipulating a half-dozen variables at one time, precise measurement, and sophisticated statistical analysis of results. In the review process for scientific journals, articles are evaluated on the basis of their theoretical relevance, methodological elegance, and statistical analysis. The view that the proper work place of psychologists is in the laboratory rather than in the outside world is reflected in the statement by Pratt (1939) that "psychologists can be most useful to society by staying in their laboratories and libraries, there to remain until they can come forth with reliable predictions and well-tested applications" (p. 179).

Allport (1968) complained that "many contemporary studies seem to shed light on nothing more than a narrow phenomenon studied under specified conditions. Even if an experiment can be successfully repeated, there is no proof that the discovery has wider validity" (p. 68). Using the distinction made by Campbell and Stanley (1966), laboratory researchers were preoccupied with internal validity (treatment effects within the bounds of the experiment) and neglected external validity (generalization of the effects beyond the confines of the experiment). Internal validity is necessary for the development of science and external validity to its application and utilization. The range of subject populations used by researchers was extremely narrow. Critics doubted the generalizability of results to other populations, especially to those in non-Western societies. To what extent were studies of leadership or group cohesion undertaken with college sophomores in Michigan generalizable to Third World nations or even to political leaders in Washington, DC? Serious questions were also being raised about the effects of the laboratory setting on the behavior of participants. Rosenthal (1966) had demonstrated that the experimenter's expectations could influence experimental results. There was growing recognition that the laboratory was a particular type of environment with its own constraints on behavior.

Academic psychology was also criticized for neglecting environmental determinants of behavior in its search for universal laws. Littman (1961) advocated that psychology seek laws applicable to all people in all places rather than to findings about particular groups in particular places. Adherents of this view were embarrassed to find that there were cultural differences even in basic sensory processes. Members of various tribes in Africa, for example, perceived optical illusions in a very different way than did Westerners (Segall, Campbell & Herskovits, 1966). If the results of basic studies of perception did not apply without qualification to other cultures, the generalization of results from social psychological investigations of group processes and interpersonal attraction to other societies was even more suspect. The neglect of environmental determinants was also an obstacle in predicting behavior within western culture. Barker pointed out that there was more similarity in the ways that two men would behave in a barber's chair or sitting in an airport than the way either individual would behave in the two situations. Yet psychologists were led by their training and research model to neglect situational variables in the search for universal laws. The question of how people behaved in airports or barber shops was considered trivial. The needs of policymakers and public officials were less for statements about all people, which were patently suspect and too general and obvious to be useful, than for information about specific groups of people in specific places. This was the sort of information that psychologists had been taught by their training to consider unimportant and insignificant.

There was a virtual absence of research on behavioral aspects of environmental stressors such as noise, air pollution, fear of crime, and crowding. Such issues did not fit neatly into fashionable psychological theories and could not be studied readily in the laboratory using accessible college sophomores as research subjects.

Those psychologists interested in social issues complained about the rewards system of the profession. The research that outsiders described as irrelevant to social problems was often highly esteemed within the field. Theories had to be abstract, elegant, and often counterintuitive in order to be accepted and experimental designs and analyses so complex that they were virtually impossible to perform beyond the confines of the laboratory. Within university departments, there was a strong antipathy to any type of application. Application was regarded as a second-rate activity in comparison to the search for universal laws of behavior. Those psychologists interested in application were unlikely to be hired at major universities, were discriminated against in the promotion process, and were looked on with disapprobation by their colleagues if they managed to stay around. These attitudes were carried over into the grant review process by academic psychologists who served on the review panels. Graduate students coming out of academic programs were trained to teach and do research. They were taught little about the constraints of problem solving in the outside world or how to persuade reluctant policymakers to take research results seriously.

Clinical psychology, the one branch of applied psychology to have obtained considerable status and public influence outside of academe, was a stepchild within the family. Its faculty and students were barely

tolerated in university departments, and the following years saw many clinical programs reduced or disbanded despite strong student demand. As a result, clinical faculty broke off from traditional universities to create independent training institutions not dominated by a laboratory-experimental orientation.

All these criticisms were, I believe, justified to a considerable degree. Stating them all in succession tends to tar an entire profession with a wide brush. It should be noted that there were some noted social psychologists such as Barker, Lewin, and Sherif whose research and teaching were directed at real-world problems who did not deserve the censure directed at the field. These individuals were as disapproving as outsiders regarding the state of their own field and remained throughout their careers largely separated from the mainstream of social psychological theory and research.

43.4. RESPONSE FROM ORGANIZED PSYCHOLOGY AND ARCHITECTURE

When pressures for change arise, they are likely to have most effect on the leadership of professional organizations that are in direct contact with elected officials and to students and younger practitioners with careers at a formative stage. New movements are less likely to have an impact on established practitioners who have developed set ways of doing things and numerous strategies for resisting change. It would be an exaggeration to say that most psychologists took seriously those criticisms directed toward their field or attempted to respond to them. The same lack of response also characterized practicing architects who tended to ignore the questions raised by environmental activists. Practitioners in a field, especially if they are associated with strong institutions or professional associations, are insulated against demands for change. This insulation is not without value because it protects professions against unwarranted outside interference into their activities, but it can also slow down the implementation of useful new ideas. The leadership of professional organizations by its visibility and contact with policymakers is more likely to be responsive to demands for change. Both the American Psychological Association (APA) and American Institute of Architects (AIA) have central offices in Washington, DC. This permits them to lobby among legislators and learn legislative concerns.

The leadership of professional design organizations reached out to their counterparts in the behavioral sciences to find answers to questions about human response to the built environment. There was some division of labor in these liaisons according to problem scale. Urban planners looked to sociologists whose research and theories dealt with the macroenvironment. Architects were more interested in the work of experimental psychologists regarding the effects of light, form, color, and sound, and the research of social psychologists upon group interaction. Private industry turned to human factors researchers for data on person–machine transactions that had expanded to encompass larger systems such as aircraft, space capsules, and undersea chambers that were simultaneously machine and environment.

The AIA sponsored workshops, obtained grants, and eventually created a research foundation with a strong behavioral orientation. The AIA leadership was far ahead of most of its membership in sensitivity to behavioral concerns, although, of course, behind where many of its younger activists members would have liked it to be. Architectural schools throughout North America sought out behavioral scientists to give lectures, organize workshops, teach courses, and participate in cross-disciplinary research projects. The AIA made space available in its professional journals for articles on behavior. Some of this activity had gone on previously but at a greatly reduced scale. Those psychologists interested in working on environmental issues were in heavy demand as speakers, consultants, and researchers. This was a tremendously exciting period for young psychologists and architects dreaming of a new field. There was more talk than action and not much money, but it created the climate out of which the institutionalized expressions of the new concern such as journals, teaching programs, and professional organizations would emerge. The continuing expansion of architectural schools during this period provided an economic basis for hiring behavioral scientists. Prior to 1960, there was probably not a single psychologist with a full-time career appointment in a school of architecture in North America. Twenty years later, such appointments were commonplace, and by 1980, it would be the atypical major school of architecture in North America that did not have at least one behavioral scientist attached to its regular faculty.[1] Such individuals were expected to teach students about human response to buildings and methods for determining user needs and behavior.

The American Psychological Association also felt the need to respond to questions of environmental quality. The APA sponsored a task force on psychology and the environment with staff support for its activities, published a monograph on psychology and the environment, and provided space in its newsletters and journals for reports on the developing field of environmental psychology. New university programs sprang up to institutionalize the new interest. These trends appeared first in the United States and Canada, then in Western Europe, and finally in Japan and the Third World. The establishment of these programs has been described elsewhere in this volume. The training programs constituted the major response of both psychology and architecture to the questions raised by the environmental and the human rights movements.

The emerging field could be viewed as (1) an independent area of study with a new title such as human ecology or envirotecture, (2) a new specialty area within psychology co-equal with existing specialty areas, (3) as part of an existing specialty area of psychology, (4) as a specialty area within design, or (5) none of the preceding. Within the academic community, there is a major difference between scientific disciplines and fields of study. A discipline reflects a common way of looking at problems; a field of study reflects a shared interest in a particular topic. Environmental studies was a field of study rather than a discipline. It was interdisciplinary and involved looking at an issue (the environment) from many different standpoints. Environmental psychology, on the other hand, is part of the discipline of psychology and therefore can be best understood as a subdiscipline. Two professional organizations, with considerable overlap in membership, have arisen as institutional expressions of these approaches. The Environmental Design Research Association (EDRA) tends to look at environmental psychology as a field of study, whereas the Division of Population and Environmental Psychology of the APA takes a more disciplinary view.

Those who argued that this was a new field were reacting to deficiencies in existing fields. Architecture and planning had been largely concerned with form and neglected behavior, whereas the behavioral sciences tended to treat people apart from the physical environment. Thus a new field with its own concepts, methods, and subject matter was necessary. Thiel (1970) gave the name *envirotecture* to the study of environmental experience and maintained that this was one of the root sciences underlying architecture and urban planning. Just as social psychology was considered by some to be a new discipline with its unique subject matter (group relations and effects) that stood midway between sociology as the study of society and psychology as the study of the individual, so environmental psychology was a new discipline midway between the studies of physical and social systems by focusing on the interaction between the two.

The study of person–environment relations could also be included under the existing umbrella of psychology as one specialty area among many. The availability of specialty programs is determined largely by the inclinations of individual faculty members, geography, and historical accident. Clinical psychology was not an appropriate model for environmental psychology because of the large amount of resources and staff required to develop an APA-approved clinical program. The more relevant model seemed those specialty areas such as organizational or industrial psychology, consumer psychology, or correctional psychology that could be created and maintained by a few core faculty with some assistance from colleagues in other departments and outside agencies. Often their status and continued existence depended on the availability of outside funds.

Environmental psychology could also be viewed as a subarea of social psychology (Singer & Baum, 1981). Supporters of this view could envisage a number of advantages to such an arrangement. It would make environmental research more respectable through its linkage with an established field and thereby obtain publication opportunities in existing journals rather than taking the time and trouble to establish new journals that would likely have, at least initially, lower status and readership than existing journals. Placing the field in social psychology would also make available a body of theory, concepts, and research that could be brought to bear on environmental issues. It would also increase exposure to environmental concepts among students and researchers in an established field. This approach also ensures that psychology graduate students interested in environmental issues will be qualified to teach in traditional areas of psychology.

Critics of this approach charged that social psychology had become a miniexperimental field that was intellectually vapid and bankrupt, without direction or purpose, and lacking in relevance to the pressing issues facing the larger society. From this standpoint, it was clearly no model for a new field that was cross-disciplinary, field oriented, and strongly committed to application (Proshansky, 1976). There was much to be gained, of course, from courses in social psychology that included sections on environmental influences, but this did not diminish the need for separate courses, curricula, and journals specifically devoted to behavioral aspects of the environment.

The argument could also have been made, although I never heard it expressed, that no new action was needed and that the environmental and human rights concerns should be embodied within the existing disciplines and fields. This would eliminate the need for new training programs, courses, textbooks, institutes, or professional associations. Nothing should be done except to encourage consideration of environmental issues and variables in psychology courses and a concern with behavioral issues in design courses. Cognitive mapping of the environment could be included in textbooks written for existing courses and papers presented at meetings of existing professional organizations.

This outcome would have meant no independent institutionalized expression of the new concerns. Though it is possible that this will be the future course of the field, that it will eventually be integrated into psychology and architecture and thereby disappear as a separate specialty, this view had few adherents among those eager to develop new courses, curricula, departments, professional associations, research institutes, and consulting firms. The first generation of people who became interested in behavioral aspects of architecture had no formal training in this area. However, they saw the need for specialty programs that provided training beyond what they had acquired and therefore helped to create programs for students and practitioners who came afterward. This situation is typical of any new specialty area. The interest comes first, and the trappings of institutionalization follow.

A view not very popular among behavioral scientists was that the field was a specialty area within design. This approach envisaged specialty programs within schools of architecture and design to train students, most of whom would have a design background, in behavioral concepts and methods. Graduate architects with bachelor's degrees, for example, might enroll in master's programs in schools of architecture and learn to do needs analysis, post-occupancy evaluation, and behavioral research. A number of programs following this model were developed in schools of architecture and urban planning. Psychologists would teach architects about the behavioral aspects of buildings, but the practice of behavioral design such as programming and building evaluation would be the responsibility of designers who had received additional training in behavioral fields.

Available career opportunities determined in large measure which approach was likely to be successful. There were few job opportunities in established architectural offices for trained behavioral scientists. Initially, it had been hoped that large architectural offices would find reason to hire graduates of the new training programs. This hope was not realized for reasons that I have discussed elsewhere (Sommer, 1980). Consultation with architectural firms remains at best a part-time interest among environmental psychologists. Nor have graduate architects with behavioral interests and training been able to find full-time positions doing programming and postoccupancy evaluation. Most of them have gone to work in architectural offices as designers first, and behavioral architects second.

43.5. SPREAD OF INFLUENCE

43.5.1. Within Psychology

Environmental psychology began at a time when it was relatively easy to start new programs. Expanding university enrollments meant that new programs could be instituted without eliminating or affecting existing programs. All this changed in the 1980s with steady-state enrollments and shrinking support funds that produced extreme competition for available resources and discouraged the creation of new programs. This makes it unlikely that new programs in environmental psychology will be started in American universities. Those programs presently in operation and supported on regular university budgets will continue. Those whose existence depends on outside funds may be eliminated.

Diminishing funds are likely to produce pressures toward conservatism and retrenchment within existing programs. This will tend to bring psychology back to core areas such as learning, perception, motivation, and social behavior. Those fields have not been able to respond to demands for relevance to practical problems. In the past, this encouraged the creation of new programs in such specialized areas as industrial psychology, community psychology, and correctional psychology, which could vent pressures for change. The dimunition of resources for new programs will close off such outlets, and the pressures for change will be felt directly on the core of psychology.

Future criticism of academic psychology will go directly to issues of validity and generalizability. The sufficiency of operational definitions will be questioned. Those who study perception in humans will need to take a serious look at how humans perceive stimuli that appear in the outside world and those who study cognition to examine how learning takes place in the outside world. The situation of two psychologies, one based on laboratory studies and another based on field studies, is intellectually and logically untenable. Integration of the two approaches will take place both at the core and at the periphery of psychology.

Early laboratory studies of human behavior were useful and important. What is likely to come under severe criticism will be the nth permutation of the same paradigm. Such an approach leads away rather than toward eventual application. Early studies of optical illusions were interesting and had heuristic value in showing that there was lawfulness to nonveridical perception. At some point, the study of optical illusions became an end in itself. Those researchers interested in, for example, the perception of highway signs will find little of interest in laboratory studies of optical illusions. If they want to learn how road signs are perceived on the highway, they will have to use road signs as stimuli.

Environmental psychologists working in applied fields such as energy or recreation will need to return to the core of psychology for sustenance and renewal. Working with sociologists, engineers, and architects brings problems of professional identity. They will not abandon their interest in applied issues but seek out concepts, theories, and methods from basic psychology that can be used to understand and predict behavior as it occurs. Hopefully, by the time that they return to the core for answers, those studying basic psychological processes will have enlarged the range of their questions and procedures to encompass many of the issues addressed by applied psychologists.

43.5.2. Linkage with Other Professions

The liaison between psychology and architecture peaked in the 1970s as the interests of the architectural profession turned away from behavior and back toward form. Architecture had a history of brief flings with art, engineering, and biology, and each time returned to form as the goal of design. Loss of interest in behavioral issues was furthered by a poor economic climate that limited new construction and the amount of money available for outside consultants. Behavioral scientists had become involved in architecture in good economic times when there was a large amount of new construction. This encouraged experimentation and some risk taking in trying new approaches. The general tightening of the economy ended most of this. Younger architectural students exposed to behavioral ideas in their training will provide the likely basis for a reawakening of interest in behavioral issues, but that is part of the future, not the present.

Interest in environmental issues among psychologists remained strong throughout the 1970s and into the 1980s. The new programs in environmental psychology were reaching maturity. They had survived earlier identity crises stemming from a heterogeneous mixture of students and faculty, diffuseness of subject matter, and a lack of standardized curricula and textbooks. By the end of the 1970s, much of the ambiguity had been resolved. The development of half a division of the American Psychological Association dedicated to environmental issues helped to institutionalize the field. The accumulation of research findings created a data base that allowed some specialization in course content. Literature in the field was beginning to coalesce into specialty areas, permitting the establishment of interest groups within the larger community of environmental psychologists. These groups or networks assemble at meetings of Division 34 or EDRA, publish their own newsletters, and maintain informal contact around such topics as energy research, pedestrian behavior, and wilderness research. Such interests take the members far beyond the earlier association of the field with architecture into such areas as transportation, urban design, appropriate technology, and recreation planning.

There has been a widely shared belief among environmental psychologists that their recommendations have not been understood or heeded by architects. It therefore seemed more efficient to attempt to reach the client directly rather than going through the architect. This has occasionally created some interesting role reversals in which the psychologist becomes a client agent and hires architects. Gary Winkel did such a good job in behavioral programming at Bellevue Hospital in New York City that he became part of the team that selected the architect to do the renovation work. I have served on the selection panel for architects on a $60-million prison construction project. My presence ensured that the architects would be sensitive to behavioral issues. At the least, it provided the opportunity to ask questions regarding the needs for color, natural light, visual stimulation, privacy, and territoriality within the institution. Role reversals in which psychologists are in a superordinate power position vis-à-vis architects have educational value. If architects believe that they need to address behavioral issues in order to obtain major contracts, it will provide an incentive for them to acquire behavioral knowledge or hire outside consultants to address these issues.

Most environmental psychologists do not see the future of their field tied directly to architecture. The architect's fee on design projects does not provide a sufficient economic base for full-time consulting by environmental psychologists. The fee structure will support occasional consultants, and over time these might develop into contractual arrangements based on a fixed number of days per year. Major architectural offices may have a "stable" of behavioral consultants just as they have consultants in other areas. This is likely to be a frustrating role intellectually because it involves brief exposure to projects without the opportunity to see the results. It can be a source of part-time income for environmental psychologists employed in other capacities or for a few who want to free-lance or work part-time. There may also be room for a few national firms to become joint partners along with architectural offices on major projects anywhere on the globe. These firms would support themselves largely on other activities, especially sponsored research that would help to pay office overhead but retain a strong commitment and available staff in such areas as user needs analysis and post occupancy evaluation and be able to respond quickly to requests for assistance on the behavioral aspects of specific design projects. The firms might maintain a registry, based on membership in EDRA or on some other basis, of local behavioral scientists interested in design issues.

The future will also see a closer liaison between psychology and the other design fields such as landscape architecture, interior design, and urban planning. There are segments of design work where the influence of environmental psychology has barely been felt. There are thousands of individuals in the United States who identify themselves as visual merchandisers concerned with product displays. These are the people who select store logos and signage, decorate store windows, and arrange interiors. Their work is most apparent during holiday seasons, but they are employed year-round to increase the visual attractiveness of retail stores. I found them eager for information about environmental psychology, particularly those aspects relating to perception and aesthetics. Such individuals lack a research tradition and know little about the intricacies of experimentation. Tact and sensitivity will be required from psychologists who want to work with them. They listen to a research report in an egocentric manner in terms of what the results can do for them personally. I am using the term *egocentric* in a nonpejorative manner in the same sense that someone buys a gardening magazine to find out how to eliminate aphids or slugs. This is the level at which busy designers will read and listen to psychologists. Often these fields do not have a strong commitment to reading as a means of discovering information. Design periodicals tend to be glossies with more pictures than words and an almost complete absence of any behavioral data, especially those data based on user response. I have had the experience of design editors removing tables of numbers and substituting graphs and diagrams. Psychologists can aid the dissemination process and also minimize the likelihood that their results will be misinterpreted by translating the information into a visual format themselves.

I can dream of an environmental psychology that learns as much from design as it contributes. Too many of our psychology buildings and offices are badly laid out for the activities that take place inside. We can profit from information on how to better use graphic aids in teaching and in the presentation of research results. We can become a visually aware segment of psychology that can influence teaching and report writing throughout the entire behavioral science community. We may also help to allay some of the rivalry and suspicion within the various design professions. Economic competition between architects and engineers, architects and interior designers, and interior designers and space planners helps to create self-serving belief systems that maintain the superiority of one group over the other. Psychologists working with these different segments may become facilitators who attempt to reduce misunderstanding and friction.

Lines of contact will be established to the various branches of engineering. This will necessarily blur the distinction between environmental psychology and human factors specialists. There may still be some division based on scale such as the design of a keyboard representing a human factors issue, whereas the layout of a building becomes one of interior design and environmental psychology, but consideration of lighting, acoustics, and color, in which people and machines are part of a single system, will necessarily involve both specialties.

43.5.3. Spread to Developing Nations

The diffusion of Western social science into the Third World has provided valuable opportunities for testing and extending theories, but it has also made clear the limitations of existing Western-oriented theories and methods. Environmental psychologists can expect to encounter many of these same problems as they move their research into the Third World, but there are also some opportunities and problems that seem more likely in person–environmental research than in other fields. Research in the Third World will bring opportunities for consultation with governments on projects at a larger scale than those possible in developed nations in helping to create new towns, new cities, and to shape regions. It will be possible to try out design innovations based on theory and past experience, evaluate them, and incorporate necessary modifications in successive projects, which themselves can be evaluated and used as the basis for further redesign. This "Volkswagen model" (Sommer, 1972) or constant fine-tuning of a basic model has been the dream of many environmental psychologists involved n postoccupancy evaluation who see their efforts restricted to a single project that is never replicated. The Third World may provide opportunities for extended involvement over aseries of projects linked together by an overall design conception.

Textbooks in environmental psychology will have to be modified to include additional examples from non-Western sources. One area of the field that has made considerable progress in this regard is mental mapping. Those researchers interested in cognitive representations of the environment have gone all over the world for examples and sites for data collection. This is due largely to the influence of geographers who have been active in this field since its inception. Part of the early history of environmental psychology was shaped at Clark University in the late 1960s where a creative collaboration was developed between departments of geography and psychology. Fieldwork for this program spanned several continents.

Diffusion to the Third World will test the validity of accepted findings in Western-oriented environmental research. There is, for example, a research literature on wilderness experience based largely on surveys of hikers and backpackers. This work must be extended beyond recreational trips to life in places where survival is a constant struggle. Western concepts of wilderness do not devote much attention to animistic perceptions of the landscape. Anyone who attempts to do mental mapping in developing nations will have to be familiar with local customs and religion. Western environmental psychologists who want to work abroad may find it useful to receive training in cultural anthropology in order to shed cultural blinders and preconceptions. At the same time, they must retain their ability to function as environmental psychologists.

The newness of the field has minimized the opportunities presently available to conduct research abroad. Universities and governments in Third World nations are unlikely to request or support visiting professorships in fields about which they are only dimly aware. To some degree, environmental psychology will have to prove its value in developed nations before it receives invitations elsewhere, even though these invitations may provide opportunities to strengthen the validity of its own theories and findings and to apply them on a broader scale than in the West. The export market for Western environmental psychology should improve as it becomes more universal in its theories, applications, and methods. The diffusion model will involve communication going in several directions. There is currently exciting work in France on the use of phenomenological inquiry in housing research (Korosek-Serfaty, 1978). This work may influence some of the more statistically minded American and British researchers as their work is transplanted into the Third World. Work on landscape form taking place in Japan provides a healthy corrective for a Western environmental psychology that has been overly concerned with the built environment (Hijuchi, 1975; Nakamura, 1980). The existing flow of environmental psychology from West to East will inevitably change into a more balanced exchange in both and other directions.

Some of the research issues largely ignored at the present time that are likely to be treated more fully as environmental psychologists begin studying in the Third World are as follows:

Space usage as affected by non-Western land-tenure systems

Kinship and space usage

Effects of industrialization on home and neighborhood interaction

Breakdown of traditional patterns of land ownership and space control

Space usage in agriculture

Attitudes toward particular geotopes such as jungle, desert, tundra, and the like

Orientation and navigation in unmarked landscapes

Oral histories of places

Plant–people relationships

Animistic perception of the environment

Religion and environmental ethics

Life in isolated settlements

Methods of preserving local culture and customs against outside intrusion

Research in non-Western nations will encourage the development of techniques that do not depend heavily on language. Although it is possible for psychologists to rely on local informants and translators, as their colleagues in anthropology have done, this is not a typical approach in psychology where investigators desire first-hand contact with their research subjects. There is too much skepticism within psychology regarding the likelihood of observer error and bias to accept the views of informants uncritically. Instead, environmental psychologists are likely to turn to observation methods and photography as a means of obtaining data.

As other cross-cultural researchers have discovered, techniques used to collect data in the West will require modification for nondeveloped and largely nonliterate societies. Mail surveys would be unsuitable in most Third World nations, as would any type of questionnaire in a situation of low literacy. Lack of familiarity with behavioral science may create a climate of fear, in which respondents are afraid to provide honest answers or cooperate with foreigners who have some government affiliation. The entire basis for an objective social science will be absent in many Third World nations. Whether any social science can be value-neutral is a continuing question even within Western social science, but in nondeveloped nations where the research is most likely to be under the sponsorship of a government agency (or perceived this way by the population) possibilities of government control and political manipulation are always at hand.

Rules for the protection and use of human subjects will have to be modified, not necessarily loosened, for use abroad. The notion of informed consent will have little meaning to people who lack understanding of the nature of the scientific enterprise. Knowledge for its own sake or for general human advancement is a very abstract notion difficult to grasp by those struggling for survival. Western conceptions of data analysis and proof are likely to be challenged in the Third World. Notions of reliability and statistical significance that are accepted as canons of faith in the West may not seem so logical in the East. Much of the statistical analysis undertaken routinely by American psychologists is considered unnecessary by colleagues in Western Europe and will probably be even less acceptable in the Third World. The widespread availability of computers in the West has encouraged the use of elaborate multivariate experimental designs and lengthy questionnaires with the expectation that the computer will sort out everything. The spread of environmental psychology to undeveloped nations lacking extensive computational facilities may compel Western researchers to seek out simpler means of data collection and analysis.

It is difficult to specify in advance which research methods will be most useful for studying life in undeveloped nations. The psychological ecology pioneered by Barker (1968) is likely to be appropriate but perhaps needs to be modified to account for the importance of natural and nonbuilt settings. Students should be trained as research generalists who have a variety of methods at their disposal.

Reform and Revolution

Those undertaking research in developing nations cannot escape the pervasive influence of ethnic and class conflict. The Third World is steeped in a history of racism and colonialism identified with the West. Currently, there is developing opposition in many African nations to Western archeologists exploring cultural history and removing irreplaceable artifacts. A clash of ideologies and cultures can be expected whenever Western social scientists undertake studies in the Third World. The nature of environmental psychology is that it is partly an applied and partly a basic discipline. Its applied aspects will necessarily have political, economic, and social overtones that prove controversial.

Occasionally researchers will find themselves in the position of opposing the government that is sponsoring their research. Researchers may find themselves allied with villagers attempting to resist centralized government control of technological changes that undermine local culture. In this role, they can find some solace and precedent in the work of advocate planners in the West who have worked with local communities to resist outside development plans.

Behavioral scientists throughout the world, because of their education, training, and social class, are likely to be identified with the ruling classes of a society on whom they depend for support. This relationship between social science and authority is likely to be perceived by the local population as intellectual subservience. The reformist assumptions of environmental psychologists are likely to be challenged as they come into contact with revolutionary

ideologies. Nor are the methods of data collection in environmental psychology appropriate to totalitarian settings where the voluntary cooperation and interests of the people studied cannot be obtained. In situations where a researcher must explicitly declare allegience to one or another warring faction, the usefulness and value of the research will be greatly diminished. When people are rushing to the barricades or fleeing for their lives, they may not want to fill out questionnaires or be interviewed. The concept of a control group does not have much meaning in the midst of a social cataclysm. When poverty and oppression are extreme, the researcher's questions will seem frivolous.

In conducting research under conditions of extreme poverty and unrest, one will not be able to use the same research methods and assumptions possible in more tranquil times. To keep aloof from endemic suffering will diminish the moral stature of the field. To study the basic effects of light and color under such conditions will make the field seem like a luxury. To quote Camus (1960):

> It is always possible to record the social conversations that take place on the benches of the amphitheater while the lion is crunching the victim.... The number of martyrs has increased amazingly over the surface of the globe. In the face of so much suffering, if art [or scientific research] insists on being a luxury, it will also be a lie. (p. 251)

It is ironic that environmental psychology, which is identified with a liberal-reformist position in the West, will be perceived as conservative or reactionary in revolutionary circles. Activists in Third World nations, even those who traditionally start out as sympathetic to social science concepts and ideals, tend to turn hostile to the analytic and reflective approach of Western social science. Environmental psychologists undertaking research in developing nations should expect some suspicion and hostility from both the far Right and the far Left.

43.5.4. Diffusion to Socialist Nations

Because other contributors to this series will be discussing the current state of environmental psychology in the U.S.S.R., I will devote most of my remarks to the future prospects of the field in Eastern Europe. As an outsider, I may be able to note trends that individuals closer to the scene may overlook. There is often value from someone from another culture serving as an observer. An outsider may also feel less constrained to discuss sensitive matters.

Ideologies change as they cross borders and become integrated into other cultures. When environmental psychology was transplanted from North American to Western Europe, it had to accommodate itself to the philosophical-speculative traditions of France and Germany. This has produced the fascinating phenomenological inquiry into the meanings of space, exemplified by the work of Bachelard (1964), Korosec-Serfaty (1978), and Moles and Rohmer (1978). Environmental psychology will also change as it moves into Eastern Europe and confronts Russian society and Marxist ideology.

At the core of Marxist philosophy is the doctrine of dialectical materialism. This is an evolutionary theory of social change emphasizing the importance of external economic forces as the primary determinants of experience. Consciousness is construed as the intensive reflection of the external conditions of society. Materialism is opposed by the doctrine of idealism that maintains that psychological forces are primary and economic forces secondary in the evolution of society. Western psychology is perceived in the East as heavily idealistic in contrast to the materialistic psychology of the Soviet Union that traces its roots to the work of Pavlov. Current Soviet psychology is considered to be a psychology of activity, based on the shaping of mental phenomena by practical activity. Activity both transforms and reflects the outside world and becomes internalized in the form of inner meanings. This unifies the subjective and the objective both in and through activity. Environment does not determine activities but sets the limits in which activities can develop (Niit, Kruusvall, & Heidmets, 1981).

Given the predispositions of Marxist ideology to environmental explanations of behavior, an explicitly environmental psychology would seem congenial. Environmental psychology arose in the West as an antidote to the mentalistic bias in psychology that ignored physical determinants of behavior. However, many of the research issues studied by Western researchers are not considered relevant or important in Socialist nations. Some of this can be traced to cultural, ideological, and political differences. There is not, for example, the same preoccupation with individual privacy in the Soviet Union as exists in the United States. In a collectivist society, privacy is not always desirable and may in fact be regarded as an impediment to collective action. Taking a sincere interest in the actions of others, even if this means violating individual privacy, is considered appropriate and necessary conduct in the U.S.S.R. This may have positive consequences in reducing litter or pollu-

tion. Soviet citizens who observe a person littering are *expected* to intervene and may be severly chastized if they do not. "Don't be a bystander" is a Soviet slogan reinforcing the idea that citizens are expected to play an active part in maintaining the public order.

Territoriality does not have the same significance in the U.S.S.R. as it does in the West, even though the core definition of territory as a space marked, controlled, and defended by an individual or group may be shared. Most of the land in the Soviet Union is owned by the state rather than private individuals. Soviet visitors to the United States often have difficulty understanding that most of the land that they see, even vast areas that are undeveloped and unused, are privately owned. Perhaps the closest analogies available to them are the vast estates formerly owned by absentee nobility during the time of the Tsars.

Environmental psychologists in socialist nations are likely to pay more attention to conditions at work than have their counterparts in the West. Because most enterprises are state owned and operated, collaboration between psychologists working in environmental research institutes and industrial planners will be possible. Psychologists should also be able to work with trade unions in improving the work place.

Western research on territories tends to concentrate on microspaces. There is little examination of actual ownership and its role in maintaining the social order. We may look forward to a future period when Soviet environmental psychologists apply a Marxist perspective to space usage and territoriality *in the West*. Thus far there has been little of this type of cross-fertilization. Each collectivity of environmental psychologists has concentrated its attention on conditions within its own sphere of influence.

In past periods, the U.S.S.R. has put great store in centralized planning, although there are trends away from this direction. If Soviet environmental psychologists become involved in the planning process, opportunities for conducting major research studies involving large samples in many locations and applying the results are manifold. Their Western counterparts perceive themselves to be distant from decision making, and their efforts are confined to lobbying architects to hire them as behavioral consultants on specific projects. The leverage available to consultants is minimal and not likely to increase. Much of the contribution of psychologists to architecture in the West has been on a trickle-down basis through research and teaching in architectural schools.

A very different structural arrangement is possible

in socialist nations with centralized planning under government control. There are currently Soviet psychologists working at the Central Research and Experimental Planning Institute of Residential Buildings, the Moscow Institute of Architecture, the Leningrad Research Institute of City Planning, and the Central Research Institute of City Planning (Niit, Kruusvall, & Heidmets, 1981). The likelihood that environmental psychologists may eventually occupy positions of authority in the building industry seems much greater in the U.S.S.R. than in the West. American researchers have dreamed of the possibility of mandating user needs analysis and postoccupancy evaluation on government projects. Even if this could be done, it would apply to only a small percentage of new construction. If building evaluation and user needs analysis could be developed in the Soviet Union, it could include all types of buildings in all locations. The potential for applied environmental psychology, especially the liaison between psychologists, architects and city planners, seems greater in the East than in the West.

Political obstacles loom ahead in a field dedicated to studies of real-world situations. The results of environmental evaluation are often critical. So long as Soviet environmental psychologists remain in universities and research centers and do "safe studies" of light, form, and color perception and avoid evaluation studies, there is not likely to be too much of a problem. Yet once Soviet environmental psychologists enter into the area of application, conflicts with the authorities are inevitable. The future of environmental psychology in Eastern Europe is likely to have ups and downs, of opening up of environmental assessments and then retrenchment when criticism of authorities is perceived. Studies of mental hospitals and jails, which are favorite topics of American environmental researchers, may be off limits to their Soviet counterparts for a very long time.

Greater exchange of information and travel between Eastern and Western environmental psychologists should enlarge the research agenda of the field. It may also provoke more interest in comparative studies of individual and group behavior in different cultures.

43.6. RESEARCH AGENDA FOR THE TWENTY-FIRST CENTURY

The concerns of most environmental psychologists have centered on microspaces inhabited by individuals and small groups. This is not unexpected in view of the background of most environmental psychologists in social psychology that defines its subject matter as the relationship between individuals and groups. Nonetheless, the most urgent environmental problems are found at larger environmental scales. The future of the field will see the involvement of environmental psychologists in efforts to solve global and eventually interplanetary problems as space travel moves into a settlement phase. This research will involve the activities of larger, superorganismic entities with jurisdictions cutting across regional, national, and planetary boundaries. The construction of a research agenda for the future is a mind-stretching activity that inevitably lays bare the naiveté and parochialism of those sufficiently foolhardy to undertake such a task. An agenda necessarily combines wish and expectation. Description of the world as it should be will have more impact if accompanied by plans for implementation.

The issue of advocacy will have to be addressed sooner or later. During most of the first century of its existence, academic psychology had the luxury of detachment from urgent social problems. The belief was also prevalent, although not universally accepted, that it could be a value-neutral science providing data on issues without taking a stand. Criticism of this value-neutral approach during the 1960s was partly responsible for the development of an environmental psychology with an implicit commitment to environmental quality. The depth and extent of this commitment will need to be explicated, clarified, and extended during the coming decades. Most Western scientists do not feel comfortable in an advocacy role. On the other hand, practitioners within applied fields such as medicine, dentistry, and engineering are much more clear as to their axiological assumptions. The physician need not be apologetic about furthering individual or public health. A civil engineer has an explicit commitment to highway safety that is not masked by any pretense about civil engineering as a value-neutral activity. The technical details of medicine and civil engineering may be objective and value neutral, but the selection of problems and the responsibilities for making recommendations are not.

Unlike colleagues in these other professions, environmental psychologists lack time-tested models of advocacy. If environmental psychology does not clarify its value assumptions and how it can function in adversarial systems, there is the likelihood that its methods and findings will be used to *justify* noxious environmental conditions. Except in the case of the most extreme stressors, it will be possible to find individuals who have successfully adapted to noise, smog, and crowding, without apparent ill effects. Some of them may appear to prosper under conditions that other individuals find abhorrent. A persistent finding in environmental research is the amazing adaptive value of our species. Unless our epistemologies and axiologies are clarified and explicated, we may find that our work becomes an impediment to change.

An agenda for the twenty-first century must include serious discussion and writing on the philosophical and moral underpinnings of the field. This task should involve active collaboration with philosophers, political scientists, and clergy. All these individuals have previously wrestled with definitions of "the good life," and now, in concert with environmental scholars and researchers, they can develop conceptions of "the good environment." The efforts and products will be steeped in value assumptions and moral dicta. Because the theologies and ideologies of the world differ sharply in their conceptions of the good life, there is no reason to expect consensus about the requisites of a good environment

Conferences to define environmental quality as well as programs to improve it at a global level should be sponsored by respected international agencies and the recommendations appropriate both for developed nations that are the source of most environmental pollution and developing nations that anticipate improvement in their standard of living through industrialization. Nations face different environmental problems even though the effects of these problems affect the entire planet. In working for international agencies and commissions, environmental psychologists can learn from colleagues in population psychology who have been working with international agencies for many years. There is an art to international consulting, which includes everything from adaptation to jet lag to competence in other languages. Efforts to train environmental psychologists for international studies must confront the issue of linguistic competence. The current situation of the hegemony of the English language in environmental psychology is probably a temporary phenomenon. English may remain an important language in the field, but it will need to be complemented by one or two additional languages. Opportunities must be available for publication of research results in multiple languages and for conferences that provide simultaneous translation.

Technological changes, natural disasters, and human-made catastrophies will markedly affect research priorities in a field concerned with people and the environment. Compared to the past and the present of environmental psychology, I predict a *relative*

lessening of concern with specialized settings such as hospitals, schools, and jails and more research on conditions such as pollution, war, unchecked population growth, and the wasteful use of resources that threaten the survival of the species. Without denying the need for research on more specialized issues, the following list of topics indicates those issues relevant to environmental psychology that I see as most critical for the welfare of the human species.

43.6.1. Pollution Effects

Problems connected with toxic waste disposal, air and water pollution, and the presence of pathogens in the environment are likely to increase over the next decades. Technical remedies will be found in some cases, but these may come too late to affect generations who must live with the effects of environmental degradation. This presents the possibility of learning to live with pollution, a process described under the headings of adaptation and habituation. Based on the past history of the human species, there is little doubt that many adjustments are possible. Advances in medical science may increase the life span in the process. This will achieve increased longevity in an objectively degraded environment, which will pose a paradox for social theorists and environmental researchers and stand as an obstacle to change. How can governments be asked to mobilize their resources when humankind seemingly thrives, at least as measured by longevity, swimming in pollution?

One role of environmental psychologists will be to measure the behavioral effects of pollutants. This work can supplement the research of public health researchers and others who rely on population statistics. Medical researchers can determine the mortality rates of those who live near toxic waste dumps or in areas with heavy smog, and behavioral scientists can measure the social psychological outcomes. These issues are politically sensitive, have major economic consequences, and important implications for the way individuals will live in the future. They also cut across national boundaries. Acid rains falling over Eastern Canada originate in the United States, and French nuclear bomb tests in the Pacific contaminate air and water in Europe. The destruction of forests in the Amazon will have a serious impact on air quality in North America.

Long-term programs to ensure the survivability of the species will require some consensus as to acceptable levels of pollution. The philosophical underpinnings of such a venture will require the assistance of behavioral scientists. General statements about environmental quality will need to be translated by engineers into technical standards and fit into a framework for implementation by governments.

In terms of prevention, there will need to be a serious assessment of existing and new technologies in terms of these pollution effects. Such an examination will be done largely by those in other professions. Environmental psychologists will have to invent roles for themselves that allow the introduction of quality-of-life indicators into the political and economic decision-making process.

43.6.2. Population

Tides of immigration beyond the control of any single nation are sweeping over various parts of the world. Demographic characteristics of regions are being altered in fundamental and perhaps irrevocable ways. Environmental psychologists will need to join with other professionals in examining the implications of shifting and expanding populations. Large concentrations of unassimilated refugees, some of the stateless, lay the basis for future turmoil. Researchers will need to identify the carrying capacity of regions and the planet as a whole. They will have to work with governments and private agencies to control population growth. Issues of territoriality as it relates to property ownership and control, national boundaries, and the oceans will need to be addressed.

Once population is brought under control, questions connected with a steady-state will arise. Little research has been done on this issue in view of the more urgent concern of controlling population expansion. Having a steady state will require international agencies to take stock of available resources, how they are distributed, and what additional resources are needed. There is much that those in the newer Second World nations such as the United States and Canada can learn from Europe and Asia about stability in the landscape and in housing. Simulation and modeling procedures may be useful in examining the behavioral implications of a steady state.

Certain current demographic trends in the United States are likely to continue and have implications for housing and land use that will involve environmental psychologists. Such trends include the increasing life span of the population, creating a higher proportion of elderly in the population. This will create demand for housing appropriate for this age group, including necessary support facilities in transportation, food service, medical care, and so forth. The proportion of women entering the work force is likely to increase; this will put more pressure on existing child care facilities and create the need for new types of facilities

such as those proximate to work places. Family size is likely to decrease as more women are working outside the home.

These population trends coupled with the rising price of land are likely to seriously limit the construction of new single-family housing. Even with both partners employed, working couples will be unable to afford to purchase new homes. This may create a new type of familial togetherness in which married couples occupy the same household as their parents. Due to continued immigration and higher birth rates, the proportion of nonwhites in the United States is likely to increase. During the 1950–1980 period this was also accompanied by a movement of nonwhites into the cities and the occupancy of the suburbs by the former residents of downtown areas. The economic disadvantages of unlimited suburbanization became apparent in the 1970s, and the high cost of suburban housing coupled with increased transportation costs and efforts will cap these trends in the future. An important research challenge for environmental psychologists will be to develop land use and housing options that bring together the diverse population groups in society, to create sociopetal rather than sociofugal neighborhoods and cities.

Much of the public housing constructed in the past three decades has been intensely segregated by age and ethnicity. Some public housing projects ended up more than 95% black, Hispanic, or Asian-American even though they were not planned to be this way. Environmental psychologists will have to join with social psychologists and city planners to assess whether practicable alternatives exist. The research agenda for the twenty-first century will have to deal directly with the politically sensitive issue of the degree to which governmental policy should support or inhibit ethnically segregated housing and neighborhoods. This may be a no-win situation for the environmental researcher who will come under criticism no matter what recommendations are made, but such research will be essential if we are not to stumble along on the road to dystopia.

43.6.3. War and Peace

Unless global conflict can be averted, all the other issues discussed here will become insignificant. Environmental psychologists have a unique perspective to contribute to peace research in emphasizing the connection between people and the physical environment. Two topics of interest to environmental psychologists that are of direct concern to peace and war are territoriality and crowding. The issues are related in that territoriality is one system for controlling intergroup hostility whereas crowding will severely tax and eventually weaken a territorial control system. The relationship between crowding and conflict needs to be explored at various environmental scales. At the level of the small group, crowding tends to lead to withdrawal and "cocooning" (Altman & Haythorn, 1965, 1967). The extent to which this occurs at larger environmental levels needs to be determined. Another relevant topic is how individuals who are not crowded themselves but who perceive their standard of living to be threatened by crowding in adjacent areas are likely to react. The research agenda must include intergroup contacts. Some work is already available on gang turf and neighborhood relationships, but the spatial factors need to be more clearly defined and the effects of density on intergroup relations need to be examined. Ethnicity should be considered as a primary variable in spatial usage. A relevant issue from the standpoint of peace research is how members of hostile groups use space to avoid contact with each other. Studies of border areas will be helpful, especially those that have been the scene of past conflicts.

43.6.4. Harmony with Other Species

The human presence on the planet has been devastating to many other species. Animals and plants adapted to living free are disappearing as their habitats are taken over by humans. The earth is moving to a monoculture based on the ability of species to tolerate the close proximity of Homo sapiens. This will probably reduce genetic diversity. Solutions must be global in scope to preserve habitats that cut across national boundaries. Large preserves are needed to protect many species. The planning must be done quickly before the situation for endangered species becomes hopeless. It will be important to learn how other species are affected by the human presence. There is no basis for assuming that the behavior of animals that currently scavenge at the fringes of human communities is similar to what it had been before the human incursion. Environmental psychologists will need to join with comparative psychologists and zoologists to identify suitable environments for captive animals. Much valuable information has already been contributed on this topic by Hediger (1950) Erwin, Maple, and Mitchell (1979), and Maple and Hoff (1982), but there are too many zoos that are poorly designed and teach erroneous lessons about animal behavior to visitors.

The effects of nature on humans have been investigated in the context of wilderness research (Lucas & Stankey, 1974), gardening (Kaplan, 1978), and

plant–people relationships (Ulrich, 1981). A model of human contact with nature requires conceptual development at a very sophisticated level. Productivity and disease models of motivation will need to be replaced by ecological models that assume the interdependence of species and the environment. The disappearance of certain plant species through industrialization and corporate farming will not have a direct and measureable impact on standards of living or health. The disappearance of the cheetah or the California condor is not going to affect the lives and livelihood of many individuals. Consideration of such issues, which have moral and spiritual dimensions, will bring environmental psychology back to its roots in the ecology movement.

Environmental psychologists have much to contribute to understanding how individuals are affected by the presence of natural elements. This is probably an issue where laboratory experimentation will be less useful than interviews, observation, and phenomenological inquiry. However, there are instances where some laboratory experimentation is possible, as in the case of Ulrich's (1981) study of physiological response to natural elements in the landscape. The epistemology of the field will need to accommodate environmental elements typically beyond the focus of awareness with minimal impact on immediate behavior.

Another topic for environmental researchers will be the effects of natural elements in the urban environment, to learn the degree to which growing plants and trees mitigate the negative effects of crowding, noise, and high stimulation. Active and passive contact with natural elements will need to be compared, that is, gardening and animal husbandry as distinct from spectator contact with plants and animals. Comparison across regions can help to show how social learning is affected by contact with nature. Developmental research can show how preferences for particular landscapes are formed. These preferences, sometimes called geotopes, seem to be imprinted at a very early age. A critical aspect of geotope formation involves early preferences for rural or urban scenes and their effects upon subsequent adjustment. Little is known about the psychological aspects of adjustment to new geotopes. Such issues need to be investigated both in the laboratory and in the field.

43.6.5. Resource Conservation

The literature on energy conservation, recycling, and litter control reflects the background of most environmental psychologists in social psychology. Investigations have dealt with resource use in apartment complexes, college dormitories, and neighborhoods (Cone & Hayes, 1980). The future is likely to see some environmental psychologists viewing these problems on a systemwide basis where the behavior of institutions and agencies, as distinct from individuals and groups, must be changed. Just as the principles of applied behavioral analysis had to be modified when they shifted from rats and pigeons in cages to applications in schools and hospitals, the principles for reinforcing desirable behavior at the individual and household levels will probably have to be adapted for use with larger institutional entities such as corporations and municipalities.

From its inception, environmental psychology has been preoccupied with urban issues to the neglect of agricultural problems. Yet in many areas of the world, some of the most pressing environmental problems such as loss of topsoil, stripping of forests, and excessive use of water are the result of wasteful agricultural practices. Environmental psychologists in the future will have to learn to work on rural problems, which may include small subsistence farmers organized in kinship networks, collective farms in socialist nations, and with large private agribusiness corporations in the West.

43.6.6. Space Travel and Settlement

Valuable information about space travel can be obtained from research on extreme environments, in which groups of people live in polar camps, submarines, isolated weather stations, and offshore oil rigs where life is characterized by isolation, confinement, and risk (Earls, 1969). Research into these settings and their effects on humans was encouraged by developments in several areas, including the deployment of nuclear submarines that could remain submerged for periods of 2 to 3 months or longer, the possibilities of developing underwater habitats for exploiting undersea resources, resource exploration in the Antarctic, and human penetration of outer space (Harrison & Connors, 1984). Behavioral scientists, including environmental psychologists, have been involved both in simulation studies (Altman & Haythorne, 1965, 1967) and in interviewing returnees from expeditions into isolated settings (Gunderson, 1963, 1968). Because much of this research was sparked by national competition and military goals, there has been some limitation on the free exchange of information.

The early research peaked during the 1960s and diminished sharply thereafter. Apparently the needs of defense planners and governments for behavioral information about life in isolated environments were

satisfied. They learned as much as they needed or wanted about the mental and physical effects of isolated environments, including the *exotic environment syndrome* that is characterized by decreased alertness and intellectual impairment, motivational decline, somatic complaints, and mood changes (Harrison & Connors, 1984). These effects can result from the monotonous daily routine coupled with imminent danger, limited facilities and supplies, and social privations.

All this is likely to change as the possibilities for space settlement, as distinct from space travel, become more feasible. It is likely that this research, too, will originate in national rivalries and the desire to gain military advantage. Semipermanent settlements will present planners with a whole new range of behavioral issues. Thus far, the high cost of payloads into space has precluded the presence of behavioral scientists on board as observers/researchers. The use of larger vehicles and more efficient propulsion systems may allow behavioral scientists to conduct firsthand observations of life in space.

Future research on these issues must broaden the range and size of populations studied. Some of the civil defense studies, in which large numbers of people lived for extended periods in simulated civil defense shelters, may be relevant (Hammes, Ahearn, & Keith, 1965; Hammes & Watson, 1965). Unlike the space simulations and polar expeditions, the shelter studies included people of varied social backgrounds, ages, and genders. It would be desirable if this research could be conducted under the aegis of the United Nations or some other international agency. Otherwise, there is the likelihood that earthly rivalries will be transplanted throughout the solar system. Hostile and suspicious nations will send up hostile and suspicious space colonies. There have been a few attempts at combined space exploration such as the joint U.S.-U.S.S.R. space mission during 1975 and the guest astronaut program initiated by the U.S.S.R. involving international crews (Oberg, 1981).

Adaptation to changes in geotope will be a critical aspect of planetary settlement. Based on images of outer space already available, individuals from lush, densely populated areas may have to adapt to sparse, bleak underpopulated landscapes. Little systematic documentation is available on the effects of such abrupt changes. It will also be necessary to protect fragile, remote environments from being overwhelmed by the human presence. The time to begin planning the physical dimensions of outer space settlements is before they have occurred. After people have moved in and established homes, roads, and businesses, it will be too late. Environmental psychologists will need to begin utopian planning in concert with architects, engineers, urban planners, transportation planners, and public health officials representing many nations. Undoubtedly, future settlements will take their own form, based on geographic and physical constraints, technical requirements, and the actions of the settlers themselves, but the planning can establish standards and set general guidelines in the forms of density, transportation, and shelter that may be useful to those who administer such programs.

Few environmental psychologists have had experience in utopian planning. This is a characteristic of training programs in the behavioral sciences that tend to emphasize the past and the present. Those utopias that have been constructed by psychologists (e.g., Skinner, 1948) are regarded more as curiosities or literary documents than planning agendas. This lack of futurism proved to be an impediment to early collaboration with architects. Whereas designers were primarily concerned with the new projects, psychologists felt most comfortable discussing available projects that could be evaluated. Institutionalizing futurism within environmental psychology through involvement in planning for outer space settlements should extend the temporal range of social science theory and research.

43.7. SUMMARY

Environmental psychology arose in the 1960s in response to the neglect of environmental variables in psychology and of behavioral variables in architecture.

Its origins can be traced to two related movements of the period, the Human Rights Movement and the Ecology Movement.

To fill existing gaps in academic psychology, which tended to be preoccupied with the laboratory approach, environmental psychology has tended to be more oriented toward field research and the application of knowledge. These differences are a matter of degree rather than kind. Environmental psychology possesses some of the characteristics of a cross-disciplinary field of study and some of the characteristics of a subdiscipline of psychology.

The future will see a return to the core of psychology by environmental psychologists working in peripheral areas and a broadening of the approach of psychology to encompass environmental variables. Collaboration and consultation with engineering and other related professions will increase, which in turn will influence the field of environmental psychology.

The diffusion of environmental psychology into the Third World will serve as a needed corrective to a Western-oriented bias in the field, and the spread of environmental psychology to socialist nations will increase concern with the conditions of work and the effects of centralized planning.

The research agenda for the next century will see the scope of the field broadened to encompass larger environmental units, clarification of the philosophical and moral underpinnings of the field, including explication of the advocacy issue, and more concern with multilingual communication. Areas within a larger research agenda will include pollution effects, population growth, war and peace, harmony with other species and with the natural environment, and space travel and settlement.

NOTE

1. According to Niit, Kruusvall, and Heidmits (1981), in the 1930s, psychologists Teplov and Shevaryov worked at the Moscow School of Architecture and co-authored textbooks with architects on the influence of color and light in architecture.

REFERENCES

Allport, G.W. (1968). The historical background of modern psychology. In G. Lindzey & E. Aronson (Eds.), *Handbook of social psychology* (Vol. 1). Reading, MA: Addison-Wesley.

Altman, I., & Haythorn, W.W. (1965). Interpersonal exchange in isolation. *Sociometry, 28,* 411–426.

Altman, I., & Haythorn, W.W. (1967). The ecology of isolated groups. *Behavioral Science, 12,* 169–182.

Bachelard, G. (1964). *The poetics of space.* New York: Orion.

Barker, R.G. (1968). *Ecological psychology.* Stanford, CA: Stanford University Press.

Bazelon, D.L. (1982). Veils, values, and social responsibility. *American Psychologist, 37,* 115–121.

Bevan, W. (1982). A sermon of sorts in three plus parts. *American Psychologist, 37,* 1303–1322.

Campbell, D.T., & Stanley, J.C. (1966). *Experimental and quasi-experimental designs for research.* Chicago: Rand-McNally.

Camus, A. (1960). *Resistance, rebellion and death* (p. 250). New York: Knopf.

Carson, R. (1962). *Silent spring.* Boston: Houghton Mifflin.

Cone, J.D., & Hayes, S.C. (1980). *Environmental problems/Behavioral solutions.* Monterey, CA: Brooks/Cole.

Earls, J.H. (1969). Human adjustment to an exotic environment: The nuclear submarine. *Archives of General Psychiatry, 20,* 117–123.

Erwin, J., Maple, T., & Mitchell, G. (1979). *Captivity and behavior.* New York: Van Nostrand Reinhold.

Grady, E.R., (Ed.).(1959). *Farmhouse planning guides: Household activity data and space needs related to design.* Ithaca, NY: Cornell University, Housing Research Center.

Gunderson, E.K.E. (1963). Emotional symptoms in extremely isolated groups. *Archives of General Psychiatry, 9,* 362–368.

Gunderson, E.K.E. (1968). Mental health problems in Antarctica. *Archives of Environmental Health, 17,* 558–564.

Hammes, J.A., Ahearn, T.R., & Keith, F.J., Jr. (1965). A chronology of two weeks fallout shelter confinement. *Journal of Clinical Psychology, 21,* 452–456.

Hammes, J.A., & Watson, J.A. (1965). Behavior patterns of groups experimentally confined. *Perceptual and Motor Skills, 20,* 1269–1272.

Harrison, A.A., & Connors, M.M. (1984). Groups in exotic environments. In L. Berkowitz (Ed.), *Advances in Experimental Social Psychology* (pp. 49–87). New York: Academic.

Hediger, H. (1950). *Wild animals in captivity.* London: Butterworths.

Hijuchi, T. (1975). *The visual and the spatial structure of landscape.* Tokyo: Gihodo.

Huntington, S.P. (1982). *American politics: The politics of disharmony.* Cambridge, MA: Harvard University Press.

Iltis, H.H. (1966). The meaning of human evolution to conservation. *Wisconsin Academy Review, 13,* 18–23.

Kaplan, R. (1978). Participation in environmental design. In S. Kaplan & R. Kaplan (Eds.), *Humanscape* (pp. 427–438). Belmont, CA: Wadsworth.

Korosec-Serfaty, P. (1978). The appropriation of space. *Proceedings of the 3rd International Architectural Psychology Conference.* Strasbourg, France: University of Strasbourg Press.

Littman, R.A. (1961). The socially indifferent science. *American Psychologist, 16,* 232–236.

Lucas, R., & Stankey, G. (1974). Social carrying capacity for backcountry recreation. *Outdoor Recreation Research, 8* 14–23.

Maple, T., & Hoff, M.P. (1982). *Gorilla behavior.* New York: Van Nostrand Reinhold.

Milgram, S. (1964). Behavioral study of obedience. *Journal of Abnormal and Social Psychology, 69,* 137–143.

Moles, A.A., & Rohmer, E. (1978). *Psychologie de l'espace.* Paris: Casterman.

Nakamura, Y. (1980). Landscape perception and man's aesthetic intervention to environment. In G. Hagino & W.H. Ittelson (Eds.), *Interaction Processes between Human Behavior and Environment, Proceedings of the Japan-United States Seminar,* (pp. 139–152).

Niit, T., Kruusvall, J., & Heidmets, M. (1981). Environmental psychology in the Soviet Union. *Journal of Environmental Psychology, 1,* 157–177.

Oberg, J.E. (1981). *Red star in orbit.* New York: Random House.

Pratt, C.C. (1939). *The logic of modern psychology.* New York: Macmillan.

Proshansky, H.M. (1976). Environmental psychology and the real world. *American Psychologist, 31,* 303–310.

Proshansky, H.M. (1981). An environmental psychologist's perspective on the interdisciplinary approach in psychology. In John H. Harvey (Ed.) *Cognition, social behavior, and the environment* (pp. 3–20). Hillsdale, NJ: Erlbaum.

Rosenthal, R. (1966). *Experimenter effects in behavioral research.* New York: Appleton-Century-Crofts.

Segall, M.H., Campbell, D.T., & Herskovits, M.J. (1966). *The influence of culture on visual perception.* Indianapolis, IN: Bobbs-Merrill.

Singer, J.E., & Baum, A. (1981). *Environmental psychology is applied social psychology.* Paper presented at the Colloquium Toward a Social Psychology of the Environment, Maison des Sciences de L'Homme, Paris.

Skinner, B.F. (1948). *Walden two.* New York: Macmillan.

Sommer, R. (1972). *Design awareness.* San Francisco: Rinehart.

Sommer, R. (1980). Environmental psychology—A blueprint for the future. *APA Monitor, 11,* 2.

Thiel, P. (1970). Notes on the description, scaling, and notation, and scoring of some perceptual and cognitive attributes of the physical environment. In H.M. Proshansky, W.H. Ittleson, and L.G. Rivlin (Eds.), *Environmental psychology.* New York: Holt, Rinehart & Winston.

Turkington, C. (1983). For farmers, failure is more than no work. *APA Monitor, 14,* 16.

Ulrich, R.S. (1981). Natural versus urban scenes. *Environment and Behavior, 13,* 523–556.

Wundt, W. (1862). *Beiträge zur theorie der Sinneswahrnehmung.* Leipzig, Germany: Winter.

AUTHOR INDEX

SUBJECT INDEX

Behavior (*Continued*)
as goal-directed, 79
individual, 1415–1416
interactional world views and, 16
levels of analysis, 1390
life span investigations and, 332
mathematical models of,
transportation and,
1006
mechanistic model of,
transportation and,
1004
molar action, emotion and, 247
narrative accounts of, 1416–
1417
objective perspectives on, 44
organization of, 254–259. *See
also* Action plan(s);
Travel
place-specificity of, 1419–1421,
1422
prosocial, mood and, 269
routine, space of setting and,
621
stream of, action theory and,
1209
subjective perspectives on, 44
tesserae, 1417
Behavioral commitment, energy
conservation and, 1065
Behavioral diversity, in cities, 1329
Behavioral ecology, natural
environments and, 795
Behavioral economics, water
conservation and, 1061
Behavioral engineering, A-B-C
model and, 372
Behavioral geography, 1366
vs. environmental psychology,
1396*n*
Behavioral mapping, emergence of
concept, 1383
Behavioral medicine, 107
Behavioral observation, in Dutch
research, 1231
Behavioral pathology, crowding
and, 63
Behavioral programming, 1501
Behavioral research, single-subject
design in, 365, 369–
370
Behavioral science research, cost-
benefit analysis and,
1005
Behavioral sciences, growth of,
1477
Behavioral sinks, crowding and,
538–539

Behavioral technology, resource
management and, in
Australia, 1149
Behavior analysis:
A-B-C model of, 364
as active research, 363–364
applied, environmental
psychology and, 362–
382
applied *vs.* experimental, 365–
366
component *vs.* package
interventions and, 368
ecology and, 378–382
evaluation issues in, 366–370
nonstatistical approach in, 369–
370
observer reliability in, 370–371
side effects and, 379–380
Behavior community psychology,
380–382
Behavior decision theory,
perception of nuclear
power risks and, 115
Behavior-environment congruence,
transactional view and,
1436
Behavior episode, 1417–1418
Behaviorism:
ecological psychology and, 1209
S-R approach and, 1441
see also Extinction; Operant
learning theory;
Reinforcement
Behavior model, *vs.* medical model,
364
Behavior modification, 371–378
A-B-A reversal design and, 372
attitude change and, 364
multiple-baseline design and,
372
social science as, 1070
Behavior object, 1418–1419
Behavior setting(s), 211, 1264,
1416
accessibility, 1430
action theory and, 1209
activity in, negotiations and,
629–630
analysis techniques, 1383
applications of concept, 616
applied psychology of, 1428
assumptions about, 616–617
background of, 615–616
Barker's theory, 623–624
contributions of, 624
growth and, 624
intrasetting events and, 624

maintenance *vs.* operating
circuits in, 623–624
occupants and, 624–625, 626
stability and, 623
as behavioral focal point, 649
boundaries of, 615
business, 617–618
central life interests and, 627
characteristics, 617–618
child development and, 288–289
coercive power of, 1428
components of, 615, 621, 624–
625, 632, 1425
concept of, 1204
concocted groups in, 618
criticism, 1431
decline of, 633–635
sources for, 634–635
definition, 30, 1416
descriptive surveys and, 617
developmental processes in,
623, 625, 630–633
channelized thinking and, 625
differentiation of, 630–633
as distinctive, 618
divergence in, 633–635
duration, 1427
ecological (E), 1416–1419, 1420,
1429, 1431
economic models, 1432*n*
emergence of concept, 1383
enigma of, 1430
equilibrium state in, 616
expanded temporal approach to,
616–617
overview of, 618–621
extraindividual behavior, 1421–
1423, 1425
facets of, 618–620, 621–643
context, 620, 637–643
environmental factors, 619,
620, 638–639
history, 620, 638, 639–640
antecedent settings and,
639
growth and, 639–640
issues related to, 638–639
linkages, 620, 635, 638,
640–643
internal dynamics, 619–620,
623–637, 639
division of labor and, 628,
629
early activities, 625
external constraints, 628,
635, 637–638
growth periods, 619
interventions, 619–620

perception of, 1174
production systems in, social
control and, 1186
research architects and, 1383
simulation of, 1235
symbolic mediations in, 1175
see also Architecture
Bureaucracy, organization
structure and, 766, 767
Bureau of Land Management, 1019
Burolandschaft, 764, 1294
Bushfires, in Australia, 1147
Business, transportation and, 988,
1001–1002, 1006
Business settings, French research
and, 1175
Bus ridership:
high-occupancy vehicle lanes
and, 993–994
reinforcement theory
terminology and, 1005–
1006
Byobu, 1159, 1160

Cabin fever, 878
Cafard, 878
California Psychological Inventory,
environmental
psychology and, 220
Campgrounds, natural resource
economics and, 797
Campground use, 893
Camping, 792
auto, visual seclusion and, 803
litter and, 1034
market research and, 799
recreational carrying capacity
and, 1031
Cancer, life expectancy and, 333
Cape Hatteras National Seashore,
1018
CAPRICODE (British Department
of Health), 1284
Carbon monoxide:
driver fatigue and, 991
imperceptible, emotional effects
of, 260
Cardiovascular disease:
heat and, 593
life expectancy and, 333
stress and, 587, 590
Car driving, *see* Driving
Car-driving simulator, use of
computer graphics in,
1266
Caretakers, in orphanages, ratio to
infants, 299

Car pooling, 64, 380
highway design and, 993–994
preferred parking facilities and,
994
Carrying capacity, 1392–1393
recreational, 1027–1032
dimensions of, 1027–1030
management approaches to,
1030–1032
Cartesian coordinates, information
storage and, 145
Cartography, mental maps and,
1286
Cataclysmic event, stress and,
575
Catecholamines, stress and, 577
Categorization, level of meaning
and, 266
Category sorting, in environmental
cognition research, 160
Causation:
Aristotle's classification of, 15
in compared world views, 13–14
theoretical approaches and, 1437
in trait approaches, 13, 15–16
see also Efficient cause; Final
cause; Formal cause;
Material cause
Cause maps, 630, 632
in behavior setting, 629
Centeredness, home and, 659
Centiurb (measure), 1427
Central America, immigration from,
population structure
projections and, 333
Centrality, dialectics of, 1185
Centralization, organizational
structure and, 767
Chairs, 754, 765. *See also* Seating
Challenge:
boredom and, 875
emotional response to, 873
extreme/unusual environments
and, 872, 873
Chance factors, environment-
behavior phenomena
and, 65–66
Change:
as aleatory process, 30
as building of new environments,
108
in compared world views, 13–14
contextualism and, 11
in Dewey & Bentley system, 9
environmental, children and, 319
in interactional world views, 10,
17–18
organicist approaches and, 11

in organismic-developmental
perspective, 1442,
1445, 1447–1448
anchorpoints and, 1447
conditions for, 1447–1448
direction of, 1447–1448
organismic world views and, 21–
22, 26
psychological processes and, 9
self-action approaches and, 9
in trait approaches, 13, 15
transactional perspective and,
101
in transactional world views, 26–
27, 35–36
vs. sameness in nursing homes,
aging/environment
models and, 339
see also Life transition;
Transformational
theory
Chemicals, imperceptible,
emotional effects of,
260
Childbirth, experience of,
environment and, 1147
Child-care facilities, women in
work force and, 994
Child development, *see*
Development, child
Childhood, early, topological
representation, studies
of, 186
Child-in-the-city project, 311, 312,
313
Child psychology, ecological, 1201
Children:
as active *vs.* passive, stimulus
environment and, 316
aerial photograph cognition in,
1287
automobile accidents and, 936–
937
in cities, life space of, 1201
cognition in, Swedish research
on, 1247
contextual behavior, normative
constraints and, 1182
customary assumptions and, 936
day-care location and, 937
defining characteristics of,
customary assumptions
and, 936
density and, 591
design for, 935–938
domestic sex roles and, 664
dwelling use by, 1261
effects of crowding on, 551–552

Mountain sickness, 883
"Muddling through," decision
    making and, 1128
Multiattribute utility theory
    (MAUT), decision
    making and, 1107–
    1109, 1126
Multidimensional scaling, 187
    in environmental cognition
        research, 158, 160,
        161–162
    limitations of, 188, 197
    river differentiation and, 805
    sorting tasks and, 1289
Multidisciplinary approach:
    emergence of, 1383
    French research and, 1172–
        1181, 1188, 1189
Multiphasic Environmental
    Assessment Procedure
    (MEAP):
    as aging/environment model,
        339–340
    elderly housing and, 842
Multiple-baseline design, 367–368,
    369, 372
Multiple sorting task, as
    methodology, 1289
Multivariate technique:
    perceived sound quality and,
        1257
    scene analysis and, 1146
Museums, way-finding in, 85–86
Music:
    arousal and, 751
    in factories, 751–752
    job satisfaction and, 765
    in offices, 751
    vigilance tasks and, 751
Musselmanism, 874, 883
Mystery:
    as environmental attribute, 785,
        805
    nature as symbol of, 789
    visual preferences and, 806

Narrative records, behavior setting
    research and, 615
National Autonomous University of
    Mexico (UNAM),
    1343, 1344–1345
National forest, as designation, 807
National Institute for Applied
    Science Research
    (TNO) (Netherlands),
    1231

National Park(s):
    behavior setting concept and,
        616
    as designation, 807, 1025
National Parks and Countryside
    Act of 1949 (United
    Kingdom), 1296
National Park Service, 1013
National Research, Development
    and Demonstration
    Council (Australia),
    1149
National Trust of Australia, 1146
Nativism, environment-behavior
    relationship and, 1373
Natural areas, *see* Community(s);
    Natural environment
Natural/artificial distinction,
    environmental meaning
    and, 810
Natural beauty, public land policy
    and, 1015
Natural categories, 230
Natural Colour System, Swedish
    research and, 1255–
    1256
Natural environment, 784–810
    aesthetic values, 1012, 1020–
        1027
    cognitive paradigm, 1021,
        1026
    coherence, 1023, 1024
    compatibility, 1022–1023
    complexity, 1022, 1023, 1024
    congruence, 1023
    experiential paradigm, 1021–
        1022, 1026
    expert paradigm, 1020–1021,
        1025–1026
    familiarity, 1024–1025
    hazard, 1023
    information, 1025
    involvement, 1023
    legibility, 1023
    making sense, 1023
    mystery, 1023, 1024
    naturalism, 1023
    perceptual set, 1025
    phenomenological paradigm,
        1020–1021
    prospect, 1023
    psychological correlates of,
        1022–1026
    psychophysical paradigm,
        1021, 1026
    refuge, 1023, 1024
    assessment of, in France, 1174

behavior in, as sociological issue,
    794–795
benefits of, 793–794
children and, 309–311
commodity values, 1015–1019
cultural perspective on, 786–787
deviant behavior in, 1012, 1032–
    1035
as dynamic, 809
early research on, 1380
ecopsychological interest in,
    1207
environmental sociology and,
    1382
ephemeral qualities of, research
    and, 809
French research and, 1188
image *vs.* function of, 807
impact of research on, 1367–
    1368
in integrated approach, 1318,
    1319–1320
integrative perspectives and,
    799–801
Japanese arts and, 1159–1161
linguistic designations and, 807
littering, 1029–1030, 1032–1035
management, 1011
    future issues and, 1026–1027
    managers, 1012, 1015–1016
        perspectives of, 1017
        training of, 1017
    user conflicts, 796, 1017–1018
mental mediations in, 1175
mental representation of, 807–
    808
multidimensional perspective
    and, 1387
noncommodity values, 1012,
    1015–1019, 1026–
    1027, 1032
non-consumptive use, 1012,
    1018
passivity in, 1328–1329
perceived value of:
    labels and, 1025
    presence of water and, 1026
perception of, in France, 1174
policy, 1011–1012
    Clean Air Act Amendments of
        1977, 1014–1015
    Endangered Species Act of
        1973, 1014
    eras, 1012
        conservation, 1014
        disposal, 1013
        environmental, 1015

multiple use, 1014
natural beauty, 1014
preservation, 1013–1014
reclamation, 1014–1015
recreation, 1014
Executive Order, 1016
Federal Administration
    Procedures Act, 1018–
    1019
Federal Land Policy and
    Management Act, 1019
Federal Water Pollution
    Control Act
    Amendments of 1972,
    1019
Freedom of Information Act,
    1019
Multiple Use and Sustained
    Yield Act, 1027
Multiple Use and Sustained
    Yield Act of 1960, 1014
National Environmental Policy
    Act of 1969, 1015
National Forest Management
    Act, 1027
National Forest Management
    Act of 1976, 1014
National Parks Act, 1027
Outdoor Recreation Resources
    Review Commission,
    1014
Recreation and Scenic Trails
    System Act, 1014
Roadless Area Review and
    Evaluation, 1019
Sagebrush Rebellion, 1014
Sunshine Act, 1019
Wild and Scenic Rivers
    Systems Act, 1014
Wilderness Act of 1964, 1014
Wildlife Refuge System, 1014
Yellowstone National Park,
    1014
Yosemite Valley, 1014
preservation of, Australia and,
    1142
reasons for use of, 791–792
recreation and, in Sweden, 1251
recreational behavior in, 1027–
    1032
recreational carrying capacity,
    1012, 1027–1032
crowding, 1028–1029
density, 1028–1029
education programs, 1031
expected outcomes, 1029
information programs, 1031

interpersonal contact in, 1029
level of technology, 1029
litter, 1029–1030
regulation of behavior, 1031
site management techniques,
    1030–1031
size of party, 1029–1030
type of use, 1029
user involvement, 1031–1032,
    1035
recreational potential of, 1329
research directions and, 809–
    810
social exchange and, 803–804
symbolic mediations in, 1175
use of, conflicting environmental
    values and, 1015–1020
users, 1012, 1015–1016
competition, 1015–1016, 1018
conflict, 1015–1016, 1018
displacement, 1016–1017
motivation, 1016, 1018
vandalism, 1032–1035
education and, 1034
information and, 1034–1035
reduction of, 1034–1035
types of, 1032
vs. artificial, 804–805
see also Landscapes; Public land
Natural gas, in Australia, 1139
Naturalistic criteria:
ecological validity and, 49
external validity and, 49
Naturalness:
degree of, setting differentiation
    and, 795
river differentiation and, 805
Natural resources management, see
    Resource management
Natural scenes, preferred,
    properties of, 806
Natural science approach, 1434
Natural selection, human
    environmental
    preference and, 785
Nature:
attitudes toward, 784
children and, 1251
in Japan, 1156–1157
Japanese vs. European, 1161
as competence builder, 788–789
as diversion, 789
human orientations toward, 786
importance of, 789–790
perception of, 1509
as restorer, 787–788, 803
as symbol, 789

urban scene preferences and,
    805
see also Natural environment
Nature preserves, passivity of
    visitors in, 1328–1329
Naval environment, occupational
    stress and, Swedish
    research on, 1255
Navigation:
cognitive mapping and, 154–155
reference points in, 138
see also Highway(s), signage;
    Map(s); Wayfinding
Navigation systems, cross-cultural
    studies of, 152
Need(s):
analysis, and government
    projects, 1506
concept of, 1175
environmental, 1181
autonomy, 1181
safety, 1181
in French research, 1177, 1180,
    1181
life-maintenance, in aging/
    environment model,
    336–337
need hierarchy, residential
    satisfaction and, 1235
psychogenic, in aging/
    environment model,
    336–337
satisfaction of, aging and, 337
as variable in aging research,
    335–336
viscerogenic, in aging/
    environment model,
    336–337
vs. wants:
cultural factors and, 1182
personality type and, 1182
Negotiated order theory, 628–629
Neighborhood organizations, 844–
    846, 850
Neighborhood Participation Project
    (NPP), 845, 846
Neighborhood quotient, sociospatial
    schemata and, 1286
Neighborhoods, 906
amenities of, commuting/stress
    relationship and, 45
change in, territorial dynamics
    and, 967
citizen participation and, 844–
    846
community development and,
    1330

Social support (*Continued*)
  public housing and, 833, 838
  stress and, 599–600, 832
  urban renewal and, 849–850
Social system(s):
  behavior settings as subunits of,
    643
  contradictions in, 636
  decline of, 633–635
  hierarchical:
    behavior settings and, 641
    coupling of subsystems in,
      641–642
    linkages with behavior settings,
      nested hierarchical
      systems, 640–641
  proximal environments and, 640
  reconstruction of, 636
  small-scale, 618
Social threat, outdoor recreation
    and, 802
Social ties, community psychology
    and, 830–832
Social traps, environmental
    problems and, 1052,
    1055, 1061, 1072, 1077
Social values, behavior settings
    and, 638
Social welfare, in Scandinavian
    countries, 1244
Societal change, extreme
    deprivation and, 877
Society for the Psychological Study
    of Social Issues
    (SPSSI), 1493
Sociobehavioral phenomena, in
    multidimensional
    framework, 1384,
    1389–1390
Sociocultural dimensions, in
    contextual analysis, 44,
    52–55, 67
Sociocultural environment:
  in holistic perspective, 1437
  orthogenetic principle and, 1445
  relocation transactions and,
    1448, 1451–1452
Sociocultural evolution, 893
  environmental assessment and,
    894, 913
Sociocultural relations, person-in-
    environment system
    and, 1443
Socioeconomic status (SES), spatial
    behavior and, 447–448,
    490
Sociofugal space, 1365

Sociogeography, Soviet
    environmental research
    and, 1313
Sociology:
  actionist, social conflict research
    and, 1175, 1186
  aging research and, 332
  behavior settings and, 618
  cities' images and, 1176
  environmental literature in, in
    France, 1179
  environmental research and, in
    Australia, 1144–1145
  environment and behavior:
    graduate programs, 1371
    literature reviews, 1380
    texts in, 1370
  in French research, 1182
  rural:
    anthropology and, in French
      research, 1186
    in French research, 1177
  social meanings of home and,
    1176
  Soviet urban studies and, 1329
  urban, in French research, 1174,
    1177
  urban planning and, in Germany,
    1205
Sociopetal space, 1365
Sociophysical system(s), in Soviet
    research, 1321–1322
Sociospatial schemata:
  neighborhood quotient and, 1286
  transport and, 1296
Sociotope, term, 1209
Sociotechnical systems, 764–765
Sociotypes, crime areas and, 980
Soft energy path, energy
    conservation and, 1048
Soil conservation, 1060
Soil erosion, 1045–1046, 1060
  in Australia, 1141
Soil salinity, grazing and, 1141
Solar energy, 1066
Solar phenomena, affective state
    and, 809
Solid wastes:
  control strategies and, 1058
  research on, 1058–1060
  types of, 1058
Solitude:
  altered states of consciousness
    and, 876
  see also Privacy
Sonic environment, semantic
    analysis and, 1246

Soul, self-action and, 9
Sound quality, perceptual
    dimensions of, 1257
South America, immigration from,
    population structure
    projections and, 333
Southeast Asia, immigration from,
    population structure
    projections and, 333
Soviet activity theory, as
    transactional world
    view, 28–29
Soviet clubs, *see* Community
    centers, use of space
    in
Soviet Union, 1312–1331
  cultural institutions in, 1328–
    1329
  environmental cognition in,
    1322–1323
  environmental perception in,
    1322–1323
  environmental viewpoint in, 1315
  guest astronaut program and,
    1510
  home environments, 1324–1327
  human spatial behavior and,
    1323–1324
  information exchange in, 1316
  interdisciplinary approach in,
    1315–1316
  neighborhoods, 1329–1330
  organizational activity in, 1315–
    1316
  philosophical background in,
    1313
  privacy in, 1505
  psychological viewpoint in,
    1314–1315
  recreational institutions in,
    1328–1329
  theoretical approaches in, 1316–
    1322
  urban space, 1329–1330
  work environments, 1327–1328
Socialökologie, 1204
Space:
  adaptation to temporal
    environmental change
    and, 1175
  appropriation of, 1175–1176
    place attachment and, 522–
    523
  architectural, assessment of,
    1246
  aspects of, in French research,
    1180